ENCYCLOPEDIA OF REAL ESTATE TERMS

To My Parents

Encyclopedia
of
REAL ESTATE
TERMS

Damien Abbott
BSc, FRICS, CDip.AF

Gower Technical Press

Published by
Gower Technical Press Ltd,
Gower House,
Croft Road,
Aldershot,
Hants GU11 3HR,
England

Gower Publishing Company,
Old Post Road,
Brookfield,
Vermont 05036,
U.S.A.

British Library Cataloguing in Publication Data

Abbott, Damien
    Encyclopedia of real estate terms.
    1. Real property—Dictionaries
    I. Title
    333.33'03'21   HD107.7

Library of Congress Cataloging-in-Publication Data
Abbott, Damien
    Encyclopedia of real estate terms.

    1. Real estate business—Dictionaries.   2. Real
property—Dictionaries.   I. Title.
HD1365.A23   1986   333.33'03'21   87–27930

ISBN 0–291–39702–6

Printed in Great Britain by
Redwood Burn Limited
Trowbridge, Wiltshire.

Contents

Acknowledgements

MAURICE K. HURRELL, B.Sc.(Econ), Dip.Ind.Admin.,A.M.C.S.T., F.R.Econ.S., who slavishly read through two drafts, the final manuscript and the proofs and supplied invaluable comments and suggested revisions.

GERARD TAVERNIER, Doctor of Law, Avocat à la Cour de Paris, who verified most of the French entries and provided comment and advice on some aspects of French law referred to in the text.

Sue East, Leslie Rogers, Hazel Daniels, Deborah Aucamp and Joan Cox, who converted an untidy and sometimes illegible handwritten text into a well typed manuscript.

The authors and publishers of the many quotations and references used throughout the book, in particular the following for permission to reproduce definitions or extracts from the mentioned publications: The Incorporated Council of Law Reporting for England and Wales for their *Law Reports* and *Weekly Law Reports*; Butterworth & Co. (Publishers) Ltd. for its *All England Law Reports*, *Crossley Vaines's Personal Property Cheshire and Burn's Modern Law of Real Property, 13th edition*, *Cheshire and Fifoot's Law of Contract 10th edition*, *Lord Denning's Discipline of Law*, *Gray and Symes' Real Property and Real People*, *Halsbury's Laws of England 4th edition* and *Barry Nicholas's French Law of Contract;* Sweet & Maxwell Ltd. for *Chitty on Contract 25th edition*, *Holdsworth's History of English Law*, *Megarry and Wade's Law of Real Property 5th edition*, *Michael Purdue's Cases and Materials on Planning Law*, *Russell on the Law of Arbitration 20th edition*, *Woodfall's Landlord and Tenant 28th edition*, *David Yates's Exclusion Clauses in Contracts 2nd edition*, the requisites of 'possession' taken from *Jowitt's Dictionary of English Law* and for the definition of 'contractor' taken from *Stroud's Judicial Dictionary;* Oxford University Press for *David Walker's Law of Delict in Scotland*, *Amos and Walton's Introduction to French Law 3rd edition*, *A.W.B. Simpson's Introduction to the History of Land Law*, Pitman Publishing Ltd., for *Merrett & Sykes's The Financial Analysis of Capital Projects* and *Keaton's Law of Trusts*, and the definition of 'trade' taken from the *Oxford English Dictionary*; Merriam-Webster, Inc., publisher of the Merriam-Webster® Dictionaries for reference to the definition of 'abut', 'appropriate', 'bond', 'exterior', and 'power' taken from *Webster's Third International Dictionary* © 1986; West Publishing Company for the definition of 'date' taken from *Black's Law Dictionary 5th edition* © 1979; The American Institute of Real Estate Appraisers for the definitions of 'appraisal', 'industrial property' and 'overall capitalisation rate' taken from *The Appraisal of Real Estate, 8th edition*; The American Law Institute for reference to the definitions of 'easement appurtenant' and 'easement' taken from *Restatement of the Law of Property* © 1936 and 'bargain' taken from *Restatement of the Law of Contract* © 1932; Prentice-Hall, Inc. for *Barlowe's Land Resource Economics 3rd edition* and *Kratovil and Werner's Real Estate Law 8th edition*, the Building Owners and Managers Association International for their definition of 'rentable area'; Surveyors Publications for the definitions of 'gross external area' and 'net internal area' taken from the R.I.C.S. & I.S.V.A.'s Code of Measuring Practice 2nd edition.

A complete list of these and other books of reference used for the preparation of this Encyclopedia is set out in the Bibliography (Appendix B).

Preface

This *Encyclopedia of Real Estate Terms* is intended primarily for those who are engaged in the field of real estate, including chartered surveyors, lawyers, bankers, accountants, builders, appraisers, and town planners. It should prove also an invaluable source of reference material for students, company secretaries, finance directors, local government officers and many others who regularly come into contact with the language of real estate. It provides more than a list of definitions: most entries contain detailed explanations, supplemented by extensive references and cross-references, thereby enabling the user to appreciate better the intent and significance of each term according to the context in which it is used. Many entries are supported by reference to legal decisions, statutory definitions and one or more bibliographical references.

A special feature of the *Encyclopedia* is its international content. Although based primarily on United Kingdom usage, it also contains terms and phrases used in the United States and France. These entries are augmented by cross-references, as well as legal decisions and appropriate bibliographical references. It is not intended as a law book, nor as a replacement for independent legal advice, but naturally use has been made throughout of legal material. In this respect, English law has taken priority. Nonetheless, it is hoped that references to the law and practice in the United States and France will be of appreciable value to anyone involved in real estate in these and many other countries whose legal systems are based on English common law or the French civil law.

The 'Notes on the use of the Encyclopedia' (p. xi) set out in greater detail the significance of the references and cross-references employed throughout the book. A list of real estate abbreviations and of abbreviations used in the text of the book is set out in Appendix A.

As far as possible, entries are current as at the end of 1986. Every care has been taken to ensure accuracy. However, the author accepts full responsibility for any errors and omissions. Comments or suggestions from users for alterations or revisions will be welcomed and fully considered.

DA

Notes on the use of the Encyclopedia

Cross-references

Terms defined elsewhere in the book are set down in bold type. This enables an extensive use to be made of cross-references which enables the reader:

1   to compare and contrast defined terms, especially those that frequently are confused or misused – eg, 'lease' and 'licence'; 'misrepresentation' and 'puffing', 'occupation' and 'possession'.
2   to examine the significance of a term in greater depth. For example, 'freehold' is better understood by reference to the feudal system; an 'indemnity' must be carefully distinguished from a 'guaranty'; *'hypothèque'* as found in French law can be compared to a 'mortgage' as found in English law; and the different forms of 'co-ownership' found in English common law can be compared to those found in the civil law.
3   to consult additional bibliographical references. Thus, for instance, 'dominant tenement' can be examined further by using the bibliographical references set out under 'easement'.

Bibliographical references

Many of the more important entries are equipped with one or more bibliographical references. This provides:

a)   a rapid but extensive means of finding further material on these entries. When there is more than one such reference, then these references are set out in an order that is based primarily on the length of the reference, with the least extensive material being put first. Thus, 'service charge' which is given three pages in *The Law of Landlord and Tenant* by David Lloyd Evans, comes before *Service Charges in Property* by Tristan McGee, which is published as four separate reports.
b)   a way of examining the meaning of a term in greater detail. Thus, a student may refer to the 'rule against perpetuities' in *The Law of Real Property* by F.H. Lawson and B. Rudden, whereas a lawyer may prefer to consult volume 35 of *Halsbury's Laws of England* or the standard text on the subject, *Gray's Rule against Perpetuities*. Similarly, the essentials for a valid lease are outlined adequately in *Adkin's Landlord and Tenant*, but are examined in much greater depth in *Woodfall's Landlord and Tenant* (which has the added advantage of an updating service).

When the year of publication is provided this indicates that there is only one edition; otherwise the number of the edition is given.

A comprehensive bibliography, which provides details of the author, title, publisher, edition, place and year of publication of all the books referred to in the text, is set out in Appendix B. (In this bibliography the latest edition of a book is indicated, which may be a more recent edition than that shown in the text of entries.)

Legal cases

These are used extensively throughout the text, being one of the primary sources of definition for legal terms. Anyone seeking a complete understanding of a term is strongly recommended to read the learned judgments that have formed the basis for some of the definitions used in this book.

Direct quotations from a law case are referenced to the page of the law report from which the quotation has been taken. All other references use the page number at which the case commences in the law report.

United States law reports are used primarily to support US entries. However, many of the terms may be used with the same meaning in England as in the United States. Accordingly, some terms are augmented by reference to English and US law reports.

Abbreviations for law reports are set out in Appendix A.

Statute law

Many terms are creatures of statute law, or are given special meaning in a particular Act of Parliament or in a Legislative Act of the US Government. As far as possible statutory definitions are included where they relate specifically to real estate. However, it is not possible to include all statutory definitions and when a term has a statutory meaning, in the context in which it is used, readers are advised to consult the relevant statute, the index of words and phrases in *Halsbury's Statutes of England, Current Law Statutes Annotated, Words and Phrases Legally Defined*, or similar reference material, or one of the bibliographical references provided in this *Encyclopedia*.

United States terms

Terms that are used primarily in the United States are denoted by (US). This does not signify any exclusivity in that respect, nor does a lack of such a denotation imply that a term may not be defined for use in the United States in the same way as in England and Wales. In the same way some terms that are not denoted (US) are augmented by reference to publications from the United States, and by the same token terms used primarily in the United States are augmented by reference to material published in England, either directly or through the cross referencing system. These arrangements are aimed at making this *Encyclopedia* of use to real estate practitioners on both sides of the Atlantic.

French terms

French terms are denoted by (F). These terms are then followed by an English translation. The use of bold type face for such a translation indicates that the English term is similar to the French term and that that English term is defined in the book. Roman type face is used for a translation when there is no equivalent English entry, or when the word or term has no English word or term that provides an adequate translation. For example, '*abandon*' can be readily translated as 'abandonment', as 'renunciation' or as 'surrender', according to the context; but '*abdication*' does not carry the same meaning as renunciation or surrender as those terms are defined in this book.

In several entries, notes on the distinction between English and French law are included to enable the user to avoid the more common misunderstandings of translation.

In conclusion, this *Encyclopedia* is designed to enable the user to understand the meaning of a term; to examine that meaning in greater detail by cross-reference to other terms; and to find easily one or more sources where that meaning is considered in still greater depth.

A

a fortiori (L)

'Much more; by or with stronger reason.'

à prendre

see **profit à prendre**

a priori (L)

'From before'. As deduced by reasoning – from cause to effect.

AAA rating (US)

see **triple A rating**.

ab initio (L)

'From the beginning'. An insurance contract that has been entered into on the basis of false information, or in breach of the **utmost good faith** (*uberrimae fidei*) required of such contracts, may be void *ab initio* i.e. from when it was entered into, not when the false information comes to light. Similarly a person who enters on to land legally and then refuses to leave when required to do so may be guilty of trespass *ab initio* – from the first moment that he or she entered on to the land. See also **adverse possession, rescission**.

ab intestatio (L)

'From an intestate'. See **intestacy**.

abandon (F)

abandonment; renunciation; surrender (of a right or claim).

(*abandon de mitoyenneté* – the relinquishment of **party wall** rights)

(*bien à l' abandon – ownerless property*, see *res derelictae*).

abandoned property

Property that has been voluntarily surrendered or vacated without any intention of reclaiming it or transferring it to another. See also **abandonment**, *res nullius*, **vacant**.

abandonment

1. The act of proscribing completely. The voluntary relinquishment of a property, or an interest in property, without any intention of resuming enjoyment or possession of that property or interest, or of vesting it in anyone else. The disclaiming of a right, expressly or by implication, without leaving any evidence of an intention to reclaim that right. A contract is said to have been abandoned when one of the parties signifies that he has no intention to fulfil or complete any of his obligations or exercise any of his rights under the contract, although such an act is taken normally as a **repudiation** of the contract.

The ownership of a title to land cannot be abandoned, although it may be lost by the **adverse possession** of another. A right to possession or use or an interest in land may be abandoned, provided there is an intention not to resume that right or interest, or some overt act or failure to act which supports that intention. Mere non-use or discontinuance of use, does not of itself constitute abandonment. There must be a clear intention to abandon, or an overt act that is repugnant to a continuing right of user. For example, in the case of an **easement**, "non-use is not of itself conclusive evidence that a private right of easement is abandoned. The non-use must be considered with, and may be explained by the surrounding circumstances. If those circumstances clearly indicate an intention of not resuming the use then a presumption of a release of the easement will, in general, be implied and the easement will be lost" – Swan v Sinclair [1924] 1 Ch. 266. Keeping a doorway bricked up for 30 years did not amount to a sufficient indication of an intention not to reopen it – Cooke v Mayor and Corporation of Bath (1868) LR Eq. 177; but removing a wall that contained a window, and then a wait of 14 years before rebuilding the wall, showed that the beneficiary had abandoned the need for light, "If a man has a right of common attached to his mill, or a right of turbary attached to his house, if he pulls down the mill or the house, the right of common or turbary will *prima facie* cease. If he shows an intention to build another mill or another house his right continues" – Moore v Rawson (1824) 3 B and C 338.

In general, a tenancy cannot be abandoned; but if a tenant leaves the premises leased to him empty and then permits the landlord to re-enter the tenancy may be said to have been abandoned (or more precisely the tenancy is surrendered) and the tenant released of his obligation to pay rent – Dodd v Acklon (1843) 6 Man. and G. 672.

In the US, the abandonment of a lease is called also an 'implied release' and is distinguished in some states from **surrender** by the lack of agreement; abandonment being based entirely on act and intent. In most states, if a tenant abandons the leased premises the landlord has a duty to mitigate the loss suffered as a result by endeavouring to relet the premises – Scheinfeld v Muntz TV, Inc. (1966)

67 Ill. App.2d 28, 214 NE 2d 506. See also **frustration, release, *res nullius***. *Modern Law of Real Property*, by Cheshire 13 edn, pp. 528–9.

2. The discontinuance of a use of land for a considerable period of time. In English planning law the abandonment of a use produces the result that the resumption of that use may constitute **development** and, therefore, require **planning permission**. In this connection factors to be considered are (i) the period of time for which the use is discontinued; (ii) whether there is any intention to re-establish the discontinued use which may be judged from the state of the property or any elected action on the part of the party seeking to reestablish the use; and (iii) any intervening user. "I [Lord Denning] think that when a man ceases to use a site for a particular purpose and lets it remain unused for a considerable time, then the proper inference may be that he has abandoned the former use. Once abandoned, he cannot start to use the site again, unless he gets planning permission: and this is so, even though the new use is the same as the previous one ... and it seems to me [Widgery L.J.] ... that it is perfectly feasible in this context to describe a use as having been abandoned when one means that it has not merely been suspended for a short and determinable period, but has ceased with no intention to resume it at any particular time." – Hartley v Minister of Housing and Local Government [1970] 1 QB 420, 421. Non-use, during a period of suspension of use, does not constitute abandonment; but a new use, even though in itself temporary, tends to mitigate in favour of an indication of an intention to aban-

don a use. "Abandonment depends on the circumstances. If the land has remained unused for a considerable time, in such circumstances that a reasonable man might conclude that the previous use has been abandoned then (the planning authority or the Secretary of State for the Environment) may hold it to have been abandoned" – *supra* at p. 420. Or, "when a use has ceased with no *intention* to resume it at any particular time ... then as a matter of fact the use has ceased." *supra* at p. 421.

Planning permission, which endures for the benefit of land, cannot be abandoned; but the benefit of a particular planning permission may be lost when, pursuant to a subsequent planning permission, a landowner builds in accordance with that permission and by such action makes the former permission intractable – Thomas Langley Group Ltd. *v* Borough of Leamington Spa (1975) 29 P and CR 358; Pioneer Aggregates (UK) Ltd *v* Secretary of State for the Environment and Peak Park Joint Planning Board [1982] JPL 371. See also **election**.

Abandonment again, by N.P. Taylor. (1983). 267 E.G. 234.

3. The act of relinquishing damaged property or salvage to an insurer with the aim of claiming a total loss.

abatement

1. Derived from the French *abattre*, 'to beat down'. The act of bringing down or taking off something in size or value. A reduction or diminution in value; a suspension of a continuing payment. For example, a tenant may receive an abatement of rent, or an owner an abatement of taxes, because of limitations placed on the full use of the property, or a purchaser may receive an abatement of purchase price because he has not received that for which he contracted. Abatement of the purchase price of a property may be granted by a court, together with a decree of **specific performance**, when the court considers it appropriate that the sale should go through, but at a reduced price, because the loss to the purchaser is not substantial. See also **frustration, rent concession, termination**.

2. The termination, removal or extinguishment of a **nuisance**. See also **abatement notice, self-help**.

3. The reduction in the entitlement to the payment of a debt when a person has insufficient assets to satisfy his creditor in full.

abatement notice

A notice, served by a local authority, that requires a person to desist from, or terminate, a statutory **nuisance**, e.g. creating noise, or air or river pollution. (Public Health Act 1936, s. 93; Control of Pollution Act 1974). See also **nuisance order, wasteland**.

Housing Law by Andrew Arden and Martin Partington (1983) pp. 447–8

abbuttals

see **abutals**.

'able and willing'

see '**ready, able and willing**'.

'able to purchase'

see '**ready, able and willing**'.

abode

A place where one lives, or intends to live. A place for dwelling. The place where a person is normally resident; usually his or her principal place of **residence**. An abode may be considered a place of shorter stay than a residence. See also **domicile, home**.

abdication (F)
renunciation; surrender.

abonnement (F)
1. Subscription. Used, for example, to refer to weekly or monthly payment, such as for parking spaces.
2. A contract at a fixed sum or rate.

aboutissant (F)
abutting; bordering.

abrogation
The action of terminating or repealing a formal act or deed, especially a statute, law or regulation. The making of a new law may abrogate an old one. cf. **subrogation**. See also **derogation from grant**.

absentee owner (or landlord)
An owner (or landlord) of land who resides away, usually at some distance, from the property to which he holds title. An owner who leaves the management and running of a property almost entirely at the discretion of an agent, making rare or no visits for the purpose of supervision and inspection. Thus ownership and management are separated, the absentee owner receiving usually an income, but taking limited interest in the use and running of the property. Frequently used to refer to a tax exile or a foreign investor. See also **passive investor**.
Legal Aspects of Alien Acquisition of Real Property, edited by Dennis Campbell (1980).

absolute assignment
The unconditional **assignment** of the whole of a chose-in-action or debt. For example, if a building contractor transfers to a lender his rights to all money due, or to become due, under a building contract as security for a debt, and empowers the lender to settle all accounts under the contract, he absolutely assigns the debts of the contract – Hughes *v* Pump House Hotel Co. [1902] 2 KB 190. See also **legal assignment**.

absolute auction (US)
see **without reserve**.

absolute estate
An **estate** in land that is not liable to be determined or modified in any way and, therefore, may well continue for ever. An absolute estate may be subject to the rights of another, e.g. a **mortgagee**.
cf. **qualified estate**. See also **fee simple absolute in possession, ownership, term of years absolute**.

absolute fee simple
see **fee simple absolute in possession**.

absolute leasehold
An **absolute title** to the rights arising out of a lease that has been registered at the Land Registry. Such a right is the securest form of leasehold interest that may be registered because the holder of the registered title is guaranteed that the lease was validly granted and that the lessor had a title which enabled the lease to be granted. The registered proprietor of an absolute leasehold holds land subject to registered encumberances; overriding interests that affect the land; any minor interest of which he has notice; and any covenant incidental to the lease (Land Registration Act 1925, ss 8, 9). cf. **good leasehold, possessory leasehold**. See also **term of years absolute**.

absolute liability
see **strict liability**.

absolute order
An obsolete term for a **compulsory purchase order**.

absolute ownership
see **absolute title, ownership**.

absolute, term of years
see **term of years absolute**.

absolute title
1. A **title** to property that is good against any third party's claim and, therefore, cannot be defeated by any other claim. An unlimited right of **ownership**. In general, an absolute title is one that is as good as can be held. In English common law there is no such right as an absolute title, or absolute ownership, so that, "where questions of title to land arise in litigation the court is concerned only with the relative strength of the titles proved by the rival claimants. If party A can prove a better title than B he is entitled to succeed notwithstanding that C may have a better title than A, [provided] C is neither a party to the action nor a person by whose authority B is in possession of the land" – Ocean Estates Ltd. *v* Pinder [1969] 2 AC 25.
cf. **possessory title**. See also **absolute estate, good title**.
2. A title to land that is registered at the Land Registry (after appropriate investigation as to its validity) and is guaranteed by the state as valid against all comers. An absolute title may be freehold or leasehold and represents the best form of such title that can exist; although it is subject to matters entered on the register; any **overriding interest** (unless the register expressly excludes such an interest); in certain cases any **minor interest** of which the registered proprietor has

notice; and, in the case of a leasehold interest, covenants, obligations and liabilities incident to the lease (Land Registration Act 1925, s.5, 9).
cf. **qualified title, possessory title**. See also **absolute leasehold, freehold absolute, Land Certificate, land registration**.
Barnsley's Conveyancing Law and Practice, 2 edn, pp. 26–9.

absolutely net lease (US)
see **triple net lease**.

absorption rate
1. The number of units of property that will be let or sold in a given period of time, e.g. 5000 sq. ft of offices per quarter.
2. The time taken for a given number of units to be absorbed (let or sold) in a particular market, e.g. the absorption rate for a new 10 000 sq. ft. building may be six months.

absque impetitione vasti (L)
'Without impeachment for **waste**'.

abstract company (US)
see **abstractor**.

abstract of title
A summary, or epitome, of the deeds, conveyances, transfers and other instruments that represent evidence of a right to a **title**, or to ownership, of a particular parcel of unregistered land, together with details of all relevant events or encumberances that may reinforce or impair that title. In England an abstract is prepared by a vendor's solicitor prior to the transfer of property and submitted to the purchaser's solicitor for examination. The abstract starts with a good **root of title**; sets out all transfers to date that affect the title to the land, such as wills and deeds of conveyance; and

provides details of any event, such as a marriage or death, that affected the title during that period. It provides no guaranty as to the validity of the title, but represents the best evidence of the validity of an unregistered title. A party who has contracted to sell an estate or interest in land is under an obligation to prove that he has a **good title** to that which he has contracted to sell and an abstract represents the best available evidence of that title. A vendor must, at his own expense, produce a proper abstract of title to the prospective purchaser, unless there is an agreement to the contrary.

Traditionally, the abstract was a written résumé of all the documents that affected a title to land. However, a modern abstract usually is made up of photocopies of all deeds, instruments or other written documents (e.g. birth, death or marriage certificates) that are relevant to a proper proof that someone has title to land, together with a list in chronological order of those documents. In addition to producing an abstract the vendor is required to demonstrate that the documents referred to therein exist and are valid, or at least to produce the best evidence in that respect.

In the US, a **title insurance** policy may be accepted, in substitution for an abstract of title as evidence that a good title is held to a property.
cf. **certificate of title, land certificate**. See also **abstractor, beneficial owner, chain of title, constructive notice, requisition**.
Contract and Conveyance, by J.T. Farrand, 3 edn, pp. 109–114.
Barnsley's Conveyancing Law and Practice, 2 edn, pp. 291–303.
Williams on Title, 4 edn, pp. 573–86.
42 Halsbury's Laws of England, 4 edn, pp. 120–30.

abstracted in chief
That which has been set out in full, e.g. a deed or event set out in full, and not merely in résumé as, usually, in an **abstract of title**.

abstracting
A term in **quantity surveying** for the process (undertaken after **taking off**) of collecting together similar items that are to be costed, usually according to trade, prior to preparing a **bill of quantities**. See also **billing**.

abstraction approach (US)
The process of determining the value of land by using the sale prices of comparable properties and then deducting, or 'abstracting', the value of buildings or improvements to ascertain the value of the land alone. Called also 'valuation by abstraction'. cf. **the 'extraction approach'**. See also **land residual technique**.

abstractor (US)
A person who specialises in examining titles to land, preparing abstracts of title and issuing certificates indicating his view on a purported title to land. An abstractor's certificate does not guarantee any form of title and, except in a case of negligence, there is no recourse against an abstractor for a defect in the title he has investigated. See also **abstract of title**.

abstractor's certificate (US)
A certificate set out at the end of an abstract of title as prepared by an **abstractor** stating which documents of title to a parcel of land have, or have not, been examined and the date on which the abstract is valid. See also **certificate of title**.

abusus (L)

In the civil law, the absolute right to dispose of property – *jus abutendi* – whether by grant or sale, or by destruction. See also *droit de propriété*, **ownership**.

abut

To adjoin or border on; usually, but not necessarily, physically **contiguous**. *Webster's Third International Dictionary* defines 'abut' as 'to touch at one end'; and 'with reference to land "abut" means to actually touch.' – Barnett *v* Covell (1903) 68 JP 69. However, in certain circumstances a building or structure may be said to abut a highway even though there is a small strip of land between that object and the highway – Stockport Corporation *v* Rollinson (1910) 102 LT 567. Abutting implies a closer proximity than **adjacent**; the former is used frequently when land borders a highway. See also **adjoining, frontage**.

abuttals

The boundaries of land, especially the frontage. Land that is in physical contact with another area of land. See also **abut**.

abutter or abutting owner

The owner of **contiguous** or abutting land. See also **abut, neighbour**.

abutting foot (US)

see **frontage**.

abutting owner

see **abutter**.

accelerated depreciation

A method of allowing for **depreciation** by which a higher amount is written-off or set aside, in the earlier years (or other periods) than would be done using straight-line depreciation. For example, the allowance may be calculated by deducting a fixed percentage from the outstanding capital each year, termed 'diminishing balance depreciation'. Other forms of accelerated depreciation include 'double diminishing balance' – by which the amount deducted is doubled each year (or, for that matter, by any other increasing amount) – and the use of the **sum-of-the-years digits method of depreciation**. See also **declining-balance depreciation**.

acceleration clause

1. A clause in a contract or deed that brings forward the right to the enjoyment of an estate in land on the happening of a particular event. A clause in a contract which provides that on the happening of a specified event an interest in land may become vested in another. See also **conditional interest**.

2. A clause in a mortgage deed which permits the mortgagor or mortgagee to advance the date for the repayment of the principal so that either party may seek to acquire an unencumbered interest. An acceleration clause is most commonly brought into effect when a mortgagor is in default in complying with a term of the mortgage agreement; the mortgagee 'accelerates' the date on which the entire loan matures, and if the debt is not then repaid in full he may take steps to foreclose. Such a right may be exercised only if expressly provided for in the mortgage deed; in the absence of an acceleration clause the mortgagee merely seeks repayment of any overdue instalments. An acceleration clause may be 'automatic' or 'optional'. An automatic clause provides that on the happening of a specified event e.g. a sale of the property,

or a default the entire loan advances to maturity. An optional clause gives the mortgagee the right to call the entire loan in if the event or default arises. An acceleration clause is construed usually against the mortgagee, especially when the provision is automatic. Referred to also as a call provision. See also **alienation clause, due-on-sale clause, foreclosure, unconscionable bargain**.

acceptance

The positive act of agreeing to an **offer**. In order for an acceptance to create a binding **contract** in English law, it must be communicated to the offeror; it must correspond with terms of the offer in its mode, time and place of operation; and there must be an understanding as to what has been accepted. "An acceptance of an offer is an indication, express or implied, by the offeree made whilst the offer remains open and in the matter requested in that offer of the offeree's willingness to be bound unconditionally to a contract with the offeror on the terms stated in the offer" – 9 Halsbury's Laws of England 4 edn p. 117. An acceptance may be implied from the words and deeds of the parties, as when a person states or implies that performance of the terms of an offer will amount to acceptance – Carlill v Carbolic Smoke Ball Co. Ltd (1892) 2 QB 484. The acceptance need not be clearly expressed, provided it is positive and unqualified; "even although parties may intend to have their agreement expressed in the most solemn and complete form that conveyancers and solicitors are able to prepare, still there may be a **consensus** between the parties far short of a complete mode

of expressing it, and that consensus may be discovered from letters or from other documents of an imperfect and incomplete description; I mean imperfect and incomplete as regards form." – Brogden v Metropolitan Railway Co. (1877) 2 App. Cas. 672.

Acceptance takes effect when communicated to, or brought to the attention of, the offeror. It must be unconditional, otherwise it is merely a **counter-offer**. Acceptance by post, as a general rule, takes effect when the letter of acceptance is posted, the post office being deemed the agent of the acceptor – Byrne v Van Tienhoven (1880) 5 CPD 344; Henthorn v Fraser (1892) 2 Ch. 27; Vassar v Camp, 11 NY 441. (Whether post is a reasonable means of communicating an acceptance, or revoking an offer, may depend on the express or implied nature of the transaction, practical considerations and the 'balance of convenience'; it will not be applied so as to create a contract that is a "manifest inconvenience and absurdity" – Holwell Securities Ltd. v Hughes (1974) 1 WLR 161. However, in some states in the US, where a writer can recover a letter before it is delivered, acceptance does not take place until the letter reaches the offeror unrevoked – Rhode Island Tool Co. v United States (1955) F. Supp. 417. Acceptance by telephone must be heard by the offeror and acceptance by telex is complete when the telex is received clearly by the offeror – "it is not until his message (that of the sender of the telex) is received that the contract is complete" – Entores Ltd. v Miles Far East Corporation (1955) 2 All ER 495 (wherein the means of communicating acceptance are discussed in full by Denning L.J.) Acceptance by telex effects a contract normally in the country where that acceptance is received. See also **auction, mistake, 'subject to contract'**.

Cheshire and Fifoot's Law of Contract 10 edn 2.32 et seq.

Anson's Law of Contract 26 edn pp. 32–45.

Chitty on Contract 28 edn paras. 54–86.

A Casebook on Contract, by J.C. Smith and J.A.C. Thomas. 7 edn, pp. 47–72.

acceptation (F)
acceptance. See also *contrat*.

acces (F)
access; approach.

access
A means or right to enter and leave a property; such as a right of access to a public highway, or a landlord's right of access to his property to inspect its state of repair. See also **easement of necessity, entry, landlord's access, right of entry, right of way, riparian rights**.

access agreement
An agreement between a local authority and an owner of open country, made under the National Parks and Access to Countryside Act 1968, s. 18, by which the general public are permitted access to an area of land for recreational purposes. A landowner is compensated for costs incurred by him, such as providing surfacing to a footpath, fencing, signs, etc. and for any diminution in the value of land resulting from the permitted access. see also **access order, footpath, right of way**.

access, easement of
see **easement of necessity**.

access order
An order made by a local planning authority and confirmed by the Secretary of State, in accordance with the provisions of the National Parks and Access to the Countryside Act 1949, s. 65 (as amended by the Countryside Act 1968, s. 17), which has the same effect as an **access agreement** when a landowner is unwilling to permit access to his land by the public. The same provisions for compensation apply as for an access agreement.

accession
The process of adding to property that is already owned so as to increase the whole. Property may be acquired by accession based on a principle derived from Roman law *accessio cedit principali*, 'an accessory thing follows the principal thing'. Accession may arise from natural growth, i.e. by **accretion**, or by artificial improvement as by annexing a **fixture** or the construction of a building on land. See also **reliction.**

accession (F)
accession;   equivalent to the English meaning: "the ownership of a thing, whether a moveable or an immoveable, gives a right to everything it produces and everything it is united with, whether naturally or artificially" (French Civil Code, art. 546). See also *immeuble*.
Précis Dalloz Droit Civil Les Biens, by Alex Weill. 2 edn, p. 36.

accessory building (US)
see **ancillary building**.

accessory use (US)
  see **incidental use**.

accident insurance
  Insurance against an occurrence that results from an accident (a fortuitous or unexpected event or an act of God), but not against an inevitability e.g. death. A term that normally excludes **indemnity insurance**, e.g. fire and marine insurance, as well as life insurance (from natural causes), but includes injury, disability and public liability insurance. Referred to also as 'personal accident insurance' or 'casualty insurance'. See also **contingency insurance, professional liability insurance**.

accommodation agent
  An **agent** who deals with the letting of residential property, especially the short-term letting of flats. Usually such agents merely maintain a register of property to let, and of tenants seeking such accommodation. An accommodation agent is not permitted to charge a fee merely for supplying details of property that is available to let, for placing the name of a tenant on a register, or issuing any advertisement or list of premises to let without proper authority (Accommodation Agencies Act 1953). However, like any other agent, they may charge a fee for successfully finding accommodation for a tenant – Sanders *v* Soper [1975] AC 239; for acting upon the instructions of a person who has power to grant a tenancy; or for the cost of displaying and advertising properties to let. The 1953 Act does not affect the charges a solicitor may make for legal work associated with the letting of residential accommodation.

accommodation density
  see **residential density**.

accommodation land
  1. Land held for future development or for an intended permanent use, but in the meantime used on a temporary basis such as for the grazing of cattle or for recreation purposes.
  2. Land obtained or improved in order to increase the value of other land, or for the more convenient use of other land. For example, land acquired in order to improve the development potential of another parcel of land.

accommodation, suitable alternative
  see **suitable alternative accommodation**

accommodation work
  Work carried out by a public authority to accommodate an owner or occupier of land that is affected by the operations or undertakings of that authority. For example, work carried out following the compulsory purchase of part of an owner's land in order to reduce the severance damage. Accommodation work may include such matters as the provision of new boundary fences, accessways, drains, bridges, etc. The only statute that stipulates the provision of accommodation work, following compulsory purchase, is the Railway Clauses Act 1845, s. 68 (which applies to railway undertakings). However, accommodation work is carried out frequently *in lieu* of **compensation for severance**, when an authority compulsorily acquires part of an owner's land, or to reduce the amount of **compensation for injurious affection**. see also **mitigation works**.

accord (F)
  agreement, in particular a general

or informal agreement.

(*accord restrictif* – **restrictive covenant**, as in a contract; a restrictive covenant on land is a *servitude*). See also *contrat*, *convention*.

accord and satisfaction

The purchase of a release from an obligation by transferring an amount of **consideration** that is less than the consideration required to fulfil the obligation. An arrangement in which a party to a contract accepts that, instead of insisting on his complete rights under the contract, he will enter into a substituted agreement and take a payment or benefit that differs from his full entitlement. 'Accord' is the substituted agreement, or **consent** thereto, and 'satisfaction' is the consideration, or that which is given, to support that agreement – British Russian Gazette and Trade Outlook Ltd. *v* Associated Newspapers Ltd. [1933] 2 KB 616. The new or substituted consideration may constitute an executory promise, i.e. it sets up the basis for a new contract, but it still discharges the original contract. The payment of a sum of money that is less than the full amount due to a creditor is not of itself sufficient consideration to prevent the creditor from pursuing a later claim for the full debt; payment of a lesser sum can be no satisfaction for a greater sum – Pinnel's Case (1602) 5 Rep. 117a. But, premature payment (or payment in a different place or in a different currency) may qualify as substituted consideration and be adequate to support an agreement to discharge the debtor's obligation. The substituted consideration may be small or unusual, but it may still be adequate to support a claim that the obligation

has been discharged, for the creditor may have a special reason to accept that which is proferred: "the gift of a horse, hawk or robe etc., in satisfaction is good, for it shall be intended that a horse, hawk, or robe etc., might be more beneficial to the plaintiff than the money, in respect of some circumstance, or otherwise the plaintiff would not have accepted it in satisfaction." – Foakes *v* Beer (1884) 9 App. Cas. 616, quoting Lord Coke. A builder who accepts a reduced price for work performed, especially because of a need for ready cash, cannot be said to have given accord and received satisfaction unless he has received something else in satisfaction of the discharge of the obligation owed – D & C. Builders Ltd. *v* Rees [1966] 2 QB 617 (or unless he has made the substituted agreement under **seal**). Similarly a builder who accepts a reduced payment because the employer maintains work is unsatisfactory does not give up his right to payment in full, unless in satisfaction he acknowledges that his obligation has been diminished or, for example, he obtains an early release of a retention sum. However, if the builder has accepted the lesser sum in satisfaction and knowingly permits the debtor to *act on* that accord he cannot then go back and claim from the debtor; he cannot change his mind and reopen a door he deliberately closed – he has set up the defence of promissory **estoppel**.

cf. **novation**.

Cheshire & Fifoot's Law of Contract 10 edn, p. 509–510.

Chitty on Contract 28 edn paras. 1471–1481.

accountant's rate of return
 see **average annual return**.

accounts method of valuation
 see **profits method of valuation**.

accretion
 1. The gradual and imperceptible increase in an area of land by natural causes e.g. by alluvial deposits resulting from movements of a river course or of the sea. Accretion can be caused by the washing up of silt or sand, **alluvion**; retreat of the water-level, **dereliction**; or subsidence of the water-level, **reliction**. (Strictly the term 'accretion' signifies the process and alluvion is the material deposited). Land created by accretion belongs to the owner of the land to which it is annexed and, where relevant, the boundary in the centre of a stream or river is adjusted accordingly, even though the original boundary may still be ascertainable – Foster *v* Wright (1878) 4 CPD 438; Southern Centre of Theosophy Inc. *v* State of South Australia (1982) 1 All ER 238. cf **avulsion**. See also **accession**.
New Law Journal, 'Accretion, Avulsion and Diluvion', by H.W. Wilkinson pp. 1164–6. (16th December 1980).
 2. An increase in a sum of money or a fund by the addition of interest. Called also an 'accrual'.
 3. The increase in an inheritance or legacy arising when a co-heir or co-legatee dies.

accroissement (F)
 accretion (to property); increase. (*taux d' accroissement* – rate of increase).

accrual
 see **accretion**.

accrual accounting
 The preparation of accounts so that income and expenditure items are brought into the accounting period in which they are earned or incurred, rather than the period in which they are actually paid or received as cash. cf. **cash accounting**.

accrue
 To come into existence by an increase in something held; to occur as a natural result. To accumulate periodically or gradually, especially as an increase in a profit or loss. See also **accretion, sinking fund**.

accrued depreciation
 1. **Depreciation** that has been accumulated already in a company's financial statement. Called also 'accumulated depreciation'.
cf. **future depreciation**.
 (US) 2. The difference between the current cost of replacing a building and the present appraised value of that structure, i.e. a loss in value due to obsolescence up to the date of an appraisal. Called also 'diminished utility'. See also **replacement cost**.

accrued estate (or interest)
 An **estate** (or **interest**) in land that will come into effect with the passage of time; the interest 'accrues' when the instrument creating it becomes operative. See also **future interest, remainder, vest**.

accrued income
 Income earned but not yet received.

accrued interest
 Interest due; interest earned but not received. Interest that has been 'rolled-up'. See also **accrued estate, compound interest, 'rolled-up interest'**.

accumulated depreciation
see **accrued depreciation**.

accumulation
The reinvestment of **interest** as it accrues. The addition of interest to capital so as to provide an ever increasing sum of money which will be payable or receivable at a future date.
cf. **amortisation**. See also **accrued interest, compound interest, rule against perpetuities, sinking fund**.

accumulation of one per period
see **amount of one per period**.

accumulations, rule against
see **rule against perpetuities**.

accumulative rate
A low-risk rate of return, especially a rate of return considered as appropriate to provide for the replacement of a capital asset at its historic cost. A rate of return incorporated in a **dual-rate capitalisation factor**, to provide a sinking fund to replace the cost of a wasting asset. Thus, if an investor acquires a wasting asset, or an investment with a limited life, he may set aside a portion of the income receivable therefrom to be reinvested at an 'accumulative' rate of interest in order to replace the original cost of the investment. The rate may be expressed before or after taking account of the investor's liability for tax.
cf. **remunerative rate**. See also **sinking fund rate**.

achat (F)
purchase.
(*prix d'achat* – **purchase price**; cost price).

acheteur (F)
purchaser. See also *acquéreur*.

achèvements (F)
finishings (of a building).
(*travail en cours d'achèvement* – work in the process of completion).

acknowledgement
A declaration, usually made in front of a notary public or before a court of law, that a formal document made by the person who has signed it has been entered into voluntarily. A testator who has not attested his **will**, i.e. signed it in the presence of two witnesses, may later acknowledge his signature in the presence of two witnesses and thereby validate the will.
cf. **affidavit**. See also **assent, attest**.

acompte (F)
instalment; down-payment; part payment (of a debt).
(*acompte mensuel* – monthly instalment)
(*acompte de préférence, sur un immeuble* – option price, on a building).

acquéreur (F)
purchaser. In French law one who acquires title to immoveable property.

acquêts (F)
Defined by the French Civil Code, art. 1401 as "the acquisitions made jointly or separately by the spouses during the marriage, and deriving from their own industry or from savings out of the fruits and revenues of their own property"; whether moveable or immoveable property. French law recognises an important distinction between separate property (*bien propres*) which is owned prior to the marriage or subsequently acquired by gift or succession (*à titre gratuit*) (unless the donor has expressed a contrary intent) and may remain in the separate ownership of a spouse after marriage; and property that

becomes part of the *communauté* or *bien communs*, and is held as common property for the duration of the marriage. Any property acquired during the marriage by either spouse, whether by purchase (*à titre onéreux)*, or with funds derived from the *communauté* is normally an *acquêts* and in the event of a dissolution of the marriage is divided between the parties.

acquiescence

A tacit or passive **agreement** or **consent** to a course of action especially when there already exists a degree of active consent. 'There can only be acquiescence where there is knowledge. The court never binds parties by acquiescence where there is no knowledge' – Weldon *v* Dicks (1878) 10 Ch. D 262.

cf. **laches**. See also **assent, estoppel, waiver**.

acquiring authority

A public body that acquires, or is empowered to acquire, property by **compulsory purchase**.

acquisition

Derived from the Latin *acquisitio*, the seeking or getting for oneself. The act or process by which something is acquired or procured, especially as a consequence of a positive act. A term of no legal import but, in common usage, acquisition may refer to the taking or acquiring of title or ownership of property as a result of **purchase** (voluntarily or compulsorily); **inheritance**; **gift**; **accession**; **assignment**; **possession**; **bona vacantia** or **escheat**; or **dedication**. It is a positive act with a permanent result and in that strict sense may preclude a gift, inheritance or similar fortuitous gain. cf. **requisition**. See also **compulsory**

purchase, eminent domain, expropriation.

acquisition (F)

acquisition; the act of purchasing a property.

(*acquisition prescriptive* **adverse possession**). See also *prescription acquisitive*.

acquisition cost

The total expenditure incurred by a purchaser of property, i.e. the actual price paid (taking into account the net value of any exchange of properties), plus fees or commission paid to agents or brokers, legal fees, stamp duty or registration duty and any other incidental costs. 'Acquisition cost' and 'purchase cost' may be used synonymously; although the latter term usually refers to the amount paid as consideration for the purchase of a property excluding any additional or associated costs. See also **purchase price, closing costs**.

acquit (F)

receipt.

(*pour acquit* – received).

acquittance

A written discharge of a debt or obligation. It may take the form of a **receipt** or a formal contractual **discharge**. See also **accord and satisfaction**.

acquittement (d'une dette) (F)

satisfaction or payment (of a debt).

act of God

A sudden act arising directly and exclusively, from natural causes, and that cannot reasonably be foreseen or controlled by man, e.g. earthquake, storm, lightning, floods; 'something in opposition to the act of man' – Forward *v* Pittard (1785) LTR 27. An action that cannot be ordained by man. An act of God cannot be avoided by foresight or any reasonable measures; it is different from an inevitable accident, even though it may have happened at least once before. "Where goods are lost, destroyed, or damaged by an act of nature to which no man contributed, the loss is an act of God.... climatic changes of temperature, decay, and deterioration from the inherent nature of goods are operations of nature and acts of God as well as storms, lightning and tempest" – Pleet *v* Canadian Northern Quebec Railway Co. (1921) 50 OLR 230. An act of God therefore, is not the liability of a party in a claim for damages or insurance – it is said to 'prejudice no one'. An act of God may preclude parties from meeting a contractual obligation and is frequently covered for by insurance; although an insurer is not liable for acts of God unless he expressly accepts that risk. cf. **force majeure**. See also **strict liability,** *vis major*.

Act of Parliament

A statute or legal code approved by Parliament. See also **bill, statute law.**

acte (F)

instrument (especially a document in writing and signed); deed; attestation.
(acte à titre gratuit – **deed of gift; deed poll**)
(*acte attributif* – **deed of assignment**)
(*acte authentique* – authenticated document prepared in the presence of a notary or any other qualified functionary)
(*acte authentique de vente* – **conveyance.** For an outline of authentic and notarial deeds see *Introduction to French Law*, by Amos and Walton. pp. 24–25; and *Manuel de Droit Civil*, by Pierre Voirin et Gilles Goubeaux.

20 edn, p. 461 *et seq.*)
(acte de cession; acte de mutation; acte de transmission – conveyance or **transfer deed**)
(*acte de notaire; acte notarié* – notarial deed)
(*acte juridique* – writ)
(*acte de vente* – **bill of sale**; conveyance)
(*acte sous seing privé* – document under private seal, i.e. one not ratified by a notary)
(*actes de propriété* – title deeds; proof of ownership)
(*acte translatif du droit de propriété* – document of conveyance).

actif (F)

asset; assets.
(*actif défectible* – wasting asset)
(*actif immobilisé* – fixed asset)
(*actif liquide* – liquid asset)
(*valeur de l'actif* – asset value).
cf. *passif*.

actio in personam (L)

An **action** *'in personam'*.

actio in rem (L)

An **action** *in rem*.

actio personalis mortitur cum persona (L)

'A personal action dies with the person'. A principle of common law, but not the civil law, that an **action** *in personam* cannot subsist after the death of the individual concerned. This rule does not apply to an action resulting from a contract nor to an action arising from misappropriation of property. As a rule this principle no longer applies and most causes of action may survive or benefit a person's estate (Law Reform (Miscellaneous Provisions) Act 1934, s. 1).

action

A civil claim for one's right brought against another in a court of law. An action is started normally by a **writ** or such other form prescribed by the court. See also **action** *in personam*, **action** *in rem*, *chose*, **foreclosure**, **forfeiture**, *lis pendens*, **recovery**, **Statutes of Limitation**.

action (F)

1. **shares** (in a company).
2. **action** (at law).
(*action possessoire* – **possessory action**, see *réintégrande*)
(*action en revendication de son bien* – action for recovery of personal property)
(*action réelle* – real action, see **action** *in rem*).

action area

An area that a local planning authority considers should be included in a **local plan** either because it requires comprehensive treatment (by development or redevelopment) or it requires an improvement to the local amenities. In particular, an area that is considered to require treatment within a period of ten years (Town and Country Planning (Structure and Local Development Plans) Regulations 1974). See also **housing action area**.

action *in personam*

An action against a person, involving his personal rights as distinguished from his rights to property. Called also a 'personal action'.
cf. **action** *in rem*.

action *in rem*

An action for the recovery of property, rather than an action against a person. An action by which a person seeks an interest in a specific thing, but not to create a direct personal liability. An action *in rem* seeks to exert a right against any claimant to the thing; it is even said to be taken 'against the whole world'. See also **ejectment**, **foreclosure**, **real action**.

action price (US)

see **asking price**.

active partner

see **general partner**.

active trust

see **special trust**.

actual age

The age of a building based on its chronological date of construction.
cf. **effective age**.

actual authority

The **authority** given by a principal to his agent, either (a) in writing or (b) by implication. Actual authority may be implied from the terms or nature of the appointment, i.e. those duties or powers that are expected from the agent based on written authority or based on **usage** or **custom**.
cf. **ostensible authority**.

actual cash value

1. The fair or reasonable price paid for a property when it is sold entirely for cash in the normal course of business; as distinguished from a price obtained on compulsory purchase or condemnation, or at a forced sale. The **market value** that should be received when a property is offered for sale, for cash.
cf. **forced sale value**.
2. In insurance, the current value of a property in terms of cash. See also **replacement cost**.

actual cash value insurance (US)

see **replacement cost**.

actual notice

Notice that has been received by direct communication, whether oral or written, i.e. notice that has been brought expressly to a person's attention. Actual notice may include also such information as a person is likely to glean, or be aware of, by the nature of a transaction; notice **implied** from the knowledge and circumstances that affect the person with whom one is dealing. Actual notice may not be inferred from general negotiation, nor casual conversation, nor by proof that a person had **constructive notice**; it must be brought to the mind of a person so that he might have an intelligent apprehension of the subject matter, "in such a way that a reasonable man, or a man of business, would act upon the information so acquired … knowledge which would operate upon the mind of any rational man or man of business, and make him act with reference to the knowledge he has acquired." – Lloyd *v* Banks (1868) 37 LJ Ch. 882.

cf. **imputed notice**.

actual occupation

see **occupation**.

actual possession

see **possession**.

actual value (US)

The **fair market value** as used when referring to the value of property in condemnation proceedings.

actual yield

see **running yield**.

actualisé (F)

(*cash flow actualisé* – **discounted cash flow**).

(*valeur actualisé* – **capitalised value**; **net asset value**).

actuarial rate of return

see **internal rate of return**.

ad coelum usque ad centrum (or, *ad inferos*) (L)

'From heaven to the centre of the earth (or to hell)'. An historical view of the limits for the ownership of **land**. However, this principle has been rejected in most countries or overruled by statute law as an unreasonable extension of the right to private property. See also **air rights, mineral rights**.

ad filum viae (L)

'To the centre of a way'. See *ad medium filum*.

ad hoc (L)

'For a special purpose; for the purpose of the matter concerned'. See **overreached interest, trust for sale**.

ad idem (L)

'Of the same mind'; agreed. See **agreement**.

ad medium filum (L)

'To the centre line'. Used in defining a **boundary line** between two parcels of land on opposite sides of a road. It is generally assumed (unless there is evidence to the contrary) that the land under a highway is owned to the centre of the way by the adjoining owner; the surface being vested in the highway authority. (This rule normally does not apply to a railway). See also *ad medium filum aquae*.

ad medium filum aquae (L)

'To the middle of a stream or river'. Where a running stream or river forms the boundary between parcels of land, in separate ownership, the bed of the stream or river belongs *prima facie* to the land owners *ad medium filum aquae*. See also **ripar-**

ian rights, water rights.

ad valorem (L)

'According to value'. An *ad valorem* tax is one assessed according to the value of a property, or as a percentage of its cost. See also **registration duty, valued added tax**.

adaptability, special

see **special suitability**.

add-on factor (US)

see **loss factor**.

'add-on' interest rate

see **nominal interest rate**.

addition

Something added or joined to another, especially something in the nature of an **improvement** to a property that permanently increases or improves its value. What constitutes an addition to an existing building, as distinguished from the creation of something new, is a matter to be determined by looking at all of the circumstances. An addition to a building normally comprises something physically annexed to the building or, at least, something used in connection and closely associated with an existing building. "The erection of a new building in place of an old building is not an addition to or alteration of that old building." – Re Leveson – Gower's Settled Estate (1905) 2 Ch. 98. See also **accession fixture**.

additional rent

Any amount paid to a landlord by his tenant over and above the principal sum fixed as **rent** at the start of the tenancy. See also **indexed rent, overage, percentage rent, service charge**.

ademption

The failure or extinction of a **legacy** because of an act of, or affecting, the testator, or a deemed revocation of the gift, during the lifetime of the testator. For example, a sale or the destruction of the subject matter of the legacy. Ademption and **revocation** are used interchangeably in relation to a will although strictly ademption arises from an act of the testator and revocation from an external act, such as a statutory provision.

adequate compensation (US)

see **just compensation**.

adequate consideration

An amount of **consideration** that represents a fair and reasonable value for a benefit received. Adequate consideration may be distinguished from 'good consideration' which has no value but represents a motive for a contract, and from 'valuable consideration' which has pecuniary value but is not necessarily adequate for, or equal to, the benefit received. See also **market value**.

adhesion contract

A contract that is very one-sided, generally favouring the party who drafted it; a contract that is offered on a 'take it or leave it basis'. A contract that is established upon terms set down by the offeror, without subsequent negotiation or variation by the acceptor; the terms of the contract "have been dictated by that party whose bargaining power, either exercised alone or in conjunction with others providing similar goods or services enables him to say: 'If you want these goods or services at all, these are the only terms on which they are available. Take it or leave it.'" –

Schroder Music Co. Ltd. *v* Macaulay [1974] 3 All ER 624. See also *contra proferentum*, **standard-form contract, unconscionable bargain.**

adjacent

Derived from the Latin *adjacere*, 'lying near'. In close proximity but not necessarily touching; near to but not necessarily next to. "Adjacent means close to or near by or lying by: its significance or application in point of distance depends on the circumstances in which the word is used." – English China Clays *v* Plymouth Corporation [1974] 2 All ER 243. "Adjacent used in contrast to **adjoining** means lying near to the land, no actual contact being necessary" – *Boundaries and Fences*, by V. Powell-Smith. 2 edn, p. 12. See also **abut, contiguous.**

adjoining

Bounding or actually touching. In its legal and primary sense 'adjoining land' means "that which lies near so as to touch in some part land which it is said to adjoin. Of necessity it connotes contiguity." – Re Ecclesiastical Commissioners for England's Conveyance [1936] Ch. 440. However, a minor barrier, such as a path or track, need not prevent one parcel of land being considered as 'adjoining' another – Coventry *v* London, Brighton and South Coast Rail Co. (1867) LR 5 Eq. 105. In some instances, adjoining may mean near by, next door but one, or 'just across the way'. Adjoining, therefore, is a word which is liable to misinterpretation and should be avoided in contracts for the transfer of land. 'There are three words, 'adjoining', **adjacent**, and **contiguous,** which lie not far apart in the meaning which they convey. But of

no one of them can its meaning be stated with exactitude and without exception. As to 'adjoining' the expression 'next adjoining' or 'immediately adjoining' is common and legitimate. This expression at once conveys that two things may adjoin which are not next to each other." – Cave *v* Horsell [1912] 3 KB 544. It may be said that "lands are adjacent to a house or a town; fields are adjoining each other; and houses contiguous to each other" – Crabb's *English Synonyms* (1816). See also **abut,** *ad medium filum.*

adjoining owner

The owner of **adjoining** or **contiguous** land. See also **boundary line, encroachment, party-wall, tree, right of support.**

adjudicataire (F)

contracting party; successful bidder (at an auction sale).

adjudication

A decision on a matter that is in dispute as reached by a court of law or tribunal
cf. **arbitration.**

adjudication (aux enchères) (F)

sale (by public auction).
(*mise en adjudication* – tender; competitive tender)
(*adjudication publique* – open tender).

adjunction

The process of adding or annexing something, especially as a subordinate part. See also **accession, subordination.**

adjustable mortgage

Any form of mortgage loan which provides that the mortgagor's regular payments may vary or be changed during the term of the mortgage, such as a **variable-rate mortgage** or a **flexible-payment mortgage**.

adjustable-rate mortgage (ARM)
1. See **variable-rate mortgage**.
2. (US) A mortgage loan which provides that the mortgagee may vary the interest rate by up to 1 per cent at fixed intervals, without changing the amount of the morgagor's regular repayments.

adjusted cost basis (US)
see **book value, basis**.

adjusted gross income (US)
see **effective gross income**.

adjusted market price
A price paid for a property, increased or reduced to take account of extraneous aspects such as personal property, need of repair, etc., and thus used as a suitable comparable when preparing a valuation. See also **comparable property**.

adjusted sale price
The sale price of a property adjusted by deducting the vendor's costs (e.g. commission, closing costs, legal costs, etc.); that is, the true consideration received for a property. See also **purchase price**.

adjusted tax basis (US)
see **basis**.

adjustment of income and charges
see **apportionment, completion statement**.

administrateur (F)
director (usually of a limited company). (*administrateur foncier* – estate manager).

administration de biens (F)
property management.

administration of estates
The procedure by which the property

of a deceased person is dealt with in an orderly manner, including the payment of debts and the distribution, by the administrator or personal representative, of any surplus property to the persons beneficially entitled. See also **intestacy, will**.

administrative charge (or expense)
A charge or item of expenditure, incurred by a property owner, that is not directly related to ownership of a property, e.g. a company administration expense.
cf. **service charge**.

administrator (fem: administratrix)
Someone appointed by a court to administer the affairs of a person who dies without leaving a will, or someone appointed when no person has been nominated or is willing and able to act as an **executor** of a will (Supreme Court Act 1981, s. 116–119). See also **personal representative**.

adopted highway (or street)
see **adoption**.

adoption
1. The taking over, by a public authority, of the responsibility for the maintenance of a **highway** or **sewer**. A highway may be adopted following agreement between a developer and a highway authority, or the authority may be required to adopt a way over land as a highway provided it is constructed to a suitable standard. However, the authority may avoid adoption if it can be shown that the way will not get sufficient use to warrant its adoption at public expense (Highways Act 1980, ss 37, 38). The authority who takes over a highway is responsible for its upkeep and maintenance and becomes the owner of the surface of the land. The ownership of

the sub-soil remains unaltered and reverts unencumbered to the original possessor if and when the highway use is discontinued. A water authority may adopt a sewer either by a declaration vesting the sewer in itself or by an agreement with the owner. The sewer may still be used by those using it before, but it is maintainable by the authority as a public sewer (Public Health Act 1936, s. 17 and 18). Ownership of a public sewer is vested in the appropriate authority for so long as the sewer exists; thereafter the land reverts unencumbered to the original owner. See also **dedication**. *Development and Planning Law*, by Barry Denyer-Green. p. 216, 228 (1982).

2. The taking over, by a trustee in bankruptcy or a liquidator, of the right to complete a contract that remains incomplete at the time of a bankcruptcy or liquidation.

advance
1. A rise or increase in value.
2. A payment made before the due date. A pre-payment or payment on account. See also **deposit, interim payment, premium, rent in arrears (or in advance)**.
3. A sum of money granted for a specific purpose, especially as a **loan**, or as part of a loan; including additional funds granted under an **open-end mortgage**. See also **construction loan, tacking**.
(US) 4. Money paid by the beneficiary of a **trust deed**, to meet real estate taxes, insurance premiums, etc., so as to protect the beneficiary's interest in the subject matter of that deed.

advance commission
see **advance fee**.

advance commitment
see **commitment**.

advance factory
A factory built before there is a known tenant or occupier, especially when this is done to entice industry to a particular area or district.

advance fee (or commission)
A **fee** or **commission** paid in anticipation of a service, but before the service is rendered, e.g. a fee paid to an agent before a property is offered for sale. Such a fee may be illegal (Accommodation Agencies Act 1953, s. 1) or may be contrary to the **code of conduct** of a professional organisation. See also **accommodation agent**.

advance refinancing
see **refinancing**.

advance service charge
An advance payment made by a tenant towards his estimated share of the **service charge** for a building. Generally this payment is made, in addition to the **rent**, when a tenant takes possession of the demised premises, or at the start of the landlord's financial year. A balancing payment is paid, or repaid, when the tenant's actual service charge liability is ascertained. See also **primary and secondary rental**.

adverse gearing (or leverage)
see **reverse leverage**.

adverse land use (US)
see **non-conforming use**.

adverse occupation
see **squatting, trespass**.

adverse possession
The open, continuous and peaceful **possession** of real property in a manner that is inconsistent with the

rights of a true owner, or of a person entitled to possession as of right; especially when that possession bars the true owner's right to recover his land. Such possession may arise *ab initio*, as when someone enters on to land as a squatter; it may arise when the paper owner apparently relinquishes possession and another takes up possession; or it may arise when a person remains in possession after his legal right has come to an end.

However, adverse possession cannot arise merely because land is vacant; a person must have taken possession of the land against the right of the legal possessor – Moses *v* Lovegrove [1953] 2 QB 533. **Title** to property may be acquired, or strictly a person's title to property may be extinguished, by a period of unchallenged and adverse possession; in particular, for a period of time prescribed by the **Statutes of Limitation**. For example, the Limitation Act 1980, s. 15 (1) provides that (except in cases of **fraud**, concealment or **mistake**) "No action shall be brought by any person to recover any land after the expiration of twelve years from the date on which the right of action accrues to him or, if it first accrued to some person through whom he claims, to that person." Thus, the effect is negative and bars the right of another to land. Unlike **prescription**, a right is not acquired by adverse possession; the possessor merely reaches a stage at which no further claim can be made against him. Land must ultimately belong to someone (in English law ultimately the Crown), therefore, the Statutes of Limitation effectively provide for a recognition of a tacit change of ownership; whereas a prescriptive right is newly created.

Adverse possession changes title to land; prescription makes or prescribes a servitude over land. Adverse occupation of the surface of land may ripen into ownership by adverse possession; adverse use of land may create a right by prescription.

The principle behind the law of adverse possession is to reinforce the possessor's ultimate title to property; *adversus extraneos vitiosa possessio prodesse solet*, 'prior possession is a good title of ownership against all who cannot show a better'. It is intended also to cure any inadvertent error in the conveyancing of unregistered land; in particular, errors relating to boundaries. Adverse possession purports to bring the reality of possession into play, rather than leaving paper title as the perpetual determinant of ownership. Accordingly, "all statutes of limitation have for their object the prevention of the rearing up of claims at great distances of time when evidences are lost; and in all well-regulated countries the quieting of possession is held an important point of policy." – Dundee Harbour Trustees *v* Dougall (1852) 1 Macq. 317. H.L. It has been said, "that it is a policy of the Limitation Acts that those who go to sleep upon their claims should not be assisted by the courts in recovering their property, but another, and I [Streatfield, J.] think, equal policy behind the Acts, is that there shall be an end of litigation, and that protection shall be afforded against stale demands." – R.B. Policies at Lloyd's *v* Butler [1950] 1 KB 81. A person who holds such a title, a **possessory title**, acquires a right to property that is good against anyone except a person with a better title and, with the failure of that better title, the possessory title matures into an **absolute title**. Title to registered land can be acquired by adverse possession but the adverse possessor cannot acquire a **legal estate** until that party is registered as the proprietor.

Adverse possession requires an intention to oust the true owner, *animus possidendi*, not the causing of inconvenience by a minor act of trespass; but, what constitutes that intent is, in the final analysis, a question of fact and degree. There must be "the intention, in one's own name and on one's own behalf, to exclude the world at large, including the owner." – Powell *v* McFarlane and Another 38 (1979) P. and CR 471. (A squatter in a Greater London Council property who paid rates was not held to be seeking to establish adverse possession – R. *v* Edwards [1978] Crim. LR 49). The period of limitation does not start to run until the true owner has been dispossessed by the intentional taking of possession by another, and therefore the possession must be continuous; although occupation by a succession of persons may be counted, provided there is a period of continuous occupation, and the successive persons are claiming one from another. However, the existence of a former adverse occupation is not available "for the possible benefit in time to come of some casual interloper or lucky vagrant." – Trustees, Executors and Agency Co. Ltd., *v* Short (1888) 13 App. Cas. 798. In summary, to acquire a good title by adverse possession it is necessary to show who was the true owner; that he has been barred by lapse of time: without fraud, deliberate concealment, or a mistake; and, in the final analysis, that a court will uphold that title.

In the US where such possession is called also hostile possession or distinct possession, or is predicated by 'open and notorious possession', the function of the Statute of Limitations is to go beyond barring an existing right, it aims to confer ownership on the adverse possessor. Most states require 10 or 20 years continuous and uninvited possession before a person can claim a possessory title. In some states the civil law requirement of **good faith** is adopted, i.e. the claimant must at the outset have gained possession honestly believing that he or she had a right to the property; otherwise a longer period (up to 30 years) of possession is required.

In French law the possessor (*possessoire*) is presumed to be the owner until rebutted by another; he must exercise his possession *nec vi, nec clam, nec precario*, 'neither by force, nor stealth, nor licence' and it must be continuous. Subject to those basic conditions, the possessor of immoveable property obtains a title by a *prescription acquisitive* ('acquisitive prescription' or '**usucapion**'). In general, in French law, a person who acquires land requires 10 to 20 years to bar any other claimant; providing he does so in 'good faith'; otherwise the period is extended to 30 years. See also **bona fide, dispossession, fraud, squatting**. Amos & Walton's Introduction to French Law 3 edn. p. 100–104.
Handbook of the Law of Real Property, by William E. Burby. 3 edn, pp. 267–280.
Real Property and Real People, by K. Gray and P. Symes. (1981) p. 93.
Megarry's Manual of the Law of Real Property 6 edn. p. 520–531.
Cheshire's Modern Law of Property 13 edn. p. 826–831.

The Law of Real Property, by Robert Megarry and H.W.R. Wade. 5 edn, pp. 1033–1056.

adverse user (US)

Use of property without licence or permission; a precursor to a claim for a right over land by **prescription**. See also **adverse possession, prescription,** *prescription acquisitive*, **squatting**.

adversus extraneos vitiosa possessio prodesse solet (L)

'Prior possession is a good title of ownership against all who cannot show a better title'. See **adverse possession**.

advertisement

A note, sign, label, showcard, announcement, representation, exhibit or any similar format used to call attention to, or warn someone (usually the general public) of, an item, product, fact or even a fiction. A means used to make something generally or publicly known, or to give public notice of something. An advertisement may be transmitted orally, in writing, in print, by sound or by light waves. It is commonly a public notice published or broadcast with the aim of enticing people to purchase goods or services, or to make some thing or fact generally known.

The placing of outdoor advertisements is controlled by the Town and Country Planning Acts and regulations made thereunder. For this purpose an advertisement is defined as, "any word, letter, model, sign, placard, board, notice, device or representation, whether illuminated or not, in the nature of, and employed wholly or partly for the purpose of advertisement, announcement or direction and (without prejudice to preceding provisions of this definition) includes any hoarding or similar structure used, or adapted for use, for the display of advertisements" (Town and Country Planning Act 1971, s. 290 (1)). The erection of an advertising hoarding and the display of an advertisement is likely to be a **material change in the use of land** (and the display of an advertisement on the external part of any building that is not used normally for that purpose is always a 'material change in the use') for which **planning permission** is required (Town and Country Planning Act 1971, s 22 (1), (4), 23). However, the display of advertisements is controlled more specifically by regulations made in accordance with the provisions of Section 63 of the 1971 Act, such as the Town and Country Planning (Control of Advertisements) Regulations 1969, as amended by the Town and Country Planning Control (Amendment) Regulations of 1972, 1974 and 1975, and if consent for the display of an advertisement is obtained under those regulations planning permission is deemed to be granted (1971 Act, s. 64). For this purpose the definition of advertisement is the same as that in the 1971 Act, s. 290 (1) but, "any such thing employed wholly as a memorial or railway signal" is expressly excluded (1969 Regulations, reg. 2 (1)). These regulations state that certain forms of advertisement are exempted from the operation of the regulations and that other forms of advertisement, are "deemed" to be authorised (unless or until the authority seeks to revoke that deemed authority "in the interests of **amenity** or public safety" by the service of a discontinuance notice, a practice sometimes known as a challenge procedure). Consent to all other forms of advertisement must be obtained from the local planning authority, although such consent may be withheld only "in the interests of amenity or public safety" (Town and Country Planning Act 1971, s. 63 (1)). The types of advertisement that are specifically excluded from the regulations are, broadly, (a) advertisements inside a building or not readily visible from the outside of an enclosed area of land; (b) advertisements (that are not illuminated or visible from outside) displayed within a building not used principally for the display of advertisements; (c) advertisements on a vehicle that is normally mobile; (d) advertisements forming part of the fabric of a building that is not normally used for advertising; (e) advertisements less than 0.1 square metres in size, on goods for sale or containers or dispensers for such goods. Consent is "deemed" to be granted by the regulations for a number of minor advertisements such as functional advertisements of a local authority; temporary estate agent's boards, business name plates; hotel or inn signs; advertisements on the forecourt of business premises; flags identifying a business owner; provided these are within specified limits as to size. Consent is not required for the display of certain special advertisements, such as election posters, traffic signs and statutory notices and such advertisements cannot be challenged by a local authority. Advertisements displayed on 1 August 1948 need not be removed provided they meet certain conditions, unless they are challenged. Stricter rules apply in an **area of special control**, or in a **conserva**tion area, where, as a rule, no advertisements may be displayed and any proposal to display an advertisement that requires consent must be advertised publicly, objections or representations considered, and usually a public inquiry held to consider any such objections or representations. See also **general offer, invitation to treat, tender, purchase notice**.

Planning Law and Procedure, by A.E. Telling. 6 edn, pp. 191–195.

An Outline of Planning Law, by Desmond Heap. 8 edn, pp. 166–175.

advocate

A person who pleads a case on behalf of another, especially a person who is learned in the law and offers advice and pleads cases in a court of law. See also **attorney, barrister, lawyer**.

advowson

In English ecclesiastical law, a right to present a fit person to a bishop so that he may be admitted to a certain **benefice**. The person holding this right, the 'patron', is considered to have a form of real property. See also **land**.

aedificare in tuo proprio non licet quod alteri noceat (L)

'No one is permitted to build on his own land so as to interfere with the rights of others'. See **ancient light, natural rights**.

aedificatum solo, solo cedit (L)

'That which is built on the **land** goes with the land'. See also **fixture**.

aesthetic

A word, derived from the Greek, originally meaning a perception of the senses. More recently it has come to mean criticism or appreciation of beauty; relating to sensual cognizance. (Kant's description of 'beauty' in *Critique of Aesthetic Judgement* conveys a similar meaning, "that which, apart from a concept, pleases universally"). A term used widely in architecture and town planning for that which is pleasing, or is considered by common opinion to be pleasing to the eye; especially that which is in unison with the environment i.e. with natural rather than purely man-made features. An authority that is in a position to grant permission for a new development generally has regard to that which is aesthetic; but, "planning authorities should recognise that aesthetics is an extremely subjective matter. They should not therefore impose their tastes on developers simply because they believe them to be superior." – Department of the Environment Circular 22/80.

affaire (F)
1. **bargain**; deal; business.
(*chiffre d'affaires* – turnover)
(*valeur d'une affaire qui marche* – **going-concern value**)
2. legal action; dispute. See also *gestion d' affaires*.

affectation (F)
appropriation; charge; allotment (of shares).

affermage (F)
lease or **rent** (especially of a farm).
(*affermer* – to lease; especially a farm at a rent independent of the produce)
See also *bail à ferme*, *fermage*, *metayage system*.

affidavit
Derived from the Latin *affidave*, 'to pledge one's faith (*fides*)'. A written declaration sworn before a notary or similar public official, of a known or believed fact or an expert opinion.

See also **statutory declaration**.

affirmation
1. A declaration or signification of what is, as of fact rather than opinion. **Acceptance**, concurrence or agreement as when a person affirms or accepts a voidable contract. Affirmation of a contract occurs in particular when a contract is entered into as a consequence of a misrepresentation and the party entitled to rescind the contract accepts, either expressly or impliedly, but in full knowledge of the facts, that he will forego his right to rescission of the contract. See also **ratification**.
2. A formal declaration that a statement is true. See also **affidavit**.

affirmative easement (US)
see **easement**.

'affixed to land'
see **fixture**.

afforestation
The turning of open land into forestry.
cf. **assart**.

after-acquired clause (US)
A clause in a mortgage deed which provides that any property acquired by the mortgagor, while the mortgage debt is outstanding, will become additional security for that debt.

after-tax cash flow (US)
see **cash flow**.

agence (F)
agency, used to refer especially to an office or a commercial service rather than, as in English law, to the relationship created.
(*agence immobilier* – **estate agency**).

agency
A relationship whereby one person (a

principal) appoints or authorises another (an **agent**), expressly or impliedly, to act on his or her behalf to bring about an agreement or transaction affecting a third party so as to alter the legal position of the principal. Agency is a relationship that goes beyond mere employment, because the consequence of the agent's action is to create a legal relationship (whether in the form of a contract or a transfer of an interest in property) between the principal and a third party. In effect, agency may give rise to two contracts; the contract whereby the agent is appointed (called as a **power of attorney**) and the contract induced by the agent. This relationship is polarised when the agent concludes a duty entrusted to him, for any gain or benefit of the agent's activity goes to the principal; the agent's appointment is then terminated or satisfied and the principal takes over any contractual liability or benefit arising thereafter.

A contract of agency is one that requires **good faith**; however, it may be considered more analogous to a trust, rather than a mere contract, in view of the type of relationship created (although a trustee is not the beneficiary's representative and, in most respects, is under a stricter duty to account for all his actions to the beneficiary). The relationship of agency may be terminated when the agent has fulfilled the duties for which he was appointed; the expiration of an agreed time limit for **performance**; by mutual agreement; by the death or incapacity of either party; if the performance of the agent's duties is frustrated; or by an express **revocation** of the agent's authority (provided the agency is not coupled with a subsist-ing interest). See also **agency of necessity, dual agency, listing, ratification, time is of the essence**.

Anson's Law of Contract, 26 edn, pp. 529–567.

The Law of Estate Agency and Auctions, by J.R. Murdoch 2 edn.

An Outline of the Law of Agency, by B.S. Markensis and R.J.C. Munday (1979).

Fridman's The Law of Agency 5 edn.

Bowstead on Agency 14 edn.

1 Halsbury's Laws of England 4 edn., paras. 701–887.

agency agreement

An agreement by which the relationship of **agency** is expressly brought into effect. An agreement by which a principal sets out the terms for the appointment of an agent. See also **power of attorney**.

agency by estoppel

see **estoppel, ostensible authority**.

agency of necessity

An action taken by one person, on behalf of another, on the grounds of urgent necessity so as to bring into existence a relationship that is akin to **agency**; especially when there is already a relationship between the parties. In particular when, on behalf of his principal, an agent takes an action that is considered to be in the best interest of the principal, but for which he has no **actual authority**; such as an action taken in an emergency and in **good faith**, when an agent is unable to communicate with his principal – China Pacific S.A. *v* Food Corporation of India, The Winston [1981] 3 All ER 688. Agency of necessity may arise also when there is no relationship between the parties but a mere stranger acts out of positive necessity, in a manner similar to an authorised agent, in order to prevent a loss by another. For example, an action taken to prevent damage or deterioration to another's property, especially when the person taking the action has some right or interest in the property such as a bailee who sells perishable goods to preserve the monetary worth entrusted to him. The necessity should arise out of something stronger than mere inconvenience; it should be more an obligation combined with a necessity to spend money. In English law the courts prefer to construe an act of an agent that binds his principal as an extension of his authority, by implication, rather than accepting that a new authority has been created 'as of necessity'. See also **quasi-contract**.

The Law of Estate Agency and Auctions, by J.R. Murdoch 2 edn, pp. 39–43.

Chitty on Contract, 25 edn para. 226.

agent

A person (the agent) authorised by another, (the **principal**) to act on his behalf, or in his place, in establishing a legal relationship, with a third party. The term 'agent' is sometimes used to refer to a principal who calls himself an agent, so that it has been said, "no word is more commonly and constantly abused than agent" – Kennedy *v* De Trafford [1897] AC 188. However, properly speaking an agent is someone appointed, expressly, impliedly, or ostensibly, to act for another, and who is authorised to act only within the limits of the terms of that appointment. An agent may even be a person who acts for another, initially without an **actual authority**, provided his actions are ratified subsequently by that other party. An act of an agent, done within the limitation of his **authority** (express or implied), is binding on his principal; thus, an agent is a person who is sandwiched contractually between two parties, his principal and the third party with whom he establishes (or endeavours to establish) a contractual relationship. However, once an agent has established an agreement on behalf of his principal, he drops out and leaves the principle as the sole contracting party; the rule is that the principal has entered into, and may sue or be sued upon, the contract made by his agent. (Exceptions to this rule may arise when there is a contrary intention; when the agent intends to be bound; or when there is an undisclosed principal or, possibly, if there is an unnamed principal).

An agent's 'authority' may arise expressly from the principal; it may arise by implication; or it may arise sometimes as a matter of sheer necessity: an **agency of necessity**. The express authority of an agent "is to be found within the four corners of the instrument (by which the authority is granted), either in express terms or by necessary implication" – Bryant, Powis and Bryant Ltd. *v* La Banque de Peuple [1893] AC 177. This instrument is called an **agency agreement** or **power of attorney**. An agent's implied authority may arise from a matter that is incidental to the proper performance of his duties; from the very nature of his position; from the **custom** or trade **usage** of the business in which he is involved; or, "when it is inferred from the conduct of the parties and the circumstances of the case, such as when the board of directors appoint one of their members to be managing director. They thereby impliedly authorise him to do all such things as fall within the usual scope of that office" – Hely-Hutchinson *v* Brayhead Ltd. [1968] 1 QB 583.

A person who purports to have authority as an agent and enters into a contract cannot later endeavour to prove that there is no contract merely because he had no authority. If an agent enters into a contract outside his authority, express or implied, without the knowledge of his principal, he is liable to fulfil that contract. However, a principal, in certain circumstances, may ratify an agent's action after the event; unless at the outset the agent failed to indicate that he was acting for another – Keighley, Maxsted and Co. *v* Durant [1901] AC 240. Further, "there is nothing to prevent an agent from entering into a contract on the basis that he is himself liable to perform it as well as his principal." – International Railway Co. *v* Niagara Parks Commission [1941] AC 342.

An agent's responsibility to his principal extends beyond that of a normal contract; there is a **fiduciary** relationship, one based on trust. An agent is responsible for keeping his principal informed of any matter that affects the authority entrusted to him and he is obliged by the nature of his position to avoid any conflict of interest or making any secret profit which may be at his principal's cost. An agent should inform his principal if he (the agent) is acting for another party who may be involved in a transaction for which the agent is appointed to act; as a rule he should not act for both sides on a sale of property (although see **dual agency**);

and he must inform his principal of any other matter that is relevant to the proper performance of his duties. An agent owes a special duty of care to his principal similar to that due from any professional advisor to his client, and an agent cannot escape a liability for his own **tort** by claiming that he is acting on behalf of another. Any money received by an agent, unless there is an agreement to the contrary, is the property of the principal and must be handed over to the principal (as to the retention of interest thereon, see **stakeholder**). An agent may be (i) 'universal' – when the authority covers all matters relating to the principal's business; (ii) 'general' – when the authority applies to a group of related matters especially when those matters arise in the ordinary course of a business or profession or out of an appointment to act for the benefit or profit of a principal in a certain area of business, e.g. the duties of a **managing agent**; or (iii) 'special' – when the agent is appointed to perform a specific task designated by the principal e.g. an agent appointed to sell a house.

An agent conducting real estate business is bound to the same formalities as his principal when entering into a contract. Thus an agent cannot execute a deed unless his appointment is made under seal – Powell *v* London Provincial Bank [1893] 2 Ch. 568.

cf. **contractor, trustee.** See also **accommodation agent, agency, auctioneer, broker, estate agent, factor, land agent, sub-agent**.

agent **(F)**

agent, in French law a term of more general application than in English law.

(*agent de location* – house agent).

(*agent exclusif* – exclusive agent).

(*agent immobilier* – estate agent). See also *exclusif*, **mandat**.

agent of necessity

see **agency of necessity**.

agglomération (F)

urban or built-up area; agglomeration. (agglomération d'unités urbaines – **conurbation**).

aggravated damages

see **damages**.

aggregation

The adding together of units to make a whole, such as adding the value of assets together for taxation purposes. See also **component valuation, hotchpot**.

agistment or egistment

An ancient term for an arrangement whereby a person, an agister, permits horses and cattle to pasture on his land in return for payment. Agistment is a form of **bailment** of cattle for the purpose of grazing and feeding of cattle. Under the **feudal system** agistment applied specifically to cattle agisted on the Sovereign's land.

agrarian

Relating to land, especially **agricultural land**.

agréé (F)

A legal representative, who normally acts in the commercial court. See also *avocat*.

agreement

An arrangement made between two or more parties by which they signify their assent, whether in writing or otherwise, to a course of action, or to a distinct intention, that affects the parties. A common understanding on an objective **cause**. The reaching of a harmonious understanding on a point of view – a concord of undertaking and intention between two or more parties. Agreement is said to be reached when there is a meeting of minds, *consensus ad idem*. "'*Aggreamentum*' (agreement) is a word compounded of two words – *viz* of *aggregatio* and *mentium*, so that *aggreamentum est aggregatio mentium in re aliqua factum vel facienda* [agreement is a combining of minds in respect of the thing to be accomplished]. And so by the contraction of two words, and by the short pronunciation of them, they are made one word, *viz aggreamentum*, which is no other than the union, collection, and copulation of two or more minds in anything done or to be done." – Reniger *v* Fogassa (1550) Plowd. 17a. An agreement may be **express** or may be **implied** from the conduct of the parties; "if, whatever a man's real intention may be, he so conducts himself that a reasonable man would believe that he was assenting to the terms proposed by the other party, and that other party upon that belief enters into the contract with him, the man thus conducting himself would be equally bound as if he had intended to agree to the other man's terms." – Smith *v* Hughes (1871) L.R. 6 QB 607. An agreement may be implied also from other circumstances, such as the normal course of dealing or trade usage. An agreement may be distinguished from a **contract** because the former is only one element in the legal relationship created by the latter and although every contract is an agreement not every agreement is a contract; i.e. an agreement need not be intended as a legally enforceable arrangement, but a contract is.

An agreement for the sale of land or an interest in land which creates a contract that is capable of being the subject of an action in a court is referred to as a **contract for sale**. A formal agreement that creates a tenancy is a **lease**, unless it is lacking in some respect and creates no more than an **agreement for a lease**. 'Agreement for sale' may be used for a contract that cannot be the subject of an action at law. An agreement for the sale of goods is a sale if absolute, but if subject to a condition it is referred to as an **agreement to sell**. An agreement may be given to the variation, putting an end to, or discharge of a contract; but, if a contract is made in **writing** it may be varied only in writing – Goss v Lord Nugent (1833) 2 LJKB 127. See also **bargain, promise**.

agreement for a lease

A **contract** entered into between two parties whereby the one promises to grant and the other to accept a **lease**, but no formal lease is brought into existence. "A contract for a lease is not in itself a **demise**, but is merely an agreement that the intending lessor shall grant a lease and the intending lessee shall accept the same. Such a contract does not of itself create a legal relationship of landlord and tenant, but it has long been established that so soon as the tenant enters under [the terms of] the agreement the relationship arises and he becomes a tenant at will. When he pays, or expressly agrees to pay, any part of the annual rent thereby reserved, his **tenancy at will** changes into a **tenancy from year to year**, upon the terms of the intended lease, so far as they are applicable to and not inconsistent with a yearly tenancy. The same rule applies to entry under a void lease." (Woodfall's *Landlord and Tenant* 28 edn. paras 1–0007). An agreement for a lease is enforceable in **equity** provided (a) there is a definite agreement between the parties (not merely an agreement to agree) on all the matters relevant to a lease (the commencement date, term, parties, property and rent); and (b) there is a **memorandum** or **note** in **writing** evidencing the agreement, or an act of **part performance** suggesting unequivocally that an agreement has been reached (Law of Property Act 1925, s. 40).

An agreement for a lease has certain shortcomings when compared to a formal lease: (a) it is dependent upon the courts exercising their discretion in granting a decree of **specific performance** to enforce the agreement – Coatsworth v Johnson (1886) 55.LJQB 220; Warmington v Miller [1973] QB 877; (b) it is enforceable only between the original parties to the agreement and, as there is no **privity of estate**, the landlord cannot enforce the covenants against an assignee i.e. the burden of the contract is not assignable; (c) any **implied easement** and other benefit granted to a tenant under a formal lease (being a **conveyance**) is not created under an agreement for a lease (Law of Property Act 1925, s. 62); (d) the agreement may not be enforceable against a *'bona fide* **purchaser'** for value of a legal estate' i.e. it may not be enforceable against the purchaser of the landlord's interest or another lessee unless the tenant's right is protected by regis-

tration as a **land charge**; and (e) an ejected tenant (being one who only had a tenancy at will and is not subject to any statutory rights protecting his occupation of the premises) may sue the landlord for damages for breach of contract, but he cannot normally recover the land. In addition, the covenants and conditions of the agreement may remain issues for continuing dispute and contention between the parties unless or until a formal lease, or some better form of agreement, is established. Further, an agreement for a lease may not be enforceable if it ought properly have been made by deed e.g. a lease by a corporation; a lease without consideration; or a lease of an incorporeal hereditament. An agreement for a lease is called also a 'contract for lease' or a 'contract for a tenancy'. See also **equitable lease, usual covenant.**
Adkin's Landlord and Tenant 18 edn, p. 34–39.
The Law of Landlord and Tenant, by D.J. Evans. 2 edn, pp. 41–56.
The Law of Real Property, by Robert Megarry and H.W.R. Wade. 5 edn, pp. 638–645.
27 Halsbury's Laws of England 4 edn, p. 48–81.
Woodfall's Landlord and Tenant 28 edn. paras. 1–0314 to 1–0436.
The Law of Landlord and Tenant by *Hill and Redman's*, 17 edn, pp. 100–25.

agreement for sale
An **agreement**, upon the principal terms for the sale of property, that has not been put into a legally binding contract; in particular, an agreement for the sale of real property set out in correspondence as **subject to contract**, or an agreement that may not have been made subject to the proper formalities. This form of agreement should be distinguished from an **estate contract**, a **conditional contract**, or a **contract of sale**, all of which, as a rule, are contracts capable of legal enforcement. See also **contract for sale, writing.**

agreement for sale and purchase (US)
see **instalment contract.**

agreement of sale
1. see **contract of sale.**
(US) 2. see **contract for deed.**

agreement, planning
see **planning agreement.**

agreement to agree
see **conditional contract.**

agreement to sell
see **contract of sale.**

agricultural building allowance
A form of **capital allowance** permitted in respect of expenditure incurred on the construction of farm buildings.

agricultural holding
In ordinary usage an area of "land used for agricultural purposes" – Kemp *v* Ballachulish Estate Co. Ltd. (1933) SC 488. In particular, "the aggregate of the **agricultural land** comprised in a contract of tenancy, not being a contract under which the said land is let to the tenant during his continuance in any office, appointment or employment held under the landlord" (Agricultural Holdings Act 1948, s. 1 (1)). A cottage used to house a farm labourer may be part of the "aggregate of the agricultural land" comprised in a tenancy and thus form part of an agricultural holding – Blackmore *v* Butler [1954] 2 QB 171. See also **agriculture, agricultural**

property, **agricultural tenancy**..
Scammell and Denshaw's Law of
Agricultural Holdings 6 edn.
Agricultural Holdings, by J. Muir
Watt, 12 edn.

Agricultural Holdings Acts

Statutes, especially the Agricultural
Holdings Act 1948 and the Agricultural Holdings (Notices to Quit) Act
1977, that set out restrictions on the
grant and termination of an **agricultural tenancy** and the rights and
duties of the parties to such tenancies.
See also **agricultural holding**.
The Law relating to Agriculture, by
Ian Stephenson (1975) Ch. 2.
Halsbury's Statutes, 4 edn, vol. 1.

agricultural land

Land used for the trade or business of
agriculture, including arable, pasture
and meadow land, land used for keeping and breeding livestock, including
poultry; as well as a **market garden,
allotment**, woodland, or orchard
(Agricultural Holding Act 1948, s. 1).
In certain English Statutes, (e.g. the
General Rate Act 1967, s. 26 and the
Agriculture Act 1947, s. 109) 'agricultural land' specifically excludes land
used for recreation or sport, land in
units under one quarter of an acre,
and any private garden. See also **agricultural holding, agricultural property**.

Agricultural Lands Tribunals

Tribunals, first established under the
Agriculture Act 1947, s. 73, Sch. 9,
whose powers were extended by the
Agriculture Act 1958, s. 8, Sch. 1.
These tribunals deal, *inter alia*, with
matters referred to them under the
Agricultural Holding Acts, in particular requests to terminate tenancies
granted statutory protection; the fixing of rent by arbitration upon the

renewal of a letting covered by the
statutes; and such landlord and
tenant disputes as claims of bad husbandry or tenant's requests to carry
out improvements. See also **agricultural tenancy**.

agricultural licence

see **grazing licence**.

Agricultural Mortgage Corporation (AMC)

A body established in 1929, under the
Agricultural Credits Act 1928, whose
principal objective is making long-
term mortgage loans for the purchase
or improvement of agricultural property, and for providing working capital secured on agricultural property.
Loans granted by the AMC are restricted to farmers and are granted for
terms of 5 to 40 years in the case of
farms, and up to 60 for forestry purposes. See also **Land Improvements
Company**.

agricultural property

Property used for the purpose of agriculture. 'Agricultural property' has
been defined by the Finance Act 1894,
s. 22 (1) (g) (a statute dealing with
estate duty) as "**agricultural land**, pasture and woodland including cot-
tages, farm buildings, farm houses,
and mansion houses (together with
land occupied therewith) as are of
character appropriate to the property".

agricultural tenancy

A **tenancy** of an **agricultural holding**;
that is, a tenancy of **agricultural land**
used for the purposes of a business or
trade. An agricultural tenancy may
arise from a letting of land, or from an
agreement for the letting of land,
(including certain leases for life) and
may be a tenancy for a term of a year
or from year to year (Agricultural

Holdings Act 1948, s. 1, 94 (1) as amended by the Agricultural Holding Act 1984, s. 1). An agricultural tenancy enjoys **security of tenure** and protection against the landlord charging an unduly high rent. This statutory protection for agricultural tenants was introduced first in the Landlord and Tenant Act 1851 and is now contained in the Agricultural Holdings Act 1948 (as amended, in particular, by the Agricultural Holdings (Miscellaneous) Provisions Act 1976, the Agricultural Holdings Act (Notice to Quit) Act 1977 and the Agricultural Holdings Act 1984).

Any letting, or agreement to let land, for use as agricultural land, made on or after 1st March 1948, (other than land forming part of agricultural **tied accommodation**, which is subject to separate statutory controls) for an interest less than a tenancy from year to year, or granted on a licence, becomes a tenancy from year to year; unless the land has been let for a specified period of less than a year for the purpose of grazing or mowing (a **grazing licence**), or the letting has been approved, as an exception, by the Minister of Agriculture, Fisheries and Food (in practice, approval is given by the County Agricultural Executive Committees). When a letting of agricultural land is made for a term of two years or more, then *prima facie* it continues at the end of the term as a tenancy from year to year. Thus, apart from a 'grazing licence'; a letting approved by the Minister; and a letting for more than one year but less than two years – Gladstone *v* Baver [1960] 2 QB 384; any other letting of agricultural land is an 'agricultural tenancy' and continues as a tenancy from year to year until

terminated by a notice to quit given in accordance with the statutory provisions and on one of the specified statutory **grounds for possession** and, in most cases, with the prior consent of the Agricultural Land Tribunal (Agricultural Holdings (Notice to Quit) Act 1977, ss 2, 3 as amended by Agricultural Holdings Act 1984, s. 6).

If the tenancy is brought to an end, the tenant may have a right to **compensation for disturbance** and either the landlord or the tenant may demand that the rent for a new tenancy be fixed by arbitration. The rent fixed by the arbitrator is to be based on the rent payable for any "comparable letting" (whether fixed by agreement or by arbitration, but disregarding (a) the fact that the tenant is in occupation; (b) any effect of an increase in value due to an improvement made or fixed equipment added, at the tenant's expense (unless carried out as a condition of the grant of the tenancy); (c) any landlord's improvement that has been grant aided by central or local government; (d) any reduction in rent arising from dilapidations, deterioration or damage to the property due to the tenant's actions; (e) any premium; and (f) any scarcity factor affecting the rent of a comparable holding; but taking account of all other relevant factors, including the "earning capacity" of the holding (Agricultural Holdings Act 1948, s. 8, as amended by Agricultural Holding Act 1984, s. 1). Any rent fixed for an agricultural tenancy (whether by agreement or by arbitration) may not be varied for three years, unless it is a variation agreed to reflect an improvement made at the landlord's expense or an agreed revision to the terms of the

tenancy (1948 Act, s.9). see also **agricultural tenant's fixtures, compensation for improvements, emblements, good husbandry, implied covenant**.
Landlord and Tenant Law, by David Yates and A.J. Hawkins, (1981) pp. 556–602.
Agricultural Holdings, by Muir Watt. 1 Halsbury's Laws of England 4 edn, paras. 1001–1154.
Woodfall's Law of Landlord and Tenant 28 edn, paras. 2–0001 to 2–0186.
Scammell & Densham's Law of Agricultural Holdings 6 edn.

agricultural tenant's fixture

A chattel or building that has been fixed to land by a tenant of an agricultural holding, but does not become the landlord's property as it may be removed by virtue of provisions in the Agricultural Holdings Act 1948, s. 13 (as amended by the Agricultural Holdings Act 1984, s. 13). Subject to certain conditions (in particular that the tenant has complied with the term of his lease; any damage done by the removal is made good; and the tenant has given one month's notice of his intention to remove stipulated fixtures to his landlord who has a right to elect to purchase such fixtures) an agricultural tenant may remove "any engine, machinery, fencing, or other fixtures . . . and any buildings" during the term of his lease or up to two months after the end of the lease. The tenant may not remove any building for which he has a statutory right to compensation from his landlord. A tenant of a market garden also has a right to remove certain items affixed to land for the purpose of his "trade or business" (Agricultural Holdings Act 1948, s. 67). See also **compensa-**

tion for improvements, trade fixture.
The Law of Real Property by Robert Megarry & H.W.R. Wade, 5 edn, p. 1094–1102.
The Law of Landlord and Tenant, by D.L. Evans, 2 edn, p. 423–468.
Landlord and Tenant Law, by David Yates and A.J. Hawkins, (1981) p. 557–602.
Woodfall's Landlord & Tenant, 28 edn, paras. 1559–1563.
Agricultural Tenancies: Practice and Precedent, by C.P. Rogers and C.V. Margrave-Jones, (1985).

agricultural tied cottage
see **tied accommodation**.

agriculture

The process, science or art of cultivating the soil; including the gathering of crops and the keeping and rearing of livestock. In particular, agriculture includes, "horticulture, fruit growing, seed growing, dairy farming, livestock, breeding and keeping, the use of land as grazing land, meadow land, osier land, market gardens and nursery grounds and the use of land for woodlands where that use is ancilliary to the farming of the land for other agricultural purposes" (Agricultural Holdings Act 1948, s. 94 (1); Agriculture Act 1947, s 109 (3) – a similar definition is included in the Town and Country Act 1971, s. 290). In the case of agricultural **tied accommodation** agriculture includes "(i) dairy-farming and livestock keeping and breeding (whether those activities involve the use of land or not); (ii) the production of any consumable produce which is grown for sale or for consumption or other use for the purposes of a trade or business or of any other undertaking (whether carried on for profit or not); (iii) the use of land as grazing, meadow or pasture land or orchard or osier land; (iv) the use of land for market gardens or nursery grounds; and (v) forestry" (Rent (Agriculture) Act 1976, s. 1).

In English planning legislation, the use of land for agriculture (or forestry) is not considered as development and, therefore, does not require planning permission (Town and Country Planning Act 1971, s. 22 (2) (e)). However, this provision is limited and may not include certain agricultural businesses, such as the sale of eggs – Hidderley v Warwick County Council (1963) 107 SJ 156, or the keeping of horses that are not part of the business of farming the land – Belmont Farm v Minister of Housing and Local Government (1962) 106. SJ 996. See also **allotment**, **agricultural property**. Ian Stephenson, The Law Relating to Agriculture (1975).

air-conditioning (a/c)

The treatment of air for the ventilation and temperature control of a room or building, including air filtration and humidity control. See also **central heating**.

air easement

see **right to air**.

air lease (US)

A lease of air-space, i.e. the lease of an **air right** over land.

air lot (US)

A specific air-space over a parcel of **land**. See also **air right**.

air right

The right to use the air space over a parcel of land. The ownership of land extends, historically, *ad coelum*, 'to the heavens'. Thus, an owner controls the space above his land; he has 'air-rights' over his land. However, it has been said in the United States Circuit Court of Appeal (and may equally be said in any court of law) that, "when it is said that a man owns, or may own, to the heavens, that merely means that no one can acquire a right to the space above him that will limit him in what ever use he can make of it as a part of his enjoyment. To this extent his title to the air is paramount. No other person can acquire any title or exclusive right to any space above him ... But any claim of a land owner beyond this cannot find a precedent in law, nor support in reason" – Hinman v Pacific Air Transport (1936) 84 Fed. (2d) 755. Thus, in English common law, he may prohibit the placing of any object, such as an advertising hoarding, that projects on to his property – Kelsen v Imperial Tobacco Co. Ltd. [1957] 2 All ER 253. A landowner may take an action in trespass to prevent aircraft flying low over his land, especially when that causes a nuisance – United States v Causby (1946) 328 US 256; Blankley v Godley [1952] 1 All ER 436, although common law and statute law recognise the right of aircraft to fly over land above a certain height, for example the Civil Aviation Act 1949, s. 40 authorises aircraft to fly over land at a reasonable height, "having regard to wind, weather and all the circumstances of the case". Similar statutes have been passed in the US (e.g. the Air Commerce Act 1926 and the Civil Aeronautics Act 1938), as well as in France where there is a similar principle regarding air rights.

A landowner may cede a right for another to occupy or take possession of a part of the air space above his land. This 'air right' may take the form of an outright sale or the grant of a lease of a strata of land, e.g. the disposal of an apartment; but the term air right is more usually applied to the grant of a mere licence or an easement, e.g. a right for a tower crane to pass over land during the period of building construction on adjoining land. A landowner may acquire a **right to air**, i.e. an **easement** permitting him to receive air along a defined channel, e.g. a ventilator, over neighbouring land. See also **avigation, transferable development rights, tree**.

air space
An expanse of space above **land**, especially a cube (or similar shape) of space that is held in different ownership to the surface of the land. See also **air right, condominium, flying freehold, partial ownership**.

aircraft, trespass by
see **air right**.

aisle
A gangway, or passageway, in a retail store or warehouse.

adjouté (F)
addition (to a document); **rider**; addendum.

aleatory contract
A contract that is dependent on an uncertain event; in particular a fortuitous or hazardous event. A wagering contract. See also **conditional contract, void contract**.

alienation
The voluntary transference of an interest in, or possession of, property from one party to another; whether during a life-time or on death. The act, or power, by which a person div- ests himself of an interest in **land** and vests that interest in another. "'Alienation' is as much to say, as to make a thing another man's; or to alter or put the possession of lands, or other things, from one man to another" – *Termes de La Ley*. The term 'alienation' may be used to refer to any transfer or disposition of an estate or interest in real property – although, the transfer of a lease; of an incorporeal right, e.g. an easement or restrictive covenant; or of a debt or mortgage is referred to especially as an **assignment**. The diverting of an estate from a person who may inherit it also may be an alienation. However, "if all that is made over is a mere personal right, and not in the nature of property, there will ... be no alienation" – Re Symon Public Trustee *v* Symon (1944) SASR 108. A right of alienation has been described as "necessarily and inseparably incidental to ownership" – Floyer *v* Bankes (1869) LR 8 Eq. 115 and, therefore, any **restraint on alienation** generally is considered void. In the US, a transfer of an interest in property against the owner's will, e.g. a foreclosure sale, is referred to as an **involuntary alienation**. See also **conveyance, forfeiture, rule against perpetuities, statutory alienation**.

alienation (F)
alienation (may be alienation of an existing right or the creation of a **partial interest** by *démembrements de la propriété*); **assignment**. See also **restraint on alienation**.

alienation clause
1. A clause in a contract setting out the rights of transference, e.g. the rights of a tenant to assign or to sublet. See also **restraint on alienation**.

(US) 2. A clause in a mortgage deed giving the lender the power to demand repayment of the outstanding balance if the mortgaged property is sold or otherwise alienated. In some states in the US such clauses are unenforceable, especially if the mortgagee is creditworthy. Called also 'due-on-sale clause' or a 'due-on-transfer clause'.
cf. **acceleration clause**. See also **assumption clause**.
Real Estate Law, Robert Kratovil and Raymond J. Werner, 8 edn, pp. 340–346.
3. A clause in an insurance policy which provides that the policy is automatically terminated if the owner disposes of the interest in the property that is the subject-matter of the policy.

alienee
One to whom property is transferred. See also **alienation, assignee**.

alienor
One who transfers property to another. See also **alienation, assignor**.

alignement (F)
alignment (of the position and direction of the boundary line of a property).
(*alignment en bordure de route* – **ribbon development**).
(*ligne d'alignement* – **building line**).

alimentary trust
see **protective trust**.

'all-in' contract
see **package-deal contract**.

all-inclusive mortgage (US)
see **wrap-around mortgage**.

all-loss insurance (US)
see **all-risks insurance**.

all-risks insurance
Insurance against all hazards of real property ownership, e.g. fire, smoke, explosion, lightning, storm, flood, collision or impact, breakage, collapse, provided that hazard is not expressly excluded. The term is confusing because it does not cover 'all risks' but only those not expressly excluded, as compared with **comprehensive insurance** which stipulates a large range of risks or perils that are covered by the insurance policy. The policy does not cover damage or loss resulting from an inevitable event, e.g. physical deterioration, or commercial risks such as a consequential loss of profit. A typical operative clause in an all-risks insurance policy might read: "the insurers will indemnify the insured against loss or physical (or material) damage to insured property however caused and occurring during the period of insurance". This would be followed by an exclusion clause for such items as wear and tear; deeds, bonds, etc.; plant and machinery; vehicles; damage by supersonic aircraft, radiation; war, etc; **inherent defect**; wilful misconduct of the insured; and such items as the parties agree to exclude, notably an **excess** or retained liability. In connection with an all-risks policy affecting deck cargo it has been said (by Lord Sumner) that "'All risks' has the same effect as if all insurable risks were separately enumerated . . . [but] there are, of course, limits to 'all-risks'. There are risks and risks insured against. Accordingly the expression does not cover inherent vice or mere wear and tear or British capture. It covers a risk not a certainty; it is something which happens to the subject matter from without, not the nat-

ural behaviour of the subject matter, being what it is, in the circumstances in which it is carried. Nor is it a loss which the insured brings about by his own act, for then he has not merely exposed the goods to the chance of injury, he has injured them himself." – British and Foreign Marine Insurance Co. *v* Gaunt [1921] 2 AC 57. In the US, called also 'all-loss insurance'. cf. **extended-perils insurance**. See also **contractor's all-risks insurance, householder's insurance**.

all-risks rate (or yield)

A single **capitalisation rate** (or a single yield) that takes account of all the risk factors that are relevant to a particular investment; usually a rate (or yield) derived from an analysis of the return obtained on comparable investments.

cf. **component capitalisation rate**. See also **composite rate, over-all capitalisation rate, remunerative rate, years' purchase**.

Assessing an all-risks yield, by Gerald Brown, 269 E.G. 700–6 (1984).

'all the estate' clause

see **conveyance**.

allegans contraria non est audiendus (L)

'He who makes statements mutually inconsistent is not to be listened to', i.e. a person cannot 'blow hot and cold'. See **election, estoppel**.

alley

A narrow passageway, especially a public **right of way** that runs between buildings to provide access to the rear. A way that is wide enough for the passage of only one vehicle.

alligator (US)

see **negative cash flow**.

allodial system

A system of land tenure by which an individual may hold land in his own right, as opposed to the **feudal system** where all land is vested in the Sovereign or land is held subject to the acknowledgement of a superior right. In English common law all land is held as a right from the Crown, i.e. there is no allodial land (Co. Litt. 1b). However, since the reforms of the Law of Property Act 1925, a **fee simple absolute** is for all intent and purpose allodial ownership, being the most absolute right recognised in modern law. In France all land has been held 'allodially' since the Revolution of 1792. In the US, since the Declaration of Independence, the fee simple is ownership under the allodial system. See also **bundle of rights theory, ownership**.

allodium

Land held under the **allodial system**, i.e. in absolute instead of servient ownership.

cf. **feodum**.

allonge

A sheet or sheets of paper attached to a **negotiable instrument** to enable endorsements to be added.

allonge (F)

allonge rider (especially to a **bill of exchange**).

allotment

1. A share or portion; that which is allotted, as with part ownership of a property or a company, granted by the party having effective control of the whole.

2. An area of land that has been subdivided, usually into small parcels, and let to individuals for horticultural cultivation either for food or plea-

sure. "Any parcel of land, whether attached to a cottage or not, of not more than two acres in extent, held by a tenant under a landlord and cultivated as a farm or garden, or partly as a garden and partly as a farm" (Allotments Act 1922, s. 3). An allotment may include an 'allotment garden' or a field garden. The expression 'allotment garden' means, "an allotment not exceeding forty poles (approx. ¼ acre) in extent which is wholly or mainly cultivated by the occupier for the production of vegetables or fruit crops for consumption by himself or his family" (Allotments Act 1922, s. 22 (1)). In certain statutes the size limitation for an allotment is extended to 5 acres (Allotment Act 1925, s. 1). A tenant of an allotment is provided with **security of tenure** and an entitlement to compensation in the event of a termination of his tenancy. A local authority also has a statutory duty to provide adequate allotments for local residents. For planning purposes an allotment is treated as land used for **agriculture** and, therefore, does not require planning permission – Crowborough Parish Council *v* Secretary of State for the Environment [1981] JPL 281. See also **compensation for improvements, enclosure, smallholding**.
The Law of Allotments, by J.F. Garner, 4 edn.
2 Halsbury's Statutes 4 edn, p. 3–79.
3. Funds made available by an institutional mortgage company for lending during a given period of time, i.e. the amount it intends to lend during that period.
cf. **commitment**.

alluvion or alluvium

Sand, silt, clay, gravel or similar material washed up by the sea or a river so as to add to the extent of the bordering land; especially when the material is deposited as a gradual and imperceptible increase. See also **accretion**.

alluvion (F)

alluvion.

alodium

see **allodium**.

alteration

1. The act or process of changing the character or fabric of a property without making something totally different in essence; in particular, changes or modifications that affect the form or structure of a property – Bickmore *v* Dimmer [1903] 1 Ch. 158. Strictly, an alteration should not change the external dimensions of a building as that would be an **addition** or **improvement**; it should not amount to building anew. "As applied to a building ... alter means to modify and change, and it presupposes an existing building of which the fabric will remain substantially unchanged after the alterations have been carried out". – Re Church of St. Jude [1956] SASR 53. Generally, an alteration is something permanent and substantial, not merely casual, short lived or *de minimis*.
2. A material change in an instrument or deed, e.g. a change of the **date**. An alteration of a deed is presumed to have been made before or at the time of execution; an alteration thereafter may be **fraud** and invalidate the deed. An alteration of a will is presumed to have been made after execution.
cf. **rectification**. See also **codicil, endorsement, supplemental deed**.
12 Halsbury's Laws of England 4 edn.

paras. 1377–1384.
Odgers' Construction of Deeds and Statutes 5 edn, pp. 18–26.

alternative accommodation
see **suitable alternative accommodation**.

alternative cost
see **opportunity cost**.

alternative mortgage loan (US)
A term that may be applied to any form of mortgage loan that differs from the traditional form of loan, i.e. from one for a fixed term, at a fixed interest rate, with level repayment to cover interest and **principal**. Examples are the **variable-rate mortgage**, the **dual-rate mortgage** and the **flexible-payment mortgage**. See also **amortisation mortgage**.
Basic Real Estate Finance and Investment, by D. Epley and J. Millar, pp. 253–284 (1980).

alternative use value
The value of land or buildings on the assumption that they are or may be put to a use that is different from the current use.
cf. **current use value**. See also **certificate of appropriate alternative development**, **highest and best use**.

altius non tollendi (L)
In the civil law and Scottish law a **servitude** by which a restriction is placed on building above a certain height, especially when imposed as a planning restriction. See also **non aedificandum**.

ambulatory
Subject to change; capable of being altered. See also **will**.

ameliorating waste
see **waste**.

amelioration
The act of improving or making something better. See also **betterment**, **improvement**.

amélioration (F)
improvement.
(*amélioration foncière* – land improvement)

aménagement (F)
zoning; **development**; management; planning.
(*aménagement du territoire* – land management; regional planning; a term applied to the control of industry and commerce, as well as to town and country planning or **land use planning**).
cf. **urbanisme**. See also **plan**.

amendement du sol (F)
land improvement, especially improving fertility.

amenity
1. The attractiveness, utility and **aesthetic** attributes of land or building, as distinguished from monetary or economic value. Amenity "appears to mean pleasant circumstances or features, advantages" – *in re.* Ellis and Ruislip Northwood UDC [1920] 1 KB370. See also **advertisement**, **amenity societies**, **building of special architectural or historical interest**, **conservation area**, **planning**, **standing amenities**, **tree preservation order**, **wasteland**.
2. A word used to describe the benefit of a **restrictive covenant**.

amenity land
Land that is used for public enjoyment or recreation; land that acts as an amenity for other land. See also **accommodation land**, **open space**.

amenity societies
see **Ancient Monuments Society, Civic Trust, Countryside Commission, Historic Buildings and Monuments Commission, National Parks Commission, National Trust, Nature Conservancy Council, Royal Fine Arts Commission, Society for the Protection of Ancient Buildings**.

amenities, standard
see **standard amenities**.

American Institute of Architects (AIA)
The national professional body representing architects in the United States. See also **architect**.

American Institute of Real Estate Appraisers (AIREA) (US)
The leading professional body in the United States representing those engaged in real estate appraisal. A member may be designated MAI (Member of the Appraisal Institute) or, if a specialist in residential property RM (residential member). The Institute is affiliated to the **National Association of Realtors**. See also **appraiser, code of ethics**.

amortisation, amortization, or amortizement
1. The gradual extinguishment of a debt or liability; especially by means of equal periodic payments at stated intervals which, in total, are sufficient to repay the capital or principal at the end of a given period, and to pay interest on the outstanding balance throughout the period. Amortisation commonly means "that payments made are equal in amount and are applied in payment of the **accrued interest** and a portion of the principal" – Price v Green [1951] 4 DLR 600. This meaning is used especially when referring to an **amortisation mort-**gage; but payments, under any agreed or established schedule, which are determined in such a way that a debt or loan is extinguished over a given period of time, may be referred to as amortisation. The extinguishment of a debt by a single payment derived from an accumulated fund, e.g. from the proceeds of a **sinking fund** is called also amortisation.

Amortisation sometimes is used synonymously for **depreciation**; however, amortisation is a deadening (from Old French *amortir* – 'to deaden') or extinguishment, being an objective process; whereas depreciation is a decline or reduction (from Late Latin *depretiare*, 'to lower a price') and is a subjective process. See also **amortisation rate, balloon payment, debt service, redemption, standing loan**.
2. The transfer of property in perpetuity to a corporation or charity, i.e. a transfer or alienation in **mortmain**.
(US) 3. In zoning, the gradual elimination of a **non-conforming user**.

amortisation fund
see **sinking fund**.

amortisation loan
see **amortisation mortgage**.

amortisation mortgage (or loan)
A mortgage (or loan) which provides for interest and principal to be repaid by means of level, or equal, annual instalments, i.e. by a constant **annuity**. These level payments are calculated so that, at the start, the annual instalment is sufficient to pay interest charged in the year on the entire loan together with a small payment of capital. As the amount of outstanding capital decreases so the amount of interest decreases, but as the total

payment remains constant the proportion of capital payment increases through the term of the loan. At the end of the period of the loan the entire capital, together with accrued interest on the outstanding balance, is totally repaid. In the UK this is a common method for repaying a mortgage loan for the purchase of a dwelling-house through a building society. (For the formula for calculating the level payments see the **annuity one will purchase.**) Called also a 'level-payment mortgage', 'constant-payment mortgage', an **annuity mortgage** or in the US an 'amortizing mortgage'. cf. 'direct-repayment mortgage'. See also **amortisation**.
Real Estate Principles, by Bruce Harwood, 2 edn, pp. 212–218.

amortisation profit
see **equity build-up**.

amortisation rate
The rate at which a loan, excluding any interest appertaining thereto, is repaid. The rate used for the **amortisation** of a loan or a sum of money. Generally, regular payments expressed as a percentage of a loan or capital. A term used synonymously with **sinking fund rate**, accumulative rate and recapture rate. See also **annuity one will purchase**, **depreciation rate**.

amortisation schedule
A schedule to a mortgage loan agreement that sets out the rate at which the debt is to be repaid. See also **amortisation mortgage**.

amortisation term
The period of time over which a loan is repaid.

amortise, or amortize
The act or process of **amortisation**.

amortissement (F)
amortisation; depreciation; redemption.
(*amortissement cumulé* – accrued depreciation)
(*amortissement accéléré* or *degressif* – accelerated or declining balance depreciation)
(*amortissement d'un emprunt* – redemption of a loan).
(*amortissement linéaire* – straight line depreciation)
(*caisse* or *fonds d'amortissement* – **sinking fund**).

amortizement (US)
see **amortisation**.

amortizing mortgage (US)
see **amortisation mortgage**.

amotion
The removal of someone from **possession** of land. See also **ouster**.

amount of one
The future worth of one (unit of money) when invested for a specified period of time with **compound interest**. Obtained by the formula:
$$A = (1 + i)^n$$
where A is the value of one unit of monetary value invested for n periods of time (or years) at a compound interest rate of i. If the interest is compounded more than once during the given periods of time (or more than once per annum), then the amount of one is given by the formula:
$$[1 + (i/m)]^{mn}$$
where m represents the number of times that the interest is credited per period of time (or in a year). Thus, if £1 is invested for 8 years at a nominal rate of 12 per cent p.a. and interest is credited to the principal (and compoun-

ded) quarterly, then it will accumulate to

$$[(1+(0.12/4)]^{4 \times 8} = £2.58$$ at the end of the period.

amount of one per period (or per annum)

The amount to which a series of payments, or deposits, of one unit of value will accumulate in a given period (or number of years) at a given rate of **compound interest**. Obtained by the formula:

$$A_n = [(1 = i)^n - 1]i$$

where A_n = amount accumulated

$i =$ interest rate for the period (or year)

$n =$ number of payments (or years)

Called also an **annuity factor** or, in the US, the **sinking fund accumulation factor**

cf. **sinking fund factor**. See also **annuity valuation tables**.

Modern Methods of Valuation 7 edn. pp. 84–85.

ampliation (F)

certified copy; counterpart.

anchor lease

A lease, usually for a long term, of part of a shopping centre to an **anchor store**.

anchor store

A major retail store or department store in a **shopping centre**, especially in a district or regional centre. In a neighbourhood or district centre the anchor store may be a supermarket or hypermarket, or a junior department or variety store. In a regional centre it would be a department store. They are considered the lynch pins to the success of a major shopping centre development and are located normally at the extremes of the centre in order to act as magnets to the pedestrian flow. Called sometimes a magnet store.

anchor tenant

A tenant who occupies an **anchor store**.

ancient demesne

Land that formed part of a **manor** and was held by the Crown during the reigns of Edward the Confessor and William the Conqueror. Such lands were recorded as the King's own **demesne** in Domesday Book (1086). Freeholders of these manors were known as 'tenants in ancient demesne' (2 Co. Inst 542). Such **tenure** was abolished by the Law of Property Act 1922, s. 128. Holdsworth's History of English Law vol. iii. p. 263.

ancient light

A **right of light** acquired by prescription. Historically a right that had existed from **time immemorial**, but since the Prescription Act 1832, s. 3., for over 20 years; unless granted expressly. (In certain cases this period may be extended to 27 years: Right of Light Act 1959, s. 1). See also **easement**.

ancient monument

A building, structure or site of considerable architectural, archaelogical or historic interest that is included in a list prepared by the Secretary of State for the Environment as being considered worthy of preservation. An ancient monument may be a scheduled monument i.e. a monument included in a schedule prepared by the Secretary of State. This schedule includes various monuments which were listed prior to the Ancient Monuments and Archaelogical Areas

Act 1979 and any other monument considered to be of national importance and subsequently added to the schedule (Ancient Monuments and Archaelogical Areas Act 1979, s. 1. The list includes over 12 000 monuments in Britain ranging from major national monuments to archeological sites, excavations, and even caves. An ancient monument may also be any other monument which the Secretary of State thinks is "of public interest by reason of the historic, architectural, traditional, artistic or archaelogical interest attaching to it" (1979 Act, s. 61 (12) (b)). It is an offence to carry out certain works to a scheduled monument, including work of demolition, destruction, removal, repair, alteration or addition or flooding or tipping operations and any such work that is likely to affect a 'scheduled monument' must be approved by 'scheduled monument consent'. Certain minor works are deemed to have such consent under the Ancient Monuments (Class Consents) Order 1981. If scheduled monument consent is refused compensation may be payable in limited instances for any resultant loss or expenditure incurred by a person having an interest in the monument (1979 Act, s. 27). The Secretary of State has power to acquire any ancient monument by compulsory purchase, agreement, or as a gift, or to place it under his own or a local authority's guardianship to ensure its proper control and management (1979 Act, s. 10–12).

Also, 'ancient monument' means "any structure, work, site, garden or area which in the [Historic Buildings and Monuments] Commission's opinion is of historic, architectural, traditional, artistic or archaelogical interest" (National Heritage Act 1983, s. 33 (8)). See also **building of special architectural and historic interest, historic building, Historic Buildings and Monuments Commission, historic structure**.

Urban Planning Law, by Malcolm Grant. pp. 477–483 (1982).
34 Halsbury's Laws of England 4 edn. paras, 595–652.

Ancient Monuments Boards

Advisory bodies that were set up for England, Wales and Scotland to advise the Secretary of State (for the Environment, for Wales or for Scotland) on the maintenance and preservation of ancient monuments. The boards were set up under the Ancient Monuments Consolidation and Amendments Act 1913 and their duties extended by the Ancient Monuments and Archaelogical Areas Act 1979. Since March 1984 their duties have been taken over effectively by the **Historic Buildings and Monuments Commission**.

Ancient Monuments Society

A voluntary organisation, originally established in 1924, to encourage interest in and to promote the conservation of ancient monuments, places of historic interest, buildings of special historical interest and fine old craftmanship in Britain. See also **Historic Buildings and Monuments Commission**.

ancient rent

An old term for the best or **rack rent** obtainable under a lease.

ancient wall

A **party wall** which has prescriptive rights attached thereto, e.g. a wall which has a right to support from a neighbour's building and, as a result of the length of time that support has been enjoyed, has fulfilled the requirements of time needed to acquire that right by **prescription**.

ancient window
see **ancient light**.

ancillary building
A building that is used in conjunction with a main building e.g. a garage or workshop; out-buildings. In the US, called also an accessory building. See also **appurtenance, curtilage**.

ancilliary use
see **planning unit**.

animals
see **damage feasant, game, negligence, nuisance, *res nullius*, strict liability, trespass**.

animus domini (L)
'The intention to hold as owner'. See **ownership**.

animus possidendi (L)
'The intention to have **possession**'; "the intention of excluding the owner (of land) as well as other people" – Littledale *v* Liverpool College [1900] 1 Ch. 23. See also **adverse possession**.

année (F)
year.
(*année de base* – base year, especially as used for calculating **indexation** increases in a price).

annex
1. To attach, join or fix an object or right to another; as in annexing a **fixture** to real property. See also **appendant, constructive annexation, servitude**.
2. An **addition** to a main building, but not necessarily physically attached. A building or structure that supplements a main building.

3. An appendix or other form of addition to a document. See also **codicil, rider, schedule**.
4. To appropriate land, as in an action by a State or a church. See also **appropriation**.

annexe (F)
appendix; rider; schedule.

annoyance
see **harassment, nuisance**.

annual
Recurring once a **year** or each year. A yearly event. See also **annuity, *per annum***.

annual capital charge
A yearly sum (**annuity**) that is sufficient to provide interest on an investment of capital and repay or recapture the amount of invested capital. A sum obtained as the product of a capital sum and an **annuity one will purchase** (or obtained by dividing that sum by the **present value of one per period**, i.e. by a **years' purchase**).

annual constant
see **mortgage constant**.

annual debt service
see **debt service**.

annual equivalent
The capital cost, or value, of an asset converted into an annual figure which if invested, over the economic life of that asset, will compound to the capital figure. An annual equivalent may be assessed simply by dividing the capital sum by the number of years for the economic life of the asset, (although that method takes no account of compound interest), or by dividing the capital sum by a **capitalisation rate** or **years' purchase** (i.e. the reverse of capitalisation – sometimes

called decapitalisation). See also **annuity**, **virtual rent**.

annual gross income
see **gross income**.

annual interest rate
see **annual percentage rate**, **effective annual interest rate**.

annual net value
see **net annual value**.

annual percentage rate (APR)
The true annual interest rate payable for a loan over a period of one year taking account of all charges made to the borrower, including compound interest, discount points, commitment fees, and taking into account the time at which principal is repaid (especially when payments of principal are made by instalments throughout the year, but interest is charged on the outstanding principal at the beginning of the year). Hire purchase loans and bank personal loans are made frequently on the basis that a nominal interest rate is charged on the original principal as if the whole balance were outstanding throughout the term of the loan, but the loan and interest is made repayable by equal instalments, usually monthly. Thus the borrower is paying interest on capital he has effectively repaid. For example, on a loan of £100 at a nominal interest of 8 per cent the borrower may pay 12 instalments during the year of $108/12 = £9.00$ per month, in arrears; on this basis the nominal or 'add on' interest rate of 8 per cent produces an APR of 14.45 per cent. The APR may be calculated by assessing an **internal rate of return** (or 'effective yield') on the lender's cash flow or, approximately (when the number of variables are limited), by

the formula:
$$X = (2\,ni)/[A\,(N+1)]$$
where X = annual percentage rate (expressed as a decimal)
i = nominal interest rate
n = number of payments in a year
N = total number of payments during the term of the loan.
A = amount of the loan
The Consumer Credit Act 1974, s. 20 (1) requires the Secretary of State to make regulations to require lenders to state clearly the true cost of credit (these regulations are contained in the Consumer Credit (Total Charge for Credit) Regulations 1980). In the US, the Federal Consumer Protection Act 1969, Part I, as extended by Regulation Z, also contains provisions requiring the publication of the real cost of credit.
cf. **effective annual interest rate**. See also **Truth in Lending Laws, usury**.

annual rent
1. The **rent** payable for one year.
2. In Scottish law, a payment of **interest**.

annual sinking fund (a.s.f.)
A **sinking fund** calculated on an annual basis.

annual value
The value or monetary worth to be derived from a property over a period of one year; the yearly income to be derived from property as a result of ownership. In English law rating 'annual value' means **net annual value**. See also **gross value, market rent, rateable value**.

annualisation
The conversion of a capital sum into

an **annual equivalent**; the reverse of **capitalisation**. See also **annuity**.

annuitant
One entitled to receive, or one who receives, an **annuity**.

annuité
annuity. See also *rente*.

annuity
1. A series of specified or determined sums of money payable or receivable yearly (or at fixed intervals during a year); whether for a particular period of time (a life or a number of years) or in perpetuity. The payment may be of equal amounts each year – a level annuity – or may increase or decrease each year – a 'variable (increasing or decreasing) annuity', and may be paid in monthly, quarterly or by any other regular instalments. An annuity may be conditional, or contingent e.g. 'until A marries'. An annuity is *prima facie* **personalty**, (although it may be paid out of a real or personal estate) and differs from **rent** which issues out of land. Annuity may mean also "the purchase of an income, and usually involves a change of capital into income, payable annually over a number of years" – Scoble *v* Secretary of State in Council for India [1903] 1 KB 504. "An annuity is a right to receive *de anno in annum* a certain sum; that may be given for life, or for a series of years; it may be given during any particular period, or in perpetuity; and there is only this singularity about annuities that although payable out of personal assets, they are capable of being given, for the purposes of devolution, as real estate" – Bignold *v* Giles (1859) 4 Drew. 346. An annuity charged against land may be registered as a **land charge** pro-

vided it is "a rentcharge or an annuity for a life or lives or for any term of years or greater estate determinable on a life or lives and created after 25 April 1855, and before 1 January 1926, but does not include an annuity created by a **marriage** settlement or will" – Land Charges Act 1972, s. 17. (1). An annuity created after 1926 is registerable as a **general equitable charge**. See also **deferred annuity**, **mortgage constant**.
2. A sum of money paid annually so that it will accumulate over a given number of years, together with accrued interest, to a specified capital sum. See also **amount of one per annum, sinking fund**.

annuity capitalisation
A method of valuing a future income stream or annuity, receivable for a limited period of time, by taking the sum of the present values of the projected periodic incomes; i.e. capitalisation by applying a factor based on the **present value of one per period** (called, in the UK, a **years' purchase** or the 'years' purchase for a term of years' or, in the US, an **Inwood factor**). Called also the **annuity method** of valuation or yield capitalisation.
cf. **straight capitalisation**. See also **discounted cash flow, dual-rate capitalisation factor**.

annuity factor
1. A figure that represents the **annuity one will purchase**.
(US) 2. See also **amount of one per period**.

annuity method
1. A method of analysing the worth of a capital investment by comparing the annual income generated by that investment with the amount required

to provide a suitable rate of return on the investment to cover interest on the capital and repay, or recapture, the capital (i.e. to provide for an **annual capital charge**). Or, by comparing the annual income generated with the **annual equivalent** cost of the capital invested (i.e. with the capital invested divided by an appropriate capitalisation factor or years' purchase). Called also the 'equivalent annual value method'.

2. A method of allowing for **depreciation** by writing-off each year, over the anticipated life of an asset, an amount based on the **annuity one will purchase**.

3. See **annuity capitalisation**.

annuity mortgage

1. See **reverse mortgage**.

2. See **amortisation mortgage**.

annuity one will purchase

An annual return, or **annuity**, receivable, over a given number of years, from an investment of one unit of value. That sum of money which if paid in annual instalments, over the period of a loan, will repay one unit of that loan, together with interest thereon; i.e. an annuity factor which provides a sinking fund to recoup the principal amount of the loan and also repays interest on the outstanding balance. The factor is given by the formula:

$a_n = i + s = i + i / [(1 + i)^n - 1]$

or $= i / \{1 - 1 / [(1 + i)^n]\}$

where i = interest rate per annum (or per period), expressed as a decimal.

s = sinking fund

n = number of annual (or regular) loan repayments (during the term of the loan)

a_n = the annuity.

This annuity figure is most commonly calculated in order to determine the level periodic instalments that will amortise a loan, i.e. to calculate a mortgage constant, and represents the reciprocal of the **present value of one per period**. For example, if a loan of £100 000 is taken out for a period of 25 years, then the constant annual amount required to repay the loan together with interest at 9 per cent per annum is:

$100\,000 \times 0.09 / [1 - (1.09^{25})^{-1}] = £10{,}180.63$

annul

To nullify or declare void; to abrogate. See also **voidable contract**.

annulation (F)

cancellation or avoidance (of a contract); **defeasance**. See also *resolution*.

annulable, *contrat* (F)

voidable contract.

ante (L)

'Before; prior'.

antichrèse (F)

A form of pledge or lien on the produce of real property as security for a loan, by which the pledgee is entitled to enter into legal possession in order to receive the rents and profits to use towards repayment of principal and interest on the loan. A form of **mortgage** that originated in Roman law when the demanding of interest, **usury**, was illegal and the lender relied on the income and profits from property (or even the benefit of occupation) as an alternative. See also *vivum vadium*, **welsh mortgage**.

anticipation (F)

(*paiement par anticipation* – payment in advance; pre-payment)

anticipation privilege (US)
see **prepayment privilege**.

anticipatory breach
see **breach of contract**.

apartment
A place of residence, comprising a room or a number of rooms, usually on one level, contained within a single building which contains two or more dwelling units that are divided from one another horizontally; normally with common rights of access and rights and obligations to **common areas**. In the UK 'apartment' generally is applied to a self-contained residence with two or more rooms; the term **flat** to smaller, and less luxurious units; and 'bedsitting room' or 'bed-sitter' to a unit comprising only one room. In the US, a building containing such residences is referred to as an 'apartment building' or 'apartment house', and in the UK as a 'block of apartments' or 'block of flats'. (In the case of Rex *v* Carson Roberts, *Ex p.* Stepney Corporation [1915] 3 KB 313 an apartment was stated to be synonymous with lodgings, although this can be explained more by the derivation of the word *ad partire* (L), 'to divide', than by the modern usage. Thus an apartment in a strict sense is a place divided up for the lodging or housing of persons; although a place of lodging is not necessarily an apartment. See also **dwelling-house, hotel, house, maisonette, multiple (or multi-family) dwelling, tenement**.
A Guide to Appraising Apartments, by E.R. Everett, 5 edn. (1979).

apparent authority
see **ostensible authority**.

apparent easement
An easement ascertained to exist from a careful inspection of a property e.g. from a well-beaten track across one parcel of land providing a right of way to another parcel or a drain taking water from the eaves of a house; as distinguished from one that is known to exist only because of the document by which it is expressly created. In the US, called sometimes a continuing easement because it exists as a result of a natural self-perpetuating circumstance as opposed to a man-made and stipulated circumstance. Called also an open easement. See also **quasi-easement**.

apparent title
see **colour of title**.

appartement (F)
apartment; flat.
(*appartement avec service* – service flat)
(*appartement meublé* – furnished flat).

appartenance (F)
appurtenance.

appeal
An application or resort to a superior court by a lower court to review the decision of the lower court (or an administrative body e.g. a tribunal, or an arbitrator), generally on judicial rather than administrative matters, in the hope of reversing the decision of the latter.
cf. **prerogative order**. See also **planning appeal**.

appel d' offre (F)
invitation to tender.

appendant
1. Something that is adjunct, or is an accessory to another thing and passes

with it, especially by inheritance.

2. Annexed to land by operation of law, as a result of use from 'time immemorial'. An appendant right is assumed to have existed since living memory and, therefore, may arise only by **prescription**, i.e. personal usage for a long time, unlike a right **appurtenant** which may be acquired by prescription or by **grant**. In English law it is possible that the only right appendant is a **right of common** which arose when a lord of a manor sub-infeudated land to a freeholder and the freeholder obtained a right of pasture on the waste land of the manor. Once a thing appurtenant has been separated from the property to which it is annexed (the principal hereditament), so as to be independent or in gross, it cannot become appendant again although it may become appurtenant. See also **annex, appurtenance, profit à prendre**.

appentis (F)
penthouse.

appointment
A **fixture**, item of furnishing, equipment and any fitting installed in a building, generally with the intention of improving its value to an occupier (but not necessarily the owner).

appointment, power of
see **power of appointment**.

apportionment
The act or process of dividing or assigning rights or liabilities proportionately. The giving by way of a portion for a particular purpose. For example, the allocation of costs, rent, rates, service charges, etc., equitably or proportionately, between different owners or occupiers of a property. The costs of occupying a property are commonly apportioned according to the area occupied. On the sale of a property apportionment is made normally according to time; thus rents, annuities and other periodic payments in the nature of income are deemed to accrue from **day** to day, and are apportioned accordingly (Apportionment Act 1870, s. 2). Under English law an annual **rent**, even if payable quarterly, is apportioned on a yearly basis, whether on sale or at the start or finish of a lease. For example, if an annual rent of £10000 is payable on the 'usual quarter days' (25 March, 24 June, 29 September, 25 December), in advance, and a property is sold on the 20 August, the purchaser will be entitled to $39/365 \times 10000 = £1068.49$ as rent for the period from 21 August to 28 September inclusive (not $39/97 \times 2500 = £1005.15$). A similar rule applies to the apportionment of rent under a lease. If a lease commences on 10 May and rent is payable on the usual quarter days, in advance, the tenant is óbliged to pay rent for the period, 10 May (inclusive) to 23 June (inclusive), i.e. $45/365$ths of the annual rent (note: if the lease commenced from 10 May the first *per diem* payment is not due until 11 May). Rent may be apportioned also according to value: for example, where part of land subject to a lease is compulsorily acquired, rent may be demanded from the lessee only for the land he retains (Compulsory Purchase Act 1965, s. 19). See also **completion statement**.

apportionment clause
see **contribution clause**.

appraisal
The act or process by which the esti-

mated value or the price of a property is determined, especially when adjudged by an impartial, independent and suitably qualified person – US *v* Crowley, 522 F 2d. 427. A term more commonly used in the US, for that which is called **valuation** in the UK. Appraisal is defined by the American Institute of Real Estate Appraisers as "an opinion of one or more specifically defined economic factors relating to adequately described property as at a specific date, supported by the analysis of relevant data". Normally this opinion is substantiated by a full report on the factors underlying the value, as assessed by the appraiser.

'Appraisal' may be used in a subjective sense to refer to the worth of a property to a particular purchaser, as distinguished from the more objective term 'valuation'.

The principal methods or 'approaches' used in the US to estimate the value of a property (with the equivalent UK terms for 'methods of valuation') are:

(a) **market comparison approach** or market data approach (comparison method)

(b) **income approach** or net income capitalisation approach (investment method)

(c) **cost approach** or replacement cost approach (reinstatement method)

(d) **abstraction approach** or land residual approach (residual method) – although this approach is encompassed generally within the cost approach. See also **appraisal report, estimate**.

Real Estate Principles by Bruce Harwood, 2 edn. Ch. 16.

The McGraw-Hill Real Estate Handbook, Robert Irwin (ed.) (1984) paras. 28–1 to 30–32.

The Appraisal of Real Estate, AIREA, 8 edn, p. 3 et seq.
See also Appendix B.

appraisal certificate (US)
see **valuation certificate**.

appraisal clause (US)
A clause in an insurance policy which provides that, in the event of loss or damage being occasioned to the insured property the insurer or the insured may call for an independent appraisal to determine the indemnity payable. See also **unvalued policy**.

appraisal correlation (US)
see **correlation process**.

appraisal date (US)
see **valuation date**.

appraisal fee schedule (US)
see **scale fee**.

appraisal report (US)
A detailed report, normally set out in writing, together with an appraisal certificate (**valuation certificate**), on a particular interest in a parcel of real estate. In the US this is commonly prepared by a qualified **appraiser**. The report outlines the purpose of the appraisal; describes the property in detail and the interest being appraised and sets down any factors and assumptions that affect its value; incorporates a summary of the appraisal process carried out by the appraiser; and sets out the **market value** of the property being appraised. See also **valuation report**.
Real Estate Valuation in Litigation, by J.D. Eaton, pp. 321–351 (1982).
Appraisal of Real Estate, AIREA, 7 edn, Ch. 26.

appraised value
The value of a property as assessed by

a qualified **appraiser**. See also **apprai-sal, market value**.

appraisement

The act of **appraisal**, especially when carried out under a court order; for example, prior to an award of com-pensation, or by a person selected by parties to a dispute. Appraisement for tax purposes is called **assessment**.
cf. **arbitration**. See also **expert**.

appraiser

A professionally skilled, trained, and experienced person who estimates the quality, worth or value of property. An appraiser has been defined as, "a person who shall value or appraise any estate or property, real or per-sonal; or any interest in possession or reversion, remainder or contingent, in any estate or property, real or per-sonal – or any goods, merchandise, or effects whatsoever kind or descrip-tion the same may be – for or in expectation of any hire, gain, fee, or reward, or valuable consideration to be therefor paid him" (Appraisers Licences Act 1806, s. 4). In the US, normally an appraiser is a Member of the **American Institute of Real Estate Appraisers**, designated MAI, or a member of the Society of Real Estate Appraisers (a Senior Real Estate Analyst, SREA). Called also a valua-tor. See also **valuer**.

appreciation

1. An increase in the **value** of a prop-erty over its purchase price or book cost. An increase that may arise as a result of an increase in demand for, or a reduction in the supply of, the prop-erty; or as a result of a reduction in the purchasing power of money, i.e. due to inflation. Appreciation may be actual or realised, when a property is

sold for a profit; or estimated or unrealised, when it results from a revaluation.
cf. **depreciation**. See also **capital gain**.
2. An assessment of the value, or the process of assessing the value, of a property. See also **appraisal**.

appreciation (F)

estimation (of value), a less precise term than *expertise*; **evaluation**.

appreciation-participation mortgage
see **equity-participation mortgage**.

approaches to value (US)
see **appraisal**.

approbate and reprobate

To approve and reject. The doctrine of approbation and reprobation requires that a person elects for one of two alternatives; one cannot appro-bate (select) and reprobate (reject) a mutually exclusive course of action, *quod approbo non reprobo*. See also **election, estoppel**.

appropriate alternative development
see **certificate of appropriate alterna-tive development**.

appropriation

1. The act or process of taking for one's own. The claiming or using of something as if one has a pre-eminent right, even though not authorised by the true owner. The taking of a thing into private ownership. The usurping of an authority. "... Pre-empt, usurp, arrogate, confiscate: these verbs all mean to seize or take over more or less dictatorially. In the order appro-priate, pre-empt, usurp, arrogate, confiscate they may be said to form an ascending scale of highhanded-ness. Appropriate has the common meaning of to set aside for a special

purpose but it signifies more generally to take over or acquire without authority or with questionable authority, usually also implying a conversion to one's use of the thing taken over…"(*Webster's Third International Dictionary*). Appropriation may be used in contradistinction to the taking of land by exercise of the power of **eminent domain**, i.e. **condemnation**; but it is sometimes used synonymously therewith to signify a form of taking of private property into public hands – N. Ward Co. *v* Bd. of Street Commissioners of City of Boston, 104 N.E. 965.

cf. **expropriation**. See also **assumption**.
2. The setting aside or application of something to a particular purpose, such as setting a property against a specific debt or setting land aside for a particular purpose. Thus, 'where the buyer owes more than one debt to the seller, and makes a payment, it is his right at the time of payment, to apply, or, in technical language, appropriate, the payment to whichever debt he pleases' – *Benjamin on Sale of Personal Property* 7 edn, p. 838. See also **dedication**.
3. The use of land acquired compulsorily for a different purpose from that originally intended. In certain cases this may entitle the previous land owner to additional compensation. Appropriation is used in a legislative sense to refer to the process by which public funds are allocated for a specific purpose; hence it is used to refer to the allocation of an area of land to a stated purpose.
4. The taking of real property into perpetual ecclesiastical use or ownership.
cf. **impropriation**.
(US) 5. A doctrine (of appropriation)

that enable a landowner to take water or divert a stream, beyond his normal riparian rights, provided he does not interfere with a prior claim to that water. See also **water rights**.

appropriation (F)
appropriation.

appurtenance
A right or privilege that is incidental or an adjunct to the ownership of a property, especially that which is necessary for the enjoyment of the property. That which is added to property and becomes, or may be considered, an inherent part of a property on transfer, unless expressly excluded. An appurtenance to land is that which is usually enjoyed with and belongs to the land; whether as a benefit to land, e.g. an **easement** or as a burden over land, e.g. a **restrictive covenant**. As a rule land itself cannot be an appurtenance to other land. "The word 'appurtenances' includes all the incorporeal hereditaments attached to the land granted or demised such as rights-of-way, of common, of piscary, and the like, but it does not include lands in addition to that granted" – Lister *v* Pickford (1865) 3 Beav. 580. Thus, if premises are leased 'with the appurtenances' that does not extend the demise "so as to include land or buildings which are used with the demised property, but are not parcel of it; nor do they include a part of the building which has been separated from it and has not been occupied with it for many years previous to the demise" (27 Halsbury's Laws of England 4 edn, p. 103). On the other hand a **conveyance** (which includes a mortgage, lease, or any other instrument that operates to transfer an interest in land, but not a

will) transfers rights and privileges appurtenant to land or any part of the land conveyed (Law of Property Act 1925, s. 62 (1)). An appurtenance may include a building, a fixture, an easement, or a servitude included in premises demised under a lease. However, when referring in the Housing Act 1957, s. 189 (1) to 'appurtenances belonging thereto' that phrase did not extend to an **easement of necessity**.
cf. **appendant**. See also **accession, appurtenant, rights of common**.

appurtenant
That which is joined as an **appurtenance**. That which belongs to, or is annexed to, a particular property, e.g. an **easement**. An appurtenant right is one that benefits a property; it cannot exist independently, **in gross**. "For this reason an exclusive **right** to grazing, or taking timber, or fishing without limit, cannot exist as appurtenant to another property." – Anderson *v* Bostock [1976] Ch. 318. A conveyance of land is deemed to include, **inter alia**, rights or advantages "appurtenant to the land or any part thereof"(Law of Property Act 1925, s. 62 (1)). Similarly, in the US, an appurtenant right belongs to and passes with the principal property – Church *v* Penna Public Utility Comm. 132 A 2d 894. See also **easement appurtenant, implied grant**.

apron (US)
An extensive hard-standing surface around a building used for parking, circulation and loading or unloading.

arbiter
An **arbitrator** or referee.

arbitrage
1. The movement of funds from one market to another to take advantage of price differences; the simultaneous purchase of something in one market and sale in another with the intention of making a profit on the different prices prevailing in the respective markets. A spread, or difference, between interest rates for similar loans but in different situations.
(US) 2. The difference between the rate on a first mortgage loan and on a corresponding **wraparound mortgage**.
3. The rendering of a judgement, or the making of an **arbitration**.

arbitrage (F)
arbitration; arbitrage.

arbitration
The hearing and adjudication of a difference, or dispute, between two parties by referring their differences to an independent and impartial third party, who is acceptable to those involved in the dispute; rather than to a court of law. The essence of arbitration is that a matter in dispute is submitted to some body or person (**arbitrator**), chosen by the parties, to make a final decision or award based on the evidence presented by the parties. An arbitrator listens to the submissions of both parties and determines the issue on the evidence; his decision is final and normally accepted as binding on the parties to the dispute. Arbitration is used usually to determine disputes on matters of fact, rather than law, although an arbitrator may have authority to express an opinion on a point of law or he may submit a matter of law to a court for its decision. Although the arbitrator is not a part of the judiciary, an arbitration procedure remains within the ambit of the law (such as the Arbitration Acts of 1950, 1975 and 1979), and

ordinary legal defences remain open to the parties (in particular a right of appeal to a court on a point of law, either when both parties request a hearing or with the leave of the court).

When a matter is submitted to a body or person who is requested to settle the dispute, usually with each party making representations, that is an arbitration; but if that party is required to fix a price using his own knowledge that is not an arbitration but a submission to an **expert** who is required to use his professional judgement i.e. to make a **valuation**. "Valuation undoubtedly precludes differences, in the proper sense of the term; it prevents differences and does not settle any which have arisen. That is the distinction ... between ... **appraisement** and arbitration" – Collins v Collins (1858) 26 Beav. 313. A submission to arbitration may arise from an **arbitration agreement** (with the parties agreeing upon the arbitrator, or agreeing that the arbitrator will be appointed by a mutually acceptable third person e.g. the President for the time being of the Royal Institution of Chartered Surveyors), or, in certain cases, from statute law, (e.g. Arbitration Act 1950, s. 31). See also **interim award**.

The Surveyor in Court, by P.H. Clarke, pp. 259 *et seq.* (1985).
Arbitration – Principles and Practice, by John Parris, (1983).
The Law of Arbitration, by W.H. Gill, 3 edn.
Arbitration: A Practical Guide, by A.T. Ginnings, (1984).
Arbitration, by M. Kay (1979).
Russell on Arbitration 20 edn.
The Law and Practice of Commercial Arbitration in England, by Michael J. Mustill and Stewart C. Boyd, (1982).

2 Halsbury's Laws of England 4 edn, paras. 501–7.

arbitration agreement

A written agreement to submit an existing or future difference to **arbitration**; whether an arbitrator is named therein or not (Arbitration Act 1950, s. 32). It may be a separate agreement, or merely a clause in a contract that disputes will be submitted to arbitration. An arbitration clause "embodies the agreement of both parties that, if any dispute arises with regard to the obligations which one party has undertaken to the other, such dispute shall be settled by a tribunal of their own constitution." – Heyman v Darwins Ltd. [1942] A.C. 373–374. An arbitration agreement is governed by statute (1950 Act, as amended by the Arbitration Act 1979) and must be in writing; or at least, evidenced in writing "by a document or documents signed by the parties which records a pre-existing agreement or authenticates or recognises the existence of an agreement to submit [a matter to arbitration]" – Frank Fehs and Co. v Kassam Jivraj and Co. Ltd (1949) 82 Ll. L. Rep. 676 (Arbitration Act 1975, s. 7 (1)).

arbitration clause
see **arbitration agreement**.

arbitrator

A person appointed to settle a matter by **arbitration**. An arbitrator is a judge appointed by individuals rather than by a government. "An arbitrator is neither more nor less than a private judge of a private court (called an arbital tribunal) who gives a private judgment (called an **award**). He is a judge in that the dispute is submitted to him; he is not a mere investigator but a person before whom material is placed by the parties, being either or both of evidence and submission; he gives a decision in accordance with his duty to hold the scale fairly between the disputants in accordance with some recognised system of law and the rules of natural justice" (Russell on Arbitration 20 edn, p. 104). An arbitrator, unlike an **expert**, does not act without receiving submissions or evidence from the parties and if he refuses to accept submissions or evidence his award may be set aside for misconduct. An arbitrator's function is governed by statute law, but he is not liable for negligence when arriving at his award. However, his decision must lie between the extremes represented by the parties. An arbitrator may be appointed as a result of an **arbitration agreement**; by the nomination of a third party e.g. the president of a professional body; or by a court decree. If the appointment is made by agreement the parties may establish any means they choose for selecting the arbitrator. For example, there may be an agreement that each party to the dispute selects an arbitrator and the arbitrators then appoint a third party, acting as an **umpire**, to decide on the dispute. Three arbitrators may be appointed with the award being established by a majority decision or two arbitrators may be appointed with the matter settled by an umpire if they are unable to agree. cf. **appraiser**.

arbitre (F)
arbitrator.

arcade
A covered passageway or pedestrian thoroughfare, commonly with rows of shops along the sides. A series of arches forming a building or gallery.

archaeological area
An area of land designated by the Secretary of State or a local authority, in accordance with the provisions of Ancient Monuments and Archaeological Areas Act 1979, s. 33, as being of archaeological importance. It is an offence to disturb the ground of such an area, or to flood or tip on the area, without previously notifying the local district council. Upon receipt of such notification the Secretary of State, or certain other bodies, have powers to enter and carry out investigatory work on such an area.

architect
Derived from the Greek *architekton*, chief artificer or master builder. A person who is skilled in the art of building; one who specialises in the design of buildings and in the control, supervision and methods for the execution of building work. "An 'architect' is one who possesses, with due regard to the aesthetic as well as practical considerations adequate skill and knowledge to enable him (i) to originate, (ii) to design and plan, (iii) to arrange for and supervise the erection of such buildings or other works calling for skill in design and planning as he might in the course of his business reasonably be asked to carry out in respect of which he offers his services as a specialist" – R. *v* Architects' Registration Tribunal *ex parte* Jaggar (1945) 61 TLR 446. An architect is employed by a client to interpret and advise on that person's requirements; to convert those requirements into plans and then into a building; to supervise the erection of that building and ensure that it is sound and comp-

lies with all codes and legal requirements; and as far as possible, to make the building aesthetically pleasing. An architect who is engaged by a building owner to supervise a contract acts as an **agent** for that purpose and has no authority to act beyond the strict terms of his engagement. An architect is responsible for exercising skill, commensurate with the standard expected of this profession, when performing his professional duties and he owes a reasonable **duty of care** to his employer. He is "not responsible for providing a perfect building in a stated time; but he is bound to use reasonable care and skill in designing and supervising the erection of a building" – Moresk Cleaners *v* Hicks [1966] 2 Lloyd's Rep. 338. In Britain a person may only use the title 'architect' provided he has reached a certain standard of qualification and experience (Architects Registration Act 1938); this standard is laid down by the Architects' Registration Council (ARCUK). The dominant body outside ARCUK is the **Royal Institute of British Architects** and the majority of practising architects are members of that institute. In the US, an architect must be licensed to practise by the state in which he works and he or she is normally a member of the **American Institute of Architects**. See also **building certificate, professional negligence**.

Architectural Practice, by J.J. Scott, (1985).

The Architect in Practice, by Arthur J. Willis and W.N.B. George, 6 edn.

4 Halsbury's Laws of England 4 edn. paras 1301–1363.

The Architect's Legal Handbook, by Antony Speight and G. Stone, 3 edn.

Longman's *Directory of Official Architecture and Planning*, annual. See also Appendix B.

architect's certificate or architect's inspection certificate
see **building certificate**

architectural interest
see **listed building**.

archive
A chamber or room for storing documents or records. A part of a building set aside as a repository.

archive (F)
archive; storage area (in an office); records.

area
The horizontal surface of a defined unit of land, or a building or defined part of a building. A flat, or relatively flat, surface, especially one that is enclosed, bounded, or set aside for a particular purpose. See also **area of comprehensive development, common areas, conservation area, development area, general improvement area, gross external area, net internal area, rentable area, sales area, site area, special area**.

area of comprehensive development
An area of land that is to be developed or redeveloped as a whole, either by a private or a public body. In particular, an area of comprehensive development was an area that a local authority defined, when preparing a **development plan** for an area under its control, as one which, in its opinion, "should be developed or redeveloped as a whole" (Town and Country Planning Act 1962, s. 4). Such an area was defined for the purpose of dealing with war damage, conditions of bad lay-out, obsolete development, pro-

viding for the relocation of population or industry, the replacement of open space, or such other purposes as the authority considered should be dealt with comprehensively, See also **structure plan**, **urban development area**.

area of outstanding natural beauty (ANOB)

An area in England or Wales designated by the Countryside Commission, under the provisions of the National Parks and access to the Countryside Act 1949, s. 87, as requiring strict standards of development control and measures to conserve or enhance its natural beauty, such as the removal of eyesores. Such an area is similar but smaller than a **National Park**. See also **article 4 direction**, **conservation area**.

area of special control

An area in England or Wales where the display of most forms of advertisement is strictly controlled, so that only special classes or specifically authorised advertisements are permitted, (Town and Country Planning Act 1971, s. 63, as amended by Local Government Planning and Land Act 1980, Sch. 15, para. 15, and regulation made thereunder). An order may be made or approved by the Secretary of State for the Environment by which strict control is exercised over the display of advertisements in areas that are considered to require special protection. These areas, sometimes called special areas, are mostly rural; although orders have been made in respect of other areas which appear to the Secretary of State "to require special protection on the grounds of amenity" (1971 Act, s. 63 (3)).

area of special scientific interest

see **site of special scientific interest**.

area research

see **feasibility study**.

area zoning

see **zoning**.

areaway

A passage or space underground intended to be used to provide light or ventilation to the basement of a building.

argentum Dei (L)

'God's money'. Money paid to secure a bargain i.e. **earnest money**.

arm's-length transaction

An agreement between two parties who have no special duty, relationship or obligation to one another. See also **special purchaser**, **undue influence**, **vested interest**.

arpentage (F)

land survey.

arpenteur (F)

land surveyor.

arrearages (US)

see **arrears**.

arrérages (F)

1. **arrears**.
2. interest; a periodic payment, in particular used in relation to Government securities or a *rente viagère* (see *rente*).
cf. *intérêt*.

arrears

A debt that is due but not yet paid. Payments (e.g. rent or interest payments) that have not been made at the appointed time i.e. on the due date. A sum of money that is in arrears remains in arrears until there is a proper **payment**. Money held in hand as a result of a prior over-payment does not automatically reduce arrears (Union Bank of London *v* Ingram (1880) 16 Ch. D. 53). In the US called also 'arrearages' or 'delinquent payments'. See also **rent in arrears (or advance), tender**.

arrent
To let land annually.

arrêt de suspension (F)
injunction, especially a preventative injunction.

arrhes (F)
earnest money; **deposit**; **key money**.

arriéré (F)
arrears.
(*interêt arriéré* – outstanding interest)
(*loyer arriéré* – **rent in arrears**).

arrogation
The act or process of taking over something without the least right or title; claiming or assuming a right to which one is not entitled. See also **appropriation**.

arrondisement (F)
administrative district, being the primary subdivision of a *département*.

article (F)
article; **clause** (of a document); condition (of a contract).

article 4 direction
A direction issued by the Secretary of State for the Environment, or the local planning authority, revoking consent to development which would be permitted development under the provisions of a **General Development Order** (GDO) (Town and Country Planning General Development Order 1977–1981, article 4). This direction requires an express planning application to be made in a particular area or for a particular form of development specified in the direction. Thus, it enables the planning authority to override the tolerances set out in a GDO, such as minor alterations or changes of use, in an area considered to be especially sensitive, e.g. in an **area of outstanding natural beauty** or in a **conservation area**. A landowner who suffers financial loss as a direct consequence of such an order may be entitled to compensation (Town and Country Planning Act 1971, s. 164). See also **compensation for planning restrictions**.

artificial person
An entity, other than a human being, that has a legal status e.g. a **company**, **trust**, cooperative. In the US called also a juristic person. See also **partnership**.

'**as, if and when' clause**
A clause in an estate agent's or broker's agreement that **commission** will be paid to the agent 'as, if and when' a sale is completed as compared to a clause that commission will be paid when a purchaser is introduced who is '**ready, able and willing**' to purchase.

'**as is', or 'as it stands'**
Accepting a property in its existing condition. 'As is' implies that the purchaser must satisfy himself by his own inspection – "for better or worse, for less or for more" – Covas *v* Bingham 23 (1853) LJ QB 29. The vendor gives no **warranty** as to the condition or suitability of the property. See also *caveat emptor*, **latent defect**.

as soon as possible (or practicable)
"To do a thing 'as soon as possible' means to do it within a reasonable time, with an understanding to do it within the shortest possible time" –

King's Old Country Ltd., *v* Liquid Carbonic Can Corporation Ltd. (Can.) [1942] 2 WWR 606. See also **time is of the essence**.

asking (or asked) price

The price at which a seller indicates his property may be acquired, e.g. the price at which he makes an **invitation to treat**. A term that implies a willingness to accept offer at a lower price. (In the US that lower price is referred to sometimes as an action price.)
cf. **reserve price**.

assart

The removal of trees by the roots so that they will not grow again, in particular when converting woodland or forestry into arable or pasture land. Differs from **waste** which is merely cutting trees that may grow again. cf. **afforestation**.

assemblage

The bringing, or the cost incurred in bringing, two or more parcels of land into single ownership or common use. cf. **plottage**.

assemblage value (US)

see **marriage value, plottage value**.

assembled land

Land, or an interest in land, that has come into single ownership by the purchase of adjoining areas of land, or of various interests in the same property. (For the purposes of assessing **development land tax** the cost of assembled land is treated as the cost of the separate interests acquired therein and the assembled land as a whole is treated as having been acquired on the date when the last part was acquired – Development Land Tax Act 1976, Sch. 2.) See also **plottage**.

assent

1. General approval; **acquiescence** in, or compliance with, something, especially a change in the conditions of a contract. 'Assent' may be considered as applying to something of minor importance or as representative of mere acquiescence. Agreement to a statement or proposition by a passive form of acknowledgement.
cf. **acceptance**. See also **election, waiver**
2. A document in writing or under seal, signed by a **personal representative**, that vests property in the beneficiary, in accordance with the wishes of a deceased person or according to the rules of entitlement on intestacy. An assent to be effective in passing a **legal estate** must be in writing; signed by the personal representatives; and must state the name of the person in whom the estate is to be vested (Administration of Estates Act 1925, s. 36 (4)). An assent must be executed even if the personal representatives are to hold land on trust. An assent represents the valid title of a **bona fide purchaser** for **value**; he need not concern himself with the will, he need only concern himself with the grant of probate or letters of administration. Generally the effective date of transfer relates back to the testator's death. See also **vesting document**.

assessed (or assessable) value

An official value placed on a property; in particular an estimate of the value of a property made for the purpose of levying an *ad valorem* tax. A value that is considered fair and reasonable by the tax authorities, but is not necessarily the market value. It may be equal to or be a percentage of the fair or market value of a property as determined by the appropriate authority or its official assessor. See also **assessment, rateable value**.

Real Estate Principles, by Bruce Harwood, 2 edn, Ch. 13.

Improving Real Estate Assessment: A Reference Manual, by Richard R. Almy (1978).

assessment

1. An evaluation, or the result of an evaluation, made in order to determine the amount of tax to be paid by an individual; in particular by an owner or occupier of land or buildings. The determination of the **assessed value** of a property.

In the US, an assessment is an official valuation made for the purpose of a local tax which is levied on the basis of individual property value. 'Assessment' as used in the US is similar to the determination of a **rateable value** as made in England and Wales. An assessment may be made for the purpose of levying a general property tax to pay for expenditure of a city, town or other taxing authority; thus, it is levied from specific properties or individuals to pay for specific expenditure, unlike general taxation. It may be called a local assessment when levied against all or most properties in a given town or area; or, a special assessment when levied against an owner of a property or properties to pay solely for the cost of public work that benefits those particular properties. A special assessment is levied on the principle that the assessed properties will be enhanced in value by the public works, such as street improvements, the cost of which is paid for by the monies raised.

When a tenant is obliged to pay 'taxes, rates and assessments' in a lease, 'assessment' means a payment which is of a similar nature to taxes and rates, but not an obligation to pay for an improvement required of a landlord, or any other special burden placed on a landlord, by a local authority – Tidswell *v* Whitworth (1867) LR 2 CP 326. See also **assessed value**.

2. The act or process by which a **tax**, **rate** or **duty** is levied by law, especially by a local or municipal authority.

3. The process by which operating costs or expenses are apportioned between the occupiers of a building. See also **apportionment**.

4. An **appraisal** or **estimate**.

Assessment Appeal Board (US)

A local government body that considers appeals against the **assessed value** placed on a property. An Assessment Appeal Board carries out functions that are similar to a **local valuation court** in England and Wales. See also **board of equalisation**.

assessment roll (US)

An official list, maintained in a local tax district, setting out a legal description of all the taxable properties in the district and the **assessed value** of each property. Similar to a **valuation list** in England and Wales.

assessor

1. An **expert** called upon to provide an opinion of value, especially in a dispute. In Roman and the civil law an assessor is also a person called on to give legal advice or assistance.

(US) 2. A public official who determines the **assessed value** of a property for taxation purposes. Similar to a rating **valuation officer** in England.

3. An adjudicator, or adjuster, called on to determine the loss suffered sub-

sequent to an insurance claim.

asset

Derived from the Norman French *assetz*, 'enough'. Any **property** that is owned and has value. That which is available to meet a debt or liability. Property, real or personal, tangible or intangible (including an interest in property, a chose-in-action, debt or even goodwill) that is available, or may be made available, to meet a debt of a person or corporation.
cf. **liability**. See also **current asset, fixed asset, wasting asset**.

asset life

see **economic life**.

asset stripping

Purchasing a company in order to sell all or a significant part of the assets at a profit, without regard to the viability of the company as a going-concern. Frequently used in a derogatory sense, although it may be a viable means of meeting all the ongoing liabilities of the company. The chance for asset stripping may arise when a company does not make a regular revaluation of its fixed assets, or when it has provided in its accounts for an excessive amount of depreciation, so that the share value is, or the **going-concern value** appears, significantly less than the **asset value** or **break-up value**.

asset value

The total net realisable value of the assets of a company after all debts (excluding the ordinary shareholders funds) have been paid. In general terms, "the value of an **asset** to a firm is the sum of money which would just compensate the firm for its loss in stated conditions" (*The Finance and Analysis of Capital Projects* by Mer-

rett and Sykes, 2 edn, p. 423). The asset value of a company is represented by the total cost required to bring it into operation; or what would be received if it were broken up and sold bit by bit. (The Royal Institution of Chartered Surveyors Guidance Notes A2 on the valuation of company assets requires that these should be assessed on the basis of the open **market value**).
cf. **net asset value**.

assign

To **transfer** to another; the process of **assignment**.

assignation (F)

writ; summons; subpoena.

assignee

A transferee or grantee; the party benefitting from the **assignment** of an interest. An assignee has been described as the person entitled to the term of a lease as between himself and the lessor, and "bound by and entitled to the benefit of the covenants, entered into by the lessee and lessor respectively, which ran with the land". Such a person may be called also the lessee's assignee or his 'assigns' – Friary *v* Singleton [1899] 1 Ch. 90. See also **privity of estate**.

assignment

The **transfer** of an interest in property, especially personal property (including a lease) or a chattel, to another. The transfer of the liabilities or rights under a contract to a person or body that is not a party to the original contract, whether as an act of a party to the contract or by operation of law. An assignment may be made as a **gift** or for **consideration**. Assignment in a lease means parting with the interest granted, not merely a part thereof – the retention of any **reversion**, however short, would create an underlease or **sub-lease**. The transfer of a freehold interest is more strictly a **conveyance**; 'assignment' is used more commonly for the transfer of a leasehold interest – although these terms are used synonymously.

"A covenant not to assign or otherwise part with the premises or any part thereof, for the whole or any part of the term is broken by a sublease; but a covenant 'not to assign, transfer, set over, or otherwise do or put away the lease of premises' is not. A covenant against subletting will restrain an assignment" – Greenaway *v* Adams (1806) 12 Ves. 395. Similarly, charging, granting a licence or power of attorney, or parting with possession of part of a property is not sufficient to constitute an assignment. However, there is no golden rule in this connection; "it is an open question . . . whether a covenant against an underletting alone precludes an assignment. Woodfall's *Landlord and Tenant* (27 edn, pp. 1–1219) states that it does. But in my [Browne-Wilkinson J.'s] judgment the decision of the Irish Court of Appeal in *Re* Doyle and O'Hara Contract [1899] 1 IR 113 shows that it is by no means a concluded question and it very much depends on the actual words used in each covenant." – Marks *v* Warren [1979] 1 All ER 31.

Either party to a contract may assign his rights or obligations, unless expressly prohibited, or unless the performance of the contract calls for the participation of the original party as with certain contracts of personal service. Thus, if a lease is silent on the matter the tenant is entitled to assign his interest. However, a lease commonly contains a covenant in some form limiting assignment or otherwise parting with possession of the demised premises. A lease must be assigned by deed, even if originally made orally, to be binding at law (Law of Property Act 1925, s. 52 (1)); although an assignment will be enforceable in equity, between the assignor and assignee only, if there is sufficient evidence in **writing** or an act of **part performance**.

cf. **novation**. See also **absolute assignment, alienation, equitable assignment, estoppel, legal assignment, privity, restraint on alienation**.

assignor

A party who assigns an interest; one who makes an **assignment**.

assigns

An **assignee**. A person substituted for another. See also **novation**.

assisted area

A generic term, derived from Assisted Areas Order 1979 (made under the provisions of the Local Employment Act 1972, s. 1 (1)), for an area or region of Great Britain that benefits from government financial assistance aimed at improving economic activity, in particular the encouragement of new investment and employment. These areas may now be classified as a **development area**; an **intermediate area**; or a **special development area**, depending on the extent of the aid available (Industrial Development Act 1972, Part I).

Business Property Handbook, The Boisot Waters Cohen Partnership, pp. 417–427 (1981).

assize of novel disseisin

A term for an ancient form of real action (introduced around 1166) to recover possession of land or tenements following **disseisin** (i.e. the wrongful dispossession of someone from land). Abolished by the Real Property Limitation Act 1883, s. 36. See also **seisin, writ of right**.

assize rent

Fixed **rent**. Rent which, under the **feudal system** of land tenure, was 'assized', that is, made certain. See also **copyhold**.

association

A body of persons who come together for a common purpose. See also **company, corporation, partnership, society**.

association (F)

association; **partnership**; society. 'An agreement by which two or more persons put together in a permanent manner their knowledge or their activities with an objective other than sharing profits' – French law of 1st July 1901, art 1. See also *société*. *Introduction to French Law* by Amos and Walton, 3 edn, pp. 52–54.

associé (F)

partner. (*associé en participation* – joint venture partner).

assumable mortgage

see **assumption**.

assumed life

see **holding period**.

assumpsit (L)

'He undertook; he promised'. "A voluntary promise made by word, by which a man assumeth and taketh upon him to performe, or pay, anything to another" – *Termes de la Ley*. A form of action in medieval English law whereby a plaintiff claimed that the defendant had undertaken (*as-*

sumpsit), in return for a sum of money which had been paid, to perform a duty; the existence of a debt being sufficient evidence for a court to assume that there was a corresponding duty to perform an action, e.g. to build a house. An action on *assumpsit* arose, in particular, when a person had a duty in the interest of public policy to perform a particular service satisfactorily, or when a person had expressly undertaken to carry out work. If the service or work was not properly completed an action arose on *assumpsit*. This form of action was brought (until it was abolished by the Judicature Acts 1873–75) to enforce a **simple contract** and provided the foundation for the means by which the English courts came to recognise the enforceability of an informal contract. *Assumpsit* was used also to refer to any contract that was not under seal. It is now used only in the US to refer to a form of action brought to recover a debt or damages for breach of a contract that is not under seal. See also **privity of contract, promise, unenforceable contract**.

Cheshire and Fifoot's Law of Contract 10 edn, pp. 4–6.

assumption

1. Laying claim to, or taking possession of, something. The act of taking upon oneself a debt or obligation, e.g. the obligations of a lease or mortgage. In the US assumption is used especially to refer to the taking over of a liability for a mortgage debt, or for the obligations of a deed of trust; as distinguished from the purchase of a property 'subject to mortgage' by which the purchaser accepts that the property is mortgaged, but takes over

no personal liability for the mortgage debt. A person who 'assumes' a mortgage becomes personally liable for the payment of the mortgage debt; the liability extending, if necessary, beyond the extent of the loss of the mortgaged property. Most mortgage deeds contain a clause prohibiting the transfer of the mortgage debt without the mortgagee's consent – called an **assumption clause** – and, if such consent is given, the morgagee frequently charges an 'assumption fee' to cover his costs or to reap part of any benefit that might accrue to a new party to the loan. See also **appropriation, novation, recourse**.

2. The acceptance of a **risk**.

3. A promise or undertaking not under **seal**. See also **assumpsit**.

assumption clause

1. A clause in a mortgage deed prohibiting the transfer of the mortgage contract without the consent of the mortgagee.
cf. **alienation**.

2. A clause in an agreement for the transfer of a mortgage loan which stipulates that the transferee or grantee accepts the personal liability for the mortgage debt. See also **assumption**.

assumption fee (US)

A charge levied by a mortgagee or lender for granting consent to his debt or liability being transferred to another. The assumption fee is payable generally when a person assumes or takes over a mortgage that was granted on terms that are now more favourable than those prevailing in the open market for a similar loan; although an 'assumption fee' may be payable merely to meet the lender's legal and administrative expenses of the transfer. See also **assumption**.

assumptions, as to planning permission
see **planning assumptions**.

assurance

1. The act of transferring property; or, "something which operates as a transfer of property" – Re Ray [1896] 1 Ch. 476. An old word for a **conveyance**. See also **beneficial owner, disentailing assurance**.

2. Synonymous with **insurance**; although generally used with reference to life assurance or a contract of indemnity that is based on a known occurance or fixed date of payment.

assurance (F)
insurance.
(*assurance au tiers* – **third-party liability insurance**)
(*assurance contre l'incendie* – **fire insurance**)
(*assurance contre la perte des loyers* – **loss of rents insurance**)
(*assurance à dotation* or *à capital* – endowment assurance)
(*assurance de responsabilité civile* – **public liability insurance** or third-party liability insurance)
(*assurance tous risques* – **all-risks insurance**)
(*assurance tous risques chantier* – **contractor's all-risks insurance**).

assured
see **insured**.

assured tenancy

A tenancy of a separate dwelling house which would be a **protected tenancy** or a **housing association tenancy**, except that the landlord is an 'approved body' as specified by the Secretary of State for the Environment, e.g. a reputable private landowner such as the Abbey Housing

Association, Wates, Costain Homes and similar private house builders or institutional landowners. An assured tenancy is given **security of tenure** by virtue of the Housing Act 1980, s. 58, but in accordance with rules that are similar to those for a **business tenancy** as provided for by the Landlord and Tenant Act 1954 (as amended by the Law of Property Act 1969), instead of the Rent Acts. Accordingly the security afforded to the tenant is less tightly controlled than an ordinary protected tenancy. In addition the rent payable for a dwelling-house let on an assured tenancy is based on the market rent (as for a business tenancy) and not a fair rent (as for a protected tenancy). An assured tenancy may be granted only for a dwelling or part of a dwelling, erected after 8 August 1980. Also, if the house had previously been occupied it must have been so occupied only by virtue of an assured tenancy and the landlord must have been an 'approved body' since the start of the tenancy (1980 Act, s. 56 (3)).

Assured Tenancies – A Guide for Landlords and Tenants, (Housing Booklet No. 17) H.M.S.O.

Residential Leases: A Draftsmans Handbook, by Charles Bennett, pp. 245–248 (1984).

The Law of Landlord and Tenant, by D.J. Evans, 2 edn, pp. 419–420.

Manual of Housing Law, by Andrew Arden, 2 edn, pp. 109–112.

Housing Law, by Andrew Arden and Martin Partington, pp. 121, 1036–1044 (1983).

at arm's length
see **arm's length transaction**.

at law
see **common law**.

at par
see **par value**.

atelier (F)
workshop.

attached
Connected to, or forming part of, something, usually on a permanent basis. Fixed or fastened to a property. In deciding whether something is attached to land or a building for the purpose of assessing its **rateable value** then it may be asked, "does the word 'attached' mean attached by some physical fastening such as screws or bolts? If it does, a thing weighing tons, which cannot be and never was intended to be lifted, would not be taken into account if not fastened to some part of the building; whereas if it were fastened it would. That, as it seems to my mind, would be a monstrous consequence. I do not think the word 'attached' does there mean 'physically fastened', so as to determine whether the thing is to be taken into account or not" – Tyne Boiler Works Co. *v* Longbenton (1886) 56 LJMC 12. See also **annex, fixture**.

attachment
A legal process or writ used for taking or seizing custody of property pending settlement of a debt. Generally used against an absconding, evasive or fraudulent debtor by a creditor who has already received a direction from the court that a debtor must meet his obligations (i.e. by a **judgement creditor**); or used prior to a formal court hearing to prevent a debtor removing property from the appropriate jurisdiction. See also **distress, lien, Mareva injunction** .

atteinte portée (F)
nuisance, especially private nui-

sance. See also *quasi-délit*.

attendance

The provision of personal services by a landlord to a tenant, as distinguished from service charges (e.g. heating, lighting, etc.). It means "service personal to the tenant performed by an attendant provided by the landlord ... for the benefit or convenience of the individual tenant in his use and enjoyment of the demised premises" – Palser *v* Grinling [1948] AC 310. Attendance may include such matters as cleaning the interior of a flat or providing linen, but it does not cover general property maintenance or upkeep of any common parts of a building. A tenant who is provided with attendance, the cost of which forms a substantial proportion of his rent, cannot claim a right to a **protected tenancy** (Rent Act 1977, s. 7); although he may have a **restricted contract**. See also **board, service tenancy**.

attest

To bear witness to a fact. To certify formally that a document is true (i.e. freely entered into or a true copy) by **signature**, or to witness another's signature on a deed. Any certified or attested copy of a document may be used as evidence in a legal action. It is not essential to attest a deed (unless it is for a **will**, a **bill of sale**, or a **transfer** of registered land), but it is a common practice. See also **certified copy**.

attestation (F)

certificate; declaration.
(*attestation de propriété* – (**abstract of title**)

attestation clause

A clause in a document that contains the signature, or declares that the document has been duly executed. A **testator** must sign, or acknowledge his or her signature to a will, in the simultaneous presence of two witnesses. If a testator has signed his or her name in more than one place the witnesses must attest the signature at the foot or end of the will – In the Estate of Bercovitz [1961] 1 WLR 892.

attorney

1. An agent or person who acts in another's place. Attorney "is an English word, and signifieth one that is set in turne, stead or place of another; and of these some be private ... and some be public, as attorneys at law" – (Co. Litt. 51a, 128a; The "private" attorney is referred to as an 'attorney-in-fact'). See also **power of attorney**.
2. A **lawyer**. In England, a term originally applied to someone who was permitted to practice in the superior courts, who is today called a **barrister**. In the US, a generic term for all members of the legal profession. See also **solicitor**.

attorney-in-fact

see **attorney, power of attorney**.

attornment

The acceptance of the coming into existence of a legal relationship; such as when a tenant recognises that another landlord, or a mortgagee, has acquired the immediate reversionary interest, i.e. has become that tenant's immediate landlord. Attornment when established between a mortgagee and a tenant creates a relationship of landlord and tenant. Attornment may arise also when a bailee (one who holds goods in **bailment**) acknowledges to the person for whom he was holding goods that he is holding them on behalf of another party. In the US, the term is used sometimes to refer to a demand for rent as made by a new owner of property. See also **attornment clause**.

attornment agreement

An agreement which establishes that, in certain circumstances, **attornment** will be accepted by the parties. For example, an agreement between a sub-tenant and a freeholder which states that if the intervening, or sandwich lease, is terminated the sub-tenant becomes the direct tenant of the freeholder.

attornment clause

A clause in a mortgage deed by which the mortgagor attornes or acknowledges that he is a tenant of the mortgagee; usually at a nominal rent. Originally such a clause was inserted to give the mortgagee a more speedy procedure in obtaining possession in the event of the mortgagor's default. This advantage no longer has such relevance, but an attornment clause enables the mortgagee to enforce covenants in the deed against an assignee of the mortgagor. See also **attornment**.

attractive nuisance doctrine (US)

see **negligence**.

auction

Derived from the Latin *auctio* – 'to increase'. A method of selling property by which a potential vendor, or his agent (auctioneer), invites open and unconditional offers, in stages, from the public at large (or, at least, from that sector of the public that attends the sale) and then accepts the highest price bid, usually by striking a hammer or gavel on a board (hence a 'sale under the hammer'). (In a Dutch or Chinese auction the auctioneer proposes the highest price, which he reduces in stages until the first bid is made and this bid is automatically accepted).

An advertisement that a property is to be offered for sale by auction is an **invitation to treat** and the property may be withdrawn prior to the auction sale without obligation (Haris *v* Nickerson (1873) 26 LT 410). When a property is put forward at an auction sale the auctioneer continues to make an invitation to treat and is at liberty to reject any bid until he signifies **acceptance** by the fall of his hammer, or any other signification of acceptance. Similarly, a bidder may retract his bid up to the same stage – Payne *v* Cave (1789) 3 Term. Rep. 148; Sale of Goods Act 1893, s. 58 (2); British Car Auctions *v* Wright [1972] 1 WLR 1519. See also **buy-in, bidding agreement, mock auction, reserve price**.
The Law of Estate Agency and Auctions, J.R. Murdoch, 2 edn, pp. 485–515.
2 Halsbury's Laws of England 4 edn paras. 360–387.
Auctions: Law and Practice, by Brian W. Harvey and Franklin Meisel (1985).

auction ring

see **bidding agreement**

auction with reserve (or with reservation)

see **reserve price**.

auctioneer

A person instructed to sell a property by **auction**; effectively a vendor's **agent**, who is authorised to submit a property for sale on a specific occasion (or a second or further occasion if the objective is not achieved on the first occasion) and then to seek the highest offer or bid. An auctioneer has an implied **authority** to effect a sale of the property entrusted to him (unless expressly instructed to the contrary) and to make representations about that property – Pickering *v* Busk (1812) 15 East 43; Smith *v* Land and House Property Corporation (1884) 28 Ch. D7. He is employed primarily to bring about a sale of the property and, therefore, it is in the nature of his responsibility to his client to see that a sale takes place at the best price possible – Fordham *v* Christie, Manson and Woods (1977) 244 EG 213. Unless expressly authorised to the contrary an auctioneer is required to offer property entrusted to him for sale to the general public and seek the best price on offer; although frequently he is permitted to withdraw a property if it does not reach a **reserve price**, as stipulated by the client, and often he is authorised to sell by private treaty if a suitable offer is received prior to the auction.

Upon acceptance of a bid, the auctioneer becomes the agent of the purchaser, as well as the vendor, in order that he may bind the parties to a sale agreement. "It is settled beyond the probability of now being disputed, that where there is a sale by auction, and the property is knocked down by the auctioneer to the highest bidder, the auctioneer is not only the agent of the vendor, but he is also the agent of the purchaser, the highest bidder; and that he is the purchaser's agent clearly to this extent, that he is entitled to sign in the name and on behalf of the purchaser, a memorandum sufficient to satisfy the **Statute of Frauds** [or now the Law of Property Act 1925, s. 40] stating the particulars of the contract" – Sims *v* Landray [1894] 2 Ch.

320. However, his ability to act as agent for the purchaser is limited to this function only. The auctioneer should check the identity of the highest bidder, obtain the bidder's signature on a memorandum giving effect to the sale within a reasonable time of the acceptance of the final bid (Bell *v* Balls [1897] 1 Ch. 663), collect any requisite deposit, and he should ensure that there is a properly executed contract. An auctioneer warrants that the vendor has no defect in the title to the property of which the auctioneer is aware and that the purchaser will receive a right to **quiet enjoyment** of the property purchased. See also **misrepresentation, without reserve**.

The Law of Estate Agency and Auctions, J.R. Murdoch, 2 edn, pp. 383–483.

auteur (F)
assignor; one who transfers a benefit or obligation to another called an *ayant cause*; a **predecessor in title**.

authentic act
In the civil law, a document that has been certified by a notary public, or other authorised public officer, or certified as a true copy of a public record. See also *acte*.

authorisation to sell (US)
see **listing, sole right to sell**.

authorised development
Development carried out with duly authorised **planning permission**.
cf. **permitted development**.

authority
1. A power or right conferred on a person or body. Approval or sanction to make a representation or to receive

a submission on behalf of another. Authority is founded only on right, unlike a **power** which may exist independently of right; authority is given but a power may be taken or usurped. A person invested with an authority frequently is called an **agent** and the person who grants that authority, a **principal**. Authority may be 'bare', 'naked' or 'mere'; or 'coupled with an interest'. A bare authority usually may be revoked at will. An authority coupled with an interest may be revoked only when the interest is revoked (Power of Attorney Act 1971, s. 4). See also **actual authority, agency of necessity, estate agent, ostensible authority**.
2. A public body or administration having local or quasi-governmental powers. A body vested with delegated power. See also **local authority, planning authority, highway authority, *ultra vires***.

autofinancement (F)
 self-financing.

automatic reinstatement clause
 see **reinstatement basis**.

autre vie (L)
 'The life of another'. See **life estate**.

avail
 An old word for the profit from the sale of land.

avance (F)
 advance; loan.
 (*loyer d'avance* – rent in advance).

avant contrat (F)
 A document that sets out the basic terms agreed prior to the preparation of a formal contract or an ***acte authentique***.

avant-projet (F)
 preliminary plan or design; **draft; estimate**.

avarie (F)
 injury; damage.
 (*clause avarie* – **average clause**).

avec droit de recourse (F)
 with right of **recourse**.

avenant (F)
 endorsement; rider; deed of variation.

average
 see **average clause**.

average annual return (AAR)
 The return from an investment calculated by taking the total return over the life of the investment, dividing that sum by the number of years the investment is held, and taking the resultant as a percentage of the initial cost of the investment. The return may be based on income, capital appreciation (or depreciation) or the combination of both. For example, if an investment costs £100 000, produces a total income over three years of £40 000 and is sold then for £120 000 the average annual return would be:
$$\frac{40000 + 20000}{100000} \times \frac{100}{3} = 20\%.$$
 This rate of return takes no account of the time at which the income is received or the capital appreciation (or depreciation) occurs, i.e. it is a non-discounted rate of return. Called also a book rate of return, an accountant's rate of return or an average rate of return.
 cf. **internal rate of return**. See also **pay-back method**.

average clause
 A condition in an insurance contract that the insured amount is 'subject to average', i.e. that if the property is

worth more than the sum for which it is insured (the property is underinsured) then, in the event of a partial or total loss, the insurer will pay only the proportion that the amount of cover bears to the actual cost of replacement. A typical average clause may read: 'if the property covered, shall, at the breaking out of any fire or at the commencement of any destruction of or damage to such property by any other peril hereby insured against be collectively of greater value than such sum insured, then the insured shall be considered as his own insurer for the difference and shall bear a rateable share of the loss accordingly' – Acme Wood Flooring Co. *v* Marten 90 LT 313. In the US commonly called a co-insurance clause. See also **co-insurance.**

average rate of return (ARR)
see **average annual return.**

aviation easement (US)
see **avigation easement.**

avigation easement (US)
An **easement in gross** for the unobstructed passage of aircraft. By law (common law and statute) civil aircraft may fly over land above specified altitudes. On the other hand private or military aircraft, or civil aircraft at an approach to a runway, may acquire an 'avigation easement' to fly over land at altitudes below those permitted by law. An avigation easement may take the form of a 'clearance easement' by which a landowner is prohibited from placing any structure on his land that exceeds a maximum height; or a flight easement by which the aircraft are permitted to fly frequently over land above a specified height. See also **air right.**

avis (F)
notice; advice; formal opinion.
(*avis de congé* – **notice to quit**) See also *notification, signification, préavis.*

avocat (F)
A legal representative, especially one who is entitled to represent a client in litigation (a term that is better not translated).
cf. *avoué*; *agréé*; *notaire*. See also **lawyer.**
Introduction to French Law by Amos and Walton, p. 22, for an outline of the French legal profession.

avoidance
The act or process of withdrawing from a **voidable contract.**

avoir (F)
credit; creditor; payment in advance.
(*doit et avoir* – debit and credit).

avoirs (F)
possessions; the total property holdings of an individual or company; assets. See also *patrimoine, propriété.*

avoué (F)
A lawyer who may be engaged in procedural matters for civil litigation in front of the court of appeal. He prepares much of the written material required by the court but, unlike an *avocat*, does not make oral pleadings at trials.

avulsion
From the Latin *avellere*, 'to tear away'. The fairly sudden and identifiable change in the limits of land due to natural causes, e.g. a change in the course of a river due to the collapse of a river bank or a flood. A change due to avulsion does not affect property ownership boundaries; unlike the gradual and imperceptible process of **accretion.** Ford *v* Lacy (1861) 7 H and

N 151; Attorney-General of Southern Nigeria *v* John Holt and Co. (Liverpool) Ltd [1915] AC 599. See also **alluvion**.

avulsion (F)
avulsion.

award
1. The decision arrived at by an arbitrator following a submission to **arbitration**. See also **interim award**.
2. The amount adjudged in court as an appropriate level of **damages**.

away-going crops
see **way-going crops**.

ayant cause (F)
assignee, in particular one who acquires property by purchase and not by inheritance. See also *auteur*.

ayant droit (F)
interested party; title holder; rightful owner; claimant.

B

back-bond or back-letter

1. A **bond** or instrument that qualifies another deed; especially an instrument in which an **indemnity** is given to a person who is in turn a surety or guarantor.

2. In Scottish law, a deed by which a party acknowledges that another transaction does not, as may appear, transfer an absolute right of ownership, but is merely a transfer of a right to a surety or mortgage against the subject matter. The signatory to the deed normally declares that he is only a trustee or mortgagee and not an absolute owner of the subject matter. Similar to a **deed of trust** in English law.

back land

Land that is situated behind an established development and generally has inadequate access for the purpose of development. See also **easement of necessity**.

backside

An ancient term for **premises**, or a yard, at the rear of a house.

back-to-back house

A house that forms part of a row or terrace of similar houses, joined together at the rear as well as the sides. The essential characteristic of a 'back-to-back' house is that it has only one external wall (the front wall); with the exception of the house at each end of the terrace which has also an external gable-end wall. "It appears that back-to-back houses in England are built in terraces, and the buildings have a solid party wall run-

ning parallel to two terraces, and the houses are built each side of the party wall, one set of houses each facing one terrace and the other facing the other. In such houses, the means of ventilation is from the front of the house except in the case of the houses at the end of the terrace, where there is ventilation on the front and one side." – Murrayfield Real Estate Co. *v* Edinburgh Magistrates [1912] SC 217. The availability of natural lighting and ventilation to a back-to-back house is more limited than for other types of houses that have exposed front and back walls. (The existence of an air shaft between the backs of the houses need not invalidate their being back-to-back structurally.)

Back-to-back houses were considered **unfit for human habitation** because of their restricted natural lighting and ventilation and as such were included in demolition or clearance schemes under the Housing Acts (Housing Act 1936, s. 22; Housing Act 1957, 3.5). However, these statutory provisions were repealed in 1980 (Housing Act 1980, Sch. 25, s. 4).

back-to-back lease

An arrangement by which an owner of one building takes over a lease from a tenant in another building and, in exchange, the tenant agrees to enter into a lease of accommodation in the owner's building.

back-to-back loan

1. An arrangement by which a loan made in one country is guaranteed by security held in another. This ar-

rangement, which is made usually through the medium of a bank in each country, may be used, for example, when the security offered is real estate that the borrower holds in a different country from where the loan is made. A premium is required normally on the amount of security pledged in order to cover the risk of any exchange rate variation up to the date when the loan falls due for repayment. No foreign currency purchases are made, unless repayment of the loan is not met by the due date.

2. An agreement by which a company or financial institution in one country guarantees a loan made to a company or institution in another country, when the domestic borrower or guarantor may not wish to be known to the ultimate lender; or when, to avoid foreign exchange control, reciprocal guarantees are given by the respective organisations.

3. A loan made to finance a series of related transactions so that the loan will eventually be granted exclusively to the final purchaser of a property.

backup offer

An offer made by a third party to purchase a property, so that if a prior, or higher, offer proves to be unacceptable or unsupported by action, the third party's offer is available for acceptance by the seller. See also **gazump, subject to contract**.

bad faith

Dishonest; an intention to deceive or misrepresent.
cf. **good faith**. See also **fraud, misrepresentation**.

bad title

A title so defective that it conveys no interest to the purchaser or holder of a property.
cf. **good title, marketable title**.

bail (pl. baux) (F)

lease (of immoveable property). In French law a lease is a personal right to the use of property; although, as in English law, a long-term lease (a *bail à construction* or a *bail emphytéotique* is generally regarded as a real right – a right which may be assigned, mortgaged or charged.
(*bail à colonat paritaire* – **sharecropper lease**. See also *metayage*)
(*bail à court terme* – short-term lease)
(*bail à long terme* – long-term lease, a lease for a term exceeding nine years).
(*bail à loyer* – residential lease)
(*bail à terme* – lease for a term of years)
(*bail à vie* – lease for a life)
(*bail d'habitation* – residential lease)
(*bail emphytéothique* – **emphyteotic lease**)
(*bail foncier* – **ground lease**, see also **droit de superficie**)
(*bail précaire* – **tenancy at will**)
(*cession de bail* – transfer of a lease)
(*preneur à bail* – lessee)
(*signer un bail* – execute a lease)
(*sous-bail* – sub-lease). See also *démembrements de la propriété, location*.
Amos & Walton's Introduction to French Law, 3 edn, pp. 109–112.
Droit Civil, Les Biens, by Jean Carbonnier, 11 edn, pp. 269–274.
Baux d'habitation et Professionnels, by Jacques Voulet, 10 edn.

bail à construction (F)

A **building lease** whereby the tenant agrees to build on the leased land and is granted a *droit de superficie*. A form of **emphyteotic lease**, introduced by a French law of 16 December 1964 No. 64–1247, that is used for urban development (law of 31st December 1975).

Précis Dalloz. Droit Civil, Les Biens (Alex Weill) 2 edn, p. 581.

bail à ferme (F)

farm **lease**. A lease to a farmer by which the tenant assumes sole responsibility for running the farm and retains the profits arising from his endeavours; in return for which the landlord receives a rent (*fermage*) that is not dependent on the profit (or loss) of the tenant's business. Such leases are granted normally for nine years, but may be granted for eighteen or over twenty-eight years. The former are renewable for periods of nine years, whereas the latter are for a single fixed term (*Code Rurale, arts.* 809–812; Laws of 31 December 1970 and 3 January 1972).

cf. **metayage system**.

Manuel de Droit Civil, by Pierre Voirin et Giles Goubeaux, 20 edn, pp. 315–316.

Baux Ruraux, by Guy Coulon et Robert Randier, 3 edn.

bail commercial (F)

commercial lease. In France applies to leases of premises for more than two years that are used for commercial or trade purposes. Such leases are subject to strict regulations under a statutory decree of September 1953; this decree gives the tenant who operates a business certain rights to renew his lease. Accordingly the *fonds de commerce* of a business includes not only the tangible assets of that business and the goodwill but also the rights under a *bail commercial*.

Commercial Leases in France, by Ronald Farrants, p. 240 E.G. 615 (1976).

bail rural (F)

A farm lease. See also *bail à ferme*.

bailee

A person who holds goods under a process of **bailment**. "Any person is to be considered as a bailee who, otherwise than as a servant, either receives possession of a thing from another or consents to receive or hold possession of a thing for another upon an understanding with the other person to keep and return or deliver to him the specific thing or to (convey and) apply the specified thing according to directions antecedant or future of the other person." – *Possession in the Common Law*, by Pollock and Wright. p. 163, 1888).

The thing or title to the thing is not transferred to the bailee.

bailleur (F)

lessor; landlord.

(*bailleur de fonds* – lender; **sleeping partner**; money lender).

bailiff

An officer of a court who is engaged to serve and enforce its orders, in particular an officer employed to levy **distress**. A sheriff's officer or a person employed by a sheriff to serve writs or to execute other legal procedures. For the purpose of levying distress no person may be employed as a bailiff unless he is so authorised by a certificate in writing from a county court judge or county court registrar (Law of Distress Amendment Act 1888, s. 7).

bailment

Derived from the French *bailler*, 'to hand over'. A delivery of **possession** of goods from the owner (bailor) to another (bailee), on trust, and on condition that they will be handed

back when a period of safekeeping, or use, has elapsed. A delivery of personal property for a specified purpose, under an express or implied contract, that after the purpose is accomplished the property will be returned to the bailor or applied according to his direction – Rich *v* Touche Ross and Co. 415 F. Supp. 95 (DCNY). Bailment must be accompanied by a transfer of actual or constructive possession of the goods; it does not arise merely because a person is given permission to leave goods on or in another's property. Bailment may take several forms such as: (i) a deposit of goods for safekeeping or repair; (ii) a means of assisting or giving an advantage to the bailee (as with goods in transit); (iii) to enable the bailee to use the goods e.g. for **hire**; or (iv) a **pawn** or **pledge**. A bailor does not transfer ownership or title to the goods to the bailee but merely a conditional right of possession. Bailment may be distinguished from a **sale** or **gift** which passes title at once, without any intention that the goods or their equivalent shall be returned. Bailment may be distinguished from a **licence** which, as a rule, places no duty or obligation on the licencee as to manner or purpose for which the licenced goods are used. See also **deposit, hire purchase, leasing**.
Mercantile Law, by Charlesworth, 14 edn, pp. 467–476.
2 Halsbury's Laws of England, 4 edn, paras. 1501–1589.

bailor
A person who hands over goods under a process of **bailment**. A bailor passes possession of the goods to another for a specific purpose but retains ownership or title.

baissier (F)
bear (on the stock exchange).

balance sheet
A statement of the financial position of a business organisation, showing its total assets and liabilities (including the owner's equity or the net worth of the organisation) at a specified point in time. See also **financial statement**.

balancing allowance (or charge)
Where an industrial building or structure is disposed of (whether as an outright sale, on receipt of compensation or insurance monies, or as a result of a lease that expires) and that property has been the subject of a **capital allowance**, a balancing allowance may be made if the proceeds of sale of the property are less than its written-down value (the 'expenditure unallowed'). Conversely, if the proceeds exceed the written-down value, a charge may be made on that excess, although the charge cannot exceed the total of the allowances given (Capital Allowances Act 1968, s. 3).

balloon mortgage (or loan)
A mortgage (or loan) incorporating a **balloon payment**, i.e. a mortgage (or loan) made on the basis that a part of the principal is repaid by a number of equal regular instalments and the balance is repaid, at the end of the mortgage term, by a single sum that substantially exceeds those regular instalments.
cf. **standing mortgage**. See also **instalment mortgage**.

balloon payment
A single lump-sum payment of the outstanding balance at the end of the term of a mortgage or loan agreement; a lump-sum that substantially

exceeds any regular instalments made towards repaying the principal during the term of the loan. For example, a mortgage of £10 000 may be granted for a term of 10 years with a provision that the capital is repaid, or amortised, by nine annual instalments of £800 and one final payment – the balloon payment – of £2800. In the US, this type of arrangement is called sometimes 'ballooning' a loan.

ballooning (US)
  see **balloon payment**.

Baltimore method of appraisal (US)
  see **corner lot**.

band-of-investment capitalisation rate (US)
  An **overall capitalisation rate** derived from a weighted average of (i) the current cost of debt service (based on an appropriate **mortgage constant**), and (ii) an appropriate rate of return on the equity invested in a property (a **cash-on-cash yield**). As an example, assume that a mortgage can be obtained to finance 80 per cent of the cost of acquiring a property investment and the 'mortgage constant' (the constant rate required to repay interest and principal by equal instalments over the term of the loan) is 15 per cent. Also assume that an investor requires an 8 per cent return on his 20 per cent equity investment. Then the overall capitalisation rate would be four-fifths of 15 per cent plus one-fifth of 8 per cent i.e. 13.6 per cent. A band of investment rate may be applied, in the same way as any other capitalisation factor, to ascertain the capital value of a projected or anticipated income from an investment. The procedure may be reversed to ascertain the required rate of return

on equity by taking away the cost of debt finance from an appropriate overall capitalisation rate deduced from comparable investments. For example, if the overall rate is assessed as 9 per cent and a 75 per cent mortgage can be repaid by an 8 per cent mortgage constant, then the cash-on-cash yield or equity dividend rate is:

$$\frac{(1 \times 0.09 - (0.75 \times 0.08)}{[0.25]} = 0.12 \text{ or } 12\%$$

A band of investment rate calculated using only the interest rate on the mortgage (and not a mortgage constant) is called also a basic rate. Called also a synthetic capitalisation rate. See also **weighted average cost of capital**.

bank draft or banker's draft
  A **cheque** or **draft** drawn by one bank on a deposit held to its account by another bank; or a cheque drawn by a bank on its own account and payable on demand, as when a branch bank draws a cheque on an account at its head office. A **bill of exchange**, where the drawer is a bank; being a negotiable instrument that is as good as cash when it is presented. A bank draft is used usually to pay for a property when the vendor requires a guaranteed payment at the time of completion.

bankruptcy
  In general, the condition of being unable to meet one's debts; the effect of a failure to have, or be able to obtain, assets to pay one's debts as they fall due. In particular, the proceeding that arises when a court resolves that a person is unable to discharge his or her debts, and that an official receiver, or trustee in bankruptcy, should be appointed to inquire into the reasons for the insolvency; to free the person from the

debts; and to distribute the proceeds from the sale of all assets to the creditors generally (unless there are any special priorities). The debtor is known as a bankrupt. If a tenant becomes bankrupt the lease automatically vests in the trustee in bankruptcy upon his appointment (Bankruptcy Act 1914, s. 53). The trustee may disclaim the lease in writing within a period of up to twelve months from the date of his appointment (a period that may be extended by the court). Until that disclaimer the landlord can claim for the full rent due.

cf. **liquidation**. See also **disclaimer, inhibition, insolvency**.

banlieue (F)
suburb.

banque hypothécaire (F)
mortgage bank; land bank.

banqueroute (F)
bankruptcy. Used when the failure is a fault of the trader (whether a fault at law or a fraud) and is consequently a criminal offence. There is no direct English equivalent.
cf. *faillite*.
Amos & Walton's Introduction to French Law 3 edn, pp. 370–371.

bare licence
see **licence**.

bare title
see **naked title**.

bare trust
A **trust** under which the trustee has no other responsibility than to hold a nominal or 'paper' title to property pending its transfer to the *cestui que trust* or beneficiary. A trust which grants the trustee such limited powers that the beneficiary has effective con-

trol over the trust property; the beneficiary being the only person able to enjoy the property and derive benefit from it and normally having the right, at any time, to require the trustee to transfer the **legal estate** to himself. A bare trust commonly comes into existence when a beneficiary reaches the age of majority and, being without disability, is able then to require the trustee to deal with the trust property as demanded. Called also a 'dry trust', 'simple trust', 'passive trust' or 'naked trust'.
cf. **special trust**.
Equity and the Law of Trusts, by P.H. Petit, 4 edn, pp. 50–51.

barème (F)
scale (of fees or charges); schedule; tariff.

bargain
From the Latin *barcaniare*, 'to change about'. An **agreement** or undertaking, negotiated between two parties, especially as struck by men engaged in trade: frequently preceding a formal contract. "A bargain is an agreement of two or more persons to exchange promises or to exchange a promise for a performance." *Restatement of the Law of Contract*, American Law Institute, (1932). para. 4. A bargain lies at the foundation of the modern concept of a commercial **contract**; that is, that someone has entered into a bargain, not a mere expression of intent – "for the intent of man cannot be tried; for the Devil himself knows not the intent of man" – Chief Justice Briar, *Anon.* (1478) YB 17 Ed. 4; although it does not create a contract without more ado. 'Bargain' is used also to refer to a process of haggling; coming to an understanding; the giving of an assurance or

pledge; or the purchase of something at a favourable price. A bargain, once reached, is not normally relinquished lightly, even though in reality it be not much more than a **gentleman's agreement**: "I'll give thrice so much land to any well-deserving friend; but in the way of a bargain mark ye me; I'll cavil on the ninth part of a hair." (William Shakespeare, *Henry IV* Part II. Act III). See also **agreement for sale, earnest money, subject to contract**.

bargain and sale

A term used to describe an **executed contract**. "Bargain and sale is when a recompense is given by both the parties to the bargain: as if one bargain and sell his land to another for money, here the land is a recompense to him for the money, and money is a recompense to the other for the land." – *Termes de la Ley*. See also **bargain and sale deed**.

bargain and sale deed

A **deed** for the sale of land which contains only the minimum essentials of a contract and no other covenants. The seller implies that he has an interest in the land and that he is transferring only that interest. This special form of deed for the transfer of land is not now known under English law; a 'bargain and sale' deed, which was a form of secret agreement for conveying land, was abolished in 1926 and all transfers of land must now be made by **deed of grant** (Law of Property Act 1925, s. 51). In the US, the use of the words 'bargain and sale' in a deed are sufficient to convey a **fee simple** title – Richardson *v* Levi, 3 SW 444, 67 Tex. 359.

cf. **quitclaim deed, warranty deed**. See also **open contract, title insu-**

rance. *Real Estate Principles* by Bruce Harwood, 2 edn, p. 95 (which sets out a typical form of bargain and sale deed).

'barring the entail'

see **base fee, disentail, entailed interest**.

barrister

A lawyer admitted to plead at the Bar. In England, a member of one of the four Inns of Court; a lawyer who gives an opinion on a client's case or 'brief' presented to him by a **solicitor**. A barrister has an exclusive right to present cases in the High Court. (A party seeking advice or being represented in the High Court does not approach a barrister directly, but always acts through a solicitor.) A practising barrister is referred to as 'counsel' and his formal legal opinion as 'counsel's opinion'. See also **advocate**.

bas quartier (F)

slum area. See also *taudis*.

base date (or period)

The point or period in time used as a reference in the future; such as in an indexation process, being either the date at which the index is first compiled, or the starting point for assessing an increase in prices in relation to an index. The start date of a lease, or construction contract, when used as a reference point for determining a future revision or escalation of the rent, or contract price.

base fee

1. An estate in land that is less than a **fee simple absolute** because it comes to an end on the happening of a contingent event. In general, a base fee is any fee estate that is not assured of

lasting for ever, i.e. it is a **qualified fee**, and it is the uncertainty as to when or if the estate will come to an end that makes the interest a base fee and not an **absolute estate**. In the US, 'base fee' is used to refer to any estate that has a qualification attached to it, whether it is a 'conditional fee', a 'defisible fee' a **'determinable fee'** or a 'contingent fee'. In English law usually 'qualified fee' is used to draw a distinction from an absolute estate; 'determinable fee' to draw a distinction from a conditional fee simple; and 'base fee' in the limited sense referred to below.

In a limited sense a base fee is "that estate in fee simple into which an estate in tail, an entail **(entailed interest)**, is converted where the issues in tail are barred, but persons claiming estates by way of remainder or otherwise are not barred." (Fines and Recoveries Act 1833, s. 1). In other words, a base fee would be an absolute estate in fee simple except that the holder of that estate risks the possibility that the person who is entitled to the immediate **remainder** (or if he is dead, his estate) may be entitled to regain the fee simple estate. A means of creating such a base fee may be illustrated by an example: assume an interest in land is held by A for his life, then the estate passes to B as an entailed interest (e.g. to B and 'the heirs of his body'), and then to C in fee simple. Then if B disposes of his entailed interest to X, X's interest would last only until B dies; but if B has disentailed his heir (i.e. defeats the claims of his heirs, or any other person claiming a right to an estate in the land) without A's consent, then X would receive a base fee. (A is referred to as the 'protector of the estate' as, in

essence, that is his function). X's base fee continues as long as B has living descendants, and the estate then passes to C – the greater the number of heirs of B the nearer X's interest approaches a fee simple. If A's consent to the disentailing had been, or is at a later date obtained, or A dies before B the interest may be enlarged into a fee simple by B executing a new deed and thereby depriving C of an interest he might have hoped would ultimately come into his possession (Fines and Recoveries Act 1833, s. 34–49; Law of Property Act 1925, s. 176). A base fee may be enlarged into a fee simple also by (a) B (or any one to whom he has conveyed his base fee) acquiring C's remainder interest; (b) by B remaining in possession of the land for 12 years after A's death (Limitation Act 1980, s. 27); or (c) in certain circumstances, by a gift by will by B provided he is in possession of the land – the grantee receiving a fee simple in a similar way as if B had made a disentailing deed (Law of Property Act 1925, s. 176 (1), (3)). See also **conditional fee**, **strict settlement**. *Introduction to Land Law*, by J.G. Riddell, 2 edn, p. 53.
Modern Law of Real Property, by Cheshire, 13 edn, pp. 254–256.
39 Halsbury's Laws of England, 4 edn, paras. 449–454.
2. A form of feudal land tenure whereby the 'tenant' held land at the will of the lord of the manor in return for base services, i.e. **villeinage tenure**. Called also 'base tenure'.

base licence
see **licence**.

base map
A map, showing the existing physical pattern of land use, used for superim-

posing planning proposals or survey information. Usually it shows limited information such as property boundaries, communication routes, etc., and the superimposition is in the form of a transparent overlay.

base period
see **base date**.

base rent
The minimum rent payable under a lease that provides for either an **indexed rent**, or a percentage or **turnover rent**. Called sometimes a 'basic rent' or 'hardcore rent'. See also **dead rent, flat rent, hardcore method**.

base tenure
see **base fee**.

base value
A value for land (based essentially on cost or current use value, with permitted adjustments) as assessed when determining a liability for **development land tax** (DLT). When determining a 'realised gain' for DLT purposes the proceeds from the sale of a property is deducted from the highest of three permitted 'base values' (the 'relevant base value') to arrive at the 'development value' upon which the tax is levied. The Development Land Tax Act 1976, s. 5 sets out these base values, which may be summarised as (i) the price paid for the land, plus any increase in its current use value since acquisition (or if the land was acquired before 6 April 1965, since that date); (ii) the current use value at the date of a disposal, plus 15 per cent; (iii) the cost of purchase, plus 15 per cent. As a rule the cost of 'relevant improvements' to the land may be treated as a price paid or cost. See also **fair value**.
Modern Method of Valuation, 7 edn,

p. 410.
Development Land Tax – a practical guide, by Clifford Joseph, 2 edn, pp. 63–69.
Development Land Tax, by Robert W. Maes, 4 edn, p. 6 *et seq*.

basement
The sub-structure of a building. A part of a building that is wholly or substantially below ground level. A basement or 'underground room' (i.e. one whose floor surface is more than 3 feet below the level of the adjoining street) is considered **unfit for human habitation** unless the average height of the room is at least 7 feet. A local authority may make regulations to secure that such rooms are properly lighted, ventilated and kept free of damp, effluvia and exhalation (Housing Act 1957, s. 18 (2)). In the US, basement is used also to refer to the lowest floor of a building, usually below ground level, or to an apartment with a ground floor entrance and rooms below ground level.
cf. **cellar**. See also **sub-basement, superstructure**.

basement house (US)
A dwelling in which the sitting rooms are at least one storey above ground level with the main entrance reached directly from ground level. The area of the building at ground level is used normally for storage or as a garage.

basic capitalisation rate
see **basic rate**.

basic rate
1. A term used in the **mortgage-equity capitalisation technique** for the capitalisation rate when there is no allowance for mortgage amortisation (i.e. for capital repayments) nor for equity build-up (i.e. for projected changes in

capital value); i.e. the rate of return on equity, before recapture and capital appreciation (or depreciation) are brought into account. To be distinguished from the **overall capitalisation rate** which allows for capital repayments and equity build-up.
(US) 2. A **band-of-investment capitalisation rate** determined using only the interest rate on a mortgage and not a mortgage constant to allow for recapture of the equity invested.
3. See **safe rate**.

basic rent
see **base rent**.

basis (US)
The cost of a property as used when assessing a liability to tax on a sale or taxable exchange of that property. The ordinary 'basis' is usually the original cost to the tax payer, but this cost may be 'adjusted' by adding the cost of capital improvements or deducting any allowable depreciation or amortisation. Capital gains tax is payable on the difference between proceeds of sale, taking account of any property received in exchange, and the adjusted basis.

basis points
One hundredth of a point i.e. 1/100 of one per cent. See also **points**.

batable land
Land that is the subject of a dispute or debate as to its true ownership, especially land on the border of two States or nations.

bâtiment (F)
building; edifice.
(*bâtiment industriel* – industrial building)
(*bâtiment en retrait* – building setback from a **building line**)

(*bâtiment de grande hauteur* – highrise building).

bazaar store
see **variety store**.

beach
see **foreshore**.

bear
One who anticipates that prices will fall. Especially applied to a speculator who contracts to sell shares he has not yet acquired expecting to acquire them in the future at a lower price; a process referred to as 'selling short' or 'short selling'.

bearer bill
see **promissory note**.

beastgate
see **cattlegate**.

bedroom community (US)
see **dormitory town**.

bedsitting room (or **bedsitter**)
A **flat** or **apartment** that consists of one room that serves as a sitting room and bedroom.

before-and-after valuation
A valuation carried out to determine a change in the value of land (or buildings) when the land (or buildings) has been or may be changed in its nature or when an interest in land is changed; as when work is carried out on adjoining land or a partial interest (e.g. an easement) has been acquired. The land is valued before and after the change and the difference represents the loss or gain to the landowner. This method is used in particular when assessing a compensatable loss (or taxable gain) in the value of land (or buildings). In the US, **just compensation** may be assessed on the basis of a before-and-after valuation, some-

times called the 'federal rule'; as compared to assessing the value of the land actually taken and adding any consequential damages, sometimes called the 'state rule'. See also **compensation for injurious affection, compensation for severance, severance damages.**

before-tax cash flow
see **cash flow.**

below par
At a price that is less than the face value or **par value**; a discounted price.

belt highway (US)
An urban by-pass.

bench mark
An official mark on a fixed or permanent object (such as a rock or major building) indicating the level of the ground relative to a given base level, usually sea-level. A reference point used in **topographical surveying.**

benefice
see **ecclesiastical benefice.**

bénéfice (F)
1. **profit**; gain; benefit (in French law a benefit or privilege granted by law rather than between two parties); premium.
(*bénéfice brut* – gross profit)
(*bénéfice net* – net profit).
2. **benefice.**
(bénéfice sécularisé – **impropriation**).

bénéficiaire (F)
beneficiary.
(note: French law does not recognise a **trust**, so this term is used only in a commercial sense).

beneficial enjoyment
Enjoyment of the benefits which real property affords a person in his own right and for his own benefit, i.e. as a

beneficiary rather than as a trustee for another. See also **beneficial owner, benefit.**

beneficial interest
1. An interest in property held by a person for his or her own use or benefit; as opposed to an interest held for the use or benefit of another, e.g. as by a trustee. The interest held by a **beneficiary** for whom property is held in trust; the rights of a **beneficial owner**. See also **equitable interest.**
(US) 2. An interest in a **real estate investment trust.**
3. An interest that arises as a result of an insurance policy and is available to the insured.

beneficial occupation
see **rateable occupation.**

beneficial owner
1. One who has the enjoyment and benefit of **ownership**, but not necessarily possession or title. When a property is held in trust, the beneficial owner is the person entitled to the financial rights and other benefits from the property itself, i.e. the **beneficiary**, rather than the trustee.

A beneficial owner of land held in trust has an **equitable interest** which is enforceable against anyone except a **bona fide purchaser** of the **legal estate** who acquires the land for **value** without **notice**. A beneficial owner has an interest in property that may be considered a real right – a right *in rem*; but it is a right that falls short of a complete form of real property because it can be defeated by a *bona fide* purchaser and the benefit transferred to the proceeds of sale of the property.

A borrower of funds who transfers a right to his property as security through a **charge by way of a legal mortgage**, is referred to also as a 'beneficial owner'.

2. Under English law, a person who conveys land for valuable **consideration** *and* is stated to be a 'beneficial owner' gives an **implied covenant** (a) that he has the full power and right to convey the property (the covenant for title); (b) that he will give **quiet enjoyment**; (c) that the property is free from any **encumbrance**, except as stated in the conveyance; and (d) that he will do all that is necessary to make good any defect in the conveyance (the 'covenant for further assurance') (Law of Property Act 1925, s. 76, Sch. 2, Part I). In the case of a transfer of leasehold property, a 'beneficial owner' implies, in addition, that he is signing a valid lease and that all the covenants therein have been complied with and that the rent has been paid. In the case of the grant of a mortgage, a mortgagor who conveys land as 'beneficial owner' implies conditions (a), (c) and (d) as for a sale and that, in the event of default on payment, the mortgagee has the power to enter into possession and then to retain quiet enjoyment. An owner of a legal estate in land who does not profess to be the beneficial owner implies only that he has not himself created any encumbrance which he has not expressly declared to the purchaser. See also **equitable interest**.

Modern Law of Real Property, by Cheshire, 13 edn, pp. 730–731.

The Law of Real Property, by Robert Megarry and H.W.R. Wade, 5 edn, pp. 159–161.

beneficial use
The right to the **use** and enjoyment of

the benefit and profit arising from property without necessarily having possession or physical occupation. See also **reasonably beneficial use**.

beneficiary
1. A person entitled to property for his own benefit and not as a **trustee**. A beneficiary includes any person who has a right to the use or benefit of property whether as a holder of a present or future interest, or a vested or contingent interest. A modern term for a *cestui que trust*. See also **beneficial owner, trust**.

2. A person who benefits under a **will**. If he receives real property he is a 'devisee' and if he receives personal property a 'legatee'.

3. A person who is in possession of an **ecclesiastical benefice**.

4. A person who is entitled to any monies paid out under an insurance policy.

(US) 5. A lender who has a right to a property as security under a **deed of trust**.

benefit
A natural or financial advantage received without need of restitution; aid or assistance received without obligation. See also **beneficial enjoyment, profit, scheme of development**.

benefit-cost analysis
see **cost-benefit analysis**.

bequest
Derived from Old English *becweath*, 'to transfer by word of mouth'. Traditionally an informal transfer of ownership. A word that came to refer to a transfer of **personal property** by will; a gift by testamentary disposition. 'Bequest', and the verb 'bequeath', are used sometimes when referring to real property in a will, but

devise is the correct word for that purpose. See also **legacy**.

best and highest use
see **highest and best use**.

best rent
The highest **rent** at which a property might reasonably be expected to let. See also **market rent, rack rent**.

best use
see **highest and best use**.

betterment
1. An enhancement in the overall value of land, or buildings thereon, brought about either by positive changes, such as road improvements, the provision of public services, the grant of consent for a new form of development, a change of user, etc. and by restrictions imposed on the use or development of other land; or by the prospect or expectation of such changes or restrictions. 'Betterment' is used especially to refer to any windfall occasioned to a landowner as a result of central or local government action (or the expectation of such action); in particular, an increase in demand and, therefore, the value of land occurring because of directly related public expenditure. Betterment when realised is considered as an appropriate subject for taxation as it is brought about by the actions, or at the expense, of the community. As a corrollary, **compensation** may be paid for a depreciation in the value of an individual's land when this is brought about by an action for the betterment of the community, e.g. the construction of a new airport or sewage works. In other words, the 'windfalls' accruing to an individual as a result of an action by the community should be taxed to pay for the 'wipeouts' caused by the community; the 'shifting values' of individual areas of land thereby being equalised by central government. See also **betterment levy, development charge, development land tax, development gains tax, recoupment, set-off, windfalls and wipeouts**.
Town and Country Planning in Britain by J.B. Cullingworth, 9 edn, Ch. 7.
2. An increase in the value of a property produced by physical improvement or alteration to the property itself.
3. In insurance, an improvement in the value of a property following its reinstatement, as a better or more modern equivalent, after damage or destruction. See also **indemnity**.

betterment levy
A levy imposed under the Land Commission Act 1967 on the **development value** of land i.e. on the **betterment** arising from the grant of planning permission. Abolished with effect from 22nd July 1970 by the Land Commission (Dissolution) Act 1971, s. 1. See also **development land tax**.
Encyclopaedia of Betterment Levy and Land Commission, by Desmond Heap, (1967).

biannual
Occurring twice a **year**.
cf. **biennial**. See also **half-yearly**.

bid
1. An **offer** to enter into a contract. An offer of a specified sum of money made by a prospective purchaser of a property, especially at an **auction**. A bid is a particular mode of offer, it is anticipatory, and aspires for acceptance. 'Bid' is used especially in com-

merce to refer to an offer to conduct or to enter into business. See also **acceptance**.

2. The price submitted by a building contractor in response to a request for a **tender** for building work. See also **quotation**.

bid bond (US)

A **bond**, or form of **surety**, given by a contractor, in conjunction with a bid to carry out building works, in which the contractor undertakes to provide a **performance bond** if he is successful in obtaining the building contract. Also, a bond provided by a surety on behalf of a bidder for a building contract to guarantee that the bidder will enter into a building contract if his bid is accepted. The sum specified in the bond, or such other sum as agreed, is forfeited if the bidder does not enter into a contract when required to do so. Called also a 'proposal bond'.

bid-in

see **buy-in**.

bidder

One who makes an offer to buy at a stated price, especially at an auction; a person who makes a **bid**. See also **puffer**.

bidding agreement

An arrangement by which a group of potential bidders agree that only one of them shall bid at an **auction**, in order that the members of the group can acquire a property at a lower price than would prevail with truly competitive bidding. If the property is acquired successfully then either the spoils are divided between the parties to the agreement on a predetermined basis, or a second auction is held with only the parties to the agreement present and any profit resulting from

that sale is divided amongst the group in an agreed proportion. A vendor, or auctioneer, may find it difficult to prove the existence of a bidding agreement, and it is not necessarily illegal. For a sale of real property English law considers that a vendor is protected adequately by being free to fix a **reserve price**; **buy-in** the property; or send a **puffer** to bid on his behalf – Heffer *v* Martyn (1867) 36 LJ Ch. 327.

It is an offence for a 'dealer' (who is defined as a person who in the course of business attends auction sales to purchase property for resale) to give a consideration or reward to anyone for abstaining, or as an inducement to abstain, from bidding for **goods** (The Auctions (Bidding Agreements) Act 1927, s. 1, as modified by a further such Act in 1969). A vendor of goods that are acquired by a person who has entered into a bidding agreement may avoid the contract under which the goods are purchased (Auctions (Bidding Agreements) Act 1969, s. 3.) Called also a 'knock-out agreement'. *The Law of Estate Agents and Auctions*, by J.R. Murdoch, 2 edn, pp. 510–515.

bienfaisance, *contrat de* (F)
deed of gift.

biennial
Occurring every two years.
cf. **biannual**.

biens (F)
property (especially in a physical sense); **goods**; assets; estate; wealth. All property that is capable of ownership, both 'things' (*res* or *choses*) and the right to things (rights *in rem*). *Biens* may be **moveables** or **immoveables**; including any right to or inter-

est in real property that is less than absolute ownership, i.e. a right arising from **démembrements de la propriété** (partial ownership). In French law the distinction between moveables and immoveables is important as there are important differences in the rights and obligations thereto.

(*biens communs* – see **acquêts**, *communauté*)

(*biens en déshérence* – **escheat**, see also **bona vacantia**)

(*biens fonciers; biens-fonds* – **real estate**; piece of land; landed property.)

(*biens immobiliers* or *biens immeubles* – **real property**; real estate)

(*biens incorporels* – **incorporeal property**)

(*biens indivis* – **undivided property**)

(*biens corporels* – **corporeal property**)

(*biens mobiliers; bien meubles* – **personal property**; **chattels**)

(*biens propres* – **several property**, under a matrimonial regime. See also **acquêts**, **communauté**. See also **propriété**).

Amos & Walton's Introduction to French Law, 13 edn, pp. 87–89.

Droit Civil, 1er année, by Jean Chevalier and Louis Bach, 8 edn, pp. 291–307.

Droit Civil, Les Biens, by Jean Carbonnier, 11 edn, p. 66 *et seq.*

Précis Dalloz. Droit Civils, Les Biens (Alex Weill) 2 edn, pp. 2–3.

Droit Civil, by Gabriel Marty and Pierre Raynaud, 2 edn, vol. 1, pp. 476–479.

Manuel de Droit Civil by Pierre Voirin and Giles Goubeaux, 20 edn, pp. 225–310.

bilan (F)

balance sheet.

bilateral contract

A **contract** that creates a reciprocal obligation – a **promise** exchanged for a promise – i.e. one where both parties have both rights and obligations both as promisor and promisee. For example, a contract of sale where one party undertakes to deliver property and the other to pay over money. In English law, where contracts are considered normally as bilateral, an **executory contract** (one where a party has performed his obligation, e.g. delivered property, but the other's obligation remains outstanding, e.g. payment of the price) may be referred to as a bilateral contract. Called also a 'synallagmatic contract' (especially when there are more than two parties exchanging promises).

cf. **unilateral contract**.

bilatéral, contrat (F)

bilateral contract. See also *contrat*.

bi-level house (US)

see **split-level house**.

bill

1. A document that evidences either a transaction in personal property or an agreement to pay money; an account rendered for goods sold, services provided, or work done. See also **bill of exchange, note**.

2. The draft of a proposed Statute that is submitted to the legislature for discussion and is intended to pass into law as an Act of Parliament. See also **statute law**.

bill of exchange

"An unconditional order in writing, addressed by one person to another, signed by the person giving it, requiring the person to whom it is addressed to pay on demand or at a fixed or determinable future time a sum certain in money to or to the order of a specific person, or to bearer" (Bill of Exchange Act 1882, s. 3). The person making the order is called the drawer, the person to whom it is addressed the drawee and the person to whom payment is made the payee. "A bill of exchange is a security, originally invented among merchants in different countries, for the easy remittance of money from one to the other ... It is an open letter of request from one man to another, desiring him to pay a sum named therein to a third party on his account; by which a man of the most distant part of the world may have money remitted to him from any trading country" (Bl. Comm. vol. ii. p. 466). A valid bill normally requires a date, a clearly specified value, and a place to be specified where it is drawn or payable. See also **banker's draft**, **cheque**, **discount**, **endorsement**, **negotiable instrument**.

bill of quantities

A detailed schedule setting out the quantity of materials required for each trade and describing the constituent parts of the work to be undertaken by a building contractor. A document that is used essentially to arrive at the price for a building or construction contract, especially one that is to be based on competitive tenders, and normally forms part of that contract. This document, which is prepared normally by an **architect** or **quantity surveyor**, is prepared from detailed drawings, specifications and other material relevant to the proposed work. It sets out in detail the work to be done, describes the type of materials required and tabulates the quantities for each trade or work-section.

The bill is divided into three main parts: (i) **preliminaries**; (ii) **preamble**; and (iii) **quantities**. A bill of quantities is prepared primarily so that a building contractor can price the work for the individual items on a uniform basis when submitting a competitive tender; the contractor sets out his price for each item and a grossed-up total and returns a completed copy of the bill as his offer for the proposed building work. During the progress of the contract the bill is used as a schedule for identifying any changes that may lead to a price variation and, at the end of the contract, as a basis for establishing the final contract price. The document may incorporate a **specification** or there may be a separate document appended to the building contract for that purpose. See also **abstracting**, **billing**, **quantity surveying**, **schedule of quantities**, **taking off**.

Architectural Practice and Procedure, by Mitchell, pp. 73–76 (1981).
Techniques for Preparing a Bill of Quantities, by Edwin P. Stewart (1971).
The Contractor's Use of Bills of Quantity by D.W.H. Skinner (1981).
Building Quantities Explained, by Ivor H. Seeley, 3 edn.

bill of sale

A written instrument that is used to transfer the ownership of goods or chattels, usually in exchange for monetary consideration. A bill of sale may be absolute if the goods are transferred unencumbered and the grantor parts with possession; or 'conditional' when the grantor retains title to or possession of the goods as security for a debt. A conditional bill of sale creates in effect a **mortgage** or **charge** on the goods.

cf. **receipt**. See also **conditional sale, sale**.

bill of variations

A schedule of all the variations made during the course of a building contract setting out details of changes in the quality or quantity of any items altered or modified and the resultant price variation. See also **variation**.

billing

The writing up of a **bill of quantities**, i.e. copying out the quantities and describing in detail the work required for a building contract. Billing is carried out after the process of **abstracting**; it divides the required work into its related constituent parts and is used then to price the building contract.

Elements of Quantity Surveying, by Arthur J. Willis and Christopher J. Willis. 7 edn, pp. 226–236.

bimensuel (F)

fortnightly.

binder

1. A written statement, usually prepared by a broker, of the terms agreed by the parties to a potential transfer of property. The binder sets out the prospective purchaser's formal offer and is submitted to the seller for acknowledgement and signature. Although containing the minimum requirements for a valid **contract** and usually supported by the payment of a **deposit**, many of the details are left to be included in a more formal contract. A receipt for a **deposit** or for **earnest money**, may be termed a 'binder' and constitute a simple form of contract. See also **conditional contract, open contract**.
(US) 2. See **cover note**.

bird-dog

A person (or a commission paid to such a person) who introduces deals, but takes no part in the consummation of the transaction. A person who is employed solely to introduce new listings or to seek out prospective purchasers. See also **broker, winkling**.

blacklist

A list of firms or individuals to be avoided, discriminated against, or with whom business should not be conducted. For example, a confidential list of uncreditworthy customers of a bank, credit company, hire purchase company or similar financial entity. Any list of firms with whom a company or State should not conduct trade. A contract to abide by the requirement that trade should be avoided with those on a blacklist may be void, as being against the public interest or in restraint of trade. See also **boycott, void contract**.

blanket deed of trust (US)

see **blanket mortgage**.

blanket insurance policy

An **insurance policy** that covers a number of an insured's properties, or a number of specified risks, up to an agreed figure at any point in time. A type of policy that is taken out commonly by an organisation that has a large number of properties. It frequently takes the form of an **all-risks insurance policy**. The policy has the advantage that the terms and conditions are standardised, except where specifically varied by a schedule or a rider to the policy. Usually the policy provides cover for any of the insured's properties from the date a property is acquired, even though the insurer may not be notified of each individual purchase until a later date. However, the insurer requires to be informed of the value of individual properties on a regular basis, and the policy provides for *pro-rata* **average** for any loss sustained on an individual property. Called sometimes a 'block policy', although that term is more strictly applicable to the insurance, against more risks, of all the goods owned by an insured, especially those of a business proprietor.

blanket mortgage (or lien)

A **mortgage** (or **lien**) secured on two or more properties. A form of mortgage that may be used to finance the development of building lots so that as individual lots are sold they are released from the mortgage. In the US, where the use of blanket mortgages is more common than in the UK, a **deed of trust** secured on two or more properties, or all the assets or properties of a debtor, may be referred to as a blanket mortgage or a 'blanket trust deed'. Called also a 'bulk mortgage'. See also **consolidation of mortgages**, **floating charge**, **release clause**.

blanket policy

see **blanket insurance policy**.

blanket trust deed (US)

see **blanket mortgage**.

blight

1. A condition, factor or influence that causes decay and stultifies growth. An external factor that causes a reduction or decline in real property values; especially when the reduction is brought about by local or central government proposals to carry out building work, such as the construction of a new highway that will affect directly the property or the surrounding area, or a proposal to compulsorily purchase land. (When assessing compulsory purchase compensation, any depreciation in the value of the interest being acquired, which is produced by an indication that the land "is, or is likely, to be acquired by an authority possessing compulsory purchase powers", is not to be taken into account: Land Compensation Act 1961, s. 9). See also **blight notice**.

2. A change in the economic or social conditions of an area or neighbourhood; in particular, one accompanied by a lowering of the general level of prosperity or a prolonged reduction in economic activity. An uncontrolled change in land use; increase in noise, congestion, etc; or the establishment of non-conforming use may well cause blight: – "Business streets lined with retail stores were invaded by factories, garages, junk shops. Localities devoted to light industry ... were invaded by heavy industry producing noise, smoke, and fumes. No land owner ... could erect a building of any sort with assurance that in ten or twenty years the building would not be obsolete by reason of an unnecessary change in the character of the neighbourhood. Sometimes these changes left a blighted district behind" – *Zoning*, by E.M. Bassett (1940), referring to New York in the 1900s.

cf. **betterment**. See also **derelict land**, **development area**, **slum**.

blight notice

A notice that may be served on a local authority by an **owner-occupier** of land when that land has become hard or impossible to sell, except at a substantially reduced price, because of

blight arising from a particular type of adverse planning proposal, or the threat of such proposal (Town and Country Planning Act 1971, ss 193–207, as extended and amended by the Land Compensation Act 1973, ss 66–82). This form of 'inverse' compulsory purchase is available to an owner of land who can prove (a) that his property is affected by one of a number of specified statutory circumstances; (b) that he has an interest in land which qualifies for protection, (in general a freeholder, or a leaseholder with not less than 3 years unexpired interest at the time of the notice, but not a mortgagee who is not in possession (1971 Act, ss 201, 203)); (c) that he has been in continuous physical occupation of the whole or a substantial part of the land for six months before the service of the notice, or for a period amounting to six months ending not more than twelve months before the service of the notice; and (d) that he has made "reasonable endeavours" to sell the property but has been unable to do so, except at a substantially reduced price (1971 Act, s. 193, as amended by the 1973 Act, s. 77). Also in the case of business premises the property must have a rateable value that does not exceed a prescribed limit of £2250 (Town and Country Planning (Limit of Annual Value) Order 1973).

The type of circumstance to which a blight notice applies includes a proposal by a local or public authority to acquire land that is shown for that purpose in a structure plan or a local plan; in a clearance area or a general improvement area; in a confirmed compulsory purchase order, provided notice to quit has not been served; in a proposed highway scheme; in an order relating to a New Town; or a similar proposal to acquire land for the functions of a public authority, government department or statutory undertaker (1971 Act, s. 192, as extended and amended by the 1973 Act, ss 68–76). The principle behind the notice is that land is affected by one of the statutorily defined circumstances and not that the land is substantially blighted, i.e. the 'blight' must take a specified form and not merely fall within the general sense of the word – Bolton Corpn v Owen [1962] 1 QB 471). The authority upon whom a blight notice has been served may object to the notice on the ground (a) that no part of the land is affected by any one of the statutory forms of blight; (b) that the person who served the notice does not have a qualifying interest in land; (c) that the server has not made reasonable endeavours to sell, or could sell at a price that is not substantially reduced by the proposal; (d) that the proposals affect only part of the land specified in the blight notice (although see **material detriment**); or (e) that the authority has no intention to acquire the land within the next 15 years (1971 Act, s 194). A person who receives such an objection may appeal to the **Lands Tribunal**, although the onus is on the claimant to prove his case. If the blight notice is accepted by the authority it acts as a deemed **notice to treat**, but if validly objected to or withdrawn it has no effect (1971 Act, ss 196–199). An authority that accepts a valid blight notice is required to acquire the subject land as if it had made a compulsory purchase order and to pay compensation discounting the effect of any blight caused by the proposal that brought about the notice. A blight notice may be served in respect of the whole of the land blighted or in respect of any part of that land.

A blight notice may be distinguished from a **purchase notice**, as the latter may be served following an adverse planning decision (generally a refusal or conditional grant of planning permission) and the former arises from positive and adverse planning proposals. See also **compulsory purchase compensation**, **inverse condemnation**.

Law of Compulsory Purchase and Compensation, by Keith Davies, 4 edn, pp. 250–262.

Encyclopaedia of Planning Law and Practice by Desmond Heap, paras. 1–237 to 1–244.

8 *Laws of England* by Halsbury, 4 edn, paras. 58–91.

blind-pool offering (US)

An arrangement whereby money is raised initially from a number of investors (i.e. the investors put their 'stakes' into a pool) and then these funds are invested in property. The investors do not know which properties will be acquired when making their commitment to the funding. Normally the investors appoint a **general partner** who is given full discretion to acquire properties on their behalf. This arrangement is illegal in certain States (notably New York), where only a **specified property offering** is permitted. Called sometimes a 'non-specified property offering'. See also **open-end fund**.

block

1. An area in a town or city, between two sets of intersecting streets, occupied by or intended for a building or group of buildings. Also the distance along one side of this area.

2. A group of terrace houses; an integrated set of buildings. A large building, or building complex, especially a commercial building comprising a number of units that are capable of occupational subdivision. See also **block of flats**.

3. A sector of a **neighbourhood**.

block of flats

A building that incorporates a number of separate units of living accommodation or flats which share common facilities, such as an entrance hall, lifts, parking, etc., but the units or flats are occupied independently, whether by tenants or co-owners. In the US, referred to usually as an 'apartment house'.

cf. **duplex**. See also **apartment**, **flat**.

block income approach

see **term and reversion method**.

block plan

A plan to a small scale which shows, in broad outline, an existing or proposed buildings, or part of a neighbourhood.

block policy

See **blanket insurance policy**.

blockbusting (US)

A method of deflating property values by introducing neighbours of a different race or class, or creating rumours to play on prejudices. The properties are bought then at a reduced price in order to resell them later at a profit when the prejudice is either removed or accepted by the newcomers. An illegal practice under the Civil Rights Act 1968. Called sometimes 'panic peddling'.

blot on title

A defect in a title to property; a defect that requires to be remedied before a vendor can grant a **good title**. See also **cloud on title**.

blue chip

A valuable asset. An investment, a company, or shares in a company, of the highest financial standing. Derived from the colour of the highest-value poker chip. See also **triple A rating**.

blue-sky laws (US)

State laws passed to protect the public against fraud in the sale of securities. In certain cases such laws may require details to be provided of mortgages, in order to ensure that the mortgagor is fully aware of the conditions of the commitments he has entered into, especially the **effective rate of interest** being charged. In some states such laws also prohibit a **blind-pool offering**. See also **truth-in-lending laws**.

board

The provision of daily meals for reward, especially the provision of meals by a landlord. "A provision by the landlord of such food as in the case of any particular tenancy would ordinarily be consumed at daily meals and would be obtained and prepared by the tenant himself, if it were not provided by somebody else." – Wilkes *v* Goodwin [1923] 2 KB 110. See also **protected tenancy, restricted contract**.

board of adjustment (US)

A body that hears appeals against a variation to a **zoning ordinance**. Called also a 'board of zoning appeal' or 'board of review'. See also **variance**.

board of equalization (US)

A local government agency whose function is to consider the **assessed value** of individual properties and the general level of assessed values in a county or other tax district in order to ensure that the tax burden is levied equitably. In particular, the board endeavours to reduce the assessed value of properties to a uniform base to ensure that one county or district does not set its level of values low in order to reduce its tax contributions to the state or another tax district.

boarding house

1. A place in which a guest has the use of a bedroom and shares other rooms in common with other guests. It has fewer facilities than an **hotel**. Unlike an hotel, a boarding house is generally a private residence with accommodation let out on a regular or a semi-permanent basis. A covenant in a lease not to use premises for any business but only "as a private dwelling-house" is breached by a tenant taking in paying guests – Tendler *v* Sproule [1947] 1 All ER 193 – and the use of a dwelling-house as a 'house-let-in lodgings' is a **material change in the use** requiring planning permission – Borg *v* Khan (1965) 17 P and CR 144. See also **lodging house**.
2. A house, or a small hotel, which provides board and lodging for holiday purposes.

boc-land or bock-land

see **charter land**.

boiler plate (US)

The fixed clauses or wording of a **standard-form contract**. See also **adhesion contract**.

bona fide (L)

'In **good faith**'. Without intention to deceive or defraud; genuinely and with honesty.
cf. **fraud**, *mala fide*. See also **utmost good faith**.

bona fide purchaser

One who acquires property in **good faith**, on the understanding that the seller has a **good title**. A person who acquires title to land knowing, expressly or impliedly, that there is a defect or encumberance against the title cannot, while acting in good faith, claim that he thought he was acquiring the land free of the defect or encumberance – Goodman *v* Harvey (1835) 4 A and E 870.

English law refers to a '*bona fide* purchaser for **value** of a **legal estate** without **notice**' as 'equity's darling', because this purchaser acquires a legal estate free of any equitable claims against the land – provided he has acted genuinely, honestly and without fraud; has no notice (express, constructive or imputed) that there is any third party who has a right or interest in the land; and has paid value (which means a sum of money, money's worth or marriage, but not necessarily the market value) for the land. A *bona fide* purchaser for value without notice has "an absolute, unqualified, unanswerable defence" to any claim against his right to the interest he has acquired in the land – Pilcher *v* Rawlins (1872) Ch. App. 259. He has acquired the most absolute estate in land and can enforce his right against the whole world. In other words a party who (a) purchases a legal estate in land; (b) pays some **consideration**, and (c) makes reasonable and genuine enquiries to establish the existence of those interests that are likely to bind him (including inspecting the property, searching for matters of which he would have constructive notice, e.g. registered land charges, and taking steps to be informed of matters which

have come to the attention of his agent or solicitor), is not bound by any equitable interest that affects the land and of which he has not become aware. In this context **purchaser** means someone who acquires land by sale or gift, including a mortgagee or lessee, but not someone who takes land by the process of law, as on intestacy. In the US, called also an 'innocent purchaser'. See also **bill of exchange**.

Manual of the Law of Real Property, by Megarry, 6 edn, pp. 64–69.
Modern Law of Property, by Cheshire, 13 edn, pp. 60–66.
Introduction to Land Law, by J.R. Riddell, 3 edn, pp. 71–80.

bona fidei emptor (L)

A **bona fide purchaser**.

bona vacantia (L)

Property that has no apparent owner. When a person dies intestate and without an heir, or there is no claimant following a liquidation, the estate becomes *bona vacantia*. In English law such property passes to the Crown (or, in certain cases, to the Duchy of Lancaster or the Duchy of Cornwall). The term *bona vacantia* may be applied also to **treasure trove**; property coming ashore after a shipwreck; **waifs** (property taken by a thief and abandoned in flight, but not retaken by the owners); **estrays** (tame animals wandering on a manor and whose owner is unknown); and the property of a dissolved corporation (Companies Act 1948, s. 354) – provided in none of the cases there is a claimant to the goods or a deliberate abandonment of the goods. See also **escheat**, *res nullius*.

8 Halsbury's Laws of England, 4 edn, paras. 1503–1504.

bond

A formal promise binding one person (an obligor) to pay a specified sum of money to another (an obligee) on a specified date or during a specified period of time. Written evidence of a debt, especially when made by a **deed** that is itself called a bond or, sometimes, an **obligation**; a contract under seal acknowledging a present or future debt. Any instrument of indebtedness issued by a company or government e.g. a **debenture, stock**. A bond may provide for the payment of a single sum or a series of payments due under a loan, whether principal or interest. A bond is secured frequently by a mortgage on property which can be enforced if the promise is not met. Bonds may be classified according to the nature of the security; the method of repayment of the debt; the issuing party; or their purposes; e.g. a 'development bond' – issued to finance the development of property; a 'mortgage bond' – secured on real property. Most bonds are conditional, i.e. they come to an end on the happening of a given condition such as the performance of an obligation or repayment of a debt. A contract "to answer for the debt, default, or miscarriage of another", which covers most types of bond, must be in **writing** (Statute of Frauds 1677, s. 4). See also **deed of trust, performance bond, promissory note**.

bonne foi (F)

good faith. In French law a person who takes possession of property in good faith, i.e. believing that he has a legal title, requires a shorter period of time to establish a prescriptive title than a person who has no such belief. See also **adverse possession**.

bonus clause

A clause in a building contract which provides for the payment of a bonus to the contractor if work is completed in its entirety on, or before, a specified date. The bonus may be a fixed sum, a percentage of the contract price, or paid at a given rate per day, per week or per month.
cf. **penalty clause**.

book cost
see **book value**.

book land
see **charter land**.

book rate of return (BRR)
see **average annual return**.

book value

The value of an asset as shown in a book of accounts. Usually the original cost of the asset, plus the cost of any additions or improvements, less any allowance made for depreciation. The book value may be adjusted to take account of any revaluation of the asset. In the US, called also 'adjusted value'. A book value before any allowance for depreciation or revaluation may be referred to as the book cost and after such an allowance as the net book cost or net book value; although after such an adjustment it is no longer a true cost. See also **going-concern value**.

boom

A period when economic activity is accelerating or expanding rapidly. The stage when an economy nears the peak of a trade **cycle**. During a boom distortions frequently occur in an economy as demand outstrips supply; usually because of pent up demand vieing with restrained supply. The result is bottle-necks in the economy so that "it becomes impossible to increase output by putting further unused resources to work, and output can be raised only by means of investment which raises labour productivity. Further rises in demand are now met more by increases in prices than by increases in production. Shortages develop in many places and there is a general excess demand for labour; prices and costs rise and business is generally very profitable. ... Investment expenditure will be very heavy, investment funds will be in short supply, interest rates may rise in the face of a heavy excess demand for loanable funds. Expectations of the future are favourable and much investment may be made which is not justified, on the basis of current prices and sales, but which requires further rises in prices and demand to render it profitable" – in *An Introduction to Positive Economics* by Richard G. Lipsey, p. 495 (1963). In the real estate market during a boom demand exceeds supply, rents and capital values rise, and investment and development activity increases. "When demand has pressed upon the existing supply sufficiently to influence real estate prices and rents, new construction will be stimulated. Potential users of space will be forced by the shortage to building directly for their own occupancy or will bid up prices and rents for existing space to a point where new building for sale or investment will be attractively profitable. The heightened construction activity will spread its influence throughout the economy and, by increasing the national income, will add further stimulus to demand for space. In an environment of rising costs and more rapidly rising prices, a

building boom develops" – in *Urban Land Economics*, by Richard U. Ratcliff, pp. 155–6, (1949). The likely consequence is that property values and new building work outstrip the level that can be sustained for any length of time, financing costs exceed the income that can sustain such costs, demand for accommodation becomes inadequate to absorb the available supply, confidence wains and the brakes are applied to the detriment of the unwary.

The Boom of the Eighties in Southern California, by Glenn S. Dumke, (1944).

The Property Boom, by Oliver Marriot, (1967).

The Property Boom and its collapse 1968–75, R.I.C.S., (1978).

boosey pasture

A right to leave cattle on pasture land to enable them to feed on last year's hay or straw, after the expiration of an agricultural licence or tenancy.

boot (US)

1. Additional cash, or other consideration, paid to make up the difference between the value of two exchanged properties, especially when paid as part of a tax-free exchange. Boot may take the form of securities, release of a mortgage obligation, or any form of property; provided it is of a different kind to the property being exchanged.

2. See **bote**.

border

Derived from Old French *bordure*, an outer edge or limit. A strip or tract of land that demarcates a frontier. A **boundary line**.

bordereau (F)

list; schedule; statement (as a summary of a deed).

borne (F)
boundary-mark; post; stone marker.

bornage (F)
A process for establishing legal boundaries to land. A process that a landowner may insist upon if an adjoining owner is unwilling to cooperate (French Civil Code, art. 646). See also **cadastre**.
Précis Dalloz. Droit Civil, Les Biens by Alex Weill 2 edn, pp. 92–98.

bote
An ancient name for **estovers** or for **compensation**. Called also 'boot'.

boundary line
A line that bounds or limits. An imaginary or natural line, or border, that divides, or indicates the limit of, two **contiguous** properties. "For every man's land is in the eye of the law enclosed and set apart from his neighbour's; and that either by a visible and material **fence**, as one divided from another by a hedge, or by an ideal, invisible boundary existing only in contemplation of the law, as when one man's land adjoins to another's"(B1. Comm. vol. iii p. 209). A boundary line may be delineated horizontally, vertically or in any direction that parties choose to divide land (or buildings).

The position of a boundary line between two properties is a frequent subject of dispute which is resolved generally by reference to the facts, and such matters as the **parcels clause** of a conveyance; any relevant **plan**; and various common law presumptions, e.g. if a boundary is delimited by a ditch, and a bank or hedge, the boundary line is denoted by the bank or hedge because a ditch is presumed to have been excavated on one's own

land – Vowles *v* Miller (1810) 128 E.R. 54. See also **abuttals, *ad medium filum, ad medium filum aquae*, encroachment, foreshore, mistake, party wall, rectification, trespass.**
4 Halsbury's Laws of England, 4 edn, paras. 831–900.
Land Law and Registration, by S. Rowton Simpson, pp. 125–156 (1984).
Boundaries, Walls and Fences, by Trevor M. Aldridge, 5 edn.
Boundaries and Fences by Vincent Powell-Smith, 2 edn.

bounds (US)
see **metes and bounds**.

boutique (F)
boutique; a small retail shop.
cf. *magasin*.

boycott
A refusal to trade or communicate or otherwise deal with a person, or body of persons, in order to try and force or prevent a course of action, especially when a concerted refusal is used towards an economic or political end. Originates from Charles C. Boycott, an English land agent of the Earl of Earne's estate in Co. Mayo, Ireland who in 1880 refused to comply with the demands of the Irish Land League to reduce rents in order to alleviate the effects of famine; Charles Parnell urged members of the league not to communicate with those who refused their demands, and consequently Boycott had to employ Ulster volunteers, with armed protection, to harvest his crops. See also **blacklist**.
Captain Boycott and the Irish, by Joyce Marlow (1973).

brandon (F)
growing crops. See also **emblements**.

breach of close
see **close**.

breach of contract
Failure, without legal cause, to perform the promise or promises that form a part, or the entirety, of a **contract**. A breach of contract may arise from a refusal or failure to perform a contract; improper, late or inadequate **performance** of a **condition** of a contract; or a failure to comply with the duties or obligations required in the contract. It may arise before the time for performance arises – an 'anticipatory breach' – if a person expresses a clear intention not to perform his obligations or takes a course of action which prevents him from properly performing the primary obligations imposed by the contract – Afovos Shipping Co. SA v Pagnan [1983] 1 All ER 455. To constitute a breach of contract, so as to enable the injured party to repudiate the contract, the default must be major or 'fundamental' and thus go to the **root** of the contract and not be just a minor failing.
cf. **breach of covenant**. See also **damages, deposit, election, injunction, *quantum meruit*, rectification, repudiation, rescission, specific performance, time is of the essence**.
Law of Contract, by Cheshire and Fifoot, 10 edn, p. 487.
Chitty on Contract 28 edn, paras. 1591–1632.

breach of covenant
The failure to perform or observe a **covenant**, or acting in a manner that is inconsistent with a covenant, especially the failure of a tenant to comply with a term of his lease. In strict terminology a 'breach of covenant'
means there is a failure that does not go to the root of the lease and, therefore, does not permit the parties to terminate the lease, but merely to claim **damages**. If the breach goes to the root of the contract it would constitute a breach of **condition**. However, 'breach of covenant' and 'breach of condition' are commonly used interchangeably. In the event of a breach of covenant a landlord may have a right to enforce **forfeiture** (provided there is an express **right of re-entry** contained in the lease); he may seek an **injunction** (especially to enforce a negative covenant); and he may also seek damages.
cf. **breach of contract**. See also **grounds for possession, repairs notice, restriction**.

breach of duty of care
see **duty of care, negligence**.

breach of warranty
1. The giving of false information that forms an essential part of a **warranty**, or failure to comply with the requirement of a warranty. A failure to comply with an executory condition of a deed. See also **warranty deed**.
2. A breach of a provision in a contract which is not fundamental to the contract and, therefore, does not entitle the injured party to repudiate the contract. See also **breach of contract**.

breach of warranty of authority
Action by an **agent** that is outside his powers or the **authority** granted by his principal. Generally the agent, and not the principal, is liable to a third party for the consequences of any such action – Collen v Wright (1857) 8 E and B 647. See also **power of attorney**.
The Law of Estate Agents and Auc-

tions, by J.R. Murdoch, 2 edn, pp. 140–148.

break an entail (US)
see **disentail**.

break clause
A clause in a lease which sets out a 'break point', if any; that is, a date on which either party may unilaterally determine a **tenancy for a fixed term** before it has run its full term. The clause may be included, for example, to permit a landlord to regain possession of a property for redevelopment, or to permit a tenant to terminate a lease at the time of a rent review, or simply to enable either or both parties to terminate a long-term lease at given dates. The right to exercise this option is subject usually to a proviso that the tenant is responsible for observing all the terms and conditions of the lease up to the break point and may be subject to the parties accepting certain requirements after the termination of the lease, e.g. that the tenant will meet the cost of putting the demised premises into a good state of repair.
cf. **rent review clause**. See also **security of tenure**, **termination**.

break-even point
The stage at which an investment produces an income that is just sufficient to cover recurring expenditure. For an investment in real property, the point at which gross income is equal to normal operating expenses, including debt service, i.e. the stage at which **cash flow** becomes positive. Called sometimes the 'default point'.

break point
1. See **break clause**.
2. In a turnover lease, the amount of sales required before a percentage or

turnover rent is charged.

break-up value
The value of a company's assets when it ceases operations. In the US, called also the 'gone-concern value'.
cf. **going concern value**.

bridge financing
see **bridging loan (or finance)**.

bridge-over loan (US)
see **bridging loan**.

bridging loan (or finance)
A short-term loan granted to cover partially or totally the cost of buying property before the proceeds from the sale of another property are available to the purchaser. In the US, called 'bridge financing' or a 'bridge-over loan'. See also **financing**, **interim loan**.

bridleway, or bridlepath, or bridleroad
A path or track along which it is permitted to ride or lead a horse (i.e. by a bridle), as well as to pass on foot or by bicycle, but from which vehicular traffic is excluded. A bridleway may, but does not automatically, include a **driftway** (i.e. a right of way to drive cattle). "A **highway** over which the public have the following, but no other, rights of way, that is to say, a right of way on foot and a right of way on horseback or leading a horse, with or without a right to drive animals of any description along the highway" (National Parks and Access to the Countryside Act 1949, s. 27 (6); Countryside Act 1968, s. 49 (1); Highways Act 1980, s. 329 (1)). Called sometimes a 'droveway' or 'horseway'.
cf. **footway**.

broad-form insurance (US)
see **all-risks insurance**.

brochure
A pamphlet or advertising document, such as one that sets out details of properties being offered for sale or lease. See also **particulars of sale**.

brochure (F)
brochure.

broker
An **agent** or intermediary who, in the normal course of his business, negotiates to bring two or more parties together with the object of their entering into a contractual arrangement and is remunerated by a brokerage fee or **commission** that normally is contingent on success. (Hence a broker is referred to sometimes as a 'commission agent' or 'commission merchant'). One who brings buyers and sellers of property together. A broker may be a firm or individual, who brings together two parties wishing to transfer property, or to finance an investment in property. The remuneration or commission is paid normally by one side or the other; although a broker may receive commission from both parties, called a 'double agency', in which case he should declare his position. "An agent who wants to make two contracts for double commission must do so in the clearest possible terms and with the clearest possible information to each of his principals what he is doing, otherwise he cannot sue under an alleged agreement" – Fulwood *v* Hurley [1928] 1 KB 504. Every broker is an agent, although an agent may not necessarily be a broker; an agent's terms of reference may be to represent a principal without necessarily having to effect a transaction in order to be remunerated, while a broker endeavours to bring about a meeting of minds in order that an agreement may be concluded and, thereby, he will be remunerated. In the US, a 'real estate broker' must hold a licence from the State in which he operates. In the UK, a party performing a real estate broker's function is more commonly referred to as an **estate agent**. 'Broker' is derived from Norman French *bronkier*, a seller of wine from the tap, or *brogour*, an untrustworthy dealer. Historically a broker was an agent for the sale of goods who did not take possession of the goods and the term was applied commonly to a dealer in secondhand furniture; thus, the term may be used in a derisory sense, although in 1878 Otto von Bismarck coined the phrase 'honest broker'.
cf. **factor**.
Real Estate Principles, by Bruce Harewood, 2 edn, Ch. 17.
Real Estate Law, by Robert Kratovil and Raymond J. Werner, 8 edn, pp. 90–120.
Real Estate Brokerage Management, by Bruce Linderman (1981).

brokerage
1. The service provided by a **broker**. A process whereby two parties to a transaction are brought together with the auspices of a third party, who is called a broker.
2. **Commission** payable to a broker.

brokerage listing (US)
see **listing**.

broker's commission
A **commission** paid to a broker or agent for his services. Called also 'brokerage'. See also **bird-dog**.

brut, (f. *brute*) (F)
(*revenu brut* – **gross income**)
(*surface brute* – **gross area**).

budget
An itemised list of the estimated income and expenditure for a person, public body or financial scheme, over a period of time; a statement of how it is planned to obtain or spend money over a given period (usually a year). See also **operating statement**.

budget (F)
budget.

budget mortgage (US)
A mortgage loan agreement which provides that the mortgagor is to pay not only interest and principal but also the taxes and insurance that are related to the ownership of the mortgaged property. A budget mortgage is intended to enable the **mortgagee** to exercise greater control over the mortgagor's total property expense budget. An arrangement more commonly used for mortgages secured on residential property. See also **piti payment**.

buffer-strip or **buffer-zone**
An area of land retained from development especially to separate conflicting users, e.g. between a residential area and a major highway. See also **building line, non-aedificandi, set-back**.

buildable area
see **building area**.

build-up method (US)
see **component capitalisation rate**.

builder
One who constructs or erects a building or other form of structure, whether on his own or another's land, for profit; in particular one who enters into a **building contract** for the repair, maintenance, or any form of building work. See also **contractor, developer**.

builder's risk insurance
Insurance provided to cover risks associated with a building that is in the course of construction. Normally such insurance is purchased by the contractor but it may be taken out by the building owner, with or without the contractor being specified as an interested party. See also **contractor's all-risks insurance**.

building
Something constructed or erected for a purpose, especially a house or similar structure. An edifice constructed of substantial material and permanently fixed to, and generally above, the soil. A 'building' is "usually understood to be some **structure** of considerable size, and intended to be permanent, or at least to endure for a considerable time whether let into the ground or not." – Stevens *v* Gourley (1859) LJCP 7; although not every structure is a building. A building is normally an enclosed, or predominately enclosed, structure built for necessity rather than convenience; "something built with a roof and walls, such as a house or factory"(*Collins English Dictionary*). However, its usage may not always be so limited. A building may be no more than a wall (provided it is of some stature), a subway or underground structure or even a roof with lateral supports. 'Building' generally excludes a fence, gate, post or any similar structure; an erection that is not intended to stay in one place, such as a caravan; and any machinery or equipment, whether forming part of a building or not. A building is normally affixed to the land for its proper enjoyment and

thereby becomes part of the realty i.e. as a **fixture**. See also **agricultural building, industrial building, listed building, obstructive building**.
4 Halsbury's Laws of England, 4 edn, p. 579.

building and loan association (US)
see **savings and loan association**.

building agreement
An agreement, between an owner of land and a builder, by which the builder is granted a **licence** to enter the land in order to erect a property or properties to an agreed specification, particularly houses, which then are sold or leased to the ultimate purchaser or lessee (who may be the builder himself). In English law this form of agreement constitutes an **estate contract**. Called sometimes a 'building licence'. See also **building lease**.

building, or buildable, area
The area of a parcel of land occupied or intended for building on, i.e. any part that is intended to be covered with buildings, as distinguished from any part that is to be left for landscaping, service roads, car parking, etc. See also **plot ratio**.

building by-laws
Regulations, first set out in the Public Health Act 1875, to control the construction of buildings and related matters. These by-laws were administered by a local authority on the basis of a central government model. In England and Wales, they were replaced by building regulations in 1966 (except in Inner London where the London Building (Constructional) Bylaws 1972, as amended by the London Building (Constructional) Bylaws 1974 and 1979, still applies).

See also **by-law**.
Building Regulations and Control, by Jan Lewkowicz, (1983).
The History of Building Regulation in London 1189–1972 by C.C. Knowles and P.H. Pitt, (1972).
Building Control in Inner London: The London Building Acts and Bye-Laws and their Interpretation, by P.H. Pitt and J. Dufton (in association with the Greater London Council) (1983).

building capitalisation rate (US)
1. A **capitalisation rate** which provides an adequate return to cover the risk of an investment in building work or improvements.
2. The capitalisation rate used in the **building residual technique**.

building certificate
A certificate, issued by an architect, a quantity surveyor, engineer or other suitably qualified third party, confirming that building works have been completed according to the terms of a building contract and that payment in respect of these works may be made by the employer to the builder. Normally 'interim' or progress certificates are issued at monthly, or other regular intervals, throughout the building contract confirming the value of work done and the interim payment, if any, due to the contractor. A 'certificate of **practical completion**' is issued when the building effectively is ready for use or occupation, although this certificate may be issued in conjunction with a schedule or certificate of outstanding defects. The certificate of practical completion transfers responsibility for the building back to the building owner and is accompanied normally by an order for the owner to pay the

full contract price, less any final retention sum. A 'final' certificate is issued when all the obligations of the building contract have been fulfilled and any defects period has passed. An interim certificate is based on a genuine estimate of the value of the work done but does not confirm that the work is satisfactory. The final certificate is intended to inform the employer that all work has been done, to the certifier's satisfaction, and should be paid for in full (or as agreed between the parties) including the release of any **retention sum**.

Practice and Procedure for the Quantity Surveyor, by Arthur J. Willis and Christopher J. Willis, 8 edn, pp. 59–66.

Architectural Practice and Procedure, by Mitchell, pp. 93–99 (1981).

building codes
1. A code or set of regulations prepared to control the standard of building work. The British Standards Institute produces codes of practice for building work based on its research and expertise, but unlike the **building regulations** these are only recommendations and have no legal application. See also **building controls, by-laws**.
(US) 2. A law, **ordinance** or government code established to regulate the standard of building and construction work and the suitability for use of buildings. Building codes may be established at local, city or state level and most states have adopted model buildings codes as the standard for such regulations. Building codes set down minimum standards for design, construction, materials, layout, etc., and are intended to preserve and protect public health, safety and welfare,

as well as to control the use and occupation of the buildings to ensure their proper maintenance. They may specify also rules for such matters as fire safety, ventilation, refrigeration, or floor loading. In addition, specialised codes have been prepared to cover particular areas of work, e.g. plumbing codes, electrical codes, or particular types of buildings or structures, e.g. schools, sports arenas, garages. See also **building permit, certificate of occupation**.

Uniform Building Code, by International Conference of Building Officials (1982).

building contract
A **contract** for the erection or extension of any building or structure. See also **bill of quantities, cost-reimbursement contract, fixed-price contract, Joint Contracts Tribunal, lump-sum contract, package-deal contract, remeasurement contract, turn-key contract**.

Business Property Handbook, The Boisot Waters Cohen Partnership, pp. 473–482 (1981).

Building Contracts – a practical guide, by Denis F. Turner, 4 edn.

Building and Engineering Contracts, by Hudson, (1970; Supplement 1979).

Building Contracts, by Keating, 4 edn.

Building Contracts and Practice, by Emden, 8 edn.

4 Halsbury's Laws of England, 4 edn, paras. 1101–1500.

building contractor
see **contractor**.

building control
A statutory control over the design, development, construction and use of a building. In the UK controls on

building may take the form of **building regulations, building by-laws,** town and country planning laws, or public health regulations, as well as any law that controls environmental pollution, working conditions in buildings (including health and safety regulations) and fire regulations. In the US, these controls take the form of **building codes** and **ordinances,** as well as **zoning ordinances** and density regulations. See also **fire certificate, listed building consent, negligence, overcrowding, planning permission, Town and Country Planning Acts.**

Business Property Handbook, The Boisot Waters Cohen Partnership, pp. 433–441 (1981).

Building Control by Legislation – The UK Experience by J.H. Granham Wright, (1983).

building finance
see **construction loan (or finance).**

building land
Land that is capable of being built on and that is likely to be developed within a reasonable period of time. Land that is ripe for building. See also **development land.**

building lease
A long-term **lease** of unimproved land on which the lessee covenants to build. Commonly the lease is for at least 99 years; although it may be as short as 50 years or as long as 999 years. Usually it is granted at a fixed **ground rent,** or a ground rent with reviews at 25 or 33 year intervals. See also *bail à construction,* **building agreement, ground lease, emphyteotic lease, leasehold enfranchisement.**

building licence
1. Permission granted to allow building work to proceed. In England and Wales, the term building licence is not used; but, a land owner must obtain **planning permission** before commencing most types of building work and such building work must conform to the **building regulations** (or in Inner London the **building by-laws**). See also **building control, licence.**
2. A term used for a licence granted by the Board of Trade between 1945 and 1951 as a prerequisite to any planning application for a new office or industrial building.
3. See **building agreement.**

building line
1. A line beyond which an owner of land is not permitted to build; in particular a line set out on a plan by a highway authority restricting the proximity of new buildings to a public **highway.** Usually the line is set at a fixed distance from the centre of the highway. A building line is intended to ensure a degree of uniformity in the appearance of new buildings, or may be fixed in the interests of road safety, and may be considered an aspect of positive planning. Called also a 'set-back line'.
cf. **improvement line.**
2. A line on a plan which shows the existing, or permitted, limit of an outer wall of a building.

building loan
see **construction loan.**

building lot
see **lot.**

building maintenance
see **maintenance.**

building of special architectural or historic interest
see **listed building.**

building operations

In determining what constitutes **development** for the purpose of deciding whether an operation requires planning permission, building operations includes "rebuilding operations, structural alterations of or additions to buildings, and other operations normally undertaken by a person carrying on business as a builder" (Town and Country Planning Act 1971, s. 290 (1)). In this context a building includes, "any structure or erection and any part of a building, as so defined, but does not include plant or machinery comprised in a building". An operation primarily means an activity that results in a physical alteration to land and has some degree of permanence in its result – Parkes v Secretary of State [1979] 1 All 213. In general, preparation work such as is necessary to prepare an estimate is not a building operation, nor is the carrying out of minor repair or decoration. Demolition of an entire building carried out independently of building construction, provided it does not materially affect the appearance of the land, is not a building operation – Iddenden v Secretary of State for the Environment [1972] 1 WLR 1433. See also **engineering operations, mining operations**.

Planning Law and Procedure, by A.E. Telling, 6 edn, pp. 64–68.
Guide to Development and Planning by R.N.D. Hamilton 7 edn, pp. 81–84.

building ordinances (US)
see **ordinances**.

building permit (US)
Written consent, granted by a local government body, for the erection of new buildings or for major alterations to, or demolition of, an existing structure. The proposed building work must conform to any local **zoning ordinance** and the **building codes** before a building permit will be granted. See also **certificate of occupation**.

building plot
see **plot**.

building preservation notice (BPN)
A notice served by a local planning authority, in accordance with the provisions of the Town and Country Planning Act 1971, 3.58, (as amended by the Town and Country Planning (Amendment) Act 1972) on any owner and any occupier of a building that in the opinion of the authority appears to be of "special architectural or historic interest and is in danger of demolition or of alteration in such a way as to affect its character as such". The notice informs the parties that the Secretary of State for the Environment will be asked to list the building. The notice has the same effect on the use of the building as if it were a **listed building**, i.e. it makes demolition, extension, or alteration, without consent, an offence. The notice takes effect as soon as it is served and remains in effect for six months, unless the Secretary of State makes a decision on the local authority's proposal beforehand. If the Secretary of State chooses not to list the building, the building is no longer protected. In that event the local authority may be obliged to pay compensation to the building owner for any loss suffered as a direct consequence of the notice (1971 Act, s. 173). No compensation is payable if the Secretary of State agrees to list the building.

building preservation order

An order, made by a local authority and confirmed by the Minister of Town and Country Planning, specifying that a building of special architectural or historic interest should not be demolished or altered without special consent. This form of order was abolished from 1 January 1969 and replaced by the **listed building consent** procedure (Town and Country Planning Act 1968, s. 40 (9), (10)).

building regulations

A code, set out by the Department of the Environment or the Welsh Office, specifying methods of construction and types of material to be used in building work in England and Wales (except Inner London which currently retains **building by-laws**, but is intended to come within the same controls at a future date). Building regulations were introduced first in 1966 (Building Regulations 1965) to standardise and consequently to replace local building by-laws. These regulations (which are made in accordance with the provisions of the Public Health Act 1936, s. 61 as amended by the Public Health Act 1961 and the Health and Safety at Work, etc. Act 1974, Part III) are contained currently in the Building Regulations 1976, as amended. They regulate the type of building material that may be used; structural design; drainage and sanitation; and lay down standards for natural lighting and ventilation. The regulations are intended to ensure the health, safety and welfare of people using buildings; the conservation of fuel and power; and prevention of waste or contamination of water. Prior to the erection of a building, or a material change in the structure of a building, the consent of the local authority must be obtained to the proposed building works, so as to ensure that they comply with the regulations.

Building regulations are produced also in the US, but these are referred to as building **ordinances** or **building codes**. See also **building control**.

The Building Regulations Explained and Illustrated, by W.S. Whythe and Vincent Powell-Smith, 6 edn.

Guide to the Building Regulations, by A.J. Elder, 7 edn.

Looseleaf Building Regulations, by Knight, (Metric Edition) (1984)

38 Halsbury's Laws of England, 4 edn. paras. 450–700.

building residual technique (US)

A method used to value buildings, or improvements, separately from the land on which they stand. An income that is assessed to represent a reasonable return on the land alone, i.e. a market ground rent, is deducted from the total net income receivable from the property, including the buildings and the difference is multiplied by an appropriate capitalisation rate, such as a rate that would amortise the building cost over its economic life.

cf. **land residual technique**. See also **property residual technique**, **residual method of valuation**.

building restriction (US)

1. See **building control, ordinances**.

2. See **restrictive covenant**.

building scheme

see **scheme of development**.

building society

An organisation established by statute, with a fixed set of rules, to make long term loans for the purchase of property, by means of mortgages secured thereon. Building societies originally developed during the late 18th and early 19th centuries to assist individuals to obtain funds to purchase their own homes. The societies received money from the general public who then became members of the society. These societies have grown appreciably in number and size but continue to provide loans predominantly for residential properties. Building societies are now strictly controlled by statute and may be established for the purpose of "raising, by subscriptions of the members, a stock or fund for making advances to members out of the funds of the society by way of mortgage of freehold or leasehold estate" (Building Societies Act 1962, s. 1 (1)). A building society is restricted primarily to these purposes and is not permitted to make direct investments in property. The societies are controlled by statute in their manner of raising money, lending powers and their general administration. At least ten members are required to form a society, but it may be a permanent or terminating body. In the US, building societies were the forerunner of the **savings and loan associations**.

The Building Society Industry, by Mark Boléat (1982).

The Building Societies, by Martin Boddy, (1980).

Building Society Law by Wurtzburg and Mills, 14 edn.

4 Halsbury's Laws of England, 4 edn. paras. 1501–1723.

Building Trust
see **equity-participation mortgage**.

built area
see **gross built or covered area**.

built-up capitalisation rate (US)
see **component capitalisation rate**.

bulk mortgage
see **blanket mortgage**.

bulk zoning ordinance (US)
see **zoning ordinance**.

bull
One who anticipates that prices will rise. A speculator who buys shares in a company expecting to make a short term profit.
cf. **bear**.

bullet loan (US)
see **gap financing**.

bundle of rights theory
A theory which propounds that **ownership** of real estate is made up of a number of rights, the sum total of which constitute absolute ownership. The theory holds that, because land cannot be transferred as a physical entity, it is represented by a set of distinct and separate rights and benefits each of which is capable of separate transfer. These rights include the right to use, to profit from, to occupy, to sell, to charge, to bequeath, to lease, to develop or to build on, and to encumber land. The holder of an unencumbered **fee simple** possesses all such rights. These rights are not unqualified, but are limited by the power of the State in the form of its right to raise taxes; to exercise the power of **eminent domain** (to take private property by condemnation); **escheat** (to take property that has no known owner or if taxes are not duly paid); and what are colourfully called the State's **police powers** (the regulation of new building, zoning ordinances, health regulations, etc.).

The bundle of rights theory is of

North American origin and owes much to the civil law concept of ownership. In English common law ownership of land is a right that one person exercises against another, one owner or title holder having a better or weaker right than another. An owner of land possesses nothing tangible and the right to land is expressed as a relationship between people in respect of real property: "once one begins to think sloppily, it is all too easy to start thinking that 'the' property owner, by virtue of being 'the' property owner, must necessarily own a particular bundle of rights over a thing, and this is to commit the error that separates laymen from lawyers. For the fact (or is it the law?) of the matter is that property is not a thing, but a set of legal relations between people governing the use of things".
Private Property and the Constitution, by Professor Bruce Ackerman, p. 27, (1977). See also *demembrement de la propriété*, **partial ownership**.

bungalow

A residential building of which the main walls are no higher than one storey, although the building may incorporate gable projections in the roof – Ward v Paterson [1929] 2 Ch. 396. A term originating from a house built in Bengalese style, that is, of a single-storey construction with a low sweeping roof.

burden

Something taken or accepted as a duty or obligation; an **encumberance**. A restriction imposed upon a freedom to use land.
cf. **benefit**. See also **restrictive covenant**.

bureau (F)

office; government office. As well as referring to an office in a building, this term covers the English equivalent 'bureau', and such groups as the executive officers, standing committees, and committees of a company.
(*bureau d'enregistrement* – registration office)
(*bureau des hypothèques* – mortgage registration office)
(*bureau d'études* – planning office, engineering office).
(note: the office of a notary is an *étude* and a lawyer a *cabinet*).

bureaux (F)

offices; office building.

business

That which keeps one busy. Any means of gaining a living or occupying a person's mind or time, especially an enterprise that involves a commercial or mercantile activity. Transactions or dealings of any kind where time and effort are utilised toward a particular end; generally, but not exclusively, to make a profit. Business entails a full level of commitment; it requires most of a person's thoughts, powers and time. Business is a general term that includes a **trade**, but a person who is involved in business is not necessarily involved in trade. A **profession** may be conducted as a business and employment may require, but does not necessitate, a business activity; but neither a profession nor employment need to be pursued as a business. Business is conducted by a person's own volition not as a consequence of a calling; it requires no special learning but only an independence of judgement and decision. Business may even include the letting of premises or the taking in of lodgers when that is a commercial activity – Bagettes Ltd. *v* GP Estates

Ltd. [1956] Ch. 290; Lewis v Weld-crest [1978] 3 All ER 1226. Thus business can mean almost anything which is an occupation, as distinguished from pleasure; "anything which is an occupation or duty which requires attention is a business" – Rolls v Miller (1884) 27 Ch. D 88; Abernethie v AM and J. Kleiman Ltd (1969) 211 EG 405. In relation to a **business tenancy** business includes "a **trade**, **profession** or employment and includes any activity carried on by a body of person, whether corporate or unincorporate". (Landlord and Tenant Act 1954, s. 23 (2)). See also **business premises**.

business cycles
see **cycles**.

business day
A normal working **day**; any day excluding a Saturday, Sunday or public holiday.

business interruption insurance
see **consequential loss insurance**.

business, loss of
see **compensation for disturbance**.

business premises
Any premises (land, houses, buildings, etc.) occupied for the purpose of **business** or **trade**. Premises that, when let, may form the subject-matter of a **business tenancy**, and therefore be subject to the protection afforded by the Landlord and Tenant Acts, including any premises occupied for the purpose of a 'business' which, in turn, "includes a trade, profession or employment and includes any activity carried on by a body of persons, whether corporate or unincorporate" (Landlord and Tenant Act 1954, s. 23 (1)). Thus a trade, business

or employment can be carried out by one person and the premises may be classified as business premises; but the "activity" must be carried on by a "group of persons". For the purposes of this statutory interpretation occupation by a business that is merely incidental to residential occupation is not occupation for the purposes of a business – Cheryl Investments v Saldanha [1978] 1 WLR 1329. The tenant does not need to use the premises exclusively for his business, he may live on the premises or make some ancilliary use of them, provided his 'business' is the predominant user – William Boyes and Sons Ltd. v Adams (1975) 32 P and CR 89. An institution that runs a private hospital or medical school carries on a qualifying activity – Groveside Properties Ltd. v Westminster Medical School (1983) 267 EG 593, as does a tennis club run by a committee – Addison Garden Estates v Crabbe [1958] 1 QB 513, but taking in lodgers for a meagre supplemental income is not likely to be considered as a business – Lewis v Weldcrest [1978] 1 WLR 1107.

In the case of a right to **compensation for improvements** the holding to which the Landlord and Tenant Act 1927 applies means any premises held under a lease, other than a mining lease, and "used wholly or partly for carrying on thereat any trade or business" (1927 Act, s. 17 (1)). This section expressly includes "premises regularly used for carrying on a profession." It excludes any part of an agricultural holding; premises let by reason of an office appointment or employment for the landlord; and premises used for the business of sub-letting residential flats. See also **commercial property**.

business property (US)

Commercial property, especially when used for the retail trade, including banks, hotels and theatres.

business tenancy

A **tenancy** of **business premises**, i.e. "any tenancy where the property comprised in the tenancy is or includes premises which are occupied by the tenant and are so occupied for the purposes of a **business** carried on by him or for those and other purposes." (Landlord and Tenant Act 1954, s. 23 (1)). It must be a tenancy in the strict sense of the word, a **licence** cannot qualify under this definition – Shell-Mex and BP Ltd *v* Manchester Garages [1971] 1 All ER 841; nor does a **tenancy at will** – Wheeler *v* Mercer [1957] AC 216; Hagee (London) Ltd. *v* A.B. Erikson and Larson [1975] All ER 234. An **underlease** or an **agreement for a lease** may create a business tenancy, but not a lease granted by way of a mortgage (1954 Act, s. 69 (1)). The tenant does not have to occupy the premises personally, nor does he have to occupy the whole of the premises; it is genuine **occupation**, or an intention to occupy the premises, for the purposes of a business carried on by the tenant, at the relevant time, that is important. Occupation through a manager, employee, agent, servant or other *bona fide* representative may be adequate – Cafeteria (Keighley) Ltd. *v* Harrison (1956) 168 EG 688; Lee-Verhulst (Investments) Ltd. *v* Harwood Trust [1972] 1 QB 204. Occupation by all or any of the beneficiaries of a trust or by a member of a group of companies is treated as occupation by the particular party that holds the tenancy (1954 Act, ss 41 (1), 42). The premises may be used partly as a residence and partly for the business of the tenant, provided the business purpose is the predominant user – Cheryl Investments Ltd. *v* Saldanha, Royal Life Saving Society *v* Page [1979] 1 All ER 5. The premises may be land only – Bracey *v* Read [1963] Ch. D 88, but a tenancy of an **incorporeal hereditament**, e.g. of an easement or a profit à prendre, cannot be a business tenancy as there are no 'premises' capable of occupation within the meaning of the Act – Land Reclamation Co. Ltd *v* Basildon DC [1979] 2 All ER 993. On the other hand, any easement or servitude that is enjoyed by the tenant as appurtenant to the premises, such as a right of access, forms part of the business tenancy (1954 Act, s. 32 (3)).

The following are expressly excluded from the provision of the 1954 Act: (i) a tenancy of an **agricultural holding**; (ii) a **mining lease**; (iii) a tenancy of on-licenced premises (a public house or the like), unless the sale of alcohol is ancilliary to another business use, such as an hotel, restaurant, theatre, place for entertainment or exhibition; (iv) a **service tenancy**, i.e. a tenancy granted by reason of the tenant holding an office, appointment or employment as stated in writing; (v) any tenancy granted for a fixed term not exceeding six months, except when the tenant (which is taken for this purpose to include any predecessor in the business) has been in continuous occupation for more than twelve months or there is an arrangement to extend or renew the term beyond six months from the commencement of the tenancy; (vi) an **extended lease** as granted under the Leasehold Reform Act 1967, s. 16

(1); (v) premises that are certified as being required in the public interest by certain public bodies, or for national security (1954 Act, ss. 43, 57–60, as amended by the Law of Property Act 1969, s. 12).

The holder of a business tenancy is entitled to **security of tenure** in that the tenancy may not come to an end unless terminated in accordance with the provisions of the Landlord and Tenant Act 1954, Part II (1954 Act, s. 24(1)). Unless terminated in that way, the tenancy automatically continues when it has come to the end of its contractual term, on basically the same terms as the expired contractual tenancy, (which includes any right for the tenant to assign or sub-let the business premises) and the landlord is deprived of any common law right to bring the tenancy to an end by **notice to quit**. Normally a 'new tenancy' is created as soon as possible after the contractual tenancy comes to an end, either by the tenant making a formal application for such a tenancy, or by the landlord giving notice to terminate the tenancy and stating that he would not oppose an application by the tenant for a new tenancy.

If a business tenancy is brought to an end in accordance with the statutory provisions the tenant may have a right (a) to **compensation for disturbance**; and/or (b) **compensation for improvements**. In the latter instance the right applies to any premises held under a lease, other than a mining lease, and "used for any trade or business", including premises used for a profession or used as an on-licence; but not an agricultural holding, premises where the tenant carries on the business of letting residential flats, nor any premises let to a tenant as

holder of any office, appointment or employment from the landlord (Landlord and Tenant Act 1927, s. 17).

The methods by which a business tenancy may be brought to an end under the 1954 Act are: (i) a landlord's notice to terminate (s. 25): (ii) a tenant's request for a new tenancy (s. 26); and (iii) a tenant's notice to terminate (s. 27). The tenant's notice to terminate may take the form of notice to quit in the usual way, or if the tenancy was granted for a fixed term, three months prior written notice that he does not wish the tenancy to continue at the end of the term (or, if the tenancy has been allowed to continue after the end of the term, three months notice, to expire on a quarter day, of his intention to quit the premises). The tenancy may be ended also by the following common law methods: (a) a **surrender** of the tenant's interest to his immediate landlord; (b) **forfeiture** due to a breach of covenant, provided there is a proviso for re-entry in the terms of the tenancy; or (c) forfeiture of a superior tenancy.

A landlord's notice to terminate does not take the form of a common law notice to quit, but must be given in accordance with the statutory provisions and in a prescribed form (Landlord and Tenant (Notice) Regulations 1983) or in substantially the same form. (Printed forms for this purpose are readily obtainable from law stationers with extensive guide notes). The notice must (a) specify a date for termination of the tenancy (being a date not earlier than six nor later than twelve months from the date of the notice, to expire not earlier than the date when, apart from the Act, the tenancy could have been determined by notice to quit or would have expired by effluxion of time); and (b) be given by the 'competent **landlord**'(who may be the immediate reversioner but must be the person capable of granting a new tenancy and either the holder of a fee simple interest or a tenancy with not less than 14 months unexpired: 1954 Act, s. 44 (1), Sch. 6). The landlord's notice must state also (i) that the tenant has two months from the **service** of the notice to notify the landlord, in writing, whether or not he is willing to give up possession on the date specified for termination; (ii) whether the landlord would oppose the grant of a new tenancy on one or more of the statutorily prescribed **grounds for possession**; (iii) if the premises comprise a house for which the tenant has a right of leasehold enfranchisement or a right to an extended lease, that the tenant has a right to state whether he intends to exercise one of those rights (in which case a separate procedure is adopted). A different form of notice is required if the premises are required in the public interest or for national security. The landlord must give also the name and address of anyone (or their agent) whom he knows or believes has a superior interest in the premises. The landlord cannot serve such a notice if the tenant has already requested a new tenancy. The tenant may then claim a new tenancy provided (i) he gives notice to the landlord within the requisite two months that he is not willing to give up possession and (ii) not less than two nor more than four months after receiving the notice he applies to the court (the county court or if the rateable value of the premises exceeds £5000 the Chancery Division

of the High Court) for a new tenancy. If the tenant fails to do either of these two things he loses his right to apply for a new tenancy and the current tenancy will determine in accordance with the landlord's notice.

The tenant has the right to request a new tenancy provided his tenancy was originally granted either for a fixed term of more than one year (whether or not it is continued by the 1954 Act); or for a fixed term and thereafter from year to year. A tenant who holds a yearly tenancy, or a shorter periodic tenancy, or a tenancy for a fixed term of less than a year may not apply directly for a new tenancy; although he may claim a new tenancy in response to a landlord's notice of termination of the tenancy.

The tenant's request for a new tenancy must (a) be in writing in the prescribed statutory form (Landlord and Tenant Act 1954, Part II (Notices) Regulations 1983), or in a form substantially to like effect; and (b) must state (i) the property to be comprised in the new tenancy, (ii) the date from which the new tenancy is to commence, being not more than twelve nor less than six months after the request for the new tenancy, and not earlier than the date on which the existing tenancy would otherwise have come to an end or could be determined (thereby putting an end to the existing tenancy from the date the new tenancy is to commence), (iii) the duration of the new tenancy requested, (iv) the rent to be payable under the new tenancy, and (v) the other terms of the new tenancy (which are usually similar to the expiring tenancy). The new tenancy requested by the tenant must not be stated to begin less than six months nor more than twelve months from the date of the request. The landlord has two months to notify the tenant if he disputes the terms proposed by the tenant or if he intends to oppose the grant of a new tenancy. The tenant must also apply to the court for the grant of a new tenancy not less than two nor more than four months after he has served his request for a new tenancy on the landlord (1954 Act, s. 29 (3)). If the landlord fails to notify the tenant within the specified time that he objects to the grant of a new tenancy it is assumed that he has agreed to the terms proposed by the tenant.

The parties may agree some or all of the terms for the grant of a new tenancy. Failing agreement an application to the court to determine the terms for a new tenancy may arise when (a) the tenant has given the requisite counter-notice to the landord's notice of termination stating that he is not willing to give up possession on the proposed termination date; or (b) the tenant has made a proper request for a new tenancy. If the landlord has not opposed the tenant's request for a new tenancy, or having opposed it has failed to establish one of the grounds for possession, the court must order the grant of a new tenancy. The new tenancy replaces any contractual or statutory tenancy that was previously in effect; although if the tenant does not wish to take the tenancy he has a right to request the court to revoke the order granting the new tenancy and terminate any future liability to the landlord after allowing a reasonable period for the landlord to re-let the premises (1954 Act, ss. 29, 36)

The premises (the 'holding') to be included in the new tenancy are those which were actually occupied by the tenant for the purpose of his business prior to the start of the new tenancy. The duration of the new tenancy is whatever the court considers reasonable in all the circumstances, but not longer than 14 years. The other terms of the tenancy are to be such as the court considers reasonable in all the circumstances, having regard to the terms of the former tenancy. If either party wishes to modify any of the terms of the tenancy the burden is on that party to provide good reason for such a modification – O'May v City of London Real Property Co. Ltd [1983] 2 AC 726. The court may insert a 'break clause' if the landlord has a *bona fide* reason to anticipate requiring the premises for redevelopment – McCombie v Grand Junction Co. Ltd [1962] 1 WLR 581; or a 'rent review clause' if appropriate to the term of the new tenancy (1954 Act, s. 34 (3), as incorporated by the Law of Property Act 1969, s. 2). The rent determined by the court is the amount which, having regard to the other terms of the tenancy, the premises comprised in the holding "might reasonably be expected to let in the open market by a willing lessor", but disregarding (a) any effect on the rent arising from the fact that the tenant, or his predecessor in title, is in occupation of the premises; (b) any **goodwill** attached to the holding by reason of the carrying on of the business by the tenant or his predecessor in the business; (c) any **improvement** carried out by the tenant or his predecessor in title, unless the improvements were carried out in pursuance of an obligation to the landlord accepted in the original tenancy or carried out more than 21 years before the application for the tenancy was made; and (d) if the premises comprise licenced premises, any value attributable to the licence held by the tenant (Landlord and Tenant Act 1954, ss. 32–36, as amended by the Law of Property Act 1969, s. 1 (1)). The number of times a business tenancy may be renewed is unlimited.

It is not possible to contract out of the provisions of the Landlord and Tenant Act 1954, Part II, unless a prior joint application is made by the landlord and tenant to the court, to exclude the tenancy in its entirety from the Act; also any agreement by which a tenant agrees to surrender a business tenancy at a future date is void unless sanctioned beforehand by the court (1954 Act, s. 38, as incorporated by the Law of Property Act 1969, s. 5). See also **bail commercial, interim rent, Landlord and Tenant Acts.**

Business Tenancies, by S.W. Magnus (1970).
Drafting Business Leases, by K. Lewison, (1980).
Letting Business Premises, by Trevor M. Aldridge 5 edn.
Landlord and Tenant, by Adkin 18 edn, pp. 371–387.
The Law of Landlord and Tenant, by D.R. Evans, 2 edn, pp. 369–418.
Landlord and Tenant Law, by David Yates and A.J. Hawkins, pp. 465–554 (1981).
Business Tenancies, by James Fox-Andrews, 3 edn.
Landlord and Tenant, by Hill and Redman, 17 edn, p. 685–860.
Renewal of Business Tenancies: Law and Practice, by Kirk Reynolds and Wayne Clark (1985).
Landlord and Tenant, by Woodfall, 28 edn, paras. 2–0630 to 2–0794.

29 Halsbury's Laws of England, 4 edn, paras. 474–557.
Handbook of Business Tenancies, by D.W. Williams, looseleaf (1985).

business trust (US)
A trust established to hold property for the profit or gain of the beneficiaries; in particular, a trust in which the trustees are also the managers who deal with the trust property for the use and benefit of the beneficiaries and are remunerated for their services. The beneficiaries receive transferable certificates of participation or shares in the trust. An entity that is more akin to a company than a strict trust. In the state of Massachusetts (where corporations were limited in their powers to hold and deal in real estate) a trust, or 'mutual fund', that invests in real estate is referred to as a 'Massachusetts trust'. Called also a 'common-law trust'. See also **discretionary trust, real estate investment trust.**

butt
To join end to end. See also **abut.**

butts and bounds system
See **metes and bounds system.**

buy-back agreement
see **repurchase agreement**

buy-in
1. The purchase of a property offered for sale by **auction** by the vendor himself or by an interested party (commonly the auctioneer acting as the vendor's agent) if the final bid is inadequate. Referred to also as 'bid-in'. See also **reserve price.**
2. To purchase a junior or subordinate interest in a property in which the purchaser already has an interest,

e.g. the purchase of a leasehold interest by a freeholder of the same property. See also **marriage value**.

buy-out
see **forward commitment (or sale)**.

buy-out rate
The capitalisation rate agreed between a property developer and a financial institution, which has agreed to purchase a development property on its completion, as the appropriate rate to capitalise the income (or prospective income) at the time of the sale. The rate is agreed normally at the time a **forward commitment** to finance the development is made by the institution.

buy-and-sell agreement
1. An agreement between two parties, especially members of a **joint venture** or **partnership**, which provides that in certain circumstances (e.g. on the termination of the partnership), one party may purchase the assets, or an interest therein, from the other. Frequently a reciprocal arrangement by which one party, usually the larger shareholder, has the first right to buy assets from the other and if this right is not exercised it is available then to the other party.
(US) 2. See **contract for sale**.

buyer
A **purchaser**, especially one who exchanges money for goods or services. See also **caveat emptor**.

buyer's equity (US)
see **down payment**.

buyer's market
A market for any single commodity or property where there are significantly more sellers than buyers so that prices are bid down; a condition in a market when the buyer is in a stronger position than the seller because supply exceeds demand.
cf. **seller's market**.

buyer's option
see **purchase option**.

by-law or byelaw
1. An **ordinance** or **code** that is applied in a specific area, such as a town or county i.e. a code of restriction on the residents in the locality to which the law applies. "An ordinance affecting the public or some portion of the public imposed by some authority clothed with statutory powers ordering something to be done or not to be done and accompanied by some sanction or penalty for its non-observance … it has the force of law within the sphere of its legitimate operation" – Kruse *v* Johndon [1898] 2 QB 96. See also **building by-law,** *ultra vires*.
2. A rule or regulation made to govern the running of an association (such as a co-ownership trust, a housing association or a condominium) or a corporation.

C

cabin
1. A small single-storey dwelling, usually of primitive design and construction, commonly used for vacation purposes. A permanent lodging built of mud or like material.
(US) 2. Sleeping accommodation, which forms part of a larger complex and is adjoined to a **motel**.

cabinet (F)
office, normally applied to a professional office and in particular a lawyer's or doctor's practice; closet; small room.

caché (F)
(*vice caché* – **latent defect**).

cachet (F)
seal. The requirement that certain documents must be sealed for authenticity is not found in French law. See also *acte*, *sceau*.

cadastral map (or plan)
A map (or plan) of an area or district delineating the boundaries of property ownership and used for title recording and taxation purposes. A cadastral map (or plan) is normally accompanied by a description of the property, by reference number, area, etc. but does not necessarily show physical features that appear on the ground, unless these correspond with the ownership boundaries. See also *cadastre*.

cadastral (F)
(*extrait cadastral* – land registry certificate).
(*plan cadastral* – **cadastral plan**). See also *cadastre*.

cadastral survey
A **survey** made to determine and record the position of property boundaries especially for the purpose of preparing an official register of land ownership. See also *cadastre*.
Cadastral Surveys within the Commonwealth, by P.F. Dale (1976).

cadastre (F)
cadastral register; **cadastral survey**. The cartographical representation of a country's territory on a common basis made to show the entire division of land ownership. "A public register of the quality, value and ownership of immoveable property in a country, compiled to serve as a basis for taxation". A form of register used in Continental Europe that is similar to the Land Registry in England; a cadastral plan indicating the legal boundaries of a valid title to land. See also **Torrens system**.
Land Law and Practice, by S. Rowton Simpson, p. 110 and Appendix A (Cadastral in France).

caducarry
Relating to **escheat**, lapse or **forfeiture**.

caeteris paribus (L)
'Other things being equal'.

cahier (F)
(*cahier des charges* – **specification**; documents for an open invitation to tender; bill of quantities; **conditions of sale**; general conditions, of any form of contract). See also *lotissement*.

caisse (F)
bank; fund.
(*caisse d'amortissement* – **sinking**

fund)

(*caisse d'épargne* – savings bank)
(*caisse des pensions* – **pension fund**)
(*caisse de retraite* – superannuation fund, pension fund)
(*caisse hypothécaire* – mortgage bank, mortgage lending office).

calendar month
see **month**.

call
1. A demand for, or right to demand, payment of money or delivery of goods, immediately or on a specified date. See also **call loan, call option**. (US) 2. An identifying mark or line on a survey plan, or on a plan attached to a conveyance, which corresponds to an object, landmark or natural boundary on the land to which the plan refers.

call loan (or mortgage)
A loan (or mortgage) repayable by the borrower upon the demand of the lender; a loan that is repayable on 24 hours' notice. The sum repayable is referred to as 'call money'. Referred to also as a 'demand loan' or 'demand mortgage'. See also **acceleration clause, alienation clause**.

call money
see **call loan**.

call option
An **option** to purchase property, stock or a commodity at an agreed price (an 'exercise' or 'striking' price) within a specified time. Normally a certain sum of money (a **premium**) is paid for the right to a call option.
cf. **put option**. See also **purchase option**.

call provision (US)
see **acceleration clause**.

'called-in' planning application
An application for **planning permission** that is considered sufficiently important for the Secretary of State for the Environment to make a direction that it be referred to him instead of being dealt with by a local planning authority. A similar action may be taken in respect of an approval of a proposal under a development order. If required by either party, the Secretary of State must hold a hearing or public enquiry before deciding whether to grant or refuse an application that has been referred to him in this way (Town and Country Planning Act 1971, s. 35). See also **planning inquiry**.

Canadian mortgage
An **amortisation mortgage** which provides for interest to be compounded half yearly but payments to be made monthly.

Canadian rollover mortgage
A mortgage loan provided on the basis that all or part of the principal may remain outstanding for the term of the loan, which is generally 20 to 25 years, but the interest rate can be adjusted at fixed intervals.

canal (F)
drain.

canalisation (F)
pipeline.

cancellation
The act of bringing to an end; **termination**. The **abrogation** of an instrument; usually accompanied by writing words of revocation across the face, or defacing or physically destroying it. See also **discharge**.

cancellation clause
see **termination clause**.

Candlemas

The feast of the Purification of the Blessed Virgin Mary, 2 February. One of the 'half quarter days' or 'term days' in Scotland. See also **quarter days**.

canon

1. An annual payment made under an **emphyteotic lease**.
2. An old term for a rent or tribute payable to a church.
3. A rule of discipline or a principle accepted as a guideline by members of an association, e.g. **a code of conduct** accepted by professional valuers.

canton (F)

An administrative district under an *arrondissement*. See also **local authority**.

capita, per (L)

see *per capita*.

capital

1. A stock of accumulated and material **wealth**. The surplus of production over consumption at a particular time, especially of goods, possessions or real assets retained for the purpose of further production, reinvestment and ultimate profit. Capital is required because production is not an instant process; it is a non-permanent resource that is used to produce or maintain income for all or a sector of mankind, i.e. it is a 'factor of production'. It may be defined as: "that part of the wealth of a country which is employed in production and consists of food, clothing, raw materials, machinery, etc. necessary to give effect to labour". – *On the Principles of Political Economy and Taxation* by David Ricardo, p. 95 (1817). Or, "all those man-made aids to further production, such as tools, machinery, plant and equipment, including every-thing man-made which is not consumed for its own sake but which is used up in the process of making other goods" – *An Introduction to Positive Economics*, by Richard G. Lipsey, 5 edn., p. 52. Capital may be classified broadly as **fixed capital** which is retained intact throughout the production process and includes buildings, plant and machinery; **working capital** which is added or reduced according to fluctuations in production levels and includes stocks and work in process; and **real capital** which is that which is finally produced. See also **capital value, fixed asset**.

2. The total **estate** of an individual or a body, including money, goods, land and buildings: "a corpus of property or assets, as distinct from periodical produce, return or income" – *Oxford Companion to Law* (1980). See also **chattel**.

3. **Money**, or **money's worth**, retained to run a company. The **net worth** (excess of assets over liabilities) of a company as owned by the proprietor(s) (sometimes called the proprietor's capital). The aggregate of the sums subscribed and paid in by the shareholders of a company, with the addition of any gains or profits realised by the use or investment of those sums. Sometimes called 'money capital' as distinguished from 'real capital' which is represented by the tangible assets of the company. See also **equity capital**.

4. The **principal** due under a loan, as distinguished from the interest payable thereon. See also **debt capital**.

capital (F)

capital.

(*capital et intérêts* – principal and

interest)
(*capital immobilisé* – **fixed capital**)
(*capitaux flottants* – **floating assets** or floating capital)
(*capital speculatif* – **risk capital**).

capital allowance
Expenditure of a capital nature that may be offset against the taxable profit of a business. In many countries expenditure incurred on acquiring capital assets may be deducted from the profit of a business prior to a liability for tax, usually in the form of an annual **depreciation** allowance. However, in the UK depreciation, i.e. the setting-off or writing down of a cost against a tax liability, is not permitted as such. Instead certain **capital expenditure** may be deducted as a capital allowance before assessing a liability to Income Tax or Corporation Tax.

The Capital Allowances Act 1968 (as amended) provides that qualifying capital expenditure may be set against taxable profits in the form of (a) a **first-year allowance** (for plant and machinery) or an **initial allowance** (for certain buildings); and (b) a **writing-down allowance** and, in certain cases on the disposal of an asset, a **balancing allowance**. See also **enterprise zone, industrial building allowance**.
Taxation of Land Transactions, by A.R. Mellows, 3 edn, pp. 112–118, 380–392, 409–410, 416–419.
Land and Tax Planning, by Patrick C. Soares, pp. 81–124.
Capital Allowances, by John W. Shock, 2 edn.

capital appreciation
see **appreciation**.

capital asset
An **asset** of a permanent nature; an asset intended for continuous use or to provide an income, rather than for trade, sale, conversion, or consumption. See also **capital, fixed asset**.

capital depreciation
see **depreciation**.

capital expenditure
Expenditure incurred to acquire property or to increase its value permanently. Expenditure for the enduring benefit of a trade or business, especially expenditure laid out to replace or improve the assets of that business, i.e. expenditure on a **fixed asset**; as distinguished from expenditure on a current or liquid asset or 'revenue expenditure' incurred in the day-to-day running of an enterprise. Thus, for example, capital expenditure may be defined to exclude "any expenditure or sum which is allowed to be deducted in computing for the purposes of tax, the profits or gains of a trade, profession, office, employment or vocation ..." (Capital Allowances Act 1968, s. 82 (1) (a)). It matters not where the money comes from but rather what the money is spent on. In general, money spent on **improvement, alteration** or **renewal** is capital expenditure, but money spent on repair and maintenance is not.

capital gain
An increase or gain in the value of a fixed asset or property from its original cost to its current value. **Profit** realised, or realisable, from the sale of a **capital asset**. A capital gain may arise from a change in the nature of a property, e.g. a change of use, resulting in a consequent increase in demand; improvement or alterations

made to a property; or a change in the purchasing power of money, i.e. inflation. It may be notional, or 'unrealised', when the asset is still held; or 'realised' when a disposal has taken place and an actual profit has been obtained. Capital gain includes profits or gains that arise other than in the normal course of business, e.g. the sale of real property by a manufacturing company, and usually a gain that arises on the sale of an asset which has been held for longer than one year, especially when so designated by statute for taxation purposes. When recorded in the financial statement of a company or when realised, it may be called a 'capital profit'.
cf. **income**. See also **capital gains tax**.

capital gains tax (CGT)

A tax levied on a realised increase in the value of a capital asset. A tax arising on the sale or exchange of an asset, (including an estate or interest in land) that, in English tax parlance, is a 'chargeable asset'. Especially a tax on a profit that does not arise in the normal course of trade or business (and, therefore, may not be liable to income tax or corporation tax). This form of tax was first introduced in the UK with effect from 6 April 1965 (Finance Act 1965) and is now provided for in the Capital Gains Tax Act 1979 (as amended by subsequent Finance Acts). In general, if a 'chargeable asset' is disposed of capital gains tax is payable on the difference between the proceeds of sale and the original cost of acquiring the asset (which since April 1982 may be increased to take account of inflation, provided the asset has been held for more than twelve months). Gains from the sale of certain assets are not

considered 'chargeable gains' and, therefore, are not taxable; such as gains from the sale of a **principal private residence** or from the sale of unit trusts. In addition, **roll-over relief** is permitted for certain industrial property and various small gains are exempt from CGT.

In the US, a distinction is made between capital gains realised within one year, 'short-term' capital gains, and gains realised over a longer period, 'long-term' capital gains. Short-term capital gains are taxed as ordinary income in the hands of the taxpayer; long-term gains are taxed more favourably as a rule. See also **capital tax, short-term capital gains tax**.

Taxation of Land Transactions, by A.R. Mellows, 3 edn, pp. 119–148.
Land and Tax Planning, by Patrick C. Soares, 2 edn., pp. 89–142.
Capital Gains Tax, by Antony Sumption, (1982).
Capital Gains Tax, by Whiteman, P. and Wheatcroft, G.S.A., 3 edn.

capital gearing
see **gearing, leverage**.

capital grant
see **grant**.

capital improvement
Any **improvement** that increases the value, or extends the useful life, of a **capital asset**.

capital investment
An investment made to acquire capital, a fixed asset or a long-term security as distinguished from an acquisition of a liquid or short-term asset. Money or resources invested in a business or enterprise for the assiduous benefit of that entity; money paid out to acquire something of permanent

use or value to a business. See also **capital expenditure**.

capital loan
A loan secured on a **capital asset**.

capital messuage
see **mansion house, messuage**.

capital money
1. Money received and held by the trustees of a **settlement**. In particular, money that is received by trustees from their sale or other dealings in **settled land**; as distinguished from income received from settled land that may be retained by the **tenant for life**. Capital money may be obtained in a number of ways, e.g. from land or heirlooms sold or mortgaged; upon the grant of a lease at a fine or premium; as consideration received for the grant of an option to purchase, or the grant of a lease of, the settled land; as damages received by the tenant for life as a result of a breach of covenant by his lessee or grantee; as money received under a fire insurance policy effected for buildings on the settled land; or as a specified portion of money received from a mining lease. Capital money must be retained for the benefit of those entitled under the settlement; it must be invested either to meet a particular purpose for which money was raised from the settled land, or in accordance with one or other of the twenty-one forms of investment or applications for the money stipulated in the Settled Land Act 1925, s. 73. These include authorised securities; an interest in land (either in fee simple or a lease for not less than 60 years); payment for authorised improvements to the settled land and its buildings; and certain forms of mortgage.

Cheshire's Modern Law of Real Property, 13 edn., pp. 189–190.
The Law of Real Property by Robert Megarry and H.W.R. Wade, 5 edn, pp. 373–375, 402–405.
Land Law: Cases and Materials, by R.H. Maudsley and E.H. Burns, 4 edn, pp. 204–205, 277–279.
42 Halsbury's Laws of England, 4 edn., para. 794–825.
2. Money arising from the sale of a **fixed asset**, or expended on the purchase or improvement of such an item i.e. **capital expenditure**; as distinguished from income or expenditure which arises on a regular or recurring basis. See also **capital gain**.

capital profit
see **capital gain**.

capital recapture
see **recapture**.

capital recapture rate (US)
see **recapture rate**.

capital recovery
see **recapture rate**

capital tax
Any tax on a change in capital value (including **capital gains tax, capital transfer tax, estate tax**); as distinguished from a tax on income.

capital transfer tax (CTT)
A tax, introduced by the Finance Act 1975, ss. 19–52 (and amended by subsequent Finance Acts), on the value of property transferred from one person to another as a life-time gift or as a settlement on death. Capital transfer tax, which since 1975 has replaced **estate duty** and **gift tax** in the UK, is levied on most gratuitous transfers (those transfers that are tax-

able being called 'chargeable transfers') that cause a reduction in the value of a person's 'estate'. An 'estate' includes most property to which a person is beneficially entitled, less any liabilities secured thereon. CTT is payable each time a chargeable transfer takes place and it is assessed on a cumulative basis, based on the net reduction in the value of the estate over the previous ten years. A final assessment is made at death when the value of all life-time chargeable transfers, made up to ten years before, are added to the value of chargeable transfers on death – a process sometimes called 'hotchpot'. Thus if a person makes life-time gifts of £10 000 and £30 000 and dies leaving £100 000, in principle, CTT is levied each time on the amounts of £10 000, £30 000; then the tax is reassessed on the entire 'estate' of £140 000 with different rates of tax applied depending on whether the transfers were on or within three years of death.

Exemptions to CTT include life-time gifts and outright transfers below a certain limit in value; a transfer that forms part of routine expenditure; a transfer for the public benefit; transfers to political parties and to certain charities; most transfers between spouses; gifts (up to a given limit) in consideration of marriage; transfers of certain works of art; and the transfer of certain business properties to the proprietor on his retirement.
Practical CTT Planning, by R.P. Ray, 2 edn.
Taxation of Land Transactions, by A.R. Mellows, 3 edn, pp. 149–173.
Tolley's Capital Transfer Tax.
Dymond's Capital Transfer Tax, 2 edn.

capital valuation
see **capitalisation, investment method of valuation.**

capital value
The **value** of a property as ascertained at one particular time, bringing into account all future income and benefits. The value of an asset as ascertained by the **capitalisation** of income, "capital, in the sense of capital value, is simply future income discounted or, in other words, capitalised," – *The Theory of Interest* by Irving Fisher, p. 12, 1930. See also **asset value, capitalised value, market value.**

capitalisation or capitalization
1. The conversion of a series of anticipated income instalments into a single current or **capital value**. The anticipated or projected income from an investment is discounted at a rate of interest that takes account of the risk of obtaining that income in the future. The process of market capitalisation means that "... every asset will be capitalized by the *price bids of buyers and sellers* in the market place at the *present discounted value* of all its future net receipts. (By net receipts we mean all the cash dollar rentals received from the asset *minus* all cash outlays for materials, repairs, etc.)" – *Economics*, by P.A. Samuelson, 4 edn., p. 593. In other words, the process involves ascertaining the market value of a future income stream as if that income were receivable at a single moment in time.

The capitalisation process may apply a single multiplier or capitalisation factor to the current income – called direct or **straight capitalisation**, or 'capitalisation in perpetuity'; or it may apply a present value factor (such as the present value of 1 per annum) to a future income stream, called, yield or **annuity capitalisation,** or 'capitalisation for a limited period of time'. Capitalisation for a limited period of time may be expressed by the formula:

$C_v = [a_1/(1+r)] + [a_2/(1+r)^2] + [a_3/(1+r)^3] \ldots [a_n/(1+r)^n]$

where C_v = the capital, or current, value

$a_1, a_2, \ldots a_n$ = the income or cash flow receipts, in each period of time, for n times.

r = capitalisation rate, expressed as a decimal.

When the income is constant straight capitalisation produces a capital value = income (a)/capitalisation rate (r). See also **investment method of valuation.**

2. In accounting, a term used to refer to additions to **capital** or reserves created in a financial statement or balance sheet. Also the act of recording **capital expenditure** in a book of accounts.

3. In finance, additions of unpaid or **accrued interest** to a total indebtedness or to the principal outstanding on a loan – the interest so added, in turn, bears interest until paid. See also **compound interest.**

capitalisation (F)
   capitalisation.
   (*taux de capitalisation* – **capitalisation rate; yield**).

capitalisation factor
   A factor or multiplier used in converting income into capital. In the UK, the term **years' purchase** is more commonly used by valuers to describe a capitalisation factor. See also **capitalisation rate, dual-rate capitalisation factor, single-rate capitalisation factor.**

capitalisation method (or approach) (US)
   see **capitalisation, investment method of valuation.**

capitalisation rate (CAP rate)
   1. A rate of discount or percentage selected as appropriate for the conversion of income into capital, i.e. for **capitalisation.** A rate that is sufficient to provide a return to an investor for accepting the risk of a capital investment as well as a return, or recapture, of the capital invested. Such a rate may be divided into 100 to produce a **capitalisation factor** for 'straight capitalisation' (i.e. multiplication by the current income), or applied in a formula, such as the **present value of one per period,** to provide a factor for 'annuity capitalisation'. A term used more commonly in the US where 'CAP rate' refers normally to a capitalisation factor rather than a capitalisation rate. See also **band-of-investment capitalisation rate, component capitalisation rate, discount rate, investment method of valuation, overall capitalisation rate, yield.**
   (US) 2. See **recapture rate.**

capitalisation table
   see **valuation table.**

capitalise (or capitalize)
   1. To convert a series of income instalments into a single capital sum; to divide income by a percentage rate (expressed as a decimal) to obtain a capital, or capitalised, value.
   2. To charge expenditure to a capital or reserve account. See also **capitalisation.**

capitalised value
   A capital value obtained by the **capitalisation** of the anticipated income from a property i.e. the value

obtained by multiplying the projected income by an appropriate capitalisation factor (or dividing by a capitalisation rate). See also **investment method of valuation**.

capitalized-income approach (US)
see **investment method of valuation**.

capitaux (F)
money.
(*capitaux errants/capitaux fugitifs* – hot money).

capite, tenant-in-
see **tenant-in-chief**.

capture rate (US)
see **catchment area**.

caravan
A covered vehicle for carrying people, especially one that can be used as a residence or place of business; a house on wheels, which may be towed or is motorised. A structure designed or adapted for human habitation which can be moved from one place to another by being towed or transported. A similar structure designed or adapted as a temporary office, particularly a construction site office, may be referred to also as a caravan.

The installation of a caravan on land (except at the rear and within the curtilage of a dwelling-house or for certain short-term stay or by certain exempt organisations (Town and Country Planning General Development Order 1977, Class I, xxii), may be **development** and require **planning permission**. In addition an occupier of land must obtain a **site licence** from the local authority before he can use that land as a 'caravan site', defined as, "land on which a caravan is stationed for the purposes of human habitation and land which is used in conjunction with land on which a

caravan is stationed." (Caravan Sites and Control of Development Act 1960, s. 1 (4)). For this purpose a caravan is defined as, "any structure designed or adapted for human habitation which is capable of being moved from one place to another (whether by being towed, or transported on a motor vehicle or trailer) and any motor vehicle so designed or adapted, but does not include: (a) any railway rolling stock which is for the time being on rails forming part of a railway system, or (b) any tent" (1960 Act, s. 29 (1)). (Exemption to the requirement for planning permission and for a site licence, as granted for the use of land as a caravan site within the curtilage and as an incidental use of a dwelling-house, certain short-term stays and for certain exempt authorities, are set out in the 1960 Act, Sch. 1.) See also **mobile home**.

caravan site
see **caravan**, **site licence**.

care, duty of
see **duty of care**.

carport
A covered area of hard-standing, usually abutting a dwelling house, used for the parking of a car. Unlike a garage, it is not entirely walled-in; commonly it takes the form of a lean-to or roofed extension to a building and is open at least at both ends.

carriageway
A **highway** over which there is a right to drive vehicles, as well as (unless prohibited by statute) a right to drive or ride animals or to pass and repass on foot. The term 'carriageway' may include a **bridleway**, but not a **driftway**. A carriageway may incorporate a **footway**, but a footway is not a

carriageway. In particular, "a way constituting or comprising a highway, being a way (other than a cycle track) over which the public have a right of way for the passage of vehicles" (Highways Act 1980, s. 329 (1)). Called sometimes a 'cartway', especially when restricted to wheeled vehicles.

carrière (F)
quarry.

carry-over clause (US)
see **extender clause**.

carrying charge
1. A recurring cost of holding a vacant property, or a property under construction; for example, an insurance premium or an interest charge on a loan. See also **front money**.
(US) 2. The regular costs of running a property; a term used particularly when assessing **closing costs**.

cart-bote
see **estovers**.

cartway
see **carriageway**.

cas fortuit (F)
A fortuitous or unavoidable event. In a general sense synonymous with **force majeure**. In a legal sense, *cas fortuit* arises from an inherent factor, e.g. a fault in the materials used in a building; *force majeure* arises from an external factor, e.g. the action of a third party or a government.
cf. **act of God**.

cash
That which readily circulates as **money**. A term that normally has a more restricted meaning than money. Cash primarily means coins of the realm and bank notes – Miller *v* Race (1758) 1 Burr. 452 – and is used commonly in that more restricted sense. However, cash can be extended in meaning to cover cheques, bank drafts or any similar instrument that can readily be exchanged for **legal tender** without reference to the credit worthiness of the payer. A coin that is treated as a curio or a collector's item is not cash or currency, but goods – Moss *v* Hancock [1899] 2 QB 111. A provision in a lease that a tenant will 'pay' or 'yield and pay' a sum of money as **rent** means payment must be made in cash, in its restricted sense. However, if a landlord accepts a cheque, or indicates that he will accept a cheque in payment of rent, thereafter he cannot refuse such means of payment; provided the cheque is honoured as soon as it is presented – Davis *v* Gyde (1835) 2 Ad. and E 623. See also **promissory note**.

cash accounting
The method of preparing accounts whereby income and expenditure items are recorded when they are actually received or paid. Thus rent is recorded when paid, rather than when legally due. Called also the 'cash basis', the 'cash receipts method', or the 'disbursement method' of accounting.
cf. **accrual accounting**.

cash allowance (US)
see **prime-cost sum**.

cash back
A financial inducement paid to a prospective tenant by a building owner as an inducement to sign a lease of vacant property. See also **rent concession, reverse premium**.

cash basis
see **cash accounting**.

cash discount
A reduction in a price or a considera-tion due under a contract for early or prompt payment.
cf. **trade discount**.

cash down (US)
1. See **deposit**.
2. See **cash out**.

cash flow
1. **Income** available to an investor in real estate, after he has paid his oper-ating expenses, debt service (interest and principal repayments on a loan), but before income tax. Cash flow may be calculated also after allowing for depreciation. Cash flow repres-ents the income available from an investment, before taking an account of the investor's own outgoings. In the US, called also 'cash throw-off'.
cf. **net income, spendable income**. See also **net cash flow**.
2. The actual movement of cash in and out of an enterprise; the gross trading profit of a business. A term used also for the difference between the income and expenses resulting from an investment, particularly when these sums are accounted for as and when paid or received (as in cash accounting), rather than when due (as in accrual accounting.)

cash-flow actualisé (F)
discounted cash flow.

cash-flow analysis
The financial analysis of a develop-ment project based on the **net cash flow** generated by the project. Cash flow analysis considers the total of all cash outflows and inflows (if any) for the project, in order to ascertain the financing requirements at any stage from its inception to completion. See also **discounted cash flow, feasibility study**.
Valuation and Development Apprai-sal, edited by Clive Darlow, pp. 53–58 (1982).

cash-flow rate of return (US)
see **cash-on-cash return**.

cash market value
see **cash value, market value**.

cash method
see **cash accounting**.

cash-on-cash return (or yield) (US)
The relationship, expressed as a per-centage, between **cash flow** (i.e. the net income receivable after debt ser-vice but before tax) and the total **equity** outlay on an investment. The cash flow includes the effective gross income less all outgoing (real estate taxes, operating expenses and interest and principal on financing); but no account is taken of capital apprecia-tion (or depreciation) or equity build-up as principal is repaid. Called also the 'equity dividend rate', 'cash-flow rate' or 'cash-flow return'.
cf. **equity-yield rate, free and clear return**.

cash on the barrelhead, or **cash on the line** (US)
see **front money**.

cash out (US)
The requirement by a seller to take the entire proceeds of a sale in cash, i.e. to require 'cash down' rather than granting a **purchase-money mortgage** or accepting an **instalment contract**.

cash receipts method of accounting
see **cash accounting**.

cash rent

1. A fixed or **base rent** payable under a lease when there is no provision for any additional payment as a contribution towards operating costs, nor any payment based on a share of the tenant's business operations such as a **turnover rent**. See also **escalation clause, primary and secondary rent**.
2. An amount of rent payable, in **cash**; usually in advance. See also **cash tenant**.

cash tenant

A tenant who pays rent as cash, especially a farm tenant whose rent is based solely on a monetary payment; as distinguished from a tenant who pays rent partially or totally on the basis of a share of his crops.
cf. **share tenant**. See also **cash rent**.

cash throw-off (US)

see **cash flow**.

cash value

The **market value** of a property on the basis of a private sale with no exchange of properties, transfer of debt or deferred payments, i.e. on the basis of an all-cash transaction. See also **actual cash value, cash out**.

casualty insurance

see **accident insurance**.

casuel (F)

contingent.

catalla (L)

'Chattels'; in the civil law any form of moveable property. See also **moveables**.

catching bargain

An **unconscionable bargain**. In particular, an agreement to lend or pay money, made on unreasonable or oppressive terms, usually because the borrower or payer is at a distinct bargaining disadvantage relative to the other party. A term which originally referred to a loan made to someone who had expectations of receiving property, especially as an heir expectant, when the lender hoped to receive a share of the property or inheritance. See also **usury**.

catchment area

The area from which a business or retail centre is assumed to derive its trade; the area over which a public service, e.g. a school, cinema, etc., exerts an influence; or the area from which any new project of development is likely to draw significant demand. The limits of this area may be assessed by considering population mobility; competitive influences on consumer demand; socio-economic trends; and factors that affect accessibility, whether physical or psychological. The content of a catchment area may be analysed on the basis of population (size, family units, age, etc.); income levels (average, frequency distribution, deviations, etc.); and other economic data (car and durable goods ownership, consumer preferences, housing, etc.), supported by market research. For a **shopping centre**, this area is determined primarily by travelling time, (the attraction of a centre decreases in geometric proportion to the travelling time for a consumer); the dynamic attraction of the centre; natural barriers, such as intervening high land or a river; and competitive retail units. As a rule, "the competitive influence of any two retail centres will be in direct proportion to the square of the size of those centres and in inverse ratio to the square of the distance from any unit of population" – (Reilly's Law).

Called also a market or 'trade area'. In the US, the percentage of the population that is likely to be drawn to a shopping centre from the catchment area is referred to as the 'capture rate'. See also **feasibility study**.
Retail Site Assessment, by R. Cox (1968).
Analysis and Valuation of Retail Locations, by Edwin M. Rams, pp. 80–98, (1976).

cattlegate
A right to graze cattle on the land of another, generally for part of the year only, one 'cattlegate' being pasture for one cow or five sheep. Called also, depending on the limitation placed on the use, 'stinted pasture', 'beastgate', or generically 'gated pasture'. See also **right of common**.

causa proxima et non remota spectatur (L)
'It is the immediate, not the remote cause, that should be considered'. See **damages**.

cause
1. Something or somebody that brings about an action, effect or event. An act that precedes, and brings about, a result. See also **commission**.
2. A ground for a legal **action**; a court action.
3. The justification for the making of a promise. A cause (*cause*) is one of the principal requirements in French law for a valid contract; but English law requires more than a cause, it requires a motive or **consideration**.

cause (F)
cause; motive for a contract; consideration. The intention to freely deliver something under a contract; the 'end pursued' in entering into a

contract. An essential requirement of a contract in French Law. (French Civil Code, arts. 1108, 1131–1133). *Cause* may be compared to the importance of **consideration** in English law, but it has a broader significance and does not require the formal exchange of benefit and detriment: "To use a much-repeated aphorism, whereas *objet* provides an answer to the question *quid debetur*? (what is owing?), *cause* answers the question *cur debetur*? (why is it owing?)" – *French Law of Contract*, by Barry Nicholas, p. 112 (1982).
(*ayant cause* – assignee). See also *contrat*, *objet*.
Amos & Walton's Introduction to French law, 3 edn., pp. 166–172.
Jean Carbonnier, Droit Civil, Les Obligations, 7 edn., pp. 91–93.
Boris Starck, Droit Civil, Les Obligations, pp. 459–477 (1972).
Précis Dalloz, Droit Civil, Les Obligations, 3 edn., pp. 294–332.

caution
A temporary means of protecting an interest in, or a charge on, land by which the person seeking protection (the cautioner) enters his claim on the Proprietorship or Charges Register at the **Land Registry**. A caution may be lodged on the register by any person interested in a parcel of unregistered land to avert a first registration; or by any person who is not the registered proprietor to avert a **dealing** in the registered land. A **minor interest** may be protected by means of a caution, but an **overriding interest** need not and cannot be so protected. The effect of a caution is to enable the cautioner to take steps to protect his interest, but it does not of itself create any interest in land. The Land Registrar

must notify a cautioner of any proposal affecting the subject land, thereby giving him the opportunity to raise an objection to a proposed registration or dealing; although this objection may or may not prove successful when examined by the Registrar. A caution is used commonly when the registered proprietor is not cooperative in producing the Land or Charge Certificate; and unlike a **notice**, a caution is a temporary and, generally, a hostile act. It may be used also in cases of fraud or deceit. A person who lodges an unreasonable caution may be ordered to pay compensation to a person who suffers consequential loss (Land Registration Act 1925, ss 53–56; Land Registration Rules, rr. 6, 7). See also **inhibition, restriction**.
Emmet on Title, 18 edn, pp. 607–609.
Concise Land Registration Practice, by Theodore B.F. Ruoff and Christopher West, 3 edn, pp. 209–212.
The Law and Practice of Registered Conveyancing, by T.B.F. Ruoff and R.B. Roper, 4 edn.

caution (F)

guaranty or **guarantor** (according to the context); **security; surety; collateral**.
(*caution solidaire* – a guaranty that preceeds the main debt, e.g. a guaranty from a third party or a parent company demanded by a lender)
Manuel de Droit Civil, by Pierre Voirin et Gilles Goubeaux, 20 edn, pp. 533–540.

cautionnement (F)

security; deposit (of money as a guaranty). See also *gage*.

cave (F)

cellar; a small storage area below ground level. See also *sous-sol*.

caveat emptor (L)

'Let the buyer beware'. A general principle of English common law that a buyer of **goods** should make all reasonable enquiries before effecting a purchase. "*Caveat emptor* in Latin or law does not mean that a buyer must take a chance, it means he must take care." – Wallis *v* Russell [1902] 2 IR 615. A vendor is obliged to disclose any defect of title of which he is aware; must not misdescribe or misrepresent any facts; and may be bound by statute as to the condition of the property (e.g. the Sale of Goods Act 1979, the Defective Premises Act 1972). Accordingly, in modern law, the principle of *caveat emptor* is limited primarily to cases of apparent, notorious or notified defects in a property.
cf. *caveat venditor*. See also '**as is**', **constructive notice, exclusion clause, misrepresentation, negligence, patent defect, undue influence, warranty**.

caveat venditor (or caveat subscriptor) (L)

'Let the seller beware'. A maxim of the civil law. However, English statute law may make a vendor liable for a defect in a property even after the date of sale. For example, the Defective Premises Act 1972, ss. 1–3 imposes a liability on builders, architects, subcontractors or others who take on work for or in connection with the provisions of dwellings to see that they use proper materials, that work is done in a workmanlike manner and that the dwelling is fit for habitation when completed.
cf. *caveat emptor*. See also **implied term, misrepresentation, negligence, puffing**.

cédant (F)
assignor; grantor.

cede
To give up, yield, **transfer**, or **surrender**. See also **assignment, cession**.

céder (F)
to **surrender**; to assign; to **transfer**.

ceiling loan
The maximum amount that a mortgagee agrees to advance as a loan against the security of a particular property or properties. Used especially to refer to the maximum amount that will be advanced when certain conditions have been met, e.g. when a building is fully let. Called also a 'top loan'.
cf. **floor loan**. See also **holdback, mortgage loan**.

ceiling price
The highest price that can be obtained for a property, or the highest price that a vendor seeks to achieve before he will conclude a bargain. A ceiling price may be equivalent to the **market value** or, if the parties agree, it may exceed that value. See also **ceiling value**.

ceiling value
The maximum amount of compensation payable for a dwelling-house that is the subject of compulsory purchase and, because it is considered unfit for human habitation, is to be acquired on the statutory basis of its **cleared site value**. (The statutory assumption is made that an 'unfit' house has no value beyond the value of the site upon which it stands; although in the open market this may not be the case). In certain instances compensation may be increased over and above the cleared site value by the addition of an **owner-occupier supplement** or a **well-maintained payment**, provided the total amount of compensation does not exceed the open market value of the house, the 'ceiling value', assuming the property had never been declared unfit (Land Compensation Act 1961, s. 10, Sch. 10). **Compensation for disturbance** and any **home-loss payment** is unaffected by this rule.

cellar
A vault or underground room. An area of a building, entirely or predominantly below ground level, used usually for storage purposes. A cellar may be distinguished from a **basement** by reason of its use; the former, normally, is left as a bare shell and is used primarily for storage, whereas the latter may be decorated in some way and used for any purpose for which any other floor in a building can be used.

central business district (CBD)
A part of a town or city where the principal retail premises and the administrative and financial offices are located; the centre of the 'downtown' area. Generally the area of highest land values, i.e. the area where economic activity is at its highest. (Based on the theory that land will tend to be used for those purposes which yield the highest net return – the **highest and best use** – the CBD is the area where competition for land is at its greatest).
cf. **civic centre**. See also **location theory, prime location**.

central core
see **service core**.

central heating
A system for heating all or most of a

building from one heat source, without any means of artificial air treatment. Usually hot water or steam from the source is circulated through pipes, or hot air through ducts, to radiators or air outlets around the building.

cf. **air-conditioning**.

Central Land Board

A body established under the Town and Country Planning Act 1947, s. 2 to administer claims for loss of development value; collect the **development charge**; and generally to administer compensation matters arising from the 'nationalisation' of land under that Act. The Board was dissolved in 1959. The Board's residual functions are now administered by the Secretary of State for the Environment. See also **claim holding**.

Town and Country Planning in Britain, by J.B. Cullingworth, 7 edn, pp. 132–134.

centre commercial (F)
shopping centre.

certain rent
see **dead rent**.

certain term
see **term**.

certificat (F)
certificate.
(*certificat de conformité* – a certificate of conformity. A certificate issued by a local authority confirming that new building works conform with a *permis de construire* – building permit.

certificat d'urbanisme (F)
planning certificate. A certificate issued by a local planning authority indicating what may be built on a parcel of land and whether there are

any restrictions on a proposed development. This certificate does not authorise building work; such authorisation is obtained by means of a *permis de construire* (building permit). (*Code de l'Urbanisme, art. R. 410*).

certificate, building
see **building certificate**.

Certificate, Land
see **Land Certificate**.

certificate of appraisal (US)
see **valuation certificate**.

certificate of appropriate alternative development

A certificate that may be issued, to assist in determining the amount of **compulsory purchase compensation**, when the land that is the subject of the compulsory purchase order neither consists or forms part of an area of comprehensive development as defined in a development plan, nor is shown in the development plan as an area allocated primarily for a use or uses which are of a residential, commercial or industrial character; so that effectively no specified form of use or development which has a market value is laid down for the area of land that it is proposed will be acquired. Such a certificate may be issued by a local planning authority stating, in the opinion of the authority, that one or more classes of development (or, if considered appropriate, no alternative form of development) is permissible for the subject land, either immediately or at a future time; assuming there were no proposal to compulsorily acquire the land. The Land Compensation Act 1971, s. 17, (as amended by the Community Land Act 1973, s. 47)

provides that the certificate may be applied for by an owner of any interest to be acquired or by the acquiring authority. The form of development specified in the certificate may be taken into consideration when assessing the appropriate amount of compensation provided the development would have been permitted if the land was not to be acquired by compulsory purchase (1971 Act, s. 15 (5)). Called also a 'section 17 certificate'. See also **planning assumptions**.
The Law of Compulsory Purchase and Compensation, by Keith Davies, 4 edn, pp. 160–163.
Encyclopaedia of Compulsory Purchase and Compensation, by Harold J.J. Brown, paras. 1–083, 2–1089, 3–108, 3–160.

certificate of charge
see **Charge Certificate**.

certificate of completion
see **building certificate**.

certificate of deposit (CD)
A receipt issued by a bank or trust company as an acknowledgement that funds have been received on deposit. The deposit may be repayable on 'demand' or after a stated period of time. A certificate of deposit usually is a **negotiable instrument**.

certificate of established use
see **established use certificate**.

certificate of estoppel (US)
see **estoppel certificate**.

certificate of fair rent
A certificate issued by a rent officer stating the **fair rent** that he considers may be charged under a regulated tenancy. This form of certificate may be obtained when there is no binding **registered rent**, either because no fair rent has been registered: for example, if the premises have not been let previously; or when a landlord wishes to ascertain the rent he may charge for premises he proposes to build, convert or improve. This only represents the rent officer's opinion of fair rent and is not binding until it becomes a registered rent. (Rent Act 1977, s. 69, Sch. 12).

certificate of indebtedness
A short-term **promissory note** issued by a company or statutory body, being an acknowledgement of a **floating charge**.

certificate of interest (US)
A certificate issued to a participant in a **joint venture** evidencing the extent of his or her participation or interest in a property held by the venture.

certificate of no defences (US)
see **estoppel certificate**.

certificate of non-listing
see **listed building**.

certificate of occupancy (CO) (US)
A document confirming that a new building meets the zoning and building codes of a state and, therefore, that it may be occupied. Called also a 'completion order'.

certificate of payment
see **building certificate**.

certificate of practical completion
see **building certificate**.

certificate of purchase (or sale) (US)
see **tax certificate**.

certificate of reasonable value (CRV) (US)
A certificate of the value of a property and its maximum loan value as issued

by a federal body such as the Veterans Administration.

certificate of reduction (US)
see **reduction certificate**.

certificate of satisfaction (US)
see **satisfaction certificate**.

certificate of search
see **official certificate of search**.

certificate of title
1. See **Land Certificate**.
(US) 2. A formal certificate of the status of an owner's or mortgagee's title to a parcel of land based on an examination of the public records. Usually issued by an attorney, an abstract company, or a government-appointed Registrar of Titles. The certificate is issued after recorded documents of title have been examined in detail stating who is understood to be the true owner of the land in question and specifying details of any encumberances affecting the land. It does not necessarily exonerate a purchaser against details of any defect of title that could be readily ascertained by his own examination of the documents or any defect of which he has **notice**. (Not to be confused with a **title insurance** document which warrants the validity of the title). In some states called a 'title opinion'.
cf. **abstract of title, Torrens certificate of title**. See also **abstractor's certificate, marketable title**.

certificate for value
A statement, usually at the end of a conveyance, certifying within which band of values for **stamp duty** purposes a transaction falls. Called also a 'certificate of value'.

certificate of valuation
see **valuation certificate**.

certificate of value
1. A formal certificate, issued by the **Lands Tribunal**, stating the value of a property when land is to be sold to a body with compulsory purchase powers.
2. See **certificate for value**.

certificate, interim
see **building certificate**.

certificate, tax (US)
see **tax sale**.

Certified Assessment Evaluator (US)
An assessor who is a member of the International Association of Assessing Officers.

certified cheque (or check)
A cheque that the bank upon whom it is drawn has certified will be honoured when it is presented for payment. The cheque is stamped on the face 'certified' or 'accepted' and signed by an officer of the bank and funds are then set aside to meet the liability. Called also a 'marked cheque'. See also **banker's draft**.

certified copy
A copy of a document or instrument that is signed and certified as being a true copy by the person having custody of the original, e.g. by a solicitor or an officer of a public records office. See also **attest**.

certum est quod certum reddi potest (L)
'That is certain which can be rendered certain'. See **lease, rent, tenancy for a fixed period**.

certiorari (L)
'To be more fully informed of'. Originally a form of **writ** issued by a higher to a lower court requesting that the

proceedings or records of a case be sent for review, with the object of reopening a case when it is considered that justice might not have been done. Since the Administration of Justice (Miscellaneous) Provisions Act 1938, s. 7 a person who considered that an administrative decision had been improperly arrived at, for example, that it is *ultra vires*, could apply to the High Court for an order of *certiorari*, which if granted would quash the decision of the administering authority. This arrangement has now been replaced by a procedure to similar effect called a 'judicial review' (Supreme Court Act 1981, s. 28–31).

In the US, a writ of *certiorari* is used also to refer to any requirement for a judicial review. For example, a request from the Supreme Court to review the validity of a statute of any state. See also **prerogative order**.

certum est ... (L)
see *id certum est quod certum reddi potest*.

cessation (F)
(*cessation de bail* – expiry of a lease).

cesser
1. The ending of a liability, annuity, or the like.
2. The **determination** of an interest in land due to the ending of a term. See also **termination**.
3. The coming to an end of a mortgage term on repayment of the mortgage debt (Law of Property Act 1925, s. 116). See also **equity of redemption**.

cession
1. The **transfer** or **relinquishment** of a right of action or a claim. The yielding or ceding of property to another. In international law, the yielding up of territory by one state or govern-

ment to another. In ecclesiastical law, the vacating or surrendering of a **benefice**.
2. In the civil law, an **assignment**. See also *cession*.

cession (F)
transfer; cession; assignment especially of a right or interest between living persons
(*cession de créance* – the surrender of a creditor's goods when he is insolvent)
(*cession-bail* – **sale and leaseback**)
cf. *disposition*. See also *vente*.

cession deed (US)
1. A deed used to transfer a right or a claim to a debt, obligation, or property. Equivalent to a deed of assignment in English law.
2. A deed by which a property owner dedicates a street to a public authority. Equivalent to a deed of dedication in England.

cessionnaire (F)
assignee; grantee.

cessment
An **assessment** or tax.

cestui que trust
Pronounced 'setty-ker-trust' and derived from Norman French, *cestui à que trust* – 'he for whom is the trust' (held). The **beneficiary** of a property held in trust.
cf. *cestui que use*.

cestui que use
Pronounced 'setty-ker-use'. A shortened form of *cestui à que oes le feoffment fut fait* – 'he to whom the use of the **feoffment** is made'. i.e. the person to whom the true benefit of land is conveyed. In old English common law if land was transferred to A to be held for the benefit of B the legal

estate was held by A who was free to deal with it as he wished. However, equity recognised B as the true owner, the *cestui que use*, or the person entitled to the benefit and profits from land. (In modern law when a trust is established to hold land for another's benefit the **beneficiary** may be referred to as the *cestui que trust*). See also **feoffee to uses, use**.
Cheshire's Modern Law of Real Property 13 edn., pp. 43–48.

cestui que vie
1. Pronounced 'setty-ker-vie' and derived from Norman French *cestui à que vie* – 'he for whose life'. A person whose life determines the duration of an estate or interest in land, especially when that interest is held by another. See also *pur autre vie*, **tenant for life**.
2. A person against whose life an insurance policy is written.

ceteris paribus (L)
'All other things being equal', which in real estate they rarely are. A term commonly employed as a basic hypothesis in financial or economic analysis.

chain of title
The succession of deeds that establish a **root of title**; the history of a title to land as traced from conveyance to conveyance or from other documents of transfer. See also **abstract of title, certificate of title**.

chain store
One of a group of **retail** stores or shops, in common business ownership, selling similar merchandise under a uniform policy. The trading outlets may be a series of small shops, supermarkets, department stores, or any other form of retail store. See also **shop**.

chalet
A small wooden house or cabin, originally found in the Alpine region of Europe (especially in Switzerland), which is characterised by overhanging eaves that provide protection from heavy snow falls.

challenge procedure
see **advertisement**.

champerty
Derived from the Latin *campi partitio* or the French *champ parti*, 'a division of land'. A bargain between a litigant and a third party that they will divide land and other proceeds of a successful litigation. A bargain that may be described as "trading in the fruits of litigation". An agreement between a lawyer and a client to divide the amount of damages awarded to the client is champerty and such an agreement is void in common law as being contrary to public policy – Rees *v* De Bernandy [1896] 2 Ch. 437; Coopers and Lybrand *v* Levitt 384 NYS 2d. 804, 52 AD 2d. 493. See also **contingency fee, void contract**.

chance bargain
A **bargain** made when both parties recognise the risks entailed, or a contract made on the basis of supposed facts which the parties acknowledge may have limited veracity.

Chancery, Court of
see **equity**.

change of use
1. See **material change in the use**.
2. A change in the use to which a leased property is put. If a lease contains no restriction as to the use to which the demised premises may be put, the tenant is at liberty to make

whatever use of the premises he chooses, provided he is not restrained by law (Yelloly *v* Morley (1910) 27 TLR 20). However, a lease normally stipulates, in the **user clause**, the purpose for which the demised premises may, or may not, be used. This covenant may take the form of an absolute prohibition of any change of use; it may specify one or more uses to which the premises may be put; it may prohibit certain types of use; or it may prohibit uses that cause a nuisance, or are offensive, noxious or dangerous or in some other way affect the value of the property or adjoining property. The covenant may provide also that the landlord's consent is to be obtained to any change of use, either giving the landlord an absolute right to refuse such consent or giving him the right to refuse consent on 'reasonable' grounds. In the event of a breach of such a covenant, the landlord may obtain an award of damages or apply for an injunction to restrain the tenant. This type of covenant runs with the land and binds any assignee or sub-tenant.

A landlord is prohibited by English statute law from requiring a **fine** (in the form of any increased rent or otherwise) merely for granting consent to a change of use. But he is permitted to obtain a payment for any reasonable loss suffered to his property, or adjoining property owned by him, as a result of a change of use by the tenant; and he is permitted to require the tenant to reimburse any reasonable expenditure he incurs in granting a licence or consent for such a change of use (Landlord and Tenant Act 1927, s. 19 (3)). A landlord may restrict any change of use in accordance with the express terms of the lease and there is no statutory introduction of words that consent will not be unreasonably withheld, unlike a **restraint on alienation** (a covenant not to assign or sub-let). On the other hand, if the covenant expressly provides that the landlord's consent shall not be unreasonably withheld, then the landlord may not refuse consent in order to obtain a collateral advantage. For example, he may not refuse consent because of the effect that a change of use might have on the value of an adjoining property that is also owned by him – Anglia Building Society *v* Sheffield City Council (1982) 266 EG 311. See also **restrictive covenant, usual covenant**.

Landlord and Tenant Law, David Yates and A.J. Hawkins, pp. 93–97, 479–481 (1981).

Hill & Redman's Law of Landlord and Tenant, 17 edn., pp. 268–274.

Woodfall's Landlord and Tenant, 28 edn., paras. 1–1214 to 1–1259.

change order (US)

A properly authorised request, usually submitted by an architect to a contractor, to make a change in the work to be carried out under a building contract or to change a term of that contract. Usually such an order permits the contractor to demand a change in the contract price. Called also a 'modification order'. See also **variation order**.

channel

The bed of a river, stream or other **watercourse**; a passageway between banks through which water is intended to flow. See also *ad medium filum aquae*.

chantier (F)

building site.

charge

1. An obligation or liability to pay money, supported by an agreement in which property is bound as **security** for the performance of that obligation, but where there is no corresponding transfer of possession or title to the property. 'Charge' is a word of general meaning and as such includes a **mortgage, lien**, or any similar burden against property; although it does not have as wide a meaning as **encumberance**. In a more restricted sense the term may be applied to any loan that includes a right to hold property, or a right to property, as security, and, therefore, a loan that is more effective than a personal debt. The chargee has no interest in the property proferred as security, but may have a right to retain the property, or may apply to a court for an order that it be sold, as satisfaction for the discharge of the debt. The principal difference between a charge and a mortgage is that a chargee cannot foreclose (i.e. acquire ownership of the property) as he has no title which can be converted into a right to own the property. However, a chargee may apply to a court for a judicial sale or may appoint a **receiver** to collect the rents and profits. See also **'charge by way of a legal mortgage', charging order, equitable charge, fixed charge, floating charge, land charge, rentcharge**.
2. An expense incurred or due; a price demanded for something. A pecuniary liability for property. See also **cost, expenditure, liability, service charge**.

charge (F)

1. **encumbrance; charge**; liability; burden; obligation.

2. **charge**; expense; cost.
(*charges communes* – common area charges)
(*charges financières* – financing charges or costs)
(*charges locatives* – tenant's charges; all service charges payable by the tenant, excluding rent)
(*à charge de* – subject to)
(*sans charges de famille* – **unencumbered**).

'charge by way of a legal mortgage'

One of the two forms in which a **legal mortgage** may be created, under English law, since 1925; sometimes called a 'legal charge'. The mortgage is created by "a charge by **deed** expressed to be by way of a legal mortgage" (Law of Property Act 1925, s. 85) and by virtue of that Act the mortgagee has "the same protection, powers and remedies" in the case of a freehold as if a mortgage had been created for a lease term of 3000 years, and for a leasehold as if the mortgage had been created for a term that is one day less than the mortgagor's term (1925 Act, s. 87). This is to all intent and purpose a **mortgage** rather than a charge, as the creditor is treated in law as if he has an interest in the land rather than a mere claim to the proceeds of sale of the secured property. This is the commonest way of creating a mortgage because (a) the form is simpler than granting a lease for a term of years (being the other form of legal mortgage); (b) the mortgagor retains his interest in the land which he may sell, provided he redeems the loan; (c) it can be applied in the same way to a freehold or leasehold interest in land (and to combined interests, if so required); and (d) the mortgagor is free usually to sub-let his property

without being bound by the formalities incumbent on a tenant.
Cheshire's Modern Law of Real Property, 13 edn., pp. 625–627.

Charge Certificate
A certificate issued by the Land Registry after a mortgagee of registered land has entered his charge on the register of the charged title to land. The certificate has the original charge deed annexed, but in other respects it takes the same form as the **Land Certificate**. It is issued to the proprietor of the charge and as long as the charge subsists the Land Certificate is retained by the Registry (Land Registration Act 1925, ss. 25, 26, 63, 65). See also **registered charge**.

chargeable gain
see **capital gains tax**.

Charges Register
see **Land Registry**.

charging clause (US)
A clause in a trust document which states that a trustee may charge for his services.

charging lien (US)
see **lien**.

charging order
1. An order, made by the High Court or any county court for the purpose of enforcing a judgement or an order of either of those courts, for the payment of money by a debtor to a creditor. The order imposes a charge on any land, or interest in land, of the debtor as specified therein (Charging Orders Act 1979, s. 1 (1)). See also **caution, equitable charge**.
2. An order, made by a local authority, which creates a charge on a property and is granted for the benefit of a tenant who has been obliged to carry out repairs following a repairs notice. The order secures the right of the tenant to recover those costs that are the responsibility of his landlord.

charity shop
A **shop** used for the sale of goods received by a charity. Such shops are entitled to relief from the liability to pay rates (General Rate Act 1967, s. 40).

charter-land
"'Charter-land' is such as a man holdeth by charter, that is to say, be evidence in writing, which otherwise is called **freehold**" – *Termes de La Ley*. Otherwise called 'bookland', 'bock land' or 'boc land', being land held from the King by 'book' or 'charter', as distinguished from **folkeland** which, before the Norman conquest (1066), was held by the common people as an inherent right. The right to hold charter-land or book land represented a free right to land and was the nearest that land tenure in England has come to an **allodial system**.

chartered surveyor
A member of the **Royal Institution of Chartered Surveyors** who has been elected an Associate or a Fellow of the Institution, designated ARICS or FRICS. A person may not call himself a Chartered Surveyor unless he is a recognised member of that Institution. See also **surveyor**.

chase
Derived from the Latin *captare*, 'to hunt'. An area of open land set aside for keeping wild beasts of chase, with an exclusive right of hunting thereover; or as a game preserve. A **forest** is normally a chase, but as a rule a chase is smaller and is left in a more natural state than a forest. A chase is bigger,

less enclosed and less formal than a **park**.

chattels

Derived from Old French *chatel*, goods or property; or the Late Latin *captale*, principal, wealth or property (from which comes *cattala*, *cattel* or cattle which were a primary form of wealth and an early means of exchange). Any kind of **goods, property** or right to property, other than a **freehold** interest in land. Historically any species of goods that could be separated from a person and his house. In particular, a right to property that is not of unlimited duration, either because of the temporary nature of the property or of the right. Chattels are classified as 'chattels real' – those associated with land or realty; and 'chattels personal' – a broad category of moveable and tangible property or personal effects, e.g. furniture, jewellery, horses, beasts. In modern usage the term is more commonly used to refer to 'chattels personal'.

Chattels real or real chattels are "interests issuing out of or annexed to real estates, of which they have one quality, *viz.*, immobility, but want of the other, *viz.*, a sufficient legal indeterminate duration, and this want it is that constitutes them chattels." (Bl. Comm. vol. ii. p. 386). In particular, chattels real includes a **leasehold interest** which was regarded in English law merely as a source of income rather than a right to land *per se*. 'Chattels personal' or personal chattels may be divided into *choses-in-action*, e.g. a debt, copyright, etc. and *choses-in-possession*, e.g. goods and money. *Choses-in-action* primarily consists of rights to things that produce a mere claim or income. *Chose-*

in-action are tangible moveables that can be transferred or held by physical possession.

Upon intestacy personal chattels means "carriages, horses, stable furniture and effects (not used for business purposes), motor cars and accessories (not used for business purposes), garden effects, domestic animals, plate, plated articles, linen, china, glass, books, pictures, prints, furniture, jewellery, articles of household or personal use or ornament, musical and scientific instruments and apparatus, wines, liquors and consumable stores, but do not include any chattels used at the death of the intestate for business purposes nor money or securities for money" (Administration of Estates Act 1925, s. 55 (1) (x)).

In modern English land law, the 'estate' of freehold and the 'interest' of leasehold (especially a term of years absolute) have moved closer together and in most respects the latter are treated as rights to real property. Thus, although a leasehold interest is technically personal property, in modern practice it has little in common with 'chattels personal'.

Trees and crops which are part of the realty before cutting, i.e. non-annual crops, are sometimes referred to as 'chattels vegetable'. See also **chose, fixture**.

chattels mortgage

A contract by which **chattels**, or a right to chattels, are transferred as security for the payment of a debt, subject to a right to reclaim the chattel when the debt is repaid. A **mortgage**, or more usually, a **charge** on chattel; in particular on pure personality or goods. A charge on 'chattels real' (a leasehold interest) is called more commonly a **leasehold mortgage**. cf. **pledge**. See also **bill of sale, promissory note**.

chattels personal
see **chattels**.

chattels real
see **chattels**.

chattels vegetable
see **chattels**.

chauffage central (F)
see **central heating**.

check (US)
see **cheque**.

chemin pietonnier (F)
footpath (especially across a piece of land).
cf. *trottoir*.

cheque
Derived from the Greek *ktasthai*, 'to acquire'. A symbolic form of **money**; the acquisition or transfer of purchasing power. A written order from one party, the drawer, to a banker, demanding the payment of money to another specified person or to the bearer of the order. A form of **bill of exchange**, drawn on a bank, that does not require acceptance by the party to whom it is submitted, but requires payment on demand (Bill of Exchange Act 1882, s. 73). A cheque is the principal means of transferring money from one individual's bank account to the bank account of another or of withdrawing cash from the drawer's own account. In the US, spelt 'check'.

chief rent
Under the **feudal system** of land tenure, rent paid to the lord of the manor, or a Sovereign, by a freeholder. In parts of England where a

rentcharge was commonly demanded when freehold land was sold, that payment was called a chief rent or a fee farm rent. The Law of Property Act 1922, ss. 128 and 138 contained provisions for the abolition of such payments (along with most other manorial incidents), although some of these survived until 1940. See also **fee farm rent, quit rent**.

chief, tenant-in-
see **tenant-in-chief**.

chiffre d'affaires (F)
turnover (especially of a retailer).
(*loyer variable indexé sur le chiffre d'affaire* – **turnover rent**).

chilling a sale (US)
see **damping a sale**.

chinese auction
see **auction**.

chirograph
A deed written by hand in duplicate on the same sheet of paper. The duplicate parts are divided by a line on which an inscription is made and the two parts are then separated along that line. Technically an indenture with *chirographum* (autograph) written along the indentation. A chirograph was made to prevent fraud so that the authenticity of the instrument could be verified by bringing the two parts together.

chirographaire (F)
Depending on a **simple contract**.
(*créance chirographaire* – unsecured debt)
(*obligation chirographaire* – simple contract). See also **chirograph**.

chose
Derived directly from the French *chose*, 'thing'. Property, in particular

a personal chattel. A chose may be 'in possession' representing anything that is tangible, moveable and can be taken by physical possession e.g. goods, animals; or 'in action' representing anything that may be claimed or recovered only by an action in law, and is not physically held, e.g. a debt, the benefit of an obligation arising out of a contract, the beneficial interest of a trust, an option to purchase land, an insurance policy, a negotiable instrument, stocks and shares in a company, or a right to compensation following compulsory purchase. Thus, a right to any thing "may be either in possession, which is when a man hath not only the right to enjoy, but hath the actual enjoyment of the thing; or else it is in action, where a man hath only a bare right without any occupation or enjoyment." (Bl. Comm. vol. ii. p. 396). A right to a chose in possession means that a person has a physical right of user or of holding something as security, whereas a chose in action is essentially a right to income or capital. See also **chattels, things**.
Cheshire & Fifoot's Law of Contract, 10 edn., pp. 493–4.
6 Halsbury's Laws of England, 4 edn., paras. 1–200.

chose(s) (F)
thing; corporeal property; action.
(note: the word *chose* is a word of common usage but in French law the words *biens*, *droit*, *res* should more strictly be used, according to the right or type of property).
(*choses communes* – **common property** see also *res commun*). See also *proprieté*.

chose in action
see **chose**.

chose in possession
see **chose**.

Christmas day
The feast of the birth of Jesus Christ, 25th December. In English law, one of the usual **quarter days** for the payment of rent.

chronological age
see **actual age**.

circulating capital
see **working capital**.

citizen-participation (US)
see **public participation**.

city region
see **urban region**.

civic centre
An area of a town or city where the principal public buildings are grouped together e.g. the town or city hall, law courts, libraries, municipal offices and other civic buildings. The civic centre commonly forms part of or adjoins the **central business district**, but may be established as a separately developed entity.

Civic Trust
A body founded in England in 1957 to promote high standards of architecture and planning and encourage public interest in the appearance of towns and villages.

civil day
see **day**.

civil law
Laws that affect the rights of the individual. Historically civil law referred to a legal system codified by the Roman Emperor Justinian covering all aspects of law in a given state, nation or city. In particular, 'the civil law' means a legal system based on a

civil code, or other state enactments, as contrasted with **common law** which develops "from precedent to precedent". In French law *droit civil* is concerned with the law of persons (or family law); the law of property and of succession; and the law of obligations, especially contract. 'Civil law' may be used also to refer to the body of laws of a state or nation (called also 'municipal law'), as distinguished from international law; or, in common usage, the law affecting private or personal rights as distinguished from criminal, military, administrative and ecclesiastical law. *A Common Lawyer looks at the Civil Law*, by F.H. Lawson, (1953).

civil wrong
see *délit*, **delict**, *quasi-délit*, **tort**.

claim
1. A demand for a **right** or **privilege**; a demand as of right or supposed right, such as a demand for compensation. A "right to payment, whether or not such right is reduced to judgment, liquidated, unliquidated, fixed, contingent, matured, unmatured, disputed, undisputed, legal, equitable, secured or unsecured." (11 United States Code, para. 101 (4) (A)).
2. An assertion of a **title**, e.g. by staking out the boundaries of an area of land. The process of asserting a right to ownership of property by taking possession and subsequent action which precludes any challenge to that right. A claim is an assertion of a right to that which belongs to another, whether legally or illegally. "'Claime' is a challenge by any man of the property or ownership of a thing which hee hath not in possession, but is withholden from him wrongfully." – *Termes de La Ley*.

claim holding
The benefit of an 'established claim' for the loss of **development value**; this loss having been sustained as a result of restrictions on future development of land which were imposed by the Town and Country Planning Act 1947. That Act contained provisions that aimed to 'nationalise' any increases in the value of land beyond its value as at 1st July 1948, on the basis that any increase over the value for the land's 'existing use' at that date belonged to the State. Any landowner who could show that his property had depreciated in value as a result of these provisions could make a claim, in accordance with the provisions of Part VI of the Act, for a loss of 'development value' against a central government fund of £300m. A 'Part VI claim', if admitted by the **Central Land Board**, which was set up to administer such claims (or, in the event of a dispute, the Lands Tribunal), was known as an established claim and the personal benefit of any such claim that had not been paid out and, therefore, subsisted at 1st January 1955 was termed a 'claim holding'. Claim holdings were increased, from that date, by the addition of one-seventh, to become an **unexpended balance of established development value** (Town and Country Planning Act 1954, s. 17, as amended by the Town and Country Planning Act 1962, ss. 88–92 and re-enacted in the Town and Country Planning Act 1971, ss. 134–138).
Encyclopaedia of Planning Law and Practice, by Desmond Heap, paras. 2-1191, 2-3017.

claim of title
see **colour of title**.

clam, vi, aut precario (L)

'Stealth, violence and entreaty'. See **nec vi, nec clam, nec precario.**

clandestine mortgage

A **mortgage** entered into, in respect of land that is already affected by a mortgage or charge, when the mortgagor does not declare the existence of a prior claim. The concealment of any instrument or encumbrance affecting a title to property that is disposed of for money or money's worth with intent to defraud, is a punishable misdemeanour; the purchaser may claim damages for the resultant loss from the person (or, if applicable his agent or solicitor) who disposed of the property (Law of Property Act 1925, s. 183). See also **fraudulent conveyance.**

class gift

A **gift** of a property, or an aggregate sum of money, to a group of persons who come within a certain category or description but whose number will not be ascertained until a future time, so that the share received by each will not be known until all the members of the class are ascertained, e.g. 'to all my children who reach 18'. When the persons who are to receive the property are known, they receive the gift in equal or other defined proportions; the share of each recipient being dependent for its amount upon the ultimate number of persons.

clause

1. A section or paragraph of a legal document. See also **covenant.**
2. A section of a parliamentary bill.

clause (F)

clause; term; proviso.

(*clause d'avarie* – **average clause**)

(*clause compromissoire, clause d'ar-*bitrage* – **arbitration clause**)

(*clause d'inalienabilité* – inalienation clause)

(*clause d'indexation* – indexation clause)

(*clause d'un bail* – lease clause)

(*clause d'echelle mobile* – cost or price revision clause)

(*clause résolutoire* – defeasance clause).

clawback

An arrangement whereby a tax benefit or relief is retaxed under a separate tax provision.

clé en main (F)

turn-key contract.

clear day

A period of twenty-four hours, from midnight to midnight; "for regularly the law maketh no fraction of a **day**." (3 Co. Inst. 53). Thus a number of 'clear days' is never less than the sum of the given number of days in their entirety. In a contract, clear days exclude the day on which the contract starts and the day on which it terminates. Accordingly 'seven clear days' notice is longer than a 'weeks notice' – between one Monday and the next there are only six clear days – Re Hector Whaling Ltd. [1936] Ch. 208. But, if something is to be done 'within' ten clear days that means it must be completed on or before the end of the tenth day from the stipulated date of commencement. See also **time, week.**

clear lease

A lease in which the tenant covenants to repay all the landlord's costs of running a building "so that the rent payable reaches the landlord clear of all the expenses and overheads [associated with the demised premises]" – O'May and Others *v* City of London

Real Property Co. Ltd (1982) 261 EG 1185. See also **full repairing and insuring lease, triple net lease.**

clear title

A **title** to land that is free of any **encumbrance** or defect. See also **free and clear title, marketable title.**

clearance area

An area considered by a local authority to contain two or more houses that are **"unfit for human habitation**, or are by reason of their bad arrangement, or the narrowness or bad arrangement of the streets, dangerous or injurious to the health of the inhabitants of the area" and which the authority considers can best be dealt with by demolition of all the buildings in the area. Before passing a resolution declaring an area as a clearance area the authority must be satisfied that alternative accommodation is, or will be, available for persons displaced from the area and that its resources are sufficient to carry through its proposals (which may include acquiring properties in the area and providing new housing) (Housing Act 1957, s. 42, 43). Clearance may be carried out piecemeal over a period of time, the intention being primarily to demolish a number of properties, unlike a **housing action area** where a more comprehensive treatment is envisaged. A local authority plan that defines a clearance area generally identifies the unfit properties by pink colouring, 'pink properties', and those properties that, although not unfit, will need to be acquired to satisfactorily clear the area by grey colouring, 'grey properties'. A clearance area cannot be defined so as to include any land in a **general improvement area**; the two

designations being mutually exclusive. See also **cleared site value, rehabilitation order, urban renewal.**

West's Law of Housing, 4 edn., pp. 103–112.

Manual of Housing Law by Andrew Arden, 2 edn. pp. 205–206.

Housing Law, by Andrew Arden and M. Partington, pp. 422–433 (1983).

clearance order

An order that a local authority was empowered to serve on an owner of an unfit house in a **clearance area**, requiring the house to be demolished (Housing Act 1957, ss. 44, 45). This procedure has been ended and the authority is now required to acquire (by agreement or compulsorily) such houses for demolition or rehabilitation. (Housing Act 1974. s. 108). See also **demolition order.**

cleared site value

The value of a plot of land excluding any buildings thereon, but assuming it can be developed in accordance with the planning and building regulations currently in force. A term used particularly to refer to the basis of valuation used for assessing the compulsory purchase compensation payable for a house that is considered **unfit for human habitation** and, therefore, is acquired on the assumption that the building has no value. (Housing Act 1957, ss. 12, 59 (2)). (Any amount payable as **compensation for disturbance** is not affected by the adoption of the cleared site value as the measure of compensation for the property itself: 1957 Act, s. 32.) cf. **existing use value.** See also **clearance area, owner-occupier supplement, repairs notice, site value, well-maintained payment.**

Statutory Valuations, by Andrew

Baum, pp. 246–253 (1983).
Law of Compulsory Purchase and Compensation, by Keith Davies, 4 edn., pp. 166–167.

clerk of (the) works

A person appointed to represent the owner or employer on a building site, usually on the recommendation of an **architect** to whom normally he reports. The clerk of works is responsible for regular supervision of building work to ensure that it complies technically with the building contract. In particular he is responsible for keeping a factual record of building work; inspecting the quality of workmanship; and resolving detailed problems on site, subject to regular reference to the architect.
Handbook for Clerks of Work, Greater London Council, 3 edn.

climatisation (F)
air conditioning.

clog (on the equity of redemption)

A stipulation or provision in a mortgage deed which prevents the mortgagor from recovering his property unencumbered after repayment of all the monies due to the mortgagee or after performance of all the obligations for which the property was given as security. A restriction, impediment, or fetter on the **equity of redemption**. Any such clog on the mortgagor's right to redeem his property is void as being alien to the nature of a mortgage. See also **'once a mortgage, always a mortgage', unconscionable contract**.

cloison (F)
partition (as a wall).

close

1. A parcel or tract of land, in particular, an area enclosed by a bank, fence or hedge. A breach of close is a form of **trespass** that arises when a person intrudes on to land that is separated from **common land** or on to land owned by a private individual. See also **boundary, cul-de-sac, enclosure**.
2. To complete a real estate transaction; the act of **closing**.

close-ended, or closed-end, mortgage (US)

A mortgage under which neither the properties nor the amount of the indebtedness may be changed. A mortgage that limits the mortgagor's ability to raise additional finance on the security of the mortgaged property. Called also a 'closed mortgage'. See also **open-end mortgage**.

close-ended, or closed-end, trust (US)

An investment trust with a fixed capital or with a fixed number of shares; its shares are bought and sold on the open market as distinguished from an **open-end investment trust** or 'mutual fund' in which shares are bought and sold by the trust itself.

closed contract

A contract for the sale of land that automatically incorporates terms set out in a **standard-form contract** (e.g. the Law Society's Conditions of Sale) except where expressly varied.
cf. **open contract**. See also **conditions of sale**.

closed-end investment trust
see **close-ended trust**.

closed mortgage (US)

1. A mortgage that cannot be repaid until its date of maturity. See also **fetter**.
2. See **close-ended mortgage**.

closer (US)

A representative of a title insurance company who attends the closing of a real estate transaction. A payment made to that representative for his attendance is called also a closer. See also **title insurance**.

closing (US)

The **completion** of the transfer of the ownership of property. Closing takes place when all the consideration is paid, mortgages secured and the title is transferred to the purchaser by the delivery of the deed. 'Closing' may be used also to refer to the stage of a sale in **escrow** when title effectively has passed from a vendor to the escrowee. *Real Estate Law*, by Robert Kratovil and Raymond J. Werner, 8 edn., pp. 175–199.
Real Estate Closings, by Raymond J. Werner, (1979).

closing adjustment (US)

see **apportionment, completion statement**.

closing costs (or charges) (US)

The costs paid on **closing** or completion of the transfer of real estate in addition to the purchase price, e.g. the title recording fees, broker's commission, attorney's fees. See also **closing statement, completion costs**.

closing fees (US)

see **closing costs**.

closing order

An order served, in accordance with the provisions of the Housing Act 1957, ss 16, 17, by a local authority upon a person having control of a dwelling-house, specifying that the house may no longer be occupied for any purpose, other than a non-residential use approved by the

authority. A closing order may be served when a local authority is satisfied that, "any house (a) is **unfit for human habitation**, and (b) is not capable at reasonable expense of being rendered so fit", but the house cannot readily be demolished. A closing order is made when a **demolition order** would not be appropriate, for example, if the building is listed as being of special architectural or historical interest or it is required for support to an adjoining property. In determining whether a house can be rendered fit for human habitation at a reasonable expense, regard shall be had "to the estimated cost of the works necessary to render it so fit and the value which it is estimated that the house will have when the works are completed." (1957 Act, s. 39). A closing order takes effect 21 days after it is served, unless there is an appeal to the county court, in which case it will become operative (unless it is quashed or revoked) when the appeal has been determined. Once a house has been made fit for habitation the local authority is bound to lift the order and there is a right of appeal against a refusal to so end the order (1957 Act, s. 27).
West's Law of Housing, 4 edn., pp. 84–90.
Housing Law, by Andrew Arden and Martin Partington, pp. 418–420 (1983).

closing statement (US)

A detailed statement of all the costs and expenses incurred at a real estate closing, showing the net amount due to the seller. Such a statement is required under the Federal Real Estate Settlement Procedure Act, 12 USC para. 2601 and in many cases must be made on a prescribed pro-forma or settlement sheet, especially if it relates to a loan to a private individual. Called also a 'settlement statement'. See also **completion statement**.

Real Estate Law, by Robert Kratovil and Raymond J. Werner, 8 edn., pp. 183–190.

clôture (F)
closing; enclosure; fence. A word that may be used for the completion of a sale or the enclosure of land, although more commonly used in the latter sense.

cloud on title (US)
A defect on an owner's title to property that could prevent an owner from providing a **marketable title**; especially an instrument which if valid would impair a title to land but upon careful examination may turn out to be invalid. For example, an option that has passed the date by which it should have been exercised but still remains on a public record, or a claim for a breach of covenant that has been rectified. A cloud on title is revealed usually on a title search. It may be removed by a **quit-claim deed** or a **quiet title action**.

cluster development (US)
A residential development in which dwellings are grouped together in a higher density than would be normal in a given district, with facilities (such as open space, recreational areas, parking, etc.) combined for common use. A zoning ordinance that permits such development as a variance to the permitted ordinance is called a 'cluster zoning'. See also **planned unit development**.

cluster zoning (US)
see **cluster development**.

co-agent (US)
see **joint agent**.

co-assurance
see **co-insurance**.

co-assurance (F)
co-insurance.

code
A set of rules or regulations produced to regulate or guide a particular group, or to provide uniformity in a field of activity. A written compilation of laws, especially a systematic preparation or consolidation of legal ordinances on a given subject. See also **building codes, code of conduct, code of ethics, ordinance, rules of conduct**.

code of conduct
A body of rules, principles and regulations established and accepted by a professional body for the conduct of their activities; in particular, a code accepted by real estate brokers, appraisers, or property managers. A code of ethics, supported by disciplinary action for a breach of the rules, is accepted by most professional bodies: Members of the **American Institute of Real Estate Appraisers** accept Regulation 10 of that Institute as their code of ethics, and the code of the **National Association of Realtors** has been adopted by several states as the basis for granting licences to Realtors. See also **canon, rules of conduct**.

codes de la construction (F)
building codes; building regulations.

codicil
An instrument made by a testator which adds to, expands, or alters in

someway, a **will**. A codicil, which may be endorsed on the will or form a separate document, must be executed and attested in the same way as the will to which it is an adjunct; it then forms part of that will.

coefficient (F)

coefficient; **ratio**; rate.
(*coefficient d'amortissement* – **sinking fund rate**; **recapture rate**)
(*coefficient d'occupation du sol* – plot ratio). See also *plan d'occupation des sols*.

coersion

The act of compelling someone to do something against their will; the application of force or a sanction to produce an agreement.
cf. **consent**. See also **duress**.

co-heirs

Two or more persons who receive property by inheritance as if they were a single **heir**.
cf. **heirs**. See also **co-parcenary**.

co-insurance or co-assurance

1. The division of responsibility for a risk between two or more insurers. Normally the insurance is accepted by a lead insurer who brings together other insurers, each of whom accepts a percentage of the risk.
2. A term applied, especially in the US, to the acceptance of part of the insurance risk by the insured. (This is the result of applying an **average clause** to an insurance policy because the insured is not strictly a 'co-insurer' in the sense referred to in 1. above.)

co-insurance clause

see **average clause**.

cold canvass

The contacting of persons who have expressed no prior interest in a pro-

duct (such as real estate) in order to solicit new business.

collateral

Derived from the Latin *con*, 'with', *latus*, 'side'; that which is granted alongside another undertaking to secure its performance, but has an independent existence. "The proper meaning of 'collateral' is not secondary but 'standing side by side'" – Athill *v* Athill (1880) 16 Ch. D 214; i.e. it is made over along with the main undertaking and in enforceable because the main undertaking is enforceable. However, collateral is used commonly to refer to any security granted to insure the performance of an agreement or pledge, but as a secondary line of defence. For example, collateral property is property, or a claim to property, made over to a lender as concurrent affirmation that the loan will be repaid; it is not intended, but nevertheless will be forfeited if the primary obligation to the lender is not duly satisfied. See also **collateral contract, collateral security, defeasance, guarantee, warranty**.

collateral agreement

see **collateral contract**.

collateral assurance (US)

An **assurance** (conveyance) made for the purpose of confirming or perfecting a title that has previously been conveyed but was lacking or defective in some respect. See also **collateral**.

collateral contract

A contract that runs side by side with a principal contract; a contract that is **collateral** to another contract and which reinforces that other contract. A collateral contract may be one entered into because another related contract has been made; as when one party in reliance on a promise given by another contracts with a third party, or one party to a contract accept that the other party to that contract may contract with a third party in a manner that has a direct bearing on the performance of the main contract. Alternatively, it may be a promise that forms the consideration or reason for another contract and would not have been given except for that other contract; a promise that becomes enforceable as a result of the enforceability of the other contract. However, "the name [collateral contract] is not, perhaps, altogether fortunate. The word 'collateral' suggests something that stands side by side with the main contract, springing out of and fortifying it. But the purpose of (a device that is referred to as a collateral contract) usually is to enforce a promise given prior to the main contract and but for which this main contract would not have been made. It is often, though not always, rather a preliminary than a collateral contract" (Cheshire and Fifoot's Law of Contract 10 edn., p. 57). Thus, a collateral contract may be one that arises out of negotiations prior to a formal contract and comes to ·fortify the main contract.

A true collateral contract is independent of, but stands parallel to, the principal contract. For example, if one property is mortgaged by A to B and then a second property is granted as collateral for the first mortgage, the debt is payable rateably out of both properties and not primarily out of the first with the second property to be used as a crutch. Similarly, if before formalising a lease a landlord maintains that a part of the property is in good condition (e.g. he gives a 'collateral warranty' or undertaking that the drains are satisfactory, even though that item is not referred to in the lease) the landlord is liable for that part of the premises which he stated was in good order as if his liability was a condition of the lease – De Lassalle v Guildford [1901] 2 K B 215. A collateral contract must be proved strictly and must not conflict with the principal contract. See also **guaranty**.

collateral security

Something of monetary value given as **security** for the performance of a contract. In particular, security for a debt provided by a third party. Collateral security for a debt is provided in addition to, rather than in lieu of, the borrower's personal liability. It is intended to remain as security unless or until the contract is performed; "any property which is assigned or pledged to secure the performance of an obligation and as additional thereto, and which upon performance of the obligation is to be surrendered or discharged" – Royal Bank of Canada v Slack [1958] OR 273. See also **collateral, mortgage**.

collateral value

The value of a property held as **collateral security** for a loan. See also **loan value, mortgage value**.

collective ownership

The ownership of one (or more) units that form part of a group of properties (hereditaments) combined with a right to use and enjoy, in common with others, certain property that is essential to the proper enjoyment of the individual units. This is not a term of any significance in English law, but may be used to make a distinction from **co-ownership**, which is a joint right to the whole of a property. Collective ownership covers such forms of ownership as a **flying freehold**; **cooperative ownership**; and the holding of all the units in trust for a number of persons with proprietory rights to individual units, as in a **housing trust**. The essential element in this form of ownership is that the owners have separate rights to part of the property (e.g. an apartment); some form of common rights to the shared parts of a building or land, e.g. the entrance areas, staircases, lifts, etc.; and, usually, a contract with each other to act as a consortium and to be bound by a set of management rules affecting their use of the property. 'Collective ownership' is not a common way of holding property in English law; instead property which is divided into a number of individual units is either held on **trust for sale** with the beneficiaries having use and occupancy rights, or is granted on a long-term lease to individual tenants, with the landlord retaining overall control of the common parts. See also **condominium, housing association**. *English Land Law (Cases and Materials)*, by Michael Harwood, pp. 203–241 (1977).

collectivités locales (or territoriales) (F)
   local authority.

co-locataire (F)
   joint tenant. Two or more tenants who have common rights under a lease. Not joint owners as in English law.

colon paritaire (F)
   sharecropper, see **metayage system**.

coloni partiarii (L)
   see **metayage system**.

color of title (US)
   A **title** that appears good but, due to some defect cannot transfer the right to land to which it purports. Called also a 'claim of title'.

combination mortgage (or loan)
   A mortgage (or loan) which combines, in the same agreement, different schemes for the payment of the interest or the principal. For example, a loan which provides initially for a variable interest rate and then, after a stated period of time, a fixed interest rate; or one which provides for the principal to be paid in the same way as in an **amortisation mortgage** and then, after a stated period, to be paid by equal instalments. See also **drop-lock debenture, variable-rate mortgage**.

combined residential density
   The **residential density** of a mixed housing development, e.g. flats, houses and bungalows; usually expressed as persons or rooms per acre.

comfort letter
   see **letter of comfort**.

commandement (F)
   writ; a form of notice sent by a huissier prior to such actions as distress for rent or by a mortgagee intending to realise his security. See also *notification*.

commanditaire (F)
   sleeping partner; silent partner.

commandité (F)
   active or **general partner**.
   (*société en commandité* – **limited partnership**).

commendation
   A process by which a person who had a right to land ceded that right to a feudal lord and relegated himself to

the status of vassal or feudal tenant, in exchange for protection from an invader or a common enemy. See also **feudal system**.

commerçant (F)
 trader, especially someone who carries on a regular commercial activity (French Commercial Code, art. 1); merchant.
 (*commerçant au détail* – retailer (*groupement de commerçants* – trader's association). See also **bail commercial**.

commercial hotel
 see **hotel**.

commercial loan (US)
 1. A loan granted against the security of **commercial property**.
 2. A loan granted for a commercial business purpose; in particular, a **short-term loan** or **overdraft**.

commercial property
 1. Real estate used for a **trade, business**, or **profession** including an office, shop, hotel, restaurant or industrial property, but excluding residential and agricultural property and any property used for public purposes, e.g. a school or hospital. Frequently, this term is used as excluding **industrial property**, especially in the US. In relation to a **capital allowance** a commercial building or structure is defined as "other than an industrial building or structure, or qualifying hotel, which is used for the purpose of a trade, profession or vocation or, whether or not for such a purpose, as an office or offices, but does not include any building in use as, or as part of, a dwelling house" (Finance Act 1980, s. 74). See also **business premises, office, shop**.
 2. Any form of income-producing or

investment **property**, or property intended to be used for profitable purposes, other than property held for use and occupation.

commercial rent
 see **market rent, rack rent**.

commingled fund
 see **commingling, commingled trust fund**.

commingled trust fund (US)
 A **trust** established to permit a number of investors, such as pension funds or insurance companies, to make common investments. A commingled trust fund that invests in real estate may be considered similar to a **property unit trust** in the UK. Called also a 'common trust fund'.

commingling (US)
 The placing of funds from different, and usually conflicting sources, into the same account. For example, placing a client's funds in the same account as an agent's personal funds; usually an illegal procedure. See also **commingled trust fund**.

commissaire-priseur (F)
 official valuer; auctioneer.

commission
 1. Remuneration paid to an agent or broker for his services in conducting a specified duty, such as introducing a purchaser of property or obtaining a loan facility. A commission is based usually on a percentage of the money received by the principal as a result of the agent's actions. Usually this remuneration is payable only on the successful conclusion of the specified function, e.g. on **completion** of a sale or the introduction of a person who is 'ready, able and willing' to purchase a particular property.

On the sale of real estate, in most instances, commission is payable to the agent who was the "effective cause of the ultimate sale" – except, under certain circumstances, in the case of a **sole agency**. Commission is not intended as a payment for work done but as a reward for achieving that which the principal required of an agent. Commission is not payable unless the principal in fact agreed to pay for a particular result and that result has been achieved in accordance with the terms by which the agent was appointed. "In order to found a legal claim for commission, there must not only be a casual, there must also be a contractual relation between the introduction and the ultimate transaction of sale." – Toulmin v Millar (1887) 3 TLR 836. It must be clear from the agent's contract that the principal intended to pay commission for the particular duties performed; and as a rule, no remuneration is payable for abortive work. Normally commission is only paid to an estate agent or broker when the transaction that he was employed to try and bring about is concluded, or at least brought to an irrevocable stage. However, "it is possible that an owner may be willing to bind himself to pay a commission for the mere introduction of one who offers to purchase at the specified or minimum price, but such construction of the contract would require clear and unequivocal language". – Luxor (Eastbourne) Ltd v Cooper [1941] AC 129. If a vendor undertakes to pay commission to an agent on completion of a sale of a property that payment is due, as a rule, when a binding contract for sale is exchanged. (In the Luxor case it was stated, *obiter dicta*, that if the vendor then withdraws in breach of contract he still remains liable to pay commission as a form of damages for loss suffered by the agent, the agent having performed the duty required of him).

An agent must act in **good faith** in order to receive a commission; "it is only an honest agent who is entitled to any commission" – Andrews v Ramsay [1903] 3 KB 638. Furthermore, it is illegal for an agent to receive a commission (or any gift or consideration) from a third party to a contract to induce him to act in a manner that would affect the affairs or business of his principal (Prevention of Corruption Act 1906, s. 1).

In the US, the rules for the payment of commission are similar generally to those established in English law, the key conditions being the terms of the agent's appointment and the performance of the requisite duties – i.e. the agent should be the 'primary and procuring cause' of the transaction required by the principal – Wilson v Schmidt and Wilson, 184 Va 642. In most states, a real estate agent or broker must be licensed at the time the service was performed and be employed under the terms of a written agreement.

cf. **fee**. See also **brokerage, dual agency, extender clause, fee, multiple agency, option, *quantum meruit*.**

Real Estate Law, by Robert Kratovil and Raymond J. Werner, 8 end., pp. 99–107.

Real Estate Law, by W.B. Milligan and Arthur G. Bowman, pp. 69–78 (1984).

The Principle of Effective Cause, by John Murdoch, 276 E.G. 742–750, 877–881, (1985).

The Law of Estate Agency and Auc-

tions, by J.R. Murdoch, 2 edn., pp. 235 *et seq.*

2. An **authority**, or request, given to another to carry out some act or duty; in particular, a formal written authority given to one party to act in place of another. See also **agency**.

3. A payment, based on a percentage of an insurance premium, made by an insurer to an agent or broker for introducing business. For property insurance, the percentage generally is between 5 per cent and 20 per cent. When insurance is arranged directly by the insured, the premium may be reduced proportionately to reflect the commission saved by the insurer.

commission (F)
  commission, especially brokerage rather than a fee for professional services; agent's fee.
  cf. *honoraires*.

commission agent
  see **broker, factor**.

Commission for New Towns
  An *ad hoc* public body, initially set up in Britain in 1959, to take over the ownership and administer the assets of a **development corporation** when the development of a new town has been substantially completed. The Commission was formally incorporated by statute in 1965 for the purpose of "taking over holding, preparing and turning to account the property previously vested in the development corporation for a new town and transferred to the Commission" (New Towns Act 1965, s. 36 (1)). It has a duty to maintain and enhance the value of the property it holds and the return obtained therefrom, having regard to "the purpose for which the town was developed and

the convenience and welfare of persons residing, working or carrying on business there". (1965 Act, s. 36 (2)). The Commission may acquire, hold, manage, dispose of, or grant interests in property. It may make contributions to the cost of providing amenities, water supplies and sewage facilities for the town. In addition it may promote and assist any business in the town, including arranging for the erection, improvement or adaptation of buildings or works. It is intended that the Commission should have a transitory role and that the assets of the new town are sold privately or transferred to the local authority in whose area the town is situated. This process is now being undertaken for the new towns that have been transferred to the Commission.

Commission, Land
  see **Land Commission**.

commission merchant (US)
  see **factor**.

commissionaire (F)
  porter.

commitment
  An **agreement** to do something. For example, an agreement by a lender to accept an application for a loan, usually subject to certain conditions. A loan commitment may be 'firm' or 'stand-by'. With a firm commitment the intention is that the loan will be made when certain conditions have been met, for example when it has been established that the borrower's financial rating is adequate. A stand-by commitment is intended as a source of finance of the last resort and, usually, is taken only if a contingent event occurs, such as when

expenditure exceeds a budgeted cost or the borrower takes up an option to purchase a property. See also **commitment fee, conditional contract, forward commitment.**

commitment fee
A charge made by a lender to an applicant for a loan at the stage when the application is accepted, i.e. at the time a **commitment** is made. The fee, which is usually a small percentage of the total amount that it has been agreed will be made available, is paid to cover the cost to the lender of holding funds available.

commitment letter
A written offer to make a **commitment**, especially to provide a loan. A letter of commitment to make a loan contains the essential terms for the proposed loan – the parties; amount of the loan; interest rate; period for which the funds will be available; property required as security – and normally specifies a date for acceptance. Called also a 'facility letter'. See also **forward commitment.**

commodo et incommodo (F)
see *enquête de commodo et incommodo*.

common
1. Held by two or more parties. cf. **several**. See also **right of common, tenancy in common.**
2. Usual, habitual; that which is accepted in the regular course of events. See also **common law, custom.**
3. An area of land in a town or city set aside for use by the general public; especially land that has been left in its natural state or for common pasturage. See also **common land, park.**
4. A right held by one person in conjunction with one or more others to enjoy the profits from the land of another; a **profit à prendre** enjoyed by several persons over **common land.**

common appendant
see **appendant.**

common appurtenant
see **appurtenant.**

common area charges
A service charge or operating cost born by the landlord for the upkeep of the **common areas** of a building.

common areas
Those parts of a property shared between the occupants of a multi-let property, or between the owners of a condominium or a building held in collective ownership, such as hallways, lobbies, lifts, staircases, plant rooms, toilets, means of access to or egress from the property, or green areas on a housing estate; but specifically excluding any areas let to or used by one occupier to the exclusion of others. Called also 'common parts', or in the US, especially when applied to a **condominium**, 'common elements'. See also **implied covenant.**

common covenants
see **usual covenants.**

common duty of care
see **duty of care.**

common elements (US)
The **common areas** of a building, especially of a property held in **condominium** ownership. The owners of a condominium have an undivided interest in these common areas.

common interest
1. An interest in property held in common with others. A term of no legal significance but it may be used to refer to any form of **co-ownership.**

2. A joint interest in a business venture. See also joint venture partnership.

(US) 3. An interest in the **common elements** of a property.

common land

Land held in separate or several ownership, but used in common. Land over which a **right of common** exists. Common land derives especially from the **feudal system** of land tenure by which, although all land was owned by the Sovereign or a subordinate lord of the **manor**, large areas of uncultivated waste land or woodland were used by the tenants of the manor in common and in a manner recognised by custom or common law. This land was part of the manor, but the lord of the manor was not permitted by law to curtail the tenant's common usage; "so much so that their rights over it became known as 'rights in common' and the land became known as 'common land'". – Corpus Christi College, Oxford *v* Gloucestershire County Council [1982] 3 All ER 999. Rights of common could persist over land retained primarily for the lord of the manor and his servants, that is, **demesne land**; or over land left for the use of other tenants, that is, **waste land**. The demesne land may have remained in the sole ownership of the lord of the manor or it may have been sold off, while the waste land may have been acquired by one or more tenants; nevertheless, the rights of common persisted. Today common land may be part of a manor; be owned privately, whether in common or severalty; or have been acquired by a public authority, such as a parish council, with the rights of common

exercisable by 'commoners' (who are usually members of the local community).

All common land in England and Wales must be registered with a county council under the Commons Registration Act 1965. For this purpose 'common land' includes (a) "land subject to rights of common" and (b) "waste land of the manor not subject to rights of common" (as defined in the Act); but not "a town or village **green** or any land which forms part of a highway" (1965 Act, s. 22 (1)). (A separate register is maintained of town or village greens.) See also **enclosure**.

English Land Law (*Cases and Materials*), by Michael Harwood, pp. 274–283 (1977).

An Outline of the Law relating to Common Land and Public Access to the Countryside, by Bryan Harris and Gerard Ryan, (1967).

The Law of Commons and Village Greens, by Ian Campbell and Paul Clayden, 3 edn.

Halsbury's Laws of England, 4 edn., para. 501–800.

common law

The system of unwritten law that derived its authority from ancient **usage**, **custom** and **precedent**: law that is, "from time to time declared in the decisions of the courts of justice; which decisions are preserved among our public records, explained in our reports, and digested for general use in the authoritative writings of the venerable sages of the law." (Bl. Comm. vol. i. p. 73). Accordingly, English common law was propogated in the courts of common law (set up after the Norman conquest in order to unify local customs into a system that was common to every man), in particular the Courts of Exchequer, Common Pleas and King's Bench; reported and recorded as judicial precedent; and, it was discussed, and its doctrines and principles refined, in early textbooks. The common law of England as distinguished from the **civil law** and **statute law** "comprises that body of principles and rules of action, relating to the government and security of persons and property, which derive their authority from usages and customs ..." It may be contrasted with equity which is (a) "grounded on the precepts of conscience and justice." (David A. Lockmiller on Sir William Blackstone (1938) p. 11n); and (b) a more fluid system of law making.

In different contexts, 'common law' can have the following meanings: (a) unwritten law, especially the Anglo-American traditions of law making, as distinguished from a written code of law; (b) law that was administered by the Courts of Common Law prior to the Judicature Acts 1873–75, as distinguished from the rules of **equity** administered in the Court of Chancery; (c) law that is common to an entire realm, as distinguished from local rules or customs accepted by a group of individuals; (d) judge-made law as distinguished from ecclesiastical law or statute law; and (e) law that was shaped in England, based on Anglo-Saxon and Norman laws, became the basis of law in the Commonwealth and formed the basis of law in most states in the US, as distinguished from an independent nation's Constitution. (In French law, the term common law (*droit commun*) is used to refer to law that applies to the entire state, as distinguished from local or regional rules).

In modern usage the term common law may be applied in a general sense to draw a distinction with the civil law; or, in a particular sense, to refer to the body of English law built up from the reign of Henry II (1154–1189) until the Judicature Acts 1873–75, by judges sent out on circuit by the King to create a common body of law throughout the realm – *la commune lay*. In either sense, common law is based on a requirement to establish solutions to particular disputes and, unlike the civil law, it does not propound universal precepts but remains in a continuous state of development.

English common law has formed an important element in establishing the foundations of modern land law so that even today, as a result of this established body of law, all land is considered to be held from the Crown; there is no absolute form of land **ownership** recognised in English law; a leasehold interest is considered **personal property** (a 'chattel real'); distinct legal and equitable interests can, and in certain cases must, be held in the same land; and the modern form of **trust** stems from the former conflict of common law with equity.

The term 'at law' or 'law' is frequently used, especially in English statutes, to refer to rules derived from common law as distinguished from principles established 'in equity'. (This distinction is made noticeably in the Law of Property Act 1925.)

common-law lien
  see **lien**.

common-law trust (US)
  see **business trust**.

common lodging-house

A **lodging-house** in which the poor are housed and boarded communally for a night, or for a short stay, normally for a modest charge. In its ordinary sense a common lodging-house is a lodging house "kept for the purpose of profit, open to all comers, whether of a certain class or not." – Booth *v* Ferrett (1890) 25 QBD 89. But in modern statute law it is defined as "a house (other than a public assistance institution) provided for the purpose of accommodating by night poor persons, not being members of the same family, who resort thereto and are allowed to occupy one common room for the purpose of sleeping and eating." (Public Health Act 1936, s. 235). The premises that constitute a common lodging-house may be part of a building, so long as there is a communal use of accommodation for sleeping and eating. The use of the premises by some residents for a week or more does not necessarily preclude them from being a 'common lodging-house' – People's Hostels *v* Turley [1939] 1 KB 149. The keeper of a common lodging-house must be registered with the local authority and must fix a notice that the premises are a registered common lodging-house to the outside of the house. Common lodging-houses are subject to local byelaws (covering such matters as overcrowding, hygene, general welfare of the occupants) and must be inspected regularly by the local authority. (1936 Act, ss. 236–248.) See also **control order**.
Housing Law, by Andrew Arden and Martin Partington, pp. 522–526 (1983).

common mistake

see **mistake**.

common of pasture

see **right of common**.

common ownership

The ownership of all the means of production by those responsible for the production process, as distinguished from **co-ownership** which applies especially to ownership of real property. See also **common property**.

common partition wall (US)

A **party wall** between two units held in **condominium** ownership.

common parts

see **common areas**.

common property

1. Property held by all the members of a community without separate or private forms of ownership. Common property is said to exist when there is a usufructuary right to property but no absolute or individual ownership of property. Called also 'communal property'. See also **collective ownership**, *res communes*.
2. Property held in public ownership. cf. **private property**.
3. Property in which one or more parties have rights in common, either apart from or together with the owner. See also **common land**.

common, right of

see **right of common**.

common socage

A form of feudal **tenure** by which the occupier of land was required to render fixed agricultural services to his lord. These services were eventually commuted to money payment, and in due course common socage came to represent the modern tenure of freehold. See also **socage**.

common, tenancy in
see **tenancy in common**.

common trust fund
see **commingled trust fund**.

common wall
see **party wall**.

commonable land
Land to which a **right of common** is attached. In particular land owned in severalty but over which a commoner could pasture beasts. Land over which common rights of pasture exist, for part of a year, especially land subject to such rights as **cattlegate**. See also **lammas land**.

commoners
see **common land**.

commons
see **common land**.

commun (F)
common.
(*chose commun* – **common property**)
(*partie commun* – **common areas**)
(*propriété commune* – co ownership; common ownership, see *copropriété*.)

communal property
see **common property**.

commune (F)
commune, the smallest form of **local authority** in France.

communauté (F)
community property. Property owned jointly by husband and wife. French law permits each spouse to retain property in separate ownership after marriage (*biens propres*), either because it was held by the parties

prior to the marriage, or it is acquired during the marriage by gift or succession, including certain property that is acquired during the marriage by one or other spouse with his or her own resources or the proceeds of other separate property (*acquêts*); all other property is held jointly by the spouses as *communauté*, or *biens communs*, i.e. it is held as common property for the duration of the marriage.
Amos & Walton's Introduction to French Law, 3 edn., p. 254

community
see **local authority**.

community apartment (US)
An apartment building held by means of a **tenancy in common**, with a right of occupancy of one or more apartments granted to each co-owner.
cf. **cooperative ownership**. See also **co-ownership**.

community association (US)
An association created to manage a condominium, in particular to maintain the common elements. See also **condominium ownership**.

community house
see **tenement**.

community land
Land acquired for the public good under the terms of the Community Land Act 1975, especially land that was ripe for development. The intention of the Act was to transfer most areas of land that were ripe for development into public ownership. A local authority was empowered to acquire any land which, in their opinion, was suitable for development with the object of obtaining planning permission for its development and

then disposing of it at a profit, i.e. reaping the **betterment**. The 1975 Act was repealed by the Local Government, Planning and Land Act 1980, s. 101.

Law of Compulsory Purchase and Compensation, by Keith Davies, 3 edn., Ch. 12.

Introduction to Town and Country Planning, by John Ratcliffe, 2 edn., pp. 363–365.

A Guide to the Community Land Act, by Frederick Corfield, (1976).

community property (US)

Marital property held by the spouses jointly but apart from, and under a different regime to, property held by either spouse in their own right. In countries or states that recognise community property ownership of any property held by the partners to a marriage may be (a) the husband's separate property; (b) the wife's separate property; or (c) community property. The separate property of the husband and wife consists of any property owned by them at the time of their marriage, and any property either received in his or her own right by gift, bequest, or devise. Any other property is considered to have been acquired by the joint efforts of both parties and to be community property. The community property system appears to have originated in the Germanic tribes and to have been established in France and Spain. It is found in eight states in the US (Arizona, California, Idaho, Louisiana, Nevada, Texas, and the State of Washington) which at one time came under Germanic, French or Spanish jurisdiction.

Any property acquired by either spouse that is not classified as separate property is held as community property, with both parties having a vested (and usually an equal) interest in the community property, despite the fact that the title to the property may be held or recorded in one name or the other. Primarily community property is that acquired by the family, in particular the family residence, or property acquired with income earned by either spouse during the marriage; excluding either parties' separate property or any property acquired from income or proceeds derived from the separate property. In general, on the death of either spouse the survivor holds his or her half interest in the community property as before, the other party's interest passing according to the testamentary disposition. If there is no will usually the surviving spouse takes all the community property. Upon dissolution of the marriage the award of property does not extend to the separate property. See also ***communauté*, homestead rights, matrimonial property, tenancy by entireties**.

Real Property, by William E. Burby, 3 edn., pp. 236–266.

Community Property, by William E. Burby, 4 edn.

community shopping centre
see **shopping centre**.

commutation

1. The **exchange** or substitution of one form of payment, remuneration, or charge for another. Money substituted for a service. See also **manor**.

2. The conversion by law of a periodic sum of money into a fixed or single sum, e.g. the conversion of an annual **tithe** into a tithe redemption annuity. See also **capitalisation**.

commuted value
see **present value**.

company
An association or collection of individuals, formed together for some common purpose or business, which carries on that business separately and distinctly from those individuals, leaving each individual generally free to dispose of his interest in that association to any other individual. "The word 'company' has no strictly technical meaning. It involves I [Buckley J.] think namely, first that the association is of persons so numerous as not to be aptly described as a firm, and secondly, that the consent of all the other members is not required to the transfer of a member's interest." – Re Stanley [1906] 1 Ch. 134.

A company may be incorporated or unincorporated. An incorporated company or corporation has at law an "existence and rights and duties distinct from those of the individual persons who form it from time to time" (Co. Litt. 250a). From the moment of its incorporation it has perpetual succession; a common **seal**; it is an 'artificial person', i.e. it has no mind or soul; it may acquire or dispose of property in its own name; and it may sue or be sued in that name. An unincorporated company has no separate existence and is not distinct from its members, but in other respects it carries on its business like an incorporated company and, unlike a **partnership**, the individuals remain free to transfer their shares, subject to the regulations adopted by the company.

In the US a 'company' may be "a corporation, a partnership, an association, a joint-stock company, a business trust, or an organized group of persons, whether incorporated or not, or any receiver, trustee, or other liquidating agent of any of the foregoing in his capacity as such." (15 United States Codes 79 (b) (2)). See also *ultra vires*.

company letting
A letting of residential property to a corporate body, usually for occupation by its employees.

comparable property
A property considered sufficiently similar in key characteristics as to be suitable for use in the **comparison method of valuation**. A comparable property should be the subject of recent transactions and ideally should be similar in location; age and design; construction and condition; and size and layout to the subject property, i.e. what is or has been available in a similar market. In practice an ideal comparable property hardly ever exists; instead a valuer extrapolates information on values from similar properties, makes adjustment and allowances, and uses his judgement to apply the resultant figure to the property he is seeking to value. So that, "the less closely analogous the object chosen for comparison is the greater the allowances which have to be made and the greater the opportunity for error." – G.R.E.A. Real Property Investments *v* Williams (1979) 250 EG 653. Properties considered suitable for a valuation are called 'comparables' or 'comps' for short.

comparables
see **comparable property**.

comparison approach (US)
see **comparison method of valuation, market approach**.

comparison, or comparative, method of valuation

A method of assessing the **value** of a property by reference to the actual price paid for a similar property or properties. The prices achieved for comparable properties are analysed and adjusted for differences in location, size, age, condition, date of sale or special suitability. This 'adjusted-price' commonly is reduced to a unit cost or rate, e.g. price per square foot, per room, per car space, (i.e. devalued); that rate is then applied to the property under consideration (i.e. re-valued). The principle applied in order to ensure consistency in this technique of appraisal is 'as one devalues so one re-values'. This method is limited by the availability of data on recent and directly **comparable property**, but it is the most reliable and accepted method of determining the value of a property and forms the basis for most other methods of valuation. However, in the final analysis, the opinion of the value arrived at is dependent on the valuer's skill and experience rather than any scientific formulation. In the US, the terms **'market approach'**, 'sales approach' or 'market-data approach' are more commonly used to refer to this method of appraisal and the term 'comparative method' is used when applying this approach to assessing the reproduction or replacement cost of a building i.e. as synonymous with **cost approach**. See also **unit cost, valuation**.

Modern Methods of Valuation, 7 edn., Ch. 4.

comparative-unit method (US)

see **project valuation, unit method**.

compensatio

In the civil law, **set-off**.

compensation

1. Something paid, or rendered, to make good a loss or injury. A return or recompense for a loss or for damage suffered, especially when the party making the payment has acted lawfully. "In the sense in which the term is usually used 'compensation' may be defined as pecuniary recompense which a person is entitled to receive in respect of damage or loss which he has suffered, other than as a result of an actionable wrong, litigated in the civil court, committed by the person bound to make the recompense. In this sense 'compensation' is distinct from '**damages**', which are recoverable in respect of an actionable wrong." (12 Halsbury's Laws of England, 4 edn., pp. 426).

In relation to land and buildings the term 'compensation' is used primarily in the sense defined above, although it may be used in a sense similar to damages in other contexts. In particular, the meaning of compensation "has been developed in relation to the compulsory acquisition of land. But the purpose of compensation is the same, whether the property taken is real or personal. It is to place in the hands of the owner expropriated the full money equivalent of the thing of which he has been deprived. Compensation *prima facie* means recompense for loss, and when an owner is to receive compensation for being deprived of real or personal property his pecuniary loss must be ascertained by determining the value to him of the property taken from him." – Nelungaloo Pty., Ltd. *v* Commonwealth (1948) 75 CLR 571.

See also **compensation for disturbance, compensation for improvements, compensation for injurious
affection, compensation for planning
restrictions, compensation for severance, compulsory purchase compensation, just compensation.**
2. In Scottish law, **set-off.**

compensation (F)
compensation; extinguishment (of a
debt); **set-off** (used more in this latter
sense).
Dédommagement is a more common
term for compensation payable by
law.

compensation for condemnation (US)
see **just compensation.**

compensation for disturbance
1. Compensation paid to a person
whose interest in property is acquired
by compulsory purchase for the loss
of use or profit as a result of having to
leave the property. A payment for
"the fact of having to vacate the premises". – Lee *v* Ministry of Transport
[1966] 1 QB 122. It is paid by the
acquiring authority for such items as
the cost of moving to new premises;
adapting fixtures to new premises;
loss on forced sale of stock; professional fees; business loss or injury, i.e.
loss of **goodwill** (whether a partial or
total loss, depending on the circumstances); and such other loss and
expense resulting directly from the
dispossession. "Any loss sustained by
a dispossessed owner (at all events
one who occupies his house) which
flows from a compulsory acquisition
may properly be regarded as the subject of compensation for disturbance
provided, first, it is not too remote
and, secondly, that it is natural and
reasonable consequence of the dis-

possession of the owner." – Harvey *v*
Crawley Development Corporation
[1957] 1 QB 494. (This case approved
the payment of costs associated with
the buying of a new house: surveyor's
fees, legal costs, travelling expenses,
which are colloquially called 'Crawley' costs. However, if a dispossessed
owner acquires another property at a
higher price he is not compensated for
that extra expenditure "because he
would be presumed to have got value
for money" – *ibid.* at p. 494). There is
no separate statutory right to compensation for disturbance, (although
it is referred to in the Land Compensation Act 1961, s. 5 (6)). The right to
such compensation follows from the
principle that an owner whose right to
land is compulsorily acquired, "has
the right to receive a money payment
not less than the loss imposed on him
in the public interest, but, on the
other hand, no greater." – Horn *v*
Sunderland [1941] 2 KB 42. In practice, it is assessed separately, but
forms part of the total amount of
compulsory purchase compensation
payable by the acquiring authority –
Manchester Corporation *v* The Countess Ossalinsky (1883) QBD unreported. "The truth of the matter is
that ... the sum to be ascertained (as
compensation) is in essence one sum,
namely, the proper price or compensation payable in all the circumstances of the case." – Horn *v* Sunderland
Corporation *supra* at p. 34.
A claimant for disturbance compensation must make every effort to
mitigate his loss, in particular by seeking out alternative accommodation.
Compensation is not payable under
this heading in respect of land that is
claimed to have a value for development, because the realisation of the

latter presupposes that the landowner would forego the former (Horn *v* Sunderland *supra* at p. 35). As a rule, compensation for disturbance is payable only for loss arising after the service of **notice to treat**, which is the action of the authority that initiates the purchase and subsequent dispossession. However, compensation is payable for expenses reasonably incurred prior to a notice to treat, provided those expenses are a natural and reasonable result of compulsory acquisition – for example, a loss of business arising because a claimant is obliged to vacate premises which are the subject of a compulsory purchase order – Prasad *v* Wolverhampton Borough Council (1983) 265 EG 1073. See also **ex-gratia payment, farm-loss payment, home-loss payment**.

Business Property Handbook, The Boisot Waters Cohen Partnership, p. 306 (1981), (for a checklist of items for a disturbance claim).
Modern Methods of Valuation, 7 edn., Ch. 30.
Compensation for Disturbance, by W.A. Leach, 3 edn.
Statutory Valuations, by Andrew Baum, pp. 209–245 (1983).
Law of Compulsory Purchase and Compensation, by Keith Davies, 4 edn., pp. 195–222.
8 Halsbury's Laws of England, 4 edn., paras. 322–342.
2. Statutory compensation paid to a tenant on determination of his tenancy as recompense for loss or expense directly attributable to the quitting of the holding. In particular, compensation paid in accordance with a statutory provision when a tenant is no longer permitted to renew his tenancy. A holder of a **business**

tenancy may be entitled to compensation based on an "appropriate multiplier" of 3 (or, in certain circumstances twice that amount) applied to the rateable value of the premises (Landlord and Tenant (Appropriate Multiplier) Order 1984) in the event that the landlord, upon certain grounds, successfully opposes the grant of a new tenancy; e.g. if the landlord requires the premises for reconstruction, for his own business occupation, or if the premises are sub-let and the landlord can let them more rationally (Landlord and Tenant Act 1954, s. 37, as amended by the Law of Property Act 196, s. 11). A holder of an **agricultural tenancy**, upon being required to vacate the holding, in certain cases, is entitled to compensation for an amount of between one and two years rent or, in certain circumstances, a further four years rent (Agricultural Holding Act 1948, s. 34, as amended by Agricultural Holding Act 1984, s. 34; Agricultural Holdings (Miscellaneous Provisions) Act 1968, ss. 9, 10). See also **tenant-right**.
Landlord and Tenant Law, by David Yates and A.J. Hawkins, pp. 551–553, 596–599 (1981).
Handbook of Business Tenancies by D.W. Williams, (1985, looseleaf) paras. 9–14 to 9–17.
Renewal of Business Tenancies: Law and Practice by Kirk Reynolds and Wayne Clarke, (1985, looseleaf) paras. 11.1.0. to 11.4.2.

compensation for improvements
Compensation paid to an outgoing tenant for an **improvement**, carried out by the tenant, or at the tenant's expense, to the leased premises during the term of the expired tenancy. In English common law any improve-

ment in the value of a property made by the tenant accrues to the landlord, without compensation, at the end of a tenancy (unless there is an express agreement to the contrary) and, in consequence, the landlord may be able to obtain an increased price for the property, either by sale or by means of a higher rent. As a result a tenant may be discouraged from making any improvements to the leased premises, unless he is paid for any benefit that accrues to the landlord.

In the case of a **business tenancy** a tenant is entitled to compensation for any improvements (including the erection of a building) not being a trade or other fixture which the tenant is by law entitled to remove, whether carried out by him or his predecessors in title, upon quitting the premises, subject to a number of statutorily prescribed conditions (Landlord and Tenant Act 1927, Part I, as amended by the Landlord and Tenant Act 1954, Part III). The conditions are (a) the premises must be held under a lease (but not a mining lease) and be "used wholly or partly for carrying on thereat any **trade** or **business**" (which includes, for this purpose, a **profession**); but not premises used as an agricultural holding, used for subletting as residential flats, or occupied by a holder of any office, appointment or employment expressly granted by the landlord (1927 Act, s. 17); (b) the improvements were not made before 25th March 1928; (c) the tenant must not have carried out the improvements under a contractual obligation for valuable consideration, whether made with the immediate landlord or a superior landlord; (d) the improvements must not have

been made in pursuance of a statutory obligation required to be met before 1st October 1954; (e) the tenant must have served notice of his intention to carry out the improvement, together with requisite plans and specifications, on his landlord (who in turn must notify any superior landlord until the notice reaches the freeholder) and the landlord must have given his prior consent or his objection must have been overruled by the court; (f) the tenant must have carried out the improvement within the time limit agreed by the landlord or fixed by the court. A claim for compensation must be made on a prescribed form, in writing, and within a period set down by statute which, depending on how the tenancy is terminated, may be up to six months before the tenancy ends or three months after (1927 Act, s. 1 (1); 1954 Act, s. 47). The amount of compensation is the lesser of (a) the net addition to the letting value of the holding as a whole, which may be determined to be the direct result of the improvement; or (b) the reasonable cost of carrying out the improvement, at the end of the tenancy, after deducting the cost (if any) of putting the work constituting the improvement into a reasonable state of repair, unless the tenant is obliged under the lease or other agreement to carry out that repair. Regard must be had also to the landlord's intended future use of the premises, e.g. the compensation may be significantly or totally reduced if the premises are to be demolished. A deduction is made for any consideration received by the tenant from the landlord for carrying out the improvement, as well as any sum due from the tenant to the landlord in respect of the expired tenancy (1927 Act, s. 1). When notified by a business tenant of an intention to carry out an improvement to the demised premises, the landlord has a right to elect to carry out the work himself, in consideration of a reasonable increase in rent. If the landlord does not elect to carry out the improvement, but does not wish the tenant to carry out the work, he has three months to object from the date of receipt of the tenant's notice of intention (accompanied by the plans and specification). If the landlord does not object within the requisite period the improvement is deemed authorised and prima facie qualifies for compensation. If the landlord objects, the tenant may apply to the court for a certificate that the improvement is a proper one, which will be forthcoming if the court is satisfied that the improvement (a) is of such a nature as to be calculated to add to the letting value of the holding at the end of the tenancy; and (b) is reasonable and suitable to the character of the holding (taking account of the effect on the amenity or convenience of the neighbourhood, looked at from the landlord's or a superior landlord's point of view); and (c) will not diminish the value of other property belonging to the same landlord, or to any superior landlord. The court may require modification to the tenant's plans or specification to achieve these objectives (1927 Act, s.3).

In the case of an **agricultural tenancy** a tenant upon the **termination** of his tenancy is entitled to compensation when he quits the holding. This right was originally granted by custom on the principle that a tenant was entitled to compensation based on any increase in the value of the holding available to an incoming tenant as a result of the outgoing tenant's improvements. This right is now governed entirely by statute (Agricultural Holding Act 1948, ss. 36–45, Sch. 2, ss. 46–51, Sch. 3, 4, s. 56). This compensation falls under five headings (i) 'old improvements' – these must have been made before 1st March 1948 and now rarely give rise to compensation; (ii) an improvement begun on or after 1st March 1948 which is generally one of a short-term nature and it does not require the landlord's approval, e.g. chalking the land, application of purchased manure; (iii) an improvement begun after 1st March 1948 which is of a more permanent nature and does require the landlord's consent, e.g. planting of hops, orchards, fruit bushes or works of irrigation; (iv) an improvement of a semi-permanent nature which requires the consent of the landlord or the Agricultural Lands Tribunal, e.g. erection of buildings, improvements to roads, reclaiming waste land, land drainage, provision of electric power; (v) **tenant right** matters which are essentially **emblements** e.g. growing crops, seeds sown and cultivations, pasture laid down. In addition a tenant is entitled to compensation when he can show that by the continuous adoption of a system of farming he has increased the value of the holding. A tenant claiming any such compensation must give notice of his claim to his landlord in writing not later than two months after the termination of tenancy. If the amount of compensation cannot be agreed the dispute is submitted to arbitration (1948 Act, Sch. 6).

A tenant of a **market garden** has a

similar, but more extensive, right to compensation for improvement than a tenant of an agricultural holding, including a right to compensation for any improvement previously paid for as an incoming tenant (Agricultural Holdings Act 1948, ss. 67–69). See also **allotment, Evesham custom.**
Adkin's Landlord and Tenant, 18 edn., pp. 372–377, 404–415.
Renewal of Business Tenancies: Law and Practice, by Kirk Reynolds & Wayne Clarke, (1985, looseleaf) paras. 12.1.0 to 12.6.5.
Handbook of Business Tenancies, by D.W. Williams, (1985, looseleaf) paras. 9–14 to 9–17.
The Law of Landlord and Tenant, by David Lloyd Evans, 2 edn., p. 414–418, 454–458.
Landlord and Tenant Law, by David Yates and A.J. Hawkins, pp. 484–492, 590–596, 599–600 (1981).
Hill & Redman's Law of Landlord and Tenant, 17 edn., pp. 688–694, 2490–2493.
Woodfall's Landlord and Tenant, 28 edn., paras. 2–0762 to 2–0773, 2–0087 to 2–0141.
1 Halsbury's Laws of England, 4 edn., paras. 1095–1128.
27 Halsbury's Laws of England, 4 edn., paras 538–553.

compensation for injurious affection

Compensation paid for depreciation in the value of land as a result of either (i) the acquisition of part of an owner's total land holding and a consequent reduction in the value of the land retained due to work carried out on the land acquired; or (ii) the carrying out under statutory powers of work on adjoining land in separate ownership, when no part of an owner's land is taken. In the first case

compensation is paid not only for the land taken but also for any damage sustained by the owner of the land as a result of the **severance** and for the **injurious affection** (noise, dirt, smell, etc.) caused by the acquiring authority (Compulsory Purchase Act 1965, s. 7). In addition if the injurious affection arises from work carried out partly on the land acquired and partly elsewhere the amount of compensation shall be assessed "by reference to the whole of the works and not only the part situated on the land acquired or taken." (Land Compensation Act 1971, s. 44 (1)). In the second case, when no land is taken but injurious affection is caused by work on adjoining land, the right to compensation is analagous to damages paid for a private nuisance, but it extends to cover damage caused by any act of the statutory authority acquiring the land that results in a physical deterioration in the value of the land. "Where by the construction of the works there is a physical interference with any right, public or private, which the owner or occupier of any property is by law entitled to make use of in connection with that property, and which right gives it a marketable value apart from the uses to which any particular occupier might put it, there is a title to compensation, if by reason of such interference, the property, as a property, is lessened in value." – Metropolitan Board of Works *v* McCarthy (1874) 43 LJCP 390. This case stated that there are four rules (the McCarthy rules) to be complied with before compensation is payable, when no land is acquired from the claimant, rules that are now effectively incorporated in the Compulsory Purchase Act 1965, s. 10: (i) the interference must result from some activity made lawful by the acquiring authority's statutory powers; (ii) the damage must be actionable at common law, if it were not authorised by statute; (iii) the loss must cause depreciation in the value of land, not personal injury or damage to a trade or business; and (iv) the interference must arise from the works executed on the land and not the subsequent use of the land. In certain cases the last requirement has been superceded by the Land Compensation Act 1973, s. 1 which provides that compensation may be payable for damage caused by 'physical factors' – "noise, vibration, smell, fumes, smoke and artificial lighting and the discharge on to the land in respect of which the claim is made of any solid or liquid substance", resulting from 'public works'. However, compensation under this part of the 1973 Act is payable only to (a) an owner (a freeholder or a leaseholder with three or more years to run) and an occupier (who meets the qualifications set out in the Act) of a dwelling; (b) an owner and occupier of an agricultural unit; or (c) an owner and occupier of other property, provided the rateable value of the property does not exceed £2250 (1973 Act, s. 2). Further, the amount of compensation may be reduced by the acquiring authority taking action to mitigate the loss, e.g. grants for double glazing, or tree planting for visual protection (1973 Act, Part II).

The amount of compensation payable for injurious affection is based on the reduction in the **market value** of the land affected and commonly is measured by means of the **before-and-after method of valuation**. See also **compensation for severance**, **set-off**.

Modern Methods of Valuation, 7 edn., pp. 512–518.

Law of Compulsory Purchase and Compensation, by Keith Davies, 4 edn., pp. 168–194.

8 Halsbury's Laws of England, 4 edn., paras. 354–393.

compensation for planning restrictions

Compensation paid for the depreciation in the value of land resulting from the loss of a right to carry out development or a right to use and enjoy land. As a general rule, in English law, a landowner is not entitled to any recompense for being prohibited from carrying out development by virtue of a parliamentary enactment – the public good of planning control is considered to take priority over the private interest. "From the earliest times the owner of property, and in particular land, has been restricted in his free enjoyment of it not only by the common law maxim *sic utere tuo ut alienum non laedas* (so use your property as not to injure your neighbours), but by positive enactments limiting his user or even imposing burdens on him ... it has been widely realised that the rights of the individual must be subordinated to the general interest." – Belfast Corporation *v* O.D. Cars Ltd [1960] 1 All ER 69. Thus, a total prohibition on the development of land, without payment of compensation, is permitted. Parliament is considered to have 'nationalised' such rights with the passing of the Town and Country Planning Act 1947. (In the US such a ruling may be considered to be in conflict with the 5th amendment of the Federal Constitution which provides that there shall be no taking of "private property for public use, without **just compensation**". Limited restriction on the use of land may be imposed without payment of any compensation; however, "if regulation goes too far it will be recognised as taking [by the exercise of the power of **eminent domain**]." – Pennsylvania Coal Co. *v* Mahon (1922), 260 US 415.

The Town and Country Planning Act 1971, ss. 134–179 (as amended by the Town and Country Planning (Compensation) Act 1985) provides that when there has been a limit placed on the existing right to use land; or a direct intervention against an authorised user or a right to use land; or an intervention by a public authority to preserve or augment the existing amenity of land, in particular, compensation may be paid: (i) when there remains an **unexpended balance of established development value** (UXB) attached to land, which resulted from a claim that was accepted for a depreciation in the value of land due to planning restrictions introduced by the Town and Country Planning Act 1947 (as subsequently amended). In this case a landowner (a freeholder, or a leaseholder with not less than 3 years unexpired) may claim for a loss in the value of his land due to a refusal (or in some cases a conditional grant) of planning permission for **new development** (excluding a material change of use) up to the amount of the outstanding UXB; (ii) when a planning permission is varied or withdrawn by a modification or **revocation order** including the modification or revocation of planning permission that was granted, or deemed to be granted, by a **development order**; (iii) following the service of a **discontinuance order** requiring the removal of an existing development from land, i.e. demolition or removal of something from land, or the putting to an end of a user; (iv) when there has been a refusal, or conditional grant, of planning permission for development that is not classified as 'new development' i.e. certain limited forms of **existing use rights** as set out in the Town and Country Planning Act 1971, Sch. 8. Part II as modified by s. 278 and Sch. 18 of that Act and by the Town and Country Planning (Compensation) Act 1985, s. 1 (2); (v) a restriction arising from a refusal of a **listed building consent**; (vi) restrictions imposed by the designation of an **ancient monument**; by a **tree preservation order**; in certain cases by a requirement to remove an advertisement; by a **pedestrian precinct** order; by a **building preservation notice**; or by a **stop notice**. In the first instance compensation is dependent entirely upon the existence of a UXB and is repayable if planning permission is granted for the 'new development' which was restricted. In the other instances compensation is payable as of right, subject to the proof of loss.

Compensation for such planning restrictions is based, as a rule, on the reduction in the **market value** of the subject property resulting from the restriction. It is commonly measured by the **before-and-after method of valuation**. See also **blight notice, police powers, purchase notice.**

Law of Compulsory Purchase and Compensation, by Keith Davies, 4 edn., pp. 291–325.

Modern Methods of Valuation, 7 edn., pp. 423–458.

compensation for severance

Compensation for damage caused "by reason of the severing of lands taken from the other lands of the owner" (Compulsory Purchase Act 1965, s. 7). It may be damage following a compulsory purchase order that results either in the total loss of part of an owner's holding or the separation of one part of an owner's land from the rest of his land by the construction of works, such as a new highway. Thus when land is acquired compulsorily compensation is paid not only for the land taken, but also for losses caused by **severance**, provided the severance results in either (a) a reduction in the market value of the land retained; or (b) other incidental losses resulting from the compulsory purchase, e.g. increased costs of running a farm, inefficiencies of scale, damage during construction work undertaken by the acquiring authority and the need for subsequent reinstatement. The amount of compensation paid for severance is based on the reduction in the **market value** of the land affected and commonly is measured by the **before-and-after method of valuation**.

In the US such compensation is called 'severance damages' which may be payable as part of the **just compensation** payable for the taking of private property for public use. There is no fixed basis for determining severance damage but, as a rule, the assessment is made on similar lines to that used in the UK, i.e. the reduction in value of the retained land as ascertained on the basis of a 'before-and-after value', taking full account of any set-off required because of the benefit of the acquiring authority's use of the acquired land – Rice *v* South Carol-ina Dept. of Highways and Public Transport., (1982) 277 SC 495. See also **accommodation works, apportionment, compensation for injurious affection, compulsory purchase compensation**.
Modern Methods of Valuation, 7 edn., pp. 504–518.

compensation notice

A registered charge against land in favour of a local authority that has paid compensation for a planning restriction. This compensation must be repaid in the event that the restriction is lifted. See also **compensation for planning restrictions, local land charge**.

competent landlord

see **landlord**.

completion (of a contract for sale of land)

The bringing of a transaction for the sale of land, or an interest in land, to finality. Completion of a sale takes place when the final account is settled between the vendor and purchaser, all legal documentation is signed, and if necessary sealed, and, in particular, there has been **delivery** of the title and of possession (whether vacant possession or possession of the rent and profits); "the complete conveyance of the estate and final settlement of the business." – Lewis *v* South Western Railway (1852) 22 LJ Ch. 209. Generally, the **date** on which good title is transferred; the actual transfer of possession takes place; and the purchase money is paid. However, when interest is "payable on completion" it is payable normally from the date fixed for completion, especially if a delay is caused by the purchaser – Kilner *v* France [1946] 2 All ER 86. Completion is usually stipulated in a contract to take place at the offices of the vendor's solicitor (or at the offices of the vendor's mortgagee) four weeks from exchange of contracts. If no date is stipulated for completion then it shall take place within a period of time that is reasonable for investigation to title and preparation of the necessary documentation. As a rule, time is not of the essence for completion of a contract for the sale of land, although it may be made so. See also **acquisition, closing, specific performance, time is of the essence.**

Contract and Conveyance, by J.T. Farrand, 4 edn., pp. 198–202.
Barnsley's Conveyancing Law and Practice, 2 edn., pp. 409–445.
42 Halsbury's Laws of England, 4 edn., paras. 125–134.

completion bond
see **performance bond.**

completion certificate
see **building certificate.**

completion costs
The costs incurred in consummating a real estate transaction; expenses incurred by a party to a transfer of an interest in land whether as a vendor, purchaser, lessor, lessee, mortgagor, or mortgagee. In particular, expenses incurred by either party to a transaction over and above the consideration set out in the contract.

The costs incurred by a purchaser may include: transfer tax or stamp duty, Land Registry search fees, (and, in the US, title examination costs), cost of registering a deed (including a mortgage, if any), title insurance premium, legal fees, and any mortgagee's commitment fee.

The costs incurred by a vendor may include: cost of registering a deed,

legal fees, brokerage commission, transfer tax (although this is usually borne by the purchaser), and any mortgage release fee.

In addition, variable expenses associated with the property (property taxes, rates, insurance premiums, service charges or operating costs, rents and other income) must be prorated between the purchaser and vendor as at the date of completion. These costs are usually set out in the **completion statement (closing statement)** prepared by the parties' lawyers. In the UK (but not necessarily in the US), broker's or agent's fees are payable after completion, while property survey fees and search fees may have to be paid prior to exchange of contract. In the US, completion costs are referred to as 'closing costs' or 'closing fees'. See also **apportionment.**

completion notice
1. Notice served by a local planning authority, in accordance with the Town and Country Planning Act 1971, s. 44, on a property owner, occupier or any other party involved in the development of property when the authority considers that development, for which the authority has granted **planning permission**, will not be completed within a reasonable time. The notice requires the development to be completed within a stated period of not less than 12 months. Permission for further development ceases to be valid when the notice takes effect. An appeal against such a notice may be made to the Secretary of State for the Environment.
2. Notice served upon one of the parties to a contract for the sale of land requiring **completion** of that contract

and thereby making time of the essence from the date the notice is deemed to take effect. See also **time is of the essence**.

3. Notice served on the owner of a newly completed property, by a rating authority, specifying that although the property may be **unoccupied** the authority proposes to levy empty rates from a date specified in the notice (General Rate Act 1967, s. 17).

completion order (US)
see **certificate of occupancy**.

completion, practical
see **practical completion**.

completion statement
A cash accounting statement of all the costs and expenses of a real estate transaction. The statement is prepared at, or immediately after, completion by the lawyer responsible for preparing the contract and conveyance of the property, or by the respective parties' lawyers. The statement shows the amounts due, or paid, by a party to the transaction, i.e. the **completion costs**. The statement also shows an **apportionment** or 'closing adjustment' of all income and expenses between the purchaser and vendor and the resultant sum due by one party (usually the purchaser) to the other.

In the UK, 'completion statement' means either (a) an account prepared by the vendor's solicitor on completion, and agreed with the purchaser's solicitor to show the amount due to the vendor from the purchaser (with the rents, charges, etc. duly apportioned); or (b) the account prepared by a solicitor after completion showing how the solicitor has dealt with the money he has handled and any bal-

ance due to the client, or to the solicitor. In the US, a completion statement is referred to as a 'closing statement' or 'settlement statement'. Some states require that such statements are prepared in accordance with set regulations, especially when they relate to loans to private individuals.
Real Estate Principles, by Bruce Harwood, 2 edn., pp. 298–320.

component capitalisation rate
A **capitalisation rate** that is made up by adding different rates to reflect the various elements of risk of an investment e.g:

safe rate	4.5% (compared to safest form of investment)
general risk	3.5% (general risk of the specific investment)
illiquidity risk	2.0% (risk of finding a ready purchaser)
rental void risk	1.0% (risk of lost income from non-letting)
component rate	11.0%

Called also the 'summation rate'. The application of a component capitalisation rate to an income is called sometimes the 'built-up capitalisation method'.
cf. **band-of-investment rate**. See also **all-risks rate, overall rate**.

component depreciation
Depreciation applied at different rates to different parts of, or interests in, the same property. For example, the structure of a building may be depreciated on a straight line basis over 30 years and the services, fixtures and fittings depreciated over 10 years.
cf. **composite depreciation**.

component financing
The financing of real estate by divid-

ing it into separate parts or interests, usually in order to increase the total value of the property offered as security. For example, creating a leasehold interest and raising a mortgage loan on the security of the freehold (subject to the lease) and also on the security of the leasehold interest. Called also 'split financing'.

composite depreciation
Depreciation applied at a single rate to an entire property, land and buildings, as distinguished from **component depreciation** where different rates are applied to different parts of the property.

composite rate
A rate of return on an investment which provides a yield to the investor that is adequate for the risk entailed and provides for the recapture of the initial capital cost. See also **all-risks rate**, **dual-rate capitalisation factor**.

composition
see **compound (a debt)**.

compound (a debt)
To agree to terms for a payment. A debtor may compound a debt by agreeing to receive a smaller sum in settlement of the debt in discharge of the full liability. Such an agreement is called a 'composition'. See also **accord and satisfaction, compound interest**.

compound amount of one
see **amount of one**.

compound interest
Interest payable or earned on both the original principal and subsequent accrued interest, i.e. on interest already due or earned. In effect, interest on interest. If a sum of money P is

invested at a compound interest rate of i per period, then at the end of n periods that sum will accumulate to a total of $A = P(1 + i)^n$.
cf. **simple interest**. See also **amount of one, discount rate, valuation tables**.

compound settlement
A **settlement** of the same land effected by two or more documents over a period of time. Such documents may be read as if they were one settlement – *Re* Ogle's Settled Estate [1927] 1 Ch. 233. See also **joinder**.

comprehensive development
The redevelopment of an area as a whole under a comprehensive planning scheme; frequently where an area has been brought into common ownership. See also **action area, area of comprehensive development**.

comprehensive development area
see **area of comprehensive development**.

comprehensive general liability insurance** (US)
see **comprehensive insurance**.

comprehensive insurance
Insurance against a large range of specified risks, as compared to **all-risks insurance** which covers all items not specifically excluded from the policy. Called sometimes 'named parts insurance' or in the US, 'comprehensive general liability insurance' or 'broad-form insurance'.

compromis (F)
compromise; arbitration agreement. (*compromis de vente* – contract for sale, used erroneously to refer to a contract that has yet to be ratified by a notary). See also *acte, avant contrat*.

'comps'
see **comparable property.**

compulsory listing (US)
see **multiple listing.**

compulsory purchase (or acquisition)
The purchase of property against the will of the owner, subject to the payment of proper compensation; the obligatory conversion of real property into money. In particular, the purchase of an interest in land for public purposes by a body possessing statutory powers, e.g. for highway construction; comprehensive redevelopment; or a statutory undertaking. In English law strictly compulsory purchase is initiated by the service of a **notice to treat** (or the issue of a **general vesting declaration**), following authorisation obtained under a **compulsory purchase order**, and is completed when **compensation** is settled and the interest in land transferred to the acquiring authority. However, in common usage and in certain statutes, the term is used to refer to any acquisition (whether by compulsion or agreement) made by an authority possessing compulsory purchase powers.

In England and Wales the land acquisition powers of public authorities are wide ranging so that land may be acquired not only for a specific statutory purpose, e.g. to facilitate the construction of a new highway, but merely for "the proper planning of an area." (Local Government, Planning and Land Act 1980, s. 91). However, "it is clear that no minister or public authority can acquire any land compulsorily except the power to do so be given by Parliament; and Parliament only grants it, or should only grant it, when it is necessary in the public interest. In any case, therefore, where the scales are evenly balanced – for or against compulsory acquisition – the decision – by whomsoever it is made – should come down against compulsory acquisition. I [Lord Denning] regard it as a principle of our constitutional law that no citizen is to be deprived of his land by any public authority against his will, unless it is expressly authorised by Parliament and the public interest decisively so demands; and then only on the condition that proper compensation is paid – see *Attorney-General v De Keyser's Royal Hotel Ltd.* [1920] AC 508. If there is any doubt on the matter, the balance must be resolved in favour of the citizen". – Prest and Others *v* Secretary of State for Wales and Another (1983) 266 EG 528.

In English law compulsory purchase requires an authorizing statute; is made currently in accordance with the procedures contained in the Acquisition of Land Act 1981; is carried through in accordance with the provisions of the Compulsory Purchase Act 1965; and compensation is paid upon the basis laid down primarily in the Land Compensation Act 1961. Although a purchase is made against the will of the individual, compensation is payable based on the presumption of a **willing seller.**

In the US compulsory purchase is referred to as the exercise of the power of **eminent domain**, or **condemnation proceedings.** (The term eminent domain is hardly ever used in English law, although it may be used to refer to the right of the Sovereign or the State to acquire land, as distinguished from compulsory acquisition which comprehends such a right being obtained with the consent of Parliament.) See also **blight notice, compulsory purchase compensation, leasehold enfranchisement, purchase notice, *ultra vires*.**

Law of Compulsory Purchase and Compensation, by Keith Davies, 4 edn., pp. 3–109.

8 Halsbury's Laws of England, 4 edn., paras. 1–55.

Encyclopaedia of Compulsory Purchase and Compensation, edited by H.J. Brown.

compulsory purchase compensation

A single sum of money paid to an individual with an interest in land, for the loss of use and benefit to be derived from that land as a result of its purchase by an authority possessing powers of **compulsory purchase**. There is a well established principle that, "unless no other interpretation is possible, justice requires that statutes should not be construed to enable the land of a particular individual to be confiscated without payment". – Attorney General *v* De Keysers Royal Hotel Ltd. [1920] AC 576. Land may be confiscated without compensation if Parliament expressly so decrees – "a statute should not be held to take away private rights of property without compensation unless the intention to do so is expressed in clear and unambiguous terms." – Colonial Sugar Refining Co. Ltd *v* Melbourne Harbour Trust Commissioners, [1927] AC 359. Thus, the Town and Country Planning Acts are considered to contain express provisions that, if a landowner is refused permission to carry out development, the planning authority is under no obligation to pay compensation, except in certain stipulated instances – (see **compensation for planning restrictions.**)

In the UK the determination of compulsory purchase compensation is no longer a matter of negotiation between the parties, supported by resort to an independent expert or arbitrator, but is a subject governed by statutory rules. In English law such rules were first set out in the Land Clauses Consolidation Act 1845 and have subsequently been incorporated in the Land Compensation Act 1961, s. 5 (except for a dwelling-house that is **unfit for human habitation** when compensation is assessed, under the Housing Act 1957, ss. 12, 59 (2), as amended by the Housing Act 1969, on the basis of **cleared site value**) as follows: Rule (1) "No allowance shall be made on account of the acquisition being compulsory" – there is no extra recompense for being forced to part with an interest in land. (Prior to 1919, 10 per cent was added to compensation on account of the element of compulsion, but this practice has been discontinued.) Rule (2) "The value of the land shall, subject as hereinafter provided, be taken to be the amount which the land if sold in the open market by a willing seller might be expected to realise" – it should be presumed, therefore, that the acquiring authority will pay the same price as the owner's interest would be likely to fetch, that is, the presumed open **market value** (subject to the other rules of compensation code enumerated below). Rule (3) "The **special suitability or adaptability** of the land for any purpose shall not be taken into account if that purpose is a purpose to which it could be applied only in pursuance of statutory powers, or for which there is no market apart from the special needs of a particular purchaser or the requirements of any authority possessing compulsory purchase powers" – a rule that applies to exclude a physical use to which land might be put by the acquiring authority, e.g. an advantage to be derived only by the acquiring authority from the extraction of minerals on the land – Pointe Gourde Transport Co. Ltd *v* Superintendent of Crown Lands [1947] AC 565, or by one exceptional purchaser, e.g. a neighbouring owner requiring land for access to a development site. This rule applies to the quality of the land itself, not the need of a special purchaser so that the **marriage value** arising from the merging of two interests in the same property, held by acquiring authority and the claimant respectively, is not wholly excluded – Lambe *v* Secretary of State for War, [1955] 2 QB 612. Rule (4) "Where the value of land is increased by reason of the use thereof or of any premises thereon in a manner which could be restrained by any court, or is contrary to law, or is detrimental to the health of the occupants of the premises or to the public health, the amount of that increase shall not be taken into account". Rule (5) "Where land is, and but for the compulsory acquisition would continue to be, devoted to a purpose of such a nature that there is not general demand or market for land for that purpose, the compensation may, if the Lands Tribunal is satisfied that reinstatement in some other place is *bona fide* intended, be assessed on the basis of the reasonable cost of **equivalent reinstatement**". This rule applies to such properties as a hospital, church, school,

etc. Rule (6) "The provision of rule (2) shall not affect the assessment of **compensation for disturbance** or any other matter not directly based on the value of land" – a rule that preserves an owner's right to compensation for disturbance.

In addition, section 6 of the Land Compensation Act, 1961 (as amended by the Local Government, Planning and Land Act 1980, s. 145) excludes increases or decreases in value arising from the development plans of the acquiring authority or due to the scheme underlying the acquisition, i.e. the value of the claimant's interest is to be assessed in a 'no-scheme world'. "It is well settled that compensation for the compulsory purchase of land cannot include an increase in value which is entirely due to the scheme underlying the acquisition." – Pointe Guarde Quarrying and Transport Co. Ltd *v* Superintendent of Crown Lands [1947] AC 572. This 'settled' principle applies to the value engendered by the scheme; the demand that results therefrom; but not to the likelihood that planning permission would be given for the scheme. When assessing the value of the subject land various **planning assumptions** may be made as to the probable form of development that would be allowed on the land, as well as any **permitted development** for which planning permission would not be required. (The 'settled principle' of the Pointe Guarde case has been challenged as in conflict with other statutory rules applied to the assessment of compensation, especially Rules 2 and 6 of section 5 of the 1961 Act, or on the grounds that it is swallowed up by section 6. "If the land was suitable for development in the first place then there will be have been no increase in value due to the scheme." (*Statutory Valuation*, by Andrew Baum, p. 149, 1983). This dichotomy is a result of 'shifting value', so that if the value of land is shifted favourably solely by the acquiring authority's scheme the claimant cannot reap that value). The Act also provides that any loss in value due to actual or prospective development, i.e. due to **blight**, is to be excluded: but the acquiring authority may **set-off** any increase in value due to the increases in the value of adjacent or contiguous land in the same ownership (1961 Act, s. 7, 8). The effect of the depreciation in value arising from an indication that, "the relevant land is, or is likely, to be acquired by an authority possessing compulsory purchase powers" must be excluded also. Finally, the amount of compensation is assessed at the date it is agreed with the acquiring authority, or failing agreement, the date it is determined by the Lands Tribunal, or the date the authority enters into possession, whichever is the earlier; or, in Rule 5 (equivalent reinstatement) cases, the date at which reinstatement becomes reasonably practicable or the date the authority takes physical possession, whichever is the earlier.

In the US, compensation payable upon compulsory acquisition (condemnation proceedings) is referred to as **just compensation**. See also **compensation for injurious affection, compensation for severance, notice of entry, notice to treat, valuation date**. *Valuer's Casebook & Approved Valuations*, by R.W. Westbrook, Vols 1, 2 (1968 and 1973). *Modern Methods of Valuation*, 7 edn., pp. 469–502.

Law of Compulsory Purchase and Compensation, by Keith Davies, 4 edn., pp. 111–222.
Statutory Valuations, by Andrew Baum, pp. 127–264 (1983).
8 Halsbury's Laws of England, 4 edn., paras. 250–317.
Encyclopaedia of Compulsory Purchase and Compensation, edited by H.J. Brown, paras. 1–074 to 1–136.

compulsory purchase order (CPO)
An order, made or confirmed by a Minister of State, in accordance with statutory authority (e.g. the Public Health Act 1936, Compulsory Purchase Order 1965, New Towns Act 1966, Highways Act 1980, Housing Acts 1957 and 1974, Town and Country Planning Act 1971, Local Government, Planning and Land Act 1980), by which a body or authority is authorised to purchase land compulsorily for a specified purpose, subject to the payment of proper **compensation**. A compulsory purchase order derives its power from an enabling statute and an authority cannot extend its powers beyond those expressly conferred by the appropriate statute. An order may be made to acquire a right that is "incidental to, or consequential upon, those things which the legislature has authorised" – Attorney General *v* Great Eastern Railway Co. (1880) 5 App. Cas. 478; but an order may not be made to acquire a right based on what appears to be authorised. "Expropriation cannot take place by implication or through intention; it is authorised or not authorised. And to see which, it is necessary to construe the authority." – Sovmots Investment Ltd *v* Secretary of State for the Environment [1977] 2 All ER 385. Once a CPO has been obtained the

powers of the acquiring authority are exercised usually under the Compulsory Purchase Act 1965. See also **blight notice, compulsory purchase, general vesting declaration, purchase notice,** *ultra vires.*
Law of Compulsory Purchase and Compensation, by Keith Davies, 4 edn., pp. 37–57.

concealed fraud
see **fraud**.

concédant (F)
licensor.

concession
1. Something given or yielded to achieve an objective. A reduction in a price made to induce someone to enter into a contract. See also **grant, rent concession**.
2. A **licence** or other grant of permission to be on land, for a particular purpose. A lease of premises for a specific purpose, especially for a purpose that is supplemental to another, may be referred to also as a concession; for example, a right to operate a demonstration booth in a retail store. See also **assent, franchise**.

concession (F)
licence; concession.
(*concession commerciale* – **franchise**).

concession immobilière (F)
"A contract by which the owner of a building, or a part of a building, built or un-built, grants a right of possession (*jouissance*) to a person, called a '*concessionaire*', for a minimum term of twenty years in consideration of an annual rent (*redevance*)." A form of contract for the right to the use of land or buildings introduced by a French law of 30 December 1967 No. 67-1253. Any form of real property

may be the subject of a *concession immobilière,* but it is usually granted in respect of commercial property. The grantee effectively receives a once and for all right to the use of a property in such manner as he may wish, except as prohibited by the contract (or by law). At the end of the contract the property reverts to the grantor, subject to a requirement that he compensates the grantee for any increase in the value of the property due to building or improvement works. The grantee has a right to terminate the agreement during the first six years, subject to six months prior notice, and may assign his right (but may not mortgage the property). During the term of the contract normally the grantee is made responsible for all repairs and maintenance of the property.
Précis Dalloz. Droit Civil, Les Biens (Alex Weill), 2 edn., p. 584–590.

concessionaire (F)
1. **licencee**.
2. The holder of a *concession immobilière*.

concièrge (F)
concierge; janitor.

concurrent interest
An interest in land held by two or more persons at one and the same time, i.e. an interest when land is held in **co-ownership**. A grant of land 'to A and B in fee simple' creates a concurrent interest, but a grant 'to A for life, and thereafter to B in fee simple' creates several and successive interests. A concurrent interest may be created by an express clause in a written contract, or implied from the nature of an agreement or the action of the parties.

cf. **several ownership**. See also **joint tenancy, matrimonial home, resulting trust, tenancy in common**.
Cheshire's Modern Law of Real Property, 13 edn., pp. 207–235.

concurrent lease
A lease granted by a landlord to run for the same term, or for the unexpired term of an existing lease, of the same premises. See also **sandwich lease**.

condamnation (F)
condemnation.

condemnation or condemnation proceedings (US)
1. A process by which a property is declared unfit for use.
2. The process of exercising the power of **eminent domain**, i.e. the right of the State to acquire property against the will of the individual subject to the payment of **just compensation**. See also **compulsory purchase, excess condemnation, inverse condemnation, police power**.

condemnee (US)
One whose land is taken in **condemnation proceedings**.

condemnor (US)
A body or authority that takes land in **condemnation proceedings**. See also **acquiring authority**.

condition
Derived from the Latin *conditio*, something agreed upon or arranged. A provision or stipulation, especially one that is a prerequisite to something else. "'Condition' is a restraint or bridle annexed and joyned to a thing, so that by the not performance or not doing thereof the partie to the condition shall receive prejudice and losse, and, by the performance or doing of the same, commoditie and advantage." – *Termes de La Ley*. Something that must occur or not occur before a right comes into existence; or something that if it occurs, or does not occur, brings an estate, right or interest to an end. Condition is used frequently to denote a component or clause of restraint in a contract that is essential to the operation of the contract; whether to bring the contract into effect or bring it to an end. A condition may be contrasted with a **warranty** which is subsidiary to the main purpose of the contract. The breach of a condition of a contract, gives rise to a right to repudiate the contract *and* sue for damages, as opposed to a breach of warranty which only gives a right to a claim for damages – Wickham Machine Tool Sales Ltd. *v* Schuler (L) AG [1972] 2 All ER 1181. However, this rule is not always clear cut and a breach of a term referred to as a condition may not necessarily permit termination of the contract; especially if it is not more or less serious or does not go to the root of the contract. Merely calling a term a condition does not make it so if the court would consider that the intention of the parties is to treat the matter as no more than a warranty.
   In a lease, whether a clause or term is a condition, and thus essential to the existence of the contract, or a **covenant** depends upon the intention of the parties. If the intention of a clause or term is that the lease shall be brought to an end in the event of a failure of the requirement, it is a condition: the lease can no longer exist because of the failure. In any other case it would be construed as a covenant, providing rights between the par-

ties other than the bringing of the contract to an end. A condition is usually preceded by such words as 'provided that' or 'on condition that' which make it clear that the lease is intended to be brought to an end if the condition is not complied with. Whereas a covenant is preceded usually by such words as 'it is hereby agreed that' or 'the tenant covenants that'. However, "it is sufficient if it appears that the words used were intended to have the effect of creating a condition. [Although] they must be the words of the landlord, because he is to impose the condition". – Doe d. Henniker *v* Watt (1828) 8 B and C 315.

In land law, in particular, a condition is a qualification annexed to an estate, either to bring an estate into effect, enlarge it or defeat it. Such conditions may be precedent, subsequent or inherent. "A condition is precedent when, unless it is complied with, the estate does not arise. It is subsequent when, if it is broken, the estate is defeated. It is inherent when the estate is qualified, restrained or charged by it." – In re Lees, *ex parte* Collins (1875) 1 Ch. App. 372.

A condition may be an **express term**, i.e. set down by the parties (sometimes called a 'condition in deed'); or an **implied term** based on the action or intention of the parties or implied by law to give efficacy to an agreement (sometimes called a 'condition in law').

In French law, "a condition is a provision which makes the existence of a judicial act ... and therefore the existence of the obligation resulting from it dependent on a future uncertain event. The condition may be either suspensive, (*suspensive*), in that the obligation will not exist

unless and until the event occurs or resolutive (*resolutoire*) in that the obligation will cease to exist if the event occurs". (*French Law of Contract*, by Barry Nicholas, pp. 150–151 1982). A condition may be distinguished from a *terme* in that a *terme* is bound to happen, though when it will happen is uncertain.
cf. **limitation, representation.** See also **breach of contract, condition precedent, condition subsequent, conditional contract, conditional interest, planning condition, repudiation, time is of the essence.**
Cheshire & Fifoot's Law of Contract, 10 edn., pp. 128–138.
Anson's Law of Contract, 26 edn., pp. 115–118.
Chitty on Contract, 25 edn., paras. 746–755.

condition (F)
condition.
(*condition d'adjudication* – terms for a sale by tender)
(*condition résolutoire* – **condition subsequent**)
(*condition suspensive* – **condition precedent**)
(*condition tacite* – **implied condition**)
cf. *terme.*

condition of sale
1. A **condition** or **term** upon which an offer for sale is made and accepted.
2. An express condition upon which a property is sold. See also **conditions of sale.**

condition precedent
A qualification or restriction that must arise or be performed before a contract becomes effective or an estate vests; a **condition** that must be fulfilled before a contract comes into existence, or before an interest in land

is created or vested in someone.
cf. **condition subsequent**. See also
conditional contract, vest.

condition subsequent

A condition that brings a contract to
an end, or changes or terminates an
interest in land, e.g. a provision that
terminates a lease in the event of the
property being destroyed by fire. A
condition that if it is not performed,
or if it does or does not happen, will
defeat an estate or interest that is
already vested in someone; "an interest upon condition subsequent arises
where a qualification is annexed to a
conveyance, whereby it is provided
that, in case a particular event does or
does not happen, or in case the grantor or grantee does or omits to do a
particular act, the interest shall be
defeated." (Cheshire's Modern Law
of Real Property, 13 edn., p. 345).
Usually, when an interest in land is
granted on condition subsequent, if
the created interest is defeated, the
right to the land reverts to the
grantor.
cf. **condition precedent**. See also **conditional interest, conditional fee
simple**.

conditional agreement

see **conditional sale agreement**.

conditional contract

A **contract** made subject to a **condition**. The contract may be subject to a
'**condition precedent**' i.e. it does not
come into effect unless or until the
condition is satisfied; or it may be
subject to a '**condition subsequent**' i.e.
it comes to an end or changes in some
way if the condition occurs. The term
'conditional contract' is used more
commonly in the former sense.
The enforceability of a conditional

contract varies from case to case. A
contract made "subject to the purchaser obtaining a satisfactory mortgage" is likely to be void for uncertainty – Lee-Parker *v* Izzet (No. 2)
[1972] 2 All ER 800. A contract subject to a "price to be agreed by the
parties", with an arbitration provision failing such agreement, is a binding contract – Foley *v* Classique
Coaches Ltd [1934] 2 KB 1; but a
price that, "shall be agreed upon from
time to time between the government
department and the purchasers" is no
more than an 'agreement to agree' –
May and Butcher Ltd. *v* R. [1934] 2
KB 17. A contract subject to the
potential purchaser obtaining planning permission, without sufficient
qualification as to the type and timing
of that permission; or a contract subject to satisfactory tenants being
obtained for a property, is likely to be
void also (unless there has been an act
of **part performance** which enables
the contract to be enforced in equity).
However, in the former case if a conditional planning permission is obtained (and the conditions are not
unduly onerous) the contract normally cannot then be rescinded –
West (Richard) and Partners (Inver-
ness) Ltd. *v* Dick [1969] 2 Ch. 424; in
the latter case, when a date was fixed
for completion this was held to mean
that, in any event, the condition no
longer applied after that date – Aber-
foyle Plantations *v* Cheng [1960] AC
115.

In the US, a conditional contract,
or one which is referred to more
commonly as a 'contingent contract',
especially if the condition may never
occur, frequently is enforceable (especially in States based on the civil
law rather than on English common

law). Thus, a contract that was contingent upon a purchaser's ability to get leases satisfactory to the buyer has been held to be valid and obliged the purchaser to make every effort, in good faith, to secure satisfactory tenants – Mattei *v* Hopper, 51 Cal. 2d. 119, 330 P. 2d. 625. Similarly, a contract contingent on the purchaser obtaining a mortgage loan for a specified sum at current interest rate is likely to be a binding contract – Barto *v* Hacks (1971) 124 Ga. App. 472, 184 SE 2d. 188.

A conditional contract may be distinguished from an **option** or a **right of preemption** because the latter forms of agreement depend upon the wishes of one of the parties, but a conditional contract depends upon some outside event.

cf. **escrow**. See also **contract of sale**, '**subject to finance**', '**subject to survey**'.

conditional fee

An ancient term for a **fee** estate in land that was limited to a man and a given class of heirs and which reverted to the original donor of the estate in the event of a failure of the requisite issue, unlike a **fee simple** estate which then passed to the general heirs of the donee. "A conditional fee, at common law, was a fee restrained to some particular heir, exclusive of others" (Bl. Comm. vol. ii. p. 110), the forerunner of the modern **entailed interest**. Sometimes called a 'fee simple conditional' as distinguished from a **conditional fee simple** which is a modern estate in land that is equivalent to a fee simple but may be cut short, usually at the behest of the grantor, if a specified condition occurs. In most states in the US a conditional fee is automatically converted into a fee simple or if granted may create no more than a life estate with the estate reverting after that life to a given heir as a fee simple. See also **base fee**, *De Donis Conditionalibus*.

Cheshire's Modern Law of Real Property, 13 edn., pp. 237–238.

conditional fee simple

An interest in land that is equivalent to a **fee simple** but may be cut short if a specified event or condition occurs. For example, a grant of land 'to A as a fee simple on condition that he does not enroll as a Chartered Surveyor' continues unaffected, unless A becomes a Chartered Surveyor at which stage it is brought to an end. A conditional fee simple is intended to be enjoyed in the same way as any other fee simple, provided that the condition does not occur; a condition that does not form a limitation on the type of estate that is granted, but may interrupt and have the effect of confiscating the estate from the grantee usually in favour, or at the option, of the grantor. (A fee simple that is granted subject to a **right of re-entry** in favour of the grantor if a certain event does or does not happen – as with the non-payment of an annual rentcharge – is a form of conditional fee simple, but for the purposes of the Law of Property Act 1925 it is classified as a 'fee simple absolute' and, therefore, may be a **legal estate**: Law of Property (Amendment) Act 1926, Sch. 1, which is added to the Law of Property Act 1925, s. 7 (1).) Called also a 'fee simple upon condition', a 'fee simple defeasible by condition subsequent' or in the US a 'defeasible fee'.

cf. **determinable interest**. See also **base fee, conditional fee, conditional interest, qualified fee.**
The Law of Real Property, by Robert Megarry and H.W.R. Wade, 5 edn., pp. 69–75.
Introduction to the Law of Property, by J.G. Riddell, 3 edn., pp. 38–44.

conditions of sale
The conditions set down by the parties to a contract for the sale of land. In particular, conditions provided by statute law or an independent body. In the event that a valid **open contract** is entered into by correspondence, the sale will be governed by the Lord Chancellor's Statutory Form of Conditions of Sale 1925 (S.R. & O. No. 779) established under the provisions of the Law of Property Act 1925, s. 46; except where those conditions have been varied by the correspondence.

Standard forms of contract (closed contracts), setting out conditions of sale, commonly are employed by solicitors e.g. The Law Society's General Conditions of Sale (current edition brought into effect on 1 September 1980, previous editions produced in 1970 & 1973); The National Conditions of Sale (now in its 20th edition, published 1 December 1981); The Conveyancing Lawyers' Conditions of Sale. These general conditions of sale are supplemented, or varied, by 'special conditions' set down by the parties as relevant or required for the property being sold. See also **auction, particulars of sale, precedent, standard-form contract.**
Contract and Conveyance, by J.T. Farrand, 4 edn., pp. 76–82.
Standard Conditions of Sale of Land, by H.W. Wilkinson, 3 edn.

42 Halsbury's Laws of England, 4 edn., paras. 82–138.

condo
Short for **condominium**.

condohotel or condotel (US)
A building held in **condominium** ownership and used as an hotel.

condominium
Derived from the Latin *condominium*, **partial-ownership**. The absolute or individual ownership of part of a building – in substance, a space within the confines of a wall, floor and ceiling – usually together with an undivided share in the ownership of the land and **common elements**. A 'condominium unit' has been defined as "an enclosed space, consisting of one or more rooms occupying all or part of one or more floors in buildings of one or more floors or stories regardless of whether it is designed for residence, for office, for the operation of any industry or business, or for any other type of independent use, and shall include such accessory units as may be appended thereto, such as garage space, storage space, balcony terrace or patio; provided that, the said unit has a direct exit to a thoroughfare or to a given common space leading to a thoroughfare". (District of Columbia Code (1973 edn.,) 5–902). Or, as an undivided interest in common "in a portion of a parcel or real property together with a separate interest in space in a residential, industrial or commercial building on such real property, such as an apartment, office or store. A condominium may include the addition of separate interest in other portions of such real property". (Californian Civil Code,

para. 783). The condominium owner has a separate interest in the 'unit' and usually an undivided interest with the other unit owners in a portion of the building called the 'common elements', e.g. corridors, stairways, elevators and the like, as well as the main walls, floors, roofs and the land – Gerber *v* Town of Clarkstown 356 NYS 2d. 926, 78 Misc. 2d. 221. The owner of a condominium has the same rights to alienate, charge, or otherwise deal with his or her property as an absolute owner of land being restrained only by the law, the terms upon which he or she bought the property, and any restriction imposed by agreement with other condominium owners in the same building. (This distinct form of ownership is recognised in Spanish law – Civil Code arts 392–406, whence it appears to have been imported into California and adopted by many other states). Normally an owner's association is formed by the condominium owners to manage and maintain the common elements and to decide on other matters that affect the owners collectively. It is not a form of ownership found in English common law, which would require the creation of separate rights of ownership of part of the building combined with **co-ownership** or lease rights to the common parts of the building, with the surface of the land held either in co-ownership or by a third party. See also *droit de superficie*, **flying freehold, master deed, planned unit development,**
Real Estate Law, by Robert Kratovil and Raymond J. Werner, 8 edn., pp. 497–528.
Condominiums and Cooperatives, by David Clurman, C. Scott Jackson and Edna L. Hebard, 2 edn.

condominium conversion (US)
The change of a building from being let as individual units to **condominium ownership**.

conduit
1. A person who acts as an intermediary or nominee for the transfer of real estate. For example, someone who acquires a property and immediately contracts to sub-sell the property to another. See also **sub-contractor, sub-sale.**
2. See **drain, sewer.**

conduit (F)
conduit; pipeline.

confiscation
see **appropriation.**

conforming use
In land use planning, a use that conforms with the permitted classification for an area or zone.
cf. **non-conforming use.**

congé (F)
permission; notice; licence; leave; dismissal.
(*avis de congé* – **notice to quit**).

consensus ad idem (L)
'Agreement as to the same thing'. See **acceptance, contract, mistake.**

conjoint (F)
jointly.
(*responsabilité conjointe et solidaire* – **joint and several liability**)

conseil expert immobilier, conseil immobilier (F)
real estate consultant; appraiser. See also **expert.**

consent
A reasoned and deliberate **agreement** to, or active **acquiescence** in, an act. A

meeting of minds or a free act of the mind; an act of being in unison with an action or idea. Consent is that which is given actively, and not taken on an understanding of another's intent; it involves "some affirmative acceptance, not merely a standing by and absence of objection". – Bell *v* Alfred Franks and Bartlett Co. Ltd [1980] 1 All ER 362. Consent cannot be said to exist when there has been **fraud, coercion, duress, undue influence** or, in certain cases, a **mistake**.

In French law, "there is no valid consent (*consentement*) if the consent has been given only by mistake, or if it has been extorted by violence or induced by fraud". (Civil Code, art. 1109). See also **restraint on alienation**.

consequential damages
1. **Damages** that do not arise as a direct result of an action or breach of promise, but follow on as a result or consequence of a principal act – e.g. loss of business resulting from fire damage to a building. Damages awarded as recompense for a loss suffered indirectly as a result of a tort or a breach of contract – called sometimes 'special damages' or 'constructive damages'. See also **consequential loss insurance**.
(US) 2. **Damages** resulting from the exercise of the power of **eminent domain**. Consequential damages may refer to loss suffered by a land owner when part of his land is taken; or when work is carried out by a public authority on adjoining land; or loss of business, goodwill or similar disturbance caused as a result of the taking of land in condemnation proceedings. The former loss is normally compensated as part of the **just compensation** paid to the land owner for the reduc-

tion in the value of his land as a direct consequence of the taking. The latter is not included in the compensation paid to the owner.
cf. **severance damages**. See also **compensation for disturbance, injurious affection, partial taking**.
Real Estate Valuation in Litigation, J.D. Eaton, pp. 175–200 (1982)

consequential loss insurance
Insurance against a loss that is not the direct result of the destruction of an insured property but arises as a subsequent result thereof, such as a loss of profit for a business; increased working costs; cost of renting alternative premises; or the payment of expenses for a property that cannot be fully utilised. Depending on the risk covered such insurance may be referred to also as 'loss of profits insurance', 'rental value insurance'; 'extra expenses insurance', 'business interruption insurance'.

consequential loss of rent
see **loss of rent insurance**.

conservation
see **amenity, amenity societies, conservation area**.

conservation (F)
(*conservation des hypothèques* – mortgage registry).

conservation area
An area designated by a local planning authority (or in certain instances the Secretary of State), originally under the provisions of the Civic Amenities Act 1967, (now covered by the Town and Country Planning Act 1971, s. 227., as amended by the Town and Country Amenities Act 1974, s. 1 (1)), as being of "special architectural

or historic interest, the character or appearance of which it is desirable to preserve or enhance". Conservation areas may take any form; "they may be large or small, from whole town centres to squares, terraces or groups of buildings. They will often be centred on listed buildings but not always; pleasant groups of other buildings, open spaces, trees, a historic street pattern, a village green, or features of archaeological interest may also contribute to the special character of the area. It is the character of areas rather than individual buildings that ... the Act seeks to preserve". (Department of the Environment Circular No. 53/67). The effect of designating a conservation area is to restrict building demolition (no building may be demolished without **listed building consent**); to strictly control all forms of new development; to require the preservation of most trees in the area; and to impose an obligation on the local authority to take steps to preserve and enhance the area. In addition the Secretary of State for the Environment is empowered to make regulations to control the placing of advertisements in conservation areas and to give directions to local planning authorities as to matters to be considered when dealing with applications to carry out development in such areas. Provisions for the control of building in conservation areas are contained in the Town and Country Planning (Listed Buildings and Buildings in Conservation Areas) Regulations 1977. See also **area of outstanding natural beauty, Historic Buildings and Monuments Commission, listed building, tree preservation order**.
Introduction to Town and Country

Planning, by John Ratcliffe, 2 edn., pp. 298–300.
Development and Planning Law, by Barry Denyer Green, pp. 102–104 (1982).

consideration
Remuneration or recompense given in exchange for a benefit or advantage conferred on one person by another. It is the legal motive, cause or reason for a **contract**; the *quid pro quo*. English law requires that a contract should comprise more than an undertaking by one party to another; a **bargain** when struck should have a motivating reason that goes beyond a moral duty. Thus a voluntary curtesy or a moral obligation is not consideration – Eastwood *v* Kenyon (1840) 11 Ad. and El. 438. Consideration must be more than a cause, it must be representative of what was considered, it must demonstrate or reinforce a practical interpretation of the cause; the legal concept of causation is not based on logic or philosophy; "it is based on the practical way in which the ordinary man's mind works in the everyday affairs of life". – McGhee *v* National Board [1973] 1 WLR 5. Consideration is the evidence that reinforces the moral and just reason behind a contract. It is the reason, or in a commercial sense the price, for which the promise, that constitutes a contract, is bought – Dunlop *v* Selfridge [1915] AC 855. A promise to pay money (but not the promise *per se*) is sufficient consideration to support a contract; as is the foregoing of a claim or right. Consideration is something that would not be given, done or foregone, but for the promise it supports.

Consideration may be 'good' or

'valuable'. Good consideration refers to something that represents a motive that has no tangible value: love or affection and which, although possibly a reasonable or moral cause for the making of a contract, will not support a contract in English common law – Tweedle v Atkinson (1861) 1 B and S 393. Valuable consideration is something that is real, not nominal or illusory; it may be pecuniary, or even the promise of marriage; it need not be adequate or sufficient; provided it can be estimated in terms of value. Valuable consideration (in land law sometimes merely called **value**) is that which is required for a valid contract; (unless the contract is under seal): "some right, interest, profit or benefit accruing to one party, or some forbearance given, suffered or undertaken by another". – Currie v Misa (1875) LR 10 Ex. 162.

Consideration may be 'executory' when it is in the form of a promise to be given at a future date and 'executed' at the stage when it accrues to the benefit of the person for whom it is intended at the time the contract is made. An amount of consideration may be expressly stipulated in the contract; or may be implied from the act or conduct of the parties, as when it is clear from the surrounding circumstances that a fair market value will be paid. A promise of payment after an act is done may be considered as a definition of the payment that it was implied would be made when that act was done and hence as an executed consideration – Lampleigh v Braithwait (1615) Hob. 105; Re Casey's Patents, Stewart v Casey [1892] 1 Ch. 104. It is not essential to the enforceability of a contract in English law for the amount of consid-

eration to be adequate recompense, provided it is 'real' (not vague) and 'sufficient' to support the bargain made. A contracting party can stipulate whatever consideration he chooses, provided it has some value in law to the promisee: "a peppercorn does not cease to be good consideration if it is established that the promisee does not like pepper and will throw away the corn". However, consideration must move from the promisee, i.e. it must be paid over, not merely promised or paid to a total stranger to the contract, in order to give effect to that contract – Tweedle v Atkinson *supra*. Past consideration, i.e. that which was wholly executed before the promise, is no consideration; although an antecedent debt or liability may be valuable consideration for a bill of exchange (Bills of Exchange Act 1882, s. 27 (1) (b)). In the event that there is no consideration, as in a transfer by **gift**, a contract may still be valid, provided it is made by **deed**.

In French law although consideration is usually supplied to reinforce a contract a *cause* may be adequate reason for the law to recognise a contract.

In the French language *consideration* has much the same meaning as in English but, because a contract in French law is an agreement, as distinguished from a promise in return for valuable consideration as in English law, consideration is not such an essential element to support the validity of a **contrat** (**consentement**, *cause* and **objet** are equally or more important elements). See also **accord and satisfaction**, **adequate consideration**, **estoppel**, **simple contract**, **value**.
Cheshire & Fifoot's Law of Contract, 10 edn., pp. 62–66.

Chitty on Contract, 28 edn., paras. 141–248.
8 Halsbury's Laws of England, 4 edn., paras. 309–328.
Anson's Law of Contract, 26 edn., pp. 78–109.

consideration (F)
consideration (under a contract). See also *cause*, *contrat*.

consolidation of mortgages
The uniting of at least two mortgages on two or more properties, granted to a single mortgagor, into a single (i.e. jointly redeemable) **mortgage**. Where a mortgagee has mortgages on several properties that are mortgaged to one party, the mortgagee may reserve the right to consolidate; that is, he may not permit any one mortgage to be redeemed in isolation. In English law, this right must be specified in at least one of the mortgage deeds and the legal date for **redemption** of all of the relevant mortgages must have passed, otherwise the mortgagee cannot prevent the mortgagor from redeeming the mortgages separately (Law of Property Act 1925, s. 93).
cf. **tacking**.
Megarry's Manual of the Law of Real Property, 6 edn., pp. 487–490.

consolidation, of rights
In the civil law, the bringing together of possession, occupation, profits, and other rights to land; in particular, the union of a right of **usufruct** with the **ownership** of the land from which that right issues. See also *pleine propriété*.

consortium (F)
consortium; *syndicat*.

constant (US)
see **mortgage constant**.

constant annual per cent (US)
see **mortgage constant**.

constant-payment mortgage
see **amortisation mortgage**.

constant-rent factor
A factor that may be applied to the rent payable in the open market to take account of the benefit of a longer than normal interval between one rent review and the next. Thus, if a tenant has a lease with a 14-year interval between reviews to market rent and the accepted pattern of rent review is 5 years, then a tenant might be prepared to pay a different rent because his initial rent is fixed for a longer period of time: a higher rent if he anticipates rising rental values and a lower rent if he anticipates falling rental values. This differential is represented by the constant-rent factor. Known also as an 'uplift factor' which may be obtained from the formula, devised by Jack Rose (1979):

$$\frac{[(1 + r)^n - (1 + g)^n]}{[(1 + r)^n - 1]} \times \frac{[(1 + r)^t - 1]}{[(1 + r)^t - (1 + g)^t]}$$

where: r = lessor's required return on capital
g = annual rate of rental growth (or decline)
n = number of years between rent reviews in the actual lease
t = number of years between normal rent reviews.

The total rent that the tenant may be prepared to pay is called the 'equated rent'. See also **interim rent**.
Statutory Valuations, by Andrew Baum, pp. 27, 36–38 (1983).
Tables of the Constant Rent, by J.J. Rose, (1979).

constituer (F)
to form; to create; to instruct.
(*constituer avocat* – to instruct counsel).

constructeur promoteur (F)
   property developer. See also *entrepreneur*, *lotisseur*.

construction
   The act or process of **building**, especially a thing out of its consituent parts. The creation or extension of a new building or **structure**. Construction includes the bringing together and assembling of materials in order to erect a building or structure; it requires more than maintaining the *status quo*. The making of an **alteration** or **addition** to a building may constitute construction, but mere repair and maintenance does not. See also **building operations**.

construction (F)
   construction; building.
   (*code de la construction* – **building control**, building code)
   (*en cours de construction* – under construction)
   (*société de construction* – construction company)
   (*coût de la construction* – building cost). See also *bail à construction*.

construction allowance (US)
   see **fitting-out allowance**.

construction bond
   see **performance bond**.

construction contract
   A contract by which one party undertakes to carry out construction or building work for another. See also **building contract, management contract**.

construction loan (or finance)
   A short-term or **interim loan** granted for the purpose of financing, and for the period of, building construction. A loan that is made upon the basis that it will be replaced on, or soon after, completion of the building

work by more permanent financing. Commonly finance available under a construction loan agreement is advanced as building work progresses and is limited to a percentage of the total expenditure incurred by the borrower at any stage during the building work. Interest is charged, usually at a variable or floating rate, upon the outstanding principal and may be payable at fixed regular intervals or when the entire loan is repaid. Called also a 'building loan'. See also **take-out loan**.

construction management (CM)
   see **management contract**, **project management**.

construction permit
   see **building permit, building controls**.

construction retainage (US)
   see **retention sum**.

constructive annexation
   The fixing of something to land by reason of its purpose or nature; for example, the lifting tackle which forms part of a gantry that is fixed to a building and, therefore, forms part of the land because it is constructively fixed as part of the whole. See also **fixture**.

constructive contract (US)
   see **quasi-contract**.

constructive damages
   see **consequential damages**.

constructive entry
   see **entry**.

constructive eviction
   Interference with a tenant's proper enjoyment of a property without necessarily depriving him of physical possession. Constructive eviction may arise when a landlord makes a prop-

erty, or deliberately permits a property to, fall into a state so that it is unfit for the purpose for which it was let, or so that the tenant is deprived, for a substantial period of time, of beneficial use or enjoyment of the demised premises. Constructive eviction actually takes place when the tenant vacates the premises, provided this was a direct consequence of an activity or inactivity of the landlord. See also **eviction, harassment**.

constructive mortgage (US)
see **equitable mortgage**.

constructive notice
Notice that is implied or imputed by law to have been given, even though the recipient may be ignorant of the fact or information that would be imparted if he or she had **actual notice**. Notice that is deemed to be given because the facts to which it relates are readily available; are obvious from inspection; or could be obtained by prudent inquiry – Hunt *v* Luck [1901] 1 Ch. 52. In relation to real property, knowledge or information that would have been revealed if such inquiries and inspections had been made (by a purchaser, his solicitors or other agent) as ought reasonably to have been made (see Law of Property Act 1925, s. 199). For example notice that would come to the attention of a purchaser in the event of proper and diligent inquiry or search; such as at a public records office, or from a proper investigation of the property and of the vendor's title. However, "the question when it is sought to affect a purchaser with constructive notice, is not whether he had the means of obtaining, and might by prudent caution have obtained, the knowledge in question,

but whether the act of not obtaining it was an act of gross or culpable negligence". – Ware *v* Lord Egmont (1854) 4 De GM and G 473.

The doctrine of constructive notice requires, therefore, that a purchaser should inspect the property; make proper enquiries as to the basis of any occupation and as to title; make enquiries of any land registration office or local government offices and, if possible, take possession of and examine carefully the title deeds. Called sometimes 'implied notice', although that term should be reserved for the form of actual notice which a person would glean from his knowledge of the facts, or the nature of the business and which does not need to be pointed out to an inquirer. Called also 'legal notice' or in the US, 'inquiry notice'.
cf. **imputed notice**. See also *caveat emptor*, **land charge, overriding interest, requisition, searches**.
Cheshire's Modern Law of Real Property, 13 edn., pp. 61–65.

constructive possession
see **possession**.

constructive trust
A **trust** that arises from an interpretation of the action of parties; in particular, a trust that arises when an owner has acquired property as a result of enrichment by another and it is only equitable for the owner to hold the property subject to the acknowledgement of the beneficial right of that other. The owner is considered to hold the property as a trustee for the **beneficiary** or *cestui que trust* who made the enrichment. "A constructive trust is the formula through which the conscience of equity finds expression. When property has been

acquired in such circumstances that the holder of the legal title may not in good conscience retain the beneficial interest, equity converts him into a trustee." – Beatty *v* Gugenheim Exploration Co. (1919) 225 NY 386. An agent who makes a profit as a result of performing the duties entrusted to him by his principal is a constructive trustee for those monies and must account to his principal in full.

"A resulting, implied or constructive trust – and it is unnecessary for the present purposes to distinguish between these three classes of trust – is created by a transaction between the trustee and the *cestui que trust* in connection with the acquisition by the trustee of a **legal estate** in land, whenever the trustee has so conducted himself that it would be inequitable to allow him to deny to the *cestui que trust* a beneficial interest in the land acquired." – Gissing *v* Gissing [1971] A.C. 905. A constructive trust does not arise out of "any express or presumed intention of the parties" (Snell's Principles of Equity, 28 edn., p. 192); in that respect it may be distinguished from an implied or **resulting trust** which arises from the implied aim or supposed intention of the parties. A constructive trust commonly arises when one person contributes towards the cost of a property that is held by another, expecting in the course of time to derive some benefit from, or obtain some interest in, the property. For example, when one party contributes towards a mortgage held by another (providing this contribution was not merely a gift, or a loan), a situation which not infrequently arises between co-habitees.

A constructive trust is considered to exist also when a binding contract for the sale of a legal estate has been executed; the vendor then holds the estate upon trust for the purchaser. The vendor is entitled to the rent and profits and must pay property outgoings up to the date fixed for completion; has a right to retain possession until the purchase monies are paid; and has a **lien** on the property in respect of any unpaid monies. However, the vendor must not wilfully damage or injure the property.

The doctrine of constructive trust originated in North America (based on the doctrine of **unjust enrichment** and **restitution**) and has been adopted by English law. Thus the Matrimonial Proceedings and Property Act 1970, s. 37 provides that where a husband or wife "contributes in money or money's worth to the improvement of real or personal property" then this contribution, provided it is of a "substantial nature", and there is no express or implied agreement to the contrary, is to be treated as creating, or enlarging, a beneficial interest in the property no matter who was the original beneficial owner. (This statutory provision may not necessarily be extended to other co-habitees or other relations, but the general principal that a constructive trust arises from contributions to the improvement of property, but not loans for the same purpose, may be applied in such cases – Hussey *v* Palmer [1972] 1 WLR 1286.

cf. **resulting trust**. See also **implied trust**, **matrimonial home**, **power of sale**.

Real Property and Real People, by K.J. Gray and P.D. Symes, pp. 477–482 (1981).

The Law of Real Property, by Robert Megarry and H.W.R. Wade, 5 edn., pp. 468–469.
The Modern Law of Trusts, by David B. Parker and Antony Mellows, 5 edn., pp. 160–175.

consuetudo est altera lex (L)
'A **custom** has the force of law'.

consumate
To bring (a transaction) to **completion**.

consumer price index (CPI)
An official index of consumer prices in the UK. Commonly used as an objective reference for adjusting lease rents to keep them in line with inflation. See also **indexation**.

contiguous
Derived from the Latin *continguus*, 'to touch closely'. In close proximity and usually, touching. A term that may be considered synonymous with **adjacent** or **adjoining** and is defined by the *Oxford English Dictionary* as 'in actual contact' or 'touching'. Although it has been said that, "there are three words, 'adjoining', 'adjacent', and 'contiguous', which lie not far apart in the meaning they convey. But of no one of them can its meaning be stated with exactitude and without exception . . . 'Contiguous' is perhaps of all three the least exact. Any one of the three may by its context be shown to convey 'neighbouring' without the necessity of physical contact." – Cave v Horsell [1912] 3 K B 544. Two properties on opposite sides of a road or river may be 'contiguous', because in such cases the ownership boundary extends *ad medium filum*, 'to the centre of the way', or *ad medium filum aquae*, 'to the centre of the river' – Micklethwait v Newlay Bridge Co. [1886] 33 Ch. D 133. See also **abut**.

contingence (F)
contingency.

contingency contract (US)
see **contingency fee**.

contingency fee (or commission)
1. A **fee** (or **commission**) payable upon the occurrence of a particular event, e.g. commission payable to an estate agent upon the introduction of a purchaser for a property who is **ready, able and willing** to buy. Called also a 'contingent fee' or an 'incentive fee'.
2. A fee payable to a lawyer or other professional advisor upon the successful outcome of litigation, especially when the amount represents a commission based on a percentage of the damages awarded to a client. The Royal Institution of Chartered Surveyors by-laws prohibit contingency fees for any matter that is "the subject of judicial or quasi-judicial proceeding". In the US, an agreement based on such an arrangement is called a 'contingency contract'. See also **champerty**.

contingency insurance
Insurance against a fortuitous, or specific contingent, liability. Insurance against a specific and foreseeable event that can be described in the policy (although the event may never happen), rather than against risks of a general nature. For example, insurance against loss due to known defects in the title to a property; or insurance against loss arising from an infringement of a long standing restrictive covenant or easement, where the beneficiary is unknown. The amount of loss payable under such a policy is normally quantified in the policy. In general all insurance is

based on a contingent event, but the term contingency insurance is more applicable to insurance against a specified loss – the insured is covering the event and the possible loss if the event occurs, rather than a property, person, or object. Called also 'contingent liability insurance'. See also **title insurance, valued policy.**

contingency reserve (US)
see **retainer.**

contingency sum
A provision in an **estimate**, for example, in a bill of quantities, to cover costs that cannot be ascertained at the time of preparing the estimate, but which are likely to occur; e.g. delays in building work due to inclement weather. See also **contingent liability, provisional sum.**

contingent business interruption insurance
see **consequential loss insurance.**

contingent contract
see **conditional contract.**

contingent debt
see **contingent liability.**

contingent estate
An **estate** that comes into effect on the happening of a 'contingent' event: that is, an event that may or may not happen. For example, a fee simple estate granted 'to A for life and then to B, or if B is not living to C', provides B with a contingent estate, or a 'contingent fee simple', which is dependent upon B outliving A. See also **contingent interest.**

contingent fee
see **contingency fee.**

contingent fee simple
see **contingent estate.**

contingent finance offer (US)
see **subject to finance.**

contingent interest
1. A **future interest** in property that depends on the fulfilment of a specified condition; an interest that arises upon the happening of an event that may or may not occur. An interest which is uncertain, either as to who will receive it or when it will arise. A contingent interest represents a prospect of having an interest in land, as contrasted with a **vested interest** which is a present or future right to land but one that will arise with the passage of time. For example, an interest granted 'to A and upon his death to X or Y, X taking in preference to Y, unless at that time Y has been accepted as a Chartered Surveyor'; or an interest granted to A 'when he becomes a Chartered Surveyor'. A contingent interest is an interest that may be disposed of (Law of Property Act 1925, s. 4 (2)), although at what value may tax the valuer's art to the extreme.
cf. **conditional interest**. See also **remainder, rule against perpetuities.**
2. Interest on a loan that is dependent on a contingent event, e.g. a given level of profit or income being available to a borrower. See also **equity participation.**

contingent liability (or debt)
A **liability** (or **debt**) that is not considered to be a definite obligation (in terms of its amount or its existence) but which will arise if a given event occurs. In accounting, a contingent liability refers to a sum set aside as a reserve against the possibility that an event that would require a payment might occur in the future. For example, a liability to pay rent as provided

by a surety on behalf of a lessee; or a payment arising as a result of an adverse decision on a legal action. There need be no certainty of the event occurring, only that a payment would be required if it occurs. Thus a contingent liability is one that may never arise as an actual debt; or it is "a debt the value of which is not ascertained". – Re. Dummelow *ex parte* Ruffle (1873) 8 Ch. App. 1001. See also **contingency insurance, guaranty**.

contingent liability insurance
see **contingency insurance**.

contingent remainder
see **remainder**.

contingent sale contract (US)
A contract of sale that is dependent upon a contingent event; in particular, a contract for the sale of a property made upon the basis that the final price or consideration will depend upon a future, uncertain, event. See also **conditional contract**.

continuing easement
see **apparent easement**.

contra bonos mores (L)
'Against public morals'. See **void contract**.

contra proferentum (L)
'Against the person who proffers.' A rule which provides that an instrument or a term of a contract shall be construed more strongly against the person who inserted, or will benefit most, from the provision. One of the cardinal rules of interpreting express contract being, "that in order to escape from the consequences of one's own wrongdoing, or that of one's servant, clear words are necessary." – Photo Production Ltd *v* Securicor Transport Ltd [1980] AC

846. See also **adhesion contract, exclusion clause, forfeiture clause**.

contract
Derived from the Latin *contrahere*, 'to draw together' or make a **bargain**. A deliberate promise or mutual agreement, between two or more parties, to do or not to do something, which is intended to be legally binding and enforceable, and is supported by consideration or evidenced under **seal**. In order that an agreement shall constitute a contract at law there must be an **offer**; an **acceptance** of that offer with the intent to bind the parties, i.e. a *consensus ad idem*; and the agreement must not infringe any rule of law. An intention to be legally bound may create an 'agreement'; the expression of a willingness to be bound may be a 'promise'; what is foreborne or foregone may constitute 'consideration'; but none of these alone constitutes a contract. In most cases, all three elements are essential to a contract; although other factors (an implication that gives effect to the intent, or a **deed** when there is no **consideration**) may support a missing element.

In summary, a contract should contain the following elements: (i) offer and unqualified acceptance; (ii) an agreement that demonstrates *consensus ad idem* and an intention to be legally committed by both parties; (iii) free and genuine consent; (iv) parties who have a legal capacity to contract; (v) an aim or intent that is legal; (vi) terms that are certain or capable of being rendered certain; and (vii) consideration of some value (however small), unless the contract is under seal.

A contract, and the terms therein,

may be **express**, that is clearly evidenced (either in writing or orally) by the parties; **implied** by the actions or conduct of the parties; or inferred from the known facts, circumstances or general language of the parties. A contract may be simple (parol); formal (speciality); or of record. A **simple contract** may be in writing, oral or implied. A **formal contract** is made by deed. A **contract of record** is one imposed upon parties *ab extra*, 'from outside', as by a court of law.

A contract may be unilateral or bilateral. With a **unilateral contract** the promisor undertakes to pay consideration to the promissee provided the latter performs, or does not perform, some action; with a **bilateral contract** (a *synallagmatic* contract) both parties accept or undertake obligations to each other. An estate agency contract frequently is unilateral as the agent only receives a remuneration if he performs the purpose of the contract, i.e. causes a sale of the property on the terms required by the principal. However, a **sole agency** contract may be bilateral where the agent will be remunerated on condition that he carries out certain duties for a specified period, e.g. advertising, negotiating, advising, etc.

In English law a contract for the sale of land differs in three important respects from most other contracts (i) it must be in **writing** or evidenced in writing and include an authorised **signature**, otherwise it may not be enforced by an action 'at law', unless there is a sufficient act of **part performance** (Law of Property Act 1925, s. 40); (ii) it is subject to the equitable doctrine of **specific performance**; and (iii) the vendor is obliged to prove

that he has a **good title** to the land he has contracted to transfer. See also **adhesion contract, assignment,** *assumpsit*, **breach of contract, building contract, contract for sale, contract of sale,** *contrat covenant*, **executed contract, executory contract, illegal contract, misrepresentation, novation, open contract, oral contract, performance, privity of contract, quasi-contract, repudiation, rescission, 'subject to contract', termination, void contract, voidable contract.**

An Introduction to the Law of Contract and Tort, by G.F. Bowden and A.S. Morris, (1978).
Cheshire and Fifoot's Law of Contract, 10 edn.
Anson's Law of Contract, 26 edn.
Chitty on Contracts, 25 edn.
9 Halsbury's Laws of England, paras. 201–699.

contract default (US)
see **breach of contract.**

contract for a lease
see **agreement for a lease.**

contract for deed (US)
A **contract** which provides that a seller will deliver a **deed** for the transfer of the subject property, i.e. will enter into a conveyance of the property when certain conditions (usually payment of the purchase price) have been fulfilled. See also **contract for sale (of land), escrow, instalment contract, land contract.**

contract for sale (of land)
1. A contract made for the sale or other disposition of land or an interest in land. Such a contract to be capable of forming the subject of an action 'at law' must be either (a) in **writing,** or some **memorandum** or **note** thereof must be evidenced in

writing; or (b) supported by a sufficient act of **part performance**, unless it is a sale made by order of a court of law (Law of Property Act, 1925, s. 40).

Upon completion of a valid contract for the sale of land, and prior to a **conveyance** of the land (or the interest therein), "the vendor becomes in equity a trustee for the purchaser of the estate sold, and the beneficial ownership passes to the purchaser, the purchaser having a right to the purchase money, a charge or lien on the estate for the security of that purchase money, and [the vendor has] a right to retain possession of the estate until the purchase money is paid, in the absence of express contract as to the time of delivering possession". – Lysaght v Edwards [1876] 2 Ch. D. 506.

cf. **contract of sale**. See also **beneficial owner, conditions of sale, estate contract, good title, open contract, 'subject to contract'**.
An Introduction to the Law of Sales of Land, by Raymond Walton, 3 edn.
Contract and Conveyance, by J.T. Farrand, 4 edn., pp. 15–227.
42 Halsbury's Laws of England, 4 edn., paras. 1–400.
William's Contract for Sale of Land and Title to Land, 4 edn., with 1983 Suppl.
(US) 2. An **executory contract** for the transfer of real estate. An agreement in writing specifying the parties, price, an adequate description of the property, and signed by the parties. A binding commitment by the parties which, after investigation of title, proceeds to a **closing** at which the purchase monies are paid and the seller usually delivers a deed of title. Called also a 'real estate contract',

'purchase contract', 'purchase and sale agreement', a 'buy-and-sell agreement' or simply an 'offer and acceptance'. See also **binder, conditional contract, instalment contract**.

Note: The definitions in paragraphs 1. and 2. are essentially the same, both indicating that a contract for the sale of land requires (a) to be in writing or evidenced in writing and (b) normally preceeds a more formal document by which the transfer is completed, title transferred and purchase monies paid (called a 'conveyance' in English law and a 'deed' – 'quit claim', 'warranty' or 'bargain and sale' – in the US). These requirements stem from English law, the former requirement from the **Statute of Frauds**; the latter from the common law requirement that real property should be transferred by a more formal manifestation than a mere contract or agreement for sale: historically there was a need for **livery of seisin**.
Real Estate Principles, by Bruce Harwood, 2 edn., pp. 149–162.
Real Estate Law, by Robert Kratovil and Raymond J. Werner, 8 edn., pp. 121–174.

contract of adhesion
see **adhesion contract**.

contract of indemnity
see **indemnity, insurance**.

contract of insurance
see **insurance policy**.

contract of record
A contract that results from an adjudication of a court of law and not from any agreement between the parties, such as a judgement of a court that a debt is owed by one party to another. The enforceability of a contract of

record depends entirely on the records of the court and not on the parties own understanding.

contract of sale

A **contract** in which a seller of property undertakes to transfer title to property, especially personal property, upon condition that the buyer completes the payment of the total consideration. A contract for the sale of goods. "A contract of sale of goods is a contract by which the seller transfers or agrees to transfer the property in goods to the buyer for money consideration, called the price ... a contract of sale may be absolute or conditional ... where under a contract of sale the property in the goods is transferred from the seller to the buyer the contract is called a **sale** ... where under a contract of sale the transfer of property is to take place at a future time or subject to some condition later to be fulfilled the contract is called an **agreement to sell** ... an agreement to sell becomes a sale when the time elapses or the conditions are fulfilled subject to which the property in the goods is to be transferred." (Sale of Goods Act 1979, s. 1). When the subject matter is land, or real property, a binding or absolute contract may be called a 'contract of sale', but to indicate that it is not a conditional contract the term 'contract for sale' is to be preferred. In the US if the contract is provisional (e.g. an earnest money contract) or conditional it may be called a 'contract to sell'. See also **contract for sale (of land), instalment contract, option.**

contract of tenancy

see **agreement for a lease, tenancy agreement.**

contract price (or sum)

The **consideration** paid under a contract. In a contract for the sale of real property, the contract price usually is the price received by the vendor before deducting any associated costs of effecting the sale. In a building contract it is the total sum paid by the employer or building owner to the contractor for performance and completion of the building works. See also **sale price.**

contract rent

The **rent** stipulated as actually payable under an existing lease. A term used to distinguish the lease rent from an **economic rent**, or from the **market rent** that could be obtained if the property were vacant and available for letting.

contract to sell (US)

see **contract of sale.**

contract time

see **'time is of the essence'.**

contract under seal

A contract made by **deed**. See also **contract for deed, seal, specialty.**

contract zoning (US)

see **planning agreement.**

contractor

Any person who enters into a **contract**. In particular, one who contracts to provide a service, to supply labour, or to perform building works. "A person who, in pursuit of an independent business, undertakes to do specific jobs of work for other persons, without submitting himself to their control in respect of detailed work." (Stroud's *Judicial Dictionary* 4 edn., citing Iron Co. *v* Dodson 7 Lea. 373), i.e., unlike an employee, a contractor is not controlled as to the detailed means by which he achieves the object or as to the exact purpose for which he is engaged. A building contractor undertakes to carry out and complete building work for an agreed financial consideration. He may be classified as a **general contractor** who undertakes an entire job, or a **sub-contractor** who performs subsidiary tasks, often of a specialised nature (e.g. tiling, plumbing), for the general contractor.

cf. **agent**. See also **builder, independent contractor**.

contractor's all-risks insurance policy

A policy of **insurance** provided to a building contractor against risks or damage that might arise during the contract period. Normally an **all-risks insurance policy** that covers all building works, plant, equipment, tools and machinery, and injury to employees and third-party liability.

A guide to the Indemnity and Insurance aspects of building contracts, by Peter Madge, pp. 138–175 (1985). *Company Insurance Handbook*, Association of Insurance and Risk Managers in Industry and Commerce, 2 edn., pp. 314–343, (1985). *Insurance for the Construction Industry*, by F.N. Eaglestone, (1979). *Contractor's All Risks and Public Liability Insurance*, by L.J. Piper, (1980).

contractor's basis

A method of **rating valuation** by which an 'effective capital value' or 'adjusted replacement cost' is estimated for the land and buildings and an **annual value** is then assessed by applying to the capital value a percentage rate of return considered appropriate for an investor in that type of property. The effective capital value for the land is based on the current cost of acquiring a suitable alternative site, and for the buildings is based on the cost of constructing a suitable alternative after allowing for depreciation or obsolescence. The intention is to ascertain the cost of a similar substitute property and decapitalise that figure to arrive at a hypothetical rental value. The use of this method of assessing the annual value of a property or 'hereditament' is based on the argument that a tenant will be unwilling to pay "more as an annual rent for a hereditament than it would cost him in the way of annual interest on the capital sum necessary to build a similar hereditament". – Dawkins (VO) *v* Royal Lemington Spa Corporation and Warwickshire County Council (1961) 178 E.G. 461. The contractor's basis is used especially when comparable rental evidence is not available, as with a property that has a limited or no ready market value, e.g. a church, school, hospital. This method is referred to sometimes as a method of "last resort" because it is used when other methods of rating valuation are unsuitable for the type of property involved. Nonetheless, "provided a valuer using this approach is sufficiently experienced, and is aware of what he is doing, and knows just how he is using his particular variant of the method, and provided he constantly keeps in mind what he is comparing with what, we [the Lands Tribunal] are satisfied that the contractor's basis provides a valuation instrument at least as precise as any other approach". – Cambridge University (Downing College) *v* Cambridge City Council and Allsop (1971) 208 EG 915. Referred to sometimes as a 'contractor's test' valuation. See also **depreciated replacement cost, reinstatement method of valuation**.

contractor's bond
see **performance bond**.

contractor's method of valuation
see **contractor's basis, reinstatement method of valuation**.

'contractor's test' valuation
see **contractor's basis**.

contractual licence
see **licence**.

contractual tenancy
A **tenancy** that arises from a contract between the parties, orally or in writing as contrasted with a **statutory tenancy** which arises by force of law. A contractual tenancy may be terminated in accordance with the terms of the contract, unless these are themselves superceded by statute. See also **express contract, lease**.

contrat (F)
contract; agreement. The French Civil Code art. 1101 defines a contract as, "an agreement by which one or several persons bind themselves, in favour of one or several other persons, to give, or to do, or not to do, something". When deciding upon the existence of a valid contract French law places greater emphasis on agreement, and the facts available to support that agreement, than on the search for the concurrence of offer and acceptance found in English common law (although the establishment of offer and acceptance are important elements in support of a *contrat*; in establishing when the *contrat* came into existence; and establishing the terms or conditions of that *contrat*). 'Hence it follows that in our [French] law we should not define a contract as it was defined by the interpreters of Roman law; *conventio nomen habens a jure civili vel causam* – "contract is a name from the civil law or given to a cause"; but that it should be defined, 'An agreement by which two parties reciprocally promise and engage, or one of them singly, promises and engages to the other to give some particular thing, or do or abstain from doing some particular act.' (*A Treatise on the Law of Obligations or Contracts*, by M. Pothier, (trans. W.D. Evans) Vol. i, p. 4, 1806). French law does not require consideration as an essential element in a contract, but article 1108 of the Civil Code sets down four requirements of a valid contract: *le consentement*, consent (autonomy of will); capacity of the parties; an *objet*; and a legal *cause*. In French law, as well as the requirements for legality, a contract must be free of a defect arising from a mistake (*erreur*) as to the object itself of the contract; fraud or misrepresentation (*dol*); and any element of duress or undue influence (*violence*). Contracts are divided in the Civil Code, arts. 1102–1107 into (i) **bilateral contracts** and **unilateral contracts**; (ii) onerous contracts and gratuitous contracts, according to the purpose of the person obliged by the contract i.e. whether or not he confers an advantage intending to receive a reciprocol advantage; (iii) aleatory (conditional) contracts and commutative contracts, depending whether or not the contract is subject to an uncertain event (an insurance contract is an aleatory contract, as it depends on an uncertain event); (iv) nominative contracts and innominative contracts, the former coming within a

form envisaged by the Civil Code and the latter being entirely dependent on the intention of the parties. Contracts also may be divided into (a) consensual, essentially all forms of bilateral contracts based on agreement: sale, hire, partnership, mandate; (b) formal, most forms of contract must be in writing to be enforceable in French law, but certain contracts must be made by notarial deed (*acte authentique*) – in particular gifts of property (*contrat de bienfaisance*), marriage, mortgages, subrogation of a debt, and assignment of a patent; (c) real, where a thing (*res*) is transferred to another upon the understanding that it will be returned, e.g. a loan for use (*prêt à usage* or *commodat*), a deposit (*dépôt*) and a pledge (*gage*).
(*contrat à prix forfaitaire*, or *à forfait* – **fixed-price contract**)
(*contrat à titre onereux* – onerous contract)
(*contrat aleatoire* – **aleatory contract**)
(*contrat d'achat* – **bill of sale**).

contrat d'adhésion (F)
   adhesion contract.
   (*contrat d'hypothèque* – **mortgage deed**)
   (*contrat de bienfaisance* or *de donation* – **deed of gift**)
   (*contrat de gage* – **bailment**)
   (*contrat de vente* – **contract of sale**)
   (*contrat leonin* – **unconsionable bargain**)
   (*contrat synallagmatique* or *bilateral* – **bilateral contract**)
   (*contrat translatif de propriété* – **conveyance**)
   (*contrat type* – **standard contract**)
   (*contrat verbal* – **oral contract**)
   (*projet de contrat* – **draft agreement**)
   (*rupture de contrat* – **breach of contract**). See also *acte, convention,*

quasi-contract.
Amos & Walton's Introduction to French Law, 3 edn., pp. 149–191.
Droit Civil 1er année, by Jean Chevalier and Louis Bach, 8 edn., pp. 365–390.
French Law of Contract, by Barry Nicholas, (1982).
Manuel de Droit Civil, by Pierre Voirin and Gilles Goubeaux, 20 edn., p. 312 *et seq.*
Droit Civil, Les Obligations by Jean Carbonnier, 7 edn. pp. 43–280.
Précis Dalloz. Droit Civil, Les Obligations, 3 edn., pp. 25–654.
Droit Civil, Les Obligations, by Gabriel Marty and Pierre Raynaud, pp. 25–286, (1962).
Droit Civil, Obligations, by Boris Starck, pp. 339–668, (1972).

contre-lettre (F)
   counter-letter, see *simulation.*

contre-mur (F)
   retaining wall.

contrepartie (F)
   1. other party (in a transaction).
   2. **counterpart** (of a deed).

contribution (F)
   contribution; tax.
   (contributions foncière – **land tax**; property taxes; real estate tax)
   (*contribution mobilière* – property tax, similar to rates in England). See also *taxe.*

contribution clause
   1. A clause in an insurance policy which provides that, when there is more than one insurer covering the same risk, liability is to be divided equitably between the insurers. Thus if a policy on a building includes cover for third-party liability, which is covered also by a separate policy

with a different insurer, the insured may not recover his loss twice. Called also an 'apportionment clause'. See also **double insurance.** (US) 2. See **average clause.**

contribution to service charge
see **apportionment, service charge.**

contributory mortgage
see **joint mortgage.**

contributory negligence
An act of **negligence** that directly causes or contributes to a person's own loss or injury and acts as a defence to a claim of negligence against another. Contributory negligence is not a complete defence but damages recoverable for negligence are to be reduced to such an extent as the court thinks just and equitable having regard to the plaintiff's share in responsibility for the loss or injury (Law Reform (Contributory Negligence) Act 1945). See also *volenti non fit injuria.*

control order
An order made by a local authority, under the provisions of the Housing Act 1964, s. 73, which enables the authority to take over the management of a **lodging house** or any other house in multiple occupation when it is considered necessary to do so in order to protect the "safety, welfare or health of persons living in the house". The order permits the local authority to take possession of the house, to control the management, and receive income from the occupiers of the building. The authority is required to prepare a 'scheme' for capital expenditure that it considers necessary to improve the living conditions of the occupiers. Such an order may take effect for a period of up to

five years. At the end of the period for which the order is effective the net cost incurred by the authority may be recovered from the dispossessed proprietor and, if unpaid, any balance becomes a **charge** on the property. There is a right of appeal against a control order to the county court, either because the proprietor considers the order unnecessary or that the works or other proposals required by the scheme are unreasonable (1964 Act, s. 82, 83). See also **local land charge.**
West's Law of Housing, 4 edn., pp. 135–138.
Manual of Housing Law, by Andrew Arden, 2 edn., pp. 255–258.

controle des loyers (F)
rent control.

controlled rent
1. Rent payable under a **controlled tenancy.** See also **standard rent.**
2. A rent that is subject to any form of **rent control.** See also **fair rent.**

controlled tenancy
A form of tenancy that was subject to stringent rent control provision as set out in the Rent Acts, in particular the Rent Act 1968, s. 52 and Rent Act 1957, s. 17. Any controlled tenancy subsisting on 28 November 1980 was either converted into a **regulated tenancy** or, if it included a predominant business user, into a **business tenancy** (Housing Act 1980, s. 64). See also **converted tenancy.**

conurbation
A loosely integrated urban area, comprising a number of towns or villages that are not totally integrated, but form a single socio-economic unit. A continuous grouping of parcels of built-up land, which may

enclose parks and rural land, but are not delimited by a significant area of agricultural land. See also **urban region**.

convenience lease (US)

A lease entered into solely to provide an income for the landlord as compared to one granted to an intending occupier. In particular, a lease to a credit-worthy tenant to provide a form of guaranty to a mortgagee. See also **component financing, head lease**.

convention (F)

agreement; covenant. In French law the term *convention* is more extensive than *contrat*; it embraces a contract, but also may cover any agreement that creates, modifies or extinguishes an obligation. (*convention de transfer de bien* – conveyance of property).

conventional mortgage (or loan) (US)

A mortgage (or loan) between two parties where no third party, such as a Federal Agency, is involved as guarantor. See also **surety**.

conversion

1. The process of turning real property into money or *vice-versa*, i.e. the sale or purchase of real property for money. The exchange of **real property** for **personal property** or *vice-versa*.

In equity certain rights to real property are regarded merely as personal property, i.e. as a right to the proceeds of sale of realty; rather than the realty *per se*, in particular when property is left under a settlement upon **trust for sale**. This premise follows from the maxim that 'equity looks on that as done which ought to be done' so that, as the intention of the settlement is that the property should be sold eventually and the proceeds of sale held by the trustees for the profit of the beneficiaries, the interest of the beneficiaries is notionally 'converted' into an interest in the proceeds of sale – this is the equitable doctrine of conversion: "... money directed to be employed in the purchase of land and land directed to be sold and turned into money, are to be considered as that species of property into which they are directed to be converted". – Fletcher *v* Ashburner (1779) 1 Bro. CC 499. In modern English law this doctrine is coming to be regarded as a fiction, so that the beneficiary is considered to retain a 'real' right to or, at least, an equitable interest in the property itself until it is actually sold – especially when the subject matter is a **matrimonial home** (Williams and Glyn's Bank Ltd *v* Boland [1980] 3 WLR 146). See also **overreached interest, reconversion**.
Real Property and Real People, by K.J. Gray and P.D. Symes, pp. 220–227 (1981).
2. The sale of real property on the instruction of a court in order to satisfy a debt.
3. An intentional and unjustifiable retention or use of another's goods in a manner that amounts to a denial or contradiction of that person's right to the goods. Wrongfully or illegally taking, receiving or keeping possession, using, altering, disposing of withholding or destroying the goods of another can all amount to acts of conversion; provided there is an intentional action that is inconsistent with the dominion and control of the goods. "Conversion consists in an act intentionally done inconsistent with the owner's right, though the doer

may not know of or intend to challenge the property or possession of the true owner." – Caxton Publishing Co. *v* Sutherland Publishing Co. [1939] AC 202. Conversion is a **tort** which is called also 'trover' and it may be contrasted with **trespass** to goods which consists of a direct interference with possession without necessarily claiming or ascertaining any title or right to the goods, e.g. removing them without permission – Fouldes *v* Willoughby (1841) 8 M and W 540. Conversion now includes **detinue** which has been abolished (although an action to recover goods wrongfully taken is referred to sometimes as an 'action for detinue'). Conversion of goods, trespass to goods, negligence so far as it results in damage to goods, and any other tort resulting in damage to goods is now called 'wrongful interference with goods' – Tort (Interference with Goods) Act 1977, s. 1. An action to recover such goods is called an action for conversion, or for wrongful interference, and an action for loss or destruction of goods by a bailee in breach of his duty to his bailor is called also an action for conversion (1977 Act, s. 2 (2)). See also **market overt**.
4. A change in the nature of a property either by a substantial change of user, or by structural works that change its function – e.g. from a single dwelling into flats; from a warehouse to a leisure centre. See also **material change in the use**.
5. A change in the form in which the ownership of property is held, e.g. from several ownership to co-ownership. See also **condominium conversion**.
6. The substitution of one form of guaranty, surety or means of financ-

ing for another. See also **refinancing**.
7. The addition of **accrued interest** to the outstanding principal on a loan so that the total debt then bears interest. See also **compound interest**.

conversion (F)
conversion.
(*conversion de saisie en vente* – official sale by public auction of a property taken by a **seizure**).

converted tenancy
A tenancy that has been converted from a **controlled tenancy** to a **regulated tenancy**. Prior to the Housing Act 1980, certain tenancies of dwellinghouses (controlled tenancies) were subject to strict rent levels – essentially based on a multiplier of the rateable value. Such tenancies could be converted to regulated tenancies in certain instances (e.g. following improvements made by the landlord) and all such tenancies were so converted in 1980 (Housing Act 1980, s. 64).

convertible mortgage (US)
A mortgage loan which provides that the lender may acquire, or increase, an **equity** share in the property held as security in lieu of accepting repayment of the principal due under the loan. A convertible mortgage agreement provides usually that the mortgagee has an option at certain intervals to replace the outstanding debt with a direct investment of his own funds in the property. After these intervals interest is payable on the outstanding principal, if any, and normally the mortgagee receives a **preferred return** on the amount of equity he has invested. A convertible mortgage is a form of joint venture between the mortgagee and the owner

or developer of the property. The arrangement frequently starts entirely as **debt financing** and is converted at a later stage into **equity participation**. See also **leveraged buy-out.**

conveyance

1. A **transfer** of property or a means by which property is transferred from one person to another; in particular, a transfer of a **legal estate**, but not the creation, or means for the creation, of a new interest or right to property.

2. An **instrument** that transfers, voluntarily, a **title** to real property from one party to another. 'Conveyance' means to purchase (in the strict sense of a positive act of acquisition and not through descent) and the instrument is referred to also as a 'deed of grant' or 'deed of conveyance'. In particular, a conveyance means a deed that effects a **sale** of land: a voluntary transaction to transfer land is called either a 'deed of gift' or a 'settlement' (according to the circumstances).

The term conveyance may be used to include, for example, "a mortgage, charge, lease, assent, vesting declaration, vesting instrument, disclaimer, release and every other assurance of property or an interest therein by any instrument except a will" (Law of Property Act 1925, s. 205 (1)). (The Land Charges Act 1972, s. 17 (1) contains a similar definition but excludes 'disclaimer'). In the US a similar broad interpretation of 'conveyance' is used so that a *lis pendens* may be a conveyance – In Putman Sand and Gravel Co. *v* Albers, 92 Cal. Rptr. 636, 14 CA 3d 722).

In English law a conveyance of land shall be deemed to include with the land "all buildings, erections, fix-tures, commons, hedges, ditches, fences, ways, waters, watercourses, liberties, privileges, easements, rights, and advantages whatsoever, appertaining or reputed to appertain to the land, or any part thereof", and land with buildings thereon conveys the buildings as well as "all outhouses, erections, fixtures, cellars, areas, courts, court-yards, cisterns, sewers, gutters, drains, ways, passages, lights ..." which go with the land and buildings, unless any of these things are expressly excluded (Law of Property Act 1925, s. 62 (1) & (2)). A conveyance transfers also the entire estate or interest held by the conveying party: prior to 1881 an 'all the estate' clause was inserted to that effect, but such a clause is no longer necessary as it is provided for by statute (Conveyancing Act 1881, s. 63, now replaced by the Law of Property Act 1925, s. 63).

Any conveyance of land or an interest in land is void for the purpose of transferring a **legal estate**, unless made by **deed**, except for (a) an assent by personal representatives; (b) disclaimers by a trustee in bankruptcy; (c) a lease for a term not exceeding three years; (d) vesting orders of the court; (e) receipts that need not be made under seal; and (f) surrenders or conveyances which operate by law (Law of Property Act 1925, s. 52 (1)). This provision applies to the grant of a **legal easement** or a **legal mortgage**, provided it is intended to transfer a right to a legal estate; in certain cases, to the grant of a **legal lease**; and in all cases, to the assignment of a legal lease.

A conveyance may contain the following clauses: (i) **parties**; (ii) **recitals**; (iii) **testatum**; (iv) **parcels**; (v) **operative clause**; (vi) **habendum, teden-**

dum, and, in a lease, a **reddendum**;
(vii) **testimonium**; (viii) **attestation**. In
addition there may be conditions or
covenants set out in the instrument
and a **certificate for value**.
cf. **assignment**. See also **beneficial
owner, contract for sale (of land),
delivery, fraudulent conveyance**.
Real Property, by William E. Burby,
3 edn., pp. 281–312.
Cheshire's Modern Law of Real
Property, 13 edn., pp. 721–735.
Contract and Conveyance, by J.T.
Farrand, 4 edn., pp. 221–330.
Practical Conveyancing, by Edward
Moeran, 9 edn.
Conveyancing Law and Practice, by
D.G. Barnsley, 2 edn.
Conveyancing, by I.R. Storey, (1983).
Modern Conveyancing, by Ruth
Annand and Brian Cain (1984).

conveyance tax (US)
A State tax imposed on the transfer
or conveyance of an interest in real
property. Called also a 'transfer tax'.
See also **registration duty**.

convivium
A form of feudal **tenure** by which a
tenant was bound to provide meat
and drink to his lord at least once a
year. See also **feudal system**.

cooperating broker (US)
see **joint agent**.

cooperative ownership
A means of holding a property, such
as an apartment, by which a corporation (or trust) is formed to hold the
land and buildings and the shareholders (or beneficiaries) have a right
to occupy part of the property. An
occupancy or **proprietory lease** is
entered into between the owning corporation (or trust) and the shareholder (or beneficiaries) permitting

them to have exclusive occupation of
a part of the property and usually
common rights over other parts of the
property e.g. entrance areas, staircases, lifts, etc. Unlike any form of
co-ownership or the ownership of a
condominium, the shareholders (or
beneficiaries) have no right of ownership to any part of the property as
ownership is vested in the corporation (or trustees). If a cooperative
owner (called in the US a 'tenant-
cooperator') wishes to dispose of this
interest he sells his shares (or assigns
his beneficial interest). This form of
ownership is more common in the US
than the UK.
In the UK cooperative ownership is
used mostly when a **housing cooperative** is created which owns, in the
form of a company (or trust) a group
of houses or flats and the shareholders (or beneficiaries) are granted
occupancy leases. However, the occupiers do not normally participate in
the growth in the capital value of the
houses as this is retained by the owning company (or trustees) and reflected in the rent charged to the
occupiers.
cf. **property trust**. See also **time-
sharing**.
Real Estate Law, by Robert Kratovil
and Raymond J. Werner, 8 edn., pp.
528–534.
Condominiums and Cooperatives, by
David Clurman, F. Scott Jackson
and Edna L. Hebard, 2 edn.

cooperator (US)
A shareholder or beneficiary in **co-
operative ownership**.

co-ownership
Ownership of an interest in one property held by two or more persons concurrently; usually as a **tenancy in**

common or a **joint tenancy**. 'Co-ownership' includes also **co-parcenary** and **tenancy by entireties**. The former is obsolete for all practical purposes and the latter was abolished in English law in 1925, although in the US it still exists in some States. Co-ownership essentially is a right to the use and possession by two or more owners of the whole of the subject property. It may be distinguished from **collective ownership** which is a right to separate ownership of one of a group of properties or units of a property (e.g. apartments), combined with a right to common user or co-ownership of certain ancilliary property, such as the common parts of a block of flats or a housing estate (open land, roads, etc.). Co-ownership should also be distinguished from successive rights to the ownership of the same property i.e. rights, which follow one another, to an estate in the same land. In the US, the term 'co-ownership' or 'co-tenancy' is used as a collective name for the forms of co-ownership originating from English common law (as referred to above), as well as for the ownership of a **condominium** and collective ownership. Called also 'joint ownership', ownership of a **concurrent interest** or, in the US, ownership of 'estates and interests in community'.

cf. **several ownership**. See also **partnership, trust for sale**.

Co-ownership Schemes for Commercial Property, by R.G. Finch and M.J. Day, 244 E.G. 280 (1977).

Real Property and Real People, by K.J. Gray and P.D. Symes, pp. 232–312 (1981).

co-ownership tenancy

A tenancy granted to a person who also has a share in the capital value of the property that is the subject of the tenancy. In particular, a tenancy of a dwelling-house granted by a **housing association** to a member of the association who, upon ceasing to be a member thereof, receives a share in the capital value of the dwelling-house (Housing Act 1980, Sch. 10, para. 1 (4)). See also **housing trust, shared ownership**.

coparcenary

An interest in land that arose in English law prior to 1925 either when land descended on intestacy to two or more persons as if they constituted one heir ('parceners', 'coparceners' or 'co-heirs') or because of the local custom of **gavelkind**. The former applied only to daughters (for whom there is no hereditary rule of primogeniture) and the latter to sons. "An estate held in coparcenary is where lands of inheritance descend from the ancestors to two or more persons ... and ... all the parceners put together make one heir; and have but one estate among them." (Bl. Comm. vol ii. p. 187). Gavelkind and most forms by which land descended to heirs on intestacy have been abolished (Administration of Estates Act 1925, s. 45 (1)). Since 1925 a coparcenary may arise only in certain cases when an owner of an **entailed interest**, being an estate that is limited to heirs of a body, dies leaving daughters to inherit. In such cases, the estate passes according to the old rules of descent on intestacy and it is held in trust for sale for the daughters who hold an equitable interest as if they were tenants in common. Called also 'tenancy by coparcenary'. See also **tenancy in common**.

The Law of Real Property, by Robert Megarry and H.W.R. Wade, 5 edn., pp. 456–460.

coparceners

see **coparcenary**.

coppice or copse

A small wood left to grow with underwood, so as to provide trees for felling as fuel. See also **tree preservation order**.

copyhold

A form of feudal tenure by which land was held by a peasant according to the custom of a **manor**. In the Middle Ages some peasants, villein tenants, were permitted to cultivate manorial land for their own use, as long as they rendered customary services or dues to the lord of the manor. They held the land on **villeinage or villein tenure**, i.e. at the will of their lord; they were obliged to render servile duties to the lord; and they had little protection from instant dismissal. However, in certain cases, the right of such a tenant to the use of land, together with details of the services to be rendered, could be entered on the manorial court rolls, a copy of which provided evidence of 'title', whence the term copyhold. "'Copyhold' is a tenure for which the tenant hath nothing to shew but the Copies of the Rolles made by the Steward of his Lord's Court." – Termes de La Ley. This right was not recognised at common law, but could be enforced by a Court of Chancery.

Copyhold could be held for a term of years; for life; or by inheritance (although copyhold by inheritance was subject to a **fine** if it passed by succession). By the 17th century servile or villein tenure had become extinct, the services being either more clearly defined or commuted to money payments; the term 'copyhold' being applied only to tenures that were recorded on the manorial rolls and benefited from the right for the land to pass to the descendants by inheritance. By the 18th century virtually all services rendered by copyholders had been commuted into money payments; many of the tenants had surrendered their 'copy' for a leasehold interest and some had acquired a freehold interest. All remaining copyholds were converted from 1 January 1926 into free and common **socage** or, as it is called today, **freehold** (Law of Property Act 1922, s. 128). See also **doctrine of tenure**.

An Introduction to the History of Land Law, by A.W.B. Simpson, pp. 145 *et seq.* (1961).

9 Halsbury's Laws of England, 4 edn., paras. 751–800.

corner plot or lot

A plot of land or a property situated at an intersection and thereby having a frontage to two streets. A plot of land or a building, especially a shop, situated on a corner of two streets, with a return frontage, is considered to have a similar value on each frontage. Thus, the 'Baltimore method of appraisal' assumes that such a plot has a value equal to the combined value of two ordinary plots. Using the **zoning method** of valuation, the front zone 'A' extends the same depth from each frontage.

corporation

An association or artificial succession of persons formed together, under one name, in such a way that they are incorporated by law into an entity that has an existence independent of the individuals who, from time to time, make up that entity. A corporation may be made up of one person – a 'corporation sole', or two or more persons – a 'corporation aggregate'. A corporation has the same capacity as an individual to acquire, hold and dispose of land.

cf. **partnership**. See also **company, mortmain**.

corporation mortgage bond

A **bond** issued by a corporation and secured as a mortgage on the fixed assets of that corporation. See also **debenture, fixed charge**.

corporeal hereditament

An inheritable right to real property; a right that is tangible, that "affects the senses, such as may be seen and handled by the body" (Bl. Comm. vol. ii p. 17), e.g. land, buildings, trees, minerals and fixtures. "All property, of whatever kind, is an incorporeal right to the corporeal use and profit of some corporeal thing" (S.M. Leake, (1857) *1 Jurid. Soc.* p. 542).

cf. **incorporeal hereditament**. See also **hereditament**.

corporeal property (or things)

Property (or **things**) that have a material existence, i.e. are tangible and palpable, such as land or goods; as distinguished from **incorporeal property** which is merely a right to property that exists in contemplation. Corporeal property, if capable of being moved, is transferred by **exchange** of physical possession; if incapable of being moved, is transferred by **grant**. See also **chattels, fixture**.

corporels, biens (F)
see *biens*.

copropriété (F)

co-ownership. (note: French law recognises no distinction between a tenancy in common and a joint tenancy as found in English law, there being no right of survivorship between co-owners in French law. Each *copropriétaire* has a distinct right to a share of the property and this right can be alienated or mortgaged by each party independently).

(*règlement de copropriété* – co-ownership regulation). See also *communauté, indivision, moityenneté*.

Amos & Walton's Introduction to French Law, 3 edn., pp. 116–118.

Droit Civil, Les Biens, by Jean Carbonnier, 11 edn., pp. 124–128, 258–268. Précis Dalloz. Droit Civil, Les Biens, by Alex Weill, 2 edn., pp. 179–187.

La Copropriété, by F. Givord et C. Giverdon, (1983).

corpus possessionis (L)

Actual **possession** of a thing. True or legal possession must include an intention to possess – *animus possidendi*.

correction deed (US)
see **rectification**.

correlation process (US)

The process in an **appraisal** of giving weight to the different factors that affect the value of a property; or, when different approaches to an appraisal have been applied, arriving at a final figure by balancing the importance of the result obtained from each approach.

correspondence, contract by
see **open contract**.

cost

The amount given, exchanged, or bartered for something that is acquired. A **price** actually paid or expended for property received or services rendered. The total expenditure or outlay, whether as money or money's worth, on acquiring possession of a property. Generally cost is measured in pecuniary terms, but it may be measured in any way that reflects the disutility or endeavour of acquiring something. A cost may be said to precede a price, because theoretically it is necessary to consider the cost before determining a price. The cost of a property may be based on an amount of money or money's worth parted with in order to acquire something – **acquisition cost**; or may be based on the amount that needs to be parted with in order to acquire something – **replacement cost**. However, a cost deduced from an amount that needs be parted with to acquire something is more akin to the **value**, than cost, to which it might bear no relation. A sum of money or outlay that has been incurred is a cost but when that amount is allocated to a person, fund or object it becomes a **charge** or expense – Re Beddoe, Downes v Cottam [1893] 1 Ch. 554. See also **basis, book cost, expenditure, historic cost, reinstatement cost, reproduction cost**.

cost approach (US)

A method of ascertaining the value of a property by assessing the **reproduction cost** or **replacement cost** of a building and adding the estimated value of the land. This method is based on the presumption that a purchaser is prepared to pay the same sum for a property as he would pay to acquire a site and reproduce or build a similar alternative. However, this presumption has limited validity and the method should be used as a last resort, i.e. when other methods have no more validity. "A building is worth its cost of replacement provided it is new, represents the highest and best use of the site, and provided its construction is justified by the expected return which it will produce." (*The Valuation of Real Estate*, by Frederick M. Babcock, p. 477, 1932). Called sometimes the 'replacement cost approach', the 'reinstatement cost approach', or the 'summation approach'. See also **reinstatement method of valuation**.
Appraisal of Real Estate, AIREA, 8 edn., pp. 441–450.

cost basis (US)

see **basis**.

cost-benefit analysis (CBA)

An analytical technique for assessing the benefits to be derived from a project, taking account of monetary and social advantages, and setting those benefits against the total financial and social cost (the **opportunity-cost**) that arises from undertaking that project. All gains and losses, arising directly or indirectly from the project, are given a unit of value (in terms of money or on a scale of importance) and are either weighed against each other or applied in a **discounted cash flow** analysis. A technique commonly applied to major government schemes or planning proposals, such as a new airport or a new town development; although the result tends to be dependent on the value-judgement of the governing body of the day. See also **feasibility study**.
The Economics of Real Property, by J. Harvey, pp. 132–159 (1981).

Modern Cost-Benefit Methods, by George Irvin, (1978)
Cost-Benefit Analysis, by E.J. Mishan, (1975).
Cost-Benefit Analysis, by D.W. Pearce, 2 edn.
Principles of Practical Cost-Benefit Analysis, by Robert Sugden and Alan Williams (1978).

cost estimating
see **quantity surveying, valuation**.

cost-in-use
The cost of a property measured according to its total recurring cost of use and occupation. Determining the cost-in-use is a means of comparing the financial implications of alternative projects by which all costs are reduced to an annual figure. The 'cost-in-use' is assessed especially to compare the cost of alternative building designs – the development costs are converted to an **annual equivalent** over the anticipated economic life of the building and the annual running costs added to arrive at the total annual cost. Alternatively the total cost of a building or project may be ascertained over a given period of time, taking into account the capital cost and all future recurring costs, and then the present annual value ascertained by means of a **discounted cash flow** analysis. See also **carrying charges, occupancy cost, virtual rent**.

cost-less-depreciation approach
see **depreciated replacement cost, reinstatement method of valuation**.

cost-of-living clause
A clause in a contract, especially a lease, which provides that the price, or rent, will be varied in line with a cost of living index. See also **indexation, rent escalation**.

cost of replacement method
see **reinstatement method of valuation, replacement cost**.

cost of reproduction
see **reproduction cost**.

cost-pass-through clause (US)
see **escalator clause**.

cost-plus contract
A form of contract (especially a **building contract**) in which the price is based on the actual cost (the prime cost of labour, materials and plant as incurred by the contractor) plus a fixed fee, or a fixed percentage, added for overheads and profit. (If the fixed fee addition is adopted the contract is called a 'cost-plus fixed fee contract'). A cost-plus contract is used especially when the extent of the building work is difficult to ascertain at the outset: for example, when part of the proposed work is inaccessible at the time of the estimate; when considerable variations in the employer's requirements may be necessary; or when there is insufficient time to make a reasonable estimate of the cost. In this form of contract a large part of the risk of cost variations is passed from the building contractor to the employer. A variant of the cost-plus contract is the 'target-cost contract' by which a target cost is stipulated and on completion the difference between the actual cost and the target cost is apportioned between the employer and contractor on the basis of an agreed formula. Called also a 'cost-reimbursement contract' or a 'prime-cost contract'.
cf. **fixed-price contract**.

cost-reimbursement contract
see **cost-plus contract**.

cost rent
see **economic rent**.

cotenancy
see **co-ownership, joint tenancy**.

cottage
1. A small **dwelling-house** situated in the country or in a village, generally with little or no land, other than a garden, attached to it; especially a house of some antiquity. Historically a cottage was "a little house for habitation of poore men, without any land belonging unto it" – Termes de La Ley, but in modern usage the term is applied to any small, and usually quaint, country or village dwelling-house, especially a dwelling that would at one time have been occupied by an agricultural labourer.
2. A small dwelling used for summer use and, generally, detached and of no more than two storeys.

cottage garden
An **allotment** attached to a cottage. See also **cottage holding**.

cottage holding
A dwelling-house, or cottage, together with not less than a quarter of an acre and not more than one acre of agricultural land which can be cultivated by the occupier of the house and his family (Agricultural Land (Utilisation) Act 1931, s. 20 (1)). Such holdings were let by local authorities to encourage the better utilisation of agricultural land, but being no longer economically viable they have mostly disappeared.

couchant
Lying down; squatting. See also **levant et couchant**.

council house
A dwelling-house owned by a local government body to meet the special housing needs of the area under its administration. Council houses are built and retained by local authorities for letting to approved tenants (generally families with low incomes or special requirements). See also **secure tenancy**.
Landlord and Tenant Law, by David Yates and A.J. Hawkins, pp. 393–426 (1981).
West's Law of Housing, 4 edn., Ch. 11.
Housing Law, by Andrew Arden and Martin Partington, pp. 702–780 (1983).
Council Housing, by D.C. Hoath, 2 edn.

counsel
see **barrister**.

counsel's opinion
see **barrister**.

counter-cyclical development process
The tendency for property development to be out of phase with general economic **cycles** due to the time lags of the planning and building processes. A developer starts planning a new project during an up-turn in the economic cycle but may not complete the building process until the cycle has ebbed; thus new buildings may continue to arrive on the market during a recession. Conversely, a general economic up-turn tends to increase interest rates, which may eventually reduce demand for property and may create bottlenecks, both of which reduces the supply of new development; thus a shortage of buildings may occur when the economy is otherwise at its most active.

counter-notice
A formal response to a **notice**, usually given in accordance with a statutory

provision. For example, notice given by a holder of a **business tenancy** in response to a landlord's notice to terminate the tenancy; or a notice served by a local authority stating that it objects to a **purchase notice** or a **blight notice**. Frequently the server of the counter-notice is claiming certain rights, such as a right to a new tenancy, or not to be bound by the original notice.

counter-offer
A response to an **offer** proposing one or more conditions or terms which are at variance with the basis of the offer. A counter-offer has the effect of rejecting the offer and, therefore, at law does not constitute an **acceptance**. It must in turn be accepted by the original offeror to create a binding contract. As a rule, a counter-offer is intended to be more than a mere request for information or a means of seeking to clarify the terms of the original offer; it may create an offer in its own right. See also **'subject to contract'**.

counterpart
Historically one of the two parts of an **indenture**, but nowadays the principal copy of a deed used when a document is executed in duplicate, especially a copy of a lease or conveyance. The original and counterpart of a document are signed and then exchanged between the parties, the grantee (or tenant) retaining the original (which was prepared by the grantor) and the grantor (or landlord) the counterpart. The original of a deed prevails as the correct document, unless there is clearly a mistake therein and then the counterpart may be brought into account.

Countryside Commission
An organisation established under the Countryside Act 1968 to review the provision of facilities for the enjoyment of the countryside; the conservation and enhancement of its natural beauty; and the need for public access. A body that replaced the National Parks Commission which had been set up in 1942 for a similar purpose. See also **area of outstanding natural beauty, national park**.
Introduction to Town and Country Planning, by John Ratcliffe, 2 edn., pp. 310–313.

county council
see **local authority**.

county matter
see **planning authority**.

'coupled with an interest'
see **agency, licence**.

coupon rate
see **nominal yield**.

cour (F)
1. courtyard.
2. court (of justice).

cours (F)
1. rate; price.
(*cours du marché* – **market price**; market value).
2. course.
(*cours d'eau* – **watercourse**; river; stream).

courtesy
see **curtesy**.

courtier (F)
broker.
(*courtier en immeubles* – land agent; realtor). See also *agent*.

courtyard
A term derived from **curtilage**, but

generally limited to an enclosed area, commonly walled-in and hard surfaced, around a dwelling-house.

coût (F)

cost.

(*coût d'acquisition initial* – **historic cost**)

(*coût d'exploitation* – **operating costs**)

(*coût de remplacement* – **replacement cost**).

covenant

1. Derived from the Latin *convenire*, 'to come together'. A **promise** or **agreement** in writing and under **seal** in which two or more parties accept an obligation to do, or not to do, something; the parties acknowledge that a certain state of affairs exists; or one or more parties stipulates the truth of certain facts. "No particular form of words is necessary to form a covenant: but, wherever the court can collect from the instrument an engagement on the one side to do or not to do something, it amounts to a covenant, whether it is in the recitals or in any other part of the instrument." – Great Northern Railway Co. *v* Harrison (1852) 12 CB 609. A covenant, because it is part of a contract or deed, must comply with the same rules as those applicable to the contract or deed. The term covenant may be used also to refer to a stipulation in writing in any agreement that should be made by deed, especially in a **lease** – Hayne *v* Cumming (1864) 16 CBNS 421.

Covenants may be **express** whether set down in writing or inferred by the construction of the entire agreement; or **implied** by law from the nature of the transaction. Covenants may be 'positive' requiring the performance

of some act or payment of some consideration; or 'negative' or 'restrictive' (a real covenant) imposing an obligation that prevents some act.

cf. *assumpsit*, **condition**. See also **express covenant, implied covenant, positive covenant, privity of contract, restrictive covenant, usual covenants, warranty**.

2. The financial standing or credit rating of a tenant or guarantor. A tenant of the highest standing (a company with a **triple A rating**, or a **blue chip company**, may be referred to as a 'prime covenant').

covenant against assignment or subletting

see **restraint on alienation**.

covenant for further assurance

see **beneficial owner**.

covenant for title

A promise or **covenant** made, by the vendor of land to a purchaser, concerning the title which is to be transferred; such a covenant normally is set out in a **conveyance**. See also **beneficial owner, implied covenant**.

covenant in gross (US)

A **covenant** that does not run with the land. See also **privity of estate, restrictive covenant**.

covenant of seisin (US)

A deed in which the vendor of an interest in land guarantees that he is the owner of the interest he purports to be selling. In English law, a covenant of seisin has been replaced by the **deed of grant** or **conveyance** which effects the same result.

cf. **quitclaim deed**. See also **warranty deed**.

cover

1. **Security**, or funds, held against a liability.

2. A factor by which one income exceeds another that is dependent on it. For example, if the interest payable on a mortgage is £1000 p.a. and the income derived from the property held as security for the mortgage is £3000 p.a., the interest is covered by a factor of 3. See also **debt-service cover ratio, loan value, margin, secured ground rent.**
3. The monetary value of a potential loss against which an **indemnity** has been obtained through an insurance policy. In the US, the policy may be called a cover and the indemnity called 'coverage'. See also **unvalued policy, valued policy.**

cover note
A memorandum of the terms of a provisional contract of insurance. The note is signed usually by an insurance agent and provides evidence of interim cover while the insurers consider details of the required insurance and prepare a formal insurance policy. In the US such a memorandum when prepared by the insurer is called a 'binder'.

cover ratio
see **debt-service cover ratio.**

coverage
see **cover, site-cover ratio.**

covered area
see **gross built, or covered, area.**

cratered property
A property investment that is a financial disaster. See also **distressed property.**

'Crawley costs'
see **compensation for disturbance.**

créancier (F)
creditor; promisee (to a contract).

(*créancier chirographaire* – unsecured creditor)
(*créancier hypothécaire* – **mortgagee**)
(*créancier nanti* – secured creditor)
(*créancier privilégié* – preferential or **preferred creditor**).

created ground rent
A rent that is fixed at a level between the value of undeveloped and developed land, i.e. between the **unimproved ground rent** and the **market rent** of land and buildings.

creative financing (US)
see **purchase-money mortgage.**

crédit (F)
loan; credit.
(*crédit de construction* – building loan or **construction loan**)
(*crédit de relais* – **bridging loan**)
(*crédit foncier; credit immobilier* – loan secured on real property)
(*crédit provisoire* – **interim loan** or **bridging loan**).

crédit-bail (F)
A lease of property granted together with an option for the lessee to purchase the property at a price that reduces throughout the term of the lease to a nominal sum at the end. For moveable property the lease is usually for five to seven years, with the option being exercisable after the first five years, and for immoveable property the lease is usually for fifteen years, with the option exerciseable after ten to twelve years.
cf. *location-vente.* See also **leasing.**
Le Crédit-Bail (Leasing) en Europe, by Mario Giovanoli, (1980).
Credit-Bail (Leasing) by Gilbert Pace, (1974).
Leasing et Crédit-Bail Mobilier, by Daniele Cremieux-Israel, (1975).

credit bargain, extortionate
see **usury**.

credit line
see **line of credit**.

credit rating
The opinion of traders, banks or rating agencies on the financial standing and the ability of a firm or individual to pay its obligations. The strength of the credit rating of a tenant has an effect on the value of a property investment to an owner. See also **covenant, triple 'A' rating**.

credit report
A report on an individual's or a company's **credit rating**.

credit-sale agreement
An agreement for the sale of goods whereby part or all of the purchase price is paid by instalments, after the date of transfer; but one that is not a **conditional sale agreement** (Consumer Credit Act 1974. s. 189 (1)). A term generally applied only to personal property. A credit sale means that title to the property has been transferred (unlike a conditional sale agreement or a **hire-purchase agreement**)'so there is no statutory right to terminate the transaction and the creditor has no right to retake possession if the debtor falls into arrears; the only remedy is an action on the debt. Called also an 'instalment sale'.

In the US a credit sale is defined as, "any sale with respect to which credit is extended or arranged by the seller. The term includes any contract in the form of a **bailment** or **lease** if the bailee or lessee contracts to pay as compensation for use a sum substantially equivalent to or in excess of the aggregate value of the property and services involved and it is agreed that

the bailee or lessee will become, or for no other or a nominal consideration has the option to become, the owner of the property upon full compliance with his obligations under the contract." (United States Uniform Code, para. 1602 (8)). See also **agreement for sale**.

criée (F)
auction.
(*chambre des criées*; *salle des criées* – auction room; sale room)
(*vente a la criée* – sale by auction). See also *enchère*.

criterion rate of return
see **target rate of return**.

critical-path analysis, or method (CPA)
A method of analysing a project by breaking it down into its component parts, or required actions, and developing a programme showing each part or action in sequence; the relationship between the various parts or actions; and the time required to complete the whole sequence. For example, a chart is prepared which endeavours to set out all the stages in a building or development process, in order to assist in monitoring the critical actions that will affect the timing of completion. The critical path is the one that shows the optimum period required to complete the process and it identifies the parts of the process that are critical to its completion.
Critical Path Analysis and Other Project Network Techniques, by Keith Lockyer, 4 edn.

croft
A small area of enclosed land, used for pasture, arable, or horticultural use, usually with a dwelling-house. See also **close**.

crop-share lease
see **sharecropping lease.**

cropper
see **sharecropping lease.**

crops
see **emblement, way-going crops.**

cross-default clause
A provision in a **blanket mortgage** agreement that, in the event of a default in the payment relating to one of the mortgaged properties, the mortgagee has a right of action against all the mortgaged properties. See also **collateral, marshalling.**

cross easement
An easement which provides recipro-cal rights of user, e.g. a joint access road. See also **party wall.**

Crown Estate Commissioners
see **Crown Land.**

Crown Land
Demesne land of the Crown, that is lands held for the use of the Crown but in her or his public capacity and which pass by succession. Land owned by the Sovereign as a body politic and which is managed in the UK by the Crown Estate Commis-sioners. Crown land also includes land belonging to the Duchies of Lancaster or Cornwall, or land held in trust for the Sovereign by a government department.

The Crown does not need to apply for planning permission in respect of its own interest in Crown land because it is not bound by an Act of Parliament; unless it is expressly or impliedly included in the Act – Minis-try of Agriculture, Fisheries and Food v Jenkins [1963] QB 325. How-ever, the Crown's representative may apply for planning permission, listed building consent, conservation area consent, or a formal determination on the need for planning permission, in respect of a development to be car-ried out on land after it is transferred to a private party or in respect of development to be carried out by a person who holds a private interest in the land (Town and Country Plan-ning Act 1984, s. 1). A private indi-vidual who has an interest in Crown land, e.g. a leasehold interest, may apply for planning permission in the usual way. See also **bona vacantia, foreshore.**

crownhold
A form of land disposal, provided for by the Land Commission Act 1967, s. 17, by which the **Land Commission** could sell a freehold or leasehold interest, subject to a restrictive cov-enant that had the effect of securing, by means of a right of pre-emption, that any future development value would go to the Commission. Crown-hold was abolished by the Land Commission (Dissolution) Act 1971.

cubing
An estimation of the cost of building work by reference to the volume of the quantities of materials required.

cujus est solum, ejus est usque ad coelum (L)
'Whose is the soil, his is also that which is above it'. See also **air rights, land.**

cul-de-sac
A **street** or alley that is closed at one end, but usually has an area for turn-ing at the closed end. Called also a 'close'. See also **dead-end street, highway.**

culvert
An underground channel for carrying water.
cf. **watercourse**. See also **drain, sewer**.

cum testamento annexo (L)
'With the **will** annexed'.

curable depreciation
Deterioration in a building that is normally repaired, or should be repaired, by a prudent owner or occupier.
cf. **deferred maintenance**.

curateur (F)
administrator (of an estate); a guardian or trustee, appointed for a particular event or transaction.

current asset
An **asset** that is fairly readily converted into cash, e.g. cash, stocks, short-term debtors, or investments that are intended to be resold in the normal course of business. Called sometimes a 'liquid asset'.
cf. **fixed asset**. See also **illiquid asset**.

current debt
see **current liability**.

current liability (or debt)
A **liability** (or **debt**) that must be met in a short period, normally within less than a year.

current price
see **market price**.

current ratio
The ratio of current assets to current liabilities in a balance sheet.

current use value (C.U.V.)
The **market value** of an interest in land assuming that it will not be used for any purpose other than that to which it is currently put, or that which is authorised by an existing planning permission or zoning regulation.

In particular, a term used, when calculating **development land tax** (DLT), for the market value of an interest in land based on the assumption that no project of **material development** (excluding certain minor forms of development – 'existing use development' – specified in the Town and Country Planning Act 1971, Sch. 8) may be undertaken, other than one for which (with some exceptions) planning permission has already been given and upon which work has already been started (Development Land Tax Act 1976, s. 7 (2), Sch. 4, Part I). Thus, in the case of DLT, where land is subject to planning permission, that permission can only be brought into account in determining current use value if (a) it relates to 'existing use development'; (b) it relates to development that is not 'material'; or (c) a resulting project of 'material development' has been commenced.
cf. **alternative use value**. See also **base value, eighth schedule development, existing use rights**.

current yield
The present yield from an investment, calculated on the basis of the current **net income** as a percentage of the **cost** or current **market value** of the investment.
cf. **equated yield, initial yield, redemption yield**. See also **running yield**.

curtail schedule
see **amortisation schedule**.

curtain principle
see **trust instrument**.

curtesy
A right of a husband to a life interest

in his deceased wife's property, if she dies intestate but leaves a child who would have inherited an entailed estate. "Tenant by the curtesy of England is where a man marries a woman seized of lands or tenements in fee simple or fee tail; that is any estate of inheritance; and has by her issue born alive, which was capable of inheriting her estate. In this case, he shall, on the death of his wife, hold the land for his life as tenant by the curtesy of England."(Bl. Comm. vol. ii. p. 125; Litt. 35). In most cases this right was abolished under English law in 1925 (Administration of Estates Act 1925, s. 45(1)). A tenancy by the curtesy can now only exist when a married woman, who has a right to an **entailed interest**, dies intestate, and thereby leaves her husband a life interest.

In the US some states still recognise the right of curtesy or have replaced it by a widower's right to a one-third interest in all the land owned by the wife during the marriage. In other states the requirement that a child must have been born to the couple, before a right of curtesy can be obtained, has been abolished. Curtesy is terminated on divorce. It cannot exist in a state that recognises **community property**.

curtilage
A courtyard or parcel of land adjoining a dwelling house, or forming part of the land fenced therein. A curtilage may include a garden, yard, or vacant land and buildings ancilliary to a house, but excludes a separate orchard and, in general, separately owned land. "In my [Buckley, L.J.] judgement for one **corporeal hereditament** to fall within the curtilage of another, the former must be so inti-

mately associated with the latter as to lead to the conclusion that the former in truth forms part and parcel of the latter.' – Methuen-Campbell v Walters [1979] 1 All ER 621. The land need not be marked off provided it can be seen, in all the circumstances, as an integral part of, belonging to, and enjoyed with, the house or **messuage** – Sinclair-Lockhart's Trustees v Central Land Board (1951) 1 P and CR 320).

custody
The care and control of a property or person. The retention of property for another but not for the possessor. Possession in accordance with a duty; especially when causing a restraint on a person's liberty. See also **bailment**.

custom
1. A practice or course of action that has been long established; something that becomes established from frequent repetition of an action or from what is done generally. **Usage** that has continued from time immemorial and, therefore, is recognised as having force of law without having been enacted as such; "the goodness of a custom depends upon its having been used time out of mind; or, in the solemnity of our legal phrase, time whereof the memory of man runneth to the contrary". (Bl. Comm. vol. i. p. 67). A custom must have been observed as a right, and cannot be in conflict with another custom, nor statute, nor common law; it must be reasonable and have been exercised peaceably. Custom is the **common law** of a locality; "it is common law because it is not statute law; it is local law because it is the law of a particular place, as distinguished from the general common law. Local common

law is the law of the country (i.e. particular locality) as it existed before the time of legal memory". – Hammerton *v* Honey (1874) 24 WR 603.

A business custom, or trade usage, is the generally accepted way of conducting a trade, business or profession. Such a custom must be certain, reasonable and generally acknowledged in the business, trade, profession to which it relates. ('Trade usage' has been defined as "any practice or method of dealing having such regularity of observance in a place, vocation or trade, as to justify an expectation that it will be observed with respect to the transaction in question". – United States Uniform Commercial Code, paras. 1–205 (2)). Thus a custom may establish an **implied term** in a contract; provided it does not conflict with an express term or the general tenor of the contract. An agent's **authority** may be implied from the custom of his market place or the established way in which he is expected to do business; "if there is, at a particular place, an established usage in the manner of dealing and making contracts, a person who is employed to deal or make a contract there has an implied authority to act in the usual way". – Bayliffe *v* Butterworth (1847) 1 Ex. 428. An agricultural tenant customarily may be required to abide by rules of **good husbandary** and customarily is entitled to compensation for the benefits he leaves on quitting the holding – Hutton *v* Warren (1836) 1 M and W 466). See also **customary right, precedent, prescription, tenant right**.
12 Halsbury's Laws of England, 4 edn., paras. 401–500.
2. An obligation of a tenant under the **feudal system** to pay rent or render services to his lord. See also **customary freehold, tenure**.

custom building, or custom-built property
A building designed to the specific requirements of the intended occupier. cf. **speculative building**. See also **package-deal contract**.

customary freehold
A form of feudal tenure by which land was held according to the custom of a **manor**, as distinguished from **copyhold** whereby land was held at the will of the lord. All customary freeholds were converted to free and common **socage** or **freehold** from 1925 (Law of Property Act 1922, s. 128).

customary right
A right over land acquired by **custom**. A right acquired by an undefined group of persons, such as the residents of a village, to use another's land; in particular a right that arose out of "the necessities of the public" (Bl. Comm. vol. ii. p. 33). For example, a right to hold a fair; a right of way to a church; or a right to enter on land to draw water. Such a right is deemed to have existed from time immemorial and to have continued uninterrupted; however, it must be certain, confined to a particular area and be a reasonable right – Mercer *v* Denne [1904] 2 Ch. 534. It is a right that is similar to an easement but there is no dominant land; it benefits a class of person and, once acquired, cannot be lost merely by non-user or waiver. See also **dedication**.

customary tenure
see **customary freehold**.

cycles

Periodic spaces of time. Intervals of time during which something moves forward, or upwards; then backwards, or downwards; beyond the starting point and finally returns to the starting point; for example, complete oscillations in an economic or business process. Phases or swings in economic activity that fluctuate between expansion, possibly leading to a **boom**, and then contraction, possibly leading to a depression or **slump**. Movements in an economy may be considered as analagous to a roller coaster so that each haul to the top is followed by the gravitational pull to the bottom. Property development, being a particularly dynamic process, tends to follow a cyclical trend: as general economic activity expands, demand for property increases, and consequently property values rise. The response is an initiation of new development, a process which tends to accelerate as further investment takes place. Eventually supply exceeds demand, values ease, new development becomes less viable and the resulting uncertainty leads to a reduction in activity. The recession in building activity is reversed only when the excess of supply is absorbed and a new phase of activity can start again. See also **counter-cyclical development process**.

Real Estate Principles, by Bruce Harwood, 2 edn., pp. 491–494.

D

damage

Derived from the Latin *damnum*, 'loss'. Harm or **injury** (physical or economic), to a person or an object; especially when arising from a wrongful act or default of another. A loss in value of property due to impact, collision, an act of God, fire etc.; a loss that may be redressed by an amount equal to the cost of restoring the property to its original condition. It has been said that, "neither in common parlance nor in legal phraseology is the word 'damage' used as applicable to injuries done to the person, but solely as applicable to mischief done to property ... We speak indeed of **'damages'** as compensation for injury done to the person, but the term 'damages' is not employed interchangeably with the term 'injury', with reference to mischief wrongfully occasioned to the person." – Smith *v* Brown (1871) 40 LJQB218. Therefore, in the context of property the word 'damage' should be used to distinguish it from personal 'injury' inflicted, or 'loss' suffered, as a result of a tort or breach of contract; but however, there is a tendency both in common and legal phraseology for the terms 'damage', 'damages', 'injury', 'hurt', and 'loss' to overlap. See also **injurious affection, insurance.**

damage feasant (or faisant)

'Doing **damage**'. Damage caused to grass, corn, wood, etc. by another's beasts, cattle or fowl trespassing on to one's land. A common law right to seize and detain such animals, 'distress damage feasant', has been abolished; but, in certain cases, an occupier of land may detain and, after 14 days (if they are not claimed), sell livestock that has strayed on to his land and is not under control (Animals Act 1971, s.47). See also **strict liability**

damages

1. A sum of money paid for the infringement of a right or neglect of a duty. Estimated compensation paid for an injury or loss that has been sustained, especially pecuniary recompense awarded by a court of law, on a once and for all basis, to a person for a wrong or injury done to her or him (whether directly or to her or his rights or property), either as a result of a breach of an obligation, or a breach of a **duty of care** owed to that person by another. This obligation, or duty, may be imposed by general law, statute, or contract. A entitlement to damages may arise because of a **breach of contract** or a **tort**. The principles for the award of damages are: (i) there should be no damages awarded in the absence of legal wrong, *damnum sine injuria*. (ii) a person is entitled only to such damages as might have been expected to arise consequentially or naturally, i.e. in the usual course of events, or such an amount as the person causing wrong might reasonably contemplate could result from his or her acts – Hadley *v* Baxendale (1854) 23 LJ Exch. 179; Victoria Laundry (Windsor) Ltd. *v* Newman Industries Ltd. [1949] 2 KB 528. In other words the

loss should not be too remote; or, colloquially, should be 'on the cards'. This rule of remoteness was enunciated in relation to a breach of contract, but a similar doctrine of 'foreseeability' applies to tort – "the essential factor in determining liability is whether the damage is of such a kind as the reasonable man should have forseen" – Re Polemis and Furness, Withy and Co., [1921] 2 KB 56. The extent of a liability for consequential losses is broader in tort than for a breach of contract because a contracting party has the ability to draw the other parties' attention to the consequences of the breach, a facility that is not normally available to a party injured by a tort – Koufos v Czarnikow, The Heron II [1969] 1 AC 350. (Other factors considered in this respect include the sequence of cause and effect; natural and probable result; and any intervening act in the chain of causation). (iii) the damages should restore, as nearly as possible by monetary recompense, the injured party to the same position as if no wrong had been suffered. (iv) the person claiming damages is under a duty to mitigate or minimize his claim – Brace v Calder [1895] 2 QB 253. (v) the award may be reduced by a failure on the part of the claimant, as when the plaintiff contributes to his own loss or does not take proper care for his own safety, usually amounting to 'contributory negligence'.

Damages may be classified as (a) 'nominal' – a token payment awarded when there has been a wrong suffered but no actual financial loss or damage; (b) 'substantial' or 'general' – based on the actual loss judged to have been suffered as a direct result of the wrong – and (c) 'special' – those losses that do not flow directly or as the inevitable result of the wrong, but can be proved to have been suffered as a natural result and which should have been contemplated by the offender as likely to arise. Special damages must be specifically alleged and proven by the claimant. In exceptional cases of tort a court may award 'aggravated' damages for extreme or malicious behaviour by the offender, such as may affect a persons feelings or dignity (although such awards are rare in English court); or 'exemplary', 'vindicative' or 'punitive' damages as a punishment to the wrongdoer whenever it is necessary to teach him or her that 'tort does not pay' or to deter the wrongdoer from commiting similar acts (for example, in a case of **nuisance** arising from harassment by a landlord), rather than merely awarding recompense to the wronged party – The term 'exemplary damages' is to be preferred in English law: Cassell and Co. Ltd. v Broome [1972] 1 All ER 825.

When determining the damages payable for a breach of contract, the amount to be paid to the party who suffers a loss may be settled when the contract is entered into – **liquidated damages**; or may be awarded at the discretion of a court – **unliquidated damages**.

In the case of damages suffered to real property, as a result of a tort or a breach of contract, the assessed amount of damages may be based on either the cost of making good the damaged property, i.e. the cost of reinstatement or repair, or the diminution or loss in value of the property. There is no established rule as to which basis a court will apply; it depends on the circumstances of the

case. In the case of a vendor or purchaser, if a vendor sells too cheaply or a purchaser pays too much due to negligent professional advice, the measure of damages *prima facie* is the difference between the price paid and market value. For example, "where there is a contract by a prospective buyer with a surveyor under which the surveyor agrees to survey a house and make a report on it – and he makes it negligently – and the client buys the house on the faith of the report, then the damages are to be assessed at the time of the breach, according to the difference in the price which the buyer would have given if the report had been carefully made from that which he in fact gave owing to the negligence of the surveyor ... So you have to take the difference in valuation". – Perry *v* Sidney Phillips and Son [1982] WLR 1301. On the other hand, where there has been **negligence** in the design or construction of a building the cost of making good the property may be a more appropriate method of providing that which had been contracted for. However, any sum awarded that is greater than the reduction in the value of the injured party's property would place the property owner in a better position than if no damage had been occasioned and would run contrary to one of the principles upon which damages are assessed.
cf. **indemnity**. See also **consequential damages, deposit, injunction, quantum meruit, specific performance, penalty, restitution**.
Anson's Law of Contract, 26 edn., pp. 491–516.
Cheshire & Fifoot's Law of Contract, 10 edn., p. 537 *et seq.*
Chitty on Contract, 28 edn., para.

1671–1749.
Street on Torts, 7 edn., pp. 434–440.
Winfield & Jolowicz on Tort, 12 edn., p. 612 *et seq.*
Salmond and Heuston on the Law of Torts, 18 edn., pp. 496–550.
The Law of Damages, by A.I. Ogus, 2 edn.
McGregor on Damages, 14 edn.
12 Halsbury's Laws of England, 4 edn. paras. 1101–1300.
(US) 2. Compensation paid for a loss in the value of land as a result of the taking of part of an owner's land as a result of the exercise of the power of **eminent domain**. Such compensation may be referred to as **consequential damages** when it arises as a consequence of the taking and/or the carrying out of work on other land or **severance damages** when it arises as a result of the severance of one area of land from another. Broadly the former corresponds to compensation for injurious affection and the latter to compensation for severance, as paid in English law. See also **before-and-after method of valuation, partial taking**.

damnum (L)
'Damage; loss'.

damnum absque injuria (L)
'Loss without wrong; loss without legal **injury**.' See **damages**.

damnum sine injuria esse potest (L)
'Damage may arise without injury'. There may be damage or loss inflicted without any act being done that the law deems an injury, and which accordingly would be compensatable.

damping a sale
An arrangement or bargain made by potential bidders, or an auctioneer, with the aim of acquiring a property

at **auction** for less than its market or fair value, e.g. telling potential bidders that a property is apparently defective when that is not the case. Such a sale normally is invalid and a court will not award a decree of **specific performance** in such an instance – Mason *v* Armitage (1800) 13 Ves. 25. In the US such a practice is called 'chilling a sale'. See also **bidding agreement**.

dangerous building (or structure)
A building or structure which is in such condition, or is used to carry such loads that it is a danger either to those in the building or those in close proximity to it. A local authority has power to require the owner of a 'dangerous building' to execute work or demolish a building, or part of a building, 'to obviate the danger' (Public Health Act 1936, s. 58). See also **negligence, nuisance, obstructive building**.

dangerous premises
see **negligence, strict liability**.

dangerous things, (escape from land of)
see **strict liability**.

data
see **datum**

date
The **time** at which an action takes place; is given or specified; or is in some way ascertained or fixed. In particular, a time as marked on a writing, either to show when something was written, or when an act is to be performed or an act done. In a deed the 'date' expresses the day, month and year on which the document was made. The date stated in a deed is presumed to be the date on which that instrument takes effect, although strictly (unless there is a clear inten-

tion that the instrument should take effect on a different date to the delivery date) the time of its **delivery** is the correct date on which a deed takes effect. "The primary significance of 'date' is not time in the abstract, nor time taken absolutely, but time given or specified; time in some way ascertained and fixed. When we speak of the date of a deed, date of issue of a bond or date of a policy, we do not mean the time when it was actually executed, but the time of its execution as given or stated in the deed itself . . . The precise meaning of date, however, depends upon context since there are numerous instances when it means actual as distinguished from conventional time" (*Black's Law Dictionary*, 5 edn.). The date of a deed, or of delivery, is not judged by reference to the hour or minute but the **day** of delivery – a day being an indivisible time for that purpose – Pugh *v* Duke of Leeds (1977) 2 Cowp. 720.

A date need not be expressed for a deed to be valid, provided the true time of delivery can be ascertained (Bl. Comm. vol. ii p. 304). The dating of a deed after its signature by the parties is not an uncommon practice; however, the practice of inserting a date after delivery is a dangerous practice in that it risks conflict with the date of execution. (A change in a date on a deed may amount to **forgery** – Forgery Act 1913, s.1, or to **fraud**.)

When time runs 'from' a particular date it begins to run at the end of that day. "The rule is now well established that where a particular time is given, from a certain date within which an act is to be done, the day of that date is to be excluded". – Goldsmith's Co. *v* West Metropolitan Railway [1904] 1 KB 5. (but, see **time**).

date (F)
date.
(date d'échéance – due date; **maturity date**)
(date de remboursement – **redemption date**) See also *échéance*.

date of acquisition
see **date, completion.**

date of appraisal or date of valuation
see **valuation date.**

datum (pl. data)
1. A point, level or line used as a point of reference e.g. a reference point indicating the height of a specific place above sea level. See also **bench mark.**
2. Any kind of detailed information, such as may be collected to assist in preparing a **valuation report** on a property; including 'general data' covering economic, demographic and social facts; 'specific data' covering details of the subject property; and 'comparative data' or comparables of similar property. See also **comparable property.**

day
A period of 24 hours, generally running from one midnight to the subsequent midnight (natural day). "The Jewes, the Chaldeans and Babylonians, begin the day at the rising of the sun; the Athenians at the fall; the Umbri in Italy beginne at midday; the Egyptians and Romans from midnight; and so doth the law of England in many cases" (Co. Litt 135a). In any event, in law, a day is an indivisible period of time, for "the law maketh no fraction of a day" (Co. Inst. vol. iii p. 53). Thus, leases or other periodic interests in land normally start and finish at midnight and most Acts of Parliament take effect from midnight

(Interpretation Act 1978, s. 4). However, a day may be divided when it is essential so to do, as when it is necessary to ascertain which of two events occurred first.

'Days' mean consecutive or 'running days' and include Sundays and public holidays; unless there is a custom to the contrary, or the word is qualified as 'working days' or in some other way. A 'clear day' means a full day (from midnight to midnight) and not any part of a day. 'Clear' days are computed excluding the first and last day; and 'at least 7 days notice' means 7 clear days, i.e. the notice expires at the end of the eighth day after the start date. However, in certain dealings a day may be any span of 24 consecutive hours or may even be shortened according to the circumstances; for example, a 'day' in banking ends at the close of working hours, and **distress** must be levied between sunrise and sunset i.e. during a 'civil day'. See also **date, time.**
Odgers' *Construction of Deeds and Statutes*, 5 edn., pp. 131–134.

day work
A method of valuing building or construction work on the basis of the **prime cost** (actual cost to the builder or contractor) of labour, materials and plant and a percentage addition for the profit of the builder or contractor.

daylight factor
A measure of the amount of natural light reaching a room whether as direct sunlight or reflected from the walls of other buildings. Generally a daylight factor is expressed as a percentage relationship between the light at an outside window sill on a clear day and the light three foot above the

floor at the darkest working area of a room. Other tests, as to the adequacy of daylight from a window, include the 'Waldram graphs'; the 45 degrees rule (light should not be obstructed above a line drawn at 45° upwards and outwards from the centre of the window or aperture), and the '50–50 rule' (50 per cent of the room receives one lumen of light at 2 feet 9 inches above floor level). However, there is no hard and fast rule for determining the adequacy of daylight, or loss of daylight, in a room; it is necessary to decide whether there is a comfortable provision of light according to the use to which a building is put – Colls *v* Home and Colonial Stores [1904] AC 179. See also **right of light**, **plot ratio**, *The Right to Light*, by Bryan Anstey and Michael Chavasse, p. 72 (1963).

days of grace
1. Days allowed for the payment of a debt after the due date, for curing a default without penalty, or for the renewal of a contract. Normally an express number of days, although custom may dictate the permitted period.
2. A specified period, after the renewal date, during which the premium to renew an insurance policy must be paid. Generally insurance remains in effect during this period unless it can be shown that there is no intention to renew the policy, as when the insured has effected an alternative policy. See also **grace period**.

de cujus (L)
'From whom'. A person from whom another claims. An attester.

de die in diem (L)
'From **day** to day'.

De Donis Conditionalibus
The title given to the Statute of Westminster 1285 (being the title of chapter 1 which dealt with **conditional fee** estates). The statute provided that when a person made a gift of land to 'A and the heirs of his body' this should be construed as expressing an intention to retain land within the family; thus the donee should not be free to alienate his estate outside the family (except for his own life time) and if there were no further issue of A then the estate reverted back to the donor or his heir. "The result of this statute was the appearance of a new kind of fee or inheritable estate, called a **fee tail**, or in Latin *feodum talliatum*, and so called because the quantum of the estate was 'cut down' in the sense that, unlike the case of the fee simple, the right to inherit was restricted to the class of heirs specially mentioned in the gift, and was not available to the heirs-general of the donee." (Cheshire's Modern Law of Real Property, 13 edn., p. 238).

de facto (L)
'In fact'.
cf. **de jure**.
see **possession**.

de gré à gré
see **gré**.

de jure (L)
'By right; by legal **title**'.
cf. **de facto**.

de minimis (L)
'Minute; insignificant'.

de minimis non curat lex (L)
'The law does not concern itself with trifles'.

de novo (L)
'Anew'.

dead-end street (US)
A street that leads nowhere; a **cul-de-sac** without an adequate turning circle at the closed end.

dead hand
see **mortmain**.

dead loan
A permanent or **long-term loan**, as distinguished from an interim loan.

dead pledge
1. see **mortgage**.
(US) 2. A mortgage that is paid on time as required or pledged.

dead rent
A rent fixed independently of any **royalty** paid for a mining right; a sum that does not vary with the yield from the mine and is payable even when the mine is not worked. Called also a 'certain rent', 'sleeping rent' or 'minimum rent'. See also **base rent**.

dealer property (US)
see **trading property**.

dealing
A transaction or transfer of registered land which requires registration at the Land Registry.

death duty (or tax)
A generic term for a tax levied or payable on the value of a person's estate at his or her death. In the UK prior to 1975, this was principally **estate duty** (or before 1949 legacy duty and succession duty). Since the Finance Act 1975 tax on the property of a deceased has been levied as **capital transfer tax** and 'death duty' as such is now obsolete.
In the US 'death tax' may refer to an **estate tax**, levied on the deceased's estate, or an **inheritance tax** levied on the benefit received by an inheritance.

debenture
A document, made usually but not necessarily under seal, that acknowledges a debt owed by a company or public body, to the registered holder or bearer, i.e. written evidence that a loan has been made. In particular, such a document issued by a company or public body. A debenture may be a simple recognition of a debt – a 'naked debenture' – or accompanied by a charge on one or more properties of the company – a 'mortgage debenture'. However, it differs from a **mortgage** in that it does not grant any interest in property to the debtor, although it may create a form of **equitable mortgage** – United Masonic Temple Corporation *v* Harris, 242 Ill. App. 296. A debenture has been defined to include "debenture stock, bonds and any other securities of a company, whether constituting a **charge** on the assets of the company or not" (Companies Act 1948, s. 455 (1)). The debenture holder may have a **fixed charge** on certain assets of the company, or a general or **floating charge** on all of the assets of the company. Debenture loans are not part of the **capital** of a company but form part of the (usually long term) liabilities of a company; although money obtained against a debenture may be called '**debt capital**'. A debenture holder is entitled to a fixed rate of interest as a priority rather than any share of a company's profits. See also **bond, drop-lock debenture, redemption**.

debenture capital
see **debt capital**.

debenture trust deed

A trust deed that vests specific property in trustees in order to give a holder of a **debenture** greater security. A debenture trust deed made against the property of a company usually provides for a **fixed charge** on the real estate owned by the company and a **floating charge** on the rest of the company's assets.

debenture with warrants (US)

A form of **debenture** which provides that the debenture holder has a right to a share in the equity of a company or in a property investment held as security. See also **convertible mortgage, equity participation, warrant**.

débiteur (F)

debtor; promisor (to a contract). (*débiteur hypothécaire* or *débiteur sur hypothèque* – **mortgagor**).

debt

Derived from the Latin *debere* – 'to owe'. Something of value, usually money, owed by one person to another. An **obligation** by a person or organisation to pay money, or money's worth, to another at present or in the future. Generally, an obligation to repay a **loan**, render a service, or supply goods. See also **accord and satisfaction, bond, chose, interest**.

debt capital

Finance for an enterprise (e.g. a business, a property investment) that is derived from a source other than the owner of the enterprise. A loan, generally on a long-term basis, to finance capital expenditure; for example, money provided by a **mortgage loan** or a **debenture**. A providor of debt capital does not receive, or accept, a share in the profit (or loss) to be derived from the enterprise to which it lends money; his reward is the receipt of **interest**, plus repayment of the debt. A provider of debt capital has priority over the owner of the enterprise – the provider of **equity capital** – in the event of the liquidation of the enterprise. Debt capital may be secured by a charge or mortgage on the assets of the borrower. Called also 'loan capital' or, when the loan is granted by means of a debenture, 'debenture capital'.

debt-coverage ratio

see **debt-service cover ratio**.

debt financing

The use of **debt capital** to acquire property.

cf. **deficit financing**. See also **financing**.

debt ratio

The ratio of debt capital to the asset value of an organisation. This ratio indicates the security in terms of the assets available to the lender of debt capital in the event of a liquidation of the organisation. Called also the 'leverage ratio'.

cf. **debt-to-equity ratio**. See also **margin**.

debt-to-equity ratio

The ratio of **debt capital** to **equity capital** in a company or an investment; i.e. the number of times the amount lent to a company or secured against a property exceeds the amount of owner's capital including reserves, or exceeds the equity used to purchase the property. Called also 'leverage ratio'.

debt service

The periodic payment required to pay a debt or mortgage loan, including interest and capital repayment. The cost of **debt capital** over a given period of time, usually a year. See also **amortisation, mortgage constant**.

debt-service constant
see **mortgage constant**.

debt-service cover, or debt-coverage, ratio (DCR) (US)
The number of times the **net operating income** from a property exceeds the annual cost of **debt service**. See also **default ratio**.

decapitalisation
The conversion of a single capital sum into an annual income or **annual equivalent** – the reverse of **capitalisation**.

deceipt
A fraudulent or deceptive representation made by words or actions, with the intention that another will act on it, so that prejudice or harm will result therefrom. Mere silence cannot amount to deceipt. Deceipt is a **tort** when the representation is untrue, is known so to be or is made recklessly without regard for the truth; is made with the intent that another will act thereon to his or her detriment; and when that party did act thereon and suffered damage or injury as a result. cf. **misrepresentation**. See also **fraud**.

decentralisation
Dispersal from a centre. A process by which population, commerce or industry is redistributed from an urban centre, usually from a congested area, to the surrounding or suburban area. Decentralisation is an active process (unlike **overspill**) encouraged by central or local government with the object of (a) redistributing employment opportunities; (b) reducing population and economic pressure in an existing area, especially when this is aimed at assisting the redevelopment of that area; (c) improving the general use of land and reducing the density of development. The term decentralisation is used also to describe a movement from an established business centre, especially when made in order to reduce property occupation costs. Decentralisation may be considered as a means of countering economic or market forces in order to achieve a political objective, for example decentralising a particular business activity in order to provide employment and thereby retain the population in another area. See also **new town**.

décentralisation (F)
decentralisation; devolution.
(*décentralisation administrative* – office relocation).

déchéance (F)
forfeiture; lapse.

declaration of condominium (US)
see **enabling declaration.**

declaration of no defenses (US)
see **estoppel certificate.**

declaration of title (US)
A judicial procedure by which a person obtains a court declaration as to the validity of a **title** to land. A procedure that may be used when a 'title holder' feels that his claim to land is threatened.

declaration of restrictions (US)
see **scheme of development.**

declaration of trust
A statement or other means by which a person acknowledges or declares that property is held in **trust;** in particular, a declaration made when the holder of property confirms himself to be the trustee. A declaration of

trust in respect of land, or an interest in land, must be "manifested or proved by some writing" and authoritatively signed; unless it arises from a resulting, implied or constructive trust (Law of Property Act 1925, s. 53 (1) (b), 53 (2)). See also **express trust, implied trust**.

declaration, statutory
see **statutory declaration**.

declining-balance depreciation
A method of calculating **depreciation** by which a fixed percentage of the total outstanding balance of the cost of a property is deducted, or written-off, each year. A form of **accelerated depreciation** which provides that the absolute amount of depreciation is higher in the early years and declines gradually. For example, if a cost of 100 is depreciated at an annual rate of 10 per cent, then the outstanding balance would reduce to 90 at the end of year 1, 81 at the end of year 2, 72.9 at the end of year 3, and so on until the cost is reduced to a scrap or residual value. Called also 'diminishing-balance depreciation' or 'reducing-balance depreciation'.

decontrolled tenancy
A tenancy of a dwelling-house which prior to 1980 had been converted from a **controlled tenancy** to a **regulated tenancy** consequent upon the provision of **standard amenities**. See also **rent control**.

decorative repair
see **tenantable repair, relief**.

decree of foreclosure
see **foreclosure**.

decrement
The process of reducing in value. A decline in property values due to economic or social factors in the area. cf. **increment**. See also **blight**.

dedication
The grant (expressly or tacitly) by a private landowner of a public right of user; such as a grant, or giving over of land, for a public **right of way, highway** or **park**. A right of way is deemed to be dedicated to the public after a continuous, open, and unobstructed user for over twenty years, unless there is evidence that it was not intended that the land should be so dedicated (Highways Act 1980, s.31 (1)). At English common law dedication may be presumed in certain cases where the user has been in existence for a shorter term and there is evidence to support an intention to dedicate the land; in this connection six years has been considered suffficient – Rugby Charity Trustees *v* Merryweather (1790) 11 East 375. Dedication may be considered also as capable of arising from the doctrine of **estoppel**, so that if a person evinces an intention that his land is to be used for a public purpose he may be estopped from denying that he had dedicated the land for that purpose. A similar principle is accepted in most states in the US – City of Cincinatti *v* White's Lessee (1832) 31 US (6 Pet.) 431, 8 L Ed.452.
The Modern Law of Highways, by Susan Hamilton, para. 6 *et seq.* (1981).
Real Estate Law by Robert Kratovil and Raymond J. Werner, 8 edn., pp. 452–460.

dédommagement (F)
damages; compensation; indemnity. See also *dommage*.

deductibles
See **excess (on insurance cover)**.

déduction (F)
deduction; allowance; **abatement**.
(*déduction fiscale sur investissement*
– **capital allowance**).

deed

A written or printed document (on
paper, vellum or parchment, but not
on any other substance) **signed,
sealed and delivered**, which conveys
or confirms an interest in property;
passes some right or title (not being a
will or codicil); or creates or affirms a
claim obligation, or an agreement
between parties. If the document
creates a contractual arrangement it
is called a 'contract under seal'; it is 'a
written promise or set of promises
which derives its validity from the
form, and the form alone of the executing instrument' (*An Introduction
to the Law of Contract*, by P.S.
Atiyah, 3 edn., p.31). A deed may be
referred to as a 'formal contract': the
form being a **signature**; a **seal**; and
delivery (A document under seal is
not necessarily a deed, for instance a
share certificate may be sealed, but
without some indication of sealing
there can be no deed – R v Morton
(1873) LR 2 CCR 27). A deed is used
especially for the transfer of property
being "the most solemn and authentic
act that a man can possibly perform
with relation to the disposal of his
property; and therefore a man shall
always be estopped by his own deed,
or not permitted to aver or prove any
thing in contradiction to what he has
once so solemnly and deliberately
avowed." (Bl. Comm. vol. ii p. 293).

A deed is required in the following
instances: (a) a **conveyance** of land, or
any interest in land, which is intended
to convey or create a **legal estate** (with
certain statutory exceptions, note-

ably a **legal lease** that is not required
to be in writing) (Law of Property Act
1925, s.52, 54 (2)); (b) the grant or
assignment of any lease of an **incorporeal hereditament** – Gardiner v
Williamson (1831) 2 B and Ad. 336;
(c) a contract made without **consideration**; (d) an express release of a right
to land (including an express **surrender** of a lease), to goods, to chattels or of a right of action; (e) in most
cases, for the appointment of new
trustees under the Trustee Act 1925;
(f) the grant of a lease of **settled land**
for more than three years (Settled
Land Act 1925, s. 42); (g) to effect a
transfer of title to registered land, in
the same way as a conveyance of
unregistered land; (h) in some cases,
for the transfer of the shares in a
company; (i) the grant of a **power of
attorney** when an agent is authorised
to execute a deed on behalf of his
principal; and (j) a **bill of sale** for the
transfer of personal chattels as security for the payment of money.

Any deed may be described (at the
commencement thereof or otherwise)
as "a deed simply or as a conveyance,
deed of exchange, **vesting deed, trust
instrument, settlement, mortgage**,
charge, transfer of mortgage, appointment, lease or otherwise according to
the nature of the transaction intended
to be effected."(Law of Property Act
1925, s. 57); i.e. calling a document
'this charge' does not prevent it being
considered as a deed – which could
have been the case prior to 1925. The
use of the word **grant** is no longer
necessary in English law to convey an
interest in land: land, or an interest in
land, may be conveyed solely by a
deed of grant (Law of Property Act
1925, s. 51).

In some states in the US a deed is

required to convey a freehold estate or when there is no consideration for the transaction. However, in most states a seal is no longer required; signing and delivery are normally deemed sufficient. A deed for the transfer of an interest in land may be described according to the form of title granted by the vendor, such as a **quitclaim deed, grant deed, warranty deed** or **bargain-and-sale deed**. See also **contract for deed, covenant, date, deed of trust, deed poll, escrow, indenture, operative part (or words), specialty contract**.

Real Estate Law, by W.D. Milligan and Arthur G. Bowman, pp. 159–170 (1984).

Real Estate Law, by Robert Kratovil and Raymond J. Werner, 8 edn., pp. 60–82.

Adkin's Landlord and Tenant 18 edn., pp. 42–43.

Chesire's Modern Law of Real Property 13 edn., pp. 725–734.

Chitty on Contract, 25 edn., paras. 18–31.

Odgers' Construction of Deeds and Statutes, 5 edn., pp. 1–17.

William's Contract for Sale of Land and Title to Land, 4 edn., pp. 631–660.

12 Halsbury's Laws of England, 4 edn., paras. 1301–1566.

deed of assignment
1. A **deed** that effects an **assignment** of a right or interest; in particular, a deed that effects the assignment of a lease. A deed by which an insolvent debtor undertakes to transfer his assets to his creditors in settlement of their claims against him.
2. A deed that is used to appoint an assignee; the deed usually states the rights and duties of the assignee.

deed of conveyance
see **conveyance**.

deed of enlargement
see **enlargement**.

deed of gift
A **deed** executed and delivered without **consideration**, i.e. a deed that conveys property as a **gift**. A gift made, without actual **delivery**, other than by deed is generally unenforceable at law. See also **conveyance, unenforceable contract**.

deed of grant
A deed that is used to effect a **grant** of property. See also **conveyance**.

deed of partition
A deed executed for the purpose of partitioning a right to property, i.e. a deed which provides for two or more parties to take separate and distinct interests in a property. See also **partition**.

deed of priorities
1. A deed executed by a lender who has a **floating charge** over the assets of a company in which it is agreed that the company may grant a fixed charge over certain assets to another lender and that the first lender will defer his priority in respect of those assets.
2. A deed that affirms a **subordination**.

deed of reconveyance (US)
see **release deed**.

deed of rectification
see **rectification**.

deed of release
see **release, release deed**.

deed of surrender
see **surrender**.

deed of transfer
see **transfer deed**.

deed of trust (US)

A deed that grants title to property, to a third party (a trustee) to be held in **trust** until a borrower has met his obligations to a lender in full. Although similar in purpose to a **mortgage**, the lender may direct the trustee to dispose of the property in the event of default by the borrower: a procedure that is intended to be less complicated than **foreclosure**. On the other hand, as soon as the debt is paid in full the trustee is obliged to transfer the property unencumbered to the borrower. Called also a 'trust deed'. See also **power of sale**.

Real Estate Principles, by Bruce Harwood, 2 edn., pp. 201–209.

Real Estate Law, by W.D. Milligan and Arthur G. Bowman, pp. 218–233, (1984).

deed poll

1. A unilateral **deed**. A term derived from a practice of 'polling', or cutting a deed evenly (rather than indenting or cutting with serration), to signify that there is only one party to the deed. A **power of attorney** is generally granted by means of a deed poll.

cf. **indenture**.

2. A form of conveyance used by an authority possessing compulsory purchase powers to vest land in itself when an owner is unable or unwilling to convey title to a property that has been included in a compulsory purchase order. See also **general vesting declaration**.

deed restriction (US)

see **restrictive convenant**.

deemed disposal

A **disposal** of property which is assumed to take place when the owner carries out a certain activity or a given event occurs, e.g. on the death of the owner. A term that is used especially to refer to a stage at which a tax liability arises. See also **capital transfer tax, development land tax**.

deemed planning permission

see **development**.

défaillance (F)

default; failure, to obey a summons.

défalcation (F)

abatement; recoupment.

default

Failure to perform a legal obligation, e.g. failure to perform a **condition** of a contract or failure to pay a sum of money when due. The default of a mortgagor (or tenant) to make payment when due may give a mortgagee (or a landlord) a right to possession of the property held as security (or of the leased property). See also **breach of contract, forfeiture, foreclosure, right of re-entry**.

default point

see **break-even point**.

default ratio (US)

The ratio of the **effective gross income** to be derived from a property to the total annual cost, including debt service, operating expenses and direct real estate taxes, of holding that property. A ratio that indicates the point at which there is a risk of default in the payment of a mortgage secured on the property.

défaut (F)

default; defect. Used more for failure to achieve something than the more formal *défaillance*.

(*défaut inherent* – **inherent defect**).

defeasance

1. Derived from the Old French *de*

faure, 'of defeat'. The rendering of a right null and void.

2. An **instrument** that may have the effect of defeating the terms or effect of another deed; a **condition** in a contract which, if fulfilled, may weaken or defeat another agreement. "A defeasance is a **collateral** deed, made at the same time with … a conveyance, containing certain conditions, upon the performance of which the estate then created may be defeated or totally undone" (Bl. Comm. vol. ii p. 327). A defeasance usually is contained in a separate instrument; if contained in the principal deed it is called a 'condition'.

In the US especially, 'defeasance' is also used to refer to a clause in a mortgage deed which provides that the mortgagee's right to a property will come to an end, or be terminated, if and when the mortgage debt is repaid in full. Or, a clause in a mortgage deed which provides that the mortgagor will reclaim an unencumbered right to property (title to which he ceded as security) as soon as the mortgage debt is repaid. Such a clause is inserted only when property is passed under a **mortgage**, and not merely as a **lien** (which does not pass title to property). In English law since 1925, as a mortgage no longer passes title to the mortgagee, 'defeasance' of the mortgagee's interest can no longer occur. See also **defeasible interest, equity of redemption, shifting clause.**

defeasance clause
see **defeasance**.

defeasible interest
1. An interest in land that may be defeated or come to an end by the happening of a future event or the operation of a **condition subsequent**, e.g. an owner's interest that may be defeated by the exercise of an option to purchase. A mortgage is said to be defeasible because of the existence of the mortgagor's **equity of redemption**. See also **defeasance**.

(US) 2. An interest that can be annulled or rendered void, e.g. an interest held by virtue of a title that may be defeated by the claim of another; but one that is not already void.

defect
A fault or failure of something: "a lack or absence of something essential to completeness" – Tate *v* Latham and Son [1897] 1 QB 506. See also **defect of title, inherent defect, latent defect, negligence, patent defect.**

defect of record (US)
An error in a public record that causes a **defect of title**.

defect of title
A **title** that does not provide what a purchaser requires or expects because of, for example, a servitude or encumberance that reduces the purchaser's proper enjoyment of the property he contracted to purchase. A vendor of property is under an obligation to point out to a purchaser any **latent defect** of title, i.e. a defect that cannot readily be ascertained by reasonable enquiry, but the vendor cannot be held responsible for "the carelessness of the purchaser who does not care to inquire" – Bowles *v* Round (1800) 5 Ves. 509. Also, in equity, a vendor is obliged to make a full and frank disclosure of any defect of title of which he is aware, in clear and concise language – Faruqi *v* English Real Estates [1974] 1 WLR 963. Thus, if a vendor of land is unable to

convey a fixture (an item that is so annexed to the land as to become part thereof), for example because another party has a lien on it, he is obliged to notify the purchaser. If he does not and the property that can be conveyed is materially different to that which he contracted to convey the vendor is unlikely to be able to obtain a decree of **specific performance** to enforce completion of the transaction. The deliberate concealment of any instrument, or encumberance, or falsification of any document relevant to the title, is a criminal offence (Law of Property Act 1925, s. 183). See also **constructive notice, contingency insurance, good title, title insurance**.

defective premises
See **negligence, repair**.

defects liability period
See **maintenance period**.

defects list
A list of matters that have not been completed in accordance with the terms of a building contract, especially defects of workmanship and materials. Usually a defects list is prepared by the architect when the building contractor claims to have substantially completed the contract. Called sometimes a 'snag list' or, in the US, a 'punch list'.

defeneration
The lending of money on **usury**.

defer
To delay in time; to delay or postpone to a future date. A term commonly used to refer to a discount in value to take account of time: a more common term in property valuation than **discount**. See also **present value**.

deferred annuity
An **annuity** or annual payment that does not come into effect or start until a future time or date, e.g. a pension right arising at a person's set age. An annual income that will be paid in the future and is provided for by the payment of a present capital sum.

deferred charge (or expense)
An expense incurred, or payment made, for a benefit that will be received in a later accounting period. An item of expenditure incurred in one accounting period but that is to be written off over a longer period of time, e.g. company formation costs that may be spread over the first two or three years of a company's profit and loss account. See also **prepaid expense**.

deferred commission (US)
A **commission** that has been earned but not yet received.

deferred income
1. The **present value** of an anticipated future income.
2. A sum of money the payment of which has been postponed to a time after the due date. See also **deferred annuity**.
(US) 3. Income received in advance of its due date; income that has been received but not earned. Deferred income is not shown in a company's balance sheet as a liability and is only entered in an income statement when it is earned or becomes due. See also **rent in advance (or arrears)**.

deferred interest
see '**rolled-up interest**'.

deferred-interest mortgage (DIM) (US)
A mortgage loan which provides that a lower interest rate will be paid in the

early years, especially one under which the federal government undertakes to pay the difference. See also **variable-rate mortgage**.

deferred maintenance (US)

Expenditure on the **maintenance** or **repair** of a property that is due to be, but has not yet been, incurred. A requirement for maintenance or repair to a building which arises primarily from a neglect of good management. This type of work often is left to be carried out as part of a scheme of **rehabilitation** or **renovation**. See also **curable depreciation**.

deferred-payment mortgage (DPM)

A mortgage loan which provides for lower repayments of capital in its earlier years, generally to assist first time house buyers. A form of **variable-payment mortgage**. Called also a 'low-start mortgage'. See also **option mortgage scheme**.

deferred-payment sale (US)

see **instalment sale**.

deferred yield

An increase in an owner's **equity** that will not be realised until a property is sold, i.e. the return from property produced by loan repayments and capital appreciation. See also **equity build-up, redemption yield**.

deficiency judgement (US)

A court order issued against a borrower when following a **foreclosure sale**, the proceeds of sale are insufficient to meet the outstanding debt.

deficit financing

1. Finance obtained to pay for a deficit, i.e. the excess of current liabilities over current assets. In particular, the issuing of government securities to provide funds to cover the budgeted excess of expenditure over revenue.
2. A loan obtained to finance an investment in property when the **cash flow** is insufficient to cover the cost of existing **debt service**; i.e. a loan required to finance a negative cash flow, or 'to feed an alligator'. A high risk form of loan which is granted normally only when there is a good prospect of increases in cash flow (from early rent increases or improved property management) or to avoid liquidation of the company owning the property. The provision of such finance is called sometimes 'pump priming'.

deforcement

1. The wrongful retention of possession of land to which another is entitled. See also **tenancy on sufferance**.
2. To eject someone from possession of property by force. See also **disseisin**.

dégradation (F)

dilapidation.
(*liste des dégradations* – **schedule of dilapidations**).

dehors (F)

outside; grounds (of a house).
(*en dehors d'un contrat* – outside the scope of a contract).

délai (F)

delay; extension of time.
(*délai-congé* – period of notice)
(*délai d'execution* – completion period)
(*délai de grâce* – **days of grace**)
(*délai de recuperation du capital investi* – **pay-back period**)

délaissement (F)

abandonment.

delay
see **laches, Statutes of Limitation.**

delayed completion
see **completion, time is of the essence.**

delegatus non potest delegare (L)
'A delegate cannot himself delegate; a person to whom power has been delegated cannot delegate further'. See **sub-agent.**

delict
In Scottish law, a civil wrong that causes injury to another but does not arise from a breach of covenant or a strict liability. "The law of delict deals with injuries, harms, losses and other damage which persons cause, wittingly or not to others living in the same organised society on whose lives their conduct in some way impinges." *The Law of Delict in Scotland*, by David M. Walker, 2 edn., pp. 4–5. *See also délit, quasi-délit.*

delinquent loan or payment
A sum of money that is unpaid when due either under the terms of a contract (e.g. rent or mortgage interest), or by law (e.g. a tax). A payment that has fallen into arrears.

délit (F)
delict; misdemeanour; offence. A wrong or injurious act against another, in particular an intentional harm caused by an unlawful action, but not a breach of contract. In French law *délit* refers to a criminal wrong or intentional harm done to another.
cf. *quasi-délit.*

delivery
1. The act of placing something in the legal **possession** or control of another. A legal act whereby control of a property is transferred voluntarily to another party. Delivery may be 'actual' when a thing is handed over physically, or 'constructive' when the law deems that possession of something has been transferred e.g. when a document evidences that possession has changed. Delivery is an essential element for a sale of goods or a conveyance of land. In the case of good "'deliver' means voluntary transfer of possession from one person to another" (Sale of Goods Act 1979, s. 61(1)). This may include 'actual' or 'physical' delivery; 'symbolic' delivery when documents of title, or a representation of a right to possession as with a key, is transferred; or an act of 'attornment' when a third party acknowledges that he holds goods on behalf of a new owner or possessor. See also **escrow.**
2. The final stage in the formalisation of a **deed** when the document is handed over to the other party, i.e. the **date** on which the deed becomes valid. "After a deed is written and sealed, if it be not delivered, all the rest is to no purpose" – Termes de La Ley. Delivery may be effected in words or by conduct and, although not essential, should be acknowledged by the recipient. "'Deliver' in this connection does not mean 'handed over' to the other side. It means delivered in the old legal sense namely, an act done so as to evince an intention to be bound" – Vincent *v* Premo Enterprises (Voucher Sales) Ltd. [1969] 2 All ER 944. Delivery may be (a) unconditional, thus taking effect without reservation or delay; (b) subject to a condition being complied with, until which time the grantor may revoke the deed – in that case there is no delivery and no valid deed until compliance with the

condition has been effected; or (c) in **escrow** i.e. it takes effect when a given time arises or a condition is performed by the recipient.

Delivery of an **abstract of title** takes place when the documents of title, or copies thereof, are delivered "with sufficient clearness and sufficient fullness" to show every instrument that contains any part of the vendor's title – Oakden *v* Pike (1865) 34 LJ Ch. 622. See also **acquisition, completion, signed, sealed and delivered, surrender.**

delivery in escrow
see **escrow.**

délivrance (F)
service, (of a notice); **delivery**. See also *signification.*

demand loan (or mortgage)
see **call loan (or mortgage).**

demand note
A **bill of exchange** or **promissory note** payable on demand.

démembrements de la propriété (F)
Literally 'dismemberments or fragmentation of property', i.e. dividing ownership of land or real property into separate or fragmented parts; **partial ownership**. A right to use real property, to have one of the benefits of ownership (*droit de propriété*), where the subject matter of that right is held by another. "Property is subject to divided interests when, for the conveyance of full ownership, the concurrence of two or more persons, having rights or powers in the subject matter, would be necessary." – Amos & Walton's Introduction to French Law, 3 edn., p. 130. These 'real rights' into which property can be divided are: *nue-propriété* (bare ownership);

usufruit (**usufruct**); a *servitude*; *usage* and *habitation*; *concession immobilière* and the right to the *superficie*; and the long leases – *bail emphytéotique* (**emphyteotic lease**) and *bail à construction*. This subdividing of ownership may be extended to include a mortgage, or a conditional interest, e.g. a life interest. However, a divided interest must be limited in its duration, as it is a rule of French law (akin to the **rule against perpetuities** in English common law) that such right should not be unduly prolonged so as to prevent absolute or complete ownership being transferred or alienated within a reasonable period of time.
cf. *remembrement*.

demesne land
1. Land held in one's own right, *in domino*, without acknowledgement to another. Thus, demesne land of the Crown is land held by the Sovereign in his or her public capacity. See also **Crown Land, doctrine of estates, domain.**
2. Land held by the lord of a **manor** for his own and his servants' use. Called also 'inland' to distinguish it from land away from the manor 'outland' or **tenemental land** which was let out or occupied by a villein tenant. A manor held by the Crown during the reign of William the Conqueror and recorded in the Domesday Book became known as an ancient demesne; or sometimes **customary freehold**, because these lands became the earliest established right of freehold. See also **feudal system.**
3. Land owned with a country house or part of a large estate.
4. **Landed property.**

densité (F)
density.
(*densité de construction* – building density)
(*densité de population* – population density).

demise

Any **transfer** or **conveyance**, especially a transfer of land for a term of years, for life or by will. A **lease** is a conveyance by means of a demise of land and the word demise is commonly used in a lease to denote the creation of a tenancy of land for a term of years; "a 'demise' or a 'lease' is the grant of a right to the exclusive possession of land for a determinate term less than that which the grantor has himself in the land." (Woodfall's Landlord and Tenant, 28 edn., 1–0003.)

The use of the word 'demise' in a lease, although not essential, implies a covenant for **quiet enjoyment** during the term of the grant – Burnett *v* Lynch (1826), 5 B and C 589 and Markham *v* Paget [1908] 1 Ch. 697 and a **covenant for title** (i.e. the lessor has the power to grant a lease, even if not the power to grant the lease he purports to grant); unless there is an express stipulation limiting the implication – Line *v* Stephenson (1838) 5 Bing. (NC) 678; Evans *v* Williams, 291 Ky. 484, 165 SW 2d. 52. See also **implied covenant**.
Hill and Redman's, *Law of Landlord and Tenant*, 17 edn., pp. 103–104.
Woodfall's Landlord and Tenant, 28 edn., paras. 1–0002 to 1–0003.

demised premises
see **demise, leased premises**.

demolition
The act of completely pulling down,

tearing down, or destroying (as a building or structure); a reduction to ruins or to a mass. The scattering of all the component parts. Although, "it can never be said that a house is not demolished because a few stones are left standing one upon another." – R. *v* Langford (1842) Car. and M 604. See also **conservation area, development, listed building**.

demolition order
An order made by a local authority, in accordance with the provisions of the Housing Act 1957, ss. 17–21, requiring the demolition of a house that is considered to be **unfit for human habitation** and is not considered capable of being made fit for habitation at a "reasonable cost". The order is served on the person "having control" of the house requiring that person to arrange for the demolition of the building. The owner of the property retains the cleared site and a person displaced from the house may be entitled to a **home-loss payment** as recompense for the loss of his or her home. In certain circumstances, an occupier of the house that is subject to a demolition order may be rehoused by the local authority. There is a right of appeal to the county court against a demolition order, which must be made within 21 days of the service of notice of the making of the order. If no appeal is made the order takes effect at the end of the 21 days and demolition of the house is then required normally within six weeks (1957 Act, s. 20). See also **clearance area, closing order**.
West's Law of Housing, 4 edn., pp. 81–99.
Housing Law, by Andrew Arden and Martin Partington, pp. 470–475

(1983).
22 Halsbury's Laws of England, 4 edn., paras. 584–591.

denoting stamp

A stamp affixed or embossed on to an instrument by the Inland Revenue to indicate the amount of **stamp duty** paid.

density

The mass of building per given area of land. A ratio that expresses the relationship between a number of units – houses, rooms, persons, etc. – and the space occupied by those units, e.g. houses per acre (or hectare), employees per square foot (or square metre). See also **floor space index, land use planning, plot ratio, population density, residential density, site coverage.**
Introduction to Town and Country Planning, by John Ratcliffe, 2 edn., pp. 397–407.
Principles and Practice of Town and Country Planning, by L.B. Keeble, 4 edn., pp. 269–285.
Urban Land Use Planning, by F. Stuart Chaplin Jr. and Edward J. Kaiser, pp. 454–50, (1979)

density zoning (US)

see **zoning ordinance**

département (F)

department, the primary administrative district in France. See also **local authority**.

department store

A large retail store selling a range of merchandise under one roof such that it is not identified with any one line of goods; although, for the purpose of promotion, advertising, control and accounting, it is divided into separate departments. A department store aims to provide for a wide range of consumer requirement while maintaining a single system of service, control and management.

Department of the Environment (DOE)

A central government department that is responsible for the control and co-ordination of land development, town and country planning, regional and local government planning, housing, and other matters relating to the national environment. This department is the central **planning authority** for matters relating to real property in the United Kingdom. Overall responsibility for the department is with the **Secretary of State for the Environment**. See also **Property Services Agency**.
Town Planning and the Surveyor, by Gerald Burke, pp. 8–11, (1980).

dépendance (F)

accessory (to property); **messuage**. (*avec dépendances* – with outbuildings).

dépense (F)

expense; **expenditure; cost**. (*dépenses d'entretien* – maintenance costs).

depleting asset

see **wasting asset**.

deposit

1. Something given for safe keeping, as security, or as an act of good faith. A sum of money, generally deemed to be a part payment of the purchase price, lodged with a person, usually a vendor's agent or lawyer, before or at the time of the signing of a contract for sale, to show the purchaser's earnest intentions.

A deposit may be made as a 'pre-contract' payment, popularly called **earnest-money**, or it may be paid as a

condition of a contract. In either case the deposit is intended to demonstrate that the purchaser means business. In the case of a pre-contract deposit it is held usually by someone who acts as a **stakeholder** and normally it is returned to the purchaser if no formal contract results – Sorrell *v* Finch [1976] 2 All ER 371. When a deposit is paid as security, i.e. as a condition of a formal contract, then if the purchaser repudiates the contract, without good reason, he surrenders the deposit; but if the contract is performed the deposit is taken into account as part of the purchase monies. It acts both as an incentive for the payer to complete his obligations under the contract and as a part payment – Howe *v* Smith (1884) 27 Ch. D 101; Ellis *v* Roberts, 98 Pa. Super. 49. However, in the final analysis, whether a deposit is recoverable depends on the construction of the agreement (express or implied) made between the parties.

A deposit may be held by a third party who is acting as an **agent** or a stakeholder, according to the terms of the contract or the implied intention of the parties. If it is held so that the holder (who may be, for example, a lawyer, estate agent or auctioneer) is acting as an agent he or she is said to be acting in a fiduciary capacity so that to all intent and purpose, it is as if the deposit is held by the vendor, who may use the monies as he or she wishes. In such an instance if the agent fails to return the deposit when the depositor is rightly entitled to receive it back, it is the vendor, and not the agent, who must be sued for the return of the deposit. However, if a deposit is held by a stakeholder, that party solely is responsible for the

money; the stakeholder acts for both parties; and the vendor cannot use the deposit towards any property he may purchase without the purchaser's consent. If there is no condition set down in a contract (either in the general or special conditions of sale) as to how the deposit is to be held a vendor's solicitor, or estate agent, holds the monies as an agent – Ellis *v* Goulton [1893] 1 QB 350; except for an **auctioneer** who holds as a stakeholder – Harrington *v* Hoggard (1830) 1 B and Ad. 577.

At common law an estate agent was entitled to retain any interest earned while holding a deposit; this rule was based on the principle that interest so earned is a reward to the estate agent for withholding a property from the market and thus foregoing the "prospect of earning a commission upon its sale to any other part" – Potters *v* Loppert [1973] Ch. 415. This common law rule has been overruled by the Estate Agents Act 1975, s. 15 which makes an **estate agent**, but not necessarily an auctioneer, accountable to the purchaser for other than *de miminis* receipts of interest on contract and pre-contract deposits. An estate agent is deemed by that statute to hold a deposit on trust, as stakeholder for the purchaser, before contracts are exchanged; and on trust, as stakeholder for the vendor, after contracts are exchanged.

If a vendor of land is in **breach of contract** by failing to provide a **good title** to the land, as a rule, the purchaser can recover his deposit (together with interest thereon), as well as the expenses of investigating title; but may not recover damages because he has lost the bargain – Bain

v Fothergill [1874] LR 7 HL 158.
However, this rule may be superseded
if the vendor just refuses to make a
good title or if there is misrepresentation or a similar action by which the
vendor seeks to avoid making a good
title. See also **escrow**.
*The Law of Estate Agency and
Auctions*, by J.R. Murdoch, 2 edn.,
pp. 190–194, 314–327, 394–400, 442–444.
Contract and Conveyance, by J.T.
Farrand, 4 edn., pp. 203–208.
Barnsley's Conveyancing Law, 2
edn., pp. 250–254.
42 Halsbury's Laws of England, 4 ed.,
paras. 244–257.
2. An amount of **collateral**, or a
premium, paid at the start of a lease.
3. A sum of money entrusted to a
bank or other financial institution for
safe-keeping, and usually for the
purpose of earning interest. See also
principal.
4. The placing of title deeds with a
lender as **security** for a loan. See also
**charge by way of a legal mortgage,
equitable mortgage, puisne mortgage**.
5. See **bailment**.

deposit receipt
A written acknowledgement of receipt of a **deposit** or **earnest money**.
This **receipt** may contain the elements
of a valid **contract** and thus can create
a legally binding contract, or, at least,
an 'agreement for sale' or an
'agreement for a lease'. See also
binder.

dépositaire (F)
bailee; trustee.
(*dépositaire d'enjeux* – **stakeholder**;
escrowee).

dépossession (F)
dispossession; eviction; disseisin.

dépôt (F)
1. depot; store
(*dépôt de marchandise* – **warehouse**).
2. **deposit; bailment**.
(*dépôt de garantie* – guaranty payment; **earnest money**; rent deposit).

depreciated cost
The cost of a property less accrued
depreciation shown in a financial
statement. See also **basis, book value**.

depreciated replacement cost (DCR)
The **replacement cost** of a property
less an allowance made to ensure that
the cost does not cover more than is
necessary to replace a property in its
depreciated state. The 'depreciated
replacement cost method of valuation' corresponds to the **reinstatement method of valuation**; the former
term being used by the Royal
Institution of Chartered Surveyors
(Guidance Notes on the Valuation of
Assets, Background Paper No. BP3)
to refer to this method of valuation
when applied to valuing a property
that has no ready market value for
company balance sheet purposes (e.g.
an oil refinery or power station). "It is
a method of using current replacement costs to arrive at the value to the
business in occupation of the property at the valuation date" – Guidance
Note No. BP3. See also **contractor's
basis**.

depreciation
1. A loss in value due to use, physical
wear and tear, or the effects of time
and neglect. A reduction in the worth
of an asset over a period of time due
to **deterioration** and/or **obsolescence**.
'Deterioration' is that which is caused
by physical changes in the state of a
property, i.e. it arises from use or consumption (depletion), or wear and

tear; whereas 'obsolescence' is that which is caused by functional changes such as changes in design and style, or by economic or environmental changes such as external changes in the neighbourhood. Depreciation may be considered as 'curable' i.e. it can be made good economically by repair and maintenance; or 'incurable' i.e. it is produced by changes that are beyond the control of the property owner and cannot be made good economically. See also **deferred maintenance, injurious affection**.
2. The writing down, and eventually writing off, of the cost of an asset over its useful or estimated economic life, in the profit and loss account of an organisation, for taxation purposes: the provision for depreciation in a valuation, a financial statement or an assessment of a liability for tax, being referred to as a 'depreciation allowance'.

The principal methods of allowing for depreciation are: the **annuity method; sinking-fund method; sum-of-the-years' digits method; straight-line method;** and any method that provides for **accelerated depreciation** or **declining-balance depreciation**. See also **accrued depreciation, capital allowance, tax shelter**.
Tax Planning for Real Estate Transaction by Jerome J. Halperin, (Coopers and Lybrand) pp. 110-149, (1978).
3. A deduction from the **reproduction cost** of a property to arrive at its current value. See also **depreciated replacement cost**.

dépréciation (F)
depreciation.
(*dépréciation par usure* – wear and tear).
(*dépréciation par vétusté*, or *dépréci-*

ation fonctionnelle – **obsolescence**).

depreciation allowance (or provision)
see **depreciation**.

depreciation recapture (US)
see **recapture of depreciation**.

depressed area
see **development area**.

depth factor (US)
A factor used in appraisal to adjust the price per foot frontage of comparable plots of land that have different depths. The price of a plot is adjusted by the appraiser using a percentage rate in order to reflect the effect on the value of the plot of its depth relative to the depths of other comparable plots. The rate of adjustment may not be proportional to the depth; as a very narrow fronted plot of land, with a relatively large depth, is likely to be less sought after than a more regular shaped plot. A depth factor may be obtained from 'depth tables' which show the percentage adjustment considered appropriate for a given depth of a plot of land compared to a standard plot in the market. See also **4—3—2—1 rule, zoning method of valuation**.

depth tables
see **depth factor**.

derelict
Personal property that has been wilfully abandoned by the owner and thereby left to be claimed by the first possessor.

derelict land
Land that has been intentionally abandoned or neglected; land gutted of use or devoid of purpose; or land damaged by mineral working, indus-

trial or other forms of development, so that it is no longer capable of beneficial use within a reasonable time without considerable improvement. Derelict land may have been neglected or damaged by man's intervention e.g. by the abandonment of a building, airfield, quarry, mine, etc.; or may be land left unattended after non-user. Derelict land does not include land, which although having a similar appearance, has been laid waste by natural causes; such as a desert, marsh land, disused farmland, or land that has now blended into, or has become part of, the landscape and is no longer detrimental to the local amenity.

Derelict land is likely to be unsightly and may well give rise to a public **nuisance**. See also **urban decay, wasteland**.

Town and Country Planning in Britain by J.B. Cullingworth, 8 edn., pp. 138–140, 190–191.

An Introduction to Town and Country Planning by John Ratcliffe, 2 edn., pp. 288–294.

Derelict Land, by Kenneth L. Wallwork (1974).

derelictae, res (L)
see *res derelictae*

dereliction
1. Material left by the gradual receding of water from land, either as a result of the sea shrinking back below its usual tidal level or a river altering its course from one bank to another. Called also 'diluvion'.
cf.**alluvion**. See also **accretion**.
2. The voluntary **abandonment** of a chattel or moveable property.

derogation from grant
Diminishing, or militating against, a

right or interest that has already been granted, i.e. doing something that takes away, grants to another, or interferes with a benefit that one person has contractually conferred on another. A term used particularly to refer to a type of **implied covenant** that is placed on a vendor of land, or a landlord, requiring that he does not use adjoining property retained by him so as to render the sold or leased land unfit, or materially less fit, for the purpose for which it was sold or let. The rule that a person must not derogate from that which he has granted is based on "a principle which merely embodies in a legal maxim a rule of common honesty". – Harmer *v* Jumbil (Nigeria) Tin Areas Ltd. [1921] 1 Ch. 225; thus, "a grantor having given a thing with one hand is not to take away the means of enjoying it with the other". – Birmingham, Dudley and District Banking Co. *v* Ross (1888) 38 Ch. D 313. For example, the following may constitute a derogation from grant: establishing a night club next to residential property; letting premises for use as a timber merchant and then building on adjoining land so as to restrict the flow of air to the timber drying sheds – Aldin *v* Latimer Clark, Muirhead and Co. [1894] 2 Ch. 437; causing vibration from machinery installed on adjoining land so as to interfere with the stability of the leased premises – Grosvenor Hotel Co. *v* Hamilton [1894] 2 QB 836. The derogation must be substantial; it does not include, for example, letting adjoining retail premises for a competing user – Port *v* Griffiths [1938] 1 All ER 295; Clarke Gamble of Canada *v* Grand Park Plaza [1967] CLR 570. Derogation may arise also when the grantor of an easement takes a course of action that limits the beneficiary's proper or full enjoyment of that easement, e.g. periodically placing obstructions over a right of way or building so as to obstruct a right of light – Pollard *v* Gare [1901] 1 Ch. 834.

cf. **quiet enjoyment**. See also **implied covenant, quasi-easement**.

Gale's Law of Easements, 14 edn., pp. 88–92.

Hill and Redman's Law of Landlord and Tenant, 17 edn.

Woodfall's Landlord and Tenant, 28 edn., paras. 1–1146 to 1–1151.

descent
The acquisition of property by **inheritance**, especially the hereditary succession to real property when someone dies **intestate**. The vesting of title in someone, upon the death of another, by mere operation of land, as distinguished from purchase (Bl. Comm. vol. ii, p. 201).

description
1. A representation given by one person which tells another, as clearly as possible, what a thing is. A description is adequate if it gives a view which enables the thing to be recognised when seen or when sensed in another appropriate way. See also **misdescription, particulars of sale, schedule of condition**.
2. The part of a deed or conveyance which describes the subject matter. See also **parcels, plan, premises**.

déshérence (F)
(*tomber en déshérence* – to **escheat**).

design and build contract
see **package-deal contract**.

design and management contract (US)
see **turn-key contract**.

designated area
An area of land delineated as liable to be purchased by a local authority or public body. An area designated for a specific form of future development, e.g. for a new town. See also **area of comprehensive development, area of special scientific interest, urban development area**.

desist
To give up a right. To forebear or refrain from an action. In the US, a 'desist and refrain order' may be issued directing a person to refrain from committing an act that violates a real estate law. See also **abandonment**.

désistement (F)
disclaimer; waiver.

dessaisir (F)
to **release**; to disseize; to transfer one's right to property to another; to dispossess. See also **disseisin**.

destination (F)
destination; purpose (to which a property is put); the nature of a property by virtue of its use, e.g. moveable property (***mobilier***) attached to land has the destination of an immoveable property (***immobilier***).
(*destination du père de famille* – a means by which a *servitude* might come into existence; when a person establishes such a right or burden between two parcels of land which are both in his sole ownership (a **quasi-easement**) then if either of these parcels comes into separate ownership the servitude comes into existence, by the nature of that which then exists and not by contract or prescription. *Destination du père de famille* only

exists "when it is proven that the two properties which now are divided had belonged to the same owner, and that it was he who brought the state of affairs into existence from which the servitude existed"(French Civil Code, art. 693). See also *immeuble*, *meuble*.

désuétude (F)
obsolescence.

detached house
A house that stands apart from any other house or non-associated building; a house separated from others and usually surrounded by unbuilt land on all sides.
cf. **semi-detached house, terrace house.**

détail (F)
retail.
(*commerce de détail* – retail trade).

detailed planning permission
see **planning permission.**

détails (F)
details; particulars.
(*détails d'un vente immobilier* – **particulars of sale**).

detainer
The act of unlawfully withholding goods from someone; a keeping of goods unlawfully in one's possession. See also **conversion.**

détention (F)
(*détention précaire* – the possession of property subject to the right of another e.g. the 'holding' enjoyed by a lessor, bailor or licensor). See also *précaire.*

deterioration
A reduction or degeneration in the quality or value of a property due to wear and tear, usage, or any other physical cause. Deterioration is the primary physical factor that causes **depreciation,** i.e. loss in value. See also **fair wear and tear, physical deterioration, waste.**

determinable fee simple
1. An estate in land that is equivalent to a **fee simple** except that it may come to an end upon the occurrence of some act or event that is specified at the time the interest is created, being an event that may never happen, e.g. a fee simple granted 'to A until she marries'. A determinable fee is created by using such words as 'for so long as', 'while' or 'until'. A determinable fee simple has a delineated and express duration and automatically comes to an end if the specified event occurs. However, if the event does not occur the estate may last for ever as with a **fee simple absolute.**
cf. **conditional fee simple.** See also **determinable interest, qualified fee.** *The Law of Real Property,* by Sir Robert Megarry & H.W.R. Wade, 5 edn., pp. 67–71, 74.
39 Halsbury's Laws of England, paras. 415–417.
(US) 2. See **base fee.**

determinable interest
1. An interest in land that is granted but may come to an end before the maximum duration allotted by the grantor due to a terminating act or event, e.g. an interest granted 'to A until B marrries' or 'to A until he becomes bankrupt'. In particular, an interest that automatically comes to an end if some event (which may never occur), specified for when the interest was created, does occur. A determinable interest is created by the use of such words as 'until', 'during', 'for as long as', and by the stipulation of determining event in one and the

same document as that which is used to grant the interest. Thus, it is an interest that is less than that which is express because it is subjected to a liability to be cut down. If the interest must come to an end at a future point (e.g. on the death of the beneficiary) it is not a determinable interest. The right to the land that forms the subject matter of a determinable interest commonly reverts to the grantor or creator of that interest, or his or her heirs.
cf. **conditional interest, executory interest**. See also **determinable fee simple**.
Cheshire's Modern Law of Real Property, 13 edn., pp. 341–344.
2. An interest in land that may be brought to an end by a prescribed event, e.g. a lease that continues from year to year 'until determined by six months notice' or 'until the tenant dies'. See also **determination, tenancy for life**.

determination

A bringing or coming to an end; usually by some deliberate act. The bringing or coming to an end of a contract, or an estate or interest in property; especially by notice as expressly provided for in a contract or as a consequence of a fundamental breach of a condition of a contract. Although, "the word determination may properly and according to legal as well as to ordinary use, signify the coming to an end in any way whatever". – St. Aubyn *v* St. Aubyn (1861) 1 Drew and Sm. 618-9. Thus, 'determination' may mean ending by effluxion of time, as with a tenancy for a term of years; or being brought to an end by any means. But it is used more commonly to convey the same meaning as

termination, i.e. the deliberate ending of an interest, rather than its **expiration** due to effluxion of time. Nonetheless, it is necessary to look at the context to ascertain whether 'to determine' or 'determination' requires an act by someone to bring the contract to an end or whether effluxion of time suffices.
cf. **rescission**. See also **breach of contract, lease**.

detinue

The withholding of goods from another, especially when this follows as a result of a legal process. A legal action to reclaim goods *in specie* which have been wrongfully detained by another against the wishes of the person entitled to their immediate possession, and to recover damages for the consequential loss of enjoyment of those goods. Detinue was abolished by the Torts (Interference with Goods) Act 1977. s.1 (1) and has been replaced by an action for **conversion**. See also **replevin**.

dette (F)

debt; liability; obligation.
(*dette hypothécaire* – mortgage debt).

developer

1. A person or body that carries on the **development** of land, especially a person or body that acquires land for building purposes and subsequent resale. See also **entrepreneur, property developer**.
2. A party that employs a **building contractor** (Town and Country Planning Act 1971, s. 90).

developer's residual approach (US)
see **residual approach**.

development

The carrying on of an activity that

changes the nature of land or buildings, especially the carrying out of an **improvement** or **alteration** to land or buildings. The making of changes in the physical environment, in particular the opening up, laying out, or changing and improving the potential of land or buildings thereon; including any change in the use, or intensity of use, of land or buildings.

Development is defined, for planning control purposes, by the Town and Country Planning Act 1971, s. 22 (1) as, "the carrying out of building, engineering, mining or other operations in, on, over or under land or the making of any **material change in the use** of any building or land" (a definition extended by the Town and Country Planning (Minerals) Act 1981, s.1 to include the removal of material from mineral workings or other deposits). Such activity generally requires **planning permission**. However, there is no one test to decide what physical characteristics constitute development. "The concept behind that definition is two-fold, first, in regard to change of use, one takes the land as it is and ascertains if it has been put to a different use, and secondly, and this is quite regardless of use, one has to ascertain whether the land itself has been changed by certain operations ... 'in, on, over or under land' .... It seems to me [Lord Parker C.J.] that the position is rather analogous to the problems which one is faced with when deciding what fixtures pass with the freehold ... one must look at the whole circumstances, including what is undoubtedly extremely relevant, the degree of permanency with which it is affected, in order to see whether the operation has been such as to constitute development." – Cheshire County Council *v* Woodward [1962] 2 QB 133-4. Thus anything that materially or permanently affects the appearance of land or the exterior of a building is likely to be treated as development.

Demolition is not necessarily development; but a material change to the landscape may be development, especially when this takes on the nature of engineering work on an appreciable scale – Coleshill and District Investment Co. Ltd. *v* Minister of Housing and Local Government [1969] 2 All ER 525. Demolition as part of a building or development scheme normally is considered to be development – London County Council *v* Marks and Spencer Ltd. [1953] AC 535. Demolition of part of a building so as to materially affect its appearance is likely to be considered as development (Secretary of the Environment Circular 67/49).

Section 22(2) of the 1971 Act also specifies certain matters that are deemed not to be development, in particular (a) "the carrying out of works for the maintenance, improvement or alteration of any building, being works which affect only the interior of the building or which do not materially affect the external appearance of the building"; (b) works by a highway authority to repair and maintain a road and repair and renew existing services (but this does not include the laying of new services); (c) incidental changes of use within the curtilage of a dwelling-house; (d) the use of land or buildings for agriculture and forestry (including afforestation); and (e) changes within the same 'use class'. The rebuilding of a house when only the foundations and some of the walls are left is not merely maintenance and improvement but development – Street *v* Essex County Council (1965) 193 EG 537. On the other hand, certain matters are declared in section 22(2) to be development (a) the use of a building as two or more dwelling-houses, when previously it was used as a single dwelling and (b) the creation or extension of a refuse tip. Certain minor matters (generally related to a change of use), although classified as development, are deemed not to require planning permission, i.e. they are **permitted development** by virtue of a **General Development Order**. In addition, any development that was authorised or started before 1 July 1948 was deemed to have planning permission, which remained valid until 1 April 1974. See also **advertisement, building operations, enforcement notice, engineering operations, existing use certificate, material development, mining operations, new development, redevelopment, Special Development Order, Use Classes Order.**

Practical Planning Law by J.F. Garner, pp. 96–105 (1981).
Cases and Materials on Planning Law by Michael Purdue, pp. 81–126 (1983).
Planning Law and Procedure, by A.E. Telling, 6 edn., pp. 63–89.
Outline of Planning Law, by Desmond Heap, 8 edn., pp. 84–102.
Urban Planning Law, by Malcolm Grant, pp. 148–178 (1982).
Encyclopaedia of Planning Law, by Desmond Heap, paras. 1–068 *et seq.*

development analysis
A financial analysis made in order to ascertain the total cost and return

from a proposed development project. See also **feasibility study, residual method of valuation.**
Property Development, by David Cadman and Leslie Austin Crowe, 2 edn.
Office Development, by Paul and Paula Marber, Ch. 5 (1985).
Valuation and Development Appraisal, by Clive Darlow (1982).

development appraisal
see **appraisal, development analysis**.

development approach (US)
see **residual approach**.

development area
An area suffering from adverse economic conditions, especially from high levels of unemployment and consequent adverse migration of its population. An area of a country considered by central government to be in need of financial assistance or other inducements, with the aim of stimulating new development, attracting further investment and thereby increasing potential employment. Such areas are designated for government assistance with the intention of 'taking work to the workers' and improving the level of economic activity.

In Britain such areas were first referred to as special areas and were designated 'development areas' in 1945. The Local Employment Act 1960 then changed the designation to 'development district', and the Industrial Development Act 1966, s. 15 reintroduced the term development area. The Local Employment Act 1972, s. 1 (as amended by the Industry Act 1972, s. 13) empowers the Secretary of State for the Environment to make orders to designate development areas as areas of the country which require special attention. The Assisted Areas Order 1979 designated a number of such areas and termed them assisted areas which in turn were divided into 'special development areas', 'intermediate development areas', or, simply, 'development areas' depending on the degree of financial or other assistance considered necessary to induce employment and to revive economic activity.

In the US this type of area is usually referred to as a 'distressed area'. See also **assisted area, enterprise zone, special area, urban development area.**

An Introduction to Regional Planning, by John Glasson, 2edn., pp. 212–217.

development charge

A tax, levied in the UK between 1947 and 1953, on any increase in the value of land due to the grant of planning permission. This tax, which was payable to the **Central Land Board**, was levied at the rate of 100 per cent on the difference between the assessed value of land without planning permission – **existing use value** – and the assessed value of the land with the benefit of a grant of planning permission – **development value**. Thus it was a tax levied on the privilege of developing land. It was abolished by the Town and Country Planning Act 1952. See also **betterment, Part VI claim.**

development control

see **advertisement, building controls, discontinuance order, conservation area, enforcement notice, listed building consent, planning permission, revocation order, tree preservation order, zoning ordinance.**

development corporation

A corporation established to layout, develop and administer a **new town**. The New Towns Act 1981, s. 4 (replacing the New Towns Act 1965, s. 3) empowers a development corporation (a) "to acquire, hold, manage and dispose of land and other property; (b) to carry out building and other operations; (c) to provide water, electricity, gas, sewage and other services; (d) to carry on any business or undertaking in or for the purposes of the new town, and generally to do anything necessary or expedient for the purposes or incidental purposes of the new town". See also **urban development corporation.**

development cost

The total cost of a project of development, including all land acquisition costs, building or construction costs (including demolition and site preparation costs), professional fees and financing costs. See also **feasibility study, residual method of valuation.**

development district

see **development area.**

development gains charge (DGC)

see **development gains tax.**

development gains tax (DGT)

A tax, introduced by the Finance Act 1974 ss. 38–40, to recoup 'development gains', i.e. capital gains which arose from the sale or letting of land that had the benefit of a right to carry out development, especially as a result of a grant of planning permission. Called also a 'development gains charge'. Effectively abolished from 1 August 1976 and replaced by **development land tax.**

Development Gains Tax, by George

Dobry, W.R. Stewart-Smith and Michael Barnes, (1975).

development land
1. Land held for planned future development. See also **development property, land bank.**
2. See **community land.**

development land tax (DLT)

A tax, or levy, first introduced by the Development Land Tax Act 1976 (and effective from 31 August 1976), which was charged on the realisation of the **development value** of land (or an interest in land) in the United Kingdom. (DLT was levied regardless of whether the taxpayer is resident in the UK.) The development value was assessed by deducting from the 'net proceeds of the disposal' (which was based on actual receipts or market value), the highest of three 'base values' (which were based on the original purchase price adjusted for changes in land value – excluding any development value; its cost plus 15 per cent; and its current use value plus 15 per cent). The development value could be realised either when an owner disposed of an interest in land; or when he was 'deemed' to have disposed of his interest by selling and immediately reacquiring it on the "commencement of a project of **material development**". ('Disposal' is defined broadly in the Act and includes a sale of a freehold or leasehold interest, or part interest, in land; the grant of a lease; and payments for the grant or release of an interest in land). Thus, an owner was taxed when he sold his land for development, started development himself or permitted another to start development on his land. Development for DLT purposes had a similar meaning to that used in

planning law, and included the making of any material change in the 'use of any buildings or other land'. In certain cases DLT was levied also when a person received compensation for a planning restriction or even compensation for injurious affection to land. Certain reliefs and exemptions from DLT were provided for: notably, the disposal of a main private residence with up to one acre of land; development of property that is to be used by a 'trader' for manufacturing or processing purposes; development begun within 3 years of an acquisition of land, provided it can be shown that no significant development value would have resulted had development started immediately after the land was acquired; development for an owner's own use and occupation subsequent to planning permission; land in an enterprise zone; and, normally, an annual exemption for the first £50000 of realised development value. Public authorities, charities, housing associations and the Housing Corporation also were granted certain exemption rights or, in certain instances, a right to defer the tax liability. Provision was made in the Act to avoid a **capital gains tax** liability leading to double taxation. As a rule DLT liability was assessed first and any other tax liability was charged against any residual gain. Development land tax was intended to be a charge on **betterment**, which arose as a result of the grant and use of planning permission, and effectively it replaced **development gains tax**. DLT was abolished with effect from 19 March 1985 (Finance Act 1985, s. 93).

Modern Methods of Valuation, 7 edn., Ch. 24.

Taxation of Land Transactions, by A.R. Mellows, 3 edn., pp. 19–77.

Development Land Tax, by D. Goy, 2 edn.

Development Land Tax Guide, by J. Matthews, T.A. Johnson and E.F. Westlake, (1984).

Development Land Tax, by Clifford Joseph, 3 edn.

46 Halsbury's Laws of England, 4 edn., paras. 551–768

Development Land Tax, by Bagnal and Lewison (updated service).

development loan or finance

A building or construction loan. A loan obtained, or finance used, for any project of development. The term may be used also to refer to a short-term or interim loan granted to a developer to cover the cost of land acquisition and preliminary development expenditure.

Valuation and Development Appraisal, edited by Clive Darlow, p. 166 *et seq.*, (1982).

development management

see **project management**.

development order

see **general development order, special development order**.

development plan

A plan prepared for a given area to show proposals for the use and development of land. A development plan shows the existing and future communication network; acts as a control for future development of the area; indicates proposals to improve the physical environment; and sets down private and public development and redevelopment priorities. A development plan is intended to act as a guide to the granting, or refusal, of planning permission. As well as defining areas for different purposes, a development plan also designates areas that may be required in the future for public purposes.

In England and Wales the term development plan was applied particularly to a plan prepared by a local authority, in accordance with statutory requirements (originally the Town and Country Planning Act 1947, s. 5), setting out the manner in which the area under its administration was to be used. Generally such plans were merely zoning maps, showing existing land uses and major development proposals, accompanied by a statement of the planning authority's principal intentions for the use and development of particular areas of land. Those plans are being superseded by the **structure plan** and **local plan**, as required by the Town and Country Planning Act 1971, Part II, as amended by the Town and Country Planning (Amendment) Act 1972, ss. 1–4 and the Highways Act, Sch. 24, s. 20, (although a development plan prepared in accordance with the provisions of the 1947 Act may remain in force until the new plans are approved). See also **town map, zoning**.

Outline of Planning Law, by Desmond Heap, 8 edn., pp. 40–46.

Practical Planning Law, by J.F. Garner, pp. 83–91 (1981).

Town and Country Planning in Britain, by J.B. Cullingworth, 8 edn., pp. 56–77.

Planning Procedure Tables, by R.N.D. Hamilton, 4 edn., pp. 1–24.

Planning Law and Procedure, by A.E. Telling, 6 edn., pp. 41–62.

Urban Planning Law, by Malcolm Grant, pp. 75–144, (1982).

development property
Property held, or capable of being used, for **development**. Property held for future development or redevelopment purposes. Property that can be increased in value by capital expenditure, in particular by the erection of a new building or buildings. See also **residual method of valuation**.
Modern Methods of Valuation, 7 edn., Ch. 18.
Property Development, by D. Cadman and L. Austin-Crowe, 1978.

development right, transferable (US)
see **transferable development right**.

development scheme
see **scheme of development**.

development valuation
see **residual method of valuation**.

development value
1. The **latent value** in a property that could be realised by carrying out development work. This value could alter significantly by a subsequent grant of consent to carry out a new form of development or a change of use.
2. A term used in various English statutes to indicate an increase in value resulting from the grant of planning permission for development, or **betterment** resulting therefrom. Especially used when the increase in value may be the subject of a tax or levy, such as **development land tax**. The Development Land Tax Act 1976, s. 4 (1) refers to the 'realised development value' which is obtained on a disposal (whether actual or 'deemed') of an interest in land and is represented by the amount (if any) by which 'the net proceeds of the disposal exceeds the

relevant base value of that interest'.

développement (F)
development; expansion.
(*zone de développement* – **development area**).

devest or divest
To deprive someone of **possession**; to take away property, or an interest in property. "'Devest' is a word contrary to 'invest'; for, as an invest signifieth to deliver the possession of a thing, so devest signifieth the taking away of possession" –Termes de la Ley.
cf. **vest**.

devis (F)
estimate.
(*devis descriptif* – **bill of quantities**).
(*devis estimatif* – preliminary estimate).

devise
1. To give land by a **will** that is duly attested by law.
2. The transfer of, or the act of transferring, property, in particular **real property** as a gift by **will** – i.e. the effective transfer of property from a dying to a living person. The devise may transfer or **'vest'** the property immediately, or the transfer may be 'contingent' on a future event such as the death of another party. It may be also a 'general devise' which transfers all the deceased's property; a 'specific devise' which transfers only specified property; or a 'residuary devise' which transfers the remaining property after one or more specific devises (A person is said sometimes to 'bequeath' personal property and 'devise' real property). Devise "when used as a noun, means a testamentary disposition of real or personal property and when used as a verb, means to dispose of real or personal prop-

erty by will." (United States Uniform Probate Code paras. 1–201 (8)). See also **bequest**.

devisee
A person who receives property by **devise**.

deviser or devisor
A person who grants or bequeaths property by **devise**.

devolution
The passing of property by transmission or succession. The transfer of property from a dying person to a person living, especially by the operation of law. See also **devise, disposal**.

dictum (L)
'A saying'; statement. See **obiter dictum**.

differential rent
A rent based on a tenant's ability to pay for the use or benefit of the leased premises rather than a **market rent**. See also **profits method of valuation**.

différer (F)
to **defer**; to postpone.

dilapidation
Derived from the Latin *di*, 'tear down', *lapidus*, 'stone'; literally to tear down stone. Originally a term for a form of ecclesiastical **waste** i.e. letting church property fall into ruin or decay. In modern terms, wastefully destroying a building or letting it slide into ruin and decay by neglect of reparation. Dilapidation may arise as a result of (a) a tort, e.g. **negligence** through failure to make a property safe for visitors; (b) a breach of contract, e.g. failure to comply with the **repair** condition contained in a lease; or (c) a failure to comply with statute

law, e.g. the Public Health Acts or Housing Acts. See also **fair wear and tear, forfeiture, schedule of dilapidations**.
The Law of Dilapidations, by W.A. West, 8 edn.
Building Surveys and Dilapidations, by Ivor H. Seeley, pp. 188–217 (1985).

dilapidations survey
see **schedule of condition, schedule of dilapidations**.

diluvion
see **dereliction**.

dîme (F)
tithe.

diminishing asset
see **wasting asset**.

diminishing-balance depreciation
see **declining-balance depreciation**.

diminution, of a claim
see **set-off**.

diminution of value
see **depreciation, injurious affection**.

direct capitalisation
see **straight capitalisation**.

direct labour
Labour employed directly by the owner of a property, for maintenance or building work, rather than by an **independent contractor**.

direct reduction mortgage (DRM) (US)
A mortgage loan which provides for the borrower to repay the principal by fixed regular amounts. The interest on the outstanding balance and hence the mortgagor's total payments decrease throughout the term of the loan. Used also synonymously for an **amortisation mortgage**.

direct sales comparison approach (US)
see **comparison method of valuation, market approach.**

direct value comparison (US)
see **comparison method of valuation.**

disbursement
The payment of money, especially in settlement of a debt. An expenditure, in particular one incurred to defray the cost of a current asset.

discharge
To complete or execute a duty or obligation in full. To make an agreement which has the effect of bringing a contract to an end; to release from a burden or obligation, e.g. to make a settlement which extinguishes a loan or debt. 'Discharge' may be used to cover any one of a number of arrangements which bring a binding agreement or contract to an end including **accord and satisfaction, repudiation, rescission, release, performance** or **frustration**. The notable feature of discharge is that the agreement is totally ended; there is no residual commitment between the parties. See also **breach of contract, estoppel, laches, merger, waiver.**

disclaimer
1. Derived from the Latin *de clam*, 'to remove utterly'. The **repudiation, renunciation** or rejection of a right or obligation. For example, an estate agent may insert a disclaimer or **exclusion clause** in the particulars of sale of a property, renouncing liability for the accuracy of the information contained therein, or stating that the particulars do not constitute an offer or form part of any contract. A disclaimer may be overruled by statute law when it is unfair or unreasonable, e.g. the Unfair Contract Terms Act 1979. See also **abrogation.**
2. Renunciation of a title to, or an interest in, property. A disclaimer by a tenant is a denial of the existence of any relationship of landlord and tenant, and effectively means that no tenancy came into existence. See also **notice to quit.**
Woodfall's Landlord and Tenant, 28 edn., paras. 1–1796 to 1–1806.
3. The notification by a trustee in bankruptcy of his refusal to be bound by an onerous contract, or to accept the ownership of onerous property, e.g. a property that is not readily saleable. The disclaimer must be made within twelve months of the trustee's appointment and must be in writing and signed by the trustee. A leasehold interest may not be disclaimed without leave of the court, unless there is an order for summary administration, or the trustee gives the lessor notice of his intention to disclaim and the lessor takes no action within 14 days, requiring the matter to be brought before the court. Damages may be awarded for any loss resulting from a rescission of a contract as a result of such a disclaimer (Bankruptcy Act 1914, s. 54).

disclosure
see **misdescription, utmost good faith.**

discontinuance
1. The termination or cessation of a right, privilege or course of action.
2. The breaking off of a use of land, especially when made for a short period of time.
cf. **abandonment**. See also **dispossession.**
3. The alienation of an estate in land so as to break any right to enjoy a continuing interest.

discontinuance notice
see **advertisement**.

discontinuance order
An order made by a local planning authority, in accordance with the provisions of the Town and Country Planning Act 1971, s. 51, requiring a use of land to be discontinued, or imposing a condition on the continuation of a use of land, or requiring a building or works to be altered or removed. Before making such an order the local planning authority must pay due regard to the provisions of any development plan for its area and should only make such an order when it is "expedient in the interests of proper planning of their area (including the interests of **amenity**)". A proposed discontinuance order must be submitted to the Secretary of State for the Environment for his consideration. The Secretary of State may give the owner or occupier of the land an opportunity of making representations against the order, or call for a public inquiry, before making a decision on whether or not to confirm a proposed discontinuance order. The order does not take effect unless or until it is confirmed by the Secretary of State. The Secretary of State may make a discontinuance order himself and he has power to vary or modify an order submitted by a local authority for his consideration. A right of appeal against the decision of the Secretary of State on a point of law may be made to the High Court (1971 Act, s. 245). Compensation is payable to any person who has suffered damage, as a result of a discontinuance order – for the depreciation in the value of his interest in land; for damage attributable to "being dis-turbed in his enjoyment of the land"; or to meet the cost of carrying out work in order to comply with the order (1971 Act, s. 170). If appropriate, the order may grant **planning permission** for an alternative use or development of the land.
cf. **enforcement notice**. See also **compensation for planning restrictions, purchase notice.**
Urban Planning Law, by Malcolm Grant, pp. 454–456 (1982).

discount
1. A reduction in the value of something. A reduction or abatement of a face value or price; in particular, a reduction allowed for prompt or early payment. A discount is a reduction given or made in advance, as distinguished from a rebate which is an amount given back after payment in full. A discount may be granted on the presumption that something is worth more at present than it may be in the future, or to take account of the risk of receiving, or not receiving, it in the future. See also **defer, discount points, discount rate, discounted cash flow, present value.**
2. A reduction from face value made when a third party buys a **bill of exchange**. The purchaser 'discounts' or buys the bill of exchange (i.e. the right to receive the face value on maturity) at a price that is reduced by an amount which takes into account the time to maturity and the financial standing of the debtor. The discount or charge made by the purchaser of the bill is expressed usually as an annual percentage rate applied to the face value of the bill, i.e. a **discount rate.**

discount house (US)
see **discount store**.

discount points

A percentage reduction in the amount of a loan, so that the amount actually advanced to the borrower is less than the nominal amount of the loan; consequently resulting in an increase in the true annual interest rate. For example, a loan of £100 is established upon which interest at 9 per cent per annum is to be charged and which is repayable at the end of the loan term; but only £98 is advanced. The lender has adjusted the loan by two discount points. (The true interest rate for one year is 11.22 per cent instead of the nominal rate of 9 per cent). Similarly, a lender may increase the loan amount for the purpose of calculating the interest rate; for example, the nominal loan amount is increased to £102, but only £100 is advanced (the true annual interest rate then becomes 11.18 per cent). See also **annual percentage rate, front loading, points.**

discount rate

1. The amount of a **discount** expressed as an annual percentage.
2. The rate of return used in the application of a **present value** factor in discounting future income. A term that is synonymous with **capitalisation rate.**
3. The rate at which a note or bill of exchange is discounted, i.e. the amount, expressed as a percentage, by which the price paid to the holder of a bill of exchange falls short of the **face value.**
4. An annual rate of interest deducted from a loan before the capital is advanced. See also **discounted-interest loan.**

discount store (or warehouse)

A retail store (or warehouse) which offers goods for sale at prices that are lower than those pertaining in the standard high street or down-town shop or in a department store. A discount store normally is divided into departments; provides more limited customer service; uses self-service techniques; and sells goods in quantities that are larger than those offered by the normal retail store. Such stores are engaged in the sale of hard goods as well as soft goods, but usually provide limited or no food sales. See also **variety store.**

discounted cash-flow (DCF)

The **present value** of the estimated future **cash flow** to be derived from an investment in a capital asset, over a given period of time (the anticipated 'economic life' or 'holding period' of the investment). The term discounted cash-flow can be applied also to the technique for analysing the viability of a capital investment project by discounting all budgeted, or projected, income and expenditure flowing from or into a project, including the initial outlay and any residual value. This type of analysis can be used either to find the difference between the present value of all income and the present value of all expenditure – i.e. the **net present value** or 'net discounted revenue': or, to find a single discount rate that makes the present value of the estimated future income equal to the present value of all expenditure over the life of an investment – i.e. the **internal rate of return**. The discounted cash flow technique is the basis for most forms of financial analysis over time, especially as a method of comparing alternative forms of investment over the same time span. Called also 'present value analysis'.

cf. **pay-back method**: See also **capitalisation**.
The Valuation of Property Investments, by N. Enever, 2 edn., pp. 83 and 100 *et seq*.
Discounted Cash Flow, by M.G. Wright, 2 edn.

discounted-interest loan
A loan upon which the interest charge is deducted from the amount of the loan before the capital is advanced, i.e. a loan subject to **discount points**. See also **annual percentage rate, discount rate**.

discounted mortgage (or loan)
A mortgage (or loan) sold by the mortgagee (or lender) for an amount that is less than the principal due under the mortgage (or loan), i.e. a mortgage (or loan) sold at a **discount**.

discounted (or discounted cash flow) rate of return
see **internal rate of return**.

discounted value
The **present value** of a future payment or income, calculated at a given rate of interest.

discounting
1. The process of ascertaining the **present value** of a sum of money that is receivable in the future.
2. The application of a **discount** to the value of something.
3. The process of selling a **bill of exchange**, before its maturity date, for a sum of money that is less than the face value of the bill.

discretionary grant
A grant by a local authority towards the cost of repair or improvement, given at the discretion of the authority. See also **improvement grant, repairs grant, special grant**.

discretionary trust
1. A trust which provides that the investment of the funds and the distribution of any income is to be left to the discretion of the trustee; although the trust deed may limit the extent of that discretion. A discretionary trust may require the trustees to distribute the entire trust property, leaving a discretion as to how the proceeds are to be distributed – an 'exhaustive trust'; or the trustees have discretion as to whether to make a distribution at all – a 'non-exhaustive trust'. See also **protective trust**.
2. An **investment company** that is not restricted to one form or class of investment. See also **open-end trust**.

disentail
To bar, or bring to an end, an **entailed interest** in a property, i.e. to convert that interest into a **fee simple** or into a **base fee** and thereby defeat the rights of those claiming an interest after a life tenant. A process that is called also 'barring the entail'.

disentailing assurance
A deed, or a provision in a will, that has the effect of converting an **entailed estate** into a fee simple absolute, i.e. a deed which removes the possibility of an estate passing to a specified or restricted line of direct descendants and enables the estate to pass without limitation.

disentailing deed
see **disentailing assurance**.

disintermination
A reduction in savings and consequently in investment; in particular, a reduction in net deposits with savings institutions and consequentially the availability of mortgage funds.
cf. **intermediation**.

dismortgage (US)

To redeem a mortgage. See also **redemption**.

dispone

In Scottish law, to convey formally.

disposal

The transference of something to the control of another by an act of a party or by law. A word of wide meaning which may extend to include any transfer of property whether by **sale, exchange, gift, lease, mortgage**, or a **grant** of any interest, easement, right or privilege. As a rule 'dispose' and 'disposition' ... "are not technical words but ordinary English words of wide meaning; and where not limited by the context those words are sufficient to extend to all acts by which a new interest (legal or equitable) in the property is effectively created." – Carter v Carter [1896] 1 Ch. 67. Disposal is used particularly to mean a transfer between living persons as distinguished from **devise**. Disposal of real property generally is taken to mean the transfer of a party's entire interest, by any means. For example, in the Town and Country Planning Act 1971, s. 290 (when referring to such matters as disposal of land by a local authority) "'disposal' means disposal by sale, exchange, or lease, or by way of the creation of an easement, right or privilege, or in any other manner, except by way of appropriation, gift or mortgage". Under the Defective Premises Act 1975, s.6 (1) disposal of premises includes "a letting, and an assignment or surrender of a tenancy and the creation by contract of any other right to occupy the premises". In capital gains tax legislation it includes a part disposal of an interest and in certain tax statutes it has been extended to include any variation or extinguishment of an interest in land. See also **alienation, deemed disposal, development land tax**.

Real Estate Investment Decision Making, Austin J. Jaffe and C.F. Sirmans, pp. 400–501 (1982).

disponible (F)

liquid asset; current asset.

disposition

see **disposal**.

disposition (F)

1. **disposal**; conveyance.
(*disposition testamentaire, de bien immobilier* – **devise**).
2. arrangement; **term**.
(*disposition d'un contrat* – term of a contract).
3. lay-out (of an estate, garden, etc.).

dispossession

The regaining of **possession** of real property by legal process, especially by a landlord on termination or expiration of a lease. The act of depriving or ousting someone from a right to possession of land. Dispossession is "where a person comes in and drives out the others from possession", as distinguished from 'discontinuance' of possession which is "where the person in possession goes out and is followed in by others" – Rains v Buxton (1880), 14 Ch. D 539–40.

cf. **expropriation**. See also **deforcement, disseisin, disturbance, ejectment, eviction.**

disregards

Factors to be ignored when assessing the market value of a property; in particular, factors to be ignored when assessing the market rent on the renewal of a **business tenancy**; the **fair** rent for a regulated tenancy; or the rent for an **agricultural tenancy**.

disrepair

The state of being in need of **repair**, either due to general decay or as a result of neglect in complying with the terms of a lease or other contractual obligation. See also **dilapidation, negligence, repairs notice, waste**.

disseisin or disseizin

The act of depriving someone of a right of **seisin**, i.e. wrongfully dispossessing or ousting the person entitled to a freehold. In the US, sometimes used to describe the injurious removal of a tenant from possession by his landlord. See also **deforcement**.

distinct possession (US)

see **adverse possession**.

distraint

The act of levying **distress**.

distress

A common law remedy of 'self-help' which permits someone (the distrainor) to remove and, after a period of time and due notice, sell the goods of another as a pledge to compel the performance of a duty or obligation (such as the payment of **rent**) or the satisfaction of a debt. The distrainor may take actual possession of the goods and remove them from the premises of their owner or prepare a list of the distrained articles and leave them on condition that they are not removed from the premises. The latter procedure is called 'walking possession'.

The procedures and the goods that may be seized are tightly controlled in English law. For example, a landlord must distrain personally or use a certified bailiff (Law of Distress Amend-

ment Act 1888, ss. 7, 8; Distress for Rent Rules 1984); he may not distrain on perishables, things in actual use, tools or implements of trade (unless there are no other goods of sufficient value), fixtures, money (except in a bag or chest), clothes, bedding, or goods of a company in liquidation; and most goods of third parties are given special protection (Law of Distress Amendment Act 1908). In the case of a **protected tenancy** or a **statutory tenancy** leave of the court is required prior to levying distress (Rent Act 1977, s. 147). Only the landlord who has the immediate reversion may distrain and he must distrain by employing a certified **bailiff**. Distress may not be levied between dusk and dawn, nor on a Sunday. Distress for non-payment of rent may be levied only after rent falls due, and the goods seized must be worth no more than the rent due. Distress may be levied for up to six years arrears of rent (Limitation Act 1980, s. 19); except in the case of an agricultural holding where the amount is limited to one years arrears (Agricultural Holdings Act 1948, s. 18). The goods distrained upon may themselves be called 'distress'.

In the US distress has been abolished in most states (Gruber *v* Pacific States Savings and Loan Co. (1939) 13 Cal. 2d 144, 8 P.2d 137; Van Ness Industries Inc. *v* Claremont Painting & Decorating Co., 129 N.J. Super 507, 324 A.2d 193); or its use is regulated by statute. In those states where it can still be levied, the action for distress is sometimes called the issue of a landlord's warrant. See also **attachment, damage feasant, replevin**.
Housing Law, by Martin Partington and Andrew Arden, pp. 283–305

(1983).
Adkin's Landlord and Tenant, 18 edn., pp. 113–142.
Woodfall's Landlord and Tenant, 28 edn., paras. 1–0792 to 1–1012
Hill and Redman's Law of Landlord and Tenant, 17 edn., pp. 364–424.
13 Halsbury's Laws of England, 4 edn., paras. 201–500.

distress damage feasant
see **damage feasant.**

distressed area (US)
see **development area.**

distressed property (US)
A property that has become an unprofitable investment for the owner, especially when the owner is faced with action by a mortgagee. Fundamentally the property may not be unsatisfactory, but it may be unsuitable to a particular investor or may have been mismanaged.

distressed sale
see **forced sale.**

distributee (US)
A person who by law receives all or part of the estate of a deceased who has left no **will**. See also **intestate.**

distribution trust
see **trust for sale.**

district council
see **local authority, planning authority.**

district plan
A form of **local plan** prepared by a local planning authority for the comprehensive planning and control of the development of an urban area, generally with a population in the range of 5000 to 75000 people. District plans are intended to include specific proposals for the development and the control of development in the area. They are the most important plans for the modern control of development and planning at county level in Britain.

district shopping centre
see **shopping centre.**

district valuer
An employee of the Commissioner of the Inland Revenue who is responsible for providing valuation advice, particularly for property taxation purposes; for assisting local authorities with matters relating to compensation; for advising on the valuation of property for rating purposes; and for providing other advice to local government bodies on financial matters including terms for development, acquisition and disposal of property, especially when central government grants or loans are involved. See also **valuation officer.**

disturbance
1. Interference with the legal enjoyment of a right "by **trespass** or **nuisance**, or in any other substantial manner" – Fitzgerald *v* Forbank [1897] 2 Ch. 96. In the case of an incorporeal right, e.g. an easement or profit à prendre, disturbance means an act that prevents the exercise of that right, such as by blocking up an ancient light or obstructing a right of way. The remedy for such disturbance is usually a claim for **damages** or to seek an **injunction.**
2. A reduction in the proper or full enjoyment of real property by the act of another. In particular, the actions of an authority possessing compulsory purchase powers that give rise to a claim for **consequential damages**; e.g. when the exercise of those powers leads to the termination or reduction

of the profits of a business against the will of the person disturbed – Horn v Sunderland Corporation [1941] 1 All ER 499. See also **compensation for disturbance.**

disturbance compensation
see **compensation for disturbance.**

divest
To deprive of a right or title; to annul. cf. **vest.** See also **devest.**

divided interest
see **partial interest.**

dividend yield
The yield obtained by calculating the relationship of the dividend payable on a share to the current share price. Similar to the **equity dividend yield** or **cash-on-cash yield** from a real estate investment, being the net return on the cash invested.
cf. **earnings yield.**

divine service
see **spiritual tenure.**

division wall
see **party wall.**

doctrine of adhesion
see **adhesion contract.**

doctrine of estates
A principle of English land law that a person does not own land outright, like a chattel, but has a mere right to an **estate,** i.e. a right to hold land for a period of time. This doctrine enables land ownership to be divided in successive holdings, but in such a way that each holding can exist at the same time: "...the land itself is one thing, and the estate in the land is another thing, for an estate in the land is a time in the land, or land for a time, and there are diversities of estates, which are no more than diversities of

time, for he who has a freehold in land has a time in land without end, or the land for time without end, and he who has land in tail has a time in the land or the land for time as long as he has issue of his body, and he who has an estate in land for life has no time in it longer than for his own life, and so of him who has an estate in the land for the life of another, or for years". – Walsingham's Case (1579) 2 Plowden 555. The word 'estate' denotes the duration of a person's ownership of land as compared to **tenure** (or, in modern terms, tenancy) which denotes the length of time for which a person may use another's land. (A distinction that in modern English land law is becoming more blurred, especially because of the increasing strength of statutory rights given to tenants to retain possession of land).

The doctrine of estates was based originally on **seisin,** i.e. the principle that any one person only has a right that is better than another's, there being no absolute right to the **ownership** of land in English law. The highest right to land that a person may possess is the **freehold,** all other rights being of more limited duration. However, each estate can have a separate marketable value, a value that is essentially deferred in time. (The French and Roman systems of land law recognise absolute ownership, or *dominium,* a right of ownership for eternity. The doctrine of estates is a unique and fundamental feature of English land law.) See also **doctrine of tenure, property,** *propriété,* **real property, remainder, reversion.**
Cheshire's Modern Law of Real Property, 13 edn., pp. 26–37.
History of English Law, by Pollock

and Maitland, 2 edn., vol. ii, pp. 10–13.
Real Property and Real People, by K.J. Gray and P.D. Symes, pp. 45–48, (1981).
The Law of Property, by F.H. Lawson and Bernard Lawson, 2 edn., pp. 88–97.

doctrine of laches
see **laches**.

doctrine of lost modern grant
see **lost modern grant**.

doctrine of tenure
An ancient principle of English land law that all land is held under some form of **tenure**, i.e. ultimately is held of the Crown, subject to certain obligations by the tenant. A theory that has greater application to the **feudal system** of land tenure than the modern form of tenure established after the reforms of the Law of Property Acts 1922 and 1925. See also **manor**.
An Introduction to the History of Land Law, by A.W.B. Simpson, p. 1 *et seq.* (1961).

documentary stamp tax (US)
see **stamp duty**.

documentary transfer tax (US)
see **transfer tax**.

document of title
A document used as evidence, or proof, of a right to possession or ownership of property. For goods a document of title, in particular a **negotiable instrument**, is used as a means for transferring the right to control those goods. For land a document of title, or strictly a **title deed**, is any evidence in writing of a **title** to that land and may include any deed, map, roll or registered document. See also **certificate of title, land certificate**.

dol (F)
fraud.

dolus (F)
(*dolus malus* – fraudulent misrepresentation; illegal deceipt, a term primarily of Roman Law).

domain
1. The total and absolute **ownership** of real property or the property so owned. Landed property held in one's own right as distinguished from property held subject to a superior lord. See also **demesne land, doctrine of estates, dominium**.
2. **Heritable property**, originally property belonging to the lord of a manor. National or 'public domain' is land owned by the government. See also **eminent domain**.

domaine (F)
domain; real estate.
(*domaine eminent* – **eminent domain**. The rights left to a landlord when the tenant has considerable security of tenure, as with agricultural property. See also **expropriation**).
(*domaine public* – public property). See also **dominium, patrimoine**.

domicil or domicile
1. Derived from the Latin *domus*, **'home'**. A person's true and permanent home. The place where someone is most likely to return to; to regard as his or her ordinary place of dwelling; or intends to be his or her fixed home, unless or until something shall occur to induce him or her (unexpectedly) to adopt some other permanent home. – Lord *v* Colvin (1859) 28 L.J. Ch. 366. A person may have a **residence** in a number of places, but, at any one time, he or she may have only one domicile. The place of a person's domicile is dependent on the acts or

deeds that lead to a conclusion as to where that person has established voluntarily a permanent place of habitation.

2. The place where a **bill of exchange** is made payable.

domicile (F)
domicile; home; residence.
(*election de domicile* – election of domicile; the place acknowledged as the residence of a party to a contract, especially for the service of a legal notice).

dominant tenament (or **dominant estate**)
The land which benefits from an **easement**, **restrictive covenant**, or any other form of **servitude**.
cf. **servient tenament**.

dominion
Property. The absolute right to the **ownership** of something, including both title and possession.

dominium (L)
1. **Ownership**. In Roman law *dominium* represents the absolute right to property, whether land or movables – the right to use; the right to enjoy and profit from; and the right to alienate or even destroy property – *jus utendi, jus fruendi, jus abutendi* – subject only to the restraints imposed by law. In Roman law a man either had *dominium* over property or he did not; there being no intervening forms of ownership or separate concurrent estates or interests in property, as in English law. Dominium may be distinguished from **possession**, because possession may be absolute but represents no more than an entitlement to property. Possession may entitle a person to a right that is protected by law, but does not, of itself, give that person a right to mastery

over property.
2. Under the **feudal system** of land tenure in Europe the relative rights to land of the lord and his tenant – a lord having a direct ownership (*dominium directum*) and a tenant having use and occupation (*dominium utile*).

dommage (F)
damage; loss; wrong suffered.
(*dommage indirect* – consequential damages)
(*dommages-intérêts* – **damages** (in law) especially as a result of a loss caused by a third party or payable as a consequence of a breach of contract). Amos & Walton's Introduction to French Law, 3 edn., pp. 182–187 (for an outline of damages for breach of contract under French law).

donatio mortis causa (L)
'A **gift** on account of death'. A gift made in anticipation of death, with the intention that it shall take effect on the donor's death.

donation (F)
gift; donation.
(*donation entre vifs* – donation *inter vivos*, i.e. a gift between living persons).

donee
The recipient of property transferred as a **gift**.

Donis Conditionalibus (L)
See **De Donis Conditionalibus**.

donor
A person who transfers property as a **gift** to another, i.e. without receiving consideration in exchange.

dormant partner
see **silent partner**.

dotard
A tree that is not suitable for **timber**,

normally because it is dead or dying. Dotards may be removed by a tenant for life without constituting an act of **waste**.

douaire (F)
dower; jointure; marriage-settlement.

double agency (US)
see **dual agency**.

double annual value
see **tenancy on sufferance**.

double decking (US)
The illegal sale of the same property to different purchasers.

double house (US)
A **semi-detached house**, or one building that contains a pair of apartments. See also **duplex house**.

double insurance
Insurance of the same risk under two separate policies, as when a policy on a building covers contents which are also covered by a separate contents policy. See also **contribution clause, over-insurance**.

double rent
see **tenancy on sufferance**.

double sinking-fund method
A method of capitalising a variable income from a property investment with a limited life, such as a leasehold interest. Unlike the application of a **dual-rate capitalisation factor (or years' purchase)**, which capitalises the income by allowing for a new sinking fund to start each time there is a change in the rent receivable, the double sinking fund method allows for a single sinking fund for capital recoupment during the entire period for which the income is capitalised.
Modern Methods of Valuation, 6 edn., pp. 487–489 (1971).

The Valuation of Property Investments, by Nigel Enever, 2 edn., pp. 136–139.

double waste
The unlawful felling of trees by a tenant for the purpose of using the timber therefrom to carry out repairs that in any event he is obliged to carry out. See also **waste**.

dower or dowery
A common law right of a wife to a life interest in a third of freehold property owned by her husband at any time during the marriage, in particular the property that her issue, if any, might inherit. A right first referred to in statute law in 1215 (*Magna Carta*, Ch.7) and more formally bestowed by statute in 25. Edw. I (*Magna Carta*) 1217, Ch.7: "and for her dower shall be assigned unto her the third of all the lands of her husband which were his during coverture, except she were endowed of less at the church door." The right to dower has been abolished in English law by the Administration of Estates Act 1925, s. 45 (2). It has also been abolished in most states in the US although a widow may have a right to claim a share of her husband's estate from his testamentary disposition. See also **curtesy, matrimonial property, widow's quarantine.**
Real Estate Law, by Robert Kratovil and Raymond J. Werner, 8 edn., pp. 254–258.
Real Property, by William E. Burby, 3 edn., pp. 188–200.

down payment
A sum of money paid as a **deposit** on the signature of a contract for sale. A sum of money paid as **earnest money**. In the US the total cash paid for a property, excluding any monies bor-

rowed upon the security of that property, is referred to as the down payment or the 'buyer's equity'.
cf. **installment**.

downside leverage (US)
see **leverage**.

downside risk
The ultimate **risk** of bankruptcy or of a project reaching a position of total loss. The risk of a loss occurring. A downside risk may be contrasted to the possible gain, or 'upside potential', from an investment. See also **leverage**.

downstroke (US)
The total cost of acquiring an investment; the **acquisition cost** of a property, including closing costs.

downzoning (US)
A change in the **zoning** on a site so as to increase the restrictions on the use and development of the property. This may be achieved by reducing the floor area ratio; limiting the type or range of use permitted; or changing the permitted use completely.

dowry
Property, real or personal, that a wife brings to her husband on marriage. A payment or gift made by a wife, or usually her father, to her husband as recompense for obligations he is assumed to have accepted on marriage. See also **dower, matrimonial property**.

draft
An order from one person to another to pay a sum of money to a named person or the bearer of the order. A draft may take the form of a **bill of exchange, a cheque** (or check) or a **banker's draft**. See also **draft agreement**.

draft agreement
A document in writing (but not the final version) setting out details of an **agreement** and prepared by one side, such as a seller or landlord, for consideration by the other side. Commonly referred to simply as a 'draft'. See also **'subject to contract'**.

drain
A ditch, channel or conduit through which liquid passes off a property (Highways Act 1980, s.100 (9)) in particular from one property to another, in order to dry or discharge foul water from the former.
Generally a drain only conducts liquid from one house, as distinguished from a **sewer** which is a large drain that serves more than one house. "'Drain' means a drain used for the drainage of one building or of any building or yards appurtenant to buildings within the curtilage" (Public Health Act 1936, s. 343 (1)). A sewer is, in every case a drain, but not every drain is a sewer. A drain may carry off rain water, but the word does not extend to gutters and down pipes. See also **fit for habitation, watercourse**.

draw down
1. The amount of money actually borrowed, i.e. used, rather than available under a loan facility.
2. To take an **advance** under a loan agreement. Called also 'takedown'. See also **draw request, tranche**.

draw request (US)
A schedule, prepared by a property developer, showing the stages at which he is likely to require to **drawdown** cash from a loan facility.

drawing area
see **catchment area**.

driftway

A right of way for driving cattle and, usually, riding a horse. Called also a 'droveway'. A term that no longer has any significance in English statute law because it has been replaced by **bridleway**, which may or may not include a driftway.

droit (F)

1. **right; equity**, a word that conveys the sense of both duty or obligation and of justice or equity.
(*droit acquis* – **vested interest**)
(*droit d'aliener; droit d'alienation* – right of alienation)
(*droit de captation d'eau* – right to water)
(*droit d'éschelle* – see *tour d'eschelle*)
(*droit de passage* – **right of way**)
(*droit de passage en cas d'enclave* – **easement of necessity**)
(*droit de parcours et vaine pâture* – common of pasture. See *vaine pâture*)
(*droit de preference; droit de priorité* – **right of first refusal**)
(*droit de pêche* – **right to fish**; piscary)
(*driot de préemption* – **right of preemption**. See also **zone** *d'intervention foncière*)
(*droit de rachat après forclusion* – **equity of redemption** – in particular a right to purchase after foreclosure, a concept originating from English common law)
(*droit de reprise* – right of repossession at the end of a lease; as with English law the right of a landlord to repossess a property at the end of a lease is restricted by statute in many cases)
(*droit de retention* – possessory **lien**)
(*droit de superficie* – surface area right, see *superficie*)
(*droit de vues* – **ancient light**; see also *vues et jour*)

(*droit littoral* – **littoral right**)
(*droit miniers* – mineral rights)
(*droit personnel* – personal right)
(*ayant droit* – interested party; rightful owner; claimant)
2. law; privilege; legal title.
(*droit civil* – **civil law**)
(*droit commun* – **common law**)
3. duty; tax.
(*droit d'enregistrement* – **registration duty**, a tax on real property transfers)
(*droit de mutation* – transfer duties, on real property)
(*droit de timbre* – **stamp duty**. Applied more to the cost of the stamps affixed to a formal document than the *droit d'enregistrement*). See also *impôt*.

droit d'habitation (F)
see *habitation*.

droit de passage (F)
see *usage*.

droit de passage (F)
see *passage, droit de*.

droit de propriété (F)
property rights; **ownership**. The central 'real right' – in the civil and French law. A term that encompasses all forms of property; the rights or benefits relating thereto; and the means by which property is acquired. Roman law considers this right to comprise three elements *jus utendi* – right of use within the law; *jus fruendi* – right to the rents or profits receivable by parting with possession to another; and *jus abutendi* – right to freely part with property, whether by destruction, alienation or consumption. In modern French law this right is everything gained by the ownership of private property (*biens*), provided the gaining of that right is not contrary to the law. See also *propriété*.

Précis Dalloz. Droit Civil, Les Biens (Alex Weill), 2 edn., p. 20 et seq.

droits réels (F)
real rights. A right to property that constitutes a right to a thing itself as distinguished from a right against another person. Real rights include absolute and conditional ownership; l'*usufruit* (**usufruct**) (including the lesser rights of *usage* and *habitation*); *le bail emphytéotique* (**emphyteotic lease**); *le bail à construction*; la *concession immobilière*; l'*hypothèque* (**mortgage**) and *les servitudes*. See also **action** *in rem*, *démembrements de la propriété*.
Droit Civil, Les Biens, by Jean Carbonnier, 11 edn., pp. 56 *et seq*.

drop-lock debenture
A form of debenture loan by which the lender agrees to make advances up to an agreed limit, in tranches, over a period of time. The interest rate is determined either when the borrower takes up the facility or when a given rate of interest (such as a bank base rate) falls below an agreed level. If the latter instance arises before any part of the facility is advanced the rate is 'locked' for the term of the loan, but if the facility is taken up before that stage the rate is based on an agreed floating rate which is only 'locked' when that rate falls below the agreed level.

dry mortgage (US)
A mortgage in which the mortgagor has no personal liability, i.e. a **non-recourse mortgage**.

dry rent
see **rent-seck**.

dry trust
see **bare trust**.

dual, or divided, agency
Agency where both sides are represented in a transaction by the same **agent** who is seeking to be remunerated by both sides. As a rule, dual agency is contrary to the principal of agency because an agent owes a **fiduciary** responsibility to his principal and is unlikely to be able to fulfil that responsibility on behalf of opposing principals. Most professional real estate bodies discourage their members from accepting or seeking dual agency. In any event, "an agent who wants to make two contracts for double commission must do so in the clearest possible terms and with the clearest possible information to each of his principals what he is doing, otherwise he cannot sue under an alleged agreement". – Fullwood *v* Hurley [1928] 1 KB 504.
    In most states in the US, dual agency is illegal, unless a broker makes it clear that he is acting solely as an intermediary and is seeking to be remunerated by both parties for establishing a common business interest; otherwise there is likely to be a conflict of interest and the broker may well have entered into a **void contract** – Duffy *v* Setchell (1976) 38 Ill. App. 3d. 146, 347 NE 2d. 218. Called also 'double agency'.
cf. **joint agency**.

dual-rate capitalisation factor (or **year's purchase**)
A **capitalisation factor** (or **year's purchase**), used to capitalise income from a depreciating investment (e.g. a leasehold interest or a wasting asset), which incorporates a mathematical adjustment so that the capital value obtained is comparable to a similar, but non-depreciating, investment.

The capital value obtained by applying this factor to a projected income from an investment is such that the investor receives both (i) a **remunerative rate** of return which is comparable to a permanent investment; and (ii) a notional **sinking fund**, which is set aside at a 'safe' or **accumulative rate** of return, to replace the original cost of the investment at the end of its useful or anticipated life. (A simple or **single-rate capitalisation factor** also provides for a notional sinking fund, but this is deemed to accumulate at the same rate as the remunerative rate). A dual-rate factor is 'adjusted' to notionally set aside extra income to replace the capital cost of the original investment, with the result that the capital value of the declining income is reduced so that the net return to the investor is comparable to the level achieved by an investor who acquires a permanent, or non-depreciating, asset. The factor may be calculated by the formula:

$r = [1/ (i + S)]$ or $i + [s/(+ s)^n - 1]^{-1}$

where r = capitalisation factor
  i = remunerative rate
  S = sinking fund factor
  s = accumulative rate
  n = number of income receipts during the term of the investment (assumed in arrears).

(In a single rate capitalisation factor $i = s$). Thus, if a wasting asset is acquired for P and produces an income of v per annum, such that $P = rv$, then the investor will receive a return on his cost of i per annum, which is less than v, throughout the term of n years, with the difference between v and i notionally invested at a rate of interest s in order to accumulate to the capital sum P to replace the

wasted asset; in other words, hypothetically, to perpetuate the income. (This formula only provides for the replacement of the original capital cost and makes no allowance for inflation or tax on the sinking fund element. For a discussion of the alternatives and a bibliography on approaches to the valuation of declining investments see *Valuation – Demand and Techniques*, by J. Ratcliffe and A. Trott, 255 EG 435 & 529 (1980). In the US this factor is called the 'Hoskold factor' or sometimes a 'sinking fund factor'. See also **internal rate of return**.

The Appraisal of Real Estate, AIREA, 7 edn., pp. 418–423.
Modern Methods of Valuation, 8 edn., pp. 110–117.
Valuation and Investment Appraisal, edited by Clive Darlow, pp. 274–283 (1983).

dual-rate mortgage
A mortgage loan which provides that interest will be payable on the basis of a short-term market rate and amortisation is calculated on the basis of a medium to long-term rate. The amount of interest is assessed on the outstanding principal at the end of each year and is deducted from the regular amortisation payments, the balance being used to repay the capital. See also **variable-rate mortgage**.

due date
see **maturity date**.

due-on-sale clause (US)
see **alienation clause**.

duplex house
A house with two separate apartments, or containing accommodation for two families, usually on different floors with separate entrances to each

unit; especially a building that would otherwise be one private residence. In the US two single-family houses connected by a party wall (called a **semi-detached house** in the UK) is referred to sometimes as a duplex – Easterly *v* Hall (1971) 182 SE 2d. 671, although it is more commonly called a **double house**. A duplex is usually divided horizontally from the other apartment in the building; whereas a semi-detached or double house is divided vertically. See also **maisonette**.

duration

The span from the beginning to the end of a period of **time**. A period of time for which an interest in property exists, e.g. the **term** of a lease. See also **estate, quantity**.

durée (d'un bail) (F)

duration (of a lease).

duress

Actual or threatened violence; an unlawful coercive act. Duress is "the compulsion under which a person acts through fear of personal suffering to himself or a near relative, as from injury to the body or from confinement, actual or threatened" (9 Halsbury's Laws of England, 4 edn., p. 172). Duress may arise also from economic pressure – Universe Tankships Inc. of Monrovia *v* International Transport Workers' Federation [1982] 2 All ER 88. A contract entered into under duress is usually of no legal effect and is voidable at the instigation of the sufferer; or, in extreme cases, it may be void at the outset. See also **harassment, unconscionable bargain, undue influence, voidable contract**.
Cheshire & Fifoot's Law of Contract, 10 edn., pp. 274–282.

Chitty on Contract, 28 edn., paras. 481–501.

dutch auction

see **auction**.

duty

1. An **obligation** to do something or refrain from doing something.
cf. **power**. See also **debt, duty of care**.
2. Something owed to another, especially to a government. See also **tax**.

duty of care

The law of **negligence** is based on the principle that it is incumbent upon any person to take reasonable care not to cause damage or injury to another who is likely to be in proximity to his actions or, in one word, to his/her **neighbour**. A principle founded on the ethic of 'mutuality of behaviour' and imbedded in modern law in the form of a requirement that a person should have in mind those in reasonable, and legal, proximity to his/her daily conduct and, thereby, that person should avoid actions that might deliberately harm others. "A legal duty so called is nothing but a prediction that if a man does or omits certain things he will suffer in this or that way by judgement of the court" (*Collected Legal Papers*, Oliver Wendel Holmes, 1920); so that a lack of reasonable care becomes a matter for sanction by a court of law.

A duty of care may be considered to arise in two stages: "first one has to ask whether, as between the alleged wrongdoer and the person who has suffered damage there is a sufficient relationship of proximity or neighbourhood such that, in the reasonable contemplation of the former, carelessness on his part may be likely to cause damage to the latter, – in which case a *prima facie* duty of care arises.

Secondly, if the the first question is answered affirmatively, it is necessary to consider whether there are any considerations which ought to negative, or to reduce or limit the scope of the duty or the class of persons to whom it is owed or the damages to which a breach of it may give rise." – Anns v Merton London Borough [1978] AC 752. Thus the duty may be limited with respect to a trespasser on land or when the offended party can be shown to have contributed, in whole or in part, to his own downfall.

A landlord who has an obligation to repair or maintain leased premises, or has a right of entry to repair and maintain premises, and therefore should be reasonably aware of any defect in the premises, owes a duty of care to any person who might be affected by that defect (Defective Premises Act 1972 s. 4). A landlord of multi-let premises has an implied obligation (unless there is an express provision to the contrary) to keep the common parts in a reasonable state of repair and maintenance and thereby owes a similar duty of care – Liverpool County Council v Irwin [1977] AC 239. See also **trespass, visitor.**

duty to convert
    see **conversion, trust for sale.**

dwelling house
    Premises that are adapted for residential use and are lived in, or are capable of being occupied for, human habitation – Lewin v End [1906] AC 304. A **house** where a person (or persons) lives, i.e. eats, sleeps and rests; especially a place where one established a **home**. A dwelling house may be a single room or a mansion; form part or the entirety of a building, including rooms that are not actually lived in

but form part of the whole, e.g. a broom cupboard, cellar, outhouse – Grigsby v Melville [1974] 1 WLR 80; be physically occupied or vacant; be a residence for one or more families, provided it is capable of providing, in its entirety, a place for human habitation. The fact that a house is rarely lived in does not preclude it from being a dwelling house, so long as the potential occupier has an intention to return, the *animus revertendi*, and the legal ability to return to the house. A house does not cease to be a dwelling house solely because the law prohibits its use for dwelling purposes, provided it has the basic characteristics expected of such a house – Baker v Huckle [1948] VLR 159. Generally 'dwelling house' refers to premises with a reasonable degree of permanence (and thus it excludes most caravans), but it may be part of a building used for other purposes.

In the case of a **protected tenancy**, the tenant must occupy a dwelling house, which may be an entire house or part of a house, provided it is 'let as a separate dwelling'. The premises must be used for living, with some degree of continuity and purpose. The 'dwelling house' includes land let with it, unless it comprises agricultural land exceeding two acres in extent (Rent Act 1977, s. 1(1), 22, 26) – Curl v Angelo [1948] 2 All ER 190. In the case of a **secure tenancy** the 'right to buy' the freehold of a dwelling house does not extend to a flat (it is limited to a right to be granted a long lease of a flat), but may include land which is or has been used, with the dwelling house (Housing Act 1980, s. 1, 3(2), as amended by the Housing and Building Control Act 1984, s. 4).

E

early redemption charge
see **prepayment penalty**.

earn-out (US)
A share of the profit, which is realised on the sale of a property, received by a person who had a charge or mortgage secured on that property. A benefit derived from a property by the vendor after it has been sold, usually as a result of a management agreement or a joint venture entered into with the purchaser. See also **equity participation**.

earnest, or **earnest money**
A payment made to secure a **bargain**. Money, or something tangible, given by a prospective purchaser on the making of an agreement, as a token of good faith; in particular, a payment made following an oral agreement. Although the term is used correctly as a synonym for **deposit**, earnest money is used frequently to refer to a smaller sum (such as a nominal sum of 1 per cent, rather than 10 per cent, of the total consideration) due under a provisional agreement to show that the parties mean business and intend more than a **gentleman's agreement**. Commonly 'earnest money' is used to refer to a sum paid, usually to a vendor's agent, prior to the signing of a binding contract. Earnest money is returned usually if a binding contract does not arise from the provisional agreement; unless that failure is a direct result of an action of the payer (Mortenson *v* Financial Growth Inc., 23 Utah 2d 54, 456 P. 2d 181, 184). In the event that a binding contract does result the earnest is treated as a part payment and then takes on all the attributes of a deposit. (For a history of earnest money see Howe *v* Smith. (1844) 27 Ch. D 89.) Called also a 'binder', 'bargain money', 'good faith money' or 'handmoney'. See also **consideration, handsel**.

earnings
Something obtained, usually in the form of money, in return for labour or the use of capital. The price of services performed. The revenue received over a period of time after deducting directly related expenses, i.e. net income received from an investment.
cf. **profit**. See also **income**.

earnings approach (US)
see **income capitalisation approach**.

earnings multiplier
see **price-earnings ratio**.

earnings yield
The percentage relationship between the net profits or earnings which a company could make available for distribution as dividends to the ordinary shareholders and the current share price. The earnings yield is calculated as follows:

$$\frac{\textit{earnings per ordinary share after tax}}{\textit{market price per ordinary share.}} \times 100$$

For a company in the UK, this is commonly expressed simply as a ratio of 'earnings per share', after corporate tax. It is the reciprocal of the **price-earnings ratio**. The earnings yield available to an ordinary shareholder in a company is comparable to the **cash-on-cash yield** available to an investor in real estate, as both measure the total return on equity (before the investor's personal liability for tax).

cf. **dividend yield**.

easement

A right or privilege which the owner of a parcel of land (the owner of the 'dominant tenement') enjoys over the land of another (the owner of the 'servient tenement'), in order to reap a benefit for the dominant tenement, but without taking any tangible profit from the servient tenement. A limited right to use, or to prevent the use of, the land of another which accommodates or improves the beneficiary's land, but grants no right to possession of land.

The essential requirements of an easement were summarised in Re. Ellenborough Park [1956] Ch. 131 (which followed Cheshire's Modern Law of Property 10 edn), namely: (i) there must be a dominant and servient tenement (an easement cannot exist 'in gross' i.e. independently of the ownership of land): (ii) an easement must accommodate or benefit the dominant tenement (and not just the owner of that land); (iii) the owners of the dominant and servient tenements must be different parties (an easement is a right in *alieno solo*, against the land of another); (iv) the easement must be capable of forming the subject matter of a **grant** whether express, implied or presumed, i.e. it is a right that must be capable of being (although it need not be) set down in a deed. An undefined or vague right, e.g. a right to view, or a right of privacy, cannot constitute the subject of an easement: "there is no such right

known to law as a right to a prospect or view" – Phipps v Pears [1964] 2 All ER 35. Nor can a right to protection from the elements form an easement – Marchant v Capital and Counties Property Ltd. (1982) 263 EG 661. The beneficiary must be able to demonstrate clearly that he has acquired a right or benefit in a positive form over the servient tenement.

An easement is an **incorporeal hereditament**; i.e. it creates no estate in land, because the dominant tenement does not derive any right of ownership over the servient tenement. It does not confer any right to possession, but merely a right to impose proprietary restrictions; therefore, it cannot form the subject of a tenancy. It is, however, a right **appurtenant** to land, so that it cannot exist as a personal right; "it is not competent to create rights unconnected with the use and enjoyment of land, and annex them to it so as to constitute a property in the grantee." – Hill v Tupper (1863) 2 H and C 127. Accordingly, it may continue even if there is a change in the ownership of either the dominant or servient tenement; it is said to 'run with the land'; although it is extinguished if both tenements come into the same hands.

An easement may be distinguished from a **profit à prendre** as there is no right for the beneficiary of an easement physically to take anything from the land, and a profit à prendre may exist 'in gross'. It may be distinguished from a **licence** which does not create any interest in land but is merely a right that is personal to the parties; although a licensee may be granted a right to occupy land. In addition, a licence, unlike an easement, may be revoked unilaterally;

need not be capable of forming the subject of a deed of grant; requires no dominant tenement; does not grant exclusive use of land; nor runs with the land; and is always an equitable right.

An easement can be 'positive' or 'affirmative'; or 'negative'. A positive easement is a right to do something positive on the servient land, but not a right to exact anything from the owner of that land. It is enjoyed for a specific purpose, e.g. a **right of way; right of light; right of support; party-wall** right; right to water, i.e. to extract it; a right of access for the purpose of facilitating repair to a building; or a right to run utilities across land, commonly called a **wayleave** (although a wayleave is frequently only a licence, there being no dominant tenement). A **negative easement** is a privilege by which the servient owner may be obliged to refrain from a certain user, or course of action, on the servient tenement, for the benefit of the dominant owner, e.g. not to build above a given height so as to obstruct the access of light to a house on the dominant tenement. In English law it has been propositioned that a negative easement cannot exist, it being merely a right to insist that a person use his land in a certain, but limited, way – Moore v Rawson (1824) 3 B and C 332: a true right or privilege to prevent the use of land, for the benefit of other land being a **restrictive covenant**. Notwithstanding that proposition negative easements are now limited in type to a right of light; a right to a free flow of air through a defined aperture; a right not to have support undermined; and a right to prevent the diversion of water run-

ning in an artificial channel. On the other hand the form that a positive easement can take is not closed; "the category of servitudes and easements must alter and expand with changes that take place in the circumstances of mankind". – Dyce v Lady James Hay (1852) 1 Macq. 305 (Scot). In 1973 a right to use an airfield was recognised as a right that could form the subject of an easement – Dowty Boulton Paul Ltd. v Wolverhampton Corporation (No. 2) [1976] Ch. 13. (In the US the dominant estate is called sometimes an 'affirmative easement' and the servient or subservient estate is called a 'negative easement'.)

An easement can be created by statute; by an express **reservation** or express **grant**, i.e. a written agreement; by implied reservation or implied grant based on the intention of the parties, e.g. a **quasi-easement**; or by presumed grant or **prescription**. An easement may arise also as 'of necessity', as when a parcel of land is 'landlocked'. However, whether expressly or impliedly, it is always granted; it cannot arise purely as an amenity or privilege, enjoyed by virtue of an informal understanding or custom. An easement commonly arises consequent upon the provisions of the Law of Property Act 1925, s. 62(1) which states that, "a conveyance of land shall be deemed to include and shall by virtue of the Act operate to convey, with the land all ... ways, watercourses, liberties, privileges, easements, rights and advantages whatsoever, appertaining or reputed to appertain to land or any part thereof, or, at the time of conveyance, demised, occupied or enjoyed with, or reputed or known as part or parcel of or appurtenant to the land or any part thereof".

An easement may be extinguished by statute e.g. a failure to register a right of common under the Commons Registration Act 1965; by an express **release**, usually by deed (but not by unilateral revocation); by an implied intention on the part of the dominant owner not to resume his right i.e. **abandonment**; by the **merger** of the tenements in question (called 'unity of seisin'); by expiration of a stipulated period of time or purpose; by an alteration in the dominant tenement in such a way that the easement is unnecessary; or by losing it to another by prescription.

In the US, a mere personal right which resembles an easement, i.e. one that has no dominant tenement to which it appertains, is called an 'easement in gross' (in English law this would normally be a licence or wayleave); and a true easement, i.e. one used in connection with specific land, is called an **easement appurtenant**. See also **apparent easement, easement of necessity, equitable easement,** *jus spatiandi*, **legal easement, natural rights, riparian rights, servitude.**

Modern Methods of Valuation, 8 edn., Ch. 32 (Compensation for Wayleaves).
Real Estate Law, by Robert Kratovil and Raymond J. Werner, 8 edn., pp. 26–50.
Real Property, by William E. Burby, 3 edn., pp. 64–93.
Introduction to Land Law, by J.G. Riddall, 3 edn, pp. 266–298.
Law for Land Management Students, by Richard Card, John Murdoch and Peter Schofield, pp. 566–582 (1981).
Land Law: Cases and Materials, by

R.H. Maudsley and E.H. Burn, 4 edn., pp. 502–596.
Megarry's Manual of the Law of Real Property, 6 edn., p. 395 *et seq.*
The Law of Real Property, by Robert Megarry and H.W.R. Wade, 5 edn., p. 834 *et seq.*
Cheshire's Modern Law of Real Property, 13 edn., p. 488 *et seq.*
Law of Easements and Profits, by P. Jackson (1978).
Gale on Easements, by Maurice and Wakefield, 14 edn.
14 Halsbury's Laws of England, 4 edn., paras. 1–239.

easement appurtenant (US)
A true **easement**, i.e. one with a dominant and servient tenement. "An easement is appurtenant to land when the easement is created to benefit and does benefit the possessor of land in his use of the land" (*Restatement of the Law of Property*, American Law Institute V 453). Thus, an easement appurtenant is annexed to, and passes with, the dominant tenement.
cf. **easement in gross**. See also **appurtenant**.

easement by implied grant
see **easement of necessity**.

easement by implied reservation
see **quasi-easement**.

easement by prescription
see **prescription**.

easement in gross (US)
A right or privilege to use property which is similar to an **easement** but where there is no dominant tenement, i.e. no land separately owned which benefits from the right. (In English law an easement, by definition, cannot exist 'in gross', such a right would be classified as either a **licence** or a

wayleave).

cf. **easement appurtenant.**

easement of access
see **easement of necessity, right of access.**

easement of convenience (US)
see **easement of necessity.**

easement of light
see **right of light.**

easement of necessity
A right of way over one parcel of land (a servient tenement) that is essential for the proper enjoyment of another parcel of land (a dominant tenement), such as access to a highway from landlocked land or a right over a staircase in a block of flats. An easement of necessity means, "an **easement** without which the property retained cannot be used at all, and not merely necessary to the reasonable enjoyment of that property." – Union Lighterage Co. *v* London Graving Dock Co. [1902] 2 Ch. 573 (Wagner *v* Fairlamb, 151 Colo. 481, 379 P 2d. 165). An easement of necessity may be distinguished from an easement that arises by implication which, once created, continues unless or until determined in the same way as an express easement: an easement of necessity lasts only as long as the necessity exists – Holmes *v* Goring (1824) 2 Bing. 76. An easement of necessity arises when land is sold without the purchaser expressly reserving a right of access over land retained by the vendor, i.e. the acquired land is 'land-locked' and the purchaser cannot benefit from the full use of the land acquired. Thus it is "a way implied from the common intention of the parties, based on a necessity apparent from the deeds." –

Nickerson *v* Barraclough [1980] Ch. 336. At the outset it is not necessarily a defined way. "A way of necessity is a way which is the most convenient access to a land-locked tenement over other property belonging to the grantor; and it is clear that the grantor has a right himself to elect in which line, in which course, the way of necessity should go." – Brown *v* Alabaster (1887) 37 Ch. D 500. However, this rule should be applied with caution as the right is exercisable only so as to provide that which is essential for the proper enjoyment of the imprisoned land and for no other purpose. The person taking an easement as of necessity should take that route which is most convenient in all the circumstances and, once having elected a route, the owner of the dominant tenement cannot change it without consent – Deacon *v* South Eastern Railway Co. (1889) 61 LT 377; nor, once the easement is established, can he extend or intensify the use made of the easement – London Corporation *v* Riggs (1880) 13 Ch. D 798.

French law provides a similar right of access from landlocked land to a public highway or from land that is sold without an adequate means of access, *droit de passage en cas d'enclave* (French Civil Code art. 682–685). Called also a 'way of necessity', an 'easement of access', or, in the US, an 'easement of convenience'. See also **quasi-easement, right of support.** Précis Dalloz Droit Civil, Les Biens (Alex Weill), 2 edn., pp. 108–118. Megarry's Manual of the Law of Real Property, 6 edn., pp. 410–411.

easement of support
see **right of support.**

échéance (F)
1. expiration date; due date (for payment of rent, a loan, etc.); **maturity date**; term (as a period of time).
(*date d'échéance de location* – date of expiry of a tenancy).
2. **lapse; forfeiture.**

échelle (F)
scale.
(*échelle mobile* – sliding scale; **escalator clause**, in a lease). See also *tour d'échelle*.

échu (F)
(*intérêt échu* – outstanding interest).
(*terme échu* – due date; expiry date, of a tenancy).

ecclesiastical benefice
Property owned or effectively controlled by an ecclesiastical authority, namely the established Church of England, which may include a rectory or parsonage house. See also **benefice.**

ecclesiastical property
"Land belonging to an **ecclesiastical benefice**, or being or forming part of a church subject to the jurisdiction of a bishop of any diocese or the site of such a church, or being or forming part of a burial ground subject to such jurisdiction." (Town and Country Planning Act 1971, s. 274 (5)).

economic depreciation
see **depreciation.**

economic life
The period of time for which something may be used profitably. The time span for which a building is expected to yield a return in excess of that obtainable from the bare land; the period for which it is economic to maintain a capital asset or an improvement. The economic life cannot exceed the **physical life** although,

due to obsolescence in design or changes in the neighbourhood, it may be shorter. Called also the 'useful life'. See also **depreciation, effective age.**

economic obsolescence
see **obsolescence.**

economic rent
1. **Rent** that is sufficient to cover all the costs of running a property including interest charges, service charges and management fees, i.e. a 'break-even' rent for the landlord. Called also a 'cost rent'.
2. The **best rent** that can be obtained in the open market, as distinguished from the contract rent payable under the terms of a tenancy agreement or lease. The economic rent may equal, exceed, or fall short of the contract rent. See also **market rent, profit rent**.
3. In economics, any sum earned by a factor of production (capital, labour, or land) that exceeds the minimum amount required to keep that factor in its existing use, i.e. any sum that exceeds the **opportunity-cost** of maintaining that factor in production. The surplus of earnings over the cost of production; "the excess value of the whole produce, or if estimated in money, the excess price of the whole produce, above what is employed" (*Principles of Political Economy*, Thomas R. Malthus, (1836), p. 136. Accordingly, economic rent is 'unearned' income, because it is derived merely from the ownership or control of the factor of production with no direct effort by the recipient of the income. When received from land, this sum is also called 'land rent', being the surplus or profit over and above the minimum cost of keeping land in operation. In theory such an amount of 'economic rent' can be sus-

tained only in the short-run because, in the long-run, alternatives will be produced which will result in a reduction in earnings to a level that barely covers the cost of production. Based on that theory economic rent was called by Alfred Marshall 'quasi-rent'. See also **marginal land**.
Land Resource Economics, by Raleigh Barlowe, 3 edn., pp. 162–164.
The Economics of Real Property, by J. Harvey, pp. 31–42 (1981).

economic value
1. The value of a property as assessed by capitalising the future anticipated net operating income for the **economic life** of the property.
2. The value of a property based on its earning potential. See also **economic rent**.

edifice
Derived from the Latin *aedificium*, 'to make a house, to construct'. A large **structure**; an imposing **building**.

édifice (F)
edifice; building.

effective age
The age of a building taking account of such factors as design, layout, standard of maintenance, equipment, amenities; rather than the age based on the building's actual date of construction. A well designed and maintained building may have a lower (i.e. younger) effective age than its actual age and thus have a longer **economic life**. The effective age of a building can be reduced by improvement or renovation. For example, a hundred year old building that has been completely renovated to modern standards ten years ago, may be regarded as having an 'effective age' of ten years and would be valued accordingly.

effective annual interest rate
The true interest rate payable over one year when interest is compounded at intervals of less than a year. The formula for converting a **nominal interest rate** to an effective annual rate is:
$$I = [1 + (i/m)]^{m} - 1$$
Where, i = nominal interest rate (expressed as a decimal)
m = no. of compounding periods per annum
I = effective rate.
Thus, a nominal interest rate of 8 per cent per annum would be an effective rate of 8.3 per cent when interest is compounded monthly. It is also called an 'effective rate'. See also **annual percentage rate, internal rate of return.**

effective capital value
see **contractor's basis**.

'effective cause'
see **commission**.

effective floor area
The floor area that is considered useable or of value to an occupier. See also **net internal area, net useable area**.

effective gross income (EGI) (US)
The **gross income** (including all rental and miscellaneous income) from a property after making allowance for vacancies and defaulting tenants, but before deducting operating expenses. See also **income**.

effective rate of interest
see **effective annual interest rate**.

effective rental rate
The true rental rate per square foot payable by a tenant, after taking into account allowances made by the landlord such as a rent free period or a

contribution made to meet the cost of an improvement made by the tenant. cf. **virtual rent.**

effective yield

The return or yield from a bond, or other instrument, based on the actual price paid and taking full account of the date income is received, or interest paid, and the date the investment matures or is sold; as contrasted with the **nominal yield** which is based on the face value or par value of the bond or instrument. See also **annual percentage rate, equivalent yield, redemption yield.**

effects

Goods and moveable property; especially corporeal **moveables**, but not **real property** (except if used in the term 'real effects'). Effects is used commonly as synonymous with goods, but strictly it is less extensive in meaning to goods, being only that which a person has and that is capable of effecting, producing or creating money – usually by sale. In a will 'effects' used *simpliciter*, will carry the whole personal estate, as a gift 'of all my effects', without more. But it is frequently used in a restricted sense, meaning 'goods and moveables', as in the common expression of "furniture and effects". In every case the court has to collect from the context the particular sense in which the testator has intended to use it." – Michell *v* Michell (1820) 5 Mad. 71. 'Real and personal effects' when used in a will embraces the testator's entire estate. See also **chattels, personal property.**

effet (F)

bill of exchange; negotiable instrument.
(*effet de commerce* – **negotiable**

instrument)
(*effet de levier* – **leverage**).

effets (F)

effects; goods; possessions; belongings; chattels; assets. See also ***biens.***

efficiency apartment (US)

A small **apartment,** usually let furnished, which comprises a combined living room, bedroom and also a kitchen and bathroom. In the UK such a unit would commonly be called a 'bedsitting room'. See also **flat.**

efficiency ratio

The ratio of the **net internal area** or **rentable area** of an office building to the **gross internal area.** See also **loss factor.**

egistment

see **agistment.**

égout (F)

sewer; drain.

eighth schedule development

see **existing use rights.**

ejectment

An ancient form of common law action used to recover possession of land when the claimant considered he had been wrongfully dispossessed of real property. Ejectment was a remedy specific to land; the claimant sought recovery of the land itself, and not merely damages (although he may also claim damages arising as a result of being dispossessed). It could not be applied to goods. The action of ejectment has been replaced in English law by the action of **recovery** (Common Law Procedure Act 1852, s. 168).

In the US ejectment may be employed as a remedy for a landlord to recover possession of his property from a tenant at sufferance; although recovery, **eviction** or **detainer** are the more usual courses of action in most States. A party seeking ejectment must show not only that he was in actual, undisturbed and quiet possession of the premises but also that he has been wrongfully ousted by another (Bradshaw *v* Ashley, 180 US 59, 21 SCt. 297). Ejectment cannot be used in a case of mere trespass. See also **dispossession, mesne profits**.

The Law of Real Property, by Robert Megarry and H.W.R. Wade, 5 edn., p. 1156.

ejusdem generis (L)

'Of the same kind or nature'. The *ejusdem generis* rule is applied when there is a particular description of property followed by some general or all-e'mbracing description; it is assumed that items covered by the general description are of the same kind or nature as the particular. For example, an insurance policy may cover things that are of a similar nature or *genus* to those set out in the contract, even if they are not specifically stated therein, but the policy does not cover things of a different *genus* – in King *v* Travellers' Insurance Association Ltd. [1931] 48 TLR 53 a fur coat was held not to be of the same nature as "jewellery, watches, field glasses and cameras and other fragile or specially valuable articles." Nevertheless "... words, however general, may be limited in respect to the subject-matter in relation to which they are used. [and] ... general words may be restricted to the same genus as the specific words that precede them" – Thames and Mersey Marine Insurance Co. *v* Hamilton, Fraser and Co. (1887) 12 App. Cas. 490. See also **words meaning of**.

election

A choice, in particular between a plurality of alternatives. In law frequently a party must elect for one alternative or another; "election is the obligation imposed upon a party by Courts of Equity to choose between two inconsistent or alternative rights or claims in cases where there is a clear intention of the person from whom he derives one that he should not enjoy both". (White and Tudor's *Leading Cases in Equity*, 9 edn., vol. i p. 373). Normally a person may elect to pursue as a remedy for a breach of contract either damages or specific performance, but not both. Election is a matter that is not based on intention but on conduct. If a person has knowingly done an unequivocal act which demonstrates that he has taken a particular course, he cannot elect to take another course which by his act he has rejected. – United Australia Ltd. *v* Barclays Bank Ltd. [1941] AC1. Thus, the third party to a contract upon discovering the identity of an **undisclosed principal** may elect to take an action against that principal, in place of the agent, but his election in that respect may preclude any right of action against the agent with whom he has contracted. Similarly, a judgement obtained against an agent precludes the third party from taking a subsequent action upon discovering the existence of the principal – Kendal *v* Hamilton (1879) 4 App. Cas. 504. A party to a contract may elect to forgo a right of **rescission** by choosing a course of action which indicates that he has no intention of taking a different course.

cf. **abandonment**. See also **approbate and reprobate, waiver**.

Snell's *Principles of Equity*, 28 edn.,

pp. 495–504.
16 Halsbury's Laws of England, 4 edn., paras. 1392–1406.

elegit

A form of action used by a judgement creditor by which he took possession of the debtor's land and held it until the debt was paid from the rent or otherwise. Abolished by the Administration of Justice Act 1956, s. 34. Since that Act a court may impose a **charge** on land for the same effect.

elevation

1. The height above a fixed level, especially the height above sea level.
2. The façade of a building.
3. A drawing that shows a side view of a building.

Ellwood capitalisation rate (US)

A **capitalisation rate** for appraising investment property, named after L.W. Ellwood MAI, which takes into account the financing used to purchase an investment and, thus, the effect of **gearing**. The calculation of the rate is based on the theory that the value of an investment is a function of (a) the amount of **debt capital** that can be obtained to acquire that investment at current mortgage rates, and (b) the amount of equity capital that would be invested at a required rate of return on that equity, i.e. value = loan available + present value of equity; where the present value of equity is the present value of the before-tax cash flow, plus the present value of the future selling price, minus the present value of the balance due on the mortgage at the time of sale. L.W. Ellwood produced a series of tables to provide a single capitalisation rate given:
  i. the mortgage coefficient at a given interest rate;
  ii. the term over which the amount of equity invested is to be recaptured;
  iii. the period of the mortgage;
  iv. the ratio of debt-to-equity:
  v. the required **equity yield rate**;
  vi. the projected appreciation or depreciation in the property over its investment life; and, if required,
  vii. the tax rate of the investor.

The application of the Ellwood capitalisation rate represents an extension of the **mortgage-equity capitalisation technique**, having been developed to take account of all the above variables.

Property Finance: Evaluations Its Effects, by Ernest Wood, 277 EG 1425 (1973).
Real Estate Investment Analysis and Taxation, by Paul F. Wendt and Alan R. Cerf, pp. 58–68 (1969).
Income Property Appraisal and Analysis, by Jack P. Friedman and Nicholas Ordway, pp. 227–243 (1981).
Ellwood's Tables for Real Estate Appraising and Financing, by L.W. Ellwood, 4 edn.

emblements

Pronounced em-blem-ents. Derived from old French *emblaer* 'to sow with grain'. An annual crop produced by cultivation; "such vegetable products as are the annual results of agricultural labour" – Chalmer's *Sale of Goods* 17 edn., pp. 280–281. Emblements are considered as identifiable with *fructus industriales*; crops that may be considered as personal property and do not form part of the land in law. The doctrine of emblements provides a common law right for a tenant of agricultural land with an uncertain interest, e.g. from year-to-year or for life, or whose interest, although for a fixed period, is unexpectedly brought to an end, to remove the crops he has sowed when they are ripe, even after his tenancy has ended, other than as a consequence of his own act – Haines v Welch (1868) LR 4 CP 91; Kingsbury v Collins (1827) 4 Bing. 202. In practice in England and Wales this doctrine no longer has any application to periodic tenants because of statutory provisions which give agricultural tenants security of tenure, or a right to **compensation for improvements** on quitting an agricultural holding.

A **tenant for life** may enter land after his life estate has come to an end and reap crops that he has sown. This applies only to artificially grown crops, such as corn, hemp, flax, carrots or potatoes; he may not return to collect fruits from seeds or plants that do not produce a crop within one year of sowing or planting and he may take only one crop – Co. Litt. 556; Graves v Weld (1833) 5 B and Ad. 119. When the tenant dies his personal representatives have a right to reap emblements that result from sowings made before his death and these form part of the tenant's estate. Emblements may not be collected if the estate if brought to an end due to a breach of a condition attached to the grant of the estate committed by the tenant. See also **way-going crops**.
Real Property by William E. Burby, 3 edn., pp. 18–21.
Woodfall's Landlord and Tenant, 28 edn., para. 2–0064.

eminent domain

Superior **dominion** over land. The power of a Sovereign, government, or a public body to take private property or an interest in a property, for public use; subject to the payment of proper and **just compensation**. The legal process of settling this action is known as **condemnation**. The term 'eminent domain' is not used now in English law where a similar process is called **compulsory purchase**. Eminent domain is a form of natural power vested in government to acquire land for public use, whereas compulsory purchase is a right obtained from parliamentary decree or statute. In the US the power of eminent domain is considered an "incident of sovereignty, and ... requires no constitutional recognition" – United States v Jones (1883), 109 US 518. However, the exercise of that right is limited by the fifth amendment to the Constitution which states that no private property shall be taken for public use without just compensation and that no person shall be deprived of property "without due process of law".
cf. **expropriation, police powers**.
Real Estate Valuation Litigation, by J.D. Eaton, pp. 1–9 (1982).
The Law of Eminent Domain, by P. Nichols, 3 edn.

emphytéose (F)
emphyteotic lease.

emphytéote (F)
lessee (of an **emphyteotic lease**).

emphyteotic (or emphyteutic) lease, or emphyteusis

A form of lease derived from Roman or the civil law and found in French law. An emphyteotic lease is defined in Civil Code of Lower Canada, art. 567 as "a contract by which the proprietor of an **immoveable** conveys it for a time to another, the lessee subjecting himself to make improvements, to pay the lessor an annual rent, and to such other charges as may be agreed upon". The law in France accepts a similar interpretation, although it is not mentioned in the Civil Code and was not given statutory effect until 25 June 1902. This form of lease was granted during the time of the Roman Empire by an owner of poorly cultivated land so that a tenant would take on the task of improving the land. The tenant paid a small rent or **canon** for this right and the owner regained the land after a number of years in an improved condition. During the period of user the holder of the lease had a form of ownership which he could alienate, create servitudes over and mortgage.

The essential elements of this form of lease are (i) the lease is long-term, commonly for 99 years but exceeding 18 years; (ii) the lessee is obliged to maintain the property and usually to make improvements to the leased property; (iii) the lease may be alienated or charged as security, providing the lessee does not cause any deterioration in the value of the lessor's reversion. See also *bail à construction, superficie.*
Droit Civil, Les Beins, by Jean Carbonnier, 11 edn., pp. 270–271
Précis Dalloz Droit Civil, Les Biens (Alex Weill), 2 edn., pp. 577–581.

empiétement (F)
encroachment; trespass.

emplacement (F)
site; location; place; piece of ground.
(*emplacement pour promotion* – **building land**)
(*emplacement de première qualité*; *emplacement de premier ordre* – **prime location**).

emprunt (F)
loan, normally for a medium to long term.
(*emprunt hypothécaire* – mortgage loan).
cf. *prêt.*

emptor (L)
'Buyer'. See *caveat emptor.*

empty rates
see **unoccupied.**

en nature (F)
in kind; *in specie.*

enabling declaration (US)
A document filed with the state government by the owner of a **condominium** (usually the developer) setting out details of each unit of ownership, e.g. each of the apartments, together with details of the **common elements** and rights thereover. Called also a 'master deed' or 'declaration of condominium', or when the units are held as leasehold interests a 'master lease'.

enchère (F)
bid.
(*enchère au rabais* – dutch auction)
(*vente aux enchères* – sale by auction).
See also *surenchère.*

enclave (F)
landlocked land.
(*droit de passage en case d'enclave* – **easement of necessity**). See also *passage, droit de.*

enclosure (or **inclosure)**
The fencing in of an area of land in order to restrict or contain its use. In particular, the closing in of an open field so as to prevent its use as **common land**. The tenure of common land requires that it will be maintained as open land and its agricultural potential restricted. The owner of

common land is subjected to the perpetual rights of the commoners who, in turn, have no right to enclose and cultivate land that does not belong to them. The purpose of enclosure is to transfer such land to private ownership and thereby aim to improve its productive capacity.

In Britain the decline of the **feudal system** of land tenure left large areas of land uncultivated and used solely as common pasture. Some of this land was appropriated into private ownership; usually by dividing the open fields, or **waste land**, of the manor into separate strips and reallocating them to individual commoners to be held in private ownership; a process that could be effected by agreement of the commoners or by private Act of Parliament. By the 15th century enclosure was a fairly extensive process and the word 'enclosure' (or inclosure) referred to three distinct movements: "the enclosure of the great open fields characteristic of midland agriculture; the enclosure of the regular town and village commons; [and] the nibbling away of forest, moor, and other waste land by what were known expressively in the North as 'intakes'" – *A Concise Economic History of Britain*, by John Clapham, p. 194, (1951).

The 16th century Agrarian Revolution accelerated the demand for further enclosures of the open fields of Britain, but the process continued sporadically. By the 18th century the increase in population, the desire of the wealthy landowner to see land in more unified ownership, and the increasing economies of scale in farming created further pressure to enclose the common land, or any other land that was considered unproductive.

Accordingly, between 1750 and 1850 a number of private Acts of Parliament were passed to simplify the procedure for the enclosure of common land; in particular the Inclosure (Consolidation) Act 1801, was passed to set out a number of general provisions that could readily be included in subsequent private Inclosure Acts. In 1845 a further Inclosure Act came to the statute book, incorporating many of the provisions of the 1801 Act, that provided for the establishment of a Board of Inclosure Commissioners for England and Wales which was responsible for further encouraging and for regulating the enclosure movement. This process was slowed down in 1852 by the passing of another Inclosure Act which limited the rate of private enclosures by requiring that all such future proposals be submitted to Parliament for its consideration.

Enclosure of common land and its transfer to several ownership is still possible; the procedure is governed by the Commons Act 1876 and the function of regulating such action has been passed to the Secretary of State for the Environment (in England) or the Secretary of State for Wales. The enclosure of common land is now rare because any such enclosure must be established as "of benefit to the neighbourhood as well as the private individual" (1876 Act, s. 7). The Commons Preservation Society has championed the public need to preserve common land; the Commons Registration Act 1965 provides a procedure for the registration and consequent preservation of common land; and local authorities have powers to take such land into their control for the public good.

The enclosure movement has been compared to the use of compulsory purchase powers in the 19th century, as the latter powers were granted to public bodies to enable them to compel recalcitrant owners to part with their land 'for the public good'. However, enclosure is more akin to **appropriation** of land by which a private Act of Parliament is used to transfer common land to individual ownership; whereas compulsory purchase aims to remove land from private ownership to enable it to be used for the public good. Nevertheless legislation for the enclosure of land was justified as being for the 'public good' or at least for the good of a 'Parliament of Landowners'; though a distinction might have to be drawn "between the ends and the means" —*Law of Compulsory Purchase and Compensation*, by Keith Davies, 4 edn., p. 8.

In France prior to the Revolution two restrictions were placed on the right to enclose open land: (i) the right of a lord of the manor to hunt upon any land outside of a town, village or hamlet; and (ii) a right of common pasture (*droit de vaine pâture*) available to local residents after the harvest. Since 1792 any landowner in France has a right to enclose (*droit de se clore*) his own land, provided that the enclosure does not impede (a) an **easement of necessity** from landlocked land (*droit de passage en cas d'enclave*); (b) an established right of pasturage (*droit de pâture*) in favour of another party; or (c) an expressly granted servitude (***servitude***).

In England 'enclosure' is used normally to refer to the surrounding of land with a fence or wall, and 'inclosure' to refer to the legal process of appropriation. In the US inclosure is preferred for either instance. However the words are interchangeable. See also **approvement, fence, manor**.
Précis Dalloz, Droit Civil, Les Biens (Alex Weill), 2 edn., pp. 98–101.
A History of English Law, by W.S. Holdsworth, Vol. iv, pp. 364–373.
Cheshire's Modern Law of Real Property, 11 edn., pp. 547–8.
6 Halsbury's Laws of England, 4 edn., pp. 280–299.
Common Land and Inclosure, by E.C.K. Gonner, 2 edn., (1966).

encroachment (or incroachment)
An illegal entry or intrusion onto the land of another, normally by an adjoining owner; in particular, when that intrusion causes injury or is an attempt by an adjoining land owner to annex land to his own. A gradual or partial intrusion on the land of another, especially that of a neighbour. "The frequent repetition of such injuries makes feelings run high, so that relations between neighbours become intolerably embittered. This is why everyone should do everything he can to avoid offending his neighbour; above all, he must always go out of his way to avoid all acts of encroachment ... If a man oversteps his boundaries and encroaches on his neighbour's land, he should pay the damage." (Plato, *The Laws*, Book 8, para. 15.) Plato suggested that a person who encroaches on to another's land should pay a fine equal to putting right damage caused by the encroachment and he denigrated the removal of boundary stones in the strongest terms as an act whereby a man tries to 'reallocate land'. An encroachment may arise also if a beneficiary of an easement extends

his rights over the servient land – Ankerson *v* Connelly [1907] 1 Ch. 678. An encroachment normally constitutes a **trespass** when the action physically takes away land or a right to land, but it may cause a **nuisance** when there is an interference with the proper use of land especially as an intrusion onto adjoining land. A landowner is under a duty to prevent anything going from his land onto his neighbours. However, "the duty is a duty to do that which is reasonable in all the circumstances, and no more than what, if anything, is reasonable to prevent or minimise the known risk of damage or injury to one's neighbour or his property." – Leakey *v* National Trust for Places of Historic Interest or National Beauty [1980] QB 524. See also **adverse possession, strict liability**.

encumberance or **incumberance**

Any **burden, claim** or other impediment on property. An encumberance does not prevent a transfer of title, but normally reduces the value of a property. An encumberance may be classified broadly as (a) one that limits a title or right to full enjoyment of a property, e.g. a **mortgage, lien, charge** or judgement to secure a debt; and (b) one that restricts the physical use of property, e.g. the burden of an **easement**, of a **restrictive covenant** or an **encroachment** from adjoining property. A tenancy, especially a protected tenancy, may be considered also as an encumberance when a vendor has contracted to sell with the benefit of **vacant possession**. The Law of Property Act 1925, s. 205 defines an 'incumberance' to include "a legal or equitable mortgage and a trust for securing money, and a lien, and a charge of a portion, annuity, or other capital or annual sum". In the US a 'cloud on title' is referred to sometimes as an encumberance. See also **adverse possession, land charge, minor interest, overriding interest**.

end loan (US)

see **take-out loan**.

end money

A sum of money which must be borrowed if the actual cost of a development project exceeds the estimated cost. A contingency fund.

endorsement (or **indorsement**)

1. The act of writing, usually on the back of an instrument, in order to transfer or assign the benefit to another. A signature placed on a document, either in order to ratify it and any alterations thereto or in order to transfer rights under the document. A bill of exchange or a cheque may be transferred to a third party by the payee signing, i.e. endorsing it, on the reverse. An endorsement of a mortgage deed may be used to transfer, or reconvey, a mortgaged property back to the mortgagor, i.e. to free the mortgage encumberance.
2. A **rider** or **memorandum** attached to an insurance policy to give effect to an alteration of the terms. For example, a rider to an insurance policy stating that a particular person has contracted to purchase property that is the subject of the policy and, therefore, that he has an interest in the property.

endos (F)
endorsement.

endossement (F)
endorsement.

endowment

1. The furnishing of someone with an income. The transfer, generally as a **gift**, of an income from property. Usually associated with an income provided by a husband to his wife (or *vice-versa*), or the provision of a permanent trust fund for the support of a person or entity. See also **dower, endowment mortgage**.

2. Any property held permanently by a charity.

endowment insurance policy

An insurance policy which provides that the insurer will pay an income or a fixed sum to a designated person at a future date, such as when the person reaches a specified age or on his or her death. Unlike the more common **contingency insurance policy**, which provides for a payment to the insured only on the happening of a stipulated but uncertain event, an endowment policy provides for a payment to the insured but leaves the date for payment as the uncertain factor. See also **endowment mortgage**.

endowment mortgage

A **mortgage loan** coupled with an **endowment insurance policy** so that the policy will guarantee payment of the mortgage debt, either on the death of the insured or when the debt falls due for redemption. The mortgagor does not repay any part of the principal he has borrowed during the term of the loan but pays only interest to the mortgagee. However, coincidental with the commencement of the loan, he takes out an endowment insurance policy (usually for the same period and amount as the loan), for which he pays regular fixed premiums to the insurer. This endowment policy may be 'non-profits', 'full-with-pro-fits' or 'low-cost'. A non-profits policy merely provides sufficient insurance to repay the loan on maturity, or on the death of the mortgagor if that occurs beforehand. A full with-profits scheme provides insurance for the amount of the loan and additionally the insurance company pays periodic bonuses, based on its investment performance, so that at maturity the insured is likely to receive more than the amount borrowed. A low-cost scheme, while providing that if the policy holder should die before the date set for repayment of the loan (the redemption date) the loan will be paid in full, only guarantees the repayment at the redemption date of part of the sum borrowed; the difference is assumed to be provided from bonuses arising from the insurance company's investment performance (The low-cost scheme is cheaper than a full profits policy; however, there is a risk that the bonuses may not reach expectations leaving the mortgagor to find the difference, although insurance companies' anticipated bonuses are calculated generally on a conservative basis).

enfeoffment

The act of investing an estate by means of **feoffment**.

enforcement notice

A notice served (or strictly 'issued', with copies served) by a local planning authority, in accordance with the provisions of the Town and Country Planning Act 1971, s.87 (as amended by the Local Government and Planning (Amendment) Act 1971), upon the **owner** and **occupier** of land (and any other person who has an interest in the land which in the opinion of the authority would be materially affected by the notice) when it appears to the authority that there has been a breach of planning control which the authority is not prepared to accept. The notice requires the breach to be remedied. An enforcement notice may be served when **development** has been carried out without planning permission or development has been carried out in a manner that contravenes a condition or limitation imposed on the grant of a planning permission. An enforcement notice requires the removal of the unauthorised development and the restoration, as effectively as possible, of the state of affairs that would have existed if the breach had never occurred. The enforcement notice grants planning permission for the use or development it is seeking to restore (1971 Act, s. 23(9); Young *v* Secretary of State for the Environment (1983) Times 28 July).

An enforcement notice to be valid must be served in accordance with strict statutory rules. It must be served on the correct person(s) (for this purpose the 'occupier' is anyone occupying the land under a lease, tenancy and, in most cases, a licence: Stevens *v* London Borough of Bromley [1972] 1 All ER 712). It must specify the alleged breach of planning control and the steps required by the authority to remedy that breach. It must state when it is to become effective (being at least 28 days after it is issued) and the period for compliance with the notice. The notice does not have to limit all unauthorised development, it may limit only a part of the development; but the authority may not use enforcement procedures to cover any development that is permitted. Thus, if there has been an intensi-

fication of use the notice may require the user to reduce the activity to its original level, but not require its total removal – Mansi *v* Elstree RDC (1965) JPL 596. A person served with an enforcement notice may appeal to the Secretary of State for the Environment, before the notice becomes effective, on the following grounds: (i) planning permission ought to be granted for the development in question or the condition(s) imposed ought to be discharged; (ii) the alleged matter is not a breach of planning control; (iii) in the case of building, engineering, mining or other operations in, on, over or under land, or conditions related thereto, or a change of use of any building to a single dwelling house, the notice has been served more than four years after the breach of planning control; (iv) in other cases to which the four year rule in (iii) does not apply, the breach of planning control occured before 1st January 1964; (v) the notice is not served in accordance with statutory requirements; (vi) the steps required to be taken by the notice exceed that which is necessary to remedy any breach of control; (vii) the period of compliance with the notice is unreasonably short (1971 Act, s. 88). In the event of an appeal the notice does not take effect (if at all) until the appeal is determined. The Secretary of State's decision on appeal is final, although there is a right of appeal against that decision to the High Court on a point of law. Failure to comply with a valid enforcement notice is an offence making the convicted party liable to a fine (1971 Act, s. 89).

cf. **discontinuance order**. See also **stop notice**.

Planning Law and Procedure, by A.E. Telling, 5 edn., pp. 173–191.
Planning Procedure Tables, by R.N.D. Hamilton, 4 edn., pp. 93–105.
An Outline of Planning Law, by Desmond Heap, 8 edn., pp. 217–240.
Urban Planning Law, by Malcolm Grant, pp. 383–429, (1982).
Encylopaedia of Planning Law, by Desmond Heap, paras. 1–177 to 1–190.

enfranchisement

Literally to 'set free', in real property, from the payment of rent. The enlargement of a lesser interest in land into a **freehold** interest, usually upon the payment of a fixed sum. "Enfranchisement of leaseholds in the eye of the tenant is the acquisition of the **fee** or the getting rid of the rent. Having got rid of that he is master of his property; it belongs to him." – Re Bruce Halsey and Bruce [1905] 2 Ch. 378. In the English law, prior to 1925, enfranchisement referred specifically to the conversion of **copyhold** tenure into freehold tenure. Today it refers to the conversion of a **long tenancy** into a freehold. See also **leasehold enfranchisement, secure tenancy**.
9 Halsbury's Laws of England, 4 edn., paras. 784–900.

engagement (F)

1. **pledge**; **hypothecation**; liability.
2. promise; commitment.

engineering insurance

Insurance of items situated in a property; e.g. boilers, lifts, electrical plant and mechanical equipment. In particular, engineering insurance covers breakdown, collapse, explosion, as well as resulting damage to other property and to third parties. Such insurance is provided usually on the condition that the insurance company undertakes regular inspections to ensure the proper upkeep and safety of the plant and equipment.
Elements of Insurance, by W.A. Dinsdale and D.C. McMurdie, 5 edn., pp. 49, 95.

engineering operation or work

In general, works for the creation of a road, highway, railway, canal, dock, harbour, or bridge and works for laying a sewer or other public utilities, especially earthworks required for such purposes. In particular, 'engineering operations' include "the formation or laying out of means of access to highways." (Town and Country Planning Act 1971, s. 290). See also **development, operations**.

English covenants of title (US)

see **beneficial owner**.

engrossment

The preparation of a **deed** in final form for execution (i.e. signing and sealing) by the parties; or a deed that is prepared for execution.

enjoyment

The receipt or retention of a benefit, advantage or reward; the exercise of a legal **right**. One may 'enjoy' or have the advantage of using an incorporeal right in the same way as one takes possession or uses a corporeal property. Thus in relation to a right of light 'enjoyed' may be taken to mean " 'having had the amenity and advantage of using' the access of light; that is nearly equivalent to 'having had the use' ". . . – Cooper *v* Straker (1888) 40 Ch.D. 27. Enjoyment of a right over land may be had by consent or agreement, but not necessarily by occupation or possession. Enjoyment normally denotes present economic benefit rather than a right to a vested interest (or estate) (US *v* Byrum, 408 US 125, 92 S Ct. 2382).

"Enjoyment as of right (in relation to a prescriptive right) means an enjoyment had, not secretly or by stealth, or by tacit sufferance, or by permission asked from time to time on each occasion or even on many occasions of using it, but an enjoyment had openly, notoriously, without particular leave at the time, by a person claiming to use the land, without danger of being treated as a trespasser, as a matter of right." (6 Halsbury's Laws of England, 4 edn., p. 223).

See also **prescription**.

enlargement

1. An increase in a right to real property. For example, an enlargement of a leasehold into a freehold by **enfranchisement**; the enlargement of a **base fee** in possession into a fee simple; the enlargement of the right of a **mortgagee** in possession, after 12 years, into a right to a fee simple. A lease for a term originally created for not less than 300 years, with an unexpired residue of 200 years where no rent or money value is payable and which is not liable to be determined by re-entry for a breach of condition, may be enlarged into a fee simple (Law of Property Act 1925, s. 153). This process is completed by the tenant executing a deed of enlargement. See also **leasehold enfranchisement, merger**.

2. To make large by **addition**; to increase the space allotted to a building (horizontally or vertically) by improvement or alteration. See also **extension**.

enquête d'urbanisme (F)

planning inquiry.

enquête de 'commodo et incommodo' (F)

public notice. In particular, notice given of a proposed expropriation of land, requesting representations from the public on the underlying project.

enquiry

see **inquiry**.

enregistrement (F)

registration; registry.
(*enregistrement d'un acte* – registration, or recording, of a deed)
(*bureau d'enregistrement* – registration office, land registry office)
(*frais d'enregistrement; droit d'enregistrement* – registration duty) See also **cadastre**.

enrichissement sans cause (F)

unjust enrichment. See **restitution**.

enrichment

see **unjust enrichment**.

ensemble (F)

building complex.
(*ensembles immobiliers* – a particular form of building complex comprising land and buildings, with common land rights. Similar to a **comprehensive development area** and subjected to the special rules of a French law of 10th July 1965).

entail

see **entailed estate (or interest)**.

entailed estate (or interest)

A **freehold** estate in land that has been limited to a person and his or her issue. A **fee** interest that is less than a fee simple; the old name for such an estate 'fee tail' being derived from *feudum talliatum* – a fee that has been 'cut down or truncated'. An entailed estate or interest comes into existence when land is settled on a person and a specified or restricted line of direct descendants. If it cannot go to further issue the estate normally reverts to the original donor or his or her heirs. An entailed estate or 'entail' aims to have a longer duration than a **life interest** but is enchained for a number of lives. "Entails are natural consequences of the law of primogeniture. They were introduced to preserve a certain lineal succession, of which the law of primogeniture first gave the idea, and to hinder any part of the original estate from being carried out of the proposed line either by gift, or devise, or alienation; either by folly, or by the misfortune of any of its successive owners." (*The Wealth of Nations* by Adam Smith, Book III, Ch. 2). An entailed estate is not intended to pass out of the specified direct line of issue without first returning to the control of the donor. It differs from an intestate succession by which, if the direct line dies out the land passes to a related line, e.g. a brother and his heirs.

An entailed interest may be (a) a 'general entail' or 'tail general' which descends without further restriction, e.g. 'to A and the heirs of his body'; (b) 'special entail' or 'tail special' which descends only to the heirs through a particular spouse, e.g. 'to A and the heirs of his body begotten by him upon X'; or (c) an entail limited to a particular sex, whether a 'tail male' or 'tail female', e.g. 'to A and the male (or female) heirs of his body.' The person entitled to the ownership of the land at any point in time is called a 'tenant in tail'. An entailed interest can be transferred to a third party but in principle, that party's interest remains liable to be extinguished by an issue of the transferor

after his death. This risk may be removed or reduced, however, by a tenant in tail disentailing or '**barring the entail**', i.e. by creating a fee simple (provided he is in possession of the estate, or obtains the consent of the protector of the estate), or by creating a **base fee** (if he has an estate in remainder or does not obtain the consent of the protector of the estate).

The terms 'entail', 'entailed interest', 'fee tail' 'estate in tail' and 'estate tail' are used interchangeably; but 'fee tail' is the correct term for an entail that was capable of existing as a legal estate prior to 1925 and could not be alienated by will, and 'entailed interest' for an entail that can be alienated, but only exists as an **equitable interest** which is now the case in English law for all entails.

Since 1925 an entailed interest may be created in **personal property**, in the same way as real property or land (Law of Property Act 1925, s. 130). See also **conditional fee, *De Donis Conditionalibus*, disentailing deed, quasi-entail, rule against perpetuities, words of limitation**.
Megarry's Manual of The Law of Real Property, 6 edn., pp. 44–51.
Cheshire's Modern Law of Real Property, 13 edn., pp. 231–256.
The Law of Real Property, by Robert Megarry & H.W.R. Wade, 5 edn., pp. 39, 40, 55, 76–92.

enter
see **entry**.

enterinement (F)
ratification; confirmation.

entire contract
A contract which provides that the entire fulfilment of the promise – the completion of all the parts of the con-

tract – is a **condition precedent** to the fulfilment of any part of the contract. For example, a building contract which provides that all the building work must be completed satisfactorily before any payment is made. The courts are likely to construe a contract as several and not entire when at all possible, but if the contract provides only for a lump-sum payment, after the duties and obligations are performed in their entirety, the contract will be enforced in its entirety – H. Daken and Co. Ltd. *v* Lee [1916] 1 KB 566. See also **lump-sum contract, substantial completion**.

enterprise zone (EZ)

An urban area where it is considered that special government assistance is required to generate economic activity; in particular, an inner-city area that has suffered from 'urban decay' and requires substantial new development to encourage new business, employment and improved social and economic conditions. The intention is to restore incentives for private investment by fiscal policies and an easing of planning constraints. In the UK, the Local Government Planning and Land Act 1980, Part XVII provides that, following submissions from local government bodies proposing appropriate areas for assistance, the Secretary of State for the Environment may designate an area as an enterprise zone. Enterprise zones are intended to be experimental and they retain their status for 10 years. These areas benefit from the following provisions: (i) exemption from general rates on commercial and industrial property; (ii) exemption from development land tax for a period of 10 years; (iii) for a similar period, 100 per cent capital allowances on commercial and industrial building; and (iv) easing of planning and other administrative controls.

In the US enterprise zones have been proposed for a number of areas of high unemployment, low economic activity and general distress. These zones are intended "to create a free market environment in depressed areas through relief from taxes, regulations and other government burdens, privatisation of some city services and involvement of private neighbourhood organisations" – Department of Housing and Urban Development (1982) The Administration's Enterprise Zone Proposal: Fact Sheet, Washington D.C., March 23. See also **special area**, **urban development area**.
Enterprise Zones, Rating and Valuation Reporter, 21 (6) & (9), pp. 144–146 and 200–201 (1981).

entire tenancy
see **severalty**.

entireties, tenancy by
see **tenancy by entireties**.

entitled
To be furnished with, or have a right to, a **title**. A term that has no strict legal meaning, but usually means a right to immediate **possession** and not merely a right in reversion or remainder. Entitled may mean any right which will come into possession; but not a right to a **contingent interest**, i.e. not a right that may never come 'into possession' – Atcherley *v* Du Moulin 2 K and J 186; Hughes *v* Young (1863) 32 LJ Ch. 137. Beneficially entitled to possession of a settled estate means being "entitled for his own benefit, if there is any

benefit to be derived from the estate, and not simply as trustee for others". – Re Jones (1884) 26 Ch. D 736. On the other hand 'entitled to possession' (in respect of a landlord seeking possession under the Rent Acts) means a legal right to possession, not a right to enforce that right through an order of the court; so that a landlord is 'entitled to possession' when he has served a valid notice to quit and acquired a legal right to possession and he has no need to wait until a court, at a later date, grants an order for possession – Hill *v* Hasler [1921] 3 K B 643. See also **beneficiary**.

entrée (F)
entry; way in.
(*entrée en jouissance* – **taking possession**).

entrepôt (F)
warehouse.

entrepreneur
Derived from the French *entreprendre* 'to undertake'. One who undertakes an enterprise or business, especially one who accepts the **risk** of a venture and employs others to further his objective. A promoter, i.e. a person who initiates, controls and steers a business enterprise. See also **developer, property developer**.

entrepreneur (F)
contractor; entrepreneur; builder as distinguished from a **promoteur** who acts as an intermediary.

entreprise (F)
business; enterprise; undertaking.
(*entreprise en participation* – **joint venture**).

entresol (F)
entresol, (literally between floors), a floor level set within the main floor

levels, or in the storey height of a building; **mezzanine**.

entretien (d'un batiment) (F)
maintenance; upkeep (of a building). (*en bon état d'entretien* – in a good state of repair; **tenantable repair**) (*frais d'entretien* – maintenance expenses). See also *reparations*.

entry
1. Obtaining possession of a property when exercising a legal right, such as **taking possession** of a property at the commencement of a lease. Entry may be made on to land only by peaceful means, a principle first enacted by the Forcible Entry Act 1381: "none from henceforth may make any entry into any land or tenements, but in the case where entry is given by law; and in such case not with strong hand, nor with multitude of people, but only in peaceful and easy manner". The term may be used also to refer to an act of going on to land to assert a legal right thereover, and may be physical entry, or constructive entry when it is exercised by law e.g. by a mortgagee exercising his right to collect the rent and profits from a property he holds as security. See also **landlord's access, notice of entry, right of re-entry, right of entry, writ of entry**.
2. An alley or path leading up to a house. A covered way between a pair of houses.

enure
To operate or take effect.

Environmental Protection Agency (EPA) (US)
A federal agency established to monitor and control environmental problems; in particular, all forms of pollution.

environs (F)

outskirts; suburbs; neighbourhood.

Epargne-Logement (F)

A scheme, designed to encourage housing construction, by which a builder can obtain an advance equal to the interest earned on a sum invested with an approved bank or savings institution or a loan at a favourable rate of interest.

épave (F)

unclaimed property; derelict; wreck.
(*épaves flottantes* – flotsam)
(*épaves rejetées* – jetsam)
(*droit d'épave* – **escheat**).
cf. *trésor*. See also *res nullius*.

epitome of title

see **abstract of title**.

épure (F)

working drawing.

equalization (US)

The adjustment, by a **Board of Equalization**, of the **assessed value** of properties in order to apportion more equitably the values, and hence the tax burdens, in an administrative area.

Equalization Board (US)

see **Board of Equalization**.

equated rent

see **constant rent**.

equated yield

A single or 'true' yield from a property investment which is let at an income that is expected to vary over a given period of time; e.g. an investment that is bought when the contractual rent (the rent actually being paid) is below the current market rental value. An equated yield represents a single yield on an investment which takes account of current income and the projected income when the current rent is reviewed to market value. The equated yield is the yield that an investor would accept from the same property if it were let at the current market rent: in other words, it is the yield from the property investment which is made equal to that which would be received from a property let at market rent. Generally, an equated yield is calculated by finding the discounted rate of return, taking account of income variations up to the time of the first rent reviews (or, for example, 5 or 7 years), but at 'current values', i.e. the **internal rate of return** on cost, over that period, at current values. When there is a single rent review, the equated yield may be obtained from the formula:

$Po = (r/e) + (R - r)/[e(1 + e)^n]$

Where Po = initial price or cost

    r = initial rental income

    R = estimated market rental value

    n = number of years to the next market rent review

    e = equated yield

In words, it is the return obtained by expressing the present income, plus the annual equivalent of the increase in income, as a percentage of the cost of an investment – that single yield which 'equates' the present value of the variable income to the capital value. A term that is used also to refer to a single yield on cost over the expected life of an investment (or a fixed term, such as 10 or 15 years) taking account of projected income at an assumed growth rate – that is a yield which is 'equivalent' to that which would be received from a similar long-term investment – although strictly this is a form of **redemption yield** and more properly is termed an

equivalent yield. Called also an 'effective yield'.

'Property Valuation: A Rational Model', *Investment Analyst*, by S.G. Sykes, p. 20 (July 1981).
The Valuation of Property Investment, by Nigel Enever, 2 edn., p. 101.

equation of rents theory
A theory that a tenant is only prepared to pay a fixed sum for the cost of occupying a property; thus if rates or service charges increase rent will decrease, more or less, pro-rata.

equitable assignment
1. An assignment that is not made in accordance with statute law and, therefore, cannot constitute a **legal assignment**. For example, the assignment of a debt or choses-in-action that is not made in **writing** or is not an **absolute assignment**.
2. An **assignment** of a lease which is only enforceable 'in equity' because it is not, as required by statute, made by **deed** (Law of Property Act 1925, s. 52(1)); or an assignment of an **equitable lease**. An equitable assignment requires no particular formality, provided the intention to transfer the lease is clear. The assignment may be evidenced in **writing**, or by some act of **part performance** (such as the assignee taking possession of the demised premises and paying rent to the lessor). An equitable assignment is enforceable between the assignor and assignee at the discretion of the court provided it is satisfied that, based on the actions of the parties, it would be equitable to do so. Even though there is a lack of a requisite formality the court will apply the maxim "equity looks on that as done which ought to be done". See also **specific performance**.

equitable charge
1. A **charge** on real or personal property created when a lender has a right to have his debt satisfied from the proceeds of sale of the property or to have a receiver appointed in the event of a default by the debtor, but has no right to possession nor any **legal interest** in the charged property – London County and Westminster Bank Ltd., *v* Tompkins [1918] 1 K.B. 528. An equitable charge need not designate specific property to be used to discharge an unpaid debt and it may be created without any particular formality, provided there is a manifest intention to charge property. "An equitable charge on land is a security which does not create a legal estate, but only confers an equitable interest in the land upon the creditor. It entitles the holder to have the property comprised in it sold by an order of the court to raise the money charged on it, but in the absence of any express provision to that effect, or unless it is a mortgage by deposit of title deeds, it does not amount to an agreement to give a legal mortgage, although it may, if duly registered, take priority over a legal estate. Even if the security provides for a legal mortgage to be granted, it is still an equitable charge as distinguished from a mortgage."– 32 Halsbury's Laws of England, 4 edn., para. 406. A formal agreement to transfer title to property as security for a loan creates an **equitable mortgage** rather than an equitable charge. Cheshire's Modern Law of Real Property 13 edn,, pp. 661–662.
Fisher & Lightwood's Law of Mortgages, 9 edn., pp. 156–158.
2. An informal **equitable mortgage** (e.g. one not protected in terms of **priority** by the deposit of title deeds).

An equitable chargee has no interest in the property charged as security for the loan and he has fewer powers than an equitable mortgagee. In particular, he has no right of **foreclosure** (but he has a right to have the property sold by order of a court), nor any right to take possession of the charged property. However, it if is made clear that the intention of the parties is to create an equitable mortgage, and there is evidence of that intent, then an equitable mortgage arises forthwith – Re Wallis and Simmonds (Builders) Ltd. [1974] 1 All ER 561. An equitable charge is founded solely on contract as distinguished from an equitable lien which is founded on a right to possession of the property. See also **general equitable charge**.

equitable conversion
see **conversion**.

equitable easement
An **easement** that is enforceable only in equity either because it is not created by the proper formalities, whether by statute, deed or prescription; or is not held "for an interest equivalent to an estate in fee simple absolute or a term of year's absolute" (Law of Property Act 1925, s.1 (2) (a)). An easement that is not created or capable of subsisting as a **legal easement**. (This interpretation must be accepted strictly: the term 'equitable easement' does not embrace such matters as a right of access for repair, or any other right that resembles an easement but arises in equity or, in particular, by **estoppel**). A common form of equitable easement is one granted for the life of the owner of the servient tenement. An equitable easement is registrable as a **land charge** if land comprising the servient

land is unregistered, or protected by a **notice** or **caution** if title to the land is registered. See also **equitable interest**.

equitable estate
1. An **estate** in land that is enforceable as a right against anyone who ought in conscience to recognise the existence of that estate, but is not as good as a **legal estate** which is enforceable against the whole world. In particular, an estate that is not capable of subsisting, or being conveyed, or created, at law because it is neither (a) an estate in **fee simple absolute in possession**, nor (b) a **term of years absolute** (Law of Property Act 1925, s.1 (1)). (These two estates, which are expressed by the Law of Property Act 1925, s. 1(1) to be the only estates capable of existing as, and usually are, legal estates, may be equitable estates, for example, if they are not created by the requisite formality, which usually means by deed). Thus, as well as a fee simple that is neither 'absolute' (e.g. a determinable or conditional fee simple), nor 'in possession' (e.g. a future right to a fee simple) and a leasehold estate that is not a 'term of years absolute' (e.g. a term of years terminable with a life or a term of years created by an agreement for a lease), any estate for a life, is an equitable estate. However, the term 'equitable estate' is no longer generally used: any estate that is not a legal estate is termed an **equitable interest** (Law of Property Act 1925, s. 1(3). An equitable estate is enforceable only against a limited number of persons. In particular, it is not enforceable against a **bona fide purchaser** of the legal estate who does not have **notice** of the existence of the equitable estate.

Any equitable estate in land must be held behind a **trust**; that is, the legal estate is held by another as trustee and the equitable estate is held by the beneficiary of that trust. (US) 2. The value of a property excluding all debt or charges against it. See also **equity**.

equitable estoppel
see **estoppel**.

equitable interest
An interest in land, originally recognised by the Court of Chancery, as enforceable against only a limited number of persons, as distinguished from a legal estate or interest which is enforceable against the world at large. An equitable interest may be defined, by exception, as any estate, interest and charge in or over land that is not a **legal estate** or a **legal interest** (Law of Property Act 1925, s. 1 (3)); or, by adopting the premise that an equitable interest is one which depends for its continued existence on the equitable doctrine of **notice**, i.e. it is enforceable against everyone, except for a purchaser acting in good faith (a **bona fide purchaser**) who acquires a legal estate in the land for valuable consideration (including money, money's worth or even a promise of marriage), and does not know, nor could reasonably have known, of the existence of the equitable interest. (As a rule, knowledge of the existence of the interest is dependent on its registration at the Land Registry). (An equitable interest is referred to merely as a right *in personam*, i.e. a contractual obligation enforceable only against certain persons, which does not grant any right to the ownership of land, as compared to a right *in rem*, i.e. to the land itself. However, as this suggests that such an interest is not a proprietary right, capable of being assigned or inherited, it may be preferable to describe an equitable interest as a right *in personam ad rem*, a contractual right to **real property**, which is limited because it is enforceable only against certain persons.)

Equitable interests may be subdivided into (a) interests which depend for their existence on a right over land; and (b) interests which can just as well exist as a claim to the proceeds of the sale of land. The former type of interest must be registered to be enforceable against a purchaser of an interest in the land; registration being automatic notice to the purchaser of the existence of the interest. The latter type of interest cannot be registered and is 'overreached' by the purchaser of a legal estate i.e. the beneficiary's right is transferred from the land to the proceeds of sale.

Equitable interests include the interest of a beneficiary under a **trust** (i.e. of a *cestui que trust*); an **estate contract**; an **equitable lease**, including an interest arising from an **'agreement for a lease'**; an **equitable mortgage**; an **equitable charge**; an equitable **lien**; an **equitable easement; a restrictive covenant**; an equitable right to a **profit à prendre**; and a mortgagor's **equity of redemption**.

An equitable interest should be distinguished from a 'mere equity' which is a right enforceable in **equity**, e.g. a right to have a mistake corrected or a right of specific performance. See also **equitable estate, land charge, minor interest, overreachable interest, tenancy in common.**

Introduction to Land Law, by J.G. Riddell, 3 edn., p. 240.

The Law of Real Property, by Robert

Megarry and H.W.R. Wade, 5 edn., p. 113 *et seq.*

equitable lease

1. A **lease** that is not capable of being enforced 'at law', because it has not been made with the proper formalities; but in all other respects is created as a valid lease. In particular, a lease for a 'term of years' (which includes a *fixed* term of less than a year) that is not created by deed; or, if the term is for a fixed period not exceeding three years, whether the lease is created in writing or orally, one that does not take effect 'in possession' (start immediately) and is not made at the 'best rent' obtainable without taking a premium (Law of Property Act 1925, ss. 1, 52(1), 54(2)). Such a lease is enforceable 'in equity' in the same way as an **agreement for a lease** (for which the term 'equitable lease' is used frequently as a synonym); provided it is evidenced in **writing** or by an act of **part performance**, (i.e. it complies with the requirement of the Law of Property Act 1925, s. 40). Either party to such a lease may apply to court for an order seeking to formalise the arrangement, i.e. to seek a decree of **specific performance**; an order that is granted at the discretion of the court when "that which is agreed to be and ought to be is treated as having been done" – Warmington *v* Miller [1973] 2 All ER 377.

Real Property and Real People, by K.J. Gray and P.D. Symes, pp. 394–400 (1981).

2. A lease granted by a lessor who holds an **equitable interest** in land, e.g. by a landlord who has a right to land held under an **estate contract** – Industrial Properties (Barton Hill) Ltd *v* Associated Electrical Industries Ltd [1977] 2 WLR 747. The holder of an equitable lease holds the tenancy subject to the equitable right of his landlord to enforce his right to the land. See also **tenancy by estoppel**.

equitable licence
see **licence**.

equitable lien
see **lien**.

equitable mortgage

A **mortgage** by which the mortgagee receives only an **equitable interest** in the property granted as security for the loan. An equitable mortgage may arise because either (a) the mortgagor only has an equitable interest in the mortgaged property; or (b) the mortgage is created informally (sometimes called an 'informal equitable mortgage or an **equitable charge**). An owner of an equitable interest may mortgage it by assigning the interest to the mortgagee, subject to a provision for a reassignment on repayment of the mortgage debt; such an assignment should be in **writing** (Law of Property Act 1925, s. 53(1)(c)). An informal equitable mortgage may arise: (i) when the parties fail to create the mortgage by **deed** as required by law (Law of Property Act 1925, ss. 52, 87); (ii) when the parties enter into an agreement to create a **legal mortgage**, either in **writing** or evidenced by an act of **part performance**, but the legal mortgage is not formalised; or (iii) when there is a mere deposit of the title deeds with the mortgagee. The last instance is the most common means by which a equitable mortgage is created. An equitable mortgagee has similar rights to the holder of a legal mortgage except that, when the mortgage is not made by deed, a receiver may be appointed only by the court and the equitable mortgagee has no strict right to possession of the rent and profits (as there is no lease of the property which grants such a right), unless expressly permitted by the mortgage agreement. An equitable mortgage created without the deposit of title deeds must be registered as a **land charge** to protect the mortgagee against a subsequent mortgagee (Law of Property Act 1925, s. 97; Land Charges Act 1972, s. 2(4)). An equitable mortgagee who forecloses on an equitable interest acquires theoretically the more restricted right to the mortgaged property; but the court will insist on the mortgagor conveying a legal title to the mortgagee in order to complete the process of foreclosure – James *v* James (1873) LR 16 Eq. 153. If an equitable mortgagee exercises a power of sale then, strictly, the purchaser acquires an equitable interest only. However, if an equitable mortgage is made by deed then the mortgagee normally has a right to require the legal estate to be transferred to the purchaser – Re. White Rose Cottage [1965] Ch. 951.

In most states in the US, the distinction between a legal and equitable mortgage is largely irrelevant because most mortgages are created by a more informal process than permitted in English law. However, a **promissory note** which expresses an intention that land should be held as security for a debt has been held to create an equitable mortgage – Trustees of Zion Methodist Church *v* Smith (1948), 81 NE 2d. 649). See also **constructive mortgage, equitable charge**.

The Law of Real Property in England and the United States: some compar-isons, by Francis R. Crane in *Ind. L. J*, vol. 36. pp. 297–299 (1961).
Cheshire's Modern Law of Real Property, 13 edn., pp. 627–629.
The Law of Real Property, by Robert Megarry and H.W.R. Wade, 5 edn., pp. 926–929.
Fisher and Lightwood's Law of Mortgage, 9 edn., pp. 11–14.

equitable owner
The holder of a **equitable interest** in land. See also **beneficiary, conversion**.

equitable right of redemption
see **equity of redemption**.

equitable rights
see **equity**.

equitable servitude (US)
see **restrictive covenant, scheme of development**.

equitable title
1. A claim to have a title to property that may be enforced only at the discretion of the courts, e.g. an **agreement for sale** or an unregistered **estate contract**. See also **equitable interest, specific performance**.
2. The interest of a beneficiary under a **trust for sale**.
(US) 3. A claim held by virtue of a **conditional contract** for sale or an **instalment contract**.

equitable waste
see **waste**.

equity
1. Derived from the Latin *acquitas*, equality or levelling. Administration according to the rules of fairness and natural justice and not solely by the application of a universal set of rules. Equity is enshrined in the maxim *jus est ars boni et acqui*, 'law is the art of what is good and fair' or, more suc-

cintly, in the maxim to which the Byzantine Emperor Justinian I reduced the basic premise of laws *honeste vivere, alterum non laedare, suum cuique tribuere*, 'to live honestly, not to hurt another, to give each his due'. Equity is the soul of a civilized legal system and is intended to mitigate the rigours of the body of law encased in books and statutes. Justice and equity are species of the same genus, being empirical assertions of what is good, but justice may be defined as that which is good at law, whereas equity is adjudged according to norms of conscience, honour or morality. Equity is good that is not constrained by the decreed law; it is not that form of law which is unduly insistent on the following of **precedent** or a written code. "It is a rectification of law in so far as law is defective on account of its generality.... It is a kind of justice, and not a distinct state of character" (Aristotle, *Ethics*, Book 5). The function of equity is to find reason, right and remedy when it is not apparent in the written law; it avoids the extreme righteousness of the letter of the law: in a way it overrides the rigours of law.

In English law 'equity' also has a specialised meaning; it refers to a body of rules derived from the Court of Chancery, rather than from the courts of **common law**. The Court of Chancery grew up in the 14th century to enable the King's Principal Minister to hear pleadings referred to the King in Council. These rules of equity were based on the equitable doctrine of fairness and natural justice, or at least the King's conscience, rather than the punctilliousness of the common and parliamentary law. Thus the 'law' may have permitted the taking

of a 'pound of flesh' but the court of equity averted the consequential shedding of blood. Equity was intended to "support and protect the common law from shifts and crafty contrivances against the justice of the law. Equity therefore, does not destroy the law, nor create it, but assists it" – Lord Cowper in Dudley (Lord) *v* Dudley (Lady) (1705) Prec. Ch. 244. Hence equity was intended to follow the law not to make it; there could be no equity without law: equity acting alone would have created almost as many rules of action "as there are differences of capacity and sentiment in the human mind."(Bl. Comm. vol. i. p. 62).

Equity developed a number of isolated remedies to bring justice or avert wrong in particular cases, and it established procedures to enforce those remedies. Equity could be used only if a claimant acted promptly, with honesty of intent; it acted on the conscience and sought equality; it sought the intent not merely the form; and it was applied entirely at the discretion of the court. Common law and equity were merged in English law by the Judicature Acts 1873 & 1875, and there is no longer a separate court of law and a court of equity, but a court of complete jurisdiction. The modern English judiciary has some latitude in deciding what is fair and just, and what accords with natural justice, but there is no longer a Court of conscience, only a Court of Law. Nonetheless, "quite apart from the natural tendency of the courts to strain to uphold just claims and reject the unjust, even if the law appears to produce other results, morals and ethics sometimes directly affect the decisions of cases". (Snell's *Equity*, 28 edn., p. 7).

The remedies and procedures developed by equity remain embedded in modern English law and have left a number of notable components that have become an integral part of modern real property law, in particular, the **equity of redemption**; the permitted enforceability of a **restrictive covenant** against a successor in title; provisions for bringing action on certain informal contracts, particularly an **agreement for a lease** and an **estate contract; relief** granted against **forfeiture** and against the charging of a **penalty** on a contract; and the determination of the **priority** of mortgages. The distinction between the legal and **equitable interest** in land; the **trust**; and the doctrine of **estoppel** are vestiges of the inherent strife between common law and equity. In addition, the remedies of **injunction, rectification, rescission** and **specific performance** are of equitable extraction, remaining discretionary, and being granted only when damages would prove an impossible or unreasonable remedy. See also **bona fide purchaser, resulting trust, use.**

The English Legal System, by Radcliffe and Cross, 6 edn., pp. 113–154. Megarry's Manual of the Law of Real Property, 6 edn., pp. 57–70.

The English Legal System, by Walker and Walker, 5 edn, pp. 21–55. Snell's Principles of Equity, 28 edn. 16 Halsbury's Laws of England, 4 edn., paras. 1201–1500.

2. In real estate, the amount of an investor's own funds paid over to acquire a property, or the difference between the present market value of a property and the amount of debt or mortgage loans outstanding against it, i.e. the net worth of an owner's interest in a property. See also **debt-to-equity ratio, equity build-up, loan value.**

3. In accounting and finance, the **equity capital** of a company, enterprise or business. The term 'equity' is used commonly to refer to the ordinary share capital of a company, i.e. the capital that is provided by the owners of the company.

equity-adjusted mortgage (US)
see **equity-participation mortgage.**

equity appreciation
see **equity build-up.**

equity build-up (or equity appreciation)
An increase in the owner's **equity** in a property resulting from the repayment by the owner of a loan, and/or the increase in the market value of that property. Upon sale of the property the 'profit' that has resulted purely from repayment of the loan is called sometimes 'amortisation profit'. See also **equity-yield rate.**

equity capital
The amount of **capital** available to the owners of an enterprise after all other liabilities have been allowed for or paid and upon which the owners expect to receive a return in the form of a share of the profits. The capital that belongs to the true owners of a company, i.e. the ordinary shareholders of that company, rather than capital loaned by creditors, namely **debt capital**. It comprises the amount of capital originally contributed by the shareholders, plus retained earnings minus any losses. See also **equity, net worth, risk capital.**

equity dividend rate (or yield) (US)
see **cash-on-cash yield.**

equity financing

The provision of a loan on the basis that the lender will receive a right to a share of the profit or **equity** to be derived from the project for which the loan is used. See also **equity capital**.

equity fund (US)

see **equity trust**.

equity investment value (US)

The amount of **equity** required by an investor in order to obtain a given rate of return over the life of property investment, after allowing for any mortgage loans or debt capital available to him and projected capital appreciation. The equity investment value represents the capital value of the net income after debt service; or the capital value of the net income less the amount of debt capital that can be secured on the property. See also **Ellwood capitalisation rate, mortgage-equity capitalisation technique**.

equity kicker (US)

see **equity participation**.

equity of redemption

A mortgagor's equitable right to the **redemption** of the mortgaged property; the right of a **mortgagor** to have his property released to him by repaying the outstanding debt (including principal, interest and costs) to the mortgagee. The equity of redemption represents the mortgagor's right to recover the mortgaged property without hinderance, after the debt is repaid in the requisite way. It may represent also a right to compel the mortgagee to release the mortgaged property, even after the mortgagor has defaulted, at any stage before **foreclosure**, or an exercise of a **power of sale**, and before any consequent transfer of an unencumbered title to

the mortgagee, or to any third party. The right to redeem mortgaged property when the mortgagor has complied with the terms of the mortgage deed is called sometimes the 'legal right of redemption'; the right to redeem after there has been a breach of a condition of the mortgage or after the contractual date for complying with the terms of the loan, is called the 'equitable right of redemption'. These rights together represent the mortgagor's equity of redemption.

Any covenant in a mortgage which unreasonably prevents redemption is regarded as a 'fetter' or 'clog' on the equity of redemption and may not be enforceable – Noakes and Co. Ltd *v* Rice [1902] AC 24; Clarke *v* Reyburn, 8 Wall. 318, 19 L Ed. 354; Peugh *v* Davis, 96 US 332, 24 L Ed. 775. The principle is that, "in natural justice and equity the principal right of the mortgagee is to the money, and his right to the land is only as a security for the money" – Thornborough *v* Baker (1675) 2 Swans. 630. Although a fetter or clog on the equity of redemption is void, the right to redeem may be postponed so that the mortgagor is not permitted to repay the principal before the time stipulated in the mortgage deed; provided the postponement is not for an unreasonable length of time and is not oppressive to the nature of a mortgage – Knightsbridge Estates Trust Ltd. *v* Byrne [1939] Ch. 441; Esso Petroleum Co. Ltd *v* Harper's Garage (Stourport) [1967] 1 All ER 699; Humble Oil and Refining Co. *v* Doerr (1973) 303 A 2d. 898. (An exception to this right of redemption applies to a debenture issued by a company which may be made irredemable: Companies Act 1948, s. 89.)

In addition, a mortgagee may obtain a collateral advantage, such as a restriction on how the mortgaged property is used while the mortgage subsists, provided that the advantage is not (a) unfair and unconscionable; or (b) in the nature of a penalty clogging the equity of redemption; or (c) repugnant to or inconsistent with the equity of redemption – Kreglinger v New Patagonia Meat Co. [1914] AC 25. An option to purchase granted to the mortgagee when a mortgage is entered into is void – Samuel v Jarrah Timber Co. [1904] AC 323; but an option granted after the mortgage has been created, as a separate and independent transaction, is valid because the mortgagor is considered to be a free agent once he has obtained the loan.

An equity of redemption may be lost by (a) an effective transfer of the right to the mortgagee; (b) a sale of the property following the excercise by the mortgagee of his power of sale; (c) a decree of foreclosure; or (d) the mortgagee entering into possession and enlarging his interest after twelve years (Limitation Act 1980, s. 20). See also **consolidation of mortgages, 'once a mortgage, always a mortgage', prepayment penalty, reconveyance**.
Introduction to Land Law, by J.G. Riddell, 3 edn., pp. 360–366.
Land Law: cases and materials, by Maudsley and Burn, 4 edn, pp. 605–635.
Megarry's Manual of The Law of Real Property, 6 edn., pp. 493–500.
Cheshire's Modern Law of Real Property, 13 edn., p. 630 *et seq.*
Fisher and Lightwood's Law of Mortgage, 9 edn., pp. 519–579.
The Law of Real Property, by Robert Megarry and H.W.R. Wade, 5 edn.,
pp. 917–919, 964–971.
32 Halsbury's Laws of England, 4 edn., paras. 407, 571–604.

equity-linked mortgage
see **equity-participation mortgage**.

equity participation
A right to share in the profits of a business, or the income from an investment, as obtained by the grantor of a loan. A share in the borrower's **equity** acquired by a supplier of **debt capital**. Generally, a provider of debt capital (or a mortgage loan) receives only interest on his money; however, the borrower may agree to provide the lender with a share of the profits, sometimes referred to as 'contingency interest', in exchange for a lower interest rate or as a means of obtaining a loan when funds are in short supply. For example, a **joint venture** is established between the equity partner or 'active partner', and the lender or 'passive partner', by which the passive partner receives a **priority yield**, or an agreed rate of interest, and a share in any profit or equity received by the joint venture (after payment of the priority yield) is divided between the participants according to an agreed formula. The formula is based on the ratio of debt to equity and an assessment of the participants' respective risks.

Equity participation may take a variety of other forms such as (a) rental or 'income participation': the lender receives a share in the income received from a property, usually over and above an agreed base level; (b) sale proceeds or 'capital value participation': the lender receives a share in the proceeds resulting from a revaluation of the property (in book form or as part of a refinancing arrange-

ment), or the proceeds resulting from a sale of the property – in the US called an 'earn-out'; (c) an option for a lender to purchase property at a future date at a previously agreed price or at a percentage of the then current market value. A loan that provides for a share of the equity is referred to in the US as a 'kicker loan' or as providing an 'equity kicker' for the lender. See also **equity-participation mortgage, equity sharing, gearing, sale and lease-back**.
Partners in Property, by B.P. Whitehouse, (1964).
The Property Development Process, edited by J. Dickinson Brown (1976), pp. 253–257.

equity-participation mortgage

A mortgage agreement which provides that the mortgagee shall receive a share of the income or profits to be derived from the mortgaged property, i.e. the mortgagee is entitled to **equity participation**. Frequently the mortgagee grants the loan at a rate of interest that is lower than the market rate and, in return, has a right to a share of the income, capital profit (in the event of a sale), or any refinancing proceeds to be derived from the property. Called also an 'equity-adjusted mortgage', an 'equity-linked mortgage', an 'appreciation-participation mortgage', a 'shared-participation mortgage', a 'shared-appreciation mortgage', or a 'participation mortgage'.

In the UK a variation of this type of mortgage takes the form of a trust, called the 'Building Trust', which receives invested capital from approved pension funds. Mortgages are granted to purchasers of dwelling houses by the Building Trust at an interest rate that is set at two thirds of the rate for comparable mortgage loans and in return the mortgagee retains a right to receive a half-share of any increase in the capital value of the house when it is sold. The house owner retains the remaining half-share in the increase in equity.
Basic Real Estate Finance and Investment, by D. Espley and J. Millar, (1980) pp. 237–238.

equity purchaser (US)

One who acquires the **equity** in a property, without necessarily assuming liability for any loan secured on the property. See also **non-recourse mortgage**.

equity rate of return (US)

see **cash-on-cash return**.

equity ratio

The ratio of the **equity** invested in a property and the market value, or purchase price, of that property.
cf. **debt-to-equity ratio, loan ratio**.

equity rent

A rent payable to a head landlord which is assessed on the basis of a proportion of the income received by the tenant from the sub-tenants or occupiers of a property; a rent that provides **equity sharing** for the head landlord. See also **gearing, sale and lease-back**.

equity sharing

An arrangement by which two or more participants share, or take a stake, in the **equity** obtained from a property investment. A common example arises when a landowner agrees to lease a site to a property developer at a nominal ground rent in return for a share in the return from the completed development. A lease granted at a rent that is below the

current market value thus enabling the tenant to obtain a **profit rent** by subletting the premises, i.e. to receive a share of the equity obtainable from the property, is called an 'equity-sharing lease'. See also **equity participation, equity rent, lease and lease-back, leverage.**
Valuation and Development Appraisal, by Clive Darlow, (1982), pp. 24–52.

equity-sharing lease
see **equity sharing.**

equity stake
see **equity sharing.**

equity trust (US)
A **real estate investment trust** that specialises in direct equity investment in property.
cf. **mortgage trust.**

equity-yield rate (US)
The rate of return over a period of time represented by the ratio of (a) the **present value** of the future anticipated **cash flow** from a property, plus **equity build-up** expressed as an annual figure to (b) the total initial cash (or **equity**) invested in that property. This return is assessed after debt service, but before building depreciation. The rate is equivalent to the **internal rate of return** from an investment, after debt service, including the discounted value of any capital gain (or loss); or the **cash-on-cash yield** (or equity dividend yield) plus the present value of the capital appreciation (or depreciation). The equity-yield rate corresponds to a **redemption yield**, after taking into account the effect of debt repayments, but before tax. Called also the 'investment rate'. See also **Ellwood capitalisation rate, mortgage-equity capitalisation technique.**

The Appraisal of Real Estate, AIREA, 7 edn., pp. 435–437.

equivalent annual value method
see **annuity method.**

equivalent reinstatement, cost of
A basis for determining **compulsory purchase compensation** as set out in the Land Compensation Act 1961, s.5, rule 5. The amount of compensation is assessed on the basis of the **reinstatement cost**, i.e. the cost of replacing or providing an equivalent property. It is applied when determining the value of a property for which there is no general demand or ready open market value, e.g. a church, school, hospital, theatre, private railway – Aston Charities Trust Ltd. *v* Stepney Borough Council [1952] 2 QB 642; Nonentities Society Trustees *v* Kidderminster Borough Council (1970) 22 P and CR 224; Birmingham Corporation *v* West Midland Baptist (Trust) Association (Incorporated) [1970] AC 874. However, in order that the 'equivalent reinstatement' rule may be applied, it is necessary to show that (a) there is no general demand or market for the purpose to which a property is put; (b) the property is devoted and, but for the compulsory purchase, would continue to be devoted to that purpose; (c) there is a bona fide intention to reinstate the subject property elsewhere – Edge Hill Light Rly. Co. *v* Secretary of State for War (1956) 6 P and CR 211; and (d) the Lands Tribunal, in the particular case under consideration, would exercise its discretion to award compensation on this basis – Sparkes *v* Leeds City Council (1977) 244 EG 56, 137–139. Called also 'rule 5' compensation.
Equivalent Reinstatement by W.A.

Leach, 253 E.G. 1331, 254 E.G. 108, 277, 391 (1980).
Boynton's Guide to Compulsory Purchase and Compensation, 5 edn., pp. 173–176.
Law of Compulsory Purchase and Compensation, by Keith Davies, 8 edn., pp. 142–4.
Encyclopaedia of Compulsory Purchase and Compensation, edited by Harold J.J. Brown, para. 2–1063.

equivalent yield

The **internal rate of return** on a property investment over a given period of time, usually the expected investment life (commonly 10 or 15 years),assuming a projected appreciation (or depreciation) of rental income over that period. The equivalent yield on a real estate investment is a form of **redemption yield** calculated after account is taken of anticipated growth (or decline) in rental values over a given period of time. It is assessed normally as a means of making a direct comparison between the projected return from a real estate investment and other long-term forms of investment, notably long-term government securities, i.e. it indicates a rate of return that may be considered 'equivalent' to the return available from other long-term investments. Sometimes used synonymously with **equated yield**.

erection

Derived from the Latin *erigere*, 'to put up straight'. The putting up or setting up of a **structure** or **building**; it covers putting up of walls, fences, scaffolding, and for town planning purposes "includes extension, alteration and re-erection" (Town and Country Planning Act 1971, s.290 (1)).

erosion

The gradual wearing away of soil due to the action of nature; the wearing away of the bank of a stream or river, usually by the action of the flowing water which slowly takes away the substance of the bank and deposits it elsewhere.
cf. **accretion**.

erreur (F)

mistake.

escalator, or escalation, clause

1. A clause in a contract which permits the price or consideration to be increased to take account of a change in conditions outside the ambit of the contract, especially to take account of inflation. In the UK, a term commonly applied to such a clause in a building contract. In the US, an escalator clause is commonly inserted in a lease of a commercial property to enable the landlord to increase (or decrease) the rent to cover increases (or decreases) in **operating expenses**. The amount by which the rent is altered may be based on actual variations in expenditure, indexation, or may be based on a fixed periodic variation. This rent variation is intended to be related to changes in operating expenses rather than changes in the market value of the property. Called also a 'cost pass-through clause', an 'increase clause', a 'step-up clause' or a 'participation clause'. See also **net lease**.
(US) 2. A clause in a lease which provides for rent to be increased (or decreased), usually at fixed intervals during the term of the lease, in accordance, with an agreed formula, e.g. an **indexed rent** or a 'stepped' or **graded rent**.
cf. **rent review clause**.

(US) 3. A provision in a lease which permits a landlord to recover rent lost because of rent control regulations imposed to limit increases in rent, when such regulations are lifted.

4. A clause in a mortgage deed which permits the mortgagee to alter the interest rate on the mortgage loan in line with the market rate of interest or any other specified rate of interest. See also **variable-rate mortgage**.

escape clause

A clause in a contract which permits one of the parties to modify or repudiate that contract, usually on the occurence of a specified condition e.g. a clause which permits a tenant to break his lease if the rent is increased at the date of a rent review.

cf. **exclusion clause**. See also **break clause**.

escape, from land

See **strict liability**.

escheat

The passing of land to the Crown, or State, in the event that there is no owner; as when a person dies leaving no competent heir. Escheat is derived from the **feudal system** of land tenure, whereby upon determination of a right of **tenure** land tacitly went back to the lord of the manor, or ultimately the Sovereign, to whom the land-holder was beholden. Escheat also arose in a case of treason or felony until the Felony Act 1870. In England, since the Administration of Estates Act 1925, s. 45 and 46, escheat has been abolished and such property is said to pass *bona vacancia* to the Crown, Duchy of Lancaster or the Duchy of Cornwall. However, the result is similar. In the US real or personal property escheats to the state or county if an owner dies intestate and no heirs can be traced. An estate that passes to a sovereign body or state in this way is called also an escheat.

escompte (F)

discount (but *cash flow actualisé* for discounted cash flow); **rebate**.

escrow, or escrow agreement

A document (or scroll) delivered by the grantor (or escrower), usually to a third party as escrow agent (or escrowee), with the intention that it will be delivered to the grantee as a **deed** upon the performance of some **condition** or the happening of some specified event (such as the payment of a purchase price, or the establishment of a proper title). A deed that has been signed and sealed but not delivered is said to be held 'in escrow'; "the vital unconditional delivery, which is essential for the proper execution of a true deed, is missing; it is replaced by a conditional delivery", (which may be an express, or implied condition for delivery) – Terrapin International Ltd. *v* Inland Revenue Commissioners [1976] 2 All E.R. 465. If the condition is performed, the deed becomes absolute; but until then it remains in suspense or 'in escrow' and is of no effect – Foundling Hospital Governors and Guardians *v* Crane [1911] 2 KB 377. However, a deed delivered in escrow cannot be recalled by the grantor, unless the grantee fails to fulfil the relevant condition. Part payment of a purchase price and delivery of a deed implies that the deed has been delivered as an escrow pending completion of the payment, unless there is evidence to the contrary – Thompson *v* McCulloch [1947] KB 447.

Strictly, an escrow is not a deed as it does not transfer any interest in property, (it only becomes a deed when all the conditions are fulfilled and delivery has taken place – Alan Estates Ltd v W.G. Stores Ltd [1981] 3 All ER 486; but it should contain the minimum requirements for a valid deed and operates as such when the conditions are satisfied. A deed need not be expressed as "delivered in escrow", providing it can be shown that there is an intention to hold delivery in suspense. Even if a document is drawn and expressed for immediate delivery, if it can be shown that a deed was delivered, "not to take effect as a deed till a certain condition was performed, it will nevertheless operate as an escrow". – Bowker v Burdekin (1843) 11 M and W 147. Upon taking effect as a deed it 'relates back', in so far as it is necessary to give efficacy to the transaction, to the date of the escrow agreement; i.e. an escrow takes effect, where applicable, at the time of the original conditional delivery and not the date the condition is satisfied – Butler and Baker's case (1591) 3 Co. Rep. 25a; Hooper v Ramsbottom (1815) 128 ER 936; although the vendor's entitlement to the rents and profits from a property until completion is not affected by this rule (and an escrowee is not entitled to lease or determine leases of the subject property until after final delivery) – Thompson v McCulloch, *supra*; Security Trust Co. v Royal Bank of Canada [1976] AC 517.

In the US, real estate is sold frequently by means of an 'escrow closing' whereby a contract for the sale of land, together with an escrow agreement, is entered into prior to verification of title and the title deeds are held and verified by an escrow agent. When the escrow agent is satisfied, he transfers the title deed to the purchaser, and pays the purchase monies he has been holding on behalf of the grantor in accordance with the escrow agreement. In the US, when the purchase price for a property is to be paid over a period of time and the title deeds are to be held in escrow until the final payment is made, an escrow agreement sometimes is referred to as a 'contract for deed' or 'instalment contract'. Property transferred to a third party under an escrow agreement sometimes may be referred to as 'escrow'.

Real Estate Law, by Robert Kratovil and Raymond J. Werner, 8 edn., pp. 192–199.

Chitty on Contract, 28 edn., para. 24.

Contract and Conveyance, by J.T. Farrand, 4 edn., pp. 322–328.

12 Halsbury's Laws of England, 4 edn., paras. 1332–1334.

escrow agent
A party to whom a contract is delivered in **escrow**; a term more commonly used in the US for an 'escrowee'.

escrow closing (US)
see **escrow**.

escrow company (US)
A company that acts as an agent for transactions which are dealt with in **escrow**. The company holds property that is the subject of an escrow transaction until the requisite condition of the transaction is fulfilled (or not as the case may be) and, if necessary, is responsible for handling the **closing** of such transactions.

escrow costs (US)
The **closing costs** paid upon comple-

tion of a transaction carried out by means of an **escrow**.

escrowee

A party to whom a contract is delivered in **escrow**. See also **escrow agent**.

escrower

The party, or grantor, who delivers a deed to a third party, or escrowee, to be held on the former's behalf in **escrow** until certain specified conditions have been met.

esculpation

Without liability or recourse. See also **non-recourse mortgage**.

espace libre (F)

open space.

essart

See **assart**.

essence of a contract

see **condition, time is of the essence**.

established claim for loss of development value

A claim that was agreed with the Central Land Board, or was determined by the Lands Tribunal, in accordance with Part VI of the Town and Country Planning Act 1947, for a loss of **development value**. The benefit of such an established claim could be converted to an **unexpected balance of established development value**. Called also a 'Part VI claim'. See also **claim holding**.

established use certificate

A certificate issued by a planning authority, under the provisions of the Town and Country Planning Act 1971, ss. 94, 95, confirming the use to which an area of land may be put by reason of (a) the use being established before and continuing since the beginning of 1964; (b) a use which contravenes a condition or limitation imposed in a planning permission, but has subsisted since the end of 1963; (c) a change of use not requiring planning permission, e.g. one within the same use class or one that amounts to permitted development; or (d) a change of use begun after the end of 1963 that falls within the existing use rights appertaining to the land, providing that there has been no change of use which would require planning permission since the end of 1963.

An application for an established use certificate is made to the local planning authority in the same way as an application for planning permission and, if refused, there is a right of appeal to the Secretary of State for the Environment. If the Secretary of State upholds the applicant's appeal he may also issue an established use certificate. If a certificate is granted the local planning authority cannot serve an enforcement notice against that user. However, an established use certificate is not a grant of planning permission, "it does not render a use lawful. To that extent it is unlike a grant of planning permission. Therefore, if, for example, the use specified in an established use certificate is abandoned, it cannot lawfully be resumed. Its function is to render the specified use, as long as it persists, immune from an enforcement". – Broxbourne BC *v* Secretary of State for the Environment [1979] 2 All ER 17. See also **abandonment**.

Outline of Planning Law, by Desmond Heap, 8 edn., pp. 198–201.

Encyclopaedia of Planning Law and Practice, edited by Desmond Heap, paras. 1-185, 2-1107.

established use

A use of land that has been in existence for a period long enough to establish that planning consent is not required for its continuation. See **established use certificate, existing user**.

estate

1. An **interest** in **land** of defined (but not necessarily ascertained) duration; the extent or nature of a person's interest in real property. An estate is merely the right to possess land for a duration; so that "all estates are but times of their continuance" (Bacon). The word 'estate' is derived from 'status' and thus it represents in essence the right to land of one person in preference to others. 'Estate' is used in place of ownership to refer to the right to hold land, because in English law there is no absolute right to the 'ownership' of land but merely a right to land for a greater or lesser duration. English law recognised an estate as a means by which ownership is detached from land and transferred to an abstract set of values. An estate is the medium for holding and transferring those values; it is a temporal division of the right to land which permits a feature that is unique to English land law – the holding of several rights to the same land at the same time.

The term 'estate' may be used in a narrow sense: "it denotes the fee simple in land and any of the various interests into which it could formerly be divided at law, whether for life, or for a term of years or otherwise". (39 Halsbury's Laws of England, 4 edn., p. 214). Thus, real estate in a technical sense denotes a person's most absolute right to land. An estate may be

either of unknown duration, a freehold: an estate in fee simple, in fee tail (an entailed interest), or for a life; or of known or ascertainable duration – a leasehold, whether for a term of years, any other fixed duration, or from year to year. An estate may be classified also as contingent or conditional; in possession or remainder; in severalty or in common; or as a legal estate or an equitable estate.

In a wider sense 'estate' may be used to denote any form of property whether real estate or personal estate.

In the US, the term estate is used frequently when tenancy would be used in English law, e.g. 'estate for a term of years', 'joint estate', 'estate in coparcenary'; effectively extinguishing the classification, found in English common law, of a leasehold as personal property rather than real property. An estate may be any real right to property; "the word estate is used to express the degree, quantity, nature, duration, or extent of an interest in land. Complete ownership is an 'estate in fee simple', but there are many other estates, such as 'life estates' and 'leasehold estates'. Each differs from the others with respect to the rights and duties of the owners of the estate in question" – *Real Estate Law* by Robert J. Kratovil, 8 edn, p. 12. See also **doctrine of estates, future estate**.

Real Property, by William E. Burby, 3 edn., pp. 4–6.
The Law of Property, by F.H. Lawson and Bernard Rudden, 2 edn., pp. 88–98.
Introduction to Land Law, J.G. Riddall, 3 edn., pp. 16–33.
The Law of Real Property, by Robert Megarry and H.W.R. Wade, 5 edn., pp. 38–109.

2. An extensive area of land or a large farm, usually encompassing a substantial residence. See also **manor**.

3. Derived from Old French *estat* 'state or condition', in particular as represented by worldly possessions. The aggregation of an individual's property; especially of a deceased person. See also **capital transfer tax, estate duty**.

4. A person's **domain**.

estate agent

A person, firm or association that deals in real property on behalf of another. In particular, an **agent** who, "in connection with the acquisition or disposal of any land or other premises, brings together or takes steps to bring together the person wishing to dispose thereof and a person prepared to acquire it, or undertakes to do either of those things, or who acts or undertakes to act as **auctioneer**, or, in the case of a proposed transaction, negotiates or undertakes to negotiate as to the terms on behalf of either party" – Restriction on Agreements (Estate Agents) Order 1970 art. 2(1); 1 Halsbury's Laws of England, 4 edn., para. 713). The Estate Agents Act 1979, s. 1(1) defines estate agent's work with certain exceptions as comprising, "things done by a person in the course of a business (including a business in which he is employed) pursuant to instructions received from another person (in this section referred to as 'the client') who wishes to dispose of or acquire an interest in land – (a) for the purpose of, or with a view to, effecting the introduction to the client of a third person who wishes to acquire or, as the case may be, dispose of such an interest; and (b) after such an introduction has been

effected in the course of that business, for the purpose of securing the disposal or as the case may be, the acquisition of that interest". An estate agent may undertake also the letting, management, surveying and valuation of all forms of property for another, and may seek to raise finance secured on property held by another.

An estate agent is usually given a general **authority** in relation to a property and "that authority ... contains also an authority to describe the property truly, to represent its actual situation, and if he thinks fit to represent its value" – Mullens *v* Miller (1882) 22 Ch. D 199. Such representations, as a rule, are not warranties and should be verified. An estate agent normally is employed to find and introduce suitable candidates or prospects for a property, so that, "the making of a contract is not part of an estate agent's business and, although, on the facts of an individual case the person who employs him may authorise him to make a contract, such an authorisation is not lightly to be inferred from vague and ambiguous language" – Wragg *v* Lovett [1948] 2 All ER 969. Thus, "when instructions are given to an agent to find a purchaser of landed property, he, not being instructed as to the conditions to be inserted into the contract as to title, is not authorised to sign a contract on the part of the vendor" – Hamer *v* Sharp (1874) LR 19 Eq. 113. However, an estate agent may be given a special authority and in that capacity may be authorised, upon stipulated terms, to bind his principal; "if an agent is definitely instructed to sell at a definite price, those instructions involve authority to make a binding contract and to sign

an agreement" – Keen v Mear [1920] 2 Ch. 579. Unless so clearly appointed, a principal may accept or reject any person introduced by the agent; although as a result he may not necessarily avoid a liability to the agent to pay **commission**. An estate agent owes a duty to act on behalf of his principal until his duties are fulfilled, or until his authority is withdrawn, and he must communicate any offer received for a property he is offering for sale to his principal, until or unless a binding contract for sale has been entered into – Keppel v Wheeler (1927) 136 LT 203. See also **accommodation agent, deposit, misrepresentation, puffing, sub-agent, surveyor**. *The Law of Estate Agency and Auctions*, by J.R. Murdoch, 2 edn., pp. 177–339.
The Practice of Estate Agency, by Nigel Stephens, (1981).

estate agent's fee
see **commission, scale fee**.

estate at will (US)
see **tenancy at will**.

estate at sufferance (US)
see **tenancy at sufferance**.

estate by the entireties (US)
see **tenancy by entireties**.

estate by purchase (US)
see **purchase**.

estate company
A private company formed to hold real estate, generally so that the shareholders may reap tax advantages and may have greater freedom to dispose of their assets.

estate contract
A contract (whether oral or in writing) by which a person has the right, at the date of the contract, to have a **legal estate** conveyed to him or created for his benefit. An estate contract may take the form of a **contract for sale**, an **agreement for a lease**, an **option** to purchase, or any other like agreement which places a person in a position to acquire a legal estate; including a contract for the purchase of a legal estate from a person who has himself a contract for the purchase of that interest from the existing estate owner. (A **right of pre-emption** does not create an interest in land and cannot form the subject of an estate contract, and is considered to be a personal right until it becomes exercisable – Pritchard v Briggs [1980] Ch. 338. Similarly a **notice to treat** subsequent to a compulsory purchase order is not an estate contract until compensation is agreed). An estate contract grants an **equitable interest** for the benefit of the intended purchaser or lessee; the legal estate remains with the grantor, who holds it as trustee until an actual conveyance or lease has been executed. An estate contract (including a right of pre-emption or any like right) may be registered as a **land charge** (Land Charges Act 1972, s. 2(4)). If not registered an estate contract is void against a subsequent **bona fide purchaser** of a legal estate for money or money's worth. Most contracts for the sale of land are estate contracts, although frequently they are not registered by solicitors because it is anticipated that a conveyance will take place within too short a space of time for the owner of the interest in the property to sell to another party and thereby override the prospective purchaser's interest.
cf. **agreement for sale**.

estate duty

A tax levied on the value of a deceased's estate, regardless of the estate's destination, but payable before the estate can pass. In the UK this duty first came into effect in 1894 and was replaced, in relation to deaths after 1975, by **capital transfer tax**. In the US, some states levy a 'death tax' or 'estate tax', based on a federal estate and gift tax, which is charged on the value of the deceased's entire estate. In other states an **inheritance tax** is levied which is payable by the beneficiary and is levied according to the value of the benefit received.

estate for life

see **life estate**.

estate for years (US)

see **tenancy for a term of years**.

estate from period to period (US)

see **periodic tenancy**.

estate in expectancy

see **future estate**.

estate in remainder

see **remainder**.

estate in reversion

see **reversion**.

estate in severalty (US)

see **severalty**.

estate in tail

see **entailed estate**.

estate in tail after possibilities

see **tenant in tail after possibilities**.

estate manager

A person retained to manage real estate, so as to ensure that the best use, profit or benefit is derived therefrom. The role of an estate-management surveyor has been defined as "to advise upon the process for which land can be used to its best advantage, and to manage landed estates – large or small – primarily for the business purpose of getting the best income out of them, but at the same time having due regard to the duties of the owner towards his tenant, his neighbours and the community, local, regional and national". (Lord Justice Scott, *Principles and Practice of Land Use*: (estate management lecture, University of London, 1948). See also **chartered surveyor, land agent, property manager**.

estate management

The art or science of directing, administering, planning, supervising and co-ordinating the responsibilities of those who own, lease, finance, occupy or use real estate in order to achieve a pre-determined objective, usually the maximization of the use and benefit to be derived therefrom. The means and activity by which land is maintained and controlled, including the study of all matters that affect land as a factor of production, in order to ensure that the best use and benefit is derived therefrom. Estate management includes control of the daily running of the property (**property management**); the planning and analysis of the present and future economic benefits to be obtained from ownership of real estate; and coordination of the responsibilities of those involved in real estate and, where applicable, the maintenance of good landlord and tenant relations. See also **land economics, highest and best use, portfolio management**.
Walmsley's Rural Estate Management, 6 edn.
Principles of Estate Management, by

M.E.T. Thorncroft (1965).
Estate Management Practice, by Tim Stapleton, (1981).

estate of inheritance
see **entailed estate, fee tail**.

estate owner
A holder of a legal estate. An estate owner may be the possessor of the legal estate in his own right, i.e. as an absolute owner (including a mortgagor); or, if land is held in trust for a beneficiary, the estate owner is the trustee who holds the legal estate and whose function is to give effect to the equitable interest of the beneficiary. An estate owner may not be an infant (Law of Property Act 1925, s. 205 (1) (v); Land Registration Act 1925, s. 3 (iv)). If land is the subject of a strict settlement the estate owner is the tenant for life, while if the land is settled under a trust for sale the estate owner is the trustee for sale. Also a personal representative or a statutory owner may be an estate owner on an interim basis.

estate *pur autre vie*
An estate 'for the life of another'. See also **life estate**.

estate rentcharge
A **rentcharge** created to enforce a **restrictive covenant**, or to meet the reasonable cost of a covenant for the provision of services repair, insurance, etc., under a **scheme of development**. Unlike other rentcharges such payments are not prohibited or extinguished (Rentcharges Act 1977, s. 2 & 3).

estate tail
see **entailed estate**.

estate tax (US)
see **estate duty**.

estate terrier
see **terrier**.

estimate
An opinion calculated approximately on the basis of probability. An assessment or evaluation of the cost of something; for example, of the probable cost of a project. An estimate by a contractor does not normally represent an **offer**, but merely an **invitation to treat**. However, a **tender** may constitute a binding offer, notwithstanding the fact that it is headed 'estimate' on the paper on which it is written – Croshaw *v* Pritchard (1899) 16 TLR 45.
cf. **quotation**. See also **bill of quantities, quantity surveying, valuation**.

estimation (F)
estimate; valuation; appraisal. See also *evaluation*.

estimator
A person who prepares an **estimate**. One who makes an assessment of the cost or value of a property. See also **quantity surveyor, valuer**.

estoppel
Derived from Norman French *estoupail*, 'conclusion'. A principle established by the English courts that it would be inequitable for a person to go back on his word, or to act inconsistently with his representations or deeds, whether these are express or implied. Estoppel may even prevent a person from stating that something is true and, therefore, should be now acted on with a legal consequence, if that statement is inconsistent with a previously accepted statement. "Estoppel is when one is concluded and forbidden in law to speak against his own act or deed, yea, though it be to say the truth" – Termes de La Ley.

(The principle of estoppel came from the Normans (Mellkenny *v* West Midland Police Force [1980] 2 All ER 235); but there is no directly related principle in modern French law.) "A man shall not be allowed to blow hot and cold – to affirm at one time and deny at another – making a claim on those whom he has deluded to their disadvantage, and founding that claim on the very matters of the delusion. Such a principle has its basis in common sense and common justice, and whether it is called 'estoppel', or by any other name, it is one which the Courts of law have in modern times most usefully adopted" – Cave *v* Mills (1862) 7 H. & N. 927–8.

"It is the first principle **upon** which all Courts of **Equity** proceed, that if parties who have entered into definite and distinct terms involving certain legal results – certain penalties or legal forefeiture – afterwards by their own acts or with their own consent, enter upon a course of negotiation which has the effect of leading one of the parties to suppose that the strict rights arising under the contract will not be enforced, or will be kept in suspense, or held in abeyance, the person who otherwise might have enforced those rights will not be allowed to enforce them where it would be inequitable having regard to the dealings which have thus taken place between the parties" – Hughes *v* Metropolitan Railway Co. [1877] 2 AC 448. A principle which may be referred to as (a) 'promissory estoppel' – when a person makes a promise not to insist on, or enforce his legal rights against another, or his clear and unequivocal representations lead another to believe that those rights will not be insisted on, and, on the strength of that promise or representation, the other party so alters his legal position, "that it would be inequitable or unfair, to permit the party claimed to be estopped from departing from the representation." – James *v* Heim Gallery Ltd (1981) P and CR 280; or (b) 'proprietory estoppel' or 'estoppel by encouragement and acquiescence' – when a person takes a certain action which is to his or her detriment or prejudice, such as taking possession of property to carry out work therein, and another clearly accepts or acquiesces in that action. For example, "if a man, under a verbal agreement with a landlord for a certain interest in land, or, what amounts to the same thing, under an expectation, created or encouraged by the landlord, that he shall have a certain interest, takes possession of such land, with the consent of the landlord, and without objection by him, lays out money upon the land, a court of equity will compel the landlord to give effect to such promise or expectation." – Ramsden *v* Dyson (1866) LR 1 HL 170. Similarly, if an owner of land invites another to spend money on that land, giving the impression that an interest in that land will be given over to the person expending the money equity "will require the owner by appropriate conveyance to fulfil his obligation ... [or if for some reason a conveyance cannot be made effectively] a court of equity may declare that the person who has expended the money is entitled to an equitable charge or lien for the amount so expended". – Chalmers *v* Pardoe [1963] 1 WLR 681–2. Estoppel may be categorised also as (c) 'legal estoppel' or 'estoppel in pais' – as a 'matter of fact' – when there is a material fact which induces an action; or (d) 'equitable estoppel' when it is based on a promise, express or implied, or when a person remains silent although he observes an action by another which is based clearly on a misapprehension or a mistake by that other party. Equitable and promissory estoppel (called also 'quasi-estoppel') are akin and may be distinguished from estoppel based on fact, action, a deed, or a record or judgement of a court. (Estoppel by a court record or judgement is the oldest form of this doctrine and is enshrined in the maxims *interest reipublicae est ut sit finis litium* – 'it is in the public interest that there be an end to litigation' – and *nemo debet bis vexari pro eadem causa* – 'no one should be in jeopardy twice on the same ground'. 'Equitable estoppel' may be used also generically to refer to any form of estoppel that arises as a principle of Equity, rather than from a court record.

Examples of the application of the doctrine of estoppel are: (i) reduction of rent during war time because a large part of a block of flats was empty – when the war was over the landlord could not insist on the lost rent for the period of the war, because previously he had already collected the reduced sum – Central London Property Trust Ltd *v* High Trees House Ltd [1947] 1 K B 130; (ii) goods shipped after the stated contract date – the receiver was sent documents stating the date of dispatch but did not examine the wording closely and, therefore, made no representations. The receiver could not refuse to take delivery of the goods on their arrival – Panchard Freres S.A. *v* Et General Grain Co. [1970] 1 Lloyd's Rep. 53; (iii) receipt from a debtor of a lesser sum than owed – the creditor clearly indicated that he accepts this as satisfactory and the debtor acts on that understanding – the creditor subsequently is bound by that settlement – D and C Builders Ltd. *v* Rees [1966] 2 QB 617 – where it was accepted by Denning L.J. that promissory estoppel can operate to extinguish an understanding that he was free of a further liability.

In summary, estoppel "is a principle of justice and of equity. It comes to this when a man, by his words or conduct, has led another to believe that he may safely act on the faith of them – and the other does act on them – he will not be allowed to go back on what he has said or done when it would be unjust or inequitable for him to do so". (*The Discipline of Law*, Lord Denning, (1979), p. 223. cf. **misrepresentation, waiver.** See also **licence by estoppel, ostensible authority, recital, tenancy by estoppel.** Cheshire & Fifoot's Law of Contract 10 edn., pp. 83–85 & 273. Anson's Law of Contract, 26 edn., pp. 100–108. *Cases and Materials on English Land Law*, by Michael Harwood, pp. 284–318 (1977). 16 Halsbury's Laws of England, 4 edn., paras. 1501–1641. Snell's Principles of Equity, 28 edn., pp. 554–563.

estoppel (or estopped) certificate (US)
An attestation that prevents a person from later acting inconsistently with what he has previously affirmed. A written statement or certificate that creates an estoppel upon the action or representations of the maker, e.g. a

certificate from the vendor of a property showing the amount of mortgage loan outstanding at the date of transfer of a mortgage (and, usually, details of future interest and principal repayment due under the loan). Called also a 'waiver of defenses', a 'no set-off certificate', or a 'certificate of no defenses'. See also **reduction certificate.**

estoppel licence
see **licence by estoppel.**

estoppel statement (US)
see **estoppel certificate.**

estoppel, tenancy by
see **tenancy by estoppel.**

estovers
Derived from the Norman French *estoffer*, to furnish and *stouviers*, necessaries; or from the Latin *fovere*, to keep warm or sustain. Timber or wood that a tenant for life or a tenant for a term of years is allowed to take from land for essential purposes. The equivalent Saxon word was *bote*. Estovers may be *fuelbote*, to fuel the house; *housebote*, to repair the house; *ploughbote* or *cartbote*, to repair agricultural implements; or *haybote*, to repair fences, ditches and walls. A tenant is not permitted to take more timber than is immediately required for the necessary repair or maintenance as that would constitute waste. See also **right of common.**

et al. (L)
Abbreviation of *et alii* – 'and others', or 'all others'.

et uxor (L)
'and wife'.

et vir (L)
'and husband'.

établissement (F)
1. establishment.
(*établissement public* – public undertaking)
2. **premises**, especially a place of business.

état (F)
1. state or status; condition.
(*état civil* – civil status, e.g. company, partnership or sole proprietor).
2. statement; schedule; inventory; account.
(*état des lieux* – **schedule of condition**; inventory of fixtures and fittings, especially as prepared prior to the grant of a lease. If a schedule of condition is prepared at the commencement of a lease the tenant is obliged to return the premises at the termination of the lease in the same condition, excluding deterioration due to fair wear and tear and *force majeure* (French Civil Code, art. 1730). If there is no schedule of condition it is assumed that the lease premises were in a good state of repair (Civil Code art. 1731).
(état des charges – schedule of charges or of incumberances)
(*état descriptif* – property description)
(*état hypothécaire* – statement of the outstanding balance on a mortgage).
3. The State.

ethics
see **code of conduct.**

étude (F)
1. **survey.**
(*étude probatoire* – **feasibility study**)
2. practice or offices, of a lawyer.
(*étude de notaire* – notary's office).

évaluateur (F)
valuer; appraiser.

evaluation

The process of estimating the monetary value of something. A general assessment of the worth or benefits to be derived from a property. A broader term than **appraisal** or **valuation** as it takes account of factors other than monetary worth. See also **cost-benefit analysis, feasibility**.

évaluation (F)

assessment; **estimate**; evaluation (less formal than *expertise*).
(*evaluation cadastralle* – cadastral or rating assessment). See also *cadastre*.

éventualité (F)

contingency.

eviction

Derived from *evincere*, 'to evict by judicial process'. In common usage eviction refers to any form of expulsion, whether by process of law or forcible re-entry, and any action against a tenant, trespasser or squatter. In particular, eviction is, "something of a grave and permanent nature done by the landlord with the intention of depriving the tenant of the enjoyment of the whole or part of the demised premises". – Upton *v* Townsend (1855) 17 CB 64, 65. Eviction may be 'actual' or 'constructive'. Actual eviction occurs when a tenant is physically deprived of possession, especially when the landlord retakes possession. Constructive eviction occurs when the landlord restricts the tenant in his proper enjoyment of the property. Usually eviction refers to a wrongful act, and in that sense, "apart from any requisite of wrongfulness, the landlord's act must (i) be of a 'permanent character', and (ii) be done with 'particular intention', *viz.*, that of disabling the tenant from continuing to 'hold' the subject of his demises, or of depriving him of the 'enjoyment' of the thing demised, or some part thereof". – Commissioners of Crown Lands *v* Page [1960] 2 All ER 729.

It is an offence to unlawfully deprive, or to attempt to unlawfully deprive, a person who is a legal occupier of a residence, a **residential occupier**, of his or her residence unless it can be shown that the person seeking the eviction believed, and had reasonable cause to believe, that the residential occupier had ceased to reside in the premises (Protection from Eviction Act 1977, s. 1 (2)). It is unlawful to enforce a right of re-entry or forfeiture of a lease of a dwelling, while any person is resident therein, otherwise than by court proceedings (1977 Act, s. 2). Again, when a tenancy of a dwelling comes to an end, even though it does not then become a statutory tenancy, the owner cannot enforce his right to recover possession without a court order (1977 Act, s. 3). Thus, any landlord (or his agent) is well advised to proceed with caution before seeking to evict any person in occupation of a residential property.

In some states in the US any act of a landlord by which he seeks to recover possession of leased premises, in particular residential premises, without due process of law and against the wishes of the tenant, is a criminal offence. An actual eviction, but not necessarily a mere interference with the enjoyment of possession, will relieve a tenant of his future obligation to pay rent – Skaggs *v* Emerson (1875) 50 Cal. 3; Smith *v* McEnary (1897) 170 Mass. 26, 48 NE 781. Actual eviction is called also 'summary possession'. See also **disposses-**

sion, ejectment, harrassment, ouster, quiet enjoyment, security of tenure.
Manual of Housing Law, by Andrew Arden, 2 edn., pp. 126–141.
Housing Law, by Andrew Arden and Martin Partington, pp. 829–863, 959–1049 (1983).
Quiet Enjoyment, by Andrew Arden and Martin Partington (1985).

éviction (F)
eviction (in a strict judicial sense); **dispossession** (of any form of property). See also *indemnité*.

evidence of title
see **certificate of title, title.**

evidence, hearsay
see **hearsay evidence.**

evidenced in writing
see **contract, memorandum, unenforceable contract, writing.**

ex contractu (L)
'Arising out of **contract**', e.g. an action arising from a contractual obligation that has not been performed.

ex delicto (L)
'Arising out of **tort**'.

ex gratia (L)
'As of favour'. Not by legal right; "without admission of liability" – Edwards *v* Skyways, Ltd [1964] 1 All ER 500. An *ex-gratia* payment is one made out of 'sympathy' and not as a result of any contractual or other legal liability for damages: the amount is left entirely at the discretion of the payer and need bear no relation to any loss suffered by the payee. For example, a person, displaced from a dwelling by an authority possessing compulsory purchase powers, who has no greater interest than a tenancy from year to year, and

who would not therefore, have any right to compensation, may receive an *ex-gratia* payment from the acquiring authority to assist that person to acquire alternative premises (Land Compensation Act 1973, s. 43). See also **home-loss payment.**

ex hypothesi (L)
'From the hypothesis'; upon the supposition'. See **hypothetical.**

ex nudo pacto none oritur actio (L)
'Out of a bare promise no action can arise'. See **naked contract.**

ex parte (L)
'On the one side; on behalf of'. An action by one party in the absence of another.

ex post facto (L)
'By a subsequent act; after the act'.

ex turpi causa non oritur actio (L)
'An action does not arise from a base cause' i.e. from an **illegal contract.**

examen (F)
(*examen des titres de propriété* – **examination of title**).

examination of title
The process of checking that a person has **good title** to a property. Normally carried out by a solicitor prior to an exchange of contract for a sale of land. See also **abstract of title, searches.**

excambion
In Scottish law, a contract by which one parcel of land is exchanged for another.

excepted risk
1. A risk that is not expressly covered in an insurance policy. See also **all-risks insurance, special perils.**
2. In a building contract, a risk that is

excluded from the contractor's liability and, therefore, one against which he does not have to insure.

exception

In conveyancing, an exclusion of part of a property, or a particular thing, from that which is the subject of a **grant**. It must be something that is severable from the grant; "a particular thing out of a general one – as a room out of a house, ground out of a manor, timber out of land, etc". – Kenson *v* Reading Cro. Eliz. 244. An 'exception' is a taking out immediately of some part of what has been granted so that it does not pass with the grant, as distinguished from a reservation which is the taking of something new out of what has already been granted. The words 'excepting and reserving', or sometimes 'subject to', in a contract for sale or in a lease, are followed either by those things that are excluded from the grant and do not pass at all, e.g. minerals; or any part of the demise which effectively is taken back or reserved, e.g. easement, sporting rights. An exception must be expressed clearly and unambiguously and words of exception are construed, *prima facie*, in favour of the grantee – Savil Bros Ltd *v* Bethell [1902] 2 Ch. 523. See also **excepted risk**.
Odger's *Construction of Deeds and Statutes*, 5 edn., pp. 189–192.
Woodfall's Landlord and Tenant, 28 edn., paras. 1-0486 to 1-0496.

exception clause

see **exclusion clause**.

excess condemnation (US)

The exercise by a public authority of the power of **eminent domain** to acquire more land than is required for a development scheme. A process that may be used to enable the authority to recoup part of its cost by selling off the surplus land at an increased price when the development work is complete. See also **condemnation, recoupment**.

excess (on insurance cover)

The first portion of a loss, being a specified sum, that the insured agrees to bear himself before any claim is paid by the insurer. Usually an excess is a small percentage of the total sum insured. It avoids the insurer having to administer small claims and results in a reduced premium for the insured. Called sometimes 'deductibles'. See also **first-loss insurance**.

excess rent

1. An amount of rent that exceeds the current market rental value, in particular when the contract rent under a lease exceeds the market rent.
cf. **profit rent**.
2. In economics, the return from cultivated land over the minimum return required to keep the land in use, i.e. the return over and above the 'marginal cost of cultivation'. See also **economic rent**.
3. Any amount of rent paid by a tenant in excess of the amount registered as the **fair rent** for a regulated tenancy of a dwelling-house. The charging of any such excess rent is illegal and, therefore, if paid may be recovered from the landlord or his personal representative (Rent Act 1977, s. 57). See also **premium, rent limit**.

exchange

The giving or receiving of one thing for another when those things are considered to be of equal worth. The reciprocal **transfer** of properties. A transfer or conveyance of one property for another like property. The term 'exchange' has no particular legal significance, but has been described as, "the mutual grant of equal interests, the one in consideration of the other". (Bl. Comm. vol. ii. p. 323).

An exchange of interests in land should be evidenced in **writing**, unless supported by an act of **part performance** or made by the court (Law of Property Act 1925, s. 40). See also **bill of exchange, exchange of contract, sale, tax-free exchange**.

exchange of contract

The stage at which a contract for the sale of land comes into formal effect. "Exchange of a written contract for sale is in my [Buckley's L.J] judgement effected so soon as each part of the contract, signed by the vendor or the purchaser as the case may be, is in the actual or constructive possession of the other party or his solicitor". – Domb v Isoz [1980] Ch. 557. Exchange may take place (a) 'face to face', usually in the office of the vendor's solicitor; (b) by post, which means it takes place when the last part is actually posted; or (c) by telephone, "after both the vendor and the purchaser sign contracts in identical form" – *supra*, at p. 560. The latter practice should only take place when partners or proprietors of the respective solicitors have agreed and recorded identical attendance notes. *Contract and Conveyance*, by J.T. Farrand, 4 edn., pp. 15–24.

exchange-value

see **value**.

excheat

see **escheat**.

excluding and limiting terms

see **exclusion clause**.

exclusif, (f.-ive) (F)

exclusive; sole.
(*agent exclusif* – **exclusive agent; sole agent**).

An *agent exclusif* may be an exclusive agent or a sole agent; his entitlement to commission depends on the express terms of his *mandat*. An estate agent's *exclusivité* is regulated by a French law of 2nd January 1970 No. 70–9 (the *Loi Hoguet*) and a law of 20th July 1972 No. 72–678.
French Law of Estate Agency (*the 'Hoguet Law'*), by Bryan Harris, in *Chartered Surveyor*, pp. 498–501 (27 April 1972).
Dictionaire Permanent, Gestion Immobilier pp. 147–166, (1981).

exclusion clause

A clause in a contract that seeks to define and limit the extent of the promisor's liability or obligation under the contract. For example, a clause which stipulates that the promisor will not be liable for such matters as a defect in goods offered for sale; for providing any **warranty** as to the quality or condition of the subject matter of the contract; or for any damage that is suffered by the promisee as a result of negligence or misrepresentation on the part of the promisor. An exclusion clause (called also an 'exception clause' or an 'exemption clause') may be regarded either as an attempt to clarify that which is set out in the contract, or as a means of circumventing the contract. It is in the latter sense that the term is more commonly used – a means of cutting the umbilical cord of the agreement. "I [Lord Wilberforce] treat the words "exclusion clause" as covering broadly such clauses in a contract as profess to exclude or limit, either quantitatively or as to the time within which action must be taken, the right of the injured party to bring an action for damages. Such a clause must, *ex hypothesi*, reflect the contemplation of the parties that a breach of contract, or what apart from the clause would be a breach of contract, may be committed, otherwise the clause would not be there; but the question remains open in any case whether there is a limit to the type of breach which they have in mind". – Willion *v* Berkley (1562) Plow. 243.

An exclusion clause which refers to the substance of the contract must be 'fair and reasonable' as "a person who makes a representation of fact cannot negative the representation by words such as those in the small print . . ." – Walker *v* Boyle (1981) 125 S.J. 724. The exclusion clause must be an integral part of the contract to which it refers, not merely something to which the promisor may point to escape an obligation, but which was not at all evident when the promisee entered into the contract, e.g. 'small print' which is not truly apparent – Chapelton *v* Barry UDC [1940] 1 KB 532. An exclusion clause may not exclude a liability for fraud – Pearson *v* Dublin Corporation [1907] AC 351. In addition, the clause must be signed by or clearly brought to the notice of the affected party; it must not be ambiguous or totally devoid of applicability to the contract; and it may not be relied upon by a party to a contract who is fundamentally in breach of a condition of contract so as to negate that condition. In summary, an exclusion clause is treated by the courts with considerable caution and

usually against the party seeking to benefit thereby: thus, "with woefully few exceptions . . . an exclusion clause is disregarded in determining what parties have agreed shall be their rights and obligation under the agreement. It is only when such rights and obligations have been ascertained that the exclusion clause will be looked at. The exclusion clause will then be treated as a completely separate entity, raising such questions as whether it is part of the rest of the contract at all; whether, on its construction, it can operate to bar a claim based on breach of the obligations already ascertained; whether, where breach of a fundamental term is alleged, there are primary obligations or core duties arising from the relationship created by the contract, regardless of the contract's specific terms and so on". (*Exclusion Clauses in Contracts*, by David Yates, 2 edn., p. 264).

Statute law has further intervened to limit the effect or to control the use of exclusion clauses especially for the purpose of consumer protection. In particular the Misrepresentation Act 1967, as amended by the Unfair Contract Terms Act 1977, which applies to contracts affecting 'business liability' – including the occupation of premises used for business purposes (excluding an occupation that is purely for recreational or educational purposes). This statute (which does not apply, *inter alia*, to insurance contracts, contracts relating to the creation, transfer or termination of interests in land and contracts relating to intellectual property such as patents, copyrights, etc.) identifies various matters that may be relevant in determining whether the term of an exclusion clause is reasonable (tests that are not applied, but would not be unreasonable to apply, to all contracts): (a) the strength of the bargaining position of the parties relative to each other; (b) whether the customer received an inducement to agree to the term; (c) whether the customer knew, or ought reasonably to have known, the existence or extent of the term; (d) whether the term excludes or restricts any relevant liability if some condition is not complied with, and whether it was reasonable at the time of the contract to expect that compliance with that condition would be practicable; and (e) whether goods were manufactured, processed or adapted to the special order of the customer. Further, section 11 of the Misrepresentation Act 1967 provides that a clause seeking to exclude or restrict a liability to **misrepresentation** must be "fair and reasonable ... having regard to the circumstances which were, or ought reasonably to have been, known to or in the contemplation of the parties when the contract was made", and "it is for those claiming that the term satisfies that requirement to show that it does". (Misrepresentation Act 1967, s. 3). Therefore, the enforceability of an exclusion clause depends on the nature of the contract. Nonetheless it must be fair and reasonable; must not of itself be the result of a misrepresentation as to its scope; must be brought to the notice of the party against whom it is seeking to operate; must not run against the fundamental intent of the agreement; and is best used to clarify, and at the same time to encase, the terms of an agreement, rather than as a means to seek to bar the fulfilment of an undertaking – a

ploy used when one party to a contract becomes aware of that which he should have been aware at the outset.

In the US, exclusion clauses are viewed with similar reservation and Uniform Commercial Codes, adopted by most states, limit the effectiveness of such clauses by setting out the exceptions or reservations that might be expected in business (but not real estate) contracts.

In French law, in general, parties are bound by the contract as it stands and exclusion clauses are brought to account as they are written (barring fraud, duress, deceit or undue influence). However, an inequality of bargaining power may be a valid reason to overturn an exclusion clause, especially if the contract relates to the sale of goods or the provision of services by a professional to a non-professional party (*Loi Schivener* 10.1.78). cf. **escape clause**. See also *contra proferentem*, **particulars of sale**, **puffing**.

Cheshire & Fifoot's Laws of Contract, 10 edn., pp. 138–173.
Anson's Law of Contract, 26 edn., pp. 137–176.
Chitty on Contract, 25 edn., pp. 465–511.
Exclusion Clauses, by Richard Lawson, 2 edn.
9 Halsbury's Laws of England, 4 edn., paras. 363–385.

exclusionary zoning (US)
Land use control regulations or zoning ordinances aimed at excluding a particular category of persons or a type of user from a given area. Exclusionary zoning may be aimed at excluding persons of a particular income level, race or economic class or as excluding a use or form of

development that will not prove to be a net contributor to local government revenue (the latter form of exclusion is called also 'fiscal zoning'). Exclusionary zoning may take the form of restrictions on such matters as high density development, low-cost housing, recreational facilities for low-income groups (e.g. communal halls, state creches), or may stipulate minimum lot-size requirements or similar density requirements.

exclusive agency
An agency granted to one party to the exclusion of any other agent, usually for a specified period of time; i.e. a **sole agency**. An exclusive agency for the sale of property does not normally preclude the principal from selling the property. Where the agent receives a fee even if the property is sold by the principal this is referred to as a **sole right to sell** or, in the US, an 'exclusive right (or authority) to sell'. In the US, called also an 'exclusive listing' or 'exclusive agency listing'.
cf. **multiple agency**. See also **listing**.
Real Estate Principles, by Bruce Harwood, 2 edn., pp. 380–384.

exclusive agency listing (US)
see **exclusive agency**.

exclusive listing
see **exclusive agency**.

exclusive occupation
The right to occupy exclusively that which is granted; a right to property which is not subordinate to another. "A person has a right to 'exclusive occupation' of a room when he is entitled to occupy it himself, and no one else is entitled to occupy it". – Luganda v Service Hotels Ltd [1969] 2 Ch. 219. ('Exclusive occupation' and 'exclusive possession' are similar

terms, the former denoting more a question of fact and the latter more a question of law; any further distinction depending on the difference between **occupation** and **possession** and the context in which the term is used.) However, neither term totally precludes someone else having rights in the property, such as a landlord's right to make occasional visits; nor does it preclude shared occupation, as in a co-ownership, where the co-owners collectively have exclusive occupation. "The expression 'exclusive possession' in relation to the occupier of a property may be used in more than one sense. It may, as I [Stamp, L.J.] see it, be used to mean that, as a factual matter, the occupant, alone or together with his family, occupies the premises and does not share them with any other person ... Or the expression may be used to mean that the occupant has a right to exclude the owner from the premises". – Heslop v Burns [1974] 1 WLR 1247. It is in the former sense that the term 'exclusive occupation' is more commonly used, especially when distinguishing a **lease** from a **licence**.

As an essential element of **rateable occupation**, in deciding whether a party has exclusive occupation, it was considered that the occupier of a railway station kiosk, who had paramount control (even though there was no permitted access at night) and thereby occupied premises that were "so let out as to be capable of separate assessment", was in exclusive occupation – Westminster Corporation v Southern Railway Co. [1936] 2 All ER 322; but many railway station bookstalls which have more limited access are not held in exclusive occu-

pation – Smith *v* Lambeth 10 (1882) QBD 327). See also **beneficial occupation, lodger, occupation.**
Landlord and Tenant, by Martin Partington, 2 edn., pp. 98–118.

exclusive possession
see **exclusive occupation**.

exclusive rent
A **rent** that is paid excluding rates, i.e. the tenant accepts the liability under the tenancy to pay rates direct to the local rating authority. See also **net rent**.

exclusive right (or authority) to sell (US)
see **sole right to sell**.

exculpatory clause (US)
1. A clause in a contract by which one party holds himself blameless from damage or injury arising out of certain circumstances relating to that contract; for example, a clause in a lease which states that a landlord is not liable for damage to any person, whether a tenant or a third party, due to any act of the landlord or his agent, or for his or the tenant's failure to repair the property. Such conditions may be difficult to enforce at law, especially when it can be shown that there was a disparity of bargaining power between the parties when the contract was entered into. Called also a 'hold-harmless clause'. See also **exclusion clause**.
2. A clause inserted in a mortgage deed by which the mortgagee agrees not to take a personal action against the mortgagor if the mortgaged property provides insufficient security for the debt. See also **non-recourse mortgage**.

executed consideration
Consideration that has been actually given in satisfaction of a contract.

executed contract
A contract that has been completed in its entirety leaving no party with any residual duty or obligation to perform. An executed contract cannot be frustrated. See also **delivery**.

executed trust
A trust arising from a settlement that can take full effect on the basis of the document by which it is established, as compared to an **executory trust** which requires further documentation to give full effect to the settler's intentions.

exécuteur (F)
executor.

execution
1. The effecting of a **deed** by signing, sealing and delivery, usually in the presence of witnesses (Law of Property Act 1925, s. 73 (1)).
2. The **performance** of the duties and obligations of a contract, such as the carrying out and completion of building work by a contractor. See also **executed contract, practical completion**.
3. The putting into effect of a judgement of a court, such as for possession of property.

exécution (F)
performance; legal seizure; distress. (*exécution d'une promesse* – performance of a promise. See *contrat*) (*exécution en nature* – **specific performance**).

executor (fem: executrix)
A person appointed in the will as the **personal representative** of a deceased person (the testator) to administer the deceased's affairs and carry out the provisions of the will. If there is no executor, a court will appoint an administrator to perform the same

effective duties. See also **probate**.
Cheshire's Modern Law of Real
Property, 13 edn., p. 783 *et seq.*

executory contract

A contract that is still to be brought
into effect or executed by the action
of the parties or by an external event,
as distinguished from an **executed
contract** which has been wholly performed. An executory contract may
be frustrated, unlike an executed contract which cannot. See also **contract
for sale, estate contract**.

executory devise

see **devise, executory interest**.

executory interest

An interest that takes effect by taking
away, or divesting, a prior interest
upon the occurrence of a future contingency. An interest which depends
on a contingent event, not on the termination of a prior interest. An interest in real or personal property which
will come into effect in the future; but
is not an interest in **reversion**, i.e. it
does not return to the original grantor
or his or her heirs.
cf. **determinable interest**. See also
contingent interest, future interest.

executory trust

A **trust** that cannot take effect on the
basis of the document by which it has
been established, but requires further
documents in order to give full effect
to the purpose of the trust, as distinguished from an **executed trust** which
gives immediate effect to the settler's
intentions.

exemplary damages

see **damages**.

exempli gratia (e.g.) (L)

'For example; for instance'.

exempt fund

A **unit trust** that is wholly or partially
exempt from a liability to pay tax on
income distributed to the beneficiaries because they have a special tax
status, e.g. a charity or pension fund.
Such organisations are referred to
generally as 'gross funds'.

exemption clause

see **exclusion clause**.

exigibilities (F)

current liabilities.

existing use

1. The use to which land is put at a
particular point in time.
2. A use of land which existed before
any introduced planning or zoning
regulation and, therefore, may continue without causing a legal infrac-
tion. See also **established use, existing
use rights**.

existing use development

see **existing use rights**.

existing use rights

1. All those rights to use property
that may be exercised without the
need for planning permission; any use
that may be undertaken without constituting **development**. See also **established use certificate, General Development Order, highest and best use,
permitted development, Use Classes
Order**.
2. Certain minor forms of **development** of land or buildings, set out in
the Town and Country Planning Act
1971, Sch. 8, as amended by the Town
and Country Planning (Compensation) Act 1985, s. 1 (2) (called 'eighth
schedule development') which, although requiring planning permission, are considered to form part of a
landowner's right in respect of his

land. These forms of development are relevant in determining whether **compensation for planning restrictions** is payable to a landowner; if planning permission is refused, or granted subject to conditions, for those forms of development set out in Part II of the eighth schedule, compensation may be payable to the landowner. In addition, upon a compulsory purchase of land, the land is valued on the basis that the forms of development set out in Part I and Part II of Schedule 8 can be carried out. Part I refers basically to rebuilding works when a building has been destroyed or demolished, together with minor additions or alterations and the conversion of any building which on 1 July 1948 was used as a single dwelling into two or more separate dwellings. Part II allows such minor developments as (i) a 10 per cent increase in the cubic capacity or floor space of an existing building; (ii) building work associated with agriculture, forestry or associated mining operations; (iii) any change of use within the same **Use Classes order**; (iv) a 10 per cent increase in a particular use of a building erected before 1 July 1948 or of other land used for a particular purpose; (v) the deposit of waste material or refuse in connection with mineral workings on a site used for that purpose.

existing use value

1. The **market value** of land with the benefit of **existing use rights** only.

2. A term introduced by the Town and Country Planning Act 1947 to mean the 'market value' of a property assuming that it may be used for its **current use** only and that no new development of that property would be permitted other than minor forms of development specified in the Third Schedule of the Act. Between August 6, 1947 and October, 3 1958 existing use value was the basis for assessing the value of land for the purpose of fixing the amount of compulsory purchase compensation.

expectancy, estate in

see **future estate (or interest)**.

expedit rei publicae ne sua re quis mal utatur (L)

'It is for the public good that no one use his property badly' (or 'so as to injure others'). A maxim of Roman law. See also **negligence, nuisance**.

expenditure

Derived from the Latin *ex-pensus* that which is paid or given up. Money or similar paid out incurred or spent, especially to acquire a benefit. Something that is used up or foreborne in order to achieve an objective or bring about a result. Expenditure is represented by actual disbursements; in particular a sum of money laid out in return for a benefit. Expenditure on property includes the cost of repair and maintenance; **operating expenses** or **service charges**; taxes or rates; insurance; management fees; and any other disbursement arising from ownership of property and the consequent need to maintain the use and value of that property. Expenditure may be taken to include a provision for depreciation although strictly this is not an actual disbursement. The payment of the cost of any loan secured on a property (principal and interest) may be referred to as expenditure, although such an outgoing is more personal to the debtor and is not necessarily any part of the cost of nor need not bear any relationship to the benefit to be derived from, the property. See also **charge, payment**.

expense ratio (US)

The ratio of expenditure to income. In particular, the ratio of **operating expenses** (excluding debt service) to **effective gross income**. See also **operating expense ratio**.

expenses

see **expenditure, operating expenses, outgoings**.

expert

A person who is knowledgeable in a particular field, from experience or by study, education or qualification. A person appointed as an expert in a dispute uses his own experience or knowledge in order to determine the basis for the settlement of that dispute and, as a rule, his decision is binding on the parties who have sought his opinion (for that is what they asked for); unless there is clearly an error on the face of that opinion or negligence by the expert. An expert is required to be experienced and actively engaged in the field in which he expresses competence and, in order that his opinion should be credible, there should be no possibility, or appearance, of bias in the views on which he is expressing expertise. An expert is required to make his own investigations and searches to ascertain the facts that affect the matter on which he is acting. In some cases he may receive submissions or evidence from the parties to a dispute on which he is to express his expert opinion but, unlike an **arbitrator**, his opinion may be outside the extremes maintained by the parties to the dispute if his own investigations and knowledge leads to

that conclusion. When a clause in an agreement specifies that a dispute is to be settled by a third party then, if that party's function appears to be one of using his expertise, he is intended to act as an expert; but if his function is to adjudicate between the opinions of the parties in dispute he is intended to act as an arbitrator. However, in which capacity a third party to a dispute is to act depends, in the final analysis, upon the context of the entire agreement – Langham House Developments Ltd *v* Brompton Securities Ltd (1980) 256 EG 719. There is no right of appeal against a determination of a dispute by an expert, although the decision may be set aside by a court of law, as when the expert is negligent or biased. In the case of a property valuation or rent review an expert is referred to also as an 'independent expert', 'independent surveyor' or an 'independent valuer'; his function being that of a valuer, but acting independently of the parties seeking the valuation or rent determination. See also **arbitration, expert witness, professional negligence**.

Handbook of Rent Review by Ronald Bernstein and Kirk Reynolds, (1982), paras. 9.4.1 – 9.4.5.

The Surveyor in Court, by P.H. Clarke, pp. 193 *et seq.* (1985).

expert (F)

expert; valuer; surveyor; appraiser.
(*expert en construction* – building surveyor)
(*expert immobilier* – valuer; real estate appraiser)
(*expert-conseil en biens immobiliers* –real estate consultant).

expert witness

A person called at a judicial proceeding to give evidence based on his/her

specialist knowledge, experience, or professional qualifications. A person who, by means of a previous course of study or habit, has obtained knowledge in a particular field that surpasses that of an inexperienced person or layman and, therefore, makes him or her better equipped to express an informed opinion. Whether a person is qualified or sufficiently knowledgeable to give evidence as an expert witness is dependent on the judge of the court; it does not depend necessarily on professional qualification – R. *v* Silverlock [1894] 2 QB 766.
Real Estate Valuation in Litigation, by J.D. Eaton, pp. 375–400 (1982).
The Expert Witness, by R.H. Mildred (1982).

expertise (F)
valuation; survey; opinion. See also *evaluation*.

expiration
Cessation. Strictly, the coming or bringing to an end, due to lapse of time. However, expiration may be used to refer to the extinction of a right by the voluntary action of the parties: that is, when the right is not forcibly brought to an end by such means as **forfeiture** or **surrender**.
cf. **determination**. See also **termination**.

expiration (d'un bail) (F)
expiration (of a lease).

exposé (F)
statement; account, report; **recitals**. (*exposé des motifs; exposé d'un brevet* – **preamble**).

exposure
The extent to which a property has been offered for lease or for sale on the open market. See also **market value**.

express
Clearly evidenced or stated; set forth in words. That which is stated clearly and definitely; the communication of information, directly or indirectly, in such a way that the information is indubitable, unambiguous and does not require inference or any support in order to ascertain what is conveyed. An express statement may be made orally or in writing, provided what has been said can be clearly established. See also **contract, covenant, express term**.

express contract
see **contract**.

express covenant
see **covenant, express term**.

express term
A term of a contract that is clear and definite; whether given by word of mouth or set out in writing. A contract wholly in writing is taken to be expressed within the pages of the written instrument. "It is firmly established as a rule of law that parol evidence cannot be admitted to, add to, vary or contradict a deed or other written instrument. Accordingly, it has been held that (except in cases of fraud or rectification and except, in certain circumstances, as a defence in actions for specific performance) parol evidence will not be admitted to prove that some particular term, which had been verbally agreed upon, had been omitted (by design or otherwise) from a written instrument constituting a valid and operative contract between the parties." – Jacobs *v* Batavia and General Plantations Trust [1924] 1 Ch. 295. How-

ever, a condition or a covenant may be treated as express if it can be 'inferred' from the written text as forming part of the express intention of the parties or when there is an ambiguity in the contract. "An express covenant is an agreement which is framed in express terms, or is inferred on the construction of the entire instrument" – Hayne *v* Cummings (1864) 16 CBNS 421 – 27 Halsbury's Laws of England 4 edn., p. 249. (Note: many real property contracts are required to be in **writing** and, therefore, that which is set down in writing is capable of stricter interpretation leaving less room for implication). cf. **implied term**. See also **oral contract, usual covenants**.
Cheshire & Fifoot's Law of Contract, 10 edn., pp. 107–115.
Chitty on Contract, 28 edn., paras. 731–833.

express trust
see **trust**.

expressio unius est exclusio alterio (L)
'The express mention of one thing implies the exclusion of another'. When a person or thing is expressly referred to in a statute or document, it may be inferred that the intention is to exclude any others of a similar nature; or, when one exception is made to a general rule, other exceptions are excluded. ('A valuable servant but a dangerous master in the construction of statutes or document.' – Osborne's *Concise Law Dictionary*, 8 edn.)

expressum facit cessare tactium (L)
'That which is express puts an end to that which is implied'. See also **express term**.

expropriation
The taking of property by the State, especially when there is no payment of compensation. Normally used to refer to powers exercised by a government over foreign owned assets, rather than to **compulsory purchase** or **eminent domain**, although it may be used in the latter senses. "Expropriation generally is used to mean a taking which conforms with the requirements of international law; 'confiscation' is used to describe a taking which is unaccompanied by compensation: 'nationalisation' is commonly used to denote an expropriation of major resources as part of a general programme of social or economic reform; and "requisition" usually means a taking for a temporary purpose." (18 Halsbury's Laws of England, 4 edn., p. 899).

expropriation (F)
expropriation; compulsory purchase; dispossession. In French law a person cannot be deprived of a right to property unless the taking is for a public purpose (*cause d'utilité publique*) and that person has received prior and just compensation (*indemnité*) (French Civil Code, art. 545). Public purpose is not defined in the Civil Code, but the economic betterment of the community is a primary consideration. In particular, property may be expropriated for housing and industrial development; slum clearance; comprehensive redevelopment; for new means of communication (roads, railways, airports, etc.); and for scientific purposes or environmental conservation. The basis for the amount of compensation for expropriation is based on the financial loss occasioned by the party expropriated, as agreed

between the owner and the acquiring authority, or if not agreed as fixed by a court of law. As in the US, the rules for assessing this loss are less formally laid down than in English law, but any effect of an underlying scheme behind the acquisition is ignored. Compensation is not paid for consequential loss e.g. for business losses.
Planning in Western Europe, Edited by J.F. Garner. (France – Prof. J. Lemaourier) p. 143 (1975).
Manuel de Droit Administratif, by André de Laubadère, 11 edn., pp. 325–337.
Précis Dalloz. Droit Civil, Les Biens (Alex Weill), 2 edn., pp. 266–280.
Précis Dalloz. Droit Administrative by (J-M Auby et R. Ducos Ader).
Petits Codes Dalloz, Code Administratif, 17 edn, pp. 917–960.
L'Expropriation pour Cause d'Utilité Publique, by Andre Homont (1975).
L'Expropriation pour Cause d'Utilité Publique, by J-M Auby, R. Ducos-Ader and J-C. Gonthier (1968).

expulsion (F)
ejectment; eviction.

extended coverage insurance (US)
see **extended perils insurance**.

extended lease
A lease that may be acquired, under the provisions of the Leasehold Reform Act 1967, s. 1, 14–16 (as amended by the Housing Act 1980, Sch. 12), by a tenant of a leasehold **house** which has been occupied as his residence under a **long tenancy** (one originally let for a term not less than 21 years), at a **low rent** (less than two-thirds of the rateable value). The tenant must have been the occupier for the past three years, or a total of

three of the past ten years, and the rateable value of the house must be below a stipulated level. A tenant who qualifies under the Act may be entitled to an extended lease of fifty years from the expiry of his existing lease on similar terms, but at a **modern ground rent**. See also **leasehold enfranchisement**.
Rent Control and Leasehold Enfranchisement, by Trevor Aldridge, 8 edn., Chs. 17, 19.
Woodfall's Landlord and Tenant, 28 edn., paras. 3–0985 to 3–1029.
Hill & Redman's Law of Landlord and Tenant, 17 edn., pp. 2330–2341.

extended perils insurance
1. A form of property insurance which extends beyond a 'standard' policy for fire cover and includes such items as impact damage, flood, storm, explosion, riot, smoke and similar perils. The policy may be extended as far as the contract specifies, but unlike an **all-risks insurance policy** the perils covered are effected by inclusion rather than exclusion. In the US, called also 'extra coverage insurance'. See **also comprehensive insurance, special perils**.
(US) 2. A **title insurance** policy that covers such aspects as encumberances, rights of occupancy, easements, etc. See also **contingent liability insurance**.

extender clause (US)
A provision in a listing contract to the effect that the principal will pay a **commission** to the broker, even after the term of the agreement has ended, provided that a sale is made to a purchaser who was introduced by the broker during the subsistence of the agreement. Called also a 'carry-over clause' or an 'override'.

extension

1. The act or process of increasing a space. An **enlargement** in size or space. The extension of a building or a use of land may constitute **development** for which planning permission is required. See also **improvement, material change in the use.**

2. The prolonging of a right, especially for an additional period of time. "Extension is a term properly used for the purpose of enlarging, or giving further duration to, any existing right, but does not import the revesting of an expired right; that would not be an extension but a recreation" – Brooke *v* Clarke (1818) 1 B. and Ald. 399.

cf. **renewal**. See also **extension agreement.**

3. An increase in the allotted time for completion of a contract. See also **delay, time is of the essence.**

extension agreement (or **clause**)

An agreement (or clause in an agreement) to prolong a right when it comes to its end. e.g. to continue a tenancy beyond its expiry date, a loan or mortgage after its maturity date, or a building contract after the completion date. See also **extender clause, time is of the essence.**

exterior

see **external.**

external

Situated or connected with the outside; out of doors. Generally the external part of a building is that part of the building exposed to the atmosphere, or not enclosed but forming the enclosure of the premises. An outer or external wall is one where at least one face is exposed to the outside elements. However, the external part of a building has been defined by Lord Denman C.J. as, "those parts which form the inclosure of premises and beyond which no part of them extends; and it is immaterial whether these parts are exposed to the atmosphere, or rest upon or adjoin some other building which forms no part of the premises". – Green *v* Eales (1841) 2 QB 237; Phelps *v* City of London Corporation [1916] 2 Ch. 255. Thus a wall that rests upon the wall of an adjoining property and would be exposed to the atmosphere if the adjoining wall were to be demolished, may be considered as an external wall – the wall *in extremus* to the house – Pembery *v* Lamdin, [1940] 2 All ER 434. Windows are not *prima facie* an external part of a building, unless they form part of the external cladding, e.g. as a curtain wall; or are looked upon as forming part of the outside frame of the building. (In order to emphasise that the intention is to refer to a part of a structure that is truly on the outside, 'exterior' may be preferred, being that which is "visible or perceptible on the outside" – *Webster's Third International Dictionary*, defining 'exterior'. "When we speak of anything which has two coats, it is usual to designate the outermost by the name of "exterior"; when we speak simply of the surface, without reference to anything behind it is denominated external; as the "exterior" coat of a walnut, or the external surface of a thing" – *Crabb's English Synonyms* (1816). On the other hand 'external' and 'exterior' may be construed as synonyms. See also **repair.**

external wall

see **external.**

extinction (F)
repayment; **termination**.
(*extinction d'une hypothèque* – repayment of a mortgage)
(*extinction d'un contrat* – termination of a contract). See also *résiliation, resolution*.

extinguishment
The act of putting to an end or causing to end. The **termination** of a right, usually by a merger of interests, e.g. the purchase of a leasehold by the freeholder or the **unity of possession** of the dominant and servient tenements associated with an easement. The destruction of a right or contract; the act by which a contract is made void or no longer enforceable or of no legal effect. A debt is extinguished when paid. An easement may be extinguished, not only by 'unity of possession', but by **release, aban-donment**, by express or implied notice, or by statute. See also **accord and satisfaction**.

extortionate credit bargain
see **usury**.

extra coverage insurance (US)
see **extended perils insurance**.

extraction approach (US)
see **abstraction approach**.

extrait (F)
epitome; abstract; summary; certificate.
(*extrait cadastral* – cadastral certificate).

extrinsic
Arising from an external act or cause; not inherent. See also **latent defect**.

exurbanisation (US)
The growth of a town or city beyond its present suburbs. See also **ribbon development**.

F

fabric

The main structure or framework of a building; the carcass or load-bearing part of a building, excluding the doors, windows, services and other finishings. See also **structure**.

fabrique (F)

factory; works.

(*prix de fabrique* – production cost; cost price).

facade

That which is made or appears as the face or front of a building; especially a face (as with a front or flank wall that gives onto a street) which is given a special architectural feature. The wall, or walls, of a building that demonstrate its primary external architectural appearance. See also **elevation**.

facade easement (US)

An easement (or, more strictly, a **restrictive covenant** or 'private zoning') by which an owner of land is prohibited from altering the facade, or exterior, of an existing building. Such a restriction may be imposed usually by a public authority on a building or structure of historic significance in order to preserve its external appearance.

face à face (emprunt) (F)

back-to-back (loan).

face interest rate

see **nominal interest rate**.

face value

1. The value stated on the face of a negotiable instrument or on an insurance policy, i.e. the amount of principal that the issuer of the instrument or the insurer undertakes to pay. The nominal or **par value**, rather than the market value. The face value is used as the basis for calculating interest on a debenture or other form of security. The face value of an interest bearing note may be stated as the principal amount plus any accrued interest.

2. The apparent value of a property, i.e. the value on first impressions.

cf. **book value**, **intrinsic value**.

facilité de credit or *de caisse* (F)

line of credit; facility, especially of a bank overdraft.

facility

A service made available by a bank to assist a customer with his or her business; in particular, an undertaking to provide a loan or overdraft up to a stipulated amount and on stipulated terms. See also **commitment**.

facteur (F)

factor.

factor

1. One who transacts business by taking possession of goods belonging to his principal for the purpose of selling them. A factor is an **agent** in a limited sense, that is, unlike an 'agent' who may transact any business in accordance with his principal's instructions, a factor only buys and sells goods on account of others. A factor may be called also a 'mercantile agent' being one who trades in goods or services, in his own name, and normally, is remunerated by a **commission** on the value of the business transacted. However, "there are two extensive classes of mercantile agents, namely: factors who are entrusted

with the possession as well as the disposal of property; and brokers, who are employed to contract about it without being put in possession". (*Mercantile Law*, by Smith, 13 edn., p. 147). The Sale of Goods Act 1979, s. 26 does not refer to 'factor', but uses the term 'mercantile agent' for an agent who, in the customary course of his business, has authority "either (a) to sell goods, or (b) to consign goods for the purpose of sale, or (c) to buy goods, or (d) to raise money on the security of goods", and such a person is deemed to have possession of the goods, even though he may have actual custody or effective control through another person. This definition excludes those who have possession of goods, such as servants, carriers and warehousemen, but are not authorised to sell them. An **auctioneer** who is entrusted with goods for sale is a factor or merchantile agent. In the US, a factor is called also a 'commission merchant'. See also **broker, lien**.

2. A bank or financial institution that specialises in credit supervision and book keeping services; in particular, the purchase of book debts (accounts receivable) and the granting of loans secured against debts. Upon the purchase of a debt by a factor the creditor receives an immediate cash payment, but the amount of that payment is discounted, i.e. the creditor receives a smaller sum than is due from the debtor, to take account of the risk to the factor of recovering the debt in full. The factor acquires the right to retain the amount actually recovered. Thus, a factor seeks to derive a profit from its more specialised ability at debt collection.

3. Any number which divides exactly into another; or a number which multiplied by one or more other numbers forms a product. A percentage figure expressed as a decimal, or the reciprocal of a **rate of return**. If I = Income, C = Capital value, the factor $F = C/I$. The number used in the capitalisation of an income. See also **capitalisation factor, valuation tables**.

factory
A building, part of a building, or a group of buildings, usually covered, used for the manufacture, assembly or repair of goods or products that generally require the employment of manual or mechanical labour. A place where goods or wares are fabricated, processed or assembled, especially from raw materials. The Factories Act 1961, s. 175 (1) defines a factory as, "any premises in which, or within the close or curtilage or precincts of which, persons are employed in manual labour in any process for or incidental to any of the following purposes, namely, (a) the making of any article or of part of any article; or (b) the altering, repairing, ornamenting, finishing, cleaning or washing or the breaking up or demolition of any article; or (c) the adapting for sale of any article". The Act also includes premises used or associated with slaughtering animals, and s. 175 (2) sets out a list of premises "in which persons are employed in manual labour" which also come within the statutory definition of a factory. The term factory is used synonymously with **workshop**, although the latter term is generally used when referring to smaller premises.
cf. **commercial property**. See also **industrial building, flated factory, overcrowding**.

20 Halsbury's Statutes of England, 4 edn., para. 411 et seq.

Redgrave's Health and Safety in Factories, 2 edn., (1976).

Factories: Planning, Design and Modernisation, by Jolyon Drury, 1981.

factum (L)
1. An act or a **deed**. A written instrument under seal.
2. A fact or statement of fact.

factum est (L)
'It is done'.

faculté (F)
option; **right**.
(*faculté d'achat* – **purchase option**).

faillite (F)
bankruptcy. Used where a *commerçant* is unable to meet his debts but there has been no serious maladministration.
cf. *banqueroute*.

Amos and Walton's Introduction to French Law, 3 edn., p. 370.

fair
A place where people gather at times set by custom or statute for the purpose of displaying, buying or selling goods. A concourse of buyers and sellers, established by Royal prerogative or **franchise**, for the purchase and sale of commodities, with the additional option of a provision for amusement – Wyld *v* Silver [1962] 1 Ch. 570. A fair is similar to a **market**, except that a market is held at more regular and frequent intervals, usually once or twice a week. A fair, therefore, is a market, but a market generally is not a fair (2 Co. Inst. 406). 29 Halsbury's Laws of England, 4 edn., para. 602 et seq.

fair actual value (US)
see **fair market value**.

fair and reasonable value
see **fair market value**.

fair annual value
see **full annual value**.

fair cash value
see **fair market value**.

fair consideration
see **fair value**.

Fair Housing Laws (US)
Federal laws passed to make it illegal to discriminate on grounds of sex, race, colour, religion or national origin when selling or letting residential property. It also made blockbusting illegal (Civil Rights Act 1968).
Real Estate Law, by Robert Kratovil and Raymond J. Werner, 8 edn., pp. 611–623.

fair market rent
see **economic rent, market rent**.

fair market value
A term that is synonymous with **market value** and in the US, is used particularly to refer to the value of property as assessed for condemnation proceedings or for tax assessment purposes. The word 'fair' imports that there is a willing buyer and a willing seller dealing in a market that is not constricted by extraneous factors such as a short-term depression – Daly *v* Nau, (Ind. App.) 339 NE 2d 71. Expressions such as 'fair actual value', 'fair cash value' or 'full cash value', 'fair value', 'fair and reasonable value', 'full market price', convey a similar meaning. See also **assessed value, highest and best use, just compensation**.

fair rent

1. A rent that is assessed by dint of the Rent Act 1977 (or previously the Rent Acts of 1968 and 1974) as being reasonable for a tenancy of a dwelling-house which comes within the ambit of that statute i.e. a **regulated tenancy**. In assessing a fair rent regard is to be had "to all circumstances (other than personal circumstances) and in particular to – (a) the age, character, locality and state of repair of the dwelling-house, and (b) if any furniture is provided for use under the tenancy, the quantity, quality and condition of the furniture". (Rent Act 1977, s. 70(1)). Further, it shall be assessed, "that the number of persons seeking to become tenants of similar dwelling-houses in the locality on the terms (other than those relating to rent) of the regulated tenancy is not substantially greater than the number of such dwelling-houses in the locality which are available for letting on such terms" (1977 Act, s. 70 (2)) – i.e. there is no **scarcity** of comparable properties available to let – Metropolitan Property Holdings *v* Finegold [1975] 1 WLR 349. Thus the rent must be "fair to the landlord and fair to the tenant, and yield on invested capital is not an essential ingredient of the determination [of fair rent]. If comparables are available which do not reflect, or are discounted so as not to reflect, scarcity value, such comparables are the best guide to a fair rent". – Western Heritable Investment Co. Ltd. *v* Husband (1983) 268 EG 266. (A decision based on the Rent (Scotland) Act 1971, s. 42(2) which contains wording akin to the Rent Act 1977). It should be assumed also that the premises are being let with vacant possession, but that the tenant will have security of tenure. When assessing a fair rent it is assumed that the tenant has complied with the terms of his tenancy, and the value of any improvement carried out by the tenant, otherwise than in pursuance of the terms of the tenancy, is disregarded (1977 Act, s. 70(3), as amended by the Housing Act 1980, Sch. 25, s. 41).

Application for the determination of a fair rent is made to the local **rent officer**. Such an application may be made at any stage, either prior to a new letting or a proposal to carry out improvements, or during the course of a tenancy. However, a fair rent is not enforceable until registered at the local Town Hall. Once registered the fair rent, (**registered rent**) is the maximum rent recoverable from a tenant who has a regulated tenancy and, except in special circumstances, this rent cannot be varied within two years of its registration (1977 Act, s. 67, as amended by the Housing Act 1980, s. 60 (1)). See also **certificate of fair rent, premium, rent limit, scarcity value.**

Statutory Valuations, by Andrew Baum, pp. 60–64 (1983).
The Law of Landlord and Tenant, by David Lloyd Evans, 2 edn., pp. 268–271.
Manual of Housing Law, by Andrew Arden, 2 edn., pp. 64–73.
27 Halsbury's Laws of England, 4 edn., para. 731.
Housing Law by Andrew Arden and Martin Partington, pp. 222–249 (1983).
Fair rents – A Practical Guide, by J. Prophet, 3 edn.

2. A rent that is considered fair and reasonable; a **market rent** as contrasted with an exorbitant or **rack**

rent (Terms such as 'fair rent', 'reasonable rent', should be avoided in leases as they are subjective; what is fair to one is not necessarily fair to another. 'Market rent' or 'open market rental value' is to be preferred).

fair value
1. A price paid that is considered fair and reasonable for that which has been obtained. When such a price is the **consideration** payable for something that is transferred under a contract it may be referred to as 'fair consideration'; although the latter term has no legal import. See also **fair market value, fair rent.**
(US) 2. An assessed value established by a public rating board or court for the purpose of determining contributions to the cost of public utilities. See also **assessment.**

fair wear and tear
Deterioration to the fabric of a property due to ageing – "the natural operation of time flowing on effects" – or normal and reasonable tenant use. "Dilapidations caused by friction of the air, dilapidations caused by exposure, and dilapidations caused by ordinary use" – Terrell *v* Murray (1901) 17 T.L.R. 570. A clause in a lease exempting a tenant from 'fair wear and tear' "exempts a tenant from liability for repairs that are decorative and for remedying parts that wear out or come adrift in the course of reasonable use, but it does not exempt him from anything else. If further damage is likely to flow from wear and tear, he must do such repairs as are necessary to stop that further damage". – Regis Property Co. *v* Dudley [1959] AC 410 (a case which restored a principle established in Haskell *v* Marlow [1928] 2 KB 45

whereby a tenant was required to carry out work to prevent further damage to a property e.g. to replace a tile that has fallen off a roof to prevent rain getting in). See also **dilapidation, repair.**

faire (F)
(*faire une avance* – to lend money)
(*faire un placement immobilier* – to make a real estate investment).

fait (L)
A **deed**.

fallow land
Land which has been ploughed and then left unseeded, usually between crop rotations.

falsa demonstratio non nocet cum de corpore constat (L)
'A false description does not vitiate a document when the thing is described with certainty'. Thus, if details contained in a will are not entirely clear this does not prevent the will taking effect if the intention of the devisee can still be ascertained. Similarly, if there is more than one description of land in a conveyance or lease a court may reject one or more of the descriptions, unless it is manifestly inaccurate or absurd so to do; but it need not reject the entire document. "As soon as there is an adequate and sufficient definition, with convenient certainty, of what is intended to pass by a deed, any subsequent erroneous addition will not vitiate it, according to the maxim *falsa demonstratio non nocet*". – Llewellyn *v* Earl of Jersey (1843) 11 M and W 189. Further, it does not matter in what order the true and untrue parts come – Cowen *v* Truefitt Ltd [1899] 2 Ch. 311.

falsification (F)
forgery.

Fannie Mae (US)
see **Federal National Mortgage Association**

farm
1. A tract of land used for agricultural purposes. In common usage, a farm is an area of land used for agriculture, usually including a farmhouse and buildings. Any parcel or parcels of land, including water, used for any form of tilling, artificial cultivation, rearing of animals or pasture. Historically a farm meant land held subject to the payment of money or the rendering of services to the owner. When used in a deed 'farm' was used to indicate that the intention is to pass the freehold and leasehold interest in the subject land and, as a rule, all houses, buildings and tenements associated therewith – Doe d. Belasyse *v* Lucan (1808) 9 East. 448. "The word 'farm' or 'ferme', called in Latine *firma*, is a compound word and doth comprehend many things. And therefore by the grant of a ferme will pass a **messuage** and much land, meadow pasture, wood etc. therunto belonging and therewith used; for the word doth properly signify a capital, or principal messuage and a great quantity of demesnes thereunto appertaining. Also by the grant of all farmes, or all fermes, it seems leases for years do pass." – Termes de La Ley. Although there may be other words in a deed of grant or a will to indicate that a leasehold interest is not to be included. See also **agricultural holding**.
2. To let out or demise for a fixed term at a stated rent. See also *ferme*.

farm-loss payment
A form of disturbance compensation, paid under the Land Compensation Act 1973, ss. 34–36, to a freeholder, or a leaseholder with at least three years unexpired lease, of an 'agricultural unit', for a loss of profit arising as a result of being displaced and obliged to take a new farm, because of action by an authority possessing compulsory purchase powers. Such a payment is assessed solely on the loss of profit due to the move to a new farm and is separate from **compensation for disturbance** paid as a result of a compulsory purchase order. A farm-loss payment is paid only to an occupier of a farm, who is displaced from his entire farm by an authority possessing compulsory purchase powers, provided he takes up a new farm in Great Britain within three years.
Law of Compulsory Purchase and Compensation, by Keith Davies, 4 edn., pp. 217–219.
8 Halsbury's Laws of England, 4 edn., paras. 338–340.

farmworker's house
see **tied accommodation**.

faubourg (F)
suburb.

fausse déclaration (F)
misrepresentation.

feasibility study
1. A financial and economic study of the viability of a proposed plan or development project. A feasibility study usually aims to show the yield or profit from the project by relating the projected revenue (net income or proceeds of sale) to the total cost. See also **appraisal, cost-benefit analysis, residual method of valuation**.

Basic Real Estate Finance and Investment, by D. Epley and J. Millar, pp. 305–323 (1980).

The Appraisal of Real Estate, AIREA, 8 edn., pp. 566–570.

Valuation and Development Appraisal, by Clive Darlow, pp. 138–165 (1982).

How to Conduct and Analyse Real Estate Markets, by G. Vincent Barrett and John P. Blair (1982).

Real Estate Investment Decision Making, by Austin J. Jaffe and C.F. Sirmans (1982).

2. A survey or study carried out to ascertain whether a given area or neighbourhood will support a proposed development project, such as a new shopping centre. See also **catchment area, market survey**.

Federal Home Loan Mortgage Corporation (FHLMC) (US)

A federal agency established in 1970 to acquire mortgages from commercial banks and savings and loan associations. The agency was established to improve the secondary mortgage market, especially for condominiums, by injecting funds into the house mortgage market without providing loans directly to home owners. Known colloquially as Freddie Mac' or 'The Mortgage Corp.'

The McGraw-Hill Real Estate Handbook, edited by Robert Irwin, paras. 6.1–6.12 (1984).

Federal Housing Administration (FHA) (US)

A section of the United States Department of Housing and Urban Development, first established in 1934, which provides private lending institutions with insurance cover on home loans and encourages improvement in housing standards and conditions.

Real Estate Principles, by Bruce Harwood, 2 edn., pp. 223–227.

federal land (US)

Land owned by the US Government.

Federal National Mortgage Association (FNMA) (US)

A federal agency established in 1938 whose principal function is to improve the secondary mortgage market for housing loans, particularly by buying existing mortgage loans and raising money by issuing government-backed debentures. The FNMA specialises in the purchase and sale of mortgages that are insured by the Federal Housing Administration or guaranteed by the Veterans Administration. Commonly abbreviated to 'Fannie Mae'.

A Guide to Fannie Mae, FNMA, (1979).

federal rule (US)

see **before-and-after valuation**.

Fédération International des Géomètres (FIG)

The International Federation of Surveyors. An organisation founded in Paris in 1978 "to group the national associations or organisations of surveyors of all countries with the object of interchanging views on matters of general interest to the profession and generally to foster relations between surveyors". A body that is particularly concerned with surveying, photogrammetry and cartography, as well as land use and land administration. In 1980 this organisation comprised 48 professional bodies throughout the world, including the **Royal Institution of Chartered Surveyors** in the UK; the **American Institute of Real Estate Appraisers** in the US; and the

Ordre des Géométres Expert in France.

Fédération Internationale des Professions Immobilières (FIABCI)

An association originally founded in Paris in 1951 under the title *Fédération Internationale des Administrateurs de Biens, Conseils et Immobiliers* (FIABCI) and now the largest international association of companies and persons practising the real estate profession. The association is now called the *Fédération Internationale des Professions Immobiliers* or the International Real Estate Federation. In 1984 FIABCI embraced 43 member countries and maintained contact with 14 other corresponding countries. The Federation's objectives are "1. Primarily, the study of all aspects of major problems with which the real estate profession is concerned in each country, and of any general solution the Federation can recommend. 2. The pooling and circulation of general and technical information to facilitate professional and public action. 3. The protection of members' interests, and assistance to members whenever the rules of the real estate profession are called into question. 4. Vocational training for the young and extension of their knowledge through international exchange of trainees. 5. Lastly, though very important, guidance of the efforts of the profession to promote the unification and development of real estate policy throughout the world, publicity and communication techniques, town planning and new social patterns."

fee

1. Historically the right of a tenant or vassal to hold land, subject to the acknowledgement of a superior owner or lord. In modern usage, an inheritable **estate** in land. A word that was the same as 'fief', 'feud', or 'feodum' and signified a feudal benefice i.e. land held of a superior lord, or the Crown, subject to the rendering of a payment in kind, such as crops or services. As the **feudal system** of land tenure in England evolved into the modern system of land ownership the word came to signify an absolute estate, in perpetuity, which on the death of an owner was capable of being transferred unconditionally to his or her heirs – the annexation of the word 'simple' signified that the inheritance was unrestricted and any alternative suffix, such as 'tail, 'tail male', 'tail female' indicated that there was a limitation on the line of inheritance. In most states in the US a 'fee' interest is equivalent to a **fee simple**, the more limited estate of a **fee tail** having been abolished, or, as in some states, it was never recognised as capable of being created. In most states the holder of the fee estate is the absolute owner of the land. "An estate of inheritance without condition, belonging to the owner, and alienable by him or transmissible to his heirs absolutely and simply, and is an absolute estate in perpetuity and the largest possible estate a man can have, being, in fact allodial in its nature – Stanton *v* Sullivan, 63 R.I. 216, 7 A. 2d 696, 698, 699." (*Black's Law Dictionary* 5 edn.) See also **base fee, conditional fee, determinable fee, fee simple absolute, manor.**

2. In Scottish law, a 'fee' or 'feu' is a right to hold land from another under a form of feudal tenure subject to the payment of a **feu duty**. The holder of a fee or feu is virtually the owner of the land, as distinguished from the

holder of land subject to a **life rent**. See also **heritable property**.

3. A recompense, normally in the form of a fixed sum of money, paid for the rendering of a professional service or for any other service demanding a special talent or skill, such as a charge for preparing a valuation report. A fee may be distinguished from a **commission** which is contingent upon success. As a rule, a person appointed to perform a professional service is entitled to be paid a reasonable fee for work done within the scope of his or her specialist skill, unless there is an express agreement to the contrary – Miller v Beale (1879) 27 WR 403; Supply of Goods and Services Act 1982, s. 15. See also **commitment fee, contingency fee, finance procuration fee, *quantum meruit*, scale fee**.

fee farm rent

A form of perpetual **rent charge** found especially in Manchester, Bath and Bristol; an annual sum payable upon the purchase of a fee simple interest, generally in lieu of all, or part, of the purchase price. A term originally used to refer to a **chief-rent**. Most forms of fee farm rents were abolished in 1935 and the remainder are being phased out under the provisions of the Rentcharges Act 1977, ss. 1–3. See also **quit rent**.

fee insurance (US)

see **title insurance**.

fee on condition (US)

see **conditional fee simple**.

fee simple

An absolute and unqualified **estate** in land; the highest **freehold** estate that a person can hold in English common law. 'Fee' indicates that the owner is free to hold the land in perpetuity and alienate it without hinderance and if the estate is not disposed of during the owner's life time it passes to the heirs of the owner. 'Simple' indicates that the **heirs** are not limited. One who holds a fee simple is "he which hath land or tenements to hold to him and his heirs for ever" (Co. Litt. 1).

In the US an estate in fee simple is defined as "an estate which (a) has a duration (i) potentially infinite; or (ii) terminable upon an event which is certain to occur but is not certain to occur within a fixed or computable period of time or within the duration of any specified life or lives; or (iii) terminable upon an event which is certain to occur, provided such estate is one left in the conveyor, subject to defeat upon the occurance of the stated event in favour of a person other than the conveyor; and (b) if limited in favour of a natural person would be inheritable by his collateral as well as his lineal heirs". *Reinstatement of the Law of Property*, American Law Institute, Vol. i. para. 14 (1936). An estate in fee simple may be **absolute**, or subject to a condition subsequent or an executory limitation.

A fee simple is the most dominant form of ownership that may be held by a private party under English law; "it confers and since the beginning of legal history it always has conferred, the lawful right to exercise over, upon, and in respect, to the land, every act of ownership which can enter into the imagination, including the right to commit unlimited **waste**". (*The Law of Real Property*, by Challis, 3 edn., p. 218). A fee simple owner, unless curtailed in some way, has the **natural rights** to land; a right of **alie-**

nation; and the right to **use** his land, within the confines of the law. On the other hand, there are limitations placed on any right to land, in particular (i) a liability for any **nuisance**, as well as a **strict liability** to a neighbour; (ii) limitations on the right to **treasure trove** and to certain **minerals** in, on or under the land; (iii) statutory restrictions such as are imposed by planning and public health laws; (iv) rights of others over the land, e.g. the beneficiary of an easement or a tenant; (v) any **restrictive covenant** that has been imposed on land; (vi) limitations on **water rights**; (vii) no entitlement to *res nullius*, things that are incapable of ownership i.e. air, water in natural channels, and wild animals; (viii) the right of alienation, which is limited by a requirement that a disposal by will is subject to a reasonable provision being made for certain relatives of the owner (Inheritance (Provision for Family and Dependants) Act 1975) and by the **rule against perpetuities**. cf. **conditional fee simple, determinable fee simple**. See also **conditional fee simple, fee simple absolute in possession**.

fee simple absolute in possession
The largest unqualified **freehold** estate in land under English law. In theory the owner of this interest has the unrestricted – or absolute – right, in perpetuity, to transfer this estate as long as he or she lives, and thereafter as long as there are heirs capable of taking and then transferring the estate. The word **fee** denotes inheritable (originally land granted "to the use of the purchaser, his heirs and assigns for ever", as a reward for services rendered); 'simple' denotes any class of heirs rather than issue of the donee of

the estate; and 'absolute' denotes that the estate is not limited in time i.e. it will continue in perpetuity, as distinguished from a **qualified fee** which is capable of coming or may be brought to an end on a given condition or the occurence of some event. ('Absolute' does not mean that there are no other rights over the land: it may be subject, for example, to a mortgage or charge). Since 1925 a 'fee simple absolute in possession' is the only form of freehold interest that can exist as a **legal estate** under English law, all other estates being equitable interests (Law of Property Act 1925, s. 1(1)). See also **absolute estate, freehold absolute, possession**.
Introduction to Land Law, by J.G. Riddell, 3 edn., pp. 38–54.
Cheshire's Modern Law of Real Property, 13 edn., pp. 147–161.
39 Halsbury's Laws of England, 4 edn., paras. 392–394.
The Law of Real Property, by Robert Megarry and H.W.R. Wade, 5 edn., pp. 123–129.

fee simple conditional
see **conditional fee simple**.

fee simple defeasible (US)
An estate in land that is equivalent to a **fee simple** but may be brought to an end on the happening of a specified condition. In the US a term that may be used synonymously with **qualified fee**. See also **conditional fee simple**.

fee simple determinable (US)
see **determinable fee simple**.

fee tail
Originally *feodum talliatum*, a fee cut down'; an **entailed interest** or 'entail' – that is, an estate in land of which inheritance is limited to the 'heirs of the body' i.e. to direct lineal

descendants of a donee of the estate. A fee tail may be limited to the male heirs only – a 'tail male'; to the female heirs only – a 'tail female'; to the heirs of a particular marriage – 'tail special'; or it may be unlimited – 'tail general' ('Fee tail' is used frequently as synonymous with an entailed interest; however a fee tail was a form of legal estate in land that existed prior to 1925 and effectively was abolished by the Law of Property Act 1925, s.1 and the term 'entailed interest' is now to be preferred in English law). In the US fee tail is a more common term than entailed interest or entail. However, the fee tail estate has been abolished in most states, having been converted into a **fee simple** or 'fee estate'. See also **base fee**, *De Donis Conditionalibus* **remainder**.

Introduction to Land Law, by J.G. Riddell, 3 edn., pp. 24–27.

The Law of Real Property, by Robert Megarry & H.W.R. Wade, 5 edn., pp. 76–92.

'feed the estoppel'
see **tenancy by estoppel**.

felling direction
An order from the Forestry Commission, requiring an owner to fell certain trees in order to improve the productivity of a forested area (Forestry Act 1967, s. 18).

femme covert (F)
A married woman.

femme sole (F)
An unmarried woman.

fence
Any kind of barrier or division designed entirely, or partially, to enclose land. A barrier or structure intended to act as a means of enclosure, protection or to mark a **boundary line**. A fence may be any visible, tangible obstruction, made of wood, iron, brick or other suitable material. A fence is erected generally by means of posts and boards, sticks, rails or wires. 'Fence' may be used sometimes to refer any barrier designed for similar effect; any thing placed or constructed around land to guard against intrusion and therefore, "in this sense the term includes not only hedges, banks and walls, but also ditches." (4 Halsbury's Laws of England, 4 edn., p. 384).

At common law an owner of land is obliged to fence his land solely to prevent cattle escaping and causing injury to his neighbour – Tenant *v* Goldwin (1704) 1 Salk. 21,360; Sutcliffe *v* Holmes [1947] KB 147. There may also be contractual, prescriptive, or statutory obligations to fence land. For example, when land is sold an obligation may be imposed on the purchaser to fence his land; an owner whose land adjoins a street is obliged to provide a fence to prevent a source of danger to anyone using the street (Highways Act 1980, s. 165); there is a **strict liability** to prevent dangerous things or dangerous animals escaping from land – Rylands *v* Fletcher (1868) LR 3 HL 330; Animals Act 1971, s. 1,2.; and a statutory liability to prevent animals from straying onto the highway (Animals Act 1971, s. 8). A right to have a fence maintained by the owner of adjoining land may arise as a form of **easement** – Crow *v* Wood [1971] 1 QB 34, but there is no automatic right available to a land owner by which he can insist on a fence being erected on adjoining land. See also **enclosure, encroachment, party wall**.

Boundaries and Fences, by V. Powell-

Smith, 2 edn., p. 2 *et seq.*
Boundaries, Walls and Fences, by
Trevor Aldridge, 5 edn.

feodum
Land granted in return for services to
be rendered.
cf. **allodium**. See also **fee, feudal
system**.

feodum talliatum (L)
'A **fee** cut down'. See also **fee tail**.

feoffee to uses
A person to whom a **feoffment** was
made upon certain conditions; one to
whom land was transferred to hold
for the benefit, or **use**, of another (the
cestui que use). At common law the
feoffee was regarded as the owner of
land, but equity came to acknowledge
the rights of any *cestui que use* or **beneficiary**. Thus a feoffee to uses may be
considered as the forerunner of a
modern **trustee**. See also **trust**.

feoffment
An ancient term for the grant of formal and open delivery of possession
of a fee interest in land by the procedure of **livery of seisin**, i.e. by a form
of tangible transfer of possession.
Under the English **feudal system** a
procedure whereby a lord of the
manor recognised the creation of an
estate in perpetuity **(freehold)** rather
than a lesser interest **(copyhold)**. Livery of seisin took place by the delivery
of a clod or twig as a symbol that land
was transferred. Since the Statute of
Frauds 1677 this process has been
replaced by the simpler procedure of
a **conveyance**. See also **deed of grant**.

ferae naturae (L)
'Of a wild nature'; animals that are by
nature wild, e.g. lions. See **strict
liability**.

fetter
To prevent someone doing something. A fetter or 'clog' on a mortgage
prevents the mortgagor exercising his
equity of redemption i.e. repaying the
loan and taking back an unencumbered right to the property. See also
'**once a mortgage, always a mortgage**'.

fermage (F)
rent, of a farm. See also ***affermage,
bail à ferme***.

ferme (F)
1. **farm**.
(*bail à ferme* – farm lease).
2. concession; exclusive licence.

fermeholt
A Lancashire term for a **farm**; an
agricultural holding.

fermier (F)
farmer; lessee or leaseholder, especially of a farm.

feu
see **fee**.

feu-duty
An annual payment for land, found
in Scotland. Similar to a perpetual
rentcharge in England. A term which
derived from a payment to a feudal or
superior lord. Feu duties are being
gradually abolished and new 'feu
rights' can no longer be created. See
also **fee, feu**.

feud or feudum
Under the **feudal system**, an estate in
land held from a superior lord subject
to an obligation to render him services. See also **fee**.

feudal system or **feudalism**
A socio-political and economic system that is based on the strength given
to a privileged class by permitting
them an absolute right to land, and

the bond or allegiance required from a weaker majority who are permitted to hold or use land only at the will of the privileged class. The feudal system depends essentially on the maintenance of the relationship of 'fiefs' and 'vassals'; the fiefs or lords, and ultimately the Sovereign, are the sole landowners and the vassals or tenants have a right or privilege to hold land only for as long as they perform services for the landowner. The feudal system is, primarily, a means by which political power is exerted through the control of the primary source of wealth and production in a rural society, namely **land**, combined with the subordination of one group of people to another. It has been defined as, "a state of society in which the main social bond is the relation between lord and man, a relation implying on the lord's part protection and defence; on the man's part protection, service and reverence, the service including service in arms. This personal relation is inseparably involved in a proprietary relation, the **tenure** of land – the man holds land of the lord, the man's service is a burden on the land, the lord has important rights in the land, and (as we may say) the full ownership of land is split up between man and lord." *Constitutional History of England*, by F.W. Maitland (1926) p. 143. The system arose from the need of small landowners to seek the protection of a more powerful landowner from a common enemy. In medieval Europe a weak landowner surrendered his land to a feudal lord; he received back a right to hold the land *in precarium* (at will) and the protection of the lord, in return for which he undertook to render various services for the

lord. "The occupiers of land were generally bondsmen, whose persons and effects were equally his [the landlord's] property. Those who were not bondsmen were tenants at will, and though the rent which they paid was often nominally little more than quit-rent, it really amounted to the whole produce of the land. Their lord could at all times command their labour in peace and their service in war". (Adam Smith, *The Wealth of Nations*, Book Two, Ch. III).

"The constitution of feuds had its origin from the military policy of the northern or Celtic nations, the Goths, the Hunns, the Franks, the Vandals, and the Lombards, who all migrating from the same *officina gentium*, as Crag very justly entitled it, poured themselves in vast quantities into all regions of Europe at the declension of the Roman empire. It was brought by them from their own countries, and continued in the respective colonies as the most likely means to secure their new acquisitions: and to that end, large districts or parcels were allotted by the conquering general to the superior officers of the army, and by them dealt again in smaller parcels or allotments to the inferior officers and most deserving soldiers. These allotments were called *feoda*, feuds, fiefs, or fees; which last appelation in the northern language signifies a conditional stipend or reward." (Bl. Comm. vol. ii. p. 45). The English system of feudal tenure had its origin in the conquest of 1066 when William, Duke of Normandy, granted to his barons land obtained as a result of his conquest in recompense for their assistance. The barons were obliged to render services to the king, such as to supply knights to keep up his standing army but these 'tenants in chief' were permitted in turn to grant a right of tenure to any number of inferior or 'villein tenants' of their own – a process known as **subinfeudation**. Thus, the holding of land from a superior lord, and ultimately from the Sovereign became the foundation of the feudal relationship. In time the rights of tenure came to be classified according to the type of service rendered. There was 'free tenure', i.e. non servile tenure, which included **knight-service; frankalmoin** or divine service; common **socage** (i.e. the performance of a certain and fixed agricultural service); and 'unfree tenure' or **villeinage** granted to the common peasant in return for servile work. Gradually the superior services were abolished; military and socage tenures were commuted for money payment; and by the Statute *Quia Emptores* 1290 subinfudation was prohibited, so that new tenures could no longer be created and only the existing rights were capable of alienation. The Tenure Abolition Act 1660 converted free tenures into 'free and common socage' or **freehold** tenure in socage. In due course villeinage became known as or was converted to **copyhold**, which might require the payment of money only, with the occupier of the land continuing to hold the land at the will of his lord (he had a copy of the manorial court rolls stating that he had a right to land as long as he performed certain customary duties). The Law of Property Act 1922 finally swept away from England the vestiges of the feudal system, converting any remaining copyhold tenure to freehold and leaving only the **fee simple absolute** as tantamount to absolute ownership of land.

However, the system remains at the root of the English system of land law; so that the principles of the feudal system are so interwoven with every part of the modern system of land law that to attempt to entirely eradicate the past would be to destroy the whole of the present system.
cf. **allodial system**. See also **doctrine of tenure, doctrine of estates, manor**.
Introduction to Land Law, by J.G. Riddell, 3 edn.
An Introduction to the History of the Law of Real Property, by K.E. Digby, 5 edn., pp. 29–61.
A History of English Law, by W.S. Holdsworth, 3 edn., vol. iii. pp. 17–19, 56–78.
The History of English Law, by F. Pollock and F.W. Maitland, 2 edn., pp. 63–73, 296–307.
39 Halsbury's Laws of England, 4 edn., paras. 304–318.

fi. fa. (L)
Abbreviation for *fieri facias*.

fiar
In Scottish law, the owner of a **fee**.

fictitious contract (US)
see **standard-form contract**.

fidelity guaranty
A **guaranty** that is good only up to a specified amount.

fidelity insurance
Insurance against the default or dishonesty of another person, e.g. of an employee or vendor of a property. Fidelity insurance provides a form of insurance and a **surety** for the insured; in a broad sense there is insurance against loss, but in a particular sense if a loss arises there is a surety to

cover that loss. See also **utmost good faith**.

fiduciare (F)
fiduciary; trustee.

fiduciary
1. An individual, corporation or association that is in a position of **trust**, or has power and authority, with respect to another. The term originates from Roman law where a fiduciary was a person who had authority to act on trust for another. In general usage a fiduciary may be a **personal representative**, guardian, **agent** or **trustee**.
2. A relationship where one party acts in good faith on behalf of another in a transaction. A person acting in a fiduciary capacity should not make a personal profit as a result of his position, but should act primarily for the benefit of the party he represents and should not be placed in any situation that conflicts with his position of trust. "It is quite clear that if an agent uses *property*, with which he has been entrusted by his principal, so as to make a profit for himself out of it, without his principal's consent, then he is accountable for it to his principal, see Shallcross *v* Oldham (1862) 2 Johns. and Hem. 609. So also if he uses a *position of authority*, to which he has been appointed by his principal, so as to gain money by means of it for himself, then also he is accountable to the principal for it, see Reading *v* Attorney-General [1951] AC 507, 516. Likewise with *information* or *knowledge* which he has been employed by his principal to collect or discover, *or which he has otherwise acquired*, for the use of his principal, then again if he turns it to his own use, so as to make a profit by means of it

himself, he is accountable..." – Phipps *v* Broadman [1965] Ch. 1018. See also **undue influence**.

fiduciary loan
An unsecured loan; a loan based entirely on **trust**. See also **fiduciary**.

fief
An estate or a lord under the **feudal system**; a **fee** or **feud**.

fief (F)
fee; fief.
(*franc-fief* – free tenure).

fief-tenant
The holder of a **fee** interest under the **feudal system** of land tenure.

field garden allotment
A small patch of land turned over to domestic horticulture and gardening; in particular, land appropriated as a form of **allotment** for the use of the labouring poor following the enclosure of lands or the regulation of a common under an Inclosure Act (Inclosure Act 1845, s. 31; Town and Country Planning Act 1971, s. 290(1)). Usually this was land that formed part of the **wasteland** of a manor and had been cultivated as a garden or fuel allotment. After the **enclosure** of the wasteland this land was let to the poor of the parish usually in plots of under a quarter of an acre.

fieri facias (L)
'Cause (it) to be made'. A writ of *fieri facias* (or *fi. fa.*) is a writ of execution requiring a sheriff to whom it is addressed to levy **distress** on goods and chattels for the amount owed by a judgement debtor. "Derived from the words in the writ by which the sheriff is commanded, **quod fieri faciat de bonis**, that he cause to be made of the goods and chattels of the

defendant the sum or debt recovered." (Bl. Comm. vol. iii. p. 417).

figuring (US)
Taking-off quantities or estimating costs from a drawing. See also **bill of quantities.**

filed plan
A **plan** used for the registration of the title to a particular parcel of land and on which the general boundaries of the subject land are usually edged red. The filed plan is sewn up with a **Land Certificate** or **Charge Certificate** and forms a part thereof. It is not intended to show the exact boundaries of the land, but only to support the written description of the registered land (Land Registration Act 1925, s. 76). Other matters affecting registered land are coloured in different ways, e.g. green edging for land removed from a title, brown tint for land over which the land has a right of way. *Registered Conveyancing*, by Ruoff and Roper, 4 edn., pp. 46–48. *Registered Land Practice Notes*, Joint Advisory Committee of the Law Society and H.M. Land Registry, (1982/83 ed.,) pp. 22–24.

filling station
A place at which petrol or gasoline is stored and supplied to the public for immediate use in motor vehicles. It may serve also as an area for the repair, service, or for the sale of motor vehicles or accessories. In the US commonly called a 'gas station'. See also **garage, service station.**

filum (L)
see *ad medium filum; ad medium filum aquae.*

final certificate
see **building certificate.**

final completion
see **substantial performance.**

finance
Money or credit supplied for a business or enterprise. The **capital** provided as a loan to a company or individual. See also **debt capital, financing.**

finance fee
see **finance procuration fee.**

finance house
A type of company that specialises in making loans for more speculative investments, e.g. hire purchase, property development, leasing. 'Finance house' may be used to refer to any merchant bank, although strictly it should be applied only to members of the Finance Houses Association.

finance lease
1. A **lease** normally of equipment, plant or machinery, granted for a non-cancellable term which is based on a major part of the asset's economic life, at a rent that is sufficient to amortise the capital cost, plus interest on the outstanding capital. The 'lessee' takes possession of the asset and is responsible for repair, maintenance and insurance throughout the term of the lease. The lease agreement normally permits the lessee to acquire the asset at the end of the term for a nominal amount. Strictly, in English law this form of agreement is not a lease but a form of **hire-purchase agreement.**
cf. **operating lease.** See also *crédit bail,* **leasing.**
Commercial Law, by R.W. Goode, pp. 833–848 (1982).
Finance Leasing, by Graham Hubbard (1980).
2. A lease by which the rent (a **finance rent**) is calculated to amortise

the cost of the subject property, together with accrued interest. Called also a 'full-payout lease'.

financement (F)
financing.

finance procuration fee
A **commission** paid to an agent or broker for arranging terms for a suitable loan which assists a person in paying for a property i.e. a fee paid to a middleman for procuring equity or debt capital. Variously referred to as a 'mortgage placement fee', 'mortgage service charge', a 'finance fee', a 'brokerage fee' or a 'finders fee'. See also **origination fee**.

finance rent
A rent that is calculated as being sufficient to repay, or amortise, the cost of a property or any other asset, together with accumulated interest, over the period during which the rent is payable, i.e. a rent calculated on the basis of a **sinking fund**. See also **leasing, finance lease**.

financial institution
An organisation established by law to conduct the business of granting finance. The organisation may be a bank, building society, trust company, public or private mortgage company or any other major institutional investor that provides capital for a business or enterprise.

financial leverage
The use of borrowed money to increase the size of investment that can be acquired, i.e. pure **leverage** as distinguished from **operating leverage**.

financial statement
A statement showing the **balance sheet**, and the profit and loss position,

of an enterprise at a point in time. See also **operating statement**.

financing
The use of borrowed **capital** or funds for a project, enterprise, company or individual. Any one of several methods used to obtain or supply money or credit for a business or venture.

The principal methods of direct real estate financing are (i) a **bridging loan** or **interim loan**; (ii) a loan secured by a **mortgage, debenture** or any other form of **bond**; (iii) a **forward commitment**; (iv) a **sale and lease-back** (and variations thereon) – or any combination thereof. In the US real estate finance is obtainable also by means of an **instalment sale** (land contract). Indirect financing may be obtained by issuing shares in a property company or any similar vehicles, such as an investment trust.
Essential Real Estate Finance, by David Sirota, 3 edn.
Financing Real Estate: Principles and Practice, by Sherman J. Maisel, (1965).
Real Estate Finance, by William Brueggeman (1981).
Real Estate Finance, by John D. Weidemer, 4 edn.
Financing Real Estate, by J.H. Boykin (1979).
Office Development, by Paul and Paula Marber, Ch. 7 (1985).

financing charges
Interest charges, but not capital repayments, incurred in purchasing or developing property. See also **carrying charges**.

financing statement (US)
A public record that a person has a

charge or **lien** on personal property. This has the effect of protecting a lender, even if the item is affixed to real property so as to become a fixture.

finder's fee

Commission paid to an agent or broker for finding a purchaser or introducing a seller of property. A **fee** paid to an individual for finding a source of finance that is made available to a third party. Called also a 'procuration fee' or 'referral fee'. See also **brokerage, finance procuration fee, prospective purchaser**.

fine

1. An amount of valuable consideration given or required as the price for something, such as the price for the grant of consent to the grant, renewal or assignment of a lease. "The phrase 'in the nature a fine', when applied to the case of obtaining consent to assign, means nothing more than 'paid as the price for' such consent." – Waite *v* Jennings [1906] 2 KB 18. A fine may include 'a premium or foregift and any payment, consideration, or benefit in the nature of a fine, premium or foregift' (Law of Property Act 1925, s. 205(1) (xxiii).

2. A payment made under the **feudal system** of land tenure to a lord. In particular, a monetary payment exacted when consent was granted to alienate land. Fines of this kind were abolished in 1660 (Tenures Abolition Act, 1660).

3. An ancient form of conveyance of land whereby an interest in land was partially brought to an end by a collusive action and then acknowledged to belong to another. Abolished by the Fines and Recoveries Act 1833.

Fine Arts Commission
see **Royal Fine Arts Commission**.

fire certificate

A certificate issued by a Fire Authority (the Greater London Council, a county council or a combination of county councils) confirming that commercial premises comply with the authority's requirements on such matters as user, means of escape and access thereto in case of fire; fire fighting equipment; fire alarms; and number of occupiers on the premises at any one time. A fire certificate is required for any premises put to a 'designated use'. That includes a factory, shop, office or railway property, where more than 20 persons are employed (and any factory where inflammable materials or explosives are kept); most hotels, hostels or similar establishments; cinemas, theatres, exhibition halls, dance clubs and the like; hospitals, residential homes and similar institutions; schools and other training establishments; and dwelling-houses where the occupants may be subject to a greater than normal risk in case of fire, e.g. boarding houses. A fire certificate must be obtained by an occupier of such premises (or the owner in the case of multi-occupied premises) and displayed on the premises. Regular occupiers of the premises must be made familiar with the means of escape from the premises in case of fire and a record kept of their instruction or training for that purpose. The certificate is intended to safeguard the day-to-day use of a property by members of the public rather than to impose controls on building construction. (Fire Precaution Act 1971, as amended by the Health and Safety at Work Act 1974,

s. 78 and extended by the Fire Precautions (Hotel and Boarding Houses) Order 1972.) See also **building regulations**.

The Property Manager's Guide to Fire Legislation in Commercial and Industrial Property (1981).

Fire and Building, by The AQUA Group, pp. 101–107 (1984).

18 Halsbury's Laws of England, 4 edn., paras. 436–446.

fire insurance
Insurance which provides protection against damage or loss of property caused by fire. Fire insurance is the principal form of insurance provided in respect of real estate. It provides an idemnity against the cost of repairing or replacing a building that is destroyed or damaged by an accidental fire, including any consequent damage to the property of a third party.

A house owner is not liable for accidental damage caused to a third party by the escape of fire unless caused by negligence or a fire that is started deliberately. (Fire Prevention (Metropolis) Act 1774, s. 86 – which, in spite of the name, applies to all of England and Wales.)

A person who has contracted to acquire (by purchase or exchange) a property is entitled to the proceeds of any payment made under a fire insurance policy upon completion of the purchase (or exchange), unless there is an express provision in the contract to the contrary, provided any requisite consent of the insurer has been obtained to the sale and the purchaser has paid the proportionate part of the insurance premium from the date of the contract (Law of Property Act 1925, s. 47). See also **consequential loss insurance, replacement cost**.

Elements of Insurance, by W.A. Dinsdale and D.C. McMurdie, 5 edn., p. 70.

Handbook of Insurance, by R.L. Carter, sec. 3.2, (1982, updated).

firebote
see **estover**.

firm
An unincorporated organisation or business entity; usually a **partnership**. The persons who collectively make up a partnership (Partnership Act 1890, s. 5).
cf. **corporation**.

firm-price contract
see **fixed-price contract**.

first and general mortgage bond (US)
A mortgage bond secured as a **first mortgage** on certain properties of a corporation and as a general or **floating charge** on the remaining properties.

first floor
The first level, being at least one full floor height, above the ground floor. In US commonly applied to the first level at, or immediately above, ground level. See also **ground floor**.

first in time
see **priority**.

first-loss insurance
Insurance that covers for losses only up to a maximum specified amount, which is less than the insured's total potential loss. The insurer is informed of the full value of the property that is the subject of the insurance policy and this is taken into account in assessing the premium, but the insurer provides an **indemnity** for only the most vulnerable percentage of the potential loss. First-loss insurance may refer also to insurance that

is provided on the basis that the indemnity is not reduced to take account of depreciation – although such insurance is more commonly called 'new-for-old insurance'. See also **excess, valued policy**.

first mortgage
A mortgage that has **priority** over all other mortgages or liens, whether taken out before or after the grant of another mortgage. In the US called also a 'senior mortgage'.
cf. **second mortgage**.

first refusal, right of
see **right of first refusal**.

first right to buy
see **right of first refusal**.

first-year allowance
A form of **capital allowance** granted for capital expenditure incurred on plant or machinery – 100 per cent of 'qualifying expenditure' may be set off against a liability to income or corporation tax in the first year of it being incurred by a person carrying on trade or profession. From 1984 first-year capital allowances are to be progressively reduced until they are phased out in 1986.
cf. **initial allowance**.

fiscal zoning (US)
see **exclusionary zoning**.

fish, right to
see **right to fish**.

fit for human habitation
Intended to be, or capable of being lived in, without having any serious effect on the occupier's health or safety. Accommodation that is 'fit for habitation' usually provides a reasonable degree of comfort, essential facilities for living and proper sanitary amenities.
cf. **unfit for human habitation**. See also **furnished tenancy, implied covenant, implied term, repair**.

fit for the purpose
As a rule in English law there is no **implied covenant** in a lease that premises are fit for the purpose for which they are let. However, there may be an implied covenant that arises as a result of the nature of the letting and there is an implied term in a contractual licence permitting someone to use a property to the effect that proper use can be made of that property. See also **fit for human habitation, repair**.

fitting-out allowance
A sum of money or concession granted to a tenant by a landlord to cover the cost, in whole or in part, of preparing leased premises for occupation. This allowance covers the cost of such items as partitioning, carpeting, electrical installations, etc. In the US, called also a 'construction allowance'. See also **rent concession**.

fittings
see **fixtures and fittings**.

fixe (F)
(*meuble à fixe demeure* – landlord's fixture; see *immeuble par destination*)
(*contrat à prix fixe* – **fixed price contract**)

fixed asset
A tangible but immovable **asset** acquired for the running of a business and which cannot be, or is not intended to be, readily converted into cash; in particular, real property, fixtures, fittings, plant, tools, machinery, etc. An asset that is required

permanently for the running of a company, as distinguished from a **current asset** which is intended for trading purposes. Called also a 'capital asset'. See also **depreciation, fixed capital**.

fixed capital

Capital acquired by a company and retained in the form of assets that are not intended to be used up, but are employed to produce the profit or income for which the capital has been subscribed. "That which a company retains, in the shape of assets upon which subscribed capital has been expended, and which assets either themselves produce income ... or ... are made use of to produce income, gain or profit." It may· be distinguished from 'circulating' or **working capital** which is intended to be "used by being temporarily parted with and circulated in business, in the form of money, goods or other assets, and which, or the proceeds of which, are intended to return to the company with an increment, and are intended to be used again and again, and to always return with some accretion". – Ammonia Soda Company *v* Chamberlain [1918] 1 Ch. 286–287. See also **fixed asset**.

fixed charge

1. A charge on a specified property e.g. on a parcel of land, or a particular asset.
cf. **floating charge**.
2. See **fixed expense**.

fixed expense

An expense of running a property that does not vary with the degree of use or occupancy of that property and must be paid when it falls due, e.g. the expense of servicing a loan, an in-surance premium and most property taxes. Called sometimes a 'fixed charge'.
cf. **variable expenses**.

fixed-fee contract
see **cost-plus contract**.

fixed lease (US)
1. A lease which provides for the payment of a **flat rent**.
2. See **gross lease**.

fixed option
An **option** to buy a property at a price that is fixed for a given period of time from when the option is granted. See also **call option, put option**.

fixed-payment mortgage
see **amortisation mortgage**.

fixed-principal-payment mortgage
A mortgage loan which provides that repayments of principal are fixed at a constant amount, with interest payable on the outstanding balance; accordingly, the total payments of principal and interest vary throughout the term of the loan.
cf. **flexible-payment mortgage**.

fixed-rate mortgage (FRM)
A mortgage loan on which interest is charged at a fixed rate throughout the period of the loan. Called also a 'flat-rate mortgage'.
cf. **variable-rate mortgage**.

fixed rent
see **base rent, dead rent, flat rent**.

fixed-term tenancy
A tenancy for a specified period of time, e.g. a tenancy for a 'term of years'. A tenancy that cannot be brought to a premature end by notice – British Broadcasting Corpn *v* Ioannou [1975] 2 All ER 1005.
cf. **periodic tenancy**. See also **short-**

hold tenancy, tenancy for a fixed period.

fixed-price contract

A contract to provide goods or services at a definite predetermined price. For example, a building contract in which the contractor accepts an obligation to complete work at an agreed and unalterable sum. A fixed-price contract may be either a single 'lump-sum contract' or a 'measurement contract'. A lump-sum contract normally provides that there will be no variation in the price, although the term may be used to refer to a contract in which the price fluctuates according to an external indicator e.g. a construction price index. A measurement contract provides a schedule of agreed prices or rates which are applied on completion of the contract to the measured quantity of work done. When there is no provision for any fluctuation in the price, or in the quantities that are considered to have been used, the contract may be referred to also as a 'firm-price contract'.

cf. **cost-reimbursement contract**. See also **package-deal contract, turn-key contract**.

fixture

An item of a personal nature that has been so attached or wrought into land, or a building on land, that it loses its independent identity and becomes part and parcel of the realty. Any chattel which has been affixed to land in such a way that, in the view of the law, it has taken on a nature that makes it part of the land loses its character as a **chattel**; it becomes a part of, and passes with, the ownership, of land. Ultimately a fixture becomes the property of the owner of

the freehold. A 'fixture' is something affixed as an accessory; it does not include materials that were made part of a building during the course of its construction – Boswell v Crucible Steel Co. [1925] 1 KB 123.

A fixture may not be removed by an occupier or a tenant of land, even though initially it was the property of that party; unless the consent of the owner, or a person who has contracted to be the owner, has been obtained or unless there is a statutory provision which overrules the dictum established by common law. The premise for the irremovability of a fixture is founded on the maxim *quidquid plantatur solo, solo cedit*, 'whatever is affixed to soil, belongs to the soil'.

In determining what constitutes a fixture, it is necessary to consider (a) the degree of annexation to land or to a building; and (b) the purpose or object of the annexation. There must be a union between the chattel and the freehold; if there is no physical annexation there is no fixture, although an object resting on the ground by its own weight alone can be a fixture provided it is clearly intended to form an adjunct to the soil or a building thereon – Holland v Hodgson (1872) LR 7 CP 335; Snedeker v Waring (1854) 12 NY 170. Thus, the second test (object and purpose of annexation) is more likely than the first (degree of annexation) to be decisive. "Perhaps the enduring significance of the first test is a reminder that there must be some degree of physical annexation before a chattel can be treated as part of the realty." – Berkley v Poulett (1977) 241 EG 913. When the intention is to improve the property permanently the chattel will become a fixture, but if it is well secured purely to ensure its proper safety, use or better enjoyment it is likely to remain a chattel – "the question is not whether the thing itself is easily removed but whether it is an essential part of the building itself". – D'Eyncourt *v* Gregory (1866) LR 3 Eq. 396. Nonetheless, the onus must be on the person who affixed it to show that it was intended all along to continue as a chattel, or (especially if the chattel is fixed only by its own weight) for the owner of the land to show that it has ceased to be a chattel (Holland *v* Hodgson, *supra.*).

In the final analysis what constitutes a fixture is a question of intention, which is to be determined by the facts in each case. An item fixed solely by its own weight generally remains a chattel; and an item moulded into a scheme of ornamentation, so that scheme would be wholly inadequate without it, usually becomes a fixture. However, both these propositions may be reversed if that would lend better credence to the predetermination of the parties. In English law items held to remain chattels include light bulbs; a valuable tapestry fixed with battens as of necessity to the wall of a private residence; an ornamental chimney piece; seats bolted in the auditorium of a theatre; an army hut bolted in sections to a concrete foundation. A plumbed in washing machine, a gas fire, a fitted carpet, and a bedroom headboard must each be fixed for its proper enjoyment, but none of these is intended normally to enhance, or become an essential part of the freehold. Items held to have become fixtures include a tapestry set into the wall as part of the design and decoration of a house; seats secured

to the floor of a cinema hall; 436 power looms installed in a mill; door and window fastenings; gratings to sinks and gulleys; and statues and stone garden seats secured by their own weight but forming part of a formal garden design. Thus, there are no hard and fast rules that may be used to decide if a chattel has become a fixture, as Lord Lindley said in Reynolds *v* Ashby [1904] AC 473–74: "My Lords, I do not profess to be able to reconcile all the cases on fixtures, still less all that has been said about them. In dealing with them attention must be paid not only to the nature of the thing and to the mode of attachment, but to the circumstances under which it was attached, the purpose to be served and . . . to the position of the rival claimants to the thing in dispute."

In most states in the US the courts have adopted the question of intention as the primary test in deciding whether an item has become a fixture. Thus, an air conditioning unit or a gas stove, although it may be easily removed, is frequently installed as an essential item in an apartment and, therefore, is clearly intended as a fixture – State Mutual *v* Trautwein (1967) 414 SW 2d. 587, 43 ALR 2d 1378; Mortgage Bond Co. *v* Stephens (1937) 181 Okl. 419, 74 P 2d. 361.

Even when a chattel has been so affixed to premises as to be classifiable as a fixture, it may be possible for the person who fixed it to remove it because of a covenant or agreement, a common law rule or, in particular, a rule of statute law. Accordingly a fixture attached to land or a building for the purpose of a tenant's trade or business – a **trade fixture** – has been considered by common law as *prima* *facie* removable; it is presumed that there is no intention to make the 'trade' fixture a permanent part of the realty – Fisher *v* Dixon (1845) 12 Cl and F 312. This common law rule does not apply to fixtures installed for the purpose of farming – Elwes *v* Maw (1802) 3 East 38, but statute law gives the tenant of an agricultural holding a right to remove certain items – **agricultural tenant's fixtures** – up to two months after the end of his tenancy (Agricultural Holding Act 1948, s. 13). Items that a tenant has a right to remove (either because they are installed for convenience, as a trade fixture, or as an agricultural tenant's fixture) are referred to as 'tenant's fixtures', and those that he may not remove, whether fixed by the landlord or the tenant, are referred to as 'landlord's fixtures'.

The right of a tenant to remove fixtures is limited to the duration of the lease (with the exception of the extended period granted to an agricultural tenant) so that, at the end of a lease, when a tenant leaves and gives up any right to possession of the leased premises, all fixtures from that time forth become the property of the landlord – Barff *v* Probyn (1895) 64 LJQB 557, whether they were affixed so as to become part of the realty, or whether they were fixed for the tenant's enjoyment or for trade purpose (generally if a lease is renewed the position remains unaltered until the tenant finally gives up possession).

A **conveyance** of land passes all fixtures (but not chattels) to the purchaser, unless they are expressly reserved by the vendor (Law of Property Act 1925, s.62 (1); as does a transfer of land by will – Re. Whaley [1908] 1 Ch. 615 – rules which apply to items which would, as between landlord and tenant, be considered as tenant's fixtures. A mortgagee's right to land includes fixtures annexed thereto, even though they are not specified in the mortgage deed, and the mortgagee acquires a right to items annexed by the mortgagor after he takes possession; again this rule includes items that would be 'tenant's fixtures' – Longbottom *v* Berry (1869) LR 5 QB 137. See also **appurtenance, compensation for improvements, emblements, Uniform Commercial Code.**

Real Estate Law, by Robert Kratovil and Raymond J. Werner, 8 edn., pp. 18–25.

Real Property, by William E. Burby, 3 edn., pp. 21–31.

The Law of Landlord and Tenant, by David Lloyd Evans, 2 edn., pp. 224–232.

Adkin's *Landlord and Tenant*, 18 edn., pp. 260–267.

Megarry's Manual of the Law of Real Property, 6 edn., pp. 19–23.

The Law of Real Property, by Robert Megarry and H.W.R. Wade, 5 edn., pp. 730–738.

Cheshire's Modern Law of Real Property, 13 edn., pp. 136–141.

Landlord and Tenant Law, by David Yates and A.J. Hawkins, pp. 38–43 (1981).

27 Halsbury's Laws of England, 4 edn., paras. 142–155

Woodfall's Landlord and Tenant, 28 edn., paras. 1–1545 to 1–1579.

Adkin & Bowen on Fixtures, 3 edn.

fixtures and fittings

A term commonly used in a contract for the sale of land, in a conveyance, or in a lease to refer to items that are the subject of sale or lease, either because they are considered in law to be fixtures or it has been expressly agreed that these items will be included as part of the realty. The term 'fittings' generally is used to refer to chattels that are not part of the realty (but pass when it is transferred) and fixtures to things that are, or have become, part of the realty (and must by definition, pass when it is transferred). See also **fixture**.

flat

1. Derived from the Old English *flet*, storey, house or building and used originally in Scotland to refer to premises on one level. In modern usage a separate set of premises, usually but not necessarily on the same floor, constructed or adapted for use as a house or building that comprises other similar premises which are divided horizontally one from another. The living accommodation may be entirely self contained or certain facilities within the building may be shared. Unlike a **dwelling-house** in which the entrance to the outside and the internal entrance to the accommodation normally is coincident, the internal entrance to the accommodation that comprises the flat is entirely separate to the outside entrance of the house or building that contains the flat. In most English statutes 'flat' is given a similar definition to that set out above (Housing Act 1964, s. 44(1); Housing Finance Act 1972, s. 90(12)). For the purpose of statutory control of service charges a flat is "a separate set of premises, whether or not on one floor which (a) forms part of a building; and (b) is divided horizontally from some other part of that building; and (c) is contained or

adapted for the purposes of a dwelling and is occupied wholly or mainly as a separate private dwelling". (Housing Act 1980, Sch.19 s. 16). In English common law (following the Scottish usage), a flat may be considered as a **house** – Grant *v* Langston [1900] AC 392; but for the purpose of leasehold enfranchisement, it is expressly excluded from the definition of a house (Leasehold Reform Act 1967, s. 2(2) (a)). See also **apartment, flying freehold, maisonette, tenement**.

Sale and Management of Flats – Practice and Precedents, by J. Cawthorn (1985)
The Sale of Flats, by E.F. George and A. George, 5 edn.
The Law of Flats, by Trevor Aldridge, (1982).

2. An area of land covered with water that is too shallow for commercial navigation.

flat cost
The cost of labour and materials, but not overheads or profit, as applied in a building estimate or contract. See also **cost-reimbursement contract**.

flat lease (US)
see **gross lease**.

flat loan
see **standing loan**.

flat-rate mortgage
see **fixed-rate mortgage**.

flat rent
A rent that is fixed for the term of a lease. Sometimes referred to as a 'fixed rent'; although a flat rent may be fixed for only part of the term of the lease. In the US, a lease containing a flat rent is referred to as a 'flat-rental lease', or sometimes a 'fixed lease'.

cf. **variable rent**. See also **base rent, dead rent, gross lease**.

flat-rental lease (US)
see **flat rent**.

flat scheme
A term for a scheme of development when applied to a block of flats. See also **flying freehold**.

flat yield
see **running yield**.

flated factory
A factory forming part of a building that is constructed or adapted by horizontal sub-division for multiple-occupation or for use as separate industrial units. Each unit or factory occupies all or part of a floor of the multi-storey building and may enjoy the use of other areas in the building in common with other occupiers. Called also a 'tenement factory'. See also **common parts**.

flexible-payment mortgage
see **variable-payment mortgage**.

flexible-rate mortgage
see **variable-rate mortgage**.

flight easement (US)
see **avigation easement**.

flip-sale (US)
see **sub-sale**.

float
The range within which a variable interest rate on a mortgage loan may be permitted to change. For example, a rate may be fixed at 3 per cent above a given base rate, but have a floor of 8 per cent and a ceiling of 20 per cent. A rate which has no such limits is called a 'full float'. See also **variable-rate mortgage**.

floating asset
An asset that is continually changing or is consumed in the course of the operation of a business, e.g. money, stocks.
cf. **fixed asset**. See also **current asset**.

floating capital
Capital used by a company to meet current or recurring expenditure. See also **working capital**.

floating charge
A **charge** on all the assets of a company, present and future, rather than on any specific property. A floating charge does not prevent a company dealing with its assets in the normal course of business. However, a floating charge may be converted, in accordance with the terms of the agreement by which it is created, to a specific or **fixed charge** if the company ceases to be a going-concern; acts outside its usual course of business; or if the party holding the charge has a right to intervene and take steps to pin down its charged assets. – Government Stock and Other Securities Investment Co. Ltd. *v* Manila Railway Co. Ltd [1897] AC 86. A floating charge "is ambulatory and hovers over property until some event occurs which causes it to settle and crystallise into a specific charge". – Barker *v* Eynon [1974] All ER 905.

"If a charge has three characteristics that I [Romer L.J.] am about to mention it is a floating charge: (1) if it is a charge on a class of assets of a company present and future; (2) if that class is one which, in the ordinary course of business of the company would be changing from time to time; and (3) if you find that by the charge it is contemplated that, until some future step is taken by or on behalf of those interested in the charge, the company may carry on its business in the ordinary way as far as concerns the particular class of asset I am dealing with." – Houdsworth *v* Yorkshire Woolcombers Association [1903] 2 Ch. 295.

A floating charge must, by its nature, be an equitable charge and cannot be registered; although it can be protected by a notice or caution entered on the Land Register. A floating charge on the assets of a company must be registered with the Registrar of Companies (Companies Act 1948, s. 95(1), (2)). See also **debenture**.

Company Law, by Ranking and Spicer, 12 edn., p. 212–229.
Commercial Law, by R.M. Goode, (1982) pp. 786–803.

floating interest rate
A rate of interest which varies at short term intervals, frequently daily, according to money-market conditions. See also **float, variable-rate mortgage**.

floor area
The surface area of a particular building measured at one level of the building or the aggregate of all such levels. The floor area of a building may be measured in a number of different ways; for example, as the **gross external area**, the **gross internal area**, the **net internal area**, or the **rentable area**. See also **gross internal area, gross lettable area, gross floor area, net floor area, net retail area, net sales area, net usable area, sales area**.

floor area ratio (or index) (FAR) (US)
see **plot ratio**.

floor loan (US)
An amount of money which a lender agrees to advance, but not to exceed

until a given condition has been met by the borrower. The residue of the advance may be withheld until certain contingencies are met; for example, until completion of the letting of a certain percentage of a building.
cf. **ceiling loan**. See also **gap financing, hold-back**.

floor lot ratio (US)
see **plot ratio**.

floor plan
A **plan** showing the detailed layout of a building or part of a building at one particular level.

floor price
The lowest price at which a vendor will contract to sell a property.
cf. **asking price, ceiling price**. See also **reserve price**.

floor space index (FSI)
The ratio of the **gross external area** of a building above ground to its total **site area** extended to include half the width of surrounding roads, i.e. the gross site area. An index established to control the density of new development on a given site, especially for high-rise buildings.
cf. **plot ratio**.

flotsam
Goods from a sunken ship that are found floating in the sea and have no apparent owner – Constable's Case (1601) 5 Co. Rep. 106a. Such property if unclaimed within a prescribed statutory period belongs to the Crown.
cf. **jetsam**. See also *res nullius*.

flowage easement (US)
A right or **easement** acquired by the State to flood an area of land either as a permanent 'easement in gross' or as temporary right for water to flow

over the land for the benefit of adjoining land. The water does not have to flow in defined water course and may vary its course or level from time to time. See also *jus spatiendi*.

fluctuation clause (US)
see **escalator clause.**

'flying freehold'
A **freehold** interest in a part of a building excluding any right to ownership of the ground, e.g. a freehold flat at an upper floor level. In English law the ownership of **land** may extend above the ground to include different storeys of a building and, therefore, the right to a freehold may be granted in stratas of a property, such a right being referred to as a 'flying freehold'. "A man may have an inheritance in an upper chamber though the lower buildings and soil be in another."(Co. Litt. 486). (Strictly, the term 'flying freehold' does not exist in English law, but is a colloquial term for a freehold interest in an upper story of a building). The owner of the freehold unit must have right of access, support and shelter and usually enters into a **scheme of development** (or 'flat scheme') whereby the other owners of the building accept mutual positive covenants, such as to repair and maintain the building, and restrictive covenants regarding user, rebuilding, etc. A management company commonly is employed to look after the building and ensure that the owners comply with their obligations. (English law does not have **condominium ownership** but recognises this form of interest in part of a building as the nearest equivalent. However, flying freeholds are rare because of the difficulty in English law of enforcing covenants between successive owners of adjoining property. A right to a part of a multi-occupied building is held more usually as a long-term lease, or the entire property is held in **co-ownership** in trust for each beneficiary who is granted a right to occupy a part of the property). See also **collective ownership, quasi-easement, right of support.**
The Sale of Flats, by E.F. George and A. George, 4 edn.

folcland or folkeland
Land which, prior to the Norman Conquest (1066), was held by the common folk or people, whether in common or severalty and, although it may have been granted for a period of time, it could not be alienated in perpetuity but eventually reverted to the community.
cf. **charter land.**

foncier (f.-ère) (F)
landed, i.e. relating to land.
(*amelioration foncière* – land improvement; **betterment**)
(*bail foncier* – ground lease)
(*bien foncier* – real estate)
(*impôt foncier* – **property tax**; land tax)
(*Credit Foncier de France* – a savings institution specialising in mortgage loans that is similar to an English building society)
(*petite propriété foncière* – **smallholding**)
(*propriétaire foncier* – landowner)
(*propriété foncière* – landed property; land holding)
(*rente foncière* – **ground rent**).

fondé de pouvoir (F)
proxy; attorney; authorised representative.

fondé de procuration (F)
proxy; agency.

fonds (F)
1. **capital; fund;** assets:
(*fonds d'amortissement* – **sinking fund**)
(*fonds de roulement* – **working capital**)
(*fonds de placement* – **investment trust, mutual fund**)
(*bailleur de fonds* – **silent partner**).
2. tenement; real estate; piece of land.
(*fonds dominant* – **dominant tenement**)
(*fonds servant* – **servient tenement**)
(*fonds et biens* – **goods** and **effects**, including a real right to property. See also *biens*).

fonds de commerce (F)
a business concern or its assets; the value of a business, especially the value of a business transferred upon the assignment of a lease of business premises; sometimes mistranslated as **goodwill**, which it includes but is not equivalent to. See also *bail commercial*.
Amos & Walton's Introduction to French Law, 3 edn., pp. 343.

fongibles (F)
fungibles

foot frontage method
see **frontage method**.

foot frontage
see **frontage**.

footpath
A path, track or part of a **highway** over which the public has a **right of way** on foot only. The Highways Act 1980, s. 329(1) draws a distinction between a footpath which crosses privately owned land and a **footway** which is incorporated in a highway. In common usage, these terms are used synonymously. In the UK, a footpath may be established over private land by statute law and a land owner is under an obligation to keep the way free of obstruction and the local highway authority is responsible for its upkeep.

footway
A **right of way** on foot whether for the public at large or a group of private individuals. "A way comprised in a **highway** which also comprises a carriageway, being a way over which the public has a right of way only" (Highways Act 1959, s. 295 – a definition reincorporated in the Highways Act 1980, s. 329). A footway generally means a paved way set alongside a highway and reserved for foot passengers; but not for vehicles, carriages or animals. In statute law a way that crosses private ground is not normally a footway – Scales v Pickering (1829) 4 Bing. 453. In the US, commonly called a 'sidewalk'. See also **footpath, walkway**.

force majeure (F)
Literally a 'superior force'. A physical or material act that is beyond human capacity to prevent. *Force majeure* is not strictly a term of English law, it owes its origin to the civil law where it resembles that which causes **frustration** as found in English law; in particular, it is used to refer to conditions that hinder performance of a contract, especially a building contract. *Force majeure* consists of an event that is entirely outside the control of the party affected by it, e.g. a war, a change of foreign government, a riot, arson, or even administrative interference. *Force majeure* must have a physical or material element, whether arising from acts of nature or man,

but it does not extend to the threat or apprehension of such an action – Hackney Borough Council *v* Dore [1922] 1 KB 431; nor does it extend to bad weather or a funeral. *Force majeure* refers to events that make performance of a contract or obligation impossible, not to those events that make performance only more onerous; the impediment must have been unforeseeable and irresistible. An administrative delay in granting a building permit is foreseeable, but a strike may be irresistible. *Force majeure* is sometimes compared to an **act of God**; however, the former includes any event that is outside the contemplation of the parties to a contract and cannot be avoided by due care and attention, including acts of God and acts of man.
cf. **cas fortuit**.
Amos & Walton's Introduction to French Law, 3 edn., pp. 214–215.
Force majeure, by P.E. Healey, Institute of Building) (1979).
French Law of Contract, by Barry Nicholas (1982), pp. 196–199.

forced sale
1. A sale made when there is a compulsion as to its time or place. A sale conducted against the wishes of the owner of a property, e.g. a sale by a mortgagee to satisfy a debt or under an order of a court. See also **foreclosure sale, power of sale**.
2. A sale when the purchaser has the power of **expropriation** or **compulsory purchase**.

forced-sale value
The value of a property assuming that the vendor is not a **willing seller**. The Royal Institution of Chartered Surveyors defines forced-sale value as the open **market value** with the proviso that the vendor has imposed a time limit for completion which cannot be regarded as a reasonable period within which to negotiate the sale, taking into account the nature of the property and the state of the market. When assessing the forced-sale value of a property the time limit should be agreed with the party for whom the valuation is being undertaken (Guidance Note on Valuation of Assets, No. GN22). See also **mortgage value**.

foreclosure
The termination of a mortgagor's **equity of redemption**, i.e. a judicial remedy that brings a **mortgage** to an end and ultimately vests the mortgagor's estate or interest in land in the mortgagee. A mortgagee in certain circumstances, has a right to begin foreclosure proceedings, when a mortgagor is in default in paying the mortgage debt (but not before), in order to try and obtain the property for himself in place of exercising his **power of sale** and merely laying claim to the proceeds of sale of the property.
A right to foreclosure arises when the date stipulated for the redemption of the mortgage loan has passed; or, if the mortgage agreement contains an **acceleration clause** (an express provision that the entire loan falls due if there is a breach of a condition of the mortgage) then from such time as the mortgagee is permitted to take advantage of that clause. If there is no specified date for redemption, or if the mortgage provides for repayment of the entire debt on demand, foreclosure proceedings may be commenced a reasonable time after the mortgagee has demanded repayment – Toms *v* Wilson (1862) 4 B and S 442. Foreclo-

sure is a remedy available to any legal or an equitable mortgagee (whether the original mortgagee or an assignee, and to any first or subsequent mortgagee); but not to a chargee, because a **charge** does not grant a right to any interest in land. Foreclosure may be instigated only by application to the High Court and the action must involve all parties interested in the mortgaged property. The court initially may issue a decree of 'foreclosure nisi' and give the mortgagor time to pay (usually six months). At that stage all subsequent mortgagees have the right also to repay the mortgage, or else lose their security i.e. be foreclosed by the prior mortgagee – hence the expression '**redeem up, foreclose down**'. If the debt is not repaid by a time specified by the court, the court may then grant a 'foreclosure absolute' which vests the mortgagor's fee simple or term of years in the mortgagee, free of the mortgagor's right to redeem and the rights of all subsequent mortgagees, although any prior or superior mortgages remain in place (Law of Property Act 1925, s. 88(2), 89(2)). Even after a foreclosure absolute the court has, for a reasonable period of time, a discretionary right to decree that the mortgagor may redeem and thus keep the property; for example, if the mortgagor has been severely impeded, but can raise the necessary finance, or if there is a significant difference between the value of the property and the amount of the loan outstanding – Campbell *v* Holyland (1877) 7 Ch. D 172–5. In addition, if the mortgaged property is a dwelling-house the court has a discretionary right to stay proceedings if it considers that the mortgagor can remedy the default which gave rise to

the foreclosure action (Administration of Justice Act 1970, s. 36). If a mortgagor in possession refuses to vacate the mortgaged property after the fee simple has been vested in the mortgagee then the mortgagee must obtain an order for possession from the court, as it is a criminal offence to physically oust a person from property (Criminal Law Act 1977, ss. 5, 6). The court is empowered to direct that the property be sold, especially when requested so to do by a party who has an interest in the mortgaged property, rather than grant a foreclosure absolute, if that is considered more equitable; this is commonly done, particularly when the property is worth significantly more than the unpaid debt or when there is rising or 'bull' property market. The sale of the mortgage property may be made on such terms as the court thinks fit, "including the deposit in court of a reasonable sum fixed by the court to meet the expenses of the sale and to secure performance of the terms". (Law of Property Act 1925, s. 91(2)).

Foreclosure is no longer a common remedy in English law due to the cost, the time it takes, the consequent loss of the right to sue the mortgagor on his personal debt if the foreclosed property proves to be worth less than the mortgage loan, and the risk that the court can always insist on a sale.

In most states in the US, **strict foreclosure**, i.e., the taking of the property by the mortgagee, is not permitted. The procedure against a delinquent mortgagor may be started by what is called an action of foreclosure or a 'foreclosure suit', but generally this is converted into a court order requiring the property to be put up for public sale if the mortgagor has not paid in the required time. Even after a public sale, the mortgagor may be entitled to exercise a statutory right of redemption. See also **foreclosure sale**.

Real Estate Law, by W.D. Milligan and Arthur G. Bowman, pp. 248–258 (1984).

Real Estate Law, by Robert Kratovil and Raymond J. Werner, 8 edn., pp. 385–390.

Mortgages, why not foreclose? by Diana Brahams, 260 E.G. 899 (1981). Cheshire's Modern Law of Real Property, 13 edn., pp. 653–655.

32 Halsbury's Laws of England, 4 edn., paras. 844–911.

foreclosure absolute
see **foreclosure**.

foreclosure nisi
see **foreclosure**.

foreclosure sale (US)
A means by which a mortgagee seeks to foreclose on mortgaged property by offering the property for public sale and reserving unto himself a right to bid for the property. In most states in the US **strict foreclosure**, i.e. taking the mortgaged property in satisfaction of the debt, is prohibited and the foreclosure sale procedure has been adopted in its stead. In the event of a default by the mortgagor, a mortgagee may have a right to sell the mortgaged property in accordance with the provisions of state laws regulating such a sale. At a foreclosure sale the mortgagee may be permitted to bid up to the amount of the outstanding debt without putting up any money. If the mortgagee is successful he effectively forecloses; however, if a higher bid is made the bidder receives title to the property. On the other hand if the property is sold to a third party for less than the mortgage debt the net proceeds of the sale are set against the debt and the mortgagee usually has a right of **recourse** against the mortgagor on his personal debt by way of a **deficiency judgement**. The right to purchase obtained by the highest bidder may be qualified by a right of the mortgagor to exercise a statutory right of redemption, i.e. to repay the outstanding debt within a stipulated period of time (which varies from two months in some states to two years in others) and reclaim the property. The right of the mortgagor to regain the property, after a foreclosure sale, is called sometimes a 'statutory redemption'. See also **certificate of sale, foreclosure**.

forclusion (F)
foreclosure.
(*droit de rachat après forclusion* – right to purchase after foreclosure; **equity of redemption**.

forecourt
An open area, enclosed or marked off, in front of a building or group of buildings.

foreign investor
see **absentee owner**.

forest
An area of land densely covered with trees and undergrowth. Historically a forest was a wooded area owned by the King and set aside for the keeping and hunting of wild beasts and game. cf. **chase, park**. See also **woodland**.

Forestry Commission
A body established in the UK in 1919 to promote the interests of forestry, the development of afforestation and the production and supply of timber.

The Commission owns and maintains large areas of forestry land, especially Crown owned forests.

foreshore

The **shore** of the sea, or of any tidal water, that lies between the limits of the high and low water marks at ordinary tides; land that is alternately wet and dry according to the flow of tides. An area of land that may extend into creeks, channels, bays, estuaries or up navigable rivers as far as the tide flows; as well as the 'sea-shore' as understood in common usage. When used in a conveyance the words 'sea-shore' and 'foreshore' have the same extensive meaning – Mellor *v* Walmesley [1905] 2 Ch. 164; Government of the State of Penang *v* Beng Hong Oon [1971] 3 All ER 1170; unless it is clear that only land bounding the open sea is being referred to.

In English law the foreshore is *prima facie* vested in the Crown; the adjoining landowner's boundary ceasing (in the absence of evidence to the contrary) at the median high water mark. The boundary of land bounded by the foreshore may well vary in accordance with the position of the median high water mark. The foreshore is subject to certain public rights of fishery, navigation and such rights as access for walking, bathing, and taking seaweed, shingle, sand and shells.

The Crown has a right to recover an area of foreshore from an adverse possessor for a period of sixty years: for this purpose foreshore means "the shore and bed of the sea and of any tidal water, below the line of the median high tide between the spring tides and the neap tides" (Limitation Act 1980, Sch. I. pt. 1 s. 11 (3)).

In the US, the ownership of land abutting the sea or tidal waters stops at the high water mark. Traditionally a dry beach belonged to the abutting landowner. However, several states have decided that this land should be enjoyed by the general public, either as a customary right or a right arising by dedication when a landowner has permitted the public onto the beach – State ex. rel. Thornton *v* Hay (1969) 462 P. 2d. 671; County of Orange *v* Chandler-Sherman Corp. (1973) 126 Cal. Reptr. 765, 5 SWUL Rev. 48; In re Opinion of the Justices (1974) 313 NE 2d. 561. See also **accretion, dereliction**.
The Law of Rivers and Watercourses, by A.S. Wisdom, 4 edn., pp. 21–36
8 Halsbury's Laws of England, 4 edn., paras. 1418–1436.

forfait (F)

fixed price; lump sum.
(á forfait – **without recourse**)
(*prix à forfait* – lump-sum contract)
(*vente à forfait* – outright sale)
(*contrat à prix forfaitaire* – **fixed-price contract**)

forfaitaire (F)

(*prélèvement forfaitaire* – withholding tax).
(*somme*, or *payement, forfaitaire* – lump sum).

forfeiture

Derived from the Latin *foris factum* or the Old French *forfaiture*, 'to do beyond what is right'; signifying an act that is outside the bounds of the law calling for a legal redress or penalty. The loss of the right to a property as a result of some negligent or illegal act or omission. The loss of an estate, privilege, benefit or right, without compensation, due to a failure to fulfil a condition or comply with a legal obligation. In old English law forfeiture was "a punishment annexed by law to some illegal act, or negligence, in the owner of lands, tenements, or hereditaments; whereby he loses all his interests therein, and they go to the party injured, as a recompense for the wrong which either he alone, or the public together with himself, hath sustained" (Bl. Comm. vol. ii, P. 1267). In particular, the loss of land by a tenant to a lord as a result of a breach of fealty, as when the tenant granted his right to the land to another against an express limitation imposed by the lord. (Forfeiture of land to the Crown used to arise following a treason, felony, murder or suicide, but this form of penalty was abolished by the Forfeiture Act 1870.)

Forfeiture of a **lease** arises when the landlord exercises his right to regain possession of the demised premises against the wishes of the tenant. A landlord may exercise this right, his **right of re-entry** either (a) if there is a breach of a **condition** of the lease by the tenant; or (b) if there is a breach of a **covenant** (i.e. a provision that is not essential to the operation of the lease) and there is also a **forfeiture clause** or proviso for re-entry inserted in the lease – Doe d. Wilson *v* Phillips (1824) 2 Bing. 13. If there is no such proviso in the lease, then the lessor's only remedy for a breach of covenant is to seek some other form of remedy (e.g. **damages** or an **injunction**) or, in the case of a periodic tenancy, to serve a **notice to quit**. However, most modern leases contain a provision that the lessor may exercise a right of re-entry in the event of a breach of any covenant contained therein.

Forfeiture of a lease is instigated normally by issuing and serving a writ for possession. Alternatively the landlord may *peacefully* re-enter the premises; unless the premises comprise an occupied dwelling-house (Protection from Eviction Act 1977, s. 2). However, the Law of Property Act 1925, s. 146(1) provides that, "a right of re-entry or forfeiture under any proviso or stipulation in a lease for a breach of any covenant or condition in a lease shall not be enforceable, by action or otherwise, unless and until the lessor serves on the lessee a notice – (a) specifying the particular breach complained of; and (b) if the breach is capable of remedy, requiring the lessee to remedy the breach; and (c) in any case, requiring the lessee to make compensation in money for the breach; and the lessee fails, within a reasonable time thereafter, to remedy the breach, if it is capable of remedy, and to make reasonable compensation in money, to the satisfaction of the lessor, for the breach" (sometimes called a 'section 146 notice'). A number of exceptions apply to this rule; in particular, the requirement does not apply to non-payment of rent; to a condition of forfeiture on the bankruptcy of the lessee; to a lease of agricultural land, a public house, or a furnished house; if the personal qualifications of the tenant are of importance for the preservation of the value or character of the property; and, in certain respects, to a mining lease. Normally, therefore, only when this procedure has been followed can the lessor proceed through the court, which still may grant an alternative form of remedy, such as an injunction to force the tenant to comply with the covenant in the lease or damages, if that is considered more appropriate.

Forfeiture is a remedy that is considered by law as a form of penalty; it is enforced against the will of the losing party, and generally is permitted only when there is a wilful act or omission that the defaulting party has not attempted to remedy. (In the case of a **protected tenancy** forfeiture of a lease is granted only at the discretion of the court, even for a breach of a condition (Rent Act 1977, s. 98, Sch. 15); and in the event of a breach of a covenant to repair, contained in a lease (other than one of an agricultural holding) granted for seven years or more with three or more years left to run, the tenant must be given a right to serve, within 28 days, a counter notice to the 'section 146 notice' if he considers the landlord's notice unreasonable (Leasehold Property (Repairs) Act 1938, s. 1). In that event the matter must be resolved by reference to the court, which has discretion to grant **relief** as it 'thinks fit' having regard to 'the proceedings and conduct of the parties ... and to all other circumstances' (1925 Act, s. 146(2)).

Forfeiture of a lease for non-payment of rent normally must be preceded by a formal demand for the exact sum due, unless the lease exempts the landlord from this requirement, or (a) there is at least half a year's rent in arrears, (b) there are insufficient chattels on the premises to provide a landlord who distrains with a possibility of recovering the arrears, and (c) the landlord has reserved a right of re-entry for non-payment of rent (Common Law Procedure Act 1852, s. 210). Further, a High Court action for possession because of non-payment of rent may be terminated if the tenant pays all arrears of rent and costs before the trial and the High Court can grant relief against forfeiture for six months after it has made the order enabling the landlord to re-enter the demised premises (1852 Act, s. 210–212). A County Court action may be terminated in the same way up to five days before the trial and the same relief may be granted after a court order as with a High Court action (County Courts Act 1984, s. 138; Administration of Justice Act 1985, s. 55).

Forfeiture is a remedy thwarted with difficulty. Re-entry may not be accompanied by violence (Criminal Law Act 1977, s. 6); it is normally necessary first to proceed through a court of law; and, even then, the tenant may seek relief through the courts. Upon forfeiture of a lease, the contract is considered to be determined and the covenants therein no longer enforceable; although obligations, especially to pay rent, up to the time of forfeiture generally are binding. See also **determination, eviction, waiver**.

Adkin's Landlord and Tenant, 18 edn., pp. 232–244.

Landlord and Tenant Law, by David Yates and A.J. Hawkins, pp. 141–145, 258–262 (1981).

Woodfall's Landlord and Tenant, 28 edn., paras. 1–1880 to 1–1966.

27 Halsbury's Laws of England 4 edn., paras. 422–443.

The Law of Real Property, by Robert Megarry and H.W.R. Wade, 5 edn., pp. 670–683.

forfeiture clause

A clause in a lease which enables a landlord, in certain specified circumstances, to terminate the lease and re-enter the demised premises. This clause uses such words as, "provided always that if the rent reserved by this deed shall be unpaid for 21 days after becoming due (whether formally demanded or not) or if the tenant commits a breach of covenant it shall be lawful for the landlord to re-enter upon the premises and thereupon this lease shall determine". A forfeiture clause generally is construed against the landlord and in favour of the tenant – based on the *contra proferentem* rule. Called also a 'proviso for re-entry'. See also **forfeiture, right of re-entry**.

forgery
Falsification or alteration of a document (or a signature to a document) with the intention that it shall appear genuine, with an intent to defraud (Forgery and Counterfeiting Act 1981, s. 1). A forged deed will not transfer property and title insurance may be arranged as a safeguard against that eventuality. See also **fraud, rectification**.

form of contract
see **deed, writing**.

formal contract
A contract in **writing**, in particular a contract which contains general and specific **conditions of sale**. Historically one under seal, but today this is not considered essential. cf. **open contract**. See also **deed, simple contract**.

formation
The act of creating a binding **contract**.

forms and precedents
see **precedent**.

formula method
A method used to value certain types of property, owned by a **statutory undertaker**, for the purpose of assessing the **rateable value**, by applying a formula laid down by statute. For example, the operational property of a gas or electricity undertaking is valued on the basis of a formula applied to the quantity of power or the output generated by a power station or similar plant (General Rate Act 1967, ss. 33–36). Ryde on Rating, 13 edn., pp. 639–647 & 1170–1174.

fortuitous event
see *cas fortuit*.

forum shopping clause (US)
A clause in a contract that specifies which state's legal jurisdiction will apply to any dispute. 'Forum shopping' is the seeking of a court of jurisdiction that is likely to give a plaintiff the most favourable judgement.

forward commitment (or sale)
An agreement to advance money as a loan, or to purchase a property, at a future date, usually subject to certain conditions such as that a building is completed and let. This commitment commonly takes the form of a binding contract between a property developer and a financial institution that a building, when completed to agreed plans and specification, will be purchased by the institution at a price calculated by reference to an agreed capitalisation rate which will be applied to a determinable income level. Referred to also as a 'prefunding commitment'. See also **financing, take-out loan**.

forward letting
see **pre-let**.

four-three-two-one rule (US)
A method of valuing a plot of land by applying a **depth factor** to four assumed depths in the ratio of 4:3:2:1, the front depth having four times greater value than the rear depth. See also **zoning**.

four unities
see **joint tenancy**.

forty-five degree rule
see **daylight factor**.

fractional appraisal (US)
The **appraisal** of part of a property. For example, the appraisal of a fractional or **partial interest**; of land excluding buildings or improvements; or of part of a structure for fire insurance purposes.

fractional interest (US)
A **partial interest** in land. This may be a physical part of a building, e.g. a condominium; a right to use part of property e.g. an air right; or a partial estate e.g. a leasehold interest or life interest.

fractionalised mortgage (US)
see **participation loan**.

fragmentation of ownership
The division of the right to the ownership of property into its component parts, i.e. into the right to use, enjoy, manage, possess, transfer or alienate, charge or mortgage, or even to destroy that right. See also *démembrements de la propriété*, **estate, partial ownership, tenure**.
The Law of Property, by F.H. Lawson and Bernard Rudden, 2 edn., pp. 77–104.

frais (F)
charges; expenses; costs; fees.
(*frais d'actes* – deed or conveyancing costs. Generally the costs of drawing up and completing a deed, as payable to a notary)
(*frais d'acquisition* – purchase or acquisition costs. Especially the expenses over and above the basic purchase price of a property)
(*frais financiers* – **financing costs**; financial expenses)
(*frais genéraux* – administrative expenses; overheads)
(*frais d'entretien* – maintenance expenses)
(*frais de gestion* – administrative expenses).

franc (F)
free; clear.
(*franc de toute servitudes* – free from all servitudes).
(*titre franc et quitte* – **free and clear** title)
(*jour franc* – clear **day**).

franchise
A right, privilege or licence granted or sold to an individual, or group of individuals, to market or distribute goods, or services, or to use the name of another upon terms and conditions that are mutually agreed upon. Historically a privilege or liberty conferred in England by Royal prerogative, or in the US, by legislative grant, permitting an individual or corporation a right that is not available to the public at large. A franchise was a right to use land for a particular purpose, whether arising by grant or prescription, in return for a service rendered to the Crown and, although the grantor may differ, the modern principle of a franchise remains the same. Generally the

grantor of the franchise (the franchisor) provides advice, marketing assistance, advertising, etc., and sometimes the goods to be sold to the other party (the franchisee). The franchise is restricted normally to a clearly defined territory. The payment made for the privilege, which may take the form of a flat fee and/or a percentage of gross sales, may be called also a franchise. A franchise is more akin to a licence than any right to real property; although the franchisee may have an independent right to occupy a property he uses for franchised sales.

Real estate brokers may use a franchising system which provides that member firms, who hold the franchise, will receive details of properties that are available on a **multiple listing** basis. The participating brokers receive assistance with advertising, sales techniques, publicity, etc. They pay a fee as members of the franchise organisation and usually a fee based on their gross sales income. In addition, franchised firms refer a prospect to firms holding the same franchise in other parts of the defined territory. See also **royalty**.

Franchising for Profit: A Guide for Professional Advisors and Businessmen, by W.A.J. Pollack and G. Golzen (1985).

Franchising, by J. Adams and K.V. Pritchard Brown (1981).

franchise (F)

franchise, in particular a percentage paid to the grantor of a franchise; privilege; exemption; excess (in insurance).

frank fee

see **free tenure**.

frank-tenement

see **free tenure**.

frankalmoin

A form of feudal **tenure** by which land was granted to an ecclesiastical body in return for prayers and religious services ('free alms'). Effectively obsolete by 1660 and any outstanding frankalmoin tenures fell into oblivion after 1925. See also **spiritual tenure**.

fraud

An intentional act of deceit or moral turpitude; a false representation by word or deed which in someway wilfully coaxes or tricks someone into a course of action that brings an unfair advantage to the person making the representation. A false statement is fraudulent when it is "made (1) knowingly, or (2) without belief in its truth, or (3) recklessly, careless whether it be true or false". – Derry v Peek (1889) 14 AC 374; Kidd v Kidd, 242 NE 2d. 385, 143 Ind. App. 648. A deliberate omission or concealment of a fact with the intention to deceive may constitute a fraud (a 'constructive fraud'); but it is not fraud to take advantage of legal rights. "Fraud, that in every conscience leaves a sting, may be by man employed on one, whose trust he wins, or on another who withholds strict confidence" (Dante, *Purgatorio* 9:55).

Fraud may be used when a person seeks to bar another's right to land by **adverse possession** by a deliberate act, as when a party, "knowing to whom the right belongs, conceals the circumstances giving that right, and, by means of such concealment, enables himself to enter and hold". – Petre v Petre (1853) 1 Drew. 397. In such a case the period of limitation on the plaintiff's right of action does not start to run until he has, or could with reasonable diligence have, discovered the fraud (Limitation Act 1980, s. 32). The concealment of any instrument or incumberance that is material to a title, or the falsification of the pedigree of any matter upon which a title depends, by any person who is disposing of property for money or money's worth, with intent to defraud, is a criminal offence (Law of Property Act 1925, s. 183). Fraud by a mortgagee who deceives a subsequent mortgagee may have the effect of deferring the prior mortgagee's rights. Fraud on a power of appointment may arise merely by the exercise of a power outside the terms of the instrument that granted that power, when the intention is to secure personal benefit. See also **clandestine mortgage, fraudulent conveyance, inhibition, misrepresentation, rectification, Statute of Frauds, undue influence.**

Frauds, Statute of
see **Statute of Frauds**.

fraudulent alienation (US)
see **fraudulent conveyance**.

fraudulent conversion
Receiving lawfully and then fraudulently withholding money or personal property from another (Larceny Act 1916, s. 1). An offence that is now treated as theft (Theft Act 1968, s. 1). See also **conversion**.

fraudulent conveyance
The transfer of property, or any contract for the sale of property, made with the intention of depriving another of his proper claim, as when a company sells assets (particularly in anticipation of a financial failure) and distributes the proceeds in order to reduce a creditor's chance of satisfying his debt. "Every conveyance of property made...with intent to defraud creditors, shall be voidable, at the instance of any person thereby prejudiced". (Law of Property Act 1925, s. 172(1)). (This section does not apply to the conveyance of an estate or interest in property to a **bona fide purchaser** for valuable consideration without notice of the fraudulent intent nor to disentailing assurances.) Further, "every voluntary disposition [i.e. a gift] of land made with the intent to defraud a subsequent purchaser is voidable at the instance of the purchaser" (Law of Property Act 1925, s. 173(1)) A transfer of property made without fair and reasonable consideration may constitute a fraudulent conveyance, especially when made so as to take advantage of a person who is in a weak bargaining position or made by one who is in a position of trust – Wright *v* Carter [103] 1 Ch. 27; Cresswell *v* Potter [1978] 1 WLR 255. In the US referred to also as 'fraudulent alienation'. See also **clandestine mortgage, Mireva injunction, misrepresentation, undervalue, undue influence.**

fraudulent misrepresentation
see **fraud, misrepresentation**.

Freddie Mac (US)
see **Federal Home Loan Mortgage Corporation**.

free and clear return (US)
The relationship, expressed as a percentage, between the **net operating income** receivable from a property and the total cost of the property,

whether paid as **debt** or **equity**; i.e. the return based on the assumption that the property is acquired 'all cash' or with 100 per cent equity.
cf. **cash-on-cash return**.

free and clear title (US)

A title to property that is not encumbered by any mortgage, lien or other encumberance. Usually a fee simple property sold without debt ('free' signifying the form of title and 'clear' the lack of debt). See also **marketable title**.

free conveyance (US)

A **conveyance** whereby the purchaser of real estate is freed of any expense of the conveyancing.

free tenure

Any form of tenure under the **feudal system** which provided that the tenant had defined services or payments to make to his lord, including socage, knight service, sergeanty, and frankalmoin; as distinguished from 'unfree tenure' or **villeinage** whereby the services or payment could be altered at the will of the lord. Called also a 'frank fee' or 'frank tenement'. See also **freehold**.

freeboard

A strip of land that runs around an ancient park, which is not necessarily owned with the park but over which the park owner can exercise rights such as the imposition of a restriction on building.

freedom to hold private property

A basic civil right of an individual to acquire and hold **private property** without restriction or confiscation except by due process of law. A right recognised in democratic liberal states but generally denied in a socialist or communist state. Such a right was recognised in Magna Carta 1215, art. 52 and extended in English law by subsequent statutes (Statute of *Quia Emptores*, Tenures Abolition Act 1660, **Law of Property Acts**, Sale of Goods Act). In English law the freedom to develop real property, without state authorisation, was removed by the Town and Country Planning Act 1947. See also **compensation for planning restrictions, compulsory purchase, expropriation, freehold, police powers**.

freehold

An **estate** in land held for a described but indefinite duration. In English law, 'estate' represents the duration of a right to the ownership of land and a freehold estate represents a right to possession of land for a time span that is incapable of exact determination. Historically, a freehold could not exist without actual possession, but in modern law a freehold may be in **possession, reversion,** or **remainder**. A freehold may be classified as 'of inheritance' i.e. one that passes so long as there are heirs; or 'not of inheritance' i.e. one that lasts only for a life. A freehold 'of inheritance' may be a **fee simple**, i.e. it passes to a person and any class of heir (so long as they persist); or an **entailed interest** (**'fee tail'**), i.e. it passes to specified heirs. A freehold 'not of inheritance' is a **life estate**, either for the life of the holder; or for the life of another, *pour autre vie*. In common usage the term freehold refers to an estate of inheritance, i.e. a fee interest (especially a fee simple absolute) and 'life interest' refers to an estate for a life.

The estate of freehold originated in mediaeval England as an interest in land granted by the lord of the **manor** to a free man, one who could not be arbitrarily dispossessed; one who had **seisin**: an enjoyment of property based on a title that could be defended by a real action, together with the right to physical possession, or a right to receive rent, for an undetermined period of time. This may be contrasted with the right held by a 'villein' – **villenage or villein tenure** – who was merely a servant of the lord; whose services could be varied at the will of the lord; who could readily be dismissed; and who had no right to let the land he occupied to another. Under the **feudal system** of land tenure a free man was considered worthy of rendering certain superior services to his lord, i.e. services that were free of any servile incidents, such as knight service or divine service; or of performing work of a certain and fixed nature, called **socage**. He was granted a lawful right to possession of land for so long as he rendered such services to the lord: "no freeman shall be taken or imprisoned, or be disseised of his freehold, or liberties, or free customs, or be outlawed or exiled, or any other wise destroyed; nor will we not pass upon him, nor (condemn him) but by lawful judgement of his peers of the law of the land" – Magna Carta (1297) Ch. 29. Thereby a freeholder was given a right to bring a **real action**, i.e. an action to recover land, as opposed to a personal action for damages, and, consequently a freehold estate was apprehended to be **real property**. With the break-up of the manorial system, the services required of a free man were commuted into monetary payment, which later became limited to a **chief rent** or **quit-rent** and in due course the title to land became a freehold: the holding of land *free* of any payment to a lord.

cf. **leasehold interest**. See also **freehold absolute, tenure**.
Cheshire's Modern Law of Property, 13 edn., pp. 30–32.
Megarry's Manual of The Law of Real Property, 6 edn., pp. 33–56.
The Law of Real Property, by Robert Megarry and H.W.R. Wade, 5 edn., pp. 33–34, 39–40.

freehold absolute
A **freehold** interest in land that has been registered with an absolute title. A registered interest in land that is equivalent to a **fee simple absolute in possession** of unregistered land. A freehold absolute title is granted by the Land Registrar when he is satisfied that an applicant's interest cannot be challenged. It guarantees to the owner that the title is the most absolute recognised in English law. Such a title is subject only to any entries shown on the register; any **overriding interest** (unless stated to the contrary on the register); and any **minor interests** of which the freeholder has **notice**. See also **land registration**.

freeholder
The holder of a **freehold** interest in land.

'from'
see **date, time**.

front-end fee
see **commitment fee**.

front-end money
see **front money**.

front foot (US)
see **frontage**.

front loading

An arrangement, especially related to a loan, by which at the outset the cost payable is significantly greater than later. For example, the whole of the interest may be payable by the borrower at the start of a loan; or a **commitment fee** or **discount points** may be charged by the lender so as to effectively increase the annual interest rate. See also **annual percentage rate**.

front money

1. The cash required by a developer to meet the cost of land acquisition, fees, survey costs, etc., prior to starting development works. Called sometimes 'front-end money', 'start-up money', 'seed money', 'cash on the barrelhead', or 'cash on the line'. See also **end money**.
2. **Short-term finance** for the development of land.

frontage

1. The distance that a parcel of land abuts a street or river. This distance when measured in feet is called the 'foot frontage'. In the US called also 'abutting foot' or when used with reference to the **assessed value** of a property, especially a special assessment, the 'front foot'.
2. The **boundary line** of a property immediately abutting a highway or street. The side of a building that faces onto a street, road, footpath or highway, or the side upon which the main entrance is situated.

frontage line

1. A line defined on a plan by a local authority beyond which new buildings may not encroach. See also **building line, improvement line**.
2. The line that represents the limit of a landowner's property where it fronts a public highway or footpath.

frontage method

A method of valuing a plot of land or a building based on its frontage to a street, mall, footway, etc. Called also the 'foot frontage method'. See also **comparison method of valuation**.

frontager

A landowner who has a boundary line onto a highway, street, river, etc. See also **riparian owner**.

fructus (L)

'Fruits'; that which springs from **land**. May be *fructus industriales*, fruits of industry, i.e. such crops or other products of the soil as are produced by man's industry through sowing and cultivation; or *fructus naturales*, fruits of nature, i.e. crops that grow naturally and independently of man's industry such as grass or trees (including the fruit from trees that do not need to have a crop taken therefrom to ensure rejuvination) especially where "the labour employed in their planting bears so small a proportion to their natural growth". – Marshall *v* Green (1875) 1 CPD 40. '*Fructus industriales*' may be **emblements** being in law goods and not any part of the land; but *'fructus naturales'* are normally part and parcel of the land and pass on a conveyance of land. See also *fruits,* **usufruct**.
Real Property, by William E. Burby, 3 edn., pp. 14–16.

fruits (F)

fruits; profits. A produce of property that is obtained without changing the substance of that property. "Fruits are defined (by *Traite Pratique de Droit Civil*, by Planiol et Ripert, 3

No. 255) as whatever the property produces at regular intervals without diminution of its substance, and are either *naturel*, such as crops, or *civil* such as rent. Fruits are distinguished from *produits*, which the possessor as such does not acquire. *Produits* include such things as stone from a quarry not regularly exploited, timber from a forest subjected to systematic cutting, and the instalments of an annuity. To acquire the fruits the possessor must reap, gather or otherwise appropriate them" (Amos & Walton's Introduction to French Law, 3 edn., p. 103 – French Civil Code, arts. 583–586.) *Fruits* may be classified also as *industriels* being those produced by man's efforts, e.g. corn, produce of a vineyard, fish from a lake; as distinguished from those that are entirely *naturels*, e.g. fruit from a tree or fruits that can be collected by foraging.

(*fruits de la terre* – **emblements**). See also *fructus*, **usufruct**.

Précis Dalloz. Droit Civil, Les Biens (Alex Weill), 2 edn., pp. 34 & 492.

frustration

From the Latin *frustra*, 'in vain'. An event or incident that prevents a purpose being performed as anticipated; such as, one that renders a contract incapable of performance. The premature determination of a contract by interrupting events, or causes, outside the expectations of the parties; such as by an **act of God**, a Government wartime decree, or destruction of the subject matter. Frustration of a contract may occur only when the interruption is of such a character and duration that it vitally and fundamentally changes the basis of the contract, and when the event or

instance could not possibly have been in the contemplation of the parties when it was made. "If the foundation of the contract goes, either by the destruction of the subject-matter or by reason of such long interruption or delay that the performance is really in effect that of a different contract, and the parties have not provided what in that event is to happen, the performance of the contract is to be regarded as frustrated." – Tatem Ltd *v* Gamboa [1939] 1 KB 139. However, the intervening circumstance must be such that the parties to the contract can unequivocally say – "it was not this that I promised to do" – and not merely that performance of the contract is onerous, extremely difficult, or more expensive to perform. "It is not hardship or inconvenience or material loss itself which calls the principle of frustration into play. There must be as well such a change in the significance of the obligation that the thing itself would, if performed, be a different thing from that contracted for." – Davis Contractors *v* Fareham UDC [1956] 3 WLR 62–3.

A contract may be frustrated if (a) the subject-matter totally disappears; (b) a particular thing or factor required in order to fulfill the contract is not and cannot be made available; (c) the whole underlying business reason is removed by circumstances that could not have been anticipated by the parties; or (d) performance of the contract is subsequently but unexpectedly made illegal. A contract relating to land is unlikely to be frustrated, as land is virtually indestructible. Nor is such a contract frustrated by a compulsory purchase order – Hillingdon Estates

Co. v Stonefield Estates [1952] Ch. 627. A building lease is not frustrated merely because all building work is prohibited for a duration by the State; and not even the intervention of war was sufficient to frustrate a ninety-nine year building lease – Cricklewood Property and Investment Trust Ltd, v Leighton's Investment Trust Ltd [1945] 1 All ER 252. A fire that makes premises unusable does not frustrate a lease; and loss of access to a warehouse for two years of a ten year lease is not sufficient grounds to frustrate the lease – National Carriers Ltd v Panalpina Ltd [1981] 1 All ER 161. However, in that case it was stated by Lord Russell, at p. 182: "I would reserve consideration of cases of physical destruction of flying leaseholds and of the total disappearance of the site comprised in the lease into the sea so that it no longer existed in the form of a piece of terra firma and could not be subject of re-entry or forfeiture. In that case I would not need the intervention of any court to say that the term of years could not outlast the disappearance of its subject matter: the site would no longer have a free holder [or] lessor, and the obligation to pay rent, which issues out of land, could not survive its substitution by the waves of the North Sea." In the US government restrictions that might reasonably be forseen, e.g. restrictions imposed during war time, have been held not to bring about the frustration of a lease even though the lessee's business is severely curtailed – Lloyd v Murphy, 25 C 2d. 48; Gordon v Slate, 233 NY1. On the other hand, several states have enacted that if a building is destroyed or rendered untenantable the tenant has no further liability for rent and if a building is totally destroyed by fire the courts will generally hold that the lease is frustrated – Teodori v Werner (1981) 415 A 2d. 31, 99 ALR 3d. 738). It may well be noted that French law accepts the intervention of *force majeure*, an unanticipated and irresistible force, as making the performance of a contract impossible, but disappearance of the foundation of a contract, economic impossibility or a change of circumstances will rarely frustrate a contract. "In no case is it open to the courts, no matter how equitable their decision may seem to them to be, to take time and circumstances into account in order to modify the agreement of the parties and substitute new terms for those which have been freely accepted by those parties" (Chanale de Crappone, Cass. Civ. 6.3.1876). Consequently, the best remedy against a loss of 'land' is insurance.

As a rule in English law the monies or consideration paid under a frustrated contract are recoverable as if the contract had not been entered into and both parties are released from any further obligation to fulfill that contract (Law Reform (Frustrated Contracts) Act 1943).

Law for Land Management Students, by Richard Card, John Murdoch and Peter Schofield, pp. 152–162 (1981).

An Introduction to the Law of Contract, by P.S. Atiyah, 3 edn., pp. 198–215.

Anson's Law of Contract, 26 edn., pp. 440–466.

Cheshire and Fifoot's Law of Contract, 10 edn., p. 516 *et seq.* (esp. pp. 522–524).

9 Halsbury's Laws of England, 4 edn., paras. 1521–1585.

Chitty on Contract, 25 ed., p. 830–875.

frustration (F)
  frustration.

frustrum terrae (L)
  A piece of **land** that stands alone.

fuel allotment
  see **allotment**.

full annual value
  1. The **best rent** or **market rent** of a property. Called sometimes a 'fair annual value'. See also **annual value, rack rent**.
  2. In rating, 'full annual value' means **net annual value** – Rose v Watson [1894] 2 QB 90.

full cash value
  The **fair market value** assuming a wholly cash transaction. See also **cash value**.

full float
  see **float**.

full floor rentable area (US)
  see **rentable area**.

full market value
  see **fair market value**.

full payout lease
  see **finance lease**.

full rent
  see **rack rent**.

full rental value (FRV)
  see **best rent, market rent, rack rent**.

full repairing and insuring lease (FRI lease)
  A lease that requires all running costs including property taxes, repairs and maintenance costs, and insurance premiums, to be paid by the lessee. See also **net lease, triple net lease**.

functional depreciation
  see **depreciation**.

functional inutility
  see **obsolescence**.

functional obsolescence
  see **obsolescence**.

fundamental breach
  see **breach of contract**.

fundamental term
  see **condition, exclusion clause**.

funding
  1. The provision of a sum of money to meet a future contingency or a known debt. See also **sinking fund**.
  2. Obtaining a loan, especially a long-term loan to replace a short-term loan. See also **financing**.
  3. The conversion of **debt** into **equity**. See also **convertible mortgage**.

fungibles
  Goods that perish by use and can be measured so as to be substituted by a similar quantity e.g. grain, sugar, oil. Land is a totally non-fungible good as each parcel is unique; a vendor cannot substitute one parcel of land for another as a means of satisfying a contractual obligation for the sale of land.

furnished premises
  see **furnished tenancy**.

furnished tenancy
  The grant of a tenancy of a dwelling-house, which is partly or fully furnished, whereby a substantial proportion of the rent includes payment for the use of furniture. Between 1920 and 1974 a dwelling-house let at a rent which included a payment for the use of furniture was treated in a different way, as regards

security of tenure and rent control, to other such tenancies. The security of tenure was limited to six, or sometimes nine months, and rents for furnished property were not controlled until 1946 (Furnished Houses (Rent Control) Act 1946). After 1946 rents for such a tenancy could be fixed by a rent tribunal, but upon a different basis to that appertaining to any other **protected tenancy**. The Rent Act 1974, s. 1(1) contained provision to convert most furnished lettings to regulated tenancies; the exception being a right to the occupation of a furnished dwelling which is let so that it comes within the definition of a **restricted contract**.

In a lease of furnished premises, there is an **implied covenant** that the property is **fit for human habitation** at the start of the tenancy – Smith *v* Marrable (1843) 11 M and W 5, although the landlord is not under any obligation to keep the premises fit throughout the term of the lease – Sarson *v* Roberts [1895] 2 QB 395. In some states in the US there is an implied warranty that a furnished property let on a short-term tenancy is fit for occupation – Zatloff *v* Winkleman, (1960) 90 RI 403, 158 A 2d. 874.

further advance

A second or subsequent advance of money by a mortgagee to a mortgagor, either against the security of the existing property held on mortgage or upon the security of another property. In equity, interest not paid when due, i.e. accrued, is considered as a further advance. See also **accrued interest, future advances clause, tacking**.

further assurance, covenant for

A covenant that a vendor of real property will execute any additional **conveyance** (assurance) that may be necessary in order to perfect or cure the title obtained by the purchaser of that property. See also **beneficial owner**.

future advances clause (US)

A clause which provides that the amount advanced under a mortgage may be increased without increasing the existing **security**. The clause may be obligatory on the mortgagee, e.g. where the mortgagee contracts to advance monies as building work progresses; or optional, e.g. where the mortgagee agrees to advance additional funds at his discretion. See also **open-end mortgage, tacking**.

future depreciation

Depreciation that it is assumed will accrue over the life of an asset and for which a provision has or will be made. cf. **accrued depreciation**.

future estate (or interest)

An **estate** (or **interest**) in land which the owner holds now, but does not take effect, as a right to enjoyment of the land, until a future date or until the happening of a future event. A future interest may be either a **vested interest**, if it will pass to an ascertained person upon the occurrence of a prior event; or a **contingent interest**, if it will pass to someone who is unascertained when the right to the interest is first granted or if the receipt of the interest is dependent on a contingent or uncertain event. In English law a future estate cannot be a **legal estate** because it does not carry a right to present **possession**. A future estate may be called an 'inchoate interest', being an interest in land that is incomplete in the benefit that may be derived therefrom. Called also an 'estate in expectancy'. See also **conditional fee, executory interest, remainder, reversion, rule against perpetuities**.

Introduction to Land Law, by J.G. Riddell, 3 edn., pp. 174–179.
Cheshire's Modern Law of Real Property, 13 edn., p. 283 *et seq.*
Megarry's Manual of the Law of Real Property, 6 edn., pp. 189–196.
The Law of Real Property, by Robert Megarry and H.W.R. Wade, 5 edn., p. 231 *et seq.*

future interest
see **future estate**.

future lease
see **reversionary lease**.

future worth or value
The value of a capital sum at a future date, or after a given period of time, after allowing for income or interest earned thereon.
cf. **present value**. See also **amount of one, amount of one per period**.

future worth of one per period
see **amount of one per period**.

G

gage

An old English term for a **pawn** or **pledge**, or an object pledged or pawned as security. In particular, a living pledge (*vivum vadium*) i.e. an arrangement by which rents and profits from land held as security for a loan are handed over to pay interest on the debt. See also **mortgage**.

gage (F)

pledge; lien; pawn; security; guaranty. Goods transferred as security for a debt, or a contract by which such goods are transferred.
(*contrat de gage* – **bailment**; pledge)
(*droit de gage* – possessory lien).
See also *antichrèse*, **mortgage**, *nantissement*.

gain

An advantage or benefit obtained by getting what one has not or keeping what one has. An increase in resources or possessions resulting from business transactions or dealings; the fruits of exertion or labour. Gain is that which accrues to man, whether of a pecuniary nature or otherwise; as compared with **profit** which results from a thing (usually by buying or selling). Gain is a general term and may include a profit, advantage or benefit; or the obtaining of the use or possession of any form of profit, whether obtained by an individual or the community. An increase in the value or worth of a property, especially the difference between the historic cost, or income, from property and its greater value at a subsequent point in time.
cf. **loss**. See also **capital gain**, **chargeable gain**.

gain (F)

gain; profit; earnings.
(*gain en capital* – **capital gain**)

gainable land

An ancient term for land that is ready for cultivation.

gale

1. A form of **gavel**, i.e. a periodic payment based on the produce of land, from which the word gale is probably derived.
2. An amount due to a superior. A payment of **rent**, tax or similar annual sum due as a form of consideration for a licence or right to land, in particular for a mining right. "The word gale is used in many senses, sometimes as the grant itself of a right to mine, sometimes as the licence conferred by the grant, and more frequently as the corporeal property affected by the grant, having a site and capable of being defined by metes and bounds." – Great Western Forests of Dean Collieries Co. Ltd. *v* Trafalgar Colliery Co. Ltd, (1887) 3 TLR 725. Gale is used particularly to refer to such a grant made by the Crown, or to the subject matter of such a grant.
3. In Ireland, a common term for rent.
4. see **rental period**.

gale-day

An old term for the day rent is payable. See also **gale**.

game

Wild birds or wild animals that are

hunted for sport. Game may include "hares, pheasants, partridges, grouse, heath or moor game, black game, bustards, woodcocks and snipes" (Game Laws (Amendment) Act 1960, s. 4(5)). (Other more, or less, extensive definitions of game are contained in the Agricultural Holding Act 1948, s. 14(4); the Game Act 1831, s. 2; and the Poaching Prevention Act 1862, s. 1.) As a rule, unless they have been tamed or are too young to escape, game belongs to nobody absolutely. The right to hunt or catch game belongs basically to the occupier or tenant of land; although a landlord frequently reserves such a right to himself.
2 Halsbury's Laws of England, 4 edn, paras. 211–213.

gangway
A way over which men pass and repass in the course of their work. A passageway in a building, especially a way opened for a particular and generally temporary purpose. See also **aisle, mall**.

gap financing
Financing obtained to cover the difference between funds that can be drawn on immediately either as equity or under a loan facility (e.g. a **floor loan**), and the total cost of a development or building project. Usually gap financing takes the form of a short-term loan or overdraft, obtained independently of construction or interim financing, and replaced, upon completion and letting of the project, by more permanent financing. See also **bridging loan, commitment, hold-back**.

garage
A building or structure used to provide shelter and protection for the storage and/or the cleaning, servicing or repairing of motor vehicles. 'Garage' may be used to refer to a building or place where motor vehicles (in particular automobiles) are taken for servicing and repair, or a building used to store a private vehicle. A private garage is usually an enclosed building providing protection from the elements. See also **carport, filling station, service station**.

garantie (F)
guaranty; warranty; security; indemnity.
(On the sale of property the word *garantie* is used when the seller provides a covenant as to title; he covenants that there are no undisclosed defects, and undertakes to provide peaceful possession of the property being sold – similar to the obligations imposed on one who sells as **beneficial owner** in English law).
(*dépôt de garantie* – **earnest money**).
See also *sûreté*.

garden
A parcel of land, usually enclosed and commonly forming part of the curtilage of a dwelling house, used for the cultivation of flowers, fruit, ornamental trees, vegetables and lawns: generally used for producing food or for the pleasure of the inhabitants of the house. A garden may be used for profit, although, unlike a nursery ground, that is not the principal objective. Land used wholly for a business purpose is not land cultivated as a garden – Cooper v Pearse, [1896] 1 QB 562. "It would appear that the ordinary meaning of 'garden' would not include an enclosure or paddock used as a horse-

paddock or cow-paddock, nor an area used as a pig-run or fowl-run. These instances are adverted to for the purpose of illustrating that the use of the word 'garden' would, probably, not of itself include all land which might ordinarily be found used in conjunction with an ordinary dwelling, not producing anything for sale or business purposes" – Dalzell v Smith [1946] N.Z. L.R. 428. See also **allotment, cottage garden, field garden, horticulture, market garden.**
Garden Law by Godfrey Sandy-Winsch, (1982).

garden apartment (US)
An **apartment** situated in a building with a garden area or with a garden setting.

garden city
A form of town designed to provide pleasant living and working conditions, surrounded by a rural belt, and large enough to provide a balanced community. This form of town was intended as a marked contrast to the paleotechnic urban jungles of the industrial revolution. "A Garden City is a town designed for healthy living and industry; of a size that makes possible a full measure of social life, but not larger; surrounded by a rural belt; the whole of the land being in public or held in trust for the community." – Garden City Association (1919). The term was first applied to a design by A. T. Thomas in 1869 for an estate on Long Island, New York. However, it is more commonly associated with model towns designed by Ebenezer Howard, of which examples are Welwyn Garden City and Letchworth. These designs were the forerunners of the post-war English new towns.

The Evolution of British Town Planning by Gordon E. Cherry, (1974) p. 34–42.
Town, City and Nation, (England 1850–1914), by P.J. Waller. pp. 176–183 (1983).
Garden Cities of Tomorrow, by Ebenezer Howard, (1898), edited by F.J. Osborn (1946).
Garden Law, by G. Sandy-Winsch, (1982).

garden suburb
A predominantly residential area or **suburb** of a town, planned and built to a low density, with adequate open spaces and green areas. A term sometimes used incorrectly for a **garden city**.

garni (F)
furnished.
(*logement garni* – furnished flat).

garnishee order
see **garnishment**.

garnishment
Derived from the French *garnir* 'to warn'. Any legal notice given to a party to a proceeding; in particular the **attachment**, by order of a court ('garnishee order'), of the monies of a judgement debtor to a third party such as a bank or judgement creditor. For example, if A owes B money which he has not repaid when due in accordance with a judgement for the debt, then a court may make a garnishee order in favour of B on money retained in A's bank account, or money due from C who is a debtor of A, for the amount of the debt.

garranty
see **guaranty**.

garth
A small enclosed area of land; a close

or yard forming part of the **curtilage** of a house, usually to the rear.

gas station (US)
see **filling station**.

gasoline service station (US)
see **service station**.

gated pasture
see **cattlegate**.

gavel
1. A periodic payment made in the nature of a rent or a duty but taking the form of produce rather than money, e.g. gavel-corn, gavel-fodder, oat-gavel; especially a feudal toll or levy due to a lord or king. The word gavel may be used also to refer to any payment extracted from a tenant, interest on money due, or usury, although these meanings are virtually obsolete. See also **gale, gavelkind**.
2. An auctioneer's hammer.

gavelkind
Derived from 'gave all kind' i.e. a custom of giving land to all sons alike (Co. Litt. 140a). Gavelkind was created so that, primarily, land passed equally to all sons, or if there were no sons to the daughters of the owner. Prior to the Norman Conquest (1066) gavelkind was the customary form of land tenure. After the Conquest the rule of primogeniture (descent to the first born) prevailed except in Kent and Kentish Town, London where gavelkind was presumed, unless there was proof of a contrary form of succession to land. Abolished by the Administration of Estates Act 1925, s. 45(1)(a). Called also 'land gavel'. See also **coparcenery**.
39 Halsbury's Laws of England, 4 edn, paras. 322–328.

Robinson's Law of Kent, or the Customs of Gavelkind, 3 edn., (1922).

gazump
Originally 'gezump', a slang word thought to be of Yiddish extraction meaning 'to swindle'. Commonly employed to refer to the withdrawal of a property after an informal bargain has been made, in expectation of selling it to another party at a higher price; the 'double-sale' of a property. The sale of a property to one party at a higher price, in spite of a previous verbal (and, therefore, non-binding) agreement to sell to someone else at a lower price. Strictly, one offer is rejected in favour of a 'better deal'. The term is used also for the practice of threatening, usually at the last minute, to withdraw a property from sale, unless a higher price is paid by the purchaser, commonly under a threat to sell to another party at that higher price. See also **gentleman's agreement, 'subject to contract'**.

geared rent
A rent that increases in a proportionate, or disproportionate relationship to some other income or rental value. For example, a tenant may agree to pay his landlord an increased rent that is geared to any increased rent receivable from his sub-tenant(s), on the basis that any percentage increase payable to the head-landlord is equal to, or higher than any percentage increase receivable from the sub-tenant(s). See also **gearing**.

gearing
1. The relationship between different forms of capital; especially between owner's capital, or **equity capital** and loans or other forms of **debt capital**

(e.g. debentures, loan stock, preference shares). In real estate, gearing is measured by the relationship between the equity capital invested in a property and the mortgage debt secured on that property. The principle of gearing is to borrow money, generally secured on certain fixed assets, at a rate of interest that exerts the least effect on the future profits of the business, so that business can expand beyond the restraint imposed by the amount of an owner's capital. In other words, to use 'other people's money' for one's own profit. The higher the amount of finance provided by a loan or debt capital, relative to the owner's capital, the more highly geared the venture is said to be and the higher the risk for the owner, or equity investors: however, as the interest payable on the debt capital does not vary with profits, then the greater the profit level (after meeting the cost of debt service) the greater the proportionate return to the owner's or equity shareholders.
2. A financial arrangement by which a movement in one factor has a disproportionate effect on another factor e.g. when an increase in the net income from an investment produces a larger increase in the income received by one investor relative to another. See also **debt-to-equity ratio, equity participation, leverage**.

general agent
see **agent**.

general building scheme (US)
see **scheme of development**.

general contractor
One who undertakes to construct or supervise the construction of an entire building, engineering or development project, rather than specified parts of a project. In particular, a **contractor** who undertakes the entire obligations of a contract, but sub-lets parts of the work to a specialist **sub-contractor** or sub-contractors. The principal contractual liability remains with the general contractor but, unless there is an express condition to the contrary (which is usually the case in a modern building contract) or the contract was entered into by reason of some special skill or quality personal to the contractor, a contractor is entitled to sub-let any part of the work to a sub-contractor – British Wagon Co. *v* Lea (1880) 5 QBD 149; Edwards *v* Newlands (Burchett (E) Ltd, Third Parties) [1950] 1 All ER 1072. Called also a 'main contractor' or, in the US, a 'prime contractor' or 'primary contractor'.

general damages
see **damages**.

General Development Order (GDO)
An order, made by the Secretary of State for the Environment, in accordance with the provision of the Town and Country Planning Act 1971, s. 24, which has the effect of granting planning permission for certain forms of **development** (the order is intended to reduce the number of planning applications for minor forms of development). For example, 23 classes of development, ranging from such matters as a minor enlargement of a dwelling-house and erection of certain temporary buildings to street repairs, are granted planning permission by virtue of article 3 of the Town and Country Planning General Development Orders 1977–1981. Such an order may be reversed or modified by the Secretary of State for the

Environment, or the local planning authority with the Secretary's consent, by means of an **article 4 direction**. A General Development Order also sets out procedures that govern planning applications.

cf. **Special Development Order**. See also **permitted development, planning application**.

Planning Law and Procedure, by A.E. Telling, 5 edn., pp. 114–120.

An Outline of Planning Law, by Desmond Heap, 8 edn., p. 103 *et seq.*

general equitable charge

A charge that may be registered as a **land charge** being a charge that is not (a) protected by a deposit of title deeds relating to the legal estate affected; (b) a charge that arises from or is affected by, an interest under a trust for sale or settlement; and (c) included in any other class of land charge. Thus, general equitable charges form a residuary class of land charges arising from statute (currently the Land Charges Act 1972, s. 2(4)) and comprise such claims as an unpaid vendor's lien, an equitable mortgage of a legal estate, certain annuities, and a rentcharge for life. The term is purely of statutory origin and covers a broader category of charges than **equitable charge** as used in common law.

general improvement area (GIA)

An area, in England or Wales, where a local authority considers that the living conditions can be bettered by making improvements to the amenities of the area or to dwellings therein, or both (Housing Act 1969, ss. 28–32, as amended by Housing Act 1974, ss. 50–51 and Housing Act 1980, Sch. 13). A general improvement area is normally in less urgent need of improvement than a **housing action area**; it is an area primarily requiring environmental improvement rather than major improvement to the dwellings. A general improvement area is proposed by the local authority, usually subsequent to a detailed report on the area prepared by a 'suitably qualified' person (whether an officer of the authority or otherwise). When an area has been designated as a general improvement area the local authority may carry out work to improve land or buildings owned by it; acquire land or houses in order to carry out improvement; or make grants to assist and encourage private owners to improve their own properties. Such an area may not cover (although it may adjoin or surround) an area that has already been declared a **clearance area** or a housing action area. It may encompass and thereby supercede a **priority neighbourhood**, and may be superceded by a housing action area (which has a still greater priority). See also **house improvement grant**.

West's Law of Housing, 4 edn, pp. 116–118.

Housing Law, by Andrew Arden and Martin Partington, (1983) pp. 635–638.

22 Halsbury's Laws of England, 4 edn, pp. 402–406.

general liability insurance
see **liability insurance**.

general lien
see **lien**.

general listing (US)
see **multiple agency**.

general mortgage
see **blanket mortgage**.

general offer

An **offer** to the public at large which, if accepted by any member of the public, creates a contract between the parties. "It is an offer made to all the world; and why should not an offer be made to all the world which is to ripen into a contract with anybody who comes forward and performs the condition? It is an offer to become liable to any one who, before it is retracted, performs the condition, and although the offer is made to the world, the contract is made with that limited portion of the public who come forward and perform the condition on the faith of the advertisement. It is not like cases in which you offer to negotiate, or you issue advertisements that you have got a stock of books to sell, or houses to let, in which case there is no offer to be bound by any contract. Such advertisements are offers to negotiate – offers to receive offers – offers to chaffer, as, I [Lindley L.J.] think, some learned judge in one case said". – Carlisle v Carbolic Smoke Ball Co. [1893] 1 QB 268. A general offer may be in respect of a specified property – e.g. on a sale by open **tender**, or a more general offer – e.g. an offer to sell a class of goods at a stated price. See also **invitation to treat**.

general partner

Any member of a **limited partnership** who is empowered to act on behalf of, and thus to bind, the other partners, but whose financial liability to the partnership may exceed his or her direct financial contribution to the partnership. "General partner, shall mean any partner who is not a **limited partner** as defined by this Act" (Limited Partnership Act 1907, s. 3).

A general partner may bind the other partners in accordance with the powers granted by those partners; he or she is personally liable for the debts or obligations of the partnership (in the same way as any partner in a **general partnership**); and he or she has a fiduciary liability to the other 'limited partners' (Limited Partnership Act 1907, s. 4). In the US any member of a general partnership may be referred to also as a 'general partner'. Called sometimes an 'active partner'.
Lindley on Partnership, 15 edn, pp. 944–946, 953–954.

general partnership

A **partnership** where all the partners accept unlimited liability for the actions of the firm and are entitled to a say in the decision making and management of the partnership, unless there is an express agreement to the contrary. A general partnership has no legal entity separate from its members and requires no special form for its establishment. However, a set of written articles, or a partnership agreement, usually is established in order to set down the respective obligations, liabilities, and duties of the partners. A general partnership is the normal form of partnership in English law.
cf. **limited partnership**. See also **general partner, joint and several liability**.

general plan

1. see **master plan**.
(US) 2. see **scheme of development**.

general power

see **power of appointment**.

general rate

see **rate**.

general tail
  see **entailed interest**.

general vesting declaration (GVD)
  A document that may be executed by any public authority possessing compulsory purchase powers, in order to expedite the acquisition of title to land (Compulsory Purchase (Vesting Declaration) Act 1981). The use of a general vesting declaration enables the authority to acquire title to land without the need for the usual procedure of serving **notice to treat**, investigating title and then taking a conveyance. A GVD enables the authority to vest title in itself, and subsequently dispose of the land, more expeditiously. Following confirmation of a **compulsory purchase order**, the acquiring authority must publish notice locally of its intention to execute a GVD and serve notice on the owner and occupier of the land affected by the order, stating that it intends to acquire the land by a general vesting declaration. Without the prior consent of every occupier of the land, a GVD may not be executed earlier than two months from the date of the notice of the authority's declared intention to use this procedure (which may be a notice incorporated with the notice that the appropriate compulsory purchase order is in force, or a separate later notice). The authority must then serve not less than 28 days notice on every owner and occupier of the land (other than the holder of a **minor tenancy** or a long tenancy that is about to expire) stating that the authority is vesting the land in itself on a specified date. The effect of the GVD is to convey the land unilaterally to the authority, as a **deed poll**, as soon as the necessary time limits have expired. On the date specified by the acquiring authority for vesting the land in itself, notice to treat is deemed to have been served and the authority then has a right to enter and take possession of the land (subject to any minor tenancies, which can be terminated in the usual way). Compensation is payable to interested parties as if the land had been acquired by the normal procedure. The date for the assessment of compensation is the date the relevant interest is vested in the authority. This procedure may not be used after a notice to treat has been served as the two procedures are mutually exclusive. Notice of the intention to execute a GVD must be registered as a **local land charge**.
  Law of Compulsory Purchase and Compensation, by Keith Davies, 4 edn., pp. 68–73.
  Encyclopedia of The Law of Compulsory Purchase and Compensation, by Harold J.J. Brown, para. 2-1811.

gentleman's agreement
  1. A **bargain** made between two persons who regard each other as honourable and who are unlikely therefore, to renege on the arrangement, even though it may not be a legally binding contract. An agreement between men (or women) of supposedly respectable and honest character; "a transaction in which each side hopes the other will act like a gentleman and neither intends to so act if it is against his material interests". – Goding v Frazer [1967] 1 WLR 293. A gentleman's agreement normally means something that is not legally enforceable and, without further evidence or an act of part performance cannot create a tenancy

– Rhodes *v* Dalby (1971) 23 P and CR 314. See also **gazump, 'subject to contract'**.

(US) 2. An agreement between a number of parties who are interested in a parcel of real estate: estate agents, property owners, landlords, etc, designed to limit the availability of that property to certain groups of people; especially an agreement to preclude dealings with racial minorities in a given area or district.

geodetic surveying

Surveying that takes account of the size and curvature of the earth and its field of gravity.

cf. **plane surveying**.

geodetic survey system (US)

see **government survey system**.

géomètre – expert (F)

surveyor (in particular a land surveyor).
(*géomètre-expert agricole* – agricultural surveyor)
(*arpenteur-géomètre* – land surveyor)

geotechnics

The science of considering methods of making the earth more habitable.

gérant (F)

manager; managing partner.
(*gérant de domaines* – **land agent**)
(*gérant d'immeubles* – property manager, housing manager)

gestion (F)

management.
(*gestion de l'immeuble* – **property management**)
(*gestion de portefeuille* – **portfolio management**)

gestion d'affaires (F)

Administration of another's affairs in that other's interest but without prior agreement, thereby creating a right to recompense as with a **quasi-contract**.

See also **restitution**.
Amos & Walton's Introduction to French Law, 3 edn, p. 192
Manuel de Droit Civil, by Pierre Voirin et Giles Goubeaux, 20 edn, pp. 407–408.

gestionnaire (F)

managing agent.

ghetto

Originally an area in Italy to which Jews were restricted to live. A term apparently first used in Venice in 1516, although Jews had been confined to areas of various cities from a much earlier date, in order to prevent their influence on the Christian communities. Now generally applied to any densely populated residential area where a race or nationality, other than the indigenous race, predominates. Any area where a socially or economically deprived group is compelled to live, e.g. Harlem, New York.

ghost tenant

A tenant in a shopping centre who rarely, if ever, trades in the leased premises thus possibly depriving the landlord of a proper level of **turnover rent**.

gift (or donation)

A voluntary and gratuitous transfer of property to another without **consideration** or expectation of consideration, or for nominal consideration. (Any transfer of property at a price which is deliberately low with the intention of conferring a gratuitous benefit may constitute a gift.) A voluntary conveyance or assignment is called commonly a **deed of gift**. A gift may be conditional but, apart from any condition, it must not be revocable or terminable. A valid gift requires: (i) a voluntary intention to

give by the donor; (ii) an act that gives effect to that intention, such as the delivery of possession, either physically in the case of a personal chattel, or by a repudiation of possession in favour of the recipient; and (iii) acceptance of the gift by the recipient (acceptance is presumed unless there is a signified rejection thereof – Dewar v Dewar [1975] 1 WLR 1532); and (iv) because there is no valuable consideration to support the contract, the gift must be made by deed or in the case of chattels by delivery. A gift should be made with an intention of benefaction and there should be no intention that, in return, any benefit passes to the donor; the recipient should be free to enjoy the property received; and the recipient should not be restrained in the manner in which he may dispose of the property – Leary v Federal Comp. of Taxation (1980) 11 ATR 145. A gift may be made *inter vivos*, between living persons; or *causa mortis*, in anticipation of death. A gift *inter vivos* must be effected by actual delivery during the lifetime of the donor, without reference to his or her death. A gift *causa mortis* is made in expectation of death but does not become effective until the donor dies. A gift may be made by **deed**; by **delivery** (provided the subject matter admits of delivery, as in the case of chattels); or by a **declaration of trust** in favour of the recipient. If a gift is made without the proper formality it may be enforceable only in a court of equity; as might arise from the doctrine of **estoppel**. See also **capital transfer tax, class gift, endowment, grant, settlement**.
20 Halsbury's Laws of England, 4 edn, paras. 1–100.

gift *causa mortis*
A **gift** in the 'cause of death'; a gift from a living person who expects to die shortly to another living person whom the donor wishes to inherit his or her property on the donor's death. Called also a 'donation', or *donatio causa mortis*.

gift deed
see **deed of gift**.

gift *inter vivos*
A **gift** made between living persons. cf. **devise**, **gift *causa mortis***.

gift tax
A tax on the assessed or deemed market value of a **gift** made during the donor's lifetime. In the UK gift tax has been replaced by **capital transfer tax**. In the US a federal or state tax is payable by a donor upon making a gift (whether a transfer without consideration or for a reduced consideration) usually on a progressive basis.

gilt-edged security
A security or bond of the highest standing; in particular, Government securities or securities of a statutory undertaking (The Capital Gains Tax Act 1979, Sch. 2. part II, as extended by subsequent statutory instruments, sets out those securities which are classified as gilt-edged securities for the purpose of exemption from capital gains tax after 12 months.)

Ginnie Mae (US)
A popular abbreviation for the **Government National Mortgage Association**.

glebe land
1. Land that belongs to a parish church. Land that forms part of, or provides income to, a parish church, rectory, vicarage or ecclesiastical

benefice (but not land that benefits from a **tithe**). In general, "the glebe of a benefice includes all land of any kind, houses or other buildings forming part of its endowments but does not include the parsonage house and grounds occupied with it". (14 Halsbury's Laws of England, 4 edn., p. 615). See also **ecclesiastical property**. 2. In Roman law, a plot of uncultivated land.

global insurance policy
see **blanket insurance policy**.

going-concern value
The value of a business as an active operating entity. The value of a business assessed on the basis of its earning power or potential profit rather than the value of its tangible assets. The going concern value may include the value, if any, of intangibles such as goodwill and any additional value to a special purchaser.
cf. **break-up value**.

going value
The **market value**. See also **going-concern value**.

good consideration
see **consideration**.

good estate management
A term used in the Agriculture Act 1947, s. 10 for a standard to which agricultural land should be cultivated and maintained "having regard to the character and situation of the land and other relevant circumstances", and a standard to which fixed equipment must be repaired, improved and maintained. See also **good husbandry, management scheme**.

good faith
Honesty of intention; "honesty in fact

in the conduct or transaction concerned". – (United States Commercial Code, para. 1–201 (19)). A lack of intention to defraud; to conceal something from another; to act with an ulterior motive; or to enter into a transaction that is clearly a sham. (An act done negligently is not one done in bad faith.) A purchaser 'in good faith' accepts that the vendor will transfer what he alleges he is selling without **fraud** and without the purchaser having to make his own searching enquiries.

A duty to act in good faith is owed particularly by an **agent** to his principal. "A principal is entitled to have an honest agent, and it is only the honest agent who is entitled to a **commission**' – Andrews v Ramsey and Co. [1903] 2 K B 638. Thus, for an agent or broker to endeavour to receive a secret profit or to obtain commission from, or act for, two parties without declaring his position would be a breach of good faith. See also **bona fide purchaser, fiduciary, utmost good faith**.

good-faith money
see **earnest money**.

good husbandry
A term used in the Agriculture Act 1947, s. 11 for a standard of management and efficiency of production required from an agricultural unit taking into account the kind of produce and the quality and quantity thereof. "Good husbandry is roughly the maintenance of a reasonable standard of efficient production having regard ... to the character of the agricultural unit and the manner in which it is being farmed." – Lory v London Borough of Brent [1971] 1 All ER 1046. This standard includes,

as applicable, proper grazing, mowing, cultivation, maintenance of fertility, proper tending of livestock, control of pests and disease, protection and preservation of harvested or lifted crops and general maintenance and repair, as well as **good estate management**. A tenant of an agricultural holding is under no statutory obligation to abide by the rules of good husbandry, unless expressly commited by the terms of a lease, but a failure to observe the rules may constitute grounds for the Agricultural Land Tribunal to approve a landlord's notice to quit (Agricultural Holdings (Notice to Quit) Act 1977, s. 2(4)). See also **grounds for possession, husband-like manner**.

good leasehold title
A title to a leasehold interest which may be registered with the Land Registry, in accordance with the provisions of the Land Registration Act 1925, s. 8(1), where that title is satisfactory to the registrar, but does not amount to an **absolute title** because there is no assurance that the lessor has a valid right to grant the lease. A good leasehold title is held subject to any estate, interest or right which may affect the freehold title or any superior leasehold title, but in other respects has the same effect as registration with an absolute title (1925 Act, s. 10). However, if the freehold title becomes registered, or can be deduced by the registrar, a good leasehold title may be converted to an absolute leasehold title. The registrar may also convert a good leasehold to an absolute leasehold title after ten years, provided the leaseholder or his predecessor has been in possession under the terms of

the lease during that period (1925 Act, s. 77(4)). See also **derogation from grant, estoppel, qualified title, possessory title**.

good record title (US)
see **good title**.

good repair
The sort of condition in which a fair-minded tenant would maintain a property; "such a state of **repair** as will satisfy a respectable occupant using the premises fairly; but not that state of repair which an owner or tenant might fancy". – Cooke *v* Cholmondesley (1858) 4 Drew. 328. In general a term in a lease which uses the words 'good repair' or 'good and substantial repair' requires a tenant to maintain the property in as satisfactory a condition as another tenant would expect of the same property, but not better. It excludes major structural repair or any improvement required to the leased property. However, the duration of the lease, the type of property and other considerations may be taken into account when interpreting such words. See also **tenantable repair**.

good root of title
see **root of title**.

good title
A **title** that enables a person to retain possession of land against any person who might present a challenge to that title; one that is free of doubt as to its legality; and can be transferred or mortgaged without fear or favour. In particular, a title that a court of equity "would adopt as a sufficient ground for compelling **specific performance** . . . such a one as would enable a purchaser to hold the property against any person who might

probably challenge his right to it". – Jeakes v White (1852) 21 LJ Ex. 269. If it is "beyond reasonable doubt" that an encumberance will not be enforced against a purchaser good title can be said to exist – MEPC Ltd v Christian Edwards and Others [1979] 3 WLR 720.

In the US, a title that is free of any publicly recorded encumberance and has been recorded as having an unbroken root of title is called a 'good record title', or a 'sufficient title'. See also **absolute title, beneficial owner, deposit, marketable title, root of title**.

goods

That which a person has at his disposal. All forms of moveable property. Anything that is tangible, may be moved and has an intrinsic value, but usually excluding **money** or **chose in action**. "Goods includes all personal **chattels** other than things in action and money, and in Scotland all corporeal moveables except money; and in particular 'goods' includes emblements, industrial growing crops, and things attached to or forming part of the land which are agreed to be severed before sale or under contract of sale"(Sale of Goods Act 1971, s. 61 – replacing a similar definition in the Sale of Goods Act 1893). – Utica Carting Storage and Contracting Co. v World Fire & Marine Insurance Co., 100 NYS 2d. 941. A term commonly used to refer to 'household' goods and items that may be severed from real property, e.g. crops and tenant's fixtures, but does not include animals, 'chattels real' (i.e. a leasehold interest), or any **fixture** (as this has become part of the realty).

In general the supply of materials as part of a construction contract is part of an agreement to execute and complete construction work and does not involve the supply of goods *per se*. See also **effects, moveables**.

The Sale of Goods, by P.S. Atiyah, 6 edn., pp. 35–38.
Chalmer's Sale of Goods Act, by Michael Mark, 18 edn., (1979).
Sale of Goods, by Benjamin, 2 edn.

goodwill

The favourable consideration that the proprietor of a business has won from the public; all the benefits attaching to, or connected with, a business as a consequence of an established and active trade. An advantageous position that, in the short run, should be sustained by a new proprietor operating from the same premises or from new premises in close proximity. The value of a business over and above the value of a similar business, due to the profits that arise from the probability that customers will return to where they are accustomed to doing business or trade; "an advantage, belonging to a house, long accustomed to carry on a particular trade" – Cruttwell v Lye (1810) 34 ER 131; Metropolitan National Bank v St. Louis Dispatch Co., 149 US 436, 13 SCt. 944. This *incremental* **profit** may be produced by the proprietor's personal abilities, or the general reputation and efficiency of the business – 'personal goodwill'; or the convenience of the location of the business to its customers – 'local or locational goodwill'; or the value brought about as a result of a monopoly position held by a business. Goodwill is an intangible asset, of an indefinite life, which attaches to the name, the proprietor, the property, an employee or other more tangible parts of a business. It has no inherent value although a property may appear to have a value in excess of its market value due to the goodwill of the occupier. Fundamentally goodwill is a personal asset rather than something inherent in the value of a property. Goodwill is a form of **personal property**, it does not automatically pass with a transfer of land, but it may be transferred separately or with the premises from which it is generated. It cannot be sold or transferred apart from the business to which it relates and even though it may be acquired at a considerable price it is ephemeral and must be nurtured by a new owner.

Goodwill is valued normally on the basis of the historic net profit of a business, after making adjustments for non-recurring or special items. Businesses are sold commonly on the basis of one to five times the 'adjusted net profit'. Also it may be valued by assessing the difference between the **going-concern value** of an enterprise and the replacement or **break-up value** of the entire enterprise. See also **business tenancy, compensation for disturbance**.

Landlord and Tenant Law, by David Yates and A.J. Hawkins, pp. 544–554 (1981).

Commercial Property Management, by A. Grear and J. Oxborough, pp. 320–344 (1970).

gore
A small, usually triangular or roughly triangular, parcel of land.

gouging
Extracting an exorbitant sum from someone; extorting an excessive price, e.g. a rent that grossly exceeds the market value. See also **duress,** **fine, premium**.

government survey system (US)
A system of land measurement and identification, first adopted in 1785, which is based on an official survey, set out on a grid system that is related to the earth's longitudinal and latitudinal lines. Called also the 'public lands survey system', the 'rectangular survey system' or the 'geodetic survey system'. See also **metes and bounds, surveying**.
The Appraisal of Real Estate, AIREA, 8 edn., pp. 156–159.
Real Estate Principles, by Bruce Harwood, 2 edn., pp. 22–27.

governmental act (US)
see **statute law**.

grace period
A period of time which may elapse after an obligation or debt falls due before there is considered to be a default. Leases and mortgage deeds commonly provide a number of days grace before the landlord or mortgagee can take action for a breach of the contract. See also **days of grace**.

graded lease (US)
A lease incorporating a **graded rent**.

graded rent
(US)1. A rent that increases (or decreases) at specified intervals in accordance with the provisions of a lease e.g. £1000 in year one, £2000 in year two, £3000 for the remaining term of a lease. Called also a 'stepped rent', particularly in the UK.
cf. **graduated rent**.
(US) 2. A rent, being paid for a property, that can be used as a comparable figure for valuation purposes, after adjustments to take account of size, location, age, etc.

graduated lease

A lease that contains provisions for a **graduated rent**.
cf. **flat-rental lease**.

graduated-payment mortgage (GPM)

see **variable-payment mortgage**.

graduated rent (US)

A rent that may be varied, usually to market rental value, at set intervals during the term of a lease. Also used synonymously with any form of variable rent, including a stepped or **graded rent**; a rent in a **revaluation lease**; or a **percentage** or **turnover rent**.
cf. **flat rent**.

grand magasin (F)

department store.

grand sergeanty

see **sergeanty**.

grant

1. In a general sense, the passing or transfer of any thing from one party to another. In a special sense, the transfer of the ownership of real or personal property in writing or by deed – a conveyance being a 'deed of grant'. (The proper legal designation for the transfer of personal property, especially a lease, is **assignment**.) 'Grant' is used in particular to distinguish the transfer of some estate or interest in land from the giving of a mere licence or of a right to personal property. (Since 1925 title to land can be transferred only by grant, i.e. such feudal means of transfer as 'livery of seisin', 'feoffment' and 'bargain and sale' were thereby abolished; but the word 'grant' is no longer necessary to transfer land or create an interest in land: Law of Property Act 1925, s. 51). A grant transfers a right to property, but it does not necessarily

effect immediate delivery. The word 'grant' is used frequently in a conveyance but, since 1925, its use does not imply any covenant or condition (Law of Property Act 1925, s. 59(2)). See also **covenant for title, demise, derogation from grant, lie in grant, lost modern grant**.
2. To give or bestow a right or privilege on someone, e.g. the grant of a right of way or easement. See also **implied grant**.
3. Financial assistance given by a public authority for a particular purpose, such as a contribution towards the cost of repairing or improving a building, improving the environment or stimulating employment. See also **home improvement grant, intermediate grant, mitigation works, repairs grant, special grant, standard grant, subsidy**.

grant; bargain; sell; convey

Words used in a conveyance to indicate that the clause thereafter forms one of the **operative parts** of the deed, e.g., 'the vendor hereby grants unto A'.

grant deed (US)

A simple form of **deed** which states that a vendor has a valid title to property which he will convey, and sets out details of any encumberances, that affect the property, but leaves the remaining conditions of sale to be governed by statute law. A grant deed does not ensure that the vendor is the absolute owner of the property and in form it falls between a **quit-claim deed** and a **warranty deed**. In some states called a 'special warranty deed'. See also **open contract**.

grantee

The party to whom a **grant** of real property is made.

granting clause (US)
see **operative clause**.

grantor
The person by whom a **grant** of real property is made. See also **vendor**.

grantor's lien
see **lien**.

grantor–grantee index (US)
A master index maintained in the Public Recorder's Office showing alphabetically all recorded instruments for the transfer of the ownership of land.

grantor trust (US)
see **bare trust**.

grasson or **grassum**
1. A **fine** that was paid for the right to transfer a copyhold estate.
2. In Scotland, a premium paid in lieu of or in addition to rent.

gratis (L)
'Without reward or consideration'. See also **gift**.

gratuit (F)
free (of charge).
(*à titre gratuit* – without consideration; as a gift).

gratuitous deed
A deed without valuable or legal **consideration**. See also **gift**.

grazing licence
A **licence** to use land for pasture or mowing for part of the year. Under the Agricultural Holding Act 1948, s. 2., a tenancy of agricultural land granted for a term that is less than 'from year to year' is converted to a tenancy from year to year and, therefore, is given **security of tenure**, However, an agreement for the letting of land or granting of a licence to occupy land only 'for grazing or mowing' during some specified period of a year may be exempt from such security; thus, such a letting may be referred to as a 'grazing licence'. See also **agricultural tenancy, common right of**.

gré (F)
agreement.
(*de gré à gré* – by private treaty; by mutual agreement)
(*au gré de l'acheteur* – at the purchaser's option).

green
An area of public open land situated in or near a town or village and put down to grass. At common law a town or village green may be common land; but for registration purposes it is defined and treated separately from 'common land'. "Town or village green means land which has been allotted by or under any Act for the exercise or recreation of the inhabitants of any locality or on which the inhabitants of any locality have a customary right to indulge in lawful sports or pastimes or on which the inhabitants of any locality have indulged in such sport or pastimes as of right for not less than twenty years" (Common Registration Act 1965, s. 22(1)). Thus the statutory definition covers recreational allotments available to local inhabitants and land that is referred to commonly as a 'village green'.

The ownership of this land is usually obscure, but probably it was waste land of a **manor** that became vested in the local inhabitants or a local body. When such land is registered it becomes common land, preserving that right of common enjoyment in perpetuity, even if the

ownership may remain uncertain.
English Land Law (cases and material), by Michael Harwood, pp. 265–274 (1977).

green belt
An expanse of countryside, surrounding or between towns or cities, in which development is prohibited or strictly controlled, with the intention of restraining the outward sprawl of urban development and preserving agricultural land. A term that originates from the Green Belt (London and Home Counties) Act 1938 which was passed, "to make provisions for the preservation from industrial and building development of areas of land" in and around London.
   A green belt is intended to provide also an area of countryside for the leisure and recreation of urban residents; therefore, it is an area which, by its nature, creates a conflict between the demands of urban dwellers and the farmer. See also **access agreement, buffer zone, garden city, open country**.
Town Planning at the Crossroads, by Lewis Keeble, p. 67 *et seq* (1961).
An Introduction to Town and Country Planning, by John Ratcliffe, 2 edn., pp. 69–74.

green field site
see **unimproved land**.

green lining (US)
A policy employed by organisations granting residential mortgages by which certain neighbourhoods are identified for favourable consideration and in which business is actively sought.
   cf. **red lining**.

greenways
Strips of landscaped land either alongside a highway or linked together in a built-up area.

grevé (F)
encumbered; burdened; entailed.
(*bien non grevé* – unencumbered property)
see also **encumberance**.

grey area
see **intermediate area**.

grey property
see **clearance area**.

grid, or gridiron, planning
A town or estate layout based on rectangular street blocks.

gros oeuvre or **gros ouvrage** (F)
superstructure (of a building) including any elements that form part of the enclosure of a building. In French law the builder, architect and *promoteur* are liable for defects in the superstructure of a new building for ten years from its completion date. See also *reception definitive*.

gross
Exclusive of any deduction; entire. A right **in gross** is one that is independent of anything else, i.e. it is not appurtenant, appendant or otherwise annexed to land. See also **gross floor area, gross income, gross lease, gross rent, gross value**.

gross adjusted income
see **effective gross income**.

gross area
see **gross external area, gross internal area, gross lettable area, gross site area**.

gross built area (GBA)
The total **gross external area** (GEA) of a building at all floor levels, based on the external dimensions without excluding the areas referred to in the

definition of GEA. An area used in calculating construction costs rather than in leasing or valuation. If those areas that are not enclosed, e.g. balconies, are excluded this area is called the 'gross covered area'. See also **gross lettable area.**

gross covered area
  see **gross built area.**

gross earnings
  see **gross income.**

gross easement (US)
  see **easement-in-common, easement in gross.**

gross effective income
  see **effective gross income.**

gross estimated rental
  A term defined for the purpose of assessing a liability to rates prior to the Rating and Valuation Act 1925 as, "the rent at which the hereditament might reasonably be expected to let from year to year free of all usual tenant's rates and taxes and title commutation rent-charge, if any". Replaced in 1925 by **gross value.**

gross external area (GEA)
  A term defined by The Royal Institution of Chartered Surveyors' and The Incorporated Society of Valuers and Auctioneers' Code of Measuring Practice (2nd edn, 1986) as the area "of a building taking each floor into account including:-

  – perimeter wall thicknesses and external projections;
  – areas occupied by internal walls and partitions;
  – columns, piers, chimney-breasts,

stairwells, lift-wells and the like;
  – lift-rooms, plant rooms, tank-rooms, fuel stores whether or not above main roof level (except for Scotland, where for rating purposes these are excluded); and
  – open-sided covered areas (should be stated separately).

  Excluding:-
  – open balconies;
  – open fire escapes
  – open covered ways or minor canopies;
  – open vehicle parking areas, terraces, and the like;
  – domestic outside WCs and coalhouses;
  – areas with a headroom of less than 1.5m (5 feet) are excluded and quoted separately".

Note: the above exclusions should be separately calculated for building cost estimating purposes.
  A term used particularly in town planning e.g. for assessing a floor space index or a plot ratio, and for rating valuations of houses and bungalows in England and Wales and industrial and warehouse property in Scotland. Sometimes used for building cost estimating. Called also the 'reduced covered area' or the 'gross floor space'. See also **gross internal area, gross built area.**

gross floor area
  The total floor areas of a building, measured from external wall to external wall. This area may be measured to include the external wall thickness – the **gross external floor area,** or to exclude that extra dimension – the **gross internal floor area.** If areas that are essential to the proper use of the building are excluded: e.g.

lift shafts, lobbies, common stairwells and other common areas – this area is referred to sometimes as the 'gross useable area'
cf. **net floor area**. See also **gross built area, gross lettable area, rentable area.**

gross floor space
see **gross external area.**

gross fund
A financial institution that is exempt from income and capital gains tax, e.g. a charity, pension fund, friendly society. See also **real estate investment trust.**

gross income
The total **income** receivable from a property investment before making any deduction for expenses, management charges, taxes, etc., or any allowance for bad debts, depreciation or repayment of capital; the total monies collected by a landlord or property owner before any expenses or outgoings. In the US the total income, including any payments received as a contribution to operating expenses, is referred to as the gross income or usually the 'gross operating income'.
cf. **net income**. See also **effective gross income, gross rent.**

gross income multiplier (GIM) (US)
see **gross rent multiplier.**

gross internal area (GIA)
The **gross external area** of a building, excluding perimeter and party wall thicknesses, external projections and finishes thereto. An area used for building cost estimation purposes, for industrial, warehouse and shop agency and valuation purposes including service charge apportionment but

excluding rating of industrial and warehouse property in Scotland. See also **gross floor area, net rentable area.**

gross leaseable area (US)
see **gross lettable area.**

gross lease (US)
A lease which provides that the lessee pays rent only throughout the period of the lease, without any 'pass-through' or **escalator clause**; the lessor paying all or most of the operating expenses, taxes, insurance costs, etc. In the US most residential and some office leases are gross leases and most industrial and shop leases are net leases. Sometimes called a 'fixed lease'.
cf. **net lease**. See also **straight lease.**

gross lettable (or leasable) area (GLA)
The total area of a shopping centre occupied by retailers – excluding all common areas such as malls, technical areas, car parking, service areas, and normally other ancillary uses such as offices, flats, etc. See also **gross retail area.**

gross multiplier (US)
see **gross rent multiplier.**

gross operating income (US)
see **gross income.**

gross population density
see **population density.**

gross profit
The profit from the sale of goods or services before the deduction of selling and administrative expenses; the profit obtained by deducting cost of goods from the actual sales price

received before the deduction of expenses.
cf. **net profit**.

gross redemption yield
see **grossed-up redemption yield**.

gross rent
The total amount payable as **rent** by all the tenants of a property, excluding any other payments, e.g. rates, taxes, service charges, etc., that a tenant may be bound to pay to the landlord under the terms of a lease, and before any allowance or deduction is made for voids or defaulting tenants. In the US gross rent and **gross income** are frequently used interchangeably, but in the UK gross rent normally refers only to payments that are strictly rent (compensation for the use and profit to be derived from land) and does not embrace other payments made by a tenant to his landlord, such as service charge contributions.
cf. **net rent**.

gross rent multiplier (GRM) (US)
A figure, based on analysis of comparable sales, used to capitalise the annual **gross income** from a property in order to estimate its capital value; or the factor which shows the relationship between the value or sale price and the annual gross income from a property. This factor may be applied either to gross income or to the **effective gross income**, provided the application is consistant with the supporting analysis. However, it is purely a rule of thumb method of valuation – a more reliable valuation is based on the capitalisation of the projected net income. Called also a 'gross income multiplier'.

cf. **net income multiplier**. See also **capitalisation factor**.

gross retail area
The total area of a retail store or shop, measured up to the perimeter of the external walls, including storage areas, staff and ancillary office accommodation, technical areas and the like, within the shop.
cf. **sales area**. See also **gross lettable area**.

gross sale price
The total consideration received by the vendor from the purchaser of a property, excluding any deduction for selling costs, fees, taxes, etc.
cf. **net price**.

gross site area
The total area of a parcel or plot of land extended to the centre of any adjoining road, which is limited to 6m (or 20 feet) in planning density calculations. See also **floor space index, site area**.

gross usable area
see **gross floor area**.

gross value (GV)
1. The **annual value**, or the estimated rent, of a property (hereditament) as assessed for rating purposes, assuming that the property is let from year to year and that the tenant undertakes to pay all the usual tenant's rates and taxes and the landlord undertakes to bear the cost of the repairs and insurance and other expenses, if any, necessary to maintain the property in a state to command that rent (General Rate Act 1967, s. 19(6)). When assessing the gross value of a dwelling house, the gross value is a hypothetical rent. "It is the rent which an imaginary tenant might reasonably be expected to pay to an imaginary

landlord for a tenancy of this dwelling in *this* location, on the hypothesis that both are reasonable people, the landlord not being extortionate, the tenant not being under pressure, the dwelling being vacant and to let, not subject to any control, the landlord agreeing to do the repairs and pay insurance, the tenant agreeing to pay the rates, the period not too short nor yet too long, simply from year to year" – R. *v* Paddington (Valuation Officer) Ex.p. Peachey Property Corporation Ltd, [1965] 2 All ER 848. 'Gross Value' is used to assess the value of all properties consisting "of one or more houses or other non-industrial buildings, with or without garden, yard, court, forecourt, outhouse or other appurtenance belonging thereto but without other land". The **rateable value** of this type of property is then determined by making a given **statutory deduction** from the gross value. (Note: The Local Government, Planning and Land Act 1980, s. 29(1) provides that when the next rating revaluation comes into force gross value will only apply to "a dwelling-house, a private garage or private storage premises"). cf. **net annual value**.
2. The **capital value** of a property excluding the cost of acquiring the property, i.e. assuming the purchaser has no such costs to bear.
3. The value of the estate of a deceased person prior to any deduction for debts, funeral expenses, estate duty or similar taxes and incumberances (Non-Contentious Probate Rules 1954, s. 2).

gross yield
The return from an investment excluding costs associated with acqui-ring and managing the investment. cf. **net yield**.

grosses reparations (F)
major or structural repairs; "structtural repairs are those to main walls and vaults, the restoration of main beams and the reroofing in its entirety; also repairing of dykes, load-bearing walls and enclosing walls in their entirety. All other repairs constitute maintenance" (French Civil Code, art. 606). Structural repairs, as a rule, are not the responsibility of a usufructuary (Civil Code art. 605). See also **usufruct**.

ground floor
The floor nearest the ground level at the place of entrance or exit from a building: where a building has two levels of entrance these are referred to commonly as the upper and lower ground floors. See also **first floor**.

ground landlord
The grantor of a **ground lease**.

ground lease
A lease of land without any building; although the lease may be 'secured' by a building or buildings erected by the tenant at a later date. A ground lease is granted usually subject to a condition that the lessee will build upon the land, i.e. a building lease, and in English law should be so construed. The lessee retains the right to the use and occupation of the buildings for the term of the lease, but at the end of the lease the land, together with the improvements, reverts to the lessor. The lessor may be a freeholder or one who is himself a lessee. In England such leases were traditionally granted for 99 years, although modern ground leases are

frequently granted for 125 years or even 999 years. See also **emphyteotic lease, enfranchisement, ground rent, leasehold enfranchisement, net lease**.

ground rent

A sum of money payable on an annual basis for the right to use and enjoy a parcel of land that belongs to another; **rent** payable for land that is let for the purpose of improvement by building. Ground rent may be used to refer to rent payable under a **ground lease** or a **building lease** (usually for a substantial term of years), or a rent based on the value of land excluding buildings and improvements. (The difference between the rent of land with the improvements and the rent of a bare site before improvement may be called the 'improved ground rent', although that term is also synonymous with **leasehold ground rent**). A modern ground lease usually provides that the initial rent is based on the annual market value of the land and that this rent is to be revised at specified intervals during the lease (commonly every 33 years during a 99-year lease or every 25 years during a 125-year lease) to a figure which maintains the same proportion that the initial ground rent bore to the rent obtained from the buildings at the start of the lease.

cf. **low rent**. See also **economic rent, security of ground rent**.

ground rent lease (US)

A form of lease used in Maryland whereby the tenant is granted a **ground lease**, usually for 99 years, and the tenant has a right to renew the lease provided he pays a specified sum of money for that right. Similar to an **emphyteotic** lease in the civil law.

ground storey

The storey of a building to which there is an entrance from the outside on or near the ground level and, where there are two such storeys, the lower of the two. The compartment of a building between the **ground floor** and **first floor**. See also **mezzanine**.

grounds for possession

The grounds available to a landlord to enable him to apply to the court in order to obtain possession of property from a tenant who has statutory **security of tenure**. English statute law provides most tenants of residential, business, and agricultural properties with a right either to the grant of a new tenancy, or a right to protection from **eviction**, when an existing tenancy comes to its contractual end.

A court will not grant an order for possession of a dwelling-house that is let on a **protected tenancy**, or that is the subject of a **statutory tenancy**, unless (a) the court considers it reasonable; and (b) either, the court is satisfied that **suitable alternative accommodation** is available to the tenant, or will be available to the tenant when the order takes effect; or, the court is satisfied that one of the cases specified in the Rent Act 1977, Sch. 15 Part I (as amended by the Housing Act 1980, s. 66. Sch. 7) is met (Rent Act 1977, s. 98). In a number of the cases specified in the Act the court is obliged to grant an order for possession provided the requisite conditions are met; for example, when a former 'owner-occupier' seeks to regain possession of a residence for his own or his family's occupation or when the premises have been let on a **protected shorthold tenancy** that has now expired. These cases apply only when the tenant had been given notice, before the commencement of the tenancy, that the landlord might seek to reclaim possession at the end of the tenancy. In the other cases the court has a discretionary right to decide whether, or not, to grant an order for possession; the onus of proof being on the landlord to show reason for his being granted possession. The discretionary cases relate to such matters as a breach of a condition of the tenancy, including non-payment of rent; causing or permitting waste or deterioration to the property or the landlord's furniture; a conviction for an illegal or immoral user or causing nuisance or annoyance to an adjoining occupier; or that the premises are reasonably required by the landlord for occupation as a residence for himself, any of his children over 18, his parents, or his spouse's parents, provided this does not cause 'greater hardship' to the tenant than to the landlord and provided the landlord did not succeed to that position with the tenant in occupation.

A landlord may not obtain possession of a dwelling let on a **secure tenancy** unless the court is satisfied that it should grant an order for possession on one of the grounds set out in the Housing Act 1980, Sch. 4, Part I. For the first six of the grounds specified in the 1980 Act the court must be satisfied that it is *reasonable* to make the order. For the next three specified grounds the court must be satisfied that 'suitable accommodation' will be available to the tenant when the order is given. For the remaining four specified grounds both of the aforementioned condi-

tions must be met.

In the case of a **long tenancy** of a dwelling granted at a **low rent**, and which falls within the rateable value limits specified by the Rent Act 1977, at the end of the contractual term the tenancy is either converted into a statutory tenancy or the landlord must obtain a court order for possession which may be granted on one of the grounds specified in the Landlord and Tenant Act 1954, Sch. 3, as amended (which correspond to those in Cases 1–9 of Schedule 15 of the Rent Act 1977).

An **assured tenancy** or a **business tenancy** does not come to an end (but may continue indefinitely) unless terminated in accordance with the provisions of the Landlord and Tenant Act 1954, Part II. It may be brought to an end by notice to quit given by the tenant, by forfeiture of the tenancy or of a superior tenancy, or by a surrender. Otherwise the tenant has a right to a 'new tenancy', unless the landlord is able to oppose an application to the court for a new tenancy on one of the grounds specified in the 1954 Act, s. 30 (as amended, in the case of an assured tenancy, by the Housing Act 1980, Sch. 5). The grounds include substantial breaches of a condition of the tenancy (e.g. persistent non-payment of rent, failure to repair); the provision by the landlord of 'suitable alternative accommodation' for the tenant; the landlord's intention to demolish or reconstruct the premises or a substantial part of the premises; the landlord's ability to obtain a higher rent by reletting premises as a whole that are currently sub-let in parts; and (except for an assured tenancy) the landlord's need of the premises for his own business, provided the landlord has not acquired or created the lease within five years of termination of the tenancy. A landlord of an assured tenancy must obtain also a court order for possession if the tenant ('**residential occupier**') refuses to vacate the premises (Protection from Eviction Act, s. 2).

An **agricultural tenancy** must be brought to an end by a duly served notice to quit and within one month after being given such notice the tenant may claim that the notice shall not take effect without the consent of the Agricultural Lands Tribunal. The Tribunal must then be satisfied in all the circumstances that it is reasonable to grant possession. The principle grounds on which the Tribunal may be satisfied that possession should be given to the landlord are (a) the land is required for a non-agricultural use that has been authorised by planning permission or for which such permission is not required; (b) the tenant has failed in his duty to abide by the rules of good husbandry; (c) the tenant is in breach of a term or condition of the tenancy; (d) the tenant is insolvent; (e) on the death of the tenant when there is no successor; or (f) the land can be amalgamated with other land to form a better agricultural unit (Agricultural Holding (Notices to Quit) Act 1977, ss. 2, 3). See also **right of re-entry**.

The Law of Landlord and Tenant, by David Lloyd Evans, 2 edn, pp. 275 – 297, 312–314, 317–318, 397–403, 443–447.

Landlord and Tenant Law, by David Yates and A.J. Hawkins, p. 334 *et seq.*, p. 507 *et seq.*, p. 575 *et seq.* (1981).

Woodfall's Landlord and Tenant, 28 edn, paras. 3–0155 *et seq.*, 2–0711 *et seq.*, 2–0038 *et seq.*

27 Halsbury's Laws of England, 4 edn, paras. 659 *et seq.*, 498 *et seq.*

1 Halsbury's Laws of England 4 edn, paras. 1053 *et seq.*

Handbook of Business Tenancies, by D.W. Williams, (loose leaf) para. 4–01 *et seq.*, (1985).

Renewal of Business Tenancies: Law and Practice, by Kirk Reynolds and Wayne Clarke, paras. 7.1.0 to 7.9.5. (1985 looseleaf).

growing crops
see **emblements**, *fructus*, **way-growing crops**.

growth rate
The annual rate at which an income or value is assumed to grow; usually as a future prediction based on past experience.

guarantee
1. A person who is entitled to the benefit of a **guaranty**.
2. A contract of guaranty or the action of giving a guaranty.

guarantor
A person who makes or gives a **guaranty**.

guaranty (or guarantee)
A **collateral** agreement by which one party gives an undertaking to a second party to be responsible for a debt or default owed by a third party. A contract by which one party (guarantor/promisor) gives a promise to another (guarantee/promisee) that if a third party (the principal debtor) does not pay a debt or meet an obligation owed to that other then the guarantor undertakes to secure that the debt is paid by the principal debtor. A

contract of guaranty is "an accessory contract by which the promisor undertakes to be answerable to the promisee for the debt, default or miscarriage of another person, whose primary liability to the promisee must exist or be contemplated". (20 Halsbury's Laws of England, 4 edn, p. 49).

A guaranty is often referred to as a 'conditional' or **collateral contract** because it is intended to lend support, or run alongside the primary liability of the third party, and not to act as an 'original' agreement; in fact it cannot exist independently of the contract, the performance of which it seeks to guaranty. In that respect a guaranty may be distinguished from an **indemnity** which is intended as a primary contract for the benefit of the party by whom a debt or obligation is owed (An indemnity requires only two parties and does not concern itself directly with the means by which the loss arises; one who gives an indemnity is not a party to any contract or arrangement by which the liability arises). Thus if one party, who is uncertain as to whether he will be paid by a company for work he is about to perform, is instructed by a manager of that company to proceed with work with the words "you go on and do the work, and I will be your paymaster. I will see you paid", then the manager has provided an indemnity (even though he may anticipate that the board will pay). But if the manager had said "you go and do the work and I shall see that the board pays you", then the manager has provided a guaranty, his liability arises only if the board fails to pay – Lake-

man v Mountstephen (1874) LR 7 HL 23. A guaranty has been described as "a promise to another as creditor to secure the payment of a debt payable to him"; and an indemnity as "a promise to another as debtor to secure the repayment of a debt payable by him" (38 SJ 577). (Although 'guarantee' may be construed to include an indemnity or cognate expressions: Companies Act 1980, s. 65(1).) A contract of guaranty, as it relates to a "debt, default or miscarriage of another" should be in **writing** or evidenced in writing and signed by the party to be held liable (Statute of Frauds 1677, s. 4); a requirement that is not essential to a contract of indemnity. (Note: Anything in writing may be construed as a guarantee "if it contains or purports to contain some promise or assurance (however worded or presented) that a defect will be made good by complete or partial replacement, or by repair, monetary compensation or otherwise". (Unfair Contract Terms Act 1977, s. 5(2) (6)) A contract of guaranty may also be called a 'contract of suretyship'.

cf. **warranty**. See also **surety**.

Anson's Law of Contract, 6 edn, pp. 67–70.

Chitty on Contract, 28 edn, para. 4406.

Charlesworth's Mercantile Law, 14 edn, pp. 481–496.

Commercial Law, by R.M. Goode, pp. 874–892, (1982).

guaranty title policy
    see **title insurance**.

H

ha-ha

An artificial boundary, which is designed to be hidden from view, between a formal garden or park and the surrounding countryside, so as to permit the garden to merge visually with the countryside beyond, while keeping cattle and other livestock out of the garden or park. The boundary is formed essentially by a sunken ditch and so the term is thought to be derived from the exclamation of surprise, 'ha!' The ditch generally has a perpendicular face on the garden side, frequently made as a stone wall, and a grassed sloping face on the outer side. See also **fence**.

habendum (L)

'To have'. The clause in a **deed** (whether a conveyance, lease or any other form of deed for the grant of an estate in land) which defines and limits the extent of the right to an estate in land that forms the subject matter of a grant. Traditionally a deed that granted a right of tenure contained the words *habendum et tedendum*, 'to have and to hold' and this section was followed by a description of the quality, i.e. the duration, of the estate being granted. For example, 'to hold unto the purchaser in fee simple' or 'to hold unto A for life, remainder to B in fee simple'. A *habendum* clause may be inserted in a lease to similar effect e.g. 'to hold unto A for a term of twenty years from the date hereof'. A *habendum* may be qualified by referring to existing encumberances that affect the property and are to be transferred with the property.

A *habendum* is not essential to a conveyance of freehold land, but if there is no *habendum* the grantee takes the freehold, the grantor's entire estate, or the estate referred to in the preceding **premises** (or parcels) clause, whichever is the lesser estate (Law of Property Act 1925, s. 60). If the duration of the estate is defined in a preceding premises clause the grantee takes that estate subject to any qualification in the *habendum*, but the description in the premises clause takes priority and cannot be contradicted or abridged by the *habendum*. However, the *habendum* may alter or vary the premises – Kendal *v* Micfield (1740) Barn. Ch. Rep. 46; or, "it may construe and explain the sense in which the words in the premises should be taken" – Spencer *v* Registrar of Titles [1906] AC 507. If an interest in land is described in the premises and a different interest referred to in the *habendum* only the former is transferred, unless the premises implies that there is an intention to pass the interest in property referred to in the *habendum* – (Gregg *v* Richards [1926] Ch. 521). In most states in the US a *habendum* is superfluous; the estate to be conveyed being clearly defined in the granting or **operative clause** or as part of the premises clause. See also ***tedendum*, words of limitation**.

habitable

Constructed or adapted so as to be inhabited. See also **fit for human habitation**.

habitable room

1. A room that is considered useable

for living purposes; i.e. a **living room**, bedroom or a kitchen used as part of the normal living space; but not a bathroom, toilet, a storage area or circulation space.

2. A room in a condition that is fit to live in, i.e is **fit for human habitation**.

habitable repair
see **tenantable repair**.

habitation
The state of dwelling or being inhabited; a **dwelling-house**, a permanent place of shelter. See also **fit for human habitation**.

habitation (F)
1. **residence; dwelling-house; domicile**. (*habitations à bon-marché*, or *à loyer modéré* – low cost, or low-rent, dwellings)
(*groupe d'habitation* – housing estate)
(*immeuble d'habitation* – residential property)
2. (*droit d'habitation* – a right to use and enjoy a dwelling house for the life time of the occupant and his family. A form of **usufruct** that is personal to the beneficiary and, therefore, is inalienable, although it is a real right. The reversionary owner remains responsible for the maintenace and repair of the house). See also *usage*.

habitation à loyer modéré (HLM) (F)
Council housing. Housing at a subsidised rent, which may be provided by a private or public body.

haeres (L)
'heir'

half a year
In general, a period which spans one half of the number of days, weeks or months in a **year**, according to the appropriate unit of measurement. However, in English law, unless indicated to the contrary, 'half a year' is taken as half the number of days of the year, not six months; i.e. a period which spans from the end of the day upon which it commences for a further period of 183 days, at least (fractions of a day being ignored in English law), to include the day upon which it ends (Co. Litt. 135b; Anon. (1515) 3 Dy. 345a). But, if a tenancy commences on one of the usual **quarter days** half a year is the period between the alternate quarter days, so that notice to quit served on the 25 June to expire on 25 December, although covering 183 days, is not half a year's notice (the notice should have been served on or before 24 June). On the other hand notice served on 28 September to expire on 25 March, although less than 183 days, constitutes half a year's notice. – Morgan *v* Davies (1878) 3 DPD 260. When a lease provides that rent is to be payable 'half yearly' the yearly sum is payable, in two equal amounts as near as possible at equal intervals in the year, i.e. at the same date every six months. See also **agricultural tenancy, tenancy from year to year**.

half-quarter days
see **quarter days**.

half yearly
see **half a year**.

halve back
see **zoning**.

ham
1. A piece of land shaped like the ham of a leg.
2. An old English word for a house, a collection of houses, or an enclosed piece of grass land.

hammer
see **gavel, under the hammer**.

hand money

see **earnest money**.

hand-over

The delivery of possession of a building site by a building contractor to the employer upon completion of the building contract. See also **practical completion**.

handsale

see **handsel**.

handsel or hansel

Cash paid over to secure a **bargain** for the sale of chattels, derived from the tradition of shaking hands on a deal. Also called 'handsale'.

hangout (US)

A period of time by which the term of a loan exceeds the term of a leasehold interest that has been given as security; thus, a **balloon payment** is required to repay fully the outstanding principal on termination of the leasehold interest. If the lease is renewed or extended the loan may remain in effect. See also **leasehold mortgage**.

harassment

Actions, words or gestures that tend to annoy, trouble or vex another. Frequently used to refer to acts calculated to interfere with the peace or comfort of a residential occupier, particularly in connection with an attempt to evict a tenant. Harassment includes such acts as locking out a tenant; cutting off essential services; assault (physical or verbal) or threats of assault; noise; and various forms of trickery. Not to be confused with an interference with a tenant's right to **quiet enjoyment**.

It is an offence to commit acts calculated to interfere with the peace or comfort of a residential occupier or a member of his household, or to persistently withdraw or withold services reasonably required for the occupation of premises as a residence (Protection from Eviction Act 1977, s. 1). See also **eviction, Rackmanism, right of re-entry**.

Landlord and Tenant, by Martin Partington, 2 edn., pp. 450–451.

Housing Law, by Andrew Arden and Martin Partington, pp. 852–860 (1983).

hard-money

1. Cash paid to acquire additional **equity** in an investment, either to repay existing debt or to take account of an increase in the value of the property. See also **convertible mortgage**.
2. Coins that have been lawfully minted for circulation as **legal tender**.

hard-money mortgage (US)

A mortgage that provides the mortgagor with cash which he intends to use to acquire goods, or finance a business, rather than directly to finance real estate; frequently taking the form of a **second mortgage**.

hardcore method

A method of assessing the capital value of a variable income stream by which that part of the income which does not vary – the 'bottom slice' or 'hardcore rent' – is capitalised at one rate of interest (for the total investment period or, if applicable, in perpetuity); each marginal increase (or decrease) in the income – the 'top slice' or 'marginal rent' – is capitalised separately (for the period during which it is receivable). The capital value of the investment is the total of these capitalised figures. For exam ple, if a property is let at a rent of £10000 per annum for 3 years and then it is estimated that the income will revert to a market rent of £15000 per annum, the capital value may be assessed as

'hardcore' rent   £10000 p.a.
capitalisation rate,
or YP, in perpetuity
at 5%   20
               £200000

'marginal' rent   £5000 p.a.
capitalised in
perpetuity at 7%
—14.29
deferred 3 years
at 7%
—0.82
14.29 × 0.82   11.72
               £58600
               £258600

(The hardcore rent is considered a more secure income than the marginal rent and, therefore, is capitalised at a lower rate of return). If the hardcore rent after the time of the reversion to market rent is capitalised at a different rate to that used before the reversion this is called the 'split reversion' method. Thus, in the above example the harcore rent could be capitalised at 5 per cent for the initial three years and then capitalised in perpetuity, deferred 3 years, at 6 per cent. Also called the 'layer or marginal method'.
cf. **term and reversion method**.
Hardcore Method of Valuation (a critical review), by W.A. Leach, 246 E.G. 475 (1978).
Modern Methods of Valuation, 7 edn, pp. 194–196.
The Valuation of Property Investments, by Nigel Enever, 2 edn., p. 127 *et seq*.

haussier (F)
bull (in stock market terms).

hardcore rent
see **base rent, hardcore method**.

'have and hold'
see *habendum*.

haybote
see **estovers**.

hazard insurance
see **liability insurance**.

head landlord
A landlord whose tenant has granted a sub-lease, as viewed by the sub-tenant. Thus if L grants a lease to T, who sub-lets to ST, and ST then sub-lets to SUT, L is the head landlord of ST and of SUT, and T is the head landlord of SUT. The lease from L to T is a head lease, as is the lease from T to ST, but in the latter case only for SUT. The head landlord may be any lessor, who has a sub-tenant, upto and including the freeholder, i.e. he may be the owner of a fee simple or a leaseholder. Called also a 'head lessee' or 'superior landlord'. See also **sandwich lease**.

head lease
A lease granted to a tenant who in turn leases the demised premises to another tenant or tenants for a shorter term, i.e. to a tenant who grants a **sub-lease**.

head lease
A lease that controls a sub-lease or any subsequent lease of a property. If a lessee, A, creates a tenancy for a term less than his own then his sub-tenant, B, is likely to be expressly required to comply with most of the terms of the lease granted to A; even though there is no **privity of contract**

between A's landlord and B. The head lease may be any 'superior lease' up to the freehold. In the US called usually a 'master lease', or sometimes an 'original or underlying lease'. See also **head landlord, privity of estate.**

head lessee
see **head landlord.**

head rent
Rent payable under a **head lease.**

heads of claim
The main titles under which a claim for **compulsory purchase compensation** is submitted, e.g. compensation for land taken, compensation for disturbance, compensation for injurious affection. When a disputed claim for compensation is submitted to the Lands Tribunal for settlement the claimant must set out "details of the compensation claimed, distinguishing the amounts under separate heads and showing how the amount claimed under each head is calculated'. (Land Compensation Act 1961, s. 4).

health and safety regulations
Regulations made under statutes, e.g. the Shops Act 1950, the Factories Act 1961, the Offices, Shops and Railway Premises Act 1963, and the Health and Safety at Work Act 1974, to govern matters such as, "saving the health safety and welfare of persons at work, for protecting others against risks to health and safety in connection with the activities of persons at work". These regulations cover also such matters as structural condition, stability of premises, fire precautions, temperature and ventilation of premises and general welfare and space facilities. See also **fire certificate, overcrowding.**
Redgrave's *Health and Safety in Fac-*
tories (1976).
Redgrave's *Offices and Shops,* 2 edn. 20 Halsbury's Laws of England 4 edn, paras. 401–801.

hearsay evidence
Testimony, not derived from a witness's personal experience; nor learned, heard or seen by the witness himself, but based on that which has been obtained or gleaned from another, usually by word of mouth. Evidence that may be presented as fact but derives its source from something that ranges from 'to the best of my knowledge' or 'what I have reason or have been given to believe', to rumour or common talk, i.e. it depends upon the veracity and competence of some person other than the bearer of the evidence. Such evidence normally is inadmissible in an English court of law, unless it is first-hand and given in accordance with strict procedural rules (Civil Evidence Act 1968, ss. 1–10); primarily because it cannot be tested directly. (It may well be admitted in a court of civil law, as in France, where the judge is left to decide on the weight to be attached to such evidence).

Evidence presented by a valuer, acting as an **expert witness,** though based on matters of which he or she does not have a first-hand knowledge, may be admissible in a hearing solely as support for the valuer's own 'opinion'; but a valuer "may not give hearsay evidence stating the details of any transaction not within his personal knowledge in order to establish them as matters of facts" – English Exporters (London) Ltd, *v* Eldonwall Ltd, [1973] Ch. 442 E. Thus, "details of comparable transactions upon which a valuer intends to rely in his evidence must, if they are to be put before a court, be confined to those details which have been, or will be, proved by admissible evidence, given either by the valuer himself or in some other way". – *ibid* at p. 442B – Town Centre Securities Ltd. *v* Wm. Morrison Supermarkets Ltd. (1982) 263 E.G. 435. In the US in condemnation proceeding similar rulings have been made as to the inadmissibility of hearsay evidence – National Bank of Commerce *v* City of Bradford, 175 Mass. 257, 56 NE 288. See also **comparable property**.

Real Estate Valuation in Litigation, by J.D. Eaton, pp. 137–139, 156–159 (1982).

The Surveyor in Court, by P.H. Clarke, pp. 44–50, 67–81 (1985).

17 Halsbury's Laws of England, 4 edn, paras. 53–77.

hebdomadaire (F)
  weekly.

hedge
  1. A boundary formed by a continuous row of low trees, shrubs or similar vegetation grown together in order to form a barrier or enclosure. See also **boundary line, fence**.
  2. A means of providing security, or reducing the risk of financial loss, in particular by acquiring rights or options that would reduce the future risk of loss.

hedge bote
  see **estovers**.

height density zoning (US)
  A **zoning ordinance** which sets limits to the maximum building height in a given area. See also **plot ratio**.

heir (fem: **heiress**)
  One who inherits real property; as distinguished from the 'next of kin' or nearest blood relation and one who benefits from a distribution under a will. A person who, based on statutory or blood descendancy, received real property when a person died **intestate**. The Administration of Estates Act 1925, s. 45, in most cases, removed the old rules and canons governing the devolution of real property on intestacy and in this context a distinction is no longer made between real and personal property. In common usage and modern English law 'heir' may be used to refer to any person who succeeds to property, whether by law or by will (although **legatee** or **devisee** are formally used to refer to a person to whom property is given by will). In the US an heir may be defined as "those persons, including the surviving spouse, who are entitled under the statutes of intestate succession to the property of a descendent". (Uniform Probate Code para. 1–201(17)). See also **heirs or heirs of the body**.

heirloom
  A **chattel** that passes by custom as an inseparable part of an inheritance e.g. a valuable painting, an ensign of honour. "Any piece of household stuff which, by custom of some countries, having belonged to a house for certain descents, goes with the house after the death of the owner unto the heirs and not the executors" – Termes de La Ley. A **tenant for life** may, under an order of a court, sell chattels settled together with land (inaccurately called 'heirlooms'), but the proceeds of sale become **capital money** which may be used to purchase other heirlooms or may be used in the same way as other capital money (Settled

Land Act 1925, s. 67).

heirs or heirs of the body

In English law prior to 1926 the word 'heirs' or 'heirs of the body' were considered to be **words of limitation** and not **words of purchase**; thus if a **freehold** estate (whether a fee simple or a fee tail) was granted to a person and "his heirs", or "the heirs of his body", then the freehold did not pass, as might be expected, to that person as a mere life estate, but as an unlimited freehold: the rule being that the life estate and the **remainder** merged together to give the recipient either the entire fee simple (if the words 'heirs' was used) or a fee tail estate (if the words 'heirs of the body' were used) (Rule in Shelley's Case (1581) 1 Co. Rep. 88b). This rule has been abolished and since 1925 the entire interest of a grantor is passed, unless an intention is expressed to the contrary (Law of Property Act 1925, s. 60). The terms 'heirs' or 'heirs of the body' are used now to indicate the size of the estate to be passed. For example, 'and his heirs' or 'heirs and assigns' are used to indicate that a fee simple is transferred, i.e. the interest is absolute and of unconditional inheritance. 'Heirs of the body' are used to indicate that an estate of limited inheritance, an **entailed interest**, is to be granted, i.e. the interest will pass to an heir begotten or borne by the person referred to or a child of such an heir, according to the rules of lineal descendancy established before 1925. In most states in the US the rule in Shelley's case has been abolished or modified by statute.

Real Property, by William E. Burby, 3 edn., pp. 338–340, 393–397.

The Law of Real Property, by Robert Megarry and H.W.R. Wade, 5 edn., pp. 48–50.

herbage

1. A licence to pasture cattle on the land of another. See also **grazing licence, right of common**.

2. The natural vegetation on land.

hereditament

Derived from the Latin *herediare*, 'to inherit' (originally the word was 'heritage'). Any form of property, real or personal, corporeal or incorporeal, that is capable of passing by inheritance (Sheppard's *Touchstone*, p. 91). "'Hereditament' is defined in the textbooks of authority to signify 'all such things, whether corporeal or incorporeal, which a man may have to him and his heirs, by way of inheritance and which, if they be not otherwise bequeathed, come to him which is next of blood, and not to the executors or administrators, as chattels do" – Lloyd v Jones (1848) 6 CB 90. In a specialist sense a hereditament is **real property**, or a right to real property, as distinguished from a **chattel**. A hereditament may be 'corporeal' or 'incorporeal'. A **corporeal hereditament** is tangible and thus traditionally capable of livery of seisin (delivery by transfer of a right of possession); it may be land, buildings or other fixtures. An **incorporeal hereditament** is intangible being annexed to or concerning a corporeal thing, but not the thing itself, and is capable of grant, e.g. an easement, profit à prendre or money held in trust to be invested in land.

A term now used almost exclusively in English rating law to refer specifically to a single unit in the **valuation list**. "Property which is or may become liable to a rate, being a unit of such property which is or would fall to be shown as a separate item in the valuation list" (General Rate Act 1967, s. 115(1)). It is used with the same meaning in English planning law (Town and Country Planning Act 1971, s. 207(1)). See also **mixed hereditament, tenement**. Ryde on Rating, 13 edn, pp. 122–144.

heritable bond
A **bond** by which land is pledged as security for a loan. See also **mortgage**.

heritable property (or heritage)
Property that is capable of being inherited; a 'heritable estate' is the Scottish equivalent of a **freehold** estate. See also **fee simple, hereditament**.

heritage (F)
inheritance; hereditament.

héritier (F)
heir, as in English law strictly as a result of intestacy although commonly used to refer to anyone who inherits property.
(*les héritiers et les ayants cause* – heirs and assigns)
cf. *ayant cause, legataire*.

heritor
In Scotland the owner of **heritable property** i.e. the equivalent to an English freeholder.

hidden defect
see **latent defect**.

hierloom
see **heirloom**.

high-rated property
1. A property which has a **rateable value** above a specified level and, therefore, is exempt from the security of tenure and rent control provisions of the Rent Acts, in particular a dwelling house that is let but not as a protected tenancy. See also **leasehold enfranchisement**.
2. see prime property.

high-ratio financing
see **gearing, leverage**.

high-rise building
In general, a building with five or more storeys above the ground level and, therefore, normally provided with a lift; the term tends to be used relative to buildings in the surrounding area.
cf. **low-rise building**. See also **skyscraper**.

highest and best use
The likely **use**, selected from a number of available choices, to which land may be put, in compliance with planning and building regulations and which, at the time of a valuation, produces the most profitable present land value. The legal use of land which, at any point in time, is likely to produce the highest return to an investor. It may be said that, "land resources are at their highest and best use when they are used in such a manner as to provide the optimum return to their operators or to society. Depending on the criteria used, this return may be measured in strictly monetary terms, in intangible and social values, or in some combination of these values". (*Land Resource Economics*, by Raleigh Barlowe, 3 edn., p. 16). This concept is not static. The use of land at any point in time is dependent on its 'capacity' – its ability to provide fruits and benefits. In turn this ability is a function of physical characteristics (slope, fertility, climate, load bearing capacity, etc.); the permitted or authorised use (agricultural, residential, industrial, mining, commercial); intensity of use (plot

ratio, planning and building height restrictions, etc.); location (access-ability, proximity to complementary uses); technological factors (building techniques, availability of plant and machinery); and the availability of other factors of production (labour, capital and management) to exploit the full potential of land. The use to which land is put is a function also of the owner's tastes and preferences and will be dependent for its succession on the demand of the end user. 'Highest and best use' thus represents a dynamic concept, a point to which land is tending. Land owners, or potential land owners, are constantly seeking to obtain a higher return from a given area of land than would be receivable by continuing the existing use. However, one use is commonly frozen at a point in time as being the use which can provide a higher or better return than any alternative. It is upon the basis of that use that an **appraisal** of land generally is carried out.

In the US 'highest and best use' is an established basis for assessing **just compensation** for condemnation, i.e. account should be taken of a reasonable probability that a zoning change would be permitted; "the sum to be awarded for real estate taken is the fair market value of the property, having reference to all the uses to which it is adapted. Its value for any special purposes is not the test, although it may be considered, with a view to ascertaining what the property is worth in the market for any use for which it would bring the most". – Sacremento Southern R. Co. *v* Helbron, 156 Cal. 408, 104 P 979. In the UK compulsory purchase compensation is based on a set of statutory assumptions as to the use to which

land may be put. Called also 'optimum use'.

cf. **existing use**. See also **residual method of evaluation**.
Real Estate Valuation in Litigation, by J.D. Eaton, pp. 62–82 (1982).
Readings in Highest and Best Use, AIREA, (1981).

highest and best use analysis (US)
see **residual method of valuation**.

highway
A strip of land or a passage, made or unmade, over which the public at large has a right of way i.e. a right to pass and repass for legal purposes. A way or road that leads along a defined route from one town or place to another; is common to the general public – Bailey *v* Jamieson 1 CPD 332; and may be used as a right of passage, without let or hinderance, at any time of the year. Essentially there must be a right of 'common enjoyment' (i.e. not just a right for a limited class of individuals), and, as a rule, there should be a duty of public maintenance.

A highway may mean more than merely a paved roadway for vehicular passage; it may include a **footpath**, **bridleway**, **drift-way**, **carriageway** or **street**: "the word highway is the genus of all public ways, as well as the cart, horse and footways" – R. *v* Saintiff (1704) 6 Mod. Rep. 255; Suffolk County Council *v* Mason [1979] 2 All ER 371. The Highway Act 1845 stated that a highway "shall be understood to mean all roads, bridges (not being county bridges), carriageways, cartways, horseways, bridleways, footways, causeways, churchways and pavements". There is no modern statutory definition, but 'highway' may extend to the whole of any part of a

highway (other than a ferry or waterway) and where it passes over a bridge or through a tunnel, that bridge or tunnel is part of the highway (Highway Act 1980, s. 328). It has been stated that, "a highway must lead from one definite place to some other definite place" – Eyre *v* New Forest Highway Board (1892) 56. JP 518; but a **cul-de-sac** or a public square may be, but should not be presumed to be, a highway. In the broader sense, 'highway' may include a way by land, sea or air – Bowke *v* Davies (1889) 44 Ch. D. 122. The land over which a highway runs may be owned by a **highway authority**, but frequently the land is owned by a private landowner or by the adjoining frontagers up to the centre line – *ad medium filum* – with the authority owning so much of the soil and the air above as is necessary for the use and upkeep of the highway. In the latter event the highway authority owns a fee simple interest in the surface of the highway, plus whatever is essential above and below to ensure its proper function. A highway once acquired as a public right, whether by **dedication**, **prescription** or statute, cannot be lost by abandonment or non-user (Dawes *v* Hawkins [1880] CB (NS) 848. However, statutory powers are available to enable a highway authority to stop up or divert a highway (Highways Act 1980, ss 116; 123; Town and Country Planning Act 1971, s. 209). In the event that a highway is legally stopped up or diverted the land reverts to the original owner. A highway authority may also stop up a private access to a highway if this is likely to cause danger or interference with traffic; subject to the payment of compensation to a landowner who is deprived of access (Highways Act 1980, s. 127). See also **adoption, building line, compensation for injurious affection, easement of necessity, improvement line, nuisance, pedestrian precinct order.**
The Modern Law of Highways, by S. Hamilton (1981).
21 Halsbury's Laws of England, 4 ed., paras. 1–996.

highway authority

A public authority, central or local, that has statutory functions for the maintenance and upkeep of a **highway**. 'Highway authority' includes the Minister of Transport in England and the Secretary of State for Wales (for trunk roads and for certain other roads placed under his authority); county councils, London Borough councils, the Common Council of the City of London, and the Greater London Council (for other roads in that authority's area) (Highways Act 1980, s. 1–3).

hire

1. To permit someone to have an exclusive right to use goods, or to obtain a service, in return for an agreed sum or reward. Ownership of the goods is retained by the grantor throughout the time that the goods are hired and remains so when the contract of hire comes to an end. The hire of goods or chattels may mean, "the long-term leasing of plant or machinery for a period equivalent to the life span of the equipment; or a monthly television rental, coupled with 'free' maintenance, that can last as long as the television itself; or the hire of a car for a weekend outing; or simply paying for the use of a deckchair, or a suit of evening clothes, for a matter of hours or even minutes".

(*Personal Property*, by Crossley Vaines, 5 edn., p. 411). See also **bailment**, **hire-purchase agreement**.
2. A payment for the use and enjoyment of moveable property; called sometimes a 'hire charge'. The terms 'hire' and '**rent**' commonly are used interchangeably when referring to personal property or goods.

hire charge
see **hire**, **hire-purchase agreement**.

hire-purchase agreement
A hybrid contract, exclusive to English law, whereby an owner of goods agrees to let them on **hire** to another and grants a right for the hirer to acquire eventually full ownership of the goods. "An agreement, other than a **conditional sale agreement**, under which (a) goods are bailed or (in Scotland) hired in return for periodic payments by the person to whom they are bailed or hired, and (b) the property in the goods will pass to that person if the terms of the agreement are complied with and one or more of the following occurs – (i) the exercise of an option to purchase by that person, (ii) the doing of any other specified act by any party to the agreement, (iii) the happening of any other specified event." (Consumer Credit Act 1974, s. 189 (1)). The price of the goods is payable by regular instalments, a 'hire charge', which are so calculated that in total they will cover the sale price of the goods, and normally interest on the unpaid balance. Full ownership of the goods passes to the purchaser upon the payment of the last instalment. Thus, a hire-purchase is a contract which combines a form of **bailment** with an **option** to purchase the bailed goods; an option that is exercised effectively when the full purchase price has been paid. It differs from an **instalment sale** or **credit-sale agreement** which transfers ownership of the goods immediately with a purely personal obligation to pay the price in stages. It differs from a pure hiring because in the latter transaction a hirer does not contract to part with ownership. Hire-purchase does not exist in Continental civil law; the nearest equivalent transaction is a *credit-bail*. In the US called usually an 'instalment credit agreement'. See also **leasing**.
The Sale of Goods, by P.S. Atiyah, 6 edn., pp. 7–12.
Charlesworth's Mercantile Law 14 edn, pp. 332–352.
22 Halsbury's Laws of England 4 edn, paras. 1–400.

historic area
see **conservation area**.

historic building
A building of sufficient antiquity or historic interest as to be considered worthy of preservation. In particular, a building over 100 years old that is associated with a notable person or event in history. An historic building may be any building considered by the **Historic Buildings and Monuments Commission** to be worthy of preservation or "any building which in the Commission's opinion is of historic or architectural interest" (National Heritage Act 1983, s. 33(8), 35(4)). See also **ancient monument, building of special architectural or historic interest, conservation area, historic structure, landmark building, listed building**.

historic building councils
Bodies set up, in England, Scotland and Wales, under the Historic Build-

ings and Ancient Monument Act 1953, to advise on historic buildings and to administer the making of grants for the upkeep and preservation of such buildings. Replaced in England in 1983 by the **Historic Buildings and Monuments Commission for England** (National Heritage Act 1983, s. 1).

Historic Buildings and Monuments Commission

A body, established under the provisions of the National Heritage Act 1983, with duties to secure the preservation of ancient monuments and historic buildings in England; to promote public knowledge and interest in such properties; and to preserve and enhance the character and appearance of any conservation area in England. The Commission may make grants in England for the repair and maintenance of buildings of outstanding historic or architectural interest; for the upkeep of land connected with such buildings; and of gardens of outstanding historic interest. The Commission may also make grants to local authorities to assist them to exercise their powers, as provided by the Town and Country Planning Act 1971, s. 114, 119 (b), (c), to acquire buildings of architectural or historic interest. See also **ancient monument, Ancient Monuments Boards, historic building**.

historic cost

The actual cost paid for an asset; the original acquisition cost, which (due to subsequent expenditure or depreciation) may be more or less than the current cost.

historic structure (US)

A structure or building that is (i) listed in the National Register of Historic Places; or (ii) located in a registered historic district and certified by the Secretary of the Interior as being of historic significance to the district; or (iii) located in an historic district which has been designated as such by a local or state law in accordance with standards laid down by the Secretary of the Interior. A 'certified historic structure' may not be demolished without authorisation. The owner of such a structure may qualify for special tax depreciation allowances (Tax Reform Act 1976).
Historic Properties: Preservation and the Valuation Process, by Judith Reynolds (1982).

historic redemption yield

The yield obtained by applying a discounted cash flow calculation to the total income and expenditure from the date an investment was acquired to the present, assuming the investment is sold at its present market value i.e. the **internal rate of return** based on past performance. A yield calculated to show the total annualised return on cost from an investment since inception, taking account of the **net income** received to date and any capital profit (or loss) resulting from a deemed sale (or any increase in equity, whether resulting from a revaluation or a reduction in debt). cf. **historic revenue yield**. See also **redemption yield**.

historic revenue yield

The **historic redemption yield** excluding any capital profit or loss (realised or unrealised), i.e. the rate of interest at which the total historic net cash flow from an investment must be discounted to equate to the original cost of that investment.

historical cost

1. The original cost recorded in books of account; the total sum of money, or its equivalent, expended in acquiring a property as established when a property first comes into a new ownership or a building comes into existence. See also **acquisition cost**.

2. The initial cost of constructing a building. To be distinguished from the original **purchase price**, or **book cost**, which is the cost to a particular buyer. However, these terms often are used synonymously.

hoarding

A **fence** or similar barrier put up around a building site to enclose and secure the land and the works thereon.

hold

To have a legal title; to keep or possess, or to retain **possession**, especially physical possession. In common law to have an estate subject to the payment of rent or rendering of service, i.e. **tenure**. A tenant is said to 'hold' of another; he has a right to possession although he does not need to have actual occupation. Possession signifies a right held unto oneself, whereas a person may hold something for another. A person may hold by force, fraud, deceit or as of right; he may keep occupation by force or as of right; but he may have possession only by exerting a right or an assumed right. See also *habendum*, **holding, holding over, tenancy**.

'hold harmless' clause (US)
see **exculpatory clause**.

hold over (US)
see **holding over**.

hold-over tenant (US)
A tenant who is **holding over**.

holdback (US)

1. A provision in a loan agreement that part of the funds will not be advanced until a certain condition has been fulfilled; for example, part of the loan is withheld until all, or at least a percentage, of a building is constructed or leased. See also **floor loan, gap financing**.

2. see **retention sum**.

holding

1. The area of land let to a tenant. See also **agricultural holding, small holding**.

2. Property that is retained or a right to retain property. Holding of land is associated with **tenure**, as distinguished from a right to occupy land. "There is a material difference between a holding and an **occupation**. A person may hold, though he does not occupy. A tenant of a freehold is a person who holds of another: he does not necessarily occupy". – R. *v* Ditcheat (1829) 9 B and C 183. See also **ownership**.

holding agreement (US)
see **land trust**.

holding company

A company that controls one or more 'subsidiary' companies by owning a significant percentage (usually more than half) of the shares (especially the voting shares), or that is in a position to control the composition of the subsidiary company's board of directors. (Companies Act 1948, s. 154). A similar company that controls one company is called also a parent company. cf. **investment company**.

holding out
see **ostensible authority**.

holding escrow (US)
see **escrow**.

holding over
The wilful retention of control of a property by a tenant following the determination or expiration of a tenancy. A tenant who holds over obtains a **tenancy at sufference** unless the landlord acknowledges his rights and creates a **tenancy at will**. If a landlord accepts rent from a tenant who is holding over that usually creates a yearly tenancy upon terms corresponding (except as to rent and duration) to the expired tenancy – Hyatt *v* Griffiths (1851) 17 QB 509; Wedd *v* Porter [1961] 2 KB 91. A tenant who holds over may become a tresspasser if given legal notice by his landlord to vacate the property; unless he is given a statutory right to remain in possession, in which case he becomes a statutory tenant. In the US called 'hold over'. See also **business tenancy, double rent, mesne profits, waiver**.

holding period
1. The period during which a capital asset is owned, especially the period of time which determines whether a gain or loss arising from a sale of the asset is subject to 'short term' or 'long term' capital gains tax.
2. In assessing the **internal rate of return** on an investment, the period for which it is assumed the investment will be held. See also **redemption yield**.

holiday let
The short-term letting of a dwelling-house for the express purpose that it be used only for accommodation during the period of a 'holiday'; although what constitutes such a letting is an issue of fact – (Buchanan *v* May [1978] 2 All ER 993). A holiday letting does not qualify as a **protected tenancy**, nor as a **restricted contract** (Rent Act 1977, ss. 9, 19 (7)). See also **grounds for possession**.
Landlord and Tenant, by Martin Partington, 2 edn., pp. 197–201.

holograph
A document (a deed or will) drawn up solely by the grantor in his or her own handwriting; particularly a non-attested **will**.

home
A place where someone lives, either permanently or temporarily: generally a person's or a family's principal place of **residence**. A house and grounds, or messuage, inhabited by any individual with his or her family, if any. Strictly a house is the structure that contains that which we make as a home. "Home is where the heart is; it is the location of the axis around which, for the present, the normal course of one's life revolves. Put another way it is the place where the gravity of one's domestic life is to be found . . ."– Geothermal Energy N.Z. Ltd *v* Inland Revenue Comr. [1979] 2 NZLR 341. A home is popularly said to be where you make it; an itinerant just makes a home more often. At any point in time a person normally has only one home, although he or she may have more than one residence, but in exceptional circumstances, e.g. when moving home or as a result of a family separation, a person may have more than one home for a time. See also **domicile, dwelling house**, matrimonial home.

home improvement grant
Financial assistance given by a local authority towards the cost of work

for the improvement, repair or conversion of a dwelling house. Such grants are intended to assist an owner or tenant of an old house or flat to bring it up to modern standards or carry out expensive repairs. A home improvement grant may take the form of an **improvement grant**, an **intermediate grant**, a **repairs grant** or a **special grant**. Intermediate grants which are for the provision of **standard amenities** (inside toilet, bath, sink, wash-basin, and hot and cold water) and associated repairs only are mandatory, the other grants are normally given at the discretion of the local authority.

HMSO (Department of the Environment Housing Booklet Number 14), Home Improvement Grants.

Manual of Housing Law, by Andrew Arden, 2 edn., pp. 207–214.

Housing Law, by A. Arden and M. Partington, pp. 581–612 (1983).

Housing Grants, by Nigel Hawkins 2 edn.

home-loss payment

A payment that may be made, under the provisions of the Land Compensation Act 1973, ss. 29–33, to a residential occupier, who has been displaced from a dwelling (which may include a caravan), on or after 17th October 1972, by a local or public authority, against his or her will. For example, when displacement results from the compulsory acquisition of an interest in a dwelling (which need not be an interest held by the claimant); from a demolition order, closing order, or clearance order; or from redevelopment proposals of an authority subsequent to a compulsory purchase. To qualify for a home-loss payment the claimant must have been in occupation of the dwelling as his only or main residence for five years prior to the displacement and he must have had a qualifying interest in the property (which may have been a freehold, leasehold, statutory tenancy, a restricted contract or a right to occupy as a condition of his employment). The payment may not be claimed if the resident leaves of his own volition, e.g. after serving a blight notice or before a compulsory purchase order is confirmed. The amount of compensation is fixed at three times the rateable value of the dwelling, with a minimum of £150 and a maximum of £1500. It is paid separately from any **compulsory purchase compensation**, being a payment made as recognition that a person is compelled to leave his home. If the strict statutory conditions cannot be met by the claimant, an authority possessing compulsory purchase powers has a discretionary power to make payments to any resident it displaces.

Law of Compulsory Purchase Compensation, by Keith Davies, 4 edn., pp. 219–221.

8 Halsbury's Laws of England 4 edn, paras. 335–337.

homestead (US)

1. A private residence, comprising a house and adjacent land, owned and occupied by a family as its **home**. In particular, land and building, used as a dwelling, to which specific legal and tax benefits apply; especially rights against debtors (the homestead right). Normally a homestead cannot be mortgaged or sold by a husband or wife without the consent of both parties and the wife enjoys certain rights to continued occupation after the

death of her husband. A homestead does not come into existence until registered as such in accordance with state regulations and the rights of a holder of a homestead differ considerably from state to state.
Real Estate Law, by W.D. Millingham and Arthur G. Bowman, pp. 289–293 (1984).
2. A right obtained by a private citizen to acquire public land after having resided on and cultivated land for a period of five or more years.

homeowner's association (US)
An incorporated, non-profit making, body formed to hold title to a number of private residential units so that the members of the association are also owners of one or more of the units. A homeowner's association is formed frequently to hold units on a planned housing estate or in a condominium and the members accept mutual rights and obligations as to the use and upkeep of the units under a 'general plan' or **scheme of development**. See also **collective ownership**.
Real Estate Law, by Robert Kratovil and Raymond J. Werner, 8 edn., pp. 484–488.

homeowner's insurance policy
A **comprehensive insurance** policy devised for an owner of a residential property to cover most perils, associated with the buildings – fire, storm, burst pipes, etc.; personal risks such as third party or public liability; liability for animals; liability to visitors and employees; and, usually, the contents of the dwelling. Called also 'householder's comprehensive insurance'. See also **all-risks insurance**.

homologation
An action by which someone agrees

or concurs; the act of **ratification**. See also **estoppel**.

homologation (F)
probate; confirmation (of a deed).

honoraires (F)
fee, generally for professional services; **royalty**.
(*honoraires d'expert* – surveyor's fees)
cf. *commission*.

hope value
An increase in the value of land produced by a belief that there is a chance that the demand for that land will change significantly; for example, when there is a prospect that planning or zoning approval will be granted for a change to a more valuable use. The price paid for land in excess of the **existing use value** when a purchaser considers there is a chance of obtaining consent to carry out an alternative and more valuable form of development; **development value** on a speculative basis. See also **highest and best use**.

horizontal lease
see **top-slice participation**.

horizontal slice participation
see **top-slice participation**.

horticulture
Traditionally the cultivation of the soil with hand tools. In modern terms the cultivation of a **garden**, **allotment** or small area of ground, including the growing of flowers, fruits, and vegetables, especially for business or profit. The cultivation of 'horticultural produce', which includes fresh fruit, fresh vegetables, fresh herbs, flowers, pot plants, fruit trees, seeds bulbs, bedding plants, as well as dried produce therefrom. (Horticultural

Act 1960, s. 8; Agriculture and Horticulture Act 1964, s. 10.)
cf. **agriculture**.

Hoskold factor (or coefficient) (US)
A factor, established in the US by
H.E. Hoskold in 1877 for the use in
annuity capitalisation, that corresponds to the **dual-rate capitalisation
factor** as used in the UK.

hostel
1. A **lodging house, inn, public house**
or similar place which provides shelter for the public, especially the travelling public. A house that provides
board or facilities for the preparation
of food and, if required, rudimentary
shared sleeping accommodation (Housing Finance Act 1972, s. 104(1); Housing Act 1974, 129(1).)
2. A rest house or temporary accommodation for the disabled, displaced,
dispossessed or deprived. "No doubt
there are a number of hostels of superior quality; and one day, perhaps I
[Megarry , V-C] may encounter the
expression 'luxury hostel'. But without any such laudatory adjective the
word 'hostel' has to my mind a strong
flavour of a building which provides
somewhat modest accommodation
for those who have some temporary
need of it and are willing to accept
accommodation of that standard in
order to meet the need". – Re Niyazi's
Will Trusts [1978] 3 All ER 788–789.
3. Historically an **hotel**, but in modern usage a place that provides over-
night lodging, especially in the form
of a supervised shelter and particularly for young people who are hik-
ing, bicycling or canoeing around a
region or country and from one shelter to another, e.g. a 'youth hostel'.
Youth hostels are affiliated normally
to the International Youth Hostel

Federation and provide shelter only
to members of national federations of
that body.

hostile possession (US)
see **adverse possession**.

hotchpot
Derived from the Old French *hoche-
pot*, a 'dish shaken up'. A mixing of
diverse things together. Any money
or property that has been granted to a
particular child during a lifetime
which must be brought into account
when determining the fair basis for the
distribution of a person's estate especially on intestacy. The purpose of
putting property in hotchpot is to
prevent someone unreasonably dis-
inheriting or favouring one or more
heirs. See also **capital transfer tax**.

hotel
A building, with many rooms, that
provides the public at large with
accommodation, food and refreshment. Traditionally "a genteel **inn** or
superior **lodging house** ... a house
where travellers are taken in to lodge"
– Formby *v* Barker [1903] 2 Ch. 548,
as distinguished from a **hostel** or an
ordinary lodging house or inn which
primarily provides refreshment and
limited, cheaper, accommodation. In
broad terms a hotel may be defined as
"an establishment held out by the
proprietor as offering food, drink
and, if so required, sleeping accommodation, without special contract,
to any traveller presenting himself
who appears able and willing to pay a
reasonable sum for the services and
facilities provided and who is in a fit
state to be received". (The Hotel
Proprietors Act 1956, s. 1(2)). A hotel
may be a commercial hotel, essen-

tially for transient visitors; or a more permanent place of residence providing the occupants with a home on a 'long-stay' basis – usually on a weekly or monthly licence. An hotel also may provide facilities such as meeting rooms, dining rooms, bars, boutiques, and entertainment; although in modern usage it need be no more than a place intended to provide good lodging – Huntley *v* Stanchfield, 168 Wis. 119, 169 N.W. 276. See also **lodging house, motel**.

Hotels, Motels and Condominiums: Planning and Design, by Fred R. Lawson, (1976).

Hotels, Motels, and Restaurants: Valuation and Market Studies, by Stephen Rushmore, (1983).

hôtel (F)
   hotel.
   (*hôtel particulier* – town house)

house
   A building capable of or intended for human habitation, i.e. primarily a **dwelling-house**. A building of permanent character that has been constructed or adapted so that it may be used for living in and usually, but not necessarily, severed from another holding. This is the common meaning, but the word house (but not dwelling-house) may be construed to include any building whatsoever, whether it is intended for use for the habitation of man or woman, or for any one purpose. "A hundred years ago there was not much difficulty in saying what was a 'house', but builders and architects have so altered the construction of houses, and the habits of people have so altered in relation to them, that 'house' has acquired an artificial meaning and the word is no longer

the expression of a simple idea; but to ascertain its meaning one must understand the subject-matter with respect to which it is used in order to arrive at the sense in which it is employed [in a particular statute]", – Grant *v* Langston [1900] A.C. 390. A complex of separate buildings constituting a hospital has been held to be a house – Governors of St. Thomas's Hospital *v* Charing Cross Railway Co. (1861) John and H. 400 – and a business user does not prevent premises from being a house. However, without prefix or suffix, outside of statutory qualification, its most common usage, a house is a building for human habitation. Also part of a building – a **flat**, an **apartment**, or a **maisonette** – or any premises used for habitation, no matter what they are called, including a **bungalow, hostel** or **lodging-house**, may be a house. A house, as a rule is a permanent structure, but the Housing Act 1957, s. 16 and s. 19 extends the meaning to a hut, tent, caravan, or other form of shelter used for human habitation. In addition, in the Housing Act 1957 it is apparent that a house means "a building which is constructed or adapted for use as, or for the purposes of, a dwelling. It need not actually be dwelt in, but it must be constructed or adapted for use as a dwelling". – Ashbridge Investments Ltd *v* Minister of Housing and Local Government [1965] 1 WLR 1324. Words such as 'house of God'; 'country-house', 'house of correction', 'guest-house' and 'work-house' indicate that any place where people are given shelter may be a house.

   For the purpose of the Leasehold Reform Act 1967, s.2(1) (which gives certain tenants a right of **leasehold enfranchisement** or a right to an

extended lease) a house includes, "any building designated or adapted for living in and reasonably so called, notwithstanding that the building is not structurally detached, or was or is not designed or adapted solely for living in, or is divided horizontally into flats or maisonettes ...". The 1967 Act provides also (a) that a building divided horizontally into flats or maisonettes may be a house, in its entirety; but the sub-divisions are not separate houses and (b) that a building divided vertically may not be a house in its entirety but any of the units into which it is divided may be. The type of building that may once have been a 'house' but has taken on the nature of a shop (at least in part) may be a house for the purpose of this statute – Lake v Bennett and Another [1970] 1 All ER 457. A house used for business purposes is a house for the purpose of the Compulsory Purchase Act 1965, s. 8 (1) – Ravenseft Properties v London Borough of Hillingdon (1969) 20 P and CR 483. The Housing Act 1957, s. 189 (1) and the Rent Act 1977, s. 86 (5) (a) extends 'house' to include, "any yard, garden, outhouses and appurtenances belonging thereto or usually enjoyed therewith" and, generally, by law, a house is considered to include the **curtilage** and outbuildings associated therewith – Co. Litt 56a; Grosvenor (Lord) v Hampstead Junction Railway Co (1857) De G and J 446. See also **back-to-back house, boarding house, cottage, duplex, mansion, messuage, semi-detached house, tenement house, terrace house**.
Legal Interpretation for Surveyors, by W.A. Leach, pp. 66–71 (1966). West's Law of Housing 4 edn., pp. 51–57.

27 Halsbury's Laws of England, 4 edn., para. 583.

house agent
see **accommodation agent, estate agent**.

housebote
see **estovers**.

householder's comprehensive insurance
see **homeowner's insurance**.

Housing Acts
Acts of Parliament that have been passed to regulate and control a variety of matters affecting private dwelling houses. In particular, Acts passed to give local housing authorities powers to provide public housing, especially for low-income families; to enter and inspect houses and, if necessary, to require the repair or even to condemn houses that are **unfit for human habitation** and to require their closure or demolition; and to control residential **overcrowding**. The first major modern Act was the Housing Act 1925 and the most recent Act was the Housing Act 1980. Housing Acts also have been passed to deal with matters that might be considered to fall within the ambit of the **Rent Acts** and the **Public Health Acts**, e.g. rent regulation, security of tenure for residential tenants, sanitary conditions. See also **clearance area, closing order, demolition order, housing action area, housing authority, repairs notice**. 22 Halsbury's Laws of England, 4 edn, paras. 401–413.

housing action area
In England or Wales, a predominately residential area considered by a local authority to require development as a whole because the existing

living conditions are unsatisfactory due to the poor social conditions and the physical state of the housing accommodation. Unlike a **general improvement area**, these areas are considered to be in need of urgent attention and to require an extensive "improvement of the housing accommodation" and "the proper and effective management and use of the accommodation" over the next five years (Housing Act 1974, ss. 34–46). A housing authority may acquire land in a housing action area; make grants to assist landowners to carry out work to improve the houses and the environment; and may carry out work itself in order to improve the area as a whole. A house action area can encompass and thereby replace, either a general improvement area or a **priority neighbourhood**. See also **clearance area**.

West's Law of Housing, 4 edn, pp. 118–121.

Manual of Housing Law, by Andrew Arden, 2 edn., pp. 218–220.

Housing Law, by Andrew Arden and Martin Partington, pp. 628–638 (1983).

22 Halsbury's Laws of England, 4 edn, paras. 620–628.

housing association

A society, body or trust set up to provide housing for its members on a non-profit making basis. The intention of the association is to construct, improve and manage housing as economically as possible for the mutual benefit of the members of the association; in particular, to provide houses for specialist members of an association e.g. members of a religious organisation, the elderly or single parent families. Many housing associations have their origins in philanthropic housing trusts established during the period of the Industrial Revolution in England to provide better housing conditions, such as the Bourneville Village Trust. Housing associations were given central government backing by the Housing Act 1957, Part VIII whereby they were entitled to government grants and subsidies and were encouraged by the financial and administrative support of the **Housing Corporation**. A new and more extensive system of financial support was introduced by the Housing Act 1974. A housing association is defined by the 1957 Act, s. 189 (1) as, "a society, body of trustees or company established for the purpose of, or amongst whose objects or powers are included those of providing, constructing, improving or managing or facilitating or encouraging the construction or improvement of houses, or hostels ... being a society, body of trustees or company who do not trade for profit or whose constitution or rules prohibit the issue of any capital with interest or dividend exceeding the rate being prescribed by the Treasury, whether with or without differentiation as between shares or loan capital". In many cases such organisations are established by large corporations to provide housing for their employees, or by a new town development corporation. Well over 2000 housing associations, private and public, had been registered by 1981. See also **homeowner's association, housing association tenancy, housing trust**.

22 Halsbury's Laws of England, 4 edn, paras. 445–464.

Housing Associations, by C.V. Baker, (1976).

housing association tenancy

A tenancy of a dwelling-house created where the landlord is a registered **housing association**, a **housing trust** or the **Housing Corporation** and the tenancy would be a **protected tenancy** but for the express statutory exclusion granted for such bodies. Prior to 1980 housing association tenancies were not granted the security of tenure applicable to protected tenancies, but were eligible to have their rents registered as 'fair rents' in the same way as a protected tenancy (Rent Act 1977, s. 67). Since 1980 most housing association tenancies have been brought within the perameters of a **secure tenancy** (Housing Act 1980, s. 28(2), (3)). See also **assured tenancy**.

housing authority

A **local authority** that is responsible under Acts of Parliament (the Housing Acts and Local Government Acts) for the administration of certain obligations relating to residential property, such as the inspection of the condition of housing in its area; provision of housing for certain members of the public; and the issue of repair notices, closing orders, demolition orders, clearance orders, and compulsory purchase orders to eliminate houses that are 'unfit for human habitation'; and the improvement of the general standard of housing in the area under its control.

In the US a housing authority usually is a corporation which provides public housing or carries out urban renewal on behalf of a state or municipal authority. See also **council housing**.
West's *Law of Housing* 4 edn, Ch.2 & 11.

housing co-operative

see **housing association, co-operative ownership**.

Housing Corporation

A body, originally established under the Housing Act 1964 and now with a constitution determined in accordance with the Housing Act 1974, s. 1, to "promote and assist the development, to publicise and to facilitate the proper performance" of housing associations and self-build societies. It may provide houses itself and acquire land and develop land for itself, or for a **housing association**, or unregistered self-build societies, as well as making loans and grants to such associations or societies. It is responsible also for maintaining a register of housing associations and for regulating associations on that register. See also **housing association tenancy**.

housing development (US)

see **housing estate**.

housing estate

A group of dwelling-houses, blocks of flats or apartments, designed and built to form a single planning entity; with the houses usually having a similar design and built by the same developer. In the US usually called a 'housing development'. See also **planned unit development, scheme of development**.

housing grant

see **home improvement grant**.

housing society

An organisation established, under the provisions of the Housing Act 1964, s. 1(7), with a similar, but more limited objective, to a **housing association**. In common usage the term housing society may be used to refer to any non-profit making society established to provide, improve or manage houses for members of the society. The term originates from the Industrial and Provident Societies Act 1893, which was passed to regulate housing charities. However, most housing societies now come with the statutory definition of housing association.

housing trust

1. A corporation or body of persons established to use all or most of its funds to provide houses predominately for persons of the lower income groups (Rent Act 1977, s. 15(5), s. 86(4); Housing Act 1980, s. 77, Sch. 10). Essentially a charitable trust established to provide accommodation for families on low incomes. See also **housing association**.
West's Law of Housing, 4 edn, pp. 289–290.
2. A private trust established to provide houses for its beneficiaries on a non-profit making basis.

huissier (F)
process-server, an officer attached to the courts who serves legal notices when so directed (similar to a bailiff); sheriff's officer. See also *notification*.

human habitation
see **dwelling-house, fit for human habitation, unfit for human habitation.**

hundred per cent location
see **prime location.**

'husband-like manner'
When a tenant of an **agricultural holding** (or similar land) is obliged to keep it in a 'husband-like manner' he is obliged to keep it in good heart and condition according to local custom –

Wedd *v* Porter [1916] 2 KB 102; to ensure that any cultivated land is in a state for efficient production; and to keep the farm house, if any, in a **tenant-like manner**. See also **good husbandry, implied covenant**.

husbandry
agriculture; the process of farming land to produce food, especially for domestic purposes or farming in a domestic or well trained manner. See also **good husbandry**.

hybrid trust (US)
see **real estate investment trust.**

hypermarché (F)
hypermarket; superstore.

hypermarket
A **retail** store that is larger than a **supermarket** and sells a large range of consumer goods (food and non-food), generally at discounted prices, and by self-service. The store is predominately on one level, free standing, with ample adjacent car parking and normally is situated in an out-of-town location with good road communications. The size that distinguishes a hypermarket from a supermarket is over 5000 square metres (50 000 square feet); although in the UK a store between 2500 square metres (25 000 square feet) and 5000 square metres (50 000 square feet) is sometimes referred to as a hypermarket.
cf. **department store**. See also **superstore.**

hypothec
A form of pledge whereby moveable property is offered as security for a loan, but the property remains freely usable by the borrower, hence, unlike a true **pledge**, neither possession nor

title is transferred to the lender. A term that strictly applies only in Roman, Scottish or civil law. In Scottish law a 'hypothec' is a form of security over moveable property where possession is retained by the debtor; a right that is similar to an equitable **lien** in English law. (A floating charge does not exist in Scottish law as it is substituted by a hypothec). See also **hypothecation,** *hypothèque.*

hypothécaire (F)
relating to a **mortgage.**
(*contrat hypothécaire* – mortgage deed)
(*créancier hypothécaire* – **mortgagee**)
(*prêt hypothécaire* – mortgage loan)
(*valeur hypothécaire* – mortgage loan).

hypothecation
The granting of a **pledge** of personal property as security for a loan, in particular the grant of a **hypothec.** A term strictly of the civil or Scottish law, but sometimes used in English law for any pledging of goods without a transfer of possession by the debtor or for the pledging of a ship or her cargo. See also **charge.**

hypothèque (F)
mortgage; a real charge over immoveable property as security for the payment of a debt (similar to the English mortgage on real property).
(*hypothèque avec amortissement cumulatif* – **amortisation mortgage**)
(*hypothèque de premier rang* – **first mortgage**)
(*hypothèque generale* – **blanket mortgage**)
(*conservation des hypothèques* – mortgage registration office)
(*grevé d'hypothèque* – burdened by, or subject to, a mortgage)

(*libre d'hypothèque* – **unencumbered**)
(*mainlevée d'hypothèque* – release or **redemption** of a mortgage)
(*purger une hypothèque* – to redeem a mortgage)
(*saisie d'une hypothèque* – **foreclosure**)
Amos & Walton's Introduction to French Law, 3 edn, pp. 123–127.
Droit Civil 1er annee, by Jean Chevalier and Louis Bach, 8 edn, p. 513 *et seq.*
Manuel de Droit Civil, by Pierre Voirin & Giles Goubeaux, 20 edn, p. 577 *et seq.*
Précis Dalloz. Droit Civil, Les Sûretés by Alex Weill, p. 238 *et seq* (1979).

hypothetical
That which depends on supposition or assumption. In particular, that which is formulated as a possible law to be tested by experiment. Something taken as given for the sake of making a testable assessment or analysis, i.e. an antecedent statement made for the purpose of argument or in order to follow through its consequences; but not necessarily something presumed to be factual.

In **rating valuation**, the 'annual value' is the amount that would be paid for a property on the assumption that there is a possible tenant, a 'hypothetical tenant', prepared to take a property upon the conditions laid down in the rating legislation. This tenant is someone who might take the premises, including an existing occupier, at the estimated rent at which the premises might reasonably be expected to let from year to year. The rent is referred to as a 'hypothetical rent'; as hypothetical as the tenant. "It is the rent which an imaginary tenant might be reasonably expected to pay to an imaginary landlord . . ." –

R. *v* Paddington (Valuation Officer) *ex. parte* Peachey Property Corporation Ltd. [1966] 1 QB 412. Thus the rating valuer has to determine the annual value of a property not necessarily on the basis of any existing tenancy, but on the basis of an *assumed* or hypothetical tenancy granted in accordance with the statutory provision. See also **gross value**, **rateable value**.

39 Halsbury's Laws of England, 4 edn, paras. 106–112.

Ryde on Rating 13 edn, Ch. 22.

I

ibid (*ibidem*) (L)
'In the same place; from the same source'.

id certum est quod certum reddi potest (L)
'That is certain which can be rendered certain'. See **lease, term, rent**.

id est (i.e.) (L)
'That is'.

idem (L)
'The same'; as previously mentioned.

ignorantia facti excusat; juris non excusat (L)
'Ignorance of the fact excuses; ignorance of the law does not excuse'. See also **mistake**.

illegal contract
A contract that, by its intent rather than its form, is contrary to the established law and, therefore, cannot be considered in a court of law. An illegal contract may stipulate for iniquity; be contrary to the general policy of the law; be against public good or public morals, *contra bones mores*; or be created for an immoral purpose, *turpis causa*. A contract may be illegal because the subject matter, the consideration, or the purpose is illegal. A lease of premises to be used for a criminal activity or to defraud the revenue is an illegal lease when the parties are aware of the intent to commit a crime. An illegal contract is void, i.e. it is treated in law as if it had never existed; but, unlike any other **void contract**, at law neither party can recover anything paid or transferred as a result of such a contract: the maxim being *ex turpi causa non oritur actio*, 'a right of action cannot arise from a base act'. See also **champerty**.
Chitty on Contract, 25 edn, paras. 1031–1193.
Anson's Law of Contract, 26 edn, pp. 292–360.

illegal interest
see **usury**.

illiquid asset
An **asset** that cannot readily be turned into cash; real property being one of the most illiquid of assets. See also **liquidity**.

immediate landlord
A landlord who obtains a right to physical possession upon the termination of a lease, as distinguished from a superior or **head landlord** whose right to physical possession depends on the termination of the lease of a person who is himself a landlord. The landlord to whom a particular tenant actually pays rent.

immediate possession
In a contract for the sale of land, possession when the contract is executed. Usually that means **actual possession** – North Staffordshire Railway *v* Lawton (1863) 3 N.R. 31. See also **vacant possession**.

immeuble (F)
building; especially an apartment building; **house**; **premises**; **real estate**; immoveable. Immeubles are classified in the French Civil Code, (a) by *nature* – being land and buildings as well as what are considered part and

parcel of the land or buildings e.g. trees, vegetation that is not cropped, water pipes, a lift in a building, etc.; (b) by *destination* – being moveables by nature but fixed to an immoveable "for the service and exploitation of the property" (French Civil Code arts. 517, 524: whether an item is immoveable by (*par*) *destination* depending primarily on the presumed intention of a vendor, mortgagor, lessor or other grantor of property); (c) by *objet* – being property that essentially comprises a 'right to property' because of the object to which it is attached i.e. a real right, less than ownership (e.g. **usufruct** or a **servitude**) and a right of action for a title to land (Civil Code, art 526).
(*immeuble commercial* – **commercial property**; commercial building, business premises)
(*immeuble d'appartement* – block of flats; apartment building)
(*immeuble d'exploitation* – **business premises**)
(*immeuble d'habitation* – **dwelling house**; residential building)
(*immeuble de grande hauteur* – **high rise building**)
(*immeuble de grand standing* – prestige building)
(*biens immeubles* – **real estate**)
(*gerant d'immeubles* – property manager)
(*vente d'immeuble* – property sale). cf. *meubles*. See also *biens*.
Manuel de Droit Civil, by Pierre Voirin and Gilles Goubeaux, 20 edn, pp. 228–234.
Traité de Droit Civil, by G. Ribert and J. Boulanger, vol. ii, paras. 2164–84.

***immobilier (f. – ère)* (F)**
immoveable; relating to **real property**.

(*agence immobilière* – estate agency)
(*agent immobilier* – **estate agent**)
(*biens immobiliers* – **real property**)
(*société immobilière* – property company; building society). See also **biens**.
Amos & Walton's Introduction to French Law, 3 edn, pp. 88–91.

***immobilisation* (F)**
conversion (of personal into real property); **capitalisation; fixed asset.**

***immovables* (F)**
immoveables. See also *immeuble*.

immoral contract
see **illegal contract.**

immoveables or immovables
Property that can be touched but cannot be moved physically because it is permanently fixed to **land**, or to a structure that itself is fixed to land, or is directly associated with land so that it cannot exist independently of the land to which it relates. An immoveable may be an estate, interest or charge over land (but not the proceeds of sale); it may be freehold or leasehold, a right under a mortgage (but not a debt *per se*); a right to minerals, or a rentcharge; the key factor being that the property has a fixed location and, therefore, is governed by the law of that place. Immoveable is also a term of the civil law corresponding roughly to **real property** in English law.
cf. **moveables.** See also **fixture**, *immeuble*.

impeachement for waste
see **waste.**

***impenses* (F)**
expenses, especially on real property; **expenditure** which improves or preserves the value of something; **capital expenditure.** See also *dépense*.

imperfect trust
see **executory trust**.

implantation (F)
establishment (of premises); layout (of a building).

implied
Gathered or necessarily deducted from the circumstances. That which may be elicited from a statement made by a writer or speaker. Something that may be presumed to exist based on conduct, intention or a state of affairs; even though it may or may not exist in fact. In particular, something that is presumed to exist in law. cf. **express**. See also **agency of necessity, constructive notice, implied covenant, implied term, implied grant, implied trust**.

implied authority
see **actual authority, agent**.

implied condition
see **condition, implied term**.

implied contract
see **contract**.

implied covenant
A **covenant** which, although not express, is deemed by law to form part of a deed. At common law a covenant may be inserted into a deed by implication, either because the covenant is considered implicit to the nature of the deed, or because it follows from the express wording used in the deed – Williams *v* Burrell (1845) 1 CB 429. Also a covenant may be implied by statute law.

The use of the words **beneficial owner** in a conveyance for valuable consideration implies certain covenants into that deed (Law of Property Act 1925, ss. 76, 77, Sch. 2). The use of the word **demise** implies certain covenants into a lease, provided the implication is not in conflict with the express terms of the lease.

A lessee implies, by entering into a lease, unless there is any express provisions to the contrary, that he will pay, in arrears, the **rent** reserved; pay **rates** and taxes that arise as a result of his occupation of property (but not those for which the landlord is statutorily liable, e.g. the landlord's income tax); not commit **waste**; maintain the premises in a **tenant-like manner** (which is the full extent of his liability under a weekly tenancy); not disclaim his landlord's title; and deliver possession to his landlord at the end of the term of the lease. A lessor implies that he will give **exclusive occupation** to the tenant for the period of the lease; grant **quiet enjoyment**; and not cause any **derogation from grant**. The law also may insert conditions into an agreement based on the conduct of the parties; based on the facts that led to the agreement; or it may infer terms in order to give 'business efficacy' to the agreement (see **implied term**).

As a rule there is no implied covenant by a landlord to **repair** – Sealfer *v* Lambeth Borough Council [1959] 3 All ER 378 but, if a landlord regularly carries out certain types of repair work, it may be inferred that he has accepted a continuing obligation in that respect. A covenant that the tenant will pay additional rent for cleaning of rooms implies that the landlord will clean those rooms – Barnes *v* City of London Corporation (1918) 2 Ch. 18; a landlord who lets premises with the express use of a lift must provide a working lift – De Meze *v* Ve-Ri-Best Manufacturing Co. 1 (1952) 160 EG 364; a landlord who retains control over the common parts (lifts, staircases, refuse chutes, etc.) of a high-rise building is expected to maintain those areas so as to ensure that the building can be utilised adequately – Liverpool City Council v Irwin [1976] 2 All ER 39; and if the tenant is obliged to reimburse the landlord for "the cost of painting in a 'workman-like manner' every third year" it can be implied that the landlord will paint the premises. Nevertheless, a covenant arises by implication because it can be said that the parties intended that the suggested stipulation should exist; not because it would be reasonable if it did exist. A landlord who lets a flat with the use of a bathroom in the building does not have an implied obligation to provide hot water to the bathroom – R v Paddington Rent Tribunal, *ex parte* Bedrock Investments Ltd [1947] KB 984. (A view that might be more questionable in the 1980's than in 1947).

Statute law implies conditions into certain leases from which the parties usually may not contract out. For example, premises let at a **low rent** are to be **fit for human habitation** at the start of the tenancy and to be so maintained throughout the duration of the tenancy (Housing Act 1957, s. 6). A landlord should ensure that any premises he permits to be used by any one are not dangerous or defective due to a want of repair on his part (Defective Premises Act 1974, s. 4). In a lease of a **dwelling-house** granted for a term of less than seven years, "there shall be implied a covenant by the lessor (a) to keep in repair the **structure** and **exterior** of the dwelling house (including drains, gutters and external pipes); and (b) to keep in repair and proper working order the installations in the dwelling house – (i) for the supply of water, gas and electricity, and for sanitation (including basins, sinks, baths and sanitary conveniences but not, except as aforesaid, fixtures, fittings and appliances for making use of the supply of water, gas or electricity) and (ii) for space heating or heating water" (Housing Act 1961, s. 32). In the case of an **agricultural tenancy** there is no implied covenant as to the condition of the land – Erskin v Adeane (1873) 21 WR 802, but either party may insist upon a written tenancy agreement at the outset (or later), with a right to arbitration on any disputed matter (Agricultural Holdings Act 1948, s. 5, Sch.1). If there is no express agreement as to responsibility for repair each party's obligations are governed by the Agriculture (Maintenance, Repair and Insurance of Fixed Equipment) Regulations 1973. cf. **express covenant**. See also **change of use, estoppel, furnished tenancy, implied term, improvement, insurance rent, negligence, restraint on alienation, usual covenant.**

Adkin's Landlord and Tenant, 18 edn, pp. 53–61.

Woodfall's Landlord & Tenant, 28 edn, paras. 1–1140 to 1–1151, 1–1465 to 1–1485.

implied easement
see **easement.**

implied grant
A **grant** of a right or interest in land that arises by implication. An implied grant may arise at common law when an owner sells part of his land and a **quasi-easement** is converted into a true easement that is apparent, continuous and necessary for the reason-

able enjoyment of the land acquired — Wheldon *v* Burrows (1879) 12 Ch.D31. Also an implied grant arises by statute when **general words** are deemed to be incorporated into a conveyance of land so as to transfer various rights, easements, fixtures, etc., which appertain, or are **appurtenant**, to the land conveyed (Law of Property Act 1925, s.62) — provided these words do not conflict with the express words. See also **easement of necessity**.

implied notice
see **constructive notice**.

implied ratification (US)
An acceptance, or **ratification**, of an agreement or action that arises from the conduct or action of a person rather than by an expressed approval, i.e. something that arises from **estoppel**.

implied tenancy
A **tenancy** that is deemed to arise from an action of two parties in relation to land, such as entry into exclusive occupation and payment of rent. See also **tenancy at will**, **tenancy by estoppel**.

implied term (or condition)
A **term** (or **condition**) of a contract which, although not express, may be read into the contract if it would be reasonable so to do, or must be read into a contract if the intention of the parties is not to be defeated; usually because it is inherent in the nature of the contract, or so obvious that it 'goes without saying'. A term may be implied to give 'business efficacy' to the contract; or as a result of **custom** or trade **usage**; or as part of the general tenor of an agreement. An implied term is what the parties *must*

have intended, normally, not what they *may* have intended – Adams *v* Adams [1943] 1 K.B. 543. The law may give effect to an implication when the result gives "such business efficacy to the transaction as must have been intended at all events by both parties who are businessmen." – The Moorcock (1889) 14 Ch. D 70. In other words to make the contract work as the parties would have intended – Luxor (Eastbourne) *v* Cooper [1941] AC 137; to insert that which would have been inserted, without hesitation (by reasonable men or women), had a defect in the contract been pointed out at the outset; "so that, if while the parties were making their bargain and an officious bystander were to suggest some express provision for it in their agreement, they would testily suppress him with a common, 'Oh, of course'" – Shirlaw *v* Southern Foundaries (1926) Ltd [1939] 2 All ER 124. A term will not be implied if it conflicts with any **express term** of the contract; if, within the context of the agreement, it acts to the undue detriment or burden of only one party to the contract; or when the express terms will suffice to make the contract effective in fulfilling the intention of the parties: "it is not competent for the court to make a contract for the parties which they have not thought fit to make for themselves, or to import a covenant which does not arise by fair and necessary implication from the language they have used." – Smith *v* The Mayor, etc. of Harwick (1857) 2 CB (NS) 669.

As a rule there is no implied term in a lease that premises are suitable for the purpose for which they are let; but if a person is merely granted a licence to occupy land or buildings, there is an implied term that the premises granted are suitable for the purpose intended by the parties – plain use and occupation arising from a licence is a different right from that granted by a lease; effectively a licence of real property is a personal contract and any implication must be considered in that light – Wettern Electric *v* Welsh Development Agency [1983] 2 All ER 629.

There is an implied term in a contract for the erection of a dwelling-house that the house is built in a good and workmanlike manner; that the house is built of suitable and proper materials; and that the house is **fit for human habitation**, after all it is a dwelling house – Miller *v* Cannon Hill Estates Ltd [1931] 2 KB 113.

The law implies terms to give the contracting parties what they would reasonably have expected, but it will not imply terms because one party has failed to make reasonable enquiries or make a proper examination of that which is offered as the subject of the contract. See also **agent**, *caveat emptor*, **implied covenant, negligence, notice**.
Odger's Construction of Deeds and Statutes, 5 edn, pp. 113–118.
Cheshire and Fifoot's Law of Contract, 10 edn, pp. 13–15, 123–127, 158–165.
Chitty on Contract, 25 edn, paras. 841–868.
9 Halsbury's Laws of England, 4 edn, paras. 351–362.
Anson's Law of Contract, 26 edn, pp. 125–135.

implied trust

1. A **trust** arising from the operation of law, especially a trust which arises as a result of an equitable need to fulfill a wish of a settler. For example, if A agrees to transfer property to B for an established price equity makes A a trustee for B. Also 'implied trust' may be used to refer to any non-express trust whether a **constructive trust**, which arises by operation of law, e.g. in a case of fraud; or a **resulting trust** which arises out of the intention of parties to a transaction.
(US) 2. A trust that arises to prevent **unjust enrichment**, especially in a case of fraud or an action that is clearly against equity (Matter of Kawczynski, (D.C.N.Y.) 442 F. Supp. 413).

implied warranty

A **representation**, not in writing, that a given condition exists or that a property is in a particular state. A term used especially to refer to a representation that a property is in an insurable condition. See also **implied term, warranty, warranty of habitability**.

impossibility of performance
see **frustration**.

impôt (F)

tax; duty. (A term that may cover most forms of tax in France)
(*impôts et contributions* – rates and taxes)
(*impôts et taxes* – rates and taxes)
(*impôt foncier* – land or **property tax**)
(*impôts locaux* – local rates)
(*impôt réel* – property tax)
(*impôt sur la plus value en capital* – **capital gains tax**)
(*impôt sur le revenu* – income tax)
(*impôt sur les sociétés* – company or corporation tax). See also *contribution*; *droit*; *prélèvement*; *taxe*.
Taxes in France, by L. Halpern, (based on '*Les Impôts en France*' by

Francis Lefebvre), 3 edn., Ch. 1.
Code Général des Impôts, by Dalloz.

impound account (US)
An account into which a borrower is required to make regular payments to meet real estate taxes and insurance premiums in respect of the property held as security for a loan.

imprest
A loan or advance of money, especially a single advance out of which a number of small payments can be made.

impropriation
The transfer of a residence that has been in ecclesiastical ownership into lay ownership.
cf. **appropriation**.

improved ground rent
see **ground rent**, **leasehold ground rent**.

improved land
Land that has been increased in value by an **improvement**, especially by the provision of roads, services, etc.
cf. **raw land**.

improved rent
Rent payable by a tenant to reflect the value of an improvement made by his landlord, especially when the total rent then exceeds the **market rent**.
cf. **virtual rent**.

improved value
1. The value of land or building taking into account any **improvement** thereto. See also **improved rent**.
(US) 2. The value of land and buildings erected thereon, as distinguished from the separate value of the land alone.

improvement
The process of making better, more desirable, or more profitable. An enhancement or amelioration in the value or quality of a property. A *permanent* **alteration** or **addition** that has the effect of raising the usefulness, price, or in any way making something more advantageous; the result of an action that makes a thing more desirable. Any form of addition to land, or buildings, that becomes part of the land, or buildings; in particular, any addition that enhances the value or utility of a property and goes beyond mere **repair** or **maintenance**; '... the provision of something new ... is, properly speaking, an improvement; but if it is only the replacement of something already there, which has become dilapidated or worn out, then, albeit that it is a replacement by its modern equivalent, it comes within the category of repairs and not improvements.' – Morcom *v* Campbell Johnson [1955] 3 All ER 206. On the other hand, if what is required in order to repair a property is a complete replacement by a modern equivalent or in a different form or structure that may well constitute an improvement. Repair may involve, and usually does, involve some degree of improvement, "in the sense of the modern substitute being better than that which has gone before." – Wates *v* Rowland [1952] 2 QB 23. But the provision of something different in kind, or something different in operation or purpose, even if it does not enhance the value, is more than repair if it ameliorates or improves the property – Woolworth *v* Lambert [1936] 2 All ER 1523; Pembery *v* Lamdin [1940] 2 All ER 434.

In English planning law improvement may come within the definition of **development**, especially when it involves the construction of roads; the construction of new buildings and associated major works; the structural alteration to an existing building, as when it alters the external appearance; or involves a **material change in the use** of a property.

For the purpose of an **improvement grant** improvement includes, 'alteration and enlargement' and work of repair that is needed to bring a dwelling-house up to the standard required by the body paying the grant (Housing Act 1974, s. 84).

In the absence of any express provision to the contrary a tenant is free to make any improvement to the premises leased to him, provided he does not commit **waste**. However, a lease may provide an absolute prohibition against improvement, especially if the improvement involves structural alteration; or the lease may provide that improvement to the premises may not be carried out without the landlord's prior licence or consent. In the latter instance any such provision "shall be deemed, notwithstanding any express provision to the contrary, to be subject to a proviso that such licence or consent shall not be unreasonably withheld" (Landlord and Tenant Act 1927, s. 19(2)). When granting such consent the landlord may impose conditions on the tenant, including a requirement that the tenant pays a reasonable sum of money in respect of the loss in value of the premises, or a loss in the value of any neighbouring premises belonging to the landlord, or of any legal or other expenses properly incurred in connection with the grant of such licence or consent. The landlord may require also that the tenant gives an undertaking to reinstate the premises at the end of the lease if the improvement does not 'add to the letting value of the holding' (1927 Act, s.19(3)). (These statutory provisions do not apply to an agricultural or a mining lease: 1927 Act, s. 19 (4)). In the last context that which constitutes an improvement is ascertained primarily from the point of view of the tenant; the landlord is "amply protected by the undertaking of the tenant to reinstate at the end of the term." – Balls Brothers Ltd. v Sinclair [1931] 2 Ch. 332.

In the case of a **secure tenancy**, a **protected tenancy** or a **statutory tenancy** a tenant must apply in writing for consent to carry out any improvement to the demised premises, but the landlord is not to unreasonably withhold such consent, and if unreasonably withheld, the consent is treated as given (Housing Act 1980, s. 81, 82). For this purpose an improvement means, 'any alteration in, or addition to, a dwelling-house and includes – (a) any addition to, or alteration in landlord's fixtures and fittings and any addition or alteration connected with the provision of any service to a dwelling-house; (b) the erection of any wireless or television aerial; and (c) the carrying out of any external decoration' (unless the landlord is liable for carrying out such decoration). See also **agricultural tenancy, business tenancy, capital expenditure, compensation for improvements, fair rent, fixture, market rent, improvement notice, listed building, tenant for life, virtual rent.**

improvement area
    see **general improvement area, housing action area.**

improvement grant

A type of **home improvement grant** made, at the discretion of a local authority, to a qualifying home owner, under the provisions of the Housing Act 1974, s. 61, to cover part of the cost of a major improvement to a dwelling (which can be a house, flat, bungalow or maisonette) in order to bring the dwelling up to a good standard of repair and amenity. An improvement grant may be made also to meet part of the cost of converting a building into a dwelling, including the cost of an alteration or enlargement. An improvement grant normally is granted only when the improved dwelling will be provided with the **standard amenities** for the exclusive use of its occupants; put into a reasonable state of repair (disregarding the state of internal decoration, but taking into account its age and character and the locality in which it is situated) and made **fit for human habitation**. The improved dwelling should also be likely to provide satisfactory housing for a period of 30 years. The local authority has power to accept a 'reduced standard' of housing if the expense of making the improvement does not warrant the 'full standard', especially if financial hardship may result to a house owner or the house is to be provided for the disabled. An improvement grant is intended to be more extensive than an **intermediate grant**.

cf. **repairs grant**. See also **special grant**.

improvement line

A line prescribed by a highway authority, in accordance with the provisions of the Highways Act 1980, s. 73, indicating the limit of an intended street widening scheme. The highway authority's intention is to purchase property up to that limit and, therefore, new building between this line and the existing highway is prohibited. There is a right of appeal to the Crown Court against a proposal of a highway authority to prescribe an improvement line. Any person whose property is injuriously affected by the prescribing of an improvement line may be entitled to compensation for the injury sustained (1980 Act, s. 73(9), (1), 307). Properties affected by an improvement line may be subject to future compulsory purchase.

cf. **building line**. See also **blight notice, compensation for injurious affection**.

The Modern Law of Highways, by S. Hamilton, para. 185 (1981).

improvement notice

Notice served by a local authority, in accordance with the provisions of the Housing Act 1974, s. 88, upon a 'person having control' of a dwelling house, which is situated in a **general improvement area** or a **housing action area**, requiring that person to provide **standard amenities**. If a house is not in a housing action area or general improvement area, the local authority has power to serve an improvement notice, provided it has received a prior written representation from an occupying tenant and it is satisfied that the house ought to be improved or is unlikely to be improved without the service of such a notice (1974 Act, s. 89). The dwelling must be capable at reasonable expense of improvement to a 'full standard' (i.e. be put into a reasonable state of repair having regard to its age, character and locality, be **fit for human habitation**, have all the standard amenities, have appropriate thermal insulation and, usually, have a life expectancy as a dwelling of 15 years) or, in certain cases a 'reduced standard'. An improvement notice normally is preceded by a 'provisional notice' to similar effect seeking an undertaking from the owner of the property that it will be improved in accordance with the local authority's requirements (1974 Act, s. 85 (1)). An improvement notice is registerable as a **local land charge**. See also **improvement grant, purchase notice, repair notice**.

Landlord and Tenant Law, by David Yates and A.J. Hawkins, pp. 199–202 (1981).

Housing Law, by Andrew Arden and Martin Partington, pp. 616–27 (1983).

improvements and betterments insurance (US)
Insurance taken out by a tenant to cover the risk of loss or damage to improvements he has made to the leased premises.

imputation (F)
appropriation; allocation.

imputed knowledge
see **imputed notice**.

imputed notice
Notice or information which a person is assumed to have received because it has been transmitted (expressly or constructively) to someone else who, it may be presumed, will remit the notice or information to the aforesaid person. For example, notice received by a solicitor or other agent for a purchaser and, therefore, assumed to be known to the purchaser. Within the law of **agency**, as a general rule, a principal is assumed to have knowledge or notice of any matter which relates to the business for which the agent is employed and which becomes known to the agent while acting within the scope of his or her authority – Hiern *v* Mill (1806) 13 Ves. 114; Mutual Life Insurance Co. *v* Hilton-Green, 241 US 215, 36 S.Ct. 676. Called also 'imputed knowledge'.
cf. **constructive notice**. See also **waiver**.

imputed value
A **value** attributed to a property which is not measured in monetary terms, such as the benefit of **use and occupation**. Value that is ascribed to something or arises from its **utility**, and not from its **intrinsic value** or from the worth of its components.

in advance
see **advance, rent in arrears or advance**.

in alieno solo (L)
'Against another's land'. See **easement**.

in arrears
see **arrears, rent in arrears or advance**.

in capite (L)
'In chief', see **tenant-in-chief**.

in chief
see **abstracted in chief, tenant-in-chief**.

in common
see **co-ownership, right of common, tenancy in common**.

in good faith
see *bona fide*, **good faith, utmost good faith**.

in gross
That which is not annexed to land. A right to land 'in gross' is not **append-**

ant, **appurtenant,** or in any other way annexed to land, but exists without benefitting land or issuing out of land. A rentcharge is a form of payment 'in gross' and in consequence does not give the payee any right to repossess the land for which it is payable. See also **easement in gross, gross, incorporeal hereditament, profit à prendre.**

in pais (L)

'In the country'. Outside legal proceedings or outside that which is contained in documents, records, based on ascertained (rather than ascertainable) fact. See also **estoppel.**

in personam (L)

'Against the person'.
cf. *in rem.* See also **action** *in personam.*

in rem (L)

'Against the thing'. "The relation between a person and a thing is called by lawyers a *real* relation, or relation *in rem* (from the Latin *res* meaning thing) and is distinguished from a personal relation or relation *in personam*" (*The Law of Property*, by Lawson and Rudden, 2 edn., p. 2). See also **action in rem, real property.**

in rem loan

A non-recourse loan.

in situ (L)

'In the place; in position'.

in specie (L)

'In actual form'. Not as a substitute or equivalent. **Money** *in specie* is coin and not paper money.

in tail

see **entailed interest, fee tail.**

inalienable

Property, or strictly a right to prop-

erty, that cannot be, or may not be freely, transferred or alienated. See also **alienation, restraint on alienation, rule against perpetuities.**

inaliénable (F)

inalienable; indefeasible.
Précis Dalloz. Droit Civil, Les Biens by Alex Weill, 2 edn, p. 302 *et seq.*

incentive fee

see **contingency fee.**

incentive zoning (US)

A provision in a **zoning ordinance** which provides that a developer will obtain more beneficial zoning, e.g. increased density or plot ratio, if he provides facilities or amenities that benefit the local community. See also **planning gain.**

inchoate interest

An imperfect or incomplete interest. An interest that has not fully come into effect, or is pending. For example, an interest in land which is about to be registered. An interest that may become a **vested interest,** provided it is not barred or extinguished by a prior event. See also **contingent interest, future estate (or interest).**

incidence

That which is **incident** or has an effect upon something else. The rate at which one cost or factor bears upon another; for example, the rate at which the cost of a parcel of land affects the total cost of a development project. See also **sensitivity analysis.**

incidence (F)

incidence.

incident

Something that follows from, appertains to or depends on another right. A privilege or burden that is accessory to an interest or estate. For example, a right of alienation is incident to an estate in fee simple (though separable in equity); distress is incident to rent; a fixture incident to the freehold. See also **incidence, incident of tenure.**

incident of tenure

A right or service that follows as part of a feudal right of land **tenure**, e.g. the provision of personal services to the Crown or a Lord. Such a right when annexed to a **manor** is called a 'manorial incident'. Most feudal incidents of tenure have been abolished; but some may continue indefinitely, unless terminated by written agreement between the lord and the tenant. Those incidents that may continue are: a tenant's right of common; a right of the lord or tenant to a mine and to minerals; a right of the lord in respect of fairs, markets, and sporting rights; any liability of the lord or tenant for the upkeep of dykes, ditches, sea walls, bridges and the like (Law of Property Act 1922, Sch. 12). *Introduction to Land Law*, J.G. Riddell, 3 edn., pp. 6–14.
The Law of Real Property, by Robert Megarry and H.W.R. Wade, 5 edn., pp. 31–36.

incidental use

A use that is dependent on, associated with, or **incident** to the principal use of premises. Therefore, a use that does not normally require planning permission or zoning consent when a principal use is already permitted. In the US referred to as an 'accessory use'. See also **material change in the use, planning unit.**

inclosure

see **enclosure.**

inclusive rent

Rent that is payable so as to include rates for the demised premises, which are in turn paid by the landlord.
cf. **exclusive rent.**

income

'What cometh in'. In general, the increase in wealth of an individual, company or other organisation over a given period of time. Recurring periodic benefits to be derived from the application of capital or labour; in particular, money or money's worth received or earned on a recurring basis. In economic terms, pecuniary advantage earned from a 'factor of production' (land, capital or labour – producing respectively rent, profit and wages as income). Gains from the sale of **capital**, but not from capital growth *per se*, may be classified as income.

Income from real property may be classified, after deduction of various expenses, as:

gross income (or, in the US, 'gross operating income') – the total receipts (gross rent, service charges contribution or operating cost receipts, licence fees, etc.) from all sources before any deductions or allowances.

effective gross income – the gross income, after allowing for losses due to voids and defaulting tenants.

net income – the gross income after deducting all operating or running expenses, service charges, property taxes, insurance costs, management fees, rent losses, etc., directly related to the property. In the US the 'effective gross income' after making these deductions is called **net operating income**, or 'net income before recapture'.

cash flow – the net income after

payment of debt service (interest and principal repayment on all loans), and usually, after an allowance for depreciation – called also 'net before tax'. (Note: income may include gains from the sale of property but this is not included in cash flow.)

net cash flow – (or 'net spendable income'). The cash flow after payment of income tax; this may be referred to as net income, or cash flow, after tax, or in the US 'net after tax'.

In relation to land law 'income' includes rents and profits (being payments received for the benefits to be derived from use, occupation or exploitation of land or buildings) (Conveyancing Act 1881, s. 2 (iii); Administration of Estates Act 1925, s. 55 (1) (v); Land Registration Act 1925, s. 3 (vi)).

cf. **outgoings**. See also **net rent**.

income approach (US)
see **investment method of valuation**.

incorporeal hereditament
A right to land that is capable of inheritance but is not tangible and does not give the owner any physical right to possession of the land, e.g. an **easement**, **profit à prendre**, **rentcharge**. 'An incorporeal hereditament is a right issuing out of a thing corporate (whether real or personal) or concerning, or annexed to, or exercisable, with the same. It is not the things corporate itself which may consist in lands, houses, jewells, or the like; but something collateral thereto, as a rent issuing out of those lands or houses ... In short, as the logicians speak, corporeal hereditaments are the substance, which may be always seen, always handled; incorporeal hereditaments are but a

sort of accident, which inhere in and are supported by that substance; and may belong, or not belong to it, without any visible alteration therein.' (Bl. Comm. vol. ii p. 20). Historically, corporeal hereditaments were said to lie in 'livery' (i.e. they may be physically transferred) and incorporeal hereditaments were said to lie in 'grant' (i.e. they may be transferred by bestowing a right on another). An incorporeal hereditament may be a right that can ripen into a **corporeal hereditament**, as where the incorporeal right is converted in time into a corporeal right; for example, land held by A for life, with the **remainder** to B, gives B an incorporeal hereditament which becomes corporeal upon the death of A. On the other hand, it may be a right that can never become corporeal; for example, a rentcharge. (Certain rights that are referred to as 'incorporeal hereditaments' are not strictly hereditaments as they are not capable of inheritance except as adjuncts to the land which they benefit.)

Incorporeal hereditaments may be classified as (i) **appendant**, that is of historical origin, e.g. advowson, a manorial incident; (ii) **appurtenant**, that is annexed to land, e.g. right of common, right of way; and (iii) **in gross**, that is they exist independently of land, e.g. rentcharge, rent-seck, common in gross, tithes, profit à prendre. See also **hereditament, incorporeal property**.

incorporeal property (or thing)
Property (or a thing) that is not tangible, cannot be seen touched or otherwise sensed, but exists as a right to tangible or **corporeal property**. Property that can never be taken into physi-

cal possession and is represented only as a right or claim, e.g. a servitude, patent, debt, goodwill, copyright.

Incorporeal property is a term derived from Roman law where it is used to make a distinction between physical things and abstract things – *res corporeal* and *res incorporeal*. "Incorporeal things cannot be possessed, since possession requires a physical holding, and they cannot therefore be acquired or transferred by any method which involves the transfer or acquisition of possession. In short, incorporeal things can neither be acquired by *usucapio* [prescription] nor conveyed by *tradito* [delivery]." (*An Introduction to Roman Law*, by Barry Nicholas, p. 106, 1962.) Incorporeal property (*incorporel*) in the civil law corresponds roughly to a ***chose-in-action*** in common law. See also **incorporeal hereditament**.

incorporel (F)
incorporeal; intangible.
(*actif incorporel* – **intangible asset**)
(*bien incorporel* – intangible or **incorporeal property**; chose-in-action). See also *biens*.

increase clause (US)
see **escalator clause**.

increment
An increase in quantity, quality or value. A gradual enlargement in area, volume or character.
cf. **decrement**. See also **accretion, enlargement**.

incroachment
see **encroachment**.

incubator unit (US)
see **nursery unit**.

incumbrance
see **encumbrance**.

incurable depreciation
Deterioration to a building that cannot be remedied, usually because it would be too expensive to restore or replace. Economic obsolescence is generally incurable.
cf. **curable depreciation**. See also **depreciation**.

indefeasible
That which cannot be defeated, forfeited, revoked or made void; especially an estate, interest or right to land that cannot be defeated by the claim of another, e.g. a right of light that has been enjoyed without interruption for over 27 years. See also **prescription**.

indemnité (F)
compensation; indemnity.
(*indemnité d'expropriation* – compulsory purchase compensation. See *expropriation*)
(*indemnité d'eviction* – tenant compensation, especially compensation awarded to a tenant who is refused a right to renew a ***bail commercial*** or a ***bail rural***)
(*indemnité forfaitaire* – **penalty**). See also ***reprise***.

indemnity
1. Derived from the Latin *in-damnum-tas* or *indemnitas*, 'non-detrimental' or 'to make free from loss'. **Compensation** or **restitution** paid by one party to another to cover a loss or injury suffered by the latter; whether arising from an agreement or otherwise. In particular, something paid or rendered to restore the *status quo ante*. An indemnity that arises from an agreement is paid because of a separate activity that affects that agreement, unlike **damages** which are paid

because of a failure to perform the agreement.

2. A **contract** by which one party agrees to accept an anticipatory loss that may fall on another. A provision of **security** against financial loss up to, but for no more than, an actual loss suffered. A 'contract of indemnity' is one entered into by a person who accepts a primary responsibility for a loss, even though he is not party to any contract or act from which the loss arises. Most contracts of **insurance** are contracts of indemnity; that is they are contracts which provide that, in the event of loss, damage or injury, an insured is placed in the same but no better position than if no privation had arisen.

A contract of indemnity may be distinguished from a contract of **guaranty** (or **guarantee**), because a guarantor accepts that he will answer for the default or debt of another only as an accessory. 'The distinction between the two contracts is, in brief, that in a contract of guarantee the surety assumes a secondary liability to answer for the debtor who remains primarily liable; whereas in a contract of indemnity the surety assumes a primary liability, either alone or jointly with the principal debtor.' – Chitty on Contract 25 edn, para. 4406. Thus, a tenant may provide a guarantee in the form of a bank deposit as security against his failure to meet his primary obligation to pay rent, but a 'tenant's default' insurance policy may be taken out by a landlord as an indemnity against the risk that the tenant cannot pay rent due to financial failure. Unlike a guarantee, an indemnity need not be evidenced in **writing**. See also **indemnity insurance**, **indemnity limit**, **reinstatement**

basis, subrogation.

Building and Engineering Contracts, by A.A. Hudson, 10 edn., pp. 306–313.

20 Halsbury's Laws of England, 4 edn, paras. 305–400.

indemnity insurance

1. **Insurance** which provides an **indemnity** against loss or damage directly occasioned by the insured; in contrast to **liability insurance** which provides an indemnity against a liability to another (or against damage caused to another's property)

2. Insurance which is based on providing an indemnity that is assessed according to the actual loss or damage suffered; as distinguished from **contingency insurance** which provides for payment when a contingent event (e.g. death) occurs, but on the basis of an amount specified in the policy. See also **replacement cost**.

indemnity limit

The maximum amount of financial loss against which an **indemnity** has been provided; in particular, such an amount as specified in an insurance policy. See also **valued policy**.

indenture

1. A document, especially a **deed**, that establishes an agreement between two or more parties and is prepared in identical form for each party to the agreement. Traditionally a deed between two or more parties was duplicated on the same sheet of paper or parchment and then cut, or 'indented' (cut with a jagged line like teeth), between the duplicates so that they could be verified as authentic copies when brought together. "If a deed be made by more parties than one, there ought to be regularly as many copies

of it as there are parties, and each should be cut or indented (formerly in acute lines *instar dentium*, but at present in a waving line) on the top or side, to tally or correspond with the other; which deed, so made, is called an indenture."(Bl. Comm. (1776) vol. ii. p. 295). The words 'this indenture' generally are found at the start of any deed involving more than one party, even when there is not actual indenting. A deed purporting to be an indenture need no longer be indented, or expressed to be an indenture, to have the effect of an indenture (Law of Property Act 1925, s. 56 (2)) "Indenture is a term peculiar to the law of this country [England] and of countries whose law is based on that of England as for example Ireland, some English colonies, and some of the United States of America), and would not be intelligible to a lawyer only instructed in the law of most continental countries." – A.G *v* Jewish Colonization Association [1901] 1 KB 143.

cf. **deed poll**. See also **counterpart**.

(US) 2. A mortgage, a deed of trust or similar instrument that acknowledges an outstanding debt of a corporation or business, or acknowledges that a corporation is bound to meet an obligation.

independent contractor

One who has a contractual obligation to perform certain acts on behalf of another, using his own methods; acting as his own master; only controlled as to the final product; and making decisions on any matters not specified in the contract by which he is appointed. "An independent contractor is one who undertakes to produce a given result, but so that in the actual execution of the work he is not under the order and control of the person for whom he does it, and may use his own discretion in things not specified before hand." – Performing Rights Society Ltd *v* Mitchell and Booker Palais de Danse Ltd, [1924] 1 KB 768 (citing Pollock on Torts, 12 edn, p. 80) – Massey *v* Tube Art Display Inc., 551 P 2d. 1387, 25 Wash. App. 792. An independent contractor is neither an employee, nor a party to a contract of service. As a rule he performs a specific act, or series of acts, in accordance with the contract, and has no continuing responsibility to act according to the master's or employer's behest: an independent contractor is neither part nor parcel of the employing organisation. Unlike an **agent**, an independent contractor makes commitments on his own behalf; in his own capacity; and is liable for any commitment made in his name. An employer is not in general liable for any **negligence** of his independent contractor. See also **contractor, main contractor, sub-contractor, vicarious liability**.

The Law of Agency, by G.H.L. Fridman, 5 edn., pp. 26–32, 269–271. *Employer's Liability at Common Law*, by John Munkman, 8 edn., p. 84.

independent valuer

see **expert**.

index animi sermo est (L)

'Words are the indication of intention'.

index lease

see **indexed lease**.

index-linked insurance policy

A property insurance policy which provides that the amount of cover against damage is adjusted automatically in line with a specified index, usually an official cost of construction or cost of living index, to allow for variations in the cost of replacing or repairing the property. This form of policy reduces the need for the insured to readjust the amount of cover by making regular revaluations and, as a rule, reduces the risk that the insurer will apply the principle of **average** to any compensation paid under the policy.

index-linked mortgage

see **price-level adjusted mortgage**.

Index Map

A map kept by the **Land Registry** showing the position and extent of every registered title to land (Land Registration Rules 1925, r. 8). An index map, or strictly a 'Public Index Map', is available for public inspection, unlike the land register itself which may be inspected only with the authority of a **registered proprietor**. See also **filed plan**, **Parcels Index**.

index method

1. Any method of valuation which adjusts the cost or value of a property by **indexation**.
2. A method of assessing the **reinstatement cost** of a property by adjusting the original, or some other historic cost, in line with a particular index. A subsequent adjustment may be made to take account of depreciation.
(US) 3. A method of adjusting the sale price of a comparable property, when applying the market comparison approach (the **comparison method of valuation**), by weighting the different factors that affect its comparative

value (location, size, age, etc.) in accordance with an index or scale.

indexation

A process of adjusting a price, or the consideration in a contract, in line with changes in a specified price index; especially in order to allow for the erosion of the price or the consideration due to inflation, i.e. to conserve the 'real value' of a sum of money. An initial price is related to a starting or base index figure (ordinarily taken as 100) and this price is adjusted in direct relationship to subsequent index numbers. The adjustment may be made at specified periods of time or specified movements in the index, e.g. every year or every time the index changes 5% from the base. For example, the rent in a lease may be adjusted by relating it to movements of an official 'cost of living' index. A building contract may be adjusted in accordance with an official 'cost of construction' index; or by an agreed formula as is commonly employed in continental Europe:

e.g. $p = P[0.40 \, (m/M) + 0.35 \, (l/L) + 0.25]$

Where, p = final contract price.

P = initial or base price at start of contract.

m and M = official index of building material costs at the start and end of the contract respectively.

l and L = the official index of labour costs at the start and end of the contract respectively.

In this example the total price is indexed on the basis of a 'weighting' of 40 per cent for materials, 35 per cent for labour, and 25 per cent for fixed costs. See also **escalator clause, weighted aggregate index.**

indexation (F)
indexation.
(*clause d'indexation* – indexation clause).

indexé (F)
indexed.
(*bail indexé* – indexed lease).

indexed lease
A lease that provides for an **indexed rent.**

indexed rent
A rent that is varied in accordance with a specified index; for example by annual adjustments based on an official cost of living or a construction index.
cf. **stepped rent.** See also **escalation clause, indexation.**

indice (F)
index.
(*indice du coût de la construction* – building cost index)
(*indice du coût de la vie* – cost of living index)
(*indice des prix à la consommation* – consumer price index).

indisponible (F)
inalienable.

individual ownership (US)
see **several ownership.**

indivisaire (F)
joint owner. See also *indivision.*

indivisible contract
see **performance.**

indivision (F)
co-ownership; joint possession; coparcenary. *Indivision* is a form of co-ownership (*copropriété*) being a right of two or more persons to hold one or more properties in common with others. However, unlike normal *copropriété*, which is a real right to property, it is more a right to a share in an undivided whole. *Indivision* arises usually from a succession to property by two or more heirs. In French law under a hereditary indivision (*indivision héreditaire*) the heirs are co-owners of an entire estate but it is a right intended to have a limited duration (usually no more than five years) after which the property is sold and the proceeds distributed among the heirs. See also *communauté.*
Précis Dalloz. Droit Civil, Les Biens by Alex Weill, 2 edn, pp. 179–187.
Manuel de Droit Civil, by Pierre Voirin et Gilles Goubeaux, 20 edn., pp. 246–247.

indorsement
see **endorsement.**

industrial building
A building used for the purpose of a trade or business that involves the manufacturing, processing, assembling or finishing of goods. A factory, mill, or similar premises; but not one used solely for the storage and distribution of goods, i.e. not the type of building that usually is called a **warehouse.** In English planning law an industrial building is defined as "a building used or designed for use – (a) for carrying on of any process for or incidental to any of the following purposes, that is to say – (i) the making of any article or of part of any article; or (ii) the altering, repairing, ornamenting, finishing, cleaning, washing, freezing, packing or canning or adapting for sale, or breaking up or demolition of any article; or (iii) without prejudice to the foregoing, the getting, dressing or preparation

for sale of minerals, or the extraction or preparation for sale of oil or brine; (b) for the carrying on of scientific research, being a process or research carried on in the course of trade of business" (Town and Country Planning Act 1971, s. 66(1)).

The Town and Country Planning (Use Classes) Order 1972 (which contains a similar definition to the 1971 Act, except that it specifically excludes a building in or adjacent to and belonging to a quarry or mine, an agricultural building, as well as a shop) categorises an industrial building according to the process carried on therein: (i) a light industrial building, which can be installed in a residential area without detriment to the local environment by reason of noise, vibration, smell, fumes, smoke, soot, ash, dirt or grit; (ii) a special industrial building which is liable to pollute the environment; and (iii) a general industrial building which is a building not included in (i) or (ii). The Local Government Act 1960, s. 21 and the Industrial Development Act 1966, s. 25, which deal with development areas, contain similar definitions to that set out in the 1971 Act. See also **capital allowance**, **industrial estate**, **industrial property**, **Use Classes Order**.

industrial building allowance (IBA)
A **capital allowance** permitted for capital expenditure incurred on an industrial building or structure which is to be occupied for the purposes of a trade. (For this purpose an extensive definition of 'industrial building' is set out in the Capital Allowances Act 1968, s. 7; this has been extended by various Inland Revenue Statements of Practice). Broadly, the building must be used for manufacturing purposes or a related trade – a 'qualifying trade' as opposed to a distributive trade – and when a building is occupied by a lessee or licensee it is the occupier's trade that is relevant. An industrial building allowance is intended to act as an incentive for new investment and to allow for depreciation. An IBA took the form of an **initial allowance** combined with a **writing-down allowance**; but, since 13th March 1984, it is limited to an annual writing-down allowance permitted until the expenditure is reduced to nil or the building is disposed of (Finance Act 1984, Sch. 12). On disposal of the building, a **balancing allowance (or charge)** may be payable. An industrial building allowance may be claimed by a property owner for capital expenditure incurred on a building that is leased, provided it is used for a 'qualifying trade' (except in an **enterprise zone** where it may be used for any purpose). For a leased building the landlord may set the allowance against his rental income. Subject to certain conditions an IBA may be claimed by a lessor and a lessee jointly or by the lessee even though the expenditure is incurred by the lessor (Finance Act 1978, s. 37).

industrial condominium (US)
An industrial building or estate held in **condominium ownership**.

industrial development certificate (IDC)
A certificate that is required in certain parts of the UK, from the Secretary of State for the Environment, authorising a change of use or the construction of an industrial building above a certain size (Town and Country Plan-

ning Act 1971, ss. 66–72). This is an additional requirement to **planning permission** and is intended to control the regional distribution of employment. This requirement has been suspended from 9th January, 1982 – Town and Country Planning (Industrial Development Certificates) (Prescribed Classes of Building) Regulation 1981.

industrial estate
An area of land sub-divided and developed comprehensively for industrial use. The estate usually has a uniformity of appearance and design and remains under one management. Typically it is developed by a single entrepreneur who provides the roads and main utilities for the estate and either sells or lets plots of land or builds a variety of industrial buildings for sale or lease. In the US the term 'industrial park' is preferred for this form of development. See also **industrial property**.

industrial park (US)
see **industrial estate**.

industrial property
1. The American Institute of Real Estate Appraisers defines industrial property as, "a combination of land, improvements and machinery which has been adjusted, synchronized and perfected into a functioning unit intended for the assembling, processing and manufacture of finished or partially finished products from raw materials or fabricated parts, such as factories; and a similar combination intended for rendering certain kinds of services, such as laundries, dry cleaners, storage warehouses, and for the production of natural resources, such as oil wells." See also **commer-**

cial property, factory, industrial building, light industrial building, warehouse, workshop.
Modern Methods of Valuation, 7 edn., pp. 339–345.
Industrial Valuations, by H.H. Karslake and A.D. Nicholls, pp. 383–395 (1974).
Industrial Real Estate, by William N. Kinnard, Stephen D. Messner and Byrl N. Boyce, 3 edn.
Industrial Development Handbook, Urban Land Institute, (1976).
2. Intangible property that is related and is of value, to business or industry, e.g. a trademark, patent, 'know-how', copyright, etc. This type of property, which exists only in the mind, is called sometimes 'intellectual property'.

industriel (F)
(*complex industriel* – industrial complex; industrial estate)
(*zone industrielle* – **industrial estate**)
(*zone industriel* – industrial zoning).

infeudation
1. The granting of a right to possession of a **freehold**.
cf. **subinfeudation**.
2. The granting of a **tithe** to a layman.

infilling
The development of an area of land between two existing built-up areas. Usually the development of small plots of land, between existing buildings, in such a way that the new development complements the existing.

informal lease
see **agreement for a lease**.

infra (L)
'below; later; underneath'.

infrastructure

The basic or underlying requirements for a new development; in particular, transport facilities, utilities or services (electricity, water, sewage, etc.), and necessary and associated land uses (shops, schools, etc.); but not buildings per se.

cf. **superstructure**.

infrastructure (F)

infrastructure.

ingrossment

see **engrossment**.

inhabitable

see **fit for human habitation**.

inhabité (F)

unoccupied; uninhabited; **vacant**.

inherent defect (or **inherent vice**)

A constituent defect in a building; an 'inborn' fault in construction which, in due course, could make a property deteriorate into a particular condition e.g. to settle or fall down. A tenant's covenant 'to **repair**' does not make him liable to improve or substantially renew the landlord's property; therefore, if that is required in order to remedy an inherent defect, he is absolved from the liability: "it is always a question of fact and degree whether that which the tenant is being asked to do can properly be described as repair, or whether on the contrary it would involve giving back to the landlord a wholly different thing from that which he demised." – Ravenseft Properties Ltd *v* Davestone (Holdings) Ltd [1979] 1 All ER 937. However, what constitutes repairing an inherent defect, and may be classified therefore as an **improvement** – giving back something better than was leased – depends on the cost,

the age and condition of the property at the start of the lease, and the duration and other terms of the lease – Brew Bros. *v* Snax (Ross) [1970] 1 QB 612. See also **defect of title**.

Landlord and Tenant Law, by David Yates and A.J. Hawkins, pp. 168–170 (1981).

Woodfall's Landlord and Tenant, 28 edn, para. 1–1437.

inheritable fee

see **fee simple absolute**.

inheritance

1. The acquisition of real property as an **heir** to another i.e. by right of succession, rather than by devise or transfer by will. However, 'inheritance' may be used to refer to the devolution of property, or any property that devolves, on the death of its owner, by will or on intestacy. In old English law an inheritance was a right to possession of land which subsisted as long as there was someone capable of taking that land as a descendant, as distinguished from a mere right of **tenure** which reverted to the landowner upon the death of the immediate holder of that right. Thus an inheritance was any property capable of passing to the purchaser's heirs (Co. Litt. 383 b.). In Roman and the civil law 'inheritance' refers to any acquisition of property, whether real or personal, by testament or by law upon the death of an owner; in common parlance the term is used in the same sense.

2. Property that is received from the estate of a deceased person.

inheritance tax (US)

A state tax levied on the value of property received by an heir; to be compared to estate, or legacy, tax which is levied on the value of the deceased's estate. An inheritance tax is not strictly a tax on the property but on the right of a living person to receive property from a deceased person – Rigby *v* Clayton, 164 SE 2d 7, 274 NC 465.

cf. **estate tax**.

inhibition

An order or entry on the proprietorship register of the **Land Registry** made to prohibit, either totally or partially, any further dealing in a registered parcel of land or land affected by a registered charge, either for a specified period of time or until a specified event occurs (Land Registration Act 1925, s. 57). An inhibition may be likened to an injunction and is made, for example, in the case of fraud, bankruptcy or when the proprietor's land certificate has been lost. An application for an inhibition may be made by any person interested in registered land, or in a registered charge, by application to the court, or to the Chief Registrar (subject to a right of appeal to the court). An inhibition is a hostile act, made in extreme cases, and is rarely encountered. See also **caution, minor interest, restriction**.

initial allowance

A form of **capital allowance** by which a person incurring capital expenditure may write-off, against taxable income, a higher percentage of the cost incurred in the first 'qualifying period' than normally would be allowed. The percentage varies from 10 per cent to 100 per cent. The balance of the expenditure may be allowed as a **writing-down allowance** in subsequent years. Initial allowances are applied broadly to expenditure on an industrial building or structure (provided it is used for an approved purpose); an hotel; mining and dredging works; a building used for scientific research; and an agricultural building. The allowance is 100% for expenditure in an **enterprise zone** and on construction of a small workshop (2500 sq. ft. or less), 75 per cent for other industrial buildings and 20 per cent for hotels. Except in an enterprise zone, initial allowances were phased out after 13 March 1984. cf. **first-year allowance**. See also **industrial building allowance**.

initial yield

The **yield** from an investment at the time of its acquisition.

cf. **running yield**. See also **cash-on-cash yield**.

injonction (F)

injunction, in particular an order given by a magistrate requiring the production of a document.

injunction

An order, granted at the discretion of a court of English law, commanding a party to refrain from, or to take, a certain course of action, usually in order to reduce or prevent injury, or the threat of injury; whether arising from a **tort** or a **breach of contract**. An injunction is either 'mandatory' (compulsive) or 'prohibitionary' (preventative, restrictive). A mandatory injunction compels someone to do something, or to undo something i.e. it is restorative in its effect; for example, an injunction may require someone to demolish a building that has been erected illegally. A prohibitory injunction restrains a party from a course of action, e.g. from committing a **nuisance** or breaching a nega-

tive promise. Most injunctions are prohibitory. An injunction may be 'perpetual'; or 'interim' (interlocutory, provisional). A perpetual injunction is made after the details of a case have been heard. An interim injunction is made to preserve the status quo until all the details of a case have been considered by the court. An injunction is an equitable remedy i.e. it is given at the discretion of the court. It acts *in personam* (i.e. it acts solely against the person) and, therefore, cannot 'run with the land'. In certain instances a court may, and will in preference, award **damages** rather than grant an injunction; for example, where (i) the plaintiff's loss is trivial; (ii) money compensation can readily be assessed and would prove an adequate remedy; or (iii) it would be oppressive to grant an injunction. A similar remedy called an 'interdict' exists in Scottish law.
cf. **specific performance**. See also **Mareva injunction**.
The Modern English Legal System, by P.F. Smith and S.H. Bailey, pp. 657–658 (1984).
The English Legal System, by R.J. Walker, 6 edn., pp. 51–53.
24 Halsbury's Laws of England, 4 edn, paras. 901–1200.

injuria (L)
'**Injury**'. An infringement that gives rise to a legal right of compensation.
cf. **damage**. See also *damnum sine injuria*.

injuria sine damno (L)
'**Injury** without harm'. See **damages**.
cf. *damnum sine injuria*.

injurious affection
An action that has a harmful or deprecatory effect; in particular, a reduction in the value of a property as a result of works carried out by a public body on adjoining property. A physical interference with any right, public or private, which the owner or occupier of any property is, by law, entitled to make use of in connection with that property – Re Masters and Great Western Railway [1900] 2 QB 687. The interference may be temporary, e.g. a restriction on access to, or disturbance to the use of, property for a limited period of time; or it may be permanent or transitional, e.g. a change in the position of a right of way or a **severance** of the ownership of land, provided the result is to confiscate an existing right and to cause a loss in value.

Compensation may be payable for injurious affection and, in this context, "the word 'injuriously' does not mean 'wrongfully' affected ... it means 'hurtfully' or 'damnously' affected ... [and] to entitle the parties interested to compensation, the injury or hurt must be such as could not lawfully be inflicted except by the powers of the Act [which authorised the works]" – MacCarthy *v* Metropolitan Board of Works 8 LR CP 208. Called sometimes 'material detriment'. See also **compensation for injurious affection, nuisance**.

injury
The act of inflicting hurt or **damage**; in particular when this arises from an intent to do harm or commit a **tort**. Injury is that which is done against a person or the rights of a person, as distinguished from 'damage' which is the loss or detriment sustained as a result of an injury. Injury may be a wrong or damage to a man's person or his or her goods and

it need not be physical in nature. It can be caused by any interference with a person's legal right to enjoy something, including his or her property, a good character, or a freedom to conduct business. Injury to land may arise from **trespass, waste, eviction,** or from **nuisance** caused by an adjoining owner or occupier. See also **dangerous premises, delict, injurious affection, negligence, strict liability.**

inland
see **demesne land, manor.**

inn
A house or similar establishment which holds itself out as a place for receiving travellers who seek food, drink and, if so required, lodging, in return for payment. 'An inn is a house, the owner of which holds out that he will receive all travellers and sojourners who are willing to pay a price adequate to the sort of accommodation provided, and who come in a situation in which they are fit to be received.' – Thompson v Lacy (1820) 3 B and Ald. 287. An inn is intended for passengers and wayfairing men – Calye's Case (1584) 8 Co. Rep. 683; as distinguished from a **lodging house** or **boarding house** which by prior arrangement provides accommodation for one or a number of nights. See also **hostel, hotel.**
24 Halsbury's Laws of England, 4 ed., paras. 1201–1255.

inner urban area
see **urban development area.**

innocent misrepresentation
see **misrepresentation.**

innocent purchaser (US)
see **bona fide purchaser.**

inquiry
Investigation to ascertain facts relating to a matter; a quest or search for information in order to ascertain truth or acquire knowledge. In real estate, 'inquiry' may be applied to (a) a **requisition** made by the purchaser of a property to clarify a doubt as to the validity of any encumberance or defect that might affect the vendor's title; (b) **searches** made to establish any matter that might affect the use or value of the property, e.g. land registry searches, local land charge searches, inspection of the property; (c) a **planning inquiry** following a refusal or conditional grant of planning permission, or a delay by a local planning authority in making a decision to grant or refuse planning permission. See also **arbitration, notice.**

inquiry notice (US)
see **constructive notice.**

inscription (F)
registration; entry, on a register.
(*inscription d'hypothèque* – mortgage registration)
(*libre de toute inscription* – unencumbered; free of all mortgage debt).

insolvency
A condition that arises when a person is unable to meet his or her debts as they fall due for payment and he cannot readily find assets to meet those debts. In the US, and in accounting parlance, insolvency is used to refer to a state when a debtor cannot pay his debts and **bankruptcy** to a legal position which arises when the debtor is subject to the provisions of a Bankruptcy Act. "A person is 'insolvent' who either has ceased to pay his debts in the ordinary course of business or cannot pay his debts as they become

due or is insolvent within the federal bankruptcy law" (United States Uniform Code, para. 1–201 (23)). Thus, insolvency normally precedes bankruptcy. See also **liquidation**.

instalment or installment
A part payment of a sum of money that is owed; one of a number of regular payments made over a period of time to meet a debt or pecuniary obligation. "The payment, or the time apportioned for payment, of different portions of a sum of money, which, by agreement of the parties, instead of being payable in gross, at one time, is to be paid in parts, at certain stated times." – *Jacob's Law Dictionary* (1797).
cf. **deposit**. See also **amortisation, hire-purchase agreement, instalment contract, interim payment**.

instalment contract (US)
A contract that provides for the sale of a property, with payment being made by portions or instalments during the term of the contract. Although the purchaser under an instalment contract may take possession of the subject property, in most States the seller retains title, as well as a **lien** on the property, until the last instalment is paid. Called also a 'land contract', an 'instalment sales contract', a 'contract for deed', a 'real estate contract', or an 'agreement for sale and purchase'. See also **conditional sale agreement, escrow, instalment sale, purchase-money mortgage**.
Real Estate Principles, by Bruce Harwood, 2 edn., pp. 164–168.
Real Estate Law, by Robert J. Kratovil and Raymond J. Werner, 8 edn., pp. 368–378.

instalment credit agreement (US)
see **hire-purchase agreement**.

instalment land contract (US)
see **instalment contract**.

instalment mortgage (or loan)
A mortgage (or loan) which provides that the debt is to be repaid by instalments over a period of time. See also **amortisation mortgage, fixed-principal-payment mortgage**.

instalment note (US)
A **promissory note** which provides for payment to be made by instalments.

instalment sale
1. See **credit-sale agreement**.
(US) 2. A specific form of sale by **instalment contract**, whereby payments are made in two or more instalments over two or more years and thereby a taxpayer postpones his tax liability from the year of sale. Provided no more than 30 per cent of the sale price is received in the year of sale and the seller receives two or more payments in two or more tax years, the seller may reduce his capital gains tax liability in proportion to the actual cash he receives in any tax year. Called also a 'deferred-payment sale'.
Basic Real Estate Finance and Investment, by D. Epley and J. Millar, pp. 453–457 (1980).

instalment sales contract (US)
see **instalment contract**.

institutional investor or lender
A large organisation or society which invests or lends funds in its own right, as distinguished from a private individual, local authority or public undertaking. The principal institutional investors are insurance companies, pension funds, trust funds, investment companies and bank. In the US 'institutional lender' is defined

more strictly to embrace only those institutions that invest depositor's money, under federal or state laws, as distinguished from institutions that invest funds held in their own right. Examples of the former are banks, savings and loan associations and of the latter pension funds and investment trusts. See also **pension fund**.
A Guide to Institutional Investment, by Angus P.J. McIntosh and G. Sykes (1985).

institutional property
1. Property owned by or used for the purposes of a public authority or a government department, e.g. a hospital, school, library, etc.
2. Property held by an **institutional investor**; in particular, investment property or property that might be considered suitable for an institutional investor. See also **prime property**.

instroke
The right to convey minerals from a **mine** that has been leased to the surface through an existing pit or shaft in an adjoining mine of the same lessor. A lessee is entitled, *prima facie*, to work minerals by instroke, unless expressly deprived of that right under his lease – Whalley *v* Ramage (1862) 10 WR 315.
cf. **outstroke**.

instrument
A written document that is authenticated normally by the signature of the author; especially one that formally records or confirms a legal act or agreement, e.g. a **bond, deed, lease, conveyance** or a **statutory declaration**. An instrument is evidence of the existence of an agreement, especially an agreement that brings a business

relation into effect. Any document under seal, as well as an Act of Parliament, may be referred to as an instrument; but a written order of a court is not normally referred to as an instrument. See also **statute, statutory instrument, trust instrument, vesting document, writing**.

instrument (F)
instrument; deed; conveyance.
(*instrument authentique* – certified instrument).

insurable interest
An interest in property that is sufficient for the holder to be able to sustain a pecuniary loss or detriment as a result of damage to, or destruction of, the property. A mortgagee has an insurable interest in the property charged to him and a trustee may have an insurable interest in trust property, provided he can be prejudiced by a loss or damage to the property; but neither a licensee nor a tenant at will (not being parties who can claim to have an interest in land) can claim to be able to suffer detriment as a direct result of the destruction of the property occupied by them. An insurable interest must exist at the time the insurance policy is effected and at the time of the loss. The interest must be more than one arising from a mere expectation that if the owner were deprived of it he would suffer a loss, otherwise the insured can suffer no loss and there is a mere wager. See also **mortgage clause**.

insurable title
A title to property that is adequate, but for which insurance may be obtained against a known, but minor, defect in the title. See also **marketable title, title insurance**.

insurable value
  see **insured value**.

insurance

An agreement which provides that one party (the insurer) will indemnify another (the insured) against pecuniary loss, damage or prejudice, arising as a result of certain events or perils – Lucena v Craufurd (1806) 2 Bos. and PNR 301. The insurer receives as consideration for this agreement, a **premium** which is assessed by him as adequate for the **risk** assumed (strictly, the insurer receives a number of premiums under similar agreements so that the total of those premiums is considered, at least, adequate to cover the risk of meeting the losses that might arise from the agreements) – Cumis Insurance Society v Republic National Bank, (Tex. Civ. App.) 480 SW 2d 762. A contract of insurance, called an **insurance policy**, provides protection or cover against the occurrence of an uncertain event – either uncertainty as to whether the event will happen at all or uncertainty as to when the event will happen.

An insurance contract is one that requires **utmost good faith** (*uberrimae fidei*) between the parties, in particular full disclosure by the insured of any facts that might affect the insurer's assessment of the assumed risk. "Insurance is a contract under speculation. The special facts, upon which the contingent chance is to be computed, lie mostly in the knowledge of the insured only: the underwriter trusts to his representation, and proceeds upon trusts to his representation, and proceeds upon confidence that he does not keep back any circumstance in his knowledge, to mislead the underwriter into a belief that the circumstance does not exist, and to induce him to estimate the risque, as if it does not exist. The keeping back such circumstances is a *fraud*, and therefore the policy is *void* ... Good faith forbids either party by concealing what he privately knows, to draw the other into a bargain" – Carter v Boehm (1766) 3 Burr. 1909. Thus, the retention of information that would lead one of the parties not to accept the bargain amounts to a fraud – a form of misrepresentation – and is sufficient to make an insurance policy void.

Insurance may be classified broadly as (i) life insurance – insurance on the life of the policy holder or another person; (ii) **fire insurance** and marine insurance – insurance against damage or destruction of property, vehicles, or marine resulting from external factors such as fire, flood, storm, riot, aircraft, etc.; and (iii) **casualty insurance** – insurance against damage or destruction to property arising from the actions of the insured or any third party. See also **all-risks insurance, co-insurance, comprehensive insurance policy, consequential-loss insurance, contingency insurance, double insurance, first-loss insurance, indemnity insurance, insurance value, liability insurance, property insurance, reinstatement basis, subrogation, title insurance, valued policy**.

Keeton on Insurance, 2 edn.
Handbook on Insurance, Edited by R.L. Carter.
Company Insurance Handbook, Association of Insurance and Risk Managers in Industry and Commerce (AIRMIC), 2 edn., (1985).
Modern Insurance Law, by John Bird (1982).

Chitty on Contract, 25 edn, paras. 3661–3741.

25 Halsbury's Laws of England, 4 edn, pp. 1–512.

General Principles of Insurance Law, by E.R. Hardy Ivamy, 4 edn.

The Law of Insurance, by Raoul Colinvaux, 5 edn.

Insurance Law, by E.J. MacGillivray and M. Parkington, 7 edn.

insurance clause

A clause in a lease which sets out the respective obligations of the landlord and the tenant for insurance of the demised premises. Each party to a lease may insure for such loss as may arise to that party in the event of damage or destruction of the leased premises. It is common practice for an insurance policy to be taken out in the name of the landlord, with the tenant being responsible for reimbursing the premium for that policy. An insurance clause frequently provides for an abatement of rent if the insured premises are rendered unusable and provides that the insurance monies will be used to reinstate the leased premises at the earliest opportunity. If leased premises are destroyed by fire, unless there is an express condition to the contrary, a landlord is not under any obligation to reinstate, but if the tenant pays the insurance premium he or she has the ability to require reinstatement and, in certain cases, an insurer may direct that money paid out is used to reinstate the premises. A covenant imposing an obligation to insure against fire is broken if the premises are uninsured for any period, no matter how short, even if a fire does not occur during that period (Penniall *v* Harborne (1848) 11 QB 368). The tenant usually covenants not to carry out any activity on the leased premises that will vitiate the policy or increase the premium payable. See also **frustration, full repairing and insuring lease, loss of rent insurance, subrogation, triple net lease**.

Woodfall's Landlord and Tenant, 28 edn, paras. 1–1153 to 1–1167.

insurance cover

see **cover**.

insurance policy

A document that sets down the terms and conditions of an **insurance** agreement. A contract whereby one party (insurer), in consideration of a premium, undertakes to indemnify another (insured) against loss or prejudice arising from a particular, but uncertain, event; an event that may be uncertain as to whether it will occur or as to when it will occur. See also **blanket insurance policy, index-linked insurance policy, long-term insurance agreement**.

insurance premium

see **premium**.

insurance rent

A payment made by a tenant to his landlord to meet the cost of the premium for an insurance policy taken out in respect of the demised premises. At common law this is not **rent** (i.e. it may not be recovered by distress) and normally it is recovered either as a separate charge, or as part of a service charge or operating expense demanded of the tenant by the landlord. A landlord who collects an insurance rent has an implied obligation to reinstate the demised premises if they are destroyed by fire (Mumford Hotels *v* Wheler [1964] Ch. 117).

insurance value
see **insured value**.

insured
A person who under the terms of an insurance policy is provided with an indemnity against pecuniary loss or damage. The 'insured' is not only the person named in the policy but may be anyone who is insured under the policy. Called also an 'assured', especially when the policy is referred to as one of assurance. See also **mortgagee clause**.

insured mortgage
see **mortgage insurance**.

insured value
The value of a property as ascertained for the purpose of an insurance policy; being a limit to the amount of indemnity provided by the policy in the event of loss. This value is ascertained normally as the **replacement cost**, assessed to be adequate as at the time when such replacement may be required. In the case of title insurance the insured value is equal normally to the purchase price or market value. Called also the 'insurable value' or 'insurance value'. See also **actual cash value, cover, insurable interest, reinstatement basis, valued policy**.

insurer
The party to an insurance policy who undertakes to accept the specified risks or underwrites the policy; the party that agrees to provide an **indemnity** in the event of loss.

intangible asset
An **asset** shown in a company's balance sheet that would have no value if the company were not sold as a going-concern; for example, preliminary setting up expenses, goodwill, copy-rights, patents, franchises. See also **going-concern value**.

intangible property
Property that cannot be physically detained, touched or handled, e.g. a debt or an easement; as distinguished from **tangible property**. Normally the only evidence as to the ownership of intangible property is a written agreement, or an oral agreement supported by tangible evidence in support of that agreement. See also **choses, incorporeal hereditament, industrial property**.

intellectual property
see **industrial property**.

intensification of use
see **'material change in the use', planning unit**.

inter alia (L)
'Amongst other things'.

inter vivos (L)
'Between living persons'. See **living trust**.

interdict
A prohibitory decree of a court. A term in Scottish or the civil law for a remedy that is similar to an **injunction**.

interesse termini (L)
'An interest in a term'. The right to property which a tenant for a term of years acquires before actual entry on to the property. The requirement that a tenant take entry on to land before a valid lease came into effect (the doctrine of *interesse termini*) has been abolished (Law of Property Act 1925, s. 149 (1), (2)).

interest
1. A **right** or **title** to something. A term that has no strict legal meaning and must be interpreted according to

the context; or by reference to a particular statute, *viz.* Town and Country Planning Act 1971, s. 134 (4); Highways Act 1980, s. 28 (5)). In relation to land or real estate an interest, in the broadest sense, means any **estate**, **claim**, or **right** in or over land. It may be a right to hold and enjoy land itself, e.g. as a **fee simple** interest, a **life interest** or a **leasehold interest**; or it may be a right to use, or to restrict the use of land, e.g. an **easement, profit à prendre** or a **restrictive covenant** – Webber *v* Lee (1882) 9 QBD 315.

In a restricted sense an interest may be any right to land that is less than an estate but greater than a mere personal right to land. Something less than a right to land itself, i.e. less than ownership, but more than a right that is exercisable against only one or a limited number of persons: it is a right to claim against the land of another to the exclusion of anyone except an owner of the land or a person with a higher or prior claim. Thus, an option to purchase a lease is an interest within the meaning of the Law of Property Act 1925, s. 56(1) (which refers to the right of a person to take an 'interest' in land even though he is not named as a party to a conveyance or other instrument by which the subject land is transferred) – Stormdale and Bath *v* Burden [1952] Ch. 223; a right to the proceeds of the sale of land that is held under a **trust for sale** is an 'interest in land' within the meaning of the Law of Property Act 1925, s. 40 (which requires a contract for the disposition of any interest in land to be evidenced in **writing**, or by an act of **part performance**, before it can form the subject of an action at law) – Cooper *v* Critchley [1955] Ch. 431; and an **option** to purchase land is

an interest for the purpose of the service of **notice to treat** under a compulsory purchase order – Oppenheimer *v* Minister of Transport [1942] 1 KB 242. On the other hand an agreement permitting a tenant to remove a fixture at the end of a lease is not an interest in land for the purpose of the 1925 Act, s. 40 (which replaces the Statute of Frauds 1677, s. 4) – Thomas *v* Jennings (1896) 66 LJQB 8. See also **beneficial interest, conditional interest, contingent interest, equitable interest, insurable interest, legal interest, minor interest, overreachable interest, overriding interest, vested interest**.

2. The price of using another's **money**; a sum paid, or accrued, by time, as compensation for being deprived of the use of money, especially when there is no right to share in the profit obtained by the person using that money. Interest is a payment received for lending a sum of money, or parting with capital; a payment received immediately as a reward for taking the risk of losing money or capital; or as a reward for foregoing the use of a capital sum for the time being – a reward for the acceptance of a delay in the return of money. In Keynesian terms the reward for parting with liquidity or for not hoarding money for a period of time; "for the importance of money essentially flows from its being a link between the present and the future" – *The General Theory of Employment, Interest and Money*, by J.M. Keynes, p. 293 (1936). Interest has been compared to "the accumulated fruit of a tree which the tree produces regularly until payment ... The essence of interest is that it is a payment which becomes due because the creditor has

not had his money at the due date. It may be regarded as representing the profit he might have made if he had had use of the money, or, conversely, the loss he suffered because he had not that use". – Riches *v* Westminster Bank Ltd. [1947] AC 398, 400.

The cost of borrowing money, the 'rate of interest', is determined by (a) the use to which a borrower can profitably put that money; (b) the loss which the lender sustains for parting with the money; and (c) the period of time for which the money changes hands – that is, the 'marginal productivity of capital' (the **internal rate of return** available to the user); the 'liquidity preference' of the lender; and the 'time preference'. This cost may be expressed by the formula, $i = Prt$; so that if a sum of money, or principal P, is parted with for a period of time t, and the charge made for parting with that money, expressed as a decimal, is r, then the total interest paid is i. Interest generally is expressed as a percentage of the principal or capital employed, i.e. as a rate of return or rate of interest, for a period of time.

In the event that a sum of money is withheld, or capital not returned when due, a benefit is foregone and recompense should be paid. This recompense normally takes the form of interest, i.e. a percentage increase in the amount finally paid. This payment is apportioned according to the period of delay, *de die in diem*, 'from **day** to day' – Re Rogers Trusts (1860) 1 Drew. and Sm. 338. See also **accrued interest, apportionment, compound interest, discount rate, effective annual interest rate, interest table, nominal interest, simple interest, usury, yield.**

interest factor
The reciprocal of a **rate of interest**. A factor used to find the present or future value of a unit of money. See also **interest table**.

interest in expectancy
see **future interest**.

interest-only loan
see **standing loan**.

interest rate
see **interest**.

interest table
A mathematical table that sets out the value of one unit of money, after allowing for **compound interest**, either as a **future value** or a discounted or **present value**. Referred to also as an 'annuity table'. See also **valuation table**.
Archer's Compound Interest and Annuity Tables, 11 edn.

interest upon interest
see **compound interest**.

intérêt (F)
interest (either on finance or in property); share; benefit.
(*intérêt courus* – **accrued interest**)
(*intérêt composé* – **compound interest**)
(*intérêt échu; intérêt exigible* – outstanding interest)
(*intérêt simple* – simple interest)
(*capital et intérêt* – principal and interest)
(*dommages-intérêts* – **damages**, see also *dommages*).

interference with goods
see **conversion, trespass**.

interior
see **internal**.

interim award
An award made by an arbitrator

prior to his final decision. An interim award may be of two kinds. "It may be an interim order made pending the final determination of the case; such as an award that an instalment under a building contract be paid pending final determination of the amount due. Or it may be an interim decision given on a particular issue or issues between the parties, pending a final determination of the whole case; such as a decision that a contract was concluded but leaving out the question of damages." – Fidelitas Shipping Co. Ltd. *v* V/O Exportchleb [1966] QB 638. Unless there is an express provision to the contrary an arbitrator may, if he thinks fit, make an interim award (Arbitration Act 1950, s. 14). See also **arbitration, interim payment, interim rent**.

interim certificate
see **building certificate**.

interim injunction
see **injunction**.

interim loan (or finance)
A **loan** obtained for a short period of time (generally one to three years) until permanent or long-term finance is obtained; in particular, a **construction loan**. See also **bridging loan, take-out loan**. See also **instalment, interim award**, *quantum meruit*, **substantial performance**.

interim payment
A payment made as part of the consideration due under a contract, usually for performance of an agreed part of the work, service or obligation required under the contract. In particular, payment made under the terms of a building contract for work completed. The most common basis for an interim payment is for the contractor to be paid the value of the estimated quantities of work done and materials supplied (usually as stipulated in an architect's **building certificate**), less any retention sum held as security against satisfactory completion of the entire contract. As an alternative the interim payment may be based on an agreed sum, or a percentage of the total contract price, which is paid at predetermined stages of the building work, such payments being referred to commonly as 'stage payments'. Even if there is no express provision for interim payments it may be considered an **implied term** of the contract that payment should be made for work at stages prior to completion of the entire contract, especially when the contract work is spread over a long period of time or when it can be shown that it is to be carried out in a number of stages and a contractor may be permitted to discontinue further work until an interim payment is made. On the other hand withholding of an interim payment does not automatically repudiate the contract and, as a rule, an interim payment does not affect any obligation to fulfill the contract in its entirety.

interim rent
A rent that the court may determine as reasonable for a tenant to pay when a **business tenancy** has come to the end of its contractual term but continues pending the establishment of the terms for a new tenancy. A landlord may apply for such a rent to be fixed (a) if the landlord has given notice to terminate the tenancy in accordance with the provisions of the Landlord and Tenant Act 1954, s. 25; or the tenant has made a request for a

new tenancy in accordance with the 1954 Act, s. 26. The Law of Property Act 1969, s. 3 (which is designated section 24A of the Landlord and Tenant Act 1954) provides that a landlord may, at the court's discretion, obtain an increase in rent from the date of expiry of the contractual tenancy until the terms of a new tenancy are established. The purpose of this provision is to ensure that the tenant does not benefit unduly from a delay in agreeing the terms of a new tenancy (either because of protracted negotiations or because of the time taken to refer the matter to the courts for determination). The 'interim rent' is fixed on the basis of **market rent**, but on the assumption that the premises are let on an annual tenancy, and having regard to the rent and terms of the expired tenancy – Regis Property Co. *v* Lewis and Peat Ltd, (1970) 3 All. ER 227. Thus an interim rent is likely to be fixed at a level between the rent payable under the expired lease and the rent that is determined for the new tenancy – English Exporters (London) Ltd *v* Eldonwall Ltd [1973] 1 All ER 726; Ratners (Jewellers) *v* Lemnoll (1980) 255 EG 987. The interim rent is payable from the date when the landlord serves notice to terminate the tenancy or the tenant requests a new tenancy, or the date on which proceeds are commenced to determine an interim rent, whichever is the later (1954 Act, s. 24A (1)).

Business Tenancies – Interpreting the Interim Rent Provisions, by D.W. Williams, 271 EG 1058–1062 (1984).
Statutory Valuations, by Andrew Baum, pp. 26–27 (1983).
Landlord and Tenant Law, by David D. Yates and A.J. Hawkins, pp. 497–499 (1981).
Hill & Redman's Law of Landlord & Tenant, 17 edn, pp. 749–753.
Woodfall's Landlord and Tenant, 28 edn, para. 2–0684.
Handbook of Business Tenancies, by D.W. Williams, para. 5.11 *et seq.*, (1985, Looseleaf).
Renewal of Business Tenancies: Law and Practice, by Kirk Reynolds and Wayne Clarke, para. 8.6.0 to 8.6.9, (1985, Looseleaf).

interlineation
Writing between the lines of a document; which has the effect of an **alteration** thereto.

interlocutory injunction
see **injunction**.

intermediate development area
see **development area**.

intermediate grant
A type of **home improvement grant**, given to meet the cost of providing **standard amenities**, and carrying out associated repair, in a dwelling-house (Housing Act 1974, ss. 65–68). An intermediate grant is made provided the dwelling will be made **fit for habitation** (as determined in accordance with the provisions of the Housing Act 1957, s. 4) when the relevant work for which the grant is given is complete; or, "it seems reasonable in all the circumstances to do so even though the dwelling ... will not reach that standard on completion of the relevant works". (1974 Act, s. 66 (b)).
See also **improvement grant**.

intermediate lease
see **sandwich lease**.

intermediate-term loan
see **medium-term loan**.

intermediation

The process whereby money is placed with savings institutions, thus enabling them to make loans.
cf. **disintermediation**.

intermingled fund (US)

see **commingled trust fund**.

internal

Relating to the inside or interior of a property; within the limits of a building structure.

A covenant in a lease to carry out internal repair is interpreted by the exception of that which forms an **external** part of a building i.e. is exposed to, or forms part of, the outside. Thus the repair of the windows (which form part of the fabric) is the responsibility of the person who has undertaken to do the 'external repairs' – Ball v Plummer (1879) 23 SJ 656; although decoration of the window frame on the inside is part of the requirement for internal repair. See also **tenantable repair**.

internal area

see **gross internal floor area**, **net internal area**.

internal rate of return (IRR)

The rate of interest that discounts a series of future cash flows to make them equal to the total cost or outlay on the investment that generates those cash flows; the one rate of interest at which the **present value** of all expenditure on an investment equals the present value of all receipts from that investment (i.e. the discount rate when the **net present value** is zero). It is called the 'rate of return over cost' by Irving Fisher, and 'the marginal efficiency of capital' by J.M. Keynes – 'that rate of discount which should make the present value of a series of

annuities, given by the return from the capital asset during its life, just equal to its supply price'. – *The General Theory of Employment, Interest and Money*, p. 135 (1936).

The internal rate of return may be calculated solving for r in the formula:

$$P_o = \sum_{i=1}^{i=n} \frac{R_i}{(1+r)^i} + \frac{P_n}{(1+r)^n}$$

Where: P_o = initial cost or 'supply price';

R_i = income during period i (or per annum), in arrears;

P_n = value of reversion in period n, (or the scrap value after n years);

n = number of periods (or years);

r = internal rate of return;

Thus, if P_o is the price paid for an investment, which produces a periodic (or annual) income in arrears of R_i for n periods (or years) and is sold at the end of that period for P_n, then the equivalent annual yield, over the life of the investment is r.

The internal rate of return is used to make comparisons between alternative investments; to decide if the return is sufficient to warrant parting with money; or to decide if it is worth borrowing money at a given rate of interest in order to make an investment. It is a measure of the inducement to invest because it measures the return of capital; i.e. it is a 'derived return'. It may be contrasted with the rate of interest incorporated in a **capitalisation factor** (years' purchase or Inwood factor) which is an 'applied return', i.e. one used to ascertain the capital value of an investment, given the interest rate or the cost of parting with or borrowing money. Called also the 'discounted (or discounted cash flow) rate of return'; the 'actuarial investment return'; the 'overall rate of return'; the 'investment or investor's rate of return', or sometimes the 'true rate of return'. See also **discounted cash flow, redemption yield**.

Real Estate Investment Decision Making, by Austin J. Jaffe and C.F. Sirmans, pp. 400–501 (1982).

The Internal Rate of Return in Real Estate Investment, by Charles B. Akerson (1976).

internal repair
see **internal, repair**.

International Real Estate Federation (FIABCI)
see *Fédération Internationale des Professions Immobilières*.

interpretation clause
1. A clause in a contract which specifies that, for the purpose of that contract, words or phrases shall have the meaning specified in that clause.
2. A part of an Act of Parliament which specifies that, for the purpose of that or a related Act, words and phrases shall have a given meaning; notable examples are the Law of Property Act 1925, s. 205 and the entirety of the Interpretation Act 1978. See also **words meaning of**.

interruption
The breaking of a continuous right of enjoyment. In relation to **adverse possession** or **prescription** an interruption must be some act or occurrence that breaks the continuity of use or possession and is clearly acknowledged as such. As a rule, interruption does not occur if the person claiming a right is under a disability, or there is

fraud, deliberate concealment or a mistake.
cf. **abandonment**. See also **disturbance**.

interruption insurance
see **consequential-loss insurance**.

interval ownership
see **time-sharing**.

intestacy
Without making a **will**. Intestacy arises when a person, who may be called an 'intestate', dies without making a will for the disposition of his or her property, or makes a will that proves to be null and void. An intestate "includes a person who does not provide for the bequeathing of some beneficial interest in his [or her] personal estate" (Administration of Estates Act 1925, s. 55 (1)(iv)). If a person dies intestate all his or her property (whether real or personal) is held on **trust for sale** by an **administrator** who is responsible for distributing the estate to the persons beneficially entitled as laid down by the Administration of Estates Act 1925, as modified by the Intestates' Estates Act 1952. In essence the beneficiaries of an intestate estate are the surviving spouse, the issue and the four grandparents of the deceased and their issue. In English law there is no longer any distinction made between real and personal property and no discrimination on grounds of sex or age. See also *bona vacantia*, **hotchpot, succession**.

The Law of Succession, by Parry and Clark, 8 edn., pp. 80–100.

The Law of Succession, by A.R. Mellows, 4 edn., pp. 151–172.

17 Halsbury's Laws of England, 4 edn, paras. 1369–1447.

intestat (F)
    intestate. See also *héritier*.

intra vires (L)
    'Within the power'. An act is *intra vires* when it is within the authority or powers of the person or company performing that act.
    cf. *ultra vires*.

intrinsic value
    The **value** of a property based on its constituents, i.e. the materials of which it is built, rather than its value as affected by 'market conditions'. A value based essentially on fact rather than opinion: a property's intrinsic value depends on "its true, inherent, and essential value, not depending upon accident, place, or person, but the same everywhere, and to every one" – 5 Ired. (NC) 698. A value that is essentially devoid of influence from such factors as geographical location (but not necessarily proximity to other property), personal preferences, future expectations and ostensible merit. The intrinsic value of a thing may be contrasted with its 'real' value, i.e. that which it will actually fetch or the benefit it will truely give.
    cf. **market value**.

introduction
    The opening words of a **deed**. The introduction is followed usually by the **recitals**. See also **preamble**.

introduction of purchaser
    See **commission**, '**ready, able and willing**'.

invalid
    Not binding; of no legal force or effect. See also **illegal contract, void contract, voidable contract**.

inventaire (F)
    inventory; schedule. See also *état des lieux*.

inventory
    1. An itemised list, or **schedule**, that describes a number of items of personal property with reasonable particularity; such as those items that are to be included in a sale; or those chattels that are to be included in a lease of real property. A personal representative is under a duty, when required to do so by the court, to exhibit in the court a full inventory of a deceased person's estate and render an account of the administration of the estate (Administration of Estates Act 1925, s. 25). See also **fixture**.
    2. A stock of goods held by a firm for the purpose of trade or production. A stock of property available for sale or lease, either as held by one company or the total amount of 'space' on the market. See also **land bank**.

inventory value (US)
    The value of an **inventory**. See also **book value**.

inverse compulsory purchase
    see **blight notice, purchase notice**.

inverse condemnation (US)
    A process by which a property owner requires a public authority to pay **just compensation** when the property is significantly reduced in value by adjoining public works or by severe restrictions placed on the use of the property. A landowner may require a government body to pay damages for the loss in the value of his land when he has been deprived of reasonable use of the land as a result of government regulation, ordinance or code; as when the effects of the government

action "are so complete as to deprive the owner of all or most of his interest in the subject matter to amount to a taking." – United States *v* General Motors Corp., (1945) 323 US 378. A person who files for an inverse condemnation suit must prove that the public agency's action amounts to a confiscation of his property, or his property right, and not merely a disturbance of his enjoyment of some attribute of the land such as a right to a view. See also **condemnation**.

invest
1. To give possession. To endow with a privilege, power or authority. See also **vest**.
2. To put out money in anticipation of income or profits – Christianson *v* State Tax Commissioners, 402 P. 743, 240 Or. 504). See also **investment**.

investissement (F)
investment.

investisseur institutionel (F)
institution investor.

investment
An addition to a stock of capital arising over time, either by an increase in the worth of the capital or by the retention of income generated by that capital. Expenditure of money to acquire property in anticipation of future income, interest or profit. Ceding of an immediate right to money, or any pecuniary benefit, in exchange for a hope that the sum laid out will accumulate to a higher sum, or produce an incremental benefit, either as income or capital appreciation, at a future date. 'Investment' includes the laying out of money as capital for a business; the purchase of securities, stocks, shares or any other form of property; or money lent against secur-

ity, or deposited in order to produce interest. An investor is considered to be a person who makes a prudent decision to lay out money for a medium to short term in search of a reasonable return for the risk entailed. He may be contrasted with a **speculator** who makes hazardous ventures with a view to short-term profit or gain. See also **risk**.

investment allowance
see **investment grant**.

investment analysis
A process by which the relative merits of alternative means or types of investment are examined. Such analysis may be broadly classified as 'fundamental analysis' and 'technical analysis'. The former analyses the intrinsic factors – income, projected earnings, comparable investment yields, etc. The latter analyses extrinsic factors – trends, general price levels, investors attitudes, market conditions, etc. See also **feasibility study**, **internal rate of return**, **net present value**, **pay-back period**, **portfolio analysis**, **sensitivity analysis**.

investment company
1. A company that uses its own capital to invest in the shares of other companies or to make investments in other enterprises without being directly involved in the management process. Frequently such a company, either by statute or under its articles of association, is prohibited from holding more than a small percentage of the shares of any one company (except another investment company) and may not distribute capital profits (Companies Act 1980, s. 41). The price of the shares in an investment company, as for any other com-

pany, is dependent on the market assessment of the performance of the company as contrasted with a unit trust whose unit price is dependent entirely on the underlying value of its investments. Sometimes an investment company is referred to as an 'investment trust', although strictly it is a **company** and not a **trust**. See also **closed-end fund, open-end investment company**.
2. A financial institution that pools the resources of a number of investors in order to make diversified investments under common management. In the US called also a 'mutual company', especially when the profits are distributed entirely to the investors.

investment credit (US)
A credit set against tax due when a 'qualifying property', such as business plant and machinery (but not real estate), is purchased. Similar to a **capital allowance** in the UK.

investment grant (or allowance)
Financial assistance, in the form of a grant or allowance, provided as an inducement to new investment. An investment grant or allowance may take the form of a cash grant, subsidy, interest-free loan, a deduction of the cost of capital expenditure from a tax liability, or any other means by which the cost of a new investment is met, in whole or in part, by a public authority. See also **capital allowance, development area**.

investment interest
Interest paid, or accrued, for a loan that is used to acquire or hold **investment property**.

investment method of valuation
A method of assessing the value of a property on the principle that capital

value is a function of:- (a) the **net income** that a property is capable of producing, and (b) the **rate of return** that a property investor requires in order to be induced to accept the risk of investing in that property. The process of valuation may be summarised as follows:- (i) estimate the total income that will be received from the investment, based on the current income receivable, or the highest income that could be obtained; (ii) estimate the projected net income by making deductions for vacancies; defaulting tenants; and expenses that the landlord is obliged to pay and will not be recovered from the occupiers, i.e. non-recoverable service charges or operating expenses, costs of management, etc.; (iii) decide on an appropriate life expectancy for the projected net income – this may be taken as perpetual for a freehold modern building, but may be limited by the termination of a leasehold interest or the economic life of a building; (iv) capitalise the total projected net income at an appropriate rate (**capitalisation rate**) to reflect the rate of return considered appropriate for the investment.

The capitalisation of income may be a **straight capitalisation** (applying an 'overall capitalisation rate' or 'years' purchase in perpetuity') if the income represents a level sum receivable for an unlimited period or in perpetuity; or **annuity capitalisation** (applying a factor that takes account of variations in the projected income, such as the 'present value of 1 per period' or 'years' purchase for a term of years') if the income represents a variable sum or is receivable for a limited period. A variable income may be capitalised also by the **term**

and reversion method, or the 'layer' or **hardcore method**. Called also, especially in the US, the 'income approach' or 'capitalized-income approach' to valuation. See also **discounted cash flow, valuation tables**.
Real Estate Investment Decision Making, by Austin J. Jaffe and C.F. Sirmans, pp. 391–397 (1982).
Property Valuation Handbook: N. Stratton (ed.).
Valuing Commercial and Industrial Property for Investment, by C.W. Jonas, (1979).
The Income Approach to Property Valuation, by A. Baum and D. Mackin, 3 edn.
Income Property Valuation, by W.N. Kinnard Jr. (1971).
The Valuation of Property Investments, by Nigel Enver, 3 edn.
Readings in the Income Approach to Real Property Valuation, AIREA (1977).
The Appraisal of Real Estate, AIREA 8 edn., Ch. 17.
Modern Methods of Valuation, 7 edn., Ch. 9.

investment property
Property acquired for retention as an investment especially property acquired in order to provide income as distinguished from property acquired for use and occupation. Called also 'income property'.
cf. **occupation property**. See also **commercial property, development property**.

investment rate
see **investment yield, remunerative rate**.

investment (or investor's) rate of return
see **internal rate of return**.

investment risk
see **risk**

investment trust
A misnomer for an **investment company**: strictly the investment vehicle is a company with shareholders and not a trust with beneficiaries, although usually it makes investment as if it were acting in the capacity of a trustee.
cf. **unit trust**. See also **real estate investment trust**.
Investment Trusts Explained, by A.A. Arnaud, 2 edn.

investment value
The value of a property that has been acquired, or is held, purely for investment; for the benefit of the income or profit to be derived therefrom; rather than for use and occupation. The term 'investment value' is used frequently to refer to the value of a property to a particular investor, as distinguished from the more objective market value or intrinsic value. See also **investment method of valuation**.

investment yield
A single rate of return or yield that an investor expects to receive from a particular form of investment; the **all-risks rate** considered appropriate for a given investment, based on a comparison with similar investments. See also **internal rate of return, remunerative rate**.

investment yield rate (US)
see **equity yield rate**.

invitation to tender
A request to one or more persons, or to the public at large, to submit an **offer** for the supply of goods, the provision of services, or the carrying out of work, especially construction work

for the person making the invitation. An invitation to tender normally is an **invitation to treat**: although sometime it is set down in a form that makes an offer submitted in response to the invitation (usually the best offer) capable of immediate acceptance. See also **tender**.

invitation to treat

An invitation or inducement to submit an **offer** with a view to entering into a contract. A declaration of a willingness to enter into negotiations; especially setting forth the terms on which an offer for sale would be considered. An invitation to treat is a precursor to an offer but does not constitute an offer; it is an offer to negotiate – an offer to receive offers – an offer to chaffer – Carlill v Carbolic Smoke Ball Co. [1893] 1 QB 268. Whether a statement constitutes an offer capable of acceptance or merely an invitation to treat is judged from the intention of the declarant, taking account of matters such as business practices, express wording and consequent actions. The most common instance of an invitation to treat arises when goods are displayed in a shop window with a price tag; these goods may be withdrawn by the shopkeeper at his own free will, without fear or favour – Pharmaceutical Society of Great Britain v Boots [1953] 1 All. ER 482; Fisher v Bell [1960] 3 All ER 731. An advertisement that an auction will be held, or an auctioneer's request for bids, constitute an invitation to treat; but submitting a property for sale at auction without a reserve price is likely to be construed as an offer – Warlow v Harrison (1859) 1 E and E 309.

In French law a public or general offer is construed normally as an offer capable of acceptance, rather than merely as an invitation to treat. "It is clear, for example, that the display of goods in a shop window constitutes an offer (provided the price is indicated, since the offer must be capable of being converted into a contract by acceptance, and there can be no sale without a determined or determinable price), and this applies *a fortiori* to such a display in a self-service supermarket." (*French Law of Contract*, by Barry Nicholas p. 61, 1982). See also **asking price**.

Cheshire and Fifoot's Law of Contract, 10 edn, pp. 27–32.

The Law of Contract, by G.H. Trietel, 6 edn., pp. 8–12.

Anson's Law of Contract, 26 edn, pp. 25–29

Chitty on Contract, 25 edn, paras. 43–51.

Halsbury's Laws of England, 4 edn, paras. 228–229.

invitee

A person who goes on to land, or into property, at the express or implied invitation of the owner or occupier who has control over that place; generally for a short time for the purpose of business, or for some other manifest reason, e.g. a customer in a shop, a visitor to an office, a passenger at a railway station. An invitee is there for the purposes of business, material interest, or communion with the occupier, and not, as with a licencee, as a matter of grace – Fairman v Perpetual Investment Building Society [1923] AC 80.

At common law an occupier of property has a **duty of care** to an invitee for the safety and condition of the property on to which he or she is invited to enter, at least so as to prevent damage to that person from an unusual danger – Indemaur v Dames (1866) LR 1 CP 288. Nevertheless, if the invitee fails to use the premises in the matter expected of him the occupier cannot remain liable for consequent injury; "when you invite a person into your house to use the staircase, you do not invite him to slide down the banisters" – The Calgarth [1927] p. 93. A similar duty is not owed at common law to a licensee; the duty to a licensee being merely to warn the visitor of concealed traps or similar dangers – Mersey Docks and Harbour Board v Proctor [1923] AC 253. However, in English law, since the Occupiers Liability Act 1957, s. 2 a 'common duty of care' is owed to all 'visitors', whether invitees or licensees. Moreover, the 'occupier' of premises to which a person is invited, or is permitted to be there, 'must be prepared for children to be less careful than adults' (1957 Act, s. 2(3)(a)), but 'may expect that a person, in the exercise of calling, will appreciate and guard against any special risks ordinarily incident to it, so far as the occupier leaves him free to do so' (1957 Act, s. 2(3)(b)). A warning may absolve an occupier from being held to have failed in his duty of care, provided it is established that the visitor clearly ignored the occupier's warning or accepted the risk of entering the premises in spite of the warning – Slater v Clay Cross [1956] 2 QB 264; 1957 Act, s. 2 (4), (5). See also **negligence**, **trespass**.

involuntary alienation (US)
The **alienation** of an interest in property against the owner's will, e.g. by a foreclosure sale or a tax sale.

involuntary conversion (US)
The **conversion** of property into cash against the wishes of its owner whether as a result of condemnation, theft, loss or otherwise.

involuntary transfer (US)
The transfer of property, or a right to property, to another against the owner's will; as in condemnation, or foreclosure.
cf. **voluntary transfer**.

involuntary trust
see **constructive trust**, **resulting trust**.

Inwood factor (or coefficient) (US)
A term for the **present value of one per period** derived from tables showing such factors, first published in 1811 by William Inwood. See also **annuity capitalisation, years' purchase**.

ipso facto (L)
'By the deed itself'.

irredeemable ground lease (US)
A **ground lease** that does not contain any provision for the tenant to purchase the land or extend the term at the end of the lease. See also **extended lease, leasehold enfranchisement**.

irrevocable trust (US)
A **trust** created to hold property which, once it has been established, cannot be terminated by the creator of the trust who grants his property to the trustees. This form of trust is used primarily when the intention is to transfer an estate as a gift prior to the death of the grantor. If properly planned the creator of an irrevocable trust is not liable to income tax, because the trust property is treated as having been transferred to the ultimate beneficiaries when the trust is created and not on the death of the

creator of the trust.

cf. **bare trust**. See also **trust property**.

isoval

A line on a map drawn to link points at which land has the same value. An isoval is similar to a contour line linking points of the same elevation.

issue

A person's descendant. Strictly a person's children, but in most contexts any person who is descended from a common ancestor. In particular, those who are left as one's children when one is dead.

J

janitor
A person hired to assist in the general day-to-day running of a building, especially general maintenance, and such functions as cleaning and making minor repairs; but not property management or leasing.

jerry-built
Built unsubstantially; not built to last, or built cheaply and with flimsy material. A term of uncertain origin; it may derive from (i) Jeremiah who prophesied that nothing was substantial unless built by the heart and that even Jerusalem would fall to the Babylonians; (ii) the walls of Jericho which fell to the Israelites under Joshua; (iii) a 'jury' mast: a temporary mast put up after a storm to enable a ship to continue its passage; or (iv) a firm of builders (the Jerry Brothers) who operated in Liverpool at the end of the 19th century and built shoddy houses. See also **inherent defect**.

joinder
A joining or putting together; as of two or more parties or documents. In order to satisfy the requirement of the **Statute of Frauds** or the Law of Property Act 1925, s. 40 (1), which require that certain agreements be evidenced in writing, it may be permissible to accept the 'joinder of documents', i.e. the reading together of related documents so as to form, in effect, a single document. For this purpose, in order to construe two documents as if they were one, it is necessary (a) for one of the documents to be in **writing** and to contain an authorised signature; (b) that there is a reference, express or implied, in that document to the second document; and (c) that the two documents when read together provide a sufficient and complete note or memorandum of the terms of the agreement.

joint adventure
see **joint venture**.

joint agent (or broker)
An **agent** (or **broker**) who undertakes to act together with, and in the same capacity as, another agent. The same authority given to two or more persons is presumed to be given to them jointly, unless there is something express or implied to indicate a contrary intention. Estate agents appointed as joint agents undertake a specific task in cooperation with one another but usually have a several liability to the principal. Normally **commission** is shared between joint agents if either one of them successfully concludes his duties. In the US it has been held that joint agents owe a duty of **good faith** to one another and that if one broker asks a second broker to cooperate or assist in the sale of a property, and the second broker receives a commission, then the first is entitled to a share of that commission; the brokers are engaged in a joint venture – Wheeler v Waller 197 NW 2d. 585. Called also a 'co agent' or in the US a 'cooperating agent' or 'participation agent'. See also **joint and several liability, multiple agency**.

joint and several liability
The liability of two or more parties

both in their individual capacities (severally) and all together (jointly); as in a partnership. A party who has a joint and several liability may be required to discharge an entire obligation, notwithstanding any right of recourse to any other party or parties.

Joint Contracts Tribunal (JCT)

A committee, comprising representatives of most of the major bodies involved in building construction in the UK, whose primary function is to establish standard forms of **building contract**. The Royal Institute of British Architects and the National Federation of Building Trades Employers first established a standard form of contract for general building work in 1909. Since then many additional bodies, including the Royal Institution of Chartered Surveyors, local authorities, the Association of Consulting Engineers, and the Federation of Associations of Specialists and Sub-Contractors, have formed the constituent bodies of the Tribunal. In addition to standard contracts, the Tribunal produces notes on building practice and various standard forms such as completion certificates and insurance contracts.

joint development company
see **joint venture**.

joint interest

A right to joint ownership of a property. See also **common interest, joint tenancy**.

joint mortgage

1. A **mortgage** granted to two or more mortgagors who are jointly liable for the entire obligation.
2. A mortgage granted by two or more mortgagees acting together. The mortgagees may have equal

rights over the mortgaged property; although frequently one mortgagee has a prior charge, but the first and subsequent mortgages are granted in one mortgage deed. Upon the death of a joint mortgagee the entitlement to a portion of the money passes to his personal representative; although a surviving morgagee may give a good receipt for money received (Law of Property Act 1925, s. 111). Called also a 'contributory mortgage'. See also **participation mortgage**.

joint ownership

Ownership by two or more parties, regardless of their relationship to each other.
cf. **several ownership**. See also **co-ownership, collective ownership, community property, joint tenancy, tenancy in common**.

joint planning board (or **joint planning authority**)

A body established by the Secretary of State for the Environment, with representatives of two or more local planning authorities, to administer development proposals that affect more than one of the authorities (Town and Country Planning Act 1971, s. 1, Sch. 1.). See also **planning authority**.

joint purchase
see **resulting trust**.

joint tenancy (or estate)

A form of **co-ownership** or 'concurrent interest' in land by which the owners (joint tenants) are all entitled at the same time to the same estate or interest in land and there is a right of survivorship so that on the death of any one owner the interest passes to the survivor; "in other words joint tenants have one and the same interest, accruing at one and the same conveyance, and commencing at one and the same time, and held by one and the same undivided possession." (Bl. Comm. vol. ii. p. 180). (In this context the word tenancy denotes **tenure** or 'holding' of land as a form of ownership and not a tenancy in the sense of a relationship of landlord and tenant.) A joint tenancy vests in each owner a right *in solido*, i.e. a right to joint possession of, and equal shares in, every part of the property and of the whole; in addition there is the essential **right of survivorship** or *jus accrescendi*, 'right of accrual'. The right of accrual means that the entire estate eventually passes to the last survivor as his sole property, at which stage the joint tenancy comes to an end (Bl. Comm. vol. ii. p. 183). The joint owners take equal shares in any rents and profits to be derived from the property and have the same, concurrent, rights of use and occupation; they are to the outside world as one.

A joint tenancy must have 'four unities' – (i) unity of title: i.e. it must be created by the same act or instrument, without 'words of severance' – words which express an intention that the owners are to take distinct and separate shares; (ii) unity of time: i.e. the joint interests must be created simultaneously; (iii) unity of interest: i.e. all the owners must have the same nature and duration of estate; and (iv) **unity of possession** i.e. each party holds a right to possession of the entire property so that no action for trespass can be brought by one owner against another. All these four elements must exist and persist, otherwise the co-ownership will be considered as a **tenancy in common**. To any third party an estate held as a joint tenancy is a single estate and can be devised or conveyed only by all the joint tenants acting together, or by the last survivor. A joint tenancy must be held subject to a **trust for sale**, with the joint owners holding the land as trustees for themselves. As trustees they have an obligation in law to sell the land, although the sale may be postponed as long as the parties agree. Any of the joint owners may apply to the court for an order for sale which will be granted, immediately or in the future, as the court thinks fit. (Law of Property Act 1925, s. 36 (1)).

English law prefers to construe co-ownership as taking the form of a tenancy in common in preference to a joint tenancy, so that if one of the joint tenants sells his interest to a stranger or obtains a larger share than the others the law considers there to be a tenancy in common. A partnership cannot hold a joint tenancy because a right of survivorship runs contrary to the nature of a partnership. In the US some states require that a joint tenancy is created only if the parties expressly state that they are creating such an interest, otherwise a tenancy in common arises. Other states have abolished joint tenancies, or the right of survivorship, so that the individual owner's interest can pass to an heir or a person named in his or her will.

A joint tenancy comes to an end if the land becomes vested in a sole owner, whether the sole survivor, a stranger or one of the joint tenants. It may come to an end also by a voluntary **partition** of the property by the owners; by an owner conveying his interest in such a way that one of the unities is broken, e.g. if another owner obtains more than an equal share; or by one of the joint tenants giving notice in accordance with the provisions of the Law of Property Act 1925, s. 36 (1) and effectively forcing a sale of the property. If there are three or more joint tenants and one of the owners disposes of his interest the new owner acquires a tenancy in common, but the remaining owners continue to hold as joint tenants *inter se*.

cf. **joint tenure**. See also **matrimonial home, tenancy by the entireties**.

Real Estate Law, by Robert Kratovil and Raymond J. Werner, 8 edn, pp. 233–241

Real Property, by William E. Burby, 3 edn, pp. 215–221.

Megarry's Manual of the Law of Real Property, 6 edn, pp. 229–301.

The Law of Real Property, by Robert Megarry and H.W.R. Wade, 5 edn, p. 417 *et seq*.

Introduction to Land Law, by J.G. Riddall, 3 edn, p. 141 *et seq*.

Cheshire's Modern Law of Real Property, 13 edn, pp. 20–20.

39 Halsbury's Laws of England, 4 edn, paras. 525–541.

joint tenure
An arrangement whereby a **partnership** is established for a short and fixed period of time; usually an informal arrangement and not commonly used.
cf. **joint tenancy**.

joint undertaking
see **joint venture**.

joint venture
A business venture between two or more parties who combine their money, skill and expertise for a specific purpose, such as the development of a shopping centre. A joint venture usually is more limited in scope than a **partnership** because with a joint venture only a single transaction or business purpose is intended and the venture terminates when that purpose if fulfilled. Normally no one of the joint venture partners can bind the other to a contract. For most legal purposes, and especially for taxation, a joint venture is treated as a partnership. Called sometimes a 'joint adventure' or a 'joint undertaking'. See also **equity participation, syndicate**.

jointure
1. Originally a joint freehold estate held by a husband and wife, but now a life estate or a sum of money granted to a wife, generally on marriage, to take effect on the death of her husband. Called also a 'legal jointure'. See also **dower, pin-money**.
2. An ancient term for an estate held in **joint tenancy**.

jouissance (F)
possession; enjoyment (of a right); **tenure**.
(*jouissance à perpétuité* – perpetual ownership)
(*avec jouissance immediate* – with **vacant possession**)
(*avoir la propriété et la jouissance des biens* – to have the ownership and enjoyment of property)
(*droit de jouissance* – **usufruct**)
(*en jouissance* – vacant possession)
(*entrée en jouissance, d'un bail* – commencement date, of a lease). See also *libre possession, propriété*.

jour (F)
day.
(*jour férié* – public holiday)
(*jour franc* – clear day)
(*quinze jours* – a fortnight)

jour, *servitude de* (F)

An opening in a wall that serves to admit daylight, but excludes air. See also *vue et jour*.

judgment creditor

A creditor who has received the benefit of a direction from a court, requiring a debtor to pay him an outstanding debt. See also **caution**.

judgment debtor

A debtor against whom a direction has been made by a court to pay an outstanding debt.

judgment lien

A statutory lien against property granted by a court order as security for the payment of a debt. See also **attachment**.

judicial dictum

See *obiter dictum*

judicial foreclosure (US)

Foreclosure carried out under the auspices of a court of law. Although called a foreclosure usually the property is sold by public auction, subject to a reserve or 'upset' price. See also **strict foreclosure**.

judicial precedent

see **precedent**.

judicial review

see **appeal**.

judicial sale (US)

A sale of property made under an order of a court by which the court is the effective vendor. See also **foreclosure sale, power of sale**.

junior financing (US)

A loan secured by means of a second or **junior mortgage**.

junior mortgage (US)

Any **mortgage** that is subordinate to

the first mortgage, whether as a second or a subsequent mortgage. See also **priority, second mortgage**.

jura in rem (L)

'Rights *in rem*'. See **action *in rem***.

jurat (US)

1. A certificate, usually issued by a government official or notary public, confirming that a writing was sworn to by the person who signed it.
(US) 2. The part of an affidavit which states where, when and before whom it was sworn – US *v* McDermott, 140 US 151, 11 SCt. 746, 35 L. Ed. 391.

jus abutendi, *jus fruendi*, *jus utendi* (L)

In the civil law, the rights to 'dispose' (or even destroy), to 'enjoy the fruits' and to 'use' property. See also *abusus*, *fructus*, **ownership**, *usus*.

jus accrescendi (L)

'A right of accrual or survivorship'. See **joint tenancy**.

jus disponendi (L)

'The right of disposition or alienation'. In the civil law, a right to goods retained after the owner has parted with possession. In common law *jus disponendi* may be used to refer to the right vested in a beneficiary to require a trustee to convey the legal estate that is held in trust. See also **bare trust**.

jus habendi et retinendi (L)

'A right to have and retain'. See *habendum*.

jus possessionis (L)

'A right of **possession**'.

jus spatiandi (L)

A right to wander at large over a defined area of land, e.g. over a garden or park. A right that may form the subject matter of an **easement** provided the area of land is sufficiently confined – Re Ellenborough Park [1956] Ch. 131.

jus tertii (L)

'The right of a third party', as where a tenant claims his landlord's title belongs to someone else. See also **estoppel**.

just compensation (US)

Compensation payable on the exercise of the power of **eminent domain**, i.e. on **condemnation** by a public authority. The Fifth Amendment to the US Constitution requires that private property shall not be "taken for public use, without just compensation". In principle, the aim of the acquiring authority is to pay just recompense (which may be more, or less, than the money value of the property taken) rather than the amount that would be payable to acquire the property at its open market value (although the term 'fair market value' is used frequently in this connection). The amount of compensation is based primarily on the benefit obtained by the appropriating authority, not merely the loss suffered by the condemned owner. It is intended to represent the full monetary value of the property taken, but not necessarily the total consequent loss suffered by the owner – US *v* Reynolds, Ky. 397 US 14, 90 S Ct. 803, 25 L Ed. 2d. 12. However, property is valued in its **highest and best use**, so that if land that is to be condemned is likely to be re-zoned in a way that will increase its value then the owner can base his claim for compensation on the higher value, pro-

vided re-zoning is probable and there is definite demand for the re-zoned land. The effect of an adverse zoning ordinance made in anticipation of condemnation is ignored; "zoning cannot be used as a substitute for eminent domain proceedings to defeat the payment of just compensation by depressing values and so reducing the amount of damages to be paid when private property is taken for public use". – Symonds *v* Buckley 197 F. Supp. 682. Compensation is not normally payable for disturbance, but it is payable for the effect of **severance**. The effect of blight caused by the appropriating authority is also ignored, but a **set-off** is made for any increase in the value of retained land resulting from the activities of the acquiring authority.

A total prohibition of new building may be considered as a 'taking' of a right to land and, therefore, entitle the landowner to a measure of compensation – Pennsylvania Coal Co. *v* Mahon (1892) 260 US 393. But a mere exercise of **police power**, e.g. a control of zoning for the public good, is not a subject for the payment of compensation. See also **before-and-after valuation, inverse condemnation**.

Readings in Market Value, AIREA, (1981).

Just Compensation: Indemnity or Market Value, by H.T. Dolan, pp. 181–187.

Market Value Approach to Value by J.L. Sackman, pp. 188–211.

Real Estate Valuation in Litigation, by J.D. Eaton, pp. 3–7, 10–26 (1982).

juste titre (F)

see *titre*.

K

'keep in repair'
see **repair**.

key money
1. A **fine** or **premium** paid for a right to acquire a property; especially a non-returnable sum paid by a tenant before he is granted possession of a property, either at the start of a new tenancy or on the assignment of an existing tenancy. Key money commonly refers to a payment made to acquire a right that has no marketable value, i.e. it is paid over and above the value of any **profit rent** or the value of any improvement made by an outgoing tenant. The demanding of key money for a right to occupy residential property is, as a rule, illegal under the Rent Acts. See also **fair rent, rent limit**.
Landlord and Tenant, by Martin Partington, 2 edn, pp. 309–314.
2. A commission paid to an agent, broker or accommodation agent for the privilege of being put forward as a potentially suitable tenant for a property.
3. A sum paid by an incoming tenant for an advantage to be derived from acquiring a lease of a property; in particular, for the right to take over fixtures, goodwill, or merely the privilege of being represented in a shopping centre.

key tenant
see **anchor tenant**.

kickback
1. A percentage payment exacted for the privilege of being permitted to take a share in a business venture. A portion of the purchase price for a property paid to one of the parties to the transaction, or his agent or representative, as an inducement to the consummation of the deal; especially when the deal is favourable to the party paying the kickback.
2. Payment made to a public official, or an employee of a major company, as an inducement, for example, to give favour to a building contractor or a seller of property; i.e. a secret rebate or bribe.

kicker, equity (US)
see **equity participation**.

knight-service
A form of **tenure** under the feudal system by which the King granted land to various lords in return for the provision of a number of armed knights or similar military service (Litt. 103). All such tenures created by the King have been converted to free and common **socage** (The Tenures Abolition Act 1660, s. 4).
Cheshire's Modern Law of Real Property, 13 edn, pp. 16–18.
History of English Law, by Holdsworth, 3 edn., vol. iii. pp. 37–46.

knock-down
The acceptance of the final bid in an **auction**, usually signified by the fall of the auctioneer's hammer. In the US referred to also as 'struck off'.

knock-out agreement
see **bidding agreement**.

L

laches

Derived from the Old French *laschesse*, slackness, carelessness, or negligence. The neglect, omission or unreasonable delay in asserting or enforcing one's rights, or in performing a duty. Laches embraces the maxim *vigilatibus et non dormientibus lex seccurit*, 'law aids the vigilant, not the indolent'. "Laches is a neglect to do something which by law a man is obliged to do." – Sebag *v* Abitol (1816) 4 M and S 463. Accordingly, "a court of **equity** has always refused its aid to **stale** demands where a party has slept upon his rights and acquiesced for a great length of time. Nothing can call forth this court into activity but conscience, good faith and reasonable diligence". – Smith *v* Clay (1767) Amb. 645. Thus, laches provides in equity, a similar end to litigation to that supplied in common law by a statutory **limitation** on a right of action. Thus it may bar an equitable remedy such as a claim for **rescission, rectification, specific performance** or an **injunction**.

cf. **estoppel**. See also **abandonment**.

Lady day

The feast of the Annunciation; 25 March. In England one of the 'usual' **quarter days** for payment of rent.

laesae fidei (L)

'Breach of faith'. See **good faith**.

lais (F)

alluvion.

(*les lais et relais de la mer* – tidal land; **foreshore**).

cf. *relais*.

lammas lands

Arable or meadow land held in fee simple subject to a right of pasturage (usually as a **right of common**) for part of the year; originally from Lammas day (1 August), or reaping time, to the following Lady day (25 March), or sowing time. Called sometimes 'half-year lands'.

Lammas day

August 1. One of the 'half **quarter days**' or 'term days' in Scotland.

land

A dry part of the earth's surface. Historically the word land meant "whatsoever may be ploughed" (Co. Litt. 4a); but in modern usage any part of the earth's crust may be classified as land (although generally 'land' excludes the oceans). Land comprises any part of the earth's surface that can be owned and exploited, whether mountain or valley, pasture or desert, town or country, dry land or land covered with water (or ice). The meaning of 'land' may be extended to all that is annexed to it, whether by man or nature, as well as its natural produce above or below the surface.

In economics, land is more than the surface of the earth; it is a natural resource, a commodity, and a primary source of wealth; it is one of the factors of production (the others being labour and **capital**) without which there can be no economic activity. It is regarded as the one economic resource that is provided by nature, as distinguished from the other resources which are provided by man. "The term 'land' often means different things depending upon the context in which it is used and the circumstances under which it is considered. Like a cut diamond it has many facets. Most important among these are the views of land as (1) space, (2) nature, (3) a factor of production, (4) a consumption good, (5) situation, (6) **property** and (7) capital (three other facets of land – concept of land as a deity, as a community, and as a store of wealth may also be noted).' – *Land Resource Economics*, by Raleigh Barlowe, 3 edn., p. 10.

In the legal sense, land is any definite space on, under, or over the earth's surface; including any **mine** or any **mineral** beneath the land, and reasonable use of the air space above. A right to the ownership of land includes the **natural rights** appertaining thereto, and anything affixed or growing on the land that has become part of the land, e.g. any **fixture**, building and *fructus naturales*. 'Land' comprehends "all things of a permanent, substantial nature, being a word of very extensive significance. . . . For land, says Sir Edward Coke (1 Inst. 4), comprehendeth in its legal signification any ground, soil, or earth whatsoever; as arable, meadows, pastures, woods, moors, marshes, furzes, and heath. It legally includeth all castles, houses, and other buildings: for they consist, it is said, of two things; land, which is the foundation; and structure thereon: so that if I convey the land or ground, the structure or building passeth with it". (Bl. Comm. (1766) vol. ii. p. 16, 17). Also land may be taken in a spatial division, "horizontally, vertically or otherwise and either below or above ground. This separate ownership may exist in strata of minerals, in the space occu-

pied by tunnels, or in different storeys of a building". (39 Halsbury's Laws of England, 4 edn., p. 263). – Newhoff *v* Mayo, 48 NJ Eq. 619, 23 A 265.

In theory, land is defined by law as a right that extends as far above and below the surface as is physically possible. A principle expressed by the maxim *cujus est solum, ejus est usque ad coelum et usque ad infernos*, 'he who possesses land, possesses to the sky above and to the depths below'. However, this historical view has been restrained by common law and statute: hence, aircraft, above a reasonable height, may fly over land, and **mineral rights** may be limited to the State.

Land is a term used interchangeably with **real property**, to refer to the distinct form of **ownership** recognised in English law: the right to hold land against others. In this sense, it is a right not merely over physical earth, and what is attached thereto but also a right to any associated intangible right, such as an easement, profit à prendre or rentcharge.

In English statutes 'land' is defined in a number of different ways. The Interpretation Act 1889, s. 3 (now repealed, but applicable to Acts of Parliament passed after 1850 and before 1979) defines it to include "messuages, tenements, hereditaments, houses, and buildings of any tenure" (unless there are words in the applicable Act of Parliament to restrict the meaning). The Interpretation Act 1978, Sch. 1 (which applies to any Act of Parliament passed after 1 January 1979) specifies that land includes "buildings or other structures, land covered with water, and any estate, interest, easement, servitude or right in or over land". The Law of Property

Act 1925, s. 205 (ix) defines it to include, "land of any tenure, and mines and minerals whether or not held apart from the surface, buildings or parts of buildings (whether the division is horizontal, vertical or made in any other way) and other corporeal hereditaments; also a manor, an advowson, and a rent and other incorporeal hereditament, and an easement, right, privilege, or benefit in, over, or derived from land; but not an undivided share in land". The Settled Land Act 1925, s. 117; the Land Registration Act 1925, s. 3; the Land Charges Act 1925, s. 20; and the Trustee Act 1925, s. 68 contain similar (but slightly varied) definitions to the Law of Property Act 1925. The Land Compensation Act 1961, s. 39 defines land to mean "any corporeal **hereditament**, including a building as defined by this section, and includes any interest or right in or over land and any right to water" (building being defined as "any structure or erection or any part of a building as so defined, but does not include plant or machinery comprised in a building"). The Town and Country Planning Act 1971, s. 290 defines land to mean "any corporeal hereditament, including a building" (and for those parts of the Act that refer to the acquisition or appropriation of land) it also "includes any interest in or right over land". On the other hand, when used in the Housing Act 1957, s. 189 (1) land does not include rights that are reasonably necessary for the enjoyment of land but that did not exist prior to a compulsory purchase of the land, i.e., in this context, it does not include a **quasi-easement** – Sovmots v Secretary of State for the Environment [1979] AC 144.

"The word 'land', when used in a lease or other assurance, includes, if there is nothing to restrict its technical meaning, all kinds of land, whether arable, meadow or otherwise, and also everything on or under the soil, all buildings erected on it, and all mines and minerals beneath it and the air space above it to such height as may be necessary for the ordinary use and enjoyment of it and the structures on it. A lease of woods includes not only the trees, but the land whereon they grow ... (but) Where the soil under the water is intended to pass the expression 'land covered with water' should be used" (27 Halsbury's Laws of England, 4 edn., p. 102).

A gift of 'land' under a will includes not only any freehold interest owned by the testator but also any leasehold interest, unless there is an express provision to the contrary (Wills Act 1837, s. 26); but it does not include land held under a trust for sale (unless included in words such as 'all interests in land' – Cooper v Critchley [1955] Ch. 431. See also **accession, accretion, accommodation land, agricultural land, air rights, building land, common land, estate, fixture, *fructus*, immoveables, land economics, mineral rights, settled land, tenements, treasure trove, waste land, water rights.**

The Law of Property, by F.H. Lawson, 2 edn., pp. 21–25.
Land Law, by Patrick J. Dalton, 4 edn., pp. 26–44.
Cheshire's Modern Law of Property, 13 edn, pp. 135–136.

land agent
1. An agent who is responsible for the management of an agricultural or

country estate and whose responsibilities extend from supervising the
physical upkeep and improvement of
the land to the maintenance of good
landlord and tenant relations. Called
also a 'land steward'. See also **estate
management**.

2. A broker who specialises in raw
land or agricultural property. See
also **estate agent**.

land assemblage (US)
see **assemblage**.

Land Authority for Wales
A corporate body initially constituted
under the Community Land Act 1975
to carry out a similar function
(excluding the collection of betterment levy) to the (now disbanded)
Land Commission in England. The
Authority's functions were revised by
the Local Government, Land and
Planning Act 1980, s. 102 (1), Sch. 18
and now include "acquiring land in
Wales which in its opinion needs to be
made available for development and
disposing of it to other persons (for
development by them)". The Authority is constituted similarly to a local
authority; it has compulsory purchase powers; and it may carry out
infrastructure work on land it has
acquired in order to make the land
more suitable for sale or development. It is not a planning authority,
although it may offer advice in this
field to a county or district authority.

land bank
1. A financial institution that specialises in making loans, usually mortgage loans, for the purchase of land,
especially farm land. 'Land banks'
were first established in England in
1695 to issue notes based on the security of land but such institutions died

out by the start of the 18th century.
Land banks to make loans were
established in the US in the 18th century and subsist today, notably in the
form of the Federal Land Banks that
specialise in long-term agricultural
loans. See also *Crédit Foncier*.

2. A stock of land held for future
development; in particular, land held
by a property development company
or a house builder to ensure a steady
programme of future development.

Land Certificate
A certificate issued, under seal, to the
registered proprietor of a parcel of
land, by the Land Registry, as evidence of title to land (Land Registration Act 1925, s. 63 (1)). A Land Certificate is a copy of those parts of the
land register that relate to the proprietor's land. It is issued in a prescribed form (Land Registration Rule
1925, r. 261. form 78); contains a description of the land and the estate
held; states the nature of the title held
(absolute, qualified, possessory, or
good leasehold); contains details of
any notices, cautions, inhibitions or
restrictions affecting the land; and
details any encumberances affecting
the land, such as a mortgage or restrictive covenant. The certificate
incorporates also a copy of the **filed
plan** appertaining to the registered
title. A land certificate, which may be
regarded as the equivalent for registered land to the deeds of title for
unregistered land, is *prima facie* evidence that a **good title** to land has
been registered (although it is only a
facsimile of the register; the actual
register being the true record of title.
If there is more than one registered
title to land, e.g. a fee simple absolute
and a lease for a term of years, then a

separate certificate may be issued to each registered proprietor. In the case of an **absolute title**, the land certificate alone is sufficient evidence of title. For a **good leasehold title**, the certificate should be accompanied by the original lease. For a **possessory title**, all relevant deeds (up to the time of first registration) should accompany the certificate in order to endeavour to show a good title. The certificate may be deposited at the Land Registry for safekeeping or it may be retained by the registered proprietor. A Land Certificate acts as *de facto* proof of title to an interest in land. As such it may be deposited with a mortgagee as security for a loan, especially as the Land Certificate must be deposited at the Land Registry prior to a transfer of the title to which it relates. Nonetheless, a lease for a term in excess of 21 years may be registered without production of the land certificate; a situation that can be guarded against by the mortgagee entering a **caution** on the land register.

A Land Certificate should be distinguished from an **official certificate of search**: the latter provides details of entries on the land charges register or a local land charges register, and may be issued to an intending purchaser of unregistered land as evidence of charges that affect the land, but it is not evidence of title. See also **charge certificate**.

land charge

A **charge** against land that places a restriction on a landowner in favour of another party. In particular, an encumberance that may be entered on the Register of Land Charges, which forms part of the **Land Charges Register**, in order to protect the beneficiary from the possibility that a purchaser of unregistered land may claim that he was not aware of the encumberance and, therefore, is not bound by it. The registration of any matter in the Land Charges Register is deemed to constitute "actual **notice** of . . . the fact of such registration, to all persons and for all purposes connected with the land affected . . . so long as the registration continues in force". (Law of Property Act 1925, s. 198 (1)). (This section does not affect the right of a mortgagee to tack a further advance on to an existing loan, in accordance with the terms of a previous agreement: 1925 Act, s. 198 (2)). The effect of registering a land charge applies only to encumberances that are required or authorised to be registered, but this does not prevent a person from entering a claim to a similar type of encumberance, which on investigation may prove to be unsubstantiated. The effect of section 198 of the 1925 Act is that any instrument or matter entered on the register is 'deemed' to be known to a purchaser, whether or not he makes enquiry. This provision applies only upon completion of a conveyance and not when contracts are exchanged (on exchange of contracts a prospective purchaser is affected only by matters of which he has, or should have, actual notice (Law of Property Act 1969, s. 24 (1)).

The various encumberances that may be entered on the register of land charges are set out in the Land Charges Act 1972, s. 2 (replacing the Land Charges Act 1925, s. 10, as amended by the Matrimonial Homes Act 1967, s. 2 (6)) and are classified in six groups, denominated classes A to F. They may be summarised as (A) an annuity, rentcharge or principal money charged against land under a statutory provision; (B) a charge on land that arises by statute law, but not as a result of any person applying to have the charge created, e.g. a claim for an unpaid contribution to the legal aid fund for land that has been recovered by a legally assisted client; (C) a **puisne mortgage**, a **limited owner's charge**, a **general equitable charge**, an **estate contract**; (D) an Inland Revenue charge for unpaid **Capital Transfer Tax**, an **equitable easement**, a **restrictive covenant**; (E) certain annuities arising before 1926; (F) a spouse's right to occupation of a **matrimonial home**. The effect of not registering a registerable land charge depends on the type of charge but, in general, non-registration makes the charge void against certain classes of purchaser of land, especially a **bona fide purchaser** for 'money or money's worth' (or in some instances a purchaser for 'value') of a **legal estate** in the land affected by the charge; even if that purchaser knew of the existence of a registrable charge, provided the purchaser acted in good faith. It is important that, before taking a conveyance of unregistered land, the prospective purchaser should make a search of the Land Charges Register, either personally or by obtaining an **official certificate of search** from the Land Registrar.

Certain equitable interests, which do not depend for their efficacy upon their continuing existance as a claim to land, but could equally well be satisfied out of the invested proceeds of the sale of land (e.g. an annuity or a general equitable charge), cannot be registered and are said to be 'overreached', i.e. following a disposition of the land the benefit of the claim is simply transferred to the proceeds of sale.

cf. **local land charge**. See also **constructive notice, overreached interest, priority notice, searches**.
Real Property and Real People, by K.J. Gray and P.D. Symes, pp. 111–153, (1981).
Cheshire's Modern Law of Real Property, 28 edn, pp. 708–718.
Megarry's Manual of The Law of Real Property, 6 edn, pp. 90–106.
The Law of Real Property, by Robert Megarry and H.W.R. Wade, 5 edn., pp. 133–136, 170–191.
Barnsley's Conveyancing Law and Practice, 2 edn, pp. 383–400.
26 Halsbury's Laws of England, 4 edn, paras. 701–770.

Land Charges Register

A register, maintained at the Land Charges Department of the **Land Registry** by the Land Registrar, which sets out details of encumberances against unregistered land that may be registered in order to give actual **notice** to an intending purchaser of the existence of the encumberance (Land Charges Act 1972, s. 1 (1)). The entire register is divided into five separate registers: (i) Register of Pending Actions; (ii) Register of Annuities (which only applied to annuities created before 1925); (iii) Register of Writs and Orders affecting land; (iv) Register of Deeds of Arrangement affecting land; and (v) Register of Land Charges (being the most significant of the five registers). The register is augmented by an index, maintained by the Registrar, where all entries can readily be traced. (The Land Charges Register applies to unregistered land and should be

distinguished from the 'Charges Register' at the Land Registry which contains details of encumberances against registered land). See also **index map, land charge, local land charges register, official certificate of search**.
Cheshire's Modern Law of Property, 13 edn, pp. 708–718.
The Law of Real Property, by Robert Megarry and H.W.R. Wade, 5 edn., pp. 171–191.

Land Commission
A body set up under the Land Commission Act 1967 to acquire land for development and collect **betterment levy**. Abolished by the Land Commission (Dissolution) Act 1971. See also **Land Authority for Wales**.

Land Compensation Acts
Statutes that set forth details of the basis for assessing **compulsory purchase compensation**. The principal current Acts are the Land Compensation Acts of 1961 and 1973.

land contract (US)
see **instalment contract**.

land development
see **development**.

land economics
An art or social science that deals with the use and allocation of the scarce resource of land and all additions or improvements to land. Land economics is concerned with the marketing, distribution and allocation of land and its products, its efficiency in the production process and its role in the welfare of the community. "It is concerned with man's economic use of the surface resources of the earth and the physical and biological, economic and institutional factors that affect, condition, and con-

trol his use of these resources" – *Land Resource Economics*, by Raleigh Barlowe, 3 edn, p. 4. It involves the study of the characteristics of land; the classification and patterns of land uses; the planning and development of land; the ownership and legal control of land; land as a commodity or as a source of wealth; the taxation of land; and economic theories of land, in terms of its price or value and the concept of **highest and best use**. See also **economic rent, land use planning, location theory**.
Urban Economics, by H.W. Richardson, (1977).
The Economics of Town and Country Planning, by K.G. Willis, (1980).
Introduction to the Economics of Urban Land Use, by M. Newell, (1977).
Urban Economics, by K.J. Button, (1976).
The Economics of Real Property, by J. Harvey (1981).
Aspects of Land Economics, by Lean and Goodall, (1966, reprinted 1973).
The Economics of Planned Development, by N. Lichfield, (1976).
Urban Land Economics, by R. Ratcliffe, (1949, reprinted 1972).
Urban Land Economics, by Paul N. Balchin and J. Kieve, 2 edn.
Urban Economics, by Alan Evans, (1985).

land gavel
see **gavelkind**.

land grant (US)
A grant of land by the federal government made to achieve a particular objective, e.g. a grant of land to a corporation for industrial development or to a university for a new educational building.

land improvement

see **development, improvement, land reclamation.**

Land Improvement Company

A British government sponsored institution, first established in 1853, that makes long-term loans for the improvement of agricultural property and certain recreational and amenity land. The Company is now governed by Special Acts of Parliament passed between 1969 and 1985.

land lease

see **ground lease.**

land leaseback

see **land sale-and-leaseback.**

land loan (US)

A loan secured against land. See also **mortgage.**

land locked

see **easement of necessity.**

land option

see **option.**

land owner

see **estate owner, owner, registered proprietor.**

land planning

see **land use planning.**

land reclamation

The winning back of land for a useful purpose. The recovery of **wasteland** for productive use. The conversion or restoration of **derelict land** so that it may be cultivated or developed for occupation or profit; including filling, levelling, draining, irrigating and any other form of land (but not building) improvement.

land register

see *cadastre*, **Land Registry.**

land registration

The recording of title to land on a formal register, so that owners may deal with land by reference to that register rather than by reference to documents of title held by existing land owners. The purpose of land registration is (a) to record all rights and interest affecting the registered land; (b) to provide that specific rights over land, in particular trusts, are excluded from the register and, therefore, on a sale of land these rights are transferred from the land to the proceeds of sale; (c) to provide a guarantee by the State as to the validity of a registered title so that, if the title proves defective, compensation is paid from a public fund to an owner who is consequently deprived of his land.

Modern land registration in England and Wales (as well as many other countries) is based on the **Torrens title system.** Under this system a landowner who wishes to register a title provides details of the interest to a public officer, together with details of any encumberances, and seeks to establish a registered title. If that title is accepted a copy of the formal record, a 'certificate of title' is issued as *de facto* evidence that the title is guaranteed (although it is the register and not the certificate that represents the title to land). Any subsequent transfer of that land is effected by registration, i.e. the cancellation of the old certificate and the issuing of a new certificate in the name of the new proprietor.

In England and Wales land registration is effected by the recording of details of titles to land and certain rights thereover at local branch offices of the **Land Registry,** and evidence of the registration is provided in the form of a **Land Certificate**. Any such registered title is then guaranteed and may be transferred without further investigation of the previous right to the land. "The object [of land registration] is to save persons dealing with registered proprietors from the trouble and expense of going behind the register, in order to investigate the history of their author's title, and to satisfy themselves of its validity. That end is accomplished by providing that everyone who purchases, in *bona fide* and for **value**, from a **registered proprietor**, and enters his deed of transfer or mortgage on the register, shall thereby acquire an indefeasible right, notwithstanding the infirmity of his author's title." – Gibbs *v* Messer [1891] AC 254. Land registration is intended to affirm titles to land; to record rights that affect, and are transferred with, a title; and to simplify land transactions: it is not intended, nor will it, validate an otherwise invalid claim to land.

Compulsory registration has been introduced in most urban areas of England and Wales, and voluntary land registration exists in certain cases in other areas. The intention is to extend the existing system to all land, but even in areas of compulsory registration the recording of a title cannot be effected until a sale of a 'registrable estate' takes place. Since 1925 the registrable estates are a fee simple absolute in possession (when registered sometimes called a **freehold absolute**) and most leases with an unexpired term of 21 years. In an area subject to compulsory registration, as a rule, every conveyance of a freehold and every grant or assignment of a lease for a term with no less than forty years unexpired (provided the transaction is made for valuable consideration), must be registered within two months of the transaction by the first or a subsequent proprietor otherwise the transaction is null and void (Land Registration Act 1925, s. 123). A lease for an unexpired term exceeding 21 years, but less than 40 years, may also be so registered and must be registered where the freehold title, out of which the lease is granted, is also registered, (1925 Act, s. 8 (1)).

A title registered at the Land Registry may be accepted by the registrar as an **absolute title** (either an absolute freehold title, or an absolute leasehold title); as a **possessory title** (either a possessory freehold title or, rarely, a possessory leasehold title), when the title is based on a claim of adverse possession; or as a **qualified title**, when the registrar is not entirely satisfied that he can register an absolute title. In addition, a **good leasehold title** may be registered by a lessee when there is no guarantee as to the title of the lessor.

Land registration provides also a means to protect certain interests in land which do not themselves represent a title to land but are capable of binding a purchaser of land when they are registered: these are **minor interests** in the case of registered land and interests or rights that may be entered on the **Land Charges Register** in the case of unregistered land. See also **cadastral register**, **land charge**, **local land charges register**, **overriding interest**.

Introduction to Land Law, by J.G. Riddell, 3 edn., pp. 420–456.
Land Law and Registration, by S. Rowton Simpson, (1976).

The Law of Real Property, by Robert Megarry and H.W.R. Wade, 5 edn.; pp. 194–230.
Concise Land Registration Practice, by Theodore B.F. Ruoff and Christopher West, 3 edn.
Barnsley's Conveyancing Law and Practice, 2 edn, pp. 13–94.
Law and Practice of Registered Conveyancing, by T.B.F. Ruoff and R.B. Roper, 4 edn.
26 Halsbury's Laws of England, 4 edn, paras. 901–1490.

Land Registry

An official organisation, first established in England under the Land Registry Act 1862, in order to permit voluntary land registration, so that a registered title to land would be virtually guaranteed by the State without the need for further investigation by a subsequent purchaser. The register was extended in use by the Land Transfer Act 1897 which made registration of title to land compulsory in the County of London. In 1925 compulsory registration was extended to a large part of England and Wales; the Register was used as a means to register a **minor interest** in registered land, which requires protection by registration if it is not to be defeated by a purchaser of a 'legal estate for valuable consideration'; and it accommodated the **Land Charges Register** which sets out details of various encumberances affecting unregistered land (Land Registration Act 1925; Land Charges Act 1925). Compulsory land registration now extends to most urban property in England and Wales and unregistered land is entered on the Register when a sale of that land takes place (Land Registration Act 1925, s. 123). The administrative headquarters of the Land Registry is situated at Lincoln's Inn Fields, London, and actual registration is made through one of twelve District Land Registries. The Register at each District Land Registry is divided into three parts: (i) a Property Register, which identifies and describes the registered land and the estate held therein and any incidental interests or benefits affecting the land (including any exemption from an overriding interest and details of easements, restrictive covenants, or other rights or privileges affecting the land); and, for leasehold land, details of the lease (principally leases for 21 years or more), together with exceptions and reservations to the lease; in addition the Property Register indicates the boundaries of the registered parcels of land by reference to a General Map; (ii) a Proprietorship Register, which contains the name and address of the proprietor, describes the form of title that is registered (absolute, good leasehold, qualified or possessory), and details of any restrictions on the proprietor's right of sale (e.g. a trust for sale or a strict settlement) together with any **restriction, caution** or **inhibition** affecting the proprietor's right to deal with the land; and (iii) a Charges Register, which details rights *adverse* to the land, such as mortgages and charges and, in general, any **notice** entered to protect lesser interests affecting registered land, as well as all such dealing with registered charges or encumberances as are capable of registration (Land Registration Rules 1925, rr. 2–7).

In general, the land register is not available for public inspection and any search thereof must be authorised by, or made by, the holder of a registered title to land. However, an **Index Map** and a **Parcels Index** is available for inspection, together with a list of pending applications, to enable an interested party to ascertain whether or not a particular parcel of land is, or is about to be, registered. See also **Charges Certificate, filed plan, Land Certificate, land registration.**

The Law of Real Property, by Robert Megarry and H.W.R. Wade, 5 edn., pp. 194 *et seq.*

Guide to Land Registry Practice, by Wontner, 13 edn.

land rent
Rent derived from land; in particular, rent from an area of unimproved land as represented by the excess of income and profits from that land over the cost of maintaining the land in its productive use. See also **economic rent, ground rent, rental value.**

land residual technique (US)
A method of valuing land, separately from the buildings or improvements standing thereon. A notional income, which is considered to represent a fair return on the building or improvements (usually a percentage of the replacement cost), is deducted from the actual or potential income receivable from the entire property and the balance, a deemed **ground rent**, is capitalised at a rate considered appropriate to the land alone.

cf. **building residual technique.** See also **abstraction approach, residual method of valuation.**

land sale-and-leaseback
A **sale and leaseback** of development land. Unimproved land is sold by a developer to a financial institution and is then leased back to the developer with a concurrent loan from the institution, secured by a mortgage on the developer's leasehold interest. The loan is intended to provide finance for the development of the site. Usually the lender provides all the financing and acquires a share of the equity to be derived from the completed development; the developer providing the design and building expertise. Called sometimes a 'land-leaseback'.

cf. **project sale-and-leaseback.** See also **equity participation, lease/leaseback financing.**

land sales contract (US)
see **instalment sale.**

land speculator
see **speculator.**

land steward
see **land agent.**

land surveying
see **surveying.**

land tax
In general, any form of tax levied on property; that is, on the rights and benefits to be derived from the ownership of real property. In particular, an annual tax levied on real property that was introduced in England in 1692 and subsisted in various forms until it was abolished by the Finance Act 1963, s. 68. See also **property tax.**

land tenant
see *terre tenant.*

land tenure
The rights to hold, use and dispose of land. See also **feudal system, tenure.**

land trust (US)
An arrangement whereby title to land is held in **trust**. The trustee of a land

trust has the power to deal with the land only in accordance with the **deed of trust** and the management and control of the trust property remains with the beneficiaries. A land trust may be used to disguise the identity of the true owners of a property; to enable land to be mortgaged without the trustees or beneficiaries having a personal liability; or to enable land to be held for the benefit of a number of co-owners or owners of a partial interest in land. A land trust is created usually for a specific purpose or for a limited period of time. The beneficiaries entitlement under the trust may be evidenced by a 'land trust certificate'. See also **bare trust**, **estate company**, **property trust**, **trust for sale**.

land trust certificate (US)
see **land trust**.

land use
see **land economics**, **highest and best use**, **use**.

land use planning
A system, usually supported by force of law, designed to control and plan the future use of land. Land use planning is effected by regulations that are intended to order and regulate the use and development of land, in particular: **zoning**, which primarily defines or restricts the type of land use; controls on **density**, which limit the intensity of land use, either in terms of building units or population; and **plot ratio** controls, which restrict the volume and height of new buildings. See also **development plan**, **land economics**, **town and country planning**.
Real Estate Principles, by Bruce Harwood, 2 edn., pp. 469–480.
Aspects of Land Use Planning, by W. Lean and B. Goodall, (1966).

Urban Land Use Planning, by F.S. Chaplin and E.J. Kaiser, (1979).
Urban Planning and Development Control Law, by Donald E. Hagman, (1975).

land value
see **economic rent**, **land rent**, **residual method of valuation**, **value**.

landed property
A popular term for **real property**. If a person devises all his 'landed property' he transfers every estate or interest in **land** that he possesses – Sharp v De St. Sauveur, 17 W.R. 1002). Used also to refer to rural as distinguished from urban property. See also **real estate**.

landlady
1. A female **landlord** i.e. a woman who owns real property which she leases to others.
2. A woman who owns or manages an inn, boarding house or a rooming house.

landlocked
An area of land, surrounded by property owned by the other parties, to which there is no right of access; in particular, no access to a public road. See also **easement of necessity**.

landlord
One who permits another (a **tenant**) to have **exclusive occupation** of land, for a certain duration, under a contract of **tenancy** termed a **lease**, in return for a right to receive rent or profits. The person between whom and the tenant the relationship of **landlord and tenant** exists. "'Landlord' implies not the mere lordship or ownership of soil, but relationship to a tenant." – Churchward v Ford (1857) 26 LJ Ex. 354. A landlord is

one who but for the tenant would be entitled to possession of the land, i.e. a person entitled to the immediate **reversion** under the lease by which his tenant was granted possession. A landlord may be the freeholder of the land; but any holder of an interest in land (including a person who is himself a tenant, or a mortgagee) who grants a lease is a landlord.

For the purpose of an **agricultural tenancy** landlord, "means any person for the time being entitled to receive the rents and profits of land" (Agricultural Holdings Act 1948, s. 94 (1)). For the purpose of a **business tenancy**, the landlord, called the "competent landlord", is either the owner for the time being of the fee simple or, basically, the tenant's immediate landlord provided he has at least 14 months unexpired tenancy; he is the landlord empowered to serve and receive notices under the provision of the Landlord and Tenant Act 1954, Part II. (Landlord and Tenant Act 1954, s. 44 (1)), as extended by the Law of Property Act 1969, s. 14). In the case of a **protected tenancy** a landlord includes any person deriving title under the original landlord (i.e. a person who is himself a tenant and has in turn created a tenancy – a 'sandwich tenant') and any person who, other than the tenant, would be entitled to possession if the existing tenant did not have statutory security of tenure (Rent Act 1977, s. 152 (1)); thus it includes anyone who can properly be called a landlord – Dudley and District Benefit Building Society *v* Emerson [1949] Ch. 707. See also **head landlord, lessor**.

landlord's access

The right of a landlord to enter on to the property that he has leased, whether to inspect the property, to carry out repairs or for any other purpose, without disturbing the tenant's possession. A lease grants a tenant a right to **exclusive occupation** of the demised premises; this includes the right to exclude the landlord for the duration of the tenancy. Thus a landlord has no right of access to leased premises, other than to levy **distress** for arrears of rent, unless there is an express provision in the lease – Barker *v* Barker (1829) 3 C and P 557. However a provision is inserted in most leases giving the landlord a right of access, at reasonable times and subject to reasonable notice, to inspect the state of the premises and to ensure that the tenant has complied with the terms of the lease.

There may be an implied right of access granted to a landlord by common law or statute. At common law a landlord has an implied right of access in order to comply with his repairing obligations – Granada Theatres *v* Freehold Investments (Leytonstone) Ltd, [1959] 1 WLR 570. A landlord of a dwelling-house who has a statutory obligation to carry out repairs may enter at reasonable times and, subject to 24 hours prior notice, to view the state of the premises (Housing Act 1961, s. 32 (4)). A landlord of a dwelling-house let on a **statutory tenancy** has a right of access at reasonable times to execute such repairs as he is entitled to execute (Rent Act 1977, s. 3 (2)). A landlord of an **agricultural holding**, or any person authorised by him, may at all reasonable times enter on the holding to view the state of the holding; to fulfill his responsibilities to manage the property in accordance with the rules of good estate management; and to provide or improve fixed equipment on the holding (Agricultural Holdings Act 1948, s. 17).

cf. **right of re-entry**. See also **entry, implied covenant, quiet enjoyment, schedule of dilapidations**.

Woodfall's Landlord and Tenant, 28 edn, paras. 1-1486/7, 1-1580.

Hill & Redman's Law of Landlord and Tenant, 17 edn, pp. 254–255.

landlord's consent
see **change of use, improvement, restraint on alienation**.

landlord's fixture
see **fixture**.

landlord's improvement
An **improvement** carried out to leased premises by the landlord or at the landlord's expense. See also **fixture**.

landlord and tenant
A relationship, created by contract, which provides that a person with an interest in land (**landlord**) will grant a right for another (**tenant**) to take exclusive possession of the land for a determinate period of time. The contract is called a **lease** or, commonly, when granted for a short period of time a **tenancy** and the consideration for that contract called **rent**. In English common law, the nature of this relationship permits the landlord to (a) demand any rent that is due; (b) levy distress; (c) bring an action for breach of covenant; (d) enforce his right of entry if necessary; and (e) regain the land at the end of the determined period (unless prevented by statute). The tenant is entitled to (a) exclusive occupation of the leased property and (b) quiet enjoyment.

Thus the tenant has the full use and enjoyment of the demised property for the duration of the lease, but he must surrender possession to the landlord upon expiry (or prior legal determination) of the lease (unless protected by statute).

In English law, the relationship of landlord and tenant is considered to create a real right, a right to land – actionable *in rem* – as compared to a right that is actionable only between the parties – actionable *in personam*. In the US, the relationship is regarded more as a personal contract; hence many States do not acknowledge a right to levy distress, and the non-performance of one covenant by the landlord (e.g. failure to repair) may give the tenant the right to be excused from performing his part of the bargain which primarily is to pay rent (or a right to carry out the repair and deduct the cost from future rents) – Marini *v* Ireland (1970) 56 NJ 130, 265 A 2d. 526. (As a rule in English law, this form of set-off is not supported readily by the courts). On the other hand, in some states, especially where it is acknowledged that a lease is a contract that cannot be brought to an end by frustration, there is an inference that the tenant has a **real** right to land, for a period of time, and not merely a personal contract. See also **attornment, bail, negligence, determination, fixture, repair, security of tenure**.

Real Estate Law, by W.D. Milligan and Arthur G. Bowman, pp. 398–425 (1984).

An Introduction to American Land Law, by George Lefcoe, Ch. 6 (1974).

Real Estate Law, by Robert Kratovil and Raymond J. Werner, 8 edn., pp. 576–610.

Leasehold Law, by T.M. Aldridge (1983).

Adkin's Landlord and Tenant, 18 edn, pp. 1–30.

Landlord and Tenant, by Martin Partington, 2 edn.

Landlord and Tenant Law, by David Yates and A.J. Hawkins, pp. 1–7 (1981).

Landlord and Tenant, by Hill and Redman, 17 edn.

27 Halsbury's Laws of England, 4 edn, paras. 1–50.

Woodfall's Landlord and Tenant, 28 edn.

Landlord and Tenant Acts

Acts of Parliament that have been passed to give the holder of a **business tenancy** a right to a new tenancy upon the expiration of his contractual tenancy, as well as a right to apply to the courts to determine the rent the tenant should pay on renewal of the tenancy or when the rent is reviewed in accordance with the terms of the contractual tenancy. These statutes provide also that, in certain circumstances, the tenant is entitled to **compensation for improvements** and **compensation for disturbance** when his tenancy comes to an end. The principal statutes currently in force are the Landlord and Tenant Act 1927, Part I, and the Landlord and Tenant Act 1954, Part II (as amended by the Law of Property Act 1969). Halsbury's Statutes of England, 3 edn, vol. 18, pp. 381–982.

landlord's warrant

see **distress**.

landmark

1. A mark or structure placed on land to designate a boundary, especially a fixed object placed conspicuously to identify an important limit.

2. A noteable building or feature on the land. See also **landmark property**.

landmark property (US)

A building of sufficient merit, in terms of historic or cultural significance, to be worthy of retention. Similar to a **listed building** in Britain. See also **historic structure**.

landowner

One who has **ownership** of land. A person who receives rent or profits from land under any form of **tenure**. A term commonly applied to a holder of a substantial area of land. See also **estate owner**, **landlord**.

Lands Tribunal

A quasi-judicial body, established by the Lands Tribunal Act 1949, whose purpose is "to strengthen and codify the statutory arrangements for settling disputes in connection with the valuation of land and to ensure that in all cases where some form of valuation under statute is required there should be a single and consistent jurisdiction, combining legal and technical experience with appeal on matters of legal importance". (Attorney General Sir Hartley Shawcross on second reading of the Lands Tribunal Bill). The tribunal deals with such matters as **compulsory purchase compensation**; **compensation for planning restrictions**; **capital transfer tax** assessments; appeals from the **local valuation courts** against rating assessments; (until the Housing Act 1980) valuations for **leasehold enfranchisement**; applications for modification or discharge of a **restrictive covenant**; disputes over a **right of light**; and a disputed **blight notice**.

The members of the Tribunal are

appointed by the Lord Chancellor and comprise a President, who has previously held judicial office or is a barrister, and other members who are lawyers, chartered surveyors or other appropriately qualified persons. The appropriate member, or members, to hear a particular case is selected by the President and a member may act either solely or, if considered necessary, with another member.

An appeal from a decision of the Lands Tribunal may be made on a point of law by the Tribunal stating its case to the Court of Appeal. See also **arbitration, Leasehold Valuation Tribunal, sealed offer.**

The Surveyor in Court, by P.H. Clarke, pp. 13–19, (1985).

8 Halsbury's Laws of England, 4 edn, paras. 223–249.

39 Halsbury's Laws of England, 4 edn, paras. 159–166.

The Lands Tribunal – a practitioner's guide, by J.H. Emlyn Jones, (1982).

lane

A narrow **road** or **street**, generally running between a constraint on both sides such as a hedge, bank, wall or row of houses.

lapse

Termination of a right or privilege as a result of a passage of time. A fall from an agreed or accepted standard. Termination, or failure, of a right or privilege due to an omission to exercise that right or privilege; especially the loss of an interest in land due to the failure to renew the interest. A lapse arises, for example, from the failure to perform a condition of a contract, such as a failure to pay rent or a failure to give notice of an intention to exercise an option. An **offer** is considered to have lapsed (a) with the passage of time, either because a prescribed delay for acceptance has passed or, if there is no delay prescribed for acceptance, within a reasonable time; (b) upon the failure to fulfil a condition attached to the offer; or (c) on the death of the offerer or offeree before acceptance.

A gift of property by **will** is said to lapse if the beneficiary predeceases the testator; in that case the property usually passes according to the general terms of the will or to the person entitled on intestacy. Exceptions to this rule arise if there is a surviving joint tenant who is a beneficiary; if the property is left in tail (i.e. as an **entailed interest**); or there is a direct descendent of the beneficiary.

cf. **abandonment, expiry**. See also **rejection, revocation, time is of the essence.**

Cheshire's Modern Law of Property, 13 edn, pp. 788–790.

latent defect

A defect that is not discoverable from normal inspection; is not obvious on examination; and may not be discovered until some further, consequent, damage or defect has become observable. In connection with a ship it has been said that a latent defect is "not simply any defect not discoverable through ordinary use and maintenance, but a defect or flaw, generally in the ... material itself, which could not be discovered by any known or customary test". – Parente (Robert A) *v* Bayville Marine Inc. and General Insurance Co. of America [1975] 1 Lloyd's Rep. 333.

'Latent defect' may refer to a defect in the structure or condition of real property, or to a **defect of title**. In either instance a vendor of property is liable for any defect of which he is fully aware but fails to draw to the purchaser's attention; but as a rule, he is not liable for a clearly apparent or **patent defect**: the maxim being *caveat emptor*, 'let the buyer beware'. A mortgage, charge, or lien on a property may be considered a latent defect if not disclosed by a vendor of the property as they are not normally apparent to the purchaser; as may be a right of way that is not physically apparent – Ashburner *v* Sewell [1891] 3 Ch. 405.

A building contractor is liable for a latent defect that arises as a result of his workmanship, until a course of action is barred by the **Statutes of Limitation**, unless there is an express contractual provision to the contrary. See also **misrepresentation, negligence, repair**.
Latent Defects: Some Legal and Insurance Considerations, by J. Douglas (1984).

lateral support
Support for land provided in a vertical plane from adjoining ground.
cf. **subjacent support**. See also **right of support**.

law
see **by-law, common law, civil law, *droit*, ecclesiastical law, equity, *loi*, ordinance, statute law**.

law day (US)
The date an obligation falls due. For example, a day set down in a mortgage deed for the repayment of the principal. See also **maturity date**.

Law of Property Acts
A set of Statutes passed between 1922 and 1926 with the intention of instituting a major reform of land law in England and Wales and, in particular,

to abolish most of the remnants of the **feudal system** of land tenure. The main object of these statutes was: (a) the simplification of conveyancing; (b) the greater protection of purchasers of land, as well as those holding equitable interests; (c) the assimilation and amendment of aspects of the law affecting real and personal property; (d) the consolidation of enactments relating to settled land and trustees; (e) the simplification of procedure for the administration of estates of deceased persons; and (f) the extension of **land registration**. This was achieved, in particular, by reducing the number of legal estates to two; codifying the number of legal interests and making any other interests equitable interests and protected by registration; making **freehold** the residual form of tenure; effectively establishing a **leasehold interest** as real property rather than personal property; creating a means by which many interests in **settled land** could be detached from land and converted to a right to the proceeds of sale primarily by introducing the **trust for sale**; and extending the system for registration of titles and charges to land.

The statutes comprise the Law of Property Act 1925 (subsequently amended by Acts of 1926, 1929, 1932, 1964 and 1969); the Settled Land Act 1925; the Administration of Estates Act 1925; the Trustee Act 1925; the Land Charges Act 1925 (now replaced by the Land Charges Act 1972); and Land Registration Act 1925 and the Court of Judicature (Consolidation) Act 1925. See also **doctrine of estates, legal estate, legal interest, overreached interest, trust**.
Real Property Law, by H. Forbes, 2 edn., pp. 31–37.

The Law of Real Property, by Robert Megarry and H.W.R. Wade, 5 edn., pp. 32–36.
Cheshire's Modern Law of Real Property, 13 edn, pp. 4–6, 81–107.
27 Halsbury's Statutes of England, 4 edn.
Sweet & Maxwell's Property Statutes, 4 edn.

Law Society Conditions of Sale
see **conditions of sale**.

lawful entry
Entry on to real property in accordance with the due process of law.
cf. **trespass**. See also **eviction, landlord's access, right of re-entry, recovery**.

lawful interest
Interest on money at a rate permitted by law. See also **usury**.

lawful money
Money, in any form, that is legally acceptable as a medium of exchange. cf. **legal tender**. See also **hard money**.

lawyer
A person who exercises the profession and practice of the law or who is learned in the law. In England and Wales encompasses a **solicitor**; a **barrister**: in the US, **attorney**; **advocate** and counsel: in France, *avocat*; *avoué, agréé*. See also *notaire*, **notary public**.

layer method
see **hardcore method**.

layland
Land that is left to lay fallow or as **pasture**. See also **fallow land**.

lease
A grant of a right to **exclusive occupation (or exclusive possession)** of property (generally, but not necessarily, of real property or land) for a fixed or definite period of time (which may be for a life, a term of years, a succession of periods or at the will of the grantor, provided the period is certain or capable of being made certain and is less than that held by the grantor) in return for a payment termed **rent** (which is usually a periodic payment, but may be a single premium). A lease of land may be considered a dual transaction, a **conveyance** of a right to exclusive occupation of land (thereby creating an interest in land), and a **contract** requiring payment for the use and enjoyment of the land. The contract (which itself is called a lease when made in writing), may be express or implied. Nonetheless by that contract a **landlord** (or, strictly a **lessor**) cedes or makes a **demise** of a right to property to a **tenant** (or, strictly, a **lessee**); a right that may be freely alienated or transferred, unless there is a stipulation in the contract to the contrary.

In English common law a lease was regarded as a personal right between the parties, which created no estate or interest in land, but was akin to the grant of a right to use goods: it was a 'chattel real'. It had no place in the **feudal system** of land tenure. However, in modern law a lease is considered more akin to a real right; a right to exclude others, including the landlord, from the land for a defined duration; that is, for so long as the contract by which the right is created remains effective (or longer if the right to possession is extended by statute).

A good and valid lease may be made only between a party who is legally capable of making a lease and a party legally capable of accepting the property demised, and the property must be capable of being the subject-matter of such a demise. The lessor must retain an interest in the property that is the subject of the demise – a **reversionary interest**; otherwise he will have no further right to regain the property, but will have created an **assignment** of his entire interest. As a rule, a lease should be made by **deed** (especially when it is intended to create a **legal lease**; when it is of an **incorporeal hereditament**; when there is no valuable **consideration**; or when it is made by a corporation). Nevertheless a lease may still be valid if made in **writing**, or even if made orally, provided there is sufficient evidence of the intention to create a lease. For example, if there is an act of **part performance**, such as entry with intent to exclude the landlord, a payment of rent; or the observance of any other condition that is prevalent to the formation of a lease.

The word 'lease' may be used especially to refer to the grant of possession of land for a term certain in excess of three years (a lease that is intended to take effect in possession for a term exceeding three years must be in writing and duly signed, otherwise it creates a mere tenancy at will: Law of Property Act 1925, s. 54). The word **tenancy** is reserved usually for short-term agreements, especially a periodic tenancy, or a tenancy at will or a tenancy at sufferance. However, the words lease and tenancy may be used interchangeably and "the term lease is used in strict law so as to include any demise, for any period however short or however long". – *In re*. Negus (1895) 1 Ch. 78. A lease may be granted by a freeholder or a person who also holds under a lease (a lease-holder); in the latter case, the lease is more commonly called a **sub-lease** or 'under lease', but nonetheless it is a lease – Camberwell and South London Building Society *v* Holloway (1879) 13 Ch. D. 759.

A formal lease, i.e. one made by deed, normally contains the following clauses: (i) the **premises** – the date, details of the parties and the subject matter; (ii) the **habendum** – the term, including the commencement date and the period for which it is fixed to run; (iii) the **redendum** – the rent reserved; (iv) **covenant**(s) – those matters agreed between the parties to the contract, such as the responsibility to repair, insure, pay rates and taxes, etc.; limitations on the tenant's right to assign, sub-let or otherwise part with possession, or to change the use of the demised premises; (v) **exception**(s) or **reservation**(s) – matters excluded or reserved from that which has been demised; (vi) **proviso**(s) and **condition**(s) – other terms imposed under the agreement, including any option on the part of either party to vary the terms of the lease e.g. a rent review clause, or a proviso for re-entry in the event of a breach of a condition of the lease by the tenant. The terms and conditions are the means by which a landowner retains control over his land in order to ensure that, when the land returns to him, it is not unduly diminished in value.

A lease that comes into effect by implication (e.g. by possession and payment of rent), or a lease that is silent as to any contrary intention, will be deemed to include certain **implied covenants**. These covenants may be implied by common law, in order to give proper effect to the intended relationship of **landlord and tenant**; or by statute law in order to ensure that a reasonable balance of responsibility is maintained between the parties.

A lease must transfer effectively an interest in land (prior to 1925 in English Law the lessee was even required to take up possession before the lease became effective, otherwise he had only an *interesse termini*, an 'interest in the term'); mere intent so to do or a simple contract to grant a lease (an **agreement for a lease**) requires further evidence to create a formal lease. Consequently 'lease' frequently is reserved for a document under seal; a less formal document is merely an 'agreement', 'tenancy agreement' or a 'contract of tenancy'. However, "an instrument is usually construed as a lease if it contains the words of present demise. Even where the instrument is called an 'agreement', and contains a stipulation for the subsequent granting of a formal lease, it may be construed as a lease if the essential terms are fixed, especially if possession is taken under it and if the covenants which would be inserted in the lease are to be binding at once ... The essential terms of an agreement for a lease are (1) the identification of the lessor and lessee; (2) the premises to be leased: (3) the commencement and duration of the term; and (4) the rent or other consideration to be paid". (27 Halsbury's Laws of England, 4 edn, pp. 49, 53).

A lease may come to an end or be determined by **expiration** of the term; by becoming a **satisfied term**; by **forfeiture**; by **surrender**; by **merger**; by **disclaimer**; by **enlargement**; by **notice to quit**; by notice exercised in accordance with an express covenant (in particular an **option** to break a lease granted for a term of years); or, rarely, by **frustration**.

A personal right to occupy land of another, with no intent to grant an interest in land (especially when there is no right to exclusive occupation of land, e.g. a right to weekly board and lodging) is a **licence**. However, whether a right to occupy land grants a lease or a licence depends on (a) the intention of the parties; (b) the exclusivity of the occupation; (c) the terms of the agreement and its mode of creation; and (d) such matters as a payment in the nature of rent, any provision for re-entry reserved by the landlord, and any obligation placed on the occupier to repair, insure, pay property taxes, etc.

In the US, in most states, a lease for a term of more than one year must be made in writing and in some states must be made by deed. Nevertheless, as in English law, if the essential requirements of a valid lease are present and there is an act of part performance, even if these formalities are not complied the existence of a tenancy will be recognised by law – Rowland *v* Cook, 179 Wash. 624, 38 P 2d. 224).

In French law a contract for the use or enjoyment of real property (*immeubles*) to the exclusion of others for a duration is a *bail*, which may be divided broadly into (i) a *bail à loyer*, which is a short-term agreement that grants a personal right that cannot be alienated or mortgaged; and (ii) a *bail emphyteotique* (**emphyteotic lease**) or a *bail à construction* which are long-term agreements incorporating obligations on the tenant to make improvements and which grant is a real right, (in English legal terms) a right

that can be alienated or mortgaged. In addition, the *droit de superficie*, which resembles a long-term building lease, is a right to use a building separate from the land for a duration (which may be fixed or indefinite) but in such a way that, although ownership of the land and building is separated, they may come together ultimately as a single right for the landowner. cf. **leasing, usufruct.** See also **building lease, counterpart, determination, flat lease, graded lease, graduated lease, gross lease, ground lease, leasehold interest, net lease, occupation lease, sandwich lease, term of years, usual covenant, use and occupation.**
Introduction to Land Law, by J.G. Riddell, 3 edn., pp. 241–265.
Landlord and Tenant, by Martin Partington, 2 edn., pp. 96–151.
Adkin's Landlord and Tenant, 18 edn, pp. 31–51.
Landlord and Tenant Law, by David Yates and A.J. Hawkins, p. 8 *et seq.* (1981).
The Law of Real Property, by Robert Megarry and H.W.R. Wade, 5 edn., p. 628 *et seq.*
The Law of Landlord and Tenant, by Hill and Redman, 17 edn., pp. 129–195.
Woodfall's Landlord and Tenant, 28 edn, paras. 1–10437 to 1–0599.

lease/lease-back financing

A form of **sale and lease-back** transaction, used to finance a real estate development project, by which the developer retains the freehold and acts as landlord to the occupational tenants, but provides a financial institution or lender with a long-term **sandwich lease** of the completed development as security for the funds

advanced. The transaction is contained in three documents: (1) a finance agreement, entered into before the development work commences, which provides that (a) the freeholder/developer will carry out a specified form of development of a site; (b) the lender will agree to provide funds for the development – this may exclude the cost of the site, which is acquired and paid for normally by the developer; (c) the developer will lease the completed development to the lender and will accept a simultaneous sub-lease back from the institution, for the same period (less a few days); and (d) the developer will agree to grant sub-underleases (occupational leases) of the completed development at open market rents: (2) a long-term (generally 99 or 125 year) head-lease of the completed development granted to the lender at a nominal rent: (3) a sub-lease back to the developer for the same term as the head-lease (less a few days) at a **finance rent**. (The finance rent is calculated to provide the lender with a satisfactory return on the total funds advanced and commonly **equity participation** in the net income received from the completed development). As an alternative the developer may carry out the development, using interim finance provided by the lender. When the development is fully let, the developer leases it to the lender at a nominal rent, and then takes a lease-back at a finance rent geared to the full occupational rent. The parties' share of the occupational rent is geared so as to provide a return to each party commensurate with their respective risk/return expectancies.

A further alternative is that commonly employed by a landowner, such as a local authority, who does not wish to be directly involved in the development process but wished to grant the occupational lease and retain control of the completed development. The landowner grants a lease of the site to the developer. The developer carries out an agreed scheme and leases it back to the landowner. The developer receives an agreed return or fee for his involvement (which may be a single premium or a rent geared to the rents received from the occupational tenants), but the landowner grants the occupational leases.

This form of transaction is used, for example, when a developer is not prepared, or is unable (as with a public authority), to part with the freehold or at times when there are restrictions on the granting of mortgage loans. Called also a 'reverse lease-back' or 'sandwich lease-back'. See also **side-by-side participation**.
Valuation and Development Appraisal, edited by Clive Darlow, pp. 45–47 (1983).

lease insurance
see **tenant's default insurance**.

lease option
see **option to purchase**.

lease-purchase (US)
see **rental purchase, sale and lease-back**.

leaseback
see **sale and lease-back, lease/lease-back financing**.

leased fee estate (US)
A **fee estate** that has been granted to another on lease, i.e. the interest of a landlord who holds a fee interest. A leased fee estate represents a right to receive rent for the term of a lease together with a fee estate in reversion. (i.e. together with the right to regain possession at the end of the lease).
cf. **leasehold estate**. See also **leaseholder's interest**.

leased premises
Premises that form the subject matter of a lease. Called also 'demised premises'. See also **demise**.

leasehold
The right to land held by virtue of a lease; a lessee's interest in land. An interest in land held from another for a defined duration, subject to the payment of rent.
cf. **freehold**. See also **absolute leasehold, good leasehold, leasehold interest, possessory leasehold**.

leasehold condominium
see **condominium**.

leasehold enfranchisement
The purchase of the freehold interest in a property by the holder of a long lease of that property (or a lease that was granted originally for a long term, generally as a **ground lease**), subject to the payment by the leaseholder of recompense for the loss by the freeholder of his right to rent from the property. The Leasehold Reform Act, 1967 (as amended by the Leasehold Reform Act 1979 and the Housing Act 1980, s. 141, Sch. 21) permits the tenant of a **house**, originally let for a term of 21 years certain or more, i.e. on a **long tenancy**, at a **low rent** (defined as one which is no higher than two-thirds of the rateable value), to acquire the superior freehold at a price determined by the Act (a price that is based on the market value of the land, but disregarding the value of the buildings thereon; 1967 Act, s. 9,

as amended by Housing Act 1969, s. 82). The house must have been occupied (in whole or in part) as the tenant's residence for the last three years, or periods amounting to three years in the last ten. The house must have a rateable value below limits set by the 1967 Act, s. 1, as amended by the Housing Act 1974, s. 118. Certain public bodies are exempt from this provision; as are houses included in an approved **management scheme**. (This type of leasehold enfranchisement is referred to sometimes as 'leasehold reform' because the 1967 Act was passed to reform the long-term ground lease system peculiar to English law: this reform is based on the principle that under a ground lease, "the land belongs in equity to the landowner and the house to the occupying leaseholder" – White Paper on Leasehold Reform (1966, Cmnd. 2916), para. 4.)

The Law of Property Act 1925, s. 153 also makes provision for the enlargement of a long lease (originally one granted for 300 years, with at least 200 years unexpired) into a freehold. However, this provision is rarely applied.

In several states in the US a long-term ground lease, although technically creating a relationship of landlord and tenant, is regarded as a transfer of the land to the tenant, subject to the payment of the annual rent; a relationship, more akin to a mortgage, which continues provided there is no default in paying the rent. In the event of a default the owner must obtain a judgement for the debt. Long term ground leases created since 1900 are redeemable by the tenant paying the landlord the value of his interest, thus redeeming the rent and becoming the owner of the freehold. See also **enfranchisement, extended lease, Leasehold Valuation Tribunal**.

Leasehold Enfranchisement – A Review, by C. Charles Hubbard, 256 E.G. pp. 809–813, 908–911 (1980).
Rent Control and Leasehold Enfranchisement, by T. Aldridge, 8 edn., Ch. 17, 18.
Leasehold Enfranchisement, by N.T. Hague, (1967).
27 Halsbury's Laws of England, 4 edn, paras. 1001–1120.
Woodfall's Landlord and Tenant, 28 edn, paras. 3–0950 to 3–1097.

leasehold estate (US)

An **estate** held by a lessee or tenant; the right to use and occupy real estate for the term of a lease, subject to the terms and conditions of that lease and subject to the payment of rent. In English law called usually a **leasehold interest**.

cf. **leased fee estate**. See also **legal estate**.

leasehold ground rent

A **ground rent** receivable by a person who holds a leasehold interest, as distinguished from a ground rent receivable by a freeholder. Anyone who is granted a ground lease may, in turn, sub-let the demised land to another and, as a rule, the sub-lease is granted at a higher rent than is payable to the superior landlord. Thus, a leasehold ground rent that is higher than the rent payable to the superior landlord is called sometimes an 'improved ground rent' (although the latter term is used more commonly to refer to the difference between the rent of bare land and land with improvements thereon).

leasehold improvement

An **improvement** made to leasehold

property by the lessee, especially an improvement that increases the value of the landlord's reversion. See also **compensation for improvements, fixture, Landlord and Tenant Acts, tenant's improvement**.

leasehold insurance

Insurance provided to cover a leaseholder against a loss of the use of the demised premises, e.g. the loss of rent receivable from a sub-tenant in the event that the premises are destroyed by fire. See also **improvements and betterments insurance, loss of rent insurance**.

leasehold interest

A right to **possession** of land for a term of years as granted by a **lease**. An interest in land, that is less than a **freehold**, and is a right to the **exclusive occupation** of land for a defined (or definable) period of time, held subject to the payment of **rent**. Usually a 'leasehold interest' means a **tenancy** granted for a fixed duration; but any form of tenancy may be referred to as a leasehold interest (including a tenancy at will or a tenancy at sufferance). A leasehold interest, unless there is evidence to the contrary, is an interest held directly from a freeholder, and not an interest held by virtue of an underlease – Re Russ and Brown's contract [1939] Ch. 34; although an interest held by an underlease is commonly referred to as a leasehold interest. In English common law a leasehold interest is referred to as a 'chattel real', because strictly it is a personal right to real property and is considered as coming within the laws relating to personal property. "The tendency, however, for several centuries has been to bring freeholds into conformity with chat-

tels real, and the process of assimilation has been carried to such lengths, especially by the legislation of 1925, that we now have substantially a common and uniform system for real property and chattels real. But ... in spite of this assimilation, leaseholds today still remain personal as opposed to **real property**." (Cheshire's Modern Law of Real Property, 13 edn, p. 37). However, in most states in the US the assimilation is more complete and a leasehold interest is considered as real estate and referred to normally as a **leasehold estate**.

A leasehold interest may be created by contract; by statute (as a **statutory tenancy**); or may arise by estoppel (as a **tenancy by estoppel**). It may be bought or sold, morgaged or charged, held for the purpose of use and occupation of the leased property, or in turn made the subject of a lease for the purpose of investment – subject only to the conditions set out in the lease by which it is created. See also **estate, landlord and tenant, term of years absolute**.

leasehold mortgage

A mortgage secured on a **leasehold interest**. Generally the mortgagee's position is subordinate to the lessor, i.e. if the mortgagee exercises a power of sale or forecloses he sells or takes only the lessee's interest.

leasehold reform

see **leasehold enfranchisement**.

leasehold title

see **absolute title, good leasehold title, possessory title**.

Leasehold Valuation Tribunal (LVT)

A tribunal established to determine values on **leasehold enfranchisement**, the rent on the grant of an **extended** lease, or related matters under the Leasehold Reform Act 1967. (Leasehold Reform Act 1967, s. 21, as amended by the Housing Act 1980, s. 142, Sch. 22). The Leasehold Valuation Tribunal is made up of members drawn from the same panel as members of the **rent assessment committee**. Prior to 1980 this function was performed by the **Lands Tribunal**. There is a right of appeal from a decision of the Leasehold Valuation Tribunal to the Lands Tribunal.

leasehold value

The value of a **leasehold interest**; the capital value of a **profit rent** receivable by a lessee: i.e. the capital value of the difference between (a) the rent contractually payable by the lessee and (b) the rent either being received by the lessee under his existing sub-lease(s) or the market rent obtainable. (This may be negative if the lessee is paying in excess of the market rent; then, as a rule, the leasehold interest may be sold only at a 'reverse premium', i.e. the lessee pays the purchaser to accept an assignment of his lease.) A leasehold interest is a wasting asset and should be valued by using a **dual-rate capitalisation factor**, i.e. a factor that provides for a 'sinking fund rate' to cover the cost of replacing the lease at the end of its term in addition to a 'remunerative rate' to provide a return on the capital value.

leaseholder

A **lessee**; one who is entitled to an interest in land in accordance with the terms of a lease. One who has the benefit of a **leasehold interest**.

lease-holder's interest (US)

The interest of a person who has leased his property to another, i.e. the interest of a **lessor** (who may be a freeholder, or a person who has a leasehold interest and, in turn, grants a lease). A lease-holder's interest is basically a right to receive a contractual rent, as specified in a lease, together with a reversionary interest at the end of that lease. 'Lease-holder's interest' is not a legally recognised term, but may be used to distinguish it from the interest held by a person who has been granted a lease – a **leasehold interest**. Called also a **leased fee estate** when the grantor of the interest holds a fee interest.

leasing

1. The grant of a **lease** of property, i.e. the creation of a right of tenancy.
2. The hiring of an asset, usually for its economic life, generally with a right for the hirer to acquire the asset at the end of the leasing period. "A lease is a contract between a lessor and lessee for the hire of a specific asset selected from a manufacturer or vendor of such assets by the lessee. The lessor retains ownership of the asset. The lessee has possession and use of the asset on payment of specified rentals over a period" (Equipment Leasing Association). In English law, such a contract is a form of **bailment**, as distinguished from a lease which creates an interest in property for an ascertainable period of time. An arrangement commonly used by companies to finance the cost of major assets – the asset is acquired by a finance company and let to the user, generally at a finance rent. See also *credit-bail*, **finance lease, operating lease**.

Leasing – The Accounting and Taxation Implications, by David Wain-

man and Howard Brown, 2 edn.
Leasing, by T.M. Clarke (1978).
Finance Leasing, by Graham Hubbard (1980).

leasing (F)
leasing, especially of personal property. See also *crédit-bail*.

legacy
Personal property left as a gift under a **will**. In its strict sense legacy is applied to money, a monetary annuity, goods, or any other personal estate, but in an extensive sense it may be understood "to comprehend any kind of estate, real as well as personal, left by the testator's will to any person". – Beckley *v* Newland (1723) 2 P Wms. 186. See also **devise**.

legal assignment
1. An **assignment** of a legal estate made by **deed** (Law of Property Act 1925, s. 52 (1)).
cf. **equitable assignment**. See also **legal lease**.
2. An assignment that is made in accordance with statute law. A legal assignment of any debt or other legal choses-in-action must be made in **writing**; made as an **absolute assignment** (not purporting to be by way of charge only); and coupled with an express notice to the debtor, trustee or any other person against whom the assignor might have had a right of action (Law of Property Act 1925, s. 136). Called also a 'statutory assignment'. See also **novation**.

legal charge
see 'charge by way of a legal mortgage', mortgage, rentcharge.
cf. **equitable charge**.

legal chose-in-action
see **chose**.

legal easement
An **easement** that is capable of being created or subsisting as a **legal interest**. A legal easement may be created or may subsist only if it is (a) held "in or over land for an interest equivalent to an estate in fee simple absolute in possession or a term of years absolute" (Law of Property Act 1925, s. 1 (2) (a)) – that is, the servient tenement must be held as a **legal estate**); and (b) created by statute, deed or prescription, in any of which three instances the easement is created by a formalised agreement, either an agreement that is visibly expressed or is presumed by law to have been so expressed. A legal easement, as distinguished from an **equitable easement**, is enforceable against any party who acquires a right to the servient land, in fact against the 'whole world', irrespective of whether that party had notice of the easement; it need not, and cannot, be registered; and, unless expressly excluded, it passes automatically upon a conveyance of the dominant land (Law of Property Act 1925, s. 62). See also **implied grant**, **overriding interest**.

legal estate
An **estate** that is capable of subsisting or being conveyed or created 'at law', as distinguished from an estate that is recognised only 'in equity'. An estate in land that is recognised in English common law as a right to retain possession and ownership of land, rather than an estate that is considered capable of being converted to monetary consideration without detriment to the holder. The Law of Property Act 1925, s. 1 (1) enacted that the only legal estates that can subsist, be conveyed, or be created are an estate in

'fee simple absolute in possession' and a 'term of years absolute'. Any other interest in land is a **legal interest** or an **equitable interest**. A legal estate is one protected by law as 'good against the whole world', i.e. any person who acquires the land that is the subject-matter of the legal estate; unlike an equitable interest which may not be binding against a *bona fide* **purchaser** for valuable consideration and, therefore, may be converted compulsorily into a monetary consideration. The holder of a fee simple absolute in possession who grants a lease remains the holder of a legal estate because the right to receive rent and profits, if any, is considered to be a right to **possession** (1925 Act, s. 205 (1) (xix)). Similarly, if the holder of a term of years absolute grants a sub-lease he remains the owner of a legal estate. Accordingly a number of legal estates may exist concurrently in the same piece of land. If A is the holder of a fee simple absolute in possession of Blackacre and he grants a lease for a term of years absolute to B who in turn grants a sub-lease for a term of years to C and A grants a 'charge by way of a legal mortgage' to D, then A, B & C have legal estates in Blackacre, and D has a legal interest.

A legal estate cannot be created or subsist as an undivided share in land i.e. as a tenancy-in-common, nor can it be held by an infant (1925 Act, s. 1 (6)); in both instances the right to the land is held in trust, the trustee holding the legal estate and the tenant-in-common or infant a beneficial equitable interest. (Note: for the purpose of the Law of Property Act 1925 those interest or charges which 'are authorised to subsist or to be conveyed or created at law', and generally are referred to as 'legal interests' are referred to as 'legal estates' in the Act: 1925 Act, s. 1 (4)). See also **legal lease**, **writing**.
Megarry's Manual of the Law of Real Property, 6 edn, pp. 84–90.
The Law of Real Estate, by Robert Megarry and H.W.R. Wade, 5 edn., pp. 123–130.
Land Law: Cases and Materials, by Maudsley and Burns, 4 edn., pp. 3–13.

legal interest
1. An interest in land that is enforceable at law, as contrasted with an **equitable interest**; i.e. an interest that binds anyone who acquires the land that is the subject of the legal interest (unless it is a registrable interest that has not been registered and, therefore, does not bind a purchaser of the land who pays valuable consideration). By the Law of Property Act 1925, s. 1 (2) the only legal interests or charges 'in or over land which are capable of subsisting or of being conveyed or created at law are:
(a) An easement, right, or privilege in or over land for an interest equivalent to an estate in fee simple absolute in possession or a term of years absolute;
(b) A **rentcharge** in possession issuing out of or charged on land being either perpetual or for a term of years absolute;
(c) A charge by way of legal mortgage;
(d) Land tax, tithe rentcharge [both these interests are now extinct and these four words have been repealed], and any other similar charge on land which is not created by an instrument;
(e) Rights of entry exercisable over or in respect of a legal term of years

absolute, or annexed, for any purpose, to a legal rent charge'.

(The interest under sub-section (e) does not include a right of re-entry reserved by an assignor of a lease, unlike the same right if it is reserved on the grant of a lease – Shiloh Spinners *v* Harding [1973] A.C. 691. (In the 1925 Act any **legal estate**, legal interest, or **legal charge** is referred to as a 'legal estate' and the owner of any such interest as an **estate owner** (Law of Property Act 1925, s. 1 (4). However, it is not uncommon to refer to the interests in sub-section 1 (2) as legal interests; and to reserve the term 'legal estate' for those interests referred to in sub-section 1 (1) of the Act). These interests *can* be legal interest, but they must be created by the proper formalities to be enforceable 'at law', usually by **deed**. See also **doctrine of estates, legal easement, legal mortgage**.

Introduction to Land Law, by J.G. Riddell, 3 edn., pp. 90–93.

2. The highest rate of **interest** that may be charged by law – a term more applicable in the US than the UK where some states stipulate a maximum rate of interest that may be charged on loans to individuals. See also **annual percentage rate, usury**.

legal lease

A lease that may be created or transferred at law, because either (a) it is a **term of years absolute** (which may be a lease for a month or 1000 years) and is made by **deed**; or (b) it is a lease "taking effect in **possession** [i.e. not in the future] for a term not exceeding three years (whether or not the lessee is given power to extend the term) at the **best rent** which can be reasonably obtained without taking a **fine**" – in

the latter case the lease will be a legal lease whether created in writing or orally (Law of Property Act 1925, ss. 1, 52 (1), 54 (2)). A legal lease may be distinguished from an **equitable lease** which is deficient in one or more of the formalities required by the Law of Property Act 1925, and, therefore, is enforceable only in equity. A legal lease no matter how short, can be assigned at law only by deed (1925 Act, s. 52 (1)). See also **agreement for a lease**.

Megarry's Manual of the Law of Real Property, 6 edn, pp. 335–336.

legal lien

see **lien**.

legal memory

see **lost modern grant, prescription**.

legal mortgage

A **mortgage** that is "capable of being effected at law" because it is made in accordance with statute. A legal mortgage may be created in two ways: (i) a lease (or sub-lease) for a **term of years absolute**, with a provision that the lease ceases when the mortgage loan is repaid in full (called a 'provision for cesser on **redemption**'); or (ii) a **charge by way of a legal mortgage** (Law of Property Act 1925, ss. 85, 86). A legal mortgage must be made by **deed** (Law of Property Act 1925, s. 52 (1)). A mortgage made in any other form can only create an **equitable mortgage**.

Before 1925 a legal mortgage was created by a conveyance of a fee simple estate to the mortgagee, with a provision that when the mortgage loan was repaid the estate was reconveyed to the mortgagor. The Law of Property Act 1925 removed this means of creating mortgages, and a first mortgage that purports to transfer a fee simple estate grants only a lease for 3000 years to the mortgagee, with a provision for cesser on redemption. A second or subsequent mortgage created in the same way takes effect as a grant of a lease for a term of years one day longer than the preceeding term (1925 Act, s. 85 (2)). A legal mortgage, of a freehold or a leasehold property, may be created by means of a lease for a shorter period, provided it is for a term of years absolute. Alternatively, and more usually, a mortgagee may adopt the simpler procedure of accepting a 'charge by way of a legal mortgage' (usually called a **legal charge**) which has a similar effect, but is made by means of a deed which stipulates simply that a legal mortgage is intended to be created but does not grant a formal lease to the mortgagee. A first mortgagee entitled to a legal mortgage must have the same right to retain possession of documents relating to the mortgaged property as if he had a fee simple estate. It is possible for any number of legal mortgages to subsist against the same property, each mortgagee having a term of years (or a right to a term of years) for a period at least one day longer than the superior mortgagee. See also **charge**.

legal notice

A **notice** prescribed by law as distinguished from one prescribed by contract – Friend *v* Shaw (1887) 20 QBD 374. A term that also may be used as a synonym for **constructive notice**. See also **notice to quit**.

legal owner

One who has a **legal estate** as distinguished from the holder of an equitable interest. (As the holder of a legal estate and the holder of an equitable estate may both be referred to as the owner in English law it is more usual to describe the former as the 'holder of the legal estate'.)
cf. **beneficial owner**. See also **estate owner**.

legal rate of interest
see **legal interest**.

legal representative
A term sometimes used for a **personal representative**. An executor or administrator.

legal right of redemption
see **equity of redemption**.

legal tender
Any form of **money** to which in law a creditor may not take exception if it is tendered in settlement of a debt. In England and Wales legal tender includes coins of the Realm up to amounts specified by statute (Coinage Act 1971, s. 2; Currency Act 1983, s. 1) and notes of the Bank of England up to any amount – provided such currency has not been called in (Bank Notes Act 1954, s. 1). (Scottish bank notes are not legal tender in England and Bank of England notes over £5 are not legal tender in Scotland.) See also **cash, tender**.

legal title
1. A title held by way of a **legal estate**. cf. **equitable title**. See also **absolute title, good title**.
(US) 2. A claim to property based on **possession** of the title deeds. See also **lien**.

legataire (F)
legatee; **heir**, under a testamentary succession.
cf. *héritier*.

legatee

A person in whose favour a **legacy** is made. See also **heir**.

legislation

The process of making written law. See also **statute law**.

legs (F)

legacy.

lender participation

see **convertible mortgage**, **equity participation**.

leonin (F)

unconscionable. See also *contrat*.

lessee

1. One who holds an interest in land as created by a **lease**; the holder of a leasehold interest – a 'leaseholder'. Strictly, a person who holds such an interest directly from the freeholder (to whom the term applies if nothing is expressed to the contrary), but 'lessee' may be used when referring to a sub-lessee, under-lessee or an assignee of a lease (Law of Property Act 1925, s. 205 (1)). Lessee is the correct term in English law for a party to a lease, especially the original party; however, in general usage, **tenant** is used more frequently when the right to hold the land is for a short term. In the case of a **restricted contract** the person who is granted the right to occupy a dwelling as a residence by virtue of such a contract, or anyone deriving title from that occupier, may be referred to as a lessee (Rent Act 1977, s. 85 (1)).
2. A **bailee**.

lessor

1. An owner of real property who grants a lease to another. Strictly, in English law the possessor of a freehold interest who creates a lease.

However, a 'lessor' may himself hold an interest under a lease i.e. he may be an "underlessor and a person deriving title under a lessor or underlessor" (Law of Property Act 1925, s. 205 (xxiii). Lessor is the correct term of English law, especially when referring to the original parties to a lease, but **landlord** is more commonly used for any party who receives rent from land or buildings. In the case of a **restricted contract** any person who grants another a right to occupy a dwelling as a residence by virtue of such a contract, or anyone deriving title from the grantor, may be called a lessor (Rent Act 1977, s. 85 (1)).
2. A **bailor**.

let

1. A grant of any interest in land, including the grant of a lease, sub-lease, licence or easement. Normally 'let' connotes the relationship of **landlord and tenant** – one who occupies premises as a bare licencee is not strictly let into possession of the premises. In English law the use of 'let' in a lease does not create any implied covenant, but it may be assumed that the lessor will grant **quiet enjoyment** – Jones *v* Lagington [1903] 1 KB 253. In the US the use of the word 'let' creates the same implied covenants in a lease as the word **demise**. – Trible *v* Seattle, 231 US 683, 34 S. Ct. 218, 58 L Ed. 435.
2. To permit another to use and enjoy property. See also **leasing**.
3. The award of a construction or building contract.

lettable area

see **net lettable area**.

letter of attorney

see **power of attorney**.

letter of comfort

A written instrument issued by one party to another whereby the former undertakes to use his best endeavours to insure that a third party fulfills his obligations to the latter, but without there being any contractual or other form of legal commitment. Commonly issued by a parent company to assist a subsidiary in obtaining a loan.

letter of credit (LC)

1. A letter addressed by a banker or other lender (the issuer) to a third party (the beneficiary) confirming that credit will be provided to a specified customer up to a given limit, or addressed to another bank authorising that bank to honour cheques drawn in favour of the customer up to a specified sum. Any advance or payment made against the letter of credit is met by the issuer of the letter and, in turn, the bank debits the customer's account.
2. A letter from a bank, issued at a customer's request, by which it is agreed that the bank will extend credit to a third party. The letter enables the recipient to obtain credit from an associated bank, usually in a foreign country. A letter of credit may be issued also to provide a mortgagee with additional security so that it acts as an indemnity for the customer/mortgagor's obligation.

letter of exchange

see **bill of exchange**.

letter of intent

A letter or **memorandum** confirming an intention to enter into a **bargain**, without creating any legally binding contract. See also **conditional contract**, '**subject to contract**', **tender**.

letting scheme

A **scheme of development** incorporated into a long-term lease.

letting value

1. See **rental value**.
2. The maximum rent that legally may be demanded under the Rent Acts. See also **fair rent**, **rent limit**.

lettre (F)

letter.
(*lettre de change* – **bill of exchange**)
(*lettre de gage* – **charge**; **bond**).

levant et couchant

Law French for 'raising up and lying down'. A trespass by cattle that arises after a period during which they have lain down on land and risen up again; generally a day and a night. A **right of common** to *levant et couchant* is a right to place such numbers of cattle for the winter as the land reasonably will take for pasturage.

level rental (US)

see **flat rent**.

lever (levée) (F)

to raise; to lift; to remove.
(*levée d'une saisie* – **replevin**)
(*lever une option* – to lift or exercise an option).
(*lever un plan* – to make a survey, in order to produce a plan).

leverage

Literally 'the action of levering or raising up'. The use of borrowed money, **debt capital**, in order to increase the total amount invested in a property. The purpose of leverage is to use debt capital, in addition to **equity capital** (that provided by the owner), so as to produce a 'gearing effect' on the equity invested. Thus leverage is referred to sometimes as 'trading on the equity' or colloquially 'using other people's money'. The higher the ratio of debt to equity, the higher the leverage on the investment. A term that has a similar meaning to **gearing**, but in the US 'leverage' is the more common term.

When the annual cost of servicing the debt (repaying interest and principal) is less than the **free and clear return** from the property the result is called 'upside' or 'positive leverage'. The reverse is called 'downside', 'negative' or 'reverse leverage'. See also **financial leverage, financing, operating leverage, positive leverage, reverse leverage, tax shelter.**

Real Estate Investment Decision Making, by Austin J. Jaffe and C.F. Sirmans, pp. 232–9 (1982).

Basic Real Estate Financing and Investment, by Epley and Millar, Ch. 20 (1980).

leverage ratio
see **debt ratio.**

leveraged buy-out
The purchase of a business mainly with borrowed money secured on the assets of the business. A type of acquisition that makes the business highly leveraged, so that the purchaser hopes to make an above-average return on his equity holding. A leveraged buy-out is commonly carried out by the management of the business – it is then called a 'management buy-out'. See also **convertible mortgage, leverage.**

leveraged investment
A property investment acquired with the use of borrowed money. See also **leverage.**

leveraged refinancing (US)
see **wraparound mortgage.**

levier (effet de) (F)
leverage.

levy
1. To raise or exact a sum of money by legal process or authority. Money collected as a **tax, assessment** or **duty.**
2. To seize in satisfaction of a legal claim; to place an attachment on real or personal property. See also **distress, seizure.**

lex loci (L)
'The law of the place'. Real property is subject to the law of the area or country in which it is situated – *lex loci situs* – but personal property is subject to the law of the place where a transaction is made; unless the parties expressly elect for a different system of law or the courts can infer their intention to adopt a different system taking into account all the circumstances.

lex loci actus or ***lex loci contractus*** (L)
'The law of a place where a contract is made or performed'. See *lex loci.*

lex loci rei sitae or ***lex loci situs*** (L)
'The law of the place where the property is situated'. See ***lex loci.***

lex non cogit ad impossibilia (L)
'The law does not compel the impossible'.

lex non scripta (L)
'The unwritten law', i.e. **common law.** cf. ***lex scripta.***

lex rei situs (L)
'The law of the situation of the thing'. See also ***lex loci.***

lex scripta (L)
'The written law', i.e. **statue law.** cf. ***lex non scripta.***

lex terrae (L)
'The law of the land'.

liability

1. A pecuniary **obligation**; any form of **debt** or obligation, especially something owed by one person to another. 'Liability' has been defined to include, "(a) any compensation for work or labour done; (b) any obligation or possibility of an obligation to pay money or money's worth on the breach of any express or implied covenant, contract, agreement, or undertaking, whether the breach does or does not occur, or is or is not likely to occur or capable of occuring, before the discharge of the debtor; (c) generally any express or implied engagement, agreement, or undertaking, to pay, or capable of resulting in the payment of, money or money's worth; whether the payment is, as respects amount, fixed or unliquidated; as respects time, present or future, certain or dependent on any one contingency or on two or more contingencies; as to mode of valuation, capable of being ascertained by fixed rules or as matter of opinion" (Bankruptcy Act 1914, s. 30 (8)).
cf. **asset**. See also **contingent liability**, **joint and several liability**, **surety**.
2. An obligation to do, or refrain from doing, something for which one would be answerable in law. The state of being required to do something by law. A person who enters into a **contract** is liable to fulfil the obligation undertaken or promise given, or to pay a sum due, or to otherwise complete his part of the contract. See also **duty of care, encumberance, strict liability**.

liability insurance
Insurance protection taken out to indemnify someone against claims for damage or injury to third parties, whether arising from a breach of contract or tort. Insurance against a liability to pay compensation, to make restitution, or to reimburse money or money's worth to a third party, e.g. to protect an employer against injury sustained by an employee, or against injury or damage caused to another's property. Liability insurance frequently arises in connection with property; also the event which gives rise to the damage or injury may cause a loss of property. Called sometimes 'hazard insurance'.
cf. **indemnity insurance**.

liability, secondary
see **contingent liability**.

libératoire (F)
(*monnaie libératoire* – **legal tender**)
(*paiement libératoire* – final payment).

libre (F)
free.
(*libre d'hypothèque* – free of mortgage debt; **unencumbered**)
(*libre d'occupation* – **unoccupied**).
(*libre possession* – **vacant possession**. See also *jouissance*. note: The words *en jouissance* in French law create a closer equivalent to **possession** as used in English law.
(*terre libre* – **allodium**).

licence (or license)
1. Permission to do something that, if not properly authorised, would be illegal. A right or dispensation granted to one party (licensee) permitting an activity to be engaged in that otherwise would be a breach of the law; or would infringe a monopoly position that has been established by another (in particular as established by the State – although, in

that case, it is usually referred to as a **privilege** or **franchise**). For example, a licence may be granted to permit a person, and that person alone, to sell alcohol; to operate a market; or to exercise a particular business or profession. It is a right that dies with the person to whom it is given. A licence may be required to carry out an activity, or perform a duty, that otherwise is prohibited by statute law, e.g. to carry out building work that is controlled by the **building regulations**. See also **building permit, planning permission, real estate licence**.

2. A personal and non-assignable consent, given by an owner or occupier of land, authorising or permitting another to be or to do some act on land that would otherwise be prohibited or unlawful; authorisation given to an action that would otherwise be a **trespass**. In particular, a dispensation or permission given in such a form that it passes no estate, nor alters or transfers any interest in property, but authorises one party (a **licensee**) lawfully to enter and stay on the premises belonging to another (a licensor) – Thomas *v* Sorrell (1673) Vaughan 351; permission that does not grant any "interest in land" – Pennine Raceway *v* Kirklees Metropolitan Council (1982) 263 EG 721 – although the recipient may well be interested in the subject land.

A licence is given to one or more specified persons as a personal right and, therefore, that right may not be assigned nor in any way transferred to another. It may be revoked at the will of the landowner (unless he is constrained by an agreement to the contrary, or the right has been combined with an interest in land, and thereby creates an **incorporeal hereditament**).

A licence to occupy land, being a personal arrangement, ceases upon the death of either party. A licence may be granted orally or in writing.

A licence may be distinguished from a **lease** as the latter grants an interest in land and always grants a right to **exclusive occupation** (although the grant of a right to exclusive occupation does not always mean that a lease has been granted). A lease creates a proprietary right, a right that may be enforced against a purchaser of the subject land: a licence, as such, does not bind a purchaser – it is purely coincidental that the subject matter is land. In order to decide whether an agreement for the occupation of land is a lease or a licence it is necessary to look at (a) the intention of both the parties (and not just such wording as is used in the agreement – Street *v* Mountford (1984) 271 EG 1261); (b) the mode of creation and the terms of the agreement (whether there is a payment of **rent** or other obligation imposed on an occupier that is more in keeping with a tenancy); and (c) "the nature and quality of the occupancy" – Marchant *v* Chartes [1977] 1 WLR 1185. "A person who is let into exclusive possession, is, *prima facie*, to be considered a tenant, nevertheless he will not be held to be so if the circumstances negative any intention to create a tenancy. Words alone cannot suffice. Parties cannot turn a tenancy into a licence merely by calling it one. If circumstances and the conduct of the parties show that all that was intended was that the occupier should be granted a personal privilege with no interest in the land, he will be held only to be a licensee." – Errington *v* Errington [1952] 1 All ER 155. Factors that mitigate in favour of a lease include the use of the word rent (or a payment that resembles rent); an arrangement that cannot readily be revoked; obligations on the occupier to carry out repairs; express prohibitions against sub-letting or altering the premises; covenants for quiet enjoyment; and provision of a rent book. On the other hand factors mitigating in favour of a licence include payment of a daily charge or a grant of land for a very short duration; absence of any express provision as to notice to vacate the premises or an arrangement for an indefinite period of time; and sharing premises with the landlord. A mere stipulation in a document that it does not create a lease or tenancy, or that it does not grant exclusive possession, is not sufficient to insure the creation of a licence. It is necessary to look at the whole document to decide whether the obligations of a Landlord or a tenant are intended (Addiscombe Garden Estates Ltd. v Crabbe [1958] 1 QB 513). Thus, "it has been said before, and it must be said again, that in the consideration of questions arising under the Rent Acts the court must look at the substance and the reality of the transaction, not its form" – Elmdene Estates Ltd v White [1960] AC 538. Similarly, the use of words such as 'let', 'lessor' etc. do not create a lease if the clear intention is to create a licence – Taylor v Caldwell (1863) 3 B and S 826.

A licence may be distinguished from an **easement** because the latter creates an interest in land, and it requires that the interest it creates benefits another parcel of land.

The permission may be given as: (a) a 'bare (or mere) licence' – without seal or valuable consideration – i.e. the person's presence on land is merely tolerated and, because there is no contractual obligation established thereby, it may be revoked at the will of the grantor; (b) a 'contractual licence', where there is a contract under seal or consideration, which may be revoked in accordance with the terms, express or implied, of the contract; or (c) a 'licence coupled with an interest' in land, such as consent given to a person with an interest in land (e.g. a tenant) to cut and remove timber or to extract minerals, which is stated to be revokable only when the interest has been terminated.

A licence, being strictly a personal agreement, is not binding on another purchaser of the land because there is no **privity of estate**. However, a contractual licence may be considered to create an equitable right to use land (an 'equitable licence') and, therefore, may be binding on a purchaser who has actual or constructive **notice** of the licence – especially when no steps have been taken to revoke the licence – Binions v Evans [1972] Ch. 359. The occupation of a room in an hotel, guest house or lodging house is usually a mere licence, but when the occupant is permitted to use his room as he wishes for a set period of time and to exclude the proprietor's 'dominion', as with a serviced flat, it is likely that a tenancy has been created. The term 'licence' may be used to refer also to the document which creates a licence. See also **agricultural licence, bare licence, grazing licence, implied term, licence by estoppel, lodger, mining lease, protected occupier, service tenancy, site licence**.
Real Estate Law, by William E. Burby, 3 edn., pp. 94–96.

The Use of Licences, by D.W. Williams, 274 EG pp. 787–796 (1985).

Law for Land Management Students, by Richard Card, John Murdoch and Peter Schofield, pp. 538–547 (1981).

Adkin's Landlord & Tenant, 18 edn, pp. 32–34.

Introduction to Land Law, by J.G. Riddell, 3 edn, pp. 306–320.

Megarry's Manual of the Law of Real Property, 6 edn, pp. 370–376.

Cheshire's Modern Law of Real Property, 13 edn, pp. 553–570.

Housing Law, by Andrew Arden and Martin Partington, pp. 48–62, 74–78 (1983).

Landlord and Tenant Law, by David Yates and A.J. Hawkins, pp. 8–32 (1981).

27 Halsbury's Laws of England, 4 edn, paras. 6–15.

Hill & Redman's Landlord and Tenant Law, 17 edn, pp. 14–33.

Landlord and Tenant, by Martin Partington, 2 edn., pp. 97–151.

The Law of Real Property, by Robert Megarry and H.W.R. Wade, 5 edn., pp. 798–812.

Licences Relating to the Occupation and Use of Land, by J. Dawson and R.A. Pearce, (1979).

licence (F)
licence.
(*droit de licence de fabrication* – **royalty**).

licence by estoppel
A licence or, strictly, a form of proprietory **estoppel** that comes into existence when a licensee has taken action, particularly involving the expenditure of money, with the consent, encouragement or acquiescence of a landowner and, as a result, has been led to believe that he may continue to exercise a privilege he has so gained. The licensor "cannot revoke the licence so as to defeat the period or purpose for which it was granted. A court of equity will restrain him from so doing. Not only will it restrain him, but it will restrain any successor in title who takes the land with knowledge or **notice** of the arrangement that has been made". – National Provincial Bank Ltd., *v* Hastings Car Mart Ltd., [1964] Ch. 686. This situation may arise when a person is permitted to build on land with the understanding that he will be permitted to reside in the premises he constructs; or when a person builds on land and encroaches on to his neighbour's land, but is given to understand by his neighbour that one wall of the building had been placed on the boundary line – Hopgood *v* Brown [1955] 1 All ER 550. Called also a 'licence coupled with an equity'.

Real Property and Real People, by K.J. Gray and P.D. Symes, pp. 484–487 (1981).

licence coupled with an interest
see **licence**.

licence coupled with an equity
see **licence by estoppel**.

licence, real estate (US)
see **real estate licence**.

licence to assign
see **fine, restraint on alienation**.

licence, under a lease
Written consent granted by a lessor permitting a lessee to vary a **covenant** or **condition** of a lease, e.g. to assign, sub-let, change user, carry out alterations, etc. See also **change of use**, **improvement, restraint on alienation**.

licensed premises
Premises that are authorised to be

used for the sale and consumption of intoxicating liquor – which may be a **public house**, **hotel**, restaurant, or an 'off-license' (which sells intoxicating liquor for consumption off the premises).
Modern Methods of Valuation, 7 edn, Ch. 33. (for valuation of licensed premises).
Valuation of Licensed Premises, by R.W. Westbrook, 2 edn.

licensee (or licencee)
1. The person who holds the rights under a **licence**; a person who has been granted a right to be on land when his or her presence would otherwise be unlawful – Thomas *v* Sewell Vaugh. 251 quoted in Frank Warr and Co. *v* London County Council [1904] 1 KB 713. A licensee has an express or implied right to enter onto another's land, but unlike a **tenant** does not have a right to exclude others (including the owner of the land) from possession. A licensee enters onto land for his own purpose and not for any purpose of doing business with the licensor. See also **invitee**, **negligence**, **visitor**.
2. A person given a privilege or franchise to engage in a business or trade. Commonly used to refer to a person who has a right to sell intoxicating liquor from licensed premises.

licensor
One who grants a right under a **licence**.

'lie in grant'
A right to property that may be transferred by **grant**; that which is capable of being transferred by deed. Interests in land 'lie in grant'; as distinguished from goods which 'lie in livery' i.e. are transferred by physical **delivery**.

lien
Derived from the French *lien* or the Latin *ligamen*, a tie or bond. A right or claim held by one person (lienor) against real or personal property belonging to another (lienee) as security for the payment of a debt or the performance of an obligation. A lien is a means by which a creditor secures a lawful right over property – reinforcing his position against general creditors – in order to coerce another to meet his obligations; although **title** to the property (but not necessarily possession) remains with the debtor. It is a right that arises generally by operation of law, especially as an equitable right, rather than a right that arises from any agreement between the parties. The usual form of lien is a 'common-law lien' (called also a 'legal', 'retentive' or 'possessory' lien); a right against property that has been transferred tacitly as security for an obligation: "a right in one man to retain that which is in his possession belonging to another, till certain demands of him, the person in possession are satisfied". – Hammond *v* Barclay (1802) 2 East. 235. A common-law lien cannot exist without possession and a person may not claim a lien over goods that are merely on his premises if another party, a tenant or licensee, has effective control. However, a possessory lien does not confer any right for the possessor to sell or otherwise deal in the property, unless there is an agreement between the parties to that effect. A possessory lien may be a general lien, or a specific (particular) lien. A 'general lien' is a right to retain property belonging to the debtor until all the debts arising from a line of business have been cleared; especially

a lien by which certain agents (e.g. solicitors, factors, bankers, stockbrokers) hold goods or documents belonging to their principal until their accounts have been settled in full. A 'particular lien' limits the right to hold property only until the debt has been paid that relates to the subject property. For example, an architect or surveyor may retain plans until the expenses or fees due for producing those plans are paid in full.

A lien may be 'equitable', that is a right which does not include possession of property and, therefore, is enforced only in equity. An equitable lien arises most frequently out of a contract when one party has not fulfilled his obligation and the law considers it fair to enforce payment by not objecting to an attachment of the debtor's property. For example, a right to a lien may arise (a) when land is conveyed to a purchaser before the purchase money is paid in full – a 'vendor's or grantor's lien'; or (b) when a purchaser has paid the purchase price but has not been granted possession – a 'purchaser's or grantee's lien'. In such cases, if the obligation is not met when due the party entitled to enforce that obligation may apply to the court either, in the former case, for a direction that the property be sold to meet the outstanding debt or, in the latter case, for an order for possession. (A vendor is not entitled to a lien if he has obtained a mortgage on the property he has sold.) Similarly, a purchaser who pays a deposit upon exchange of contracts may have a lien on that sum until the conditions of the contract have been satisfied. When a lien arises by statute it is called sometimes a 'statutory lien'. A lien does not create any interest in property, nor a right of action to claim property; it does not arise directly from any contractual arrangement, but from the maxim that 'equity looks on that as done which ought to be done'. Thus, unlike a **mortgage** or **charge**, it creates security against a property that has previously been the subject of a transaction between the parties. (In certain instances, especially in the US, what is called a mortgage or charge may take a form that creates a mere lien i.e. there is no grant of an interest in the property).

Common examples of a lien are the right of a solicitor to hold documents until his account is settled; of a banker to hold deeds until a loan is repaid; of a tax authority to exercise a claim to property until tax is paid; of a carrier to hold goods until their cost of carriage has been paid; or of a factor to retain goods until the principal's accounts have been paid, either for those goods, i.e. a particular lien, or until the factor's account is settled, i.e. a general lien.

A lien on land does not bind a purchaser of the land who acts in good faith and does not have **notice** of the existence of the lien. However, a lien may be protected by registration as a **land charge**, if the land is unregistered, or by an entry of a **minor interest** on the Land Registry, if the land is registered.

In the US a statutory lien held by a building contractor against material or machinery on the building site, as security for a payment due under the contract, is called a 'mechanic's lien'. See also **bailment**, **contract for sale**, **general equitable charge**, **seizure**.

The Law of Estate Agency and Auctions, by J.R. Murdoch, 2 edn., pp.

73–76, 471–474.

28 Halsbury's Laws of England, 4 edn, paras. 500–600.

Personal Property, by J.C. Vaines, 5 edn., pp. 137–144.

lien (F)

(*lien de droit* – **privity**).

lien theory (US)

see **mortgage**.

lienee

A person whose property is subject to a **lien**.

lienor

A person who has a **lien** over another's property.

lieu (pl. lieux) (F)

place; locality; house; premises.

(*lieu de séjour* – **residence**)

(*état des lieux* – **schedule of condition**)

(*vider les lieux* – to vacate the premises).

life annuity

An annuity that is payable for a person's lifetime. Called sometimes a 'rental annuity'. See also **reverse mortgage**.

life estate (or interest)

An **estate** in land which, although equivalent to a **freehold**, is limited for the life of a person and thus carries no right of inheritance. A life estate may subsist for the life of the holder of the estate in land; or for the life of another person: an estate *pur autre vie*. (In the latter instance the other person, the *cestui que vie*, determines the length of the life even if he outlives the holder of the interest – a grant 'to A for the life of B' lasts as long as B lives, regardless of A's life span.) A life estate is the shortest form of free-

hold and although it can be transferred to another the right to hold the estate ends with the death of the person for whose life the estate was created. It is not a fee estate.

The term 'life *estate*' particularly refers to a right to hold land under the feudal system; the commonest form of tenure whereby a lord permitted a vassal to hold land for life; a right that could not be alienated but, upon the death of the life tenant, reverted to the lord. This form of 'estate for life' was not an estate of inheritance and was called a 'mere freehold', or 'freeholds', as opposed to a freehold of inheritance or fee interest. This form of life estate, effectively, was abolished in 1925 and the modern 'life **interest**' has a different parentage being a right created under a **settlement**.

In modern English law a life interest usually arises when the holder of a fee simple grants land to another **(tenant for life)** for a life – either the life of the grantee or the life of another (*cestui que vie*, 'he for whom the life subsists'). The holder of a life interest is called a 'tenant for life' i.e. a person who has tenure for life; but is not a tenant in the sense of one of the parties to any relationship of landlord and tenant. A modern life interest is similar to a feudal life estate except that the estate need not revert to the grantor on the death of the tenant for life, but may then pass to another person nominated by the grantor. The essence of a life interest is to grant for a lifetime a right for a person or persons to enjoy the benefits or fruits of land and then to direct the right to those benefits to a third party. A tenant for life may take the annual profits from land, "but he must not take or destroy anything that is part

of the inheritance. He is entitled to fruits of all kinds, but must leave unimpaired the source of the fruits". (Cheshire's Modern Law of Property, 13 edn, p. 260). Thus, a 'tenant for life' may sell his interest (which is of value only for as long as he, or the *cestui que vie*, survives); grant leases; or mortgage the land for all or part of his life, although he may require consent to such actions; but he must not commit **waste** and thereby impair the interest of the person who comes after him. See also **conditional interest, curtesy, determinable interest, tenancy for life, tenant in tail after possibilities, usufruct**.
Real Estate Law, by William E. Burby, 3 edn, pp. 188–200.
Cheshire's Modern Law of Property, 13 edn, pp. 257–265.
39 Halsbury's Laws of England, 4 edn, paras. 459–480.

life interest
see **life estate, tenancy for life**.

life of a building
see **depreciation, economic life, wasting asset**.

liferent
In Scottish law, a right to use another's property (moveable or immoveable) for the grantee's life in the same way as if one were the owner; a form of personal servitude for life over another's property. Similar, in respect of realty, to a **life estate** in English law.

life tenant
A person who has an estate in land for a life, either his or her own life or the life of another; the holder of a **life estate**. See also **tenant for life**.

life tenancy
see **tenancy for life**.

light, right of
see **right of light**.

light industrial building
A building used for an industrial purpose that generally would not be detrimental to a residential area, i.e. it would not cause excessive environmental disturbance such as noise, vibration, smell or air pollution. See also **industrial building, Use Classes Order, warehouse**.

light, ancient
see **ancient light**.

ligne d'alignement (F)
building line.

limit of credit
see **line of credit**.

limit of indemnity
see **indemnity limit**.

limitation
1. The act of defining the extent of something. A certain time allowed for an action to take place or to be brought. A 'limitation of action' means a period of time, specified by statute law, within which proceeding to enforce a right must be brought to a court of law. A 'limitation of estate' means the period of time for which an **estate** is specified to endure. See also **conditional interest, determinable interest, Statutes of Limitation, words of limitation**.
2. The marking out of a limit or **boundary line** of a property.
3. A restriction placed on the use to which a property may be put. See also **change of use, restrictive covenant**.

Limitation Acts
see **Statutes of Limitation**.

limite (F)
boundary line.

(*limite de construction* – **improvement line**; building line).

limited common elements (US)

The **common elements** in a **condominium** which are limited to certain owners to the exclusion of all others, e.g. parking spaces, areas that are the sole responsibility of certain owners, party walls between individual apartments.

limited fee

A fee interest in land that is less than a **fee simple**; a fee simple interest that may be defeated or come to an end for any one of a number of reasons. A term that has no strict legal meaning but may refer to any form of **qualified fee**, a **base fee** or a **fee tail**.

limited liability company

A business organisation in which the liability of the shareholders is limited for the amount of their paid-up shares and up to, but not beyond, any shares not paid up. See also **company**, *société anonyme*.

limited owner

In general, an **owner** of property who has an estate or interest less than absolute ownership. In English law, any owner of an estate in land, other than the owner of a fee simple absolute, including the possessor of a life estate (**tenant for life**), or an entailed interest (**tenant in tail**). cf. **estate owner**. See also **statutory owner**, **usufructary**.

limited owner's charge

An **equitable charge** that is acquired by a **tenant for life** or a **statutory owner** who has discharged his liability to capital transfer tax or other liabilities. Thus, if a tenant for life pays tax in respect of the estate from whence his interest is derived, he acquires a charge over settled land as if he had lent money to the estate as a mortgagee. The tax normally is payable out of the proceeds of sale of the estate. Such a charge is registrable as a **land charge**.

limited company

see **limited liability company**.

limited partner

A **partner** whose liability is limited to his or her capital contribution to a partnership. A member of a **limited partnership** who provides the capital, but takes no active part in the management and cannot bind the partnership by his or her acts or conduct (Limited Partnership Act 1907, s. 6 (1)). In English law a limited partner "shall at the time of entering into such partnership [a limited partnership] contribute thereto a sum or sums as capital or property valued at a stated amount, and ... shall not be liable for the debts or obligations of the firm beyond the amount so contributed". And, "A limited partner shall not during the continuance of the partnership, either directly or indirectly, draw out or receive back any part of his contribution, and if he does so draw out or receive back any such part shall be liable for the debts and obligations of the firm up to the amount so drawn out or received back". (1907 Act, s. 4 (2), (3)). A body corporate may be a limited partner. Called also a 'special partner', a 'sleeping partner' or a 'dormant partner'. cf. **general partner**. See also **passive investor**.

limited partnership

A **partnership** in which one or more

partners, **general partner**(s), are appointed to manage the partnership business and to accept full responsibility for the conduct of the firm, and one or more partners, **limited partner**(s), contribute capital to the partnership but take no active part in its management (Limited Partnership Act 1907, s. 4 (2)). The limited partners are liable only up to the amount of the capital they have contributed. The general partners are remunerated normally as salaried employees and the limited partners receive the profits (or share in the losses) of the enterprise. In English law (but not in most States in the USA, nor in the civil law) a limited partnership can have no distinct legal status, apart from that of the individual partners, and consequently the general partners are liable for any losses over and above the contributed capital of the limited partners.

In the US this form of partnership is commonly used for real estate investment. Most states have adopted a Uniform Limited Partnership Act to regulate such partnerships. See also **joint venture**.

limited period permission
Planning permission that has been granted for a limited period of time. A planning authority may grant planning permission for a specified period when the authority does not consider it expedient to permit the development to be a permanent feature (Town and Country Planning Act 1971, s. 30 (1) (b)). At the end of the specified period the subject property must be restored to its original condition or revert to its original user. Also, the Town and Country Planning General Development Order 1977, Class IV permits the use or erection of certain temporary buildings in connection with an operation that has been authorised by a valid planning permission e.g. site huts. See also **planning condition**.
Encyclopaedia of Town and Country Planning, by Desmond Heap, paras. 2-2661-2.

line
A demarcation, **boundary line**, or limit; especially of a plot of land. See also **building line, improvement line**.

line of credit
An amount of credit made available by a bank to an established customer to cover day-to-day business needs, usually subject to an agreed maximum. This facility usually is intended to supplement, but not replace, an interim loan; it commonly takes the form of an overdraft; and is subject to regular review by the lender. For example, a developer may be granted a line of credit to cover unexpected variations of expenditure for a building project. Called also a 'credit line' and the agreed maximum facility the 'limit of credit'. See also **facility**.

linear city
A form of city design where development has been planned along one principal axis or thoroughfare.
cf. **ribbon development**.
Introduction to Town and Country Planning, by John Ratcliffe, 2 edn., pp. 45-47.

liquid asset
Cash, or an asset that is readily convertible into cash.
cf. **fixed asset**. See also **current asset**.

liquidated damages
A particular sum of money, set out in

a contract, which represents a fair pre-estimate of **damages** to be paid in the event of a default by one of the parties to the contract. That sum, no more or no less, is payable in the event of a **breach of contract**; if there is no such specified sum in a contract the injured party may claim such damages as are occasioned. For example, a building contract may specify a fixed sum, as liquidated damages, to be paid by the contractor, for each day that building work remains outstanding after the agreed completion date. Liquidated damages are a genuine pre-estimate of the loss that can result from a breach of contract and as such are recoverable in a court of law, as contrasted with a **penalty** which is intended to be a burden or punishment imposed to ensure completion of a contract and is likely to be set aside by a court – Law v Redditch Local Board [1892] 1 QB 132; J.E. Hathaway and Co. v US, 249 US 460, 39 S Ct. 63, 63 L Ed. 707. A clause in a contract specifying for liquidated damages should set out the items which the damages are intended to cover so that, in the event of a dispute as to whether the sum represents liquidated damages or a penalty, a court can ascertain the loss sustained by the injured party. See also **deposit, unliquidated damages**.

liquidation
1. The 'winding-up' of the affairs of a business or a company. The sale of a company's assets for cash and the repayment, as far as possible, of all its debts, especially when a company has ceased trading as a result of **insolvency**. Liquidation may arise compulsorily, usually at the instigation of the creditors, as when a bankrupt person seeks to obtain as much cash as possible to repay his debts. It may arise voluntarily when the owners have achieved the purpose for which the company was established or when they agree that they wish to discontinue trading. In either case a liquidator is appointed to assume control of the company, arrange for the orderly sale of its assets and discharge its liabilities. Liquidation is the process required prior to the winding-up of a company.

Liquidation by one party to a contract does not necessarily terminate or cause a breach of a contract as the liquidator may continue running the business until it is effectively wound up. However, the other party to the contract may seek rescission of the contract or may claim damages if a loss arises from the liquidation. A formal lease frequently contains a condition that the landlord may terminate the tenancy in the event of the tenant's liquidation. In that event the landlord must enter a claim to the liquidator for his entire loss. On the other hand the landlord is at liberty to refuse to terminate the lease but may instead enter a claim for the rent due under the lease.
cf. **bankruptcy**.
2. The process of converting an asset into cash. See also **conversion, liquidity**.

liquidation (F)
1. liquidation; winding-up.
(*liquidation d'une société* – winding up of a company)
(*valuer de liquidation* – break up value).
2. settlement (of a debt).

liquidation value (US)
see **forced-sale value**.

liquidité (F)
liquidity.

liquidity

The state of holding liquid assets. The ease with which assets may be converted into cash. In the case of a property investment, the ease with which an investor anticipates being able to convert that investment back into cash, the degree of liquidity, is one of the factors which affects the capital value of the investment; thus a sizeable investment in one property is likely to demand a higher return for an investor than an investment in a smaller, more liquid, but otherwise comparable property. In the case of a business, liquidity refers to the ability of that business to raise cash to pay its debts as they arise, without unduly affecting the operation or purpose of the business. See also **current asset**, **risk**.

liquidity ratio

A ratio that measures an organisation's ability to meet its current obligations; e.g. the ratio of current assets to current liabilities. See also **liquidity**.

lis pendens (L)

'A pending action'. In England and Wales a *lis pendens* may be registered as a **land charge** (Land Charges Act 1972, s. 5); or, in the case of registered land it may be protected by a **notice**, **caution**, or **inhibition** (Land Registration Act 1925, s. 59). In the US called also a 'notice of pendency'.

listed building

A building considered to be of "special architectural or historic interest" and, therefore, included in a list of such buildings prepared for and approved by the Secretary of State for the Environment. A building is included in the list because it, or part of it, may be worthy of preservation on its own merits; because it forms part of a group of buildings that may be worthy of preservation as a whole; or because it contains a particular feature that may be worthy of preservation (Town and Country Planning Act 1971, s. 54, as amended by the Local Government, Planning and Land Act 1980, Sch. 15. para. 5). The inclusion of a building in this list does not automatically make it worthy of preservation, but the owner must apply for a **listed building consent** before any alteration or demolition of the building may be carried out that would affect its character as a building of special interest. The buildings included in the list are classified as Grade I or Grade II. The appropriate grade depends on whether the building is considered of exceptional interest, or merely worthy of consideration so as to warrant further examination if alteration or demolition is likely (Department of the Environment Circular 102/74 on Historic Buildings and Conservation). It is a criminal offence to carry out any work on a listed building without consent (1971 Act, s. 55) and if an owner of a listed building deliberately lets it fall into disrepair the local authority has power to acquire it compulsorily (1971 Act, s. 117); in that event the amount of compensation paid may be severely restricted. In the event of an unauthorised interference with a listed building the local planning authority, or the Secretary of State, may serve a 'listed building enforcement notice' on the owner of the building (1971 Act, s. 96). The fact that a building is listed must be entered on the **local land charges reg-**

ister and the owner and any occupier of a listed building must be notified of a proposal to list a building. When an application has been made, or granted, for planning permission to alter, extend or demolish a building, any person may apply to the Secretary of State for the Environment for a certificate that there is no intention to list the building. If such a certificate is granted the Secretary of State is precluded for five years from including the property in the list of buildings of special architectural or historic interest. See also **ancient monument, building preservation notice, conservation area**.

Development and Planning Law, by Barry Denyer-Green, pp. 97–102 (1980).

Practical Planning Law, by J.F. Garner, pp. 166–170 (1981).

Planning Law and Procedure, by A.E. Telling, 6 edn., pp. 181–191.

Guide to Development and Planning, by R.N.D. Hamilton, 7 edn., pp. 281–292, 427–428.

An Outline of Planning Law, by Desmond Heap, 8 edn., pp. 202–214.

Urban Planning Law, by Malcolm Grant, pp. 462–465 (1982).

Planning Procedure Tables, by R.N.D. Hamilton, 4 edn., pp. 118–129.

34 Halsbury's Laws of England, 4 edn, paras. 653–687.

Listed Buildings – The Law and Practice, by Roger W. Suddards, (1982).

listed building consent

Approval obtained from a local authority, (or, in the event of an appeal, from the Secretary of State for the Environment), in accordance with the provisions of the Town and Country Planning Act 1971, s. 55 (2), to make alterations; to extend; or to demolish a **listed building**. (It is an offence to demolish a listed building without consent and a grant of planning permission for works that would alter a listed building does not imply listed building consent, unless expressly stated in the permission.) Application for listed building consent is made to the local planning authority and, if it is intended to demolish a listed building, certain national organisations must be notified and the Royal Commission on Historical Monuments must be given one month's notice to enable them to make a record of the building. The Secretary of State must be informed of a proposal to grant listed building consent and, if he wishes, he may then call in the application for his consideration. Listed building consent may be given unconditionally or on condition that part or parts of a building are preserved. There is a right of appeal against a refusal or conditional grant of listed building consent to the Secretary of State. An appeal may be made also if the local authority fails to give a decision on an application for consent within a statutorily prescribed period of two months. In the event of a refusal of consent to alter or extend (but not to demolish) a listed building, compensation may be paid to recompense the owner for such financial loss as he has sustained (this amount generally is based on any reduction in the open market value as a result of the refusal); or the owner may serve a **purchase notice** on the authority if the refusal makes his property incapable of "reasonable beneficial use' (1971 Act, s. 190). A grant of planning permission may operate as a listed building consent when the development authorised by the permission requires the alteration or extension of the building and the permission expressly describes the permitted work (1971 Act, s. 56, as extended by the Local Government, Planning and Land Act 1980, Sch. 15 para. 5). A listed building consent is valid for a period of five years or such other period as the local authority may specify. See also **compensation for planning restrictions**, **conservation area**.

listing (US)
The placing of a property by an owner with a real estate agent or broker, under the terms of an agreement which provides that the agent will endeavour to secure a purchaser, or tenant, for that property in return for which the agent will receive a **commission**. The agreement may take the form of an 'open or general listing' (**multiple agency**); an 'exclusive listing' (**exclusive agency**); or a '**multiple listing**'. Called sometimes an 'authorisation to sell'. See also **agency**.
Real Estate Law, by W.D. Milligan and Arthur G. Bowman, pp. 62–68 (1984).
Real Estate Law, by Robert Kratovil and Raymond J. Werner, 8 edn., pp. 96–99.

listing (F)
1. listing, of a building of special architectural or historical interest – a procedure similar to that used in the UK exists in France for listing certain buildings of merit.
Planning in Western Europe, Edited by J.F. Garner (France – Prof. L. Lemasurier), p. 142, (1975).
2. **listing**, of a property for sale.

literal meaning
The meaning given to a word in its ordinary, commonly-understood sense. A literal construction of a contract takes account of the words alone without regard to the intent of the parties or extrinsic factors; "the grammatical and ordinary sense of the word is to be adhered to, unless that would lead to some absurdity, or some repugnance or inconsistency with the rest of the instrument, in which case the ordinary or grammatical sense of the word may be modified, so as to avoid that absurdity and inconsistency, but no further". – Grey v Pearson (1857) 26 LJ Ch. 481. A similar rule, the 'literal rule' applies to the interpretation of statutes and "when the language of the Act is clear and explicit, we must give effect to it, whatever may be the consequences, for in that case the words of the statute speak the intention of the legislature". – Warburton v Loveland (1831) 2 D and C 489. It must be assumed that words in statutes are used precisely and exactly, not loosely or inexactly; if a word has one probable meaning, it is given that meaning – its primary or literal meaning – unless that creates an absurdity or a manifest hardship; it is for the judges to construe judical construction of parliament's language but not to legislate for parliament's meaning. When interpreting a statute, the 'literal rule' provides that a word with one meaning only is given that meaning, notwithstanding the result. See also **term of art**, **words, meaning of**.

littoral (F)
(*droits littorals* – **littoral right**).

littoral rights
The rights concerning land abutting the **shore** of the sea or a lake. In English common law the sea-shore

belongs to the Crown and in most states in the US it is vested in the state. The adjoining 'littoral owner' has a right of access to the shore, but may not remove any sand as of right. cf. **riperian rights**. See also **accretion, foreshore, water rights**.

livery

The transfer of title to land by giving physical **possession**. See also **delivery, livery of seisin**.

livery of seisin

A feudal process for the delivery of possession of land. Livery of seisin was either 'in deed' or 'in law'. Livery in deed was an invitation to enter on to land accompanied by a symbolic transfer of a sod or twig; "livery in law is when the feoffor (grantor) saith to the feoffee (grantee), being in view of the house and land, "I give you yonder land to you and your heirs, and go enter into the same, and take possession thereof according; and the feofee doth accordingly in the life of the feoffor enter." (Co. Litt. 486). In English law since 1925 land, or an interest in land, is no longer conveyed by livery of seisin but must be transferred by a 'deed of grant' or **conveyance** (Law of Property Act 1925, s. 51 (1)). See also **feoffment, seisin**.

living room

A room in a residence that is used for habitation, especially as part of the more permanent process of living, as contrasted with a room available for ancillary uses. A living room may be a room used for social activities during a considerable part of the day, including a sitting room, kitchen or bedroom; but not a bathroom, toilet, storage area, hall or garage – Kenyon v Walker, Stevenson v Kenyon,

[1946] 2 All ER 595. However, "a living room is not something which can be identified objectively without regard to the situation of its particular occupant, occupants or users. What, indeed, may be a living room if in single occupation, as for instance a kitchen, is not necessarily a living room if it has to be made available for use of several distinct households; and I [Lord Radcliffe] should say the same of a bathroom and, again, of a spare bedroom". – Goodrich v Paisner [1956] 2 All ER 187. A kitchen that is so small that it is only possible to use it for cooking is not a living room in the proper meaning of that term – Marsh Ltd. v Cooper [1969] 2 All ER 500. See also **habitable room**.

living trust

A **trust** by which property is transferred to a trustee during the lifetime of the owner, as distinguished from a 'testamentary' trust which arises upon death. As soon as the property is placed into a living trust the trustees have responsibility for its management and control in accordance with the terms of the trust instrument. Called also an '*inter vivos* trust'. See also **special trust**.

load factor

see **loss factor**.

loan

A transaction by which one person (creditor or lender) delivers something of value – goods, money or anything of pecuniary worth – to another (debtor or borrower) on the understanding that it, or its equivalent, will be returned, or repaid, in the future. The thing delivered also may be called a loan. When a loan takes the form of money (**principal**) usually it is repayable, whether by instalments or as lump sum, with a reward for its use, called **interest**. A loan of money may be secured by a **lien**, **charge**, or **mortgage** on property owned by the borrower, in order to give the lender some form of security against non-payment of the debt owed to him. The process of entering into this form of agreement is called **financing**, funding, or obtaining an advance. An instalment sale is not a loan because the money paid over is not intended to be paid back; although it may create a debt. See also **bailment**.

loan capital
see **debt capital**.

loan commitment
see **commitment**.

loan constant
see **mortgage constant**.

loan cover
see **cover**.

loan fee
A charge made by a lender for making a loan, over and above the interest rate. See also **commitment fee, front-end loading**.

loan origination fee
see **origination fee**.

loan participation
see **convertible mortgage, participation loan**.

loan points
see **discount points**.

loan ratio
see **loan-to-value ratio**.

loan service
see **debt service**.

loan-to-value ratio
The ratio of the amount granted as a **loan** to the **market value** of a property held as security for that loan.
cf. **debt-to-equity ratio**. See also **discount points**.

loan value
The value of a property as determined for the purpose of granting a loan against the security of that property. The amount advanced against the security of a property generally is less than its loan value (which in most instances would be the same as the **market value**). Many lending institutions are restricted by law as to maximum percentage of the loan value of a property they may advance against the security of that property. See also **mortgage value**.

local (pl. locaux) (F)
place; premises.
(*local commercial, local d'affaires* – commercial or **business premises**. In particular the premises to which a ***bail commercial*** applies).
(*local d'habitation* – dwelling-house)
(*locaux pour magasin* – retail premises)
(*impôts locaux* – rates).

local assessment (US)
see **assessment**.

local assessment committees
Bodies which, until 1948, considered similar matters to those now considered by **local valuation courts**.

local authority
A corporate body that is responsible for the administration of government in a restricted area (such as a parish, town, city or county) of a state, nation or country, and normally is required to provide local services under spe-

cific powers conferred by central government. Primarily this body is a decentralised authority elected by suffrage of the population of that area, although the extent of decentralisation and suffrage is mutable. (In its purest sense local government should be totally autonomous, but central government control and support of local government varies by degrees, a higher degree of central power being exercised, for example, in France than in the UK or in the US). Local authorities derive their income from local taxes or **rates**, usually supplemented by central government grants. The Finance Act 1974, s. 52 defines a local authority as "(a) any authority having power to make or determine a rate; (b) any authority having power to issue precept, requisition or other demand for the payment of money to be raised out of a rate". Generally local authorities are created by statute and are subordinate to statutory, judicial and ordinant controls.

The principal areas of local authority responsibility that affect real estate are town and country planning; housing; building control and regulation; public health regulation; highway construction and maintenance; drainage, and sewage and refuse collection; national parks and protection of the countryside; the compulsory or purchase condemnation of land for local purposes; and the maintenance of a local land charges register.

The local authorities in England and Wales comprise the Parish (in England) or Community Councils (in Wales); County Councils (metropolitan and non-metropolitan); District Councils (metropolitan and non-metropolitan); the Common Council of the City of London; and the London Boroughs (The Local Government Act 1972, s. 270 (1)). In certain statutes a local authority may be more strictly defined, for example a parish council may be excluded from the definition.

In the US, the local authorities vary from State to State, but may be classified broadly as County or Parish; County or Township; and City. In France the local authorities, in ascending order of importance are *communes*, *cantons*, *arrondissements* and *départements*. See also **development corporation**, **highway authority**, **housing authority**, **planning authority**.

Directory of Local Authorities, Oyez Longman Publishing Ltd., annual.
Local Government Law, by Keith Davies, (1983).
Principles of Local Government Law, by C.A. Cross, 6 edn.

local land charge

A charge, burden or restriction that arises from an action of a local or public authority and binds successive owners of the land for as long as it remains in force (Local Land Charges Act 1975, s. 1). Local land charges may be categorised broadly as: (i) financial charges – for work done by a local authority under a statute which the authority seeks to recover, e.g. repair works carried out pursuant to a repair notice; repair works to private streets; maintenance work on sewers and drains; and land compensation charges; (ii) restrictions – imposed by a local authority, Minister of the Crown or government department, on the use of land, e.g. a planning charge (such as an enforcement notice, a compensation notice, a building preservation notice, a tree preservation order), a condition imposed in a listed building consent, a closing order or a demolition order; (iii) positive obligations affecting land, e.g. a planning agreement; and (iv) acquisition proposals, e.g. a compulsory purchase order. Proposals for future compulsory purchase, road widening, etc., also may be entered on the register, as well as certain orders emanating from other public authorities or from a statutory provision such as a New Town Order, Civil Aviation Order, a land drainage scheme and an open-cast coal mining scheme. Certain matters are expressly excluded from the statutory definition of a local land charge – (i) a prohibition, restriction, or a positive obligation, arising between a lessor and lessee; (ii) various restrictions enforceable by the Crown, or central or local government, in respect of their own land; (iii) conditions imposed on the grant of planning permission prior to 1st August 1977; (iv) prohibitions arising from forestry dedication covenants; (v) prohibitions affecting all of England and Wales (Local Land Charges Act 1975, s. 2). A local land charge normally is recorded in the **local land charges register** maintained by the local authority and details of such a charge may be obtained by a personal search of the register, or by obtaining an **official certificate of search** from the local authority. A local land charge that is not registered still binds any person who acquires the land. However, if a purchaser obtains an official certificate of search which does not reveal the charge, then he is entitled to compensation for any loss sustained from the authority who could have registered the charge (Local Land Charges Act 1975, s. 10). A local land charge is registered against the land itself and not, as with a **land charge**, in the name of the estate owner.

Local Land Charges, by J.F. Garner, 9 edn., pp. 7–11.
Barnsley's Conveyancing Law and Practice, 2 edn, pp. 189–196.
26 Halsbury's Laws of England, 4 edn, paras. 771–795.

local land charges register
A register of local land charges maintained by a district council in England and Wales, a London Borough council or the Common Council of the City of London. A register of local land charges is maintained by each local authority containing details of various charges, burdens or other restrictions against land (whether registered or unregistered land) arising from the authority's own actions or the action of certain public authorities. The register is divided into twelve parts and entries are made against the land itself.

Details of items on a register may be obtained by a prospective purchaser of land either by a personal search or by a request to the registrar for an **official certificate of search** (Local Land Charges Act 1975; Local Land Charges Rules 1977). See also **local land charge**.

local ordinance (US)
see **ordinance**.

local plan
A plan prepared to guide the development of a part of a town or district. In particular, a map or set of maps, supported by a written statement, prepared by a local planning authority (generally the appropriate District

Council) in England or Wales to guide development in a particular area. These plans cover such matters as traffic management, general improvement of the area and conservation. (Town and Country Planning Act 1971, ss 11–15). There are three distinct types of local plan (i) a 'district plan' for a town, part of a town or a district; (ii) an 'action area plan' for a specific area (an **action area**) that requires special attention; and (iii) a 'subject plan' prepared for a specific development proposal or building. A local plan fills in, and should follow, the proposals of a **structure plan**, which usually has been prepared beforehand by the county council. (In an area where a local authority has serious inner urban problems, a local plan may be adopted before a structure plan has been approved by the Secretary of State for the Environment, provided the local plan conforms with the general form of the draft structure plan submitted to the Secretary of State (Inner Urban Areas Act 1978, s. 12).) See also **development plan, public participation.**

An Introduction to Town and Country Planning, by John Ratcliffe, 2 edn., pp. 94–100.

Urban Planning Law, by Malcolm Grant, pp. 115–132 (1982)

Encyclopaedia of Planning Law and Practice, by Desmond Heap, paras. 1–046 to 1–049.

Local Plans in British Land Use Planning, by P. Healey (1983).

local planning authority
see **planning authority.**

local rates
see **rates.**

local search
An enquiry made to ascertain details of any **local land charge** registered against a parcel of land. Any person may search, or requisition a search of, a local land charges register. The search may be made in person; or by requesting an **official certificate of search**, for which a fee is payable (Land Charges Act 1975, ss. 8, 9; Local Land Charges Rules 1977, 5. 11). See also **searches.**

Conveyancing Searches, by A.R. Mellows, pp. 30–34 (1975).

local valuation courts
Tribunals in England and Wales, first established under the Local Government Act 1948 to replace local assessment committees, with the function of hearing appeals at first instance, against proposals for the alteration of a rating assessment on a property included in the **valuation list**. If a **proposal** is made to alter the assessment on a property, or an objection is made to a proposal to alter an assessment, and the proposal is not withdrawn, the matter automatically goes to the local valuation court. The tribunal is made up of a chairman and two other members (or sometimes a chairman and only one member) who are usually lay people drawn from a local valuation panel selected by the local authority. Normally hearings are held in public and evidence on matters of fact or law relating to valuation of the property under consideration may be submitted by the appellant, the valuation officer, the owner or occupier, the rating authority or an objector to the proposal. Such evidence may be submitted also by an expert witness called on behalf of one of the parties

appearing before the court. There is a right of appeal against the decisions of a local valuation court to the **Lands Tribunal**. (General Rate Act 1966, ss. 76, 77, 82–92, as amended by the General Rate Act 1970, s. 1 & the Local Government Act 1970, Sch. 13, paras. 29, 30).
Ryde on Rating, 13 edn, pp. 710–726.

locataire (locatif, -ive) (F)

tenant; lodger; lessee.
(*locataire à bail* – leaseholder, lessee)
(*immeuble locatif* – tenement house)
(*locataire principal* – head-lessee)
(*réparations locatives* – tenant's repairs)
(*co-locataire* – joint tenant)
(*sous-locataire* – sub-tenant)
(*valeur locative* – rental value, especially of a dwelling-house).

location

1. The situation of a property in relation to other properties and to the facilities that serve the property such as roads, public transport, complementary uses, etc. In real estate, 'location' is used commonly to refer to the economic rather than geographical position i.e. it reflects the relative importance and hence the value attached to the property. Synonymous with '*situs*'. See also **location theory, prime location**.
Office Development, by Paul and Paula Marber, Ch. 4, (1985).
2. A site or building occupied or available for occupation.
3. A parcel or tract of land, particularly an area marked out for official purposes. Also the act of staking out an area of land, especially an area that forms the domain of a new settlement.
4. A contract for the letting or hiring of personal property. Also the act of letting or hiring personal property.

location (F)

letting; hiring; renting; a contract for the letting of any form of property, including a fonds de commerce; tenancy.
(*location indivise* – joint tenancy)
(*agent de location* – letting agent; estate agent)
(*prix de location* – rental value)
(*sous-location* – sub-lease; sub-letting).

location plan

A plan showing the location of a site or building and drawn to a sufficiently large scale to show a site in relation to the surrounding area, normally to a scale of 1/2500 or larger.
cf. **site plan**.

location theory

An economic theory devised to explain the factors which account for the **location** of a particular economic user and the associated hierarchy of land values. Location theory seeks to explain where consumers and producers will settle and establish an economic activity; to explain the preference for one site or location compared to another; and to produce an explanation of relative land values and to explain movements in land values over time. The basis of most location theories is the principle of 'comparative advantage' – land is fixed in space and limited in quantity (at least in the short run) and in a free economy each area of land tends to produce those products, or to be used for the purpose, for which it has the greatest ratio of advantage or the least ratio of disadvantage compared to any other area of land. See also **highest and best use, land economics**.
Aspects of Land Use Planning, by W.

Lean and B. Goodall, pp. 153–172 (1966, reprinted 1973).

location-vente (F)
A **rental purchase**. A contract by which one person lets a property to another at a rent that is higher than normal, but with a provision that at the expiration of the lease the lessee has an option to acquire the property. cf. *crédit-bail*. See also **leasing**.

locational obsolescence
see **obsolescence**.

lock-in period
A period of time during which a lender is prohibited from repaying a loan. See also **equity of redemption, repayment penalty**.

locus in quo (L)
'The place in which' something is claimed to have been done, as in **trespass**.

locus regit actum (L)
'The place governs the act'.

locus sigilli (**LS**) (L)
'The place of the **seal**'. The words or initials that are sometimes inserted in a circle at the end of a document to indicate the place for fixing a seal.

lodger
Originally a person who lived in a tent. One who lives or dwells in a place for a short time. A person who passes the night in a given place; one who occupies hired rooms in a **lodging house**; especially a temporary resident, or licensee, who resides in and in some way shares and has permissive occupation of a property which is also the place of residence of the owner. A lodger is a person who pays to live in another's house, may have exclusive occupation of part of the house, but is subordinate to the owner in terms of mastery of the house; it matters not whether any payment for the use of the property covers board and lodging, or board alone – Smith *v* M'Caldon, (1948) SLT (Sch. Ct. 20–21). "Generally speaking, a lodger is a person whose occupation is of part of a house, and subordinate to and in some degree under the control of a landlord or his representative, who either resides in or retains possession of or dominion over the house generally, or over the outer door, and under such circumstances that the possession of any particular part of the house held by the lodger does not prevent the house generally being in possession of the landlord." – Thompson *v* Ward (1871) 40 LJCP 188. A person who has exclusive control over the outside door of a house is not a lodger, but a householder. A lodger normally is not a tenant but a **licensee** of the premises he occupies. See also **licence, resident landlord, restricted contract**.

lodging house
A house where rooms are let as temporary lodgings; especially a place where living accommodation is provided as furnished accommodation with limited or no **board**. In a lodging house, primarily, there is no definite intention that the residents shall have any right to stay more than a few nights and, as a rule, lodging houses are not occupied as separate dwellings. In the US, called also a 'rooming house'.
cf. **apartment**. See also **common lodging-house, lodger**.

logeable (F)
tenantable.

(*maison logeable* – house in tenantable condition).

logement (F)
accommodation; housing; lodging.
(*logement garni*; *logement meublé* – furnished rooms, furnished flat)
(*logement insalubre* – slum housing)
(*crise du logement* – housing shortage)
(*logement ouvrier* – tenament house).

logeur (F)
landlord (of furnished residential premises).

loi (F)
law, especially statute law.
cf. *droit*

long lease
see **long-term lease**, **long tenancy**.

long tenancy
"A **tenancy** granted for a term of years certain exceeding twenty-one years, whether or not subsequently extended by act of the parties or by any enactment." (Landlord and Tenant Act 1954, s. 2 (4)). A long tenancy of a residential property, if granted at a **low rent** (defined as less than two thirds of the rateable value of the demised premises) – as is commonly the case with a **ground lease**, is not capable of being a **protected tenancy** and thus benefitting from the protection afforded by the Rent Acts. However, the 1954 Act, Part I provides that a long tenancy at a low rent will qualify for similar protection if it would have been a protected tenancy apart from the 'low rent'. Such a tenancy does not come to an end on expiration of the contractual term. To terminate such a tenancy the landlord must serve notice, in accordance with the statutory provisions, upon one of

a number of permitted **grounds for possession**. If the tenant contests the notice the landlord must apply for a court order. If the court will not grant possession the tenant is entitled to a **statutory tenancy** under the Rent Acts. Alternatively, the landlord may propose a statutory tenancy at the end of the contractual term by giving notice in the prescribed statutory form (1954 Act, s. 4). The tenancy may be brought to an end also by the tenant giving one month's **notice to quit**, by **surrender**, or by **forfeiture**.

The Leasehold Reform Act 1967 extends the statutory rights of a holder of a long tenancy by enabling a tenant who occupies a house on a 'long tenancy', at a low rent, to acquire an **extended lease**, or to have a right of **leasehold enfranchisement** i.e. to acquire the freehold. In this context a long tenancy is one granted for the same term as stipulated in the Landlord and Tenant Act 1954 'whether or not the tenancy is (or may become) terminable before the end of that term by notice given by or to the tenant or by re-entry, forfeiture or otherwise'; and that includes any successive tenancies (whether arising by statute or contract) that are granted or are renewable for a term of over twenty-one years (Leasehold Reform Act 1967, s. 3). The provisions of the 1954 Act and the 1967 Act do not apply merely because a tenant has been in occupation for 21 years; the lease must have been granted originally for a period in excess of 21 years. See also **long-term lease**.
Long Tenancies at a low rent; the statutory code by Mark Pawlowski, 274 EG 104, 106, 116, (1985).
Housing Law, by Andrew Arden and Martin Partington, pp. 82–85 (1983).

Landlord and Tenant Law, by David Yates and A.J. Hawkins, pp. 375–392 (1981).
The Law of Landlord and Tenant, by David Lloyd Evans, 2 edn, pp. 346–364.
Law of Landlord and Tenant, by Hill and Redman, 17 edn., pp. 2171–2474.

long-term capital gains tax
see **capital gains tax**.

long-term insurance agreement
An insurance policy for a fixed number of years, commonly 3 to 5 years; in return for the commitment to one insurer for that term the insured generally receives a reduction in the annual premium. Called also a 'term policy'.

long-term lease
In general, a lease granted for a fixed initial term (not being a **periodic tenancy**) of twenty years or more; although, especially in the US, a lease for five years or more may be referred to as a long-term lease.
cf. **short-term lease**. See also **long tenancy, tenancy for a term of years**.

long-term loan (or financing)
A loan granted for a fixed term, generally in excess of ten years, as contrasted with an **interim loan**. Such a loan may take the form of a mortgage, debenture or sale and lease-back financing. Called also a 'permanent loan (or financing)'.
cf. **short-term loan**.

long-term policy
see **long-term insurance agreement**.

lord of the manor
see **manor**.

loss
1. An amount by which the proceeds from the sale of an asset falls short of the cost of acquiring that asset; or an amount by which the aggregate expenditure incurred in running a business exceeds the aggregate income generated by that business, over a given period of time.
cf. **profit**.
2. The condition of ceasing to return possession of something.
cf. **gain**. See also **ademption, consequential loss insurance**.

loss factor (US)
The difference between the **net useable area** and the **rentable area** of an office building expressed as a percentage of the rentable area. This factor expresses the percentage of floor space for which a tenant pays rent but cannot derive benefit therefrom due to columns, air conditioning units, etc. within the area leased to him. Called also a 'load factor' or 'partial floor factor' or, when expressed as a percentage of the net useable area, an 'add-on factor'. See also **efficiency ratio**.

loss of profit
see **compensation for disturbance, damages**.

loss of profits insurance
see **consequential-loss insurance**.

loss of rent insurance
Insurance obtained by a landlord to cover the loss of rental income from an investment, following damage caused by fire or special perils, until the building is restored and tenant(s) can retake possession. In the US, also called 'rent insurance'.
cf. **rental value insurance, tenant's default insurance**.

loss rent
An amount by which the market ren-

tal value of a property exceeds the contractual rent due from the tenant, i.e. a negative **profit rent**. See also **reverse premium**.

lost modern grant, doctrine of
A doctrine of English Law that may be applied when establishing a right to an easement or profit à prendre by **prescription**. Under this doctrine, it is assumed that (a) if a right over land has been enjoyed, without interruption, for an extensive period (usually more than 20 years) then this right must have been in existence since the start of 'legal memory' (taken to be 1189 – the start of the reign of King Richard I); (b) a deed of grant was made after 1189 (a 'modern grant') but presumably it has been lost; and (c) as a result the user has a lawful right to continue to enjoy the easement or profit – Dalton *v* Angus and Co. (1881) 6 App. Cas. 773; Tehidy Minerals Ltd. *v* Norman [1971] 2 QB 528. This doctrine was introduced as a fiction to circumvent a situation which arose when a right to land had been established by common law prescription (based on the rule that it had been enjoyed for as long as anyone could remember i.e. since 1189), but the person who had been deprived of that right was able to demonstrate that the user must have commenced at some time after 1189 (for example because a building that benefits from the easement or profit à prendre must have been erected after 1189) and, therefore, was able to defeat the claimant's right. The doctrine of lost modern grant seeks to demonstrate that, nonetheless, the extensive period of user is sufficient to support the view that the right must have been granted, but only the

evidence of grant is missing. A claim to a 'lost modern grant' is available only when common law prescription cannot be applied and it must be based on stronger evidence than common law prescription. It is rebutted if it can be shown that the right is of a type that is not capable of being acquired by **grant**; that the user has not been enjoying it 'as of right' (i.e. because it was taken by force, secretly, or without permission); or that at some stage during the period of enjoyment the right could not have existed, as when the person who would have made the grant was not at that time capable of making it.

lost property
see **treasure trove**.

lot
1. A parcel or **plot of land**, especially one out of several parcels into which an area of land has been divided. See also **allotment, parcelling, plottage**.
2. That which fortuitously determines what we are to acquire.

lot (F)
1. **lot**; parcel or plot of land.
(*lot à batir* – building plot or site; building lot); One of the plots of land into which an area has been subdivided, either by *lotisement* or *partage*. See also **parcelling, plottage**.
2. a share of an estate.

lot and block system (US)
A system of land identification used in towns laid out on a grid system; each street block, and a lot within that block, is allocated a number – thus Lot 7, Block 10, identifies a specific parcel of land. This system may be used for land registration and land transfer.
cf. **metes and bounds**. See also **plot**

map.
The Appraisal of Real Estate, AIREA,
8 edn., pp. 161–162.

lot line (US)
see **boundary line**.

lotissement (F)
parcelling; plottage;   the subdivision
of land into separate building plots.
"A transaction, and the result of a
transaction, which has the object or
effect of a voluntary subdivision of
land into one or more plots (*lots*) for
simultaneous or successive sales or
lettings with the aim of creating dwellings, gardens or commercial or
industrial premises" (Law of 31
December 1958 No. 58–1466 *Code de
L'Urbanisme, art R. 315-1*). Such
subdivision of land for sale or letting
must receive the prior approval of the
local authority, otherwise the transaction is null and void. In the event
that a *lotissement* is authorised, the
land developer is responsible for laying out and carrying out such work as
is stipulated by the authority prior to
the disposition of individual plots of
land. A purchaser of such plots may
develop the land only in accordance
with the approved development plan
and a specification (*cahier des
charges*) for the entire area.
Planning in Western Europe, edited
by J.F. Garner, (France – Prof. J.
Lemasurier), pp. 137–139 (1975).
Précis Dalloz. Droit Civil, Les Biens
(Alex Weill), 2 edn, pp. 173–176.
*Les Grands Arrêts du Droit de L'Ur-
banisme*, by J.-P. Gilli et H. Charles,
nos. 30–80 (1974).
Petit Code Dalloz, Code de l'Urbanisme, 3 edn, pp. 406–449.

lotisseur (F)
property developer; land developer,
especially a person or company that
buys undeveloped land and, having
provided roads and services, sells off
individual plots. See also *lotissement,
promoteur*.

louage (F)
letting; renting; hiring, may be the letting or hiring of property, a thing, or
labour; although the term *louage*
generally is not used for real property.
(*louage de terres* – farm lease). See
also *bail, location*.

louer (F)
to rent; to hire out.
(*louer à bail* – to lease)
(*à louer* – available to let)

loueur (F)
lessor.

low rent
A yearly **rent** reserved under a lease
(leaving out of account any payments
for maintenance, repairs, insurance,
rates and services) which is less than
two-thirds of the **rateable value** of the
property in respect of which the rent
is payable (Leasehold Reform Act
1967, s. 4 (1)). A tenancy of a dwelling
house at a low rent is not capable of
being a **protected tenancy** (Rent Act
1977, s. 5 (3)). In the case of a progressive or graded rent, as a rule the question of whether there is a low rent is
determined by reference to the highest rent payable under the lease
(Woozley *v* Woodall [1950] 1 KB
325). See also **fit for human habitation, leasehold enfranchisement, long
tenancy, low-rent tenancy**.

low-rent tenancy
see **low rent**.

low-rise building
A building of four storeys or less, i.e.

one generally not requiring a lift. cf. **high-rise building**.

low-start mortgage
see **deferred-payment mortgage, variable-rate mortgage, variable-payment mortgage**.

loyer (F)
rent, the price paid periodically under a lease (*bail*). *Loyer* refers to the sum paid for the possession under a lease; it normally excludes any payment for service charges, as well as any form of turnover rent, a payment for a right of **usufruct** or for a *concession immobilière*.

(*loyer d'avance* – rent in advance)
(*loyer de bureau* – office rent)
(*loyer de l'argent* – interest rate)
(*loyer symbolique* – nominal rent)
(*loyer modéré* – fair rent; see *habitation à loyer modéré*)
(*loyer variable* – variable rent; graded rent)
(*loyer variable indexé sur le chiffre d'affaire* – **turnover rent**)   ,
(*loyer minimum garanti* – minimum guaranteed rent; **base rent**)
(*arriéré de loyer* – rent arrears)
(*bail à loyer* – lease, of a house). See also *location, affermage, fermage, redevance, rente*

lu et approuvé (F)
read and approved; a formal acknowledgement, placed before a signature, that the signatory has understood the preceding text.

lump-sum adjustment
A single sum added to, or deducted from, the value of a property to make it a suitable **comparable** for assessing the value of another property. See also **quantity allowance**.

lump-sum contract
1. A form of **building contract** in which the contractor submits a single (all-inclusive) price for building works. Normally this form of contract is entered into only after competitive prices have been obtained by tender; or, at least, when the employer has been able to satisfy himself that the sum is reasonable and that the work can be properly completed by the contractor at that price. Failure to complete a lump-sum contract usually prevents the contractors from recovering the agreed price or any part thereof – Appleby v Meyers (1867) LR 2 CP 651. "On any lump-sum contract, if the work is not substantially performed and there has been a failure of performance which goes to the root of it, as for instance where the work has only been half done, or is entirely different in kind from that contracted for, then no action will lie for the lump sum. The contractor can then only succeed in getting paid for what he has done if it was the employer's fault that the work was incomplete, or there was something to justify the conclusion that the parties have entered into a fresh contract, or the failure of performance is due to impossibility or **frustration**." – Hoenig v Isaacs [1952] 2 All ER 182. Called also a 'stipulated-sum contract'. See also *quantum meruit*, **substantial performance**.
2. A contract that provides for the consideration to be paid in one sum (usually on completion) rather than by instalments.
cf. **instalment contract**.

M

made land
Land that is reclaimed from the sea or a lake by filling or tipping.

made-up land
Land that is brought up to the level of the surrounding area by artificial means. In particular, an area of land the level of which is raised by tipping waste material. See also **land reclamation**.

magasin (F)
shop; store; warehouse.
(*magasin à succursales multiples* – multiple store; chain store)
(*magasin discount* – **discount store**)
(*grand magasin* – **department store**).

magnet store
see **anchor store**.

mail (F)
mall; shopping mall.

main contractor
see **general contractor**.

main residence
see **domicile, home, principal private residence**.

mainlevée (F)
release; withdrawal.
(*mainlevée de saisie* – releases of an attachment or seizure; **replevin**)
(*mainlevée d'hypothèque*; *mainlevée d'une inscription hypothècaire* – release of a mortgage).

mainmorte (F)
mortmain.

maintenance
The act or process of keeping something in a particular or proper state or condition; especially keeping a property in good order, and in a state of efficiency, by **repair**. Maintenance is a continuous process which may involve repair, but requires a greater degree of attention to general upkeep than does repair. Maintenance is not intended to extend the useful life or improve the efficiency of a building; that would constitute **improvement**. It does not include significant works of rebuilding; nor does it include making material alterations; but it may include repair works that result in a minor element of improvement. In a lease 'to maintain' the premises primarily means to keep in the same condition as when the lease was granted (fair wear and tear excluded); although the term is used generally in a broader text e.g. "to maintain in a good (or reasonable) state of repair".

In a building contract the requirement to carry out "maintenance works" may have two meanings; it may mean, "keeping in the same state" or "keeping in the same state and improving the state, always bearing in mind that it must be maintenance as distinguished from alteration of purpose". – Sevenoaks, Maidstone and Tunbridge Rly. Co. v London, Chatham and Dover Rly. Co. (1879) 11 Ch. D 634, 635. Whether or not the contract calls for 'improving the state' of the work depends on the nature and intent of the contract; although a builder's liability during a defects liability period or **maintenance period** is to make good any faults arising from inadequate workmanship or materials and not merely the type of maintenance for which a tenant normally is liable. See also **deferred maintenance**.

maintenance bond

A **bond**, or contract of insurance, which provides an **indemnity** against poor or defective workmanship in a building.

maintenance expense

Any cost or expense incurred on the **maintenance** of a building. See also **operating expenses, service charge**.

maintenance fee (US)

A charge payable by a property owner for the cost or expense of maintaining that property; in particular a charge levied against the owner of a condominium property. See also **management fee**.

maintenance period

A period, stipulated in a building contract, during which a builder is obliged to make good any defect of workmanship or materials in order to comply with the terms and conditions of the contract. Usually this period is twelve months from **practical completion** of the building work and generally the employer holds back part (commonly 10 per cent) of the contract price – a **retention sum** – to ensure that the outstanding work is completed satisfactorily. However, this is not the entire period during which the contractor can be liable for building defects; he may be liable for negligent workmanship or a **latent defect** until such an obligation is barred by statute. Called also a 'defects liability period'. See also **maintenance, negligence, Statutes of Limitation**.

maintien dans les lieux (F)

enjoyment of **possession**, of a property (following a legal adjudication); **hold over**. See also *reprise*.

maison (F)

house; dwelling-house.
(*maison d'habitation* – **dwelling-house**)
(*maison de pactille* – **jerry-built** house)
(*maison de prêts sur gage* – pawnshop)
(*maison de rapport* – **tenement** house)
(*maison, dependances et terres* – messuage)
(*maison jumelée* – **semi-detached house**).

maisonette

1. A small **house**. A two-storey house that has the appearance of a single house but is divided internally into independent dwellings or flats with separate means of access at ground floor level. See also **duplex**.
2. A self-contained dwelling, normally on two or more levels, forming part of a house or apartment building (or block of flats). See also **flat**.

maître (F)

The formal title applied to an *avocat* or *notaire*.

maître d'oeuvre (F)

A person employed to supervise and coordinate building work on behalf of the owner of the building (*maître d'ouvrage*) – usually the architect of the project. See also **responsibilité decennale**.

maître d'ouvrage (F)

building owner, in particular the party responsible for commissioning new building work under a *marché d'enterprise*.

major retail centre (MRC)

A concentration of retail stores, in an urban or suburban location, that draw custom not only from the immediate neighbourhood, but also from an area that extends well beyond. The stores may be located in a planned **shopping centre** or in an older, street or neighbourhood, development. The United States Bureau of Census (1966, pt. V) uses the term 'major retail centre' to refer to major centres of retail stores, provided they do not form part of the **central business district**.

major tenant
A tenant of a high financial standing who occupies a major or significant amount of space in a property. See also **anchor tenant, prime tenant**.

'make good'
To **repair** so as to make as good as new, or the best approximation thereto. To restore a damaged property to the condition it was in before damage was occasioned, not merely to pay compensation or to provide something similar – Crofts *v* Haldane (1867) LR 2 QB 194; City of London Real Property Co., Ltd, *v* War Damage Commission [1957] 1 All ER 526. See also **restore**.

mala fide (L)
'Bad faith'.
cf. *bona fide*. See also **misrepresentation**.

mall
1. A covered or shaded area set aside for pedestrian use. A term commonly used to refer to a public walkway in a shopping centre, i.e. a 'shopping mall'.
(US) 2. A large or regional **shopping centre**.
Shopping Malls: Planning and Design, by Barry Maitland (1985).

man-land ratio (US)
see **population ratio**.

management
see **estate management, management contract, portfolio management, project management, property management**.

management agreement
A contract between a property owner and a **managing agent** setting out the duties to be performed by the agent; the terms and conditions of appointment; and the agent's remuneration. See also **power of attorney**.

management contract
1. A form of **building contract** in which a 'management contractor' undertakes to act only as a supervisor and does not directly carry out any of the building work. The management contractor employs sub-contractors to actually carry out the work or brings together a number of sub-contractors who are employed directly by the building owner. His primary responsibility is to plan, coordinate and organise the construction of a project without directly undertaking any of the work. Usually the management contractor is remunerated by a fee based on a percentage of the total cost of the building work. The management contractor accepts a form of **project management** role but also accepts responsibility for ensuring that the building work is completed for an agreed total price. A form of building contract that is more common in the US and Continental Europe than the UK.
2. See **management agreement**.

management fee
The **fee** charged by a **managing agent** for his services. Usually a fee based on a percentage of the total income collected by the managing agent from

the property under his management. In the US called sometimes a 'maintenance fee'.

management scheme

A scheme by which a landlord of a large leasehold estate of dwelling-house sought to establish that it was in the best interests of 'good estate management' that he should have the right to retain the freehold (or a long leasehold interest) rather than the tenants having a statutory right of **leasehold enfranchisement** (a right to acquire the freehold and extinguish the leasehold interest). The Leasehold Reform Act 1967, s. 19 provided that certain landlords could retain the freehold (or in certain cases a long leasehold interest) of a housing area where the tenant would otherwise be able to exercise a right of leasehold enfranchisement; this exemption was permitted where it was considered that, "in order to maintain adequate standards of appearance and amenity and regulate development" ... it was "in the general interest that the landlord should retain power of management in respect of the houses". This arrangement only applied to an area that was occupied directly or indirectly under tenancies held from the same landlord. In order to benefit from this provision, the landlord must have established a 'management scheme' for the housing area under his control; he must have obtained a 'certificate' from the Secretary of State for the Environment (or in Wales, the Secretary of State for Wales), within two years of the Act coming into force, confirming that it is in the general interest that the landlord should retain powers of management in respect of the houses; and then he must have applied to the High Court for approval to the scheme. Generally schemes were approved only for landlords of large well established housing estates, e.g. estates owned by Housing Trusts, Housing Associations, New Town Corporations, the Church Commissioners.

Leasehold Enfranchisement, by N.T. Hague. pp. 53–62 (1967).

managing agent

An **agent** appointed by a property owner to control and direct the day-to-day running of a property. His duties include, *inter alia*, collecting rents and service charges; payment of outgoings and management expenses; keeping proper accounts for the properties under his control; supervising problems that arise between landlord and tenant; and arranging for routine property repairs and maintenance. A managing agent is vested with general powers: that is, he is to exercise his duties with judgement and discretion, using his own expertise and acting with limited direction from his principal on matters within the nature of his appointment. However, his duties remain those of an agent, not an **independent contractor**, and he must not decide on matters of policy without reference to his principal. See also **estate manager, management fee, property management**.

mandamus (L)

'We command'. A **prerogative order or writ** from a court of superior jurisdiction compelling some person, body, tribunal, or court to perform a duty imposed on them by public law, such as an order to an authority or public officer requiring the fulfillment of a statutory duty. In particular, an order from the High Court of

Justice requiring action so that "justice may be done", especially when there is no other suitable remedy. For example, in an extreme situation, a landowner who has been served with notice to treat subsequent to a compulsory purchase order may apply to the High Court requesting an order of mandamus, in order to compel the acquiring authority to take steps to determine the amount of compensation payable for his property. The grant of the order is made at the court's discretion and is made only in relation to matters of a public or semi-public nature. An application for any prerogative order is known in English law as an "application for judicial review" (Supreme Court Act 1981, s. 31 (1)). In the US an order of mandamus may be called also an 'order of mandate'.

cf. **specific performance.**

mandant (L)
see **mandator.**

mandant (F)
principal (of an agent); one who gives a *mandat* to another.

mandat (F)
1. **power of attorney;** agency agreement.
2. **principal** (in a transaction).
(*mandat et mandataire* – principal and agent)
(*mandat non divulgé* – **undisclosed principal**)
(*exclusivité du mandat* – exclusive agency). See also *exclusif.*

mandataire (F)
authorised agent; **mandatory attorney** (in-fact); **proxy.**
(*mandataire général* – general agent).
cf. *mandant.*

mandate
1. An **authority** given by one person (the mandator) to another (the mandatory), to act on his or her behalf; e.g. the authority given to an agent, or employee, to perform specified duties on behalf of a principal, or employer. A signed document used to grant such authority also may be called a mandate. See also *mandat,* **power of attorney.**
2. The gratuitous transfer of goods to another under a contract which provides that certain actions will be performed with the goods, i.e. a form of **bailment** without reward for the bailee.

cf. **deposit.**

mandate, order of (US)
see *mandamus.*

mandator
One who gives a **mandate** to another. Called also a 'mandant'.

mandatory
One to whom a **mandate** is given.

mandatory injunction
see **injunction.**

manoir (F)
manor; manor house.

manor
A large estate that formed an economic unit of rural society in medieval England. After the Norman conquest manors were established by those who owed direct fealty to the King (knights, the Church, etc.) and by the 11th century a manor was any unit owned by a lord, subject to an ultimate fealty to his Sovereign. Generally a manor comprised a principal residence (manor house) and its immediate surround – **demesne land** or 'inland' – which was retained for

the lord and the personal use of his servants. Beyond was **tenemental land** or 'outland', occupied by those who were termed villeins because they rendered various services, at the will of the lord, in return for their continued right (termed **villenage**) to hold or 'tenant' the land. The remainder of the land was waste land (woods and scrubland) occupied mostly as common land. – Corpus Christi College, Oxford v Gloucestershire County Council [1982] 3 All ER 998–9. The modern English system of land ownership is, to some extent, derived from this manorial system. Thus, in time, the villein had his rights recorded or copied into the manorial rolls, obtaining a form of **tenure** called **copyhold**. Much of the waste land, together with land held directly or sold off by the lord and any land outside the system (allodial land) that came into the hands of freemen, provided the form of tenure that became known as **freehold**. Some land, whether forming part of the demesne land or the waste land, remained in the common occupation of the tenants and forms the majority of modern day 'common land'. The modern manor is the residue and strictly is any such land owned by a barony or lordship since the Statute of **Quia Emptores** 1289 (when the process of **subinfeudation**, i.e. creating a number of tenures of the same land, was abolished).

The manor essentially became a system of government by which the ruling class, represented by a lord or great personage, controlled a natural unit of settlement; generally this unit was centred on the lord's main residence, the manor house, and its immediate lands. However, the manor was never universal and its manner of administration varied considerably according to the diversity of its origin.

The manorial system was probably imported into England by the Anglo-Saxons in the 8th century, although it has been suggested that it developed from the Roman 'vill' which was established at a much earlier date to control serf labour. Nevertheless it developed to form the kernal of a political and administrative regime that prevailed in much of Western Europe from around the 8th century until it started to breakup in the 14th century. It was "a graduated system of jurisdiction based on land tenure, in which every lord judged, taxed and commanded the class next below him . . . in which private war, private coinage, private prisons took the place of the imperial institution of government". – *The Constitutional History of England*, by William Stubbs. Vol. 1 p. 292.

The objective of a well run manor was self-sufficiency; no person had any right of land ownership, the serfs were dependent on and tied to the land, and ultimately were subservient to a feudal lord. The essentials of the manorial system were, "the economic dependency of a man on his lord; the relationship of the grantor of bookland to the inhabitants of the land so granted; the relationship created by the tie of commendation; the relationship created by the granting of soke and other judicial privileges . . . No doubt the terms 'manerium', 'mansio' or 'halla' originally meant a house or building; and they are sometimes used in their original sense. But at the end of the Anglo-Saxon period, the term 'manor' was coming to mean an estate in the land, or a group of persons cultivating such an estate, which could be looked at as an economic whole...." (*History of English Law*, 3 edn., by W.S. Holdsworth, Vol. 1, pp. 23–24).

The manorial system was the nucleus of the **feudal system** of land tenure, a system organised under aristocratic administration and based on 'fief' – land held by a tenant as an inferior right (the word fief being *feudum* in Latin and *feud* or *fee* in Old English). The system gradually broke up as a result of (a) the substitution of money payments for labour services (**commutation**) – leading toward a system of rent payments; (b) the alienation of the lord's demesne (i.e. parting with a right to services in return for money) in order to secure labour, especially after the Black Death, leading eventually to the modern leasehold system in English law; (c) the use and development of the **enclosure**, extending the ownership of private property; and (d) the establishment of a central judicature, superceding the manorial courts.

The manorial system was particularly prevalent throughout Western Europe in the 10th–13th centuries and was even adopted as the basis for the administration of estates in America in colonial times. (In the US, a manor was an estate of inheritance, subject to a **fee farm rent** payable to a representative of the colonial power.) The system was not broken in the US until the Declaration of Independence in 1776 and in France until the Revolution of 1792. It has continued in a diluted form in England and is still not entirely extinct as certain property continues to maintain the right to be called a manor house and to carry certain manorial rights or **incidents of tenure** over adjoining land, the most important being mineral and sporting rights.

The manorial system may be considered to have formed a fulcrum for a steady evolution of land tenure from one based on labour service, or serfdom, with a dependency that denied any true right to private property; to a modern system of ownership, whereby land can be held freely; (whether in perpetuity, as with a fee simple absolute, or for a more limited duration, as with a periodic tenancy) and during the period for which it is held the holder's right may not be impeded by a superior lord (whether the Crown or a private landlord) without due process of law.

9 Halsbury's Laws of England, 4 edn, pp. 482–496.

History of English Law, by Holdsworth, 3 edn., pp. 23–32, 179–184.

manor house
see **manor**.

manorial incidents
see **incidents of tenure**.

manse
The residence of a clergyman (especially in Scotland the residence of a Presbyterian clergyman) together with the **glebe land** attached thereto.

mansion house
1. A large dwelling-house, especially one that forms part of an estate. See also **messuage**.
2. An important residence on a **manor**; the chief residence of the lord of the manor being the 'principal mansion house'.

In the case of a settlement of land, the main house, if any, and the land occupied therewith (provided it is not a farmhouse or a house with 25 acres or less of accompanying land) is deemed to be the 'principal mansion house' or 'capital messuage'. If a **tenant for life** wishes to dispose of the principal mansion house he must obtain the consent of the trustees of the settlement or an order of the court, if (i) the settlement was made before 1926, unless there is a provision expressly dispensing with this requirement; or (ii) the settlement is made after 1925, and there is an express provision requiring such consent or order to be obtained (Settled Land Act 1925, s. 65). See also **settled land**.

manus mortua (L)

'A dead hand'. See **mortmain**.

map

A representation or picture on a flat surface of certain features of a given area of land, prepared in order to show their relative positions; especially a representation that shows lines of communication, administrative boundaries, landmarks, key locations, etc. A **plan** showing relief and other landscape features as established by a survey of an area.

march or marches

A property limit or **boundary line**. A territory of official jurisdiction; to 'march' with another county or state means to have a common border, as Scotland borders on England.

marchand de biens (F)

property trader. Under French law one who habitually deals in property and is entitled to acquire property without paying registration duties, provided the property is resold within 5 years. On resale, within that time limit, the purchaser pays registration duty and the *marchand de biens* pays

taxe sur la valeur ajoutée (value added tax) on his profits.
Taxes in France, by Lionel Halpern, 3 edn., p. 123.

marché (F)

market; **bargain**; contract.
(*marché à forfait absolu* – fixed or **lump sum contract**)
(*marché à forfait relatif* – fixed-price building contract, based on a schedule of prices)
(*marché à bordereau de prix* – **remeasurement contract**, a building contract based on a schedule of rates and prices and a basic form of bill of quantities)
(*marché au comptant* – cash purchase)
(*marché d'enterprise* – building contract; a contract by which a *maître d'ouvrage* employs an *entrepreneur* to undertake building or construction work (French Civil Code, arts. 1787–1799))
(*marché fait* – fixed price)
(*marché immobilier* – property market)
(*prix du marché* – **market price**).

Mareva injunction

A form of interlocutory **injunction**, which derives its name from the case of Mareva Compania Naviera S.A. of Panama *v* International Bulk Carriers S.A. [1975] 2 Lloyd's Rep 509 and is now given statutory force by the Supreme Court Act 1981, s. 37 (2) which provides the High Court with the power to restrain "a party to any proceedings from removing from the jurisdiction of the High Court, or otherwise dealing with, assets" which might be disposed of in order to avoid their being used later to meet an obligation that might be enforced by the court. A Mareva injunction permits a plaintiff to request a court to freeze assets up to the maximum amount he is claiming in an action. It may be granted *ex parte*, but is granted only "when it appears that there is a combination of two circumstances. First, when it appears likely that the plaintiff will recover judgment against the defendant for a certain or approximate sum. Second, when there are also reasons to believe that the defendant has assets within the jurisdiction to meet the judgment, in whole or in part, but may well take steps to ensure that these are not available or traceable when judgment is given against him" – Z Ltd., *v* A and another [1982] 1 All ER 572.

marge de reculement (F)
 set back, the distance between a building line and a property boundary.

margin
 1. A sum of money that exceeds what is absolutely necessary. An amount by which the **market value** of an asset, offered as security or collateral for a loan, exceeds the amount of the loan. This excess is the borrower's **equity capital** and represents the lender's margin of safety. If the value of an asset falls below the amount of the loan, the margin is said to 'run-off'. The amount of margin required by a lender depends on (a) the credit rating of the borrower; (b) the type and liquidity of the **collateral**; and (c) the degree of risk in realising the market value of the asset. See also **debt-to-equity ratio, gearing, mortgage value**.
 2. A loan made by a stockbroker or commodity broker to enable a customer to acquire securities or commodities for a higher amount than the capital available to the customer, with the securities or the commodities

being held as security for the loan.
 3. An area of land left undeveloped between a property boundary and a new building. A **zone non-aedificandi** or 'set-back' area.
 4. An obsolete term for a **boundary line**.

marginal efficiency of capital
 The increased return that may be obtained by investing one unit of capital; the return engendered by a marginal increase in investment. The marginal efficiency of capital reflects the propensity to invest; thus if the discounted income generated by an investment is greater than its cost, the investment will be profitable and, other things being equal, it should be undertaken. See also **internal rate of return**.

marginal income
 Income received, or capable of being received, from an investment above a given base level. For example, the amount by which the market rent of a property exceeds the amount payable contractually by an existing tenant. See also **hardcore method, top-slice income**.

marginal land
 Land that, at any point in time, (given a particular level of supply and demand) is just worth cultivating; land that yields an income marginally higher than the cost of producing that income. Land that is not quite worth exploiting is called also marginal land. See also **economic rent**.

marginal method
 see **hardcore method**.

marginal note
 A heading or brief description set out in the margin of a statute or legal

document. Such a note is not intended to form any part of the document and does not have any legal effect. It is intended only for guidance or reference, except in cases of complete ambiguity or contradiction.

market

1. A public place where people meet, at an appointed time, in order to conduct business either in one or a variety of goods. 'A place to which sellers who have not found buyers take their goods in the hope of finding buyers, and to which buyers resort in the hope of finding the goods they want.' – Scottish CWS Ltd, *v* Ulster Farmers' Mart Co. Ltd [1959] 2 All ER 495. Any **shop**, or shopping centre, constitutes a market; however, the term is used commonly to describe a number of stalls set up in a public square, on certain days, for the sale of goods or provisions at the most competitive price.

2. A public place where buyers and sellers are permitted to gather to trade in goods; as authorised by a **franchise** from the Crown, by Act of Parliament, or as a result of an established right of use. "The franchise right of holding a concourse of buyers and sellers to dispose of commodities in respect of which the franchise is given" – Marquess of Devonshire *v* O'Brien (1887) 19 LR Ir. 390. The holder of the franchise has a real property right that may be leased or sold – that is a right to hold a market within a designated area, on given days of the week, for the sale of particular commodities. The franchiser has a monopoly for the specific form of market and receives his profit by charging for the use of space to erect stalls (**stallage**) or levying a charge on the value of the items sold (**toll**). cf. **fair**.

Law of Markets and Fairs, by Pease and Chitty, 2 edn.
29 Halsbury's Laws of England, 4 edn, paras. 601–716.

3. Any aggregation of potential buyers and sellers, or any network that brings together potential buyers and sellers, so that a **price** is established at which goods or commodities are traded. In this sense a market does not require a fixed place. When buyers and sellers come together, or are brought together (for example, by a **broker**) with the intention of making a bargain, so that the ownership of goods may be transferred at a price fixed by consensus, there is a market.

A 'perfect' market is said to exist when 'buyers have no preferences as between the different units of the commodity offered for sale, sellers are quite indifferent to whom they sell, and both buyers and sellers have full knowledge of prices in other parts of the market'. (*Introduction to Economics*, by Alec Cairncross, 3 edn., p. 271). Most markets are considered to be 'imperfect' because, for the same goods, transactions take place in diverse places; restraint may be placed on certain buyers or sellers; and the goods may not be readily divisible, so that a unit price cannot be created. The market for land is highly imperfect. It is distorted by the heterogeneous nature of land; the imbalance of knowledge and negotiating skills of buyers and sellers; the lack of readily available information on real estate transactions; the illiquidity of land as an asset; and the differences in extraneous factors that affect buyers and sellers of real estate e.g. tax, government rent controls. The free exchange and availability of information in a perfect market makes the price of goods – the **market price** – readily ascertainable; the more imperfect the market the more unpredictable and speculative the price. See also **market value**.

market approach (US)
see **market comparison approach**.

market area
see **catchment area**.

market comparison approach (US)
A method of appraising or estimating the value of a property by making reference to the value of similar or **comparable property**. Called also the 'market value approach', 'market-data approach', 'market-comparison approach' or the 'sales comparison approach'. See also **appraisal, comparison method of valuation**.
The Appraisal of Real Estate, AIREA., 8 edn., pp. 309–331.

market-data approach (US)
see **market comparison approach**.

market garden
An area of land, together with buildings thereon (greenhouses, potting sheds, etc.), used as a **garden** or nursery for the growing, cultivation and production of fruit, hops, seeds and vegetables, on a modest scale, for the purpose of trade or business. A market garden may be a domestic garden or it may be larger than a domestic garden, but it is more intensively cultivated, and is operated on a smaller scale, than an agricultural holding or farm – Purser *v* Worthing Local Board of Health (1887) 18 QBD 820. A tenant of a market garden is entitled to more extensive compensation in the event of the termination

of his tenancy. See also **allotment, compensation for improvements, Evesham Custom**.

market method
see **comparison method of valuation**.

market overt (or ouvert)
A public and open **market**. A market which in England is authorised and regulated by law, so that anyone who buys goods, according to the usage of the market, acquires a good title to the goods, provided he buys them in good faith and without notice of any defect or want of title on the part of the seller (Sale of Goods Act 1979, s. 22). This section applies, for example, to an agent who sells goods without his principal's authority: it does not apply to a sale of stolen goods that may be recovered if a thief is convicted and ordered to return the goods; nor does it apply to a sale to a trader or a sale by sample, because the entire transaction must be conducted in the market – Crane *v* London Dock Co. (1864) 33 LJQB 244. A market overt is held only between sunrise and sunset (Market Overt Case (1596) 5 Co. Rep. 336). It may be held on any day except Sundays and public holidays and, outside the City of London, it must be held in a place established by custom or legal authority. In the City of London every shop is a market overt when open to the general public to sell such goods as the shopkeeper normally trades in. This rule as to a market overt does not apply in Wales or Scotland.

market price
The **price**, or consideration, actually paid in a particular **market**; the price at which, in a given market, it is con-

sidered that supply and demand are equal. (There must be a market in order to set such a price – "the expression market price is inapplicable to beer, for there is no beer market". – Courage *v* Carpenter [1910] 1 Ch. 262. In economics, the cost of producing a commodity is referred to as the 'cost price' or 'natural price' and "the actual price at which any commodity is commonly sold is called its market price. It may be above, or below, or exactly the same with its natural price". (*Wealth of Nations*, by Adam Smith, Book I, Ch. 7). Market price is used sometimes synonymously with **market value**, although the market price is the sum actually paid (or demanded) and market value the real or estimated worth.

market rent

The **market value** for renting purposes. The **best rent** at which a property might reasonably be expected to let with vacant possession in the open market when offered by a willing lessor to a willing lessee, taking full account of the terms of the tenancy offered. See also **agricultural tenancy**, **business tenancy**, **economic rent**, **fair rent**, **rack rent**.
Handbook of Business Tenancies, by D.W. Williams, paras. 11.25–11.38 (1985, looseleaf).

market survey

A survey of an area to ascertain the demand and competition for a property and to determine the general market conditions as they may affect that property. See also **feasibility study**.

market value

The price that a property might reasonably be expected to realise if offered for sale in a particular **market** in the normal course of business. The amount that a property should realise, usually expressed in money terms, when it is offered for sale, for a reasonable period of time, by a **willing seller**, so as to enable the property to be brought to the attention of all potential and willing buyers. 'Market value' is the amount that a property might be expected to bring, as distinguished from **market price** which is the amount that the property can be sold for at a given time. Market value is established by reference to the transactions in the normal and regular course of business; it is based on evidence from private treaty sales. It is an estimate of worth based on certain implicit assumptions; namely, (i) neither the buyer nor the seller is under any undue influence or duress to consummate the bargain; (ii) a reasonable time is allowed to negotiate a bargain, given the type of property and the state of the market; (iii) no account is to be taken of an additional bid from any **special purchaser**; (iv) the bargain is concluded subsequent to an arm's length transaction; and (v) the sale is concluded as a simple cash (or equivalent) transaction.

The term 'open' market value may be used to emphasise that the market is to be overt and available to every person who might constitute a buyer in the market in which the property might normally be sold, and not limited or restricted to any selected group of purchasers. When assessing compulsory purchase compensation, "the market is to be the open market, as distinguished from a limited class only, such as members of a family. The market is not necessarily an auction sale. ... (The value) is such amount as the land might be expected to realise if offered under conditions enabling every person desirous of purchasing to come in and make an offer, and if proper steps were taken to advertise the property and let all likely purchasers know that land is in the market for sale." – Inland Revenue Commissioners *v* Clay and Buchanan [1914] 2 KB 466. An 'open market' requires that the property is brought to the attention of any person who might (a) wish to know that the property is being offered for sale; (b) be willing or desirous of purchasing the property; and (c) be prepared to submit an offer for the property.

The Royal Institution of Chartered Surveyors define 'open market value' as "the best price at which an interest in property might reasonably be expected to be sold by Private Treaty at the date of valuation, assuming: (a) a willing seller; (b) a reasonable period within which to negotiate the sale, taking into account the nature of the property and the state of the market; (c) values will remain static throughout the period; (d) the property will be freely exposed to the market; and (e) no account will be taken of an additional bid by a special purchaser,"(Guidance Note No. GN22).

In English statutes the term market value is defined in a variety of ways, e.g. "the price which that property might reasonably be expected to fetch on sale in the open market" (Income and Corporation Tax Act 1970, s. 167 (1)); "the market value at any time of an interest in land is the consideration which that interest might reasonably be expected to fetch on a sale at that time in the open market; but that consideration shall not be assumed to be reduced on the ground that the inter-

est in all the land in question is to be placed on the market at one and the same time" (Development Land Tax Act 1976, s. 7 (1)). See also **fair market value, highest and best use, value.**

Readings in Market Value, AIREA, pp. 68–74 (1981).

Guidance Notes on the Valuation of Assets, The Royal Institution of Chartered Surveyors (1982).

market value approach
see **market approach**.

marketability study
see **feasibility study**.

marketable title
A **title** to property that is sufficiently free from defect so that a reasonable person would acquire the property without requiring any discount on its market price. A title that is free from any material defect or doubt; is not subject to legal dispute; and would be supported in equity if the vendor seeks a decree of **specific performance** requiring the purchaser to accept it – Sinclair *v* Webb, 104 A 2d. 561, 204 Md. 324. A title that is not only an established right, i.e. a **good title**, to that which is being transferred, but is free from any encumberance of defect not specified in the contract for sale. A term used more commonly in the US where it is called also a 'merchantable title'.
cf. **unmarketable title**. See also **cloud on title, free and clear title.**
Real Estate Law, by Robert Kratovil and Raymond J. Werner, 8 edn., pp. 135–144.

marriage value
An increase in value, or a release of latent value, brought about either by the merging of two interests in the

same property or the merging of two adjoining or contiguous properties into common ownership. The most common instances of marriage value arise when a property is let at less than its market rental value and the respective interest of the landlord and tenant are merged, or when a small undevelopable site is added to a larger site.
Modern Methods of Valuation, 7 edn., p. 119.

marshalling
Arranging or disposing in order, especially of assets according to their **priority** for creditors. The equitable doctrine of marshalling permits a creditor, or mortgagee, to claim simultaneously against all properties held as security, provided that he does not unreasonably deprive any other party, who may have a claim against only one of the properties, of his right to security – Aldrich *v* Cooper (1803) 8 Ves. 382; Meyer *v* United States, 375 US 233, 84 S Ct. 318, 11 L. Ed. 2d. 293. The doctrine is intended to permit all creditors of a single debtor to be satisfied in the most equitable way possible. Thus, if A mortgages Stone House and Timber Cottage to B (as a first charge) and subsequently mortgages Stone House (as a second charge) to C., then B must satisfy his charge from Timber Cottage first; only then, if his debt is still not satisfied can B claim against Stone House. Thereafter, C has a right to claim against Stone House.

Martinmas
The feast of St. Martin of Tours, 11 November. In Scotland one of the half **quarter-days** or 'term days'.

Massachusetts trust (US)
see **business trust**.

master deed (US)
see **enabling declaration**.

master lease (US)
A lease that is in a standard form and is intended to act as a guide when granting new leases in a particular building or development scheme. See also **enabling declaration, head lease, standard-form contract**.

master mortgage (US)
A standard form of mortgage contract that is recorded at a public records office by a mortgagee as representative of the basic terms upon which a number of separate mortgages may be granted. A master mortgage is recorded to save the expense of duplicating most of the mortgage contract every time a mortgage that is granted on similar terms is recorded, as on a housing estate. When a new mortgage is granted only the basic terms are recorded (term, property secured, interest rate, etc.) and the remaining conditions are indicated by reference to the recorded master mortgage.

master plan
An overall plan, usually accompanied by a detailed written text, prepared as a guide to proposals for the future long-term growth and planning of an area. The plan sets out such matters as demographic growth projections, infrastructure proposals, land use zoning, etc.; more detailed plans are intended to be fitted into its framework. A particular example of a master plan is one prepared to regulate the entire development of a new town. Called also a 'general plan'. See also **regional plan, structure plan**.

material breach
see **breach of contract, condition**.

'material change in the use'

A term inserted originally in the Town and Country Planning Act 1947, s. 12 (2) and now incorporated in the Town and Country Planning Act 1971, s. 22 (1) that refers to an activity considered to be a form of **development** and, therefore, to be subject to planning control. The term is not defined further in the Act but, based on case law, it covers a change in the character of land or a building; a substantial change of use; or a significant intensification of the use of land or a building. Whether an intensification of use is a 'material change' is a matter of degree, and "matters of degree are for the Secretary of State [for the Environment] to decide" – Brooks and Burton v Secretary of State for the Environment [1978] 1 WLR 1294.

"A change of *kind* will always be material – e.g., from house to shop or from shop to factory. A change in the *degree* of an existing use may be 'material', but only if it is very marked. For example, the fact that lodgers are taken privately in a family dwelling house would not in the Minister's [now the Secretary of State's] view constitute a material change of use in itself so long as the use of the house remains substantially that of a private residence. On the other hand, the change from a private residence with lodgers to a declared guest house, boarding house or private hotel would be 'material'" (Ministry of Town and Country Planning Circular No. 67, 15 February 1949. This circular does not have force of law, but as it has never been withdrawn, it reflects substantially the wishes of central government.) The effect of a change of use on the general planning requirements of an area may be relevant when determining if the change is material; " ... the increasing intensity of use or occupation may involve a substantial increase in the burden of the services which a local authority has to supply, and that, in truth, might in some cases at least, be material in considering whether the use of the land has been materially changed". – Guildford RDC v Fortescue [1959] 2 QB 112.

When deciding what constitutes a material change in the use of land or buildings, what is termed a **planning unit** (an area considered as a whole for planning purposes) must be looked at, i.e. it is necessary to consider the entirety; not just a part of the whole, or a part of a building within the unit – Williams v Ministry of Housing and Local Government (1967) 65 LGR 425; De Mulder v Secretary of State for the Environment [1974] QB 792. A mere cessation of user *per se* cannot be construed as a material change (that would mean that a landowner would require planning permission to cease an activity); but if one of a number of uses of a parcel of land ceases and a remaining use is intensified there may well be a 'material change of use' – Wipperman v Barking London Borough Council (1965) 17 P and CR 225. See also **permitted development, Use Classes Order**.

Outline of Planning Law, by Desmond Heap, 8 edn., pp. 89–93.
Development and Planning Law, by Barry Denyer-Green, pp. 17–26 (1982).
46 Halsbury's Laws of England, 4 edn, para. 89.
Guide to Development and Planning, by R.N.D. Hamilton, 7 edn., pp. 87–139.
Encyclopaedia of Planning Law and

Practice, by Desmond Heap, para. 1–071.
Urban Planning Law, by Malcolm Grant, pp. 159–172 (1982).
Cases and Materials on Planning Law, by Michael Purdue, pp. 67–120.

material considerations
see **planning application**.

material detriment
see **injurious affection, severance**.

material development
Any significant change in the state, nature or use of land; in particular, **development** that is more than *de minimus* in nature. The term 'material development' was introduced into the Land Commission Act 1967, s. 99 (2) to cover those forms of development which gave rise to a potential liability to a levy on development value, i.e. it was used to describe an action that gave rise to a liability for **betterment levy**. With the exception of certain 'permitted development', it included most forms of development as defined in the Town and Country Planning Acts. This Act was dissolved by the Land Commission (Dissolution) Act 1971. The Development Land Tax Act 1976, s. 7 reintroduced the term material development and defined it to include most forms of development that require planning permission (as defined in the Town and Country Planning Act 1971, s. 22). Thus, 'material development' excludes development permitted by a **general development order** (but not development excluded from an order by an Article 4 direction nor a condition attached to a specific planning permission) and a number of tolerances set out in Part II of the 4th Schedule of the 1976 Act (the

most notable being a 10 per cent alteration or enlargement of a building). Material development is relevant to the assessment of **development land tax** in two respects (a) in determining the **current use value**, which was the value on the assumption that only development which was not material could be carried out and (b) in determining when there had been a 'deemed disposal' of land, which arose upon the start of a 'project of material development'. The start of a project of material development included various 'specified operations', including the digging of a trench to contain the foundations of a building, the laying of any underground pipe or main, and the making of any material change in the use of land (1976 Act, Sch. 1 para. 2 (1) (2)). However, when starting such development there must have been a reasonable expectation of being able to carry it on to completion – R. *v* IRC, *ex parte* Harrow LBC [1983] STC 246.

'Material development' was used also in the Finance Act 1974, Sch. 3, s. 6 with reference to a potential liability for **development gains tax**, where it was given a broader meaning than in the aforementioned statutes, with exceptions set out in section 7 of the 1974 Act. This tax was effectively replaced by Development Land Tax in 1976 (Development Land Tax Act 1976, s. 35) which was in turn abolished by the Finance Act 1985, s. 93.

matrimonial home
Property owned and lived in by the parties to a contract of matrimony. A place where a man and woman have established a **home** together as husband and wife.

Until the Married Woman's Property Act, 1870 it was considered that, by marriage, the husband and wife became one party in law, and that the one party was the husband – hence, the husband acquired on marriage, not only a wife as property but also any property owned by her. During the marriage the parties jointly could dispose of any real property; the husband had power to dispose of his own interest without the concurrence of his wife (although he was obliged to maintain a 'matrimonial home'); but the wife alone had no power to dispose of any real property, even that which she brought to the marriage. If she predeceased him, the husband was entitled, in certain circumstances, to a life interest in any freehold (fee simple or fee tail) land of his deceased wife – he became entitled to a **tenancy by the curtesy**. If he predeceased her, the wife was entitled to a life interest in one third of his freehold property, her right of **dower**, provided she could show that she might have had an issue capable of inheriting that estate. Divorce was virtually unheard of so a wife effectively, from the date of her marriage, had no right to separate property other than a right to a roof over her head. In the 19th century the Court of Chancery recognised a wife's claim to such property as she brought to the marriage and, in limited instances, divorce was permitted. To meet these changes various statutes were passed to extend a wife's entitlement to real property, in particular the Married Woman's Property Act 1882, s. 1 (1) which recognised the right of a wife to acquire, hold or dispose of real and personal property as if she were a *femme sole* (a single woman). However, a wife's right to own property upon the same basis as her husband was not finally granted until the Law Reform (Married Women and Torfeasors) Act, 1935.

In modern English law husband and wife, like any individuals, have separate rights to any property held in their sole name. On the other hand, the matrimonial home may be held in accordance with an express agreement for the benefit of both parties as a **joint tenancy** or, more commonly, as a **tenancy-in-common**. When the property is held in the sole name of one party, then, in the words of Lord Denning M.R. "it is entirely appropriate to describe (husband and wife) as equitable tenants in common of the land – that is of the land itself – until sale: and then after sale, in the proceeds of sale". – Williams and Glyn's Bank Ltd *v* Boland [1979] Ch. 331. The entitlement of each party to the proceeds of sale depends upon (a) their respective contributions to the cost of acquiring the property, whether as a direct payment of the initial price, a contribution to repayment of a mortgage, or, in exceptional cases, by indirect contributions – Re Rogers' Question [1948] 1 All ER 328; and (b) any contribution in money or money's worth to the improvement of the property, provided that the contribution is of a "substantial nature" and provided there is no agreement to the contrary, express or implied (Matrimonial Proceedings and Property Act 1970, s. 37). In the case of (a), a **resulting trust** or a **constructive trust** is said to arise, with the husband and wife as beneficiaries according to the amount of their respective contributions; in the case of (b), statute imposes a trust to the same effect.

In the event of divorce it is not necessary to decide upon the spouses' strict rights to an interest in the matrimonial home, because the court has power to distribute such property as is owned by the spouses, taking into account such factors as any previous contribution in terms of care of the home and bringing up children, and the loss that accrues to the respective parties as a result of the dissolution. In the process the court endeavours "to place the parties, so far as it is practicable . . . in the financial position in which they would have been if the marriage had not broken down . . ."(Matrimonial Causes Act 1973, s. 24 (2)).

Husband and wife each have the same rights to occupy a rented matrimonial home in so far as it affects third parties – National Provincial Bank Ltd *v* Ainsworth [1965] A.C. 1175. Between the spouses if one spouse has a right to occupy a dwelling-house (by virtue of any form of contract) the other spouse is given "rights of occupation" of that house. Thus, (a) if one spouse is in occupation he or she has a right not to be evicted or excluded from the dwelling-house or any part thereof by the other spouse except under a court order and (b) if a spouse is not in occupation, he or she has a right with the leave of the court to enter into and occupy the dwelling-house (Matrimonial Homes Act 1983, s. 1). The Matrimonial Proceedings and Property Act, 1970 and the Matrimonial Homes Act 1983 apply to spouses only and the same provisions and protection are not given to a mistress or co-habitee. However, a mistress or co-habitee may have a right to a share in the proceeds of sale of a property because

there is a resulting trust which has arisen as a consequence of contributions made by the mistress or co-habitee toward the cost of purchasing or improving the property; or because a similar action has brought about a tenancy-in-common. Alternatively, a mistress or co-habitee may have some form of licence to occupy based on financial contributions, or a promise supported by the doctrine of **estoppel**.

An equitable interest arising out of the Matrimonial Proceedings and Property Act 1970, or the rights arising under the Matrimonial Homes Act 1983, may be protected by registration as a **land charge** (Land Charges Act, 1972 s. 2 (7)); or, if the property is registered, by entry of a **notice** or **caution** (Land Registration Act 925, s. 101 (3)). See also *communauté*, **community property, constructive trust, co-ownership, homestead**, overriding interest.

Manual of Housing Law, by Andrew Arden, 2 edn., pp. 142–151.

Introduction to Land Law, by J.G. Riddell, 3 edn., Appendix 1.

Real Property and Real People, by K.J. Gray and P.D. Symes, Ch. 11, 16. (1981).

Matrimonial Property and Finance, by P. Duckworth, pp. 1–64 (1980).

22 Halsbury's Laws of England, 4 edn, paras. 1026–1062.

Matrimonial Finance and Taxation, by J. Jackson and D.T.A. Davies (1980).

maturity date

The date on which an obligation, such as a bill of exchange, bond, mortgage, etc., becomes due for final repayment. See also **redemption date, yield to maturity**.

'McCarthy rules'
see **compensation for injurious affection**.

meadow land
An area of grass land, especially a field in which grass is grown for hay or pasture. See also **agricultural land, grazing licence**.

means of access
see **access, easement of necessity**.

measure-and-value contract
see **fixed-price contract**.

measurement contract
see **fixed-price contract**.

mechanic's lien (US)
see **lien**.

medium filum (L)
see ***ad medium filum***.

megalopolis
Derived from the Greek, *megalou*, 'great', and *polis*, 'city'. A very expansive city; a densely populated area that is larger than a conurbation, usually comprising more than one city; or a city and a major urban area around that city. 'Megalopolis' was used by Epaminondas of Thebes in 371 B.C. to describe the joining together of many small cities into a large city for administrative purposes and also by Jean Gottmann in 'Megalopolis, the Urbanised North-eastern Seaboard of the United States' (1961) to describe the multitude of cities on the east coast of the US.

meliorating waste
see **waste**.

memorandum
Derived from the Latin *memorare*, 'to remember'. A written summary or brief note of the terms of an agreement.

In English law a memorandum may be an element in establishing a valid **contract**, and if the contract relates to "the sale or other disposition of land or any interest in the land" then, if it is sought to bring an action under that contract, that which has been agreed, or some note or memorandum thereof, must be in **writing** and signed by the party, or an authorised agent acting for the party, against whom the action is to be brought (Law of Property Act 1925, s. 40 (1)). The memorandum need not be in any particular form, provided it contains the essential elements to support a valid contract: the parties, an adequate description of the property, the consideration, the date and details of any other matter that may be material to, or form a condition of, the contract that the memorandum is intended to support (Re. Hoyle [1893] 1 Ch. 84): and it may even be contained in more than one document. It need not form a contract in its own right, i.e. it may be made '**subject to contract**', provided there is other evidence that a contract has been established, e.g. a subsequent oral contract which waives the written constraint (but, not an oral contract followed by a written contract made 'subject to contract') – Griffiths *v* Young [1970] Ch. 675. This requirement, for a written and signed memorandum, does not affect the law relating to **part performance** (1925 Act, s. 40 (20); nor any other rights between the parties other than the right of action on the contract. See also **agreement for a lease, binder, endorsement, joinder, rider, Statute of Frauds**.
The Law of Real Property, by R. Megarry and H.W.R. Wade, 5 edn, pp. 577–578.

mensuel (*f.- elle*); **mensuellement** (F)
monthly.
(*mensualités* – monthly instalments)

merchandise
Goods or chattels that are normally bought and sold, but generally not real property. The subject matter of trade.

merchantable title
see **marketable title**.

merchantile agent
see **factor**.

mere equity
A right that may be enforced between two parties in **equity**, and concerns land, but does not create any interest in land, e.g. a right to rectification of a contract or a right to an injunction.
cf. **equitable interest**.

mere licence
see **licence**.

merger
The absorption of one estate in land by another. The combining of two or more interests in the same property into the hands of the same person, at the same time, so as to extinguish all but one of the interests. In particular, the absorption of a lesser estate into the hands of one party by joining it with a greater estate held by that party, without there being any intervening estate. A situation that most commonly arises when a landlord acquires the interest of his direct tenant, the smaller interest is then said to be 'sunk or drowned in the greater estate' – Bl. Comm. vol. ii p. 177; i.e. it is extinguished by operation of law. A merger cannot take place if there is a mortgage on a leasehold interest; nor if the lease and the reversion are held in different capaci-

ties, e.g by a trustee and a beneficiary respectively – Chambers *v* Kingham (1878) 10 Ch. D 743. At common law the merger of a term of a lease into the reversion was considered to have the effect of destroying the covenants of any underlease; but since 1925 the head lessor becomes in effect the landlord of the under tenant (Law of Property Act 1925, s. 139 (1)).

A merger takes place between a contract for the sale of land and a conveyance so that the former is extinguished by the latter. However, the contract is extinguished "only to the effect that the deed [conveyance] is intended to cover the same ground". – Palmer *v* Johnson (1884) 13 QBD 351. The contract may remain as a **collateral** agreement to the conveyance if it covers a separate matter.
cf. **surrender**. See also **marriage value**, **merger clause**, **satisfied term**, **termination**, **unity of possession**.
Cheshire's Law of Real Property 13 edn, pp. 851–853.

merger clause (US)
A clause in a written agreement which specifies that the writing shall constitute the entirety of a contract and that there is no **warranty**, representation or agreement that can have any effect on the agreement, other than that which is **express**. As a rule, a contract in writing does not require a merger clause because the terms agreed between the parties are contained in the document and all previous oral agreements are merged into the written instrument – Hawkins *v* United States, 96 US 689, 24 L. Ed. 607). See also **express term**.

mesne
Intermediate; that part in between a

beginning and end in time. See also **mesne lord, mesne profits, sandwich lease**.

mesne assignment
1. The creation, or assignment, of a **sandwich lease**.
2. An assignment of a lease that takes place between the time of the grant of the original lease and a more recent assignment. For example, if A grants a lease to B, B assigns to C, and C assigns to D the assignment by B is a mesne assignment.

mesne charge (or encumberance)
A charge (or encumberance) that is situated in time between two other charges or encumberances, e.g. a charge that does not rank as a first charge but ranks ahead of another charge in terms of **priority**.

mesne lord
Under the **feudal system** of land tenure a lord who held land from a **tenant in chief** and granted that land to an inferior lord or **tenant in demesne**. See also **tenure**.

mesne profits
Profits arising during an intervening period. For example, profits lost as a result of being wrongfully dispossessed from land; or profits obtained when a party has wrongfully retained possession, such as by a tenant who retains a property after the termination of his lease. "A claim for mesne profits can be joined with an action for the **recovery** of the land, and mesne profits is only another term for damages for **trespass**, damages which arise from the particular relationship of landlord and tenant". – Bramwell *v* Bramwell [1942] 1 All ER 138. The claim is brought to remedy a tort and not for a breach of contract (as any

contract has been satisfied). A payment of mesne profits is based on the equivalent to the "fair value of the premises" for the period of wrongful occupation. In the case of a tenant who retains possession after the end of his lease the amount is based usually on the former rent, but it may be higher (or lower) if justifiable – Clifton Securities *v* Huntley [1948] W.N. 267. Mesne profits represent a claim for **unliquidated damages**, as compared to **rent** which is a liquidated sum. See also **mistake, tenancy on sufferance, use and occupation**.

mesne tenancy
see **sandwich lease**.

messuage
A **house** together with any outbuildings, courtyard, garden or orchard, occupied therewith – Doe d. Clements *v* Collins (1788) 2 Term Rep. 498. In particular, a dwelling-house, together with the **curtilage** and land and building appurtenant thereto. A property that is lived in, together with the premises used at the same time and as an essential part of the occupancy – Kerkslake *v* White (1819) 2 Star. 509. The transfer by will of a 'messuage' also passes the curtilage, even if there is no provision to that effect – Borrows *v* Ellison (1871) 24 LT 365. A 'capital messuage' is the principal **mansion house** of an estate.

metayage (F)
metayage system.

metayage system
A form of land **tenure** by which a landowner permitted his land to be occupied and cultivated in exchange for a share (usually one half) of the produce of the soil. The farmer had no right to the land itself, but only to

the produce. A system that developed in France in the 18th century (where it is called a *bail à colonate paritaire*) as well as in the southern United States, but was rarely found in England. 'To the slave cultivators of ancient times gradually succeeded a species of farmers known at present in France by the name Metayers. They are known in Latin, *Coloni Partiarii*. They have been so long in disuse in England that at present I know no English name for them. The proprietor furnished them with the seed, cattle, and instrument of husbandry, the whole stock, in short, necessary for cultivating the farm. The produce was divided equally between the proprietor and the farmer' (*Wealth of Nations*, by Adam Smith, Book III, Ch. 2 (1776)). See also **share-cropping**.

mete
1. To distribute by subdivision.
2. A boundary. See also **metes and bounds system**.

metes and bounds system (US)
A method of describing a plot of land by specifying the dimensions of its boundaries (*metes*) both by distances and compass measurements, and identifying certain landmarks (*bounds*). A system that is used especially for showing title to newly settled land before any more formal system of land referencing is established. Called also the 'butts and bounds system'.
cf. **lot and block system**.
Real Estate Principles, by Bruce Harwood, 2 edn., pp. 18–22.

methods of depreciation
see **depreciation**.

methods of valuation
see **valuation**.

métreur-vérificateur (F)
construction surveyor; **quantity surveyor**, although generally less qualified or specialised than a quantity surveyor in the UK, and more commonly employed in an architect's office.

metropolis
Literally a 'mother city'. A capital or major city. In the UK the Inner London area is referred to as the metropolis.

metropolitan area
The area in and around a city (especially a capital city); but not necessarily extending as far as the surrounding **conurbation**. A densely populated area around a dominant commercial centre, e.g. the area in and around the **central business district**. In the UK the 'Metropolitan Area' is the whole of Greater London, in contradistinction to the City of London.

meubles (F)
moveables; personal property; furniture. *Meubles* may cover all things capable of ownership that can be moved, whether on its own account (*meubles par nature*), e.g. animals; or by an external force, e.g. goods, furniture (commonly called *meubles meublants*). In French law the distinction that is drawn between *meubles* and ***immeubles*** creates one of the fundamental ways in which property (***biens***) is classified (the other primary division is between *biens corporels* and *biens incorporels*). All property is either *meubles* or *immeubles*. *Meubles* have no fixed destination or territory, they may be readily moved from place to place; are not so unique that they cannot be replaced by a similar object; and they can be hidden or destroyed. However, a *meuble* may

become an *immeuble* if it so affixed to land as to become part of that land – an *immeubles par destination*, similar to a **fixture** in English law.
(French Civil Code, art. 527–536).
(*meubles meublants* – furnishings; moveables as opposed to fixtures)
(*biens meubles* – chattels; moveables; personalty.
(*appartement meublée* – furnished apartment). See also *mobilier*.

mews

A cobbled alleyway or yard, originally leading to stables or accommodation for carriages, commonly with workers residences above; now containing garage accommodation and high-class residential accommodation over. Found predominantly in London.

mezzanine

A storey between two principal storeys of a building; a floor level inserted within an established envelope in order to provide additional floor space, but one that usually covers a smaller area than the floors above and below.

Michaelmas

The feast of St Michael the Archangel and all the angels, 29 September. One of the usual **quarter-days** in England and Wales.

Midsummer day

The feast of St. John the Baptist, and the summer solstice, 24 June. One of the usual **quarter-days** in England and Wales.

mine

An underground working made, as a pit or other form of excavation, for the purpose of extracting ore, precious stones or any other **mineral**. In its primary signification a mine is an underground operation, although generally it is taken to include structures, machinery, minerals, etc., placed on the surface and associated therewith. A surface or an opencast working to extract minerals from the earth's crust also may be termed a mine – Midland Railway *v* Haunchwood Brick and Tile Co. (1880) 20 Ch. D 552. 'Mine' may be used to embrace the stratum, vein, seam, as well as the space left when the mine has been worked – Batten Pooll *v* Kennedy [1907] 1 Ch. 256. The essence of what constitutes a mine is the mode in which the extraction is made, and not the geological or chemical nature of the extracted material – R. *v* Bretel (1832) 3 B and Ad. 427. cf. **quarry**. See also **mining lease, mining operations, right of support**.
31 Halsbury's Laws of England 4 edn, paras. 1–1000.

mine (F)

   mine.

mineral

A naturally occuring inorganic substance, normally in solid crystalline form, which may be a single element, but usually is a compound or comixture of compounds. In general 'minerals' include, "every substance which can be got from underneath the surface of the earth for the purpose of profit". – Hext *v* Gill (1872) 7 Ch. 699.

Whether a particular substance is a mineral depends on the context in which the term is used and the custom adopted therein. In the scientific world 'mineral' "is a loose and inexact term that may be defined chemically as any element, inorganic compound or mixture occuring or originating in the earth's crust and atmosphere, including all metals or non-metals (except carbon), their compound and ores". (*The Condensed Chemical Dictionary* 10 edn., Van Nostrard Reinhold Company). Sand, sandstone, brick-earth, and clay soil are not normally classified as minerals. In a conveyance, when minerals are made a **reservation**, this means "everything except the mere surface, which is used for agricultural purposes; anything beyond that which is useful for any purpose whatever, whether it is gravel, marble, fireclay, or the like comes within the word 'mineral' when there is a reservation of the mines and minerals from a grant of land". – Midland Ry. Co. *v* Checkley (1867) LR 4 Eq. 19.; North British Railway Co. *v* Budhill Coal & Sandstone Co. [1910] AC 125. In English planning law 'minerals' includes, 'all minerals and substances in or under land for removal by underground or surface working, except that it does not include peat cut for purposes other than sale'. (Town and Country Planning Act 1971, s. 290 (1)). See also **mine**, **mineral rights**.

mineral lease
see **mining lease**.

mineral rights
The right to minerals found under the surface of **land**. Normally these are owned and conveyed with land; unless specifically excluded, or reserved by law, as (in English law) with the right to gold or silver in mines which go to the Crown – The Case of Mines (1568) 1 Plowel. 310; A-G *v* Morgan [1891] 1 Ch. 432. Oil and natural gas in underground strata belong to the Crown (Petroleum (Production) Act 1934, s. 1) and coal is vested in the National Coal Board (Coal Industries (Nationalisation)

Act 1946). When land is acquired by compulsory purchase, as a rule, the right to minerals passes to the acquiring authority and the interested party is compensated for any loss in value sustained thereby. Certain statutes, e.g. the Railway Clauses Consolidation Act 1845, the Acquisition of Land (Authorisation Procedure) Act 1946, enable an acquiring authority to acquire land and leave the vendor with a right to exploit the minerals under the land. See also **mineral**, **mining lease**, **profit à prendre**.
Modern Methods of Valuation, 7 edn., Ch. 34 (for valuation of mineral rights).

mineral royalty
see **royalty**.

minimum rent
see **base rent**, **dead rent**.

mining lease
A contract by which a landowner grants or permits another a right to work a **mine** and extract minerals therefrom. (Frequently the right granted is not strictly a **lease** because there is no demise of an interest in land, but merely the grant of a right to remove material under the soil. In general a 'mining lease' may be no more than a licence, a **profit à prendre**, or an **easement** for access combined with the right to the extracted material; however, a grant of an exclusive right to occupation of a mine for a period of time at a fixed charge, in part or whole, may well be construed as a lease.) In the Law of Property Act 1925, s. 205 (1) (xiv) 'mining lease' "means a lease for mining purposes, that is, the searching for, winning, working, getting, making merchantable, carrying away, or

disposing of mines or minerals, or purposes connected therewith, and includes a grant or licence for mining purposes". Similarly, the expression 'mining lease' may mean "a lease for any mining purposes or purposes connected therewith, and includes a grant or licence for any mining purposes", and 'mining purposes' include "the sinking and searching for, winning, working, getting, making merchantable, smelting or otherwise converting or working for the purposes of any manufacture, carrying away, and disposing of mines or minerals" in or under land, and "the erection of buildings, and the execution of engineering and other works suitable for those purposes" (Landlord and Tenant Act 1927, s. 25 (1); Settled Land Act 1925, 117 (1) (xv)). Generally the landowner receives a fixed sum or **dead rent** from the tenant or licencee, together with a **royalty** based on the quantity of mineral extracted. A mining lease terminates after a specified or determinable period of time, or when the mine is exhausted, i.e. when the purpose for which the lease was granted is satisfied. See also **instroke, mineral, outstroke, satisfied term.**

mining operations
Work in connection with the operation of a **mine**. In English town planning law 'mining operations' means "the winning and working of minerals, other than excepted minerals in, on, or under land, whether by surface or underground working". (The Town and Country Planning (Minerals) Regulations 1971, s. 1 – The Town and Country Planning General Development Order 1977, s. 2 (1)). Development (as defined in the Town and Country Planning Act 1971, s. 22)

includes the removal of material from mineral-working deposits, deposits of slag, fuel ash or clinker, as well as the extraction of minerals from a disused railway embankment (Town and Country Planning (Minerals) Act 1981, s. 1 (1)). See also **mineral.**

mining rent
Rent payable under a **mining lease.** Rent, or a payment in the nature of rent including a **rentcharge, royalty** or licence fee paid for a right to extract and remove material from a mine.

minor interest
An interest in registered land that is not binding on a purchaser who pays "valuable **consideration**" for a **legal estate,** unless it is entered on the register of the land affected. Minor interests, by definition, comprise all interests in registered land other than (a) the registered title *per se* (a registered freehold or registered leasehold title); (b) an **overriding interest** (which requires no protection by registration and binds a purchaser of the registered land, unless the register expressly provides for an exception); and (c) an interest entered on the register prior to 1926 (Land Registration Act 1925, s. 3 (xv)). Thus minor interests are a residual group of rights to land which are neither created or transferred by registered dispositions, nor are likely to be discovered (at least in theory) by a thorough examination of the land itself or by reasonable enquiry.

Minor interests include family and commercial interests in land, and may be categorised as (i) the equitable interest of the beneficiary of a **trust for sale** or a **strict settlement**; and (ii) most of the type of interests that, in the case of unregistered land, would be recorded as a **land charge**, e.g. a restrictive covenant, an estate contract, a rent charge, a legal lease for a term exceeding 21 years, a legal charge, a spouse's right to a matrimonial home. The first category of minor interest is entered on the register for the protection of the beneficiary, but upon a sale of the registered land the interest is said to be 'overreached' i.e. the beneficiary's interest is transferred into a claim against the proceeds of sale. The second category of registered minor interests remain binding against a purchaser of the registered land in the same way as a land charge binds a purchaser of unregistered land.

A minor interest may be protected by an entry on the charges or proprietorship register at the Land Registry, either by a **restriction** or **inhibition** or, usually, by a **caution** or **notice** (Land Registration Act 1925, s. 101 (3)). An intending purchaser of registered land can obtain details of minor interests entered on the land register by means of a personal search, or by obtaining an 'official search certificate' which is valid up to 30 days from its date of issue. See also **overreachable interest**.

The Law of Real Property, by R. Megarry and H.W.R. Wade, 5 edn., p. 209 *et seq*.

minor tenancy
A tenancy for a term of one year or less. In connection with the service of notice effecting a **general vesting declaration**, a 'minor tenancy' means "a tenancy for a year or from year to year or any lesser interest" (Compulsory Purchase (Vesting Declarations)

Act 1981, s. 2 (1)). See also **short-term tenancy**.

minute (F)
draft; original (of an *acte*).
(*minute d'un acte* – original of a deed)

misdescription
A description of property, especially in an agent's **particulars of sale**, that does not give a clear and precise statement of fact and, therefore, does not represent the truth. Misdescription may be considered as synonymous with **misrepresentation**; however, the term 'misdescription' is applied usually to a statement that comes to form part of a contract, rather than a statement which merely induces someone to enter into a contract. A misdescription may make a contract void if it amounts to **fraud** or if it produces a substantially different contract to that which would have been intended by the parties had a true description been made. "Where the misdescription is wilful or designed, it amounts to fraud, and such fraud, upon general principles of law, avoids the contract altogether. Where the misdescription, although not proceeding from fraud, is in material and substantial point, so far affecting the subject-matter of the contract, that it may reasonably be supposed, that, but for such misdescription, the purchaser might never have entered into the contract at all, in such cases the contract is avoided altogether, and the purchaser is not bound to resort to the clause of compensation. Under such a state of facts, the purchaser may be considered as not having purchased the thing which was really the subject of the sale." – Flight *v* Booth (1834) LJ 4 CP 69. However, if a mis-

description is not substantial a court may enforce a contract, or grant a decree of **specific performance**, and award damages for any loss suffered by a purchaser. Non-disclosure of facts, known to a vendor or his agent, may in certain circumstances constitute an implied misdescription. Cases in which misdescription has been held to have occurred include: describing leasehold land as freehold land – Re Russ and Brown's Contract (1934) Ch. 34); calling an underlease a lease – Re Thompson and Cottrell's Contract [1943] Ch. 97; describing premises let on tenancies protected by the Rent Acts as decontrolled – Ridley *v* Oster [1939] 1 All ER 618; describing land as suitable for building when an underground culvert was discovered later which prevented building – Re Puckett and Smith's Contract [1902] 2 Ch. 258.

A misdescription in a deed does not invalidate the document if it is clear from the rest of the text what is intended. The maxim of law is *falsa demonstratio non nocet cum de corpore constat*, 'a false description does not vitiate a document when the thing is described with certainty'.

cf. **puffing**. See also **exclusion clause; good faith, mistake, latent defect, professional negligence, voidable contract**.

Contract and Conveyance, by J.R. Farrand, 4 edn., pp. 52–55.

The Law of Estate Agents and Auctions, by J.R. Murdoch, 2 edn., pp. 518–531, 549–551.

mise (F)

placing; putting stake; **bid**.

(*mise à prix* – **reserve price**; upset price)

(*mise aux enchères* – bid at auction)

(*mise en demeure* – formal notice; to put on **notice**, i.e. to inform a party of a failure to fulfil an *obligation*; in French law a prerequisite to an action for damages for breach of contract since, 'a creditor who does not take steps to compel a debtor to fulfil his obligation is presumed to acquiesce in the delay' – Amos & Walton's *Introduction to French Law* 3 edn., p. 183. There is no exact equivalent in English law cf. *notification*).

(*mise en exploitation* – open up for development)

(*mise en gage* – **hypothecation;** pledging)

(*mise en oeuvre d'un plan* – implementation of a plan)

(*mise sous séquestre* – **sequestration**)

(*mise en valeur* – exploit; opening up for development).

mismatching

The use of short-term finance for a long-term investment, most notably the use of an overdraft for the purchase of a real property investment. Also the use of a loan in one currency to finance an investment acquired with another currency.

misrepresentation

A presentation of false or misleading information, especially when made recklessly or with intention to deceive. A false or misleading statement made by one party to a contract (or his agent) which, although not forming part of the contract, induces another to enter into the contract upon terms or conditions that are different from those actually in existence. A misrepresentation must relate to matters of fact, not law, intention or opinion; thus using such statements as 'desirable location', 'excellent view', is not a representation of fact but only a salesman's personal opinion – usually referred to as **puffing**. But, a representation of opinion may involve a representation of fact: "if the facts are not equally well known to both sides, then a statement of opinion by one who knows the facts best involves very often a statement of a material fact, for he impliedly states that he knows facts which justify his opinion". – Smith *v* Land and House Property Corporation (1884) 28 Ch. D 15. (In that case a description of a tenant, who was in arrears with his rent, as a desirable tenant was considered a misrepresentation.) In general, if the person making a representation knows, or ought to know, that the statement is false and likely to mislead there is a misrepresentation. Misrepresentation must induce someone to enter into a contract to constitute an actionable wrong. Thus, an agent is not liable to the party who contracts with his principal when it is the misrepresentation of the agent that induced the contract; because the agent is not a party to the contract (although he may be liable for **fraud**, **deceit** or **negligence** as a result of deception or recklessness). On the other hand an agent's misrepresentation, if known or acknowledged by the principal, is tantamount to a misrepresentation by the principal himself, which may make the principal liable to the other party to the contract and the agent liable to his principal for a breach of the agency agreement. The agent may be liable also for the misrepresentation if it is established that he has entered into an implied or **quasi-contract** with the other party.

A misrepresentation may act as a bar to an exemption or **exclusion clause** inserted in a contract if the representation is such as to mislead the other party about the existence or extent of the exemption or exclusion: "if it conveys a false impression, that is enough. If the false impression is created knowingly, it is a fraudulent misrepresentation; if it is created unwittingly, it is an innocent misrepresentation; but either is sufficient to disentitle the creator of it to the benefit of the exemption". – Curtis *v* Chemical Cleaning & Dyeing Co., Ltd., [1951] 1 KB 808–9.

A statement does not constitute misrepresentation if the person accepting it is aware that it is untrue; does not take any account of it when deciding to enter into a contract; or uses his own judgement or expertise when assessing the representation – Attwood *v* Small (1838) 6 Cl. and Fin. 232. Furthermore, no one can plead misrepresentation if he never hears the claims being made. On the other hand, a person who makes a false representation cannot claim that he thought the other party would know better. "No one is entitled to make a statement which on the face of it conveys a false impression and then excuse himself on the ground that the person to whom he made it had available the means of correction." – Nocton *v* Lord Ashburton [1914] AC 962.

At common law, in order that a party to a contract may claim misrepresentation and rescind the contract or claim damages, the representation should be fraudulent, i.e. there must be an intention to deceive. If the person making the representation believed the statement to be true he may be culpable of 'innocent misrepresentation' but, as a rule, the contract remains binding. However, "if a man, who has or professes to have special knowledge or skill, makes a representation by virtue thereof to another – be it advice, information or opinion – with the intention of inducing him to enter into a contract with him, he is under a duty to use reasonable care to see that the representation is correct, and that the advice, information or opinion is reliable. If he negligently gives unsound advice or misleading information or expresses an erroneous opinion, and thereby induces the other side to enter into a contract with him, he is liable in damages". – Esso Petroleum v Mardon [1976] 2 All ER 801, Hedley Byrne v Heller [1964] AC 465. Further, a person may still be liable for damages, "notwithstanding that the representation was not made fraudulently, unless he proves that he had reasonable ground to believe, and did believe, up to the time the contract was made that the facts represented were true". (Misrepresentation Act 1967, s. 2 (1)). The latter provision does not apply to an **auctioneer** who is liable only for common law 'fraudulent misrepresentation'; although an auctioneer may be liable for **negligence**, if his representation is clearly of that nature.

Silence or non-disclosure may constitute misrepresentation when it might reasonably be expected that a party to a contract would make a declaration on a substantive matter affecting the contract – in particular, when silence distorts a positive representation, when there is a **fiduciary** relationship between the parties; when the silence arises from a professional person with specialised knowledge who might reasonably be expected to draw an innocent party's attention to a known defect; or when

there is a contract made in ***uberrimae fidei***, in '**utmost good faith**'.

In the US the common law distinction between innocent misrepresentation and fraudulent or known misrepresentation is no longer of particular significance. If damage is suffered and there was a factual misrepresentation the loser has a prima facie right to recompense, either to damages or a right to rescind the contract. As in modern English law, a party who has the greater knowledge or experience has the higher duty to take care in his or her representations – "The old law was *caveat emptor*, "let the buyer beware." The buyer had to investigate before buying. If he failed to discover defects in the building, that was his bad luck. Nowadays the courts are getting away from this primitive rule." (*Real Estate Law*, by Robert Kratovil and Raymond J. Werner, 8 edn., p. 164).

cf. **estoppel**. See also **misdescription, professional negligence, rescission, voidable contract, warranty**.

Law for Land Management Students, by Richard Card, John Murdoch and Peter Schofield, pp. 193–212 (1981).

Anson's Law of Contract, 26 edn, pp. 209–239.

Cheshire & Fifoot's Law of Contract, 10 edn, pp. 235–273.

Chitty on Contract, 25 edn, paras. 391–472.

31 Halsbury's Laws of England, 4 edn, paras. 1001–1137.

mistake

Something that is taken amiss; an erroneous or misconceived notion of a fact. In relation to a contract a mistake generally arises when there has been no *consensus ad idem* on an important aspect of the agreement, i.e. no precise meeting of the minds; when there is a different perception of the existence, nature, identity of the subject matter, or even of the parties to a contract. In order to nullify a contract, a mistake must be of such a nature that it may be said that no contract would have resulted had the parties realised the true situation. It is not sufficient that the parties merely took a different view from each other as to the respective benefit or burden arising from the contract. There must be "some mistake or misapprehension as to some facts ... which by the common intention of the parties, whether express or more generally implied, constitute the underlying assumption without which the parties would not have made the contract they did" and ... "if mistake operates at all, it operates so as to negative or in some cases to nullify **consent**." – Bell *v* Lever Brothers, Ltd., [1932] AC 206, 217; Grymes *v* Sanders, 93 US 55, 23 L Ed. 798. A mistake is "an omission made not by design, but by mischance and one not calculated to mislead" – Sandford *v* Beal (1896) 65 LJ QB 74.

When, as the result of a mistake, a contract is fundamentally different from that intended by the parties it is voidable at the instigation of the aggrieved party, i.e. the contract may be treated as if it had never come into existence. However, in English law mistake is narrowly defined and generally the courts will seek to enforce a contract, especially when the parties can achieve substantially what they contracted for, and award damages for any loss suffered by an aggrieved party. If there is a mutual mistake but the parties act in such a way as to "infer the existence of an agreement or licence" the parties are, by the doctrine of **estoppel**, unable to claim that there is no contract – Cornish *v* Abington (1859) 4 H and N 549. A mistake of fact, when significant, may provide a ground for relief from the obligations of a contract, but normally a mistake of law does not. A serious mistake, one that is so serious that it cannot be rectified, renders a contract void; but, if the mistake is insufficiently serious to render the contract void the contract may be voidable, for example, if there is a common mistake as to whether a tenancy is subject to the Rent Acts – Solle *v* Butcher [1950] 1 KB 671. The most common forms of mistake are mistakes as to the identity of the subject-matter; as to the existence of the subject-matter; as to the essential contractual assumptions; and as to the identity of one of the parties to the contract.

If an authority in pursuance of a confirmed compulsory purchase order enters land and "it appears that they have through mistake or inadvertence failed or omitted duly to purchase or to pay compensation for any estate, right or interest in or charge affecting that land", they may remain in undisturbed possession, but the authority must purchase the interest and must pay compensation and **mesne profits** for the loss suffered by the party entitled to the omitted interest (Compulsory Purchase Act 1965, s. 22).

A clear distinction should be drawn (although the distinction may be a fine one) between a mistake, **misrepresentation, misdescription**, misunderstanding (see *caveat emptor*) and ignorance of the law (see *ignoran-*

tia juris neminem excusat). Thus if A sells a parcel of land to B, and a boundary dispute subsequently arises, this may be due to (i) a mistake, if a previous owner had moved the evidence of the true boundary, a fact that A and B are both ignorant of; (ii) a false representation or a misdescription (depending on whether it induces the contract or subsequently comes to form part of the contract) made by A to B that certain landmarks represented the boundary (possibly in order to increase the price) knowing that, on further investigation, this would prove false; (iii) a misunderstanding as to the true position of the boundary fence even though this may be clearly shown on the title deeds (although this may constitute a mutual mistake); or (iv) B may not have apprised himself of the fact that the land is registered at the Land Registry and that by law the description of the land incorporated in the Land Certificate indicates the true title rather than documents obtained by him during preliminary negotiations.

In French law a mistake (*erreur*) may arise from two causes, an '*erreur sur la substance*' i.e. a mistake which relates to 'the fundamental object (*objet*) of the agreement'; or an '*erreur sur la personne*' i.e. a mistake as to the person with whom it is intended that the contract would be made, and in that case the contract is not void "unless the question of the person was the principal cause of the agreement" (Civil Code, art. 1110). Thus, a mistake as to the area of land being acquired, provided it is substantial e.g. it makes it unsuitable for the purpose for which it was acquired; as to the substantial qualities of authenticity and origin of a work of art; as to

the solvency of a person being granted a surety; and in limited cases a mistake as to the value of the subject matter, may be sufficient to make a contract void. But a mistake of the identity of a vendor of land is unlikely to produce the same result. See Civil Code, art. 1674

French Law of Contract, by Barry Nicholas, pp. 80–96 (1982).

Barnsley's Conveyancing Law and Practice, 2 edn, p. 605–608.

Law for Land Management Students, by Richard Card, John Murdoch and Peter Schofield, pp. 181–192 (1981).

Anson's Law of Contract, 26 edn, pp. 252–291.

Cheshire & Fifoot's Law of Contract, 10 edn, pp. 199–234.

Chitty on Contract, 25 edn, paras. 311–379.

32 Halsbury's Laws of England, 4 edn, paras. 1–100.

mitigation of loss
see **compensation for disturbance, damages**.

mitigation works
Works carried out by a public authority to reduce or abate the **injurious affection** caused by its activities, e.g. insulation work carried out to a house adjoining a highway or an airport in order to reduce the effect of noise on the occupiers of the house. Various statutes impose a duty on or give power to public authorities to carry out mitigation works to reduce the effect of their actions on adjoining landowners. The Land Compensation Act 1973, Part II gives a highway authority, or other appropriate authority powers and imposes duties to reduce the injurious effect of their works by sound-proofing, tree plant-

ing, etc. The Civil Aviation Act 1971 provides for the making of grants to meet the cost of sound-proofing buildings near to an airport.

mitoyen (F)

common boundary.

(*mur mitoyen* - **party wall**). See also *mitoyenneté*.

mitoyenneté (F)

party wall rights; the owner of a party wall. In French law any common wall that serves to separate buildings in separate ownership is presumed to be a party wall, unless there is evidence to the contrary and a party wall is deemed to be held in *copropriété* (co-ownership) (French Civil Code, art. 653–673).

Précis Dalloz. Droit Civil, Les Biens (Alex Weill) 2 edn, pp. 193–207.

Droit Civil, Les Biens, by Jean Carbonnier, 11 edn, pp. 210–221.

mixed action

An action which involves both a real and a personal action. See also **action *in personam*, action in *rem***.

mixed fund

A trust or company that invests in both **real property** and **personal property**. See also **hybrid real estate investment trust**.

mixed hereditament

A **hereditament**, not being a dwelling-house, that is occupied partly as a dwelling so that the proportion of its rateable value attributable to the purposes of a private dwelling is greater than the proportion attributable to other purposes (General Rate Act 1967, s. 48 (5)). A mixed hereditament, like a dwelling-house, may be liable to a lower rate in the pound than other property. See also **rates**.

mixed property

A right to or over property that has a status compounded of real and personal property, e.g. a right to a lease of a building and machinery therein.

mixed tenancy

A **tenancy** of a property that is used for two or more purposes. For example, a shop with living accommodation in the same building and let to the same tenant. A determination as to which is the dominant user may have important ramifications when considering the statutory provisions that apply to the tenancy. If the property that is the subject of the tenancy comprises **business premises**, it may be governed by the Landlord and Tenant Acts; if essentially a **dwelling-house**, it may be governed by the Rents Acts, or if it is an **agricultural holding**, it may be governed by the Agricultural Holdings Acts.

cf. **multiple tenancy**.

mobile home

A structure that is used as a dwelling and is capable of being moved from place to place. A **caravan** or similar single-storey dwelling, which is someone's **home**; is capable of being moved; but usually is situated on a semi-permanent site and normally is connected to mains electricity and water. Generally such a dwelling affords more spacious accommodation than a touring caravan; has more limited mobility; is designed for longer term occupation and, commonly, is the owner's only or main residence.

The Mobile Homes Act 1975, as amended by the Mobile Homes Act 1983, gives a licencee or tenant of such accommodation, who occupies it as his or her only or main **residence**.

(provided it is placed on a "protected site", i.e. essentially a site for which a **site licence** is required and that is used for permanent stationing of mobile homes or caravans) limited rights of tenure and protection from eviction and a right to a written statement from the owner of the site of the terms upon which it has been agreed that the occupier of the mobile home has been permitted to station the dwelling (Mobile Homes (Written Statement) Regulations 1983). For this purpose a mobile home has the same meaning as 'caravan' as defined in the Caravan Sites and Control of Development Act 1960, as amended by the Caravan Sites Act 1968 (Mobile Homes Act 1975, s. 9. (1)). See also **fixture**.

Real Estate Law, by Robert Kratovil and Raymond J. Werner, 8 edn., pp. 571–575.

Landlord and Tenant, by Martin Partington, 2 edn., pp. 464–465.

Mobile Homes, by Clive Brand, 276 E.G. 1339–1348 (1985).

Housing Law, by Trevor Aldridge and Martin Partington, pp. 1111–1126 (1983).

mobilier, *(f.- ère)* (F)
　　personal property; **moveables.**　Any form of property that is not classified as *immobilier.*
　　(*biens mobiliers* – personal effects; chattels; moveables)
　　(*contribution mobilière* – a local property tax replaced in 1974 by *taxe d'habitation*)
　　(*propriété mobilière* – chattels)

mock auction
　　A sale by **auction** at which a genuine effort to sell a property at the highest price bid is thwarted or made a sham. For example, holding an auction of cheap goods and making the pur-chase of such items a condition of entry to bid for more expensive items, or inducing bids from parties who have been deliberately introduced to bid up the price, but have no intention of making the final bid. The Mock Auctions Act 1961 makes it an offence to promote or conduct, or to assist in the conduct, of a mock auction for the sale of certain chattels. For this purpose a mock auction takes place if (a) goods are sold to the final bidder at less than the final bid, or a discount or credit on part of the purchase price is paid to the pur-chaser; (b) the right to bid at an auc-tion is restricted to persons who pre-viously have bought or agreed to buy one or more articles; or (c) articles are given away or offered as gifts at the auction (1961 Act, s. 1 (3)). At com-mon law any fraudulent or unreaso-nable act, e.g. the introduction of sham bidders, who pretend to be real bidders, used to prevent the proper price being realised at a sale by auc-tion, may amount to a conspiracy and enable the sale to be set aside – R. *v* Lewis (1869) 15 Digest (Repl) 1179. See also **bidding agreement.**

modalité (F)
　　restrictive clause.
　　(*modalités de paiement* – methods of payment)

'**mode or category of occupation**'
　　see *rebus sic stantibus*, **tone of the list.**

model house (US)
　　see **show house.**

modern grant, lost
　　see **lost modern grant.**

modern ground rent
　　The **ground rent** of a site, based on the current market rental value of that

site, assuming that it is cleared of buildings and is to be let on a long-term (usually 50 years or more) ground lease. In particular, the rent that is considered to represent the letting value of the site of a house, excluding the value of any buildings thereon, but assuming that the site can be used for any purposes for which it had been, or could lawfully have been, used during the period of an existing tenancy (Leasehold Reform Act 1967, s. 15 (2)). A 'modern ground rent' is the amount that is payable, under the provisions of the Leasehold Reform Act 1967, either when a **long tenancy** that is subject to the provisions of the Act is made into an **extended lease**; or when it is assumed that the lease will be extended and the capital value of a site is being asessed for the purpose of **leasehold enfranchisement**.

Statutory Valuations, by Andrew Baum, pp. 95, 98–102 (1983).

Valuation: Principles and Practice, by W.H. Rees (ed.), 2 edn., p. 61 *et seq*.

modernisation

The act of bringing a property up to current standards of usage, design, layout and facilities. Modernisation includes putting property into a good state of **repair** and decoration, providing modern finishings and replacing outdated mechanical equipment with modern equipment. See also **improvement**, **refurbishment**, **renovation**.

modification order

see **change order**, **revocation order**.

modified fee

see **qualified fee**.

moiety

A half interest, e.g. a half interest held under a **joint tenancy**, a **tenancy-in-common**, or as a right to a **party wall**. When a person bids successfully at auction for a 'moiety' of a piece of ground he will purchase that half of the ground, and if his bid is based on a price per square yard the purchase price will be that price multiplied by the number of yards – not half that amount – Chamberlain *v* Lee (1840) 8 LJ Ch. 266. 'Moiety' is used sometimes to refer to any fractional part of a property, e.g. a third or quarter.

moins-value (F)

capital loss; **depreciation** (in value); **obsolescence**.

(*moins-value de cession* – realised capital loss)

cf. *plus-value*.

mois (F)

month.

(*mois calendaire*; *mois commun*; *mois civil* – calendar month)

(*mois legal* – thirty days)

money

Believed to be derived from *Moneta*, the temple of the Roman goddess Juno, which was used as a mint in ancient Rome. Anything that passes from hand to hand as a readily acceptable medium for the exchange of articles of value, or is kept as a store of value. An item or commodity used to express debts or liabilities; or that is acceptable as a means to discharge debts or liabilities. 'The natural and primary meaning of money is **cash** or coin of the realm...Still, in the common acceptation of the word there is a more extensive meaning given to it .....' – Barrett *v* White (1885) 24 LJ Ch. 726. Money has been defined in a literal sense "by Mr. Walker in *Money, Trade, and Industry* as that which passes freely from hand to hand through the community in final discharge of debts and full payment for commodities, being acceptable equally without reference to the character or credit of the person who offers it and without the intention of the person who receives it to consume it or apply it to any other use than in turn to **tender** it to others in discharge of debts or payments for commodities" – Moss *v* Hancock [1899] 2 QB 116.

In economics, money is reputed to serve four basic functions; (i) as a unit of **exchange** – 'it is a machine for doing quickly and commodiously, what would be done, though less quickly and commodiously, without it' (*Principles of Political Economy*, by John Stewart Mill, Book III, Ch. VII, para 3; 1848) (ii) as a measure of **value** or **wealth** – "in the first place money appears in the function of a mere instrument for measuring the value of individual parts of wealth ... But money also appears in a second or higher function, that is, it embraces the value itself that is measured by it .... Therefore money gives its owner a general power of wealth...and... appears as an independent bearer of such power" (*Obligationenrecht*, by Savigny, vol. i. p. 405, 1851); (iii) as a store of value or purchasing power – "it is not for its own sake that men desire money, but for the sake of what they can purchase with it" – (*The Wealth of Nations*, by Adam Smith, Book IV, Ch. I, 1776). Although it may be asked, "why should anyone outside a lunatic asylum wish to use money as a store of wealth? Because ... our desire to hold money as a store

of wealth is a barometer of the degree of our distrust of our own calculations and conventions concerning the future... The possession of actual money lulls our disquietude" (*The General Theory of Employment*, by J.M. Keynes, *Quart. J. Econ.* p. 216 1937); (iv) as a standard or means for deferred payment, a link between the present and the future – money "acts as a guarantee that we may have what we want in the future: though it is not needed at the moment, it insures the possibility of satisfying a need when it arises" – Aristotle, *Ethics*, Book 5. Money may take the form of coins, bank notes or similar currency; negotiable paper money, promissory notes (e.g. cheques, postal orders, money orders); precious metals; or any goods that are accepted by society as readily exchangeable, without question and without being used up in the process.

In law, money must be acceptable as a medium of exchange and must be capable of being expressed authoritatively as a recognised unit of account; in particular, it means **legal tender**. It includes, "all chattels which, issued by the authority of the law and denominated with reference to a unit of account, are meant to serve as a universal medium of exchange in the State of issue" (*The Legal Aspects of Money*, by F.A. Mann, 4 edn, p. 8). "A medium of exchange authorised or adopted by a domestic or foreign government as a part of its currency." (United States Uniform Commercial Code, para. 1–201 (24)).

In its contemporary usage money, or 'money supply', refers to the sum total of cash and credit available in the economy, including cash, legal tender, demand deposits at the bank (or similar guardians of such liquid assets), accountable credit extended to facilitate the acquisition of goods, and, sometimes, time deposits.

The precise meaning of money depends on the time, place and context: in execution of a debt it may be limited to legal tender; in a third world country to coins; in economic management it may mean all or part of the money supply; and in a will it may, if the content so implies, extend to the worth or value of a person's total estate – Re Mellor [1929] 1 Ch. 46; Re Barnes's Will Trusts; Prior *v* Barnes [1975] 1 WLR 515; Haynes *v* Henderson (Tex. Civ. App.) 345 S.W. 2d 857). See also **capital money**, **interest**.

Droit Civil, Les Biens, by Jean Carbonnier, 11 edn., pp. 22–55.

32 Halsbury's Laws of England, 4 edn, paras. 101–400.

money weighted rate of return
see **internal rate of return**.

money's worth
Anything that can achieve or procure the same purpose as **money**. Something that "can be turned into money" – Tennant *v* Smith [1892] AC 150, i.e. land, chattels, goods, shares which can be converted into cash, coin of the realm, bank notes or bank demand deposits. 'Money's worth' is a term used in English land law to refer to some present **consideration**, as referred to in contract law. "The price or consideration given for property where property is acquired in return for something other than money, such as services or other property, where the price or consideration which the acquirer gives for the property has got to be turned into money before it can be expressed in terms of

money." – Secretain *v* Hart [1969] 3 All ER 1199 (although it need not equate to the value of the property acquired – Midland Bank Trust Co. *v* Green [1981] 2 WLR 28). 'Money's worth' may mean also that which is given in satisfaction of an existing debt.

month
A period of **time** that may be approximately four weeks; 30 days; 1/12th of a year; or any similar period that is a measure of the moon's time of revolution or cycle of its phase changes. Alternatively, the time taken for the sun to pass through one sign of the zodiac, or a twelfth of the time required for the earth to go round the sun. In law the actual time-span of a month depends on the context; (i) at common law, it is "a lunar month, or 28 days, unless otherwise expressed" (Bl. Comm. vol. ii p. 141), and is to be so construed in any contract prior to 1926 and in any statute prior to 1851; (ii) in statutes since 1850 (Interpretation Act 1978, Sch. 1, replacing the Interpretation Act 1889, s. 3), unless there is a contrary intention, and in ecclesiastical matters at any time, it is a 'calendar month' (based on the Gregorian calendar). Also, "in all deeds, contracts, wills, orders and other instruments executed, made or coming into operation after the commencement of this Act, unless the context otherwise requires – 'month' means calendar month" (Law of Property Act 1925, s. 61); thus, mortgages and leases made after that statute are considered to run on the basis of a calendar month, unless there is evidence to the contrary; (iii) in mercantile or commercial contracts, it is a calendar month, especially in the City

of London, unless there is evidence to the contrary – Turner *v* Barlow (1863) 3 F and F 950, but in many contracts effecting loans, especially in the US, it is a 'business month' of 30 days (so that annual interest is apportioned on the basis of a 360 day year).

A 'calendar month' is strictly one of the twelve spans on the calendar e.g. all of June or all of September, but the term is used more usually to span two parts of consecutive months. Thus, when a period of time is required to cover a given number of months, that period ends on the day of the month which bears the same number as that on which it begins; so that, within four months of 30 September is on or before 30 January, not 31 January – Dodds *v* Walker [1981] 2 All ER 609. The time span does not extend into a subsequent month, so that 'three months from 30 November' ends on 28 February, and 'one month from 29 January' ends on 29 February in a leap year. Rent payable 'every three months, commencing with 30 November' is due on 28 February, 30 May, 30 August and 30 November; but rent payable 'every three months hereafter' under a lease 'from 30 November' is due on 1 March, 1 June, 1 August, 1 November, as the **day** of the date is excluded in law.

monthly, or month-to-month, tenancy

A **periodic tenancy** that continues until determined by one month's notice, normally to expire on the anniversary of the commencement date or the date on which rent is normally due. A monthly tenancy may be created expressly, or may arise by implication when a tenant enters into possession of a property, or holds over at the end of a lease, and pays rent on a monthly basis. See also **month**.

monument

1. A visible landmark, structure or building, especially a structure erected to mark a notable event or person. See also **ancient monument, landmark building.**
2. A permanent object serving as a **boundary line** or limit.

monument historique (F)

ancient monument.

moral obligation

A duty or obligation which a person ought rightly to perform, but is not legally bound to fulfil. See also *assumpsit, gentleman's agreement.*

morceler (F)

to divide; to partition; to parcel out. See also *lotissement.*

mortgage

A transaction whereby one party (**mortgagee**) accepts a claim or title to property from another (**mortgagor**) as security for the payment of a debt, or the discharge of some obligation, for which the property is given; subject to a proviso that when the loan is repaid, or the obligation discharged, the property is released or returned to the mortgagor free of the mortgagee's claim. A mortgage secures for the mortgagee, in respect of the property charged, a **priority** over any other creditors for the satisfaction of an unpaid debt, but leaves the mortgagor with a right to recover his property by repaying the debt, called his **'equity of redemption'**. (The term mortgage is derived from the Old French *mort-gage* meaning a 'dead-pledge' because at common law the mortgagor's right to regain his property effectively was mortified, until equity intervened to redress the balance in his favour). A mortgage comprises two transactions, (i) a personal **contract** for the payment of a debt (in the US called the 'mortgage note') and (ii) a **conveyance** or charge of property, or an interest in property, as security for that debt. The property offered as security may be real or personal, although the term mortgage is more commonly used to refer to a claim over real property.

A mortgage may be effected by a lease or sub-lease of land; by transfer of possession of a chattel; by an assignment of a choses-in-action or debt; or by a charge on any interest in property (including an agreement to create a charge). In English law a mortgage of real property is created usually by (i) a lease for a term of years; (ii) a '**charge by way of a legal mortgage**'; or (iii) by a deposit of title deeds, accompanied by an agreement setting out the loan terms.

A mortgage may be distinguished from a **pledge**, or pawn of personal property, as the pledgee, or pawnbroker, gains possession but ownership remains with the pledger; from a **lien** which may or may not grant possession to the lienor, but does not grant any title or right to deal with the property; and from a **charge** which conveys no interest in property but gives merely a right to take certain steps involving the charged property: usually, in the event of default by the borrower, to enforce a sale of the property and claim settlement of the debt from the proceeds.

In the US some states adopt the view that a mortgage grants the mortgagee title to the mortgaged property and other states consider that he has no more than a lien on the property; these are known respectively as 'title theory' states and 'lien theory' states, while other states adopt an approach to analysing a mortgage which falls between these extremes. The title theory, which is a distillate of the old English common law mortgage, propounds that property is conveyed, together with a strict right to possession, to the mortgagee with a reconveyance upon satisfaction of the debt – Pongetti v Bankers Trust S and L Association (Miss.), 368 So. 2d. 819. The lien theory, which is more akin to modern English law, propounds that neither title nor possession is granted to the mortgagee, but only a right to satisfy the debt from the proceeds of sale of the property – United States v Commonwealth Title Ins. and T. Co., 193 US 651, 48 L. Ed. 830; Zeigler v Sawyer, Tex. Civ. App., 16 SW 2d. 894, 896. In most States the 'hybrid', or intermediate, form of mortgage is adopted. This hybrid falls between the title theory, whereby in the event of default by the mortgagor in paying his debt the mortgagee forecloses (i.e. extinguishes the mortgagor's equity of redemption) and the lien theory, whereby the property is sold at public auction and the mortgagee's debit repaid from the proceeds of sale. In the US a mortgage may be classified also as (a) a **regular mortgage**, when an interest in land is conveyed to the mortgagee, subject to an equity of redemption held by the mortgagor; (b) a mortgage made by way of a **deed of trust**, whereby the secured property is held by a third party unless and until the debt is repaid; and (c) an **equitable mortgage**, which arises where it can be shown that it was intended that property should be held as security for a debt but no formal deed to that effect was prepared.

In modern English law, the intervention of the mortgagor's equity of redemption; the doctrine that **'once a mortgage, always a mortgage'**; the stringent statutory regulations that govern a mortgagee's right to possession; the strict limits on the right of **foreclosure**; and the common practice, of accepting a deposit of the title deed or a 'charge by way of a legal mortgage' as adequate security; blur the clear distinction between a mortgage and a charge.

A mortgage may come to an end or be discharged by **redemption**; by the mortgagee exercising his **power of sale**; by foreclosure; by **merger**; or by operation of law, i.e. a **receipt** endorsed on, or annexed to, the mortgage, signed by the mortgagee, acknowledging that someone has paid the debt in full (Law of Property Act 1925, s. 115 (1)).

In French law a mortgage, (*hypothèque*), is similar to the English 'charge by way of legal mortgage' (or may be said to follow the 'lien theory') with the mortgagee having a right to exercise a power of sale by auction in the event of default. See also **amortisation mortgage**, *antichrèse*, **assumption, blanket mortgage, bulk mortgage, close-ended mortgage, consolidation, debenture, first mortgage, leasehold mortgage, legal mortgage, puisne mortgage, purchase-money mortgage, sub-mortgage, tacking, Welsh mortgage.**
Real Estate Law, by Robert Kratovil and R.J. Werner, 8 edn., pp. 264–313.
Modern Mortgage Law and Practice, by R. Kratovil and R.J. Warner, 2 edn.

Law for Land Management Students, by Richard Card, John Murdoch and Peter Schofield, pp. 584–604 (1981).
Introduction to Land Law, by J.G. Riddell, 3 edn., pp. 352–388.
Land Law: Cases and Materials, by R.H. Maudsley and E.H. Burn, 4 edn., pp. 596–689.
The Law of Real Property, by R. Megarry and H.W.R. Wade, 5 edn., pp. 913–1014.
Mortgages, by P.B. Fairest, 2 edn.
32 Halsbury's Laws of England, 4 edn, paras. 401–1052.
Fisher & Lightwood's *Law of Mortgage*, 9 edn.

mortgage (F)
chattel **mortgage**. See also *mortuum vadium*.

mortgage assumption (US)
see **assumption**.

mortgage banker (US)
A company or other form of financial institution that specialises in making mortgage loans but, unlike a **savings and loan association**, it uses its own funds rather than money received from depositors. Normally these organisations only grant interim finance, i.e. loans for a maximum period of 5 years.

mortgage bond
see **bond**.

mortgage broker
A **broker** who specialises in procuring finance secured by means of a mortgage; one who, for gain or reward, acts as an intermediary between a party seeking a mortgage loan and a supplier of mortgage money.

mortgage certificate (US)
An instrument that evidences the

existence of a mortgage and states the principle terms of the mortgage, especially one that refers to a fractional portion of a mortgage loan.

mortgage clause
A clause in a fire insurance policy, as taken out by a mortgagor, that refers to the interest of the **mortgagee** in the mortgaged property. The clause may require only that the mortgagee is informed if any claim is made under the policy; or it may require that any money paid under the policy goes direct to the mortgagee to the extent of his interest in the mortgaged property. A mortgagee has no claim upon money paid under an insurance policy taken out solely in the name of the mortgagor – Halifax Building Society *v* Keighley [1931] 2 KB 248. However, if a mortgage is made by deed the mortgagee has the power to insure the mortgaged property against loss or damage by fire, and to add the premium to the mortgagor's debt with equal priority (Law of Property Act 1925, s. 101 (1)); unless there is a declaration in the mortgage deed that no insurance is required or the mortgagor has accepted an express obligation, or has agreed with the mortgagee, to maintain the insurance (1925 Act, s. 108 (2)). Called also a 'mortgagee clause' or in the US an 'open-mortgage clause'.
cf. **union mortgage clause**. See also **reinstatement basis**.

mortgage commitment
see **commitment**.

mortgage company
see **mortgage banker**.

mortgage constant
1. A constant sum of money which if paid in regular instalments, over the period of a loan, will repay the principal amount of the loan, together with interest accrued thereon. A mortgage constant is usually expressed as a factor which represents the periodical payment required to repay one unit of the loan principal, plus interest. Each payment, as calculated by applying the mortgage constant, consists partly of interest and partly of capital repayments. This constant is given by applying the formula for the **annuity one will purchase**. Called also a 'debt service constant', a 'loan constant', a 'k-factor' a 'partial payment factor', or 'constant' for short.
2. The percentage relationship between the regular amount required to pay capital and interest under an **amortisation mortgage** and the initial amount of the capital.

Mortgage Corporation, The (US)
see **Federal Home Loan Mortgage Corporation**.

mortgage debenture
see **debenture**.

mortgage debt
The total debt that is owed by a party who has mortgaged property as security for that debt. See also **mortgage money**, **recourse**.

mortgage deed
A written instrument which records the terms of a **mortgage** loan. A **deed** that specifies the property granted as security, the obligations and duties of the mortgagor and mortgagee and the terms for redemption. A mortgage deed conveys or grants an interest in the property, to be held as security for a debt, and creates a binding personal contract between the parties, i.e. if made in respect of real estate it is both a **conveyance** or **demise** of land and a

loan document. See also 'charge by way of a legal mortgage', deed of trust.

mortgage discount
Discount points payable by a mortgagor.

mortgage duty
A tax payable on the registration of a mortgage deed. See also registration duty, stamp duty.

mortgage endowment insurance
see endowment mortgage.

mortgage-equity capitalisation technique (US)
A method of valuing an income-producing property which takes account not only of the return required on the property but also existing or available mortgage finance appropriate for the property. This form of valuation is based on the principle that the price that will be paid for an income-producing property is equal to the sum of the amount of equity capital available to purchase the property and the amount of debt capital that can be raised using the property as security, i.e. unlike the conventional 'income approach' (investment method of valuation) it considers the effect of 'leverage'.

The projected net operating income from the property to be valued is capitalised by a single factor (an 'overall rate') derived from a formula that takes account of some or all of the following: (i) the return on equity required by a purchaser (equity yield rate); (ii) the mortgage interest and amortisation rate; (iii) the loan period; (iv) the ratio of debt to equity (loan ratio); (v) capital appreciation (or depreciation); (vi) the holding period. This technique may be used also as a method of investment analysis to ascertain any one of these variables in particular the equity yield rate – given the other variables. See also band of investment capitalisation rate, Ellwood capitalisation rate.

An Introduction to the Mortgage Equity Concept and Ellwood Tables, by Frederick S.C. Young, 22 *Appraisal Institute Magazine*, pp. 20–36 (1978).

Income Property Appraisal and Analysis, by Jack P. Friedman and Nicholas Ordway, pp. 207–223 (1981).

The Instant Mortgage-Equity Technique, by Irvine E. Johnson, (1972).

The Appraisal of Real Estate, AIREA, 8 edn, pp. 426–439.

mortgage guaranty bond
see mortgage guaranty insurance.

mortgage guaranty insurance
Insurance taken out by a mortgagee to provide protection against a default by the mortgagor in meeting his obligations. Usually cover is provided against the risk that the mortgagor might be injured, become bankrupt or lose his employment. A mortgage guaranty insurance policy or 'mortgage guaranty bond' may be taken out also when the property held as security is likely to provide insufficient cover in the event of the mortgagee having to exercise his power of sale to realise the debt. See also mortgage insurance.

mortgage insurance
Insurance taken out on the life of a mortgagor to repay the outstanding balance on a mortgage loan, in the event of his death prior to the final date for redemption of the mortgage. Called also 'mortgage redemption insurance' or 'mortgage protection insurance'.

cf. **mortgage guaranty insurance**. See also **endowment mortgage**.

mortgage lender
see **mortgagee**.

mortgage loan
A loan secured by a mortgage. A term used to emphasise that a loan is secured by a mortgage on property. If the property is real estate called also a 'real estate loan'. See also **debt capital**.

mortgage loan insurance
see **mortgage insurance**.

mortgage note
see **secured loan**.

mortgage money
"**Money** or **money's worth** secured by a **mortgage**" – (Law of Property Act 1925, s. 205 (1) (xvi)).

mortgage out (US)
see **equity out**.

mortgage participation (US)
see **equity-participation mortgage**, **participation mortgage**.

mortgage placement fee
see **finance procuration fee**.

mortgage policy
A **title insurance** policy taken out by a mortgagee to provide an indemnity in the event that the title to the property held as security proves to be defective. See also **mortgage insurance**.

mortgage protection insurance
see **mortgage insurance**.

mortgage redemption insurance
see **mortgage guaranty insurance**.

mortgage sale
A sale of a property when a mortgagor has defaulted on his obligations and either the mortgagee has exer-cised his **power of sale** or a court order has been granted, subsequent to a request for an order of **foreclosure**. See also **foreclosure sale**.

mortgage trust (US)
see **real estate investment trust**.

mortgage value
The value of a property for the purpose of accepting it as security for a loan. Strictly, this is equivalent to the **market value** and an advance by way of a mortgage is restricted usually to a percentage (generally no more than 80 per cent) of that value, unless there is additional collateral or insurance. However, a valuer commonly adopts a conservative approach to a valuation prepared for mortgage purposes (although this is not required to comply with the standards laid down by the Royal Institution of Chartered Surveyors). Furthermore, in a bullish property market he "can reasonably be required to be aware of the fact that the market is "high" or unusually buoyant, when such are the circumstances, and to guard against over-confidence in such market conditions. He can reasonably be required to consider what the position of the property may well be in circumstances of forced-sale within six to twelve months of his valuation." – Corisland Investments Ltd., *v* Druce and Co. (1978) 248 EG 315.
cf. **forced-sale value**.
Royal Institution of Chartered Surveyors, Guidance Note no. A. 3 (on mortgage valuations).

mortgagee
One who receives or holds the benefit of a **mortgage**; a lender who accepts an interest in, or a claim over, property as security for a debt or obliga-

tion owed to him. A mortgagee may be a person who receives a lease, a sub-lease, a 'charge by way of a legal mortgage', or any person who obtains title to a property under a mortgage (Law of Property Act 1925, s. 205 (1) (xvi)).

A mortgagee has a right to **possession** of the mortgaged property, either actual possession, or possession in order to grant leases (provided he has a **legal mortgage** or a legal or registered charge, but not merely an equitable charge); "the mortgagee may go into possession before the ink is dry on the mortgage unless there is something in the contract, express or by implication, whereby he has contracted himself out of that right. He has the right because he has a legal term of year [a lease] in the property or its statutory equivalent [a 'charge by deed expressed to be by way of a legal mortgage']" – Four-Maids Ltd. v Dudley Marshall (Properties) Ltd [1957] Ch. 320. However, normally the mortgagee forgoes this right in favour of the **mortgagor** and does not take possession unless and until there is a default which enables him to enforce his right to possession of the secured property. A mortgagee who takes possession is accountable for the proper running and reasonable repair of the property; he must account to the mortgagor for the rents and profits he receives; and must obtain no advantage other than what is necessary to pay principal, interest and any costs due to him. A mortgagee in possession may grant any lease provided it is authorised by the Law of Property Act, s. 99. Basically the types of lease that are so authorised are an agricultural or occupation lease for any term not exceeding fifty years, and a building lease for any term not exceeding nine hundred and ninety-nine years; provided the lease is granted to take effect in possession not less than twelve months after its date at the "best rent that can reasonably be obtained" (without any **fine** being taken). A mortgagee who seeks possession of the mortgaged property, in order to enforce his right to the security, usually must proceed through the courts to obtain an order for possession and the courts may refuse such possession "except when it is sought *bona fide* and reasonably for the purpose of enforcing the security and then only subject to such conditions as the court thinks fit to impose". – Quennel v Maltby [1979] 1 WLR 322. In addition, the right to actual possession may be overruled by a tenant's statutory right to protection from **eviction**. Further, the court has a discretion to adjourn a mortgagee's action for possession of a dwelling-house if satisfied that the mortgagor is able to pay any sums due to the mortgagee within a reasonable period of time (Administration of Justice Act 1970, s. 36; Administration of Justice Act 1973 s. 8).

In the event of default by the borrower (mortgagor) in paying the loan when due, the mortgagee has a right to require a sale of the property that is the subject of the mortgage and, thereby, have the debt discharged: i.e. a right to exercise his **power of sale**. In addition to the power of sale, a mortgagee may sue on the personal debt owed to him; appoint a **receiver** to collect income from the mortgaged property; or, subject to certain strict conditions, he has a power of **foreclosure** (i.e. to acquire the property for himself). These rights of the mortgagee generally are cumulative; hence having exercised his power of sale, if the proceeds are insufficient, the mortgagee may sue on the mortgagor's personal debt, provided thereby he does not claim for an overpayment of what is due to him. See also **consolidation**, **recourse**, **mortgage clause**, **tacking**.

mortgagee clause
see **mortgage clause**.

mortgaging out (US)
Payment of the entire purchase price for a property with funds borrowed by way of a mortgage secured on the property. Obtaining a mortgage for an amount that equals, or exceeds, the total cost or market value of a property, thereby enabling an owner to release his own **equity**.

mortgagor
One who offers an interest in, or claim over, a property to a lender (**mortgagee**) as security for a debt, i.e. one who grants a **mortgage** of property. A mortgagor of land retains the beneficial interest in the mortgaged property and is entitled to reclaim his interest on repayment of the debt: called his **equity of redemption**. A mortgagor "includes any person from time to time deriving title under the original mortgagor or entitled to redeem a mortgage according to his estate, interest or right in the mortgaged property" (Law of Property Act 1925, s. 205 (1) (xvi)). A mortgagor is not entitled to **possession** of the mortgaged property, but generally is let into possession by the mortgagee. In addition, unless restricted by the mortgage deed, a mortgagor in possession is entitled to grant leases and subsequent mortgages, and to accept a surrender of any lease in order to grant a new lease (Law of Property Act 1925, s. 100 (1)).

mortis causa (L)
'On account of death'. See **gift**.

mortmain
Literally a 'dead hand'. Under the **feudal system** of land tenure, land that was held only as a personal right, e.g. **villein tenure**, and which on the death of the villein, or servant, reverted automatically to the lord of the manor. A term that was applied later to land held by an ecclesiastical or charitable organisation which, "always had its hand open to acquire and its hand closed to **alienation**". In modern usage land, or an interest in land, held by a body with an indefinite life e.g. a Corporation, the Church. Since the possessor of the land cannot die, in that sense the interest therein is said to be inalienable.

mortuum vadium (L)
'A dead pledge'. A form of **mortgage** by which the lender received a fee estate in land as security for the loan, on condition that if the mortgage debt was repaid in full the estate would be reconveyed to the borrower. It was called a 'dead pledge' because the estate was retained by the mortgagee, and dead to the mortgagor, if the debt was not discharged on time (Bl. Comm. vol. ii. p. 157). A feature of a *mortuum vadium* was that the lender usually had a right to the rent and profits from the land in order to discharge only the interest on the debt. cf. **vivum vadium**.

motel
An abbreviation of 'motor hotel'. An **hotel**, usually located near a major highway and with ample car parking,

that caters particularly for the motorist. Generally, a motel provides medium to low price facilities for one-night residents and tourists, and caters for small conferences and meetings. However, some modern motels provide facilities similar to full-scale hotels, with restaurants, meeting and assembly rooms, swimming pools, telephones, telex, and full room service.

movables (F)
moveables.

moveables or movables
Property that is not affixed to the soil and, therefore, can readily be transported from one place to another. In the civil law, any property that is not immoveable i.e. it is not land or that which is fixed to land. Although not a term of English law, in common usage moveables may be applied to any tangible and **personal property**; excluding such interests in real property as a leasehold interest or an easement.
cf. **immoveables**. See also **chattel**, **goods**.

mowing licence
see **grazing licence**.

multiple agency
The placing of property for sale with more than one **agent**, on a non-exclusive basis, at any one time. The agents act independently of each other and only the one who introduces a purchaser '**ready, able and willing**' to purchase the property receives a commission. Called also a 'mixed agency', or in the US, a 'general listing' or 'open listing'.
cf. **multiple listing, sole agency**. See also **joint agent, agency**.

multiple, or multi-family, dwelling (US)
A **dwelling-house** designed to accommodate three or more families. See also **apartment house, tenement house**.

multiple listing (US)
A **sole right to sell** given to members of a multiple listing organisation in a particular area. Instructions to sell a property are submitted by the principal to a broker who, as a member of the listing organisation, is obliged to make details available to other members. He does this either through a central bureau or by circulating a list of properties on which he is retained to the other members. In the event of a successful sale the commission is divided either (a) between the broker who introduced the purchaser (selling broker) and the broker to whom the listing was given (listing broker); or (b) between all the members of the organisation on an agreed basis. Multiple listing is used sometimes (incorrectly) as synonymous with **multiple agency**. Referred to also as a 'compulsory listing', especially when the brokerage fraternity in a particular area are predominatly members of an organisation that has a virtual monopoly on conducting property sales.
cf. **exclusive agency listing**. See also **franchise**.
The Practice of Estate Agency, by Nigel Stephens, p. 387 (1981).
Real Estate Principles, by Bruce Harwood, 2 edn, pp. 285-286.

multiple occupation
see **control order, common lodging house, overcrowding**.

multiple tenancy
A **tenancy** of premises that normally

would form the subject of two or more lettings; for example, two separate apartments, a shop with adjacent office premises, a dwelling-house and an adjoining workshop. cf. **mixed tenancy.**

multiplier
A factor used to capitalise income. In the US a multiplier may be a **gross income multiplier** or a **net income multiplier.** See also **capitalisation factor, years' purchase.**

multipropriété (F)
multi-ownership, property owned by two or more co-owners; **time sharing.**

multi-storey building
A building comprising two or more storeys, especially one that exceeds four storeys. See also **high-rise building, storey.**

municipalité (F)
municipality.

municipality
1. A predominately urban area (a city, town or other form of urban district) that has a corporate or statutory right of self-government.
2. An urban **local authority** that has political responsibility over a defined area.

muniments
Written documents that evidence, fortify, or otherwise relate to, an owner's title to property; **title deeds.** "'Muniments' are evidences or writings concerning a man's possession or inheritance, whereby he is able to defend the estate which he hath" – Termes de la Ley. See also **abstract of title, Land Certificate, official certificate of search.**

mur (F)
wall.
(*mur de séparation* – dividing wall; **partition**)
(*mur de soutènement* – retaining wall)
(*mur mitoyen, mur commun* – **party wall**)
(*gros murs* – main walls, see **grosses reparations**). See also **mitoyenneté.**

mutation
A change. The transfer of a right to property from one person to another.

mutation (F)
change, especially of ownership, conveyance; **transfer**; alteration.
(*mutation immobilière* – land transaction; property trading)
(*droit de mutation* – transfer tax, especially on property). See also **simulation.**

mutatis mutandis (L)
'The necessary changes being made', i.e. things are to remain the same except for what is essential. For example, a lease may be renewed at a different rent *mutatis mutandis*, that is, the other terms and conditions of the lease remain unaltered.

mutual company (US)
see **investment company.**

mutual consent
see **contract.**

mutual fund (US)
1. See **open-end investment company.**
2. The equity capital held by an **investment company.**

mutual investment company (US)
An **investment company** that raises its share capital by buying and selling its own shares according to the demand of its investors.

mutual investment trust
   see **mutual investment company.**

mutual loan association (US)
   see **savings and loan association.**

mutual mistake
   see **mistake.**

mutual option
   see **option.**

mutual trust (US)
   see **open-ended trust.**

N

naked contract

1. A bare promise; a **bargain** that has not been consummated in proper legal form. See also **agreement for a lease, agreement for sale**.

2. A **contract** that is lacking in some essential element – in particular, **consideration** – and, therefore, is void. Generally referred to as a ***nudum pactum***; a term which derives from Roman law and signifies a "bare pact (i.e. an agreement which does not fall within the limits of any recognized contract) [and, therefore] begets a defense but not an action" (*An Introduction to Roman Law*, by Barry Nicholas, p. 192 (1962)). See also **void contract**.

naked debenture

A **debenture** that contains only an acknowledgement of a debt and does not provide a mortgage or charge on any of a company's properties. Called also an 'unsecured note'.

cf. **mortgage debenture**. See also **floating charge**.

naked possession

Possession of property without any apparent right or pretence to ownership.

cf. **seisin**. See also **adverse possession**.

naked title (US)

1. The title granted to a trustee when a mortgage is created by means of a **deed of trust**.

2. A title granted when the transferor makes no representation, or gives no guaranty, as to the validity of that title. Called also a 'bare title'. See also **quitclaim deed**.

naked trust

see **bare trust**.

named insured

A party specified in an **insurance contract** as the person protected; in a fire insurance policy, this may be the property owner and/or a mortgagee. See also **insurable interest, mortgage clause**.

nantissement (F)

pledge; security; bailment; hypothecation. The granting of goods as security for a debt is termed a ***gage*** and the granting of a right over real estate may be an ***antichrèse*** or a ***hypothèque***.

(*titres de propriété remis en nantissement* – title deeds lodged as security)

(*droit de nantissement* – **lien** on goods).

National Association of Realtors (NAR) (US)

The largest real estate organisation in the United States, first formed in 1908 under the name National Association of Real Estate Boards and renamed in 1972. It now comprises over 500 000 members drawn from members of the major appraisal, brokerage and real estate management organisations in the United States. Members of the NAR are designated Realtors R or Realtors-Associates R; a designation that may be used only by its members. The organisation includes among its members real estate agents and brokers, property managers and appraisers. Members of the NAR subscribe to a **code of ethics** and the organisation is the prime body for the control of licencing of real estate brokers and sales persons at State level.

National Conditions of Sale
see **conditions of sale**.

national domain
see **domain**.

National House Building Council (NHBC)
A voluntary non-profit making body established with British government approval to encourage improved building standards for dwelling-houses and to provide warranties against certain building defects for houses or flats approved by the Council: in particular, against structural defects, subsidence, settlement or heave, appearing within ten years of construction. The Council also provides independent building inspectors and assists in arranging arbitration for disputes that relate to houses covered by its warranty. The Council members include representatives from the Building Societies Association, building employers' organisations, the Royal Institution of Chartered Surveyors, the Royal Institute of British Architects, building trades unions and consumer protection bodies. A builder or developer who is a member of the Council and builds a new house enters into an agreement with the first purchaser and warrants that the house is built in a workmanlike manner, built of proper materials, fit for human habitation and complies with the NHBC regulations. During the first two years of the warranty (the 'initial guarantee period') the builder undertakes to make good any defects in the property; during the remaining eight years he is responsible for "damage to the building requiring

complete or partial rebuilding or repair work". In addition, the NHBC provides insurance to cover the first purchaser against a failure of the builder to rectify a defect (by reason of his bankruptcy or liquidation) or to meet the cost of an award obtained against the builder.
Guarantee for New Homes – a Guide to the NHBC Scheme, by A.P. de B. Tapping and R. Rolfe, 2 edn.

national park
An area of countryside considered to be of special importance because of its outstanding natural beauty or scientific interest and set aside and maintained by the government essentially for recreation or study. A term of North American origin where the Federal Government owns and manages the land and restricts public access in order to preserve the natural environment and wildlife. (The first such park was the Yellowstone Park, Wyoming, which was established formally in 1872; although Yosemite Valley and the Mariposa Big Tree Grove, California, were declared by Congress in 1864 as, "premises to be held for public use, resort and recreation ... inalienably for all time". There are now over 150 such parks in the United States of America. In Britain national parks are designated by the **Countryside Commission** (formerly the Nationl Parks Commission) by an order confirmed by the Secretary of State for the Environment under the National Parks and Access to the Countryside Act 1949, s. 5, (as extended by the Countryside Act 1968) as areas of particular national beauty and suitability for public enjoyment and recreation. Notable examples are parts of the

Lake District, Dartmoor, Exmoor, the Peak District, the Norfolk Broads, the Yorkshire Dales, North York Moors, Snowdonia, Northumberland and Brecon Beacons. Generally such areas are in private ownership with arrangements made to facilitate public access and ensure preservation of the landscape. The county planning authority in whose area a National Park is situated is required to prepare a map of the Park for sale to the public and the authority has power to make grants in respect of any activity that conserves or enhances the amenity of the Park (Wildlife and Countryside Act 1981, ss. 43, 44).

In France there are five national parks (*parcs nationaux*): la Vanoise, Port-Cros, Pyrenees occidentales, Cevennes and les Ecrins. See also **access agreement, area of outstanding natural beauty, area of special control.**

Introduction to Town and Country Planning, by John Ratcliffe, 2 edn., pp. 308–313.

United Nations' List of National Parks and Equivalent Reserves.

National Parks Commission

A body established under the National Parks and Access to the Countryside Act 1949 to administer national parks. Superseded in 1968 by the **Countryside Commission.**

National Trust

The National Trust for Places of Historic Interest or Natural Beauty. A charitable trust established in 1895 by Octavia Hill, Sir Robert Hunter, and Canon Hardwicke Rawnsley, and incorporated by the National Trust Act 1907, "to promote the permanent preservation for the benefit of the nation of land and buildings of beauty or historic interest". Its powers were extended by the National Trust Acts of 1937 and 1939 so that it may now acquire buildings of national or architectural interest or importance, as well as similar chattels, and make these available for public viewing and enjoyment. The National Trust is a private charitable trust that raises finance from the public, but also benefits from Government aid. Property owned by the Trust may be declared 'inalienable' so that such property may never be sold or given away without express Parliamentary authorisation. The National Trust (together with the allied National Trust for Scotland) is now the third largest landowner (by area) in Britain behind the State and the Crown.

The National Trust Guide, edited by R. Fedden and R. Joekes, 2 edn.

nationalisation

see **expropriation.**

natural rights

Rights that are considered an ordinary incident of the ownership of any area of **land** in its natural state; unless such a right is curtailed by agreement or statute or lost to another by prescription. A natural right cannot be acquired by grant (whether express, implied or presumed) and cannot be derived from any artificial addition to land. "Natural rights of property must be rights which attach to property in its primitive state; and cannot, without a contradiction in terms, be applied to an artificial subject matter, like a house". – Angus *v* Dalton (1878) 4 QBD 169. In particular, (a) a right to receive air that comes through a defined passage, in an unpolluted state (but not the free passage of air itself: Webb *v* Bird (1862) 13 CB (NS) 841; (b) a right not to have the support of land itself undermined by an owner of adjacent or subjacent land (a right that does not extend to man-made additions to land per se); (c) a right of a riparian owner to the free flow of water in a natural stream (subject to reasonable rights of extraction by an upper riparian owner); (d) a right to the unimpeded passage of fish from neighbouring land when running in a natural watercourse. There is no natural right to light recognised in English law, such a right must be acquired as an easement or preserved by a restrictive covenant. See also **riparian rights, right of air, right to fish, right of support, water rights**.

Nature Conservancy Council

A body that superseded the 'Nature Conservancy' which was established by Royal Charter in 1949 to provide advice on the conservation and control of flora and fauna and to establish and manage nature reserves. The Nature Conservancy Council as such was established in 1973 for, "the purposes of nature conservation and fostering the understanding thereof" (Nature Conservancy Council Act 1973, s. 1 (1)). The Council is responsible for establishing and maintaining nature reserves; providing advice to (amongst others) the Secretary of State for the Environment on nature conservation; commissioning and supporting research on related matters; and disseminating knowledge of nature conservation. See also **site of special scientific interest**.

néant (F)

of little or no value; nought.

nec vi, nec clam, nec precario (L)

'Not by violence, stealth, or entreaty'. An essential requirement for establishing a right over land by **prescription** is that the right has been used or enjoyed *nec vi, nec clam, nec precario*; that is the right must not be claimed as a result of force, secret user, nor must the right have been obtained without consent. Thus, the claimant of a prescriptive right is endeavouring to establish that the person against whom he is seeking to establish that right voluntarily and openly acquiesced in the user. See also **adverse possession**.

necessity, agency of

see **agency of necessity, quasi-contract**.

necessary easement

see **easement of necessity**.

necessary repair

see **implied covenant, tenant-like manner, tenantable repair**.

negative cash flow

A situation where the gross income from a property investment is insufficient to meet operating expenses and the annual cost of debt service, i.e. the **cash flow** is negative. In the US, an investment that generates a negative cash flow is called sometimes an 'alligator'. See also **deficit financing, leverage**.

negative covenant

see **restrictive covenant**.

negative easement

An **easement** by which the owner of land limits a right or benefit over adjoining land, e.g. a right not to have an adjoining land owner obstruct the flow of light or air or not to remove a right of support. In English law, as a rule, the creation of new negative easements is regarded with disfavour, the law preferring to consider such a right as a positive easement, e.g. a right to receive light across a given area of land, or as a **restrictive covenant**, – Phipps v Pears [1965] 1 QB 76. In the US, called also a 'subservient easement'.

negative leasehold (US)
see **profit rent**.

negative leverage
see **leverage**.

negative profit rent
see **profit rent**.

negligence
An omission, failure, or a statement that a reasonable man would not perpetrate because it might result in loss or injury by a person to whom a **duty of care** is owed. "Negligence is the omitting to do something that a reasonable man, guided upon those considerations which ordinarily regulate the conduct of human affairs, would do or the doing of something which a reasonable man would not do." – Blyth v Birmingham Water Co. (1856) 11 Exch. 784; Union PR Co. v McDonald 152 US 262, 14 SCt. 619, 38 LEd 434. Negligence covers both acts that a man or woman would not commit and statements that would not be made, for fear that they might cause financial hardship to another. A layman is expected to conduct himself so that a 'person on a Clapham omnibus' would not consider that he was oblivious to such harm as he might cause his fellow being. Thus "whenever one person is by circumstances placed in such a position with regard to another that everyone of ordinary sense who did think would at once recognise that if he did not use

ordinary care and skill in his own conduct with regard to those circumstances he would cause danger or injury to the person or property of the other, a duty arises to use ordinary care and skill to avoid such danger." – Heaven v Pender (1883) 11 QBD 502. A failure, whether knowingly, wilfully or intentionally to exercise that ordinary care or attention which, in all the circumstances of the case, might foreseeably cause harm, damage or injury is negligent behaviour and is a breach of that duty which any person owes to another – to have reasonable regard and care for the interests of other persons. In order to be able to claim negligence an offended party must demonstrate that he was owed a duty of care; that there was a breach of that duty; that he has suffered damage, which is not too remote from the negligent act or statement; and that he himself was not acting in an unreasonable manner.

Negligence is a **tort**; it may arise from an omission, miscarriage or a false statement but, unlike **misrepresentation**, it does not arise directly from a contractual relationship, (although it may flow from a breach of an express or implied obligation arising out of a contract that requires reasonable care or skill; when that obligation arises in the course of a business, or from the occupation of premises for business purposes (Unfair Contract Terms Act 1977, s. 1, as amended by the Occupier's Liability Act 1984, s. 2). It is a separate tort from, but may arise together with, a **nuisance**; for example, when a property owner fails to repair and maintain premises his neighbour may suffer injury from falling material, and also be obstructed in the proper use and enjoyment of his property.

Negligence may arise in a number of instances that specifically relate to real estate. For example: (i) a landowner permitting something to escape from land when he knows, or should know, that danger is likely to arise therefrom – a **strict liability** owed by a landowner to the public at large, (ii) a liability owed by an occupier of premises to exercise a "common duty of care" towards any **visitor** to those premises (Occupiers Liability Act 1957, s. 2.); in this context the duty is one to take reasonable care to see that the visitor will be safe while on the premises and, if there is a danger that the visitor might be injured, the duty of care must have regard to the "nature of the danger, the length of time that the danger was in existence, the steps necessary to remove the danger and the likelihood or otherwise of an injury being caused." – Sawyer *v* H. and G. Simmonds Ltd, (1966) 197 EG 879, (iii) a landowner's liability for a failure to take steps to prevent injury to children who are likely to **trespass** on his land; the landowner is expected to provide an obstacle to any child who might approach something dangerous on the land, an obstacle that should be "sufficiently difficult to surmount as to make it clear to the youngest unaccompanied child likely to approach the danger that beyond the obstacle is forbidden territory" (in the US called the 'attractive nuisance doctrine') – Herrington *v* British Railway Board [1972] AC 877, (iv) a failure of a person who takes on work for, or in connection with, the erection, conversion or enlargement of a dwelling-house (which may include a contractor, subcontractor, architect, engineer, surveyor or any other professional person) to ensure that the work is carried out in a workmanlike or professional manner; that proper materials are used; and that the house is fit for human habitation when completed (Defective Premises Act 1972, s. 1) – this duty, which applies to work carried out after 1st January 1974, applies to tenants and purchasers of the house and is additional to any common law duty of care owed by the same persons, (v) the failure of a landlord, who is under an obligation to his tenant for the **repair** or **maintenance** of the demised premises, whether an express obligation or an obligation that is implied (for example from his right of entry to carry out repairs or maintenance), to carry out his obligations and thereby risk harm being occasioned to a user of the premises (Defective Premises Act 1972, s. 4) – a duty that arises when the landlord knew, or might reasonably have known, of the defect, (vi) a local authority's failure to carry out its statutory duties, for example to inspect a property in the course of construction in order to see that it accords with the **Building Regulations** – Anns *v* Merton London Borough Council [1978] AC 728, (vii) a building contractor's failure to take reasonable care to make access to a house safe for visitors – AC Billings and Sons Ltd., *v* Riden [1958] AC 240. This list is not exhaustive but illustrates the need for any person having control of land, buildings or anything attached thereto, to take reasonable care that the property is safe for any intending or likely user; a liability that extends to owners and occupiers, their agent and managers, and their professional advisers. In this branch of the law, which has developed rapidly in the past 25 years, the courts are trenchant when seeking to protect the weak from the strong; especially the ordinary man against a possessor of real estate who fails to maintain his asset in a safe and secure condition, but still expects or invites others to enter thereon.

A person cannot escape a liability for negligence merely by giving notice that he is not liable to anyone for a negligent act or omission, unless that is reasonable. "A person cannot by reference to any contract term or to a notice given to persons generally or to particular persons exclude or restrict his liability for death or personal injury resulting from negligence" (Unfair Contract Terms Act 1977, s. 2(1)). See also **contributory negligence, laches, professional negligence, trespass, *volenti non fit injuria*.**

Law for Land Management Students, by Richard Card, John Murdoch and Peter Schofield, pp. 297–350, (1981).
Civil Liability for Defective Premises, by Holyoak and Allen, (1982).
Liability in Negligence, by J.C. Smith (1985).
The Law of Defective Premises, by Antony Speight and Gregory Stone, (1982).
The Law of Torts, by Harry Street, 7 edn., pp. 93–205, pp. 259–276.
Tort, by Winfield and Jolowicz, 12 edn., pp. 93–205, 259–276.
Charlesworth & Percy on Negligence, 7 edn.

négligence (F)
negligence; carelessness. A word not used generally in French law where the closest equivalent to the English tort of negligence is *quasi-délit*.

négociation (F)
negotiation.

negotiable instrument
A written document that may be assigned or transferred in the normal course of business; in particular, an unconditional order or promise to pay a definite sum of money (but not a mere **receipt**), signed by the maker of the **instrument**. A written instrument that constitutes an obligation to pay money (or, sometimes, to deliver a security for money) and passes a good title merely by **delivery**, or by **endorsement** and delivery. A person who accepts a negotiable instrument in **good faith** and for **value** (the '*bona fide* holder'), without **notice** of any defect, obtains an indefisible title and a right of action in his or her own name, even if the transferor's title was defective. Thus a negotiable instrument does not rely on **privity of contract** and is not affected by the maxim *nemo dat quod non habet*, 'no one can give what he does not possess'. A negotiable instrument may take the form of a bank note, **cheque, bill of exchange, certificate of deposit, promissory note** or a bearer bond or bearer share. See also **negotiation**.

negotiation
1. A discussion or bargaining process between two parties conducted with a view to concluding an **agreement** or settling a dispute on a matter of mutual concern. Negotiation does not of itself aim to produce a binding contract, but a contract may result thereafter as a means of cementing any agreement or settlement. The process of negotiation may be conducted directly between the parties or through an intermediary. In real estate, an **estate agent** or **broker** is the

most common intermediary negotiator. When the intermediary has been appointed to negotiate and 'arrange' a sale of property, then negotiation may be described as that process "which passes between parties or their agents in the course of or incident to the making of a contract; and if the negotiation is brought to such a close as leaves the principal at liberty to say, 'I accept the offer' – then the agent has done all that a negotiating agent can do, and within the meaning of the rule he has arranged the sale, the sale afterwards being effected." – In re Macgowan, Macgowan v Murray [1891] 1 Ch. 116. See also **bargain, commission, 'subject to contract'.** 2. The transfer of a **bill of exchange** or **negotiable instrument** from one person to another, whether by delivery, or endorsement and delivery, in such a manner that the transferee becomes the possessor of the document. See also **negotiable instrument.**

neighbour or neighbor
One who lives in an adjoining house. Any **adjacent** or **adjoining** owner or occupier of land. In relation to a right of support for land a neighbouring landowner 'must be the owner of that portion of land, whether a wider or narrower strip of land, the existence of which in its natural state is necessary for the support of my land'. – Birmingham Corporation v Allen (1877) 6 Ch. D 289. When considering a liability for a **tort**, neighbours have been defined as, 'persons who are so closely and directly affected by my act that I ought to reasonably have them in contemplation as being so affected when I am directing my mind to the acts or omissions which are called in question'. – Donaghue v

Stevenson [1932] AC 580. See also *ad medium filum*, **boundary line, negligence.**

neighbourhood or neighborhood
1. The immediate vicinity; an area in close proximity. See also **adjacent, neighbour.**
2. An area of a town or city that makes up a distinct community.
3. A number of people who form a cohesive unit usually within a larger area or district. See also **neighbouring unit, shopping centre.**

neighbourhood shopping centre
see **shopping centre.**

neighbourhood unit
A homogeneous urban or suburban area of predominately residential property which has grown up or, more usually, has been created in order to provide ease of access to essential facilities and to provide a balanced and identifiable community. A neighbourhood unit is a distinct and territorial grouping of people established as a self-contained entity, i.e. with shops, schools, meeting halls, service industries, recreation areas, etc. This form of urban planning grew in popularity in the US in the interwar period and was adopted for many of the new towns and many new housing developments in Britain during the immediate period after World War II. Such units of development have been termed 'neighbourhoods', 'districts', 'residential communities' or even 'villages'. The ideal size for such communities is a subject of controversy but is commonly considered to fall in the range of 1000 to 10000 persons.
An Introduction to Town and Coun-

try Planning, by John Ratcliffe, 2 edn., pp. 49–52.
Principles and Practice of Town and Country Planning, by Lewis Keeble, 4 edn., p. 218 *et seq.*

nemo contra factum suum proprium venite potest (L)
'No one can go against his own act or deed.' See **derogation from grant, estoppel.**

nemo dare potest quod non habet (L)
'No one can give that which he has not'. See **covenant for title, estoppel, sub-lease.**

nemo dat qui (quod) non habet (L)
'No one can give who possesses not'; i.e. no one can be given a better **title** than he has himself.
See also **negotiable instrument.**

nemo plus juris ad alium transferre potest, quam ipse habet (L)
'No one can transfer a greater right to another than he himself has'. Thus the title of an assignee can be no better than that of his assignor. See also **assignment.**

net after tax (US)
see **income.**

net annual value (NAV)
The **annual value** of a property as assessed for rating purposes on the assumption that the tenant undertakes "to pay all the usual tenant's rates and taxes and to bear the cost of the repairs and insurance and other expenses, if any, necessary to maintain the **hereditament** in a state to command a rent". (General Rate Act 1967, s. 19(3)). The **rateable value** of a property may be determined directly by assessing the 'net annual value'; or by assessing the **gross value** and then making given **statutory deductions** to

cover "repairs, insurance and other expenses" to arrive at the net annual value. Net annual value is determined directly for most industrial properties, for cemeteries, racecourses, caravan sites, most operational property of statutory undertaking and properties where the value of land, rather than buildings is being assessed. For other types of property it is derived from the gross value. When there is no indication to the contrary rateable value and net annual value are synonymous.

net asset value
The **net worth** of the ordinary shareholder's funds expressed as the price per ordinary share. Not to be confused with the **asset value** per ordinary share which is based on the current market value of all assets assuming a break-up of the company; although the terms 'asset value per share' or 'net tangible assets per share' are used sometimes to refer to the net asset value of a company. See also **break-up value.**

net assets
see **net worth.**

net book value
see **book value.**

net capital
The present or **net worth** of a business.

net cash flow
Cash flow after deducting any liabilities for tax, loan interest and principal payments and allowing for depreciation. **Income** that may be distributed free of all liability. When assessing the financial liability of a capital project, net cash flow has been defined to comprise "the net cash

receipts to which a project gives rise. Formally they comprise profits less taxes when actually paid, plus depreciation provision less replacement capital expenditures when actually made, plus net changes in working capital, plus the recovery of any net residual values from assets at the end of a project's life, plus miscellaneous cash receipts which fall into none of the preceding categories." (*The Finance and Analysis of Capital Projects*, by Merrett and Sykes, 2 edn., pp. 29–30.) Called also 'net spendable income' or 'net operating cash flow'. cf. **net income**.

net cost
The actual amount paid, or the cost, of a property after taking account of any benefit or income received in return.
cf. **gross cost**. See also **acquisition cost, equity**.

net current assets
see **working capital**.

net discounted revenue
see **net present value**.

net discounted value
see **net present value**

net floor area
The total floor area of a building capable of use for the purpose for which the building is intended and which is measured from the inside finish of the structural, external or party walls; excluding any impediment to its proper use (internal partitions, columns, pillars, air-conditioning units, etc.) and any common or shared areas (lift shafts, stairwells, toilets, plant rooms, corridors, etc.). See also **net internal area, net sales area, net usable area, rentable area**.

net income
The annual **income** received, or likely to be received, from investment in a property, after deducting all operating costs and expenses directly related to that property. Net income may be expressed as before or after tax. Net income is calculated before any allowance for depreciation.
cf. **gross income, net cash flow.**

net income before recapture (US)
see also **net operating income.**

net income multiplier (NIM) (US)
A **capitalisation factor** used to convert a net income stream into a present capital value. The reciprocal of the **overall capitalisation rate.**
cf. **gross income multiplier**.

net income ratio (US)
The ratio of **net operating income** to **effective gross income** – the complement of the **operating expense ratio.**

net internal area
A term defined by the Code of Measuring Practice of The Royal Institution of Chartered Surveyors and The Incorporated Society of Valuers and Auctioneers (2nd edn, 1986) as: "The usable area within a building measured to the internal finish of perimiter or party walls, ignoring skirting boards and taking each floor into account, excluding:
– toilets, toilet lobbies, bathrooms, cleaners' cupboards and the like;
– lift-rooms, plant-rooms, tank-rooms, other than those of a process nature, fuel stores and the like;
– stairwells, lift-wells and those parts of entrance halls, atria, landings and balconies used in common or for the purpose of essential access;

– corridors, where used in common with other occupiers or of a permanent essential nature (e.g. fire corridors, smoke lobbies etc);
– areas under the control of service or other external authorities;
– internal structural walls, walls enclosing excluded areas, columns, piers, chimney breasts, other projections, vertical ducts and the like;
– the space occupied by permanent air-conditioning, heating or cooling apparatus and ducting which renders the space substantially unusable, having regard to the purpose for which it is intended (where such apparatus is present its area may be quoted separately for valuation purposes)."
Car parking areas and floor space with a headroom of less than 1.5m (5 feet are excluded and treated separately. In applying this term to shops the depth is measured from back of pavement or forecourt to back of sales area, assuming as a rule that the depth is reasonably constant.

An area used for office and shop agency, valuation and rating practice (including service charge apportionment) other than ancillary offices in warehouses and industrial property, as well as industrial agency, valuation and rating practice for buildings in multi-occupation. Called sometimes the 'effective floor area.'
cf. **gross internal area**. See also **rentable area, net sales area.**

net leasable area (US)
see **rentable area.**

net lease or net-net-lease (US)
A lease that requires the lessee to pay the **operating expenses** resulting from his occupation of the premises including repairs, maintenance, taxes, insurance premiums, utility costs, etc.

Under a 'net lease' the lessee generally pays operating and maintenance expenses; under a 'net-net-lease' he pays also the cost of insurance; and with a 'net-net-net' or **triple net lease** he pays real estate taxes as well. However, the term net lease is used commonly in a generic sense for any lease which provides that the lessee is to pay all or most of the property outgoings. (The US Internal Revenue Service places limitations on the deductions permitted from taxable income derived from a 'net lease' property and for this purpose a net lease exists if either (a) the lessor's total deductions for business expenses (excluding rent, interest, taxes, depreciation, non-business deductions and certain other reimbursements) are less than 15 per cent of rental income; or (b) if the lessor is guaranteed a specific return or is permitted to pass all expenses through to the tenant).
cf. **gross lease**. See also **escalator clause.**

net lettable area (US)
see **rentable area.**

net listing (US)
A form of agency **listing** which provides for the principal to receive an agreed price for a property and for the estate agent or broker to retain as commission any sum received above that price. Called also a 'net sale contract'. Net listing is illegal in many states. See also **contingency fee.**

net-net lease (US)
see **net lease.**

net-net-net lease
see **net lease, triple net lease.**

net operating cash flow
see **net cash flow.**

net operating income (NOI)

Net income receivable from a property before payment of capital or interest on any loans, i.e. before 'debt service'. Called also 'operating income' or 'net income before recapture'.

cf. **cash flow**.

net operating profit

see **net profit**.

net option

An **option** that grants a right to purchase property at a specified price to the vendor. See also **put option**.

net population density

see **population density**.

net present value (NPV)

The difference, at a given discount rate, between the **present value** of (i) the total net income to be derived from an investment and (ii) the total expenditure and outgoings incurred in making and maintaining that investment, taken over the projected life of the investment. Net present value is calculated as a means of assessing the viability of alternative investments by reducing all income and expenditure for each alternative to a common base, i.e. to a single value obtained by discounting to the present day (or the date of the initial investment) the amounts receivable over and above the amounts payable for each investment. A positive NPV indicates that an investment is profitable and the higher the NPV the better the profitability of that investment (The net present value of the **net income** receivable from an investment is equivalent to the **capital value** of that investment). Called also the 'net discounted value' or the 'net discounted revenue'.

cf. **internal rate of return**. See also **capitalisation, discounted cash flow**. *The Valuation of Property Investments*, by Nigel Enever, 3 edn., pp. 80–82.

net price

The **price** paid for a property excluding any fees, commissions, discounts, taxes, i.e. the true consideration paid for the property. See also **acquisition cost**.

net profit

Profit after deducting, selling and administrative expenses and depreciation, which may be measured either before or after tax. Net profit may be classified before the cost of debt finance – 'net operating profit', or after all costs – 'clear, or net, profit for distribution'.

cf. **gross profit**. See also **net income**.

net redemption yield

A **redemption yield** after tax.
cf. **grossed-up redemption yield**.

net rent

1. The total amount payable by the tenant(s) of a property as specified under the lease(s) as **rent**; excluding any other payments the tenant may make to his landlord, such as service charge contributions, rates, insurance premiums, interest on late payments. See also **net income**.

2. An amount of rent stipulated in a lease as payable without the tenant having any right to make deductions from that rent; "when a party stipulates to receive a *net* rent, that means a rent clear of all deductions to which it would otherwise be liable." – Bennett *v* Wormack (1828) 6 LJ (OS) KB 176.

(US) 3. The rent receivable from the tenant or tenants of a building after an appropriate deduction or allowance for voids or defaulting tenants, or occasionally after deducting non-recoverable operating expenses, i.e. the rent that goes into the landlord's pocket for his permanent retention. See also **effective gross income, income.**

net rentable area (US)
see **rentable area.**

net residential density
see **residential density.**

net retail floorspace
see **net sales area.**

net return
see **net yield.**

net sale contract (US)
see **net listing.**

net sales area
The **net internal area** available in a retail store or shop exclusively for display and sale of merchandise; excluding storage, equipment areas, offices, toilets, rest rooms, lifts, staircases, etc. The area normally used to calculate the ratio of turnover to selling area. Called also the 'net retail floorspace'.
cf. **gross retail area**. See also **sales area.**

net spendable income
see **net cash flow.**

net usable area
The area that a tenant or occupier may actually use for the purpose for which he is occupying a building. In an office, the area that could be carpeted and upon which furniture can be placed. In the US the net usable area is equivalent to the **rentable area**, on the assumption that an office floor is to be let to more than one tenant, but

excluding columns, stantions, and any air-conditioning units or similar items that obstruct the full use of the space. See also **net internal area, net sales area.**

net worth
The value of the total assets (excluding fictitious assets) of an organisation, less the total liabilities (excluding the owner's capital), i.e. the total value of the owner's share of a business. In accounting normally taken as the book value of the equity and preference shareholders' interest, including retained reserves, although this basis of valuation may not fully take account of the current market value of the assets. Called also a company's 'net assets' or 'total equity'.
cf. **asset value, break-up value**. See also **equity capital, net asset value.**

net yield
The yield represented by expressing the **net income** receivable from an investment as a percentage of the total **acquisition cost** of that investment. The return on an investment after taking account of cost of managing that investment and any losses incurred during the holding period. Net yield may be expressed as before or after tax, and before or after **debt service**. Called also the 'net return'. See also **cash-on-cash return, free and clear return, net redemption yield.**

network analysis
A technique for planning and controlling a project by which the stages in the project are set out in sequence and inter-related by means of a diagrammatic representation, in order to determine the sequence of work that produces the optimum use of time at the minimum cost. See also **critical-**

path analysis, programme evaluation and review technique.

new development
Development of land that is essentially outside the scope of a landowner's 'existing use rights'. Defined by The Town and Country Planning Act 1971, s. 22 (5) as, 'any development other than development of a class specified in Part I or II of Schedule 8' (eighth schedule rights). If planning permission is refused, or granted subject to conditions, for 'new development', the owner may be entitled to a payment from any unexpended balance of established development value attached to the land. See also compensation for planning restrictions.
Guide to Development and Planning, by R.N.D. Hamilton, edn, pp. 403–8.

'new-for-old' insurance
see replacement cost.

new tenancy
see business tenancy, extended lease.

new town
A town that is developed as an entity over a relatively short time span (10–20 years) usually to meet an urgent housing need, as compared to a town that develops by natural growth, over several generations. In British urban development the post-war new towns are commonly regarded as a direct descendant of the garden cities: a concept which today comprises an urban development area with a comprehensive range of services including housing, shopping, industry, social facilities, etc., that make the area reasonably self-contained.
'New Town' specifically refers to an area designated for development under the provision of the New Towns Acts 1946 and 1965. These new towns have been designated since 1946, although from 1977 the creation of further New Towns has been curtailed because of reduced housing needs and the increasing importance being placed on the redevelopment of inner city areas. See also Commission for the New Towns, designated area, development corporation, garden city.
The British New Towns, by M. Aldridge, (1979).
New Towns, by Pierre Merlin (1971).
The New Town Story, by F. Schaffer (1970).
New Towns, by Osborn and Whittick (1977).

New Towns Commission
see Commission for the New Towns.

new town development corporation
see development corporation.

'no-buy' pledge (US)
An agreement entered into by tenants of a multi-let building, when it is proposed to convert the building to co-operative or condominium ownership, by which the tenants promise not to proceed with the purchase of their units until the majority of those who signed the agreement have accepted that the best deal has been reached by the promotors (usually a tenant's association) of the proposed change in the form of ownership.

'no-compete' clause (US)
see non-competition clause.

'no-deal, no-commission' clause
see 'no-job, no-fee' clause.

'no-job, no-fee' clause
A clause inserted in an agency agreement that no fee or commission will

be paid by the principal unless a particular result is achieved by the agent; for example, the introduction of a party who completes the purchase of a property as compared to a purchaser who is only '**ready, able and willing**' to purchase the property. Called also a 'no-deal, no-commission' clause.

no set-off certificate (US)
see **estoppel certificate**.

no-scheme world
see **compulsory purchase compensation**.

noise
see **derogation from grant, mitigation works, non-conforming user, nuisance**.

nominal company
see **nominee company**

nominal consideration
Consideration that has no significant value but is included in a contract that is not made by deed to preserve its apparent validity under English law; or is included in a contract to indicate that an outright gift is not intended. See also **peppercorn rent**.

nominal damages
see **damages**.

nominal interest rate
1. The interest rate payable for a period of one year assuming the entire principal remains outstanding during the year and interest is accrued only once a year, as compared to the **effective annual interest rate** which is the true rate payable when interest is compounded at intervals of less than a year.
2. The basic annual interest rate quoted on a promissory note or on a loan agreement and levied through-

out the term of the loan on the initial amount of principal, not withstanding that the interest is compounded other than annually or repayments of principal are made by instalments during the term of the loan. Thus, if a sum of £2000 is borrowed for one year at a 'nominal interest rate' of 10 per cent per annum, and the principal is repayable monthly by equal instalments, then £200 is payable as interest even though the total amount of principal is not available for the full year. Called sometimes an 'add-on interest rate' or 'face interest rate'. See also **annual percentage rate, face value**.

nominal return
see **nominal yield**.

nominal share capital
The capital that a company is authorised to raise rather than the amount actually paid-up by the shareholders. The total **face value** of the share capital of a company. See also **nominal value**.

nominal value
1. A value stated as a matter of form, which bears no relationship to **market value**.
2. The face value as indicated on a share in a company, i.e. the **par value**.

nominal yield (or rate)
1. The **dividend yield** when related to the **nominal value** of a share, as contrasted with the same yield when related to the market value of the share.
2. The rate of return specified on a bond, or other financial instrument as a percentage of the nominal or **par value**. The nominal yield is the basis normally used by a company for expressing its rate of dividend return

Called also the 'nominal return' or 'coupon rate'.
cf. **effective yield**.

nominale (F)
nominal.
(*valeur nominale* – **nominal value; face value**).

nominated sub-contractor
A **sub-contractor** or supplier appointed because of the wishes of the employer as distinguished from one appointed at the sole discretion of a building contractor. Usually a nominated sub-contractor is appointed or selected to carry out specialist work and frequently, at the time that a main contractor is invited to tender for work, the employer specifies that certain parts of the work will be undertaken by a specialist contractor of the employer's choice. However, in spite of the intervention of the employer there is **privity of contract** between only the main contractor and the sub-contractor, and not between the employer and the sub-contractor unless the employer makes an express stipulation to the contrary. Nonetheless the employer usually remains responsible for renomination if the sub-contractor fails to fulfill his obligations. Some building contracts provide the main contractor with a right of objection to a nominated sub-contractor.

nominee company (or trust)
A **company** (or **trust**) formed to hold investments in name only, i.e. as a **fiduciary** (or trustee) for another party such as an overseas resident who wishes to conceal his identity. A company that is effective in name only. Called also a 'nominal company'.

non-aedificandi (L)
'No building'. An area of land where all building is prohibited, such as alongside a highway or between buildings.

non altius tollendi (L)
A form of negative easement in the civil or French law by which an owner is prohibited from building above a certain height. A term that may be used also to refer to a similar planning or zoning restriction. See also **servitude**.

non-assumption clause (US)
see **alienation clause**.

non-competition clause
A clause in a lease, especially a lease of retail premises, by which the lessee agrees not to carry on a competing use within a specified radius of the subject property, either during or for a reasonable period after the expiry of the lease. A form of a **restrictive covenant** in a lease. In the US called also a 'no-compete' clause.
cf. **user clause**.

non-conforming use
A permitted use of a property which, although started legitimately, is now in conflict with the current zoning or land use regulations for the area. A user that is no longer considered to be compatible with the surrounding area, especially when that user causes a nuisance, in terms of noise, fumes, smell, etc., that would not be permitted if the use were introduced into the area anew. For example, a light industrial property in a residential neighbourhood. See also **discontinuance order, nuisance**.
Handling the Land Use Case, by Schnidman, Abrams and Delaney, pp. 503–508 (1984).
American Law of Zoning, by Robert

M. Anderson, 2 edn., para. 6.01 *et seq.*

non-derogation from grant
see **derogation from grant**.

non-disclosure
A failure to reveal facts or important information that has a direct bearing on a transaction. See also **latent defect, misdescription, misrepresentation, utmost good faith**.

non est factum (L)
'It is not (his) deed'. A plea made by someone in whose name a deed is executed that the document is not his; for example, because he was totally misled as to the effect of the contents, or because of fraud, forgery or other falsehood. The plea may apply to a **mistake** as to the essence of the deed, but not its content; i.e. the plea is that there was never a meeting of the mind on what was purportedly agreed – Muskham Finance *v* Howard [1963] 1 QB 904. For example, if a person who is unable to read signs a document based on a false representation as to its contents, it is possible for that party to declare *non est factum*.
Carlisle and Cumberland Banking Company *v* Bragg [1911] 1 KB 489 – Sanders *v* Anglia Building Society [1971] AC 1004.

non-free tenure
see **villeinage**.

non périmé (F)
unexpired.
(*terme d'un bail non périmé* – **unexpired term** of a lease).

non-recourse loan (or mortgage)
A loan (or mortgage) granted on the basis that the lendor's right of action in the event of default by the borrower (or mortgagor) is limited to the property held as collateral; there being no right of **recourse** against the borrower personally. In the UK a mortgage agreement rarely precludes the right of the mortgagee to sue on the personal debt. In the US mortgages are granted frequently on the basis that the only recourse for the **mortgagee** is a claim against the proceeds of sale of the mortgaged property; thereby facilitating the transfer of a mortgage with the mortgaged property held as security for that mortgage.
The use of the words 'without recourse' (or the French equivalent *sans recours*) by the drawer, or an indorser, of a **bill of exchange** precludes that person's own liability to any subsequent holder of the bill, in the event that the bill is not paid when it matures. See also **exculpatory clause**.

non sequitur (L)
'It does not follow'.

non-specified property offering (US)
see **blind pool offering**.

non user
see **abandonment, discontinuance**.

nondisturbance clause (US)
A clause inserted in a mortgage agreement which specifies that in the event of **foreclosure** the mortgagee undertakes not to terminate any lease or tenancy of the subject property. In the US (but not in English common law) any lease created after a mortgage is granted may be liable to termination if a mortgagee acquires title to a property by foreclosure. See also **attornment**.

nonfeasance
The neglect or failure of a person to

do that which he ought to do. See also **laches, negligence**.

nonvalued policy (US)
see **unvalued policy**.

nook of land
An area of land of uncertain dimensions. A purchaser of a 'nook of land' is unsure of the area he has acquired.

normal wear and tear (US)
see **fair wear and tear**.

noscitur a sociis (L)
'Know it from its associates'. The meaning or interpretation of a word can be gathered from the context: "English words derive colour from those that surround them". – Bourne *v* Norwich Crematorium Ltd [1967] 2 All ER 578. See also *ejusdem generis*, **implied term**, **words meaning of**.

notaire (F)
notary. A lawyer with a particular responsibility for conveyancing, attesting wills, as well as duties similar to an English **notary public**. A *notaire* prepares and authenticates documents in accordance with the law but does not represent any of the parties; he cannot act if the parties are not in agreement.
(*acte de notaire* – notarial deed)
(*étude de notaire* – notary's office).
See also *avocat*.

notarié acte (F)
notarial deed. See also *acte*.

notary public
A public officer authorised to administer oaths; to certify copies of documents; and to attest deeds and other written documents, particularly when these are required for legal proceedings. In England and Wales usually a **solicitor**. See also *notaire*.

note
1. An unconditional **promise**, evidenced in writing, to pay a sum of money at a specified time to a particular person or the bearer of the written evidence. Commonly called a **promissory note**, or when secured by a mortgage, a 'mortgage note'.
2. A brief written record. A short account of an event, action, information or something similar, especially when made to assist the memory or as a summary to be used later in a more detailed report. "The only difference between an '**agreement**' and a note of an agreement is that, in the one instance a formal agreement is meant, and in the other, something not so particular in form and technical accuracy, but still containing the essentials of the agreement." – Williams *v* Lake [1859] 29 LJQB 3.

note (F)
note; bill. See also *lettre*.

note financing
see **secured loan**.

note mortgage
see **secured loan**.

notice
1. Information, advice or a warning brought to a person's knowledge or attention. An act, advice, or other means, whereby one party is appraised of some fact or proceeding by another. "Notice is a word which involves that knowledge may be imparted by notice, but 'notice' and 'knowledge' are not the same thing, although loosely one sometimes talks as if to act with notice and to act with knowledge were indeed the same." – Cresta Holdings Ltd. *v* Karlin [1959] 3 All E.R. 657. "A person has 'notice' of a fact when (a) he has actual

knowledge of it; or (b) he has received a notice or notification of it; or (c) from all the facts and circumstances known to him at the time in question he has reason to know that it exists. A person 'knows' or has 'knowledge' of a fact when he has actual knowledge of it. 'Discover' or 'learn' or a word or phrase of similar import refers to knowledge rather than to reason to know." (United States Uniform Commercial Code para. 1-201 (25)). In law notice may take three forms: (a) express notice or **actual notice** – directly given or brought to a person's attention, usually in writing; (b) **constructive notice** – deemed by law to have been acquired, as with a fact that a person would discover by making reasonable inquiry, such as examining a land register or inspecting a property – Hunt *v* Luck [1901] 1 Ch. 45. (Called sometimes 'statutory notice' when statute law imparts that information has been brought to a person's notice); (c) **imputed notice** – received by an agent or solicitor (as actual or constructive notice) and thereby assumed for the purpose of a transaction in hand, to be known to the principal or client. See also ***bona fide* purchaser, blight notice, building preservation notice, completion notice, counter-notice, enforcement notice, notice of entry, notice to quit, notice to treat, purchase notice, stop notice.**
2. An entry on the charges register at the **Land Registry** of an estate, interest, right or claim to land; especially a **minor interest**, or a registrable lease or charge created by a registered proprietor of land. Such an entry may be made to protect certain lesser interests or rights affecting registered land (or claims to such rights) which

might otherwise not be binding on a purchaser of registered land. (Land Registration Act 1925, ss. 48–52). Such a notice prevents a purchaser from taking the land free of the registered interest, but it does not make an invalid claim valid. See also **land charge**.

notice of assessment (US)
A notice given, by a state or local tax agency, to an owner of real property of the **assessment** placed on his property.

notice of completion
see **completion notice**.

notice of entry
Notice given by an authority possessing compulsory purchase powers, served with or subsequent to a **notice to treat**, stating that the authority intends to exercise its right to enter and take possession of land (Compulsory Purchase Act 1965, s. 11(1) Sch. 3). A notice of entry is served on a party who has an interest in land when an authority wishes to enter and take possession of the land before compensation is agreed or determined and before the authority has acquired title to the land. The notice must be served on the owner (including a mortgagee in possession) and any lessee or other occupier of the subject land not less than fourteen days before the authority intends to enter and take possession. Interest, at a set statutory rate (see Acquisition of Land (Rate of Interest after Entry) Regulations), is payable on the finally agreed or determined compensation from the date entry is taken by the authority. Also, entry may be taken on to land by the authority lodging in court an appropriate sum for com-

pensation, for each party interest in the land, and giving a bond to pay proper compensation, when this is finally agreed or determined, with interest thereon (1965, Act s. 11(2)) although this procedure is rarely used. See also **general vesting declaration, right of entry, valuation date.**

notice of objection to severance
see **severance.**

notice of pendency (US)
see *lis pendens.*

notice to quit
Express notice given by an existing landlord to his existing tenant stating that an existing tenancy is brought to an end and that the landlord intends to regain **possession** – Lower *v* Sorrell [1962] 3 All ER 1083. A term that may be applied also to notice from a tenant to his landlord, stating that the tenant intends to deliver up possession of the premises when permitted by the lease. Notice, which on its expiry, is intended to bring to an end the relationship of **landlord and tenant**. A valid notice to quit must be given strictly in accordance with the terms of the agreement by which the tenancy is created. It must be plain and unequivocal and must (i) state the premises to which it relates (and relate to the whole of the premises, unless the lease, or a statute, permits partial termination); (ii) specify, in accordance with the terms of the letting, the correct date for the termination of the tenancy, or the correct date must be ascertainable with certainty; (iii) be properly delivered; and (iv) be unconditional. As a rule, notice to quit need not be in any particular form; it is a good notice "if it be so expressed that a person of ordinary

capacity receiving the notice cannot well mistake its nature; it must be clear and unambiguous." – Bury *v* Thompson [1895] 1 QB 696. It need not necessarily be in **writing** – Timmins *v* Rowlinson (1765) 3 Burr. 1603 – unless the tenancy is created in writing or written notice is required by statute; but, to avoid dispute, it is preferable for the notice to be in writing. Notice to quit is necessary to terminate a **weekly tenancy**, a **tenancy from year to year** (yearly tenancy), or any other **periodic tenancy**. It is not required to terminate a tenancy for a term of a year, unless expressly stipulated for in the lease; or unless a notice is required by statute.

In English law, various statutes require that notice to quit be given for a particular period of time, or that the notice conveys certain information to a tenant, in particular his right to continued occupation or to a new tenancy – e.g. for a **business tenancy** – Landlord and Tenant Act 1954, s. 25(2)); for a **residential tenancy** – Protection from Eviction Act 1977, s. 5(1), The Notices to Quit (Prescribed Information) (Protected Tenancies and Part VI Contracts Regulations 1975); for an **agricultural tenancy** (Agricultural Holdings Act 1948, ss. 2, 4, 23 and Agricultural Holdings (Notices to Quit) Act 1977 as amended by Agricultural Holdings Act 1984, ss. 5, 6, 7). A notice to quit part of any leased premises is void, unless permitted by an express term of the lease. However, the Agricultural Holdings Act 1948, s. 31 permits a landlord to terminate a lease for part of an agricultural holding in certain circumstances (e.g. if the landlord requires land for development) and, in that event, the tenant may treat the notice as notice to quit the entire holding (1948 Act, s. 32). See also **protected tenancy, security of tenure, service, time**.

Cheshire's Modern Law of Property, 13 edn, pp. 443–445.

The Law of Landlord and Tenant, by David Yates and A.J. Hawkins, pp. 250–257 (1981).

The Law of Landlord and Tenant, by David Lloyd Evans, 2 edn., pp. 196–200.

Hill & Redman's Law of Landlord and Tenant, 17 edn, pp. 475–496.

Woodfall's Landlord and Tenant, 28 edn, paras. 1–1967 to 2–2032.

27 Halsbury's Laws of England, 28 edn, paras. 182–201.

notice to repair
repair notice, repairs notice, schedule of dilapidations.

notice to treat
A formal notice served, pursuant to a **compulsory purchase order**, upon an owner who is believed to have an interest in land stating the intention of an authority possessing the compulsory purchase powers to acquire that interest. Notice to treat is given to "all the persons interested in, or having power to sell and convey or release, the land, so far as known to the acquiring authority after making diligent inquiry." (Compulsory Purchase Act 1965, s. 5 (1)). A mortgagee, and a person with an equitable interest arising either from an option or a contract to purchase, is entitled to notice to treat. Any tenant, no matter how short his interest, is entitled to notice to treat (although in the case of a periodic tenancy for a year or less the authority may acquire the landlord's interest and then terminate the tenancy by service of notice to quit).

Notice to treat is not served on the beneficiary of an easement, a restrictive covenant, or a licence affecting the land. The notice need not be in any particular form but must describe the land to which it relates; request details of the owner's precise interest in the property and the amount of his claim for **compensation**; and stipulate that the acquiring authority is willing to treat and pay compensation for the purchase of the interest to which the notice relates (1965 Act, s. 5(2)) – Hull and Humber Investment Co. *v* Hull Corporation [1965] 2 QB 145.

A notice to treat is a clear indication of an authority's intention to acquire the land and goes further than an **invitation to treat** in the law of contract; it binds the parties to a contract, at a price to be agreed – Mercer *v* Liverpool, St. Helens and South Lancashire Rail Co. [1904] AC 461. When coupled with an agreement of the proper compensation to be paid, a notice to treat constitutes a binding **contract**; however, "it is not until compensation is agreed or assessed that the equitable title in the land (i.e. the right to acquire the interest in land) passes to the party who has served the notice to treat" – West Midlands Baptist (Trust) Association (Incorporation) *v* Birmingham Corporation [1966] 1 All ER 216. An owner of land is free to deal with his land as he wishes after the receipt of notice to treat and before the acquiring authority acquires title or takes possession. A notice to treat is not an **estate contract** and, therefore, is not registerable as a land charge, but after it has been served either party can seek a decree of **specific performance** to enforce the arrangement.

A notice to treat may be withdrawn

within six weeks from the receipt of the claim for compensation. If it is not withdrawn, it fixes the interest in land to be acquired, so that thereafter the owner of the interest being acquired cannot increase his entitlement to compensation by creating a new interest, e.g. by granting new leases, or otherwise dealing with the land (Mercer *v* Liverpool, St. Helens and South Lancashire Rail Co., supra). However, notice to treat does not fix the date for deciding on the amount of compensation (the **valuation date**) – that is determined either when the parties reach agreement (or the matter is settled by the Lands Tribunal); or when the authority takes possession following a notice of entry (West Midland Baptist Trust case, supra); or, in a case where compensation is assessed on the basis of the cost of **equivalent reinstatement**, the date when reinstatement is first practical (usually when reinstatement commences) or the date of entry by the authority, whichever is the earlier. Following receipt of a notice to treat the recipient must submit a claim for compensation to the acquiring authority within 21 days. If no claim is received the authority may submit the question of determining compensation to the Lands Tribunal. See also **blight notice, compensation for disturbance, general vesting declaration, purchase notice**.
Law of Compulsory Purchase and Compensation, by Keith Davies, 4 edn., pp. 58–65.
Encyclopaedia of Compulsory Purchase and Compensation, by Harold J.J. Brown, paras. 1-1041 to 1-1053.
8 Halsbury's Laws of England, 4 edn., paras. 121-142.

notification (F)
notification; **notice**. Notification may be by post or an official process server (*huissier*). In general the term is used more in the sense of bringing to a person's attention, rather than the legal service of notice e.g. by notice to quit.
cf. **mise en demeure**. See also **congé, préavis, signification.**

notorious possession
Possession that is so conspicuous and open that a diligent owner would be presumed to be aware of it – a requisite of **adverse possession**. In the US used also as a synonym for adverse possession.

novation
The substitution of a new **contract** in place of an existing contract; or a third party in place of an existing party to a contract, and the discharge of the existing contract or the person who was a party to the old contract. Novation means, "that there being a contract in existence, some new contract is substituted for it, either between the same parties (for that might be) or between different parties; the **consideration** mutually being the discharge of the old contract." – Scarf *v* Jardine (1882) 7 App. Cas. 351; Edward Petry and Co. *v* Greater Huntingdon Radio Corpn, (DCWVa) 245 F Supp. 963). The old party is released from all obligations and is replaced by the new party; or the old contract is completely replaced by the new one. This 'exchange' of contracts must be performed with the concurrence (express or implied) of all the parties; unlike an **assignment** which may, in some cases, be effected without the concurrence of the party who is not assigning his rights under the

contract. Novation may be distinguished from the assignment of a contract because, although the assignor may transfer the rights (and possibly the liabilities) of an assignment, the assignor remains liable if the assignee fails to perform the contract. A contractual obligation or benefit (especially one relating to real estate) is more usually transferred by an assignment, but novation arises frequently in relation to a contract to pay a debt, a contract of service, or a partnership contract. See also **privity of contract**.
Chitty on Contracts, 24 edn, pp. 1193 and 1375.
Cheshire and Fifoot's Law of Contract, 10 edn, pp. 468, 471.

novation (F)
  novation.

novel disseisin, assize of
  see **assize of novel disseisin**.

novus actus interveniens (L)
  'A new act intervening'. See **damages**.

noyau (F)
  service core (of a building).
  (*noyau central* – central core).

nu (F)
  naked; without consideration. See also **naked contract**.

nu-propriétaire (F)
  bare-owner; a person who has a right of ownership but does not derive any benefit therefrom, i.e. a person who has granted the **usufruct** to another.
  cf. *usufruitier*.

nude contract
  see **naked contract**.

nudum pactum (L)
  'naked contract'.

nue-propriété (F)
  bare-ownership; **ownership** without a right of enjoyment, i.e. where the use and benefit is held by a *usufruitier*.
  cf. *pleine propriété*. See also **usufruct**.

nuisance
  A cause or source of annoyance, vexation or inconvenience. An action or conduct, or lack of action or conduct, that results in an interference with another's reasonable enjoyment of, or legal right to enjoy, the use of a property or a right thereover. "Nuisance, *nocumentum*, or annoyance, signifies any thing that worketh hurt, inconvenience, or damage". (Bl. Comm. vol iii, p. 216). A term that cannot be precisely defined but includes (1) 'public nuisance': acts that cause damage, inconvenience or annoyance to the public generally, or a class of the public. "A public nuisance is a nuisance which is so widespread in its range or so indiscriminate in its effect that it would not be reasonable to expect one person to take proceedings on his own responsibility to put a stop to it, but it should be taken on the responsibility of the community at large". – Att.-Gen. *v* P.Y.A. Quarries [1957] 2 QB 169. An obstruction of a highway, or the carrying on of any activity that endangers the use of a **highway**, is a public nuisance; this includes erecting a hoarding or scaffolding, excavations, leaving unattended overgrown trees, undermining support, depositing materials, failing to repair dangerous premises, etc. Public nuisance must affect a substantial sector of the public, not just a few people. (2) 'statutory nuisance' – acts that contravene a particular statute. Or, (3) 'private nuisance' – acts

that affect an individual or group of individuals, in particular "the unreasonable use by a man of his land to the detriment of his neighbour". – Miller v Jackson [1977] 3 All ER 344. A nuisance must violate the rights of another, i.e. cause **injury** and the injured person must suffer actual loss or **damage**, otherwise an action for nuisance will fail.

In real estate nuisance means, especially, the use of a property so as to interfere with a person's use and enjoyment of another property; something which diminishes the value of a property – for example, the obstruction of a right of way, or allowing something to escape and encroach on to another's land such as water, smoke, noise, animals, trees, etc. Nuisance is not finite, it depends on surrounding circumstances, so something that may be a nuisance in Grosvenor Square may not be one in Smithfield market – Bamford v Turnley (1862) 3 B and S 77. A person cannot commit a nuisance unless he or she is aware or should be aware of the inconvenience or annoyance created. Thus "if the nuisance is created, not by want of repair but, for example, by the act of a trespasser, or by a secret and unobservable operation of nature, such as a subsidence under or near the foundations of the premises, neither an occupier nor an owner responsible for repair is answerable, unless with knowledge or means of knowledge he allows the danger to continue". – Wringe v Cohen [1940] I KB 229.

The word 'nuisance' frequently is found in leases and, in combination with the words 'annoyance', 'grievance' or 'inconvenience', extends beyond normal nuisance and imparts a particular obligation to act in a more restrained manner between landlord and tenant and between neighbours.

If a tenant causes a nuisance from the premises he occupies, normally he is liable, unless a landlord is himself responsible for creating the nuisance e.g. by failure to meet a landlord's repairing obligation or when the letting clearly was contemplated to cause a nuisance. In the latter instance both parties may be liable for the nuisance – Smith v Scott [1973] Ch. 314. Where a landlord reserves a right to enter and repair the demised premises, or where a landlord is liable by statute to carry out repairs (e.g. a dwelling let for a term of less than seven years: Housing Act 1961, s. 32), a landlord is liable for a nuisance arising from his failure to repair (Wringe v Cohen, *supra*). See also **abatement, damages, derogation from grant, disturbance, encroachment, injunction, negligence, strict liability, trespass.**

Law for Land Management Students, by Richard Card, John Murdoch and Peter Schofield, pp. 381–396 (1981).
Law of Nuisance, by R. Buckley (1981).
Winfield and Jolowicz on Tort, 12 edn, p. 377 *et seq.*
Salmond and Heuston on Tort, 18 edn, pp. 47–86.
34 Halsbury's Laws of England, 4 edn, paras. 301–400.

nuisance order
An order issued by a magistrates' court ordering a person to comply with an **abatement notice** or **prohibition notice** (Public Health Act 1936, s. 94). The order may be issued when a person has failed to abate a statu-

tory nuisance or when a nuisance is likely to render a house **unfit for human habitation**.

nuisance value

The price of tolerating the continuation of a **nuisance**, or the reduction in the value of a property due to the existence of a nuisance.

nuisances (F)

nuisance, as used in the general or physical sense e.g. the creation of pollution, rather than in the legal sense. See also *délit, quasi-délit*.

nul (F)

void.

(*nul et de nul effet* – **null and void**).

null and void

Of no legal effect; unenforceable. See also **void contract**.

nullity

An act that has no legal effect whatsoever. See also **void contract**.

nursery finance

Finance granted by a bank to a company upon terms that include **equity participation**, usually in the form of a minority shareholding in the company.

nursery unit

A small unit of property made available to meet the needs of new businesses, especially a small **workshop**. In the US called also an 'incubator unit'.

nut (US)

A slang term for overheads, or the total expense involved in undertaking a project.

O

obiter dictum (L)

'A saying by the way'. An observation made by a judge, when expressing his decision on a case, that is not intended as a binding statement of law because it does not relate directly to the facts before him. An *obiter dictum* does not form part of the *ratio decidendi* or reason for the decision, although it may be of persuasive authority in a future case.

objet (F)

subject or purpose (of an action); article; thing. In French law, the transaction or legal subject-matter of a contract. The object or subject of an obligation; every obligation arising from a contract must, in French law, have an *objet*. Every contract must have as its *objet* a thing (*chose*) which a party is obliged to transfer or something it must do or not do. The *objet* must be determined or determinable i.e. it must exist; it must be licit; and it must be capable of private existence. For example, the *objet* of a contract may be the sale of land, the pledging of goods or the performance of a service. See also *cause, contrat*.

objets (F)

objects; **things**. See also *propriété*.

obligataire (F)

debenture holder, bondholder.

obligation

1. A tie or **bond** that commits one person to another. Something that one is bound to do, or one agrees to refrain from doing. A personal promise given by one party (an obligor) to another (an obligee) to perform a par-ticular duty or to pay a sum of money e.g. a debt. 'Obligation' is a generic term that refers to any duty, whether arising from contract, law, a bare promise, a gentleman's agreement, or a moral commitment. Specifically, it is "a bond with a condition annexed and a penalty for nonfulfillment". (*Webster's Third New International Dictionary*; Co. Litt. 172a). An obligation may be 'personal', where it binds an individual; or 'real' where it binds real property, such as arises from an easement or mortgage. See also **liability**, *obligation*.

2. An instrument that sets out the terms of a promise, or any agreement enforceable by law. See also **bond**.

obligation (F)

bond; **debenture**; **obligation**; condition; liability; debt; privity.

(*obligation contractuel* – **privity of contract**)

(*obligation hypothécaire* – mortgage debenture)

(*obligation réelle* – a charge secured on real property, i.e. one enforceable by an action *in rem* rather than against the debtor or charger in his personal capacity, e.g. a non-recourse mortgage).

Amos & Walton's Introduction to French Law, 3 edn, pp. 137–148.

Manual de Droit Civil, by Pierre Voirin et Gilles Goubeaux, 20 edn., p. 310 *et seq*.

obligation bond (US)

A **bond** entered into by a mortgagor in which he provides a personal surety to the mortgagee, separate from the mortgage obligation, for non-payment of real estate taxes and insurance premium in respect of the mortgaged property.

obligatory advance clause (US)
see **future advances clause**.

obligee
The beneficiary of an **obligation** or bond. See also **creditor, mortgagee**.

obligor
The person bound to perform an **obligation**. See also **debtor, mortgagor**.

obsolescence
Derived from the Latin *obsolescere*, 'to grow old' or 'fall into disuse'. A process whereby a property falls into disuse, or becomes worn-out or unproductive, due to changes in design, style, economic' activity or public need. A decline in the market value of a property due to extrinsic and not inherent factors, i.e. due to causes that go beyond physical **deterioration** or wear and tear. Obsolescence may be 'economic' or 'functional'. Economic obsolescence (sometimes called 'environmental' or 'locational' obsolescence) is caused by changes arising outside the property's immediate parameters, e.g. changes in local planning, in the neighbourhood, or a shift in demand to substitutes. Functional obsolescence (sometimes called 'physical obsolescence') arises from changes in consumer demand or in the suitability of property for its existing use; especially when there is a more cost-effective alternative available or there is deficiency in the property itself so that it no longer meets modern requirements, e.g. a lack of central heating or of an automatic lift in an office building. In the US, called sometimes 'inutility' – a thing is obsolete when it

is of no further use – Real Estate Land Title and Trust Co. *v* US, 309 US 13, 60 SCt. 371, 84 L.Ed. 542. See also **depreciation, economic life**.

obsolescence (F)
obsolescence.

obstructive building
A building which, due to its contact with or proximity to other buildings, may be dangerous or injurious to health (Housing Act 1957, s. 72 (4)). The Housing Act 1957, ss. 72–74 gives a local authority power to order the owner of an obstructive building to demolish the whole or part of that building. The owner has a right to make representations to the authority; to require the authority to purchase the property; or to be paid compensation for any loss resulting directly from the order.

A building may not be erected over a public **highway** without a licence granted by a highway authority (Highways Act 1980, s. 177). An obstruction or projection from a building that prevents the proper use or passage along a **street** may be removed by order of a highway authority or local authority, subject to a right of appeal to a magistrates' court (Highways Act 1980, s. 152). See also **dangerous structure, demolition order, purchase notice**.

occupancy
1. The taking and holding of physical **possession** of a property, especially one that has no apparent owner; the type and character of the use of property. Occupancy and **occupation** derive their meaning from the verb 'occupy'; "the former being used to express the state of holding or possessing any object, the latter to

express the act of taking possession. He who has the occupancy of land enjoys the fruits of it" (*Crabb's English Synonyms* 1816). See also **entry**.

2. The taking and holding of property under a **tenancy**. See also **occupancy agreement**.

occupancy agreement

An agreement which permits a person to enter into **occupation** of a property prior to completion of the proper legal formalities for the transfer of that property – in English law an occupancy agreement normally creates a **licence** to use land. See also **agreement for a lease, tenancy at will**.

occupancy cost

The total cost to a tenant of occupying a property; including rent, property taxes, repairs, service charges or operating expenses, and any other **outgoings** directly resulting from his use and enjoyment of the property. See also **cost-in-use, equation of rents theory**.

occupancy lease

see **proprietory lease**.

occupancy permit

see **certificate of occupancy**.

occupancy rate

1. The percentage of a property that is let or occupied. See also **absorption rate, vacancy allowance**.

2. The ratio of population to an amount of occupiable accommodation, e.g. persons per habitable rooms or persons per dwelling. See also **density, population density**.

occupant (F)

occupier; one who has **possession**, especially one who holds over at the end of a lease.

occupation

The act of taking **possession** for the purpose of use or enjoyment. The ability to hold property so as to enjoy the fruits therefrom; to have uninterrupted user; or to exercise control thereover. A person in occupation has control, or a degree of control, over a property and essentially actual possession; but unlike a 'possessor' he exerts no claim to ownership, which is a wholly independent right. "Occupation includes possession as its primary element, but it also includes something more. Legal possession does not, of itself, constitute an occupation. The owner of a vacant house is in possession ... If, however, he refurbishes it, and keeps it ready for habitation whenever he pleases to go into it he is an occupier though he may not reside in it one day of the year. On the other hand, a person who ... takes actual possession of a house ... whether by leave of the owner or against his will, is the occupier of it." – R *v* St. Pancras Assessment Committee (1877) 2 QBD 588. Thus, occupation is a question of fact, unlike title which is a question of law and 'possession' which is a right that may be enforced by law.

'Occupation' may suggest that there is a legal right to possession, but it may denote "nothing more than physical presence in a place for a substantial period of time ... Its precise meaning [in any particular statute]... must depend on the purpose for which, and the context in which it is used." – Madrassa Anjuman Ismalia of Kholwad *v* Municipal Council of Johannesburg [1922] 1 AC 504.

In a lease, occupation does not mean personal use and occupation, but the right to occupation of all that passes under the lease – Whittington *v* Corder (1852) 20 LTOS 175. Occupation may even be "enjoyed vicariously through furniture and caretakers and constructively through the exercise of control of the subject-matter" – Reeve and Another *v* Hartlepool BC (1975) 30 P and CR 524. On the other hand, a person who parts with the use and enjoyment of premises is considered, *prima facie*, to have parted with occupation (Brown *v* Brash [1948] 2 KB 247). A tenant who must "occupy premises for the purpose of a business" (in order to have a statutory right to a new tenancy – a new **business tenancy** – under the Landlord and Tenant Act 1954, Part II) cannot be said to be in occupation if he grants a licence for the use of the premises to another person (Hancock and Wills (a firm) *v* GMS Syndicate Ltd. (1983) 265 EG 469; "in order to apply for a new tenancy under the 1954 Act a tenant must show either that he is continuing in occupation of the premises for the purposes of a business carried on by him, or, if events over which he has no control have led him to absent himself from the premises [e.g. a fire], that he continues to exert and claim his right to occupancy." – Morrison Holdings *v* Manders Property (Wolverhampton) Ltd. [1976] 2 All ER 205.

Any person in actual occupation of land is deemed to create an **overriding interest** in the land which is binding on any person who purchases a registered interest in the land, even though the purchaser does not have **notice** of the occupation and even though the existence of that interest is not entered on the land register. The existence of such a right is based on the actual condition, not upon any other interpretation of the meaning of occupation. A wife is in occupation of premises that are legally occupied by her husband; two partners in a business can be in actual occupation. Such occupation does not depend on title; even a squatter can be in occupation for this purpose. – Williams and Glyn's Bank *v* Boland [1979] Ch D 331, 332).

In insurance, a requirement that a property is occupied or in occupation is satisfied if the property is intended, arranged or designed to be occupied; but not if the property is left unoccupied for any length of time, without any immediate intention to regain occupation. See also **occupancy**, **occupier**, **rateable occupation**.

occupation (F)
occupation; possession (of real property)
(libre d'occupation – **vacant possession**).
In French law *occupation* imparts a similar general meaning to occupation in English law, i.e. it is something more than physical possession; however, the word *occupation* is used in particular to refer to a means of acquiring title to *res nullius* – personal property that has no owner.
Précis Dalloz. Droit Civil, Les Biens (Alex Weill), 2 edn, pp. 368–378.

occupation lease
A 'lease' granted to a person in conjunction with his employment or trade; in particular when the employment is related directly to the subject matter of the lease, e.g. a lease of a cottage to an agricultural worker. In practice, this is likely to be a **licence** connected with employment; a personal right, and not an interest in land.

cf. **occupational lease**. See also **service tenancy, tied accommodation, tied house**.

occupation property
Property acquired or let for use or occupation by the holder.
cf. **investment property**. See also **occupational lease, owner-occupier**.

occupation trust
see **trust for sale**.

occupational lease
A lease granted for the purpose of personal occupation and enjoyment. In particular, a lease granted to a tenant who intends to use a property for his own purposes, as compared to a building lease or a lease granted to a person who intends to grant a sublease and derive income from the property. 'Occupational lease' and **occupation lease** are used interchangeably, although the latter term refers more usually to a lease granted to a tenant who intends to use the property in conjunction with his or her employment or trade. In the US an occupational lease is called also a 'space lease'. See also **business tenancy, occupation, proprietory lease**.

occupied
see **occupation, occupier**.

occupier
A person who has a right to take or maintain possession of property, without necessarily having an estate, interest or claim to the property. One who has a right to **occupation** of land. 'Occupier' is a term of imprecise meaning; in common usage it means a person living or physically using a property on a more than transient basis. In law it may mean any person who has a right to exercise control over a property. For example, in connection with a **duty of care** owed to a **visitor** it has been said, "wherever a person has a sufficient degree of control over premises that he ought to realise that any failure on his part to use care may result in injury to a person coming lawfully there, then he is an 'occupier'" – Wheat *v* E. Lacon and Co. Ltd. [1960] AC 578.

For the purpose of serving an enforcement notice on an 'occupier' of land, a **licensee** whose 'occupancy' is not too transient is such a person – Stevens *v* Bromley London Borough Council [1972] Ch 400. However, as a rule a licensee is not an occupier, unless he has some permanent right to control or use land. A person who leaves a property ready for use or habitation may be an occupier for rating purposes, because he has beneficial occupation; and a person who evinces an intention to return to a residence remains an occupier for the purposes of the Rent Acts – Roland House Gardens Ltd *v* Cravitz (1974) P. & C. R. 432). See also **residential occupier, squatter**.

occupier's liability
see **negligence, visitor**.

occupy
see **occupancy**.

oeuvre, gros (F)
see *gros oeuvre*.

offer
To declare a willingness to enter into a **bargain**. A proposal put forward voluntarily by one party for **acceptance** or **rejection** by another. A proposition by one party (offeror) which, if unconditionally accepted by another (offeree), constitutes an agreement.

"In the ordinary sense of the term in business matters an offer is something which by acceptance creates a bargain." – Bennett Walden and Co. *v* Wood [1950] 2 All ER 137. An offer must be certain in all its terms and not merely an indication that a property may be available for sale, or simply an indication of price (especially when an offer is related to real estate – Clifton *v* Palumbo [1944] 2 All ER 497). There should be a clear intention on the part of the offeror to be bound by an acceptance of that offer.

An offer may be withdrawn at any time until it is accepted unconditionally – Payne *v* Cave (1789) 3 Term Rep. 148, but an offer remains capable of acceptance until the offeree is made aware of its withdrawal – Henthorn *v* Fraser [1892] 2 Ch 27. (It may be implied that the offer is revoked upon the offeror's death or incapacity). An offer sent by mail (unlike an acceptance sent by mail) is not effective until it reaches the other party. A conditional offer is not accepted unless all of the conditions attaching to the offer are accepted. An acceptance that is subject to a variation in a condition of the offer constitutes a counter-offer; that is, it creates a new offer which, in turn, must be accepted to create an agreement.

cf. **invitation to treat**. See also **bid, general offer, quotation, repudiation, revocation, specific performance, 'subject to contract', tender**.
Anson's Law of Contract, 26 edn, pp. 25–32.
Cheshire and Fifoot's Law of Contract, 10 edn, pp. 26–32
Chitty on Contract, 25 edn, paras. 42–53.
9 Halsbury's Laws of England, 4 edn, paras. 227–244.

offer and acceptance
see **contract**.

offer price
see **asking price**.

offer to sell
see **invitation to treat**.

offeree
A person who receives an **offer**.

offeror
A person who makes an **offer**.

office
Premises used primarily for the administration of a business, society, or a commercial or charitable enterprise. A place where the functions of a public office are conducted; premises that are ancilliary to an industrial building user and are used principally for administration; or the place of work of a professional man.

Under English planning law office "includes a bank and premises occupied by an estate agency, building society or employment agency or (for office purposes only) for the business of car hire or driving instruction, but does not include a post office or betting office." (Town and Country Planning Use Classes Order 1972, s. 2 (2)).

For the purpose of statutory provisions relating to the health, safety and welfare of persons employed to work in "office premises" that term means a building or part of a building, used for office purposes, and office purposes "includes the purposes of administration, clerical work, handling money and telephone and telegraph operating" (Offices, Shops and Railway Premises Act 1963, s. 1 (2)(a)(b)). This statute (as amended

by the Health and Safety at Work, etc., Act 1974 and ministerial orders made thereunder) provides that office premises, where persons are employed, are, *inter alia*, to be kept clean, ventilated and properly lit, maintained at a reasonable temperature, during working hours, and provided with proper washing and sanitary facilities, as well as first-aid facilities. See also **commercial property, fire certificate, overcrowding, shop.**
Modern Methods of Valuation, 7 edn., pp. 345–51 (for the valuation of office properties).
Planning Office Space, by Francis Duffy, Colin Cave & John Worthington, (1976).
Office Development, by Paul & Paula Marber, (1985).
Offices Today and Tomorrow, by Antony Salata, (1985).

office copy
An exact copy of an official document certified as such by the holder of the original. For example, a copy of subsisting entries recorded at the **Land Registry** as issued to an intending purchaser by the Land Registrar. See also **land certificate.**

office development permit (ODP)
A permit that was required from the Secretary of State for the Environment for any erection, extension, or alteration, of an office building in certain parts of England and Wales (especially the more densely populated areas). The permit was required before any application for planning permission could be made and was intended to ensure proper distribution of office employment. This requirement was abolished from 9th August, 1979.

office exclusive (US)
see **exclusive right to sell.**

official certificate of search
1. A certificate issued by an officer of the **Land Registry** pursuant to an application from an authorised purchaser of unregistered land who is seeking to ascertain whether there is an encumberance that has been registered in the name of the **estate owner** of the land he is seeking to acquire and of which he is not aware. In effect, this certificate gives a *bona fide purchaser* of a **legal estate** freedom from liability for any registrable **land charge** that is not disclosed (or not pointed out by the present owner prior to exchange of contracts). It gives protection from any subsequent entry on the register (except for a **priority notice** given to the registrar when a rapid sequence of transactions takes place and it is not possible to register a particular land charge), for a period of 15 working days from the date that the application for a search is deemed to be delivered at the Registry (Land Charges Act 1972 ss. 10, 11). An official certificate of search provides a purchaser, or an intending purchaser, with a guarantee that he has been notified of any encumberance registered against the land to which it relates, even if the certificate is made in error or contains an omission (Land Charges Act 1972, s. 10 (4)).
cf. **land certificate.** See also **index map, minor interest, search.**
Conveyancing Law and Practice, by D.G. Barnsley, 2 edn., pp. 404–407.
26 Halsbury's Laws of England, 4 edn, paras. 1094–1101.
2. A certificate issued by a Registrar of a Local Land Charges Register

pursuant to an application for details of any **local land charge** registered against a parcel of land (Local Land Charges Act, 1975, s. 9). Such a certificate is valid only at the date of issue.

offrant (F)

bidder (at an auction, especially the highest bidder).

offre (F)

offer; **bid**; **tender**; supply.

(*offre réelle* – official tender of money in payment of a debt; cash offer)

(*offre sans condition, sans reserve* – unconditional offer). See also *contrat*.

Amos & Walton's Introduction to French Law, 3 edn, p. 154.

off-shore company (or trust)

A company (or trust) that has established its place of registration in a country – an 'off-shore' country – that has low rates of taxation and, usually, limited legal regulation. Normally an off-shore company (or trust) conducts business in different parts of the world to its place of registration, but aims to be subject to the taxes and regulations of the 'off-shore' country only. If the principal activity of the company (or trust) is in a particular 'on-shore' country, or the shareholders (or beneficiaries) are resident in an 'on-shore' country, then that country will claim, especially for taxation purposes, that the company (or trust) is not 'off-shore' but should be liable to the appropriate fiscal and legislative policy of the 'on-shore' country. See also **tax haven**.

off-site cost

A cost incurred in developing a parcel of land that is not directly related to the site itself, such as the cost of providing access across adjoining land or the cost of a mains sewer serving several sites.

'old-for-old' insurance

see **replacement cost**.

olographe (F)

holograph

omission

1. The failure to fulfil or complete a required action; neglect of a duty. See also **laches, negligence**.
2. Something left out by accident. A part of a document left blank. See also **misrepresentation, 'slip rule', utmost good faith**.

omne quod solo inaedificatur solo cedit (L)

'That which is built on to the soil becomes a part of the soil'. See **fixture**.

'on or before'

see **time**.

one hundred percent location (US)

see **prime location**.

onerous covenant

A **covenant** requiring the performance of an obligation that is more onerous to perform than the benefit or advantage to be derived therefrom, e.g. a covenant in a lease which, if performed, would add far less to the value of the lessee's interest than the cost of undertaking the obligation. A covenant that is unduly one-sided. See also **frustration, undue influence**.

'once a mortgage, always a mortgage'

A maxim which stresses the principle that a **mortgage** is intended solely as security for a loan and not as a means to secure a collateral advantage for the mortgagee; in other words that once the mortgagor has paid back his debt to the mortgagee the purpose of the mortgage has come to an end – Seton *v* Slade (1802) Ves. 273. "The principle is this – that a mortgage must not be converted into something else; and when once you have come to the conclusion that a stipulation for the benefit of the mortgagee is part of the mortgage transaction, it is but part of his security, and necessarily comes to an end on the payment off of the loan." – Noakes and Co. Ltd. *v* Rice [1902] AC 33, 34. Thus if a petrol company lends money on condition that the mortgaged property is used only for the sale of the mortgagee's products, he cannot insist on this tie continuing when the mortgage is redeemed, or prevent redemption for fear of loosing that tie – Samuel *v* Jarrah Timber and Woodpaving Corporation [1904] AC 323. In order to maintain the tie the mortgagee must show that the sales agreement is entirely separate from the mortgage agreement. See also **equity of redemption**, **solus agreement**.

onéreux (F)
(*à titre onéreux* – for valuable consideration; subject to certain liabilities).

op. cit. (opus citatum) (L)
'The work cited before; as previously mentioned', e.g. a book or article referred to earlier in a text.

open and notorious possession (US)
see **notorious possession**.

open easement (US)
see **apparent easement**.

open contract
A **contract** left open for interpretation by implication of law. A valid contract that contains only the mini-

mum requirements for validity – the names of the parties, the subject matter and the **consideration**. An open contract rests on the principle *id est certum quod certum reddi potest* – 'that is certain which can be rendered certain'. Thus it does not rest on the need to spell out every detail of the parties requirements. "Even though one or more terms are left open a contract for sale does not fail for indefiniteness if the parties have intended to make a contract and there is a reasonably certain basis for giving an appropriate remedy." (United States Uniform Commercial Code para. 2–204(3)).

In particular, a **memorandum** in **writing** for the sale of land which satisfies the formal requirements for a valid agreement for such a sale, but leaves all other terms to be implied by law. A contract may be entirely open; or, it may be partly open to the implications of the law with some details contained in a **formal contract**. A vendor who enters into a contract for the sale of land that is left completely open (and not made by correspondence) implies, in particular, that (a) he will provide, at his own expense, evidence of his **title** to the land; (b) he is selling a **fee simple** estate, with **vacant possession**, free of any **encumberance**; (c) upon completion he will convey a **good title** to the property; (d) all matters reasonably required for, or enjoyed with, the estate are to be conveyed to the purchaser; (e) **completion** of the conveyance of the property will take place within a reasonable time, subject to receipt of the purchase monies; and (f) he requires no payment, as a deposit or otherwise, prior to completion (Law of Property Act 1925, ss. 42–45, as amended by the Law of Property Act 1969, part III).

An open contract made by correspondence (which means any contract contained in a letter or letters that have passed between the parties) is governed by the Statutory Conditions of Sale 1925, subject to any contradictory condition set out in the correspondence (Law of Property Act 1925, s. 46). See also **conditions of sale, contract for sale**.

Contract and Conveyance, by J.T. Farrand, 4 edn, pp. 77–82.

William's Contract for the Sale of Land and Title to Land, 4 edn, p. 565 *et seq*.

Emmet on Title, 18 edn, pp. 70–71.

open country

In relation to the provision of public access to the countryside by means of an **access agreement** or **access order**, 'open country' is defined as an area consisting wholly or predominately of mountain, moor, heath, down, cliff or foreshore, including any bank, flat or other land adjacent to the foreshore, and any river, canal and land associated therewith, and any woodlands (National Parks and Access to the Countryside Act 1959, s. 59(2), as amended by Countryside Act 1968, s. 16) See also **national park**.

open-end clause

see **future advances clause**.

open-end fund (US)

see **open-end investment company**.

open-end investment company (US)

An **investment company** that is not limited as to the amount of its share capital and may issue and redeem shares on a regular basis, usually by reference to its net asset value. Generally the shares of an open-end invest-

ment company are not traded on the open market; instead, the company itself buys back the shares that a shareholder wishes to relinquish. The company funds the share purchases by realising assets, and acquires new assets as and when it sells new shares. Thus, in its mode of operation, it is similar to a **unit trust**. Called also a 'mutual fund' or sometimes an 'open-end fund'.

cf. **closed-end investment company**.

open-end mortgage

A mortgage which provides that the mortgagor has the facility to increase his borrowing up to a specified limit without offering additional security. Normally all advances under the terms of an open-end mortgage rank with the same priority as if they had been made at the outset.

cf. **close-ended mortgage**. See also **future advances clause, tacking, subordination**.

open-ended trust

A **trust** that permits the trustees to make or vary investments or the size of the trust at their discretion. An open-ended real estate trust may invest in any type of real estate, unless specifically restricted by the trust deed, and may acquire and dispose of assets without reference to the beneficiaries. See also **protective trust, special trust**.

open land

An area of land that is not totally enclosed and is not used for any intensive purpose. Generally vacant land that is not built on and on which no business is regularly carried out.

When the term 'open land' was used in a statute (Town and Country Planning Act 1949, s. 33 (1)) which provided that a local authority had power to serve an **abatement notice**, because the land is injurious to the amenity of the area, it was said that a definition of the term 'open land' had to depend on 'all the circumstances of the case'. Land that was open to the air and unbuilt on, but fenced and used for the purposes of a business of a car breakers' yard, which was annexed to buildings used in connection with that business, was not 'open land' – Stephens *v* Cuckfield Rural District Council [1960] 2 All ER 716. See also **common land, open space, waste-land**.

open listing (US)
see **multiple agency**.

open market
see **market overt**.

open market value
see **market value**.

open market rental value
see **market rent**.

open mortgage (US)
A **mortgage** that permits the mortgagor to repay the principal in full at any time, without a **prepayment penalty**. A mortgage that has passed its date of maturity, but has neither been terminated by the mortgagee requesting payment of the outstanding balance in full nor extended formally. See also **equity of redemption**.

open mortgage clause (US)
see **mortgage clause**.

open offer
see **general offer**.

open planning
Arranging the interior of an office or residence with the minimum use of walls or partitions between the main areas of activity.

open space
Land that is left undeveloped; is not intended to be built on; and is reserved for landscaping, agricultural or recreational use. For example, a public park, square, common, heath, garden or a burial ground. "The essential quality which is connoted by 'an open space of land' is the quality of being unbuilt on." – Re Bradford City Premises [1928] Ch. 143.
Various statutes provide public authorities with the power to acquire (by agreement or compulsion) and hold land as open space for the benefit of the public (Open Spaces Act 1906; Housing Act 1957, s. 150; Local Government Act 1933, s. 174; Town and Country Planning Act 1971, ss. 121, 129; New Towns Act 1965, s. 7). See also **green belt, open country, open land**.
34 Halsbury's Laws of England, 4 edn, paras. 401–561.

operating costs
see **operating expenses**.

operating expense ratio (OER) (US)
The ratio of **operating expenses** to **effective gross income**, expressed as a percentage – the complement of **net income ratio**. Called also the 'operating ratio' for an investment.

operating expenses (US)
The **expenses** or **outgoings** that arise from running and maintaining a building. Periodic expenditure that is necessary in the long run to maintain a given level of income from a property and to ensure the proper upkeep and operation of that property. Operating expenses include the costs of maintenance and repair,

insurance (both of the property and other associated risks), public utilities, cleaning, refuse collection, heating or air-conditioning, salaries, wages and other payroll costs, management fees, and, frequently, a sinking fund to provide for the replacement of obsolete equipment. 'Operating expenses' correspond broadly to '**service charges**' in the UK. Called sometimes 'operating costs'. See also **fixed charges, outgoings, net operating income**.

International, Downtown and Suburban Office Building Experience Exchange, Building Owners and Managers Association Annual Report, Washington D.C.

Dollars and Cents of Shopping Centres, Urban Land Institute Triannual Report, Washington D.C.

The Appraisal of Real Estate, AIREA, 8 edn., pp. 362–370, 726.

operating income (US)
see **net operating income**.

operating lease
A **lease** of **personal property** granted for a period that is significantly shorter than the economic life of the property, with the lessor retaining responsibility for repair and maintenance. Unlike a **finance lease** the lessor remains actively concerned with the upkeep of the property; the lessee may terminate the agreement at relatively short notice, without paying a penalty; and the lessor derives his profit primarily from re-leasing the property to a succession of users. See also **leasing**.

The Appraisal of Real Estate, by AIREA, 8 edn., pp. 362–370, 726–727.

operating leverage (US)
A means of increasing the return from

an income producing property by arranging for as many operating expenses as possible to be fixed (eg, by entering into long-term service contracts) so that as the income from the tenants increases, the net income to the investor increases in a greater proportion.
cf. **financial leverage**. See also **leverage**.

operating ratio (US)
see **operating expense ratio**.

operating statement
A statement of the income and expenditure of a business, or a property investment, over a period of time. See also **budget**.

operational land
Land, or an interest in land, held by a **statutory undertaker** for a normal purpose or activity of that particular body (Town and Country Planning Act 1971, s. 222).

operations
Activity on land that is considered by the Town Planning Acts to change the physical characteristics of the land and, therefore, to constitute **development**, for which planning permission is required. In particular, an activity that results in "some physical alteration to the land, which has some degree of permanence to the land itself" – Parkes *v* Secretary of State for the Environment [1978] 1 WLR 1308. Such activity may comprise **building operations, engineering operations,** or **mining operations**.
cf. **material change in the use**.

operative clause
1. The clause in a **conveyance** that effects the transfer of the property, e.g. "the vendor hereby conveys Blackacre unto the purchaser in fee

simple". In the US called also the 'granting clause'. See also **operative part, words of limitation**.

2. The clause in an **insurance policy** that sets out the obligations of the insurer.

operative part (or words)

The part (or words) of a **deed** that give effect to the agreement intended, or which sets out the principal object effected; as contrasted with details of the parties, the date and the **recitals** which are essentially supporting statements. The operative parts of a deed are introduced commonly by the words, 'Now this deed witnesses'. See also **covenant, *habendum,* parcels.**

opportunity cost

The cost foregone in following one course of action instead of another. The expenditure that would be incurred in producing or acquiring alternative goods or services. The advantage or benefit surrendered in order to acquire something else. "If the choice lies between the production or purchase of two commodities, the value of one is measured by the sacrifice of going without the other." – *The Formula for Sacrifice*, by Davenport, J.P. Econ, pp. 567–8 (1893). Thus, the true cost of an office building may be the number of houses that could be constructed for the same price. The opportunity cost of capital to an investor is the rate of return that is foregone when one form of investment is made in place of another. See also **cost-benefit analysis.**

opportunity-cost rate of return
see **target rate of return**.

optimum use
see **highest and best use**.

option

A choice. A right to do or not to do something; such as a right to accept or reject an **offer** within a specified or reasonable period of time. Generally the beneficiary of an option (offeree) has sole control over the choice he or she is permitted to make and may withdraw therefrom at will. The grantor of the option (offeror) is precluded from withdrawing so long as the option remains exercisable; "an option on a proper analysis is no more than an ordinary offer coupled with a **promise** not to withdraw the offer during the period of the option." – Mountford *v* Scott [1974] 1 All ER 254.

An option may be 'mutual' when either party has the right to exercise the right upon the happening of a specified event or at a particular time, for example when each party has a right to terminate a lease at the end of a given number of years. Or, it may be 'unilateral' when it may be exercised by only one party. The most common forms of unilateral option are the 'option to purchase' and the 'option to sell', called also, respectively, a **call option** and a **put option**. An option to purchase is a promise to sell given by an owner of property which is kept open for a defined or definable period of time. An option to sell is a right available to an owner of property to require another party to purchase that property within a defined or definable period of time.

An option, to be enforceable, must contain the requirements of any valid **contract**; in particular, the price to be paid must be ascertained, or be capable of being ascertained, with certainty, on or before the time fixed for exercising the option.

An option to purchase land is an **equitable interest** in land, unlike a **right of pre-emption** which is considered to be a personal contract between the parties – Pritchard *v* Briggs [1980] Ch. 338. An option to purchase a legal estate is an **estate contract** and must be registered – either as a **land charge** if the land to which it relates is unregistered, or by a **notice** if the land is registered – in order to be enforceable against any third party who acquires the land for money or money's worth.

An option to purchase entered into as part of a mortgage agreement may be void if it seeks to fetter the mortgagor's **equity of redemption** (i.e. his right to regain the mortgaged property, free of the mortgagee's rights, after the debt has been repaid in full) – Samuel *v* Jarrah Timber and Wood Paving Corporation Ltd. [1904] AC 323; but this rule does not apply if the option is part of a later, and independent, transaction between the mortgagor and mortgagee (Reeve *v* Lisle [1902] AC 461).

The completion of an option agreement does not give an agent a right to a **commission** for 'effecting a sale' of the subject property (unless there is an express provision in the agency agreement to that effect), because a sale of the property is contingent on the decision of the option holder to exercise or not to exercise his right to purchase. In the US called also a 'time bargain'.
cf. **conditional sale contract**. See also **hire-purchase, renewal**.
The Law of Landlord and Tenant, by David Lloyd Evans, 2nd edn., pp. 166–170.
Land Options, by C.G. Barnsley, pp. 1–3 (1978).

option (F)
option.
(*option d'achat* – purchase or **call option**)
(*option de vente* – sale or **put option**).

option listing (US)
The **listing** of a property with a broker combined with an **option** granted to the broker to purchase the property on specified terms. A broker who is granted an option listing has a particular fiduciary responsibility to his principal. As a rule he should act in the **utmost good faith** to ensure that he is not taking advantage of his privileged position by comparison with any other independent broker.

option money
Money paid to secure an **option**. Normally this sum is lost if the option is not exercised, but sometimes it may be set-off against the total consideration for any property acquired.

option mortgage scheme
A scheme, that came into operation in the UK on 1 April 1968, by which a mortgagor could opt to forego his right to set off the interest on his mortgage loan against personal tax in exchange for a lower rate of interest; the difference in the rate of interest was paid to the mortgagee by the government. The purpose of the scheme was to assist house purchasers who pay income tax at less than the standard rate. The mortgagor could not opt out of this arrangement for the first four years, even if his tax situation changes during that time. This scheme applied only to loans for the purchase of a property that was intended as a main residence. Since 1982 a qualifying borrower can pay his interest net of income tax and

accordingly this scheme has lost its effect for new loans and, therefore, is to be abolished (Finance Act 1982, s. 27(1)).

cf. **flexible-payment mortgage**.
West's *Law of Housing*, 4 edn, pp. 313–317.

option period

The period of time for which an **option** remains exercisable. As a rule, the longer the period during which the holder of an option may exercise his right, to buy or sell, the more valuable the option.

option to purchase

see **hire purchase option**.

oral contract

A verbal or unwritten **contract** (A contract made 'of many words' could be verbal, but unless done by word of mouth, or conveyed by speech, it is not oral). A contract for the transfer of real property generally must be in **writing** or evidenced by an act of **part performance**. See also **open contract, simple contract, Statute of Frauds**.

oral lease

see **parol lease**.

order

See **closing order, compulsory purchase order, demolition order, possession order, prerogative order**.

order of mandate

see *mandamus*.

ordinance

A decree or order made by an authoritative body; in particular, by a body that is subordinate to the Sovereign or State. For example, regulations made by a municipality that affect the use of property in the area under its control, e.g. a **zoning ordinance** or a building code. See also **building regulations, police powers**.

ordinary annuity capitalisation (US)

The capitalisation of a series of future regular incomes by the application of a **single-rate capitalisation factor**, i.e. a single-rate years' purchase or Inwood factor; to be distinguished from the application of a **dual-rate capitalisation factor**, i.e. a dual rate years' purchase or Ellwood factor. See also **annuity capitalisation**.

ordinary interest (US)

Interest calculated or charged on the basis of 360 days to a **year** (12 months of 30 days each).

ordinary meaning rule

A rule for the construction of contracts, especially contracts of insurance, when the meaning of a word or term is in doubt. If there is no other rule for interpretation, words are to be understood "in their plain, ordinary and popular sense". – Robertson *v* French (1803) 4 East. 135. When in doubt interpretation should be based on the context, and the most commonly accepted meaning as understood by men or women of the world of reasonable intelligence; although technical words must be given their strict technical meaning. See also **literal rule, term (or word) of art, words meaning of**.

ordinary repair

see **tenantable repair**.

ordnance survey map

A map of a part of Great Britain produced by the **Ordnance Survey**. Such maps are produced under the provisions of the Ordnance Survey Act 1841 (Interpretation Act 1889, s. 25) and are currently published at scales ranging from 1: 1250 to 1: 625 000.

The Ordnance Survey produces small and large scale maps. The small scale maps, which are intended for route planning and general purpose uses, are published to a scale of 1: 625 000 (1 in to 10 miles or 1 cm to 625 km) called Routeplanners; 1: 250 000 (1 in to 4 miles or 1 cm to 2.5 km) called Routemasters; 1: 63 360 (1 in to 1 mile or 1 cm to 0.63 km) called Tourist maps; 1: 50 000 (1¼ in to 1 mile or 2 cm to 1 km) called Landrangers; 1: 25 000 (2½ in to 1 mile or 4 cm to 1 km) called Pathfinders or Outdoor Leisure maps; and 1:10 000 (6 in to 1 mile or 1 cm to 100 m) called Town and City maps. The Routeplanners and Routemasters are ideal for motoring and touring. The Pathfinders are intended for walking. The Town and City maps, although strictly not small scale, are useful for visitors, public service and public use.

The large scale maps are published to a scale of 1: 10 000 (or in some areas 1:10 560); 1:2500 (25 in to 1 mile or 1 cm to 25 m); and 1: 1250 (50 in to 1 mile or 1 cm to 12.5 m). The 1: 10 000 maps cover the entire country and provide, in particular, contours at 25 feet, or 10 metre or 5 metre, vertical intervals. The 1:2500 maps cover rural areas and the 1:1250 maps cover urban areas. The 1:1250 maps are an essential source of detailed information for such things as the planning of new development road and property management, land transfer and land registration, the emplacement and maintenance of telecommunications, electricity, gas and water pipelines. The Ordnance Survey maps are being continuously up-dated. In addition, even prior to publication, the Ord-

nance Survey makes its surveys for large scale maps available to the public under a service called "SUSI" – Supply of Unpublished Survey Information. Also, 1: 1250 and 1: 2500 maps may be obtained on microfilm to reduce map storage needs.

Ordnance Survey maps are Crown Copyright for a period of 50 years from the end of the year in which they were made (Copyright Act 1956, s. 39). Permission to produce Ordnance Survey maps may be obtained on each occasion a copy is required; or, in the case of public bodies, various professional and business firms, educational institutions and printers by means of a standard licence. Applications for a specific consent or a licence are made to Copyright Branch, Ordnance Survey, Romsey Road, Maybush, Southampton SO9 4DH. Ordnance maps are distributed by retailers and authorised agents.

Land Law and Registration, by S. Rowton Simpson, pp. 115–118 (1976).

Ordnance Survey (O.S.)
A body founded in 1791 to be responsible for surveying and mapping Great Britain and for the publication of official topographical maps of the Country. See also **ordnance survey map.**

ordonnance (F)
ordinance; order (of a judge); enactment.
(*ordonnance d'éxpropriation* – vesting order, an order of a court vesting title to land in an expropriating authority and converting any right over that land into a claim for an *indemnité d'expropriation*)
(*ordonnance relative à l'utilisation du sol* – land use ordinance)

ordre (F)
order; injunction; priority.
(*ordre public* – public policy; law and
order)
(*ordre utile* – priority, of creditors).

original, or originating, contractor
see **main contractor**.

original cost
see **acquisition cost, book cost**.

original lease (US)
see **head lease**.

**original unexpended balance of estab-
lished development value**
see **unexpended balance of established development value**.

origination fee
A fee charged by a lender to cover the
lender's costs of granting a loan.
cf. **finance procuration fee**. See also
commitment fee, discount points.

origine de propriété (F)
root of title.

ostensible authority
Authority that someone holds out as
having but that has not truly been
granted; authority that has a pretence
of being real. Ostensible authority
may arise when (a) a principal allows
his agent to act in such a way that a
third party would believe that the
agent had the required authority to
perform the act he is performing and,
if appropriate, to bind the principal;
(b) a principal allows his agent to act
as if he still had authority after an
agency relationship has been terminated; (c) a principal knowingly permits his agent to give the impression
of having more authority than he has
been actually given; or (d) the principal fails to inform a third party, with
whom he knows the agent is treating,

that the agent's authority has been
strictly limited. Ostensible authority
may act as a form of **estoppel** so as to
bind the principal to the agent's acts
in the same way as if actual authority
had been given, because the agent,
with his principal concurrence, may
permit the third party to alter his
position in reliance on the agent's
representations or actions; thus,
ostensible authority has been termed
"agency by estoppel" – Rama Corporation *v* Proved Tin and General
Investments Ltd. [1952] 2 QB 150.
(**Agency by estoppel** may arise also
when the doctrine of estoppel creates
a contract of agency; as distinguished
from the true application of the doctrine of ostensible authority, by which
the agent is permitted to bind his
principal). Ostensible authority may
be called also 'apparent authority',
although the latter term refers especially to that authority which a principal has never given but he permits
the agent to exercise. See also **agency
of necessity**.

ouster
The wrongful **dispossession** or exclusion of someone from real property,
in particular from freehold property
or a right of inheritance.
cf. **eviction**. See also **deforcement,
disseisin**.

outbuildings
see **ancilliary buildings**.

outdoor advertising
see **advertising**.

outgoing tenant's valuation
see **tenant right**.

outgoings
Charges or **expenditure** arising from
the use and maintenance of property.

A term frequently used as a 'catch-all' for any disbursement or payment made by an owner or occupier of real property. To an owner or landlord 'outgoings' include all costs arising as a result of ownership; in particular, if a property is let, that expenditure which is not recoverable from a tenant, as well as management expenses and income lost due to voids and defaulting tenants. To an occupier or tenant 'outgoings' include any expenditure arising as a result of use and occupation; in particular, **rent**, **service charges** or **operating expenses** payable to a superior landlord, **rates**, taxes, insurance costs (includes any premium payable for insurance maintained by a landlord), repair and maintenance costs.

A clause in a lease requiring a tenant to pay 'outgoings' extends to cover such expenditure as may be incurred by a landlord in order to maintain the income a property is capable of producing, whether of a recurring or non-recurring nature – including paving or drainage charges, repairs, rates, taxes, and any other payment necessary to achieve the landlord's objective of maintaining (but not improving or renewing) his property – Aldridge *v* Ferne (1886) 17 QBD 212; Smith *v* Smith [1939] 4 All ER 315. A tenant, who agrees "in perfectly clear and unambiguous terms" that he will pay for all outgoings, cannot limit his responsibility in that connection – Stockdale *v* Ascherberg [1904] 1 KB 450. However, in the case of a short-term tenancy, if doubtful wording is used when referring to the tenant's liability for outgoings the position will be construed against a landlord of a short-term tenancy; it being considered "fantastic in the case of a statutory or of an ordinary weekly, monthly or yearly tenant that, in addition to an increase in rent, he should be asked to make some contribution towards the capital expense, since he can have no real interest in the capital value of the land." – Harrington *v* Croydon Corporation [1968] 1 QB 8.
cf. **income**. See also **duties**.
Modern Methods of Valuation, 7 edn., pp. 57–65.
The Law of Landlord and Tenant, by David Lloyd Evans, 2 edn., pp. 134–137.
Woodfall's Landlord and Tenant, 28 edn, para. 1–1335.
Hill and Redman's Law of Landlord and Tenant, 17 edn, pp. 311–313.

outhouse
A building adjoining, or that is part of, a dwelling-house. A building within the **curtilage** of a house. See also **appurtenance, ancilliary building**.

outland
see **tenemental land**.

outline planning permission
see **planning permission**.

outstanding natural beauty
see **areas of outstanding natural beauty; national park**.

outstanding term
The period remaining until the expiration of a lease that has been granted for a term of years; a period of time remaining when the purpose for which a lease was granted has been achieved. See also **satisfied term**.

outstroke
A right granted to a lessee of a **mine** to work through into an adjoining mine. A lessee of a mine generally is allowed to work an adjoining mine of the

same landlord, without express consent, provided he does not need to go outside the leased area to extract the minerals. A royalty for a right of outstroke is called a **wayleave** or 'wayleave rent'.

cf. **instroke**.

ouvrage (F)

main structure (of a building)
(*les gros ouvrages* – main walls, see *gros ouvrages, grosses reparations*).

'over the mortgage' (US)

An expression used to indicate the price that a purchaser must pay for a property above the amount of a mortgage loan that is to be transferred with the property. See also **assumption, equity**.

over-insurance

Insurance of a property for more than its 'actual cash value' or **replacement cost**, or for a sum that exceeds the maximum loss that might be sustained in the event of a claim (even after taking full account of projected inflation). Over-insurance has no advantage for the insured as the insurer is not obliged normally to pay more than the true loss suffered by the insured, i.e. the insurer has only contracted to provide an **indemnity**. Over-insurance merely results in the payment of an excessive premium by the insured. A property may be over-insured, however, to avoid the risk of the application of an **average clause**. cf. **under-insurance**. See also **double insurance, valued policy**.

overage

That part of the rent which exceeds the base rent or guaranteed minimum rent in a percentage or turnover lease. In the US called also 'override'. See also **turnover rent**.

overall capitalisation rate (US)

A single **capitalisation rate** used in the income approach to appraisal. "An overall capitalisation rate is an income rate for a total property that reflects the relationship between one year's net operating income and total price or value." (*The Appraisal of Real Estate*, AIREA, 8 edn., p. 339). This rate is selected, or calculated, to provide a rate of return that is sufficient to recapture the capital cost of an investment and provide a satisfactory return to the investor (i.e. it includes a **sinking fund rate** and a **remunerative rate**). However, unlike a **dual-rate capitalisation factor** ('Hoskold factor') the overall rate is not determined purely by a mathematical calculation but by reference to 'overall' returns on comparable investment sales or by application of a **band of investment rate**. A term that may be considered synonymous with **years' purchase**. See also **straight capitalisation**.

The Appraisal of Real Estate, AIREA, 8 edn., pp. 388–390, 423–428.

overall rate of return (US)

1. The rate of return on an investment obtained by dividing the **net operating income** by the **purchase price**.
2. See **internal rate of return**.

overbuild

To build more properties than normally are demanded in a particular market. See also **boom**.

overcrowding

A condition where more people occupy property than is considered healthy. The Housing Act 1957, s. 77, Sch. 6, specifies standards, which if exceeded, constitute overcrowding in a dwelling-house (one that is occupied by "members of the working class or of a type suitable for such use"). These standards stipulate a permitted ratio of persons per room and per floor area of living accommodation. In addition, a dwelling-house is deemed to be overcrowded if two or more persons, aged 10 or over, of the opposite sex, not being husband and wife, have to sleep in the same room.

The majority of shops, offices and factories must not, while work is going on therein, be so overcrowded "as to cause risk of injury to the health" of the persons employed or working therein (Factories Act 1961, s. 2 (1); Offices, Shops and Railway Premises Act 1963, s. 5(1)). The Acts stipulate also the minimum amount of space to be allocated for each person employed, or working in the premises. See also **common lodging house**, **rent book**.

Manual of Housing Law, by Andrew Arden, 2 edn., pp. 243–247.

Housing Law, by Andrew Arden and Martin Partington, pp. 481–490 (1983).

Redgrave's Health and Safety in Factories, 2 edn, pp. 39–40.

Redgrave's Offices and Shops, 2 edn, pp. 18–19.

20 Halsbury's Laws of England, 4 edn, paras. 614, 785.

overhead

An expense of running a business that is incurred independently of the level of activity e.g. rent, a property tax, insurance.

overimprovement

An **improvement**, or work of improvement, to a property that costs more than the amount it adds to the market value of the property.

overreachable interest

An interest in land that is considered capable of being detached from land and converted into a claim against the proceeds of sale if land is sold; in that way the purchaser of a **legal estate** in land can acquire that estate free of the overreachable interest (whether or not he has notice thereof) without adversely affecting the benefit enjoyed by the holder of that interest. In particular, the right of a beneficiary under a **strict settlement** or a **trust for sale** (in the latter instance, the beneficiary is considered effectively to have a claim against the proceeds of sale at the outset). The beneficiaries of an overreachable interest lose their rights to enjoy the land itself; their rights are transferred to the monies accruing from the sale – i.e. an *ad hoc* trust for sale is created – and the beneficiaries' equitable interest is said to be 'overreached'. An interest is overreached only provided that (a) the statutory provisions regarding the sale and distribution of the proceeds of sale are complied with; and (b) the interest is one that is statutorily capable of being overreached. An interest that is considered by statute as incapable of being overreached is one that enjoys a benefit which cannot be transferred to the proceeds of sale; or an interest that a purchaser might expect to acquire with the legal estate – for example, an equitable interest protected by a deposit of documents; an estate contract; most registered equitable interests; and a restrictive covenant (Law of Property Act 1925, s. 2).

An interest of a mortgagor may be

considered also as an overreachable interest if, having failed in an obligation under the mortgage agreement, the mortgagor thereby permits the mortgagee to exercise his power of sale and convert the interest into a right to the proceeds of sale.

cf. **overriding interest**. See also **conversion, land charge, minor interest**.

Cheshire's Modern Law of Real Property, 13 edn, pp. 77–78, 161–164.
Megarry's Manual of the Law of Real Property, 6 edn, pp. 283–290.
The Law of Real Property, by Robert Megarry and H.W.R. Wade, 5 edn., pp. 136–139, 398–410.
Land Law: Cases and Materials, by R.H. Maudsley and E.H. Burn, 4 edn., pp. 26, 187–191, 258–261.

override

1. To render an interest in land void. An interest is said to be overridden when a **legal estate** is acquired by a *bona fide* purchaser for **value** without **notice**, i.e. by a purchaser who, acting in good faith, is not informed, and is unable reasonably to ascertain, that the interest exists and has paid valuable consideration for the legal estate. In that event the holder of the 'overridden interest' cannot enforce his right against the new owner of the legal estate. See also **bona fide purchaser, overriding interest**.

(US) 2. See **overage**.

(US) 3. See **extender clause**.

4. A share of a **commission** received by a principal agent and paid to a sub-agent.

overriding interest

An interest, right, power or encumberance that affects registered land and binds a purchaser of the land, or any interest in the land, even though he has no knowledge of the interest and even though the interest is not entered on the land register (Land Registration Act 1925, s. 3 (xvi). This is the kind of right that a purchaser of registered land is assumed by law to be able to find by making proper enquiries and searches; for example, by inspecting the property, making appropriate requisitions to the vendor, and examining the local land charges register. An overriding interest includes in particular (a) a right of common, a right of way, a right of water, a profit à prendre, and any other legal easement; (b) various liabilities to repair a highway, a chancel of any church and an embankment, river or sea wall; (c) a lease for any term not exceeding 21 years, provided it was granted at a rent without payment of a premium; (d) a local land charge (unless protected by an entry on the register); (e) "the rights of every person in actual **occupation** of the land or in receipt of the rents and profits thereof save where enquiry is made of every person and the rights are not disclosed" (including a right to purchase the freehold granted to an occupying lessee: Webb *v* Pollmount [1966] 1 All E.R. 481); (f) a right acquired or in the course of being acquired by an adverse possessor or squatter; (g) a mining right of the National Coal Board (Land Registration Act 1925, s. 70 (1), as amended). A particular object of the provision referred to in (e) (which extends to cover a right of a spouse to the **matrimonial home**) "is to protect a person in actual occupation from having his [or her] rights lost in the welter of registration. He [or she] will be protected. No one can buy the land over his [or her] head and thereby take away or diminish his [or her] rights. It is up to every purchaser before he [or she] buys to make inquiry on the premises. If he [or she] fails to do so, it is at his [or her] risk." – Strand Securities Ltd *v* Caswell [1965] Ch. 968.

An overriding interest may be entered on the register for convenience, but need not be so for protection. (However, if entered on the register it ceases to be an overriding interest and is protected by that entry, i.e. it becomes a **minor interest**). cf. **overreachable interest**.

The Law of Real Property, by Robert Megarry and H.W.R. Wade, 5 edn., pp. 204–209.

Cheshire's Modern Law of Real Property, 13 edn, pp. 739–745.

Real Property and Real People, by K.J. Gray and P.D. Symes, pp. 331–348.

Concise Land Registration Practice, by T.B.F. Rouff and C. West, 3 edn., pp. 36–43.

26 Halsbury's Laws of England, 4 edn, paras. 987–993.

overriding lease
see **concurrent lease**.

overspill
Population, originating from a crowded conurbation, that spills out into the surrounding countryside; or is relocated to an area away from the main centre such as a new town. People who, due to a shortage of living accommodation, or a lack of employment, move out of an urban area into the surrounding countryside to establish new communities. Overspill emanates especially from a population that is considered surplus to the normal capacity of a town or city to maintain, without unduly stretching

its available facilities. See also **decentralisation**.

overt
Open to public view; not disguised or secret. See also **market overt**.

owner
1. One who has **ownership** of property. A person in whom a property is beneficially vested and who has the occupation or control of it.

An owner of real property may be any person who has an estate or interest in land, whether a legal or equitable estate or interest; provided he has a right to exclusive enjoyment, and not a mere licence. A mortgagee not in possession and a tenant holding under a periodic tenancy, or any short-term lease, normally is not considered an owner.

In English land law there is no absolute owner, but rather 'holders' of land who have greater or lesser rights against other holders. Thus there may be more than one owner of the same property; for example, there may be a holder of a fee simple absolute, a tenant for life and a tenant for a term of years, each having differing degrees or durations of ownership. However, in common parlance and as a primary meaning in law the owner of land is the holder of a **fee simple**, or the freeholder.

In statute law an owner is usually the person entitled to receive the **rack rent** from land, e.g. "'owner in relation to any land' means ... a person other than a mortgagee not in possession, who, whether in his own right or as trustee for any other person, is entitled to receive the rack rent of the land, or, where the land is not let at a rack rent, would be entitled if it were so let" (Town and Country Planning

Act 1971, s. 290 (1)). (This section does not apply to the requirement to notify an owner about a planning application nor a representation to a local planning authority that may be made by an owner following a planning application – in those cases, the owner is the estate owner of the fee simple or the holder of a tenancy with not less than ten years unexpired: 1971 Act, s. 27 (7), 29. The Housing Act 1977, s. 189 (1); the New Towns Act 1965, s. 54; Land Compensation Act 1961, Sch. 2, s. 2 (b); and the Highways Act 1980, s. 100 (a) defines an owner as the person, other than a mortgagee not in possession, entitled to dispose of a fee simple (whether in possession or in reversion) or a person entitled to the rents and profits under a lease with more than three years unexpired. For the purpose of compulsory purchase an owner is, "any person having power to sell and convey the land to the authority" (Compulsory Purchase Act 1965, s. 1(b)). In English rating law an owner is the "person for the time being receiving or entitled to receive the rack rent" (General Rate Act 1967, s. 115).

Prima facie, an owner has a right to possession, a right of alienation, and has a right to recover a property from all others; but any one, or all of these rights, may be restrained or fettered for the present. An owner may part with possession to a bailee, pledgee, thief or squatter; his right of alienation may be restrained under a deed of settlement; and his right to recover the property may be shackled by law. Nevertheless he remains the owner until the power of control is transferred, voluntarily or involuntarily, to another. See also **beneficial owner**, **estate owner**, **reputed owner**.

2. In a building contract, the owner may be (a) the party who owns the land upon which the building work is carried out; (b) the principal party to the contract, who pays the **contractor** for the building work; or (c) the client of a professional advisor employed in connection with the building work.

owner-occupier

A person who is both the **owner** and the **occupier** of a property. For the purpose of the right to serve a blight notice or purchase notice, 'owner-occupier' is defined as a freeholder or any person who holds a lease with at least three years to run; provided he or she has been in **occupation** of the whole or a substantial part of the 'owner's interest' for six months prior to the service of the notice, or at least six of the twelve months prior to the service of the notice (Town and Country Planning Act 1971, s. 203). In the case of a right to **compensation for injurious affection** (as payable when an interest in land is depreciated by 'physical factors' caused by the use of public works) an owner-occupier is one who has a substantial interest in the land affected by the public works and occupies a substantial part of the land or, if the land is an agricultural unit, occupies the whole of the land (Land Compensation Act 1973, s. 2(5): cf. definition in the 1973 Act, s. 41 (9) which relates to advances made to assist a displaced residential occupier to acquire or construct a dwelling in substitution for one taken by an authority with compulsory purchase powers). An 'owner-occupier' of a dwelling, who may have a statutory ground for possession against a protected tenant, is, "a person who occupied the dwelling-house as his residence" and lets it on a **regulated tenancy** (Rent Act 1977, Sch. 15, case 11). See also **grounds for possession, leasehold enfranchisement, owner-occupier's supplement, resident landlord.**

owner-occupier's supplement

A supplementary payment made, in accordance with the provisions of the Housing Act 1969, s. 68 and Sch. 5., to an owner-occupier who has a qualifying interest in a private dwelling-house that is considered unfit for human habitation and for which compulsory purchase compensation normally would be based on the **cleared site value**. The payment, which is made only when certain strict conditions are met, is based on the difference between the market or **ceiling value** of the house and the cleared site value. The purpose of this provision is to ensure that a residential owner-occupier who normally would be compensated upon compulsory purchase as if his unfit house had no value (except as a site), receives a reasonable market price for the premises. The owner for this purpose is any person entitled to receive a **notice to treat** under a compulsory purchase order. The occupier, as a rule, needs to have been in actual occupation for a period of two years, but a person may succeed to a previous occupation, and a shorter period may be adequate provided that the person did not take up occupation in the knowledge of a likely right to the increased compensation. See also **well-maintained payment.**

West's Law of Housing, 4 edn, pp. 241–245.

Housing Law, by Andrew Arden and Martin Partington, pp. 1074–1078 (1983).

owner's, landlord's and tenant's public liability insurance (O, L & T insurance) (US)

see **property owner's liability policy.**

owner's policy (US)

see **title insurance.**

ownership

The right of one person to exercise power and control over property to the exclusion of others. In less absolute terms, a right to the exclusive use, possession and enjoyment of a thing for a period of time, together with a right to transfer that thing to others; subject to any rights or duties owed to others and limitations imposed for the public good. The maintaining of a rightful **title** to property, with or without **possession**, especially a title that is protected by law. Ownership is, 'the greatest possible interest in a thing which a mature system of law recognises' – (Ownership, by A.M. Honoré, in *Essays in Jurisprudence*, p. 108, 1961).

Ownership includes a right of physical user, a right of possession, a right to derive financial benefit therefrom, a right to dispose in whole or in part, and, in theory, a right to waste or destroy. In its most absolute form, ownership is made up of the rights described in Romanistic legal terms as *utendi, fruendi* and *abutendi*, use enjoyment and abuse, i.e. to do as one likes. Put another way, ownership may comprise all or most of the rights attaching to property; namely occupation, possession, use, transfer, alienation, gift, management, charge, or even destruction. Absolute ownership (*dominium*) is the combination of all these rights.

In English common law, ownership of land is not recognised as being capable of forming the subject of an absolute right. Ownership was removed effectively from the substance of land and common law created an abstract right called an **estate** – a right to maintain a better title than another. This concept, which is founded on the feudal system of **tenure**, makes an owner no more than a holder of land from another; ultimately from a tenant of the Crown or some other Lord. "The truth is that English law has never applied the concept of ownership to land. 'Ownership' is a word of many meanings, but in the present context we can take it to signify a title to a subject-matter, whether moveable or immoveable, that is good against the whole world …" – (Cheshire's Modern Law of Real Property, 13 edn, p. 26). However, in modern law, when a person holds land as an estate of **fee simple absolute in possession** there is no significant difference from the form of ownership recognised by the Romans (although in Roman Law, which recognised no distinction between real and personal property, ownership could more truthfully be described as 'absolute' in law). Thus it has been said that, "by slow degrees, the statement that there is no absolute ownership of land has been deprived of most of its important consequences." (*Collected Papers*, F.W. Maitland, vol. i. p. 196 (1911).

In the United States, with its base of English common law, interlaced with civil law and a federal constitution, ownership is described in terms of the **bundle of rights theory** – an 'absolute owner' has a complete bundle of rights, a right to possess, use, occupy, enjoy, lease, charge, sell, etc.; a 'lesser owner' has one or more of the

items in the bundle removed. Thus, "a person who has the totality of the rights, powers, privileges and immunities which constitute complete property in a thing is the 'owner' of the 'thing', or 'owns' the 'thing' … The owner may part with many of the rights, powers, privileges and immunities that constitute complete property and his relationship to the thing is still termed ownership both in this Restatement and as a matter of public usage". (American Law Institute, Restatement of the Law of Property (1936) vol. i. p. 26).

In French law ownership (*propriété*) resembles the right recognised in Roman law and is defined as, "the right to possess and dispose of things in the most absolute way, provided they are not used in a matter prohibited by laws and regulations". (Civil Code, art. 544).

Ownership, as well as being absolute, may be limited in quantity or quality; may be corporeal or incorporeal; may be present or future; may be exercised in respect of real property or personal property; and may be a real right or a personal right. Nevertheless, whatever form it takes ownership is subject to the powers of government and the laws of the land (especially taxation, compulsory purchase and eminent domain, building and planning restrictions, 'police powers', and escheat or *bona vacantia*); any obligations or duties owed to the public at large; any constraint imposed by a person who has a greater or more absolute form of ownership; and any limitation imposed by the grant of a lesser right or interest. See also **co-ownership, collective ownership, co-operative ownership, several ownership**.

Amos & Walton's Introduction to French Law, 3 edn, p. 98–100.

Principles of Real Estate, by Bruce Harwood, 2 edn, pp. 39–44.

Real Property and Real People, by K.J. Gray and P.D. Symes, p. 3 *et seq.* (1981).

35 Halsbury's Laws of England, 4 edn, paras. 1127–1148.

P

pacage (F)
pasturage.
(*droit de pacage* – grazing rights).

package-deal contract
A **building contract** which provides
that the contractor will be responsible
for all the professional design services
(architectural, engineering, etc.) as
well as the building work. Under this
form of contract the person for whom
the work is carried out accepts the
completed building according to the
contractor's design and specification,
rather than according to the standard
demanded of his own architect or
other professional advisors. Called
also an 'all-in' contract or a 'design
and build' or 'design and construct' contract.
cf. **turn-key contract**.

package mortgage
A mortgage (or more usually a
charge) that is secured on real and
personal property. In the UK this
type of mortgage is rare; but in the US
it is not uncommon for a mortgage on
domestic property to be secured on
the house and major items of
equipment.

package insurance policy
An insurance policy that covers a
number of different risks of loss, or
different types of property. See also
blanket insurance policy.

packing
Filling a building with tenants upon
terms that are inferior to those obtainable in open market conditions, usually in order to present a 'fully-leased'
building to a prospective purchaser.

pacte (F)
agreement; contract.
(*pacte commissoire* – an agreement
for the sale of property which reserves
the right for the vendor to terminate if
the purchaser fails to pay the price
within a specified period)
(*pacte de réméré* – option to repurchase)
(*pacte léonin* – **unconscionable bargain**)
(*pacte nu* – **naked contract**).

pactum, nudum (L)
see **nudum pactum**.

pactum est servanda (L)
'An **agreement** is to be kept'. See **gentleman's agreement**.

pad sale
The sale, or grant of a long-term
ground lease, of a site in a shopping
centre, usually to an **anchor tenant**.
The tenant is responsible for erecting
and maintaining his own building,
which is integrated physically into the
centre.

paiement or payement (F)
payment; settlement of a debt.
(*paiement à compte* – part payment,
in advance)
(*paiement d'avance*; *paiement par
anticipation*; *paiement anticipé* –
payment in advance)
(*paiement à temperament* – payment
by instalments).

pais, **estoppel in**
see **estoppel**.

panic peddling (US)
see **blockbusting**.

pannage, common of

An ancient right by which, for certain times of the year, swine are permitted to forage for food in a commonable wood or forest.

paper

Written evidence of a debt. A **bill of exchange, promissory note, mortgage,** or similar contract for the payment of a sum of money, usually on or by a specified date. 'Paper' may be sold, usually at a discount, to a lender or factor, or may be pledged as security for a loan. See also **instrument, negotiable instrument**.

par value

1. The nominal or **face value** of a share or security.

cf. **market value**.

2. The **principal** outstanding on a mortgage loan at a given point in time.

paradis fiscaux (F)

tax haven.

paramount lease (US)

see **head lease**.

paramount title

A **title** that is superior to another. A stronger or better title to that claimed in opposition thereto.

parc national (F)

national park.

parcel of land

A specified area, or plot of land, usually in single ownership; especially one that forms part of a greater area of land. A single area of land held in the possession of one party, without in any way being separated by another's land. See also **hereditament**.

parcelle de terrain (F)

parcel of land; in particular, one of the parcels of land defined on the *cadastre* (cadastral register).

parcels clause

The section of a **deed** (a conveyance, lease or other deed dealing with property) that describes the subject property.

The parcels clause of a **conveyance** should contain a single, certain and unambiguous, description of the property: "as long as only one species of description is resorted to in describing parcels, no harm is done ... If, however, several species of description are adopted, risk of uncertainty at once arises, for if one is full, accurate, and adequate, any others are otiose if right, and misleading if wrong." – Eastwood *v* Ashton [1915] AC915–916. A description of a parcel of land solely by reference to a **plan** is good, provided the plan is to an adequate scale, and has been prepared and clearly marked for the purpose. A precise verbal description of the boundaries and appropriate land marks (**metes and bounds**) is good; but a description by name, by address, or by a mere statement of a land area tends to be too vague or uncertain. A mixed form of description may be disasterous. The parcels clause frequently starts with the words "All that ...". See also **'all estates' clause, exceptions and reservations, description, general words, premises**.

Parcels Index

An index of every parcel of land registered at the **Land Registry**. See also **index map**.

parcelling

The act of dividing land into separate plots for sale or development.

parcenary – parol lease

637

cf. **assemblage**, **plottage**. See also **plat**.

parcenary
see **coparcenary**.

parcours (F)
passage; path; course (of a river etc.).

parcours, *droit de* (F)
right of common; right of pasture; pasturage. See also *vaine pâture*.

pari passu (L)
'With equal step; without preference; at the same rate; equally'.

parish
1. An area that falls within an administrative boundary of the established church; a district committed to the charge of one incumbent "having the cure of the souls therein."(Bl. Comm. vol. i p. 110).
2. In England, the smallest area of local government, having been originally an ecclesiastical parish. See also **local authority**.

park
1. Derived from the French *parc*, 'enclosure'. An enclosed area of ground, held by royal grant or prescription, that is stocked with beasts for hunting.
cf. **chase**, **forest**. See also **enclosure**.
2. A tract of land set aside for public recreation, pleasure, rest, or enjoyment.
3. An area of forest or land preserved in its natural state for public enjoyment.
4. A privately owned and enclosed area of countryside, especially gardens, woodlands and pasture attached to a country house or manor house.

Parker Morris standards
A set of standards proposed, following the Parker Morris report *Homes for Tomorrow and Today* (1961), as a minimum for local authority house building in the UK when central government grants were required. These standards included minimum requirements for space, heating and standards of equipment. The requirement that council houses comply with these standards was abolished from April 1981.

parking lot
An open area of land used for the stationing of motor vehicles, generally for an appreciable period of time in a day. See also **garage**.

parking ratio
The ratio of the number of parking spaces provided for a building to the gross lettable or rentable area of that building.

paroisse (F)
parish.

parol
Oral; executed by word of mouth only, not in **writing** or under **seal**. Sometimes parol denotes something that is in writing, but not under seal. See also **parol lease**, **simple contract**.

parol, or parole, contract
A contract made by word of mouth, but not put in **writing** or set under **seal**. See also **simple contract**.

parol lease
A **lease** that is not made by **deed**. A parol lease is enforceable in the same way as one made by deed provided it takes effect immediately; it is made for a term not exceeding three years; and the tenant pays the best rent reasonably obtainable, without being obliged to pay a fine or premium (Law of Property Act 1925, s. 54 (2)).

(Strictly, a parol lease is one made by word of mouth – an 'oral lease' – but the term is used also for any lease in writing, but not under seal). See also **agreement for a lease, legal lease.**

Parry's valuation tables
see **valuation tables.**

parsonage
A house for a parson or incumbent of a **parish**. A certain portion of land established for the maintenance of a minister of the church, usually being the entire **benefice.**

The house, land, parish church, tithes, etc., that are set aside to provide fruits and benefits for a parish priest. See also **glebe.**

part (F)
share; part; portion.
(*part de copropriété* – share in coownership.

part VI claim
see **claim holding.**

part VI contract
A tenancy that came within Part VI of the Rent Act 1968; i.e. a tenancy granted at a rent which included a payment for the use of furniture or for board or attendance. The Rent Act 1974 effectively abolished the distinction between furnished and unfurnished premises in respect of rent regulation and security of tenure and since the Rent Act 1977 such a tenancy may come within the classification **regulated tenancy**, unless it is a **restricted contract**. See also **furnished tenancy.**

part owner
1. A person who holds an interest in property in **co-ownership** or **common ownership**. See also **coparcenary, joint tenant, tenant-in-common.**

2. One who has a **partial interest** in land.

part payment
1. The **payment** of a sum of money, that is less than the total amount due to discharge a debt or liability under a contract. In general, part payment does not constitute **satisfaction** of the whole of a debt (Pinnel's case (1602) 5 Co. Rep. 117). See also **accord and satisfaction, deposit, lien.**
2. A payment, being one of a number of payments to be made, generally at fixed intervals, under an **instalment sale** or a **mortgage loan**. In the US, more commonly called a 'partial payment'. A part payment of a loan is first applied to pay interest and the balance, if any, is used to reduce the principal debt. See also **amortisation mortgage, instalment.**

part performance, doctrine of
A doctrine, originating in the English Court of Chancery, which provides that although an agreement for the sale or other disposition of land has not been put into **writing**, or evidenced in writing, and duly signed, and, therefore, would not be enforceable 'at law', if one of the parties to the agreement acts to his detriment, based on a reasonable presumption that there is an enforceable agreement, the other party cannot accept the benefit of that action and then claim the agreement is unenforceable, merely because it is not in writing. The principle of the doctrine is that "equity imputes an intent to fulfil an obligation"; so that, if one person takes a course of action 'relying on the promised performance of another' the court may exercise its discretion to enforce the commitment to that promise, notwithstanding the lack of

proper formality. The doctrine of part performance arose to remedy injustices when contracts for the sale of land did not comply with the **Statute of Frauds**. It is now endorsed by the Law of Property Act 1925, s. 40 (2), which provides that the statutory requirement for written evidence of contracts relating to land (*viz*: 1975 Act, s. 40 (1)) is not affected by the "law relating to part performance."

A common instance of the application of the doctrine of part performance arises when a tenant enters into possession of a property, pursuant to an oral contract, and carries out structural alterations thereto; if the only reasonable explanation for that action is the existence of the oral contract, the court will enforce the contract (Broughton *v* Snook [1937] Ch. D 505). Similarly, if a landlord carries out structural alterations to a property on a verbal undertaking, supported by frequent representations, that a particular person will take a lease of the property when the alterations are complete the court will enforce that understanding, because the landlord's action is a clear case of part performance carried out in reliance on the other person's representation – Rawlinson *v* Ames [1925] Ch. 26. Taking possession in anticipation of a lease may be a sufficient act of part performance, but merely retaining possession at the end of a lease is not – Re. National Savings Bank Association (1867) 15 WR 753. On the other hand, the retention of possession and a payment of rent, which is accepted by a landlord, has been held to be a sufficient act of part performance – Miller and Aldworth Ltd. *v* Sharp [1899] 1 Ch. 622. In the US a similar view has been adopted so that mere retention of possession may be considered as referrable to the old tenancy, and not necessarily to any new tenancy – Lapedus *v* Weinberg, (1940), 292 Mich. 439, 290 NW 859; but if hardship would result from not acknowledging the new tenancy the courts will normally grant a decree of specific performance – Halsey *v* Robinson, 1942, 19 Cal. 2d. 476, 122 P. 2d. 11.

It is fundamental to the application of the doctrine that (a) there is evidence of the essential terms of the contract; (b) the intention of the parties can be clearly ascertained; and (c) the action that has been performed unequivocally refers to, and is consistent with, the alleged contract – Steadman *v* Steadman [1974] 3 WLR 56. In other words an act of part performance, to be accepted by a court, requires "that the acts in question be such as must be referred to some contract and may be referred to the alleged one; that they prove the existence of some contract, and are consistent with the contract alleged." – Fry on *Specific Performance*, 6 edn., p. 278 – Maddison *v* Alderson (1883) 8 App. Cas. 485. In addition, the contract in question must be capable of enforcement, i.e. it must not be illegal or arise from fraud or misrepresentation. The doctrine of part performance is applied frequently to support a request for a decree of **specific performance**, when there appears a proper and justifiable contract to support.

cf. **estoppel**. See also **agreement for lease**.

Real Property, by William E. Burby, 3 edn., pp. 288, 289.

Introduction to Land Law, by J.G. Riddell, 3 edn., pp. 222–231.

Hill and Redman's Law of Landlord and Tenant, 17 edn, pp. 116–119.
The Law of Real Property, by Robert Megarry and H.W.R. Wade, 5 edn., pp. 589–599.
Land Law: Cases and Materials, by R.H. Maudsley and E.H. Burn, 4 edn., pp. 62–71.
Megarry's Manual of the Law of Real Property, 6 edn, pp. 141–146.
Cheshire's Modern Law of Property, 13 edn, pp. 117–122.
42 Halsbury's Laws of England, 4 edn, paras. 44–45.

partage (F)
partition, as in the division of an estate held in co-ownership into separate or several ownership; **apportionment**; share; portion. See also *lot*.

partiaire, bail à colon (or *à colonat*) (F)
sharecropper lease. See also **metayage system**.

partial floor factor (US)
see loss factor.

partial interest
An interest in land that is less than a fee simple absolute. A partial interest in land may be created as a result of a physical subdivision of land (horizontally or vertically); the grant of a limited right of user, whether in terms of time, type or person; or the grant of a financial charge or mortgage over land. Partial interests include also the benefit of land held in trust; a right to land held in co-ownership or collective ownership; the right to an easement or any other form of servitude; a leasehold interest; and a life interest. The term 'partial interest' is more common in the US than in the UK and it derives its origin from the **bundle of rights theory** by which land is considered as a collection of rights to land, the fee owner having a complete bundle of rights and any other owner has a partial interest. French law acknowledges a similar group of real rights – usufruct; real servitudes; an emphyteotic lease; etc. – the creation of any one of which is termed *demembrements de la propriété*. See also **doctrine of estates, fractional interest**.
Appraisal of Real Estate, AIREA, 8 edn., pp. 531–552.

partial payment (US)
see **part payment**.

partial payment factor (US)
see **mortgage constant**.

partial reconveyance deed (US)
see **partial release**.

partial release (US)
The release of certain properties from a **blanket mortgage**, generally upon repayment of a specified part of the principal. A deed that gives effect to a release of part of the property held under a mortgage is called a 'partial release deed' or a 'partial reconveyance deed'.

partial taking (US)
The taking of part of an owner's land, or a partial interest in land, by an exercise of the power of **eminent domain**, i.e. the compulsory **severance** of a right of ownership. See also **severance damages**.

participating mortgage
see **participation mortgage**.

participation
see **equity participation, public participation, slice**.

participation (F)
participation; share; interest (in a partnership or joint venture).

(*association en participation* – sleeping partnership)
(*société en participation* – joint venture partnership). See also *société*.

participation agent (or broker) (US)
see **joint agent**.

participation clause (US)
see **escalation clause**.

participation lease
see **equity participation, slice**.

participation mortgage (US)
1. A mortgage provided by several lenders who act together so as to spread their risk. Usually the mortgaged property is held in trust for the participating mortgagees. Called also a 'participating mortgage' or a 'fractionalised mortgage'.
2. See **equity-participation mortgage**.

particular agency
see **agency**.

particular estate
1. An **estate** in land that is carved out of another estate and precedes a **remainder** or **reversion**.
2. Any estate less than a **fee simple**.

particular lien
see **lien**.

particular partnership
A **partnership** established for a specific purpose or enterprise, as distinguished from a partnership established for general business. See also **joint venture**.

particular purchaser
see **special purchaser**.

particular tenant
The holder of a **particular estate**.

particulars of sale
1. Written details of a property that is to be offered for sale or to let, normally setting out a brief description of the property and the terms upon which it could be acquired. In particular, details of a property that is to be sold by **auction**. The particulars of a property that is to be offered for sale may be submitted by a vendor, or his agent, to prospective purchasers; but, as a rule, such particulars do not constitute a formal **offer**, but merely an **invitation to treat**. However, particulars of sale issued prior to a sale by auction are deemed to form part of the contractual terms upon which the property is to be offered for sale. Particulars of sale should be interpreted as if they were addressed to a layman and "should accordingly be interpreted in accordance with what they, on a fair reading mean to an ordinary person" – Mustafa v Baptist Union Corporation Ltd. (1983) 266 EG 813. In the US, called also 'property brief'. See also **exclusion clause, misdescription, misrepresentation, puffing**.
2. The part of a contract for the sale of land that describes the subject-matter of the contract, i.e. it sets down a physical description of the property and the interest to be sold.
cf. **conditions of sale**. See also **plan, premises**.

parties
Those who have entered into a formal contract; "they that make a deed and they to whom it is made are called parties to the deed" – Termes de la Ley.

parties communes (F)
common areas, especially in a building held in *copropriété* (co-ownership).
cf. *parties privatives*.

parties privatives (F)

private areas, especially in a building held in *copropriété* (*co-owner-ship*), being those areas used exclusively by the property owners, e.g. an apartment, garage.

cf. *parties communes*.

parting wall

see party wall.

partition

1. The division of real property held in co-ownership into separate, or several, ownership. The splitting of a right to joint possession of land so that the respective parties have separate rights of ownership: a means by which co-ownership is destroyed. Partition of an interest in real property can only be enforced with the consent of all the co-owners, or by order of a court. Partition does not create or transfer a new interest, but merely severs the unity of possession. See also condominium, joint tenancy, severalty, tenancy-in-common.

2. A light-weight wall used to divide areas of a building internally. Generally, a partition is not part of the structure or carcass of a building; it is non-loadbearing; and extends vertically only between floor and ceiling. See also party wall.

partner

A member of a partnership. One who joins with another, or others, in an unincorporated business with a view to profit. Any person who represents himself to be a partner in a particular firm is liable as a partner to anyone who on the faith of such representation has given credit to the firm (Partnership Act 1890, s. 14 (1)). Thus, a person need not be an actual partner to be liable for a partnership debt that he has occasioned. See also active partner, general partner, sleeping partner.

partnership

A voluntary, but unincorporated, business relationship established by two or more persons (partners) who act together in order to carry on a trade, profession or occupation, with a view to making and sharing profits arising from their endeavour. The partners contribute their property, skill, experience, toil and energy (or some or all of those) towards the joint aim of profit; while accepting the common risk and possibility of loss.

In English law, an arrangement cannot be a partnership if the partners are, in effect, formed together as a company or the relationship is registered as a company. The receipt by a person, with others, of the profits of an unincorporated business is *prima facie* evidence that he or she is a member of a partnership; but does not, of itself, confirm a person as a partner. The sharing of the gross returns, or "the receipt of such a share, or of a payment contingent on or varying with the profit of a business" does not, in isolation, create a partnership; nor does the receipt of a share of the profits by a lender of money to a business; nor does the receipt of a share of the profits received as a result of the sale of the goodwill of a business. These factors may indicate that a partnership exists, but it is necessary also to consider the intention of the parties to the relationship and any contract entered into between them (Partnership Act 1890, s. 2 (2) (3)). In addition, co-ownership of property (whether as a joint tenancy, a tenancy-in-common, common property, or a part ownership of any form) does not create a partnership (although property acquired by a partnership is held as a **tenancy-in-common** by the partners; and any property brought for the purposes of the business, or with partnership money is held in the same way, as partnership property (1890 Act, ss. 2 (1), 20, 21).

A partnership may take the form of a **general partnership** in which each and every partner shares in the profits and losses of the partnership and is involved in the management and conduct of the partnership and is liable for the debts of the partnership to the full extent of his property ownership, as if he were a sole proprietor; or a **limited partnership** in which one or more partners (general partners) are responsible for the debts of the partnership in their entirety, and one or more partners (limited partners) contribute capital, under the terms of the partnership agreement, but are not liable for debts beyond the amount of their contribution (Limited Partnership Act 1907, s. 4). Limited partnerships are rare in England, but are not uncommon in the US, especially for real estate ventures.

'General partnership' may mean also a partnership established for a general purpose or business, e.g. an estate agent or solicitor's practice as distinguished from a 'particular' or 'special partnership' established for a particular transaction or purpose.

English law does not recognise a partnership as a separate legal entity; property must be held by the partners; and each partner is treated as having **joint and several liability** to third parties. In French law there is

no distinction made between a 'company' and a 'partnership', both being embraced by the term *société* (although the definition of a *société* in the French Civil Code, art. 1832 is similar to that applied to a partnership in English law: a *société anonyme* being close to an English limited company). In most states in the US a partnership follows the English pattern and is governed by a Uniform Partnership Act. However, in some states a partnership may be recognised as a legal entity, similar to a corporation, and may enter into a lease in its own name – termed a '**tenancy-in-partnership**'.

In English law real property that is acquired by a partnership is held in trust for the partners as tenants in common; the property cannot be held as a joint tenancy because the latter form of co-ownership requires a 'right of survivorship' amongst the partners, a right that is inconsistent with the commercial nature of a partnership – Lake v Craddock (1732) 3 PW158. See also **joint venture**.

Modern Partnership Law, by D. Milman and T. Flanagan, (1983).
Partnership Law and Practice, by R. Burgess and G. Morse, (1980).
Law of Partnership, by Charles D. Drake, 3 edn.
Underhill's Principles of the Law of Partnership, 11 edn.
35 Halsbury's Laws of England, 4 edn, paras. 1–300.
Lindley on Partnership, 15 edn.

partnership property
see **partnership**.

party
1. One who has entered into a transaction, either as a sole party or with others.

2. A person who is involved in a legal action or transaction, e.g. a landlord, tenant, vendor, purchaser, mortgagor, mortgagee, agent, principal, etc.

party structure

A **structure** that separates buildings, stories, or rooms and belongs to two persons as part owners. The structure may be a partition, floor, or any other form of structure. Thus, a party structure is like a **party wall** except that it occupies a greater space or has a more substantial form.

party wall (or party fence)

A wall (or fence), erected on the boundary of adjoining parcels of land, which "belongs to two persons as part owners or divides two buildings one from another". – Weston *v* Arnold [1873] 8 Ch. App. 1089. A party wall is used normally for the mutual benefit of both parties. The term may be used in four senses: (i) a wall that is held under a **tenancy in common**; i.e. it is held equally by co-owners; (ii) a wall that is considered to be severed vertically, one half belonging to each of the neighbouring owners (although the wall may be placed physically on the boundary line, or entirely on one side or the other); (iii) a wall owned entirely by one of the adjoining owners but with an **easement** to have it maintained in position in favour of the other land owner; or (iv) a wall divided vertically into halves or moities with cross-easements in favour of each party – Watson *v* Gray (1880) 14 Ch. D 194–5.

In English law since 1925 the first category can no longer exist, such a form of ownership of a party wall is now considered to be in the fourth category (Law of Property Act 1925,

s. 38) and, in the absence of evidence to the contrary, it may be presumed that any party wall falls into that category. If the wall falls entirely on one side of a boundary it is presumed to fall in the third category, except that any easement may be rebutted by evidence to the contrary. A party wall is constructed in some cases as ostensibly an external structural wall of a building, but as an economy, it has been made to serve the same purpose for two adjacent structures.

A dispute affecting a party wall right – loss of support, alterations to a building, etc. – is dealt with normally by agreement between the parties, with matters affecting financial losses being referred to arbitration. In the areas within the old London County Council boundaries precise arrangements in this respect are set out in the London Building Acts, e.g. The London Building Acts 1930–1939. (For this purpose two slightly separate definitions of party wall are set out in the 1939 Act, s. 4 and s. 44). Called also a 'common wall', especially in the US, or sometimes a 'parting wall'. See also **terrace house**.

The Law of Boundaries and Fences, by Vincent Powell-Smith, 2 edn., pp. 143–164.

4 Halsbury's Laws of England, 4 edn, paras. 889–896.

Party Wall Legislation and Procedure, RICS, (1982).

pass

To change hands, especially on death. To **transfer** or be transferred. See also **vest**.

pass-through (US)

A provision made by the Internal Revenue Service whereby income, profits, depreciation, etc. may be passed through a partnership to the individual partners free of tax. Called also 'flow through'. See also **real estate, investment trust**.

passage, *droit de* (F)
right of way.
(*droit de passage en cas d'enclave* – **easement of necessity**. The French Civil Code, arts. 682–686 gives an owner of an *enclave* (landlocked land) an easement of necessity to a public way to enable him to use the land. The right may be exercised for as long as the necessity exists. It may be established along a route agreed with the neighbouring landowner (the owner of the servient tenement) or, failing agreement, by a legal judgement. An appropriate *indemnité* (compensation) may be payable to the owner of the servient tenement, either as a single capital sum or as an annual sum. See also *servitude*.
Droit Civil, Les Biens, by Jean Carbonnier, 11 edn., pp. 224–226.
Précis Dalloz. Droit Civil, Les Biens (Alex Weill), 2 edn, pp. 108–118.

passage, right of
see **right of passage**.

pass-through clause (US)
see **escalation clause**.

passation d'un acte (F)
execution of a deed.

passif (F)
liability; liabilities; **debt**.
(*passif éventuel* – **contingent liability**)
(*passif exigible* – **arrears**).

passim (L)
'In various places; here and there'.

passing rent
see **contractual rent**.

passive investor
An investor who does not take any active part in the management of his investments, but merely invests his funds in order to receive an income or capital gain. See also **absentee owner, limited partnership, sleeping partner**.

passive trust
see **bare trust**.

past consideration
see **consideration**.

pasture
An area of land covered with grass or herbage to be eaten by cattle or other livestock; land used or set aside for grazing animals. See also **agricultural land, common land, right of pasture**.

patent defect
A defect that is clearly visible or obvious; "... in considering what is a **latent defect** and what a patent defect, one ought to take the general view that a patent defect, which can be thrust upon the purchaser must be a defect which arises either to the eye, or by necessary implication from something which is visible to the eye" – Yandle and Sons *v* Sutton [1922] 2 Ch. 210. See also **defect of title**.

path
see **footpath**.

patrimoine (F)
patrimony; estate; heritage. A person's *patrimoine* represents his or her entire estate, especially that which can pass by inheritance. *Patrimoine* may be used to refer to all the *propriété* (property) of an individual (whether owned now or capable of being owned in the future), or, more usually, to all the assets and liabilities (net worth) of an individual. Thus, it

includes assets (*actif*) and liabilities (*passif*), i.e. it includes anything that may be converted into money terms including a duty to perform an act or the benefit of such a duty. *Patrimoine* includes all forms of property, *biens réels*, *biens personnels* and *droits intellectuels.* It is the indivisible, totality of a person's worth so that, "it is thus in the *patrimoine* that property and obligation meet and merge". (*French Law of Contract*, by Barry Nicholas, p. 29, 1982)
Amos & Walton's Introduction to French Law, 3 edn, p. 19.
Droit Civil, by Jean Chevallier and Louis Bach, 8 edn, pp. 34–36.
Droit Civil, Introduction, by Boris Stark, pp. 140–144 (1972).
Droit Civil, Les Biens, by Jean Carbonnier, 11 edn., p. 1 *et seq.*
Précis Dalloz. Droit Civil, Les Biens, (Alex Weill) 2 edn, p. 1 *et seq.*
Droit Civil, Introduction, by Gabriel Marty and Pierre Raynaud, 2 edn., p. 462 *et seq.*

patrimony
1. Property inherited from a father's estate or that of his paternal ancestors. See also *patrimoine.*
2. The ancient estate of an institution, corporation or church.

pâturage (F)
pasture.

pâture, vaine (F)
see *vaine pâture.*

pavement light
A form of window or light set into a pavement so as to let daylight into a basement or cellar. Usually it is made of solid glass blocks set in a cast-iron frame. See also **ancient light.**

pavilion
Derived from the Old French *pavillon*, 'butterfly-like'. Originally a large tent rising to a peak. A light or temporary building, usually with a peaked roof, especially one used for the purpose of ornament or as a shelter for those engaged in a sport or recreation. A pavilion also may be erected for the purpose of an exhibition, and, although intended to be of a temporary nature, sometimes may be left in place after its original purpose has been fulfilled. In many cases such buildings are of elaborate design and themselves become exhibits.

pawn
1. The actual or constructive delivery of personal goods to another as security for a loan, debt or engagement, i.e. a form of **bailment**. The person who delivers the goods (pawnor) retains title thereto, and the holder of the goods (pawnee) is obliged to take good care of the goods while they are in his possession. If the debt is not paid when due the pawnee has a right to dispose of the goods, but must account to the pawnor for the net proceeds of sale if any, that exceed the amount of the outstanding debt. See also **pledge**.
(US) 2. In Louisiana, USA, 'pawn' is used to refer to an *antichrèse* (Civil Code La. art 3101).

pawnee
One to whom goods are delivered in **pawn.**

pawnor
One who delivers goods to another to be held in **pawn.**

pay-back analysis
A method of **investment analysis** that measures the time required for the

total net income or cash flow, generated by an investment to equal the initial capital cost of that investment. A simple method of comparing investments that takes no account of the stage at which income is received over the pay-back period; nor of the discounted value of money over the life of the investment; nor of the interest that could be earned on the income received during the life of the investment. The period of time taken for the income to equate to the initial cost is called the 'pay-back period'. For example, if an investment of £1000 produces a net income of £200, £300, £500 in the first, second and third years after the investment is made the pay-back period is three years. See also **discounted rate of return, recapture**.

pay-back period
see **pay-back analysis**.

pay-off penalty
see **prepayment penalty**.

payment
Something given or delivered as remuneration for goods or services or to discharge a debt or obligation. Money, or any other form of pecuniary benefit, made over to a seller by a purchaser of property. "The word 'payment' in itself is one which, in an appropriate context, may cover many ways of discharging obligations. It may even . . . include a discharge, not by money at all, but by what is called 'payment in kind'." – White v Elmdene Estates Ltd., [1959] 2 All ER 610–1. In the case of the discharge of a debt or obligation "payment is **satisfaction** of a claim made by or on behalf of a person against whom the claim is made" – Halsbury's Laws of

England vol. 42, 4 edn, p. 241. cf. **set-off**.

payment in advance
see **advance payment, rent in advance (or arrears)**.

'peaceably and quietly'
A term used in a lease to describe the tenant's right to **quiet enjoyment** of property, i.e. without interruption of possession, and not, as may seem, a right to be undisturbed by noise – Jenkins v Jackson (1889) 40 Ch. D 74.

peak pitch
The best retail location in a shopping centre and, therefore, the position that generates the highest rental value. Called also the 'prime trading location' or 'prime pitch'. See also **highest and best use, prime location**.

pecunia (L)
In the civil law and old English law any form of property; **things** in general. (In the Domesday Book *pecunia* is used to refer to cattle or beasts, which were a primary source of wealth or property; hence, the derivation 'cattle' – 'chattel' – **'capital'**.) See also **pecuniary consideration**.

pecuniary consideration
Consideration that takes the form or relates to money, whether as a cash payment or as a gain in monetary worth. See also **good consideration, money's worth, premium**.

pedestrian precinct
see **precinct**.

pedestrian precinct order
An order made by a local authority, under the provision of the Town and Country Planning Act 1971, s. 212, by which the authority states that it intends to convert a highway, other

than a trunk or principal road, into a footpath or bridleway so as to restrict its use only to pedestrians, cyclists and certain service vehicles. A party that suffers damage, or a loss in the value of their interest in land, as a result of a loss of lawful access to a highway is entitled to compensation for any damage or loss or depreciation in value of the interest which is directly attributable to the order.

pedestrianisation

The conversion of a public highway or street into an area with limited or no vehicular access. See also **mall, pedestrian precinct order, precinct**.

penal rent

1. A rent that substantially exceeds the **market rent** of a property. See also **rack rent, rent limit**.
2. A charge for late payment of rent which exceeds the loss suffered by the landlord to whom the payment is due and, therefore, may be construed as a **penalty**.

pénalité (F)

penalty.

penalty

A sum of money payable as a redress for a fault, error or injury. Something inflicted, for example, to secure the due performance of a contract. A sum of money, or a **fine**, specified in a contract as payable in the event of a breach of a condition of that contract. A sum that is intended to exceed any reasonable loss or damage suffered, or likely to be suffered, as a result of a breach of a contract. A penalty may be contrasted with **liquidated damages** which is a sum that is intended to equal the actual loss suffered. "The essence of a penalty is a payment of money stipulated as *in terrorem* of the offending party (to act as an inducement to the performance of a contract); the essence of liquidated damages is a genuine pre-estimate of damage." – Dunlop Pneumatic Tyre Co. Ltd., *v* New Garage and Motor Co. Ltd., [1915] AC 86. The payment of a penalty is not enforceable in a court of law because it is considered that a party should not be paid more than his true loss. Thus, if a building contract is completed late the employer may not be able to recover a penalty if no loss has been suffered as a result of the delay. Similarly, if interest on a loan is paid late the charging of a higher interest rate for late payment may be considered as penal interest, because the lender is receiving a higher amount than the actual loss suffered for parting with the money; although charging interest on interest at the same rate is not penal – Holles *v* Vyse (1693) 2 Vern. 289; Wallingford *v* Mutual Society (1880) 5 AC 685. On the other hand, it is permissible to charge a higher interest rate and provide that it will be reduced if prompt payment is made (this is considered to be equivalent to fixing a higher interest rate for the loan at the outset) – Strode *v* Parker (1694) 2 Vern. 316. A reasonable or market interest rate (but not a usurious rate) may be charged on rent that is in arrears. The intention should be to cover the creditor's loss without unreasonably penalising the debtor: "a penalty covers but does not assess the damages". Any sum, or provision in a contract, which permits one party to recover more than the true loss, or to retain more than a reasonable entitlement, in the event of default on that contract, is likely to be construed as a penalty. See also **forfeiture, prepayment penalty, usury**.

pennage
A payment for the right to erect pens at a **market** or **fair**. See also **stallage**.

pension fund (or trust)
An institution that holds and invests funds which it has received from individuals on trust with the intention that those individuals will receive an income or lump-sum payment on their retirement in later years. In the UK pension funds are one of the major direct investors in real estate. In the US pension funds are controlled as to the forms of investment by the Employment Retirement Income Security Act (ERISA) and their investments in real estate are restricted primarily to mortgage loans. See also **institutional investor**.
The McGraw-Hill Real Estate Handbook, by Robert Irwin (ed.), paras. 3-1 to 3-19 (1984).
Pension Funds and Their Advisors, A.P. Financial Registers Ltd. (annual).

penthouse
1. A self-contained apartment, or flat, or any other enclosed area located on the top floor of a building; normally a separate floor added to the main structure with a recess, walkway, or balcony around the perimeter. "Structures built above the main roof line and recessed behind the exterior wall line, to house water tanks, elevator machinery ... and, in more recent times, living quarters of a luxurious nature" – Great Lakes Hotels Ltd. *v* Noshery Ltd. (1968) 56 CPR 169. A penthouse apartment or flat is commonly considered to be the most prestigious and, therefore, most valuable apartment, or flat, in a build-

ing. Derived from Old French *pentis*, 'attached on', or Middle French, *pente*-'slope'.
2. An annex, or structure joined on to another building with a lean-to roof; especially a form of shelter over a passage or arcade.

peppercorn rent
A token **rent** provided for in a lease, theoretically as an acknowledgement of a higher estate in land, i.e. of the relationship of landlord and tenant. A **lease**, being a document that strictly must be made by deed, requires no **consideration** and, therefore, stipulating for such a rent is intended merely to indicate that the landlord is retaining a right to regain the property at the end of the lease term. In practice, the peppercorn rent is never demanded.

per (L)
'As stated by'.

per annum (L)
'Yearly; on an annual basis; every year'. *Per annum* means a payment for a complete **year**, and is not apportionable; unlike a payment "at the rate of" so much a year. – Salton *v* New Beeston Cycle Co. [1899] 1 Ch. 779. See also **per cent**.

per autre vie (L)
'For the life of another'. See **life interest**.

per capita (L)
'By heads; according to the number of individuals'. A term used in the law of succession to denote that the descendants take property in equal shares, i.e. as so much 'per head'.
cf. ***per stirpes***.

per cent (or *per centum*)
'By a hundred; parts of a hundred'; a

percentage. If a rate is stated as a 'per cent', without any further qualification, either expressly or as can be implied from the context, "that rate means *per cent per annum* just as if the words *per annum* were written in". – London and Harrogate Securities, Ltd. *v* Pitts [1976] 3 All ER 815.

per cur: per curiam (L)
'By the court'. A decision of a court, as distinguished from a decision delivered by one judge; or a decision given but not written.

per diem (L)
'By the **day**; daily'.

per mensum (L)
'Per **month**; by the month'.

per my et per tout (L)
'By the half and by all'. Used to refer to the right vested in a joint tenant to have a half and an entire interest in land, but no right separate from the other party. See also **joint tenancy**.

per pais (L)
'By the country'. See **estoppel**.

per pro: per procurationem (L)
'By proxy or procuration; as an agent' "A simple 'p', 'pro' or 'for', expresses an authority generally, and 'per pro' or 'p.p.' express an authority erected by procuration or **power of attorney**." – Ulster Bank *v* Synnott [1871] IR 5 Eq. 612.

per se (L)
'By itself; in its own right'.

per stirpes (L)
'By stock; by roots'. A term used in the law of succession to denote that the property is distributed according to the right of representation, so that the children of any one descendant receive their share in accordance with

their parent's entitlement as if he or she had been living and not equally with other members of the same generation. Taking property *per stirpes* is known also as taking by right of representation.
cf. *per capita*.

per year
see *per annum*, **year**.

percentage
A rate **per cent**; part of a whole expressed as the unit fraction of a hundred.

percentage lease
A lease that provides for the payment of a turnover or **percentage rent**, i.e. a rent based, in whole or in part, on the value of the tenant's sales or turnover. In the UK, more commonly called a **turnover lease**.
Leases: Percentage, Short and Long Term, by Stanley L. McMicael and Paul T. O'Keefe (1974).

percentage rent
A **rent** based on a percentage of a tenant's sales or turnover made on the leased premises, as defined by the lease. In the UK more commonly called a **turnover rent**. See also **base rent, overage**.

percolating water
see **water rights**.

péremption (F)
limitation (in time); **abatement** (of a right of action); **extinguishment** (of a right), e.g. of a right to build after a certain period of time from the grant of a *permis de construire*.

perfect title (US)
see **good title, marketable title**.

performance
The carrying through of something to

completion. The discharge of a **promise, obligation** or duty *in toto*. The completion of all the requirements, or fulfillment of all the terms, of a contract, the effect being to **discharge** the contract. Strictly, a contract is discharged by performance only when the performance complies exactly with the terms of the contract – Re Moore and Co., Ltd. and Landaur and Co. [1921] All ER Rep 466. However, the court may accept that performance has taken place if what has been done fulfills substantially the intentions of the parties and, if only a comparatively minor part of the contract remains incomplete, may award **damages** for the loss suffered by the beneficiary of the contract; rather than grant an **injunction** to insist on completion down to the last detail. Thus, if a builder substantially completes a building, but leaves some paintwork unfinished, the contract would be treated as performed and, "the builders are entitled to recover the contract price, less so much as it is found ought to be allowed in respect of the items . . . found to be defective" – H. Dakin and Co. Ltd. *v* Lee [1916] 3 KB 566. This equitable doctrine of **substantial performance** does not apply in cases where precise performance of the entire contract is a condition precedent to the effective performance of any part of the contract; for example, in the case of a **lump-sum contract** for the construction of a building.

The performance of the obligations of a contract may be 'divisible', or 'indivisible' ('entire'). A divisible obligation permits the one party to insist upon performance without necessarily permitting the other party also to require performance. For example, a landlord may insist on a tenant paying rent in full, when due, even though the tenant has no prior right to insist on the landlord carrying out a repairing obligation. An indivisible obligation means that one party cannot insist upon performance unless he has, or is clearly willing, to fulfil his side of the bargain. See also **accord and satisfaction, commission, part performance, set-off, specific performance, tender**.

Anson's Law of Contract, 26 edn, pp. 419–427.

Cheshire & Fifoot's Law of Contract, 10 edn, pp. 476–501.

Chitty on Contract, 25 edn, paras. 1385–1456.

9 Halsbury's Laws of England, 4 edn, paras. 472–527.

performance bond

A **bond** given by one party to another as a surety for the proper performance of a contract by a third party. The bond takes the form of a **guaranty** so that, if the third party fails to meet his obligation or contractual duty, the guarantor undertakes either to complete the obligation or duty or to pay damages up to an amount specified in the bond. In the event of default, as a rule, the bond must be complied with or monies paid "on demand without proof or condition" – Edward Owen Ltd *v* Barclays Bank Ltd. [1977] 3 WLR 764. Called also a 'completion bond' or 'surety bond'. See also **bid bond**.

performance mortgage (US)

A mortgage which provides that the cost of **debt service** will be met by income from the mortgage property. See also **equity participation, participation mortgage**.

periodic estate (US)
see **periodic tenancy**.

periodic repayment (US)
see **amortisation mortgage, part payment**.

periodic tenancy
A generic term for a **tenancy** that continues for a succession of fixed and regular periods, until determined by **notice to quit**. The periods may cover any time span – week to week, month to month, quarter to quarter, year to year – but the tenancy remains as one continuous tenancy; it is not a series of renewable contracts. A periodic tenancy may be created expressly; may arise by implication, as when a person takes, or retains, exclusive possession of land and pays a regular rent; or may be created by statute, as when a tenant of a dwelling-house obtains a right to a **statutory tenancy** (although a statutory tenancy is not a tenancy in the strict sense). The notice to terminate the tenancy must cover an entire period and unequivocally expire at the end of that period. If the period is not expressed in a lease it is implied from the manner in which the **rent** is calculated; but not from the regularity by which it is payable. Thus, a rent of so much per year creates a yearly tenancy, even if payable quarterly. On the other hand, a tenancy that commences on one of the **quarter days**, at a rent payable four times a year, will normally be construed as a quarterly tenancy terminable on a successive quarter day.

A **tenancy from year to year** (yearly tenancy) may be terminated at the end of the first, or any subsequent year, and, unless there is anything expressed to the contrary, **half a year**'s notice to quit, expiring the day

before the anniversary date of commencement, is adequate to determine the tenancy. In the US called also an 'estate from period to period' or a 'periodic estate'.
cf. **tenancy for a fixed period**. See also **agricultural tenancy, business tenancy, monthly tenancy, tenancy at sufferance, tenancy at will, weekly tenancy**.
Hill and Redman's Law of Landlord and Tenant, 17 edn, p. 50 *et seq.*

permanent commitment
A **commitment** by a financial institution, or any other potential lender of money, that it will provide a permanent or **long-term loan** at a future date. Commonly applied to a commitment granted to a property developer that funds will be available to replace an **interim loan** when a development is completed and/or fully let.

permanent financing
see **permanent loan**.

permanent loan
A long-term loan used to finance a completed development or an investment, as distinguished from **interim financing**.
cf. **construction financing**. See also **take-out financing**.

permis (F)
licence; permit.
(*permis de démolir* – demolition permit)
(*permis de lotir* – parcelling permit). See also ***certificat de conformité***.

permis de construire (F)
building permit. A *permis de construire* is intended to control urban planning, standards of building work and all aspects of building security, safety and public health. It is required

for all forms of development (excluding certain minor forms of development; certain forms of development carried out by the State; and development in areas covered by a *zone d'aménagement concerté*, by an approved *lotissement* or by a *plan d'occupation des sols* where development is controlled in accordance with the plans prepared for those areas). A *permis de construire* is required for an external or major internal alteration to a building, as well as for any change of user. (*Code de l'Urbanisme, arts. 421, 422*).
Précis Dalloz, Droit Administratif (J.M. Auby & R. Ducos-Ader), 6 edn, para. 507 *et seq.*
Droit Administratif, by André de Laubadère, 12 edn, pp. 378–382.

permission
see **permit, planning permission, licence.**

permissive waste
see **waste.**

permit
To give leave to an action. A written order or **licence** granted by a person or organisation, especially a government body, formally approving an activity by another. See also **building permit, certificate of occupancy, franchise, planning permission.**

permitted development
Development that may be undertaken without a need for planning permission because it is included in one of the classes of permitted development set out in a **general development order** – this order has the effect of granting planning permission for a specified class or type of development. (This 'permitted development' should be distinguished from certain forms of development which are specifically excluded from being classified as 'development' by virtue of the Town and Country Planning Act 1971, s. 22 (2).) See also **article 4 direction, eighth schedule development, established use certificate, special development order, use class.**
Business Property Handbook, The Boisot Waters Cohen Partnership, pp. 387–391 (1982).

perpetually renewable lease
A lease that provides the tenant with a right to renew his tenancy for as long as he desires. Such a lease is automatically converted into a lease for a term of 2000 years, or a sub-lease for one day less than the term out of which it derives (Law of Property Act 1925, s. 145, Sch. 15, para. 5).
In the US a perpetually renewable lease is not normally enforceable or it may be barred as contrary to the **rule against perpetuities.**

perpétuité (F)
perpetuity. See also **rule against perpetuities.**

perpetuity
The quality of continuing forever, or for an indefinite period. An interest in land may be said to be created 'in perpetuity' if the interest is so created that it will continue for an unlimited period of time, e.g. a **freehold.** Alternatively, it may be created to come into effect after the expiry of a perpetual or inalienable interest; "that is to say, an estate unalienable, though all mankind join in the conveyance" – Scatterwood v Edge (1699) 1 Salkeld, 229. See also **rule against perpetuities, year's purchase in perpetuity.**

perquisition (F)
search; enquiry.

perquisitor

One who acquires property other than by inheritance; "one who acquired an estate by sale, by gift, or by any other method, except only that of descent" – Bl. Comm. vol. ii. p. 220. cf. **purchaser**.

personal accident insurance

see **accident insurance**.

personal action

see **action in personam**.

personal chattel

see **chattel**.

personal covenant

A **covenant** that is enforceable only between the two parties; a covenant of which neither the benefit nor the burden may be assigned, i.e. a covenant that does not 'run with the land'. cf. **real covenant**. See also **privity, restrictive covenant, recourse**.

personal estate

The **personal property** of an individual, including money (but not money's worth when represented by **real estate**), goods, debts, choses-in-action, stocks, shares and loans. Personal estate may be considered as synonymous with a personal chattel if the context so admits, i.e. it may include a leasehold interest. If a person devises his "personal estate and property", "personal property, estate or effects" or "personal estate and property whatsoever and wheresoever" it may be taken that he intends to pass all personal property, but not any real estate – Buchanan v Harrison (1861) 31 LJ Ch 74. A mortgagee's claim may be classified as personal estate; at least until such time as he exercises a right of foreclosure and thereby acquires the mortgagor's estate. See also **bequest, chattel, estate, moveables**.

personal liability

The liability of an individual for a debt or obligation either apart from, or in addition to, security given for that debt. If necessary, a personal liability may necessitate the realisation of a person's entire assets to satisfy the debt. See also **limited (liability) company, recourse**.

personal liability insurance

see **accident insurance**.

personal property (or personalty)

Property that is not classified as **real property**, i.e. any form of property that is not land or an interest in land. Personal property includes goods, chattels, debts, shares, etc. (sometimes called 'pure personalty' or 'chattels personal'); as well as leasehold interests (sometimes called 'chattels real'). Personal property, or 'personalty', may be corporeal, i.e. tangible and moveable – furniture, clothing, etc; or incorporeal, i.e. intangible – debts, goodwill, patents, etc. It may be divided into 'choses-in-possession' – property that can be recovered by physical possession; and 'choses-in-action' – property that can be recovered only by an action at law. Unlike real property, personal property can be the subject of absolute ownership; title to pure personalty is transferred by a **bill of sale**; and the period of limitation on a right of action to recover personal property, under the Statutes of Limitation, differs from those for real property.

A **leasehold interest** is referred to as personal property because historically it is enforceable as a right between the parties to the lease and not as an action to recover land (although the hiring of land is treated as a branch of real property law and the hiring of pure personalty as a branch of **bailment**, contract or tort). 35 Halsbury's Laws of England, 4 edn, paras. 1101–1200.

personal representative
Any legally appointed representative. A person appointed to administer the affairs of another, especially to deal with the estate of a deceased person, either in accordance with the terms of a will (as an **executor**) or in accordance with the rules on intestacy (as an **administrator**). "'Personal representative' means the executor, original or by representation, or administrator for the time being of a deceased person ..."(Administration of Estates Act 1925, s. 55 (1) – Law of Property Act 1925, s. 205 (xviii)). The estate of a deceased person devolves on to the personal representative until it is wound up. Called also a 'legal representative'.
17 Halsbury's Laws of England, 4 edn, para. 704 *et seq.*

personal residence
An individual's **home** or place of **abode**. See also **homestead, principal private residence, residence**.

personal servitude
A **servitude** 'in gross', i.e. one belonging only to the beneficiary and not **appurtenant** to any land.
cf. **real servitude**. See also **profit à prendre**.

personalty
see **personal property**.

physical deterioration
Deterioration of property due to decay of the materials of which it is made. See also **obsolescence**.

physical life
The period for which a building may be used before **physical deterioration** or **obsolesence** end its viable existence.
cf. **economic life**.

physical value
The value of a building as determined by assessing its reproduction or **replacement cost**, after allowing for depreciation. See also **inherent value**.

piccage or pickage
A toll or levy imposed for the privilege of breaking ground to install a booth or stall at a market or fair. See also **pennage, stallage**.

pick of land
A narrow parcel of land that runs into a corner.

picle
From the Latin *piccolo*, 'small'; a small **close** or enclosure.

piecemeal development
The development of an area in a gradual, sporadic or *laissez-faire* manner. Development carried out in an area where there is no overall planning or development control.
cf. **comprehensive development**. See also **ribbon development**.

pied-à-terre
A small home or flat, especially when used as a place of short-term resort. Commonly refers to a second place of residence, such as an apartment maintained in a city by a country dweller. See also **apartment**.

piggyback loan (US)
A loan made by two lenders as one party to a mortgage agreement. Normally one lender has priority over the other; although, unlike a standard first and second mortgage arrangement, the 'piggyback' lenders join in a

single mortgage agreement. See also **joint mortgage**.

pignus

In the civil law, a pledge or security for a debt. Under a pignus there is delivery of possession to the pledgee unlike **hypothecation** where the pledgor retains possession of the property pledged.

pink properties

see **clearance area**.

pin-money

An allowance made to a wife, by her husband, for her personal expenses (originally money for such costs as dressmaking, etc.). In particular, a provision made in a **strict settlement** to the same effect.

pipe, drainage

see **drain, sewer**.

pipeline

A conduit, usually underground, for the transportation of oil, gas or water. Generally, a means of conveying a liquid substance from a store to a place of consumption; unlike a **drain** which conveys waste materials away to a point of disposal. A pipeline is defined by the Pipe-lines Act 1962, s. 65 (1) as a pipe or system of pipes for the conveyance of anything other than air, water, water vapour or steam and that definition specifically excludes a drain or sewer and most pipes within a building. See also **culvert, easement, wayleave**.

Agricultural Valuations: A Practical Guide by R.G. Williams, pp. 73–80, (1985).

The Valuation of Pipe-Line Easements and Wayleaves, by R. and P.M. Poole, (1962).

Pipes, Mains, Cables and Sewers, by

H. Wilkinson, 4 edn.
38 Halsbury's Laws of England, 4edn, paras. 1043–1102.

piscary

1. A right to take fish, for personal consumption, from waters belonging to another; either as a personal **profit à prendre** or, more especially, as a **right of common**. See also **right to fish**.

2. A fishing ground.

piti payment (US)

A payment under a loan agreement which includes 'principal', 'interest', 'taxes', and 'insurance'. See also **budget mortgage**.

place of abode

see **abode**.

placement

1. The granting of a loan or mortgage. The making of an investment. See also **financing, funding**.

2. The offering of new shares in a company to a number of selected investors rather than to the public at large.

placement (F)

investment.

(*placement de père de famille* – safe or blue chip investment).

plafond légal de densité (*PLD*) (F)

A limit on the right to build above a given density without payment of a local tax (*versement pour dépassement du plafond légal de densité*). A limit that corresponds to a *coefficient d'occupation du sol* of 1, or 1.5 in major cities, is imposed as the permitted limit. Above that limit a person seeking to carry out development must pay a tax which is intended to contribute towards the cost of financing local services and the provision of open spaces. (French Law of 31st December 1975; Code de L'Urbanisme, arts. L. 112–1 to 112–7 & R. 112–1 to 112–2).

Petits Codes Dalloz, Code de L'Urbanisme.

Manuel de Droit Administratif, by André de Laubadère, 12 edn, p. 403.

plan

1. A large scale **map** of a small area. A means of indicating the boundaries of a parcel of land in a horizontal plan, especially to show the extent of an area of land that is the subject of a transfer.

A plan merely annexed to a document has little significance and a plan expressed to be "for identification only" will not prevail over a written description. But if land is expressed to be "more particularly described" or "delineated" on an attached plan, then that plan prevails over the written description in a conveyance – Eastwood *v* Ashton [1915] AC 900. A plan made to too small a scale, or for another purpose other than the conveyance in question, normally will be ignored by the courts. Hence a plan to a scale of 1:2500 is "worse than useless" for the purpose of defining the boundary between a divided parcel of land – Scarfe *v* Adams [1981] 1 All ER 843; as is a plan to no scale at all. Thus a plan should be intended to form or substantiate a **description** in a deed only when it has been professionally prepared and in no way is at odds with the description; otherwise it will be otiose or misleading. A purchaser cannot insist on a vendor going to the expense of preparing a plan unless it is necessary – Re Sharman's Contract [1936] Ch. 759; but in many cases a well prepared plan is not only beneficial, it is essential. See also **filed plan, parcels**.

Conveyancing: The Use of Plans by Sandi Murdoch, 258 EG 927 (1981).

Odger's Construction of Deeds and Statutes, 5 edn, pp. 180–183.

2. A line drawing, diagram or sketch of a building, or a proposed building, taken as a horizontal section and shown on a flat surface. The term 'plans' commonly refers to a set of drawings of a new or proposed building, especially those that form part of a building contract.

cf. **elevation**. See also **specification**.

3. An overall scheme or layout for the future development of an area. A proposed means of achieving a development objective as set out in a written report, incorporating maps and diagrams. See also **development plan, local plan, planning, structure plan**.

plan (F)

plan; drawing; scheme; map; diagram; project; design.

(*plan cadastral* – **cadastral plan**; cadastral survey)

(*plan d'aménagement* – **development plan**)

(*plan d'amortissement* – redemption table)

(*plan de financement* – financing plan)

(*plan de situation* – site plan)

(*plan directeur d'urbanisme* – **master plan**).

plan d'alignement (F)

highway alignment plan. A plan that shows a proposed major realignment of the highways in a city; it represents in effect a number of *lignes d'alignement* (building lines) in front of which no new building work may be carried out.

Plan d'Aménagement Rural (PAR) (F)
Rural Development Plan. A plan prepared to control the land use in a rural area that is likely to be affected by significant future urban development which is planned for the neighbouring or surrounding area.

Plan d'Aménagement de Zone (PAZ) (F)
Development plan prepared for a *zone d'aménagement concerté* (ZAC) that does not have a prescribed *Plan d'Occupation des Sols*, setting out general land use and development restrictions (*Code de l'Urbanisme, arts. R. 123–23*).

Plan d'Occupation des Sols (POS) (F)
land use or density plans. Plans that set out detailed rules and planning restrictions for urban areas. Such plans vary in content but essentially fix traffic circulation routes; limits for future development; areas required for open space or green areas; density limits (*coefficient d'occupation du sol*); building regulations (type, size, external appearance etc.); and any similar restriction on the use or development of land, as considered appropriate. A POS must be submitted for public comment and inquiry before it can be brought into effect. (*Code de l'Urbanisme, art. L. 123–1 et seq.*). See also *plan d'urbanisme, schéma directeur d'aménagement et d'urbanisme*.
Précis Dalloz. Droit Civil, Les Biens, 2 edn, pp. 161–163.

plan de sauvegarde (F)
a conservation plan. A plan prepared to limit demolition and provide for the improvement of an area of special historic or architectural interest.

plan d'urbanisme (F)
urban development plan. In French urban planning since 1967 development plans comprise *schéma directeur d'aménagement et d'urbanisme* (SDAU), which is a broad based plan and report that resembles a **structure plan** as prepared under English planning law; and a *plan d'occupation des sols* (POS), which sets out planning constraints for a smaller area in greater detail and resembles a **local plan** as prepared in English planning law (*Loi d'Orientation Foncière*, 30 December 1967; *Code de l'Urbanisme, art. L. 124–1 et seq.*).
Urban Development in France and Germany, CALUS, pp. 18–25 (1974).
Précis Dalloz. Droit Civil, Les Biens, (Alex Weill), 2 edn, p. 161 *et seq*.
Planning in Western Europe, France – by J. Lemasurier. Edited by J.F. Garner, pp. 117–154 (1975).

plane surveying
Surveying in order to define an area on the earth's surface, disregarding the curvature of the earth.
cf. **geodetic surveying**.

planification urbaine (F)
town planning.

planned development project (US)
see **planned unit development**.

planned unit development (PUD) (US)
A development, for the most part of residential properties, which is planned so as to provide an above average density by establishing building clusters and shared areas of open space. Usually the development is carried out by a single developer and the properties sold to individuals or 'unit holders'. The unit holders are also shareholders in a corporation, which holds title to the common areas. The

owners are free to use the interior of the properties as they wish, but accept mutual restrictions on the use and management of the common areas and constraints on the maintenance and appearance of the exterior. Called also a 'planned development project'. See also **scheme of development**.

Real Estate Law, by Robert Kratovil and Raymond J. Werner, 8 edn., pp. 535–542.

planning
1. The preparation of a plan, diagram or scheme. The organisation of details for the design and implementation of a development or building project.
2. A system, normally backed by the force of law, for the control and regulation of the use and development of land; more commonly referred to as **town and country planning**, land use planning or, when appropriate, 'city planning'. See also **amenity**, **Town and Country Planning Acts**, **zoning**.
3. The process by which a government authority controls and directly intervenes in the normal economic forces rather than relying on a free market mechanism; normally referred to as 'economic planning'. A process whereby the State co-ordinates and channels the actions of individuals in the interest of the common good. See also **police power**.

Planning Acts
see **Town and Country Planning Acts**.

planning advantage
see **planning gain**.

planning agreement
An agreement between a local planning authority and any person inter-

ested in carrying out **development** of land by which the authority secures commitments as to the form of the intended development, "for the purpose of restricting or regulating the development or use of land either permanently or during such period as may be prescribed by the agreement" (Town and Country Planning Act 1971, s. 52). A planning agreement is made prior to, and as a condition of, the grant of **planning permission** and represents a bargain by which conditions that would otherwise be attached to the permission are avoided; a means by which a landowner voluntarily subjects his land to restrictions in order to secure the type of scheme that he prefers. The power of a local planning authority to enter into such an agreement is given by the Town and Country Planning Act 1972, s. 52 (thus it is sometimes referred to as a 'section 52 agreement'). Similar powers are contained in the Local Government Act 1972, s. 111 and the Housing Act 1974, s. 126. A planning agreement is frequently entered into when the planning authority is seeking a **planning gain**, such as a benefit for the local community provided by the landowner; or when the authority wishes to impose a **planning condition** that otherwise it might not be able to enforce, either because it does not relate to the permitted development or it is not a matter for normal planning control.

A planning agreement may be enforced in much the same way as a **restrictive covenant**, "as if the local planning authority were possessed of adjacent land and as if the agreement had been expressed to be made for the benefit of such land" (1971 Act, s. 52 (2)). Thus it is enforceable against any person who derives title to the land from the party who originally entered into the agreement. In practice a planning agreement is made normally by deed and it is registrable as a planning charge in the **Local Land Charges Register**.

In the US a similar form of agreement between a planning authority and a private developer is referred to as a 'contract zoning'. See also **betterment**.

Planning Agreements in Practice, by J.N. Hawke, JPL 5, 86 [1981].

planning appeal

An application to the Secretary of State for the Environment made, in accordance with the Town and Country Planning Act 1971, s. 36, by a party who (a) has been refused **planning permission** to carry out development; (b) has been granted planning permission subject to certain conditions; (c) has been refused consent to matters reserved by an outline planning permission; (d) is aggrieved by a decision reached following an application to determine whether an activity is **development** and needs planning permission; or (e) has not received a decision from the local planning authority within the prescribed statutory time limit. The appeal is made against the decision of the local planning authority in order to obtain the Secretary of State's ruling on the original planning application. The procedure is administrative, i.e. is based on facts placed before the Secretary of State and is not concerned with points of law (for which the application would be to a court of law). The Secretary of State may reach his decision after he has considered written statements from both sides, or he may appoint an inspector to hear the appeal at a public hearing (a **planning inquiry**) and then make his decision after he has considered the inspector's report. (In some cases the inspector may be authorised to make the final decision and this is merely vetted by the Secretary of State.)

A person aggrieved by the Secretary of State's decision may appeal, within six weeks of the Secretary's decision, to the High Court on the grounds of a substantial error of law or procedure in the decision reached by the Secretary of State (Town and Country Planning Act 1971, s. 245). See also **called-in application**.

Challenging Conditions, by Antony Bowhill, 258 EG 230–231 and 319–320 (1981).

Practical Planning Law, by J.F. Garner, pp. 143–151 (1981).

Planning Appeals, RICS (1982).

Planning Procedure Tables, by R.N.D. Hamilton, 4 edn., pp. 62–70.

Urban Planning Law, by Malcolm Grant, p. 553 *et seq.* (1982)

Fighting Planning Appeals, by Lewis Keeble (1985).

Planning Appeals and Inquiries, by L.A. Blundel and George Dobry, 3 edn.

planning application

A formal request to a local **planning authority** for **planning permission**. Such a request may be made by any person, but if the applicant is not the owner of the subject land (a freeholder or holder of a lease with not less than seven years unexpired), the owner must be informed (or reasonable steps taken to inform him) of the application. In addition, if the land constitutes or forms part of an agricultural holding, any agricultural tenant must be informed of the application.

A planning application must be submitted on the forms issued by the local planning authority for the purpose; be accompanied by suitable plans and such other information as the authority may reasonably require; be accompanied by the requisite **planning fee**; be accompanied by an appropriate certificate that the applicant is the owner of the land or that the owner and, if applicable, any agricultural tenant has been informed of the application; and, in certain cases, be accompanied by a certificate confirming that application has been publicised (by a proper notice posted on the site) (Town and Country Planning Act 1971, s. 26, 27; Town and Country Planning General Development Orders 1977–81). A planning application must be acknowledged by the planning authority and, unless there is an agreement to the contrary, determined within eight weeks.

When dealing with the application the authority shall have regard to the provisions of any **development plan** in force, and to any "other material considerations"; including any representation relating to the application (Town and Country Planning Act 1971, s. 29). What constitutes "other material considerations" depends on the circumstances; they cover a wide field and may include "the effect of a proposal on road safety or the beauty of the surroundings, the effect on public services such as drainage and water supply, conflict with public proposals for the same land . . . and many other factors. They must be genuine planning considerations i.e. they must be related to the

purpose of the planning legislation, which is to regulate the development and use of the land and not some extraneous purpose". – Secretary of State's Development Control Policy Note No. 1 (1969).

When the planning authority has fully considered the application it may (a) grant permission, either unconditionally or subject to such conditions "as they think fit" or (b) refuse planning permission (1971 Act, s. 29 (1)). The decision must be in writing and if permission is refused or granted subject to conditions reasons must be stated. A register of all applications is kept for public inspection (1971 Act, s. 34). See also **called-in planning application, established use certificate, planning appeal, planning certificate.**

Planning Procedures, by John Stephenson, pp. 114–124 (1982).
Planning Procedure Tables, by R.N.D. Hamilton, 4 edn., pp. 31–47.
Development and Planning Law, by Barry Denyer-Green, pp. 59–78 (1982).
Planning Law and Procedure, by A.E. Telling, 6 edn, pp. 99–105.
Practical Planning Law, by J.F. Garner, pp. 107–114 (1981).
An Outline of Planning Law, by Desmond Heap, 8 edn., p. 116 *et seq.*
Urban Planning Law, by Malcolm Grant, p. 196 *et seq.* (1983).
Encyclopaedia of Planning Law and Practice, by Desmond Heap, paras. 1–077 to 1–083.
46 Halsbury's Laws of England, 4 edn, paras. 155–161.

planning assumptions
The statutory assumptions that may be made when assessing **compulsory purchase compensation** as to the type of planning permission that could be

granted for the development of the area of land in question. These assumptions are set out in the Land Compensation Act 1971, ss. 15–16 and "any planning permission which is to be assessed in accordance with any of the provisions of those sections is in addition to any planning permission which may be in force at the date of the **notice to treat**" (1971 Act, s. 14 (2)). Basically this provision enables the landowner, when the open **market value** of his land is being assessed, to bring into account (in addition to any authorised or **permitted development**; or **eighth schedule development**: 1971 Act, s. 15 (3)) any 'prospect' of obtaining planning permission for (a) such development as accords with the proposals of the acquiring authority; (b) a use or development of a specific description shown on the current development plan; (c) a use that might reasonably be permitted by the planning authority in accordance with proposals shown for an area designated for comprehensive redevelopment or as an action area; (d) development referred to in a **certificate of appropriate alternative development**. However, factors such as the likelihood that planning permission reasonably might be granted for a use shown on the development plan; the availability of sewage facilities; the time at which the permission would be granted; and any **planning condition** that the planning authority would be likely to impose, must be taken fully into account in deciding on these assumptions. In addition, if **compensation for a planning restriction** has been paid subsequently to a refusal of planning permission for a form of 'eighth schedule development', it may not be assumed that that

form of development would be permitted. These assumptions are made to assist a landowner in determining the planning permission that would be granted if no compulsory purchase was proposed, but they do not preclude any other reasonable assumption as to the likely form of planning permission that a prospective purchaser might anticipate (1971 Act, s. 14 (2)). Thus, it may be assumed that planning permission for certain alternative forms of development would be available, but this does not mean that there will be a demand for that development: "It is not planning permission by itself which increases value. It is planning permission coupled with demand." – Viscount Cambrose *v* Basingstoke Corporation [1966] 3 All ER 164. Any *demand* for the land produced solely by the acquiring authority's proposed scheme of development must be ignored. See also **highest and best use, hope value, special suitability**.
Compulsory Purchase and Compensation, by Barry Denyer-Green, 2 edn., pp. 121–131.
Law of Compulsory Purchase and Compensation, by Keith Davies, 4 edn., pp. 156–166.
8 Halsbury's Laws of England, 4 edn, paras. 258–284.
Encyclopaedia of Compulsory Purchase and Compensation, ed. Harold J.J. Brown, para. 1–078 *et seq.*

planning authority
A public body responsible for considering, formulating and implementing local or central government policies and proposals for the use and development of land. The primary responsibilities of a planning authority are to (i) consider a strategy and policy

for the future planning and development of the area under its control; (ii) prepare plans (including **structure plans** and **local plans**) for the future use and development of land in its area, and to consult with the general public and all interested parties on those plans (a process commonly called '**public participation**'); (iii) consider proposals submitted to it for the development or changes in the use of land and buildings or, more specifically, to consider applications for **planning permission**; (iv) control the development of land, including the service of enforcement notices in respect of unauthorised development or discontinuance orders in respect of 'non-conforming uses'; (v) acquire or dispose of land for planning purpose, or for certain development or redevelopment purposes and, generally, to administer **town and country planning** at a national and local level. In England the central planning authority is the **Secretary of State for the Environment** and in Wales the Secretary of State for Wales, who act through the Department of the Environment and the Welsh Office respectively. The Secretary of State is responsible, generally, for the creation of a national planning policy and, specifically, for the approval of such matters as local development plans prepared by a local authority; planning appeals; confirmation (or otherwise) of compulsory purchase orders; grants for local authority development projects; and making various planning regulations.

The local planning authority primarily is the council of the county council or of the district council (metropolitan or non-metropolitan); the council of a London borough; and

the Common Council of the City of London (Local Government Act 1985, s. 3).

New Town Development Corporations and Urban Development Corporations have wide powers in connection with planning and development within their designated areas. A parish council (or in Wales, a community council) is not a local planning authority, but, is entitled to be consulted and make representations on all or specified planning applications and in certain cases to be consulted on general planning matters. See also **development corporation, joint planning committee, local authority, planning commission**.
Local Government Law, Charles Cross (ed.), para. 2–431 (1980, loose leaf).

planning blight
see **blight, blight notice**.

planning certificate
A term that is not used specifically in English planning law, but could be applied to various certificates issued in connection with planning and development, including (i) an **established use certificate**; (ii) a **certificate of appropriate alternative development**; (iii) a certificate obtained from a planning authority under the provisions of the Town and Country Planning Act 1971, s. 53 specifying whether a landowner's proposals constitute **development** and, if so, whether planning permission is required; (iv) a certificate accompanying a **planning application**, as required by the Town and Country Planning Act 1971, s. 27, specifying that the applicant is the owner of the subject land; or has notified the owner(s) (being the freeholder and the owner

of any lease with not less than 7 years unexpired) that the application has been made or, if the owner is not known, has taken appropriate steps to trace the owner by advertising locally or placing a notice on the land. See also **industrial development certificate**.

planning charge
see **local land charge**.

planning commission (US)
A board established by a city, county or other local government body to control the use and development of land. A planning commission is responsible for preparing master plans for consideration by the state legislature; reviewing development and rezoning proposals; initiating comprehensive zoning proposals; and generally advising and administering land planning proposals.

planning condition
A restriction or restraint imposed by a planning authority when it approves an application to carry out development, i.e. a condition that is made a prerequisite to the carrying out of development pursuant to a grant of **planning permission**. The Town and Country Planning Act 1971, s. 29 provides that in determining a planning application a local planning authority "shall have regard to the provisions of the **development plan**, so far as material to the application and to any other **material considerations** ... and may grant permission either unconditionally, or subject to such conditions as they think fit". A local planning authority may impose conditions also "for regulating the development or use of any land under the control of the applicant (whether

or not it is land in respect of which the application was made) or requiring the carrying out of works on any such land, so far as appears to the local planning authority to be expedient for the purposes of or in connection with the development authorised by the permission". (1971 Act, s. 29 (1)). Such conditions, which must be reasonable, may take the form of (a) regulations to control the appearance, layout, design, etc. of the development; (b) restrictions on the time for which a consent is valid – 'permission for a limited period only' – including a requirement that thereafter buildings be removed, a use discontinued or land reinstated; or (c) a stipulation as to the time within which the development must be completed. "Nevertheless the law says that those conditions, to be valid, must fairly and reasonably relate to the permitted development. The planning authority are not at liberty to use their powers for an ulterior object, however desirable that object may seem to them to be in the public interest" – Pyx Granite Co. Ltd *v* Ministry of Housing and Local Government [1958] 2 WLR 371. From the various cases considered in relation to planning conditions, in summary, "four main principles govern the validity of conditions 1. They must serve a valid planning function: i.e. conditions must not be imposed for ulterior purposes no connected with planning. 2. They must fairly and reasonably relate to the permitted development. 3. They must not be totally unreasonable. 4 They must not be so uncertain that they can be given no sensible or ascertainable meaning". (*Cases and Material on Planning Law*, by Michael Purdue, p. 261, 1977). Certain conditions are expressly permitted by statute, e.g. the preservation of trees; control on the use of other land of the applicant; the restoration of a site after a specified period; and, in certain cases, that the permission is personal to the applicant. See also **planning agreement, planning appeal, planning gain.**

Conditions in consents, by Antony Bowhill, 256 EG 993–994, 1085–1089 (1980).

Use of Conditions in Planning Permissions, by Susan Nott and Peter Morgan, 276 EG 536, 539 (1985).

Outline of Planning Law, by Desmond Heap, 8 edn., pp. 143–149.

Planning Law and Procedure, by A.E. Telling, 6 edn., pp. 120–132.

planning consent
see **planning permission.**

planning control
see **enforcement notice,** *permit de construire,* **planning permission, zoning ordinance.**

planning decision
see **planning permission.**

planning enforcement
The means of control exercised by a planning authority over unauthorised development; normally as exercised by the serving of an **enforcement notice.** See also **discontinuance order.**

planning enquiry
see **planning inquiry.**

planning fee
A payment to cover the cost of processing a **planning application.** Such fees may be charged in accordance with regulations made by the Secretary of State (Local Government Planning and Land Act 1980).

planning gain
A benefit secured for the 'community as a whole' at the expense of a recipient of planning permission. A 'planning gain' is extracted from the recipient of planning permission, by the local planning authority, as a *quid pro quo* for the right to carry out a particular form of development, or to change the use of land; especially when such development or change of use would not be readily approved. A planning gain may take any form (a concession, surrender of an existing right, or even expenditure) provided there is a true benefit for the community; it is directly relevant to the development for which planning permission is being sought; and it is "fairly and reasonably related in case and kind" to the proposed development. It should be related to the needs of the new development and not sought "as an opportunity to obtain some extraneous benefit or advantage or as an opportunity to extract a payment for the benefit of the rate-payers at large" – Town and Country Planning Act 1971 – Planning Gain: Circular 22/83. 'Planning gain' is a means by which the local authority endeavours to recoup, for the public in general, some of the **betterment** that is presumed to accrue to a landowner when he is granted planning permission.

The gain is secured either by the imposition of a **planning condition** or by means of a **planning agreement.** For example, consent may be given for an office development, provided the developer agrees to incorporate shops and residential units which he might not have intended to provide; or he agrees to a grant of land to the planning authority for road widening, public car parking or recreational

purposes. A planning authority may not refuse planning permission on the grounds that the applicant will not provide a 'gain' by carrying out development that the authority is statutorily responsible for providing, e.g. supplying houses for persons on the authority's housing waiting list – R v Hillingdon LBC *ex parte* Royco Homes Ltd [1974] 2 All ER 643. Called also 'planning advantage'. In the US a similar arrangement is referred to as 'incentive zoning'.
Planning Gain – an overview, by John Ratcliffe, 258 EG 407–413 (1981).

planning inquiry

1. In Britain, a quasi-judicial hearing of a case for the grant or refusal of **planning permission** held by an inspector appointed by the Secretary of State for the Environment, following an appeal against a local planning authority's decision on a planning application.

In France a similar public hearing may be held before an inspector (*commissaire-enquêteur*) to consider proposals for the development of an area, but there is no right of appeal combined with a public inquiry following a refusal of a *permit de construire* (building permit). See also **planning appeal**.
Development and Planning Law, by Barry Denyer-Green, pp. 171–177 (1982).

2. A search or inquiry made to obtain details of planning consents, and conditions attached thereto, which relate to a particular parcel of land. The Town and Country Planning Act 1971, s. 34 requires a local planning authority to maintain at its offices a register of all planning applications, and decisions and to make the register available for public inspection. See also **enquiries**.
Guide to Development and Planning by R.N.D. Hamilton, 7 edn., Ch. 20 (Investigation of Planning Title).

planning permission

The written legal consent given by a **planning authority** (whether a local planning authority or the Secretary of State for the Environment) to a proposal for the **development** (or a **material change in the use**) of land (R. v Yeovil Borough Council, *ex parte* Trustees of Elim Pentecostal Church (1972) 23 P. & C.R. 39). Planning permission is required for any activity that is included within the statutory definition of 'development', excluding (a) **permitted development**; (b) a change of use that is not material; (c) certain changes of use that relate to the user in 1948; and (d) the resumption of a prior use of land upon expiration of a temporary planning permission (Town and Country Planning Act 1971, ss. 22–24). Consent may be given as 'detailed' or full planning permission, or in 'outline'. Detailed planning permission approves all matters relating to the development and no further consent is required, although the permission may be granted subject to a **planning condition** (and every detailed planning permission must impose a condition that development is to be commenced within 5 years, or such other period as the authority considers appropriate: Town and Country Planning Act 1971, s. 41). Outline planning permission is granted, "with the reservation for subsequent approval by the local planning authority or the Secretary of State of matters (referred to ... as 'reserved matters') not particularised in the application" (Town and Country Planning Act 1971, s. 42 (1)). Usually 'outline' planning permission is sought so that a landowner may have an indication of the category of development that will be permitted and of basic aspects that are relevant to that development, such as the plot ratio or density. Details of the final form of the development – siting, design, external appearance, construction materials, drainage, etc. – may be approved in one or more subsequent applications to the authority (no limit is placed on the number of such applications that may be made, once outline consent has been obtained and as long as it remains in force: Heron Corporation Ltd *v* Manchester City Council [1978] EGD 953. However, the proposed development should not be varied radically from that approved in outline).

Whether a particular 'development' requires planning permission may be determined by an application to the local planning authority for a ruling under the Town and Country Planning Act 1971, s. 53. If consent is required, such an application is treated as an application for planning permission. See also **completion notice, enforcement notice, general development order, planning agreement, planning appeal, planning certificate, revocation order.**

Business Property Handbook, The Boisot Waters Cohen Partnership, pp. 381–413 (1981).

Land Law: Cases and Materials, by R.H. Maudsley and E.H. Burn, 4 edn., pp. 793–811.

The Need for Planning Permission, R.I.C.S., 2 edn.

Practical Planning Law, by J.F. Garner, pp. 115–133 (1981).

Planning Law and Procedure, by A.E. Telling, 6 edn., pp. 90–134.

Notes on the Need for Planning Permission, by C.M. Brand and D.W. Williams, 3 edn.

An Outline of Planning Law, by Desmond Heap, 8 edn., pp. 103–163.

Cases and Materials on Planning Law, by Michael Purdue, pp. 127–189 (1977).

Urban Planning Law, by Malcolm Grant, pp. 263–271 (1982).

Encyclopaedia of Planning Law and Practice, by Desmond Heap, para. 1–074 *et seq.*

46 Halsbury's Laws of England, 4 edn, paras. 93–154.

planning purpose

A term used in the Town and Country Planning Acts to signify one reason that may be used by a local authority to justify the **compulsory purchase** of land. A term that is not defined precisely, but includes the acquisition of land for such purposes as comprehensive redevelopment; the proper planning of an area; the relocation of population or industry; improvement of environmental facilities, etc.

Law of Compulsory Purchase and Compensation, by Keith Davies, 4 edn., pp. 225–240.

planning register

see **planning inquiry.**

planning restrictions compensation for, see **compensation for planning restrictions.**

planning title

see **planning inquiry.**

planning unit

A physical area of a building, or a piece of land, that is to be considered as a single unit when determining whether there has been a **material change in the use** of a property and, therefore, a breach of planning control. In English planning law, when seeking to establish whether a property has undergone a material change of use, it is necessary to look at an area used for a particular purpose as a whole: to consider the entire 'planning unit'. The planning authority should exclude from its deliberations any area used for a different or unrelated purpose, but must include as part of the planning unit those areas whose user is ancilliary or incidental to the primary purpose. "It is essential to look at the unit as a whole, that is to say, the whole area on which a particular activity is carried on: and see what is the primary purpose for which the whole area is used. It is the primary purpose which determines the character of the user and not the ancilliary uses." – Brazil (Concrete) Ltd v Amersham RDC (1967) 18 P and CR 399. The essential criterion in deciding whether the planning unit has materially changed its use is whether there has been a significant change in the use of the entirety – a change in the total character of the property and not merely a change in one section of the unit.

When considering the parameters of a planning unit, a building or an area of land may be categorised in one of three ways: (i) a property where it is possible to recognise a single main user, to which all other uses are incidental or ancilliary – as in a factory with administration offices and a canteen; (ii) a property where there are a number of uses, but it is not possible to say that one use is incidental or ancilliary to another nor that one use

is contained in a separated or unrelated area – as in an hotel or a department store, with a restaurant and storage areas; and (iii) a property where there is a number of distinct and unrelated uses, confined to separate and distinct areas – as with a lock-up shop with a dwelling over and a workshop at the rear (even though they are all part of the same unit of occupation). In the first two instances the entire area represents a distinct planning unit. In the third instance, because each area is used for a different main purpose (together with its incidental and ancilliary activities), they are considered as separate planning units – Burdle v Secretary of State for the Environment [1972] 1 WLR 207. As a rule, a building that forms the subject of a single planning permission is one planning unit. In addition, an entirely new building normally constitutes "an entirely new planning unit" – Petticoat Lane Rentals Ltd v Secretary of State [1971] 1 WLR 1112.

A dwelling-house may constitute a planning unit and would remain as one unit even if one room is used as a professional office; "it can rarely if ever be right to dissect a single dwelling-house and to regard one room in isolation as being an appropriate planning unit ..." – Wood v Secretary of State for the Environment [1973] 2 All ER 404. However if the upper floor is converted into flats and the ground floor into offices (following a grant of planning permission) then two (or more) planning units come into existence and must be treated as such when considering whether any further material change of use has taken place, and, therefore whether planning permission is re

quired for that change.
Land Use – The Planning Unit, by
Antony Bowhill, 255 EG 141–145
(1980).
Planning Law and Procedure, by
A.E. Telling, 6 edn., pp. 84–86.

plantation (F)
planting (of trees etc.); erection (of a
structure etc.). The proximity of a
tree to the boundary of a neighbour's
land is strictly controlled in French
law so as to limit encroachments by
roots and branches (French Civil
Code, arts. 671–672). See also **encroachment**.
Droit Civil, Les Biens, by Jean Carbonnier, 11 edn., pp. 227–228.
Précis Dalloz. Droit Civil, Les Biens
(Alex Weill), 2 edn, pp. 103–105.

plat or plat map (US)
A plan or map of an identified area or
district, usually based on an official
government survey, showing the location and detailing boundaries of individual plots or parcels of land. Plat
maps are prepared for most urban
areas and are usually the means of
indicating the legal boundaries of
land, especially the legal boundaries
of land, especially when a large area
of land is sold off in lots. Individual
plots are identified usually by reference to a **lot and block system**, e.g.
Lot 6, Block 2. A plat map may be
prepared by a local tax assessor's
office to show the boundaries of land
ownership for taxation purposes: a
'tax plat'. It may be prepared for identification purposes following a detailed survey of an area: a 'plat of
survey' or 'identification plat'; or prepared to show an area of land that is
to be subject to a subdivision: a 'plat
of subdivision'.
cf. **plot plan**.

pledge
A transaction by which goods, or
documents of title to goods, are transferred to a creditor as security for a
debt or obligation owed to him. On
the grant of a pledge, ownership
remains with the borrower (pledgor),
but in the event of default the property may be sold by the lender (pledgee). "The contract of pledge is a
bailment or delivery of goods and
chattels by one man to another, to be
held as a security for the payment of a
debt or performance of an engagement, and upon the express or
implied understanding that the thing
deposited is to be restored to the
owner, as soon as the debt is discharged, or the engagement has been
fulfilled. The thing deposited as security is called a **pawn** or pledge; the
party making the deposit, the pawnor
or pledgor, and the person who
receives it in his possession, the pawnee or pledgee. The contract is to be
distinguished from the contract of
hypothecation, by the transfer of the
possession or the actual tradition or
delivery of the thing intended to be
charged, to the creditor, and from the
contract of **mortgage**, by the absence
of a transfer of the ownership or right
of property thereof to the pawnee
during the continuance of the trust." –
Addison on Contracts (1856) pp. 317–
318. A pledge arises from the agreement of the parties; unlike a **lien**
which arises by operation of law as a
means of coercing one party into
meeting an obligation; but, as with a
legal lien, a pledge grants possession.
An essential element of a pledge is
that there must be delivery, actual or
constructive, of possession of the
property to the pledgee, together with
a right for the pledgee to assign the

property, as necessary, to satisfy the debt. However, as with a mortgage, payment of the debt entitles the pledgor to redeem the property before it is capable of being assigned by the pledgee. The deposit of title deeds to land, creates an **equitable mortgage** or an **equitable charge** and not a pledge – the subject-matter being a right to real property.
cf. **warranty**. See also **promise, security**.
Chitty on Contracts, 25 edn, paras. 2424–2442.
Crossley Vaines' *Personal Property*, 5 edn., pp. 459–462.
36 Halsbury's Laws of England, 4 edn, paras. 101–200.

pledgee
One who obtains a **pledge**.

pledgor
One who makes or gives a **pledge**.

pleine propriété (F)
see *propriété*.

plot, of land
A small area or parcel of land; especially an area demarcated for a particular use or purpose. A parcel of land delineated for a particular purpose on a plan, normally representing land held in single ownership; especially one of a number of similar parcels each of which is intended for separate development. In the US, generally called a 'lot', the word plot being synonymous with **plat** (from which the word plot is derived).

plot plan
A plan showing the subdivision of an area of land into separate plots or lots. Normally the plan also shows estate roads, parking areas, areas of landscaping, areas for building and such other details as services or utilities. A plot plan is prepared usually prior to **parcelling**. See also **plat map**.

plot ratio
The relationship between the total **gross external floor area** of a building and the **site area** of the land (excluding the surrounding roads, if any) on which that building stands. In the US, called the 'floor area ratio' or 'floor lot ratio'. A plot ratio is defined in order to restrict the volume and thereby the height of buildings that can be placed on land.
cf. **floor space index**. See also **density, site coverage**.

plottage (US)
1. The consolidation of two or more adjoining plots of land into one larger plot to be held in the same ownership or control; especially with the intention of increasing the usefulness or value of the whole. Called also assemblage'.
cf. **parcelling**. See also **plottage value**.
2. The area of a **plot of land**.

plottage value (or increment) (US)
The increase in value resulting from **plottage**, i.e. from the bringing of two or more areas of land into the same ownership. Called also 'assemblage value'. See also **marriage value**.

ploughbote
see **estovers**.

plus-value (F)
capital gain; betterment; appreciation; increase in value.

Pointe Gourde rule
see **compulsory purchase compensation**.

point
1. The smallest unit by which a variation in a price is measured – a point

may be one unit of value, e.g. £1 or $1; 1/32nd of a unit; 1/100th of a unit; or even 1/10,000th of a unit, e.g. the exchange rate of a currency may change by 25 points from 1.7600 to 1.7625. See also **basis point**.
2. A unit of measurement used to indicate variations in a price or stock, especially one unit of measurement that is related to a base or index number. An increase of an index from 105 to 110 is 5 points, and a fall from 50 to 45 is also 5 points (but a true fall of 10 per cent); hence a point is called sometimes an 'absolute percentage'.
3. In financing, one percent of the amount of a loan. In particular a 'point' refers to a **discount point** added on the principal, rather than to the interest rate, the latter being referred to as a 'percentage point'. The addition of one point to a loan adds approximately 1/8 per cent to the interest rate. See also **effective interest rate, origination fee**.

police (F)
policy. police.
(*police d'assurance* – insurance policy).

police power (US)
The power of promoting the interests of society as a whole by limiting the freedom of an individual to act or use his property at will; in particular the power available to a sovereign authority to legislate so as to impair the use or value of private property for the benefit of the public at large. A power that may be exercised, without compensation, provided it is intended for the public good and is not aimed specifically at one parcel of land. The right of a government (especially one of the states of the United States) to restrict, regulate and control the indi-

vidual's free use of land by law and precept – as by taxation, public health and building regulations, zoning ordinances, and pollution or environmental controls.
"'Police power' is a right that arises from the judiciary rather than from the constitution; it is based on the maxim *sic utere tuo et alienum non laedas*, 'so use your own property as not to injure another's; and has developed into the power of the state to limit the unhindered use of land – "the power of government inherent in every sovereignty ... to govern men and things within the limits of its dominion" (*Licence Cases*, 5 Howard 583, 1847). Police power may be distinguished from **eminent domain**, for the latter involves "the 'taking' of property because of its need for public use while the former involves the regulation of such property to prevent the use thereof in a manner that is detrimental to the public interest. The police power may be loosely described as the power of the sovereign to prevent persons under its jurisdiction from conducting themselves or using their property to the detriment of the general welfare" (Nichols on *Eminent Domain,* 3 edn. Vol. I sec. 1. 42). See also **building controls, bundle of rights theory, ordinance**.

policy of insurance
see **insurance policy**.

poll, deed
See **deed poll**.

pond
see **land, water rights**.

pooled fund
An arrangement whereby a number of investors place funds collectively into a common form of investment; a

vehicle for investment used frequently when a number of investors combine their resources to acquire a larger investment than could be acquired by any one investor. See also **blind-pool offering, investment company**.

population density

The ratio that expresses the relationship between a unit of land area (acre, square metre) and the average number of people occupying that area. Population density may be considered a function of accommodation or **residential density**, i.e. the number of residential units on a given area of land, and **occupancy rate**, i.e. the number of persons per residential unit of accommodation. See also **density**.

portefeuille (F)

portfolio; negotiable instrument.

porteur (F)

holder; bearer.
(*porteur d'action* – shareholder)
(*porteur de créance hypothécaire* – mortgagee)
(*titre au porteur* – **negotiable instrument**).

portfolio

1. Derived from *porto-folio* or the Italian *portofaglio*, papers carried together or, in commerce, securities held together. All the investments or securities held by a person or body.
2. Investments held indirectly, e.g. through a **mutual fund, investment trust** or **unit trust**, rather than directly.

portfolio investment

Investment in the shares of a company or a range of investments, as distinguished from a direct investment made by the purchase of assets or real property. The investment of funds into a number of diversified areas or diversified properties.

portfolio management

The overall management, control and supervision of a number of investments (a **portfolio**) with the aim of maximising the **return** and minimising the **risk**. Portfolio management involves a continuous and active process of review to determine areas where action can be taken to improve the return and reduce the risk, both on the individual investments and on the entire portfolio. Portfolio management is carried out within given risk-return parameters; in particular, within the objective criteria of the investor in terms of liquidity, finance, diversification, preferences for income or capital growth, etc. The art of portfolio management is to optimise the return on the entire group of investments while acknowledging the level of risk that is acceptable to the investor. Portfolio management of real estate includes such matters as supervision of **property management**; analysing the composition of the portfolio (the **portfolio mix**); examining the performance of individual investments relative to one another as well as to objective targets and to alternative forms of investment; and reviewing the entire portfolio relative to targets or to other investments.

A Guide to Institutional Property Investment, by Angus P.J. McIntosh and Stephen G. Sykes, p. 221 *et seq* (1985).

Real Estate Portfolio Analysis, by Chapman M. Findlay III, Stephen D. Messn and Rocky A. Tarantello (1983).

portfolio mix

The composition of an investor's **portfolio** of investments. A portfolio mix may be expressed, for example, as the percentage invested in different geographical areas; different sectors, (bonds, equity shares, property, cash); different dates of maturity; different degrees of liquidity; or different sizes of investment.

portier (F)

porter; **janitor**.

portion

A part or share of an estate received by will or inheritance; in particular, a share left under a **strict settlement** for children upon their attaining majority, or, for a female, if she marries before that age. See also **dower**, **endowment**.

positive covenant

A **covenant** that requires rather than limits an action; i.e. a covenant that requires some positive action in order that it may be complied with. A positive covenant does not need to be worded in a positive fashion, provided the intention is to call for an action e.g. "not to allow the boundary hedge of Whitelands to become overgrown" is a positive covenant requiring the hedge to be cut. At common law, a positive covenant affecting land is considered to be a personal commitment and, therefore, strictly only the benefit and not the burden is enforceable upon the disposition of a freehold interest in the land to which the covenant relates. A positive covenant does not 'run' with the covenantor's land, so that a purchaser or successor in title to the land, against which the covenant is imposed, may (provided the covenant 'touches or concerns' the land) take such advantage as the covenant offers, but he is not obliged to accept the imposition required of the covenant – The Prior's Case (1369) YB 42 Ed. III, Pl. 14; Smith and Snipes Hall Farm Ltd, *v* River Douglas Catchment Board [1949] 2 All ER 179. However, this rule may be circumvented in a number of instances; in particular (a) by requiring an indemnity from a subsequent purchaser prior to the disposition of the land so that a contractual chain is established between the original covenantor and subsequent purchasers of the land – a chain that remains effective so long as it is not broken either by the death or disappearance of the original covenantor or a new purchaser failing to continue to accept the chain of covenants; (b) a provision in the Law of Property Act 1925, s. 153 and the Leasehold Reform Act 1967, s. 8 which stipulates that such covenants may be enforceable upon **enfranchisement** i.e. conversion of a long leasehold to a freehold; (c) the doctrine of 'mutual benefit and burden' applied to a **scheme of development** (i.e. a person who accepts and continues to enjoy the benefit of a covenant should endure the burden associated therewith – Halsall *v* Brizell [1957] Ch. 169. (d) when there is a **right of re-entry** in the event of a violation of a positive covenant; or (e) statutory provisions which enable a local planning authority to enforce such covenants when they arise in a **planning agreement**.

A positive covenant in a lease is enforceable between any person who takes an estate in the land (whether by acquiring the reversion or an assignment of the tenant's interest) provided the covenant affects the subject-matter of the lease, i.e. it 'touches and concerns' the land demised, and there is **privity of estate** between the parties taking action on the covenant.

cf. **negative covenant, restrictive covenant.**

Cheshire's Modern Law of Property, 13 edn, pp. 572–576.

Real Property and Real People, by K.J. Gray and P.D. Symes, pp. 612–613 (1981).

positive easement
see **easement.**

positive leasehold (US)
A **leasehold interest** that has a marketable value, i.e. one where the rent payable under the lease is less than the current market rental value; a leasehold interest from which a **profit rent** may be obtained by the tenant. See also **leasehold value.**

positive leverage (US)
see **leverage.**

possession
The physical detention and control of property, together with the continuous and expressed intention to retain that property to the exclusion of other persons. Possession may be held irrespective of ownership or title; it consists primarily of "actual **occupancy** as distinct from **ownership**" (*The Shorter Oxford English Dictionary*). In English law it may be physical possession, protected by **right**; or a right in itself – a right to exclude others. "There are, therefore, [in law] three requisites of possession. First, there must be actual or potential physical control. Secondly, physical control is not possession, unless accompanied by intention; hence, if a thing is put into the hand of a sleeping person, he has not possession of it. Thirdly, the possibility and intention must be visible or evidenced by external signs, for if the thing shows no sign of being under the control of anyone, it is not possessed; hence if a piece of land is deserted and left without fences or other signs of occupation, it is not in the possession of anyone, and the possession is said to be **vacant.**" (*Jowitt's Dictionary of English Law*, 2 edn., vol. 2. p. 1386).

English law does not contain an exhaustive definition of possession as it depends on the circumstances and the object, or right, that is said to be in someone's possession. Roman law draws a useful distinction between *corpus* and *animus.* One acquires possession by an act of the mind and an act of the body – *corpore* et *animo.* *Corpus* indicates the tangible possession of something, the physical control over the entirety, including the right to use, enjoy, detain, and if one wishes (providing there is no opposing or repugnant interest) the right to destroy or change the character of the property. *Animus* is the intention to benefit from possession: that which may be derived as a consequence of possession without destroying or altering the nature of the property; such as is enjoyed by the beneficiary of an easement or by a usufructury. If I lose something I do not have the *corpus*, but would retain the right or intention to possession: the *animus.* On the other hand, if I have something on my property of which I am not aware, because it is hidden, I have the *corpus*, but not the right or *animus* to possess it. In English law, it has been said that "possession is a deceptively simple concept. It denotes a physical control or custody of a thing plus knowledge that you have it. You may possess a thing without knowing or comprehending its nature; but you do not possess it unless you know you have it" – R v Boyesen [1982] 2 All ER 163. This simplification recognises the need for 'detention' as the substance of possession; emphasises the prerequisite of cognizance; but understates the requirement of intention to possess, *animus possidendi*. An **occupier** controls, and knows that he controls, his domain, but recognises that as soon as he parts with actual control, he has lost an important element of occupation – the ability to hold the property; whereas a 'possessor' may give up actual possession without affecting his *animus possidendi*.

'Possession' may be considered in four senses: firstly, physical or 'actual possession'; secondly, possession as attributed to someone by law; thirdly, a right to possession, with the authorisation of another; and fourthly, 'constructive possession', the legal right and intention to possession. In its most common usage possession implies *de facto* or 'actual possession' – "the word *actual* merely emphasises that what is required is physical presence not some entitlement in law." – Williams and Glyn's Bank v Bolland, Williams and Glyn's Bank v Brown [1980] 2 All ER 413. 'Actual' possession is considered to be the most basic form of possession. Possession as attributed to someone by law is that right to retain control which is protected when there is **title**. The adage "possession is nine-tenths of the law" only "places in a stronger light the legal truth that every claimant must succeed by the strength of his own title and not by the weakness of his antagonist" (*Wharton's Law Lexicon*, 14 edn.). Possession with the authorisation of another is that right which arises, for example from a licence or a lease permitting the use of land; it creates a form of title but one that endures only for a certain period of time. Constructive possession is a right to land by a party claiming, or who proposes to claim, a right to **adverse possession**, e.g. by a squatter (although mere **entry** onto land cannot constitute a legal right to possession: Doe d. Baker v Coombes (1850) 9 CB 718).

'Possession' upon purchasing real property does not mean necessarily personal or physical entry into possession but, if a property is tenanted, a right to the rents and profits – Lake v Dean (1860) 54 ER 499. When used in defining the legal estate of a '**fee simple absolute in possession**', possession means the right to the present enjoyment of land, not merely the right to actual possession; as distinguished from a right to a **reversion** or **remainder**: "'possession' includes receipt of rent and profits or the right to receive the same, if any" (Law of Property Act 1925, s. 205 (xix) – Land Registration Act 1925, s. 3 (xviii) and the Settled Land Act 1925, s. 117 (1) (xix)).

In relation to goods, possession may be satisfied by the ability to exercise control: "a person shall be deemed to be in possession of goods or documents of title to goods where the goods or documents are in his actual custody or are held by any other person subject to his control or for him or on his behalf (Factors Act 1980, s. 1 (2)). (In other words a person may have only the corpus or only

the *animus* and still be in possession.)
Goods may be in the physical possession of one party, a finder, but the
person who misplaced them may
have a superior legal right to possession of those goods. See also **bailment, constructive notice, custody,
dominium, eviction, holding, occupation,** *possession, propriété,* **seisin,
taking possession, vacant possession.**
An Introduction to Roman Law, by
Barry Nicholas, pp. 107–115 (1962).
Précis Dalloz. Droit Civil, Les Biens
(Alex Weill), 2 edn, p. 317 *et seq.*
Possession in The Common Law, by
F. Pollock and R.S. Wright (1888).
A History of English Law, by W.S.
Holdsworth, 3 edn., vol. vi, pp.
447–481.
35 Halsbury's Laws of England, 4 edn,
paras. 1111–1126 (possession of
chattels).
39 Halsbury's Laws of England, 4 edn,
para. 487 (possession of land).

possession (F)
possession. In French law possession indicates the legal right to property and the intention to retain that
property, or the physical possession;
"possession is the retention and
enjoyment of a thing or a right which
we hold or we exercise by ourselves,
or by another, who holds that thing or
right, or who exercises it in our name"
(French Civil Code. art. 2228). However, although it has a similar meaning to English law, the mere right to
the benefit or enjoyment of property
may be referred to as *jouissance* and a
right of user, without any legal title or
right, as *usufruit (***usufruct**). "Possession, in its primary meaning is the *de
facto* exercise of such control over an
object as would be justified by ownership, supposing the possessor to be, as

of course he generally is, the owner.
From this primary meaning, which
can only apply in respect of corporeal
things, the idea is extended to such
more limited enjoyment as corresponds, for example, to a real right less
than ownership (such as a servitude)
over a corporeal thing, and to the
possession of an incorporeal thing
such as personal status. The possession must have the *animus domini* ...
the intention to exercise the material
mastery on his own behalf ... Where
the physical control or occupation of
the thing is exercised by one person
on behalf of another, as lessee, bailee
or bare licensee, the former has only
détention précaire or *possession précaire,* the true possession being in the
principal – the lessor, bailor or licensor ... The possessor is presumed to
be the owner unless and until a better
title is shown by another person. In
the case of movables this presumption is ... rebuttable only in comparatively rare cases. In the case of
immovables it may always be rebutted. Possession carries with it three
other important consequences: (i) it
may lead to the acquisition of title by
prescription; (ii) it may confer the
right to the **fruits;** (iii) in the case of
immovables it gives the right to exercise the possessory actions." – Amos
& Walton's Introduction to French
Law, 3 edn, pp. 100–101.
(*possession de fait* – actual or **adverse
possession**)
(*possession paisible* – **quiet enjoyment**)
(*possession trentenaire* – thirty year's
possession; a requirement in French
law for a claim to absolute title following adverse possession)
(*possession vaut titre* – possession [of
personal property] amounts to title:

similar to the English maxim 'possession is nine tenths of the law')
(*libre possession* – **vacant possession**)
(*prise de possession* – occupation; act of taking possession)
(*titre de possession* – **title**). See also *possessoire, prescription acquisitive, propriété*.
Manuel de Droit Civil, by Pierre Voirin et Gilles Goubeaux, 20 edn., pp. 252–264.
Droit Civil, Les Biens, by Jean Carbonnier, 11 edn., p. 173 *et seq.*, p. 327 *et seq.*
Précis Dalloz. Droit Civil, Les Biens (Alex Weill), 2 edn, pp. 321–338.

possession order

An order granted by a county court consenting to the termination of a **statutory tenancy** of a dwelling-house which would otherwise continue to benefit from security of tenure. Such an order will not be granted unless the court is applying one of the mandatory grounds for possession; or, if it is exercising one of its discretionary **grounds for possession**, the court "considers it reasonable to make such an order" (Rent Act 1977, s. 98 and Sch. 15, as amended by the Housing Act 1980, ss. 66–67 and Sch. 7). The court may grant a possession order that (a) takes immediate effect, although such instances are reserved primarily for trespassers; (b) is outright but its final effect is deferred for a set period of time; or (c) is conditional, as when it takes effect only after a tenant has moved to alternative accommodation or as when it ceases to have effect if the tenant pays arrears of rent within a stated period of time. See also **ejectment, eviction**.
Landlord and Tenant, by Martin Partington, 2 edn., pp. 425–440.

possession, unity of

see **joint tenancy**.

possessions

Things that are owned or capable of being owned; the aggregate of a person's tangible wealth; goods and chattels. See also **chattel, chose, goods**.

possessoire (F)

possessory title. Under French law *possession* (**possession**) imputes a greater claim to ownership than under English law, i.e. the possessor is assumed to be the owner until shown to the contrary. See also **adverse possession**.

possessory action

An **action** to recover possession of property. In particular, a real action to recover possession of a freehold. 'Action for possession' was abolished in 1833. See also **possession order**.

possessory interest

1. See **possessory title**.
(US) 2. An interest in property held by a person who has the use and occupation of property under a lease, licence, concession, or any other grant of a right to possession of property.

In US appraisal practice, the value of a 'possessory interest' is represented by the total value of parting with the use and occupation of property for the term of a lease; it includes the value of the lessor's right to receive the contractual rent, plus the value of the lessee's right to any **profit rent** he may be able to obtain during the term of his lease. It represents the value of the **leaseholder's interest**, excluding his reversion, plus the value, if any, of the **leasehold interest**.

possessory leasehold

A leasehold title to land that is registered at the Land Registry based on **adverse possession**; either as a period of possession that is adverse to the leaseholder or adverse possession of land that forms an accretion to an existing lease. See also **possessory title**.

possessory lien
see **lien**.

possessory title
1. A **title** to property based on a period of actual possession rather than on a deed, will or similar document. Title claimed after a lengthy, uninterrupted, period of **adverse possession**. In particular, a title established when it can be shown "that there has been such a long uninterrupted possession, enjoyment and dealing with the property, as affords a reasonable presumption that there is an absolute title in fee simple". – Cottrell *v* Watkins (1839) 48 ER 980 – provided such possession has been exercised without force, stealth or consent.
2. A title that may be registered at the Land Registry by a person who is claiming to have acquired an interest in land by **adverse possession**. If the Land Registrar is satisfied as to the applicant's title he may enter the applicant as proprietor either with absolute title or, if appropriate, a qualified or good leasehold title, but subject to any rights to the land existing or capable of arising at the time of first registration. Thus the registered possessory title is guaranteed as far as all dealings after the date of first registration, but no guarantee is given as to the validity of the title prior to that date. A possessory title may be converted to an absolute title (or, if appropriate, a good leasehold title),

without the qualification, in the event that the land is transferred subsequently for value. The Registrar grants an absolute title to freehold land after 15 years, or a good leasehold title after 10 years, unless he is dissatisfied as to the possessor's right to such a title. (Land Registration Act 1925, ss. 75, 77). A person requesting registration of a possessory title must produce such deeds or other evidence of title as are available, and may be required to provide a **statutory declaration** to support his claim. See also **possessory leasehold**.

possibility
A future event that may, or may not, happen; an event that is contingent on another event or action. An interest in land that is dependent on an event the occurrence of which is uncertain, e.g. the death before a given date of a tenant for life. See also **contingent estate**.

possibility of a reverter
An interest in land that arises when a person grants a **freehold** interest in land to another subject to a contingent event which, if it arises, would return the freehold to the grantor. For example, if A grants land "to B on condition that he never marries Y", A has the possibility of the land reverting to him if B marries Y. See also **determinable interest**, **reversion**.

post
see **acceptance**, **offer**, **service**.

post office
see **office**, **shop**.

potential gross income (PGI) (US)
The maximum **gross income** that can be derived from an investment in property assuming it is fully leased

and there are no defaulting tenants. cf. **effective gross income.**

pouvoir (F)
1. **power; power of attorney**; possessory lien.
(*fondé de pouvoir* – attorney in fact; agent, holding power of attorney).
2. manager.

power
1. Ability to do, or control, something; especially an ability that arises out of a position of ascendency. The force or influence, for good or evil, available or given to a person or persons to affect the course of another's plight; "...power indicates possession of the ability to wield coercive force, permissive **authority** or substantial authority..." – *Webster's Third International Dictionary.*

An ability, usually derived from one person and given to another, to exert an influence over a third party; especially a legal authority or capacity to act for another. An authority given by one person (donor) to another (donee) whereby the donee is permitted to deal with or dispose of real or personal property, either for the benefit of the donee or others. The authority may be absolute or limited by the donor.

The word 'power' is normally used in connection with real property "in the sense of an authority given to a person to dispose of property which is not his" – *The Law of Real Property*, Megarry & Wade, 5 edn, p. 489. It is a right to deal with property in a special way and is distinct from a right of **use, trust**, or **ownership** i.e. it is not a form of property *per se*: "A power is an individual personal capacity to do something. That it may result in property becoming vested in him [the

holder of the power] is immaterial; the general nature of the power does not make it property" – *Ex parte Gilchrist* [1886] 17 QBD 521.
cf. **dominium, duty.** See also **power of alienation, power of appointment, power of attorney, power of sale.**
36 Halsbury's Laws of England, 4 edn, paras. 801–985.
2. A document that grants legal authority.

power appendant (or appurtenant)
An ability to deal with property that arises entirely out of the nature of the estate over which a **power** exists, e.g. a power held by a life tenant to dispose of the land he holds for life.

power of alienation
An authority given to someone permitting that person to grant, sell, assign, or otherwise transfer an interest in property. See also **alienation, restraint on alienation.**

power of appointment
An authority given, by deed or will, to enable a person to select or choose who is to receive a benefit from property; whether it be the enjoyment of an estate or the income therefrom. The person granting the authority is called the donor, the person to whom that authority is given is the 'donee' or 'appointor', and the person who receives the benefit, or in whose favour the appointment is made, is the 'appointee' or 'object of the power'. A power of appointment, which can arise upon the creation of a **strict settlement** or a **trust for sale**, may be distinguished from a **trust**, because the former gives a discretion to the appointor (who is not compelled to make any appointment); whereas it is imperative that a trustee

appoints the beneficiary, otherwise this duty may be effected by a court of law. A power of appointment may be 'general' when the donee has an unrestricted ability to select the beneficiaries, or 'particular' or 'special', when he must choose from a class of beneficiaries. See also **power**.

Real Property, by William E. Burby, 3 edn, pp. 398–411.

Cheshire's Modern Law of Property, 13 edn, pp. 268–281 & 307–310.

Land Law, by P.J. Dalton, 3 edn., pp. 184–188.

Land Law: Cases and Materials, by R.H. Maudsley and E.H. Burn, 4 edn., pp. 327–331.

The Law of Real Property, by Sir Robert Megarry and H.W.R. Wade, 5 edn., pp. 491–499.

power of attorney

A written instrument in which one person or persons (**principal** appointor, or constituent) authorises another (**attorney** or agent) to act on his behalf, or represent him or her, in a general or specified manner. A power of attorney may be 'general' or 'special'. The holder of a general power may act in any manner that the principal would be likely to adopt, so that, as a general rule, "when the authority is general it will be construed liberally; but also . . . it must be construed according to the usual course of business in such matters." – Pole *v* Leask (1863) 33 LJ Ch. 892. In contrast the holder of a special power may act only in accordance with limited and express authority.

An attorney-in-fact may not act for his own benefit, thus he is not permitted to pay his own fees from the principal's account, and he is required to make his position clear to third par-

ties. The creation of powers of attorney is strictly controlled by statute, especially by the Power of Attorney Act 1971. 'Power of attorney' may refer also to the authority granted by the principal to the attorney. The instrument is referred to sometimes as a 'letter of attorney'. See also **authority**.

Powers of Attorney, by Charles Caplin and Arnold Wexler, 4 edn.

1 Halsbury's Laws of England, 4 edn, paras. 730–732.

power of sale

1. The right of a mortgagee to sell property, secured by a **mortgage**, upon default of the mortgagor. Any mortgagee, provided the mortgage is made by **deed**, has a power, when the mortgage money becomes due and is not paid by the mortgagor, to sell the mortgaged property (Law of Property Act 1925, s. 101 (1)). In the case of an instalment mortgage the money is "due" when any instalment remains unpaid in accordance with the terms of the deed – Payne *v* Cardiff RDC [1932] 1 KB 241. Subject to certain conditions this right may be exercised without the necessity of applying to a court of law; unlike **foreclosure**. However, the Law of Property Act 1925, ss. 101–107 sets out detailed conditions that must be met prior to the exercise of a power of sale. The principal conditions are that the mortgage is made by deed; the mortgage debt is due; and there is no contrary intention expressed in the deed. Further, when the power of sale has arisen, and prior to exercising this power, (a) proper written notice must be given to the mortgagor requiring payment of the mortgage money and default in payment of the money, or part thereof, must subsist for three

months after service of the notice; or (b) interest must be at least two months in arrears; or (c) a condition of the mortgage deed or a statutory duty, other than payment of the mortgage money or interest, must be breached by the mortgagor, e.g. the mortgagor has leased the property without the mortgagee's prior consent. In certain circumstances a mortgagee may be obliged to apply to a court before exercising his power of sale, e.g. if the property is subject to a tenancy protected by the Rent Acts. This power is the most common remedy available to a mortgagee on default of a mortgagor and is ordered frequently by a court of law in place of foreclosure. If the mortgage is not made by deed the mortgagee may not sell the mortgaged property without the mortgagor's consent, or without recourse to a court to ask for a sale in order to discharge the mortgage debt.

The proceeds of sale of a mortgage property are used to discharge any prior encumberance to which the sale is not made subject; to meet the costs of the sale; to pay the mortgagee's debt – principal, interest and costs; to pay the due debts of other mortgagees; and the balance, if any, goes to the mortgagor. Any attempt by the mortgagee to recover more than his debt will be struck out by the equitable principle, "once a mortgage, always a mortgage".

Once a power of sale has accrued, the mortgagee may exercise that power as he chooses. He need not wait for the market to improve, nor need he give the mortgagor's interest greater importance than his own – provided he does not seek to cheat the mortgagor. On the other hand when exercising that power of sale the mortgagee owes a duty "to take reasonable precautions to obtain the true **market value** of the mortgaged property at the date on which he decides to sell ... [and] the sale must be a genuine sale by the mortgagee to an independent purchaser at a price honestly arrived at." – Cuckmere Brick Co. v Mutual Finance Ltd. [1971] Ch. 968, 969. The duty to obtain the "best possible price that the circumstances permit" is owed not only to the mortgagor, but also to any guarantor "since they are both in close proximity to the circumstances of the sale." – Standard Chartered Bank v Walker and Ano. (1982) 264 EG 345. A mortgagee is in a similar position to a pledgee of goods; "although he may choose his time to sell, he must conduct the sale properly and must sell at a fair value and he should not sell to himself." – Nash v Eads (1880) 25 Sol. Jo. 95. A sale by auction is frequently considered the best method of obtaining a fair price, but "sale by auction does not necessarily prove the validity of the transaction ... for the price obtained at any particular auction may be less than the price obtainable by private treaty and may depend on the steps taken to encourage bidders to attend" – Tse Kwong Lam v Wong Chit Sen [1983] 3 All ER 54. Accordingly adequate professional advice should be taken on the best means of sale. If a property is subject to more than one mortgage any mortgagee may exercise a power of sale, but a second or subsequent mortgagee sells the property subject to any prior mortgage.

A mortgagee will normally seek to obtain vacant possession of the mortgaged property prior to exercising his power of sale; unless there is a third party entitled to a right to retain possession, e.g. a statutorily protected tenant or a spouse in a **matrimonial home**.

When a mortgagee has exercised a power of sale he is considered to be a trustee of the mortgagor for any monies that remain after the payment of the outstanding principal, interest and any costs (Law of Property Act 1925, s. 105).

In the US, 'strict foreclosure' is almost non-existent and a public sale of the mortgaged property is the mortgagee's usual remedy. French law does not recognise foreclosure and the public sale of the mortgaged property is the primary remedy against a defaulting mortgagor, especially when a personal action on the debt would prove fruitless. See also **deed of trust, receiver of rents**.

Real Estate Law, by W.D. Milligan and Arthur G. Bowman, pp. 251–258 (1984).

Real Estate Law, by Robert Kratovil and Raymond J. Werner, 8 edn., pp. 386–388.

Cheshire's Modern Law of Real Property, 13 edn, pp. 649–653.

The Law of Real Property, by Robert Megarry and H.W.R. Wade, 5 edn., pp. 936–942.

Fisher and Lightwood's Law of Mortgage, 9 edn, pp. 359–381.

32 Halsbury's Laws of England, 4 edn, paras. 708–741, 847–853.

2. The right of a **tenant for life** to sell settled land at the best price obtainable. See also **capital money, overreachable interest**.

power of termination
see **right of re-entry, termination**.

powers of mortgagee
see **mortgagee**.

practical completion
The **completion** of building construction work to a point at which a building or structure can be used for the purpose for which it is intended. Called also 'substantial completion'.

prairie value
The value of an area of land in its natural and unimproved state. See also **raw land, waste land**.

preamble
The introductory part of a document, statute or ordinance; e.g. a general explanation of the purpose and effect of an Act of Parliament or a description of the general requirements of each trade in a bill of quantities. A preamble sets out the spirit or intent of the document, but is not intended to have any legal effect. See also **recitals**.

préambule (F)
preamble.

préavis (F)
notice; advance notice; warning. See also *notification*.

précaire (F)
at will; precarious.
(*détention précaire* – holding of possession, subject to the recognition of the right to ownership by another. The *détenteur précaire* (the 'precarious holder') has physical control over an object, but has a right of possession which is transient because "normally, the owner has delivered the object at the demand, on the entreaty, of the holder, that is to say the holder must, at a future date, restore it to the owner" – Précis Dalloz. Droit Civil, Les Biens (Alex Weill), 2 edn, p. 333. Forms of *détention précaire* include a right under a lease,

pledge, or bailment, or a right of a usufructuary. See also **possession**. (*titre précaire* – **tenancy at will**).

precarious possession
Possession at the will of another. See also **tenancy at will**.

precario (L)
'Entreaty; will of another'. See *nec vi nec clam nec precario*, **prescription**.

precatory words
Words of entreaty; in particular, words in a will requesting (but not directing) that something be done.

precedent
1. A judgment of a court that acts as a basis for determining future legal decisions. A precedent may be 'original' and create new rules, or be 'declaratory' and apply existing rules. In English **common law** a single precedent, in particular one that is reasoned by a court of superior jurisdiction as a rule, is binding on a court when considering a similar case. In the **civil law** normally a series of precedents is required to have the same weight. (In French law the doctrine of precedent is called the *jurisprudence* of the courts).

The doctrine of precedent, (or, more strictly, the doctrine of *stare descisis*, 'to abide by decided cases'), that is the extent to which a court (in particular a court of appeal) is bound by its previous decisions, remains controversial. Or at least, "let it not be thought that I am against the doctrine of precedent I am not. It is the foundation of our system of case law. This has evolved by broadening down from precedent to precedent ... All I am against is its too rigid application" (*The Discipline of Law*, by Lord

Denning, p. 314 (1979)) – Gallie *v* Lee [1969] 2 Ch. 37. See also **condition**, **custom**, *ratio decidendi*.
Precedent in English Law, by Rupert Cross, 3 edn.
2. A draft document that is used as a guide for others e.g. a **standard-form contract**. In the US called also a 'short-form document'. See also **conditions of sale**, **fictitious document**.
Butterworth's Encyclopaedia of Forms and Precedents, 4 edn., updated.

precinct
1. An area or part of a territory (e.g. a town) that has definite bounds or functions, especially one demarcated by an imaginary line or a physical limit such as a wall. Often used to refer to an area set aside for shopping and associated pedestrian areas; especially an area that is traffic free, i.e. a pedestrian precinct. See also **pedestrian precinct order**.
2. A part of a town or city set aside for government purposes. See also **civic centre**.

preclosing (US)
An arrangement prior to a **closing** by which the parties to a real estate transaction agree the principal issues that might arise at the closing, such as the form of documents, apportionment of costs, etc.

predecessor in title
One who previously held title to a property and through whom another has established his **root of title** to that property.
"The expression 'predecessor in title' in relation to a tenant or landlord means any person through whom the tenant or landlord has derived title, whether by assignment,

by will, by intestacy, or by operation of law" (Landlord and Tenant Act 1927, s. 25 (1)).

précedant (F)
precedent.

précompte (F)
tax, especially when withheld at source.
(*précompte immobilier* – property withholding tax). See also *taxe*.

préemption, droit de (F)
right of preemption. See also *zone d'aménagement differé, zone d'intervention foncière*.

pre-emption, right of
see right of pre-emption.

pre-entry
A customary right of a tenant, who is to take over a farm in the spring, to enter on to land before his tenancy begins in order to prepare the land and sow crops.
cf. entry.

preference, droit de (F)
right of first refusal.

preferred creditor
A creditor with a claim which takes precedence over one or more other creditors. See also priority.

preferred return (US)
see priority yield.

pre-funding commitment
see forward commitment.

prejudice
Injury or damage to a person's rights. A tendency to favour one side, or one view point, to another. See also without prejudice.

prelease (US)
see pre-let.

pre-let
An agreement to grant a lease of premises before a building is ready for occupation. This agreement is commonly entered into before, or while, a building is under construction. In the US called also a 'prelease'. See also agreement for a lease, licence.

prélèvement (F)
drawdown; levy, especially a deduction made from legal expenses before dividing an estate; deduction in advance.
(*prélèvement forfaitaire* – withholding tax).

preliminary enquiries
see enquiries.

preliminaries
An introduction to a specification or bill of quantities. The preliminaries, or strictly the 'preliminary clause', sets out items that are not a direct part of the physical work of a building work, but are essential to the execution of that work. In particular, a section that sets out matters which do not affect any particular trade. For example, the names of parties to a building contract; a description of the site; the respective liabilities of the employer and contractor; an outline of the work involved; work to be undertaken by nominated sub-contractors; general conditions of the contract; and contingencies.
cf. preamble. See also provisional sum.

premises
1. Derived from the Latin *praemittere*, 'to set or put before'. Those parts which have gone before. Proposition or statements made as a preface to something else.
2. In a conveyance or lease, the 'pre-

mises' is the property itself, i.e. the 'parcel' of land to be conveyed or transferred; the subject-matter of the **grant** or **demise**. Thus, the **parcels clause** in a conveyance (a deed of grant, lease, mortgage or similar deed of transfer) may be referred to as if it were the premises clause. 'Premises' may refer also to any part of a conveyance that precedes the *habendum* which, in turn, describes the duration of the interest to be granted. In the latter sense it includes an introduction, the date, details of the parties and the subject-matter, and sometimes a statement of the facts and reasons for the grant. See also **recitals**.
3. A description of a definite property; especially a structure or building. A distinct part of a property, or that which is closely associated with, or is appurtenant to, a property, e.g. the **curtilage**, or land surrounding a property and used in connection therewith. "The word 'premises' is commonly used as comprising land and houses and other matters." – Doe d. Hemming *v* Willets (1849) 7 CB 715.

In the case of **leasehold enfranchisement**, 'premises' refers to any garage, outhouse, garden, yard and appurtenance let and occupied with a **house** (Leasehold Enfranchisement Act 1967, s. 1 (3)). See also **appurtenance, business premises, hereditament, tenements**.

premium

1. An amount that exceeds the proper or reasonable **consideration** for an agreement. A payment made as an inducement to action or as a reward for loss. In particular, a sum of money payable merely for the privilege of obtaining a right to property,

e.g. a capital sum payable at the start, by a lessee, for the right to take the lease. A premium may represent a **fine** required for a right to property; it may be a capitalised **prepayment** of rent; or it may be a deposit as **security** for unpaid rent or damage to the demised premises. In English Common Law a premium is strictly not **rent**, even if it is payable by instalments (although a rent may be expressed as payable by way of a single advanced sum that is termed a premium – Regor Estates Ltd *v* Wright [1951] 1 KB 689. A premium usually takes the form of cash, but it may take any other form that represents money's worth e.g. goods, services, acceptance of a loan.

It is illegal for anyone to require (either directly or through a third party) the payment of a premium for the grant, renewal, continuance, or assignment of a **protected tenancy** (a provision that only applies to a **restricted contract** if there is a registered rent) and a tenant who has made such a payment can sue for its return (Rent Act 1977, ss. 119, 120 and 125). Demanding an excessive price for furniture as a condition for the granting, renewal, continuance, or assignment of a protected tenancy, or the right under a restricted contract, is considered equivalent to demanding a premium (1977 Act, s. 123). For this purpose a premium includes "(a) any fine or other like sum; (b) any other pecuniary consideration in addition to rent; and (c) any other sum by way of a deposit, other than one which does not exceed one-sixth of the annual rent and is reasonable in relation to the potential liability in respect of which it is paid". (Housing Act 1980, s. 79 – amending the definition in the Rent Act 1977, s. 128 (1) which did not include the exception in (c)). Whether a sum is a premium or an advanced payment of rent depends upon the facts of the case and the transaction as a whole – Reger Estates Ltd., v Wright [1951] 1 KB 689; but the onus of proof that the payment is not illegal lies with the landlord. A payment demanded as consideration for a right to surrender a protected tenancy is not illegal. cf. **discount**. See also **key money**.

Modern Methods of Valuation, 7 edn., pp. 127–130 or *Statutory Valuations*, by Andrew Baum, pp. 7–10 (1981) (for the assessment of premiums payable as a condition for the grant of a lease).

Housing Law, by Andrew Arden and Martin Partington, pp. 356–370 (1983).

The Law of Landlord and Tenant, by Hill and Redman, 17 edn.

Woodfall's Landlord and Tenant, 28 edn, paras. 1–0693, 3–0593 to 3–0601.

27 Halsbury's Laws of England, 4 edn, para. 759.

2. Consideration paid for a chance to receive a reward or bonus; e.g. an amount paid above the par value of a share, or the price paid for an option. An amount charged by the lender for the grant of a loan.

3. Consideration to be paid, at one time or from time to time, by an insured party under a contract of insurance; the sum of money that is set down in an **insurance policy** as the price the insured pays for the undertaking by the insurer to pay for a loss sustained by the insured as a result of an event against which the insurance is provided – the price of an **indemnity**.

4. The consideration paid for the assignment of a leasehold interest,

normally as represented by the capitalised value of the **profit rent**. Premium may be used also to refer to any payment made upon taking over a lease above the market value of the leasehold interest or the value of tenant's fixtures and fittings; including any consideration paid for **goodwill**. See also **reverse premium**.

premium rent
see **constant rent**.

premium value
The amount by which the capital value of the market rent of a property exceeds the capital value of the rent receivable under an existing lease of the property, i.e. the capital value of the **profit rent** of a property. See also **leasehold value**.

preneur (à bail) (F)
lessee.
(*bailleur et preneur* – lessor and lessee). See also *locataire*.

prepaid expense
An expense paid before it is due, or paid for a benefit not yet received; in particular, one that covers a future period such as a new tax year or the period after the date for a transfer of property. For example, an insurance premium paid for a forthcoming year or rent paid in advance. In the US such a payment, i.e. one made for a benefit to be received over more than one accounting year, may be called also a 'deferred charge' or 'deferred expense'.

prepaid rent
Rent paid in advance of the due date. See also **rent in arrears or advance**.

'prepared to purchase'
see **prospective purchaser**, '**ready, able and willing**'.

prepayment

A **payment** in advance. See also **prepaid expense, rent in arrears or advance**.

prepayment clause

A clause in a mortgage deed which provides that the mortgagor can repay the outstanding principal before the due date.

cf. **acceleration clause**. See also **equity of redemption**.

prepayment penalty

A special charge or penalty demanded of a mortgagor when a mortgage is repaid before it becomes due. If the amount is excessive it may be regarded as a clog or fetter on the mortgage, i.e. it unduly hampers **redemption** of the mortgage, and legally may not be demanded. In the US, such a payment is limited in many States to one per cent of the outstanding principal. Called also a 'pay-off penalty' or 'early redemption charge'. See also **clog on the equity of redemption**.

prepayment privilege

The right of a mortgagor to repay the outstanding principal, in full or part before the normal maturity date, without paying a **penalty**. Called also an 'anticipation privilege.' See also **acceleration clause, equity of redemption**.

prerogative order or writ

Historically any order that emanated from the Crown. An order submitted, at the discretion of a superior court, to an inferior court or public official, when the superior court seeks to review a matter of law because it is considered that there may have been a miscarriage of justice. The order may take the form of *certiorari* (to quash); *prohibition* (to prevent); or *mandamus* (to compel), depending on the nature of the injustice the court is seeking to redress. Since the Administration of Justice Act 1938 such commands are 'prerogative orders' and not 'prerogative writs'; the only remaining prerogative writ is that of *habeas corpus*.

cf. **appeal**.

prescription

The acquisition, or extinguishment, of a right over another's land (in particular, a **servitude**) by the uninterrupted use and enjoyment of that right for an extensive period of time. Prescription arises from the legal maxim *omnia praesumuntur rite et solemonitur esse acta*, 'all rights are presumed to be correctly and duly done'; so that a person who exercises a right over land, openly and notoriously, is presumed to have obtained that right correctly, until the contrary is proven. Prescription, like **custom**, results from established user and reaches a point at which the law says that the user is sufficient evidence that it was properly obtained and should continue unabated: "prescription and custom are brothers, and ought to have the same age, and reason ought to be the father, and congruence the mother, and use the nurse, and time out of memory to fortify them both". – Rowles *v* Mason (1612) 2 Brownl. & Golds. 198. However, prescription (unlike custom) is claimed as a personal right and not by the public at large.

The acquisition of a right by prescription is called 'acquisitive prescription' and the extinguishment of a right 'negative or extinctive prescription'. (In the civil law it is known as *usucapio* and in French law *acquisition prescriptive*).

Prescription may be distinguished from **limitation** in that prescription applies only to incorporeal hereditaments and similar intangible rights, whereas limitation, or **adverse possession**, applies to land or other corporeal hereditaments. Prescription creates a new or substituted right to an intangible claim over land; limitation destroys one person's right to claim that the law should protect his right to hold land: "the latter merely extinguishes existing titles whereas prescription has the effect of generating new rights. Limitation has a negative and extinctive effect, whereas prescription is positive and acquisitive in its mode of operation". (*Real Property and Real People*, by Gray and Symes, p. 598, 1981).

The acquisition of a right by prescription requires (a) a period of actual and continuous user – Dare *v* Heathcote (1865) 25 LJ Ex. 256, although minor interruptions are permissible; (b) that the use was acquiesced in and enjoyed as of right 'not by force, not in secrecy, not with permission', *nec vi, nec clam, nec precario*; (c) to be claimed against an incorporeal hereditament and, normally, against a fee simple estate.

In modern English law a prescriptive right may be claimed at common law; by **lost modern grant**; or based on statute law. At common law it was necessary to show that the use had existed from time immemorial, 'time out of mind', which came to be taken as from 1189 (the start of the reign of Richard I). In practice the courts recognise that if it can be shown that the right has been enjoyed for living memory it is likely to support a prescriptive claim (unless rebutted by proof that the right could not have existed in 1189 or did not exist at some defined time since 1189, as when a building that forms the essential object of the right has been erected since 1189). Lost modern grant supposes that there was a grant of the right before 1189 but the deed of grant has been mislaid; again this presumption is now normally contained within a twenty-year time span. The more usual means of establishing a prescriptive right is to rely on the Prescription Acts.

The Prescription Act 1832, ss. 1–3 basically makes the following provisions (a) uninterrupted enjoyment, as of right, of a **profit à prendre** appurtenant for 60 years becomes absolute and indefeasible, but enjoyment for a period of 30 years can be defeated only by a user which can be shown to have existed before 1189, although it may be defeated by one of the ways recognised by common law, e.g. because the right was enjoyed by *vi* (force), *clam* (secrecy), or *precario* (permission) or because the right could never have been granted in the first place; (b) uninterrupted enjoyment of an **easement** as of right, (other than a right of light) for 40 years becomes absolute and indefeasible, but 20 years' enjoyment can be defeated only by the same means as for a profit à prendre; and (c) uninterrupted enjoyment of a **right of light** to a building for 20 years becomes absolute and indefeasible, unless enjoyed by written consent or agreement. (In the case of light there is no need to prove the enjoyment was 'as of right', merely that it was an 'uninterrupted' user; there is no presumption that the right was ever granted). In practice a person may accept a shorter period of use when acquiring land and arrange **contingency insurance** to cover any loss that might arise in the event of a valid challenge to that right before it becomes absolute.

In the US the English common law rules and the doctrine of lost modern grant have been largely superceded by statute law. The periods of time required to acquire a right by prescription are broadly the same as those required to acquire title by adverse possession. An easement for light and air or lateral support normally cannot be acquired by prescription. Other easements and profits à prendre require 5, 10 or 20 years, according to the State. The basic principles of *nec vi, nec clam, nec precario* and the need for actual, adverse, open, continuous and uninterrupted user follow the same basic rules of English law Stevenson *v* Williams (1958) 188 Pa. Super. 49, 145 A 2d. 734; Scott *v* Weinheimer (1962) 140 Mont. 554, 374 P 2d. 91.

Called sometimes a 'presumed grant'.
Real Property, by William E. Burby, 3 edn., pp. 76–83.
Megarry's Manual of the Law of Real Property, 6 edn, pp. 415–427.
Cheshire's Modern Law of Real Property, 13 edn, pp. 515–525.
The Law of Easements and Profits, by Paul Jackson, pp. 110–318 (1978).
6 Halsbury's Laws of England, 4 edn, paras. 72–109, 259–264.

prescription (F)
prescription; limitation (in time).
(*prescription extinctive* – extinctive or negative prescription)
(*prescription est interrompue* – time already run is disregarded; in French

law a prescriptive claim to adverse possession must not have been interrupted either by a natural cause, i.e. by abandonment, or by a civil cause, i.e. by a legal action of another; although it may be suspended, e.g. by a minor's inability to enforce his rights. See also *prescription acquisitive, usucaption*.
Amos & Walton's Introduction to French Law, 3 edn, pp. 101–102.
Précis Dalloz. Droit civil, Les Biens (Alex Weill), 2 edn, pp. 379–406.

prescription acquisitive (F)
adverse possession. "Acquisitive prescription or *usucapion* is a way to acquire a primary real right to property, whether ownership, usufruct, or a servitude, by the exercising of a right for a continuous period, which in principle is thirty years, but frequently is a lesser period" – *Précis Dalloz. Droit Civil, Les Biens* (Alex Weill), 2 edn, p. 379.
Manuel de Droit Civil, by Pierre Voirin et Gilles Goubeaux, 20 edn., pp. 271–276.
Droit Civil, Les Biens, by Jean Carbonnier, 11 edn., pp. 231, 232, 275 *et seq.*
Droit Civil, Les Biens, by Gabriel Marty and Pierre Raynaud, p. 199 *et seq.* (1965)

present
To **offer, tender** or deliver, for example, a document or instrument for payment. See also **delivery**.

present estate
An estate in **possession**; an estate in land vested-in-possession.
cf. **future estate**. See also **vested interest**.

present value (PV)
1. The value of a right to future income after allowing for a **discount**,

or reduction in value, due to the effluxion of time. The present value of £108 discounted at 8 per cent over one year is £100. Called also 'present worth'. See also **net present value**.

2. The current value of something after taking full account of depreciation, or appreciation, and any improvement or wear and tear. See also **market value**.

present value of one

A sum of money which if invested now at a rate of **compound interest** will be worth one unit of value at the end of a certain period of time (e.g. a number of months or years). This sum may be calculated by the formula

$$V = [(1 + i)^n]^{-1}$$

where: V = the sum invested

    i = the interest rate

    n = the number of periods of time.

This calculation may be used to discount a sum of money to take account of its erosion in worth over time. Thus, if £100 is receivable in 5 years and is assumed to reduce in 'real value' at the rate of 12 per cent per annum that sum is worth:

$100 \times [(1 + 0.12)^5]^{-1}$ or £56.74 today (alternatively, if £56.74 is invested today with compound interest at 12 per cent per annum it will be worth £100 in 5 years). The present value of one is the reciprocal of the **amount of one per period**. In the US, the terms 'present worth of one dollar' or 'reversionary factor' are more commonly used. See also **true interest rate**, **valuation tables**.

Modern Methods of Valuation, 7 edn., pp. 80–84.

present value of one per period (or per annum)

The **present value** of a series of future payments, or instalments, of one unit of value, that are to be invested at a fixed compound interest rate over a given period of time (or number of years); or, the discounted value of a future level income, i.e. of an annuity certain. Represented by the formula:

$$PV = (1 - [(1 + i)^n]^{-1})/i$$

where: PV = the value today of a right to receive one unit of value, for n periods of time (or years), discounted at an interest rate of i per period (or per annum). The present value of one per period is the reciprocal of the amount that will be purchased by an annuity of one unit of value. In the UK called also a **year's purchase** and in the US a 'present worth factor' or an 'Inwood factor or coefficient'. See also **capitalisation factor**, **discounted cash flow**, **internal rate of return**, **net present value**.

Modern Methods of Valuation, 7 edn., pp. 88–93.

present value ratio

The ratio of the **present value** of the cash flow receivable from an investment and the present value of the expenditure incurred making that investment; the ratio of the present value of 'cash inflows' to 'cash outflows'. See also **net present value**.

present worth (PW)

see **present value**.

present worth factor (US)

see **present value of one per period**.

'presents'

A word used in a **deed** to refer to the deed itself, e.g. "and now by these presents it is agreed that . . .".

preservation area

see **area of outstanding natural beauty**, **conservation area**, **preservation district**.

preservation district (US)

An area of land or district that is designated to be maintained in substantially its present condition. Similar to a **conservation area** in UK, but extends to cover open spaces, scenic areas, beaches, forestry, etc.

preservation order

An order that was made by the Ministry of Works, under the provisions of the Historic Buildings and Ancient Monuments Act 1953, s. 11, to provide for the protection of an ancient monument. The provision effectively has been superseded by the inclusion of such buildings or structures in the list of 'scheduled monuments' under the provisions of the Ancient Monuments and Archaelogical Area Acts 1979. See also **building preservation order, tree preservation order.**

presumed grant

see **prescription.**

presumption

1. The taking of **possession** or **occupation** of something without due right. A 'presumptive title' is one based solely on actual occupation, without any apparent legal right to possession. See also **seizure.**
2. An inference, or taking of something for granted, based on other established facts; a presumption continues until rebutted by other evidence. See also **constructive notice, hearsay evidence, lost modern grant.**

presumptive title

see **presumption.**

prêt (F)

loan.

(*prêt hypothécaire* – mortgage loan)
(*prêt à tempérament* – instalment loan).

prêteur (F)

lender.

(*prêteur sur gage* – pledgee; bailor).

preventative injunction

see **injunction.**

preventative maintenance

Maintenance or **repair** carried out to a building in order to prevent, or in anticipation of, excessive deterioration or need of repair at a later date. See also **deferred maintenance.**

prévision (F)

provision; contingency allowance; forecast.

(*prévision de rentabilité* – **cost-benefit analysis**).

price

That which is given for something bought. The **cost** at which something is obtained, expressed in terms of **money** or its equivalent. The amount or worth (generally in the form of money) paid or demanded for, or placed on, something. A measure, in terms of money or **money's worth**, of the exchange **value** of goods or services. "The real price of everything, what everything costs to the man who seeks to acquire it, is the toil and trouble of acquiring it" – Adam Smith's *Wealth of Nations*, Book I, Ch. 5. Wages are the price of labour; **interest** the price for the use of money; **profit** the price of capital; and **rent** the price for use and occupation of land. The price when set out in a contract is called the **consideration.** Price, cost and value are given a similar meaning when converted to a pecuniary unit, but a clear distinction should be drawn between these terms because a property may cost one amount, then be priced at another, but valued at a third figure – it is important to know the value of property and not just the price, for therein lies a profit (or loss). See also **custom, fair price, open market value, purchase price, reserve price**.

price–earnings multiplier
see **price–earnings ratio**.

price–earnings ratio (p/e ratio)
The ratio of the market value of an ordinary share in a company to the net earnings after tax available for distribution to the holder of one ordinary (equity) share in the company. Effectively, a p/e ratio represents the number of years required for the earnings of a company, which are available for distribution to the ordinary shareholder (i.e. after the payment of any dividends due to preference or minority interest shareholders), to 'pay-back' the cost of acquiring a share in the company. When applied in reverse, to the earnings of a company, in order to assess the capital value of a share, the ratio is called a 'price earnings multiplier', or 'earnings multiplier' (in principle this multiplier is equivalent to the **years' purchase** applied to capitalise the income from a property). The p/e ratio is the reciprocal of the **earnings yield**. See also **capitalisation factor, yield**.

price-level adjusted mortgage (PLAM)
A mortgage loan in which the repayments are linked to a measure of changes in prices, usually retail prices, by reference to a cost-of-living index. If the interest is fixed (or varies with market conditions) and the outstanding principal is adjusted the mortgage is called usually a 'price-level adjusted mortgage' or an 'inflation-adjusted mortgage'. If the interest rate is adjusted the mortgage

is called an 'index-linked mortgage'. See also **variable-rate mortgage**.

prima facie (L)
'On first appearances; on the face of it': Based on appearance, without better evidence or explanation. *Prima facie* evidence is that which is accepted in law as fact, unless or until rebutted by evidence to the contrary.

primary and secondary rental (US)
A payment in the nature of **rent** that includes both a fixed figure for the property – true or 'primary rent' – and a figure which is determined periodically to cover **operating expenses** – a 'secondary rent'. See also **advance service charge**.

primary contractor
see **general contractor**.

primary financing (US)
A loan that has the first **priority** in the event of a default, e.g. a first mortgage.

primary use
see **planning unit**.

prime (F)
premium; allowance.
(*prime d'assurance*– insurance premium).
(*prime de remboursement* – redemption cost)
(*prime pour lever* – **call option**)
(*prime pour livrer* – **put option**)
(*lever la prime* – to take up an option)
(*vente à prime* – seller's option).

prime contractor (US)
see **general contractor**.

prime cost
The direct cost or expense of a commodity, excluding general overheads and profit. The actual cost incurred by a contractor on labour and mate-

rials. Specifically, the sum paid to a sub-contractor or supplier for work done or material supplied. See also **prime-cost sum**.

prime-cost contract
see **cost-plus contract**.

prime-cost sum (pc sum)
A sum of money included in a **bill of quantities** or **building contract** to cover the cost of acquiring certain articles which have not yet been decided upon, e.g. ironmongery fittings, but which will be paid for on the basis of the supplier's cost. In particular, a sum set down as an estimate of the cost of works or services to be provided by a **nominated subcontractor** or nominated supplier. The contractor is not paid a stated sum but only the actual cost as determined when the applicable work is completed. In the US called also a 'cash allowance'.

prime covenant
see **covenant**.

prime lease
see **head lease**.

prime location
The most sought after location for a particular purpose. As a rule a 'prime location' is that part of an urban area at which land values are at their highest; the location where a business might expect to achieve the highest profit relative to any other location (sometimes called a 'one hundred percent' location). A property may be considered to be in a prime location if it is in the very best position by virtue of demand from prospective occupiers, communications, and associated uses. Strictly, for any one use, 'prime location' should be applied to only

one location, but it tends to be used to describe any good, well established, location; thus making strict definition irksome.
cf. **secondary location**. See also **highest and best use**, **peak pitch**.

prime parcel (US)
see **prime property**.

prime pitch
see **peak pitch**.

prime property
The choicest or most sought after property. A property considered by an investor to be of the best quality due to such factors as location, age, condition, and tenancy. Strictly, prime property is confined within the definition of a property located in a **prime location**; suitable for the most discerning occupier; constructed to a modern standard of design and finish; in a good state of repair and maintenance; and, if applicable, let to first-class tenants (e.g. triple 'A' or blue chip companies, major institutions or government bodies) at the current market rent with the tenant paying all the cost of maintaining and repairing the building. Owing to the dearth of such properties the term 'prime property' is used sometimes to embrace properties that lack one or more of these qualities or characteristics, but in most respects are close to this definition. A prime investment property is one that would be valued by adopting the lowest yield (or the highest capitalisation rate) applicable to the category of investment. In the US, called also a 'prime parcel'. See also **investment property**.

prime tenant (US)
1. The largest single occupier of a property, or a tenant of good finan-

cial standing and reputation who occupies a substantial part of a building. Frequently in the US it is an essential requirement to the financing of a new development project that a prime tenant has been secured. In a shopping centre a prime tenant may be a departmental store and in an office building a corporation with a high credit rating.
2. See **head lessor**.

prime trading location
see **peak pitch**.

primogeniture
The first born of the parents; the right to succeed to property as the first born, especially as the eldest son. The feudal rule of primogeniture provides that the eldest son takes all the real estate of intestate parents to the total exclusion of all others; if there is no male heir, females take equally as coparceners. This rule was abolished in English law in 1925. See also **coparcenary**, **entailed interest**, **intestacy**.

principal
1. One who accepts a primary liability as a consequence of an undertaking given to provide an indemnity for an undertaking or burden accepted by another.
2. A person who, being competent to act in his or her own right, appoints another to act as an **agent**. See also **agency**, **undisclosed principal**.
3. The capital sum of a debt, as distinguished from the **interest** charged or earned thereon. A capital sum invested with interest.

principal (F)
principal; capital sum.
(*principal et intérêt* – principal and interest).
(*locataire principal* – head lessee).

principal mansion house
see **mansion house**.

principal moneys
The amount advanced under a mortgage loan as distinct from the interest or any other sum arising out of the agreement; in particular, the capital advanced as distinguished from **accrued interest**.

principal of substitution
see **opportunity cost**.

principal private residence
The place of **residence** in the UK accepted by the Inland Revenue as being a person's 'main' home and thus generally eligible for exemption from capital gains tax. An individual may claim such exemption upon disposal of an interest in "(a) a dwelling-house or part of a dwelling-house which is, or has at any time in his period of ownership been, his only residence, or (b) land which he has for his own occupation and enjoyment with that residence as its garden or grounds up to the permitted area" (Capital Gains Tax Act 1979, s. 1011). The 'permitted area', as a rule, is one acre (including the site of the dwelling-house). Where someone owns two or more private houses he may elect that one be treated as his 'principal private residence' or failing an election the Inland Revenue will judge which house falls within that definition. Capital gains tax will be payable on the sale of any other residence which belongs to that person.

prior charge (or mortgage)
A charge (or mortgage) that has **priority** over other (subordinate) obligations. See also **first mortgage**.

priorité (F)
   priority.
   (*priorité d'hypothéque* – mortgage priority)
   (*droit de priorité* – **right of first refusal**)

priority
   see **priority of a mortgage**.

priority caution
   A **caution** entered at the Land Registry to protect the priority of **minor interest**; such a caution when lodged determines the priority between assignees and incumberancers of life interests, remainders, reversions and executory interests (Law of Property Act 1925, s. 102). See also **priority of a mortgage**.

priority of a mortgage
   The order in which competing claims of mortgagees are met when one mortgagee is entitled to exercise his claim to the mortgaged property and, thereby, excludes another mortgagee from satisfying his claim to the property; especially when the net proceeds from the sale of property prove insufficient to satisfy all the competing claims. The claims of competing mortgagees are not paid pro-rata to the amount of their debt. Although *prima facie* a mortgage may rank according to its time of creation – *qui prior est tempore potior est jure*, 'he who is first in time has the strongest claim in law' – English law requires that a mortgagee should make the existence of his claim ascertainable to any subsequent mortgagee who is prepared to make reasonable inquiries or searches. This may be done in three ways. First, by retaining the title deeds so as to make it obvious to anyone contemplating a mortgage

that the mortgagor is not free to deal with the property as he chooses. Secondly, by registering the mortgage at the Land Registry. Thirdly, if the mortgagee has been offered only an equitable interest in land as security for his loan, by informing the holder of the legal estate of the mortgage that has been entered into.

   The complex rules of English law for determining the priority of mortgages may be summarised thus: (i.) a mortgage protected by a deposit of the title deeds relating to the **legal estate** (a form of mortgage transaction that is not registrable as a **land charge**), depends for its priority on the date on which the mortgagee obtained a deposit of the deeds; except that a person who holds only an **equitable mortgage** of the legal estate, even though he may have received a deposit of the deeds first, will have his priority postponed if the legal estate is charged, in good faith, as a **legal mortgage** and the legal mortgage does not have **notice** of the equitable mortgage – Pilcher v Rawlins (1872) 7 Ch. App. 259 (ii.) a mortgage not protected by a deposit of the title deeds relating to the legal estate should be registered as a land charge (either as a **puisne mortgage**, if a legal mortgage, or a general equitable charge, if an equitable mortgage) and priority is determined by the date of registration (Law of Property Act 1925, s. 97). Failure to register makes a registrable charge void (i.e. effectively posponed in priority) against a mortgagee who takes an interest in the land at a later point in time (Land Charges Act 1925, s. 4 (5)). On the other hand, if A registers his mortgage as a land charge he takes priority over any mortgage (whether legal or equitable) that is granted to B at a later date, even if the mortgage to B is accompanied by a deposit of the title deeds because, by the prior registration, the later mortgagee has notice of the charge (Law of Property Act 1925, s. 198 (1)); unless A is grossly negligent in not seeking to obtain the title deeds because, in all the circumstances, he should have taken such action before taking the charge. (iii.) a mortgage of an **equitable interest** is governed by the date upon which the holder of the legal estate (e.g. the trustee of a settlement of a trust for sale, or the estate owner) is given notice of charge – Dearle v Hall (1823) 3 Russ. 1, as amended by the Law of Property Act 1925, s. 137; except that a mortgagee who has actual or constructive notice of a prior mortgage cannot alter his later priority merely by giving notice to the holder of the legal estate. (iv.) the priority of a mortgage protected by the deposit of title deeds, and of a mortgage of an equitable interest, may be upset by fraud, gross negligence (especially in seeking the title deeds), misrepresentation, or by estoppel. (v.) if the land is registered, the priority of a mortgage of the legal estate depends on the date upon which a **registered charge** is created, or, if the mortgage is not registered, the date of entry of a **caution** in the proprietorship register of the Land Registry, and not according to the date of creation of the mortgage (Land Registration Act 1925, ss. 29, 106). A mortgage of an equitable interest in registered land is protected by a prohibitory 'caution' or 'inhibition' according to the date on which such a caution or inhibition is lodged at the Land Registry (Land Registration Act 1925, s. 102). (vi.) a mortgagee may, in certain circumstances, be able to add a further advance to an existing mortgage and maintain his priority as if the total advance had been made at the outset (Law of Property Act 1925, s. 94). Thus, a prospective mortgagee should (a) if the land is unregistered, seek out the **title deeds** relating to the legal estate or, if the land is registered, obtain a copy of the **Land Certificate**; (b) enquire of any existing mortgagee whether he has agreed or undertaken to tack on a further advance to his existing mortgage loan; (c) if the land is unregistered, search the Land Charges Register or, if the land is registered, the Charges Register of the Land Registry; (d) if the property offered as security is an equitable interest only, notify the holder of the legal estate that he has taken a charge on that interest; and (e) make reasonable enquiries and inspect the property to ascertain whether there are any rights or interests that patently might affect his security, e.g. a person in possession. See also **marshalling, priority notice, subordination, tacking**.

Cheshire's Modern Law of Real Property, 13 edn, pp. 662–685.

The Law of Real Property, by Robert Megarry and H.W.R. Wade, 5 edn., pp. 986–1005.

priority neighbourhood

A predominately residential area considered by a housing authority to require improvement, both of the social and physical conditions, but not with the same urgency as a **housing action area** (Housing Act 1974, ss. 52–55). A priority neighbourhood is typically established adjoining or surrounding a housing action area, or a

general improvement area, and is indicative of an area that will require action or improvement when the area requiring more urgent attention has been dealt with.

priority notice

1. A notice entered on the Land Registry, on a prescribed form 17, to protect a person who intends to acquire land and apply for registration of the title as the first **registered proprietor**. The notice is normally effective for 14 days from the date it is lodged at the Registry and if, during that period, the intending proprietor or his solicitor applies to register title he takes priority over any other party from the date the priority notice is lodged (Land Registration Act 1925, s. 144; Land Registration Rules 1925, r. 17).
2. A notice lodged at the Land Charges Department of the Land Registry against a parcel of unregistered land by a person who intends to register a **land charge** that he contemplates making. The notice must be lodged on form K.6 not later than 14 clear days before the charge is intended to take effect and has the effect that if the charge is made, and provided it is registered within 30 days of the priority notice, it takes effect as if it had been registered at the time the priority notice was lodged (Law of Property (Amendment) Act 1926, s. 4 (1); now the Land Charges Act 1972, s. 11 (1) and the Land Charges Rules 1974, r. 4). Such a notice is used when a rapid succession of transactions take place, as when a restrictive covenant is placed on land and the land is then immediately mortgaged before the covenant is properly registered.

priority yield

The percentage return or yield that one joint venture partner (usually the passive investor) or a lender, by agreement receives from an investment before any income is paid to any other investor or lenders. So that, if an investor in a joint venture is guaranteed a priority return of 7 per cent he will receive all the income while the investment yields 7 per cent or less; if, or when, the investment yield exceeds 7 per cent, the partners divide the income over and above the priority yield according to the terms of the joint venture or loan agreement. A priority yield should be distinguished from a 'guaranteed yield' as with the latter one partner guarantees to make up the difference between the income received from the investment and the guaranteed yield stipulated in the agreement between the parties. Called also a 'preferred return'.

prisée (F)

appraisal, especially before an auction sale. See also *estimation, expertise*.

private dwelling-house

A **dwelling-house** occupied by a private person, a family, or closely connected or related persons, but not one divided into separate dwellings or flats, nor one occupied for business purposes – G.E. Stevens (High Wycombe), Ltd. *v* High Wycombe Corporation [1961] 2 All ER 741. The use of premises as a 'private dwelling-house' may include sharing with friends or with a paying guest, but does not encompass the granting of a lease or licence to a stranger. Premises used, or converted, to a lodging house are unlikely to be classified as a 'private dwelling house', because then there may not be privacy of entry and exit. See also **principal private residence**.

private nuisance
see **nuisance**.

private offering
The offering of a real estate investment to a limited number of investors, as distinguished from an offer to the public at large. Such an offering may well be exempt from statutory regulation.

private property
Property held in private ownership, whether held by an individual (or individuals) or a corporation, as distinct from property held by a state body. Property held by one or a number of individuals to the exclusion of all others. The right of an individual or a group of individuals to acquire and hold private property without restriction or confiscation, except by due process of law, is one of the basic civil rights recognised in democratic–liberal states, but denied in socialistic–communist states. Thus, private property is regarded by some as a means to deprive the community as a whole of its natural right to the ownership of the means of production, or **wealth**, in favour of a privileged minority. However, once acquired, whether by venture, stealth, force, purchase or exchange, the right to its retention is protected normally by government; is a right that is dependent for its existence on Sovereign or Government power, "without the protection whereof, every man would have equal Right to the same". — Thomas Hobbes, *Leviathan* (1651) Ch. XXIX.

The right to hold private property is recognised in the Old Testament (Kings I, xxi); in Magna Carta 1215 (Ch. 39); in the French Declaration of the Rights of Man and the Citizen 1789 (art. 17); in the fifth amendment to the Constitution of the United States; and in the United Nations Universal Declaration of Human Rights 1948: "1. Every one has the right to own property alone as well as in association with others. 2. No one shall be arbitrarily deprived of his [or her] property". – (art. 17).
cf. **communal property, public property**. See also **community property, compulsory purchase, eminent domain, expropriation, just compensation, ownership, possession**.

private residence
see **principal private residence**.

private right of way
A **right of way** that is limited to one or a number of persons but not to the general public.
cf. **highway**.

private zoning (US)
see **restrictive covenant**.

privilege
A benefit, exemption, or advantage enjoyed by one person, as distinct from that which is enjoyed as a common advantage or could be enjoyed by the world at large. See also **easement, franchise, priority, profit à prendre**.

privilège (F)
privilege; lien; charge; licence.
(*créance privilégiée* – preferred charge)
(*créancier privilégié* – **preferred creditor**).

privity
A tie between two parties that is recognised by law, e.g. that of **contract, tenure, covenant**, blood etc.; a mutual or successive relationship to the same right, interest or property. In particular, the mutual relationship that exists between two parties, either as

parties to a contract – **privity of contract**; or as parties having a bond to the same estate in land – **privity of estate**. Privity may arise also between an heir, executor or certain other persons who succeed to the rights and benefits of a contract.

privity of contract

The relationship that exists and extends only between the parties to a **contract**. Privity of contract means that "a contract cannot (as a general rule) confer rights or impose obligations arising under it on any person except the parties to it". Chitty on Contract, 28 edn, p. 662 – Tweedle *v* Atkinson (1861) 30 LJ QB 265. Privity of contract represents the notion of the right of the parties to the contract to sue or be sued; a right, or burden, that persists even though one of the parties has assigned the benefit or obligation of the contract to another: in a lease, "the rule is that a lessee remains liable upon his express covenants, notwithstanding an assignment and acceptance of rent from the assignee ..." – Baynton *v* Morgan (1888) 22 QBD 82. This rule applies to the original lease rent and to any increase arising from an express rent review clause in the lease – Centrovincial Estate plc *v* Bulk Storage Ltd (1983) 268 EG 59. A contract once entered into must be performed, or discharged by subsequent agreement.

In English common law there must be privity of contract between the parties to enable an action to be sued upon; so, strictly a third party cannot sue any of the parties to a contract, even though he may have suffered a loss because the contract has not been performed. However, this doctrine is tainted by a number of qualifications.

In the first place the ancient principle of **assumpsit** permitted one party to claim that another had undertaken (*assumpsit*, 'he assumed responsibility') to do something or pay for something in return for a benefit received. This principle evolved to permit the enforcement of an implied promise or **quasi-contract** so as to prevent an unjust benefit or enrichment arising from the mere lack of a proven contract between the parties. On a similar premise, an executor is permitted to assume the position of a debtor and thereby enable a debt to be satisfied from a person's estate. Secondly, a person may take another's place as party to a contract if he can demonstrate that the other was contracting on his behalf, even though the intervening party was unknown to the other original party to the contract at the time the bargain was struck – the doctrine of **undisclosed principal**. Thirdly, in the law of property, if two parties have a mutual interest in the same land, e.g. a lessor and an assignee, there is said to be **privity of estate** and those parties each may have a right to sue or be sued by the other on matters that 'touch and concern the land'. Fourthly, in certain circumstances, if a right under a contract is assigned to a third party that party may enforce his right against the remaining original party to the contract – as with a **statutory assignment** or an **equitable assignment**. Fifthly, statute law has intervened to make available rights of action for third parties to a contract; e.g. the Law of Property Act 1925, s. 56 (1) stipulates that a person may acquire the benefit of a right to land or other property, although he is not named as a party to a conveyance or other instrument, provided that the deed purports to confer that benefit on him.

Even though there is no right of action on a contract between two parties, there may be another course of action available, e.g. an action of **tort**. See also **novation, trust**.
Cheshire & Fifoot's Law of Contract, 10 edn., pp. 404–406.
Anson's Law of Contract, 26 edn, pp. 363–389.
Chitty on Contract, 25 edn, paras. 1221–1266.
9 Halsbury's Laws of England, 4 edn, paras. 329–343.

privity of estate

A mutual relationship that is considered as present between two parties who have an interest in the same estate in land; as between lessor and lessee, tenants-in-common, and between a tenant for life and a remainderman. There is said to be **privity of contract** and privity of estate between the original parties to a **lease**: the former relationship arising as an incidence of the contract and the latter as an incidence of the lease creating a tie to an estate in land (it should be noted that there is privity of contract between the parties to an **agreement for a lease** but no privity of estate until the lease is formally executed).

Privity of contract and privity of estate persist simultaneously between a lessor and lessee as long as a lease continues, so that the existence of the latter has no practical significance, unless either party assigns their interest to another. If either the lessor or lessee makes an **assignment** of his interest to a third party the privity of estate between the original parties is broken, but a privity of estate comes into existence between the remaining lessor or lessee and the third party; in other words, if there is a right to the same property as landlord and tenant there is privity of estate. On the other hand, a tenant who sub-lets land does not transfer his estate to the sub-tenant, but merely carves a shorter estate out of his interest; there is no privity of estate between a head lessor and a sub-lessee. These relationships may be illustrated diagrammatically, as shown opposite.

The effect of privity of estate is that most covenants in a lease are enforceable between those parties who are linked by privity of estate; even though there is no privity of contract to enable an action on the contract to be used on. A lessor can enforce a covenant in a lease against an assignee; but not against a sub-lessee (unless the sub-lessee has directly covenanted with the lessor to observe the terms of the lease). Those covenants that may be enforced as a result of the relationship of privity of estate are said to 'touch and concern the land', or 'have reference to the subject matter of the lease' so as to be capable of running therewith or with the reversion – Horsey Estate Ltd v Steiger [1899] 2 QB 89; Breams Property Investments Co Ltd v Stroulger [1948] 2 KB 1; Law of Property Act 1925, ss. 141, 142. A covenant that is purely personal – such as one to pay money to a third party or that the landlord will not operate a competitive business near the demised premises – does not 'touch and concern the land' and cannot be the subject of privity of estate – Thomas v Hayward (1869) LR 4 Ex. 311; Los Angeles Terminal Land Co. v Muir (1902) 136 Cal. 36, 68 P. 308. See also **restrictive covenant**.

1. L ——Pc—— T
      —Pe—

2. L ——Pc—— T ——Pc——→ A
     | |
     L----------Pe----------J

3. L ——Pc—— T ——Pc—— A
   | |
   ↓ |
   R ------- Pe ---------J

4. L ——Pc—— T ——Pc—— A ←—Pc—→ ST
   | |
   R ---------Pe---------J

L = original lessor

T = original lessee

A = assignee of lessee

R = assignee of lessor

ST = sub-tenant

Pc = privity of contract (but not necessarily the same contract)

Pe = privity of estate

——→ assignment   ←——→ sub-letting

Megarry's Manual of the Law of Real Property, 6 edn, pp. 377–389.
Cheshire's Modern Law of Real Property, 13 edn, pp. 437–440.
The Law of Real Property, by Robert Megarry and H.W.R. Wade, 5 edn., pp. 740–757.
Land Law: Cases and Materials, by Maudsley and Burns, 4 edn., pp. 420–427.
27 Halsbury's Laws of England, 4 edn, paras. 391–398.

prix (F)

price; **consideration**; quotation; cost; value.

(*prix d'achat* – **purchase price**)

(*prix d'adjudication* – knocked-down or actual sale price, at auction)

(*prix de détail* – retail price)

(*prix de location* – **rental value**; letting price)

(*prix du marché* – **market price**)

(*prix de remplacement* – **replacement cost**; **reinstatement cost**)

(*prix de revient* – cost price; prime cost)
(*prix de revient comptable* – book cost)
(*prix de revient effectif* – actual cost price)
(*prix de revient réel* – historic cost).

pro emptore (L)

'As the buyer: by the title of a purchaser'.

pro forma (statement)

A statement 'according to form', i.e. one that shows how a situation might develop, e.g. a schedule of the projected income and expenditure from a real estate investment over a given period. See also **feasibility study**.

pro rata (L)

'In proportion; at the rate of'. See also **apportionment**.

pro tanto (L)

'For so much; to that extent; as far as it goes'. A payment made *pro tanto* is a part payment or a payment on account. A purchaser *pro tanto* acquires something less than a complete interest – a **partial interest** e.g. a lease.

probate

1. A certificate granted by a court or the Probate Office signifying that a will has been proved, thus enabling the executor to administer the effects.
2. The formal procedure by which an executor proves the validity of a will.

proceeds

The **income** or **revenue** from a property investment; the price or consideration received on the sale of a property. See also **yield**.

procès-verbal (F)

minute(s); an official record of terms agreed between parties; statement.
(*procès-verbal de vente* – record of a forced sale).

procuration (F)

procuration; proxy; power of attorney.

procuration fee

see **finance procuration fee, finder's fee**.

procuring cause (US)

see **effective cause**.

produit net (F)

net return; net yield.

produits (F)

products of land which, unlike *fruits*, are not obtained on a regular basis and are used up in the process, e.g. stone from a quarry that is not regularly exploited. See also **usufruct**.

profession

A vocation or occupation, by which a person earns his or her living, that requires the application of educational knowledge and specialised skills; especially when that skill is of a mental or intellectual nature, rather than purely of a physical or manual nature (Inland Revenue Commissioners *v* Maxse [1919] 1 KB 657). Historically the only 'professions' were the learned professions of divinity, law and medicine; but today 'profession' extends to any occupation that requires extensive educational training, the use of an intellectual skill and usually the maintenance of certain standards of conduct. Profession is impossible to define precisely; carrying on a **trade** is not a profession; merely selling property, real or personal, is not a profession. "Ultimately one has to answer this question: Would the ordinary man, the ordinary reasonable man – the man, if

you like to refer to an old friend, on the Clapham omnibus – say now, in the time in which we live, of any particular occupation, that it is properly described as a profession?" – Carr *v* Inland Revenue Commissioners [1944] 2 All ER 167. For the purpose of assessing a liability to income tax in English law an architect, a journalist, and a headmaster, have been held to be carrying on a profession, but an insurance broker and a stockbroker have not. Accordingly a valuer, a property investment analyst and a quantity surveyor may be said to be carrying on a profession, but a real estate broker may not.
cf. **business**. See also **professional negligence**.

professional indemnity insurance
see **professional liability insurance**.

professional liability insurance
A form of insurance that provides an **indemnity** to a person engaged in a profession against claims for financial loss arising from **professional negligence**, or other errors or omissions that might arise in the normal course of business. Solicitors, architects, chartered surveyors, chartered and certified accountants are required by their respective professional associations to maintain such insurance in respect of advice which, in their professional capacity, they give to their clients. Called also 'professional indemnity insurance'.
A Guide to Insurance of Professional Negligence, by Digby C. Jess (1982).

professional negligence
Negligence that occurs when a person, using his professional skill and judgement, fails to perform his duties according to the standards expected

of him. "Every person who enters into a learned profession undertakes to bring to the exercise of it a reasonable degree of care and skill. He does not undertake if he is an attorney that at all events you shall gain your case, nor does a surgeon undertake that he will perform a cure, nor does he undertake to use the highest degree of skill. There may be persons who have a higher education and greater advantages than he has, but he undertakes to bring a fair, reasonable and competent degree of skill" – Lanphier *v* Phipos [1838] 8 C and P 475. Anyone who claims to be, or is held out to be, an expert in an area where others acknowledge a far lesser proficiency, must accept that those others may come to rely on that expertise; so that, "if in a sphere in which a person is so placed that others could reasonably rely upon his judgement or his skill or his ability to make careful inquiry, a person takes it upon himself to give information or advice to, or allows his information or advice to be passed on to, another person who, as he knows or should know, will place reliance upon it, then a **duty of care** will arise" – Hedley Byrne and Co Ltd *v* Heller and Partners Ltd [1964] AC 503. See also **misrepresentation**, **valuer**.

professions liberales (F)
professional occupations, e.g. lawyers, accountants, architects, etc.

profit
A benefit, advantage, or gain that can be measured in monetary terms. An amount by which **income** exceeds the **expenditure** committed in order to earn that income, measured over a period of time, commonly a year. The amount by which the proceeds of sale

of an asset exceeds the cost of that asset; the excess of return over outlay. A 'fortuitous advantage' or a 'risk premium', i.e. a monetary gain in net worth over a specified period of time owing to a change in supply or demand; that which accrues from fortune or chance rather than as a result of exertion. In economics, profit is considered as the reward for **risk**, the financial benefit or remuneration for enterprise. It arises from uncertainty, unlike **interest** which arises from a contractual obligation, or **rent** which is a return to be derived merely from land ownership. Although in business ventures, interest and profit are interrelated, interest can be considered as the profit to be derived from the risk of parting with money, and 'rent' can be considered as the profit to be derived from making an improvement to property.

In land law 'profits' denote produce or part of the soil, whether as trees, crops, mines, herbage, etc. (Co. Litt. 4b). 'Profit' may be used also to refer to rent or service due to a lord by a tenant; or as an abbreviation for a **profit à prendre**. See also **beneficial occupation, economic rent, mesne profit, price, profit rent**.

profit à prendre

A right to enter on to the land of another in order to take something from the soil that is capable of ownership, such as minerals, timber, crops, pasture, turf, game or even the soil itself. A profit à prendre is not an interest in land, but the subject matter must emanate from the land and be capable of ownership. Thus, game and fish from land are capable of ownership when killed and can form the subject of a profit à prendre.

Something blown, washed or brought onto land cannot form the subject of a profit à prendre because it is not part of the produce of land; nor can water from a spring or a right to water cattle at a pond, because the water when taken (unless stored in a container) is not deemed to be capable of ownership *per se* by anyone. A profit à prendre may be distinguished from an **easement**; the latter does not permit the taking of anything from land, but must benefit another interest in land whereas a profit may exist as a right **'in gross'** i.e. independently of a right to land.

A profit à prendre may be enjoyed by one person alone – a 'several profit'; or in common with others – a 'profit in common' or 'right in common' (although it cannot be enjoyed by a fluctuating class of persons such as the inhabitants of a village). It may be **appurtenant** i.e. attached to land that is benefitted by the right and only capable of being enjoyed for the needs of the dominant few; or **appendant** i.e. attached to land by operation of law (although such a right must have come into existence before the Statute of *Quia Emptores* 1296).

A profit à prendre may be acquired by statute; express **grant** or express **reservation**; **implied grant**, in accordance with the provisions of the Law of Property Act 1925, s. 62; or by **prescription**. It may be extinguished by express **release**; implied release, e.g. by **abandonment**; by the product being exhausted or otherwise ceasing to exist; by approvement; or by unity of the beneficiary and the owner or possessor of the land from which the produce arises (**unity of seisin**). (Note: although the term is of apparent French derivation there is no such right as a profit à prendre in French law and such rights as resemble a profit à prendre or an easement, are classified as a **servitude**). See also **overriding interest**, **right of common**, **usufruct**.

Real Property, by William E. Burby, 3 edn., pp. 62–93.

Cheshire's Modern Law of Real Property, 13 edn, pp. 530–542.

The Law of Real Property, by Robert Megarry and H.W.R. Wade, 5 edn., p. 850 *et seq.*

The Law of Easements and Profits, by Paul Jackson, pp. 28–38 (1978).

14 Halsbury's Laws of England, 4 edn, paras. 240–269.

profit in common
see **right of common**.

profit rent
The difference between the rent reserved under a lease, i.e. the contractual rent, and the rack rent or market rent of the demised property. In the US, called usually 'positive leasehold' if the market rent exceeds the contractual rent or 'negative leasehold' or if the market rent is less than the contractual rent. See also **leasehold value**, **top-slice income**.

profit sharing
see **equity participation**.

profits
see **profit**.

profits basis of assessment
see **profits method of valuation**.

profits insurance
see **consequential loss insurance**.

profits method of valuation
A method of valuing property based on the tenant's ability to pay for the benefit to be derived from the use of that property, i.e. the ability to pay a portion of the commercial profits or receipts which are derived from the use of the property. Generally, this method of valuation is applied only to premises that are used for a trading purpose, such as a petrol filling station; a retail shop; a public-house; an hotel; or a restaurant. The simplest way of applying this method is to assume that a tenant can pay as rent a certain percentage of the profits of the business. If a capital value is required, it is assessed by capitalising the assumed rent.

This method of valuation is employed commonly to assess the **rateable value** of a property for which there is little comparable evidence of similar premises let on the open market, but for which there is comparable evidence of turnover and trading profits. "'Profits basis', in relation to the valuation of a hereditament, means the ascertainment of the value of that hereditament by reference to the accounts, receipts or profits of an undertaking carried on therein" (General Rate Act 1967, s. 115 (1)). However, the rateable value is based on what a hypothetical tenant could reasonably afford to pay and does not have regard to whether an actual tenant is a flourishing trader or is carrying out business at a loss – Mersey Docks *v* Liverpool Overseers (1873) LR 9 QB 97. Called also the 'accounts method of valuation', and in rating valuation the 'profits test', or 'profits basis of assessment'. See also **percentage rent**.

profits test
see **profits method of valuation**.

program evaluation and review technique
see **project evaluation and review technique**.

progress payments

Periodic payments made, in accordance with the terms of a construction contract, for the cost of work carried out by the contractor. A **retention sum** is normally deducted from such payments to safeguard against inadequacies of the work. See also **instalment**.

progressive rent

A rent that increases automatically during the term of a lease, whether by reference to a particular time or by reference to a particular contingency, e.g. a **graduated rent** or an **indexed rent**.

prohibition

A **prerogative order** from a superior court to an inferior court or to a tribunal demanding that judicial proceedings be discontinued, especially when the proceedings may be *ultra vires*, or against the law of the land. cf. *certiorari*.

prohibitory injunction

see **injunction**.

project analysis (or appraisal)

A comprehensive analysis of the financial viability of a development project. An assessment that takes account of economic demand, cost, design, finance, marketing, cash flow and any other factors likely to indicate whether or not a project would be profitable. The analysis includes establishing criteria against which the project may be assessed and the means for judging the results as the development progresses. See also **feasibility study**.

Valuation and Development Appraisal, edited by Clive Darlow (1982).

project evaluation and review technique (PERT)

A form of **network analysis** used to ascertain, and control, the most efficient way of allocating resources to a project. PERT aims to plan and schedule events but not necessarily to monitor the activities or actual work to be done. It does not relate cost to time, but aims to set down alternatives in order to show the optimistic, pessimistic, or the most likely, course that a project will take. This technique of evaluation depends more extensively than **critical-path analysis**, on feed-back, for the control of variations in the project. Called also a 'project-network analysis' or 'program evaluation and review technique'. See also **project management**. *A Management Guide to PERT/ CPM*, by Jerome D. Wiest and Ferdinand K. Levy, 2 edn.

project management

The systematic planning and control of a project from inception to completion. The organisation of the resources required for a project, in terms of materials, equipment and skills, so that the requisite items are available at the right time and in the right place, and so that the project is carried through with the maximum efficiency and at the minimum cost. The aim of effective project management is to focus the decision making process on to one person or group of persons – the project manager – so as to facilitate communication, reduce misunderstanding and to enable the project manager to report succinctly to the principal or employer and report back and instruct those who are responsible for carrying through the project. See also **management con-**

tract, **project evaluation and review technique**.

Office Development, by Paul and Paula Marber, (eds.), (1985).

Design of Project Management Systems and Records, by A.T. Peart (1971).

Building Production and Project Management, by Burgess and White (1979).

Project Management for the Design Professional, by Frank Stasiowski and David Burnstein (1983).

Project Management Handbook, by David I. Cleland and William R. King (1983).

Project Management, by Dennis Lock, 3 edn., (1984).

Total Project Management, by E.A. Stallworthy and O.P. Kharbanda (1983).

Project Management in Construction, by Antony Walker (1984).

Advanced Project Management, by F.W. Harrison, 2 edn., (1983).

project sale-and-leaseback

A **sale and leaseback** of developed property, both land and buildings; especially of a newly completed development.

cf. **land sale-and-leaseback**.

project valuation

A simplified form of **residual valuation**, that uses only unit costs. A rough method of valuation used especially to value a development site. The valuation is made on the basis of the permitted plot ratio for the site; then the rent per unit of permitted development is capitalised and the unit cost of the building work is deducted, leaving a balance available which represents the estimated unit price for the purchase of the site. (A method of valuation which was accepted by the Lands Tribunal when determining a claim for compulsory purchase based on a before-and-after valuation in the case of The Trustees of the St. Clement Danes Holborn Estate Charity *v* The Greater London Council (1966) 198 EG 1045.

Valuer's Casebook of Approved Valuations, by R.W. Westbrook, Vol. 1, pp. 53–55 (1968).

projection period

see **holding period**.

projet (F)

project; plans; scheme; draft.

(*projet d'aménagement* – development project)

(*projet de loi* – Government bill).

promesse (F)

promise; promissory note.

(*promesse d'achat* – sales option)

(*promesse de vente* – purchase option)

(*promesse synallagmatique de vente* – contract for sale; **bilateral contract**)

promise

1. A declared intention or undertaking given by one person (promisor) to another (promisee) that one will do or not do something. An undertaking that something shall happen, or shall not happen, in the future. An undertaking to bestow something on another, or an assurance that something will be brought about. Usually an assurance which, when acted upon, will bestow a benefit on the person receiving the promise. A bare promise does not create a **contract** in English law, unless supported by consideration or evidenced under seal – Tweddle *v* Atkinson (1861) 1 B and S 393. Promise is used also to refer to any pledge, or earnest, given or received.

cf. **agreement**, **representation**. See

also **bargain, oral contract, warrant**.
2. The mutual undertakings given and received by the parties to a **bilateral contract**. A promise in a contract may be a **condition** thereof; but a condition is not necessarily a promise. See also **covenant**.

promisee
One who receives a **promise**.

promisor
A person who gives a **promise**.

promissory estoppel
see **estoppel**.

promissory note
"An unconditional promise in writing made by one person to another, signed by the maker [or promisee], engaging to pay, on demand or at a fixed or determinable future time, a certain sum of money, to, or to the order of, a specified person or bearer" – Bill of Exchange Act 1882, s. 83. The written document may be referred to as a 'promissory note', a 'bond' or simply a 'note'. A bank note is a promissory note with the bank as promisor. A mere acknowledgement of a debt, e.g. an IOU, is not a promissory note, nor is an offer of employment that promises payment. A promissory note, to take effect, must be delivered to the promisee (1882 Act, s. 81). A promissory note may be payable by instalments, but it is invalid if made payable on the occurrence of a contingent event. The promisee may retain it until payment is due or he may transfer it to another. The recipient must act in **good faith** when he acquires the note, without knowledge of any defect, if he in turn is to claim the payment when due.

A **mortgage** may be set out in two separate documents; the 'promissory note' which sets out the terms of the loan and the 'mortgage instrument' which sets out details of the property charged as security for the loan.
cf. **bill of exchange**. See also **negotiable instrument**.
Real Estate Principles, by Bruce Harwood, 2 edn., pp. 180–184.
Guide to Negotiable Instruments and Bills of Exchange, by Dudley Richardson, 7 edn., pp. 156–162.

promoter
1. A person or body that initiates a business venture, such as a scheme for the development of property. One who conceives and brings about new business and provides or obtains the requisite finance. In particular, a person who takes an active part in forming and raising finance for a new company. A person or body that provides finance for a new venture, in anticipation of deriving a profit therefrom, may also be referred to as a promoter. Professional advisors – lawyers, accountants, chartered surveyors, etc. – are not regarded as promoters when acting in their professional capacity. See also **property developer**.
2. A party authorised by Act of Parliament to execute works or undertake certain duties.

promoteur (F)
promoter; developer.
(promoteur immobilier – **property developer)**. See also *maître d'ourage*.

property
Anything that by its nature is capable of **ownership**, i.e. that which belongs or could belong to some person or persons. A right that a person has to withhold something from others, and is so protected by law. A thing or right

that has a monetary value and is capable of transfer. "Property is the most ambiguous of categories. It covers a multitude of rights which have nothing in common except that they are exercised by persons and enforced by the State. Apart from these formal characteristics, they vary indefinitely in economic character, social effect, and in moral justification. They may be conditional like the grant of patent rights, or absolute like the ownership of ground rents, terminable like copyright, or permanent like a freehold, as comprehensive as sovereignty or as restricted as an easement, as intimate or personal as the ownership of clothes or a book, or as remote and intangible as shares in a gold mine or rubber plantation." – *The Acquisitive Society*, by R.H. Tawney, pp. 56–57 (1921). In common parlance property is considered to be any object *per se*, i.e. a tangible thing; or the right to use, possess, enjoy and dispose of a thing. However, in jurisprudence and ethics it is referred to frequently as a benefit, or burden that one person receives, or bears, against another:
– "that low, bestial instinct which men call the right of property" (Leo Tolstoy, *Story of a Horse*).
– "what ever gratifies the passion for possession in one and disappoints it in another" (Ambrose Bierce, *Collected Works*, 1911).
– "that sole and despotic **dominion** over the external things of the world, in total exclusion of the right of any other individual in the universe" (Bl. Comm. vol. ii. p. 2).
– "the right to use and abuse. It is the absolute, irresponsible domain of man over his person and his goods. If it ceases to be the right to abuse it would cease to be property" (*Système*

des Contradictions Economiques, by P.J. Proudon).
Or, more analytically, "the term property may be defined to be the interest which can be acquired in external objects or **things**. The things themselves are not, in a true sense, property, but may constitute its foundation and material, and the idea of property springs out of the connection and control or interest which, according to law may be acquired in them or over them" – *The Institution of Property*, by C.R. Noyes, p. 357 (1936). (Magna Carta, the Declaration of Human Rights, the Constitution of the United States and the French Civil Code all refer to 'property' as something of which a person may not be deprived without due process of law; thus, it is a private right, a right of an individual, which is protected against any overriding power of the community).

Property, as a right of ownership, may mean **corporeal property** (e.g. land, a chattel, goods) or **incorporeal property** (e.g. a right of way, profit à prendre, choses-in-action). Or, in English law, because no proprietory interest can be more than a right or claim to ownership, all property may be considered as "an incorporeal right to the corporeal use and profit of some corporeal thing" – S.M. Leake, 1 Jurid. Soc., p. 542 (1857). Property may be classified also as **real property** – land or any right appertaining to land; and **personal property** – any property that does not relate to land.

English statute law provides various definitions which generally denote that 'property' includes real and personal property: any estate or interest in property; money or any debt; and anything that may be the subject of an action either *in rem* or *in personam*. For example, "'property' includes any thing in action and any interest in real or personal property" (Law of Property Act 1925, s. 205 (1) (xx)). In Hale *v* Hale [1975] WLR 931 – in connection with a matrimonial cause – 'property' was even held to include an assignable weekly tenancy.

In the US property is defined by the Uniform Property Act para. 1 (a) as, "one or more interests either legal or equitable, possessory or non-possessory, present or future, in land, or in things other than land, but excluding powers of appointment, powers of sale and powers of revocation"; and in the Uniform Probate Code para 1–201 (33) as, "both real and personal property or any interest therein and means anything that may be the subject of ownership". See also **bundle of rights theory, possession, private property, trust property.**

property bond
A form of property 'unit trust' that is administered by an insurance company. In the UK a **unit trust**, which accepts money from the general public, cannot be 'authorised' to invest directly in real property (although it may invest in the shares of property companies), due primarily to the illiquidity of such investment (Prevention of Fraud (Investment) Act 1958). However, since 1966 an investor may acquire a single-premium life assurance policy with profits linked to investment in real property, termed a property bond. The premium may be payable as one lump sum or by regular premiums over the life of the policy. In practice this investment is treated as if it were a purchase of units in a trust, the price of the units being related to the value of the underlying assets.
cf. **property unit trust.**
Valuation and Investment Appraisal, edited by Clive Darlow pp. 141–146 (1983).

property brief (US)
see **particulars of sale.**

property company
A company that invests primarily in land and buildings.
cf. **property unit trust.** See also **property investment trust.**

property developer
A person or body with an interest in real property that undertakes development or redevelopment, including the overall control of the building, financing and letting process. Commonly 'property developer' refers to any organisation that acquires land with the intention of building and reselling at a profit, as compared to an **institutional investor** who may undertake property development but with the intention of retaining the completed investment. See also **speculator.**

property development
see **development, development analysis, residual method of valuation.**

property insurance
Insurance against a **risk** associated with the ownership, use and occupation of property. Insurance of real estate is obtained to provide an **indemnity** against loss or damage arising from such matters as (a) fire (whether occasioned by explosion or otherwise), but excluding spontaneous combustion, and fire resulting from earthquake, subterranean fire, riot, civil commotion, war, rebellion,

revolution, and similar risks; (b) lightning and thunderbolts; (c) explosion (with similar exclusions to fire cover), unless caused by boilers; (d) vehicular impact, aircraft and articles falling therefrom: (e) storm, tempest, flood and burst pipes. The exceptions mentioned and damage resulting from subsidence, landslip and structural defect may be covered by an extended policy. (However, damage caused by radioactivity and nuclear explosion is not normally insurable). In addition, insurance may be taken out to cover loss of rental income as well as service charges that may be incurred even though a building may be unusable while undergoing repair. Injury to the public is covered usually by a separate **public liability insurance**. See also **all-risks insurance, comprehensive insurance, consequential loss insurance, engineering insurance, special perils**.
Real Estate Law, by Robert Kratovil and Raymond J. Werner, 8 edn., pp. 212–227.
Property Insurance, RICS (1983).

property line
see **boundary line**.

property management
The specialised function of supervision and control of real property. This includes, *inter alia*, the collection of rent and other income; verification and payment of expenses; if applicable, the apportionment and collection of service charges; repair, maintenance and cleaning of the property; liaison with tenants and occupiers; notification of rent reviews and lease renewals; the keeping and rendering of accounts; if necessary, the appointment of caretaking staff; regular inspection of the property; liaison with local and public authorities; and any other matters which affect the efficient running of the property. These responsibilities may be carried out directly by the owner or by a property manager acting as his agent. A **managing agent** may be responsible for all aspects of management, (or may be appointed to perform only specific functions e.g. collect rent), but normally he is not responsible for major building works, valuation, rating assessment, tax returns, negotiating rent reviews, reletting of vacant space, or planning matters, unless specifically so appointed. See also **estate management, portfolio management**.
Property Management, by Robert Kyle, 2 edn., Real Estate Education Company, Chicago.
Managing Business Property – A Legal Handbook, by T.M. Aldridge and T.A. Johnson (1978).
The Management of Urban Property, edited by T.A. Johnson (1972).
Commercial Property Management, by A.C.L. Grear and L. Oxborough (1970).
Property Management in Real Estate Decision-Making, by Austin J. Jaffe (1979).
Property Management, by Douglas Scarrett (1983).
Principles of Real Estate Management, by James C. Downs Jr., 11 edn.

property manager
A party appointed to carry out the responsibility and exercise the function of **property management**. See also **managing agent**.

property owner
A person who has **ownership** of property. See also **estate owner, landlord, landowner, owner**.

property owner's liability insurance
see **public liability insurance**.

property investment trust
An **investment company** that raises money by the sale of shares and invests the proceeds either in the shares of property companies or directly in real property. Generally investment is made on a discretionary basis, so that although the investment vehicle is a company, it performs its functions in the same manner as a trust.
cf. **property unit trust**. See also **property bond, real estate investment trust**.

property register
see *cadastre*, **land registration, Land Registry**.

property residual technique (US)
1. The valuation of land and the buildings thereon as a single entity, rather than as separate elements as in the **land residual technique** or the **building residual technique**. See also **residual method of valuation**.
The Appraisal of Real Estate, AIREA, 8 edn., pp. 395–396.
(US) 2. A method of valuing an income producing property by either (a) capitalising the **net income** attributable to the land, i.e. by deducting from the total income an amount that will accumulate, at compound interest, to replace or recapture the cost of buildings, and then adding an estimate for the **replacement cost** of the buildings. This method is applied only when the buildings or improvements that are to be recaptured represent a fairly insignificant part of the total value e.g. a farm building; or (b) capitalising net income, before

recapture, for a fixed term (e.g. the remaining term of a lease) and adding the **reversionary value** as a capital sum based on an assessment of comparable properties. This is not a separate method of valuation but merely a combination of two approaches adapted so that in the first instance the residual value of the land, and in the second instance the reversionary value, is the more significant factor. See also **term and reversion method**.

Property Services Agency (PSA)
A body first established in 1972 to act as an agency for the **Department of the Environment** and to be responsible for providing, equipping and management of property for Government Departments in England, Wales, Scotland, Northern Ireland and for the Foreign Office world wide. The PSA's activities fall into four main categories: design of new buildings and supervision of construction; maintenance of buildings, military and other installations; estate management; and the supply of furniture, fuel, domestic equipment, engineering plant, vehicles and transport, and office design services. The PSA also performs these services for a number of Government–related bodies.

property tax
Money levied by the government against the deemed value or against the income arising from property, rather than against an individual or a legal entity. A tax levied against real property may be referred to as a **land tax**, a real estate or realty tax, or simply a property tax. In the UK, the principal property taxes are **capital taxes** (e.g. capital gains tax, capital transfer tax, development land tax);

local **rates** (although strictly rates are payable by the occupiers of property); and **stamp duty**. In the US taxes on real estate include capital gains tax, documentary tax, inheritance tax and gift tax, as well as a state property tax on the assessed value of a property.
Handbook of Taxation of Land, by J. Graham, (1982).
Taxation of Land Transactions, by A.R. Mellows, 3 edn.

property unit trust (PUT)
A **unit trust** that invests in real property. In the UK, a unit trust scheme (as defined by the Prevention of Frauds (Investments) Act 1958, s. 26 (1)) to invest directly in real property must be authorised by the Secretary of State for Trade and Industry. Such trusts are authorised only to accept funds from organisations whose business is to invest in securities; in general these organisations have widely drawn investment powers and are exempt, or partly exempt, from income and corporation tax e.g. pension funds, charities, etc. (Private individuals are not permitted to invest directly in these trusts, because of the illiquidity and special nature of real property as an investment vehicle, but they are restricted to investment in **property bonds**.
   A unit trust that specialises in the purchase of shares in property companies may be called also a property unit trust, although it is more precisely called a 'property share unit trust', the term property unit trust being reserved for the more specialised trust referred to above.
cf. **property investment trust**.
Unit Trusts: the Law and Practice, by Martin Day and Paul Harris, pp. 122–124 (1974).

proposal
1. Something put forward for acceptance or rejection. An expression of a desire or willingness to perform an undertaking or to enter into a contract. It may be in the form of an **invitation to treat** or an **offer**.
2. A written proposal that an alteration should be made to the rating **valuation list**. Effectively, a proposal is a challenge to the rating assessment placed on a property. A proposal to alter the rateable value of a hereditament in the valuation list may be submitted by the valuation officer, or an "aggrieved person" who may be the owner, occupier, or the rating authority. Such a proposal may be made at any time but a reason must be given for the challenge; although almost any reason may be given, e.g. that the assessment is 'excessive, incorrect or wrong in law'. A proposal may be objected to by the owner, occupier, rating authority or the valuation officer and if agreement on a new assessment cannot be reached the matter is submitted to the **local valuation court** for determination.

proposal bond
see **bid bond**.

propriétaire (F)
owner (of property); **landlord**; **proprietor**.
(*propriétaire indivis* – joint owner)
(*propriétaire* – occupant; owner-occupier)
(*propriétaire sous condition* – limited owner, a right to property ownership subject to a **condition precedent**).

proprietas (L)
'**Property**; **ownership**'.

proprietary estoppel
see **estoppel**.

proprietary interest
A right to the **ownership** of property; an interest that is actionable *in rem*, against the thing, and not merely *in personam*, against the person. A right to property that represents an **estate** or **interest** in land; as distinguished from a personal right granted by a **licence** which is not an 'interest in land'. (A 'proprietary interest' may mean a right held by any person 'interested in land' – Pennine Raceway Ltd, *v* Kirkless Metropolitan Council (1982) 263 EG 721). See also **bundle of rights theory**.

proprietary lease
A lease between the company that holds a property in **co-operative ownership** and the tenant/shareholder who is granted a right to occupation of a particular unit. Called also an 'occupancy lease'.

proprietary rights
The rights which arise from the ownership of a property; especially the **natural rights**, as distinguished from acquired rights such as easements or leases. See also **proprietary interest**.

propriété (F)
property; ownership; estate. In French law property is an absolute right to the ownership of property (real or personal), "the right to enjoy and dispose of things in the most absolute way, provided that they are not used in a manner prohibited by laws or regulations" (French Civil Code, art. 544). Thus, ownership is the central element of French law of property (accordingly *propriété* may be translated both as 'property' and 'ownership'). French law does not recognise a **doctrine of estates** as in English law i.e. a succession of right to real property. In French law ownership attaches to land itself; there is no distinction between legal and equitable interest; and no trust or settlement can apply to real property – hence possession is a more important representation of ownership in French law compared to English law. Therefore, in French law an owner may, in theory, use property to a point of destruction without concern for any other person, provided his actions are not "prohibited by laws or regulations". *Biens, effets, avoirs, choses* and *objets* also are used to mean property and to draw distinctions between the types of property.
(*propriété commerciale* – business premises, a term that specifically refers to the right of a tenant of business premises to the renewal of his lease. See also *bail commercial*)
(*propriété commune* – ownership in common; co-ownership)
(*propriété foncière* – landed property; land ownership)
(*propriété individuelle* – severalty)
(*propriété industrielle* – industrial property. Used both in the sense of industrial buildings and industrial patents, trade marks, names, etc. – Sometimes called intellectual property.)
(*propriété louée à bail* – leasehold property)
(*propriété mobilière* – chattels)
(*propriété non bâtie* – building plot)
(*propriété viagère; propriété en viager* – life interest)
(*titres de propriété* – title deeds; deeds of conveyance)
(*pleine propriété* – bare ownership, absolute ownership, the nearest equivalent to an English **freehold**). See also *droit de propriété*, **real property**,

nue-propriété, **things, usufruct.**
Droit Civil 1ère année, by Jean Chevallier and Louis Bach, pp. 307–356.
Précis Dalloz. Droit Civil, Les Biens (Alex Weill), 2 edn., pp. 19–31.
Droit Civil, Les Biens, by Jean Carbonnier, 11 edn., p. 107 *et seq.*
Droit Civil, Les Biens by Gabriel Marty and Pierre Raynaud, p. 35 *et seq.*

proprietor
1. One who has **title** to a property; one who exerts control over something; a legal **owner** of a property. A proprietor has a full right to dispose of the thing he possesses, but that right might be deferred in time.
2. A person who derives **profit** from an enterprise, including a landlord. See also **land owner, registered proprietor.**

proprietorship
A term used synonymously with **ownership.**

proprietorship register
see **Land Registry.**

prorate
To assess proportionately. See also **apportionment, closing-cost adjustment, quarterly.**

prorogation (F)
extension (of time).
(*prorogation de bail* – **renewal** of a lease)
(*prorogation de terme* – **days of grace**).

prospect
see **prospective purchaser.**

prospective purchaser
A potential or interested purchaser (or seller) of real property. "The word 'prospective' does not connote neces-sarily either the term 'ready' or 'willing' or 'able'; it means a man who has the question of buying property in prospect or in contemplation and is prepared to make an offer with regard to it. This means that there must be a *bona fide* prospect" – Drewery and Another *v* Ware – Lane [1960] 3 All ER 532. On the other hand, when an estate agent is retained to "introduce a purchaser" for a property that means a person who enters into a binding contract to purchase and not a person "who was **ready, able and willing** to purchase, but who did not in fact proceed to the signing of a binding contract" – Jones *v* Lowe [1945] KB 75. (unless the principal clearly expresses a contrary intention).

protected furnished tenancy
see **furnished tenancy.**

protected long tenancy
see **long tenancy.**

protected occupier
see **eviction, residential occupier, tied accommodation.**

protected shorthold tenancy
A **protected tenancy** that, because it fulfills certain conditions, can be brought to an end after the term for which it was granted has expired by the landlord being able to seek a mandatory order for possession under the provisions of Case 19 of the 15th Schedule of the Rent Act 1977 (Housing Act 1980, ss. 51–55). The conditions that must be fulfilled are: (a) the tenancy must be granted for a fixed term, and not as a periodic tenancy, of not less than one nor more than five years; (b) there must not be any provision enabling the tenancy to be brought to an end during the term, except by way of **forfeiture** for a

breach of covenant; (c) *before* the grant of the tenancy the landlord must have given the tenant a notice, in the prescribed statutory form, stating that the tenancy is to be a protected shorthold tenancy; and, in London, (d) at the time the tenancy is granted, either (i) a **fair rent** must be registered for the dwelling house in question, or (ii) a certificate of fair rent must have been obtained and an application for the registration of the fair rent must be made (and not withdrawn) not later than 28 days after the beginning of the term. A protected shorthold tenancy cannot be granted to a person who, immediately before the tenancy was granted held a protected tenancy or a **statutory tenancy** of the dwelling house. A shorthold tenancy can be created only after 28 November 1980.

The holder of a protected shorthold tenancy has an absolute right to bring the tenancy to an end by (a) one month's notice, if the term was granted for two years or less; or (b) three month's notice if the term was granted for more than two years (1980 Act, s. 53). As a rule, a protected shorthold tenancy cannot be assigned (1980 Act, s. 54). Before the landlord who has granted a protected shorthold tenancy can take proceedings to recover possession of the dwelling house, he must have given at least three month's notice prior to the end of the fixed term (or, if given after the term has expired, during the same three months of any succeeding year) and the notice must be given and served in the prescribed form. Provided the statutory requirements are complied with, the court must then grant the order for possession as requested by the landlord (1980 Act, s. 55).

The Law of Landlord and Tenant, by David Lloyd Evans, 2 edn., pp. 314–318.
Residential Leases: a Draftsman's Handbook, by Charles Bennett, pp. 240–245 (1984).
Real Property and Real People, by K.J. Gray and P.D. Symes, pp. 449–451 (1981).
Woodfall's Landlord and Tenant, 28 edn, paras. 3–0186 A, 3–0207, 3–0746 to 3–0750, 3–0857/29.

protected tenancy

A **tenancy** of a **dwelling-house** (either an entire house or part of a house provided it is "let as a separate dwelling"), that is governed by statute law, so that the tenant is given the benefit of **security of tenure** and a right to apply for a **fair rent** to be fixed for the dwelling (Rent Act 1977, Part I, as amended by the Housing Act 1980). 'Protected tenancy' is the term applied to a contract of tenancy that is afforded this statutory protection, i.e. one that cannot be terminated except by the grant of a court order in accordance with the particular statutory provisions; and when that contract of tenancy comes to an end or expires the tenant is entitled to a **statutory tenancy**. (Since the Housing Act 1980 the term regulated tenancy is applied both to the protected tenancy and the statutory tenancy that arises thereafter). In précis, a protected tenancy is "a tenancy of a dwelling-house which qualifies for inclusion as being let as a separate dwelling and having a rateable value within the limits laid down by the Act" – Smalley *v* Quarrier [1975] 2 All ER 688. Basically, the rateable value limits currently exclude dwelling-houses with a rateable value in excess of £1500 in Greater

London and £750 elsewhere (Rent Act 1977, s. 4).

Apart from dwelling-houses that do not fall within the above definition, a tenancy of a dwelling-house does not normally qualify as protected tenancy if: (a) it is let with a substantial quantity of land (so that the land and not the house is the dominant subject of the tenancy); (b) it is let as **business premises**, including, as a rule, premises that are partly used for business and partly as a residence; (c) it forms part of an **agricultural holding** and the tenant is the farmer of the holding; (d) it forms part of, or is let with, **licenced premises**; (e) it is occupied by an incumbent of an ecclesiastical benefice of the Church of England; (f) the landlord is an exempted body, e.g. the Crown, a local authority, a New Town authority, a registered housing association, a housing trust, the Housing Corporation (although most tenants of such bodies are protected by having a **secure tenancy**); (g) the premises are let with living accommodation that is shared with the landlord; (h) the premises are let on or after 14 August 1974 by a **resident landlord**; (i) the tenant is pursuing a course of study at one of certain educational institutions (primarily universities or colleges of further education) and that institution is the landlord; (j) the premises are let as a holiday home; (k) no rent is charged, or the rent is less than two thirds of the rateable value; (l) the dwelling is let, *bona fide*, with **attendance** or **board** so that the cost of attendance forms a "substantial part of the whole rent" or the board is more than *de minimus*; (m) the tenancy qualifies as a **protected shorthold tenancy** or an **assured tenancy**;

(n) the premises are exempt by virtue of a ministerial order. Finally, there is no security of tenure so long as a dwelling-house is overcrowded or unfit for habitation; thereby enabling a landlord to comply with statutory requirements enforced by a housing authority in this respect. See also **furnished tenancy, grounds for possession, long tenancy, restricted contract, secure tenancy**.

Manual of Housing Law, by Andrew Arden, 2 edn., pp. 44–52.

Landlord and Tenant Law, by David Yates and A.J. Hawkins, pp. 279–300 (1981).

The Law of Landlord and Tenant, by David Lloyd Evans, 2 edn., pp. 238–322.

Housing Law, by Andrew Arden and Martin Partington, pp. 88–116 (1983). Woodfall's Landlord and Tenant, 28 edn., paras. 3–0007 to 3–0021.

protection from eviction
see **eviction, security of tenure**.

protective covenant (US)
see **restrictive covenant**.

protective trust
A **trust**, especially one established to hold property for the life time of the beneficiary, which contains a provision that it may be terminated on the occurrence of a specified event, because that is considered to be in the best interest of the beneficiary, e.g. if the beneficiary tries to sell his interest or becomes bankrupt – at that stage the trust income is applied for a better purpose such as the support of the beneficiary's family. Called also a 'spendthrift trust' or 'alimentary trust'.
cf. **bare trust**. See also **determinable interest**.

provisional agreement

An **agreement** reached between two or more parties which, although normally creating a binding contract, requires that certain details or formalities are still to be arranged. Generally the means of agreeing these points is outlined in the agreement, with a reference to arbitration for disputed matters. See also **conditional contract, gentleman's agreement**.

provisional notice

Notice served on the owner of a dwelling-house by a local housing authority, prior to an **improvement notice**, specifying work to be done in order to provide the requisite **standard amenities**, and seeking an undertaking from the owner that such amenities will be provided (Housing Act 1974, s. 85 (1)).

provisional sum

A sum of money included in a building cost estimate, or set down in a **bill of quantities**, for an item that cannot readily be priced (which may or may not be required), or as a general contingency. It is understood by the parties to a building contract that this amount is provisional and the sum will be adjusted or agreed upon at a stage when more information is available, e.g. when soil tests are available or when the actual time taken for certain work can be ascertained. See also **contingency sum, prime-cost sum**.

proviso

A clause in a written contract, usually beginning with words such as 'provided always that', that imposes a **condition, limitation** or qualification on the operation of the agreement, e.g. a clause in a lease giving the landlord a right of re-entry in the event of a breach of covenant. In particular, a proviso is a qualification to a previous stipulation, covenant or condition. "This word hath divers operations. Sometimes it worketh a qualification or limitation, sometimes a condition, and sometimes a **covenant**." (Co. Litt. 146b). "In a lease the terms 'proviso' and condition are synonymous, and signify some quantity annexed to an estate, by virtue of which it may be defeated, enlarged or created upon an uncertain event." (Woodfall's Landlord and Tenant, 28 edn, para. 1-0530).

cf. **exception**. See also **usual covenant, warranty**.

proviso for redemption

see **equity of redemption**.

proviso for re-entry

see **forfeiture clause, right of re-entry**.

proxy

A contraction of procuracy – a letter or **power of attorney**. A person, or the document appointing a person, to act on behalf of another; in particular, an appointment to vote at a meeting. See also **mandate**.

public auction

The sale of a property by **auction** following extensive advertising to attract public attention. A public auction is used most commonly in uncertain market conditions; for the sale of unusual property; for the sale of small investment properties or farms where the potential purchasers may be widespread geographically; or following the exercise by a mortgagee of his **power of sale**. In the US frequently called a 'public sale'.

public dedication
see **dedication**.

public domain
Land owned or controlled by the government. See **domain**.

public easement (US)
A **right of way** over land for the benefit of the public. (In English law, an **easement** cannot exist as a right for the public). See also **easement in gross, footpath, highway**.

Public Health Acts
A series of Statutes, especially the Public Health Acts 1875 and 1936, passed to control new building, by providing minimum standards of design, layout, sanitary conditions and amenities. See also **Town and Country Planning Acts**.

public highway
see **highway**.

public house
A place licenced to sell intoxicating liquor to the public at large for consumption on the premises. Unlike an **hotel**, a public house does not essentially offer sleeping accommodation. See also **inn, licenced premises, tied house**.

public housing (US)
Housing provided by the government for low-income families. Similar to council housing in the UK. See also **council house**.

public index map
see **index map**.

public land
Land owned by a public authority or government. See also **open space, public domain, public property**.

public lands survey system (US)
see **government survey system**.

public liability insurance
Insurance against the risk of damage or injury to members of the public (other than employees) or another's property from matters that arise from the ownership of property or from the conduct of a business. Called also 'property-owner's liability insurance', 'third-party liability insurance', or merely 'liability insurance'.
cf. **property insurance**. See also **professional liability insurance**.

public notary
see **notary**.

public nuisance
see **nuisance**.

public open space
see **open space**.

public park
see **open space, park**.

public participation
A process whereby new development proposals, especially for areas of comprehensive development, new highways, and major public works, are presented to the public for their comment to give them the chance of sharing in the formulation of planning policies and proposals. Such participation is used increasingly to obtain public reaction to a development or planning proposal outside the requirement for a public hearing. See also **planning inquiry**.
Department of the Environment Circular 52/72 on the Town and Country Planning Act 1971, part II.
Practical Planning Law, by J.F. Garner, Ch. 12 (1981).
Land, Law and Planning, by Patrick McAuslan, pp. 97–141 (1975).

The Ideologies of Planning Law, by
Patrick McAuslan, pp. 11–74 (1980).

public path
"'Public path' means a highway being
either a **footpath** or a **bridleway**."
(National Parks and Access to the
Countryside Act 1949, s. 27). See also
bridleway, footpath.

public property
Property owned by a State or
government body. Property that may
be enjoyed by the public at large, or a
large sector of the public.
cf. **private property**. See also **public
domain, highway, open space**.

public recorder's office (US)
An office wherein details of documents relating to the transfer of an
interest in land are recorded. Called
also a County Recorder's office, a
Registrar's office or a Bureau of Conveyances. See also **land registration**.

public road (or roadway)
see **highway**.

public sale
A sale of property conducted with
due notice that any member of the
public may attend and may buy. See
also **public auction**.

public sector tenancy
see **secure tenancy**.

public trustee
A government official, originally
established under the Public Trustee
Act 1906, who is appointed as a **trustee** when a trust exists but no person
has been appointed to administer that
trust, as when there is no will made by
a deceased or no trustee is nominated
under a settlement. See also **trust
corporation**.

public utilities (US)
see **utilities**.

public utility company (US)
A private company that provides utilities for the public at large.

public utility easement
see **wayleave**.

public utility undertaking
see **statutory undertaker**.

public way
see **highway**.

publici juris (L)
'Of public right'. Used to describe
property that may be used by any
member of the public, e.g. a highway
or public footpath, or a right to light
or air. See also **natural rights, *res
nullius***.

puffer
One appointed to bid on behalf of an
owner at a sale by auction in order to
excite interest and force up the bidding. The secret employment of a person to bid up the price of goods, by
making people think that someone is
prepared to purchase when he has no
such intention, is a **fraud** – Green *v*
Baverstock (1863) 32 LJCP 181.
However, at an auction for the sale of
land, provided that it is made known,
in the particulars or conditions of sale
available to all potential bidders, that
the vendor, or a person acting on his
behalf, is bidding there is no such
fraud (Sale of Land at Auctions Act
1867, s. 6). In the US called also a
'by-bidder'.
cf. **buy-in**. See also **mock auction,
reserve price**.
*The Law of Estate Agents and Auc-
tions*, by J.R. Murdoch, 2 edn., pp.
486–493.

puffing

1. Exaggerated statement about a property, usually one that is being offered for sale, so as to enhance the attributes of the property; the exaggeration is obvious as such to an interested party e.g. "superior residence", "much sought after location". Such a statement can be seen to be highly subjective and, provided it is not a statement of fact, does not constitute misrepresentation. This form of statement is found frequently in an estate agent's or broker's particulars of sale. See also **representation**.

2. The act of employing a **puffer** to bid up prices at an auction.

puisne mortgage

A **legal mortgage** of unregistered land that is not protected, in terms of **priority**, by the mortgagee holding the title deeds to the legal estate. Usually the first legal mortgagee holds the title deeds and all other legal mortgages are puisne mortgages. The priority of a puisne mortgage depends on its date of registration as a **land charge**, not on the date of its creation. If a puisne mortgage is not registered it loses its priority (Law of Property Act 1925, s. 97; Land Charges Act 1972, s. 2).

In English law, prior to 1925, puisne mortgage meant any mortgage that was subordinate to a first mortgage. In the US it still has the same meaning.

cf. **equitable mortgage**. See also **overreachable interest, tacking**.

puller tenant (US)
    see **anchor tenant**.

punch list (US)
    see **defect's list**.

punitive damages

Damages that exceed the actual loss suffered and are intended to have the effect of a **penalty**. Called also 'exemplary damages'.

cf. **liquidated damages**.

pur autre vie (L)

(Pronounced "per ohter vee"). 'For the life of another'. See **life interest, tenant for life**.

purchase

To procure or acquire ownership of something voluntarily and in exchange for valuable consideration; to buy or acquire for money or an equivalent. The consummated action of a **purchaser** "The word purchase (*perquisitio*) is applied in law to any lawful mode of acquiring property by the person's own act or agreement, as distinguished from acquisition by acts of law, as descent, escheat and the like. A purchase in the above sense includes **acquisition**, not only under contract of sale for a valuable consideration, but also by gift or without consideration, and by devise." – *Property in Land*, by Leake, p. 117. "'Purchase' includes taking for sale, discount, negotiation, mortgage, pledge, lien, issue or re-issue, gift or any other voluntary transaction creating an interest in property." (United States Uniform Commercial Code para. 1–201 (32)). See also **estate contract, sale, words of purchase**.

purchase agreement
    see **agreement for sale**.

purchase and leaseback
    see **sale and leaseback**.

purchase contract (US)
    see **contract for sale**.

purchase cost
see **acquisition cost**.

purchase money
The **money** or **money's worth** required as **consideration** to acquire a property or an interest in property. On the **completion** of a purchase of land payment should be made in legal currency, unless there is an agreement to the contrary. Strictly, a cheque or banker's draft is unacceptable on a conveyance of land (although these forms of payment frequently are accepted, the former usually emanating from a solicitor). See also **purchase price**.

purchase-money deed of trust (US)
see **purchase-money mortgage**.

purchase-money mortgage (US)
A mortgage obtained by a vendor of land from the purchaser as security for all or part of the purchase monies, the mortgage obtained pursuant to an **instalment contract**. Since the mortgage deed is entered into concurrently with the conveyance of the property, it usually takes priority over all other mortgages. If the mortgage is obtained on terms that are more favourable than the purchaser would acquire elsewhere, this is termed 'creative financing'. Called also 'seller financing'. A similar arrangement secured by means of a deed of trust is called a 'purchase-money deed of trust'.
cf. **cash out**. See also **financing, lien**.
Real Estate Law, by Robert Kratovil and Raymond J. Warner, 8 edn., pp. 351–357.

purchase notice
A notice served by an owner of land on a local authority, in accordance with the provisions of the Town and Country Planning Act 1971, s. 180, requiring the authority to acquire his property, following a refusal of planning permission or a grant of conditional planning permission. The server of the purchase notice must be able to demonstrate that, as a result of the refusal of the permission applied for or because of the conditions imposed, his land is incapable of "reasonably beneficial use in its existing state", after taking full account of any form of **permitted development**. The notice is served on the county borough, London borough or county district council for the area in which the land is situated, who may accept it (either directly or by referring it to another authority who has agreed to purchase the land), in which case the council or authority is "deemed to be authorised to acquire the interest of the owner compulsorily" (Town and Country Planning Act 1971, s. 181), i.e. the purchase notice has much the same effect as a notice to treat served by an authority possessing compulsory purchase powers. Alternatively, the council may reject the notice by submitting a copy to the Secretary of State and notifying the owner of its reasons. The Secretary of State then must adjudicate on the validity, or otherwise, of the notice.

A purchase notice may be served also if a local authority issues (i) a notice requiring the demolition of an obstructive building; (ii) an improvement notice; (iii) a revocation order or modification order; (iv) a discontinuance order; (v) a tree preservation order; (vi) a refusal of consent to the display of an advertisement on land; (vii) a notice refusing (or conditionally approving) listed building consent; or (viii) a refusal of consent for certain minor forms of development

(development considered as part of the '**existing use rights**' of land as set out in the Country Planning Act 1971, Part I, Sch. 8). In all but the first two cases (which are covered by the provisions of the Housing Act 1974, ss. 74, 101), the purchase notice procedure is the same as for a refusal or conditional grant of planning permission and the land-owner must be able to demonstrate that his land is "incapable of **reasonably beneficial use** in its existing state". See also **blight notice, inverse condemnation**. *Modern Methods of Valuation*, 7 edn., pp. 459–463.

Boynton's Guide to Compulsory Purchase and Compensation, 5 edn, pp. 107–112.

An Outline of Planning Law, by Desmond Heap, 8 edn., pp. 271–276.

Law of Compulsory Purchase and Compensation, by Keith Davies, 4 edn., pp. 241–249.

Encyclopaedia of Compulsory Purchase and Compensation, by Harold J.J. Brown, paras. 1–030 to 1–033, 2–2122 *et seq.*

purchase offer
see **offer**.

purchase option
An **option** to **purchase**; often used to refer to the right of a tenant to purchase the landlord's interest on the expiry of a lease. See also **call option**.

purchase price
The cash, or monetary equivalent, actually paid by a purchaser to acquire a property. Consideration paid consequent upon a contract for the sale of property. See also **acquisition cost**.

purchaser
One who acquires property, or a right to property, by **purchase**. A person (buyer) who obtains something for valuable consideration from another (seller). "'Purchaser' may ... mean any one of four things. First, it may bear what has been called the vulgar or commercial meaning; purchaser may mean a buyer for money. Secondly, it may include also a person who becomes a purchaser for money's worth, which would include the case of an exchange. Thirdly, it may mean a purchaser for valuable consideration, which need not be money or money's worth, but may be, say, a covenant or the consideration of marriage. Fourthly, it may bear that which in the language of real property lawyers is its technical meaning, namely, a person who does not take by descent." – Inland Revenue Commissioners *v* Gribble [1913] 3 KB 218. A person who acquires property by adverse possession, by testament, as a result of intestacy and, as a rule, by gift, is not a purchaser.

English statute law contains a variety of definitions of purchaser which includes anyone who obtains property, other than by operation of law, provided there is something of value given in exchange. "'Purchaser' means a purchaser in good faith for **money** or money's worth and includes a lessee, mortgagee or other person who in good faith acquires an interest in property for money or money's worth; or in reference to a legal estate includes a chargee by way of a legal mortgage" (Law of Property Act 1922, s. 188 (27)). The Law of Property Act 1925, s. 205 (xxi) contains a similar definition except that for the purpose of certain parts of the statute "valuable consideration" replaces "money or money's worth"; and "where the context so requires purchaser includes an intending purchaser". (For this definition valuable consideration includes a covenant in consideration of marriage, but does not include a nominal consideration in money.) In land registration "'purchaser' means a purchaser in good faith for valuable consideration and includes a lessee, mortgagee, or other person who for valuable consideration acquires any interest in land or in any charge on land" (Land Registration Act 1925, s. 3 (xxi)); and for the registration of land charges "'purchaser' means any person (including a mortgagee or lessee) who, for valuable consideration, takes any interest in land or in a charge on land" (Land Charges Act 1972, s. 17 (1)).

purchaser for value
see **bonafide purchaser, value**.

purchaser's lien
see **lien**.

purchaser's policy (US)
see **title insurance**.

purger (F)
(*purger une hypothèque* – to pay off, or redeem, a mortgage).

purposes of a valuation or appraisal
see **valuation**.

put option
An **option** available to a holder of property, stock, or a commodity to sell to another at a previously agreed price at a future date. Normally the party who has agreed to purchase the subject matter has paid a certain sum of money (a premium) for the benefit of being able to buy at the agreed price; usually because the buyer expects to make a profit when the subject matter is acquired.
cf. **call option**.

Q

qua (L)

'In the capacity of; considered as', e.g. *qua* trustee – 'as a trustee'.

qualification certificate

A certificate that a local authority granted to the landlord of a dwelling-house which was let as a **controlled tenancy** confirming that the property had been rendered fit for human habitation by the provision of **standard amenities**. The certificate was a prerequisite to the conversion of a controlled tenancy to a **regulated tenancy** (Housing Finance Act 1972, s. 27). The Housing Act, 1980 converted any remaining controlled tenancy to a regulated tenancy and, therefore, such certificates are no longer applicable.

qualified acceptance

Acceptance of an offer made subject to certain reservations or conditions. Such an acceptance does not constitute complete acceptance of the offer and, therefore, is effectively a **counter-offer**. See also **'subject to contract'**.

qualified estate

see **qualified fee**.

qualified fee

A **fee** interest in land that is limited or modified in some way, so that it will not endure to the holder for ever. "A base or qualified fee is such a one as has a qualification subjoined thereto, and which must be determined whenever the qualification annexed to it is at an end." – Bl. Comm. vol. ii. p. 109. A qualified fee may, for example, be a **conditional fee simple** (one that comes to an end upon the occurrence of a condition precedent) or a **determinable fee simple** (one that may come to an end on the occurrence of a contingent event specified when the estate is granted). Called also a 'modified fee' or 'qualified estate', or in the US a 'defeasible fee' or 'qualified fee estate'.

cf. **absolute estate**. See also **base fee, fee simple defeasible, qualified title**.

qualified fee estate (US)

see **qualified fee**.

qualified land

Land against which an **unexpended balance of established development** value has been registered.

qualified property

1. A limited right to property, e.g. personal property against which a bailee has a right to possession. A precarious form of ownership that lasts only as long as it is enjoyed, as with a right of light.
2. Property that has no owner, e.g. wild game, fish, water, but may be reduced to private ownership in certain circumstances (Bl. Comm. vol. ii p. 391). See also *res nullius*.

qualified title

A registered title to property granted when an **absolute title** has been applied for but the Land Registrar is unable to accept the application due to a defect in the title. When an owner of land applies to register an absolute title, but can only prove a limited right, due to some defect or prior claim, the registrar may accept the title subject to a specified prior claim or subject to an "excepted estate, right or interest" (Land Registration Act 1925, s. 7, 12). A qualified title arises frequently when a document or evidence of title has been mislaid.

quality of estate
The nature of an **estate** in land according to its certainty, e.g. freehold or leasehold, present or future; or according to its manner of enjoyment, e.g. solely or in common.
cf. **quantity of estate**.

quantitatif (F)
bill of quantities.

quantities
The part of a **bill of quantities** that sets out a description of the individual items to be costed and provides a place to insert the quantity of each item required.

quantity allowance
An allowance or deduction made when assessing the value of one property, as compared to another, to take account of a significant difference in size. As a rule, a larger property has a lower value per unit area compared to a smaller one. Thus, a deduction (usually as a percentage) may be made from the unit value of a **comparable property** before applying that unit value to the property to be valued. It is a means of giving account to the view that there is greater competition for smaller properties, or *vice versa* – Marks and Spencer Ltd *v* Chandler (V.O) (1959) R and IT 639. A quantity allowance should be made only when there is evidence that demand for large properties is likely to be more limited than for smaller ones, and not when supply and demand are reasonably in balance or when there is a shortage of larger properties. See also **zoning**.

Mainly for Students, Quantity Allowances 200 EG 920 (1966).

quantity of estate
The nature of an **estate** in land according to its term or duration, e.g. life interest or lease for 99 years.
cf. **quality of estate**.

quantity survey (US)
see **quantity surveying**.

quantity survey method (US)
A method of estimating the **replacement cost** of a building by adding together the cost of every component required to construct that building – materials, labour, overheads, profit, etc. See also **cost approach**, **quantity surveying**.

quantity surveying
The economic and financial measurement, analysis and control of building or construction work. A process whereby the cost of building work is estimated by breaking down the building work into its component parts – materials, labour, time, overheads, profit, etc. – and ascertaining a price for each of these parts in order to arrive at a cost for the whole. This process may be divided into three basic stages (i) measuring the dimensions of the proposed building or construction work from the architect's drawings (called **taking-off**); (ii) working out the volumes, areas, etc. of the building (called **squaring** the dimensions); (iii) working up the totals (including **abstracting** i.e. grouping similar items together) and pricing the work by applying appropriate cost rates. These detailed workings generally are set out in a **bill of quantities** which may be used by a building contractor to establish a contract price. Quantity surveying may include also

related work, such as considering the most economical form of layout, materials and methods of construction; estimating the time for building work; cost planning in conjunction with all members of the construction team; advising on alternative forms of building contract and building contractor; preparing tender documents; project control; valuation of completed construction work; preparing and agreeing accounts with contractors; settling cost disputes; and any similar work undertaken by a **quantity surveyor**. In the US referred to usually as a 'quantity survey'.
Quantity Surveying: Practice and Administration, by D.F. Turner, 3 edn.
The Anatomy of Quantity Surveying, by G.A. Hughes, 2 edn.
Elements of Quantity Surveying, by Arthur J. Willis and Christopher J. Willis, 7 edn.
Advanced Quantity Surveying, by A. Ashworth and B.C. Heath, (1983).
More Advanced Quantity Surveying, by Christopher J. Willis and Leonard Moseley, (1984).

quantity surveyor
One who advises on construction costs; estimates the cost of building work; advises, analyses and supervises the cost aspects of a building contract; and carries out other work associated with the process of **quantity surveying**. A quantity surveyor is employed by the building owner or the architect. He has no contractual relationship with the builder, unless there is a clear intention to create such a relationship. His primary duty is to prepare detailed quantities, based on plans prepared by the architect, to enable the builder to estimate the

amount for which building work can be executed – Taylor *v* Hall (1870) IR 4 CL 467.

In the UK, a quantity surveyor is a separate professional advisor from an architect or engineer (which is not normally the case in the US and most European countries) and most practitioners are members of the **Royal Institution of Chartered Surveyors**, the Institute of Quantity Surveyors or the Incorporated Association of Architects and Surveyors. A person may not describe himself as a 'chartered quantity surveyor' unless he is a member of the Royal Institute of Chartered Surveyors – Royal Institute of Chartered Surveyors *v* Shepherd (1947) 149 EG 370.
Practice and Procedure for the Quantity Surveyor, by Arthur J. Willis and Christopher J. Willis, 8 edn.

quantum (L)
'Amount'. See **quantity of estate**, ***quantum meruit***.

quantum damnificatus (L)
'The amount of damage suffered'. See also **damages**.

quantum meruit (L)
'As much as he has earned (or deserved)'. A principle that owes its origin to the doctrine of ***assumpsit***, 'he promised', i.e. that a person undertook work on the understanding that he or she would be paid for the effort. "If I employ a person to transact any business for me, or perform any work, the law implies that I undertook, or assumed to pay him for so much as his labour deserved. And if I neglect to make him amends, he has a remedy for this injury by bringing his action on the case upon this implied *assumpsit*" – Bl. Comm. vol.

iii. p. 161. A action for *quantum meruit* may arise (a) from a **quasi-contract**, i.e. a contract that is not made expressly, but arises when the actions of the parties demonstrate that there is an intention to accept the mutual benefits and burdens that are in the nature of a contract; or (b) when it can be shown clearly that a person is to be paid for work done, or services rendered, but the appropriate amount of that payment has not been expressly set out in a contract, or cannot readily be ascertained by reference to any agreement. There is an established equitable principle that one party to a contract (express or implied) should be reimbursed for the benefit rendered to the other party to that contract, even if the contract has not been fulfilled in its entirety – Planche *v* Colburn [1824–34] All ER Rep. 34. In that case, it was stated that three sets of circumstances may give rise to a *quantum meruit* payment: (i) when there is an agreement that a 'reasonable', but unspecified, payment should be rendered; (ii) when it is intended that work should be paid for, but no sum of money is specified; (iii) when a contract has been cut short due to unforseen circumstances (as when it has been recognised as void), but it is reasonable that a payment should be made for work done up to that stage.

A principal whose liability to pay a **commission** to an agent is expressed to be contingent upon success, promises to pay only if the agent's objective is achieved: "There is no promise to pay reasonable remuneration if the principal revokes the authority to the agent. And it is a further objection to a claim on a *quantum meruit* that the employer has not obtained any bene-

fit. The agent has earned nothing until the event materialises" – Luxor (Eastbourne) Ltd *v* Cooper [1941] AC 141. There can be no implied liability to pay an agent for services when there is an express liability to pay only for success – Lott *v* Duthwaite (1803) 10 TLR 76.

A person who is induced to provide a service in anticipation of receiving a contract, e.g. a builder who makes estimates and obtains quotations beyond what would normally be expected of him, may be entitled to a payment for the benefit he has rendered – William Lacey (Hounslow) Ltd. *v* Davies [1957] 1 WLR 932. cf. **unjust enrichment**. See also **part performance**, **void contract**.

The Law of Estate Agents and Auctions, by J.R. Murdoch, 2 edn, pp 69–70, 462–463.

Anson's Law of Contract, 26 edn, pp 596–600.

Chitty on Contract, 25 edn, paras 2047–2052.

Hudson's Building and Engineering Contracts, 10 edn, pp. 62–63.

9 Halsbury's Laws of England, 14 edn paras. 692–699.

quarry

Derived from the Latin *quarriere*, a place where a person cuts stones into 'quarters'. A place where mineral is extracted but, unlike a **mine**, one that is not below ground. "An excavation or system of excavations made for the purpose of, or in connection with, the getting of minerals (whether in their natural state or in solution or suspension) or products of minerals, being neither a mine nor merely a well or borehole or a well and a borehole combined" (Mine and Quarries Act 1954, s. 180).

quarterly (or every quarter)
Four times a year. This may be every 91 days (Co. Litt 91b), every quarter day, or at three monthly intervals. If nothing is expressed to the contrary, an annual sum payable 'quarterly' is due every quarter of a year from the commencement date, taking the most probable quarterly interval; unless the commencement date is one of the **quarter days** and then it is payable every quarter day – Vanaston *v* Mackarly 2 Lev. 99.

quarter days
Days accepted by legal custom as being appropriate when payments are due 'quarterly' or on the 'usual quarter days'. In England and Northern Ireland these days are: 25 March (Lady day); 24 June (Midsummer day); 29 September (Michaelmas); 25 December (Christmas day). In Scotland the 'half-quarter days' or 'term days' are used: 15 May (approximately) (Whitsunday); 1 August (Lammas day); 11 November (Martinmas); 2 February (Candlemas) (although it is more common for half-yearly payments to be made on Whitsunday and Martinmas). In the US and many Continental European countries, the commonly accepted 'quarter days' are 1 January: 1 April: 1 July: 1 October (although there is no legal custom in this respect).

quasi (L)
'As if it were; similar to'.

quasi-contract
An **agreement** that parties purport to enter into by their actions, resulting in one party being enriched at the expense of the other, so that the former is under an obligation to make **restitution** to the other as if a contract

had been established between them. An arrangement that manifestly is not a **contract** and does not arise from a tort, but one that the law is prepared to enforce. "It is clear that any civilised system of law is bound to provide remedies for cases of what has been called **unjust enrichment** or unjust benefit, that is, to prevent a man from retaining money of, or some benefit derived from, another which it is against conscience that he should keep. Such remedies in English law are generically different from remedies in contract or in tort, and are now recognised to fall within a third category of the common law which has been called quasi-contract or restitution" – Fibrosa Spolka Akeyjna *v* Fairbairn Lawson Combe Barbour Ltd. [1943] AC 61. Thus, for example, the owner of a ship is bound to pay for its rescue from peril. "It is a legal liability, arising out of the fact that property has been saved, that the owner of the property who has had the benefit of it shall make remuneration to those who have conferred the benefit upon him, notwithstanding that he has not entered into a contract on the subject" – The Five Steel Barges (1890) 15 PD 146. It may be considered that a similar principle applies to someone who expends money, as a matter of necessity, and not solely as a voluntary act, in order to save another's home from an imminent peril.

Quasi-contracts arise most frequently when a person has received a pecuniary benefit by a mistake of fact; as a result of an ineffective or incompleted contract; arising from a necessity; when money is paid for something, but another should have made the payment, as where as surety pays in place of the principal debtor; or where an unfair advantage or duress has been used to secure a pecuniary benefit.

The principle of payment for unjust enrichment is well established in Roman law; "if one man has managed the business of another during the latter's absence, each can sue the other by the action on uncommissioned agency; the direct action being available to him whose business was managed, the contrary action to him who managed it." – 3 Just. Inst. 27, 1. Similarly it has been adopted by French law (Civil Code, art. 1370) and is widely acknowledged in the US; but it is treated with some reservation in English law which will seek first to tie an obligation to a contract (as an **implied contract**) or to a tort (e.g. a failure to fulfil an obligation or waiver of a right arising from a tort). In the final analysis the distinction between an implied contract and a quasi-contract is one of degree of intent. See also **agency of necessity, constructive trust, estoppel,** *quantum meruit.*

Amos & Walton's Introduction to French Law, 3 edn, pp. 192–199.

Anson's Law of Contract, 26 edn, pp. 571–578.

Chitty on Contract, 25 edn, para. 10.

Cheshire & Fifoot's Law of Contract, 10 edn, pp. 574–601.

9 Halsbury's Laws of England, 4 edn, paras. 630–750.

quasi-contrat (F)
quasi-contract; implied contract.

quasi-delict
see **delict,** *quasi-délit.*

quasi-délit (F)
quasi-delict. A wrong or injury caused to another, in particular by an unintentional harm caused by failure to act within the confines of the law. Similar to tort in English law. See also *délit.*

quasi-easement
An **easement** that arises by implication, e.g. an easement acquired with land as being necessary for the reasonable enjoyment of that land. A quasi-easement is that form of right over one parcel of land in favour of another parcel of land which has all the elements for a valid easement, except that both parcels of land are in the same ownership. This right comes to life when one of the parcels of land is transferred to a new owner who would expect to continue to enjoy the land in the same manner as his predecessor. A quasi-easement is one that can be seen to belong, or to be detectable as belonging, to the property granted, such as drains or watercourses that are in existence; a right over a made track; or a right of light to an existing window. Such a right is not expressly granted and, although it may include an **easement of necessity** that is not apparent, it will not include a right of way that has to be established anew. "On the grant by the owner of a tenement of part of that tenement as it is then used and enjoyed, there will pass to the grantee all those continuous and apparent easements (by which, of course, I mean quasi-easements), or, in other words all those easements which are necessary to the reasonable enjoyment of the property granted, and which have been and are at the time of the grant used by the owners of the entirety for the benefit of the part granted". – Wheeldon *v* Burrows [1879] 12 Ch. D 49.

A term that may be used to refer also to an easement that is lacking in some essential element, although this is more strictly an **equitable easement**. See also **implied grant**.
Land Law: Cases and Materials, by R.H. Maudsley and E.H. Burn, 4 edn., pp. 524–529.
Cheshire's Modern Law of Real Property, 13 edn, pp. 506–511.
Gale on Easements, 14 edn, pp. 92–106.

quasi-entail
An **entailed interest** (or entail) granted for the life of someone other than the holder of the interest. An estate in land that arises when an interest in land is granted to a person and the heirs of his body *pur autre vie*, 'for the life of another', i.e. it is granted to that person and his descendant only for as long as the other person, the *cestui que vie*, lives. For example, if a **tenant for life**, A, settles *his* interest in land on "B and the heirs of his body and thereafter on C", B has a quasi-entail which comes to an end on the death of A; in effect A did not have a sufficient interest at the outset to grant a true entailed **interest**.

quasi-estoppel
see **estoppel**.

quasi-possession
Possession of a right, as compared to possession of a thing; in effect the **enjoyment** of the right, as with an easement.

quasi-possession (F)
right to an **easement**.

quasi-rent
1. A payment for the use of personal property, e.g. a payment made under a leasing agreement. (Strictly **rent** is a

payment for the use of real property, but 'rent' is employed commonly to refer to a payment under a hire purchase or a similar agreement relating to personal property).
2. see **economic rent**.

quasi-tenant at sufferance
A sub-tenant who continues to occupy land after his own and his landlord's lease has come to an end, without the head-landlord consenting or dissenting. See also **tenancy at sufferance**.

quasi-usufruct (F)
see **usufruct**.

que estate (F)
Norman French for 'whose estate'. Land in which an interest, in the nature of an easement or profit à prendre, has been acquired by prescription: "those whose estate he has; which last is called prescribing a *que estate*." – Bl. Comm. vol. ii. p. 264.

qui approbate non reprobat (L)
'He who accepts cannot reject'. See **election**.

qui facit per alium facit per se (L)
'He who acts through another is deemed to act in person', i.e. the authorised acts of an agent are the acts of a principal. See also **agency**.

qui prior est tempore potior est jure (L)
'He who is first in time has the strongest claim in law'. A maxim that may be upheld, in equity, where the merits of a claim for **priority** are equal – Rice *v* Rice (1853) 2 Drew. 78. "But where the merits are unequal, as for instance where conduct on the part of the owner of the earlier interest has led the other to acquire his interest on the supposition that the earlier did not exist, the maxim may be displaced

and priority accorded to the later interest." – Latec Investments Ltd *v* Hotel Terrigal Pty Ltd. (In Liquidation) (1965) 113 CLR 276.

qui sentit commodum sentire debet et onus (L)

'He who enjoys the benefit ought also to bear the burden'. See **restrictive covenant**.

Quia Emptores (L)

'For as much as the purchasers'. The title given to a statute passed into English law in 1290 which made major reforms of land law. It permitted free men to sell land without the consent of the lord of the manor and restricted a fee simple estate to one person, i.e. it abolished **subinfeudation** (Bl. Comm. vol. ii. p. 91). (The statute was the Statute of Westminster III 18 Edw. I c. 1. and it commenced with the words *Quia emptores terrarum et tenementorum de feodis magnatum*, 'For as much as purchasers of lands and tenements of the fees of great men'). See also **feudal system**.

quicquid plantatur solo, solo credit (L)

'That which is fixed to the soil, becomes a part of the soil'. See **fixtures, leasehold, enfranchisement**.

quid pro quo (L)

'Something in return for something'. See **consideration, contract**.

quiet enjoyment

The right of a purchaser, or lessee, not to have his proper use and enjoyment fettered or interrupted by any act of the vendor, or lessor, or any lawful act of someone rightfully claiming under or in trust for the vendor, or lessor – Howell *v* Richards (1809) 11 East. 642; Trimble *v* Seattle, 231 US 683, 34 S.Ct. 218, 58 LEd 435. The right of quiet enjoyment refers in the main to such matters as denial of a proper title or of a right of possession, rather than to noise or physical disturbance. It does not refer to acts of strangers. A landlord who covenants to give quiet enjoyment "promises not to interfere with the tenant's exercise and use of the right of possession during the term. I [Pearson L.J.] think the word 'enjoy' used in this connexion is a translation of the Latin word *fruor* and refers to the exercise and use of the right and having the benefit of it, rather than to deriving pleasure from it" – Kenny *v* Preen [1962] 3 All ER 819. A landlord must not subject a tenant to persistent intimidation, or continually obstruct access to the premises, or otherwise prevent a tenant from peacefully using the premises for the purpose for which they were let. A mere "temporary inconvenience which does not interfere with the estate, title or possession" is not a breach of covenant for quiet enjoyment – Phelps *v* City of London Corporation [1916] 2 Ch. 255; Manchester, Sheffield and Lincolnshire Railway *v* Anderson [1958] 2 Ch. 394. There is an **implied covenant** for quiet enjoyment in every grant of a tenancy of land, even if there is no such provision expressed in a lease – Markham *v* Paget [1908] 1 Ch. 697.

If a vendor sells land as **beneficial owner** he implies that the purchaser will receive a right to quiet enjoyment of the land granted (Law of Property Act 1925, s.76, 72, Sch. 2. Pts. I & II) cf. **derogation from grant, harassment**. See also **constructive eviction demise, eviction, peaceably and quietly, re-entry**.

Adkin's Landlord & Tenant, 18 edn

pp. 77–79.
Landlord and Tenant Law, by David Yates and A.J. Hawkins, pp. 98–101 (1981).
The Law of Landlord and Tenant, by David Lloyd Evans, 2 edn., pp. 89–91, 137.
Hill and Redman's Law of Landlord and Tenant, 17 edn, pp. 196–206.
Woodfall's Landlord and Tenant, 28 edn, paras. 1-1282 to 1-1316.
27 Halsbury's Laws of England, 4 edn, paras. 322–335.

quiet title action (US)
An action brought in a court of law to establish a **good title** to real property, especially an action taken to remove a **cloud on title**. The action is brought against any person who maintains a claim to the subject property in order to establish the validity, or otherwise, of his claim(s). See also **quitclaim deed**.

quiete clamare (L)
'To give up all claims'. See also **quitclaim deed**.

quietus redditus (L)
Quit rent.

quit
To set free or release; to leave or give up possession permanently. Free and clear. See also **notice to quit**.

quit rent
A form of rent, payable under the **feudal system** of land tenure, that enabled a tenant (being a freeholder or ancient copyholder) to discontinue his obligation to render services to the lord of the manor i.e. he was permitted to go 'free and clear' of all services (Bl. Comm. vol. ii. p. 42). Quit rents were abolished in England in 1926. A term used sometimes to refer to a chief rent or **fee farm rent**.
In the US, the term quit rent may be used to refer to the final payment by a tenant before he gives up possession of real property, or to a perpetual payment or **rentcharge** reserved by the seller of a fee simple interest. See also **mesne profits**.

quitclaim deed (US)
1. A deed by which a person acknowledges that he has given up any action or claim to land that he might have against another. A term that has been superceded by a **deed of release**. See also **deed of grant**.
(US) 2. A deed of conveyance that transfers such interests in a property as the grantor has, without giving any guarantee that the grantor has any title or right to possession of the property. The grantor cedes or 'quits' any claim or title that he has, or claims to have, to a property i.e. it is a release of an interest or right to land – Moelle *v* Sherwood, 148 US 21, 13 SCt 426, 37 LEd 350. The deed does not contain any covenants and is used only when the grantor purports to have certain rights to land and thereby may be lifting a **cloud on title**. Called also a 'release of deed'.
cf. **bargain and sale deed**, **warranty deed**. See also **title insurance**.
Real Estate Principles, by Bruce Harwood, 2 edn., p. 96 (for an example of a quitclaim deed).

quittance
1. The discharge of an obligation or debt. See also **accord and satisfaction**.
2. A document that acknowledges the discharge or payment of a debt.

quittance (F)
discharge (of a debt); **receipt**.

(*quittance de loyer* – rent receipt, in French law an important element in establishing the existence of a tenancy).

quitte (F)

free, of debt.

quitus (F)

discharge; receipt in full.

quod aedificatur in area legata cedit legato (L)

'That which is built on ground that is granted by will passes to the devisee.' See **fixture**.

quod meum est sine me auferri non potest (L)

'What is mine cannot be taken away without my consent'; but see **compulsory purchase** and **eminent domain**.

quod vide (q.v.) (L)

'Which see'.

quotation

A document by which a person gives a prospective customer or employer an indication of the terms upon which the former is prepared to undertake specific business. A statement of the price at which a contract may be entered into; commonly used in relation to building work. A quotation, in general, is not intended to constitute an **offer**; but, "a quotation might be so expressed as to amount to an offer to provide a definite article, or to do certain works, at a defined price. But the ideas of quotation, and of an offer to sell are radically different". – Boyers *v* Duke [1905] 2 IR 624. An offer is intended to form a basis for a contract; a quotation is intended to be used for comparison, further analysis, or negotiation; but not for acceptance as the basis of a contract.

cf. **estimate**. See also **invitation to treat**.

R

rabais (F)

reduction (in price); **rebate**; **discount abatement**; allowance.

(*vendre au rabais* – to sell at a discount)

(*vente au rabais* – sale by dutch auction).

rachat (F)

repurchase; redemption; release; surrender.

(*rachat d'une obligation* – redemption of a debenture)

(*droit de rachat* – option to purchase cf. **droit de préemption**)

(*valeur de rachat* – **surrender value**; redemption price).

rachmanism

The exploitation of a tenant of residential property by taking advantage of a position of weakness due to his or her income, age, race, etc. The term is derived from Mr Perec Rachman who, in London between 1954 and 1960, "is alleged to have used hired bullies to intimidate statutory tenants by violence and threats of violence into giving vacant possession of their residence and so placing a valuable asset in the hands of the landlord". – Cassell and Brown [1972] AC 1079. A term now used to refer to any form of **harassment** or exploitation of residential tenants, which seeks to extract exorbitant rents or to evict the occupants so as to realise a higher price for a property by selling it with vacant possession. See also **eviction**.

The Limits of Legal Process: a Study of Landlords and Crime, by David Nelken, pp. 1–28 (1983).

Rachman, by Shirley Green (1981).

rack rent

The highest annual rent at which a property can be let. Historically, and still in the US 'rack rent' means the highest rent a landlord can obtain in the open market. In particular, an extortionate or exorbitant rent ("to oppress men by rack-renting land is particularly detestable" – *The Agrarian Problems in the Sixteenth Century*, by R. H. Tawney, 1921). In old English law it was used also to signify a rent that had been freely negotiated between a landlord and tenant, as distinguished from a charge for the privilege of land tenure under the **feudal system**: "a rent of the full value of a tenement, or near it" – Bl. Comm. vol. ii. p. 41). In modern usage rack rent merely signifies the best **market rent** obtainable for a property especially as distinguished from a lower rent payable under an existing contract of tenancy; "the value at which the premises are worth to be let by the year in the open market – that is to say, what a tenant, taking one year with another, may fairly and reasonably be expected and required to pay" – Gundry *v* Dunham (1916) 85 LJKB 422. If the maximum rent recoverable from a tenant is limited by statute, for instance to a **fair rent** as registered under the Rent Act 1977, then that rent is the rack rent for the premises at the time of the letting – Rawlance *v* Croydon Corporation [1952] 2 All ER 543; Newman *v* Dorrington Developments [1975] 1 WLR 1642. In English statute law 'rack rent' is used frequently to mean a rent that is "not less than two-thirds of the full

annual value", especially as distinguished from a **low rent** or **ground rent** (Public Health Act 1936, s. 343; Housing Act 1957, s. 39 (2); Highways Act 1980, s. 329 (1)).

Radburn

A form of layout for a residential estate, originally designed for the town of Radburn, New Jersey, USA, in which pedestrian access is segregated almost entirely from vehicular access by means of bridges and underpasses, and by means of a network of footpaths that lead to the front of the houses but do not abut on to the road as on a conventional estate. Vehicular access is provided by feeder roads from which a series of cul-de-sacs give access to the rear of the houses where parking areas and garages are located. An adaption of this type of layout commonly was used for the design of many of the housing estates developed in the postwar English new towns. Although, "the famous Radburn development in New Jersey was based on the principle of the super-block, an area surrounded by through roads into which a number of culs-de-sacs thrust their way like sperm into an ovum. On one side the houses fronting these culs-de-sacs had a short garden, beyond which was the cul-de-sac carriageway. On the other side was the main garden, at the end of which ... there was a space occupied by footways. The kind of layout loosely described as 'Radburn' ... constructed in Coventry, Basildon New Town and a number of places is really not like this at all. The front garden, or small garden, abuts upon the footpath and greenway, while the main garden, or back garden, abuts upon the cul-de-sac carriage way" (*Town Planning at the Crossroad*, by Lewis Keeble, p. 121 (1961)).

radiation (F)

(*radiation d'inscription* – termination of a mortgage, by repayment)
(*radiation d'hypothéque* – the official annulment of a mortgage registered against a property by the registrar of mortgages).

rang (F)

order; class; priority.
(*rang hypothécaire* – mortgage priority)
(*capacité de remboursement en premier rang* – first-class covenant)
(*hypothéque en deuxième rang* – second mortgage).

ransom strip

A strip of land that fronts a public highway and, because it is in separate ownership, prevents an owner of another parcel of land from obtaining access to the highway, i.e. a piece of land that prevents a landlocked owner from fully exploiting his land, thus placing him in a position of being held to 'ransom' by the owner of the strip of land. See also **easement of necessity**, **marriage value**.

rapport (F)

1. **return**; profit ratio.
(*immeuble de rapport* – investment or income producing property)
(*maison de rapport* – tenement house).
2. reimbursement; restitution.
3. report.
(*rapport d'expert* – expert's report; survey)
(*rapport d'expertise* – **valuation report**; survey)

ratable property
see **rateable property**.

rate
1. In proportion. A direct relationship between amounts, e.g. a **ratio** of income to capital value, or interest to principal, expressed as a percentage. cf. **factor**. See also **interest rate, rate of return**.
2. According to **value**; a charge, payment or estimate made according to an assessed quality or value, especially when measured against some other unit. For example, a charge made by a contractor for an amount of work done.
3. To estimate the worth or value of something; to place a value on an item or commodity.
4. A local tax to which the occupier of a property is subjected; in particular, a tax based on the **rateable value** of a property and levied by an authority that has jurisdiction over a district in which the property is situated in order to pay for services provided by that authority. The General Rate Act 1967, s. 115 (1) defines 'rate' as basically equivalent to the 'general rate', being a single levy made by a **rating authority** on any occupier of land, houses, mines of any description, woodlands, sporting rights or advertising rights to pay for services provided by that authority, but excluding certain 'excepted rates' referred to in section 115 (1).

rate of interest
The rate at which a sum of money earns **interest**, i.e. the rate, usually on an annual basis, at which a price is paid for borrowed money. See also **compound interest, discount rate**.

rate of return
The relation, expressed as a percentage, between the net income or profit derived from an investment and the amount of capital invested – usually calculated at an annual rate. See also **accountant's rate of return, amortisation rate, capitalisation rate, discounted rate of return, cash-on-cash return, internal rate of return, overall rate of return, sinking fund rate, true rate of return, yield**.

rateable hereditament
see **hereditament**.

rateable occupation
Occupation of property which is of such a nature that it is deemed sufficient to create a liability for the occupier to pay **rates**. This term is not defined by statute, but English case law has established that it requires four elements or 'tenets of rating': (i) **actual occupation**, i.e. physical possession by which the occupier derives some benefit from the tangible use thereof, a mere intention to occupy a property is not sufficient to constitute rateable occupation – Hampstead Borough Council *v* Associated Cinema Properties [1944] KB 412; (ii) **exclusive occupation**, or sufficiently exclusive for the purpose of the person having that right, i.e. a right to exclude others from the property in the same way as the occupier; (iii) occupation that is of value to the occupier, i.e. 'beneficial occupation' – Kingston-upon-Hull Corporation *v* Clayton [1963] AC 28; (iv) occupation of a reasonably permanent nature. (An itinerant showman has only transient occupation and not rateable occupation: R *v* St. Pancras Assessment Committee (1877) 2 QBD 581; but a trespasser may have the benefit of rateable occupation.). "First, there must be actual occupa-

tion; secondly, it must be exclusive for the particular purposes of the possessor; thirdly, the possession must be of some benefit to the possessor; and fourthly, the possession must not be for too transient a period" – John Laing and Sons Ltd, v Assessment Committee for Kingwood Assessment Area [1949] 1 KB 344 (a case which decided that the occupier of a builder's hut was in rateable occupation). **Unoccupied** property, as a rule, is not liable to rates if no benefit can be derived therefrom; but a property that was left unoccupied because there was no winter trade was deemed to be beneficially occupied, taking the year as a whole – Mayor, etc., of Southend-on-Sea v White (1900) 65 JP 7. Rating law treats such occupation like fruits of a tree and looks at the overall benefit to be derived from a property.

Ryde on Rating, 13 edn, pp. 20–121. 39 Halsbury's Laws of England, 4 edn, paras. 15–42.

rateable occupier
A person who is in **rateable occupation** of a property.

rateable property
Property that is capable of being the subject of a rating assessment, including **unoccupied** property; as distinguished from property that is incomplete or under reconstruction. See also **hereditament, rateable occupation**.

rateable value
1. The value of something estimated according to a proportionate rate.
2. The annual value of a hereditament as determined for the purpose of levying a local tax; in particular, the value as assessed for the purpose of charging rates. Rateable value may be assessed as a **gross value** or a **net annual value**, depending on the type of property. Unless there is some indication to the contrary 'rateable value' means 'net annual value' – Waller v Thomas [1921] 1 KB 541. Called also an 'assessed value'. See also **rating valuation**.

rates
A tax paid to a local authority by an occupier of property on the basis of the assessed annual value (the **rateable value**) of that property. The amount of this tax is expressed at a uniform amount per pound of rateable value as determined for each property (General Rate Act 1967, s. 41 (a)). The tax is paid by the occupiers of most properties in the local authority's area of jurisdiction and the revenue is used to finance the needs of the authority levying the charge or the needs of any authority that has levied a precept on that authority. Similarly, a levy made by a statutory body to pay for local utilities also may be called rates, e.g. water rates, drainage rates. A rate represents a charge for the benefit of occupying a property to which the authority provides a service: it is payable by anyone who is deemed to be in **rateable occupation** of a property. Rates are an imposition spread over a district to cover expenses in that district, as distinguished from a levy or assessment imposed on a particular property to pay for an expense directly related to that property.

If a property is let and there is no express provision in the lease or tenancy agreement as to who shall pay the rates, the liability rests with the tenant in rateable occupation. If there is a covenant in the lease that one party is to pay "all rates" that includes a liability to pay water rates – Direct Spanish Telegraph Co. *v* Shepherd 13 QBD 202; unless the covenant indicates that the word 'rates' is intended to be limited to a local tax imposed for the benefit of occupation, rather than for a service available to the tenant personally. Thus a covenant to 'bear, pay, and discharge all rates, taxes, and impositions whatsoever whether parliamentary, parochial, or imposed by the corporation of the City of London or otherwise' was interpreted to exclude water rates – Badcock *v* Hunt (1888) 22 QBD 145. See also **duty, rate, tax, usual covenant**.

Business Property Handbook, The Boisot Waters Cohen Partnership, pp. 283–295 (1981).

Hill and Redman's Law of Landlord and Tenant, 17 edn, pp. 305–314.

Woodfall's Landlord and Tenant, 28 edn, paras. 1-1327 to 1-1355.

ratification

The approval, confirmation or sanctioning of an act or agreement; especially an act or agreement made by another, that did not have prior authorisation. For example, a person may ratify a prior action, which has been performed on his account, so as to give effect to that action as if it had been authorised originally – Bolton Partners *v* Lambert (1889) 41 Ch. D 295. In particular, an act of an agent that is approved by a principal after the event, even though, at the time the act was carried out, it was outside the agent's normal duties or was not expressly incorporated in the terms by which the agent was appointed. As a rule, in order for ratification to be

effective (a) the principal must be fully aware at the time of the ratification of all the circumstances and facts surrounding the agent's action; (b) the agent whose act is sought to be ratified must have purported to act as an agent; (c) at the time the act was done the principal must have been in existence, be capable of being ascertained, and have been competent to act as principal; and (d) at the time of the ratification the principal must be capable legally of doing the act himself – Firth *v* Staines [1897] 2 QB 75. A company cannot ratify an action done prior to its formation and an agent remains personally liable for any contract that he enters into on behalf of a company that is to be formed – Kelner *v* Baxter (1866) LR 2 CP 174; European Communities Act 1972, s. 9 (2). (However, in certain cases, a company that acts *ultra vires* may be liable to a third party who contracts in good faith believing that the directors had capacity to bind the company: European Communities Act 1972, s. 9 (1).

An **undisclosed principal** cannot ratify an agent's action – Keighley, Maxted and Co *v* Durrant [1901] AC 2400; but an unnamed principal may be able to ratify an agent's action, provided the principal can be identified in due course by the third party and the third party knew that there was a relationship of agency affecting the transaction. There is no restriction as to the type of act that may be ratified and the ratification may be express, or implied from the conduct of the principal after the event. However, the act must be ratified in its entirety. A ratified act takes effect from the date it took place, not the date of the ratification. Ratification of a deed must be made itself by deed. See also **agency, authority, estoppel**. Anson's Law of Contract, 26 edn, pp. 530–533.

Cheshire and Fifoot's Law of Contract, 10 edn, pp. 425–429.

The Law of Agency, by G.H.L. Fridman, 5 edn., p. 73–96.

Bowstead's Law of Agency, 15 edn, pp. 51–83.

ratification (F)
ratification; approval.

rating
1. The process of assessing the value of a property for local property taxation purposes. See also **rates, rating valuation**.
2. See **credit rating**.

rating authority
A local authority that determines the amount of rates to be levied in an area and uses the proceeds therefrom to finance the expenditure it considers appropriate for that area. The rating authorities for England and Wales are district councils, the councils of the London Boroughs, the Common Council of the City of London, the Sub-Treasurer of the Inner Temple and the Under-Treasurer of the Middle Temple (General Rate Act 1967, s. 1 (1) as amended by the Local Government Act 1972).

rating list
see **valuation list**.

rating valuation
The **valuation** of a property for the purpose of levying rates thereon; the assessment of the **rateable value** for a property. The value of a property (**hereditament**) for rating valuation purposes represents the deemed annual value of the property (whether the **gross value** or the **net annual value**) at the appropriate **valuation date**, assuming (i) the hereditament is vacant and available for letting, and (ii) the premises are as they stand at that date – *rebus sic stantibus* – but are basically in good repair. Regard also should be had to the general level of assessed values for other properties on the valuation list – the **tone of the list**.

The principal methods used for this form of valuation are (i) the comparable or **rental method**; (ii) the **contractor's basis**; (iii) the **profits test**; (iv) the **formula method**. The valuation is carried out by the **valuation officer** for the area in which the property is situated. It is submitted to the person who has the benefit of **rateable occupation** of the property, who may accept the assessment or appeal by way of the **local valuation tribunal**. Each hereditament is separately assessed; although a property that is sub-divided or has a mixture of uses but is occupied as a whole, generally is valued as a whole. See also **proposal**.

Valuation for Rating, by R.R. Smith (1979).

Ryde on Rating, 13 edn, p. 442 *et seq.*

The Principle and Practice of Rating Valuation, by Roger Emeny and Hector M. Wilkins, 4 edn.

39 Halsbury's Laws of England, paras. 97–168.

Encylopaedia of Rating Law and Practice, ed. Harry Sales (1985).

ratio (L)
'Reason; cause'. See also *ratio decidendi*.

ratio
A rate or proportion. The relationship of one number to another; the

result of dividing one number by another. Ratios frequently are used as management tools – for example, a ratio may be calculated to indicate the financial standing of a company; for example, (i) a financial ratio, e.g. **debt-to-equity ratio, debt ratio, liquidity ratio**; (ii) an investment ratio, e.g. **price/earnings ratio, dividend yield** (a ratio expressed as a percentage); (iii) operating ratio, e.g. profit/turnover, profit/capital employed, debtors/sales.
cf. **factor**.
Business Ratios: A Guide to Interpretation, by Leon Hopkins, 2 edn.
Company Accounts: A Guide, by David Fanning & Maurice Pendlebury (1984).
Interpreting Company Reports and Accounts, by Geoffrey Holmes and Alan Sugden, 3 edn.

ratio (F)
ratio.
(*ratio d'endettement* – **gearing**)
(*ratio de levier* – **leverage ratio**)
(*ratio de liquidité* – **liquidity ratio**).

ratio decidendi (L)
'The reason or ground for a (judicial) decision'. The *ratio decidendi* of a case is the ruling that is binding as a **precedent** on an inferior court.
cf. *obiter dictum*. See also *stare decisis*.

ratione soli (L)
'By reason of the soil'. See **land, fixture**.

ratione solis (L)
'By reason only'.

ratione tenure (L)
'By reason of **tenure**', i.e. because a person holds land.

rattachement (F)
tacking.

ravalement (F)
cleaning and repointing (the exterior of a building). A term derived from French statute law, first brought into effect by a Paris law of 1852, which provides a right for a local authority to enforce the upkeep of the exterior of buildings by a property owner.

raw land
Land in its natural state; land that has never been cultivated, built on or improved. See also **agricultural land, unimproved land, wasteland**.

raze
To tear down a building; lay level with the ground; to carry out **demolition**. Raze, like erase, signifies complete removal, or making even with the ground.

re (L)
'In the matter of'.

'**ready, able and willing**'
An expression used to describe a **prospective purchaser** who is in a position to sign a *binding* contract. An estate agent's **commission** may be payable upon condition that he procures a purchaser who is 'ready, able and willing' to acquire a property on terms acceptable to the seller. If the agent fulfils that condition then, even if the seller withdraws the property, he has earned his commission. The 'ability' to purchase depends primarily on financial ability; "it is sufficient if it is proved by the agent or by the purchaser that the circumstances are such that if the vendor had been willing and ready to carry out his contract, he [the purchaser] on his part at the proper time could have found the

necessary money to perform his obligation." – James v Smith [1931] 2 KB 322; Pellaton v Brunski (1924) 69 Cal. App. 301, 231 Pac. 583. 'Ready' may be considered as interchangeable with 'able' and both may be impeded by an outside factor, such as the fact that a prospective purchaser of a lease was not a suitable assignee for the existing landlord – Comley v Wellman 65 WN (NSW) 268; Dellafiora v Lester [1962] 3 All ER 393. 'Willing' means that the purchaser should be prepared to put his signature to a binding contract; "for the words 'ready and willing' imply not only the disposition, but the capacity to do the act" – De Medina v Norman (1842) 11 LJ Ex 322. Moreover, if a purchaser offers to buy at less than the asking price, (and the vendor initially accepts) and fulfils the criteria outlined above, even though the sale does not proceed (for example, because the vendor then decides to sell to another at a higher price) the prospective purchaser, is considered as 'ready, able and willing' – Christie Owen & Davis v Rapacioli [1974] QB 781. "He must be a person who is 'able' at the proper time to complete; that is, he must have the necessary financial resources. He must also be 'ready'; that is, he must have made all necessary preparations by having the cash or a banker's draft ready to hand over. He must also be 'willing'; that is, he must be willing to hand over the money in return for the conveyance"... I (Lord Denning) can see no sensible distinction between instructions to 'find a purchaser', 'find a party prepared to purchase', 'find a purchaser able and willing to complete the transaction' and 'find a person ready, willing and able to purchase'. The right and liabil-

ities of house owners in these cases should not depend on fine verbal differences. If estate agents desire to get full commission not only on sales, but also on offers, they must use 'clear and unequivocal language': See Luxor (Eastbourne) Ltd., v Cooper [1941] AC 108, 129 per Lord Russell" – Dennis Reed Ltd. v Goody [1950] 2 KB 287–8. In many states in the US, in the case of house sales, the accepted view is that an agent or broker is the best party to judge whether a prospective purchaser can obtain satisfactory financing and, therefore, if this proves not to be possible the agent cannot claim to have introduced a party who is able to purchase – Ellsworth Dobbs Inc. v Johnson, 50 NJ 528. A person is not 'willing' to purchase if all he has done is sign an agreement 'subject to contract' or 'subject to survey' – Graham and Scott (Southgate) Ltd v Oxlade [1950] 2 KB 257. However, two agents may be capable separately of introducing a purchaser 'ready, able and willing' and in that event they would both be entitled to commission: "where a prospective vendor binds himself to more than one estate agent, he may find himself liable to pay more than one commission." – Christie Owen and Davis Ltd, v Rapacioli supra at p. 790. In order to avoid such double commissions a vendor should not instruct more than one agent using this form of wording. The word 'prepared' may be considered to incorporate all three of the requirements of 'ready, able and willing'.

Real Estate Law, by Robert Kratovil and Raymond J. Werner, 8 edn., pp. 99–102.

The Law of Estate Agency and Auc-

tions, by J.R. Murdoch, 2 edn., pp. 243–261.

real action

1. An ancient common law action by which a freeholder sought to recover his land. A real action sought to recover possession or **seisin** of land and not merely damages for loss of a right to land. Most forms of real actions were abolished in 1833 and land is now recovered by **ejectment** (Real Property Limitation Act 1833, s. 37; Judicature Acts 1873–75). See also **action in rem, real property, recovery, writ of right.**

2. In Roman and the civil law an action taken to recover moveable or immovable property or proving a title to such property.

real asset

see **fixed asset, real estate.**

real chattel

see **chattel.**

real contract

In the civil law a contract that creates an obligation affecting a thing (*res*) and not merely a personal contract. In Roman law these contracts were *mutuum* (loan); *commodatum* (loan for use); *depositum* (deposit) and *pignus* (pledge). See also **action in rem.**

real covenant

A **covenant** that touches and affects land and therefore 'runs with the land' i.e. the benefit and burden is enforceable between parties who have an interest in the same land.

cf. **personal covenant.** See also **privity of estate, restrictive covenant.**

real effects

see **real property.**

real estate

Land and anything permanently fixed thereto, as well as any rights or interests in land. A right or claim that attaches to the very substance of land, as distinguished from **personal estate** which belongs to a person and as such is temporary and moveable. Historically 'real estate' meant property that was capable of being recovered by a *real* action (i.e. an action which sought to recover true possession of the property and not merely a bare claim supported by recompense). Thus, in a strict legal sense, real estate does not include a leasehold interest, which is regarded in English common law as personal estate (a 'chattel real') and is capable of recovery only by a personal action between the parties – Butler *v* Butler (1884) 28 Ch. D 71. However, this common law anacronistic interpretation of 'real estate' is superceded by the more common view that a leasehold interest is real estate. (Accordingly, in the US, real estate may even include a gas or oil lease; US *v* Texas Eastern Transmission Corp. (DCLa) 254 F.Supp. 114.)

In connection with the devolution of property on to a personal representative on a person's death, real estate includes "chattels real and land in possession, remainder or reversion, and every interest in or over land to which a deceased person was entitled at the time of his death; and real estate held on trust (including settled land) or by way of mortgage or security, but not money to arise under a trust for sale of land, nor money secured or charged on land" (Administration of Estates Act 1925, s. 3(1)). See also **chattel, fixture, real property.**

real estate agent

see **estate agent.**

real estate appraisal

see **appraisal, valuation.**

real estate broker
see **broker**.

real estate credit (US)
A loan grant against the security of **real estate**. See also **financing**.

Real Estate Commission (US)
A board established at state level to control the licensing of persons engaged in business connected with real estate. See also **commission, real estate license**.

real estate contract (US)
see **instalment contract, contract for sale (of land)**.

real estate investment trust (REIT) (US)
An unincorporated trust, or association, established under a law passed in 1961, that pools the funds of a large number of investors in order to place money exclusively in real estate, by direct investment, by granting mortgage loans, by leasing arrangements or by a combination of such methods. The trust is a passive investment vehicle; control is vested in the trustees and its income must accrue from such sources as rent and mortgage interest and not from property trading and development. Provided that the trust follows a strict set of rules laid down by the Internal Revenue Service; has not less than 100 investors or beneficiaries; is not more than 50 per cent owned by five or fewer individuals; and distributes 95 per cent of its income; then it is not taxed as a separate entity – Internal Revenue Code, ss. 856–860, 26 USCA para. 856. The investors are taxed only in their individual capacities.
A REIT that specialises in mortgage lending is called a 'mortgage trust', one that specialises in direct property investment an 'equity trust', and one that undertakes both forms of investment a 'hybrid trust'.
REIT Fact Book, National Association of Real Estate Investment Trusts (annual).

real estate licence (US)
A licence required by a person who wishes to act as an **agent** or **broker** in real estate. Any person who wishes to act as a real estate agent must have a state licence. Many states require a person who carries on any form of business relating to real estate to have a licence e.g. an appraiser, property manager, mortgage broker.
Real Estate Principles, by Bruce Harwood, 2 edn., pp. 411–438.

real estate listing
see **listing**.

real estate syndicate
A **syndicate** that specialises in real estate investment.

real estate tax
see **assessment, land tax, property tax**.

real property
Property that can be recovered by a real action, i.e. **land**, an interest in land and anything annexed to land that has become part of that land. A right to land or to anything that 'touches and concerns' land. Historically 'real' property was that which could be recovered *in specie* and land was that form of property; a real action could be brought only by a **freeholder**, i.e. one who had *seisin* of land – thus land became known in English law as real property. It may be distinguished from **personal property** which is recoverable only by means of a personal action for the

recovery of damages. "The term 'property' is used to denote either rights in the nature of ownership or the corporeal things, whether land or goods, which are the subjects of such rights. 'Real' denotes that the thing itself, or a particular right in the thing, may be specifically recovered; and, since originally specific recovery was only allowed in cases where the claimant was entitled to a freehold interest, that is an estate for life or a greater estate, 'real property' denotes (1) land and things attached to land so as to become part of it, and (2) rights in the land which endure for a life or were, under the law before 1926, inheritable, whether these involve full ownership or only partial enjoyment of land or the profits. On the other hand, rights in land which endured for a term of years only were not originally specifically recoverable and were described as 'chattels real' (39 Halsbury's Laws of England, 4 edn, para. 301). Thus, a right to a **lease-hold** is not strictly real property as it was regarded as no more than a personal right between parties that if infringed upon could be replaced by damages. However, in modern English practice, real property embraces land, as well as all interests or rights that extend to land itself – including a leasehold. Called also 'realty'. See also **chattel, corporeal property, hereditament, incorporeal property, ownership, real estate.**
Holdsworth's History of English Law, vol. iii, p. 3 *et seq.* & vol. vii, p. 3 et seq.
Megarry's Manual of the Law of Real Property, 6 edn, pp. 17–19.
The Law of Real Property, by Robert Megarry and H.W.R. Wade, 5 edn., pp. 10–11, 1147.

real representative
see **personal representative.**

real right
A right to property that entitles the person vested with that right to take possession of the property, as contrasted with a personal right which entitles a person only to exert a claim against another in order to compel performance of an obligation. In the civil law called a *jus in re*. See also **action in rem.**

real security
A **mortgage** or **charge** secured on property (real or personal) as contrasted with a personal obligation or guaranty which only grants contractual rights against a third party to a debt or obligation. See also **lien, pledge, rentcharge, security.**

real servitude
A **servitude** that restricts or limits the use of land, as distinguished from a personal servitude which is enforceable only between particular persons. See also **easement, restrictive covenant.**

real value
Value excluding changes in the purchasing power of money. The real value of a property may change due to physical changes, e.g. improvements to the property; changes in the neighbourhood; or changes in the supply and demand for the property rather than changes in the purchasing power of money. See also **intrinsic value.**

realisation or realization
The process of disposing of an asset, business or property, especially by converting it into money. See also **liquidation, sale.**

realised development value
see **development land tax**.

Realtist (US)
A member of a body affiliated to the **National Association of Real Estate Brokers** (NAREB).

Realtor (US)
A real estate broker who is an active member of the **National Association of Realtors** (NAR) (formerly the National Association of Real Estate Boards). 'Realtor' is a registered trade mark of that association and the use of the designation is governed strictly by the rules and regulations of the association.

realty
see **real property**.
cf. **personalty**.

realty reappraisal (US)
The periodic **revaluation** of a property. See also **revaluation lease**.

realty tax (US)
A tax on real property. See also **assessment, property tax, rate**.

reappraisal
see **revaluation**.

reappraisal lease (US)
see **revaluation lease**.

reasonable care
see **duty of care**.

reasonable market value
see **fair market value, market value**.

reasonable rent
The rent at which a property might reasonably be expected to let; the **market rent** for a demised property. Unless there is evidence to the contrary a reasonable rent is "assessed on an objective basis without reference to the particular landlord or the par-

ticular tenant or to the history of how the premises came to be built or paid for" – Ponsfor *v* HMS Aerosols Ltd, [1979] AC 83. See also **fair rent, restricted contract**.

reasonable time
see **time**.

reasonable wear and tear
see **fair wear and tear**.

'reasonably beneficial use'
A term, derived from the Town and Country Planning Acts (currently contained in the Town and Country Planning Act 1971, s. 180), that is used to denote the ability (or lack thereof) of a property to produce a modicum of profit to its owner. A use that, in all the circumstances, is of some particular benefit to the landowner. In the event that an owner of land is refused planning permission for development (or granted planning permission subject to conditions) and, as a consequence of that refusal (or the imposition of those conditions), his land, or a part thereof, is incapable of "reasonably beneficial use in its existing state" (or "cannot be rendered capable of reasonably beneficial use by the carrying out of the permitted development ... in accordance with those conditions") the owner may require the appropriate local authority to acquire the affected land by serving a **purchase notice** on the authority. The purpose of the purchase notice is "to enable a landowner whose use of his land has been frustrated by a planning refusal to require the local authority to take the land off his hands. The reference to 'beneficial' use must therefore be a reference to a use which can benefit the owner or a prospective owner of

the land and the fact that the land in its existing state confers no benefit or value upon the public at large would be no bar to the service of a purchase notice," – Adams and Wade Ltd., *v* Minister of Housing and Local Government and Another (1965) 18 P and CR 67. However, the land in question must be virtually useless and not "less useful ... in its present state than if developed" – R *v* Minister of Housing and Local Government *ex parte* Chichester RDC [1960] 1 WLR 587. There must be no reasonable prospect of deriving a benefit from the land even after taking full account of any form of development that may be permitted, either because it is authorised by a general development order or use classes order, or because it does not require planning permission. Thus an agricultural use, which does not require planning permission, or use as a sports field, may be beneficial and, therefore, in this context may take the land outside the application of a purchase notice. However, in the final analysis, what constitutes reasonably beneficial use is primarily a matter of fact and degree; to be determined by the Secretary of State for the Environment if the local authority refuses to accept the purchase notice (General Estates Co. Ltd, *v* MHLG [1965] EGD 98). See also **revocation order**.
Law of Compulsory Purchase and Compensation, by Keith Davies, 4 edn., pp. 242–245.
Cases and Materials on Planning Law, by Michael Purdue, pp. 437–445 (1977).
Encyclopaedia of Compulsory Purchase and Compensation, by Harold J.J. Brown, para. 2-2125 (1960 loose leaf).

reassessment
The process of fixing a new or a revised **assessment**;a **revaluation** of a property for local taxation purposes. A reassessment may be made when it is considered that a particular property is out-of-line with the value of comparable properties, or when all the properties that are liable to a particular tax are considered to need revaluation in order to bring them up to their current value. See also **proposal**.

rebate
A repayment or refund; a **discount**. A return of part of the interest due on a loan because of early payment of the loan. See also **abatement, kickback, rent concession**.

rebuilding
The process of replacing or restoring a building or structure to its original, or near its original, state or condition; in particular the demolition and reconstruction of the whole, or a substantial part, of a building in a similar, but not necessarily identical, form. It is possible to rebuild without producing a replacement in the same style or shape; it is not necessary that the replacement is used for the same purpose; and it may be possible as part of the process of rebuilding to make minor alterations or additions that were not part of the original building or structure. However, the process must go beyond mere alteration or repair; there must be a 'building anew'. Structural alteration and repair alone cannot amount to rebuilding. "To rebuild might mean to pull down entirely, and to re-edify in the same shape as before; or it might signify rebuilding in some parts and repairing the rest: but taking it in

either way, rebuilding and repairing must be something different from repairing merely" – Doe d. Dymoke *v* Withers (1831) 2 B and Ad. 902. In planning law, the construction of a building to a different design or size from the one that is being replaced does not constitute 'rebuilding' and, therefore, is likely to require planning permission – Bragg *v* Hurstville Municipal Council 21 LGRA. See also **reconstruction, reinstatement.**

rebus sic stantibus (L)

'The thing as it stands' When making a **rating valuation**, the assessment is made *rebus sic stantibus*. The property is valued in its existing state, and according to the circumstances, as at the date of the valuation, and not as it might be or could be made to be – Port of London *v* Orsett Union [1920] AC 273. Thus the valuer must ignore benefits that would arise if the property were altered, and any benefit that would arise from another "mode or category of occupation" – Fir Mill Ltd. *v* Royton UDC and Jones (VO) (1960) 175 EG 1029. However, full account is to be taken of any intrinsic factor that might affect the value: the property is to be valued "as it in fact is" – Robinson Brothers (Brewers) Ltd., *v* Houghton and Chester le Street Assessment Committee [1937] 2 KB 469. Repairs that a landlord might reasonably undertake prior to a letting are assumed to have been carried out (especially when assessing the gross value); unless the cost of those repairs is out of proportion to the rent obtainable for the premises, when it may be assumed that a landlord would let the premises in their existing state at a commensurately low rent – Saunders

v Maltby (1976) 239 EG 205.

In assessing **compulsory purchase compensation** the interest being acquired is to be valued *rebus sic stantibus*, just as it occurred at the date of **notice to treat**; thus the claimant may not seek recompense for changes he may bring about at a later date – for example, by granting a new lease at an enhanced rent. See also **tone of the list.**

recaption

The act of peacefully retaking goods or chattels that have wrongfully been retained by another.

recapture

The recovery of invested capital by the use of **net income**, by mortgage amortisation, or by equity appreciation. See also **net operating income, recapture clause, recapture of depreciation.**

recapture clause (US)

1. A clause in a lease that permits the landlord to terminate the lease and regain possession upon a stipulated condition; for example, if the tenant seeks to assign the lease or, in a turnover lease, if the tenant fails to maintain a given level of turnover. The latter instance normally applies only to a lease that provides for no minimum or base rent. See also **right of re-entry.**
2. A clause in a **ground lease** that provides the tenant with a right to purchase the landlord's interest at a specified time during the lease.

recapture of depreciation (US)

A provision whereby the Internal Revenue Service may recover tax underpaid by a taxpayer who has used a higher depreciation rate than is permitted. As a rule, on the sale of

real property, any capital gain that results from the application of depreciation at a rate that exceeds straight-line depreciation is taxed at income tax rates. Only gains due to appreciation from the original cost, after allowing for straight-line depreciation, are taxed at capital gains tax rates.
Tax Planning for Real Estate Transactions, by Jerome Y. Halperin, pp. 136–144 (1978).

recapture rate (US)
The annual rate at which the capital invested in a property is recovered from the net income the investment generates, after payment of interest on any loans secured on the property. Called also the 'capital recovery rate' or 'capitalisation rate'. See also **sinking fund rate**.

recasting (US)
Rescheduling, or rearranging the **priority** of, an existing loan.

receipt
A written acknowledgement, submitted by a recipient to a payer, that a payment has been made or goods delivered. Written evidence that one person has paid money or money's worth to another. In a contract for the sale of land, receipt is used to refer only to the acknowledgement of the consideration given for the property, not the acknowledgement of a grant of property *per se*.
A receipt clause, or words such as "the purchaser hereby acknowledges receipt", in a **deed** is sufficient recognition that the consideration money has been paid when the deed is executed, without the need for a separate receipt or for an endorsement on the deed (Law of Property Act 1925, s.

67); and to a subsequent purchaser such a receipt clause is sufficient evidence that the monies due have been paid in full (1925 Act, s. 68). A receipt is not required to be given in a ready-money transaction because, in effect, there is no debt – Bussey *v* Barnett (1842) 9 M & W 312. However a receipt, although *prima facie* evidence that a sum of money has been paid, is not conclusive evidence to that effect and may be rebutted by evidence that the money has not wholly or partly been paid – Skaiffe *v* Jackson (1824) 3 B and C 421.
A receipt endorsed on, written on the face of, or annexed to a mortgage deed by the person in whom the mortgage is vested, mentioning the person who owed the debt and acknowledging that the debt has been paid, normally acts as a reconveyance, surrender or release of the mortgaged property and discharges the mortgage (Law of Property Act 1925, s. 115).
cf. **release**. See also **deposit**.

receipt clause
see **receipt**.

réception (des travaux) (F)
Acceptance (of work under a building contract by the ***maître d'ouvrage***); Certificate (for building works). *Réception* may be express, or implied as when the owner takes possession of the building. *Recéption definitive* (the issue of a final certificate) is generally the point from which the ten year guarantee (***responsabilité decennale***) by the architect, *maître d'oeuvre* and *entrepreneur* (builder) commences.
(*réception définitive* – final certificate)
(*réception provisoire* – interim certificate).

recette (F)
receipt; **income**; **revenue**; **cash flow**, return.
(*recettes et depenses* – income and expenditure).

receiver

1. A person appointed by a court to administer and deal with property when it is considered that an independent party should take control in place of the person currently holding the property. A receiver may be appointed in the event of bankruptcy or on the dissolution of a partnership. A receiver, as a rule, is not appointed to manage a business, but to realise the assets and pay the debtors; although he may be permitted to manage a business in order to obtain the best return for the debtors.

2. A person appointed by a court to hold and conserve property that is the subject of litigation, or when the property is owned by someone who is mentally incapable, and to administer that property as agent for the court.

3. A person appointed by a **mortgagee** to collect income and manage property; usually pending the exercise of the mortgagee's **power of sale**. A receiver may be appointed without prior application to the court provided the mortgagee is empowered by the mortgage deed or a separate instrument to make such an appointment and provided the mortgage money has become due (Law of Property Act 1925, s. 101). The power to appoint a receiver arises and must be exercised in much the same way as a statutory power of sale. A 'receiver of rents' is deemed to be the agent of the mortgagor, to whom he must account, and his actions are regulated by statute law, in terms of his power

of appointment, remuneration, general powers and duties, and the order in which he must apply any rent he collects (Law of Property Act 1925, s. 109). Any order appointing a receiver or sequestrator of unregistered land may be registered as a **land charge** in the name of the estate owner of the land (Land Charges Act 1972, s. 6 (1) (b)); or in the case of registered land may be entered as a **caution** or **notice** against the registered title (Land Registration Act 1925, ss. 49, 54, 59).
32 Halsbury's Laws of England, 4 edn, paras. 742–748, 839–843.
The Law of Real Property, by Robert Megarry and H.W.R. Wade, 5 edn., pp. 947–949, 952–953.

reciprocal contract
see **bilateral contract**.

recitals
Statements, normally forming the introduction to a **deed** or other formal **instrument**, that set out its purpose and matter. 'Recitals' may be 'narrative' or 'introductory'. Narrative recitals are statements of fact such as a statement of the history that led up to the making of a deed, or an exposition of the subject matter of a deed or a previous related deed. Introductory recitals are statements of the motive or necessity for the rest of the document. Recitals usually start with the word 'whereas'; for example, a statement at the start of a conveyance – "whereas the owner is seised of an estate in fee simple absolute in Whiteacre...".

A recital is not essential to a contract or conveyance, but it is common practice to explain the reason or object for entering into an agreement. Recitals are not a substantive part of that which is agreed, i.e. they are not

operative parts of the document. The operative parts of a deed when expressed in clear and unambiguous language "are not to be controlled, cut down or qualified by a recital or narrative intention" – Mackenzie *v* Duke of Devonshire [1896] AC 408. However, a recital may clarify an ambiguity in an operative part of a deed and, in the absence of any contrary statement or fact, a recital may have the effect of an **estoppel** to any thing or action that clearly conflicts with it. In a conveyance such an estoppel may have the effect of reinforcing the title that is transferred, especially if at the time of conveyance a vendor does not hold the title referred to in the recital, but acquires that title at a later date: the title passes under the doctrine of 'feeding the estoppel'. A recital in a lease may have the effect of creating a **covenant** when there is nothing expressed on a particular point; for example, it may confirm that which constitutes a **usual covenant**.

In an insurance policy, a recital may be a statement that a premium has been paid or that the insurer has received a proposal to insure a certain risk.

cf. **preamble**. See also **premises**.

recits (F)
　recitals.

reclamation of land
　see **land reclamation**.

réclame (F)
　advertising.
　(*réclame tapageuse* – **puffing**)
　(*en réclame* – on offer).

recompense
　see **compensation, damages, *quantum meruit*, unjust enrichment**.

récompense (F)
　recompense; reward; compensation. See also **indemnité**.

reconciliation (US)
　The process by which an appraiser determines the final value of a property based upon estimates made by different **approaches to value**. Called also 'correlation'.

reconditioning
　The act of giving a new lease of life; restoring to a good condition. Reconditioning generally does not include replacement of structural materials, plant or equipment, or making improvements and, therefore, does not go as far as **renovation** or **refurbishment**. Reconditioning of a building is intended to extend the economic life of a building and includes carrying out neglected or deferred maintenance, but it does not include providing anything new or substantially different.

reconduction (F)
　renewal, of a lease or hiring agreement.
　(*reconduction tacite* – see ***tacit***).

reconstruction
　The act of **rebuilding**, or of reforming a structure, in a similar manner. The act of constructing anew; especially all or a substantial part of something that existed but has lost its entity. Reconstruction is carried out after demolition or destruction (in part or in total) of a building, or group of buildings, and essentially requires a substantial replacement or recreation of that which has been demolished or destroyed. See also **construction, rehabilitation**.

reconversion

The reverse of the process of **conver-. sion**; in particular the changing of money into real property, especially when the law had presumed that a property has been converted into money. Thus, if land is held on **trust for sale** the law presumes that the beneficiary's interest is no more than an entitlement to the proceeds of sale; reconversion arises if the beneficiary regains a right to claim the land itself as a legal estate.

reconveyance

1. A deed that transfers an interest in property back from the mortgagee to the mortgagor upon discharge of a mortgage debt. A **receipt** or **memorandum**, annexed to the deed that transferred a right to property as security for a debt, normally provides sufficient evidence that the debt has been discharged and the property reconveyed to the mortgagor (Law of Property Act 1925, s. 115). See also **discharge**, **redemption**.
2. A transfer of a title to property back to the original or former owner. See also **sale and buy-back**.
(US) 3. A transfer of property that is held under a **deed of trust** back from the trustee to the trustor when the debt secured by the deed of trust has been paid.

record owner (US)

One who is recorded as the holder of a registered title to land.

recordation (US)

The act of recording a document at the offices of a government recorder. See also **constructive notice**, **land registration**.

recorded plat or **recorded survey** (US)

see **plat**.

recording

see **land registration, recordation**.

recoupment

1. The recovery of that which has been expended. The recovery of a loss by a subsequent gain. For example, a public authority may seek to recoup part of the cost of a development project by acquiring more land than it requires for the project and, when it has completed the development, selling the surplus land at a price that has been enhanced by the development.
cf. **recapture**, **set-off**. See also **abatement**, **betterment**.
2. A cross claim under a contract for damages; thus when one party claims damages for breach of contract the other party may seek to recoup part of the amount claimed by making his own claim. "Recoupment is distinguished from **set-off** in these three essential particulars: (1) in being confined to matters arising out of and connected with the transaction or contract; (2) in having no regard to whether such matters are liquidated or unliquidated; (3) in not being the subject of statutory regulation but controlled by law" – 3 Mich. 281. A term used more in the US than in English law.

recourse note (US)

A note or memorandum that provides a lender with a personal right of **recourse** against a borrower, apart from any right of recourse to property held as security for the loan.

recourse, right of

Literally, a right of 'running back'. A right to demand payment; in particular, the right of a lender, or **mortgagee**, to take a personal action against the borrower, or mortgagor, if the proceeds from the sale of a property offered as security are inadequate. In English law, because a mortgage is both a conveyance of an interest in land and a contract for a debt, a mortgagee may exercise a right of **foreclosure** or a **power of sale**, in order to satisfy the payments due to him, and if not satisfied he may still sue under the contract for the personal debt owed by the mortgagor. As a result of the personal right of recourse, the mortgagee may sue the mortgagor even though he has transferred his interest in the mortgaged property to a third party and the mortgagee may have recourse to other property of the mortgagor. In the US, generally a right of recourse is available to the mortgagee only if he has expressly reserved that right in the mortgage deed or some other express form, e.g. in a **recourse note**. See also **non-recourse mortgage**.

recours (F)
recourse.
(*recours contentieux* – appeal, against a tax assessment).
(*assurance contre le recours de tiers* – **third-party liability insurance**)
(*sans droit de recours; sans recours* – **without recourse**)
(*recours contre un tiers* – with recourse).

recovery
1. A form of action that replaces **ejectment** and is brought by a party who has been wrongfully dispossessed to enable him to regain possession of land.
cf. **right of re-entry**. See also **adverse possession, eviction, Statutes of Limitation**.
2. The act of regaining that which has

been lost or is missing. See also **restoration, subrogation**.
3. A form of common law action (an action of 'common recovery') brought by a tenant in tail to bar an **entailed interest** and thereby enable the owner of that estate to sell a fee simple estate. Abolished by the Fines and Recovery Act 1833 and replaced by the use of a **disentailing assurance**.

rectangular survey system (US)
see **government survey system**.

rectification
1. Derived from the Latin *rectificare*, 'to put right'. The act of putting something right that was made faulty by accident or inadvertence. The correction of something, as a matter of discretion, that is erroneous or doubtful. For example, the correction of a document when the parties to an agreement realise that it does not state what they had intended; usually due to a **mistake** or a clerical error. Rectification of a document does not create a new agreement or vary the bargain reached, it merely records that which had been agreed previously. "The essence of rectification is to bring the document which was expressed and intended to be in pursuance of a prior agreement into harmony with that prior agreement ..." and "what you have to find out [prior to rectification] is what intention was communicated by one side to the other, and with what common intention and common agreement they made their bargain." – Lovell and Christmas Ltd. *v* Wall [1911] 104 LT 88, 93. Rectification does not create two agreements — an agreement and a rectifying agreement, nor an agreement with a rider effecting a correction, but one agreement "to be read as if it had been

originally drawn in its rectified form". — Johnson v Bragge [1901] 1 Ch.37.

Before a court will order rectification of a document it is necessary to establish, beyond reasonable doubt, that something had been agreed and that what has been agreed should be inserted in place of that which subsists. As a rule, it is necessary to show that the error arose from the mutual mistake of the parties. However, rectification may be made in a case of **fraud** or **misrepresentation**; when it is clear that there has been a clerical blunder or grammatical mistake; or "where the words of the document were purposely used but it was mistakenly considered that they bore a different meaning from their correct meaning as a matter of true construction". — Re Butlin's Settlement Trusts [1976] 1 Ch.260, (but not if the words end up recording what the parties had intended — Rose v Pimm [1953] 2 QB 450. Rectification may be ordered also if one party mistakenly believed a particular term was included in a contract and the other party knew of the mistake but permitted it to be excluded from the contract when it is put in writing — A. Roberts and Co. v Leicestershire County Council[1961] Ch.555. Nevertheless, rectification is an equitable remedy and is granted only at the discretion of the court.

In the US, called also 'reformation' and the deed that effects the new agreement is called a 'deed of reformation' or a 'correction deed'. See also **deed of rectification**, *non est factum*, **rescission**.
Cheshire & Fifoot's Law of Contract 10 edn, pp. 214–216.
Anson's Law of Contract 26 edn, pp. 283–285, 287.

Chitty on Contract 25 edn, para. 352 *et seq.*
2. An alteration to an entry at the **Land Registry**, pursuant to an order of a court or at the instigation of the registrar, when the entry has been made by error or omission or obtained by fraud. An indemnity may be payable to any interested party affected by such a rectification (Land Registration Act 1925, s.82, 83). See also **'slip rule'**.
Megarry's Manual of the Law of Real Property 6 edn, pp. 532–546.

rectification (F)
    rectification.

recul (sur rue) (F)
    set-back (from a road).
    (*zone de recul* — set-back area).

reculement, servitude de (F)
    A **servitude** imposed by a highway authority by which new building is prohibited in anticipation of a road widening scheme (*un plan d'alignement*).
    (*ligne de reculement* — **building line**; set-back line)
    see also *zone non aedificandi*.

reddendum
    'That which is to be paid or rendered'. The clause that specifies in a lease the **rent** payable (or the basis for calculating the rent payable) and its due date. In the event of a conflict between the reddendum and the **habendum** (which specifies the commencement date and term of a lease) the habendum prevails — Matthews v Smallwood [1910] 1 Ch. 784.

redditus (L)
    Rent.

'redeem up, foreclose down'
    A maxim that applies when there are

several mortgages on the same property and one of the mortgagees seeks to redeem a superior mortgage. A mortgagee who wishes to redeem a prior mortgage (i.e. pay off the debt owed to a prior mortgagee and step into his shoes) must redeem any mortgage situated in terms of priority between his own mortgage and the prior mortgage – 'redeem up' and also he must foreclose on all subsequent or junior mortgages and on the mortgagor's interest – 'foreclose down'. Thus, if a property is mortgaged by M_0 to M_1, M_2, M_3, M_4 and M_5 (in that order of priority) and M_4 wishes to redeem M_2's mortgage, he must redeem the mortgage of M_3 and foreclose on M_4 and M_0. Only M_1's mortgage can remain in force. The maxim applies only to court proceedings and is based on the principle that before a court will permit redemption the entitlement of any prior mortgagee, whose claim would be affected by the redemption, must be ascertained and any subsequent mortgagee, and the mortgagor, must be foreclosed upon – i.e. given the opportunity of redeeming the debt of their respective prior mortgages – or, if they fail to take that opportunity, lose their claim against the property. The maxim does not apply in reverse, a mortgagee who forecloses does not need to concern himself with prior, but only subsequent, mortgages. See also **redemption**.

redemption

1. Derived from the Latin *redimere*, 'to buy back'. The recovery of one's unfettered rights; the process of 'buying-back' a property by discharging in full a debt secured on that property. The process by which a **mortgage** on land is cancelled, by repaying the total debt (including principal and interest), and the land is released to the mortgagor. A mortgaged property may be reclaimed, as appropriate, (i) by the mortgagor physically retaking **possession**, (ii) by the return of the title deeds or an annulment of a registered charge; (iii) by a **reconveyance** of the title to the mortgagor; or (iv) a **receipt** for the monies paid endorsed on the mortgage deed.

A right to redeem a mortgage is not confined to the mortgagor (or anyone to whom he has transferred his **equity of redemption**); it may be exercised by any other person who has an interest in the mortgaged property or who is liable to pay the mortgage debt. Such a person does not necessarily acquire the property unencumbered but he 'steps into the shoes' of the mortgagee who has been redeemed and becomes a mortgagee himself. Redemption may take place on the date set down in the mortgage deed – 'legal redemption', or, in certain circumstances, at a later date – 'equitable redemption'. A mortgagor who transfers his right to redeem – his equity of redemption – to another loses that right unless he is sued subsequently on any personal covenant or privity of contract with his mortgagee. A right of redemption of mortgaged land is lost by a mortgagor if a mortgagee has been in possession of the land for a continuous period of twelve years (Limitation Act 1980, s. 16). See also **foreclosure**, '**redeem up, foreclose down**'.

2. The **repurchase** of a property at the same or an enhanced price.

3. The repayment of a loan at the end of a specified period of time, "as dis-

tinct from the mere payment of periodic sums as they become due". – Re Sandbach [1951] Ch. 803. The repurchase of a note, bond, debenture or other instrument of debt by paying its value to the holder. The redemption of a debenture, whether secured or unsecured on the assets of a company, may be made subject to a condition that the repayment of the debt does not immediately entitle the company to the return of secured property, i.e. the 'equity of redemption' may be postponed for a long time; until the occurrence of some remote contingency; or even indefinitely (Companies Act 1948, s. 89). See also **release**, **redemption yield**.

redemption date
1. The date on which a fixed-term loan is repaid at 'par value'; or an investment is sold after a specified or assumed holding period. In the former case the date is called also the 'maturity date'. A term most commonly applied to the repayment date on government stock or bonds. See also **redemption yield**.
2. The date on which a mortgage debt is repayable in full, or the date on which the final repayment of capital is due. See also **acceleration clause**, **equity of redemption, redemption**.

redemption fund
see **sinking fund**.

redemption yield
The average annual rate of return from an investment or loan, over its assumed life or holding period (up to the **redemption date**), taking account of the total projected net income and any capital profit (or loss) on resale of the investment or redemption of the loan. A redemption yield on an investment is the same as the **internal rate of return**; but redemption yield generally is used when referring to bonds or government securities, or when the profit on resale of the investment represents a significant factor in determining the average annual return over the life of the investment. In the case of a real estate investment a redemption yield may be calculated to take account of the projected income and capital gain (or loss), assuming future inflationary growth, over a number of years (commonly 10 or 15 years), in order to make a comparison of the return obtainable from long-term government securities. See also **equivalent yield**.

redevance (F)
royalty; dues; fees; rent; quit-rent; land tax. A more generic term than *loyer* – the latter covering only **rent** for the right to possession of land – as in the strict sense of English law. *redevance* may cover *charges locatives* and such payments as a turnover rent or a royalty, i.e. the total amount paid by a tenant. *Redevance* in old French law covered any due to a landlord, whether payable as money or in any other form.
(*redevance annuelle* – yearly rent)
(*redevance emphytéotique* – rent paid under an **emphyteotic lease**).
(*redevance foncière* – ground rent)
(*redevance tréfoncière* – mining royalty).

redevelopment
The act or process of **rebuilding** an area, especially an area that has reached the end of its economic life or a blighted area that requires complete renovation and renewal. The **development** of an area of land as an

entity by replacing existing buildings or groups of building, usually with entirely new buildings that are constructed on a new layout and to a different design. (Within the meaning of the Land Compensation Act 1973, s. 29, which refers to land held for 'redevelopment', demolition prior to building is considered to be part of the process of redevelopment – R. *v* Corby District Council, *exp*. McLean [1975] 1 WLR 735). See also **comprehensive development, urban renewal**.

reditus (L)
  rent.

reditus quieti (L)
  quit rent.

reditus siccus (L)
  rent-seck.

redlining (US)
  A practice by which an investor or lender demarcates an area that he considers to be unsuitable for property investment or lending.
  cf. **greenlining**.

reduced covered area
  see **gross external area**.

reducing-balance depreciation
  see **declining-balance depreciation**.

reduction (F)
  reduction; abatement.

reduction certificate (US)
  A certificate prepared by a mortgagee, usually prior to the transfer of a mortgage loan, setting out details of the rate of interest on the loan and the outstanding balance due from the mortgagor.
  cf. **estoppel certificate**.

réel (f.réelle) (F)
  real; actual

(*action réelle* – real action, i.e. an **action in rem**)
(*droit réel* – a right to real property, see **droit**)
(*intérêt réel* – true interest rate)
(*offre réel* – cash offer)
(*saisie réelle* – attachment of real property)
(*sûreté réelle* – charge, on real property; secured debt).

re-entry, right of
  see **forfeiture, right of re-entry**.

réestimation (F)
  reassessment; **revaluation**.

réévaluation (F)
  revaluation.

re-evaluation lease (US)
  see **reappraisal lease**.

réfection (F)
  restoration; refurbishment

referral fee (US)
  see **finder's fee**.

refinancing
  1. Renegotiating the terms of an existing loan or taking out of a new loan to replace an existing loan; especially the replacing of an interim loan with a long-term or permanent loan. Referred to also as 'refunding'. In the US, if a new mortgage is taken out and the proceeds utilised to repay an existing mortgage before it is due this is referred to as 'advance refinancing'. See also **financing, wrap-around mortgage**.
  2. The sale of a loan or debt by the original lender, in advance of its due date for repayment, as a means of recovering the amount outstanding. See also **discounting**.

reformation (US)
  see **rectification**.

reformation deed (US)
see **deed of rectification**.

refunding
see **refinancing**.

refurbishment
The process of making as good as new, including essential modernisation and **renovation**. The restoration of a building in order to give it a new lease of life; in particular, to restore a former usefulness and style. Refurbishment does not aim to alter the essential fabric and design of a building but to modernise and repair in order to preserve the building, while replacing worn or outmoded components. Refurbishment generally goes further than reconditioning, but does not extend to **reconstruction**. See also **rehabilitation**.

regional plan
A non-statutory form of **development plan** prepared for a large area of a country or region. In the UK, regional plans are prepared usually by a planning commission established for the purpose, or by a group of local planning authorities, acting under central government direction and supervision. The primary intention of a regional plan is to link together plans prepared by local planning authorities; e.g. structure plans, with national plans prepared by central government. Regional plans for the UK were prepared especially in the 1960's, e.g. the South East Regional Plan; however, such large scale plans are now no longer in vogue. The structure plans are considered to be adequate means of governing town planning on a macro-scale, with the control of planning on a national scale left entirely to the Secretary of State for the Environment. Called also a 'strategic plan'. See also **structure plan**.
Introduction to Regional Planning by John Glasson, 2 edn.

regional shopping centre
see **shopping centre**.

régisseur (F)
manager; agent; steward; bailiff. (*régisseur de domaine* – **land-agent**).

register
see **Land Registry, local land charge register**.

register of writs and orders
see **land charges register**.

registered charge
A **charge** over registered land entered on the charges register of the **Land Registry** in the name of the proprietor of the charge (Land Registration Act 1925, s. 25, 26). A registered charge is the usual means by which a mortgage of registered land is effected and once registered operates as a **charge by way of a legal mortgage**.
cf. **land charge**. See also **charge certificate, legal charge**.

registered encumberance
An **encumberance** on land that is registered or recorded so as to remain binding on a purchaser of the land or any interest therein. Such an encumberance is registered for its own protection. If not registered it is normally not binding on third parties, so that any person who subsequently acquires the land is freed of the encumberance. See also **equitable interest, land charge, local land charge, minor interest, registered charge**.

registered land
An area of land that forms the subject

matter of **land registration**; in particular, any estate or interest in land registered at the Land Registry (Land Registration Act 1925, s. 3 (xxiv)).
Registered Land, by D.J. Hayton, 2 edn.

registered land certificate
see **land registry certificate**.

registered proprietor
The party entered on the Proprietorship Register at the Land Registry as the holder of a registered title to land (Land Registration Act 1925, s. 3(xx)). A registered proprietor who has acquired an area of land in good faith is guaranteed a good title to the land; subject only to any **entry** (which may be a caution, notice, inhibition or restriction) on the register and any **overriding interest**. See also **priority notice**.

registered rent
1. A **fair rent** established by a rent officer, or a Rent Assessment Committee, for a residential property that is subject to a **regulated tenancy** and registered at the local town hall. An application to register a rent may be made by the landlord or the tenant, and must be made in the prescribed form. A local authority also may apply to the rent office for a fair rent to be assessed for a dwelling-house in its area, if no such rent has previously been fixed. A registered rent is the maximum amount, the 'rent limit', (exclusive of rates) that may be charged by the landlord of a regulated tenancy and cannot be changed without reference to a rent officer (Rent Act 1977, ss. 62–75, as amended by Housing Act 1980, ss. 59–62). A new rent may not be registered within two years from the initial registration,

unless there is a change in the property itself, as when the landlord carries out improvements. See also **certificate of fair rent**.
The Law of Landlord and Tenant, by David Lloyd Evans, 2 edn., pp. 271–275.
Landlord and Tenant, by Martin Partington, 2 edn., pp. 60–61 and 272–275.
2. A rent payable under a **restricted contract**, as determined by a **rent tribunal**, and registered by a local authority, which has a duty to keep an up-to-date register of such rents. The register must contain details of the rent, the contract and the dwelling to which the contract applies (Rent Act 1977, ss. 79–81).

registered title
see **land registration**.

registrable interest
see **land registration**.

registrar
One who compiles and maintains a register, e.g. an official appointed to maintain records at the Land Registry.

registrar of deeds (US)
A **registrar**, or recorder, of deeds.

registration duty
A tax payable on the registration of a formal document; especially an *ad volorem* tax payable on the registration of title following the transfer of an interest in property. In the US, registration duty is used to refer to a 'conveyance tax' or a 'transfer tax'.
cf. **stamp duty**.

registre (F)
register; record.
(*registre du cadastre* – land or cadastral register)

(*registre foncier* – land register; terrier).

règle proportionelle (F)
average clause (in an insurance contract).

règlement (F)
1. regulation; statutes (of a company); rules.
(*règlement administratif* – **by law**) (*règlements de copropriété* – co-ownership regulations, a document that sets out details of the common parts and details the areas held by each co-owner; stipulates the basis for the apportionment of charges; and sets down the regulations for the use of the common parts, see ***copropriété***) (*règlement du lotissement* – parcelling regulations. Regulations that are attached as an integral part of a consent to sub-divide land for sale and development: *Code de l'Urbanisme, art. R. 315–329*, see ***lotissement***).
2. payment; settlement (of an account).

regress
Going back; the act of retaking **possession**. See also **right of re-entry**.

regression of value theory
A theory that the value of any one property tends to be drawn to the lowest level of property values in the neighbourhood (A theory that may be considered akin to Gresham's law: "bad money drives out good").

regular mortgage (US)
A mortgage that conveys an interest in land to the mortgagee; as distinguished from a mortgage that grants a mere right over property as security for a debt e.g. an **equitable mortgage**, a **deed of trust**, or a mere deposit of title deeds. The nearest equivalent in English law would be a **legal mortgage**. Called also a 'technical mortgage'.

regulated tenancy
A tenancy of a dwelling-house that is either a **protected tenancy** (i.e. a contractual tenancy that is afforded statutory security of tenure and rent regulation) or a **statutory tenancy** (i.e. a tenancy that comes into existence when a protected tenancy comes to an end contractually) (Rent Act 1977, s. 18). Prior to the Housing Act 1980, 'regulated tenancy' meant any tenancy of a dwelling-house that specifically came within the ambit of the Rent Act 1977, provided it was not a **controlled tenancy**. Since 1980 all controlled tenancies have been converted into regulated tenancies and 'regulated tenancy' now has the broader meaning defined above (Housing Act 1980, s. 64).

regulation Z (US)
see **Truth-in-Lending Act**.

rehabilitation
The process of restoring to a habitable condition, especially restoring a property to its original condition without changing the design or style. Rehabilitation is carried out generally as part of a programme for the improvement and restoration of buildings in a specific area. The rehabilitated buildings are returned, as far as possible, to their original condition, but with the provision of modern amenities, both for the buildings and for the area as a whole, together with an upgraded standard of accommodation. In particular, rehabilitation refers to the process of improving the living conditions in a residential area that has fallen into a state of urban decay, especially when government assistance is provided. Rehabilitation may include partial reconstruction and redevelopment, in order to

improve the environment in which the buildings are situated; but does not extend to changing the basic character of the area, its form, or the structure of the buildings. See also **general improvement area, refurbishment, rehabilitation order, renovation, urban renewal**.

rehabilitation order
An order made by a local authority, in accordance with the provisions of the Housing Act 1974, s. 114, Sch. 10, specifying that a house that is **unfit for human habitation** must be improved to a "full standard", instead of being included in a **clearance area** and demolished. A "full standard" is fulfilled by the provision of the **standard amenities**; putting the house in reasonable repair; providing proper thermal insulation; making it fit for habitation and usable, as a rule, for 15 years. The owner of a house that is included in a clearance area, because it is unfit, may request the local authority to make a rehabilitation order and thereby exclude the property from being demolished as part of the clearance area. A rehabilitation order must be confirmed by the Secretary of State before it comes into effect. See also **intermediate grant**.
West's Law of Housing, 4 edn, pp. 110–111.
Housing Law, by Andrew Arden & Martin Partington, pp. 430–431 (1983).

Reilly's law
see **catchment area**.

reinstatement
1. The replacement or restoration of a property to its original condition. The act of **rebuilding** a property that

has been demolished or destroyed, has collapsed, or has fallen into a state of ruin or dilapidation. "To reinstate the Church of Saint Jude ... means to build it up again when it has collapsed or become ruinous or dilapidated past repair, so that it has to be demolished; to put it back as it was before, not necessarily of the same materials, but according to the same design, so as to be easily recognisable by those who knew the fallen or ruined church when it was stable and standing upright". – Re. Church of Saint Jude [1956] SASR 53.

In an insurance policy, the meaning of 'reinstate' depends on whether the property in question is a building or a chattel: "from the collocation of the words it would seem that 'reinstate' is used with reference to property which has been damaged, and 'replace' for property which has been destroyed. But when one is dealing with chattels the term 'reinstate' means to replace the chattels not *in situ* but *in statu*" – Anderson *v* Commercial Union Assurance Co. (1885) 55 LJQB 149. Thus, reinstatement of a building requires, as far as is possible, that the damage is made good where the building stands; but with chattels reinstatement requires that the chattel *per se* is put back as it was, but not necessarily where it was. However, an insurer has no greater obligation when reinstating a building after a fire than to put the building substantially in the same state as it was before it was damaged; the insurer is not bound to pull down the old walls and replace them entirely on account, for example, of defects in the foundations – Times Fire Assurance Co. *v* Hawke (1858) 1 F7F407. See also **repair, reinstatement basis**.

2. The act of restoring a loan to its agreed contractual status, i.e. paying arrears up to date.

reinstatement basis

A basis on which an insurance policy is accepted so that, in the event of a total loss, the insurer agrees to meet the **replacement cost** for an equivalent property. As a rule, the insurer undertakes to pay the cost of replacing or reinstating the property with the nearest equivalent, but no better, and limits his total liability to the insured value stated in the policy. The insurer may elect to reinstate the property itself, in any manner he thinks fit, especially if that can be done more cheaply; such reinstatement may be effected by providing an equivalent property or by putting the damaged property in the same condition as before the loss – Anderson *v* Commercial Union Assurance Co. (1885) 55 LJ QB 148. However, the insurer is expected to 'reinstate' and he cannot restrict this liability merely because the end result may produce a better property for the insured; conversely, if the reinstated or replaced property is inferior to that which is lost, the insurer is obliged to make good the full loss suffered.

In certain circumstances an insurer may be obliged to reinstate, rather than pay monetary compensation: (a) when the policy expressly so requires; (b) when the property is held in trust or by a mortgagee in possession, or is an ecclesiastical property; (c) if the insurer suspects arson or fraud, or when requested by the person interested in the property (Fire Preventions (Metropolis) Act 1774, s. 83: this Act in spite of the title, applies to the whole of England, but not to Lloyd's underwriters). In addition, a mortgagee may be able to insist that any monies received under a policy effected on the property that is the subject matter of his security, be applied in or towards the discharge of the mortgage debt (Law of Property Act 1925, s. 108 (4)). An insured cannot, without giving prior notice, reinstate of his own accord and then ask to be reimbursed by the insurer with the cost he has incurred. See also **average, indemnity, insurance rent, new-for-old insurance**.

General Principles of Insurance Law by E. R. Hardy Ivamy. 4 edn, pp. 486–495.

The Law of Insurance, by Raoul Colinvaux. 4 edn, pp. 176–180.

reinstatement cost

1. In valuation terms, the total **cost** of a property obtained by assessing the cost of acquiring an equivalent area of land (or the value of the land on which any building stands) and adding the estimated cost of replacing the building, after allowing for depreciation. See also **equivalent reinstatement, reinstatement method of valuation**.

2. In insurance, especially when assessing the costs of restoring damaged (rather than destroyed) property, reinstatement cost is synonymous with **replacement cost**. See also **reinstatement, reinstatement basis**.

reinstatement cost approach (US)

see **cost approach**.

reinstatement method of valuation

A **valuation** of a property based on an assessment of its **reinstatement cost**, i.e. the cost of acquiring an alternative site and the cost of rebuilding a similar, but not necessarily identical, building. This method of valuation is used in particular to value a property for which there is no ready market, e.g. a school, hospital, church, and although, strictly, the assessed amount is not a **market value** it is taken as the best approximation thereto. Called also the 'cost of replacement method' or, in the US, the 'cost approach'. See also **contractor's method, depreciated replacement cost, equivalent reinstatement**.

reinstatement value

see **equivalent reinstatement, reinstatement cost**.

réintégrande (F)

A form of action for ejectment or recovery of possession of land (*action possessoire*); in particular by someone who has been dispossessed by force.
cf. *revendication*.
Précis Dalloz. Droit Civil, Les Biens (Alex Weill), 2 edn, pp. 354–356.

reinvestment rate

The rate at which income received from an investment is assumed to be reinvested; this need not be the same as the rate of return on that investment.

rejection, of an offer

Declining to accept an **offer**. Rejection of an offer occurs if and when (a) the notification of rejection is received by the offeror; (b) an offer is made subject to conditions; or (c) a **counter-offer** is submitted to the offeror.
cf. **acceptance**. See also **lapse, revocation**.

relais (F)

reliction. The material left by the gradual retreat of the sea or the meandering of a river. In general such

material belongs to the owner of the land upon which it is deposited; except in the case of the sea (where it belongs to the state), or a lake or pond (where the water itself belongs to the riperian landowner) (French Civil Code, arts. 557–388).
cf. *lais*.
Précis Dalloz. Droit Civil, Les Biens (Alex Weill) 2 edn, pp. 52–54.
(*credit de relais* – **bridging loan**).

re-lease

To grant a new **lease** of property that previously has been let, either to a tenant whose period of occupation has come to an end or to a new tenant. Synonymous with 're-let'.
cf. **release**. See also **renewal**.

release

1. The act of giving up or relinquishing a right, claim or privilege, especially one arising from a contract. The extinguishment of a debt or claim by payment. A release may be distinguished from a **receipt** as "a release extinguishes the claim, and when given in itself annihilates the debt; but a receipt is only evidence of payment, and if there be proof that no payment was made, it cannot operate as evidence of payment against such proof". – Bowes *v* Foster (1858) 27 LJ Ex 266. The release of a mortgage debt means that the total debt, including interest and principal, has been paid and the property held as security has been returned to the mortgagor unencumbered. A document that acknowledges the discharging of a debt or the extinguishment of a right also may be called a release, or a 'deed of release'. See also **accord and satisfaction, surrender**.
2. The giving up of a legal right of action. "The giving or discharge of

the right or action which any hath or claimeth against another, or his land" – Termes de la Ley. See also **renunciation**.

3. The **relinquishment** of an interest in land to one who currently has possession; especially the surrender of a right to a larger estate, which may be either a **remainder** or a **reversion**, to the holder of an inferior estate in the same land. For example, the ceding of a landlord's right to a reversion to his tenant or a remainderman's right to a tenant for life.

cf. **re-lease**. See also **abandonment, quitclaim deed, lease and release**.

release clause

A clause in a **blanket mortgage** that enables one or more of the charged properties to be freed from the mortgage upon repayment of part of the debt. The clause normally specifies an amount that can be repaid at any particular time during the agreement and the secured property that is thereby released. Partial release is not permitted normally if the mortgagor is in default under any of the terms of the mortgage agreement. A release clause is usually inserted in a mortgage secured on an area of land that is to be developed in stages and then sold off as separate plots, thus enabling the plots to be sold unencumbered by the developer's own mortgage commitments. See also **partial release clause**.

release deed (US)

A deed that frees a debtor's claim over a property that has been charged or granted as security for a deed, especially a deed that terminates a **deed of trust** so as to free the property to the debtor (trustor). Called also a 'deed of reconveyance' or 'deed of release'. See also **release, reconveyance**.

relessee

One to whom a **re-lease** is given.

re-let

see **re-lease**.

relevé (F)

survey; summary; register; abstract. (*relevé hypothécaire* – mortgage certificate, stating whether a property is mortgaged or not).

reliction

The process by which land is left permanently exposed when the sea, a lake or a river recedes gradually. Also, the land so left, which comes into the ownership of the abutting owner provided the land has been exposed by a gradual, but permanent, process. See also **accretion, dereliction**.

relief

1. A legal remedy or redress; in particular, a remedy obtained from a court of equity against a grievance, wrong, or injustice. A remedy granted at the discretion of a court to redress an injustice when a claim to a **penalty** or a right of **forfeiture** has arisen. Relief may take the form of an **injunction**, a decree of **specific performance**, relief against **forfeiture** of a lease, or **rescission** of a contract.

A tenant may apply to a court for relief against a landlord's right of re-entry or forfeiture under a lease and the court may grant or refuse relief as it thinks fit, having regard to the circumstances and the conduct of the parties (Law of Property Act 1925, s. 146 (2)). Whether such relief is granted depends, *inter alia*, on (a) the nature of the breach; (b) whether the tenant is able and willing to remedy the breach; (c) whether the tenant's default was wilful; (d) the gravity of the breach; and (e) "the disparity between the value of the property of which forfeiture is claimed as compared with damage caused by the breach" – Shiloh Spinners *v* Harding [1973] AC 724. However, the court generally will grant relief against a landlord's notice seeking to enforce re-entry or forfeiture when the following conditions are met: "in the first place the applicant must, so far as possible, remedy the breaches alleged in the notice, and pay reasonable compensation for the breaches which cannot be remedied. In the second place, if the breach is of a negative covenant, such as not to carry on a particular business on the demised premises, the applicant must undertake to observe the covenant in future, or at least must not avow his intention to repeat the breach complained of. In the third place, if the act complained of, though not a breach of a negative covenant, is of such a nature that the Court would have restrained it during the currency of the lease on the ground of **waste**, the applicant must undertake to make good the waste, if it be possible to do so. In the fourth place, if the act complained of does not fall under either the second or third head, but is one in respect of which damages, other than nominal, might be recovered in an action on the covenant, the applicant must undertake not to repeat the wrongful act or to be guilty of a continuing breach". – Rose *v* Spicer [1911] 2 KB 241–2. On the other hand, as relief is based on equity, the person seeking relief must come to the court 'with clean hands'; thus relief will not be provided, for example, to a squatter.

Relief may be granted also against a requirement that a tenant carry out internal decorative repairs to a house or other building, after the court has had regard to "all the circumstances of the case" (Law of Property Act 1925, s. 147 (1)). This provision does not apply if the decoration is necessary for the maintenance or preservation of the structure; to keep the premises in a habitable or sanitary condition; to comply with a statutory requirement; or when the tenant is expressly required to decorate at the start of the lease or yield up the premises in a specified state of repair at the end of the term (1925 Act, s. 147 (2)). Relief against forfeiture of a lease has the effect of extinguishing any effect that the forfeiture might have had, so that a **sub-tenant**, who might have lost his right to the demised premises because the head-lease was to have been forfeited, is reinstated as if the forfeiture was deemed not to have taken place at all – Dendy *v* Evans [1910] 1 KB 263.

2. A reduction or removal of a liability or obligation, e.g. a reduction in a liability to pay a tax or levy.

3. A payment made under the **feudal system** of land tenure by a tenant to the lord of the manor upon succeeding to land by descent.

4. The topography of a land surface.

relinquishment
The act of giving up, surrendering, or abandoning a right or thing. See also **abandonment, release, surrender, waiver.**

relocatio (L)
Re-lease. In the civil law the renewal of a lease on its determination upon the same terms as before; either by an express grant or by the landlord permitting a tenant to holdover. See also *reconduction.*

relocation

1. The removal to a new location. See also **suitable alternative accommodation**.

2. In Scottish law, the tacit renewal of a lease on similar terms when a tenant holds over after the original lease has expired. See also *relocatio*.

relocation (F)

renewal, of a lease; reletting. See also *tacit*.

relocation clause

A clause in a lease that enables the landlord to require his tenant to move to alternative accommodation.

relogement (F)

rehousing.

rem (L)

'Thing'. See **action in rem**.

remainder

1. An **estate** in land that comes into effect, as a right to possession, upon the determination of an immediately preceding estate; was created at the same time and by the same instrument as the preceding estate; but does not revert to the original grantor of the estate that has come to an end. Thus if a person creates two or more estates in land that follow in time, e.g. a grant to "A for life, then to B for life, then to C in fee simple", the estate preceding the remainder (B's interest) is called a **particular estate** (from the Latin *particula*, a 'small part') and the interest thereafter (C's interest) is the remainder. If, by operation of law, the estate passed back to A, after B, then A's interest would be a **reversion** (A being the original grantor) and not a remainder. If the estate was granted merely "to A for life and then to B", B's estate would be a remainder.

A remainder may be 'vested' or 'executed'; or 'contingent' or 'executory'. A vested remainder requires that the person who will hold the remainder is ascertained at the outset and takes effect as soon as the particular estate ends. A contingent remainder takes effect upon the occurrence of an event that might never happen (especially when the person who will ultimately take the remainder is unascertained when the estate is granted), or a designated, but uncertain, period of time after the particular estate ends – "it is not the uncertainty of the enjoyment in the future, but the uncertainty of the right to that enjoyment, which marks the difference between a vested and a contingent interest" – 4 Kent, Comm. 206. A contingent remainder may become a vested remainder when the contingent event occurs or when the person who will obtain the future estate is ascertained. The person who holds the interest in the remainder is termed the 'remainderman', but his interest is called a 'reversionary interest'. See also **future interest**.

Real Property, by William E. Burby, 3 edn., pp. 338–344.

Cheshire's Modern Law of Property, 13 edn, pp. 284–288.

39 Halsbury's Laws of England, 4 edn, para. 482 *et seq.*

The Law of Real Property, by Robert Megarry & H.W.R. Wade, 5 edn., pp. 44–45, 231–233, 1176–1189.

2. The ultimate **beneficiary** under a trust. See also *cestui que trust*.

3. An estate or interest in real property, or an entitlement to the proceeds of sale thereof, left after the expenses of administering a will and the express wishes of the testator have been satisfied.

cf. **residue**.

remainder person
see **remainderman**.

remainderman
One whose interest in land comes into effect, as a right to possession, after another interest has expired, but who was not the grantor of the interest that has come to an end, i.e. one who holds or is entitled to an interest in remainder.
cf. **reversioner**.

remaining economic life
The period of time before a property reaches the end of its **economic life**: effectively, for an investor, the time left for him to recover (or recapture) the capital he has invested in the property.

remboursement (F)
repayment; redemption; reimbursement.
(*rendement sur remboursement* – **redemption yield**)
(*délai de remboursement* – **pay-back period**).

remeasurement contract
A form of **building contract** in which the price is based initially on approximate quantities (of material and labour) and an agreed schedule of rates for the work. Work is carried out and paid for during the contract period on a basis of 'best estimate' and the final price is established when all the work is completed. However, unlike a **cost-reimbursement contract** many of the elements that make up the price are fixed, or capable of being fixed, at the commencement of the contract. This contract is used when the exact work and, therefore, the quantities cannot be determined precisely; for example, when, at the commencement of a contract, the extent of the building work is concealed.
cf. **lump-sum contract**. See also **fixed-price contract**.

remembrement (F)
land consolidation; **assemblage**. A process by which a number of land owners proceed, by exchange or reallocation of land ownership, to make a more rational pattern of land ownership – usually with a view to economics of scale or in anticipation of a development project. *Remembrement* may be either *remembrement rural* – the consolidation of small plots of farm land in order to improve agricultural efficiency; or *remembrement urbain* – the acquisition of land or interests in land to assist comprehensive redevelopment.
cf. *démembrements de la propriété*, *lotissement*.
Le Remembrement Rural, by D. Linotte, (1980).
Précis Dalloz. Droit Civil, Les Biens. (Alex Weill), 2 edn, pp. 149, 206.
Droit Civil Les Biens, by Gabriel Marty and Pierre Raynaud, vol. ii, pp. 335–358 (1965).

remedies
see **accord and satisfaction, damages, distress, injunction, prerogative order, rectification, relief, rescission, specific performance**.

rémeré, faculté de (F)
repurchase **option** to. In particular, a clause in a contract for sale by which the vendor has a right to repurchase the subject matter within a maximum period of five years at the original price, plus the purchaser's expenses.
(*vente à rémeré* – conditional sale).
cf. *droit de préemption*.

remise

To give up, **surrender**, or **release** a claim. The terms 'remise' and 'remit' are used in a deed of surrender of an estate in land to signify that the grantee gives up all rights or claims to the land.

cf. **demise**. See also **quitclaim deed**.

remise (F)

remission; discount, delivery.
(*remise de dettes* – remission or cancellation of a debt)
(*remise en état* – put into repair).

remit

1. To send money, especially to pay for goods or services. To annul a debt or fine by payment. See also **remise, tender**.
2. To refrain from exacting something; to desist from extracting a penalty. See also **release, surrender, waiver**.

remittance

1. Money sent by one person to another, usually as a payment or settlement (in whole or in part) of a debt.
2. An instrument by which money is remitted from one person to another.

remoteness of damage

see **damages**.

remoteness, rule against

see **rule against perpetuities**.

remplacement (F)

replacement; reinstatement.
(*coût de remplacement* – **replacement cost**).

remuneration

see **commission, compensation fee,** *quantum meruit*.

remunerative rate

1. A rate of interest that provides an investor with an acceptable return on

his investment taking account of the risk, but makes no allowance for recovery of the invested capital. Called also the **'investment rate'**.
cf. **accumulative rate**. See also **dual-rate capitalisation factor**.
2. The rate at which profit is generated from an investment.

rendement (F)

yield; return; profit.
(*rendement boursier* – dividend yield)
(*rendement brût* – gross income; gross return)
(*rendement marginal du capital* – marginal return, or efficiency of, on capital; **internal rate of return**)
(*rendement sur remboursement* – **redemption yield**)
(*taux de rendement* – **rate of return**).

render

1. To yield, return or pay. A statement of the **rent** to be paid under a lease frequently is preceded by the words 'rendering and paying'. See also **reddendum**.
2. A **royalty** paid in kind.

renegotiable-rate mortgage (RRM)

see **variable-rate mortgage**.

renewal

1. The granting of something anew. The grant of a new lease following a surrender or an expiry of an existing lease. A 'renewal option', i.e. a right to a new lease upon the expiration of an existing lease, grants a tenant a right to a new lease on the same terms as the old lease, except where expressly modified; but, unless expressly stated, grants no further automatic right of renewal – Lewis *v* Stephenson (1898) 67 LJQB 296.

A perpetually renewable lease is converted into a lease for a term of 2000 years, and any contract made

after 1925 to renew a lease for a term of over 60 years from its termination is void (Law of Property Act 1922, Sch. 15).
cf. **extension**. See also **business tenancy, novation, reversionary leasehold**.
2. The replacement of a loan that has been granted for a fixed period of time and that has come to an end.
cf. **refinancing**. See also **roll-over loan**.
3. Restoring to the same condition as new; putting something as far as possible into the same state or condition as before damage, destruction, deterioration or dilapidation. Renewal requires that the substituted item or property is new, as distinguished from **reinstatement** which may entail putting back an old item or property but in serviceable or useable condition. Renewal may involve the replacement of all or a substantial part of a property, but replacement of a small part of the whole cannot amount to a renewal of that whole. See also **rebuilding, renovation, repair**.

renonciation (F)
renunciation; abandonment; disclaimer (of a right without conferring it on anyone else); **waiver; surrender** (of a lease).
(*renonciation à prescription* – abandonment of a prescriptive right).

renouveler (un bail) (F)
to renew (a lease)

renovation
The process of restoring or putting back to a former state; especially something that has been substantially impaired by time and neglect. A process that may include **repair** and **improvement**, but not reconstruction

in a different design or style or with a substantial modification or alteration. See also **refurbishment, rehabilitation, renewal**.

rénovation (F)
renewal (of a contract); **renovation; restoration**.
(*rénovation urbaine* – **urban renewal**).

rent
1. Derived from the Latin *reditus* or Old French *rente*, 'to render' or 'to yield'. A periodic payment or return that a tenant makes to an owner of land, as recompense for a right to use and profit from the **exclusive occupation** of that land, or any other corporeal property, for a determinable period of time: "The word, rent, or render, *reditus*, signifies a compensation, or return; it being in the nature of an acknowledgement given for possession of some form of inheritance – Co. Litt. 144. It is defined to be a certain profit issuing yearly out of land and tenements corporeal" – (Bl. Comm. vol. ii p. 41; (Woodfall's Landlord and Tenant, 28 edn, 1–0679 – M.E. Blatt Co. *v* US, 305 US 267, 59 S.Ct. 186, 83 L Ed. 167). Historically, rent was considered as a service paid by one person to another in return for a right to enjoy the possession of that other's land – a burden rendered by one person in return for the benefit of depriving another of occupation for a period of time; it was regarded as one of the principal incidents of land ownership. It represented the means by which the tenant acknowledged his fealty to the landowner while the landowner countenanced the tenant's existence on his land. However, that notion of rent, which is rooted in the **feudal system** of land tenure, has been

replaced by a modern view which regards rent as no more than a contractual payment (whether in a monetary form or otherwise) for the use of land; remuneration that a tenant is bound to make for the exclusive right to receive the fruits and benefits of land: "the medieval concept of rent as a service rendered by a tenant to the landlord has been displaced by the modern concept of a payment which a tenant is bound by his contract to pay the landlord for the use of this land". – United Scientific Holding Ltd. *v* Burnley Council [1977] 2 All ER 76. Thus, in a modern sense, rent is the **consideration** for a contractual right to property – the contract being called a **lease**.

Rent is a payment that stems from the relationship of **landlord and tenant** and is an acknowledgment of that relationship. Such a payment was termed **rent service**, as distinguished from a **rentcharge** which is a burden due by an owner of land to another party with whom there is no relationship of landlord and tenant. However, the term rent may be used sometimes to cover both forms of payment: "'rent' includes a rent-service or a rentcharge, or other rent, toll, duty, **royalty**, or annual or periodic payment in money or money's worth, reserved or issuing out of or charged upon land, but does not include mortgage interest" (Law of Property Act 1925, s. 205 (xxiii)). (The Administration of Estates Act 1925, s. 55 (1) and the Land Registration Act 1925, s. 3 contain similar interpretations, although the former excludes a royalty.) Rent is payment for land, but if buildings or fixtures are attached to the land and thereby are included in the total 'price', that

payment is rent for land in toto.

Rent must be certain in its character, or must be expressed in such a way as to be capable of being made certain, both in respect of the amount due and the time when it is due. In this respect the maxim adopted is *certum est quod certum reddi potest*, 'that is certain which can be rendered certain'. A rent that is "to be agreed" is uncertain; but a rent that is to be determined "having regard to the market value" is capable of being made certain – Brown *v* Gould [1972] Ch. 53. Normally rent is a pecuniary payment, but it may be made payable in goods or services; provided it does not take the form of a share of the produce of the soil, as that would not represent true fealty for the land. (Even under the Rent Acts, rent may be made payable in services, provided the service can be quantified in terms of money – Montague *v* Browning [1954] 2 All ER 601. It must be a periodic payment, although the amount may be varied during different periods of the same lease.

Rent should be made payable to the landlord, or his agent, not to a third party and in English common law it is payable on the demised premises, annually in arrears and in **cash** (although if a landlord indicates that he will accept a cheque the landlord cannot refuse such a form of payment at a later date, so long as the cheque is honoured – Henderson *v* Arthur [1907] 1 KB 10). However, it may be specified that rent is to be payable at any named interval, in any form, and at any place agreed between the parties. Commonly rent is payable at weekly, monthly, or quarterly intervals, in advance. A tenant should seek out his landlord and **tender** rent, and rent sent by post is paid at the tenant's risk (although if it is agreed that rent can be paid by post payment is made when the payment is posted – Beevers *v* Mason (1978) 37 P & CR 452). In practice a landlord normally demands rent in the same way as any other debt, but his failure so to do does not diminish the tenant's obligation. Upon an assignment of the landlord's interest rent remains payable to the assignor, until the tenant has been given notice of the change. A **premium**, or lump-sum payment, may be construed as rent: "I [Evershed M.R.] cannot, for my part, think that the area of the law would be so short as to disable it from dealing appropriately with such a case as that last suggested, if it appeared that the so called premium was, in truth and in substance, nothing more or other than rent qualified and provided for in 'an abnormal form'" – Woods *v* Wise [1955] 2 QB 45.

A feature of rent, at common law, is that if it is not paid when due the landlord has a right to levy **distress**, i.e. to enter on to the demised premises to seize certain goods of the tenant in order to elicit payment. However, the usual remedy for non-payment of rent is a simple court action against the tenant for the sum due or, if expressly permitted under the lease, an action of **forfeiture** and recovery of possession of the demised premises. Strictly, rent is a payment for corporeal property (on which goods may be situated) and is not a payment for an incorporeal right, such as an easement, licence, or profit à prendre, nor is it a payment for goods alone (although in common usage this limited interpretation is not always applied). A payment outside the terms of a lease (excluding a payment subsequent to a rent review) or made after a lease has expired, e.g. **mesne profits**, strictly is not rent.

Rent is by nature the effective recompense for the use of land and, on the grant of a tenancy there is normally an express provision for the payment of rent; but in the absence of an express provision, there is an **implied covenant** that a reasonable rent will be paid for that land. The amount of such payment is dependant on the intention of the parties, based on the relationship established, i.e. upon the terms and conditions by which the land is used.

Whether the entire amount paid by a tenant to his landlord represents rent depends on the nature of the agreement. As a rule, any payment in respect of what is let, whether described as rent or not, is rent. Thus, if rates and rent together are paid to the landlord – i.e. as an **inclusive rent** – then, even though the landlord is acting solely as a conduit for the rates the entire sum is rent and, therefore, may be distrained for. A sum reserved as additional rent to cover the fire insurance premium for the leased premises has been held to be rent – Breadalbane *v* Robertson (1914) 51 Sc. LR 156. But, a collateral payment to a landlord for specified services, e.g. lighting, heating, cleaning, which is not stated to be rent and does not represent a payment for what is let cannot be construed as rent and, if unpaid, would not carry a right to levy distress. However, in most leases the *reddendum* stipulates those payments that are constituted as rent and leaves no grounds for doubt: "the lease contains a reddendum, and whatever services or suits are thereby reserved partake of the character of rent" – Vyryan *v* Arthur (1823) 1 B and C 410.

The obligation to pay rent terminates when the relationship of landlord and tenant comes to an end which may be (a) when a lease for a term of years comes to an end; (b) when a tenant is evicted; (c) if a lease is surrendered or frustrated; or (d) if the tenant abandons the premises and the landlord re-enters and re-lets the premises.

The term 'rent' and 'rental' are synonymous; the latter being more common in the US. See also **apportionment, base rent, best rent, chief rent, constant rent, contractual rent, dead rent, double rent, equity rent, excess rent, exclusive rent, fair rent, fee-farm rent, graded rent, graduated rent, gross rent, ground rent, head rent, improved rent, insurance rent, interim rent, leasehold ground rent, market rent, net rent, penal rent, percentage rent, peppercorn rent, primary and secondary rent, profit rent, quit rent, rack rent, registered rent, rent control, rent in advance (or arrears), rent review clause, rent roll, rent-seck, rental, tonnage rent, turnover rent, virtual rent.**

Real Property, by William E. Burby, 3 edn., pp. 164–180.
Adkin's Landlord and Tenant, 18 edn, pp. 87–111.
The Law of Landlord and Tenant, by David Lloyd Evans, 2 edn., pp. 108–134.
Landlord and Tenant Law, by David Yates and A.J. Hawkins, pp. 115–158 (1981).
Hill & Redman's Law of Landlord and Tenant, 17 edn, pp. 315–363.
Woodfall's Landlord and Tenant, 28

edn, paras. 1–0679 to 1–0785.
27 Halsbury's Laws of England, 4 edn, paras. 211–257.
2. In economics, rent is the excess of income over and above the minimum required to keep a factor of production in its present use; i.e. it means **economic rent**. The uniqueness of rent for land is that land tends to be in short supply, and so rent may be considered as "that portion of the produce of earth, which is paid to the landlord for the original and indestructible powers of the soil" (*Principles of Political Economy and Taxation*, by David Ricardo, p. 33, 1917); or "the economic return that accrues or should accrue to land from its use in production" (*Land Resource Economics*, by Raleigh Barlowe, 3 edn., p. 162). See also **quasi-rent**.

rent achivement (US)
see **holdback**.

Rent Acts
Acts of Parliament passed to control the relationship between a landlord and a tenant of residential property; in particular, to provide **security of tenure** for the tenant and to limit the amount that a landlord can charge as rent for property that comes within the ambit of the Acts. "The policy of the Rent Acts was and is to protect the tenant in his house, whether from the threat to extort a premium for the grant or renewal of his tenancy, to increase his rent, or to evict him ... The Rent Acts have throughout their history constituted an interference with contract and property rights for a specific purpose – the redress of the balance of advantage enjoyed in a world of housing shortage by the landlord over those who have to rent their homes." – Horford Investments

Ltd *v* Lambert [1976] Ch. 52.

'Rent Acts' were passed initially to control the letting of dwelling-houses in the period of acute housing shortage that developed during the two world wars, e.g. the Increase of Rent and Mortgage Interest (War Restrictions) Bill 1915 and the Rent and Mortgage Restriction Act 1939. Since the Second World War a succession of Acts have passed on to the statute book with the aim of tightening the legislative controls that affect the letting of residential property (with the exception of the Rent Act 1957 which sought to 'de-control' such lettings). The Rent Act 1965, as consolidated into the Rent Act 1977, extends the controls to most private lettings, and the Housing Act 1980, although providing some exceptions to earlier Acts, brought most public sector lettings within a similar form of security of tenure to that which applies to private lettings. In addition, the Landlord and Tenant Act 1954, Part I provides that when a **long tenancy** comes to an end the tenant has similar protection to that provided for other tenants of residential property and the Protection from Eviction Act 1977 provides that a landlord cannot obtain possession of a dwelling-house against the will of the occupier without resorting to a court for an order for possession. Referred to also as the 'Rent Restriction Acts'. See also **assured tenancy, eviction, fair rent, protected tenancy, regulated tenancy, rent control.**

Hill and Redman's Law of Landlord and Tenant, 17 edn, pp. 867–870.

Landlord and Tenant, by Martin Partington, 2 edn., p. 152 *et seq.*

27 Halsbury's Laws of England, 4 edn, paras. 564–575.

rent allowance

A form of grant paid to a tenant of a dwelling-house to assist with the payment of rent when the tenant's income is deemed to be inadequate. In the UK, local authorities are empowered by the Housing Finance Act 1972, Part II and Rent Act 1974, s. 11, Sch. 4 to make such grants. cf. **rent concession.**

rent assessment committee

A body that hears appeals against the decisions of a **rent officer** on the determination of the **fair rent** for a regulated tenancy of a dwelling house. A rent assessment committee normally comprises three members drawn from a rent assessment panel (appointed for a particular area by the Lord Chancellor and the Secretary of State for the Environment) – usually, a surveyor, a layperson and a legally qualified chairman (Rent Act 1977, Sch. 10). It is a tribunal and not a court and is concerned only with determining the rental value of dwellings that come within its jurisdiction. A rent assessment committee does not need to take account of the decision of the rent officer but acts as an independent **expert** for the purpose of determining a fair rent. An appeal against a decision of a rent assessment committee, on a point of law only, lies to the High Court. See also **Leasehold Valuation Tribunal, rent tribunal.**

rent assessment panel

see **leasehold valuation tribunal, rent assessment committee.**

rent book

A book, or similar document, that records rent and other tenancy details. In particular, a document that must be provided to any person who is granted a right to occupy premises as a **residence** and is charged a weekly rent (Landlord and Tenant Act 1962, s. 1 (4), replacing various earlier statutes to similar effect). The book must set out details of the landlord's name and address; the amount of rent payable; details of any local authority statutory rent allowance scheme; details of other letting terms; and a statement of the maximum number of persons permitted to occupy the house with a summary of what constitutes an overcrowding offence. All weekly tenants – that is, those to whom a rent per week is quoted even if it is not paid weekly, or is paid weekly but is quoted at other intervals – must have a rent book provided by the landlord. The duty does not exist if the rent "includes a payment in respect of **board** and the value of that board to the tenant forms a substantial proportion of the whole rent". The requirement is not limited to premises covered by the Rent Acts but applies to any tenant or licencee provided "rent is payable weekly" for a right "to occupy any premises as a residence". It is a criminal offence for a landlord not to provide the requisite rent book, but due to ignorance of the law by many tenants, the requirement frequently is not complied with. Full details of the particulars to be included in a rent book are set out currently in the Rent Book (Form of Notice) Regulations 1982, S.I. No. 1474.

The Law of Landlord and Tenant, by David Lloyd Evans, 2 edn., pp. 332–334.

Landlord and Tenant, by Martin Partington, 2 edn., pp. 58–68.

Housing Law, by Andrew Arden and Martin Partington, pp. 210–212 (1983).

rent-charge
see **rentcharge**.

rent concession
A discount from an established or market rent granted as an inducement for a particular tenant to enter into a lease. Such a discount may take the form of a direct reduction in the rent for part of the term of the lease, or some other concession granted by the landlord to a prospective tenant, e.g. the provision of partitioning or an agreement to maintain a fixed level of service charge. A rent concession is intended to be a temporary provision; it should not amount to a straight rent reduction for the term of the lease, because it is the landlord's intention to maintain the general rent level, or to create that illusion, in order to maintain the apparent value of the property – especially when he is negotiating rent reviews with other tenants.

cf. **rent allowance**. See also **cash back,** **fitting-out allowance, virtual rent**.

rent control
The regulation by law of the maximum level of rent that a landlord is permitted to charge for a particular property. Statutory rent controls, in one form or another, have been introduced in most countries, especially for residential properties, in order to protect tenants (who are considered to have more modest means than their landlords) against being charged exhorbitant rents when there is an undue shortage of properties available to let. (Such controls frequently exacerbate the position by reducing the incentive for landlords to provide properties to let and thereby forcing up the rent for existing properties still further; on all the evi-

dence this legislation "sacrifices the right of the landlord to that of the tenant" (*General Theory of Law*, by Jean Dabin, para. 149 (1944)).

The forms that rent controls take include temporary restrictions on rent increases (usually as an anti-inflation measure); linking rent levels or rent increases to an artificial statutory formula; or establishing a procedure for determining the maximum level of rent that may be charged based on a **fair rent**, **market rent**, or some other 'rental value'.

In the UK 'rent control' is used sometimes to refer to a freeze or severe limitation placed on rent increases; in particular, the term was applied to the strict form of control exercised over certain residential tenancies, between 1920 and 1980, when a property was subject to a **controlled tenancy**. 'Rent regulation' is used in contradistinction to refer to any statutory form of intervention in the free market that would otherwise exist between landlord and tenant.

In the UK and France rent regulation applies to most residential property, business premises and agricultural holdings. In the US, certain states and cities (notably Baltimore, Boston, Miami Beach, New York City and some towns and cities in Alaska, California, Connecticut, Maryland, Massachusetts and New Jersey) have statutory rent control or regulation that applies to residential properties. See also **Rent Acts**, **registered rent**.
Verdict on Rent Control: Essays on the Economic Consequences of Political Action to Restrict Rents in Five Countries, by Frederick A. Hayek, *et al.* (1972).
Rent Control and Leasehold Enfranchisement, by Trevor Aldridge, 8 edn.

rent day
A day appointed for the payment of rent. See also **quarter day**, **rent in advance (or arrears)**.

rent escalation
see **escalation clause**.

rent gradient
A graphical representation of the relationship between the rent paid for a unit of property and its distance from a given point – usually from the central business district or a commercial centre. The rent for a parcel of land may be considered to decline in inverse proportion to the square of the distance from the place of highest value. See also **catchment area**.

rent in advance (or arrears)
Rent is payable in **arrears**, unless expressed to the contrary. Rent is 'in arrears' at the end of the day on which it is due and a landlord may distrain on the following day. Rent is due on the date specified in the lease (or the appropriate anniversary of the commencement date), unless that day is a public holiday when the liability for payment is postponed to the next day. Any sum paid before the due date is an advance or prepayment to the landlord and technically is not properly paid; thus, if a landlord sells his interest before the due date then, as a rule, the new landlord may still claim rent on the due date because the right to sue for arrears of rent (and any other sum due from the tenant) passes to a purchaser of the reversion – De Nicholes *v* Saunders (1870) LR 5 CP 89 (Law of Property Act 1925, s. 141). See also **distress**.

rent insurance
see **loss of rent insurance**.

rent limit

see **registered rent**

rent (or income) multiplier (US)

A factor applied to the rent (or income) receivable from a property to determine its capital value, i.e. a **capitalisation factor**. See also **gross rent multiplier, net income multiplier**.

rent officer

A person appointed by, but independent of, a local authority to determine the **fair rent** for a dwellinghouse, in accordance with the provisions of the Rent Acts (originally the Rent Act 1965 but now the Rent Act 1977, s. 66). An appeal against the decision of a rent officer may be made to a **rent assessment committee** by either party to the tenancy. See also **certificate of fair rent, registered rent**.

rent policy

See **loss of rent policy**.

rent reduction

A reduction in the amount of rent contractually due to a landlord under a tenancy. A rent reduction is a permanent facility granted to a tenant. cf. **rent concession**. See also **accord and satisfaction, set-off**.

rent registration

see **registered rent**.

rent regulation

see **rent control**.

rent restriction

see **rent control**.

Rent Restriction Acts

see **Rent Acts**.

rent review clause

A clause in a lease which permits the lessor or lessee to seek a reassessment of the rent of the demised premises at a specified interval or intervals, without any corresponding right for the lease to be determined at that stage. A rent review clause provides for the rental value of the demised premises to be reassessed, usually by reference to the then current **market rent**; as distinguished from a 'rent variation' or escalation clause by which, "with or without the landlord being required to initiate the process of calculation, the amount of rent is varied by reference to some other rent, cost, price or index … A rent review clause properly so called is a clause which permits the lessor (or lessee) to call for the reconsideration or reassessment of the rent. At stated intervals, and in accordance with the procedure laid down by the clause, the new rate of the rent is agreed by the landlord and the tenant or determined by the process laid down in the lease, the new rate applying until the next review date or the expiry of the term." (27 Halsbury's Laws of England, 4 edn, p. 166).

A rent review clause is intended to keep the landlord's return in line with market conditions prevailing at the time of the review, while enabling the tenant to have secure possession for the term of the lease. It provides the tenant with a certainty as to his level of rent during the intervals between the rent review dates and still enables the landlord to combat the eroding value of the income he receives. The clause is "for the benefit of the tenant because without such a clause he would never get the long lease which he required; and under modern condition it would be grossly unfair that he should. It is for the benefit of the landlord because it ensures that for the duration of the lease he will receive a fair rent instead of a rent far below the market value of the property which he demises". – United Scientific Holdings v Burnley Borough Council [1976].

The operation of a rent review clause is a matter of law and valuation; "it is a question of law which must be determined by the court in order that the surveyors may know what is the subject-matter which they are required to value ... it is not the function of the court to give the surveyors directions as to how they shall make their valuation; that is to say, what factors to take into account and what weight to give to them". – Compton Group Ltd v Estates Gazette (1977) 244 EG 801. Thus in essence it is a question of valuation and negotiation, supported if necessary by reference to an **expert** or **arbitrator** to determine the rent in cases when the landlord and tenant are unable to agree.

In the UK, leases of commercial property have traditionally been granted for long terms, up to 20 or more years, and rent review clauses were introduced to combat the high level of inflation that has prevailed since the last world war. Originally reviews were provided at 14- or 7-year intervals, but the norm has been reduced now to 5 years, with 3-year intervals being not uncommon. In the US, leases of commercial property are granted generally for shorter periods (5 or 10 years) and so a rent review or 'revaluation clause' is a less prevalent feature of such leases. In France, annual escalation clauses, tied to the cost of living, are normally introduced into any commercial lease (*bail commercial*), with any rent review provision (one based on a

review to market rent) being tied by law to a right for the parties to terminate the lease at three yearly intervals. See also **graduated rent, indexed rent, revaluation lease, time is of the essence**.

Modern Methods of Valuation, 7 edn., pp. 326–330.
Statutory Valuations, by Andrew Baum, pp. 31–41 (1983).
The Law of Landlord and Tenant, by David Lloyd Evans, 2 edn., pp. 114–120.
Letting Business Premises, by Trevor M. Alrdidge, 5 edn., pp. 10–16.
Handbook of Business Tenancies, by D.W. Williams, para. 4.01 *et seq* (1985, looseleaf).
Rent Reviews and Variable Rents, by D.N. Clarke and J.E. Adams, 2 edn.
Handbook of Rent Review, by R. Bernstein and K. Reynolds, (1981).

rent roll

A schedule of the total **rent** received or receivable from a particular property, or the total rent received or receivable by a particular investor from his real estate portfolio, over a stipulated period of time.

rent-seck

A **rentcharge** formerly created with no express right, if the rent fell into arrears, for the landlord to levy distress (Bl. Comm. vol. ii p. 42). Since 1730 the recipient of such a payment has been given the statutory power to distrain for an unpaid rent-seck (Landlord and Tenant Act 1730, s. 5; Law of Property Act 1925, s. 121). Called also 'dry rent' or 'barren rent'.

rent service

A payment made to an owner of land for the right to use and occupy his land. Historically, a payment made to a feudal lord in the form of a service rendered and, at common law, carrying an automatic right of **distress** for non-payment.

In modern law, rent service is a payment for a right to tenancy, i.e. a relationship created between a landlord and a tenant; as distinguished from a **rentcharge** which is a periodic payment for land, but one that is not paid as a consequence of a landlord and tenant relationship, i.e. the recipient has no interest in the land. See also **rent**.

rent tribunal

A tribunal that was responsible for fixing reasonable rents and granting limited security of tenure for residential premises which came within the Rent Acts and were let at a rent that included a payment for furniture and services. Since 1980 the rent payable for such premises is assessed in the same way as for unfurnished premises, i.e. as a **fair rent**; the rent tribunals as such were abolished and their function transferred to a **rent assessment committee**. However, when carrying out a similar function to the former rent tribunals (i.e. when dealing with a matter arising under a **restricted contract**), the committee is known as a 'rent tribunal' (Housing Act 1980, s. 72).
Manual of Housing Law, by Andrew Arden, 2 edn., pp. 93–103.

rent unit factor
see **factor**.

rent-up
To fill up a new building with tenants.

rent variation clause (US)
see **escalation clause**.

rentable (F)
profitable.
(*loyer rentable* – **economic rent**).

rentabilité (F)
financial analysis; profitability.
(*taux de rentabilité* – **rate of return**).

rentable area (US)
The area let, or available for letting, in a commercial building. The area for which a tenant is deemed to pay rent. A term most commonly applied to such an area in an office building when the rent payable by a tenant is determined by applying an amount per unit area. In the US, a typical definition of 'rentable area' is that of the Building Owners and Managers Association International, the area "computed by measuring from the inside surface of the outer masonry building wall (but where the outer building wall is 50 per cent or more of glass, the rentable area shall be measured from the inside of glass area) to the finished surface of corridor side of partitions, or to the opposite outer masonry wall or glass surface whichever is applicable to the letting, including columns or projections necessary to the building". Ancilliary areas, e.g. toilets, closets, etc., generally are included for single tenancy floors or where a tenant has exclusive use thereof. A number of exclusions are made for shared areas; in particular, stairs, elevator shafts, ventilation stacks, air or service ducts, flues, etc., together with their enclosing walls. Air-conditioning ducts and areas taken up by associated equipment, toilets, closets, etc. enclosed within an area let exclusively to one tenant are considered part of the rentable area. The American National Standards Institute defines rentable

area in a similar way. It refers to the rentable area of a single tenancy floor as the 'full floor rentable area', and the rentable area of a multiple tenancy floor as the 'net rentable area' being the sum of all rentable areas on that floor i.e. excluding areas not exclusively let to one tenant.

In the UK, the terms **net internal area**, 'net lettable area' or 'effective floor area' (with the corresponding definition) are more commonly used when referring to the area for which a tenant pays rent. See also **net usable area**.

rentage (US)

1. The **base rent** in a lease, excluding any payment of a turnover rent; that is, the fixed minimum rent payable under a turnover or percentage lease. cf. **overage**.

(US) 2. A true or primary **rent** for land as paid under a lease, excluding any other payment made by a tenant to his landlord, such as operating cost contributions. See also **primary and secondary rent**.

rental

1. A corruption of rent roll; the sum total of rent.

2. An amount paid as **rent**. A periodic payment for the use of property; in particular an annual payment for the hire of goods. See also **rental value**.

(US) 3. Something that is granted in return for rent.

rental agreement

A **lease**; an express form of tenancy agreement. A term that is applied mainly to a short term tenancy agreement, particularly when granted for residential property.

cf. **agreement for a lease**.

rental annuity

see **life annuity**.

rental escalation charge (US)

A payment made by a tenant, as required under an **escalation clause**, to cover an increase in operating costs.

rental method

A method of valuation used to determine the net annual value, of a building by reference to rent paid for comparable properties. In particular, the valuation of a property for rating purposes using the **comparison method of valuation**. See also **investment method of valuation, rating valuation**.

rental multiplier (US)

see **rent multiplier**.

rental period

1. The period of time covered by a payment of **rent**. Called also 'gales'.

2. 'A period in respect of which a payment of rent falls to be made' (Rent Act 1974, s. 7 (6)).

rental property (US)

Property that is subject to a lease (or leases), i.e. an income producing or **investment property**. Property for which rent is paid or received.

rental purchase

A means of purchasing a property by which the whole or part of the purchase price is paid in three or more instalments and the vendor retains the deeds to the property until all, or a specified part, of the purchase price is paid. The vendor enters into a contract for the sale of the property conditional upon payment of the purchase price by instalments; until the final instalment is paid the purchaser is permitted to occupy the property as a licensee; and title to the property is not transferred until the conditions of the contract are met in full.

Rental purchase agreements have been used as a sham means of, in effect, leasing a dwelling-house in order to avoid the **Rent Acts**. However, since 1980 any person who occupies a dwelling-house under a rental purchase agreement (whether to acquire a freehold or a leasehold interest) upon terms that require the whole or part of the purchase price to be paid in three or more instalments has a similar right to protection from **eviction** as any other residential occupier (Housing Act 1980, ss. 88, Sch. 25). Called also 'lease-purchase'. See also **conditional contract**, *crèdit-bail*, **instalment contract**.

rental value

The annual sum at which a property might reasonably be expected to let in the open market assuming that the terms upon which it is let are similar to those upon which properties of a similar nature are normally let. See also **market rent**.

rental value insurance

Insurance to cover an occupier of property against the cost of renting alternative premises in the event of fire. Called also 'use and occupation insurance'.

cf. **loss of rent insurance**. See also **consequential loss insurance**.

rentcharge

An annual or other periodic payment made for land when there is no relationship of landlord and tenant between the payer and payee, i.e. a payment made in the nature of rent but "where the owner of the rent hath no future interest, or **reversion**

expectant in the land; as where a man by deed maketh over to others his whole estate in fee simple with a certain rent payable thereout" – Bl. Comm. vol. ii p. 42. A periodic payment made by a substituted owner of land to the former owner of the same land, due payment of which is secured by a right of **distress** either as expressly reserved or as allowed by statute. In particular, "any annuity or periodic sum of money charged upon or payable out of land, except a **rent service** or interest on a mortgage on land" – Limitation Act 1980, s. 38 (1). A rentcharge arises most frequently when the price for the purchase of land is made payable in whole or in part as an annual equivalent. It is a form of charge on land which, if it falls into arrears, enables the payee to take a personal action for the money; may entitle him to levy distress, or take possession of the land until the payment is made; but does not entitle him to regain the land as for a **rent service**.

No new rentcharge can be created after 22nd August 1977, except (a) one that relates to a **building scheme** – an 'estate rentcharge'; (b) one that has the effect of making the land upon which it is charged **settled land**; (c) certain forms of statutory rentcharge; and (d) a rentcharge created under an order of the court. All existing rentcharges are to be redeemed by not later than 22nd July 2037 (Rentcharges Act 1977, ss. 2, 3.) In this context a rentcharge is defined as, "any annual or other periodic sum charged on or issuing out of land, except – (a) rent reserved by a lease or tenancy, of (b) any sum payable by way of interest". (Rentcharges Act 1977, s. 1). This definition effectively covers a **fee farm rent**, a **chief rent** or any payment of a similar nature, whatever it is called. See also **general equitable charge**, **legal interest**, **quit rent**, **rent-seck**.

Megarry's Manual of the Law of Real Property, 6 edn, pp. 390–395.

Cheshire's Modern Law of Real Property, 13 edn, pp. 603–614.

The Law of Real Property, by Robert Megarry and H.W.R. Wade, 5 edn., pp. 818–829.

39 Halsbury's Laws of England, 4 edn, para. 1201 *et seq.*

rente (F)

income, especially unearned income; revenue; annuity; rent; stock (in a company).

(*rente foncière* – ground rent; a rent payable for an indefinite period as distinguished from *loyer* which is payable for a fixed-term lease)

(*rente viagère* – life annuity; life interest)

(*bail à rente* – **finance lease**, a grant of a charge on immoveable property in exchange for an annuity – there is no exact equivalent in English law. See also *crédit-bail*)

(*servitude de rent* – **rentcharge**).

renter

One who holds land subject to the payment of rent, i.e. a **tenant** or **lessee**.

rentier

Originally a person whose income was derived solely from interest earned on government securities; the word being derived from the French *rentes*, a particular form of interest-bearing government bond. In modern terms, rentier is applied to any person whose income is unearned, i.e. is derived solely from the ownership of capital, rather than one whose income

is derived from his own labour. A rentier may be a person who inherits wealth; a retired person; or an institution that specialises in fixed interest investments. See also **economic rent**.

rentier (F)

rentier; fundholder; a person of private means.

(*rentier viager* – holder of life annuity)

(*petit rentier* – small investor).

renting (F)

rental; hiring (of moveable property).

rentrée (F)

re-entry; receipt.

rents and profits

Income to be derived from land; the total of **rent** and **profit** accruing from a property on an annual basis.

rents insurance (US)

see **loss of rent insurance**.

renunciation

1. Derived from the Latin *renunciare*, 'to pronounce against'. The stating of an intention to give up an available right or privilege. The **repudiation** of a contract, "when one party by words or conduct, evinces an intention not to continue to perform his part of the contract". (Chitty on Contract 28 edn, p. 883). Renunciation must go beyond refusal or omission to perform some part of the contract; it amounts to a refusal to perform the outstanding obligations of the contract in their entirety. An agent renounces his authority to perform the duties entrusted to him when he indicates expressly or impliedly that he does not intend to continue to act for his principal.

cf. **abandonment**. See also **termination**.

2. The act of giving up, surrendering,

abandoning or releasing a right, interest or title; especially when nothing of value is received in exchange. A term that, strictly, is not used in English law where it is replaced by **surrender** or **release**. (In Scottish law it is equivalent to 'reconveyance' or 'release', i.e. a mortgagee may renounce his right to property or a tenant may renounce his tenancy).

repair

The process of making good, fixing or mending defects. Restoring a property to a good condition following deterioration through use, misuse, damage, decay or dilapidation. Repair includes **maintenance**; **restoration**; and when necessary, **renewal** of parts of a property. It requires also some element of anticipation to prevent future deterioration – Day *v* Harland and Wolff Ltd [1953] 2 All ER 388. Normally repair does not include **reconstruction, alteration, improvement, renewal** in toto or any other such work that would improve the value or change the character of a property. Nevertheless, "repair and renew are not words expressive of clear contrast. Repair always involves renewal; renewal of a part, a subordinate part ... Repair is restoration by renewal or replacement of subsidiary parts of a whole. Renewal, as distinguished from repair, is reconstruction of the entirety, meaning by the entirety not necessarily the whole but substantially the whole subject-matter under discussion". – Lurcott *v* Wakeley [1911] 1 KB 923. When a tenant is liable under a lease 'to repair' a property then a "diminution of value, resulting from the natural operation of time and the elements, falls on the landlord; but the tenant must take care that the premises do not suffer more damage than the operation of these causes would effect; and he is bound by responsible application of labour, to keep the house as nearly as possible in the same condition as when it was demised" – Gutteridge *v* Munyard (1834) 1 Mood. and R 336.

The exact extent of a tenant's obligation under a lease is dependent on the type of building, its condition, as well as the exact wording of the repairing covenant in the lease. For example a covenant 'to repair' includes putting dilapidated property into a good state of repair – Proudfoot *v* Hart (1890) 25 QBD 42, but it does not necessitate renewal or rebuilding: "if a tenant takes a house which is of such a kind that by its own inherent nature it will in course of time fall into a particular condition, the effects of that result are not within the tenant's covenant to repair" – Lister *v* Lane and Newsham [1893] 2 QB 216. Whether what is required of a tenant is repair or renewal is a question of fact and the degree of work involved; "however large the words of the covenants may be, a covenant to repair a house is not a covenant to give a different thing from that which the tenant took when he entered into the covenant. He has to repair that thing which he took; he is not obliged to make a new and different thing". – Lister *v* Lane *supra* at p. 217; Ravenseft Properties *v* Davstone (Holdings) [1919] 1 All ER 929. (In the Ravenseft case it was stated that the cost that the work of repair bears to the value or cost of the whole premises may sometimes be a useful guide).

An obligation to repair is commonly preceded by such words as 'good', 'proper', 'sufficient', 'necessary', 'substantially' or 'habitable' and such words convey much the same meaning as **tenantable repair**, i.e. to put, keep and leave a property in such condition as a new tenant might expect to find it having regard to the type of property. However, such words do not extend the requirement to making good deterioration arising from **fair wear and tear**, nor, for example, repairing a small hole made in order to hang a picture – Perry *v* Chotzner (1893) 9 TLR 488. Thus when interpreting a repairing covenant in a lease "the correct approach is to look at the particular building, to look at the state which it is in 'at the date of the lease', to look at the precise terms of the lease, and then come to a conclusion whether, on a fair interpretation of those terms in relation to that state, the requisite work can fairly be termed repair. However large the covenant, it must not be looked at *in vacuo*". – Brew Brothers Ltd. *v* Snax (Ross) Ltd. [1970] 1 All ER 602.

A weekly tenant has an **implied covenant** to use a property in a **tenant-like manner** – Warren *v* Keen [1954] 1 QB 15 – and a yearly tenant has also to keep the premises wind and water tight – Wedd *v* Porter [1916] 2 KB 91; but such tenants have no further obligation. At common law a landlord has no obligation to keep leased property in repair, although he may have an implied or statutory obligation. For example, in most cases, there is an implied covenant that the landlord (excluding certain bodies as specified in the Housing Act 1980, s. 80) of a dwelling-house, let after 24th October 1981 on a lease that was originally for less than 7 years, must keep the exterior and structure in repair and maintain the installations and services (Housing Act 1961, s. 32), and a dwelling-house let at a **low rent** must be made **fit for human habitation** (Housing Act 1957, s. 6). The landlord may be obliged to carry out certain repairs in order to insure that the leased premises comply with building, safety, and public health regulation, unless such an obligation is placed expressly as an onus on the tenant.

cf. **renewal**. See also **clear lease, full repairing and insuring lease, good repair, inherent defect, relief, repairs notice, right of entry, set-off**.

Housing Disrepair, by N.C. Martyn and E. Lloyd-Jones, (1985).

The Law of Landlord and Tenant, by David Lloyd Evans, 2 edn, pp. 95–98, 152–166.

Adkin's Landlord and Tenant, 18 edn, pp. 157–186.

Hill & Redman's Landlord and Tenant, 17 edn, pp. 219–259.

Woodfall's Landlord and Tenant, 23 edn, para. 1–1432 *et seq*.

27 Halsbury's Laws of England, 4 edn, paras. 264–317.

repairing lease
see **full repairing and insuring lease, net lease, repair, triple net lease**.

repairs grant
A grant made by a local authority, under the provisions of the Housing Act 1974, ss. 71–72, towards the cost of repairing or improving a dwelling in a **housing action area** or a **general improvement area**; provided it is not work associated with the provision of a new dwelling (1974 Act, s. 56(2)(c)).

cf. **improvement grant**.

West's Law of Housing, 4 edn, p. 273.

repairs notice

1. A notice served by a local authority, under provisions of the Housing Act 1957, s. 9, on a person "having control of a house" that is considered **unfit for human habitation**, requiring that person to render it fit. The notice must specify the work required to render the house fit for habitation and it must be possible to carry out that work at a "reasonable expense". The Housing Act 1969, s. 72 (subsequently entitled the Housing Act 1957, s. 9 (1A)) provides also that a local authority may serve notice upon the person having control of a house in case of "substantial disrepair", requiring that person to execute works to rectify the defects. In addition, if an occupying tenant makes representation that a house is in such a state of disrepair that, although it is not unfit for human habitation, the occupying tenant is suffering material personal discomfort a local authority may serve a repairs notice on the person having control of the house (Housing Act 1980, s. 149, subsequently entitled the Housing Act 1957, s. 9 (1B) (1C)). In the latter instances the local authority must have regard to the "age, character and locality" of the property when serving the notice. A repairs notice has a dual purpose, for, "it seems to me [Lord Denning] that the policy of Parliament was to make the owners of houses keep them in proper repair. Not only so as to keep up the stock of houses but also to see that protected tenants should be able to have their houses properly kept up" – Hillbank Properties Ltd *v* Hackney Borough Council [1978] 3 WLR 268. See also **charging order**, **closing order**, **improvement notice**.

West's Law of Housing, 4 edn, pp. 76–81.
Housing Law, by Andrew Arden and Martin Partington, pp. 399–414 (1983).

2. A notice served by a landlord on his tenant indicating that repairs, which are the tenant's express responsibility under a lease, have not been carried out and that the landlord intends to enter into the demised premises, carry out the repairs himself, and reclaim the cost from the tenant; or a notice served by the landlord after the work has been carried out in order to recover the cost of the repairs from the tenant. Such a notice may be enforced only if provided for in the lease; either as an express right, or a right that is implied because the landlord has covenanted to **repair** the demised premises – Yellowly *v* Morley (1910) 27 TLR 20; Granada Theatres *v* Freehold Investments (Leytonstone) [1959] 1 WLR 570. (A landlord who has a statutory duty to repair a dwelling house let on a regulated tenancy, or to maintain an agricultural holding, has a right to enter to perform that function: Rent Act 1977, ss. 3 (1), 112; Agricultural Holding Act 1948, s. 17.)

The Leasehold Property (Repairs) Act 1938, s. 1, as extended by the Landlord and Tenant Act 1954, s. 51, provides that a landlord may recover damages for a breach of covenant to repair only provided he has served at least one month's notice of the breach specifying the repair work required; claiming compensation to which he is entitled; and requiring the tenant to carry out the repairs. The tenant must be given a reasonable time to carry out the repairs and also be given the right to serve a counter-notice claiming relief if the landlord's requirement is unreasonable. A landlord who decides to enter and carry out repairs himself waives his right to claim **forfeiture** of the lease for disrepair. The amount of damages that a landlord can recover from a tenant as a result of a breach of covenant to repair is restricted to the diminution in the value of the landlord's reversion (Landlord and Tenant Act 1927, s. 18).

In the case of an **agricultural tenancy**, if a tenant fails to repair or maintain the holding the landlord should serve notice on the tenant on a Form 1 Notice, in accordance with the Agricultural (Forms of Notices to Remedy) Regulations 1978, specifying the works required to remedy the defect and giving not less than six months for the work to be carrried out. The tenant has a right to challenge the notice and in that event the matter may be submitted to arbitration (Agricultural Holdings (Arbitration on Notices) Order 1978). See also **right of entry, schedule of dilapidations, specific performance**.
Landlord and Tenant Law, by David Yates and A.J. Hawkins, pp. 209–210 (1981).
3. Notice served on the owner of a **listed building** by a local planning authority, in accordance with the provisions of the Town and Country Planning Act 1971, s. 115, specifying work that is necessary for the proper preservation of the building. The notice is a prerequisite to the compulsory purchase of such a building when the owner has failed to repair or maintain the building.

réparation (F)
repair; damages; redress.

(*réparations civiles* – compensation; civil damages)
(*réparation d'entretien* – keeping in repair)
(*réparations locatives* – tenant's repairs).
Dictionnaire Permanent: Gestion Immobilière, pp. 1211–1218.

repartition (F)
assessment (of taxes); **apportionment** (of costs or expenses); distribution (of income among creditors).

replacement cost (or value)
The cost of providing a substitute property that is equally useful to that replaced; the cost of **rebuilding** a property at current prices. For the purpose of fire insurance, the cost of replacing a building that has been destroyed so as to provide, as far as possible, a suitable replacement in terms of design and efficiency. Such cost may be based on the assumed provision of an equivalent modern building, either without any allowance for depreciation of the original building at the time of destruction – 'new-for-old'; or after an appropriate allowance for depreciation – 'old-for-old'. (Old-for-old insurance is called also **indemnity insurance** because it provides a true indemnity for the actual loss suffered). However, if there is no provision as to which basis to adopt, the insurer need pay for no more than an equivalent property 'as was', i.e. the policy is made on a **reinstatement basis**. In the US, insurance provided on the basis that the insured will receive no more than the actual loss, after due account has been taken of depreciation, is called sometimes 'actual cash value insurance'.
cf. **reproduction cost**. See also **cost approach**.

replacement cost approach (US)
see **cost approach**.

replevin
Derived from the Latin *replegiare*, to 'repledge' or deliver out of pledge or surety. A form of legal action that may be used to recover goods that have been unlawfully taken; in particular, to recover specific goods that were taken in an action of **distress** that was wholly illegal (Bl. Comm. vol. iii p. 14). A form of action used especially when the true owner requires the goods rather than damages. If a person is seeking only damages he would take an action in **trespass**. See also **detinue**.

répondant (F)
surety; guarantee; financial reference.

report, valuation
see **valuation report**.

repossession
1. The retaking of **possession**. A word that has no import in English law. It is used in the US for the reclaiming of a right to possession of property when the possessor has ceased to pay for the right to continue in possession; for example, when a purchaser fails to keep up his payments under an instalment contract. See also **dispossession, recovery, right of re-entry**.
2. The regaining of goods that have been sold under a **hire-purchase** agreement when the hirer has defaulted in paying for the goods.

representation
An oral or written statement being an assertion of fact, as compared to an expression of an opinion; a statement on a matter of law or an expression of an intention. In particular, an account that is made with the clear intention of influencing an action, especially one on the faith of which a party enters into a contract. A representation implies a matter of *factum* (fact) and not a question of *faciendum* (the happening of a fact) relating to what might happen in the future. A representation may form part of a contract, i.e. it may be a **term** or **condition**, or it may be a 'mere representation'. A 'mere representation' is intended as a statement of opinion and is clearly not intended to entice the recipient into a contract or legal obligation without further investigation. A distinction between a representation of fact that is intended, or should be known will be relied on, as part of a contract and a 'mere representation', or **puffing**, is a question of degree dependent on the surrounding facts and the relative position of the parties. "Mere silence cannot amount to a representation, but when there is a duty to disclose silence may become significant and amount to a representation". – Greenwood *v* Martins Bank Ltd [1933] AC 57. A representation falls short of a **warranty**; it may amount to a clear expression of fact but, of itself, it is not intended to form a promise as to the validity of the fact. See also **agency**, *caveat emptor*, **estoppel, misrepresentation, utmost good faith**.

représentation (F)
agency.
(*représentation exclusive* – **sole agency**)

representative, personal
see **personal representative**.

reprise (F)
retaking; recovery.
(*reprise locative* – fixture, especially a

tenant's fixture)
(*droit de reprise* – statutory right of renewal of a lease; **security of tenure**).

reprobate
To refuse to accept; to reject.
See also **approbate and reprobate, estoppel**.

reproduction cost
The cost, at current prices, of making a copy or replica; in particular, the cost of rebuilding an identical building or structure, irrespective of the usefulness of such a process, i.e. the cost of providing a facsimile. The cost of a building that is as close as possible to an original both in design, appearance, style and materials. A cost that may be expended, for example, to replace an ancient monument or a listed building.
cf. **replacement cost**.

repudiation
The act of refusing to accept or of disclaiming something; in particular, the action of refusing to discharge a duty or obligation. **Renunciation** or **disclaimer** of a right or privilege. An intimation, by words or conduct, of an intention not to perform the obligations of a **contract** *in toto*; a denial of the existence of a contract; or a claim that a contract is not binding due to some fact such as **fraud, mistake, duress, undue influence** or that an essential **condition** has been breached by the other party. "Repudiation of a contract may mean that, having admittedly made a contract, you decide to break it and to break it in such a way that you intend not to proceed with it. Another use of the word 'repudiation' is where you say: 'There never was a contract between us'. If it turns out that there was a

contract, the act of one party denying the existence of it is to repudiate it . . . Or it may mean: a mere contention that under the terms of the contract the defendant is completely free from liability by reason of some fact." – Toller *v* Law Accident Insurance Society Ltd [1936] 2 All ER 956, 958. A party to a contract may repudiate it in express terms; or it may be repudiated by implication, as when a course of action is embarked on which prevents the party from proceeding with the promise or obligation contained in the contract. The repudiation of a contract by one party entitles the other party to treat the contract as ended and to claim **damages** suffered as a result.
cf. **abandonment, frustration**. See also **breach of contract, rescission, time is of the essence**.
Cheshire & Fifoot's Law of Contract, 10 edn, pp. 483–493.
Chitty on Contract, 25 edn, para. 1601 *et seq*.

répudiation (F)
repudiation; relinquishment.
Précis Dalloz. Droit Civil, Les Biens, (Alex Weill), 2 edn, pp. 280–281.

repurchase
The **purchase** of a property that has been owned previously by the purchaser. See also **redemption, repurchase agreement**.

repurchase agreement
A contract that gives a vendor a right to repurchase a property on specified terms; especially an agreement between a vendor and purchaser of property to the effect that if the purchaser desires to resell within a specified period of time the vendor may reacquire, or have an **option** to reac-

quire, the property. Called also a 'buy-back agreement' or 'sale and buy-back agreement'. See also **right of pre-emption**.

reputed owner
1. A person who appears to be, may be inferred to be, or claims to be the owner of goods; usually by having physical possession, even after he may have sold them or lost his rights to another. In particular, a person who conveys to the minds of the world at large a reputation of ownership, based on "such facts as are capable of being, and naturally would be, the subject of general knowledge to those who take any means to inform themselves on the subject". – Re Couston, *Ex p.* Watkins (1873) 8 Ch. App. 529.
2. A person, believed to be the owner of a parcel of land, upon whom an authority must serve notice, such as notice of a compulsory purchase order or notice of a liability to pay a local property tax. For the purpose of serving a notice of the apportioned cost of **street works** upon the owner of premises fronting the street (under the Highways Act 1980, s. 250 (5)), the reputed owner means "the person whom the local authority really believes to be the owner, and a person who has been the owner, and whom the local authority has dealt with as such, is certainly a reputed owner" – Wirrall Rural District Council v Carter [1903] 1 KB 651. Alternatively, the reputed owner is the person who, after diligent enquiry, is believed by the local authority to be the owner of the land in question. If a local authority cannot ascertain the owner of a parcel of land it may well serve notice on the last known owner and fix a notice in a prominent position on the land. See also **notice to treat**.

required rate of return
see **target rate of return**.

requisition
1. The taking of property or a right to property, especially possession of property, as a temporary measure by a government authority. Commonly used to refer to the taking of goods or housing to meet the needs of a military authority. Requisition should be distinguished from **expropriation** or **compulsory purchase** which are a permanent means of taking property.
2. An **inquiry** made to elucidate a matter affecting a property that is to be transferred or charged; in particular, an inquiry, usually made by a prospective purchaser's or mortgagee's solicitor of a vendor's or mortgagor's solicitor, relating to an **abstract of title**. A requisition may require the vendor or mortgagor to demonstrate that a particular matter that appears to be a **defect of title**, is not, or to explain how he intends to rectify a doubt or defect of title. A requisition is strictly an inquiry relating to a matter of title, in particular a matter arising from a perusal of the abstract of title; however, at the same time as requisitions on title are made it is not uncommon to seek to clarify any other matter affecting the subject property, or the arrangements for completion of the transfer. Requisitions are normally made after a contract for the sale of land has been exchanged, but "it is now not uncommon for such requisitions, under the name of preliminary inquiries, to be made before the contract are exchanged". (Williams on Title, edn, p. 683).

cf. **searches**, **time is of the essence**.
3. A request made to the Registrar of the Land Registry or to a local authority for an official **certificate of search** to ascertain details of any encumberances registered against a particular parcel of land.
4. In the civil law or Scottish law, a formal request to perform an obligation, usually as made by a notary.
5. A formal demand for something to be done. For example, the demand for the provision of a public utility, as when a request is made for a statutory undertaking to provide a water supply or a public sewer in accordance with the provisions of the Water Acts of 1945 or 1972.

requisition (F)
requisition; levy.

res (L)
'A **thing**'. Any thing that may be the subject matter of **ownership**, whether corporeal or incorporeal; personal or real; moveable or immoveable. A term used especially to refer to a particular thing as object *qua* object; rather than a right or interest in that object. See also **action in rem**, **chattels**, *res communes*, *res derelictae*, *res nullius*.

rescision (F)
rescission; avoiding a contract (due to a mistake or misrepresentation).

res communes (L)
'Common property', in the sense of property that belongs to everyone. In the civil law, "those things which, though a separate share of them can be enjoyed and used by everyone, cannot be exclusively and wholly appropriated; as light, air, running water" (Compendium of Mackeldey,

Civil Law (1845) para. 156). See also *res nullius*.

res derelictae (L)
Property that has been abandoned and has no apparent owner: e.g. flotsam and jetsam, **treasure trove**. Such property may become the property, or pass into the ownership of, the first finder – 'finder's keepers' – subject to compliance with certain statutory obligations. See also **abandonment**, *épave*, **possession**, *res nullius*.

res extincta (L)
A thing that has ceased to exist. In particular, the subject matter of a contract that has ceased to exist as a result of a mistake.

res inter alio acta (L)
'A transaction between others, or strangers'.

res ipsa loquitor (L)
'The thing speaks for itself'. In a claim for **negligence** the onus of proof is placed on the plaintiff, but the facts of a particular accident may provide *prima facie* evidence of a negligent act on the part of the defendant; for example, if a person is injured by a roof tile that falls from the defendant's property, it may be claimed that the defendant was clearly in a position to prevent the accident and, therefore, was negligent in not doing so.

res nullius (L)
A term of Roman law, and used in the civil law (including French law) to refer to property that has no owner. A thing that does not belong to anyone; property that does not have an owner, either because it never had an owner, such as wild animals or fish in the ocean, or because it has been aban-

doned by its owner (*res derelictae*) or left on intestacy without a successor. In particular, property that never had an owner or is not considered capable of ownership, e.g. air and waters of the ocean. See also *épave*, **possession**, *res commune*, **treasure trove**.

res permiit domino (L)
'The loss falls on the owner'.

res sua nemini servit (L)
'No one can have an **easement** over his own property'. See also **quasi-easement**.

resale
1. The sale of property that has been acquired from another, generally within a short period of time. cf. **sub-sale**.
2. The sale of property to a third party after it has been sold to another, such as when a person sells goods because the purchaser is in default in paying the full purchase price. See also **power of sale**.

réserve (F)
reserve; **reservation** (from what is granted with land).
(*réserve foncière* – land bank)
(*fonds de réserve* – reserve fund)
(*sous réserve* – **without prejudice**)
(sous réserve de ... – subject to ...
note: French law does not recognise the same limitation placed on words that convey the sense of '**subject to contract**' as in English law). See also **conditional contract**.

rescheduling agreement
An agreement between a borrower and a lender by which the parties modify the terms of a loan when the borrower is in default or is likely to default. Usually the agreement establishes a new repayment schedule and possibly revises the loan interest rate or the property held as security. In the US called also a 'work-out agreement'.

rescind
To cut off, take away or remove. To cancel, annul or abrogate a contract by **abandonment, rescission, or revocation**.

rescission
The act of terminating, annulling, cancelling, or abrogating a **contract** so as to restore the parties to their respective positions before any agreement was entered into, i.e. 'undoing' a contract *ab initio*, as if the contract had never existed. A contract may be rescinded as a consequence of a **mistake, fraud, undue influence, or misrepresentation**. It may be possible also for a contract to be rescinded if there is an express provision entitling one party to terminate the agreement when the other party cannot, or will not fulfil the terms of the agreement, as when the vendor of a property cannot or will not provide adequate replies to the requisitions on title. In the latter sense, when a contract has come into existence but is brought to an end by a failure on the part of one of the parties, the action is more usually referred to as **repudiation**.

Rescission of a contract *ab initio* is an equitable remedy; that is, it is given at the discretion of the court, and it is granted only when **restitution** can be effected as if the contract had never existed, i.e. *restitutio in integrum* 'rescission in full' – must be possible "To put a very simple case: suppose that a person goes and buys a cake which is afterwards eaten, and then he finds that a fraud has been practised on him, he cannot set up the fraud and rescind the contract, because he cannot return the cake." – Clarke *v* Dickson (1858) 27 LJQB 225. Restitution may not be granted if the offended party chooses to affirm the contract; if a third party would lose thereby, for example, if the subject matter of the contract has been resold to a *bona-fide* **purchaser** without notice of a fraud; or if, due to a lapse of time, the offended party is estopped from continuing to exercise his rights. Further, if a contract has been entered into as a result of innocent misrepresentation, then if the court is of the opinion that it would be equitable to do so, "the court may award damages in lieu of rescission and declare the contract subsisting" (Misrepresentation Act 1967, s. 2(2)).

Rescission should not be confused with the **termination** of a contract by one party when an essential condition of the contract has not been performed. With termination there is no element of restoring the *status quo ante*, because part of the contract may have been performed – a terminated contract had an existence that has been brought to an end, usually prematurely. By comparison, a rescinded contract is treated as if it never existed. "Where one party to a contract expresses by word or act in an unequivocal manner that by reason of fraud or essential error of material kind inducing him to enter into a contract he has resolved to rescind it, and refuses to be bound by it, the expression of his election, if justified by the facts, terminates the contract, puts the parties in *status quo ante* and restores things, as between them, to the position in which they stood before the contract was entered into". – Abram Steamship Co. *v* Westvill Shipping Co. [1923] AC 781.

A claim that a contract should be rescinded generally is not compatible with a claim for **damages**, because the rescinded contract is treated as never having come into existence. However, if one party deliberately prevents a contract from coming into effect, damages may be claimed in addition to rescission of the contract. In the case of an **agreement for a lease** where there has been a breach of the agreement, rescission may be used to refer to the claim of the party who is not in breach that the agreement is terminated; such a claim is not inconsistent with a claim for damages – Johnson *v* Agnew [1980] – AC 367. See also **election, revocation, voidable contract.**

Anson's Law of Contract, 26 ed., pp. 222–227, 431–433.
The Law of Real Property, by Robert Megarry and H.W.R. Wade, 5 edn., pp. 618–623.
Cheshire's Modern Law of Real Property, 13 edn, pp. 131–133.
Cheshire & Fifoot's Law of Contract, 10 edn, pp. 253–262.
Chitty on Contract, 25 edn, paras. 374–379, 1482–1487.
9 Halsbury's Laws of England, 4 edn, paras. 535–559.

reservation
1. A right or interest retracted from the subject-matter of a grant of property, such as something taken back by a landlord from the subject-matter of a lease, e.g. a **right of entry** on to the premises demised in order to carry out repairs. **Rent** is the principal item reserved by a landlord upon the grant of a lease. A reservation is something new taken back from that which has been granted, or, strictly, something regranted to the grantor; something

"newly created or reserved out of the land or tenement demised" – Co. Litt. 47a. It may be distinguished from an **exception** which is something that exists but it not granted. A reservation arises from the nature of the right or interest regranted and not from the words used; so that a statement such as, "reserving unto the vendor" does not necessarily create a reservation – Re Dance's Way [1962] 1 Ch. 490. A reservation normally only arises by an express re-grant, although it may arise by implication in the form of an **easement of necessity**.

A **right of way** or a **profit à prendre** in favour of a landlord over the premises he leases, strictly, are neither exceptions nor reservations (although they are sometimes referred to as such), because they were not part of the original grant or part of the premises as granted, but newly created rights granted to a landlord. "It was long settled at common law that an 'exception' is only properly allowed of things *in esse*, such as trees or minerals; a 'reservation' is properly admitted of services to be rendered by the tenant, such as paying rent or providing a beast (heriot), whereas a right to come and kill and carry away wild animals is only a liberty or licence – a profit à prendre – which can take effect only by grant and not by exception or reservation. Words of reservation of sporting rights, operate, therefore, not by way of reservation proper, but by way of re-grant by the tenant" – Mason *v* Clarke [1954] 1 All ER 191.

cf. **grant**.

2. An area of publicly owned land set aside for a particular purpose, e.g. for a school, for future development.

3. An area of land (administered by the Bureau of Indian Affairs) that has remained in the ownership of an American Indian tribe or that has been set aside for their use and enjoyment.

reservation price (US)
see **reserve price**.

reserve price
The minimum price that must be bid at a sale by **auction** before the vendor will sell; if this reserve price is not reached the property is 'brought in' by the vendor. During an auction, when a bid has been made that is equal to or exceeds the reserve price, the auctioneer will state, usually, that the property is 'on sale' i.e. is put on **offer**. If a principal submits a property to an auctioneer for sale "subject to a reserve price", he "gives no power to the auctioneer, either expressly or impliedly, to accept a less price" – McManus *v* Fortescue [1907] 2 KB 6. Until the reserve price is reached every price suggested by the auctioneer, and every bid or offer, including the final one (acceptance of which is signified by the fall of the hammer) is conditional on the final sale price being "equal to or higher than the reserve price" – McManus *v* Fortescue *supra* at p. 7. However, a vendor may only place a reserve price on a property that is offered for sale by auction when he has expressly stated that intention in the conditions of sale, or it is made clear that the sale may be subject to reserve so that a prospective purchaser is put on notice to make inquiry as to whether the reserve is being maintained at the time of sale; otherwise the law presumes that the sale is without reserve. In the US called also a 'reservation price.

The Law of Estate Agency and Auctions, by J.R. Murdoch, 2 edn., pp. 387–392, 487–504.

'reserved matters'
see **planning permission**.

résidence (F)
residence.

resettlement
see **barring the entail**.

residence
1. A form of **abode** or place of habitation, whether temporary or permanent, to which a person most frequently resorts for living purposes, i.e. a place where he sleeps most usually but not necessarily on successive or regular days or weeks. A person has his residence wherever he normally lives: "that is where he has his bed and where he dwells ... the (normal) place of residence of a person is a place where he eats, drinks and sleeps" – Stoke-on-Trent Borough Council *v* Cheshire County Council [1913] 3 KB 705, 706. A residence is a place where a person actually lives as distinguished from a **domicile** which is the place that he or she considers, or is deemed to consider, as a permanent **home** – although a person's main residence is a primary factor in deciding a domicile. A person may be 'ordinarily resident' where he or she resides in the normal course of life, as opposed to a temporary residence, and may be 'habitually resident' where there is a regular physical presence for a significant period of time.

In the case of a **statutory tenancy** or a **restricted contract** a dwelling-house occupied by a person as his or her 'residence' is the place to which he or she intends to return for the purpose of living there as a home. A person may cease to remain in actual possession or actual occupation, but still continue to treat the place as his or her residence (and thereby remain as a statutory tenant or protected occupier) provided there is an intention to return coupled and clothed with some "formal, outward and visible sign" of that intent – Brown *v* Brash [1948] 2 KB 255. A tenant may have two places of residence, if he can manifestly show that he occupied both places as a home – Langford Property Co. Ltd *v* Tureman [1949] 1 KB 29; Beck *v* Scholz [1953] 1 QB 570. However, in this context the need for reasonable permanency is necessary, so that the occupation of an hotel room for a temporary stay is not occupation as a residence – R *v* Bethnal Green and Paddington Rent Tribunals, *ex parte* Rowton Houses Ltd (1947) SJ 255. But a person may be resident in an hotel when he stays there on a more than transient basis – Luganda *v* Service Hotels Ltd [1969] 2 Ch. 209.

A 'place of residence' when used in statute law must be construed according to the object and intent of the particular legislation. It is used normally in its commonly accepted sense as the place where a person usually sleeps and lives, but it may refer to the place where a person has a business abode or is to be found daily – R. *v* Fermanagh Justices [1897] 2 LR 563; R. *v* Tyrone Justices [1901] 2 LR 511. As a rule, a company has its residence for tax purposes where its central management and control is to be found (De Beers Consolidated Mines Ltd *v* Howe (Surveyor of Taxes) [1906] AC 455). See also **principal private residence**.
2. A place used as a **home**. In particular, dwelling-house of some standing

or pretention.

3. A building used to house students. Called usually a 'hall of residence'.

resident landlord

A landlord of a dwelling-house who, at the time he grants a tenancy, occupies as his residence another dwelling-house within the same building but one that is not a purpose-built block of flats. The Rent Act 1977, s. 12 (as amended by the Housing Act 1980, s. 65) provides that a tenancy of a dwelling-house let by a resident landlord shall not be a **protected tenancy** (although it may be a **restricted contract**). The provision is intended to exclude a tenant, who rents part of a person's home, from having the security of tenure that would be afforded to a similar tenant, if the landlord was not resident in the same building. A 'resident landlord' must have occupied the dwelling at the time he granted the tenancy and a person cannot qualify under this provision merely by moving into a building and later granting a new tenancy to an existing tenant. See also **grounds for possession**.

Rent control and Leasehold Enfranchisement, by Trevor Aldridge, 8 edn., Ch. 4.

Housing Law, by Andrew Arden and Martin Partington, pp. 109–114 (1983).

residential density

A ratio that expresses the average relationship between a unit area of land and the number of residential or household units occupying that unit, e.g. houses per acre, dwellings per hectare, bedspaces per acre. Residential density may be expressed as: (a) 'overall residential density' – the average number of units per unit of land contained within a total area, in particular the entire area of a town; (b) 'gross residential density' – the average number of units per unit of land contained within a given residential area (e.g. within a neighbourhood, housing estate), including all residential land, and land used for roads, primary schools, local shops and associated open space, but excluding land that is used for secondary schools, for institution property (hospitals, central libraries etc.) and for any other purpose that is considered to serve another residential area; (c) 'net residential density' – the average number of units per unit of land contained within a given residential area, including land used for ancilliary open space, gardens, etc., and the area taken up to the centre line of any surrounding roads, but excluding land used for any non-residential purpose (e.g. local shops and schools). Residential density is called also 'accommodation density'. cf. **population density**. See also **density**.

residential occupier

A person who occupies premises as a residence, "whether under a contract or by virtue of any enactment or rule of law giving him the right to remain in occupation or restricting the right of any other person to recover possession of the premises". (Rent Act 1965, s. 30 (5); Protection from Eviction Act 1977, s. 1 (1)). See also **eviction harassment**.

residential tenancy

A tenancy of a **dwelling-house** (which may include a flat). See also **assured tenancy**, **controlled tenancy**, **protected tenancy**, **secure tenancy**, **shorthold tenancy**, **statutory tenancy**.

residual approach (US)

see **residual method of valuation.**

residual estate

see **residuary estate.**

residual method of valuation

A method of ascertaining the value of land, excluding buildings, especially a site that is available, or intended, for development or redevelopment. A method of **valuation** that is based on the premise that the price a purchaser will pay for a parcel of land for development depends on that person's assessment of the present value of the estimated future income from the completed development, less the cost of all construction and building work (including all ancilliary costs, e.g. finance and administration and an appropriate allowance for the developer's profit) required to complete the development. The residual method may be used to estimate the value of a development site which is to be offered for sale; to ascertain the anticipated return or profit from a development project; or to establish a budget for a construction project.

The residual method of valuation, by its nature, contains a considerable number of variables (rent, construction costs, yield, building period, letting or sale period, financing costs, fees, and other ancilliary costs and taxes) and these must be assessed on the bases of the valuer's expectations of the future. It is a highly subjective method of valuation and should be used with caution. It has been said, in connection with an application to the Lands Tribunal to determine **compulsory purchase compensation**, that, "it is a feature of the residual valuation that comparatively minor adjustments to the constituent figures can

have a major effect on the result …" and "… once valuers are let loose on residual valuations, however honest the valuers and however reasoned their argument they can prove almost anything". – First Garden City Ltd *v* Letchworth Garden City Corporation (1966) 200 EG 123. It is accepted therefore, by the Lands Tribunal as a method of 'last resort'. However, in practice, it is the principal means of development analysis and forms the basis for assessing and monitoring the profit to be derived from a property development. Called also a 'development valuation' or in the US the 'abstraction approach' 'valuation by abstraction', the 'residual approach' or sometimes 'highest and best use analysis'. See also **building residual technique, development property, land residual technique, project valuation, property residual technique.**
Property Valuation Handbook, edited by A. Straton.
Development Properties and Residual Valuation, by B.A. Jolly (1976).
The Appraisal of Real Estate, AIREA, 8 edn., pp. 395–398, 435–438.
Modern Methods of Valuation, 7 edn., Ch. 12.
Valuation and Development Appraisal, edited by Clive Darlow, pp. 1.–28 (1982).

residual process (US)

A method of appraisal, based on the **income approach**, used to estimate the value of a plot of land excluding any buildings thereon or a building separate from the land. An income is assessed that is considered appropriate to the plot of land or the building; usually by deducting from the income receivable from the land and buildings together, an income estimated as appropriate for the land, or building, alone. This income is then capitalised at a rate that is appropriate to the element being valued, i.e. the land excluding the buildings thereon or the buildings excluding the land. See also **building residual technique, land residual technique, residual method of valuation.**

residual valuation
see **residual method of valuation, residual process.**

residual value
1. The value of an interest in property for the remaining, or residual, term of a lease; the **present value** of the right to receive the rent and profits reserved under a lease for the rest of its term.
cf. **reversionary value.**
2. The value of a property at the end of its useful or **economic life**. See also **scrap value.**
3. The value of land as determined by the **residual method of valuation.**
4. The value of land used for mining or as a quarry, after extraction work has been completed.

residuary clause
see **residue.**

residuary estate
see **residue.**

residue
That which remains, what is left, after something is withdrawn or deducted. The residue of an **estate** is that interest which is left after the estate that was granted is terminated; or, the value of an estate after all debts, legacies and expenses have been met. In a 'residuary clause' in a will, such as, "all the remainder and residue of my property", the term 'remainder' refers to

real property and 'residue' to personal property. See also **remainder, residual value.**

resiliation (F)
cancelling; annulment; **termination** (of a contract or lease).

resoluto jure concedentis resolvitur jus concessum (L)
'The grant of a right comes to an end on the termination of the right of the grantor'.

resolution (F)
annulment; termination; **rescission** (especially following a breach of contract and a consequent court order). A remedy that is similar to the common law remedy of rescission, but in French law a party must apply to a court for the *resolution* of a contract and the remedy is provided at the discretion of the court. "*Resolution* differs essentially from *rescision*. The former presupposes the contract to be valid, and it is owing to a cause posterior to the agreement that the resolution takes place; while *rescision*, on the contrary, supposes that some vice or defect annulled the contract from the beginning. *Resolution* may be by consent of the parties, or by the decision of a competent tribunal; *rescision* must always be by the judgement of a court" – Tropl. de la Vente, note 689).

resort property (US)
A real estate development that caters primarily for vacation and recreational activities.

résoudre (F)
to cancel; to rescind.

respondeat superior (L)
'Let the **principal** answer'. A maxim that arises from the principle that a

master is liable for the actions of a servant who is pursuing his proper employment duties. See also **agency, vicarious liability**.

responsibilité (F)
responsibility; liability.
(*responsibilité conjoint et solidaire* – **joint and several liability**)
(*responsabilité decennale* – ten year building work guaranty. French law provides that the architect, builder and the ***maître d'oeuvre*** are liable for defective building work for which they were responsible for a period of ten years from the date of completion – ***réception definitive*** – of those works. This liability extends primarily to the superstructure – *gros oeuvre* – and the external edifice of a building (French Civil Code, arts. 1792, 2270, as amended by a law of 3rd January 1977)).

restitutio in integrum (L)
'Restoration to the original position'. See **damages, rescission**.

restitution
1. In its common usage, the act of restoring something, either to its owner, or to its former physical state. See also **rebuilding, reinstatement, restoration**.
2. In English law, an equitable remedy that may permit money or property to be recovered when it has been obtained dishonestly, officiously, unconscionably or under duress; for example, from an infant who has obtained property by misrepresenting his age. Restitution arises from a principle of natural justice, "the foundation of it being a retention by one man of the property which he had unduly received from another, or received for a purpose, the failure of

which rendered it improper that he should retain it" – *Essays on Money Had and Received*, by Evans, pp. 6–7 (1802), commenting on Lord Mansfield's decision in Moses *v* Macferlan (1760) 2 Bur. 1005. A principle enacted in the American Law Institute's Restatement of the Law of Restitution: Quasi-Contract and Constructive Trusts (1937) para. 1: "A person who has been unjustly enriched at the expense of another is required to make restitution to the other".
cf. **recovery**. See also **quasi-contract, rescission, unjust enrichment**.
An Introduction to the Law of Restitution, by Peter Birks (1985).
Anson's Law of Contract, 26 edn, pp. 571–607.
Chitty on Contract, 25 edn, paras. 1931–2057.

restitution (F)
restitution; reinstatement.

restoration
The act of returning something, either to a person, or to its former original and, as far as possible, identical state or condition. Putting all or part of a property back into its original state whether by **rebuilding, renewal** or **reconstruction**. See also **reinstatement, renovation, restitution**.

restraint on alienation
A restriction placed on the right of a person to transfer property to another. Generally any condition that permanently restricts a person's right to transfer an absolute right to property or a fee interest is void, because it is repugnant to the interest held by that person – Re. Dugdale (1888) 38 Ch. D 176; Bonnell *v* McLaughlin (1916) 173 Cal. 213, 159 p. 590.

Any tenant (except a tenant at will) is free to assign or sub-let, the whole or any part of the property leased to him, unless there is an express restraint on alienation. However, most leases contain an express covenant restricting, in some way, the assignment, sub-letting, charging or otherwise transferring the demised property without the landlord's prior consent. Such an express covenant frequently provides that the landlord's consent to an alienation of the property will not be *unreasonably* withheld. Further, the Landlord and Tenant Act 1927, s. 19(1) provides that in any lease (except a lease of an agricultural holding) containing a covenant or condition against assignment, sub-letting, charging, or parting with possession of a demised premises or any part thereof without consent or licence, there will be a "proviso to the effect that such licence or consent is not to be unreasonably withheld". A landlord may not demand a **fine** or **premium** for granting such consent, although he may require a reasonable sum for any legal or other expenses incurred in this respect (Law of Property Act 1925, s. 144). What constitutes withholding consent unreasonably depends on the nature of the property; the type of tenant; the other terms of the lease; and any effect on the landlord's interest. In effect it is impossible to formulate strict rules as to how a landlord can exercise his power to reasonably refuse such consent. "The utmost the court can do is to give guidance to those who have to consider the problem. As one decision [on the question of reasonableness] follows another, people get to know the likely result, in any set of circumstances. But no one

decision will be a binding precedent as a strict rule of law. The reasons given by the judges are to be treated as propositions of good sense – in relation to the particular case – rather than propositions of law applicable to all cases." – Bickel *v* Duke of Westminster [1977] QB 524. In deciding whether there has been an unreasonable refusal of consent to assignment or any other form of alienation of a lease, "it is not for the defendants to prove that they were justified in withholding their consent but for the plaintiff to prove that it was unreasonably withheld ... It is not enough to show that other lessors might have accepted the proposed assignees: the lessors were not to be held to have withheld the licence unreasonably if in the action they took they acted as a reasonable man might have done in the circumstances". – Shanly *v* Ward (1913) 29 TLR 715. However, a lessor whose consent is sought to an underletting "is not unreasonable in asking for what purpose a proposed undertenant is going to use the premises, and in stipulating for a covenant between the under-tenant and himself with regard to under-letting similar to that which already exists between himself and his own tenant" – Berger *v* Jenkinson [1905] 1 Ch. 456. The reason for refusal of consent should be directly related to the letting; it should not be wholly independent of the relationship of landlord and tenant as created by the subject lease – Houlder Bros and Co. Ltd *v* Gibbs [1925] 1 Ch. 583; and account should not be taken of some other matter that might be of collateral benefit to the landlord. The landlord may not seek to prevent a tenant from parting with his tenancy merely because the change might have an adverse affect on neighbouring premises owned by the same landlord – Anglia Building Society *v* Sheffield City Council (1983) 266 EG 311. Instances in which consent has been held to have been withheld *reasonably* include (a) the complete inadequacy of the financial standing of the assignee, when related to the level of rent under the lease; (b) an adverse effect on the landlord's own trading interest; (c) a significant effect on the value of the landlord's interest or the letting value of the rest of the same property, but not solely on the ground that it might create management problems. Instances in which consent has been held to have been withheld *unreasonably* include (a) a refusal when a parent company was not prepared to act as surety; (b) a refusal for fear that the proposed assignee would vacate other property owned by the landlord and that those premises would be difficult to relet; (c) the refusal of the consent of a superior landlord; (d) a refusal by the landlord in an attempt to regain possession before the end of the lease. In the case of a building lease, originally granted for more than forty years, which has more than seven years to run, the landlord cannot prohibit in any event an assignment or underletting; in that case the tenant only need give six months prior notice of the intended alienation (Landlord and Tenant Act 1927, s. 19 (1)). It is unlawful to discriminate on the ground of sex, race or religion against an intended assignee or sub-lessee (Race Relations Act 1976, s. 24 (1)).

In the US, there is no similar statute law but, if a condition is imposed on a consent to alienation so as to make the interest in property of no use or benefit to the assignee, this would be an unreasonable restraint on alienation. Not to withhold unreasonably consent to alienation permits no arbitrary considerations of personal taste, sensibility, or convenience; nor may a landlord rely on mere whim or caprice, no matter how honest his judgement (Weisner *v* 791 Park Avenue Corp. (1958) 180 NYS 2d 734, 7 App. Div. 75).

When a property is given as an absolute right of ownership but to be held in trust, a restriction on the beneficiary's right to require a sale of the property at any time; a limitation that the property be assigned only to one particular person; or a similar restriction that substantially prevents a beneficiary from deriving the full benefits of ownership (including the freedom to lease or charge the property) is void.

Landlord and Tenant Law by David Yates and A.J. Hawkins, pp. 221–226 (1981).

27 Halsbury's Laws of England, 4 edn, paras. 363–375.

Woodfall's Landlord and Tenant, 28 edn paras. 1–1168 to 1–1212.

restraint of trade
  see **non-competition clause, restrictive covenant**.

restricted contract
  A contract whereby one person grants to another a right to occupy a dwelling-house (which may be an entire house, part of a house, or even a room in an hotel) as a **residence**, in consideration of rent that includes payment for the use of furniture or for services (Rent Act 1977, s. 19 (2)). For this purpose services includes **attendance**, the provision of heating and lighting, the supply of hot water and

any similar facility related to the occupation of the dwelling, but not merely cold water supply, sanitary accommodation or simply access. A restricted contract also exists if a tenant would have had a **protected tenancy** but is excluded from the normal Rent Act protection that applies to such tenancies either (a) because he shares living accommodation with his landlord or (b) because there is a **resident landlord**, notwithstanding that the rent does not include payment for the use of furniture or for services (1977 Act, ss. 20, 21). A restricted contract may be a tenancy or a licence, provided the occupier is entitled to **exclusive occupation** of a least some part of the accommodation within the dwelling (1977 Act, s. 19 (6)). A contract is not a restricted contract if (a) the rateable value is above a statutorily specified limit (1977 Act, s. 19 (3) (4); (b) it is a **regulated tenancy** (1977 Act, s. 19 (5) (a)); (c) the landlord is the Crown (but not in the case of property that is only managed by the Crown Estate Commissioners), a government department, a registered housing association, a housing trust, the Housing Corporation, a housing co-operative, a local authority, the Commission for New Towns, a development corporation, or the Development Board for Rural Wales; (d) the total rent includes a substantial payment for **board** that is provided to the occupier; (e) it is let to a "protected occupier" under the Rent (Agriculture) Act 1976, s. 19 (5) (e); (f) it is a holiday letting (1977 Act, ss. 19 (5) (aa) – (e), (7)); or the occupation is granted rent-free (1977 Act, s. 19 (2)).

A grantor or holder of a restricted contract or the local authority is entitled to request the **rent tribunal** to fix a "reasonable rent" for the dwelling and once fixed that rent may not be varied for a period of two years, except by a reference to the tribunal by both parties to the contract or when there has been a substantial change to the dwelling, to the furniture or services provided or the terms of the contract. A holder of a restricted contract has no security of tenure as such. However, if the contract was made before the Housing Act 1980, at the request of the holder of the restricted contract, the rent tribunal has powers to postpone a notice to quit for up to six months; or, if the notice to quit is given by the landlord and the tenant applies to the rent tribunal for a reduction in rent, the notice is automatically deferred for six months from the date of the tribunal's decision. If the contract was made after the 1980 Act the court has power to postpone the notice for up to three months (1980 Act, s. 69., subsequently referred to as the Rent Act 1977, s. 106A). The tribunal may reduce or remove this deferment of the notice to quit in the event of a default by the occupier (Rent Act 1977, s. 106). In addition, an **owner-occupier**, who gave notice on or before the contract was entered into that he was an owner-occupier, may regain possession immediately the contract comes to its agreed end if the dwelling is required as a residence for that **owner-occupier** or any member of his family who resided with him when he last occupied the dwelling as a residence (1977 Act, s. 105). See also **eviction, furnished tenancy, tied accommodation**.

Real Property and Real People, by Gray and Symes, pp. 455–459 (1981).

Manual of Housing Law, by Andrew Arden, 2 edn., pp. 93–103.

Housing Law, by Andrew Arden and Martin Partington, pp. 116–119 (1983).

Landlord and Tenant Law, by David Yates and A.J. Hawkins, pp. 354–361 (1981).

restricted tenancy
see **restricted contract**.

restricted value
see **claim holding**.

restriction
1. A **limitation** or prohibition placed on the actions of someone. A limitation placed on the use of property, e.g. an **encumberance**; a **restrictive covenant**; a **planning condition**; a **restraint on alienation**; **a user clause**. See also **building controls, covenant, qualification, planning permission, zoning ordinance**.
2. A means by which any transfer, charge, disposal or other form of **dealing** in registered land is prevented until certain conditions or requirements, which are specified on the land register, have been dealt with, such as the consent of the registered proprietor is obtained or money arising from the transaction is directed to be paid to a beneficiary of settled land. A restriction is entered on the Proprietorship Register at the **Land Registry** (Land Registration Act 1925, s. 58). A restriction is used most commonly to protect a **minor interest**.
cf. **caution, inhibition**. See also **overreachable interest**.

restrictive covenant
1. A **covenant** in a contract that restricts or regulates a course of action. In particular, a covenant contained in a deed which restricts or limits the use of real property. Restrictive or negative covenants are found commonly in leases whereby the landlord seeks to limit the tenant's freedom to use or enjoy the demised premises, e.g. a clause that limits the right of user (a **user clause**) or limits the tenant's right to transfer his interest in the demised premises (an **alienation clause**).

A covenant in a lease, although enforceable between the original landlord and the original tenant throughout the term of the lease (because there is **privity of contract** i.e. the parties have bound themselves personally on the terms of the lease), may not be enforceable against a party who takes an assignment of the interest held by either the landlord or the tenant. Nevertheless, upon an assignment of the landlord's or the tenant's interest the benefit or advantage of a restrictive covenant can be expressly assigned, thereby enabling the assignee to enforce that benefit against the remaining original party. On the other hand, the burden or sufferance imposed by the covenant (i.e. the right to be sued on it) cannot be assigned and, as a rule, it is the assignor who remains liable. Nonetheless, the relationship of landlord and tenant is considered to subsist if the covenant 'touches and concerns' the demised premises (i.e. is reasonably incidental to the relationship of landlord and tenant, rather than being merely a personal covenant). In other words, if the covenant affects the landlord *qua* landlord or the tenant *qua* tenant, then an assignee may be liable for the burden of the covenant. Thus, "if L leases land to T, and T assigns the **legal lease** by deed to A, the common law rule laid down in Spencer's Case (1583) 5 Co. Rep. 16a is that A is entitled to the benefit, and the subject of the burden, of all covenants and conditions touching and concerning the land for there is **privity of estate**. In short, both the benefit and the burden of the covenants run with the land" (Megarry's Manual of the Law of Real Property, 6 edn, p. 380). And, although this common law rule does not apply in the same way if the landlord assigns his reversion, statute has enforced the same principle for all covenants and provisions that "have reference to the subject-matter of the lease" (Law of Property Act 1925, ss. 141 (1), 142(1)). Most covenants in leases 'touch and concern' the land or 'have reference to the subject-matter of the lease' but, for example, a tenant's option to purchase his landlord's interest or a tenant's liability to pay money to a third party, is considered personal to the parties and the burden may not bind an assignee; i.e. a purchaser of the landlord's interest who does not have notice of the option is not bound by it – Re. Leeds and Batley Breweries Ltd. v Bradbury's Lease [1920] 2 Ch. 548 – and a purchaser of the tenant's interest is not bound to continue the payment – Mayho v Buckhurst (1617) Cro. Jac. 438. See also **agreement for a lease**, **equitable lease**.

The Law of Landlord and Tenant, by David Lloyd Evans, 2 edn, pp. 82–83, 148–152, 179–181.

Woodfall's Landlord and Tenant, 28 edn, paras. 1–1132 to 1–1139, 1–1214 to 1–1259.

2. An agreement by which a holder of a parcel of land (covenantor) undertakes to accept a restriction, or **covenant**, placed on the use to which he may put his land for the benefit of the holder of another parcel of land (covenantee). (Such an agreement being a 'covenant' strictly should be made by deed and the holders of the land parcels normally are freeholders; although such an agreement may apply just as well between leaseholders). Such a covenant is referred to commonly as a vendor and purchaser covenant, because it is the form of covenant that is entered into when a landowner sells part of his land and wishes to prevent the new landowner from carrying on an activity or developing the land in a way that would be detrimental to the value or amenity of the land he has retained. The land sold with the burden of the covenant is called the 'servient tenement' and the land that is held to benefit from the covenant is called the 'dominant tenement'.

A restrictive covenant is passive in nature; it restricts the owner of the servient tenement in his freedom to use his land; but it is negative in that it does not require the expenditure of time, labour or money – Haywood v Brunswick Permanent Benefit Building Society (1881) 8 QBD 410. A restrictive covenant is described sometimes as a 'negative easement'. However, unlike an **easement** a restrictive covenant may be entered into only by express agreement and may not be acquired by implied grant or prescription; it is only capable of existing as an **equitable interest** (whereas an easement can, and normally does, create a legal interest); and it does not require the same certainty as to the subject matter as an easement.

As with a restrictive covenant in a lease (see 1. above) vendor and purchaser covenants are enforceable at common law between the original parties; unless there is an express provision to the contrary, the original covenantor is liable for any breach, even if he has parted with his interest in the servient tenement; i.e. he is personally liable for any breaches committed by subsequent owners of the land (Law of Property Act 1925, s. 79; – Tophams Ltd. *v* Earl of Sefton [1967] 1 AC 50). Furthermore, the covenant may be enforced by any other person for whom the covenant is intended to grant a benefit (e.g. an adjoining landowner), even if that person is not named as a party to the original conveyance or other form of instrument by which the covenant was created (Law of Property Act 1925, s. 56; – Beswick *v* Beswick [1968] AC 58). In addition, since 1925, any person claiming under the covenant (e.g. a lessee or successor in title) may enforce the benefit of the covenant, provided the covenant was made for the benefit of the land owned by the covenantee (Law of Property Act 1925, s. 78; – Smith *v* River Douglas Catchment Board [1949] 2 KB 500).

Historically, English common law did not consider that a restrictive covenant was enforceable by an assignee of the dominant or servient tenement, because there is not normally, 'privity of contract' with the assignee and, unlike a restrictive covenant in a lease, there is no 'privity of estate'. However, the courts of equity and statute have intervened to provide that in many cases covenants that 'touch and concern' the land and are intended to bind an assignee will be enforceable by or against that assignee. In particular because equity considered that, as a restrictive covenant may affect the purchase price of land, "nothing could be more inequitable

than that the original purchaser should be able to sell the property the next day for a greater price in consideration of the assignee being allowed to escape from the liability which he had himself undertaken" – Tulk *v* Moxhay (1848) 2 Ph. 777 – and, as in the case of a **scheme of development**, it is normally the intention that the lands will change hands regularly but that the covenants should continue to be enforceable.

In the case of unregistered land, a restrictive covenant should be registered as a **land charge**, otherwise it will not be binding on a purchaser (including a mortgagee or lessee) for money or money's worth of the legal estate in the land or an interest in the land held by the covenantor (Land Charges Act 1972, s. 4 (b), replacing similar provisions in the Land Charges Act 1925, s. 13 (2). (For this purpose a restrictive covenant is defined as "a covenant or agreement (other than a covenant or agreement between a lessor and a lessee) restrictive of the user of land created or arising on or after 1 January 1926 and being merely an equitable interest.) In the case of registered land the covenant is protected by entry on the Land Register of a **notice** (or in cases of difficulty a **caution**) against the affected land (Land Registration Act 1925, s. 50).

A restrictive covenant may be discharged or modified by express or implied **release**; by unity of ownership, i.e. the land that is burdened and the land that is benefitted come into the same ownership ('**unity of seisin**'); by a declaration of the court; or by order of the **Lands Tribunal** following an application by the owner of the land burdened. The Lands Tribunal has power to discharge, wholly or partly, or to modify a restrictive covenant affecting freehold land, or leasehold land where the term created was for more than 40 years of which at least 25 years have expired, except for mining leases (Law of Property Act 1925, s. 84). In such cases the Tribunal must be satisfied (a) that by reason of changes in the character of the property or neighbourhood, or other material circumstances, the situation has so materially changed that the restriction "ought to be deemed obsolete"; (b) that the continuation of the restriction would impede some reasonable use of the land, and either there is no practical benefit to be derived from its continuance or it is contrary to the public interest (although for an application to succeed on the grounds of public interest. "it must be shown that the interest is so important and immediate as to justify the serious interference with private rights and the sanctity of contract" – Re Collins' Applications (1975) 30 P and CR 527) and that money will be adequate compensation for the loss or disadvantage that might be suffered by the discharge or modification; (c) the persons entitled to the benefit of the restriction (being of full age and capacity) have agreed, either expressly or by implication, by their acts or omissions, to the covenant being discharged or modified; (d) when it is considered that a discharge of the covenant "will not injure the persons entitled to the benefit of the restriction". (Law of Property Act 1925, s. 84(1), as amended by the Law of Property Act 1969, s. 28.)

In the US a restrictive covenant is called also a 'private (restrictive) zon-ing', an 'equitable servitude', an 'equitable land burden' or a 'deed of restriction'. See also **planning agreement.**

Real Property, by William E. Burby, 3 edn., pp. 100–109.

Discharge or Modification of Restrictions on Land, by W.A. Leach, 214 EG 421 (1970).

Cheshire's Modern Law of Property, 13 edn, pp. 571–602.

Megarry's Manual of the Law of Real Property, 6 edn, pp. 439–459.

16 Halsbury's Laws of England, 4 edn, paras. 1345–1367.

Land Law: Cases and Materials, by R.H. Maudsley and E.H. Burn, 4 edn., pp. 693–778.

The Law of Real Property, by Robert Megarry and H.W.R. Wade, 5 edn., pp. 739–798.

Preston & Newson's Restrictive Covenants affecting Freehold Land, 7 edn.

3. A condition contained in a contract which restricts the right of one of the parties, for the benefit of the other party, to act freely after the contract has come to an end. For example, a clause in a lease which provides that a shop keeper is not to trade for a specified period of time and within a defined radius of the premises leased to him after the expiration of that lease; or a condition of employment that prevents an employee from engaging in an activity or soliciting business in competition with his former employer in the event of the termination of the employee's contract of employment. "Any contract which interferes with the free exercise of (a person's) trade or business, by restricting him (or her) in the work he (or she) may do for others, or the arrangements that he (or she) may make with others, is a contract in restraint of trade. It is invalid unless it is

reasonable as between the parties and not injurious to the public interest". – Petrofina *v* Martin [1966] Ch. 146.

restrictive injunction
see **injunction**.

restrictive zoning (US)
1. **Zoning** rules imposed by a local government body which limit the use of land, or a building, to one particular user e.g. to storage warehousing only.
2. See **restrictive covenant**.

resulting trust
A **trust** that is not created expressly but is presumed by law to arise from the intention of parties who are associated in a property transaction. A resulting trust may arise when (a) a purchase is made by one person but the money is provided (in whole or part) by another on the understanding that the other will receive an interest in the property; or (b) on a disposal of a property the owner omits to transfer some **equitable interest** to the purchaser. In either case an interest in the property is held on trust for the benefit of the party who should have received that interest. A resulting trust may be considered as similar to, or as a form of, an **implied trust**. A resulting trust terminates if an express trust is created or declared to the same effect.

resumption of possession
The taking back of premises granted under a lease. See also **right of re-entry, repossession**.

rétablissement (d'un édifice) (F)
repair; **restoration** (of a building).

retail
Derived from the Middle French *retailler*, 'to cut up' or 'divide into

pieces'. The sale of goods in small quantities, especially to an ultimate consumer. The sale may be transacted in a **shop, department store**, retail **market** or similar outlet, or by mail order; as well as by **auction** (Shops Act 1950, s. 74). To be contrasted with wholesale, which consists of the sale of goods to a person who intends to resell them. (The receipt and return of goods for dry cleaning with some of the cleaning carried out on the premises, was not considered a "retail trade or business" for the purposes of the Shops (Early Closing Days) Act 1965, s. 1 – Boyd *v* Bell [1970] SC 1.

retail buyer
A person who purchases property for use and occupation, as contrasted with a purchaser who buys purely for the income or profit to be derived from property. See also **investment property**.

retail centre
see **major retail centre, shopping centre**.

retail lot sale (US)
The sale of a plot or lot of land to the ultimate customer, e.g. to a person who intends to build a house thereon for his or her occupation; in particular, a sale of a number of plots to the same party.

retail store
see **shop**.

retail store mix (US)
see **tenant mix**.

retainage (US)
see **retention sum**.

retained agent
see **agent, sole agency**.

retainer
1. A fee paid to a professional advisor, consultant, or lawyer to retain that person's services.
2. A document that expresses the terms upon which a lawyer has been engaged; in particular, a document given to a barrister by a solicitor engaging the barrister to act and appear for a party in litigation.
3. see also **retention sum**.

retard (F)
delay.
(*en retard* – in arrears)
(*intérêt de retard* – arrears of interest).

retention
The withholding of possession of property that has been sold to another, until payment of the sale price has been made in full. See also **lien, retention sum**.

rétention, droit de (F)
possessory **lien**, on goods for an unpaid sum i.e. a vendor's lien.

retention period
see **maintenance period, retention sum**.

retention sum
Part of the total money due to a building contractor for work done, but held back by the employer to ensure satisfactory completion of the terms of a **building contract**. Usually the sum held back is based on a percentage (commonly 10 per cent, or 5 per cent for large contracts) of each progress payment that is due during the course of the contract. These accumulated retentions generally are held until the employer's supervising architect (or quantity surveyor) certifies that the building works have been completed satisfactorily. Sometimes called a 'retainer' or 'contingency reserve'; or, in the US, a 'retainage' or 'holdback'. See also **completion certificate, maintenance period**.

retentive lien
see **lien**.

retour (droit de) (F)
redemption (right of); **reversion**.

retrait (F)
repayment; withdrawal (of a right); repurchase (as distinguished from pre-emption); redemption.

rétrocession (F)
reconveyance, especially when land has been acquired by a public authority but is no longer required and is sold back to the original owner.

return on capital
see **profit, rate of return, yield**.

return on equity
see **cash-on-cash yield, earnings yield, recapture**.

revaluation
The making of a new assessment of the value of a property. "A revaluation connotes an existing **valuation**. The ordinary meaning of valuation is an estimate of the worth of a thing. The ordinary meaning of a revaluation is a fresh estimate of the worth of the same thing". – Commissioner of Taxation (NSW) *v* Hardie Investments Pty Ltd (1946) 73 CLR 505. The updated value may be obtained, for example, for incorporation in a company's balance sheet; for taxation purposes (especially for local taxation, i.e. rates); or to induce a lender to provide additional finance by using the new value as security for a higher, or new, loan. Called also, especially in

the US 'reappraisal'. See also **reassessment**.

revaluation clause (US)
see **rent review clause**.

revaluation equity
An increase in the **equity** of a property that arises as a result of a revaluation.

revaluation lease
A lease that provides for the rent to be revised during the term by means of a revaluation. 'Revaluation lease' may refer to a lease that contains a provision for the rent to be revised by reference to the **market rent** of the demised premises, or by reference to an agreed percentage of the reassessed capital value of the premises. In the US, the latter is called also a 'reappraisal lease' or a 'revaluation lease'. See also **rent review clause, turnover lease**.

revaluation reserve
An amount, set out in the financial statement or balance sheet of a company, that represents an increase in the value of a property following a **revaluation**.

revalorisation (F)
revaluation.

revendeur (F)
retailer; broker.

revendication (F)
recovery, a similar form of action to that in English law, although in French law may be used to recover real and personal property.
cf. *réintégrande*.
Precis Dalloz. Droit Civil, Les Biens (Alex Weill), 2 edn, pp. 456–460.
Droit Civil, Les Biens, by Jean Carbonnier, 11 edn., pp. 296–299.

revenu (F)
revenue; income; yield.
(*revenu brut* – gross income)
(*revenu du sol* – ground rent)
(*revenu foncier; revenu cadastral* – property income, especially for tax assessment purposes)
(*revenu locatif* – rental income).

revenue
That which comes back; income that is received back as a result of an investment. The total return from any form of property; in particular, investment income as distinguished from wages or salaries. See also **profit, recapture, yield**.

revenue stamps
see **stamp duty**.

réversion (F)
reversion; remainder.

reverse annuity mortgage (RAM)
see **reverse mortgage**.

reverse leaseback
see **lease and leaseback**.

reverse leverage
see **leverage**.

reverse mortgage
An arrangement by which an **annuity** is paid against property granted as security under a mortgage deed; the mortgagor receives annual income for a specified period of time, or for life, and the mortgagee obtains the repayment of capital as a lump sum either at a specified future date, usually from a life insurance policy upon the death of the borrower, or upon the resale of the mortgaged property. Called also an 'annuity mortgage' or 'reverse annuity mortgage'.

reverse premium

A sum of money paid by an assignor of a lease to a prospective assignee as an inducement to take over the liabilities under the lease. A reverse premium may be paid when the contractual rent exceeds the market rent, i.e. when there is a 'negative' **profit rent**.

reverse yield gap

see **yield gap**.

reverser

see **reversioner**.

reversion

1. Derived from the Latin *revertor*, 'returning again'. The part of an **estate** in property which remains when a person grants an estate (a **particular estate**) to another for a shorter period of time to that which he holds, e.g. the interest retained by an owner of a fee simple who grants a life interest to another or by a freeholder who grants a tenancy for a term of years. Reversion may be used also to refer to the process by which an estate in land returns to a person who had granted a shorter estate to another; "the return of land to the grantor and his heirs after the grant is over" – Co. Litt. 1426. "A reversion has two intendments, the one is an estate left continuing during the particular estate, which is the most common sense; the other is the returning of land after the particular estate has ended, which is the natural sense of the word, according to the definition of the Latin tongue, so that the reversion of the land, and the land when it reverts, is all one" – Throckmerton *v* Tracy (1555) 1 Plwd. 160. A reversion is not created by the grant of an estate or interest in land, but comes into exist-

ence when another estate or interest is carved out of the same land and, thereby, the grantor defers his right to actual or physical possession of the land. A reversion may be distinguished from a **remainder** which is an estate that is granted but comes into effect, as a right to possession, after another estate has come to an end; a remainder is an estate that cannot return to the grantor. "A reversion in law is not a remainder, the difference being that a reversion is what is left and the remainder is that which is created by the grant after the existing possession" – Symonds *v* Leaker (1885) 15 QBD 632. There may be only one reversion in an estate (i.e. the estate returns only to the original grantor), but there can be any number of remainders (i.e. the estate can pass to a continuing succession of persons). (A reversion frequently is referred to as a 'future estate', although strictly that is not the case because in English law the grant of a leasehold interest is the grant of a personal interest and does not affect the 'estate' of the grantor). Called sometimes a 'reverter' or a 'right of 'reverter'. See also **reversionary interest**, **reversionary value**.

2. The rights of a beneficiary under a trust who obtains the absolute interest in a property on the death of a **tenant for life**.

reversion factor (US)

see **present value of one**.

reversionary income

see **reversionary investment**.

reversionary interest

1. An interest in land that is deferred either as a **remainder** or as a **reversion**. The right to the future use and

enjoyment of real property upon the termination or expiration of an existing right to possession; as upon the expiration of a current lease or a life interest. A reversionary interest held by a lessor may be a **legal estate**, but a reversionary interest that follows any other interest must be an **equitable interest**. See also **tenancy, vested estate**.

2. A **future interest** in land (whether vested or contingent) created under a settlement. (Finance Act 1975, s. 51 (1)).

reversionary investment

An investment that has a prospect of a substantial increase in its income and, therefore, its capital value. In particular, property that is currently let at less than its **market rent**, but has a foreseeable prospect of being let at the full annual value. For example, a property leased at a rent that is fixed for a number of years, but which can be let at the full annual value at the end of that period of time (the 'reversionary period'), either because there is a provision in the lease for a rent review or the landlord then will be free to grant a new lease. The income that arises at the end of the reversionary period is called the 'reversionary income'.

cf. **reversionary interest**. See also **equated yield, hardcore method, term and reversion method**.

reversionary lease

A lease that is restricted so as not to commence until a future date; in particular, one that will come into effect with the benefit of actual **possession** when another lease ends. In English law a lease, or any contract to create a lease, at a rent or granted in consideration of a fine, that does not take effect for more than 21 years from the date it is created, as a rule, is void if made after 1925; although an option in a lease for over 21 years to renew the lease for a further 22 years is valid (it is the commencement date of the lease that is important, not of the contract itself) (Law of Property Act 1925, s. 149). Called also a 'future lease' especially when it is not dependent on the prior determination of another lease. See also **legal estate, renewal, reversion**.

reversionary value

The value of a property assuming that it is resold after a set period of time; or the amount an owner receives on resale of an interest in property after a period of ownership. The **present value** of a property at the end of a specified period of time, especially upon the expiration of a lease. The value of a **reversionary interest**. See also **redemption yield**.

reversioner

One who has a right to an interest in land, such as a right to physical possession, after the interest that he has granted in the land has come to an end; i.e. one who holds an interest in **reversion**. Called sometimes a 'reverser'.

cf. **remainderman**.

reverter

see **reversion**.

revest (US)

1. The act of returning property to its owner; the vesting of property again. See also **reconveyance, vest**.

2. To reinvest income or capital received from a property, i.e. by the act of reinvestment.

revient, prix de (F)
  cost price.

revision de loyer (F)
  rent review.

revocable trust
  see **bare trust.**

revocation
  Derived from the Latin *revocare*, to recall. "'Revocation' is the calling back of a thing granted"(*Jacob's Law Dictionary*). The recalling of an act or deed that has been made; which may be the revocation of an order, an **offer**, a **will**, an agent's **authority**, a **power of attorney** or any similar withdrawal of that which has been granted. An **offer** (unless forming an option) may be revoked, as a rule, at any stage before it is accepted – Payne *v* Cave (1789) 3 Term. Rep. 148, but it remains in effect until a clear notice of revocation has reached the offeree. Thus, if revocation is made by post it takes effect when the letter is received, not when it is posted – Dickinson *v* Dodds (1880) 5 CPD 344. Revocation may not be effected if the party seeking to withdraw has indicated, expressly or impliedly, an intention to be bound by the original offer or commitment.

  An agent's authority may be expressly revoked, or revoked by implication as when a principal appoints another party to perform the same act and, thereby, prevents the original agent from continuing to perform his duties. The authority may be revoked at the will of the principal, unless (a) it was stated to be irrevocable and the agent has an interest in completing his duties; (b) the authority is coupled with an interest; or (c) it is essential that the original agent carries out or completes a particular obligation. An agent's authority, as a rule, is not revoked until he has received notice to that effect and the authority can be revoked only in accordance with the original terms of appointment. When an agent's authority is revoked, legally he is no longer able to bind his principal, unless there is some need or authority which follows from the nature of the terminated contract; although if a third party concludes a transaction, without knowing that an agent's authority has been revoked, that party's rights remain intact (Powers of Attorney Act 1971, s. 5 (2)). An agent is not entitled to a **commission** for a service performed, such as introducing a purchaser, after his authority has been revoked, unless the service clearly was performed during the period of the authority. However, an agent cannot be deprived of his existing rights and an agency agreement for the sale of land usually provides that a commission is payable upon the introduction of a purchaser during the term of the agreement, even if a resultant sale to that purchaser does not occur until a later date. See also **extender clause, 'subject to contract'.**

révocation (F)
  revocation; rescission.
  cf. ***abrogation.***

revocation order
  An order made by a local authority, in accordance with the provision of the Town and Country Planning Act 1971, s. 45, by which **planning permission** that already has been granted is revoked. Such an order may be made at any stage before the development that had been authorised is

completed, but it cannot affect building or other operations already carried out. Any person upon whom such an order is served has a right to a local inquiry or hearing if he objects to the order. Compensation is payable to an affected landowner for financial loss suffered as a direct result of a revocation order, or a landowner may have the right to serve a **purchase notice** on the authority requiring the local authority to acquire the subject property provided the land as a result of the revocation order, is rendered "incapable of **reasonably beneficial use**".

A similar order – a 'modification order' – may be served modifying (or, in effect, partly revoking) any planning permission that already has been granted. Revocation and modification orders are rarely served because of the resultant compensation that may be payable and the rights of appeal; as an alternative, if planning permission is not taken advantage of, it is cheaper for a local planning authority to wait until the permission expires, usually, after 5 years. See also **compensation for planning restrictions, discontinuance order**.

revolving credit (or loan)
Credit (or a loan) that is renewable on a cyclical basis up to a set maximum limit, i.e. a loan that may be paid back or drawn down as the borrower wishes within a specified limit. See also **commitment, roll-over loan**.

rezone
To change the **zoning** allocated to an area of land. See also **special use, permit, spot zoning, variance**.

ribbon development or **ribbon building**
The development of a succession of predominately residential buildings along the frontage of a major highway leading to a town or city, with individual properties having direct access to the highway. This form of development is restricted almost entirely to the highway frontage, with land to the rear of the buildings left undeveloped. Ribbon development is the antithesis of modern **town and country planning**; it comprises a succession of residential buildings developed *laissez-faire*, with an anarchy of driveways, road junctions and crossroads, interspersed with retail units, garages, warehouses, factories, etc. The only common factor is the array of buildings and the highway that serves the whole. This type of development provides little social cohesion and it is regarded commonly as being a wasteful and undesirable system of land use. In general, design is left to the vagaries of an individual owner or builder; the height of a building is dependent on a developer's anticipation (or 'mis-anticipation') of demand and the use of one plot of land bears only a random relationship to its neighbour. In Britain, ribbon development became commonplace during the period between the two world wars along highways leading to the major cities. This resulted in the passing of the Restriction of Ribbon Development Act 1935, in order to limit further building along the frontage of certain major highways. In the US, where such development is called also 'roadside development' or 'string development', many modern towns demonstrate this form of urban growth. See also **strip development**.

rider
An addition or amendment attached

to a legal document, often taking the form of a separate sheet of paper. See also **codicil, endorsement**.

right

1. A proper, open, and just claim to something. An **interest, privilege** or other claim to property. 'Right' is a much over-used word, but it may be employed broadly to denote either (a) that which is just and equitable; or (b) a claim or privilege enjoyed by a person or persons, especially when given the protection of the law. For example, "no one shall be subjected to arbitrary interference with his privacy, family, home or correspondence, nor to attacks upon his honour or reputation. Everyone has the right to the protection of the law against such interference or attacks ... Everyone has the right to property alone as well as in association with others. No one shall be arbitrarily deprived of his property" (Universal Declaration of Human Rights, art. 12 and 17: adopted by United Nations General Assembly on 10 December 1948). A right, in its abstract sense, is independent of man-made law and regulation; it is that which benefits man (as with a right to freedom of speech or expression), unlike a **title**, privilege or similar claim which is dependent on the support of the law. See also **ownership, private property, writ of right**.

2. A legal claim of **title** to a thing, i.e. a claim that can be sustained against others. "'Right' is where one hath a thing that was taken from another wrongfully, as by disseisin, discontinuance, or putting out, or such like, and the challenge or claime that he hath who should have the thing, is called right" – Termes de la Ley.

An "enjoyment as of right" (as related to a prescriptive claim to property) means "an enjoyment had, not secretly or by stealth, or by tacit sufferance, or by permission asked from time to time, on each occasion or even on many occasions of using it; but an enjoyment had openly and notoriously, without particular leave at the time, by a person claiming to use it without danger of being treated as a trespasser ..." – Tickle *v* Brown (1836) 4 AD and E 382. Something enjoyed 'as of right' is freely held; held *nec vi, nec clam, nec precario*, 'not by violence, nor stealth, nor permission'. See also **prescription**.

right of access

A legal right to enter upon particular premises. See also **access, easement of necessity, landlord's access, right of entry, right of way**.

right of action

A right to bring an **action**. See also **choses-in-action**.

right of buy-back

see **right of pre-emption**.

right of common

One of a number of rights which "one or more persons may have, to take or use some portion of that which another man's soil naturally produces" (Cooke's Inclosure Acts (4th Edn) cited in Halsbury's Laws of England, 4 edn, p. 177). A right of common is a form of **profit à prendre** enjoyed by one or more persons as a customary right, in common with others. The right may be (i) common of **pasture** – a right to graze cattle; (ii) common of **pannage** – a right for pigs to forage in a wood; (iii) common of **pescary** – a right to fish; (iv) common of **turbary** – a right to cut peat; (v) common of **estovers** – a right to take timber for agricultural building or repair; (vi) common in the soil – a right to take sand, gravel, stone, minerals for use on the commoner's holding.

For the purpose of registering common land, rights of common includes "cattlegates and beastgates (by whatever name known) and rights of sole or several vesture or herbage or of sole and several pasture, but does not include rights held for a term of years or from year to year" (Commons Registration Act 1965, s. 22 (1)). A right of common may be **appendant**, i.e. limited to certain ancient rights to plough and manure the land; or it may be **appurtenant**, i.e. have been acquired by grant or by prescription. A right of common may be held in gross, when it is not held to benefit another parcel of land. Also, it may have arisen *pur cause de vicinage*, being a customary right for cattle to stray on to adjacent unfenced common land. Called sometimes a 'profit in common'. See also **cattle gate**, **levant and couchant**.

Cheshire's Modern Law of Real Property, 13 edn, pp. 532–536.

right of entry

1. The right peacefully to take or resume **possession** of land; especially a right to enter on to land for the first time, whether as a purchaser of an interest in that land or at the start of a tenancy. A right to enter on land as a **licencee**, **visitor** or **invitee**. cf. **trespass**. See also **taking possession**.

2. A right that a landlord might reserve to himself to enable him to go on to land granted under a tenancy; especially a right to enter on to a property to carry out repairs or improvements. A landlord has no implied right of entry on to leased property during the subsistence of the tenancy, although if he covenants to **repair** he has an implied right of entry for that purpose. A right of entry may involve entering on to land but it need not exclude the tenant's continued right of possession; unlike a **right of re-entry** which is adverse to the tenant's continued possession. See also **implied covenant**, **landlord's access**.

3. The right of an authority that has powers of **compulsory purchase** to enter and take possession of land, without the consent of the owner, in pursuance of those powers. An authority also may have statutory powers to enter on land to survey it (Local Government (Miscellaneous Provisions) Act 1976, s. 15; Compulsory Purchase Act 1965, s. 11 (3); Town and Country Planning Act 1971, s. 280; Highway Act 1980, s. 289). See also **notice of entry**.

right of first refusal

A right to be permitted an opportunity to acquire property before it is offered to another, but on similar terms. A right that can be exercised only when the owner has received a bona fide offer for the property from a third party. The term is colloquial and connotes that the owner of a property, before selling to someone else, will intimate to the person holding the right the price at which it will be sold to that other person and, if requested, the owner will sell at that price to the person having the right of first refusal – Manchester Ship Canal Co. *v* Manchester Racecourse Co. [1900] 2 Ch. 352. The term 'right of first refusal' is used synonymously with a **right of pre-emption**, but the latter right is more certain in its effect and does not require the finding of a potential purchaser as a precondition of the offer or as a basis for determining the price. A right of first refusal arises frequently as a right granted to a tenant to acquire his landlord's reversionary interest, or as a right of one co-owner to acquire another co-owner's interest in the same property. cf. **option**. See also **void contract**.

right of light
The right to the continuous passage of light through an opening or window. In practice, a right of light is a negative **easement**; it gives an owner or occupier of a building the right to prevent the owner or occupier of adjoining land from building or placing anything that obstructs the passage of light to his land (it is not a right to view, as might be obtained by a **restrictive covenant**). A right of light, as a rule, should be sufficient for the comfortable enjoyment of a dwelling or use of business premises, i.e. it is based on the needs of ordinary user – Colls *v* Home and Colonial Stores Ltd. [1904] AC 179. In the case of a greenhouse sufficient light is required for its ordinary use as a greenhouse, not merely reasonable illumination – Allen *v* Greenwood [1980] Ch. 119. A right of light may be obtained by **express grant** or **implied grant**; or by **prescription**. It may be terminated by express **release**, **waiver** or **abandonment**. See also **ancient lights, daylight factor**.
The Right to Light, by Bryan Anstey and Michael Chavasse (1963).

right of necessity
see **easement of necessity**.

right of occupation
see **matrimonial property, protected occupier, security of tenure, statutory tenancy**.

right of passage
Specifically, a right to be ferried across a stretch of water, but also a right to pass or repass along a **highway**, street, or any similar **right of way**. See also **easement**.

right of pasture
A right, normally given by licence, to graze cattle or sheep on another's land that is laid down permanently to grass or wild herbage. The ploughing up of any land laid down as meadow or pasture may be a form of agricultural **waste**. See also **grazing licence, right of common**.

right of possession
see **possession**.

right of pre-emption
The right to acquire a property before it is offered to others. Unlike an **option**, this right does not create an interest in land and is purely a personal contract – at least, until the property is offered for sale. It cannot be exercised unless and until the vendor decides to offer the property for sale. "Under an option, only one step is normally needed to constitute a contract, namely the exercise of the option. Under a right of pre-emption two steps will be necessary, the making of the offer in accordance with the right of pre-emption, and the acceptance of that offer" – Brown *v* Gould [1972] Ch. 58. Unlike a **right of first refusal**, which may be too vague or uncertain to constitute a legally binding **contract**, a right of pre-emption should comprise an offer to sell upon specified terms; at a time to be deter-

mined by the vendor or offeror; and a right at that stage for the offeror to accept or reject the offer.

A right of pre-emption, being a personal contract, does not bind a purchaser of the land affected by it, unless he has **notice** of its existence. However, it may be registered as a **land charge** for the protection of the holder of the right, so that as soon as the vendor indicates an intention to sell the land the right crystallises into an interest in land in the form of an option (Land Charges Act, 1972, s. 2 (4) (iv) – Pritchard v Briggs [1980] Ch. 338).

A right of pre-emption reserved by a vendor who sells land that is intended for development, but which is not developed within a specified period of time, may be called also a vendor's 'right of buy-back'.

right of recourse
see **recourse (right of)**.

right of redemption
see **equity of redemption, redemption**.

right of re-entry
1. The right of a person to regain **possession** of land that has been granted to another; in particular, the right of a landlord to regain possession from his tenant, whether following notice to quit or otherwise. A right of re-entry may be exercised 'peacefully' or 'by process of law'. Peaceful re-entry arises when a landowner physically retakes possession of the land without legal proceedings, as when a tenancy has been brought to an end and the tenant voluntarily quits the demised premises. The process of law is exercised against the wishes of the possessor, as when a landlord takes an action to recover

possession from his tenant pursuant to a claim for **forfeiture** of the lease.

A proviso for re-entry is inserted into any well drawn lease, empowering the lessor to seek to re-enter the demised premises when rent is in arrears for a stipulated period of time (commonly 14 or 21 days), or when the lessee is otherwise in breach of covenant. If there is no such proviso the landlord has no right of re-entry during the course of the lease, unless the tenant is in **breach of condition** of the lease.

cf. **right of entry**. See also **eviction, relief, security of tenure, usual covenant**.

2. An interest in land held by a person who has transferred an **estate** in that land on condition subsequent, i.e. a future right to that land which may be converted into an immediate right if the transferor exercises a right he has reserved (the right of re-entry to regain the estate). See also **conditional fee simple**.

right of reverter
see **reversion**.

right of support
1. An **easement** for the support of land, or a building, received from neighbouring land, or buildings. See also **party wall**.
2. A right by which an owner of land is entitled to subjacent and lateral support from adjoining land, either for the soil or sub-soil; a common law right that is a natural incident to the ownership of land – Dalton v Angus (1881) 6 App. Cas. 740. A landowner may not dig up or mine his land so as to cause his neighbour's land to collapse; although he can divert water flowing in an undefined channel without being liable for a consequent

land slippage (but not water with silt or brine as that is equivalent to removing land – Jordeson *v* Sutton Southcoates and Drypool Gas Company [1889] 2 Ch. 217; Lotus Ltd. *v* British Soda Co. Ltd and another [1972] Ch. 123). This natural right does not extend to a right of support for a building on the land (although a landowner can acquire an easement for that purpose) and does not impose an obligation to provide extra support to combat the extra load imposed by a building – Wyatt *v* Harrison (1823) 2 B and Ad. 871. See also **natural rights, quasi-easement**.
Real Property, by William E. Burby, 3 edn., pp. 40–44.

right of survivorship
     see **joint tenancy**.

right of way
     The right to pass and repass over the land of another. It may exist as a private right, i.e. as a **licence** or an **easement**; or a public right i.e. a **highway** – a right for the public at large to pass over a set route without having a set origin or destination. A right of way make take several forms, e.g. a right on foot, on horse back, in a vehicle or to drive cattle. A public right of way may be created by statute, usually be a highway authority acquiring such a right; or by the land being dedicated and accepted as a highway (Highways Act 1980, s. 31). In the US, a public right of way is often referred to as an easement; although it has been said that the term imports an easement, and not a public highway (2 Barb. (N.Y.) 432). See also **easement of necessity, right of passage**.
Rights of Way, by J.F. Garner, 4 edn., pp. 1–10.

Rights of Way – A guide to Law and Practice, by Paul Clayden and John Trevelyan (1983).

right to air
     A right to the passage or air over land or building to or from adjacent property. A right to air through a defined aperture or channel can be acquired as an **easement**; but a landowner has no general or natural right to the flow of air to, or from, his land. However, if a landowner enjoys a right to the flow of air over his land, the polluting of that air (except when authorised by statute, by express or implied grant, or by prescription) creates a **nuisance** – Chastey *v* Ackland [1897] AC 155 HL. See also **derogation from grant, natural rights**.

right to buy
     see **leasehold enfranchisement, secure tenancy**.

right to fish
     An owner of land has an absolute right to take any fish in water entirely on his land, unless limited by statute law. A riparian owner (one who owns land adjoining a watercourse) owns the bed of a stream or non-tidal river to the middle of the watercourse and has a right to fish up to that boundary. In a tidal river all members of the public have a right to fish up to the point where the tide ebbs and flows. A right to fish may be granted to another as a **profit à prendre**, either as a several or sole right or as a right of common (called a 'common of fishery' or a 'common of piscary'). A right to fish may be granted to another to the exclusion of the grantor of that right or in common with the grantor. See also ***ad medium filum aquae***.

right to view
see **easement, right of light.**

rights, natural
see **natural rights.**

rights to water
see **littoral rights, riparian rights, water rights.**

ring, auction
see **bidding agreement.**

riparian owner
see **riparian rights.**

riparian rights
The rights appertaining to land that adjoins or abuts a **watercourse** or river running between banks, in particular a non-tidal watercourse. An owner of land that adjoins a non-tidal watercourse – a 'riparian owner' – owns the bed of the watercourse up to the centre – *ad medium filum aquae.* (The bed of a tidal river belongs to the Crown unless it has been expressly granted to a subject.) The riparian owner also has various rights at common law in connection with the water. These riparian rights are (a) a right of navigation on the water up to the point where the tide ebbs and flows; (b) an exclusive **right to fish**; (c) a right to draw water for 'ordinary' domestic or agricultural use connected with the land adjoining the watercourse (but not spray irrigation); (d) a right to receive a free flow of water unaltered in quality and quantity, subject to the 'ordinary' use by an upper riparian owner. In addition, a riparian owner may extract water for 'extraordinary' purposes in any quantity, provided its use is reasonably connected with the riparian land and it is restored substantially undiminished in volume and unal-

tered in character – Embrey *v* Owen (1861) 6 Ex.353. A riparian owner's right to extract water (otherwise than for domestic or agricultural purposes, excluding 'spray irrigation', and isolated extractions of not more than a thousand gallons), or to pollute water, is limited by statute (Water Resources Act 1963, ss. 23–25, as amended by the Water Act 1973. s. 9; Rivers (Prevention of Pollution) Act 1951).
cf. **littoral rights.** See also **accretion, injury to land, water rights.**

risk
The possibility of loss, destruction, or injury; the relative uncertainty of an event occurring. Risk is a function of lack of knowledge; the less that is known about the probable turn of events, the greater the risk: "risk varies inversely with knowledge". – The Theory of Interest, by Irvine Fisher, p. 221 (1930). In general usage, risk denotes a chance of loss; either loss arising from chance or the wind of fortune, or loss as distinguished from gain or **profit**. In investment, risk is equated with the sacrifice of something at the present, especially money, in the hope of a better outturn or profit in the future; it implies a choice of alternatives.

Real estate development and investment is concerned with speculative risks, such as the possibility of an increase or decrease in income or capital value; the possibility of a change in the cost or availability of finance; the possibility of a change in taxation; the possibility of a change in the value of money; and the possibility of adverse government intervention, e.g. compulsory purchase or rent control.

In insurance, risks are divided into

those that are 'speculative', e.g. one that arises from a business venture and, therefore, could result in a loss (or profit), and those that are 'pure', e.g. one that arises from an **act of God**, theft, fire, etc., which will only lead to a loss. An insurer normally is prepared only to provide an **indemnity** against pure risks; insurance being a business that concerns itself with factors that are entirely beyond the insured's control. In an insurance policy 'risk' may be used to refer to the peril insured against; the subject-matter that is at risk; or the circumstances in which a claim would be met. See also **all-risks insurance, downside risk, risk capital, sensitivity analysis, speculator**.

risk capital

Capital invested in a project, that is likely to be lost in its entirety in the event of failure. Capital invested in a project of a speculative nature. Generally **equity capital** rather than debt capital, the latter normally being secured on the assets of the borrower. See also **risk, venture capital**.

risk premium

An increase in a price or rate of interest made in order to take account of a particular risk, especially when determining a **capitalisation rate**. See also **component capitalisation rate, risk rate**.

risk rate

A **rate of return** on an investment that is sufficient to induce someone to part with money in order to make that investment. The price of accepting a **risk** expressed as an annual percentage of the total amount of money that might be lost; the rate of return that an investor considers appro-

priate for an accepted risk. See also **component capitalisation rate, remunerative rate**.

risque (F)

risk.

(*risques du recours de tiers* – third-party liability risks)

(*risques locatifs* – tenant's third-party risks)

(*assurance tous risques* – '**all-risks insurance**)

(*assurance au premier risque* – **first-loss insurance**).

river

see **riparian rights, right to fish, water rights**.

river authority

A body originally charged under the Water Resources Act 1963 with maintaining rivers and water resources. River authorities were abolished in 1973 and their functions transferred to water authorities (Water Act 1973, ss. 9, 33). See also **water rights**.

riverain (F)

fronting (a river or road); riperian owner; abbuter.

(*droits riverain* – **riperian rights**).

road

A public route for the passage of vehicles. A line of communication, thoroughfare, or way over land that is accessible to the general public. A road is used for the passage of vehicles, animals and persons and normally is a hard surfaced or paved route that leads from one place to another. 'Road' may refer loosely to any way or thoroughfare that is surfaced artificially, whether used as a private or public right of way, including a public or private drive or even a cul-de-sac – Spackman *v* Secretary of

State for the Environment [1977] 1 All ER 257. A road may include a bridge, lane, footpath or other forms of passage over land. In connection with road traffic offences, 'road' is defined to mean "any **highway** or any other road to which the public has access, and includes bridges over which a road passes" (Road Traffic Act 1972, s. 196 (1) 1). See also **street**.

roadside development (US)
see **ribbon development**.

roll (US)
see **tax roll**.

roll-over expenses (US)
Expenses associated with reletting a property, such as leasing commission and redecoration costs.

'roll-over' mortgage (or loan) (ROM)
A mortgage or **loan** granted subject to a condition that permits the lender to vary the rate of interest at stipulated times or on specified conditions, such as every quarter or in line with a given rate of interest. Usually a roll-over loan is a short or medium-term loan, where the interest rate is reviewed at the end of each set period, i.e. it 'rolls over' from one period to another. It may be distinguished from a **variable-rate mortgage**, which continues as a long-term loan but with a provision that the rate of interest can be varied at specified times.

roll-over relief
A provision which enables a **capital gains tax** liability on an asset (including land, buildings, fixed plant and machinery and goodwill) to be deferred when the proceeds of sale are used to acquire a similar replacement asset in order to continue a business. The replacement asset must be

acquired one year before the sale, or three years thereafter. (Capital Gains Tax Act 1979, ss. 115–121).

rolled-under loan (US)
A loan that is renewed at a lower interest rate to that appertaining to the one that has matured.

rolled-up interest
Interest that is not paid at its due date, but is added to the outstanding principal. Future interest is paid on the aggregate of the principal and the 'rolled-up' or **accrued interest**. See also **compound interest**.

rompre (un contrat) (F)
to cancel (a contract).

room
An interior part of a house or building given aside for a particular purpose, especially as part of a dwelling. A particular area or space. See also **bed sitting room**, **living room**.

rooming house (US)
see **lodging house**.

root of title
A document or instrument that starts a claim of **title** to unregistered land. A *good* root of title, unless stated otherwise in a contract for the sale of land, is, "a document purporting to deal with the entire legal and equitable estate and interest in the property, not depending for its validity upon any previous instrument, and containing nothing to throw any suspicion on the title of any of the disposing parties". (Williams on Title 4 edn, p. 574). The document should show clearly the extent of the estate to be transferred (both in terms of its quality and quantity); must have no 'cloud' over it; and must not be

dependent on extrinsic evidence. The best root of title is a **conveyance** made for valuable consideration or a deed creating a first legal mortgage of a **fee simple** absolute, or if applicable a comparable document dealing with a lesser estate, that was made at least 15 years beforehand. A deed of gift of a freehold, and a specific devise in a will of a testator who died before 1926 with an assent drawn up by the executors after 1925, are both good roots of title. A lease, equitable mortgage, and a general devise leave other interests to be ascertained, or do not show the full extent of the estate to be passed, and are not good roots of title. As a rule, a purchaser of land may require a root of title to be traced back at least 15 years in order to be satisfied that the seller has a 'good' root of title (Law of Property Act 1969, s. 23). See also **abstract of title**, **chain of title**, **good title**.

The Law of Real Property, by Robert Megarry and H.W.R. Wade, 5 edn., pp. 607–609.
Contract and Conveyance, by J.T. Farrand, 4 edn., pp. 96–98, 101–103, 121.
Barnsley's Conveyancing Law and Practice, 2 edn, pp. 286–291.
Conveyancing, by I.R. Storey, pp. 47–49 (1984).
42 Halsbury's Laws of England, 4 edn, paras. 143–181.

row house (US)
see **terrace house**.

Royal Fine Arts Commission
A body established in 1924 to offer advice on matters of aesthetic design, especially on the design of buildings in historic areas or on major building projects. The Commission offers advice on planning and design to Government departments and may call upon expert witnesses in connection with development proposals or planning applications.

Royal Institute of British Architects (RIBA)
The principal body of architects in Britain. Founded in 1834 to promote "the general advancement of Civil Architecture and for promoting and facilitating the acquirement of the knowledge of various Arts and Sciences connected therewith". An **architect** may be a Fellow or Associate of that institute and accordingly is designated FRIBA or ARIBA.

Royal Institution of Chartered Surveyors (RICS)
The principal professional body of surveyors in Britain. Founded in 1868 and incorporated by Royal Charter in 1881 as The Surveyors Institution, its name was changed in 1947 to The Royal Institution of Chartered Surveyors. The objects of the Institution are, "to secure the advancement and facilitate the acquisition of that knowledge which constitutes the profession of a surveyor, namely, the arts, sciences and practice of: (a) determining the value of all descriptions of landed and house property and of the various interests therein; (b) managing and developing estates and other business concerned with the management of landed property; (c) securing the optimal use of land and its associated resources to meet social and economic needs; (d) surveying the structure and condition of buildings and their services and advising on their maintenance, alteration and improvement; (e) measuring and delineating the physical features of the Earth; (f) managing, developing

and surveying mineral property; (g) determining the economic use of resources of the construction industry, and the financial appraisal and measurement of construction work; (h) selling (whether by auction or otherwise) buying or letting, as an agent, real or personal property or any interest therein; and to maintain and promote the usefulness of the profession for the public advantage".

Membership of the Institution consists of four classes, namely Fellows, Professional Associates, Associates and Honorary Members; and there are classes of Probationers and Students attached to but not Members of the Institution. Fellows and Professional Members may use after their name the initials FRICS or ARICS and the designation 'Chartered Surveyor'. Associates and Honorary Members are appointed to assist with the profession, its professional knowledge and objects; the former are not surveyors by profession and the latter are not engaged in practice as a surveyor in Great Britain, Northern Ireland or the Republic of Ireland. All Members of the Institution are subject to the Bye-Laws of the Institution.

royalty
A share of the profits or produce paid for the privilege of using another's property. Originally a right to exploit land or a similar privilege granted by royal prerogative, in return for a payment. In modern usage a royalty is any payment made for the use of property (real, personal or intellectual) and is paid in relation to the income received therefrom. A royalty paid for land is normally a part of the *reddendum* under a lease, i.e. it is a

true rent, even though it is paid by reference to the produce rather than the value of the land itself – R. *v* Westbrook, R. *v* Everist (1847) 10 QB 203. Under a **mining lease** it is a form of variable rent; the variable being the quantity of natural resource or mineral extracted from the mine. See also **dead rent**, **escheat**.

rue (F)
road; street.
(*rue entretenue par la municipalité* – adopted street).

ruelle (F)
mews.

ruine (F)
decay; deterioration or falling down (of a building).

rule against accumulations
see **rule against perpetuities**.

rule against perpetuities
A rule of law which provides that an interest in land is void if it is created so that it will not take effect, or **vest**, until a date that is too far into the future. It restricts the creation of any interest in land subject to a contingent event that prevents someone from having an absolute right to possession until a point in time considered by law to be too remote. A perpetual postponement of a right to possession of land is considered contrary to public policy because it 'ties up' the use of land and prevents its free alienability. Accordingly, the law has sought to define a 'perpetuity period' within which an interest in land must vest, and a **contingent interest** is void if it might vest after the end of the 'perpetuity period' – Duke of Norfolk's Case (1683) 1 Cas. in Ch. 1.

The 'perpetuity period' is basically an existing (human) life or lives in being (whether they have an interest in the land or not) plus 21 years, including an allowance for gestation, from the date the interest is granted (in the case of a grant *inter vivos*) or the date of a testator's death (in the case of a devise). "No interest is good unless it vests, if at all, not later than twenty-one years after some life in being at the creation of that interest" (The Rule against Perpetuities, by J.C. Gray, 4 edn., p. 201). Normally, "it is not sufficient that it *may* vest within that period, it must be good in its creation; and unless it is created in such terms that it cannot vest after the expiration of a life or lives in being, and twenty-one years, and the period allowed for gestation, it is not valid, and subsequent events cannot make it so" – Dungannon (Lord) *v* Smith (1845) 12 Cl. and Fin. 563. A similar 'rule against inalienability' provides that land cannot be transferred in such a way that it is perpetually restricted from being freely transferrable. Before the defined 'perpetuity period', the land must come into the hands of someone who is entirely free to convey the land. Similarly a 'rule against accumulations' prevents a person from providing that the income from property left under a will is made to accumulate for too long a period in favour of a future person or persons (generally a person unconceived 21 years hence) (Law of Property Act 1925, s. 164 (1)).

The modern rules for determining whether the 'perpetuity period' has been exceeded are complex and now depend on whether the instrument creating the interest is made before or after 1 July 1964. Since the Perpetuities and Accumulations Act 1964 the rules have been reformed and, to a degree clarified, in particular by the introduction of a period for which it is permitted to "wait and see" whether the land will vest within the required period. In addition, a testator may specify for a period of 80 years within which the interest will vest.

In the US, in certain states, a period of 'wait and see' to ascertain if the interest did vest, is permitted and in several states the 'perpetuity period' is limited to 99 years.

In French law, successive rights to land are restricted and, in general, land must not be made to pass beyond a life in existence (or, at least, one conceived).

The principle behind this rule is that it would be unreasonable to create remote interests because (i) it withholds property from free commercial use and, therefore, reduces the return from land – no one who is unsure of the length of his tenure is likely to make the maximum investment in an asset; (ii) it encourages the concentration of wealth in the hands of a few; (iii) it favours the survival of the fittest to the detriment of the feeble; (iv) it may encourage capricious or eccentric gifts to a few who may be reticent in making the best use of their land; "it seldom happens, however that a great proprietor is a great improver ... To improve land with profit, like all other commercial projects, requires an exact attention to small savings and small gains, of which a man borne to great fortune even though naturally frugal is very seldom capable. The situation of such a person naturally disposes him to attend rather to ornament which pleases his fancy than to profit for

which he has so little occasion"
(Adam Smith, *Wealth of Nations*,
Book 3, Ch. 11); (v) it may lead to the
favouring of a side of a family as yet
uncreated against, on the other side,
the present generation – the dead
should not be permitted to dictate to
the living, or rather the unconceived
should not rule over the living; (vi) as
with **mortmain** it retains a 'dead-
hand' on land so that it is not freely
transferable and thus enabled to tend
towards its **highest and best use**.
Called also the 'doctrine of remoteness' or the 'rule against remote vesting'. See also **barring the entail**,
vested interest.
Amos and Walton's Introduction to
French Law, 3 edn., pp. 129–136.
Real Property, by William E. Burby,
3 edn., pp. 412–426.
Future Interests, by Lewis H. Simes,
2 edn., p. 163 *et seq.*
The Law of Property, by F.H. Law-
son and Bernard Rudden, 2 edn., pp.
177–187.
Real Property and Real People, by
K.J. Gray and P.D. Symes, pp. 185–
211 (1981).
Cheshire's Modern Law of Real
Property, 13 edn, pp. 290–339.
The Law of Real Property, by Robert
Megarry and H.W.R. Wade, 5 edn.,
pp. 238–310.
Land Law: Cases and Materials, by
R.H. Maudsley and E.H. Burn, 4
edn., pp. 290–350.
The Rule against Perpetuities, by
J.H.C. Morris and W.B. Leach, 2
edn.
The Rule against Perpetuities, by J.C.
Gray, 4 edn.
The Modern Law of Perpetuities, by
R.H. Maudsley, (1979).
35 Halsbury's Laws of England, 4
edn., paras. 901–1100.

rule against remote vesting
see **rule against perpetuities**.

rule of 72
A rule of thumb that the number of
years required for an investment to
double in value can be found by dividing the annual compound interest
rate into 72. For example, an investment providing a 12 per cent annual
compound return will double in value
in 6 years.

rule of 78
A rule of thumb for calculating the
outstanding portion of an annual
payment due under an **amortisation
mortgage** that is repayable monthly.
The sum of the number of months
outstanding is divided by 78 (being
the sum of the digits 1 to 12) to
express the proportion of the annual
payments outstanding. For example,
at the end of month 7, 50/78ths of the
total annual payment is outstanding
(8 + 9 + 10 + 11 + 12 = 50). See also
sum-of-the-years' digits method.

rule in Rylands *v* Fletcher
see **strict liability**.

rules of conduct
Rules laid down by the governing
body of a professional organisation
by which a member of that organisation is required to conduct his professional duties e.g. the rules or bye-laws
laid down by the **Royal Institution of
Chartered Surveyors**, the **Royal Institution of British Architects**, or the
Law Society. These rules are published by the appropriate organisation and incorporate details of disciplinary powers and procedures to be
adopted to enforce such rules. See
also **code of ethics**, **duty of care**,
solicitor.

rules of good husbandry
see **good husbandry**.

'run off' of a margin
see **margin**.

'run with the land'
see **easement, privity of estate, restrictive covenant**.

running costs
see **operating costs, service charge**.

running expenses
see **operating expenses**.

running repairs
Repairs that arise during the day to day use of a property, such as mending fuses, replacing tap washers, replacing a broken window pane. See also **repair, tenantable repair**.

running yield
The yield from an investment at a particular point in time, i.e. the relationship of the income at that time to the original cost, or the ten market value, expressed as a percentage. Called also the 'flat yield', 'straight yield' or, if taken at the present point in time, the 'actual yield' or 'current yield'.
cf. **initial yield**. See also **cash-on-cash yield**.

rupture (d'un contrat) (F)
breach (of a contract).

rural property
Agricultural, farming or non-urban property, i.e. property in the country or outside a built-up area. 'Rural property' may include a small settlement such as a village or isolated community. See also **agricultural land**.
The Appraisal of Rural Property AIREA (1983).
Walmsley's Rural Estate Management, 6 edn.

rurban property
Property, situated outside the limit of a town or city, which is in the process of transition from being **rural property** to becoming urban in character. Generally an area situated just beyond **suburban** property.

S

safe rate

The **rate of return** from an investment that is considered to have the lowest level of risk. Generally taken as the rate of interest receivable from a government bond or security, or the return represented by a well secured ground rent let on a long lease to a company of the highest financial standing. See also **risk rate**.

safety clause (US)

see **extender clause**.

saisie (F)

seizure; **sequestration**; attachment. (*saisie-immobilière, saisie-réelle* – seizure on real property)
(*saisie-arrêt* – **attachment**; **garnishment**.
(*saisie hypothécaire* – **foreclosure**)
(*saisie pour loyer* – **distress**)
(*conversion-saisie* – official sale by public auction of a property taken by seizure).

saisine (F)

seisin.

sale

The **transfer** of property, or a title to property, from one party (a seller or vendor) to another (a buyer or purchaser) for a consideration paid or agreed to be paid. "The passing of title from the seller to the buyer for a price" (United States Uniform Commercial Code, para. 2–106 (1)). The execution of any contract for a change of ownership of property may be considered a sale, even though it is conditional or will not be completed until actual **delivery** of the property. A sale is made usually for monetary consideration but an **exchange** of one property for another may be classified as a sale: "sale or exchange is a transmutation of property from one man to another, in consideration of some recompense in value for there is no sale without recompense; there must be a *quid pro quo*. If it be a commutation of goods for goods, it is more an exchange; but, if it be a transferring of goods for money, it is called a sale" (Bl. Comm. vol. ii. p. 446). (In the case of a sale of goods, if the goods are freely transferred the transaction is called a 'sale'; if the contract is to be performed in the future, or subject to some condition, it is called an 'agreement to sell'; and the instrument that transfers the goods is called a **bill of sale**: Sale of Goods Act 1979, s. 2 (1).)

In the case of real property, generally, a sale requires a **conveyance** or deed of grant and the sale does not take place until **completion** of the transaction). "A sale (of land) is, properly speaking a conveyance, that is, a transfer, of property in consideration of a price in money, and accordingly a contract for the sale of land is a contract whereby one legal person, called the vendor, agrees to convey (or transfer) by the appropriate legal method, to another legal person, called the purchaser, some land, or some interest in land in consideration of a sum of money, which is called the purchase price" (*The Law of the Sales of Land* by Raymond Walton. 3 edn, p. 47. A transfer of land in exchange for an agreement to relinquish a debt is not a sale of property properly so called, but merely an agreement to extinguish a debt – Simpson *v* Connolly [1953] 2 All ER 477.

The term 'sale' is used principally to refer to a transfer of corporeal property and **cession** or **assignment** to refer to a transfer of incorporeal property, or a lease which, in English law, is (at least historically) a personal right to use and enjoy property. (In French law *vente* is used in a similar way to 'sale' and **cession** for the ceding of an incorporeal right or the transfer of a lease). However, the grant of a long-term ground lease, or a lease combined with an option for the lessee to purchase the lessor's interest, may be regarded as akin to, or a simulation of, a sale; especially when considering the treatment of a transaction for tax purposes. cf. **gift**. See also **auction, conditional sale agreement, conditions of sale, contract for sale, grant, instalment sale, power of sale, public sale, purchase, sell, trust for sale**.
41 Halsbury's Laws of England 4 edn, (Sale of Goods) para. 601 *et seq.*
42 Halsbury's Laws of England 4 edn, (Sale of Land) paras. 1–400.

sale and buy-back
A sale of property to a financial institution or investor with concurrently a contract for sale by which the vendor agrees to repurchase the property under an **instalment contract**. See also **repurchase agreement, sale and lease-back**.

sale and lease-back
A form of real estate financing whereby an owner sells his property and simultaneously takes a long-term lease of the property from the purchaser. The purpose of the transaction is to enable the vendor to realise the immediate capital value of his property and at the same time to retain possession. He may retain physical possession, as with a retailer or an industrial company; or the right to receive rent and profits, as with a developer. Sale and lease-back financing is used most frequently when mortgage finance is in short supply or when a property owner considers that the annual cost (in the form of rent) will be lower than for an alternative form of finance (although in the long run, increasing rental payments, and the foregoing of possible capital appreciation may make the arrangement more expensive than a mortgage loan. The alternative between ownership and leasing may be analysed by means of a **discounted cash flow** appraisal, especially after giving full weight to the tax implications). Synonymous with 'purchase and lease-back'. See also **land sale-and-leaseback, lease/lease-back financing, project sale-and-leaseback, slice**.
Real Estate Law, by Robert Kratovil and Raymond J. Werner, 8 edn., pp. 272–276.
The Property Development Process, CALUS, pp. 91–96, 267–272 (1976).
A Guide to Institutional Property Investment, by Angus P.J. McIntosh & Stephen G. Sykes, pp. 99–108 (1985).
Valuation and Development Appraisal, edited by Clive Darlow pp. 209–233 (1982).

sale-buyback (US)
see **sale and buy-back**.

sale 'off-plan'
The sale of a building or part of a building before it is complete, especially the sale of flats in a block before

the entire complex is finished. See also **self-financing development**.

sale, power of
see **power of sale, tenant for life**.

sale price
1. The total **price**, in money or money's worth, paid over on the transfer of property. Usually the **consideration** in a contract; although the proceeds of sale received by a vendor, after deducting all costs directly associated with the sale, e.g. lawyer's fees, agent's commission, etc., may be referred to as the 'net sale price'.
2. The price at which a property is expected to sell in the open market. See also **market value**.

sales area
"The **net internal area** (NIA) usable for retailing purposes, but excluding storerooms, unless they are formed by non-structural partitions, the existence of which should be stated if applicable."(The Royal Institution of Chartered Surveyors' Code of Measuring Practice, 1979). For this purpose the depth of a retail store or shop should be measured from the back of the pavement, or forecourt, to the back of the sales area, and should include any recessed entrances, arcade displays, etc.
cf. **gross retail area**. See also **net sales area**.

sales comparison approach (US)
see **comparison method of valuation, market comparison approach**.

sales contract
see **contract for sale**.

sales mix
see **tenant mix**.

salvage value
An amount realised, or estimated to be realised, upon the sale of a property that has reached the end of its **economic life**. A sum of money that is received for a property that otherwise would be destroyed, given away, or 'written-off' because it is considered to have no further value.

salvo jure (L)
'Without prejudice'.

sandwich house (US)
see **terrace house**.

sandwich lease
The interest held by a lessee (or tenant) who himself has granted a lease; the 'sandwich party', being both a lessor and a lessee, but neither a freeholder nor occupier. If the owner A of a freehold (or a fee estate) leases his property to B, who in turn leases it to C, A has a freehold subject to a lease (or a leased fee estate), B has a sandwich lease and C holds a sublease. Called also a 'mesne tenancy' i.e. a tenancy held by an intermediate party. See also **head lease, lease/lease-back financing**.

sandwich lease-back
see **lease/lease-back financing**.

sans recours (F)
without recourse. A term used especially on a **bill of exchange** to indicate that the drawer or an endorser of a bill of exchange has repudiated his liability to the holder.

satellite town
A town that is dominated by, or is dependent on, another town or city. For example, a town separated from a major city or metropolis, usually by a green belt or any other form of protected countryside, but to a large extent economically and socially

dependent on that city. See also **garden city**, **new town**.

satisfaction
1. The termination of an obligation or a contract by **performance**, i.e. by the discharge of what is due, such as by repayment of a loan. The execution or performance of an agreement. "The donation of a thing with the intention that it is to be taken either wholly or in part in extinguishment of some prior claim" – Lord Chichester v Coventry (1867) 36 LJ Ch. 673. Recompense for an injury done or a debt owing. See also **compensation**.
2. Something given in part or entire **settlement** of a prior claim by the donee. The equitable 'doctrine of satisfaction' provides that if a person makes a payment or performs an act that has an unclear intention, but is aimed apparently at satisfying a debt or performing an obligation, the court may accept that the settlor has discharged the debt or obligation, provided the payment or act is a sufficient substitute. See also **accord and satisfaction**, **ademption**.

satisfaction certificate (US)
A formal written acknowledgement from a mortgagee confirming that a loan has been repaid in full (including any arrears of interest), that all the terms and conditions of a mortgage agreement have been complied with, and that the property charged will be released. See also **release deed**.

satisfactory title
see **marketable title**.

satisfied term
A **tenancy for a term of years** that has come to an end before its normal expiration date because the purpose for which the tenancy was granted has been fulfilled. A tenancy for a term of years that has become a satisfied term merges with the interest held by the landlord and ceases accordingly. Where the purpose is satisfied for part of the land comprised in the term, the tenancy terminates as if a separate term had been created originally for that part of the land (Law of Property Act 1925, s. 5). See also **merger**, **outstanding term**.

savings and loan (S and L) association (US)
An association, formed under federal or state law, that accepts savings from the public, in return for which it grants shares in the association and grants mortgage loans, primarily on residential property, to the shareholders. A savings and loan association performs a similar function to a **building society** in the UK and is one of the principal sources of home loans. The savings and loan associations are essentially local in their operations, but are regulated at a national level by the Federal Home Loan Bank Board (FHLB). Called sometimes a 'thrift association'.

scale fee
A fee paid in accordance with an authorised or recommended scale. In particular, a **fee**, or **commission**, based on a level of charges recommended by a trade or professional body; for example, the Royal Institution of Chartered Surveyors' 'scale of professional charges'. Generally a scale fee is based on a percentage of the value of the property involved in the work to which the fee relates. In view of the suggestion of a monopoly in the provision of professional services by a body that publishes such fee

scales, increasingly these publications are prohibited by law.

scarcity value

The extra **value** attached to something due to an exceptional shortage in its supply relative to wants or demands. Although scarcity is a primary determinant of value, 'scarcity value' is the extra premium attached to something on account of a short-term dearth or deficiency in its availability. It represents an increase in value which arises because, in the short-run, demand for something substantially exceeds the available supply – a value that theoretically cannot be sustained in the long-run. In economic theory, scarcity value cannot be sustained because a high price will induce extra production, increased supply, and drive prices down or alternatively, a substitute will be found. However, production difficulties (as with land), combined with the propensity to consume rising with supply – the more we have, the more we want – can sustain an element of scarcity almost indefinitely. See also **economic rent, fair rent, market value.**

sceau; scelle (F)

seal. *Sceau* is an official mark on a document and *scelle* is an official closure of a property.

schedule

A detailed list, inventory or table set down in writing. A formal list added or appended to a document, especially a legal or financial document or statute. A 'schedule' is usually a sheet or sheets of paper annexed to a contract, deed, statute, deposition, or other instrument, extending the terms that are mentioned in a principal document; especially those terms that are at variance with the general or standard terms of a document. A schedule frequently is attached to a lease setting out details of fixtures or fittings or services to be provided by one of the parties. A schedule may be added to an insurance policy (especially to a **blanket insurance policy**) to enumerate the risks covered, or excluded from the policy, or to specify the properties covered by the policy. See also **schedule of dilapidations, schedule of quantities, schedule of rates.**

schedule of condition

A written survey that sets down a description of the physical condition and state of repair of a property which is to be altered in some way, for example by renovation, or is to be the subject of a lease.
cf. **schedule of dilapidations.**

schedule of dilapidations

A list of items of **repair** or **maintenance** that a landlord requires a tenant to make good in order to comply with the terms of a lease. An interim schedule of dilapidations may be submitted to a tenant at any time during the term of a lease, when the landlord determines that a tenant has not fulfilled his repairing obligations, providing there is a covenant in the lease permitting the landlord (or his agent or surveyor) to enter the demised premises in order to view their state of repair. A final schedule of dilapidations may be submitted on expiry of the lease setting out repairs that should have been carried out by the tenant during the term of the lease.
cf. **schedule of condition.** See also **dilapidation, landlord's access, repair,**

right of entry.
The Law of Dilapidations, by W.A.
West, 8 edn., pp. 143–144, 195–204.
*Agricultural Valuations: A Practical
Guide*, by R.G. Williams, pp. 53–71
(1985).
*Building Surveys, Reports and Dilap-
idations*, by Ivor H. Seeley, pp. 218–
244 (1985).
Woodfall's Landlord and Tenant, 28
edn, paras. 1–1580 to 1–1583.

schedule of quantities
A schedule that describes the work or
duties to be performed by a building
contractor and against which the cost
of the work can be marked, particularly when submitting a tender for
building work. A term more commonly used in the US.
cf. **schedule of rates**. See also **bill of
quantities, fixed-price contract.**

schedule of rates
A schedule to a building contract that
sets out the agreed rates to be charged
for work done and against which the
quantity of materials and labour can
be marked.
cf. **schedule of quantities**. See also **bill
of quantities**.

schedule rights
Those **existing use rights**, available to
a landowner by virtue of the Town
and Country Planning Act 1971, Sch.
8 ('eighth schedule development'),
which although requiring planning
permission may not be restricted without a right arising to compensation.

scheduled area
An area of Great Britain that is considered to require special economic
attention and positive inducements to
industry. See also **assisted area,
development area.**

scheduled gross (US)
The projected **gross income** that can
be expected from a property investment.
cf. **effective gross income.**

scheduled monument
see **ancient monument.**

scheduled property
1. In insurance, an individual property described in a schedule to an
insurance policy that covers a number
of other properties. Normally the
insured value is set down alongside
the description or address of the
property. See also **blanket insurance
policy.**
2. See **ancient monument, listed
building**.

*schéma directeur d'aménagement et
d'urbanisme (SDAU)* (F)
land use plan. A form of development plan which falls between a central government plan and a local development plan. Similar in scope to
an English **structure plan**. Detailed
land use plans – *'plans d'occupation
des sols'* – are prepared to fit in the
general guide lines established by
these 'structure plans'.

scheme of development
A scheme by which an owner of a
defined area of land divides it up for
sale as separate building plots and
imposes on the purchasers restrictions as to the use and development of
the land with the intention that the
area as a whole, and each and every
plot, will benefit thereby. For example, a scheme that requires each purchaser of a plot of land on a housing
estate to use the land only for the
erection of a dwelling-house, in accordance with plans and specifications approved by the original

vendor. A scheme of development establishes a form of 'local law' by which the development and management of the estate is controlled for the benefit of all the purchasers and their successors; a scheme that is for the mutual benefit of all the purchasers, enabling "each purchaser to have, as against the other purchasers, in one way or another the benefit of the restrictions to which he has made himself subject" – Re. Dolphin's Conveyance [1970] Ch. 662. The principle behind a scheme of development is that each purchaser (or his successor), as well as the common vendor, has a right to enforce the restrictions for his own benefit, and by the same token, accepts the burdens imposed on his use of the land; thus "reciprocity is the foundation of the idea of a scheme... [and a purchaser] must know both the extent of his burden and the extent of his benefit." – Reid v Bickerstaff [1909] 2 Ch. 319.

Strictly a scheme of development requires five conditions to be satisfied for there to be the 'mutuality of enforcement' that is an essential element of the scheme: (i) the area to which the scheme applies must be clearly defined – Reid v Bickerstaff supra; (ii) the land owner seeking to enforce the scheme must have derived title from a common vendor (or from a successor in title who is bound in equity to the common vendor); (iii) the common vendor must have laid out the area for sale with the intention that the restrictions, drawn up in accordance with some general plan, would be imposed on the use and development of all the plots; (iv) each purchaser must have accepted the restrictions on the understanding that similar restrictions would be imposed

on every other purchaser; and (v) the restrictions must be intended by the vendor to be, and are, imposed for the benefit of each and every plot (although the restrictions imposed on each plot need not be identical – Elliston v Reacher [1908] 2 Ch. 384). However, a scheme of development is likely to bind any owner of land on the estate where (a) it is clear that the common vendor's intention was to impose substantially the same restrictions on all the plots in the defined area; (b) the purchasers acquired their plots on the understanding that the 'laws' of the estate would be binding on them and would benefit the entire estate; and (c) it was intended that the purchasers would have reciprocal rights to enforce the law against the other owners – Re Wembley Park Estate Co. Ltd's Transfer [1968] 1 All ER 457; Eagling v Gardner [1970] 2 All ER 838. A scheme of development may apply in the same way if the land is let on long-term ground leases. The term 'scheme of development' is a genus; a particular instance of such a scheme is referred to as a 'building scheme' for the area – Brunner v Greenslade [1970] 3 All ER 836, and a similar scheme applied to a block of flats may be referred to as a 'flat scheme'.

In the US such a scheme is referred to as a 'general scheme of development', or in a particular instance a 'general building scheme' and it is enforceable on much the same principles as in English law; the reciprocal benefits and burdens being referred to as 'equitable servitudes' (as they are rights originally arising from an English Court of Equity – Weigman v Kusel, 270 Ill. 520. The restrictions are referred to as 'general plan restrictions' and are set out usually in a 'declaration of restrictions'. See also **planned unit development, restrictive covenant**.

Real Estate Law, by Robert Kratovil and Raymond J. Werner, 8 edn., pp. 391–410.

Introduction to Land Law, by J.G. Riddell, 3 edn., pp. 340–343.

Cases and Materials on Land Law, by E.L.G. Tyler, 2 edn., pp. 262–267.

Megarry's Manual of the Law of Real Property, 6 edn, pp. 454–456.

The Law of Real Property, by Robert Megarry and H.W.R. Wade, 5 edn., pp. 790–793.

Land Law Cases and Materials, by R.H. Maudsley and F.H. Burns, 4 edn., pp. 742–752.

Preston and Newson's Restrictive Covenants affecting Freehold Land, 6 edn, pp. 53–55.

scheme of management
see **management scheme**.

scheme world
see **compulsory purchase compensation**.

science park
A mixed industrial and office development that is intended for use by firms involved primarily in advanced scientific research, development and production of scientific instruments. The 'park' is a form of campus, usually sited near a university, which aims to provide modern premises in a pleasant environment with readily accessible support facilities for the users.

scutage
A monetary levy or fine exacted from a feudal tenant by his lord or the Sovereign to pay for military services. In most cases scutage or 'escutage' came to replace the provision of **knight-service** from the middle of the twelfth century.

seal
A mark or impression used to ratify, confirm or authenticate a document or signature. In particular, a formal mark affixed in order to effect a **deed**. Originally a seal was embossed in wax, but today it may take any form that can be considered as sufficient authenticity of the maker's mark: "to constitute a seal, neither wax or wafer, nor a piece of paper, nor even an impression is needed" – Re Sandilands [1871] 6 CPD 413. Even a signature over words such as 'sealed with my seal' or a witnessed signature in a circle on a document demarked *locus sigilli* (or LS), 'place of the seal', will suffice – First National Securities *v* Jones [1978] Ch. 109; Jacksonville MPR and Nav. Co. *v* Hooper, 160 US 514). Traditionally a seal was used to circumvent illiteracy, because of a lack of any adequate means of proving the authenticity of a signature. Also, the addition of a seal affected the type of action that could be brought to enforce the contract. Today it has little relevance to the prevention of fraud, a **signature** being the more usual means to authenticate a document. However, in addition to those cases when a deed is a statutory requirement, the use of a seal may still make a contract enforceable 'at law' rather than 'in equity', i.e. it makes certain contracts enforceable as of right, rather than at the discretion of the courts. Every company is required to have a seal and every instrument to which a seal is affixed must be signed by a director, and countersigned by

the secretary or another director (Companies Act 1948, s. 108 (1), Sch. 1, Table A, art. 113). In most states in the US, the common law effect of a seal has been abolished and it is rarely encountered except in certain cases to authenticate a contract executed by a corporation. See also **'signed sealed and delivered'**.

Chitty on Contract, 25 edn, paras. 18–31.

9 Halsbury's Laws of England, 4 edn, paras. 210–211.

sealed bid

A **bid** made under seal i.e. placed in an envelope and sealed until the time set for its consideration. A sealed bid is a common requirement when competitive offers are made in response to an **invitation to tender** for building work or for the provision of services. The sealed offers are submitted before a specified time and then opened for consideration at that time.

sealed offer

An unconditional **offer**, submitted by one party to a dispute to the other, that is placed in a sealed envelope to be opened after the dispute has been settled by an independent expert or an arbitrator. The offer is not intended to take precedence over the independent determination of the dispute. It is indicative of the final offer made prior to the submission of the dispute for independent determination and it may be taken into account prior to deciding on a fair allocation between the parties of responsibility for payment of the expert's or arbitrator's costs.

A sealed offer is submitted usually by an authority that is acquiring land compulsorily, prior to a reference to the **Lands Tribunal** to determine the amount of compensation payable for the land. The offer is submitted to the Tribunal, in a sealed envelope to be opened after the Tribunal's award, as a representation of the final figure the acquiring authority was prepared to offer as compensation. As a rule, if the Tribunal's award exceeds the authority's sealed offer costs are paid by the authority and in the reverse case by the claimant. This rule applies only to costs incurred after the sealed offer is submitted to the Tribunal and, in order to take advantage of this provision, the claimant must have previously submitted a detailed claim for compensation to the acquiring authority (Land Compensation Act 1961, s. 4; Lands Tribunal Rules 1975, r. 50). In any event, the award of costs remains a matter of discretion for the Lands Tribunal. Called sometimes an 'unconditional offer'.

search certificate

see **official certificate of search**.

searches, title

Enquiries made by a prospective purchaser of land, or an interest in land, to determine the existence or otherwise, of any encumberance that affects the vendor's title to the land. In particular, searches of a land register to ascertain details of any matter that is recorded as affecting a parcel of land. Such searches may be made in person or by requesting an **official certificate of search** from the HM Land Registry or the Land Charges Department. In addition, searches should be made of the **local land charges register** and, where appropriate, of a register of common land, an Area Coal Board Office, or any statutory body that may have a right that affects the land e.g. British Rail.

'Search' may refer also to an inspection of the **Land Registry** to establish if a title to land has been registered. cf. **requisition**. See also **constructive notice, index map, Land Charges Register, overriding interest planning inquiry, priority notice.**
Conveyancing Searches, by A.R. Mellows (1975).
Handbook of Conveyancing Searches and Enquiries by E.O. Bourne (1984).

seashore
see **foreshore, shore.**

seasoned loan
A loan that has been outstanding for a number of years, during which time the lender has substantially complied with the terms of the loan agreement.

seck-rent
see **rent-seck.**

second-hand evidence
see **hearsay.**

second mortgage
A mortgage granted against the security of a property that already has been charged with a **first mortgage** and, therefore, a mortgage that ranks as a lower **priority** in the event of any claim against the secured property. A mortgage may be ranked as first, second, third, etc., according to its priority. In practice, any mortgage that is subordinate to a first mortgage may be termed a second mortgage or, especially in the US, a 'junior mortgage'. A second mortgagee should give notice of his charge to the first mortgagee and, normally, the latter's consent is required to the creation of a subsequent charge. See also **general equitable charge, puisne mortgage, subordination, tacking.**

secondary approach to value (US)
Any method or approach to an **appraisal** that is used as a check on the principal or 'primary' method of valuation. A secondary approach is used either to lend support to the primary valuation or to verify the **highest and best** use for a property.

secondary easement (US)
A right that is required or is available to accomplish the intended purpose of a primary or existing **easement**, such as a right to enter on land to clean a ditch that runs across the servient tenement and forms the subject matter of an existing easement; or, a right to go on land that forms the subject of an easement for the extraction of minerals to test for the presence of the minerals – Beckwith *v* Rossi (1961) 157 Me. 532, 175 A. 2d 732.

secondary financing (or loan)
Financing (or a loan) secured by means of a **second mortgage**. See also **Federal Home Loan Mortgage Corporation, Federal National Mortgage Association, finance house, Government National Mortgage Association.**

secondary location
A relative term, although generally it is used to describe any position that is inferior to a **prime location**; especially a location that is significantly disadvantaged. A location, within a given town or neighbourhood, that does not secure the highest value or one that is located on the fringe of the **central business district.**

secret profits (or commission)
see **agent.**

Secretary of State for the Environment
One of Her Majesty's Principal

Secretaries of State who is responsible in England, as head of a department (the Department of the Environment which was first established under the Secretary of State for the Environment Order 1970, No. 1681), for local government administration and finance, including rating; housing and construction; highways; town and country planning and land use; environmental control; inner city renewal and new town development; royal parks and palaces; historic buildings, buildings of special architectural interest and ancient monuments; and sport and recreation. In particular, the Secretary is responsible for the introduction of new planning legislation; for making regulations, orders and statutory instruments as necessary to implement his general responsibilities; for the consideration and approval of development plans submitted by local planning authorities; for hearing and approving appeals against compulsory purchase orders; for hearing and approving planning appeals and appeals against enforcement notices; for making grants to government departments for the reclamation and improvement of agricultural land and rural industries; as well as for overseeing the **Property Services Agency**.

The Secretary of State is assisted by the Minister of State for Local Government, the Minister of State for Housing and Construction and Under-Secretaries of State. See also **highway authority**, **planning authority**.

section of land (US)

One of the portions into which public land is divided for sale to individuals. A section of land has an area of one square mile (640 acres), being one thirty-sixth part of a 'township'.

section 52 agreement

see **planning agreement**.

section 146 notice

see **forfeiture**, **repairs notice**.

secure tenancy

A tenancy of a dwelling-house, 'let as a separate dwelling', by a local authority, or one of various other public housing authorities, to an individual (or individuals) for occupation as his or her 'principal or only home'. By virtue of the Housing Act 1980, ss 28–34, a secure tenancy continues until terminated by a court order for possession given on one of the grounds specified in the 1980 Act, Schedule 4, Part I. A 'secure tenancy' may be no more than a mere licence, provided a separate dwelling-house (which may be a house or part of a house) is let to an individual (or a number of individuals as a joint tenancy) for use as that person's (or one of the person's) principal or only home. A secure tenancy may be created by a local authority; the Housing Corporation; certain housing associations, housing trusts, or housing co-operatives; a new town development corporation; the Commission for New Towns; an urban development corporation; or the Development Board for Rural Wales; but not the Crown. The 1980 Act, Schedule 3, specifies a number of forms of tenancy that are not secure tenancies. These include: a tenancy for a fixed term exceeding 21 years; in certain cases, a tenancy granted to an employee of the landlord or one of the public authorities to whom the Act applies, who is required to occupy the premises for the express purpose of his or her employment; in most cases, a tenancy granted to a student attending a designated course at a university or a college of further education; tenancy of an on-licence (a public house or the like); certain temporary or short-term tenancies, notably a tenancy granted to a homeless person or of a house that is held pending development; a **business tenancy**; an **assured tenancy**; and tenancy of a dwelling that forms part of an **agricultural holding** and occupied by a person who is responsible for control of farming. In addition, if either the landlord or the tenant ceases to meet the requirements that are essential to create a secure tenancy the letting will cease to be a secure tenancy; for example, if the tenant ceases to occupy the house as his 'principal or only home' or if the landlord ceases to fall into one of the designated categories (although the tenancy may then become a **protected tenancy**).

Thus, a 'secure tenancy' brings about a measure of security of tenure for most occupiers of council houses, or houses owned by quasi-public authorities, by requiring the landlord to serve proper notice of its wish to terminate the tenancy, and then to prove in the court that it has grounds for possession. The 1980 Act, s. 34, Sch. 4, as amended by the Housing and Building Control Act 1984, sets out sixteen grounds upon which the court may grant an order for possession. Broadly these are: (a) serious neglect or fraud on the part of the tenant, e.g. non-payment of rent, serious neglect of the property or furniture therein, or creation of nuisance to a neighbour; (b) the dwelling-house is overcrowded; (c) the landlord needs the premises for demolition or reconstruction; or (d) the housing priority of the landlord, e.g. the premises are more extensive than is required by the tenant or the local authority has a special need for the house to rehouse another family. Before granting an order for possession the court must be satisfied (i) if the ground falls in category (a) that it is reasonable to do so; (ii) if the ground falls in category (b) or (c) that **suitable alternative accommodation** will be available when the order takes effect; or (iii) if the ground falls in category (d) that it is both reasonable to make the order and that suitable alternative accommodation will be available.

A secure tenancy granted by a local authority is not subject to any statutory rent regulation and a local authority may "make such reasonable charges for the tenancy or occupation of the houses as they may determine" (Housing Act 1957, s. 111 (1)). In the case of any other landlord of a secure tenancy, the rent may be limited to a **fair rent** in a similar way to a letting by a private landlord.

A person who has held a secure tenancy of a dwelling-house for at least three years (even if not of the same dwelling) has a 'right to buy' either the freehold, if the property is a house, or a long-leasehold interest, if the property is a flat (Housing Act 1980, ss 1–4). The price at which he may buy is reduced by between 30 per cent and 60 per cent of the **market value** depending on the length of time for which the tenant has occupied the dwelling (or dwellings). This discount may be repayable, in whole or in part, if the property is resold within five years of the purchase. A person who is a secure tenant and has a 'right to buy' has a right to a mortgage from his landlord, or where the landlord is a housing association, from the Housing Corporation.

If the holder of a secure tenancy dies, his or her spouse, or otherwise a member of the family who at the death was occupying the house as his or her principal or only home and has lived in the house for 12 months prior to the tenant's death, may succeed to the tenancy.

Manual of Housing Law, by Andrew Arden, 2 edn., pp. 77–92.

Landlord and Tenant Law, by David Yates and A.J. Hawkins, pp. 404–426, 433–437 (1981).

Public Sector Housing Law, by David Hughes pp. 99–111 (1981).

The Law of Landlord and Tenant, by David Lloyd Evans, 2 edn., pp. 471–479.

Hill and Redman's Law of Landlord and Tenant 17 edn, pp. 2067–2101. Woodfall's Landlord and Tenant, 28 edn, paras. 3–0314 to 3–0320 and 3–0723 to 3–0745.

Residential Leases: A Draftsman's Handbook, by Charles Bennett, pp. 249–270 (1984).

Encyclopaedia of Housing Law and Practice, edited by Arden and Cross, paras. 2–2782 to 2–2822.

secured creditor

A creditor whose debt is secured by a charge, lien or mortgage on property, or any part thereof, owned by the debtor (Bankruptcy Act 1914, s. 167). cf. **unsecured creditor**. See also **recourse**, **secured loan**.

secured ground rent

A **ground rent** paid for land upon which a building or buildings have been erected. The ground rent is said to be 'secured' because, in the event of the ground rent not being paid, the landlord has the benefit of a right to the extra value provided by the additions to the land. If the buildings are let, the security of a ground rent may be measured by the ratio of the ground rent to the market rental value, or the contractual rent receivable for the property. Thus, if the market rent is £50000 and the ground rent £10000 the ground rent is five times secured – the higher the security the lower the risk of the ground rent not being paid and, therefore, the higher the capital value of the ground rent. The ratio may be termed also 'cover', i.e. in the above example the ground rent is five times covered.

cf. **unsecured ground rent**. See also **security of ground rent**.

secured loan

A loan against which property has been pledged or mortgaged as **security**. In the US, a document that evidences a personal loan secured by a **mortgage** on property normally is called a 'mortgage note' and the document that creates the mortgage as such a 'mortgage deed'. In English law, these documents are contained in one instrument: the mortgage.

security

1. Something given, deposited, or pledged as an assurance that an obligation will be met, or as a safeguard against a loss. Property (real or personal) or good faith, pledged, mortgaged or hypothecated to underwrite the repayment or recovery of a debt. In the event that the obligation is not met the holder (grantee) of the security resorts to the property for the amount of the debt. In general, in the

event of a sale of the security, the balance of the proceeds remaining after the debt has been repaid in full belongs to the grantor or debtor. A personal guaranty to answer for the debt or debts of another may be referred to as a 'personal security', as distinguished from a 'collateral security' which may be given in addition to the borrower's personal liability. Security may be classified also as 'active' or 'passive'. Active security means that the debtor has a right to sell the property to meet his claim. Passive security means that the debtor holds the property until the claim is met in full, as with a possessory lien or pawn. See also charge, debenture, deposit, lien, mortgage, pledge, warranty.

2. The expectation or degree of confidence that something will happen, e.g. of an income being received at a future date. A factor that may be considered to be inversely related to risk; thus, the greater certainty of something happening the lower the risk of it not happening. Security is an important factor when determining the value of a property.

3. "A debt or claim the payment of which is in some way secured." – Re. Douglas's Will Trusts, Lloyd's Bank v Nelson and Others [1959] 2 All ER 620. Written evidence, or an instrument, which shows that assets have been given as a guaranty or warranty for a debt; a written confirmation that the holder has a right to property or assets not in his possession. Such an instrument is negotiable and usually marketable.

4. A generic term for stocks, debentures, shares or funding certificates of a similar nature. "'Securities' include stocks, funds and shares" (Law of

Property Act 1925, s. 205 (1) (xxv); Settled Land Act 1925, s. 117 (1) (xxiii)). (Strictly shares are not a security, the shareholder being the owner of the assets.) A more extensive definition of securities is given in statutes that concern taxation, fraud, etc., e.g. the Income Tax Act 1952, s. 234 (5); the Finance Act 1968, s. 55 (1); the Prevention of Fraud (Investments) Act 1958, s. 26 (1); and, in the US, the Securities Act 1933 and 15 United States Code para. 77 (b) (1), 78 (c) (10), 79 (b) (16). See also bond, negotiable instrument, stock.

security capital
Capital that is secured by means of a pledge, lien or mortgage. See also debt capital, fixed charge, security.

security of tenure
The right of a tenant to retain possession of a property at the end of a contractual period of tenure; notwithstanding the expiration of a lease or the service of a notice to quit by the landlord. In particular, a statutory right of a tenant to the grant of a new or continuing tenancy, or to protection from eviction.

In many countries the law has intervened to alter the contractual rights of a landlord and tenant; especially to redress a supposed imbalance between the bargaining position of a landlord, who is considered capable of protecting his own interests, and a tenant, who is considered to be in need of shelter. In English law, the equitable relief given to a tenant against a landlord's strict right to forfeiture of a lease, for breach of covenant, may be considered a form of security of tenure. The most effective security given to a tenant is a prohibition against a landlord evicting a 'residential occupier' without recourse to a court of law (Protection from Eviction Act 1977, s. 1). Such an action is a criminal offence; as is the use or threat of violence for the purpose of securing entry into any premises when there is known to be someone opposed to the entry (Criminal Law Act 1977, s. 6).

English statute law contains extensive provisions for security of tenure; either by requiring a landlord to proceed to a court of law in order to secure possession of demised premises, or by enabling a tenant to request a new tenancy from his landlord and if this is opposed requiring the matter to be referred to the court. The form that the statutory security of tenure takes depends on the type of tenancy that exists. Thus, the **Landlord and Tenants Acts** provide that a holder of a **business tenancy** has a right to apply to court for a new tenancy; the Agricultural Holdings Acts provide that before an **agricultural tenancy** can be brought to an end the landlord must require the court to approve his reason for seeking possession; the Rent Acts and the Housing Acts provide differing forms of security for residential tenants depending on whether the occupation is classified as a **protected tenancy**; an **assured tenancy**; a **secure tenancy**; a **shorthold tenancy**; a **restricted contract**; or a **long tenancy**. In addition an occupier of an agricultural **tied accommodation** has security of tenure, if his employment is terminated, provided he or she qualifies as a 'protected occupier'. See also **extended lease, grounds for possession, leasehold enfranchisement, matrimonial home, statutory tenancy, tenure**.

see-through building
A building that is vacant; especially an office building with a glass facade and that has not been fitted out with internal partitioning. Colloquially, a building that is devoid of tenants.

seed money
see **front money**.

seigneurie (F)
manor. See also *manoir*.

seignory
The right or authority of a feudal lord; the land that comprises a **manor**.

seing (F)
signature.
(*acte sous seing privé* – **simple contract**; signed but not sealed or notarised; private agreement).

seisin or seizin
1. Derived from the Latin *saisire* or Old French *saisir*, 'to take **possession**; to seize or sit on land'. A word associated with feudal possession, in the sense of an enjoyment of land to the exclusion of others; as contrasted with a right to actual possession or **occupation**. In particular, seisin represented the right to a freehold in possession (Co. Litt. 266b), being the most absolute form of estate that a person could hold under the Crown; a right that is better than bare possession as held by a leaseholder or by an owner of personal property. Seisin as held by a freeholder is not lost by the grant of a lease, because the right to receive rents and profits is a form of possession. In a general sense, seisin represents ownership of land by an individual in the highest form recognised by English common law; a right to possess land and, with proof of

title, to exclude others. "Seisin is a root of title, and it may be said without undue exaggeration that so far as land is concerned there is in England no law of ownership, but only a law of possession."(Cheshire's Modern Law of Property 13edn, p. 27).

There is said to be **unity of seisin** or **unity of possession** when an owner of land that is burdened by an easement or restrictive covenant acquires the land benefitting from the easement or restrictive covenant and thereby extinguishes that encumberance (or vice versa), i.e. when the dominant tenement and servient tenement come into common control.

In the US, a general **warranty deed** is said to contain a 'covenant of seisin' by which the grantor is deemed to own and to convey the estate or interest that he or she undertakes to convey. See also **disseisin**, **livery of seisin**. *History of English Law*, by Pollock and Maitland, 2 edn., vol. 2 pp. 29–80.

2. The act by which a new freeholder was invested with a right to land subject to the right of fealty to a lord or the sovereign.

seizure

1. The act of taking **possession**, especially by legal authority or warrant. The act of taking hold or capturing property by force. The forceable taking of possession, in particular by a civil authority or an individual. Taking possession of goods as punishment for a hostile or wrongful act.

2. Under the **feudal system** of land tenure, the retaking of possession of **copyhold** land by a lord as a result of a default by the tenant.

3. The state of having **seisin**, i.e. possession as a feudal right.

self-amortising mortgage
see **amortisation mortgage**.

self-build housing association (or society)
A form of **housing association** in which the members join together in a co-operative to acquire land and build houses for purchase or occupation by its members. The labour is provided chiefly by the members of the association, rather than any firm of building contractors. "A housing association whose object is to provide, for sale to, or occupation by, its members, dwellings built or improved principally with the use of its members' own labour" (Housing Act 1974, s. 12).

self-financing development
A development that is financed before completion by the proceeds from its sale or by the income generated over a short period of time, so that it does not require permanent or long-term financing. For example, an apartment building where individual apartments are sold before or during construction to provide funds for the cost of the building work. Similarly an investment that generates funds to pay for itself in a short period of time is called a 'self-liquidating investment'.

self help
Action taken by an individual to redress a wrong committed against that person; such as an action taken to prevent an irritation, **nuisance, trespass** or similar inconvenience, or to recover goods that have been wrongfully taken or withheld, without recourse to a court of law. See also **abatement, distress, eviction, recaption, squatting**.

self-insurance
Insurance, in part or in whole, pro-

vided by the insured himself. The insured may set up a special fund or accept, in whole or in part, the risk of financial loss. See also **average, co-insurance**.

self-liquidating investment
see **self-financing development**.

self-liquidating loan
see **amortisation loan**.

sell
To transfer property to another for money or valuable consideration – Paine *v* Cork Co. (1900) 69 LJ Ch. 158. To dispose of property by **sale**. An authority given to an agent to sell a property, in the absence of anything narrowing the meaning of the word 'sell', means "not only to negotiate for but to sign an **agreement for sale**" – Rosenbaum *v* Belson [1900] 2 Ch. 271.

seller
One who offers goods or property for **sale**. In particular, a person who performs the physical act of transferring property for money or valuable consideration. For the purpose of a sale of goods a seller may be defined as a person who sells goods, as well as a person who "agrees to sell goods" (Sale of Goods Act 1979, s. 61 (1)). Also any person who sells goods on behalf of another may be referred to as a seller; thus a seller has been said to be "the person carrying on the business" (of selling) – Edwards *v* Pharmaceutical Society of Great Britain 2 KB 77d. The term 'seller' is used generally in the context of a sale of goods, and **vendor** when there is a sale of land.

seller financing (US)
see **instalment contract**.

seller's lien
see **lien, purchase-money, mortgage**.

seller's option
see **purchase option**.

selling short
see **bear**.

semestriel (F)
half-yearly; six-monthly.

semi-annual
see **biannual**.

semi-detached house
One of a pair of dwelling-houses linked together by one common or **party wall**. In the US, called also a 'double house', or sometimes **duplex house** – Stephenson *v* Perlitz (Tex. 1976) 537 S.W. 2d 287).

senior mortgage
A mortgage, especially a **first mortgage**, that has priority over one or more other mortgages.
cf. **junior mortgage**.

sensitivity analysis
A method of evaluating risk by which an analysis is made of the effect of changes in one of a number of variables on the overall profitability of a proposed investment or development project, i.e. an analysis of the sensitivity of profit to changes in any one factor that might affect that profit. For example, each of the variables in a development project (rent, or land and construction costs, or finance costs, or the letting period, or sale price) is assumed, in turn, to change by a given percentage; the percentage change in the total profit of the project then is calculated in order to establish which variable has the greatest impact on the overall profitability. Alternatively, an **internal rate of**

return for a project may be calculated after adjusting each of the variables in turn. This sensitivity analysis may be used also to assess changes in each variable given differing fixed sums for each of the other factors; or to show the interdependence of any one variable on any other, given a fixed amount for the remaining functions – for example, to show the effect of different rent levels upon the letting periods, or the effect of different selling prices on the internal rate of return for the project. Sensitivity analysis aims to identify the critical variable but it does not take account of the probability of a change in any one of the variables.

Property Development, by David Cadman and Leslie Austin-Crowe, 2 edn., pp. 48–51.

Valuation and Development Appraisal, by Clive Darlow, pp. 89–103 (1982).

The Evaluation of Risk in Business Investment, by J.C. Hull (1980).

Risk, Uncertainty and Decision-Making in Property Development, by Peter Byrne and David Cadman, (1984).

separate property (or estate)
1. An estate or interest in property the ownership of which is enjoyed by a person in his or her own right, without any right or part thereof being shared with others.
cf. **common property**. See also **several ownership**.
(US) 2. In a state where a married couple may hold some of their property as **community property**, separate property is that which is owned by either the husband or the wife in an own right rather than jointly. It might be property owned before a marriage

or property acquired, by inheritance, will or as a gift, during marriage. See also ***acquêts***.
3. A separately owned area or unit in a **condominium**.

sequestration
1. A legal process by which a person is temporarily deprived of possession, or of his right to property, until he has performed an action required by a court of law, e.g. the repayment of a debt. In the case of real property the right to rents and profits may be sequestered by a court of law or other competent authority, such as a sheriff or commissioner, until a debt is paid.
2. In Scottish law, the act of taking control of the property of a bankrupt in order to arrange for its disposal for the benefit of the creditors.
3. In international law, the **seizure** of private property for use by the state.

sequestration (F)
sequestration; illegal detention.

sergeanty
A form of feudal **tenure** by which the tenant was obliged to perform some service for the Sovereign, such as carrying a banner or leading an army. This form of tenure was personal to the Sovereign and was granted only to a **tenant in chief** (Litt. 153, 161). Called also 'grand sergeanty' as distinguished from **knight service** which could be held from a mesne or intermediary lord.

service
1. The act of bringing something to a person's attention, especially in a fashion prescribed by law, whether actively or constructively. The act of formally delivering a **notice, writ**, summons, or any other form of document relating to court proceedings.

Service may be 'personal' i.e. showing the original or leaving a copy with someone; or 'substituted' i.e. brought to a person's knowledge by advertising, sending, leaving, or affixing a notice to a person's place (or last known place) of residence. If notice is to be 'given' or 'received' it may be submitted either in writing or orally, but if it is to be 'left' or 'served' then, as a rule, it should be in writing.

The Law of Property Act 1925, s. 196 requires that any notice under that Act (except a notice served in proceedings in the court) should be in **writing** and any notice required or authorised by that Act to be served shall be sufficiently served "if it is left at the last-known place of abode or business in the United Kingdom of the lessee, lessor, mortgagee, mortgagor or person to be served ..." or in the case of a lessee or mortgagor "is affixed or left for him on the land or any house or building comprised in the lease or mortgage ..." and "shall also be sufficiently served if it is sent by post in a registered letter" or in a similar manner, provided it "is not returned through the post-office undelivered". The notice is deemed to be made when it would normally be delivered. The Landlord and Tenant Act 1927, s. 23 (1) and the Law of Property Act 1954, s. 66 (4) state that a notice under either of those Acts shall be in writing and may be served "either personally, or by leaving it for him (the person on whom the notice is to be served) at his last known place of abode in England or Wales, or by sending it through the post in a registered letter addressed to him there". In the case of a public authority or company, notice is served on the secretary or other principal officer at the principal or registered office of that body. In the case of a landlord service on an authorised **agent** may constitute proper service on the landlord. If the notice can be shown to have been given and actually received that constitutes good service – Stylo Shoes Ltd v Prices Tailors Ltd [1960] 2 WLR 8.

"Where any Act authorises or requires any document to be served by post (whether the expression 'serve' or the expression 'give' or 'send' or any other expression is used) then, unless the contrary intention appears, the service is deemed to be effected by properly addressing, pre-paying and posting a letter containing the document and, unless the contrary is proved, to have been effected at the time at which the letter would be delivered in the ordinary course of post" (Interpretation Act 1978, s. 7; this provision does not apply to court proceedings). In certain instances notice may be served adequately if left at the last place of abode or business or affixed to a property. However, the safest method of ensuring proper service of a notice is to send it by registered post (or recorded or personal delivery) and to request an acknowledgement of receipt. A notice placed in a letter box may not necessarily be served adequately – Kaene v Jackson (1981) SLT (Sch. Ct.) 32; and sending a letter to the wrong address will definitely not be served adequately – White v Weston [1968] 2 WLR 1459. See also **debt service, reputed owner**. 2. The rendering of something, in money or in kind, to a lord in return for a feudal right of **tenure** (Bl. Comm. vol. ii p. 60). See also **rent-service, services**. 3. In the civil law, a **servitude**.

service (F)
1. service.
(*service d'un emprunt* – **debt service**)
(*services fonciers* – service charge or operating expense on real estate).
2. administrative authority.
(*services publics* – public utilities).

service business (or trade)

A business (or trade) that provides a service to the general public. An establishment that is involved primarily in selling services, especially one located in retail premises rather than an office e.g. a bank, estate agent, insurance broker, travel agent, building society, betting office, café. See also **service industry**.

service charge

A periodic charge made, or incurred, for the cost or expense of running a building, especially a cost or expense that benefits more than one party (whether a tenant or owner-occupier) in a multi-occupied building. In particular, such costs as are regularly recharged by a landlord to a tenant in accordance with the terms of a lease and which vary from time to time according to the actual expenditure incurred on running the building – but not **rent** payable for the demised premises *per se*. A service charge may include expenditure on repair, maintenance, cleaning and refuse collection, lighting, heating or air-conditioning, staff costs, property management expenses or fees, contributions to a sinking fund for replacement of plant and machinery, including those charges incurred in the upkeep of the common areas of a property. (Insurance premiums may be included in a lease as part of the 'service charge' for a building, but if not so expressed insurance is not included automatic-

ally as a cost of servicing the building – Property Holding and Investment Trust *v* Lewis (1969) 20 P and CR 808). The total cost borne by the landlord is certified usually by the property manager (or sometimes an independent auditor) and recovered as additional rent, on a proportional basis, as provided for in the leases. A service charge, if not paid when due, does not form part of the **rent** under a lease, unless expressly reserved as such, and, therefore, may not be recovered by an action for **distress**.

The Housing Act 1980, s. 136, Sch. 19 entitles a tenant of a private flat to receive a properly audited statement of the service charges to be made by the landlord and permits the tenant to insist on the landlord only charging for the "reasonable" cost of such services. For the purpose of this Act a service charge is "an amount payable by the tenant of a flat as part of or in addition to the rent – (a) which is payable, directly or indirectly, for services, repairs, maintenance or insurance or the landlord's costs of management"; and which varies, in whole or in part, according to the sum expended or estimated to be expended by the landlord, including his overheads (1980 Act, Sch. 19, s. 1 (1)). In addition, the tenant may insist that the landlord obtains at least two estimates for repairs and services for which the tenant is expected to bear the cost. This provision does not apply to a local authority, a new town development corporation, The Commission for the New Towns and the Development Board for Rural Wales. No such statutory right is given to a tenant of any other type of property and in such cases the liability for the payment of service charges is entirely dependent on the provisions contained in the lease. Called also 'tenant's contributions' or in the US, **operating expenses** (although generally in the US, there is no presumption as to recovery). See also **advance service charge, apportionment**.

The Law of Landlord and Tenant, by David Lloyd Evans, 2 edn., pp. 342–345.

Woodfall's Landlord and Tenant, 28 edn, paras. 1-1325 to 1-1326.

Drafting Business Leases, by Kim Lewison, pp. 84–97 (1980).

Residential Leases: A Draftsman's Handbook, by Charles Bennett, pp. 81–91 (1984).

Housing Law, by Andrew Arden and Martin Partington, pp. 371–376 (1983).

Service Charges in Flats, by Brian J. Harding, 247 EG 707–713, 799–805 (1978).

The Law of Flats, by Trevor M. Aldridge, pp. 18–31 (1981).

Service Charges in Property, by T. McGee, (1984).

service core

A part of an office building, frequently in the centre or on one side of the carcass of the building, in which the principal mechanical services are grouped together, e.g. lifts, service or utility ducts, etc. The 'service core' of a building may include also the area containing common toilets, staircases and landings around the main core. See also **common areas**.

service flat (or apartment)

A flat or apartment let at a rent that includes a payment for services such as internal cleaning, linen, cooking facilities, etc., but not for **board** (although prepared meals may be provided on request).

cf. **boarding house, hotel**. See also **restricted contract, service tenancy**.

service industry

An organisation or enterprise involved in work, or in carrying on an operation, that is aimed primarily at providing a service to the public or for the benefit of another. In particular, a business that receives goods for the purposes of repair, treatment or maintenance; or a business that carries on a similar activity by visiting the owners of such goods. For example, motor vehicle repairing, laundry, dry cleaning, photographic processing, fuel delivery, window cleaning, repairing and servicing of domestic appliances, hiring of goods. Such an enterprise can operate from a location that acts as a receiving house for the goods to be serviced, etc., or a location that acts as a base for those providing the service. See also **service business, industrial building**.

service licence

see **service tenancy**.

service life

see **economic life**.

service occupancy

see **service tenancy**.

service property (US)

A property that is used for the operational purpose of a business, trade or occupation and has little use for any other purpose e.g. a clubhouse, restaurant, school. See also **service flat, special suitability**.

service station (or facility)

Premises used predominately for the repair and servicing of motor vehicles; although a part of the premises may be set aside for the sale of vehicles or component parts. A term that may be used also to refer to a petrol-filling or gasoline station.

service tenancy

A **tenancy** granted to a person who is an employee of his or her landlord, usually to enable that person to perform better his employment; or a tenancy of a **service flat (or apartment)**. The term 'service tenancy' is used frequently to refer to a form of occupation that is not a tenancy at all, but merely a licence granted to an employee – commonly called a 'service occupancy'. In this context the expression service tenancy is ambiguous and should be avoided – "sometimes 'service tenancy' is used as a synonym for a licence in contrast to a tenancy; elsewhere it is the phrase used to describe a tenancy (or licence) under which services are provided by the landlord to the tenant or occupier, as in the phrase 'service apartments'. Alternatively, the expression is used to describe those tenancies to which the provisions of the Rent Act 1977, s. 98 (1) (b), Sch. 15, Case 8 apply in contrast to those tenancies where the fact that the landlord is or was the tenant's employer is merely coincidental to the existence of the tenancy. The phrase 'service occupancy' is clothed with almost as much ambiguity as it is so often used in contrast to 'service tenancy'. There would appear to be no need for the use of expressions other than 'licensee' or 'tenant' in this context, and the use of those two terms only may help to avoid confusion" (27 Halsbury's Laws of England, 4 edn, pp. 12, 13). The Rent Act 1977, s. 98 (1) (b), Sch. 15, Case 8 refers to one of the discretionary grounds upon which a court may grant an order authorising a landlord a right to regain possession of premises let on a **protected tenancy** namely that the premises are required reasonably for occupation by a new employee in place of a former employee who has occupation of the premises. See also **occupation lease, restricted contract, tied accommodation**.

Landlord and Tenant, by Martin Partington, 2 edn., pp. 458–462.

service tenant

A person who is granted a **service tenancy**.

service trade

see **service business**.

serviced flat

see **service flat**.

serviced office

An **office** where the occupier is provided with services over and above those available to normal office tenants, such as the use of telex facilities and secretarial facilities. Such premises are usually let on short term tenancies or licences. See also **licence**.

services

1. Provisions made by a landlord or management company for the benefit of the occupier of a building; such as maintenance of common parts, heating, electricity, water, window cleaning, porterage, etc. See also **board, service charge**.

2. Piped or ducted facilities provided to a building, e.g. water, electricity, gas, telephones, drainage. Services may be classified as 'private' when situated within a site boundary and 'public' when situated off-site. Called also **utilities**, especially when provided by a public undertaking.

servient tenement (or estate)
Land that is burdened with an encumberance, such as an **easement** or restrictive covenant created for the benefit of another parcel of land.
cf. **dominant tenement**. See also **right of way, tenement.**

servitude
Any liberty, privilege, right or advantage annexed to, and adversly affecting, land; in particular, a right *in rem*, annexed to a piece of land, which entitles the owner of that land to do something or prevent the doing of something on another's land. A term that is not strictly one of English law, but is used to refer to any burden over land, including an **easement, profit à prendre** or **restrictive covenant**.
cf. **positive easement**. See also **encumberance,** *servitude.*

servitude (F)
easement; servitude; encumberance; charge (on real estate). "A *servitude* is closely analogous in character to an easement: it is a right *in rem* , attaching to one immoveable, the dominant tenement, and imposing a burden upon another, the servient tenement" (Amos and Walton's Introduction to French Law, 3 edn, p. 119). It is defined in the French Civil Code, art. 637 as, "a charge imposed on a tenement [a parcel of land] for the use and utility of a tenement belonging to another". Thus, a servitude possesses the same characteristics as an easement in English law and it may, similarly, be positive (authorising one party to use another's land for the benefit of land held) or negative (restricting the use of land for the benefit of land held). However, in French law it is a perpetual right that 'runs with the land' (i.e. the burden and the

benefit are enforceable against subsequent landowners of either the dominant or servient tenement) and, therefore, the complexity which English law has created in deciding on the enforceability of an easement (or a restrictive covenant) on the assignment of either the dominant or servient tenement is unknown in French law. Further, French law makes no distinction between an easement and a **profit à prendre** (the latter privilege, i.e. one that has no dominant tenement, in French law is likely to take the form of **usufruct** or a **lease** – the term profit à prendre, although apparently of French origin, is not found in French law). A *servitude* may be imposed also on land by a public authority in the interest of the general public (a *servitude d'utilité publique*), although such restrictions on the use of land do not necessarily benefit another area of land (*Code de l'Urbanisme, art. L. 160*).
(*servitude d'appui* – right of support from an adjoining building or for an electricity wayleave stay)
(*servitude de passage* – **right of way**)
(*servitude de reculement* – see *reculement*)
(*servitude d'urbanisme* – planning servitude, i.e. a restrictive covenant imposed by a planning authority. See also *non altius tollendi*)
(*servitude de visibilité* – vision splay)
(*jour de servitude* – right of light , see also *vue et jour*). See also *zone non aedificandi.*
Manuel de Droit Civil, by Pierre Voirin et Gilles Goubeaux, 20 edn., pp. 301–310.
Droit Civil – Les Biens, by Jean Carbonnier, 11 edn., p. 221 *et seq.*
Précis Dalloz. Droit Civil, Les Biens (Alex Weill), 2 edn, pp. 131–141,

528–576.

Droit Civil, by Gabriel Marty and Pierre Raynaud, vol. ii, pp. 155–191, (1965).

set

An old word for 'let' or **lease**.

set-back

1. The space, usually required by planning or highway regulations, between the **boundary line** and a **building line** that affects a property, i.e. an area that must be left free of all buildings. A requirement or **ordinance** to 'set-back' buildings may be prescribed in order to keep new buildings a set distance from a highway, or to maintain a uniform frontage.

2. The placing of an upper storey of a building further back, in the horizontal plan, from the floor below. Planning regulations commonly require the upper storeys of a high-rise building to be set back a distance that is equal to, or exceeds, the height between storeys in order to improve the appearance of the building from ground level and to provide adequate light to the lower levels of adjoining buildings.

set-back ordinance (US)

see **set-back**.

set-off

1. An act by which one party to a contract sets all or part of the cost of performing his obligations under the contract against the cost of an obligation or duty owed to him by the other party to the contract, either as a result of the same or a closely related contract. In particular, the discharge or reduction (in whole or in part) of a monetary sum owed by a debtor by an amount due from his creditor. In effect the one party acknowledges the justice of the demands of the other party, but sets up a demand of his own to counterbalance or discharge the other's demand, in whole or in part (Bl. Comm. vol. iii p. 304). Set-off may be applied only as a result of a direct relationship between two parties and not by the involvement of a third party who happens to have a debt with both parties. As a rule a tenant may not refuse to pay rent on the premise that he is setting this off against repairs that have not been carried out by his landlord. However, if a tenant has given prior and proper notice and then discharged a landlord's repairing obligation – especially when this results from a defect in a new building or an obligation the landlord cannot deny, so that a tenant has not received what he contracted for – "the tenant may be entitled to set off the cost he incurs against rent due" – British Anzani (Felixstowe) Ltd *v* [1979] 2 All ER 1063; Lee-Parker *v* Izzet [1971] 1 WLR 1688.

Set-off, although distinguishable in practice from a reduction in the consideration payable under a contract due to a failure of **performance**, may be considered akin to the latter; the financial effect being similar.

Landlord and Tenant Law, by David Yates and A.J. Hawkins, pp. 186–188 (1981).

Hill and Redman's Law of Landlord and Tenant, 17 edn, pp. 337–340.

Woodfall's Landlord and Tenant, 28 edn, para. 1-0755.

42 Halsbury's Laws of England, 4 edn, paras. 401–513.

Law of Set-Off, by R. Calnan (1986).

2. A reduction in the compensation payable for land acquired by an authority possessing compulsory purchase powers because of an increase

in the value of adjoining land retained in the same ownership, as a result of the actual, or the prospect of, development by the acquiring authority; for example, as a result of the authority providing access to a new highway. Where a person owns other land that is "contiguous or adjacent" to land being acquired "there shall be deducted from the amount of the compensation ... the amount (if any) of such an increase in the value of the interest in that other land" as is attributable to the intended development by the acquiring authority (Land Compensation Act 1961, s. 7). This provision is qualified by a number of conditions set out in Part I of the First Schedule of the 1961 Act as amended by the New Towns Act 1966, s. 2. A similar provision is contained in the Highways Act 1980, s. 261, and most other statutes by which powers of compulsory purchase are granted. Set-off may be applied also when compensation for injurious affection is paid if the value of the affected land, or other adjacent or contiguous land, is increased by the activity of the authority paying the compensation (Land Compensation Act 1973, s. 6). If the amount by which the land is increased in value exceeds the amount of compensation no compensation is paid, but the acquiring authority cannot recover any betterment that has accrued to the owner of the land. cf. **recoupment**. See also **betterment, compulsory purchase compensation**. *Law of Compulsory Purchase and Compensation*, by Keith Davies, 4 edn., pp. 146–148. *Encyclopaedia of Compulsory Purchase and Compensation*, by Harold J.J. Brown, para. 1–105.

settled estate
An estate in land which passes in accordance with the provisions of a **settlement**. "The meaning of a 'settled' estate, whether in legal or popular language, as contradistinguished from an estate in fee-simple, is understood to be one in which the power of alienation, of devising, and of transmission according to the rules of descent, are restrained by the limitation of the settlement" – Micklethwait *v* Micklethwait (1858) 4 CBNS 858. See also **settled land**.

settled land
Land conveyed to several persons in succession. Land, or any estate or interest in land, that is the subject of a **settlement** (Settled Land Act 1925, s. 2). Settled land may be held (a) in trust for any person by way of **succession**; (b) as an **entailed interest**; (c) as a **determinable interest**; (d) as a **conditional interest**; (e) on behalf of a minor until he or she attains majority; or (f) as part of a marriage or family settlement. Each party entitled to land under the settlement may use the land only on condition that he does not limit the other parties' future rights of enjoyment. As a rule, a purchaser of a **legal estate** in settled land does not need to concern himself with the terms of the settlement provided he deals with the **tenant for life** (or the **statutory owner**) acts in **good faith**, and the document that transferred the land to tenant for life (or the statutory owner) – the "principal vesting instrument" – is seen to contain the requisite statutory information (Settled Land Act 1925, s. 110). See also **settled estate, strict settlement, trust instrument, vesting document, waste**. Megarry's Manual of the Law of Real

Property, 6 edn, p. 238 *et seq.*
The Law of Real Property, by Robert
Megarry and H.W.R. Wade, 5 edn, p.
317 *et seq.*
Land Law: Cases and Materials, by
R.H. Maudsley and E.H. Burn, 4
edn., p. 250 *et seq.*

settlement
1. Any **disposition** of real or personal
property, made by deed, by will (or, in
rare cases, by statute) with the intention that the property is to be enjoyed
by a number of persons or classes of
persons in succession. Any instrument by which property is limited to
several persons in succession may be
called a 'settlement', especially when
it is intended that no one person can
deprive the others of their future
rights of enjoyment as stated in the
instrument (Settled Land Act 1925, s.
1, 117 (xxiv). The creator of the settlement, the 'settlor', places the property in **trust** and designates the beneficiaries and the terms on which they
may take the property.

In English law a settlement made
with the intention that the land itself
should pass to the successors is called
a **strict settlement**; but if the land is
intended to pass only as a form of
investment and could just as well be
converted into money, immediately
or at a future date, a **trust for sale** is
created. When the word settlement is
used alone it is taken, by common
usage, to mean a 'strict settlement',
unless the context implies reference
to, or creation of, a trust for sale.

For the purposes of **capital transfer
tax**, 'settlement' is widely defined so
as to include any disposition, however
made, which results in a trust or annuity being charged on property; including a lease for life (unless it is granted at

a full consideration) (Finance Act
1975, Sch. 5, s. 1; Capital Transfer Tax
Act 1984, s. 43 (2)). See also **doctrine
of estates, settled land, trust.**
*Law for Land Management Stu-
dents*, by Richard Card, John Murdoch and Peter Schofield, pp. 512–
524, (1981).
Cheshire's Modern Law of Property,
13 edn, p. 165 *et seq.*
Settlements of Land, by B.W. Harvey, (1973).
42 Halsbury's Laws of England, 4
edn, paras. 601–1100.
2. The act or process of resolving a
dispute between parties, especially a
civil dispute, without recourse to a
determination by a court of law. An
agreement by which parties to a dispute ascertain what is due from one to
the other.
3. **Determination** of a contract by
agreement; in particular, the payment
of a debt or account in full. The fulfilment of an obligation to another by
means of monetary recompense. See
also **accord and satisfaction.**
4. The payment of the balance due
on the transfer of real property or an
interest in property in accordance
with the **completion statement.** See
also **closing.**
5. A formal **grant** or **conveyance** of
property or something that is granted
or bestowed on another.

settler
see **squatting.**

settlor
1. One who creates a **settlement**,
either by will or by a disposition of
property, during his or her lifetime.
See also testator.
2. One who creates a **voluntary trust.**

several
Relating to one individual; having a

separate existence. 'Several' is opposed usually to 'joint' or '**common**'. See also **joint and several liability, several ownership**.

several pasture
see **sole common of pasture**.

several ownership
Ownership held by a person as a sole right; an estate or interest in land owned separately, i.e. entirely by one party without any other party joined therein. "He that holds lands or tenements in severalty, or is **sole tenant** thereof, is he that holds them in his own right only, without any person being joined or connected with him in point of interest during his estate therein" (Bl. Comm. vol. ii p. 179). A several interest may be an absolute right or a successive right to land. It may be distinguished from a **concurrent interest**; the ownership of **common land**; and any form of **co-ownership** where an interest in land is shared at the same time. Called also an 'estate in severalty', a 'several tenancy', a 'tenancy-in-severalty', an 'entire tenancy' or in the US 'individual ownership' or 'sole ownership' (the word tenancy is used here to indicate a right of '**tenure**' or ownership and not a right to hold land for a limited duration from a landlord).
cf. **joint tenancy, tenancy-in-common**.

several tenancy
see **several ownership**.

severalty
see **several ownership**.

severance
1. Division into part. For example, the division of an area of land held in one ownership into areas of separate ownership, especially when part of the land is retained by the original owner. See also **partition, severance of a reversion**.
2. Acquisition of part of an area of land, or part of a building, so as to separate it from other land, or another part of a building, with which it was held; especially when the acquisition is made by an authority possessing compulsory purchase powers. In particular when the land compulsorily acquired contributed to the value of the land retained and the severance thereby results in a reduction in the value of the retained land.

When land (or a building) is acquired compulsorily an owner of a "house, building or manufactory" shall not be compelled to sell part only of that property if the severance resulting therefrom causes "**material detriment**" to the remainder; nor shall the owner of a "park or garden belonging to a house" be compelled to sell a part thereof if the severance seriously affects "the amenity or convenience of the house." (Compulsory Purchase Order 1965, s. 8 (1)). – 'Material detriment' in this context means that the remaining part must be "less useful or less valuable in some significant degree" – Ravenseft Properties Ltd v Hillingdon LBC (1968) 20 P and CR 493. Similarly, if only a small area of land (less than half an acre), situated outside a town or not built up on, is to be left after a proposed compulsory acquisition, or part of a farm is left so that it cannot be farmed effectively, the owner of the residual area of land may serve a 'notice of objection to severance' requiring the authority to purchase his interest in the whole area (Compulsory Purchase Act 1965, s. 8 (2), (3); Land Compensation Act 1973, ss

53–57). Any dispute on such matters of severance is determined by the **Lands Tribunal**. See also **compensation for severance, injurious affection**. *An Outline of the Law of Compulsory Purchase and Compensation*, by Barry Denyer-Green, 2 edn. 8 Halsbury's Laws of England, 4 edn, paras. 318–321.

3. The conversion of an equitable **joint tenancy** into a **tenancy-in-common** by severing the interest of one of the joint tenants i.e. the destruction of the 'unity of interest' that is essential to a joint tenancy. The use of '**words of severance**' in a deed of grant, e.g. "in equal shares", "equally", "to be divided between", "amongst", which indicate that each tenant is to take a distinct share in a property, are sufficient to show that there is no unity of interest and that a tenancy-in-common is to be created. Severance may arise (a) if one of the joint tenants transfers his interest during his life time to another party (who because he did not acquire his interest at the same time, or as part of the same title deeds, becomes a tenant-in-common); (b) by agreement between the joint tenants; or (c) when it is clear from the nature of the dealings of one of the joint tenants that the intention is to destroy the essential 'unity' of a joint tenancy, e.g. bankrupcy of one of the parties. See also **partition**.

4. "The rejection from a contract of objectionable promises or the objectionable elements of a particular promise, and the retention of those promises or those parts of a particular promise that are valid." (Cheshire & Fifoot's Law of Contract 10 edn, p. 373). Severance of a contract may arise when the contract is void because it is contrary to statute law, but the court considers that a part of the contract nonetheless should be performed as envisaged by the parties.

5. The act of removing something attached to land; in particular, the removal of a **fixture** from land.

severance compensation

see **compensation for severance**.

severance damages (US)

Compensation paid for the loss or reduction in the value of a parcel of land resulting from the **partial taking** of land from an owner by the exercise of the power of eminent domain. Severance damages may arise from the taking and the resultant severance, or from the works carried out on the land taken by the expropriating authority. The compensation is based on the difference between the value of the land retained by the owner as assessed before and after the taking. See also **before and after valuation**, **compensation for severance**.

severance of a reversion

A transfer of part of a **reversionary interest** to another party, as when a landlord sells part of the land that is the subject of a lease to another. When such a severance has taken place every condition of the tenancy is apportioned and becomes annexed to the severed part (including the right to determine the lease by notice to quit or otherwise), so that every landlord may enforce those conditions that relate to the severed part (Law of Property Act 1925, s. 140). However, the tenancy continues as one agreement i.e. there are not a number of separate tenancies brought into existence.

severance tax (US)

A tax charged on the value of an extracted natural resource e.g. on timber, coal, oil or minerals.

sewer

A conduit, usually underground, constructed for the discharge of storm water, waste water, waste matter, effluent or similar noxious matter. A sewer is intended to serve more than one building or yards appurtenant to buildings, unlike a **drain** (Public Health Act 1936, s. 343 (1)). It may take waste or effluent to a sewerage treatment plant, or it may be a conduit for water from land, generally on a large scale, to a river or to the sea – Sutton *v* Norwich Corporation (1858) 27 LJ Ch. 742.

A 'public sewer' is a sewer constructed or adopted by a local authority for the drainage of a number of properties (1936 Act, s. 20).

Development and Planning Law, by Barry Denyer-Green, pp. 213–218 (1982).

38 Halsbury's Laws of England, 4 edn, paras. 339–398.

Law of Sewers and Drains, by J.F. Garner, 6 edn.

Pipes, Mains Cables and Sewers, by H. Wilkinson, 4 edn.

shack land

1. An area of arable land that is owned solely or severally but is thrown open for use as **common land** by the individual owners when the crop has been collected. 'Common of shack' existed also "over those parts of the **manor** which according to the course of cultivation there pursued were for the time being laying fallow. During these periods the cattle of the village pastured promiscuously over open fields" (Holdsworth's History of

English Law, 3 edn, vol. iii p. 144). cf. **lammas land**. See also **right of common**.

2. Land that is let for pigs or chickens to feed on after the harvest.

share

1. A partial use or enjoyment of something in conjunction with another. Any one of the parts into which a property, or invested capital, is divided.

2. A joint right to a part of the **equity capital** of a corporation; the monetary interest of a shareholder in a limited company or partnership. When used in a will 'shares' include '**stock**' in a company – Morrice *v* Aylmer (1875) LR 7 HL 717). A deposit of a company's shares, together with an expression of intent to charge those shares, creates an **equitable mortgage** over the shares.

share capital

The amount of shares issued, or authorised to be issued, by a company. See also **capital, equity capital, stock**.

share lease (US)

see **sharecropping lease, percentage lease**.

share rent

A rent calculated to provide the landlord with a share of the benefit received by the tenant from his use of the leased land. See also **metayage system, percentage rent, royalty, sharecropping lease, slice**.

share tenant

see **sharecropping lease**.

sharecropping lease (US)

A form of lease granted to a tenant farmer, especially in Middle Western and Southern states, by which the landowner provides machinery, seeds and stock and the tenant (called a 'share-tenant' or 'cropper') undertakes to provide a percentage of the crop, or proceeds from the sale of livestock, as a form of rent. This form of arrangement derives from the **metayage system** which originated in Europe.

shared-appreciation mortgage (SAM) (US)

see **equity-participation mortgage**.

shared-ownership lease

A form of co-ownership whereby two parties acquire shares in a property, as joint owners or 'tenants-in-common', where one party grants a lease of his share to the other. The lessee generally has an option to acquire the remainder of the property from the other owner in the future at market value. An arrangement usually entered into between an investor or mortgagee and a home owner; the arrangement reduces the home owner's initial capital outlay, but enables him or her to have occupation of the entire property and an opportunity to acquire the entire property at a later stage. In the UK the landlord/mortgagee usually is a housing association or a local authority. See also **equity-participation mortgage**.
The Law of Flats, by Trevor Aldridge, pp. 89–96 (1982).
Shared Ownership – A Stepping Stone to Home Ownership, by P. Allen (1982).

shell property

An unfinished or 'shell' unit in a new development, especially in a shopping centre; a building or similar structure in which a tenant, or other intending occupier, is responsible for the installation of all fixtures and fittings, including any interior partitioning, plumbing, heating and electrical works, and decoration. See also **fixture**.

shelter, tax

see **tax shelter**.

shifting clause

A clause in a deed of **settlement** which provides that, in certain stipulated circumstances, the settled property will devolve in a different way to that primarily prescribed; for example, "to A for life unless B becomes a Chartered Surveyor". See also **conditional interest, defeasance**.

shifting interest (or use)

An interest in land that may be transferred from one **beneficiary** of a settlement to another in the event that a stipulated contingent event arises (such an interest was referred to also as a 'shifting use', because the beneficial right to enjoy land was at one time referred to as a **use**).

shop

Premises to which members of the public or some section of the public are invited and do resort, for the purpose of buying goods for their ultimate consumption; a place, comprising a building or part of a building, normally of a permanent character, used for any trade or business of a **retail** nature. A place or centre of activity for the reception, storage and distribution of goods, merchandise or even ideas; an establishment to which people resort for the purpose of exchange. (The term retail is derived from the French *retailler*, 'to cut off' divide into small pieces, hence a shop is a place where goods are sold predominately in small quantities.

"'Shop' includes any premises where any retail trade or business is carried on" (Shops Act 1950, s. 74) In this definition, which relates to health and safety at work, 'retail trade or business' may include a service trade or business, provided the activity is similar to that carried on in a retail shop – M. and F. Framley Ltd. *v* Ve-Ri-Best Manufacturing Co. Ltd [1953] 1 All ER 51.

"'Shop' means a building or structure permanent in its location from which the occupier can at will exclude persons and in which such occupier stores, displays, offers for sale and sells over the counter his goods to persons seeking to purchase such goods by way of comparison with a **warehouse** in which goods are sold in bulk at wholesale prices to persons requiring the same for resale to consumers in small quantities at retail prices" – Plummer and Adams *v* Needham (1954) 56 WALR 1. Premises used for the storage of goods intended for retail sale, as well as for the repair and service of such goods, may be included within a broad definition of a shop (e.g. Offices, Shops and Railway Premises Act 1963, s. 1, which deals with health and safety at work); but premises found in a shopping area or **shopping centre** which are not used for the retailing of goods, such as a bank or estate agent's office, are not generally classified as shops.

In English planning law, the term 'shop' is considered to cover premises where any business in the nature of retail, or what is related or appropriate thereto, is carried on and is defined in the Town and Country Planning (Use Classes) Order 1972 as "a building used for the purpose of carrying on of any retail trade or retail business wherein the primary purpose is selling goods by retail, and includes a building used for the purposes of a hairdresser, undertaker, travel agency, ticket agency or post office or for the reception of goods to be washed, cleaned or repaired, or for any other purpose appropriate to a shopping area, but does not include a building used as a fun-fair, amusement arcade, pintable saloon, garage, laundrette, petrol filling station, office, betting office, hotel, restaurant, snack-bar or café or premises licenced for the sale of intoxicating liquors for sale on the premises". For rating purposes a shop encompasses any premises to which the public resort for retail trade, or "any premises of a similar character where retail trade or business (including repair work) is carried on" (Rating and Valuation (Apportionment) Act 1928); also any premises used in association therewith, are treated as a retail shop. For the purpose of the above definitions, premises are not necessarily precluded from being classified as a 'shop' merely because the customers resell the goods purchased, or because the goods are not on the premises at the time of sale, but the presence of these factors tends to suggest that they are not truly retail in character; thus mail order is not retail because the public cannot 'resort' to the premises from where the goods are dispatched. See also **market, market overt, office, Use Classes Order**.

20 Halsbury's Laws of England, 4 edn, para. 419.

Shop: A Manual for Planning and Design, by David Munn, (1983).

Design and Planning of Retail Systems, by David Gosling and Barry Maitland, (1976).

shopping centre

A concentration of **retail** stores, shops and premises of a similar character. A term applied most commonly to a group of such premises, together with service facilities and a pedestrian mall, constructed usually in accordance with a uniform building plan, to serve a particular community, neighbourhood, district or region. A shopping centre generally incorporates a mixture of retail units or shops, together with associated facilities such as banks, restaurants, cinemas, petrol filling stations and ample off-street car parking. Frequently such a centre is maintained under the control of a single owner or manager.

Shopping centres may broadly be classified as:

'Local' centres – comprising a small group or parade of shops, predominately independently run, primarily serving a population of under 2000 and with a built area of under 2500 square metres or under 25 000 square feet).

'Neighbourhood' or convenience centres – comprising a supermarket, a small variety of general stores, and a number (about 10 to 20) of specialist shops principally selling convenience goods, serving a neighbourhood of around 10 000 people situated within a radius of under five miles. These centres have a built area from around 2500 square metres up to 5000 square metres (or around 25 000 to 50 000 square feet).

'District', 'secondary' or 'subregional' centres – similar to a neighbourhood centre but larger and containing additional facilities such as a minor or junior department store and serving a wider trade area – up to 200 000 people. These centres are intended to serve a district, part of a major region, or a small town and have a built area from around 10 000 square metres up to 25 000 square metres (or around 100000 to 200000 square feet). In the US a similar size shopping centre is referred to as a 'community centre'. 'Regional' centres – generally characterised by providing 'one stop' shopping, i.e. providing a similar range of goods to that found in a **central business district**, incorporating an enclosed mall, two or more major department stores, a complete range (up to 100 or more) of small retail shops, as well as ancilliary facilities, such as banks, cinemas, restaurants, etc. A centre that is intended to serve a population of over 250 000 people and ranging in size from a built area of around 25 000 square metres to well over 100 000 square metres (or 250 000 to over 1 million square feet). In the US such a centre is referred to also as a 'mall'.

A shopping centre also may be a number of retail units in the central area of a town or city; for example, one developed at random over a period of time – the traditional 'high street' centre; or a centre that has the same facilities as a regional centre and is part of the central business district. In the lay sense a shopping centre is any group of shops which provide most forms of convenience shopping and a degree of comparison shopping; in the professional sense it is normally a planned development. See also **anchor tenant, catchment area shop, strip centre, tenant mix**.

Shopping Centre Management, by Peter G. Martin (1982).
Design for Shopping Centres, by N Beddington (1982).

Enclosed Shopping Centres, by C. Darlow (ed.), (1982).
Shopping Centre Development Handbook, by Frank H. Spink Jr., (1977).
Shopping Centre Design and Investment, by M.A. Hines, (1983).
The Valuation of Shopping Centres, by Robert L. Garrett *et al.*, (1976).
Shopping Centre Management: Principles and Practices, by Horace Carpenter Jr., (1984).

shopping mall
see **mall**.

shore
Land bordering a large body of water, especially bordering the sea. Land that is alternately wet and dry between the 'ordinary' high and low water marks – Port of Seattle *v* Oregon and WR Co., 255 US 56. The sea-shore is such land that is ordinarily washed by the sea; land that *prima facie* belongs to the Crown or State. Thus, for land that is bounded by the sea, the 'shoreline' is the boundary line between private and public property. In most states in the US this line is set by the mean high water mark – Borax Consolidated *v* Los Angeles, 296 US 10; although in a few states it is taken as the highest point washed by the sea and in other states it is taken as the mean low water mark so that the sea-shore is owned privately by the adjoining land owner. Land that borders the sea-shore may alter its limit of ownership as the mean high and low water mark moves. See also **accretion, foreshore**.
Real Property, by William E. Burby, 3 edn., pp. 46–48.
Real Estate Law, by Robert Kratovil and Raymond J. Werner, 8 edn., p. 479.

short-form document (US)
A written document that sets out the basic terms and conditions of an agreement and refers to a **standard-form contract**, or related documents, for the other terms and conditions. A short-form document is intended primarily as a summary of the principal document and is prepared in order to keep the principal document secret. See also **open contract, precedent**.

short-term capital gains tax
see **capital gains tax**.

short-term lease
A lease for a term of ten years or less, and especially a **periodic tenancy** for a year or less. A lease that need not be in **writing** to be enforceable in a court of law; in English law, one for less than three years and in most states in the US, one for less than a year, is referred to usually as a short-term lease.
cf. **long-term lease**. See also **protected shorthold tenancy**.

short-term loan (or financing)
A loan that may be recalled within a period of one year or less.
cf. **long-term loan**. See also **current liability, financing, interim loan, roll over loan**.

shorthold tenancy
see **protected shorthold**.

show house
A house presented for viewing and inspection, especially a dwelling-house completed ready for occupation and made available for inspection by persons who may be interested in acquiring a similar property. A house to which prospective purchasers can resort in order to look at that which is representative of what they may buy; commonly a new house that

is a model for another which is to be built to a similar design and specification, but on a different site. In the US, called also a 'model house'.

sic ultere tuo ut alienum non laedas (L) 'So use your property as not to interfere with that of others'. See **encroachment, nuisance, strict liability**.

side-by-side lease
see **side-by-side participation**.

side-by-side participation
A form of **equity participation** whereby the partners in an investment project or joint venture share, in an agreed proportion, the *total* cash flow received from that investment. When a property is leased to a tenant on a long-lease and he, in turn, sub-lets to occupational tenants upon terms which provide that the head landlord will receive a proportionate share of the rents payable by the occupiers, then the head lease sometimes is referred to as a 'side-by-side', 'income-sharing' 'vertical' or 'back-to-back' lease. Called also 'vertical-slice participation' or in the US, 'straight-up participation'.
cf. **top-slice participation**. See also **lease and lease-back financing**.
A Guide to Institutional Property, by Angus P.J. McIntosh and Stephen G. Sykes, pp. 93–99 (1985).

sidewalk (US)
A **footway** or pavement generally running alongside a street or road and commonly in front of properties that give on to the thoroughfare. Called sometimes a 'pedestrianway' or '**walkway**'. See also **footpath**.

signature
A person's name or mark written with his own hand as evidence that he

intends to be bound by or accepts that which goes before. A signature is the accustomed mode in which a person places his mark – Morton *v* Copeland (1855) 16 CB 535. (In English law prior to 1925 a **seal** was the more usual method of authenticating a deed, but now signing or placing of a mark on a document is deemed sufficient: Law of Property Act 1925, s. 73). A signature need not be, but usually is, placed at the end of a document (except in the case of a **will**, which should be signed at the end and witnessed by two parties; Wills Act 1837, s. 9). What is essential is that it indicates the intention of an individual to authenticate a document *in toto*. – Durrell *v* Evans (1862) 1 H and C 191. A seal with a testator's initials has been held sufficient to signify that a will has been signed (In Emerson (1882) 9 LR 1r.). A printed signature may be valid, providing it can be ascertained that a person intends to be bound by it. When an agreement, memorandum or note of a contract for the sale of land or other disposition of land or any interest in land requires to be "signed" to be capable of forming the basis of an action at law, any writing that has the effect of authenticating the whole of the document is sufficient – Ogilvie *v* Foljambe (1817) 3 Mer. 53. See also **execution, *non est factum*, 'signed, sealed and delivered', Statute of Frauds, subscribe**.

'signed, sealed and delivered'
A phrase which indicates that a **deed**, a 'contract under seal', has been entered into; that is, that these three actions have been completed. The most complete form of evidence that a person has agreed expressly to be

bound by an agreement or commitment. Any deed made after 1 January 1926 must bear the **signature** or mark of the parties to the contract (not just a seal) (Law of Property Act 1925, s. 73); certain documents must be made under **seal**; and "where a contract is to be made by deed, there must be **delivery** to perfect it" – Xenos *v* Wickham (1863) 14 CB (NS) 473. See also **acknowledgement**.
Chitty on Contracts, 25 edn, paras. 18–24.

signification (F)
    service (of notice).
    (*signification d'un congé* – the giving of notice to quit)
    (*acte de signification* – writ). See also **huissier, notification.**

silent partner
    A partner who supplies capital but takes no active part in the general management of a business. Called also a 'dormant partner' or 'sleeping partner'.
    cf. **general partner**. See also **limited partnership, passive investor.**

simple contract
    A contract made orally or in writing, but not by **deed**, by special instrument, or created by a court record (B Comm. vol. ii p. 465). A simple contract may be express or implied, or partly express and partly implied. Liability under a simple contract is founded on the objective appearance of the agreement, rather than the formalities employed. Called also an 'informal contract'.
    cf. **specialty contract**. See also **agreement, consideration, equitable lease, parol contract, Statutes of Limitation.**

simple interest
    Interest paid or computed only on the original principal of a loan and not on the aggregate of the principal and any accrued interest.
    cf. **compound interest**.

simple licence (US)
    see **licence**.

simple trust
    1. See **bare trust**.
    2. A trust not created by any formal instrument but brought into effect in a manner prescribed by law.
    cf. **special trust**. See also **constructive trust, implied trust, statutory trust for sale.**

simulation (F)
    simulation; fictitious sale (of real property). An arrangement whereby, although an interest in property is transferred, the transaction effecting that transfer takes place by an ostensible or secret document which disguises a true conveyance; for example, the shares of a company that holds a property may be transferred, giving the impression that no property has changed hands with an actual transfer of title being effected by a separate, secret, document. The law may look at the true nature of the transaction, especially tax laws, and any secret contract, or 'back-letter' (*contre-lettre*) takes effect "only as between the contracting parties – they have no effect as regards third parties". (French Civil Code, art. 1321). Amos and Walton's Introduction to French Law, 2 edn, pp. 177–179.
    Précis Dalloz. Droit Civil, Les Biens, (Alex Weill), 2 edn, pp. 295–296.

single-rate capitalisation factor (or years' purchase)
    A **capitalisation factor** (or **years' purchase**) used to capitalise a level annual income without any provision to

recapture capital; a factor that is equivalent to the **present value of one per period**. A single-rate capitalisation factor is used to convert an income into a capital value, so that the income represents a return *on* the capital value, but, unlike a **dual-rate capitalisation factor (or years' purchase)**, it does not provide for any part of income to be set aside to provide for replacement *of* the capital value at the end of a given duration, i.e. it does not provide that a **sinking fund** is set aside to replace the capital value. In the US, called also the 'Inwood factor (or co-efficient)'. See also **annuity capitalisation**.

sinking-fund (sf)

A fund created by setting aside a series of regular sums of money, over a given period of time to accumulate (generally with interest accrued thereon) to a predetermined amount. A sinking fund is created usually in order to meet the cost of a specific obligation or to repay a known debt at a future date. A charge or allowance made against the profits of an organisation in order to make a provision for the cost of replacing an asset at the end of its useful or economic life. A number of equal periodic payments that will accumulate to one unit of value when invested with compound interest; the amount of these payments being calculated by the formula:

$$Sn = i/[(1 + i)^n - 1]$$

where: Sn = the periodic payment or 'sinking fund factor'.

i = compound interest rate or sinking fund rate.

n = number of periodic payments.

A sinking fund is used commonly to replace the cost or value of a wasting asset; to repay a debt or obligation at a future date – to build up a 're-demption fund'; or to retire a debt. Called also an 'amortisation fund' or 'redemption fund'. (A sinking fund factor is the reciprocal of the **amount of one per period**.)

cf. **amortisation, annuity**. See also **depreciation, dual-rate capitalisation factor**.

Modern Methods of Valuation, 7 edn., pp. 85–88.

sinking fund accumulation factor (US)

see **amount of one per period**.

sinking-fund factor

see **sinking fund**.

sinking-fund method of depreciation

A means of allowing for depreciation by deducting or writing-off from the capital cost or value of an asset an amount equivalent to a **sinking fund**. Called also the 'reinvestment method of depreciation'.

sinking-fund rate

The rate of compound interest applied when assessing a **sinking fund**. Generally the rate will be one that is considered 'safe', as the intention is to accumulate capital at the minimum risk. Called also the 'accumulative rate', 'amortisation rate' or 'recapture rate'.

cf. **remunerative rate**. See also **dual rate capitalisation factor, safe rate**.

sit-in

Occupation of a property for the purpose of protest or obstruction to its use. In law a sit–in may amount to **trespass**. See also **squatting**.

site

1. The **location**, position or situation of a parcel of land. The place or

which something is situated or a particular use is carried on, especially in a local sense. "The site is the spot on which anything stands or is situated; it is more commonly applied to a building or any place marked out for a specific purpose; as the site on which a camp has been formed." (*Crabb's English Synonyms*, 1816). The 'location' represents where something is to be found; it indicates the position of a site relative to other uses of land. Thus a site can be surveyed but a location is merely assessed or analysed. See also **situs**.

2. An area of land delineated for a particular use or purpose; especially land available for improvement, development or redevelopment. In the US, called more commonly a 'plot'. See also **lot**.

site analysis

An assessment of the potential of unimproved land, or of land that may be capable of or may benefit from development or redevelopment. In particular, the examination of the suitability of a site for a particular development proposal. See also **feasibility study**, **highest and best use**, **residual method of valuation**.

site area

The total area of a given parcel of land, or plot, measured in a horizontal plane. In particular, the total area within an owner's title boundary, or the total area of land within the boundaries of a site intended for development or redevelopment and, in general, contained within the limits of a highway. See also *ad medium filum*, **gross site area**.

site coverage

The proportion of a plot of land that is covered by building improvements. See also **plot ratio**.

site development

The provision of infrastructure to an area of land before buildings are erected thereon. Site development may include the provision of roads, main services or public utilities, as well as clearing and levelling the site.

site licence

A licence granted by a local authority, under the provision of the Caravan Sites and Control of Development Act 1960, s. 1, authorising an occupier of land to use his land as a **caravan** site for touring caravans (that is, for caravans that are capable of being moved from one place to another). Before a site licence may be granted, **planning permission** must be obtained for the siting of a caravan or caravans. Once planning permission has been obtained a local authority (the district or borough council) may not then refuse a site licence, but it may impose conditions relating to the siting of the caravans. Section 5 of the 1960 Act provides that the local authority may impose conditions on the occupiers of land to which the licence relates – in particular, to control the number of caravans on a given site; the length of stay permitted; the type of caravans (but not the materials of which they are made); the positioning of the caravans; the stationing of other structures, vehicles or tents; landscaping requirements; fire safety; and the provision of adequate sanitary facilities. The licence may stipulate also that the site owner is obliged to carry out work on the relevant land to improve the site prior to the stationing of the caravans thereon. These conditions may be amended or varied by the local authority at any time but must have full regard to the interests of the caravan dwellers, other persons directly affected and the public at large; as well as the Secretary of State's 'Model Standards for Caravans' (1960 Act, s. 8 (4)). A site licence is not required in certain cases, e.g. stationing a caravan within the curtilage and associated with a private dwelling-house, provided the caravan is used as incidental to the enjoyment of the house; specific short-term stays; stationing a limited number of caravans for part of the year; building site caravans; seasonal accommodation of agricultural and forestry workers on agricultural and forestry land; caravans used by certain 'exempt bodies' or travelling showmen (1960 Act, Sch. 2).

Guide to Development and Planning, by R.N.D. Hamilton, 2 edn., Ch. 13.
Encyclopaedia of Planning Law and Practice, by Desmond Heap, paras. 1–125 – 1–137.
46 Halsbury's Laws of England, 4 edn, paras. 317–343.

site (or area) of special scientific interest (SSSI)

An area of land considered to be of value for scientific purposes by reason of its flora, fauna, or unusual geological or physiological features. These areas are proposed as such by the Government financed **Nature Conservancy Council**. The Council must notify its proposals to the local authority, Secretary of State for the Environment and every owner and occupier of any area deemed to have special scientific interest. Any person notified of such a proposal may make representations or objections to the Council and such representations or objections must be considered before an area is designated formally as a site of special scientific interest.

Normally, public access is severely limited to any area formally notified to be of special scientific interest and no development or potentially harmful operation may be carried out in such an area without the Nature Conservancy Council being formally notified and giving its consent, or until a period of three months elapses from the date the owner or occupier gave notice of its intention to carry out work (Wildlife and Countryside Act 1981, ss. 28–33).

Urban Planning Law, by Malcolm Grant, pp. 310–313 (1982).
Encyclopaedia of Planning Law and Practice, by Desmond Heap, paras. 2–2074 – 2–2083.

site value

The value of an unimproved area of land taking into account the benefit of any permission to build in accordance with planning or zoning regulations. Sometimes referred to as the **residual value** of a plot of land. See also **cleared site value**.

site value tax

A tax that is levied solely on the basis of the value of a parcel of land, excluding any buildings erected thereon. See also **land tax**, **property tax**.

sitting rent
see **virtual rent**.

sitting tenant

1. A tenant who is in physical possession of a property, particularly one who remains in possession upon expiry of a lease. In the US, in the latter instance, called also a 'holdover tenant'. See also **holding over**,

tenancy at will.
2. A tenant who has an immediate right to **possession** of property, as distinguished from a tenant who has a **reversionary interest**.

situation (F)
situation; report.
(*situation du marché* – market report)
(*situation nette* – **net worth**).

situs
1. The **location**, situation or **site** of a property (real or personal). The place to which intangible property is deemed to belong for legal or tax jurisdiction purposes. Real estate always has a fixed situs, i.e. a particular property cannot change its legal or fiscal jurisdiction.
2. The preferred location for the establishment of a business or a new building, especially from an economic point of view.

six months
A period of time equivalent to six successive periods of a **month**, not necessarily **half a year**; it may be six calendar months or six lunar months. In English law, prior to 1926, six months could be limited to six lunar months (Rogers *v* Kingston-upon-Hull Dock Co. (1864) 34 LJ Ch. 165). However, since 1926, in all deeds, contracts, wills, orders or other instruments 'month' means calendar month (Law of Property Act 1925, s. 61). In the case of a yearly tenancy, unless there is an express agreement to the contrary, notice of termination is, at common law, half a year (to expire on the anniversary of the date on which the tenancy commenced), but in English law if the tenancy started on one of the usual **quarter days** notice must coincide with the second succeeding quarter day. A **grazing licence** granted for 'six months' periods' is effectively a letting for one year and cannot be excluded from the provisions of the Agricultural Holdings Act 1948, s. 2.

sky factor
see **daylight factor**.

sky lease (US)
see **air lease**.

sky sign
see **advertisement, air space**.

skyscraper
A building that appears to touch the sky, or at least one that obliterates a view of the sky from street level. A **high rise building**, usually at least fifty storeys high.

sleeping partner
see **silent partner**.

sleeping rent
see **dead rent**.

slice
A portion of a sum of money or income received by one of a number of investors, especially a part of the total income received by the investors under an **equity participation** agreement. By way of illustration, the net income, or cash flow, from a property investment may be divided so that an institutional or passive investor receives all the income up to an agreed percentage return on cost – a **priority return**; an agreed percentage over and above the 'priority return' is received by a developer or managing partner; and any residue or **top-slice** is divided between the investors in an agreed proportion based on the relative sums invested and the risks entailed by the respective investors – both parties

receiving different slices of the total income. See also **side-by-side participation, top-slice participation**.

slice method
see **layer method**.

sliding-scale rent
see **graded rent, graduated rent, indexed rent**.

'slip rule'
A rule that gives the registrar of the Land Registry a discretionary right to correct "any clerical error or error of a like nature" on the register or on any plan or document referred to therein, provided the correction can be made without detriment to any registered interest (Land Registration Rules 1925, 5. 13). See also **rectification**.

slum
An urban area, neighbourhood or residential property that is characterised by squalid or excessively dilapidated property and, therefore, is dangerous to the health of the resident population. Property characterised by overcrowding, decay, decrepitude, poor arrangement or layout, and a lack of proper sanitary conditions: frequently occupied by very poor or socially deprived or repressed families. See also **back-to-back house, clearance area, ghetto, housing action area, improvement area, unfit for human habitation**.

slum clearance
A process of clearing decrepit or **slum** property, especially residential property that is **unfit for human habitation**, usually combined with the building of modern property as a replacement. In Britain, this is accomplished principally by the local housing authority declaring an area

to be a **clearance area** or **housing action area** in order to deal with either individual dwelling-houses or with the area as a whole. In the US, the Department of Housing and Urban Development (HUD) is the principal public body responsible for slum clearance. See also **urban renewal**.

slump
A sustained and, frequently, sudden decline in prices or economic activity. The period in a trade **cycle** when economic activity declines at its fastest rate. 'Slump' is used to refer especially to a sudden fall in prices and activity and is commonly a precursor to a recession or, if the decline is prolonged, a depression.

small holding
A piece of land, not being or forming part of a farm, generally detached from a residence, that is used for agricultural production in order to supplement the income of a private individual or family. English statutory definitions of a small holding limit the size to greater than one acre, but not more than fifty acres, – or to no more than seventy five acres (viz: Small Holdings and Allotments Act 1908, s. 61 (1); Small Holdings and Allotments Act 1926, s. 16; Agriculture Act 1947, s. 67; Agriculture (Miscellaneous Provisions) Act 1954, s. 3). The Agriculture Act 1970, ss 37–65, (which contains no separate definition of smallholding), as amended by the Agriculture (Miscellaneous Provisions) Act 1972, s. 9, 26, Sch. 6 and the Local Government Act 1972, ss. 131, 272, Sch. 30, contain provisions for the reorganisation, encouragement and management of smallholdings by certain local authorities (called 'smallholding authorities').

cf. **allotment**. See also **agricultural holding**.
2 Halsbury's Laws of England, 4 edn, paras. 94–135.

smoke
see **nuisance**.

socage
A form of feudal tenure whereby a freeman was permitted the right to possession of an area of land, which formed part of a **manor**, in exchange for various services rendered to the lord of the manor. Generally, the services were of a fixed non-servile and non-military nature. (Socage may have meant that the tenant rendered services arising from the 'soke' or ploughshare; or a form of 'soc' or free tenure.) However, the principal feature of this form of tenure was that the tenant had a defined and certain duty to the lord of the manor; "a tenure by any certain and determinate service" (Bl. Comm. vol. ii p. 79). Thus, it may be distinguished from **villeinage** (or villein tenure) by which the services could be varied at the whim of the lord). The services might have been of an agricultural nature (common socage) or of a non-personal nature, such as providing footmen or equipment for battle (petty sergenty). By the end of the 15th century most services of this nature had been commuted into money payments. The Tenures Abolition Act 1660 converted most forms of free (non-servile) tenure into 'free and common socage' and those holding such tenure commonly made a single payment or **quit rent** to the lord and acquired a freehold tenure. With effect from 1 January 1926 all such forms of feudal tenure were converted into free and common socage held from the crown, now usually called **freehold** (Law of Property Act 1922). cf. **knight-service**. See also **copyhold, gavelkind, doctrine of estates**.
Holdsworth's History of English Law, vol. iii p. 51 *et seq.*
39 Halsbury's Laws of England, 4 edn, paras. 307–309, 318–319.

société (F)
company; firm; partnership; society. A *société* in French law differs from a company in English law, because *société* extends from a partnership to a company. "'La *société*' is a contract whereby two or more persons agree to place something in common with the object of sharing the profits or benefits which may arise therefrom. Every '*société*' must have a lawful object and the contract must be in the common interest of the parties thereto. Each member of the *société* must contribute either money or some kind of property or his [or her] effort" (French Civil Code, art 1832, 1833). A société may not have to be created for the sole purpose of profit, but it must have a *but lucratif*, i.e. it must intend to benefit the proprietors financially which distinguishes it from an **association**.
(*société à responsibilité limitée*; *société limitée* – limited company, in particular a private limited company)
(*société anonyme* – limited liability company)
(*société commerciale en nom collectif* – general partnership)
(*société de gerance* – management company)
(*société d'investissements* – **investment company**)
(*société en commandité* – limited partnership)
(*société en nom collectif* – partnership)

(*société en participation* - **joint venture**)
(*société fiduciaire de placements* - **investment trust**)
(*société immobilière* - real estate company; building society).
French Company Law, by J. Le Gall, edited by R. Pennington (1974). Petits Codes Dalloz. Code des Sociétés 5 edn.

société civile immobilière (F)

A type of company that is formed solely for the purpose of acquiring land, building thereon and selling the completed properties (French Civil Code, art. 1832 *et seq*; law of 16 July 1971).

société immobilière pour le commerce et l'industrie (SICOMI) (F)

property company for commerce and industry. A form of company established solely to invest in real estate. A SICOMI is exempt from income and capital gains tax, provided it is authorised by the Ministry of Finance; it complies with certain rules regarding capitalisation; distributes 85 per cent of its income as dividends; and invests 100 per cent of its funds in commercial property (French Law of 28 September 1967). It is intended to act as a long term investor and not a trader or developer of property. Frequently the tenant of a SICOMI is granted an option to purchase the property after 15 to 25 years i.e. a lease granted by a SICOMI takes the form of a *crédit-bail.*
Petits Codes Dalloz, Code des Sociétés, 5 edn, pp. 1062–1063.

society

A group or association of individuals formed together voluntarily for a common interest or purpose. A commercial society is one formed for a business purpose but generally, unlike a **company**, not for the prime object of making a profit; it has no legal status *per se*, but is created to outlast the life of any individual member. A society may be constituted as a club, institution, or any other organisation or association of persons, especially when those persons accept a common rule, share a common belief, or are involved in a common trade or profession. See also **building society, partnership**, *société*, **syndicate**.

Society for the Protection of Ancient Buildings

A private organisation first established in 1887 by William Morris to fulfil the purpose explicit in its name. The society maintains records of historic and important buildings and makes efforts to find uses for any such building that is under threat of demolition. See also **ancient monument**.

soft loan

A loan on which interest is charged at a rate that is well below the market rate.

soft money (US)

1. Money paid that does not augment the amount of **equity** invested in a property e.g. interest payments on a mortgage loan. See also **carrying charges**.
(US) 2. Money paid for a property by means of a **purchase-money mortgage**.

soil

The surface of the earth; especially dry land that may be ploughed or dug. The removal, with a view to sale, of more than five cubic yards of soil in any three months from agricultural land, if it constitutes **development** for which planning permission is required, but has not been obtained, (excluding the cutting of peat and turf), is an offence (Agricultural Land (Removal of Surface Soil) Act 1953). See also **fixture, mineral, profit à prendre, right of support**.

sol (F)

ground; soil

(*sol de construction* – foundation soil).

solar day (month, or year)

see **day, month, year**.

sole agency

An agency agreement whereby an **agent** is appointed to buy, sell or let a property on the understanding that the principal will not enter into any other agency agreement in respect of the subject property (usually for a given period of time or in a given district). A 'sole agent' normally accepts that he will "use his best endeavours" to sell or let the property and generally is appointed for a fixed period of time. During the period of appointment he is responsible for marketing the property; negotiating with prospective purchasers; reporting fully to his principal; and, usually, making every effort to introduce a person who is **'ready, able and willing'** (or a similar person) to purchase or rent the property. In the event of a sale of the property, a payment is due to the agent, even if the purchaser or tenant is introduced to the vendor by another agent. (The assumption is that the sole agent was appointed to negotiate with all prospective purchasers or tenants and in all probability would have concluded a 'bargain' with the taker.) However, he may not be entitled to the same **commission** as if he had concluded the transaction

unaided, because the agent was not the 'effective cause' of the transaction – the agent's entitlement to commission depends upon the precise terms of his appointment and the extent of the duties performed – Hampton and Sons *v* George [1939] 3 All ER 627. On the other hand, if a sale or letting results directly from a contact by the principal with the purchaser a sole agent is precluded normally from receiving any payment – Bentall, Horsley and Baldry *v* Vicary [1931] 1 KB 253. Called also a 'sole selling agency', an 'exclusive agency' and in the US, an 'exclusive agency listing' or an **'exclusive listing'**.

cf. **sole right to sell, multiple agency**. See also **estate agent, *quantum meruit***.

The Law of Estate Agency and Auctions, by J.R. Murdoch, 2 edn., pp. 217–220, 272–275.

The Practice of Estate Agency, by Nigel Stephens, pp. 64, 83 *et seq.*, (1981).

sole agent

see **sole agency**.

sole common of pasture

A right of pasture available to commoners alone, rather than the owner of the land. Called also 'several pasture'. See also **right of common**.

sole ownership (US)

see **several ownership**.

sole right to sell

An agency agreement whereby an agent is appointed on the basis that the marketing of a property is left solely in the hands of the agent; therefore, during the period of this appointment, the agent acts to the exclusion of any other person, including the principal/vendor. A sole right to sell is similar to a **sole agency** except that if a sale results from the actions of the principal the agent is still entitled to a payment – Chamberlain and Willows *v* Rose [1931] 1 KB 261 n. This payment may not be equal to the full **commission** the agent would have earned had he introduced the purchaser himself and generally is based on the loss suffered by the agent. Called also a 'sole selling right' or in the US, 'exclusive right to sell' or an 'exclusive authority to sell'.

sole selling right
see **sole right to sell**.

sole tenant
One who holds property in his own right only, without any other party being joined as owner of the same property. See also **severalty**.

solicitor
In England and Wales a person who advises on legal matters, prepares legal documents, conducts litigation, and may make representations in a lower court of law on behalf of another (matters submitted to the High Court are presented by a **barrister**). A solicitor must be admitted as such by the Master of the Rolls after having qualified by examination, completed the Law Society's training and have been accepted as of good and suitable character. A solicitor is enrolled at the Supreme Court of Judicature and is certified by the Law Society (by means of an annual practising certificate) as authorised to practice (Solicitors Act 1974). He is bound to exercise reasonable care and skill in performing his professional duties; he owes a special duty of care and has a **fiduciary** responsibility to his client; and is bound by

various rules, or codes of practice and conduct (Solicitors' Practice Rules), as laid down by the Law Society. See also **professional negligence**.

solicitor's lien
see **lien**.

solidarité (F)
joint liability.
(*responsabilité conjoint et solidaire –* **joint and several liability**).

solo cedit quod solo implantur (L)
'What is planted in the soil belongs to the soil'.

solo cedit quod solo inaedificatur (L)
'That which is fixed to the soil becomes part of the soil'. See **fixture**.

solus agreement
An agreement by which a retailer or distributor of merchandise ties himself to buy goods from only one supplier. A form of agreement that is entered into frequently in conjunction with a loan or mortgage agreement between a retailer and a supplier; especially for the retail supply of petroleum products. A solus agreement may be void if it unreasonably restrains the trading activity of a retailer or is considered to be prejudicial to the public interest – Esso Petroleum Co. Ltd *v* Harper's Garage (Stourport) Ltd [1968] AC 269; Amoco Australia Pty. Ltd *v* Rocca Bros Co. Engineering Pty Ltd [1975] AC 561. See also '**once a mortgage always a mortgage**', **void contract**. Cheshire and Fifoot's Law of Contract, 10 edn, pp. 356–360, 366–367.

sommation (F)
notice (requiring someone to perform an obligation). See also *notification*.

souffrance (F)
sufferance; tacit permission.
(*bail à souffrance* – **tenancy on sufferance**)
(*jours de souffrance* – **days of grace**).

sous (F)
(*sous-bail* – **sub-lease**)
(*sous-bailleur* – **sub-lessor**)
(*sous-entrepreneur* – **subcontractor**)
(*sous-ferme* – sub-lease, of a farm)
(*sous-location* – sublease; subletting)
(*sous-locataire* – subtenant)
(*sous-louer* – to sublet)
(**sous réserve** – on condition; 'subject to'. See also *réserve*)
(*sous seing privé* – under private seal. cf. *acte authentique*)
(*acceptation sous réserve* – qualified acceptance, i.e. a **counter-offer**).

sous-traitant (F)
sub-contractor.

souscrire (F)
to subscribe; to sign; to give consent.
(*souscrire un acte* – to sign a deed).

space lease (US)
see **occupational lease**.

space plan
A preliminary layout plan of an office floor showing proposed partitioning and internal office arrangements etc. and prepared in accordance with the requirements of a prospective occupier.

special adaptability
see **special suitability**.

special agent
see **agent**.

special area
1. An inner urban area of Great Britain where it is considered by central government that special social needs exist and where the appropriate local authority is authorised to (a) make loans for site preparation and site development work; (b) make grants to assist a person taking a lease of premises intended for industrial or commercial purposes; (c) make grants to assist a small firm (one employing no more than fifty employees) to pay interest charges on loans taken out to finance the purchase and development of land (Inner Urban Areas Act 1978, ss 8–11). See also **urban development area**.
2. A term first used in Britain, by the Special Areas (Development and Improvement) Act 1934, for a **development area** i.e. an area subject to government assistance because of depressed economic conditions. In 1945, such areas were extended and renamed 'development areas'. In 1972, development areas were subdivided into 'development areas', 'intermediate areas', and 'special development areas'. See also **assisted area**.
3. See **area of special control**.

special assessment (US)
see **assessment**.

special benefit (US)
see **betterment**.

special charge (or lien)
A **charge** (or **lien**) secured on specified property.
cf. **floating charge**. See also **fixed charge**.

special condition (US)
A condition in a contract for the sale of land, that must be satisfied before the contract becomes binding. For example, a condition which provides that the purchaser must obtain suitable finance, or satisfy himself of certain facts provided to him by the vendor, before the purchaser will proceed with the transaction. See also

contingency contract, 'subject to contract', 'subject to finance', 'subject to survey'.

special conditions of sale
see **conditions of sale.**

special contract
see **specialty contract.**

special damages
see **damages.**

special development area
see **development area.**

Special Development Order (SDO)
An order made by the Secretary of State for the Environment, in accordance with the provisions of the Town and Country Planning Act 1971, s. 24, by which the Secretary intervenes directly in connection with a proposal for the development of an area of land and grants **planning permission** in place of the local planning authority. A Special Development Order is reserved usually for such major projects as a new town, a nuclear power station or an inner urban development project. It may be made also to limit the application of a **General Development Order** (1971 Act, s. 22 (3)).

special grant
A grant made usually at the discretion of a local authority, in accordance with the provisions of the Housing Act 1957, s. 69–70, to the owner of a house in multiple occupation for the purpose of providing **standard amenities.**
cf. **intermediate grant, standard grant.** See also **improvement grant.** West's Law of Housing, 4 edn, p. 273.

special industry
An industrial use specified in a **Use Classes Order,** as being one that is especially liable to create pollution; in particular, a use that is liable to result in the emission of poisonous waste, fumes or smell. See also **industrial building.**

special investment area
A rural area in Britain where the population has declined over a number of years and, as a result, government aid may be made available to stimulate the establishment of a nucleus of small industries that it is hoped will reverse the decline.

special, or specific, liability insurance
1. Insurance against a specific risk of a claim from a third party, e.g. a claim made by a client as a result of professional negligence, as contrasted with insurance against a claim from the public at large. See also **liability insurance.**
2. **Contingency insurance** against a specified risk.

special lien
see **lien, special charge.**

special partner
see **limited partner.**

special perils
Any risk associated with the ownership or control of property that may be insured against, other than fire. "Those perils which are not covered by, or which are excluded from, the normal fire policies issued by insurers" – *Special Perils Insurance*, by M.G. Eagle, p. 2 (1963). Property insurance policies frequently are provided against fire, and against 'special perils' which covers such matters as explosion, storm, flood, riot and civil commotion, impact (vehicular or aircraft), malicious damage, subsidence,

accidental breakage. See also **all-risks insurance, comprehensive insurance.**

special power
see **power of appointment.**

special property
A right to the ownership of property that is subordinate to an absolute or unconditional right of ownership. Called also 'qualified property'. See also **special use property.**

special purchaser
A purchaser, or prospective purchaser, who pays or is prepared to pay a higher price for a property because of his particular position; such as a person who has an interest in an adjoining property; another interest in the same property, e.g. a tenant who is seeking to acquire his landlord's interest; or a person with a vested interest in a property.

When assessing **compulsory purchase** compensation no account is to be taken of the "**special suitability or adaptability** of the land for any purpose" that arises solely from the needs of one particular purchaser, especially the needs of the authority possessing the compulsory purchase powers (Land Compensation Act 1961, s. 5 (3)). In other words, any increase in **market value** caused by a special purchaser, over and above the 'open' market value, are to be ignored. However, the mere existence of only one prospective purchaser does not automatically bring this rule into account; nor is an increase in value due to the merger of a leasehold and a freehold interest necessarily precluded – Lambe *v* Secretary of State for Air [1955] 2 QB 612. It is necessary to show that the 'special purchaser' has created a market for

the land that otherwise would not exist. See also **marriage value.**

special purpose
see **special suitability or adaptability.**

special purpose property (US)
see **special use property.**

special scientific interest, site of
see **site of special scientific interest.**

'special suitability or adaptability'
An attribute that arises as a direct consequence of a proposal by a public authority to acquire land for a purpose for which it has obtained statutory compulsory purchase powers. When assessing **compulsory purchase compensation** "the special suitability or adaptability of the land for any purpose shall not be taken into account if that purpose is a purpose to which it could be applied only in pursuance of statutory powers, or for which there is no market apart from the special needs of a particular purchaser or the requirements of any authority possessing compulsory purchase powers" (Land Compensation Act 1961, s. 5 (3)). An authority with statutory powers to purchase land for a particular purpose is not expected to pay a price based on special suitability "merely by reason of the fact that it was easy to forsee that the situation of the land would lead to compulsory powers being some day obtained to purchase it" – Re. Lucas and Chesterfield Gas and Water Board [1909] 1 KB 16.

Clearly, any area of land may be specially suitable for the purpose to which it is put, or may be specially suitable or adaptable for a use to which it could be put – special suitability or adaptability being a factor that contributes to determining its

market value – but if that special attribute arises solely as a result of the acquiring authority's underlying reason for purchase, it must be ignored when determining the appropriate amount of compensation.

In the US, in condemnation proceedings the adaptability of land for a special purpose or use is an element to be considered when determining **just compensation**, but not if that purpose or use arises only as a result of the proposed condemnation – State by State Highway Commission *v* Stumbo, 222 Or. 62, 352 P. 2d 478. See also **special purchaser**.

special tail

A **fee tail** or **entailed estate** that is limited to the children of specified parents.

special tax assessment (US)

see **assessment**.

special trust

A **trust** created by an express instrument, or for a specific purpose. In particular, a trust in which the trustees have active and substantial duties and powers in relation to the management, control and disposal of the trust property in accordance with the settlor's intentions. This is the most common form of trust. Called also an 'active trust'.

cf. **bare trust**. See also **trust for sale**.

special use (US)

see **special suitability or adaptability**.

special use permit (US)

A permit consenting to a particular exception to a **zoning ordinance** e.g. consent to the erection of a church in an area zoned residential.

cf. **variance**. See also **non-conforming use**.

special use property

Property that is designated, equipped and used for a particular purpose; or a property that may be used readily for only a single purpose, e.g. a church, filling station, hospital. Such property is not generally bought and sold in the open market and cannot be said to have a market value in the ordinary sense of the term. In the US, called also 'special purpose property' or 'specialty property'. See also **equivalent reinstatement cost of**.

Readings in the Appraisal of Special Use Property, AIREA, (1981).

special warranty deed (US)

see **warranty deed**.

specialty

see **specialty contract**.

specialty contract

A **contract under seal**; in particular, an obligation to pay a debt accepted under **seal**, due from the Crown, or arising under statute – R *v* Williams [1942] AC 555. Called also a 'formal specialty'.

cf. **simple contract**. See also **deed**.

specialty property (US)

see **special use property**.

specialty store

A retail store or shop that restricts its products to a particular type of goods, in particular high quality or unusual goods.

cf. **variety store**.

specie

see *in specie*, **money**.

specific charge

A **fixed charge**, as distinguished from a floating charge.

specific performance, order or decree of

An order, made by a court of law,

compelling a party to perform a contract in accordance with, or substantially in accordance with, its agreed terms; especially when the court considers it equitable that the contract be carried through to a conclusion, rather than one party merely paying **damages** for his neglect in abiding by the terms of the contract. "The specific performance of a contract is its actual execution according to its stipulations and terms; and is contrasted with damages or compensation for the non-execution of the contract" (Fry on Specific Performance, 2 edn, p. 2). A decree or order of specific performance is a remedy granted when a contract would not otherwise be enforceable due to a lack of proper formality. This form of order is awarded on the basis of the maxim that 'equity looks on that as done which ought to be done'. Specific performance was granted – Walsh *v* Lonsdale (1882) 21 Ch. D 9 – in order to enforce an **agreement for a lease** for seven years which, although not recorded in writing, had been partly acted on by the tenant entering into possession and paying rent subsequent to an oral agreement.

A decree of specific performance is an equitable remedy and, therefore, is granted at the discretion of the court; although the basis on which the discretion is exercised is now fairly well settled by precedent. For example, the court will not grant specific performance when there has been misrepresentation, duress, fraud, unreasonable delay; when to do so would cause hardship; or if the contract is illegal. In general, a decree of specific performance is granted only when (i) the intention of the agreement can be clearly ascertained; (ii) the contract can be properly performed by both parties to the contract (it is not available when one party, e.g. a minor, cannot perform the contract – Flight *v* Bolland (1818) 40 ER 817 – and the party seeking to enforce the contract is willing and able to perform his or her part of the bargain; (iii) the party seeking to enforce the contract has acted reasonably, i.e. has come to court 'with clean hands', and the contract is legal; (iv) no serious loss or hardship would be incurred by enforcing the agreement; in other words, a plaintiff "should not be permitted to insist on a form of relief which will confer no appreciable benefit on himself and will be materially detrimental to the defendant." – Charrington *v* Simons and Co. [1970] 1 WLR 730. In addition, specific performance is a remedy that is granted only when common law can provide no other remedy; in particular, "a specific performance is only decreed, where the party wants the thing *in specie*; and cannot have it any other way." – Errington *v* Aynesley (1788) 2 Bro. CC; Flint *v* Bandon (1803) 8 Ves. 159. Thus, it is normally used only in cases when the subject matter of the contract is unique or has a special character and, therefore, damages would be inappropriate; in particular, a contract relating to land. However, the court may order specific performance and also award damages if it is equitable so to do: Judicature Act 1925, s. 86; and if a court refuses to grant specific performance of a contract for the sale of land it has power to order the repayment of any deposit paid (Law of Property Act 1925, s. 49).

Specific performance will not be granted when it would require a continuing intervention by the court; for example, when there is a requirement that a landlord provide a resident porter in a building – Ryan *v* Mutual Tontine Westminster Chambers Association (1893) 62 LJCh 252. It will not be granted to enforce a contract for personal services or a contract where there is no consideration; "the courts have never dreamt of enforcing agreements strictly personal in their nature whether they are agreements of hiring and service, being the common relation of master and servant or whether they are agreements for the purpose of scientific pursuits or for purpose of charity and philanthropy." – Rigby *v* Connol 1880 14 Ch. D 487. Similarly, specific performance will not be granted to enforce an agency or partnership contract. Normally this remedy would not be provided to enforce a contract to erect or repair a building, because generally this would require supervision by a court and normally damages will provide an adequate remedy; however, in certain circumstances, the court may enforce a covenant under a ground lease to erect a building – Wolverhampton Corporation *v* Emmons [1901] 1 KB 515. The courts also may enforce a landlord's obligation to repair due to the "balance of inconvenience" caused – Jeune *v* Queens Cross Properties Ltd [1974] Ch. 97. In addition, a tenant of a dwelling-house may seek specific performance against a landlord for breach of a repairing covenant (Housing Act 1974, ss. 125, 129 (1)). See also **part performance**.

The Law of Landlord and Tenant, by David Lloyd Evans, 2 edn., pp. 51–56.

An Outline of the Law of Contract, by G.H. Treitel, 3 edn., p. 388.

Cheshire's Modern Law of Property, 13 edn, pp. 129–131, 377–378.

Anson's Law of Contract, 26 edn, pp. 517–520.

Cheshire & Fifoot's Law of Contract, 10 edn, pp. 559–565.

Land Law: Cases and Materials, by R.H. Maudsley & E.H. Burn, 4 edn, pp. 76–82, 421–4.

Chitty on Contract, 25 edn, paras. 1761–1818.

specification

A detailed written or printed description of the materials, size, workmanship, finishes etc. of a building or structure that has been or is to be erected. A specification is prepared normally by an architect, quantity surveyor or consulting engineer for the guidance of a building contractor and may form part of the **building contract** documents. See also **bill of quantities**.

Specification Writing, by A.J. Willis and C.J. Willis, 8 edn.

Specifications and Quantities, by D. Burchess, 2 edn.

The Practical Specifier: A Manual of Construction Documentation for Architects, by Walter Rosenfeld, (1985).

Specifications, by David Martin, (annual).

specified-property offering (US)

An investment in property to be held by a syndicate when the members of the syndicate are aware of the particular properties to be acquired at the time of their initial investment.

cf. **blind-pool offering**.

spéculateur (F)

speculator.

(*spéculateur à la baisse* – bull, syn. **baissier**)

(*spéculateur à la hausse* – bear, syn. **haussier**).

speculator

A person who ponders on the future course of events; engages in reasoning *a priori*; or ventures into matters that are fanciful or unreal. In business, a person who participates in hazardous ventures, or exceptional risk-taking, with the hope of realizing extraordinary profit; especially someone who buys and sells in anticipation of short-term profit. One who is "largely concerned, not with making superior long-term forecasts of the probable yield of an investment over its whole life, but with foreseeing changes in the conventional basis of valuation a short time ahead of the general public" (*The General Theory of Employment, Interest and Money*, by J.M. Keynes, p. 154 (1936)).

Commonly used in a deprecatory sense to describe anyone who indulges in highly risky or rash trading as contrasted with ordinary trade or business. A speculator is considered as someone who acts contrary to common sense, investigation and nature, and who bases his actions on chance, fortune and his own divining – "Oh! Speculators on things, boast not of knowing the things that nature ordinarily brings about; but rejoice if you know the end of those things which you yourself devise ... Beware of the teaching of these speculators, because their reasoning is not confirmed by experience." (*The Notebooks of Leonardo da Vinci*, (c. 1550)). A speculator is someone whose activity falls between that of a gambler and a merchant adventurer; his actions are normally 'hazardous' but with a fair prospect of financial gain if the results of those actions are successful. On the other hand the actions of a speculator frequently have a limited prospect of

success and they are then described as "rash and hazardous" ... "a speculation which no reasonably careful man would enter into, having regard to all the circumstances of the case – Re. Keays, *ex parte* Keays (1891) 9 Morr. 22.

A property speculator, commonly, is considered to profit by "buying and selling land for the purpose of making a quick profit" – Ken Wilson's Enterprises Ltd. *v* Inland Revenue Comr. [1975] 2 NZLR 180. He may hope to benefit from high rates of inflation or a change in the use to which he can put the land. He is accused even of pushing up prices by withholding land from the market; a view that requires a presumption that speculation can have a major determining effect on the property market. In general a view that is misplaced. On the other hand "sudden fortunes, indeed, are sometimes made in such places by what is called the trade of speculation. ...A bold adventurer may sometimes acquire a considerable fortune by two or three successful speculations; but is just as likely to lose one by two or three unsuccessful ones." (*The Wealth of Nations*, by Adam Smith, Book I, Ch. 10 (1776)).

Land speculation has been defined as "the holding of land resources, usually in something less than their **highest and best use**, with the primary managerial emphasis on resale at a capital gain rather than on profitable use in current production. Traditionally, the land speculator has shown little interest in the returns he could secure from the operation of his real estate resources. He tends instead to regard property as a commodity that he can buy and sell at a profit" – *Land Resource Economics*, by Raleigh

Barlowe, 3 edn., pp. 201–202.

Thus taxes that are levied on the gains arising from 'land speculation' (e.g. short-term gains tax in the US and, prior to 1985, development land tax in the UK) are considered a justifiable means of exacting a return to the community of at least part of the gain accruing to a speculator as the result of a shade of fortune. See also **bear, bull, property developer, risk**.

spendable income

The income available to an investor, either after taking account of all outgoings and taxes, or after making a provision for a **sinking-fund** to replace the cost of a wasting asset. See also **net spendable income**.

spendthrift trust (US)

see **protective trust**.

spes successionis (L)

'A hope of succeeding to property'.

spiritual tenure

A form of feudal **tenure** granted by a lord in return for prayers or devine services provided by the tenant. It could be **frankalmoin** by which an ecclesiastical body (a bishop or monastery) was required to pray for the lord's soul or 'divine service' by which the tenant undertook certain duties such as saying mass once a month or providing alms for the poor (Litt. 135–139).

split-financing

Separate financing obtained (a) for the purchase of land and (b) for the construction of buildings, or improvements to buildings, on that land; or for the purchase of different interests (a freehold and a leasehold) held in the same property.

split-level house

A house with two overlapping storeys designed for occupation by one family. In particular, one where the living areas are on different levels; or where the upper and lower areas only partially overlap as where the lower level is left void or is used as a garage. A house that is built partly on one storey and partly on two storeys. In the US, called also a 'bi-level house'. See also **maisonette**.

split rate

1. A separate **capitalisation rate** applied to land and buildings, or applied to different parts of an income. See also **hardcore method**.
2. The rate of interest on a **wrap-around mortgage**.

split reversion method

see **hardcore method**.

spot zoning

Specified area to be made an exception to a general plan. Spot zoning may be invalidated by a court of law if it can be shown that the municipality has favoured one land owner to the unreasonable detriment of the surrounding area or so as to prejudice the intention of a general plan. See also **special use permit, variance**.

square foot, rate per

see **unit cost or value**.

squatter

"One who, without any colour of right, enters on an unoccupied house or land, intending to stay there as long as he can." – McPail *v* Persons Unknown, Bristol Corporation *v* Ross [1973] 3 All ER 395. A person who enters on to land, legally or illegally, and refuses to leave when he or she has no right to stay. See also **squatting**.

squatting

The seizure of physical **possession** of real property belonging to another without any title or authority. An intrusion on to unoccupied land with a view to claiming title by **adverse possession** or at least staying there as long as the squatter can. A **squatter** was originally a settler on colonial land; "a person who has taken possession of a piece of land and occupied it by building and by cultivation, and has, by so taking possession of it, asserted a right to it" – Hoggan *v* Esquimalt and Nanimo Railway [1894] AC 429. A 'squatter's title' arises from an illegal entry into possession, which is not acknowledged by the payment of rent or in any similar manner and which remains unchallenged so that the possessor acquires a title that is good against anyone but the true owner. In time the squatter will endeavour to prove that he has a good title due to the failure of the true owner to protect his rights, i.e. to prove that he has established title by 'adverse possession'.

In a modern sense, 'squatting' is used to refer to any entry on to a vacant property with the intention of taking up residence; generally starting as a form of **trespass**, whether by a person or persons seeking a home, or by a person who entered the property under a licence which has been revoked e.g. a worker in a factory engaged in a sit-in. In law squatting is a trespass and the true owner may enforce his right to possession by an action in tort. In addition, the Criminal Law Act 1977, s. 7 makes the use of violence to gain entry on to land an offence, and an offence is committed by a person(s) who fails to leave premises when requested to do so by a "displaced residential occupier" or a "protected intending occupier". See also **Statutes of Limitation**.
Squatting, by A.M. Pritchard (1981).

stabilised net income (US)

The average **net operating income** that is generated by a property excluding extraneous or non-recurring income and expenditure. The stabilised net income shows the revenue excluding distortions, such as the costs of substantial capital improvements or a high level of vacant accommodation during the initial renting period.

stage payment

see **interim payment**.

stakeholder

A third party who holds money or property on behalf of two or more parties to a contract until certain conditions have been met; or on behalf of parties who are in dispute with one another, until that dispute has been resolved.

A payment made to another party as a form of **deposit**, or **earnest money**, prior to a formal exchange of contract for the sale of land, is held by that party acting as a stakeholder and normally it must be returned to the prospective purchaser if no contract results; the proposed vendor having no responsibility for the stakeholder's failure to repay the deposit – Sorrell *v* Fitch [1977] AC 728. This may be contrasted with a payment made to another party when a contract is signed which, if there is no evidence to the contrary, is held by that party acting as **agent** for the vendor, and the purchaser must take action against the vendor when seeking a return of the deposit – Edgell *v* Day (1865) LR

1 CP 80. However, it is common practice for the deposit to be paid to ·a solicitor on an express condition that it is held by him acting as a stakeholder. A stakeholder, unlike an agent, may not apply the money in any way proposed by the vendor and at common law is not accountable for any interest earned on the deposit – Harrington *v* Hoggart (1830) 1 B and Ad. 586. See also **conditions of sale**, **escrowee**.

stallage

A payment made for the privilege or convenience of placing a stall on the soil, or using standing room for cattle or goods, in a **market** or **fair** – Great Yarmouth Corporation *v* Groom (1862) 1 H and C 102; A.-B. *v* Colchester Corporation [1952] Ch. 586. See also **pennage**, **piccage**.

stamp duty

In English law, originally a duty raised by requiring stamps acquired from the government to be affixed to most legal or official documents (Bl. Comm. vol. i. p. 323). Stamp duty may be of a fixed amount; or *ad valorem*, that is, in proportion to the value of the property that forms the subject matter of the document. An *ad valorem* stamp duty is now payable on most instruments by which property, or an interest in property, is conveyed or sold (Stamp Act 1891, as subsequently amended). As a rule the amount of the duty is assessed on the basis of a percentage of the consideration stated in the **instrument**, subject to exemptions for small transactions. (Leases at no rent and no premium are subject to a fixed duty of £2.) Every transfer on sale of a fee simple estate, agreement for a lease or lease for seven years or more, and a transfer on sale of a lease, or the benefit of an agreement for a lease for seven years or more, must be submitted to the Inland Revenue, and be stamped, within thirty days of the date thereof, unless the total consideration is below the amount set from time to time (Finance Act 1931, s. 28, as subsequently amended). An appropriate **denoting stamp** is embossed on the instrument to indicate that the duty has been paid. A document that is not covered by the proper duty may not be entered in civil proceedings and, therefore, is unenforceable at law. In the US, a similar form of duty is called a 'stamp tax'. See also **certificate of value, conveyance tax, registration duty**.

Taxation of Land Transactions, by A.R. Mellows, 3 edn, pp. 187–203.

Land and Tax Planning, by Patrick C. Soares, 2 edn., pp. 253–276.

Tolley's Stamp Duties, 2 edn.

44 Halsbury's Laws of England, paras. 601–800.

Sergent and Simms on Stamp Duty, 8 edn.

The Law of Stamp Duties, by J.G. Monroe and R.S. Nock, 5 edn.

stamp tax (US)

see **stamp duty**.

standard amenities

Facilities considered essential to a residential property so as to make it **fit for human habitation**. The term 'standard amenities' was introduced in the Housing Act 1959 and these amenities are now specified in the Housing Act 1974, Sch. 6 as a fixed bath or shower (normally in a separate bathroom), a wash-hand basin, a sink, a hot and cold water supply and a water closet. In general, where these amenities are absent, a grant may be

obtained from the local authority toward the cost of providing them. See also **improvement notice, intermediate grant.**
West's Law of Housing, 4 edn, pp. 268–269.

standard conditions of sale
see **conditions of sale.**

standard contract
see **standard-form contract.**

standard depth
see **standard unit.**

standard-form contract
A printed contract in which the terms and conditions are set out in a standard form so that it may be used for any number of contracts relating to similar business or similar types of transfer. For example, a 'standard lease' which contains general conditions and covenants and leaves only details of the parties, the subject property, duration and consideration to be completed. Standard form contracts, or 'standard contracts' are produced usually by authoritative bodies to assist those that use such documents by being time saving, consistent and, theoretically, less liable to misinterpretation. See also **adhesion contract, conditions of sale, precedent.**

standard grant
A grant made by a local authority, prior to the Housing Act 1974, toward the cost of providing **standard amenities** in residential property. Subsequently replaced by an **intermediate grant.**

standard lease
see **standard-form contract.**

standard mortgage clause
A clause in a fire insurance policy,

which provides that, in the event of loss, payments by the insurer shall be made to the mortgagee. See also **mortgagee clause.**

standard rent
The maximum rent that could legally be charged for a **controlled tenancy** prior to the Rent Act 1957. A rent that was initially fixed by reference to the contractual rent at a particular date and could be varied only in limited circumstances and was subsequently based on a multiple of the gross annual value of the property for rating purposes. Since all controlled tenancies have been converted to regulated tenancies such rents are no longer relevant. See also **fair rent, rent limit.**

standard unit
A unit of property of given dimensions, especially one taken as a standard for units in a new development or as a standard when applying the **comparison method of valuation.** A term most frequently applied to a shop unit: commonly a unit with a frontage of 20 or 25 feet (6.10 or 7.62 metres) and a standard depth of 60 or 100 feet (18.29 metres or 30.48 metres). See also **unit cost, zoning.**

standby commitment (or loan)
see **commitment.**

standby fee
A fee paid by an applicant for a loan as an act of earnest intent.
cf. **commitment fee.**

standing loan (or mortgage)
1. A loan requiring the payment of interest only during its term. The total amount of the principal is repayable at the end of the term. Usually a short-term or medium-term loan

granted at a fixed rate of interest. Called also a 'straight loan', a 'term loan', a 'flat loan' or simply an 'interest-only loan'. cf. **amortisation loan**.

2. A short-term loan made available as a temporary measure until an alternative and more permanent loan can be obtained; in particular, a loan granted to cover a period from completion of a development project until long-term financing is available or the project is sold.

stare decisis (L)

'To abide by a decided case'. A principle that if the same point comes forward for judicial consideration a previous decision will be applied. See also **common law, precedent**.

start-up money

see **front money**.

State Board of Equalisation (US)

see **Board of Equalisation**.

state rule (US)

see **before-and-after valuation**.

statement of condition (US)

see **balance sheet**.

'stats'

see **statutory deductions**.

status quo (L)

'The state in which things are'. See **rebus sic stantibus**.

status quo ante (L)

'The same state as before'. See **restitution**.

statut (F)

statute; by-law; regulation; ordinance. See also *loi*.

statute barred

see **Statutes of Limitation**.

Statute of Frauds

A statute, first enacted in England in 1677 to prevent the use of **fraud** and perjury as means of enforceing supposed agreements. The statute provided that certain types of contracts could not be brought before a court of law, unless evidenced by some **note** or **memorandum** in **writing** which was duly signed. The purpose of the Statute of Frauds was not to overturn contracts between parties merely on the ground of a lack of proper formality, but to prevent a claim to the benefit of a contract that has been brought about by perjury, fraud or similar action. In English law, this statute has been largely repealed or replaced by other enactments – notably, with regard to land, by the Law of Property Act 1925, s. 40 and ss. 52–54. A similar statute has been adopted by most States in the US, providing in particular that for any contract for the disposition of real estate to be legally enforceable it must be "in writing and signed by the person to be charged therewith", or some note or memorandum of the agreed terms must be in writing and duly signed. Leases for a term of one year or less are generally excluded from this requirement. See also **estoppel, part performance, signature, will**.

Real Property, by William E. Burby, 3 edn., pp. 287–289.

Cheshire & Fifoot's Law of Contract, 10 edn, p. 174 *et seq.*

Chitty on Contract, 25 edn, paras. 264–298.

statute law

Law which derives its origin from rules made by a legislative branch of government – in the UK, Parliament with Royal Assent; in the US, for Federal laws the Senate and House of Representatives with Presidential Assent, and for State laws the State Senate and Assembly, with the assent of the Governor. (In the US 'statute law' refers particularly to a state law or enactment, as distinguished from a federal law or a municipal ordinance.)

A proposed law is initiated in the form of a draft (or **bill**) which is presented to the legislature for consideration and debate. If the law is passed, in accordance with various prescribed means, it becomes a statute or Act of Parliament in the UK (or that part of the United Kingdom to which it is made applicable – for example statutes for England and Wales frequently are made separately from those applied to Scotland or Northern Ireland) and a Governmental or Legislative Act in the US (or for lesser bodies, a local law or ordinance). Frequently referred to simply as 'legislation'.

cf. **civil law, common law**. See also **Agricultural Holdings Acts, Landlord and Tenant Acts, Housing Acts, Law of Property Acts, police powers, Public Health Acts, Rent Acts, Statute of Frauds, Statutes of Limitation**. *Statute Law*, by Francis Bennion. *Statute Law*, by W.F. Craies, 7 edn.

Statute *Quia Emptores*

see *Quia Emptores*.

Statutes of Limitation

Statutes passed to fix a period of time within which proceedings must be taken in order to enforce a legal right of action. If proceedings are not taken within the specified statutory time limits, a right of action is barred. The principal time limits for actions in connection with real property are now consolidated in the Limitation Act 1980 and may be summarised as : (a) actions on a simple contract; for arrears of rent; and in tort (ss. 2, 5, 19) – six years. (b) actions on a contract under seal (s. 8) – twelve years. (c) actions to recover money (whether principal or interest) secured by a mortgage or charge, or to recover the proceeds of the sale of land (s. 20) – twelve years. (d) action to redeem land from a mortgagee in possession (s. 16) – twelve years. (e) action to recover an estate or interest in land (s. 15) – twelve years.

It should be noted that "where in the case of any action for which a period of limitation is prescribed by this Act either – (a) the action is based on **fraud** of the defendant; or (b) any fact relevant to the plaintiff's right of action has been deliberately concealed from him by the defendant; or (c) the action is for relief from the consequences of a mistake; the period of limitation shall not begin to run until the plaintiff has discovered the fraud, concealment or mistake (as the case may be) or could with reasonable diligence have discovered it" (Limitation Act 1980, s. 32 (1)). This postponement of the running of time in cases of fraud, concealment or mistake does not apply to an innocent purchaser of land for valuable consideration (1980 Act, s. 32 (3)).

In the US, the statutes of limitation vary from state to state and as to the period provided for different forms of action. See also **adverse possession, laches**. Megarry's Manual of the Law of Real Property 6 edn, pp. 520–531. *The Law of Real Property*, by Robert

Megarry and H.W.R. Wade, 5 edn., pp. 1030–1057.

statutorily protected tenant
A tenant who has the benefit of **security of tenure** conferred on him by statute and usually some form of statutory rent control. In particular, a "'statutorily protected tenancy' means (a) a **protected tenancy** within the meaning of the Rent Act 1977 or a tenancy to which Part I of the Landlord and Tenant Act 1954 applies; (b) a protected occupancy or **statutory tenancy** as defined in the Rent (Agriculture) Act 1976; a tenancy to which Part II of the Landlord and Tenant Act 1954 applies; a tenancy of an agricultural holding within the Agricultural Holdings Act 1948" (Protection from Eviction Act 1977, s. 99). See also **agricultural tenancy, business tenancy, eviction, long tenancy, protected occupier.**

statutory assignment
see **legal assignment.**

statutory conditions of sale
see **conditions of sale.**

statutory declaration
A written statement of facts signed by the person making the declaration and attested by a notary public, a Justice of the Peace, or Commissioner for Oaths. The Interpretation Act 1978, Sch. 1 states that such a declaration is one made in accordance with the Statutory Declarations Act 1835, which has the effect of making a false declaration akin to perjury. A statutory declaration may be used in extrajudicial proceedings to much the same effect as a declaration made in court under oath. A statutory declaration is made frequently when it is not possible to find the true owner of an interest in land; when it is necessary to establish a fact relating to any claim that might affect that interest e.g. the period of time for which a person has been in possession of land; or when title deeds have been lost.

statutory dedication
see **dedication.**

statutory deduction
In a rating valuation a deduction made from the **gross value** of a property to arrive at the **net annual value.** The amount of this deduction is set out in the Valuation (Statutory Deductions) Orders 1962 and 1973. For a property with a gross value in excess of £430 the amount is "£100 plus 16⅔ per cent of the amount by which the gross value exceeds £430". A slightly larger percentage is applied to lower value properties. Referred to as 'stats' for short.
Ryde on Rating, 13 edn, p. 1339.

statutory estate (US)
An estate or interest in land created by statute law e.g. a homestead right, dower, curtesy or community property.

statutory foreclosure (US)
Foreclosure that is carried out by a sale of the mortgage property in direct satisfaction of the debt.
cf. **strict foreclosure.** See also **foreclosure sale.**

Statutory Form of Conditions of Sale
see **conditions of sale.**

statutory formula
see **formula method.**

statutory instrument (SI)
A document that brings into effect a rule, order, regulation or by-law that has been made by a delegated authority pursuant to statute law; in particu-

lar, a document that has the effect of putting into effect a power to make, confirm, or approve an order, rule, regulation or other subordinate legislation that has been conferred on Her Majesty the Queen by Order in Council, or on a Minister of the Crown or Secretary of State (Statutory Instruments Act 1946, s. 1.). Such instruments have the same force of law as the statute from which they derive their authority. Over 2000 such instruments are issued every year covering matters which Parliament considers it would be more appropriate to delegate to a Minister. These instruments are published on behalf of a Minister by Her Majesty's Stationery Office.

statutory land use plan
see **development plan**.

statutory law
see **statute law**.

statutory lien
see **lien**.

statutory mortgage (or charge)
A **mortgage** (or **charge**) made by deed in one of the forms set out in the Fourth Schedule of the Law of Property Act 1925. Such a mortgage may be made, or transferred, merely by reference to the statute thereby reducing the length of the mortgage document (1925 Act, ss. 117, 118). See also **charge by way of a legal mortgage**.

statutory notice
Notice given or served in accordance with a statute, e.g. notice given by a landlord, under the Landlord and Tenant Act 1954, s. 25 stating his intention to terminate a **business tenancy**. See also **forfeiture, notice to quit**.

statutory nuisance
A **nuisance** that is laid down as such by statute, especially statutes passed to reduce environmental pollution or to ensure that property is not maintained in "such a state as to be prejudicial to health ... (or) injurious, or likely to cause injury, to health" (Public Health Act 1936, s. 92). See also **abatement notice**.

statutory order
see **statutory instrument**.

statutory owner
A person who has the powers of a **tenant for life** when a life interest has been created by a **strict settlement** and there is no person who has been granted the powers of a tenant for life, or who is qualified to act as tenant for life as when the land has been left to a minor. The statutory owner may be a person of full age designated by the settlement; or the trustees of the settlement (except where they have power to convey the settled land in the name of the tenant for life); or, when the beneficiary of a will is under 18 and no **vesting instrument** has been made, the personal representative of the testator until the property is independently vested in the beneficiary (Settled Land Act 1925, ss. 23, 26, 117 (1) (xxvi)).

statutory protection (of tenants)
see **security of tenure**.

statutory redemption period (US)
see **foreclosure sale**.

statutory rules
see **statutory instrument**.

statutory tenancy
A right of occupation that is brought into effect by statute law after a tenancy comes to the end of its con-

tractual term. In particular, a personal right to remain in occupation of a dwelling-house (whether a house or part of a house) when a **protected tenancy** comes to an end, or is brought to an end, in accordance with the terms by which it was created (which may be by forfeiture or any other common law method of terminating a contract of tenancy) (Rent Act 1977, s. 3). Strictly, the right is not a tenancy at all but a "status of irremovability" – Keaves v Dean [1924] 1 KB 686. It is a personal right of occupation available to a protected tenant, or a **protected occupier** who has been in possession of the dwelling immediately before termination of the tenancy; it cannot be assigned or sold and does not pass to the personal representatives of a deceased statutory tenant nor to a trustee in bankruptcy; and it continues only so long as the tenant "occupies the dwelling-house as his **residence**". It has been said that "a new *monstrum horrendum, informe, ingens*, has come into our ken, the conception of a statutory tenancy: the conception that a person may have such a right of exclusive possession as will entitle him to bring an action for trespass against the owner of that property but which confers no interest whatever in land." – Marcroft Wagons Ltd v Smith [1951] 2 KB 501. A tenant who ceases to occupy the premises and shows a clear intention not to return, or who sub-lets or endeavours to part with the entire premises loses his right to a statutory tenancy. A statutory tenancy continues, as far as applicable, on the same terms and conditions as the original contract of tenancy, unless (a) the tenant unequivocally gives up residential occupation and the tenancy

is then brought to an end by **notice to quit** given in accordance with the terms of the original contract of tenancy; (b) the court makes an order for possession against the tenant on one of the **grounds for possession** set down by statute (a landlord who obtains such an order is not required to give notice to quit to the tenant as the order automatically brings the tenancy to an end); (c) a new contractual tenancy is agreed between the parties; or (d) the tenant gives notice to quit in accordance with the terms of the original contract of tenancy (or if no notice is so required not less than three months notice) (Rent Act 1977, s. 3).

On the death of a statutory tenant the right of irremovability may be transmitted either to the surviving spouse (if any) of the original tenant or otherwise a "member of the tenant's family", providing the successor was residing in the dwelling immediately before the death of the original tenant (and for six months prior thereto if the successor was not a spouse). This right of succession (a 'statutory tenancy by succession') can take place twice after the death of the original tenant, with a spouse taking priority in the succession (Rent Act 1977, Sch. 1, as amended by the Housing Act 1980, s. 76).
cf. **contractual tenancy**. See also **business tenancy**, **grounds for possession**, **long tenancy**, **regulated tenancy**, **tied accommodation**.
Real Property and Real People, by K.J. Gray and P.D. Symes, pp. 433-443 (1981).
The Law of Landlord and Tenant, by David Lloyd Evans, 2 edn., pp. 290-297.
Landlord and Tenant Law, by David

Yates and A.J. Hawkins, pp. 300–307, 328–330 (1981).
Landlord and Tenant, by Martin Partington, 2 edn., pp. 207–220.
Woodfall's Landlord and Tenant, 28 edn, paras. 3–0192 to 3–0211.
27 Halsbury's Laws of England, paras. 590–604.

statutory tenant
A person who holds a **statutory tenancy** i.e. a tenant who has a statutory right to retain occupation of a dwelling house after a contractual tenancy has come to an end. See also **statutorily protected tenant**.

statutory trust
A trust that arises as a result of a statutory provision. In particular, a trust created to hold land "upon trust to sell the same and stand possessed of the net proceeds of sale ..." (Law of Property Act 1925, s. 35). See also **implied trust, statutory trust for sale**.

statutory trust for sale
A **trust for sale** that expressly or impliedly comes into existence by virtue of statute. A statutory trust for sale may arise if (i) land is transferred (by devise or conveyance) to two or more persons as tenants in common (Law of Property Act 1925, s. 34 (2)); (ii) land is transferred (by devise or conveyance) for the benefit of two or more persons as joint tenants (Law of Property Act 1925, s. 36 (1): (iii) a person dies **intestate** and personal representatives are appointed to administer that person's estate (Administration of Estates Act 1925, s. 33 (1)); (iv) a legal estate is conveyed to two or more persons jointly – not as mortgagees or trustees – of whom at least one is an infant (Law of Property Act 1925, s. 19 (2)); (v) trustees

have taken property that has been freed of a mortgagor's right to repay the debt, as by **foreclosure** (Law of Property Act 1925, s. 31); (vi) in certain cases, when trustees of a settlement invested the proceeds of sale of personal property in land (Law of Property Act 1925, s. 32 (1)). Unlike an express trust for sale created to deal with settled land, a statutory trust for sale requires the trustees, as far as possible, to respect the wishes of the beneficiaries; the trustees are required to give effect to the rights of those who are interested in the land, as opposed to those who were interested in the land e.g. the settlor. See also **joint tenancy, statutory trust**.
Cheshire's Modern Law of Real Property, 13 edn, pp. 198–199.
The Law of Real Property, by Robert Megarry and H.W.R. Wade, 5 edn., pp. 412–421.
The Law of Succession, by E.R. Mellows, 4 edn., pp. 151–152, 489–490.

statutory undertaker
A body authorised by statute law to provide services to the general public – in particular, transport by road, rail, water or air, e.g. British Rail, British Waterways, public utilities, e.g. Postel; the Electricity, Water or Gas Boards; responsibility for canals, docks, harbours, piers or lighthouses, e.g. the Port of London Authority; or excavation of minerals, e.g. the National Coal Board. (Acquisition of Land (Authorisation Procedure) Act 1946, s. 8; Housing Act 1957, s. 189 (1)). A statutory undertaker is usually, but is not necessarily, a public authority. See also **general development order, highway authority**.

step-rate mortgage
A mortgage loan granted for a long

term (usually 20 or 25 years) at an interest rate that varies at predetermined stages during the period of the contract. Such a mortgage, although rare, may be granted to ease the mortgagor's costs in the early years. See also **variable rate mortgage**.

step-up clause (US)
see **escalator clause**.

step-up (or step-down) rent
A form of **graduated rent** that starts at a low (or high) level, especially a level that is well below (or above) market value, and increases (or decreases) automatically at stages during the term of the lease, normally until it reaches the market rent then current at the time the lease was entered into.

stepped rent
see **graded rent**.

stet (L)
'Let it stand'.

stinted pasture
The right to turn out as many, but no more, cattle on to **common land** as is sufficient to manure and stock the land. A common of pasture 'without stint' means that the number of cattle is not 'unmeasured' i.e. not properly ascertained (Bl. Comm. vol. iii p. 239). The right of pasture may also be 'stinted', i.e. limited, in respect of time. See **cattlegate**.

stipulation
1. A **condition** in a contract that restricts the action of the parties. See also **restrictive covenant**.
2. **A bargain**.

stipulation (F)
provision, covenant.
(*stipulation pour autrui* – a contract

by which one person obtains from another an obligation or profit for a third party. In French law a *contrat* (contract) generally cannot affect third parties (a similar principle to **privity of contract** found in common law) but, "one may stipulate for the benefit of a third party when this is the condition of a stipulation which one makes for oneself or of a gift which one makes to another. He who has made the stipulation cannot revoke it if the third party has declared that he desires to take advantage of it" (French Civil Code, art. 1121). This provision enables a mortgagee to claim a debt from a purchaser of a property when the latter has acquired the property subject to an undertaking given to the vendor that he will pay off the mortgage.
Manuel de Droit Civil, by Pierre Voirin et Gilles Goubeaux, 20 edn., pp. 385–390).
(*stipulation, d'un contrat* – provision or clause, of a contract).

stirpes (L)
see *per stirpes*.

stock
1. Capital invested in or lent to a business or enterprise. A term that normally covers the shares (ordinary or preferential) and **debenture** stock, but not the unsecured loans of a company. Stock may be distinguished from shares in a company by having to be fully paid up, and being transferable in any amounts, i.e. by not being distinguished by numbering. See also **security, share**.
2. A fixed-interest security granted by a government authority.
3. Property held for sale or for processing. See also **inventory, land bank**.

4. An estate or property that produces income.

5. A family, or a line of descent. The first person to hold property that is to be transmitted by **succession**.

stop list

see **black list**.

stop notice

A notice served by a local authority, in accordance with the provisions of the Town and Country Planning Act 1971, s. 90, as amended by the Town and Country Planning (Amendment) Act 1977, upon any person who has an interest in land, or any person who is carrying on an activity on land, that is the subject of an **enforcement notice**, stipulating that an "activity" being carried out on the land must be stopped within a specified period (being not less than three days nor more than twenty one days). A 'site notice' may be placed also on the land giving details of the stop notice. A stop notice may be served after an enforcement notice has been served in order to prevent further activity until the outcome of the enforcement notice has been decided, but the stop notice must be served before the enforcement notice takes effect. The effect of a stop notice is to bring an enforcement notice into immediate effect and thus require the suspension of all further activity on the land. It continues in effect until the enforcement notice procedure is completed; the enforcement notice is withdrawn, expires or is quashed; or the stop notice is withdrawn. A stop notice is a temporary expedient against which there is no appeal. A local authority may be liable to pay compensation if a person with an interest in the land has been deprived of a benefit as a

direct consequence of the notice, as when subsequently the enforcement notice is not upheld or is modified; or either the enforcement notice or the stop notice is withdrawn and the stop notice has caused the interested person to suffer financial loss. The compensation may cover such matters as the cost arising from a breach of a building contract when building work is interrupted by a stop notice. A stop notice may not be applied to prevent (a) the use of any building as a dwelling-house; (b) the use of land as the site for a caravan that is used as a main or only residence; or (c) to prevent any action that is essential to comply with a requirement of the enforcement notice.

Guide to Planning and Development, by R.N.D. Hamilton, 7 edn., p. 342.
An Outline of Planning Law, by Desmond Heap, 8 edn., pp. 228–230.
Urban Planning Law, by Malcolm Grant, pp. 423–425 (1982).
Encyclopaedia of Planning Law and Practice, edited by Desmond Heap, paras. 1–183, 4–180 to 4–182.

store

see **retail store, warehouse**.

storey, or story

All those parts of a building on the same floor level, especially at a level above the ground. The space in a building between consecutive floor levels. "Each of a number of tiers or rows (of orders, columns, window mullions or lights, etc.) disposed horizontally one above another" *The Shorter Oxford English Dictionary*). Probably derived from a practice in medieval times of painting a series of pictures on mullions or horizontal bands set out between windows to depict a tale or story.

straight capitalisation (US)

The **capitalisation** of an income by the application of a single factor, or multiplier, which assumes that the income is receivable in perpetuity; as compared with **annuity capitalisation** which applies a factor, based on the present value of one unit, for a period of time. Called also 'direct capitalisation'. In the UK the application of a **years' purchase** (YP) in perpetuity is equivalent to straight capitalisation and the application of a YP for a period of time is equivalent to annuity capitalisation. See also **overall capitalisation rate**.

The Appraisal of Real Estate, AIREA, 8 edn., pp. 341, 387–401.

straight lease (US)

A lease with a rent that is fixed throughout its term, i.e. with a **flat rent**.

straight-line method of depreciation

A method of allowing for **depreciation** by which the cost of an asset, or the total amount to be written off, is divided by the number of years over which the asset is to be depreciated, and the resulting quotient deducted each year from the initial amount; i.e., in accounting, an allowance of an equal amount, or a fixed percentage, each year against the profits of a company to provide for the replacement cost of an asset at the end of its economic life. This method of depreciation assumes that the asset being depreciated declines in value at a constant rate over its estimated life. Called also the 'age-life method of depreciation'.

cf. **accelerated method of depreciation**.

straight-line recapture

The **recapture** of the cost of an investment by equal periodic amounts.

straight loan (or mortgage)

see **standing loan (or mortgage)**.

straight rent (US)

see **flat rent**.

straight-term loan

see **standing loan**.

straight-up participation (US)

see **side-by-side participation**.

straight yield

see **running yield**.

strategic plan

see **regional plan**.

stream

A **watercourse** that runs in a defined channel on or under the surface of the ground; in particular, a narrow, natural course of water forming a small river or brook. "A stream of water, in law, is water which runs in a defined course. It is that which is capable of diversion; and it has been held that it does not include the percolation of water below ground" – Taylor *v* St. Helen's (1877) 6 Ch. D 273. See also **riparian rights**, **water rights**.

street

A thoroughfare or roadway, which generally is paved and provides a public right of access for passengers or vehicles; but not necessarily a **highway**. In particular, a way that has houses or other buildings running in a more or less continuous row along one or both sides. "What one has to find before one can determine that the highway in question is a street, is that the highway has become a street in the ordinary application of the word, because by reason of the number of houses, their continuity and proximity to one another, what would be a road or highway has been converted into a street" – Attorney General *v* Laird [1925] 1 Ch. 318. The term 'street' may be used to encompass the footpath and normally includes the houses or buildings on either side. A street may be distinguished from a **road** where the emphasis is on the coming and going, whereas in a street the primary concern is with access to and from houses or buildings. Thus a **cul-de-sac** is a street.

In statute law 'street' is given a more extended meaning to encompass a way or area that would not necessarily be covered in the ordinary meaning of the word; for example, a street "includes any highway and any road, lane, footpath, square, court, alley, or passage, whether a thoroughfare or not, and includes part of a street" (Highways Act 1980, s. 329 (1)). A similar definition is contained in the Public Health Act 1936, s. 343 (1) and in various statutes dealing with public utilities and road traffic.

street works

Works carried out, normally by a highway authority, in order to provide or maintain a **street**, including drainage work, surfacing or resurfacing, paving, making good a street and the provision or repair of lighting (Highways Act 1980, s. 203 (3)). (For this purpose a street is not defined according to the popular meaning of the word but by statute: Warwickshire CC *v* Atherstone Common Rights Proprietors (1964) 65 LGR 439).

The Law Relating to Private Street Works, by H. Parris (1979).

strict foreclosure (US)

Foreclosure on mortgaged property when, after the mortgagor has been given a fixed time (usually six months or less) to repay his outstanding debt and the debt remains unpaid, the property is vested in the mortgagee without the mortgagor having a subsequent right of **redemption** or a right to insist on a **foreclosure sale**. The effect of strict foreclosure is to vest title to the property in the mortgagee and bar the mortgagor's **equity of redemption**. Strict foreclosure, which originated from the English common law right of foreclosure that gave little redress to the mortgagor, is no longer common in the US and the courts normally intervene to permit the mortgagor a stay of execution or a right to a foreclosure sale. See also **legal foreclosure**.

strict liability

A liability for damage or injury for which a person is culpable, irrespective of any intentional, inadvertent or meditated neglect. A liability that arises because a person is involved with an exceptional or hazardous activity, or because he or she exerts control over dangerous property. Strict liability if a form of **tort** for which the liability is not absolute but, because there is an unnatural element of danger attached to certain activities or properties, the law allows little scope for an evasion of blame. The law expects that a person who knows, or ought to realise, that he is more likely to cause injury or harm as a result of a "non-natural" enterprise or operation, will exercise a more marked degree of care than is required in the course of any normal daily activity.

Strict liability may arise from (i) the bringing or keeping of something on land which is likely to cause damage or injury if it escapes; (ii) the keeping of animals, especially those that belong to a dangerous species; or (iii) the ownership or use of dangerous or defective property, or the conducting of hazardous operations on land. In respect of (i), it was said by Blackburn J., when establishing the 'Rule in Rylands *v* Fletcher', that "a person who for his own purposes brings on his lands and keeps there anything likely to do mischief if it escapes, must keep it in at his peril, and if he does not do so, is *prima facie* answerable for all the damage which is a natural consequence of its escape." – Rylands *v* Fletcher (1868) LR1 Ex. 279–280 (LR 3 HL 330). This liability extends for example, to the escape of water from a reservoir (as in Rylands *v* Fletcher); the escape of noxious waste, gas, vibration or even noxious persons; and the escape of fire (except when a fire starts accidentally, and without gross negligence: Fire Prevention (Metropolis) Act 1774, s. 86. In respect of (ii) common law holds that a person is liable for the escape of a dangerous animal (*ferae naturae*) or any animal that is known to have a tendency to cause harm. This common law liability has been extended by the Animals Act 1971 to animals that belong to a "dangerous species" i.e. a species "which is not commonly domesticated in the British Islands, and whose fully grown animals normally have such characteristics that they are likely, unless restrained, to cause severe damage or that any damage that they may cause is likely to be severe." (1971 Act, s. 6 (2)). In addition, a person is strictly liable for an animal that causes injury if he knew, or could be taken to know, that it had abnormal characteristics. A person is strictly liable if an animal

under his control or care strays on to the highway and causes injury (unless the highway crosses common, waste or unenclosed land). In respect of (iii) a person is strictly liable for injury if he (a) keeps explosives, poisons, etc.; (b) is responsible for dangerous premises or (c) carries on any dangerous activity on land. "If a man does work on or near another's property which involves danger to that property, unless proper care is taken he is liable to the owners of the property for damage resulting to it from failure to take proper care, and he is equally liable if, instead of doing the work himself, he provides another, whether servant, agent or otherwise to do it for him. A like principle applies to work done in or near a highway involving danger to those who use it.... It was the defendant's duty to take care that the dangerous operation which he had undertaken was done safely" – Brooke *v* Bool [1928] 2 KB 587–8.

A defence to a strict liability may be raised by establishing that the plaintiff was wholly at fault (i.e. contributed to the accident); that the escape was due to *vis major* or was an **act of God**; in certain cases, that the plaintiff was a trespasser or the injury was caused by a third party's neglect; or that the act was authorised by statute. *Animal Law*, by Godfrey Sandys-Winsch, 2 edn., pp. 6–8.

Law for Land Management Students, by Richard Card, John Murdoch and Peter Schofield, pp. 397–416 (1981)

Tort, by C.D. Baker, 3 edn., p. 172 *et seq*.

The Law of Torts, by J.F. Clerk and W.H. Lindsell, 15 edn., para. 1–11 *et seq*.

The Law of Torts, by John G. Flem-

ing, 6 edn., pp. 300–337.
Winfield and Jolowicz on Tort, 10
edn, pp. 358–402.
Strict and Vicarious Liability, by
L.H. Leigh, (1982).

strict settlement

A form of **settlement** of land created
when a person wishes to ensure that
his or her estate will be preserved
intact for future generations, i.e. so
that land itself may be 'kept in the
family'. A strict settlement of land
(called the **settled land**) may be made,
by deed or will, when a landowner
wishes to ensure that a succession of
persons will enjoy the benefits of owning land; not just a claim over the
proceeds of sale, as with a **trust for
sale**. The most usual form of strict
settlement arises when land is "limited
in trust for any persons by way of
succession"(Settled Land Act 1925, s.
1 (1) (i)).

The Settled Land Act 1925, which
governs the creation and disposition
of settled land, provides that a
number of similar interests in land,
however created, are to be treated as
strict settlements (referred to in the
Act merely as a "settlement"). These
include (a) an **entailed interest** to be
held in possession (whether or not it is
capable of being barred or defeated);
(b) a **conditional fee simple**; (c) a
determinable fee simple, or any corresponding interest in leasehold land;
(d) a **contingent interest** that is equivalent to a fee simple or term of years
absolute; (e) land subject to a family
charge, e.g. "to A for life in fee simple
subject to a payment of £1000 to the
grantor's widow for her life time"; (f)
a right to possession of a fee simple
interest or a term of years absolute
granted to an infant or minor. An
interest in land held under a **bare
trust**, or an interest that resolves itself
into a bare trust (as when an infant
reaches full age and consent), cannot
be a strict settlement, because the
beneficiary can require that the land
is transferred to himself and thereby
bring the successive right to land to an
end.

A strict settlement requires (a) a
legal estate (a fee simple absolute in
possession or a term of years absolute) that is vested in a **tenant for life**
or, if there is no tenant for life appointed, a **statutory owner**; (b) two
instruments for its creation – a **vesting
document** (a 'vesting deed' or 'vesting
instrument') and a **trust instrument**;
and (c) the holder of the legal estate
to have unrestricted power (but not
the duty) to sell the settled land
(although in exercising the power he
must consider the terms upon which
the settlement was created and the
best interests of the beneficiaries).

A common form of strict settlement arises as a marriage settlement.
For example, the husband grants
himself a life interest (to take effect on
his marriage) with the remainder to
his eldest son, if any, of the marriage
(as an entailed interest) and then, if
the eldest son dies without an heir, an
interest is granted in succession to the
other sons in order of age – ultimately, if there is a failure of issue to
take the estate, the land reverts to the
husband or his successors in title. An
annual rencharge or **jointure** may be
provided for the wife if she survives
her husband and capital sums, secured on the land may be granted to
any younger children. The husband is
the tenant for his life and holds the
legal estate, and that estate and the
tenancy for life passes to the eldest

son or such other person nominated in the trust instrument.

Strict settlements are rarely made today because of (a) the complex statutory rules that govern such settlements; (b) the wide powers available to the tenant for life when dealing with the land and the possibility that the eldest son (for example) may disentail, i.e. bar the rights of those claiming after the tenant for life; and (c) the high level of taxation that can be payable upon the value of the estate of each tenant for life on his or her death. See also **rule against perpetuities**.

Strict Settlement – A Guide for Historians, by Barbara English and John Saville, University of Hull (1983).

Land Law, by P.J. Dalton, 4 edn., p. 140 *et seq.*

Real Property and Real People, by K.J. Gray and P.D. Symes, pp. 154–184 (1981).

Introduction to Land Law, by J.G. Riddall, 3 edn., pp. 95–125.

Land Law: Cases and Materials, by R.H. Maudsley and E.H. Burn, 4 edn., pp. 248–289.

Cheshire's Modern Law of Real Property, 13 edn, pp. 166–196, 789–795, 797–799.

The Law of Real Property, by Robert Megarry and H.W.R. Wade, 5 edn., p. 311 *et seq.*

Settlements of Land, by B.W. Harvey (1973).

strip centre
A form of planned **shopping centre** that is made up of a row of shops along a street, pedestrian way or mall and is designed usually to serve a small district or neighbourhood area.

strip development (US)
see **ribbon development**.

structural repair
Repair to the **structure** or main fabric of a building – Granada Theatres *v* Freehold Investment (Leytonstone) [1959] Ch. 592. A covenant in a lease to carry out structural repairs is limited to that effect: it does not require the carrying out of repair to the finishes nor decoration – Granada *v* Freehold Investment (Leytonstone) Ltd *supra*). Similarly, structural repair includes repair of the foundations, main walls, roof, main water supply and the drains, but (arguably) not the fixing of a mere leak from a pipe – Blundell *v* Osdale Ltd (1958) 171 EG 491). See also **external,** *grosses réparations*, **implied covenant, latent defect**.

structure
Derived from the Latin *stuere*, 'to heap together'. Something raised or set together; constructed or built. Any **building** or **construction**; or something that is built or constructed in the nature of a building. Commonly 'structure' is used to refer to the main frame or load-bearing parts of a building; as well as to hoardings and erections of various kinds, especially when an adjunct of or an ancillary to a building. In particular, a structure is something of a substantial nature; built as a whole, usually from a number of different parts or components; and, generally, erected as a permanent edifice. The structure comprises the primary parts of a building, which may include the water supply, drainage, etc., but not the internal fitments, finishings and decorations. "A structure is something which is constructed but not everything which is constructed is a structure ... A structure is something

of a substantial size which is built up from component parts and intended to remain permanently on a permanent foundation; but it is still a structure even though some parts may be moveable, as, for instance, about a pivot" – Cardiff Rating Authority *v* Guest, Keen Bladwin's Iron and Steel Co. Ltd [1949] 1 KB 396. Any building is a structure and anything permanently attached to a building may become part of the structure; but anything that can be moved from place to place, although in the nature of a structure, in general is not regarded as a structure. When a building is completed by a landowner the components are essentially a structure but anything added subsequently, which does not alter the building, is not normally a structural element, although it may be a fixture and thus become part of the structure. See also **infrastructure**.

structure (F)
   structure.

structure plan
   A written statement with maps, illustrations and diagrams that a local planning authority (normally a County Council) or a number of neighbouring authorities is expected to prepare, in accordance with the provisions of the Town and Country Planning Act 1971. s. 7, for an area under its jurisdiction. The structure plan for an area is prepared in order to set out, *inter alia*, (a) the local planning authority's policy and major proposals for the development and other use of land in that area (including measures for the improvement of the physical environment and the management of traffic); (b) the relationship of those proposals to general proposals for the

development and other use of land in neighbouring areas that may be expected to affect the area; and (c) such mattters as may be prescribed or as the Secretary of State for the Environment may in any particular case direct. The structure plan should indicate any part of the area that has been selected for comprehensive development, redevelopment or improvement. It should include also proposals for the protection of the countryside; the improvement of communications; the location of industry; the maintenance and improvement of leisure activities; and any general proposals for increasing economic activity. These plans are intended to form a link between a national or a **regional plan** and detailed plans for a more limited area of land e.g. a **local plan**. Structure plans should be based on a prior survey of the principal physical and economic characteristics of the area of the authority and, as appropriate, any neighbouring area; including a survey of such matters as land use, population, communication, housing needs, employment, industrial and commercial activity. The local planning authority should consult with other authorities who might be affected by the proposals contained in the structure plan. Survey material and draft plans should be published to provide for a fair degree of public participation in the formulation of structure plans. When prepared, a structure plan is submitted by the local authority to the Secretary of State for the Environment (via the Department of the Environment) for his comment and ultimate approval. At that stage the plans should be made available for inspection and opportunity given for objections to the plans to be submitted to the Secretary of State. The Secretary of State, having considered the information before him, may approve the structure plan, or he may require the local planning authority to provide further details or to modify the plan, and then resubmit it (1971 Act, s. 8). When approved, a structure plan is intended to act as a broad means of development control, but should be continually reviewed to take account of the needs of the community. See also **development plan**.

Introduction to Town and Country Planning, by John Ratcliffe, 2 edn., pp. 86–94.

Cases and Materials on Planning Law, by Michael Purdue, pp. 30–59 (1977).

sub-agent

A subordinate **agent**; a person, or organisation, appointed by one who is himself an agent in order to carry out the duties or responsibilities, or a part thereof, entrusted to that agent. An agent, the main agent, may not appoint another, as sub-agent, to perform duties or act in a capacity beyond the powers conferred on the main agent. The maxim is *delegatus non potest delegatum*, 'delegated power cannot be delegated' – which "imports that an agent cannot, without authority from his principal, devolve upon other obligations to the principal which he has himself undertaken to personally fulfil; and that, in as much as confidence in the particular person employed is at the root of the contract of agency, such authority cannot be implied as an ordinary incident in the contract" – De Busche *v* Alt (1878) 8 Ch. D 310.

However, that case indicated that there may be instances where delegation is an acceptable part of the nature or custom of a particular business or it may be necessary in an emergency.

An agent who instructs a sub-agent normally cannot claim a **commission** if the sub-agent performs the function required of the main agent, unless it can be shown that the principal accepted, expressly or impliedly, that there would, or might, be a sub-instruction – John McCann and Co. *v* Pow [1975] 1 All ER 129. Unless there is an agreement to the contrary, or the agent was authorised to employ a sub-agent, there is no **privity of contract** between a principal and a sub-agent; thus the principal cannot sue the sub-agent for **negligence** (unless the sub-agent was employed in a special capacity for which he may owe a **duty of care** to the principal); and the sub-agent cannot claim a commission from the principal; he must claim from the agent who employed him. See also **subcontractor, power of attorney**.

sub-basement

A storey, or one of several such storeys, situated below the first basement of a building.

sub-charge

A **charge** issued against the security of an existing charge or mortgage debt.

subcontractor

1. A person or firm that undertakes to perform a duty or obligation, in whole or in part, for which another has been employed. In particular, a **contractor** who carries out work on behalf of a main or **general contractor**; especially a person or firm employed for special work or to carry

out part of a main contract, e.g. plumbing, heating and ventilation, or finishing work under a building contract. A subcontractor has an obligation, or **privity of contract**, with his principal, master or employer (the main contractor); but as a rule has no contractual relationship with the party (the main employer) for whom the work or duty ultimately is being performed. A specialist subcontractor may be liable to the main employer for **negligence** in the performance of his duties, if he is considered to be in such close "proximity" as to owe a **duty of care** to the main employer – Junior Books Ltd *v* Veitchi Co. Ltd [1982] 3 WLR 377. A contracting party is free to transfer work to another, i.e. to enter into a new contract (a sub-contract), unless expressly prohibited or unless it is clearly contrary to the basis for the foundation of the contract; but in so doing he cannot assign his duties. "In many contracts all that is stipulated for is that the work shall be done and the actual hand to do it need not be that of the contracting party himself – the other party will be bound to accept performance carried out by somebody else. The contracting party, of course, is the only party who remains liable. He cannot assign his liability to a sub-contractor, but his liability in those cases is to see that the work is done and if it is not properly done he is liable. It is quite a mistake to regard that as an assignment of the contract; it is not" – Davies *v* Collins [1945] 1 All ER 248. See also **sub-agent**.

2. See **sub-purchaser**.

subdivision
The division of an area of land into

two or more plots for sale or development. Called also 'parcelling'. See also *lottisement*, **partition**.

subinfeudation
A process by which under the **feudal system** of land tenure innumerable rights to a **fee** or **feu** interest were granted in the same land by a succession of mesne or intermediate lords or landowners. Under the feudal system the ultimate or 'superior' land owner is the Sovereign who grants the land to 'inferior' owners or Crown vassals. By subinfeudation the inferior owner, adopting the position of a mesne lord, granted the right to the land to another vassal who in turn, by adopting a similar position, granted the land to yet another vassal. Each mesne lord demanded services or payment from his inferior and retained the right to regain the land if any such obligation was not met – Re Holliday [1922] 2 Ch. 698. The process of subinfeudation was prohibited in England and Wales by the Statute of **Quia Emptores** 1290, c. 1. Thereafter a fee interest could only pass by substitution i.e. one owner conveying his **tenure** to another. The replacement of substitution by subinfeudation paved the way for the holder of the fee simple to be limited to one person who in turn held directly from the Crown.

subjacent support
The support that land receives from the underlying strata.
cf. **lateral support**. See also **natural rights**, **right of support**.

subject plan
A form of **local plan** prepared by a local planning authority setting out details of special development mat-

ters in its area. These plans are not intended to deal with such matters as comprehensive development (these come within the ambit of an **action area plan**), but with such matters as detailed land use policy and urgent development control, e.g. green belt policies, land reclamation schemes.

'subject to average'
see **average**.

'subject to contract'
Words used to indicate that something set down in writing is not intended to commit the writer until a binding and concise form of contract is entered into: "the matter remains in negotiation until a **formal contract** is settled and formal contracts are exchanged" – Keppel *v* Wheller [1927] 1 KB 584 Winn *v* Bull (1877) 7 Ch. D 29. Words such as "subject to preparation of a formal contract", "subject to a proper and binding contract", or "subject to a contract to be prepared and approved by the parties' solicitors" are used, especially when an initial offer or an acceptance of an offer is made for a property, but the party to that offer or acceptance does not wish to be legally bound until such matters as title, leases, building consents, mortgages, etc., have been verified and all relevant searches completed. "Where parties enter into an agreement whether oral or in writing, which is expressly made 'subject to contract', or to a stipulation having the like effect, they demonstrate by this sipulation that they have no immediate intention of contracting" – Law *v* Jones [1973] 2 All ER 445. Thus, the parties, in using such words, are stating that whatever is said within the context of their negotiations may contain an element of equivocation. Correspondence made 'subject to contract' does not constitute a valid memorandum in **writing** for the purpose of the Law of Property Act 1925, s. 40 and, therefore, is not normally capable of creating an enforceable contract for the sale or other disposition of land or any interest in land (Tiverton Estates Ltd *v* Wearwell Ltd [1974] 1 All ER 209). Such a qualification continues to affect the agreement until both parties clearly demonstrate their intention to expurgate it, or until it can be implied that the parties have demonstrated their mutual understanding that a legal commitment has been entered into – Cohen *v* Neesdale Ltd (1982) 262 EG 437. The use of the words 'subject to contract' may also have a negating effect on the intention of the parties; for example, if a notice served by a landlord to increase the rent payable by a tenant is made 'subject to contract', the tenant could take it that the landlord's intention as to the rent he will seek to charge is based, not on the figure in the notice, but on a figure ascertained after negotiation – Shirlcar Properties Ltd *v* Heinitz and Another (1983) 268 EG 362. Also, the words may have no effect if used after terms have been agreed and nothing remains other than formal documentation – Richards (Michael) Properties *v* Corporation of Wardens of St Saviour's Parish [1975] 3 All ER 416). (The use of such words to indicate an intention not to be contractually bound is uniquely recognised in English law and may be of little effect elsewhere. Thus, in the Scottish case of Erskine *v* Glendinning, 9 Macph. 656, an acceptance of an offer of a lease "subject to lease drawn in due form"

was not precluded from being construed as a binding contract, albeit a **conditional contract**. In the US some states recognise that parties may express an intention not to be bound until formal or detailed contracts are executed – Scott *v* Fowler, (1907) 227 Ill. 104, 81 NE 34), but if parties proceed as if a binding contract exists their initial reservations may be precluded – Sewel *v* Dalby, (1951) 171 Kans. 640, 237 P 2d.366). See also **agreement for a lease, gazump, gentleman's agreement, oral contract, 'subject to finance', 'subject to survey'**.

Subject to contract – magic words? by Harold Wilkinson, 262 EG 1055 (1982).

The Standard Conditions of Sale of Land, by H.W. Wilkinson, 3 edn., pp. 111–170.

Land Law: Cases and Materials, by R.H. Maudsley and E.H. Burn, 4 edn., pp. 58–62.

42 Halsbury's Laws of England, 4 edn, para. 24.

'subject to finance'

An agreement between two parties for the transfer of an interest in property, subject to a condition that the purchaser can obtain satisfactory finance or a mortgage loan. A form of conditional (or even contingent) contract that in English law is unlikely to have any greater effect than a contract **'subject to contract'**, or is likely to be considered void for uncertainty – Lee-Parker *v* Izzet (No. 2) [1972] 2 All ER 800. (In England, it is more common for the purchaser to enter into an option to purchase, the option to extend for such a period of time as is considered adequate to obtain the requisite finance.) In the US, and in the many Commonwealth countries, the courts have tended to enforce a contract 'subject to finance' when (i) the type and terms of the loan being sought are specified (usually within set criteria); (ii) a time limit is set in which the finance must be sought and obtained; (iii) the purchaser undertakes to use his best endeavours to secure a reasonable loan on the terms specified; and (iv) a provision is made whereby the seller has the ability to procure a loan on behalf of a purchaser if the purchaser has not taken steps to do so. French law of contract tends to follow a similar view, taking a more subjective view of whether a contract exists. However, it is necessary for the parties to provide a clear indication of the basis of their agreement as the court will not make a contract for the parties. In the US, called also a 'contingent finance offer'. See also **conditional contract**.

Agreements 'Subject to finance', by Brian Coote, 40 (1) Conv. and Pr. Lawyer 37–50 (1976).

Real Estate Law, by Robert Kratovil and Raymond J. Werner, 8 edn., pp. 147–148.

'subject to mortgage'

1. See **subject to finance**.

(US) 2. A clause in a contract for the sale of property by which the purchaser agrees to take over responsibility for the payment of interest and principal under a mortgage loan secured on the property, but does not accept any subsequent personal liability in the event that the mortgagee has reason to foreclose or exercise his power of sale. Thus the purchaser accepts that if the vendor/mortgagor defaults in meeting his obligations the property can be lost to the mortgagee or disposed of by a foreclosure sale; accordingly the purchaser normally obtains a right to the **'equity of redemption'**, i.e. to repay the loan in full if the mortgagee seeks to foreclose or exercise his power of sale.

cf. **assumption**. See also **acceleration clause, reduction certificate, transfer of a mortgage**.

'subject to prior sale'

A term used, especially by real estate agents, to signify that a property may be withdrawn from the market or from a proposed **auction** sale at any stage if a contract for sale is entered into with another party, i.e. the vendor is not bound to accept an offer or submit the property for sale by auction if he chooses to retain it or dispose of the property to another party. See also **gazump**, **'subject to contract'**.

'subject to survey'

A phrase that may be added to an offer, or incorporated in an agreement, to buy property, to indicate that the purchaser does not intend to acquire the subject property unless he is able to obtain a survey report that he deems satisfactory. The contractual effect of such a phrase (or similar phrases such as 'subject to a satisfactory survey' or 'subject to a surveyor's report') depends on the intention of the parties. It may be taken to indicate (a) that the parties have entered into a **conditional contract** with the proviso that when the purchaser has obtained the survey report he is able to insist, at his choice, that the property is conveyed to him, the vendor then being committed to convey the property – Ee v Kakar (1979) 40 P

and CR 223); (b) that there is a binding contract, the purchaser has undertaken to obtain a formal survey of the subject property, and that he may withdraw from the contract only if the survey reveals something that he would not reasonably have bargained for, e.g. a major structural defect; or (c) that neither party had ever intended to be bound by any form of contract until the survey has been obtained, so that it may be said that the purchaser has "reserved unto himself the absolute and undisputed right to say whether he liked the surveyor's report" – Marks v Board (1830) 46 TLR 424. However, if there is no strong evidence that the parties intended to be bound contractually (nor had they established any basis for resolving what constitutes a satisfactory survey) it is likely that the court will treat the qualification 'subject to survey' in the same way as the qualification **'subject to contract'**. In the US, a contract subject to the purchaser obtaining a soil compaction report to his satisfaction may be enforceable provided the report proved satisfactory to a reasonable person – Collins v Vickter Manor, 47 Cal. 2d 875; 306 P. 2d 783.

If an agent introduces a purchaser of a property and that person agrees to proceed "subject to satisfactory survey", the agent cannot be said to have introduced a "willing" purchaser and thereby be entitled to a **commission** – Graham and Scott (Southgate) Ltd v Oxdale [1950] 2 KB 257.

Williams on Title, 4 edn, p. 21 & 4th Commulative Supplement D4, D5.

'Subject to Survey', by Henry E. Markson, 124 SJ 871–872 (1980).

The Standard Conditions of Sale of Land, H. Wilkinson, 3 edn, p. 38.

sub-lease

A **lease** granted by an existing lessee for a term that is shorter (by at least one day) than that held by the grantor; a grant of part of the interest held under a lease, but with the retention by the grantor of some part of the unexpired term of that lease. The portion held by the grantor is termed the **reversion**. A sub-lease of all or part of the demised premises may be granted for the entire term of the lease (less one day) or a shorter term; but it is essential that the grantor retains an interest in the land granted, otherwise the grant will be an **assignment**. "Where a lessee, by a document in the form of a sub-lease, divests himself of everything that he has (which he must necessarily do if he is transferring to his so called sub-lessee an estate as great as, or purporting to be greater than his own) from that moment he is a stranger to the land, in the sense that the relationship of landlord and tenant, in respect of tenure cannot any longer exist between him and the so called sub-lessee. That relationship must depend on **privity of estate**" – Milmo v Carreras [1946] 1 All ER. Even a periodic tenant may sub-let for periods that are similar to those for which he holds the tenancy, providing there is a provision for termination prior to the termination of the landlord's interest – Wheeler v Smith [1926] EGD 194 (DC).

A covenant in a lease not to "assign or sub-let" will be breached if there is a grant of any right of **tenancy**, but the grant of a licence, or otherwise permitting someone into possession without payment, is not a breach of such a covenant; unless there is added such words as "in any other way part with possession" – Horsey v Steiger

[1898] 2 QB 259. A covenant "not to sub-let" the demised premises is not breached by a sub-letting of only part of the premises – Cook v Shoesmith [1951] 1 KB 752, unless words such as "any part thereof" are added. Strictly, it is a **misdescription** to refer to a 'sub-lease' as a 'lease'. Called also a 'sub-tenancy', 'underlease', or sometimes a 'derivative lease'. See also **head lease, privity, relief, restraint on alienation, sandwich lease, sub-lessee, surrender.**

sub-lessee

A lessee or tenant who holds an interest in property by virtue of a **sub-lease**, i.e one who holds a right under a lease from a lessor who himself holds an interest by virtue of a lease. If L grants a lease of land to T and T sub-leases the land to ST, then at common law ST's interest comes to an end if T's interest is brought to an end by forfeiture (but not if it is surrendered) – Great Western Ry Co. v Smith (1876) 2 Ch. D 235. However, in that event ST may apply for **relief** to the court and may be granted a new lease for a term that is not greater than the unexpired term of the former lease to T and upon such other terms as the court may decide (Law of Property Act 1925, s. 146 (4), as amended by the Law of Property (Amendment) Act 1929, s. 1). If a sub-tenant is granted relief he usually enters into a direct lease with the lessor of the forfeited lease on similar terms to the old sub-lease, although he may be permitted to extend his term to one that corresponds to the forfeited lease. Called also a 'sub-tenant'.

sub-lessor

A lessee or tenant who grants a **sub-**

lease to another; one who holds a lease and grants a lease of the same property to another, retaining to himself a **reversionary interest**.

sub-let

1. To grant a **sub-lease.** Synonymous with underlet.
2. To enter into a contract with a **sub-contractor.**

sub-mortgage

A **mortgage** granted upon the security of an existing mortgage, i.e. a mortgage of an existing mortgagee's interest in a property. In English law a sub-mortgage may be created by a 'charge by way of a legal mortgage' secured against the mortgagee's rights or, alternatively if the original mortgage was created by a lease, by a sublease for a term that is shorter (usually by a few days) than that held by the original mortgagee. An equitable sub-mortgage may be made by a deposit of the title deeds, if held by the head mortgagee, with the sub-mortgagee. Normally, a sub-mortgagee takes over the mortgagee's right and remedies available under the original mortgage. Alternatively, he may exercise his rights against the original mortgagee and, to satisfy his claim, take that mortgage direct.

subordination

An agreement to move a mortgage (or lien) to a lower **priority**, i.e. an agreement by which a mortgagee (or lienee) agrees to defer his right of recourse to a property in favour of another party who has, or may have, a lower ranked or even no charge or claim against the property.

sub-purchaser

A person who acquires property from another immediately after that other aquires the property. A purchaser contracts to purchase a property then, simultaneously, undertakes to resell that property to another, a 'sub-purchaser'; thus the first purchaser acts purely as a conduit for the sub-purchaser. A sub-purchaser acquires a **lien** on any interest in the subject property acquired by the purchaser and on any sum paid by the purchaser as a deposit.

subrogation

Literally 'to ask in another's place'. The substitution of a third party for an existing party to a contract so that the third party may enforce a claim arising from that contract, in the same way as the existing party. The principle of subrogation provides that if one person discharges the debt or liability of another then the former may take the place of the latter for any resultant claim against a third party. Thus, if A owes money to B, and C discharges that debt, then C has a right to recover money from any third party who owes money to A, as if he were in A's place for that purpose. C must have been under some obligation regarding the debt, or have some interest to be protected when paying the debt; but by paying the debt equity acknowledges C's right to be reimbursed by taking over rights, remedies or claims available to A; even though those rights and claims have not been expressly assigned or ceded to C – Norfolk and Dedham Fire Insurance Co. *v* Aetna Casualty and Surety Co., 132 Vt. 341, 318 A. 2d 659 – Orakpo *v* Manson Investments Ltd [1977] 1 All ER 666. The substituted party takes over all the rights and duties of the original party, even though effectively the contract may not have been formally assigned to him. "What it does is provide specific remedies in particular cases of what might be classified as **unjust enrichment** in a legal system based on the civil law.... It is a convenient way of describing a transfer of rights from one person to another, without assignment or assent of the person from whom the rights are transferred and which takes place by operation of law in a whole variety of widely different circumstances" – Orakpo *v* Manson Investments Ltd [1977] 3 All ER 7 HL. "Subrogation differs from a **transfer** or **assignment** of a debt, and from delegation, in the circumstances that it does not, necessarily, depend upon the creditor, but may be made independently of him. It is, properly speaking, but a fictitious cession made to one who has a right to offer payment; it is not a true cession nor sale of a debt, but such as is conceded by law and may have effect by operation of law and the act of the debtor, even without the consent of the creditor from whom the debt proceeds."(Dixon on Subrogation (1862) p. 1).

In **insurance**, the insurer has a right of subrogation, that is a right to pursue the insured's claims against a third party in order to reduce or mitigate the amount of loss or residual liability of the insurer; in particular, a right to take over property for which the insured has paid the owner an adequate **indemnity** to cover the loss thereof. The doctrine of subrogation requires broadly that "the insurer must be placed in the position of the assured"... the insurer "is entitled to the advantage of every right of the assured, whether such right consists in contract, fulfilled or unfulfilled, or

in remedy for tort ... the doctrine does not arise upon any terms of the contract of insurance; it is only another proposition which has been adopted for the purpose of carrying out the fundamental rule (i.e. indemnity) which I have mentioned, and it is a doctrine in favour of the underwriters or insurers in order to prevent the assured from recovering more than the full indemnity; it has been adopted solely for that reason" – Castellian *v* Preston (1883) 11 QBD 38. The insurer is entitled to step into the insured's shoes and benefit from any right or claim that would be available to the insured in respect of the subject matter of the insurance, provided that any sum so recovered is limited to the loss for which the insurer has provided an indemnity, i.e. he may recover only what he has actually paid by way of indemnity to the insured.

In French law subrogation arises also when property that is destroyed or disposed of may be replaced by a suitable alternative property, rather than the property *in esse*. For example, if a person sells goods upon which another has a lien, the seller may be permitted to substitute, or subrogate, similar goods, based on value, to preserve the lienor's rights – this is termed *subrogation réelle* – "subrogation signifies replacement, *subrogation réelle* is therefore, the replacement of one property by another which takes the place and character of the former" (Précis Dalloz. *Droit Civil, Les Biens* (Alex Weill) 2 edn, p. 258). See also **guarantee**.

cf. **abandonment, novation.**
Manuel de Droit Civil, by Pierre Voirin and Gilles Goubeaux, 20 edn, pp. 483–489.
Chitty on Contract 25 edn, paras.

3728–3729, 3734.
The Law of Insurance, by Raoul Colinvaux, 4 edn., pp. 135–141.
General Principles of Insurance Law, by E.R. Hardy Ivamy, 4 edn., pp. 496–513.
MacGillivray and Partington on Insurance Law, 7 edn, pp. 471–510

subrogation (F)
subrogation; substitution.
(*subrogation réelle* – see **subrogation**).

sub-sale
The **sale** of a property immediately it is acquired (or, strictly, immediately after it is acquired), usually as a result of an agreement entered into simultaneously with the original purchase contract. In the US, called sometimes a 'flip-sale'. The sale of the rights under a purchase contract is known also as 'trading on the equity'. See also **sub-purchaser**.

subscribe
1. To place one's **signature** at the end of a document; literally 'to write under'. Subscribe may be used sometimes to refer to the giving of assent to or attesting a document, especially a will. See also **attest**.
2. To agree to purchase shares in an undertaking; especially a newly formed company (Companies Act 1948, s. 445 (1)).
3. To agree to make an investment.

subsequent condition
see **condition subsequent**.

subsidised rent
A rent that is reduced effectively by a payment made to the tenant, generally by a party other than the landlord. For example, a grant by a government agency to a local authority enabling the authority to charge a lower rent for a house than would normally be considered economic, or to charge a rent that is below the market value. In the US, called also a 'subsidy rent'.
cf. **rent concession**.

subsidy
A grant of financial assistance which may take the form of a gift of money or pecuniary benefits such as a price reduction. In particular, aid given by central or local government to a private individual or company, especially when such aid is given to assist that party in achieving a government's economic objectives. In Britain, the most common examples of subsidies that affect real property are the **improvement grant**; the **option mortgage**; central government subsidies made to local authorities or New Town Corporations toward the cost of public housing; a tax allowance in a **development area** or **enterprise zone**. See also **capital allowance**.

subsidy rent (US)
see **subsidised rent**.

subsoil
see **subsurface rights**.

substantial completion
see **substantial performance**.

substantial performance
Completion or **performance** of a contract in good faith to a point when it may be said that the beneficiary has received or obtained substantially that which he had contracted for. The legal 'doctrine of substantial performance' may discharge a promisee to a contract from an obligation to perform that contract, as literally interpreted, when performance would be inequitable. The principle of the doct-

rine is that if a party (the promissee) to a contract has completed his obligations to all intent and purpose, but has failed in a minor way only, the promisor may not repudiate the contract and refuse all payment as if the contract had not been properly performed. However, the doctrine may not relieve the promisor of his right to claim damages for a loss suffered as a result of the non-completion of that which was contracted for. For example, if a builder completes a house but has used different, but adequate, materials to those set out in the specification, the owner of the house may be obliged to accept that the house is completed – subject to a right to **set-off** any loss in value he has suffered against the final contract price. This doctrine is one of equity and, therefore, is a matter for the discretion of the court. See also **part performance**. *Real Estate Law*, by Robert Kratovil and Raymond J. Werner, 8 edn., pp. 553–555.
Cheshire and Fifoot's Law of Contract, 10 edn, pp. 479–480.
Hudson's Building and Engineering Contracts, 10 edn, pp. 245–255.

substantial repair
see **repair**, **tenantable repair**.

substitué, bien (F)
entailed estate; remainder; reversionary interest.

substitution of liability
see **novation**.

substitution value
The value of a property based on the cost of a suitable alternative. A basis for the objective valuation of any property, especially when applying the **comparison method of valuation**,

or when assessing the reinstatement cost. See also **opportunity cost**.

subsurface right
The right of a landowner to the stratas or sub-soil underneath his **land**. Strictly, an owner of land owns the subsoil *ad centrum*, 'to the centre of the earth' (excluding certain minerals) and, therefore, he may grant a right for another party to use the subsoil or substrata as a right (i) to remove material (as a **profit à prendre**); (ii) to use and enjoy a passage under the land to or from adjoining land (as an **easement**); or (iii) to enter and use a space under the land, e.g. a mine passage (as a **lease** or **licence**). See also **mineral rights**, **mining lease**, **right of support**.

sub-tenancy
see **sub-lease**.

sub-tenant
see **sub-lessee**.

subtopia
A word compounded by the architect Ian Nairn (in *'Outrage'*, Architectural Press, 1955) from 'suburbia' and 'utopia' to denote "the world of universal low density mass ... an even spread of abandoned aerodromes and fake rusticity, wire fences, traffic roundabouts, gratuitous notice boards, car parks, and 'Things-in-Fields'"; i.e. uncontrolled surburban sprawl, or any form of urban development that is ill-conceived, ill-designed and unsightly.
cf. **urbanity**. See also **ribbon development**.

suburb
Derived from the Latin *sub*, 'close to' and *urbs*, 'town'. An area on 'he outskirts of a town or city. Commonly

used to refer to a predominately residential area, that has developed on the fringe of an urban area adjacent to the countryside; especially an area from where many of the residents commute to work in a town or city. Historically the 'suburbs' were situated just outside the city or town walls or boundary; in general they were less intensively or formally developed than the town centre; and were considered less salubrious than the town itself – "In the suburbs of a town ... lurking in corners and lanes blind" –Chaucer.

suburbia
A word used, commonly in a derogatory sense, for a **suburb** of a town or city.

succession
The taking over of property by **inheritance** or by **will**, but not by grant or purchase. A process by which an interest in property passes, on the death of its owner, to another. See also **devise, intestacy, settlement**.
The Law of Succession, by A.R. Mellows, 4 edn.
The Law of Succession, by D.H. Parry and J.B. Clark, 8 edn.

succession (F)
succession; inheritance; estate. The transfer of property from a deceased person or the *patrimoine* transferred. (*droit de succession* – estate duty).

succession tax (or duty) (US)
A tax levied against the value of property received from a deceased person; a tax on the benefit of acquiring property by inheritance. See also **capital transfer tax, estate tax, inheritance tax**.

successor
One who follows in place of another. A person who acquires land by **succession**.

sufferance
Consent to, or acceptance of, an action that has not been expressly authorised, but is implied by the failure to condemn or interfere with that action.
cf. **estoppel**. See also **tenancy on sufferance**.

sufficient repair
see **tenantable repair**.

suggestio falsi (L)
'A statement of a falsehood'; an active misrepresentation.
cf. *suggestio veri*.

suggestio veri (L)
'The suppression of truth'; a passive **misrepresentation**. (*suppressio veri, suggestio falsi* – 'suppression of the truth is a suggestion of falsehood'). See also **utmost good faith**.

sui generis (L)
'Of its own kind' i.e. the only one of its kind.
cf. *ejusdem generis*.

sui juris (L)
'Of his own right' i.e. subject to no legal incapacity.

suitable alternative accommodation
Premises to which it might reasonably be expected that an occupier would move in order that an existing property can be vacated and used for another purpose; in particular, a dwelling-house to which it would be reasonable to require a tenant to move in order that he or she can vacate an existing dwelling and, as a result, the landlord can obtain a court

order for possession of the dwelling under the Rent Acts (or the Housing Act 1980 in the case of a secure tenancy). The Rent Act 1977, s. 98 provides that a court may make an order for possession of a dwelling-house, which is or would become subject to a **statutory tenancy**, if it is satisfied that "suitable alternative accommodation is or will be available to the tenant". This requirement may be satisfied by a certificate from the local housing authority that it will provide such accommodation; or when the court is satisfied that the alternative accommodation is reasonably suitable to the needs of the tenant and his family as regards "proximity to place of work", and that the accommodation is (a) similar as regards rental and extent as the local housing authority may provide in the circumstances or (b) "reasonably suitable to the means of the tenant and to the needs of the tenant and his family as regards extent and character", which, if applicable, includes the provision of furniture (Rent Act 1977, Sch. 15, Part IV). The accommodation should be judged, then, according to the means of the tenant; his or her housing needs; the extent and character of the accommodation (it should not be such that it may be considered overcrowded); the location of the premises; the prospect of the tenant having equivalent security of tenure; and the entire circumstances of the tenant's existing accommodation. The tenant should be able to live in a "reasonably similar way" – Hill and Another *v* Rochard and Another (1983) 266 EG 631. Environmental considerations may be taken into account, so that if a house is especially noisy, compared to the previous house, it may not be 'suitable alternative accommodation' – Redspring *v* Francis [1973] 1 WLR 138). However, it need not be in all respects as good; the tenant's cultural and social aspects are not factors that necessarily need to be considered – Siddiqui *v* Rashid [1980] 1 WLR 1018; and "the alternative accommodation need not be a dwelling-house in which all the fads and fancies and preferences of the tenant shall be gratified to the full" – Sheriff Chilholm at Jedburgh, 16 July 1920 in Clark *v* Smith (unreported), quoted in Hill *v* Rochard, *supra*.

A landlord of premises that are subject to a **business tenancy** where the tenant has a statutory right to a new tenancy, may oppose the tenant's application for a new tenancy when "the landlord has offered and is willing to provide and secure the provision of alternative accommodation". The accommodation must be "suitable for the tenant's requirements (including the requirements to preserve goodwill) having regard to the nature and class of business and to the situation and extent of, and the facilities afforded by, the holding". Regard must be had also to the "terms of the current tenancy and all other relevant circumstances" (Landlord and Tenant Act 1954, s. 30 (1) (d)). See also **grounds for possession**.

Woodfall's Landlord and Tenant, 28 edn, para. 2–0715.

How Suitable is Suitable? by D.W. Williams, 268 EG 882–4 (1983).

Cases and Materials on English Land Law, by Michael Harwood, pp. 27–35.

Landlord and Tenant Law, by David Yates and A.J. Hawkins, pp. 335–336, 508–509 (1981).

sum-of-the-years-digits method of depreciation (SYD depreciation)

A method of allowing for **depreciation** that provides for a greater rate of depreciation in the earlier years. The total amount to be depreciated is divided by the summation of the number of years over which the asset is to be depreciated (the sum-of-the-years-digits) and the result is multiplied each year by the number of years outstanding. For example, if depreciation is to be allowed over 6 years, in year 1 the depreciation would be

$$6/(6 + 5 + 4 + 3 + 2 + 1)$$

or $6/21$ths of the total; in year 2, $5/21$ths of the total, and so on. The sum-of-the-years-digits, D, may be obtained by the formula:

$$D = n(n + 1)/2$$

where n = the number of years.

summary possession (US)
see **eviction**.

summation method or approach (US)

An approach to an appraisal of a property based on the addition of the value of all components utilised to create the whole, e.g. the **cost approach** when used to assess the worth of a property by calculating the cost of all the labour and materials, plus the profit, required to rebuild that property. See also **quantity surveying**.

summation rate (US)
see **component capitalisation rate**.

superette
see **supermarket**.

superficie (F)

surface area (of a building or part thereof); ground lease.

(*droit de superficie* – "The right of an owner (called a *superficiaire*) to an area of property, of which the underneath or '*trefonds*' is owned by another property owner (called a *tréfoncier*) ... the '*droit de superficie*' can relate to the entire surface of ground, only the sub-soil escaping its hold" – Précis Dalloz, *Droit Civil, Les Biens* (Alex Weill) 2 edn, p. 591. A right which is similar to a modern English building lease whereby the building is granted for a long-term but strictly the land is retained by another, and at the end of the period of grant the entirety reverts to the grantor or landowner).

cf. **emphyteotic lease**. See also **condominium**, *concession immobilière*, *démembrements de la propriété*.

Droit Civil, Les Biens, by Jean Carbonnier, 11 edn., pp. 306–316.

superficies

1. In Roman or the civil law, the grant of a right to the surface of land to enable the grantee to build thereon, subject to the payment of an annual sum. See also *droit de superficie*.
2. The surface of the earth and what is on top of it.

superficies solo cedit (L)

'A structure attached to the land becomes part of the land'. See **fixture**.

superfluous land

Land acquired by compulsory powers but not required for the purpose of the undertaking envisaged – Hobbs *v* Midland Railway Co. (1882) 20 Ch. D 431. Originally land acquired by a railway undertaker that the undertaker was obliged to sell or, if it did not, was automatically returned to the previous owner (Land Clauses Consolidation Act 1845, s. 127). See also **recoupment**.

superior landlord
see **head landlord**.

superior lease
see **head lease**.

supermarché (F)
supermarket.

supermarket
A self-service retail establishment, usually on one level, selling predominately food, convenience goods and household supplies. Normally these goods are arranged in open display, with goods of a similar type being grouped together in the same area, and purchases are paid for at a number of checkout counters near the exit. As a rule a supermarket has a sales area between 400 square metres (or about 4000 sq. ft.) and 2500 square metres (or about 25000 sq. ft.) A smaller store of this type may be called a 'superette' or self-service shop and a larger one a **superstore** or **hypermarket**. See also **shopping centre**.

superstore
In the UK, a retail store that sells predominately food, convenience goods and household supplies and that falls in size between a **supermarket** and a **hypermarket**, i.e. between 2500 sq.m, (25000 sq. ft) and 5000 sq.m (50000 sq.ft). (In France, this size of store falls within the definition of a hypermarket.)

supplemental deed (or instrument)
A **deed** (or **instrument**) that is added to and becomes part of an existing deed (or instrument). For example, a deed that effects an increase in the area of a property that is the subject of an existing lease. A supplemental deed does not affect the main deed, except for such modifications as those set out in the supplement; i.e. it acts as if it were endorsed on to the original deed. "Any instrument ... expressed to be supplemental to a previous instrument, shall, as far as may be, be read and have effect as if the supplemental instrument contained a full recital of the previous instrument ..." (Law of Property Act 1925, s. 58).

support, right of
see **right of support**.

supra (L)
'Above; prior to'.

sur-arbitre (F)
umpire.

surenchère (F)
higher bid.
See also *echère*.

sûreté (F)
surety; **warranty**.
(*sûreté mobilière* – charge)
(*sûreté immobilière* – **mortgage**)
(*sûreté réelle* – charge, on real property; secured debt; see also *gage, hypothèque*).

surety
1. An undertaking given to answer for the debt, default or omission of a creditor of a third party in the same way as that creditor, i.e. to answer to the third party just as if the person giving the undertaking had pledged his or her own credit. A surety is a form of insurance for the debt or obligation, i.e. it resembles an **indemnity**; it may be distinguished from a **guarantee** which is given as support for the debtor's solvency or ability to pay. However, in many cases surety is used as synonymous with guarantee; especially in a lease where a person is

unlikely to indemnify the landlord for all losses arising out of the tenancy (Associated Dairies Ltd *v* Pierce (1983) 265 E.G. 562). See also **letter of credit**.

2. A person who gives a commitment to meet an obligation, liability or debt of another in the event that the other fails to meet his or her obligations direct. A surety gives a commitment or indemnity at the same time and, usually, in the same document as the primary obligation, unlike a guarantor; a surety gives an undertaking that the debt will be paid, a guarantor undertakes to see that the debtor shall pay what is due (although surety is commonly used synonymously with guarantor – as it is in the United States Uniform Commercial Code, para. 1–201 (4)). A surety is liable, therefore, at the same time as, and not after, the party being assisted. A person who gives a surety, and is then called upon to fulfil his obligation, has a right of action against the person to whom he gave the undertaking – Badeley *v* Consolidated Bank (1887) 34 Ch. D. 536.

cf. **warranty**. See also **indemnity**, **subrogation**.

Tenants, Assignees and Sureties – I & II, by Sandi Murdoch, 272 EG 732–736, 857–866 (1984).

surety bond
see **performance bond**.

surety insurance
see **guaranty insurance**.

surface (F)
surface.
(*surface batie* – **built area**)
(*surface brute* – **gross area**)
(*surface de plancher hors oeuvre* – built floor area, which may be gross

or net. The **gross external floor area** of a building – which excludes balconies, basement areas that are not fitted out, and similar areas – is used to calculate the *coefficient d'occupation du sol*: code de l'urbanisme, art. R 123–22–2)

(*grande surface* – **hypermarket**; **superstore**). See also ***Plan d'Occupation des Sols***.

surface right
The right to use the surface of **land**. Land may be divided into stratas of ownership with a landowner retaining only the right to use or occupy the 'surface' (to a given height above the ground or depth below the ground). cf. **air rights**, **sub-surface right**. See also **ground lease**, **minerals**, **right of support**, **soil**, **superficies**.

surrender
The act of yielding or giving up a right or claim to possession of something to another; especially a voluntary act by which the holder of a particular estate in land gives up that right to the holder of the immediate **remainder** or **reversion** so that the particular estate merges with the remainder or reversion (Co. Litt. 337b). The giving up of the interest held by a tenant to his landlord, with the landlord's consent, so that the tenant's interest is lost in favour of the landlord prior to the termination of the tenancy by effluxion of time. Upon surrender the interest given up becomes absorbed or swallowed up by the greater estate (the remainder or reversion); as distinguished from a **release** which operates by the greater estate descending, or being given up, to the holder of the lesser estate. A surrender arises from the agreement of the parties, express or implied, as distinguished from

abandonment whereby the tenant merely illicits an intention not to continue with his right of possession. A surrender does not relieve the tenant of his past obligations, unless it is brought into effect by **accord and satisfaction**; however, it does relieve him of future obligations to the landlord. Thus a tenant is liable for any increase in rent prior to the surrender, even if the amount of that increase has not been quantified at the time of the surrender – Torminster Properties Ltd. *v* Green [1983] 1 WLR 676. A surrender must be of the tenant's entire estate or term; but only part of the demised premises may be surrendered. The transfer of a lease to a superior (but not the immediate) landlord is not a surrender, but operates as an **assignment** of the lease.

Surrender may be express or by operation of law. A surrender of any lease, even one created orally, should be made by **deed** (Law of Property Act 1925, s. 52). However, a surrender made orally for value and supported by evidence in **writing** or an act of **part performance** is likely to be enforceable in equity. Surrender by operation of law arises when it can be implied from the circumstances that the parties have put an end to the relationship of landlord and tenant. For instance, a surrender will be implied when the tenant during the course of the lease gives up possession with the consent of the landlord or the landlord re-lets the premises with the consent of the tenant. A surrender also may arise, based on the principle of **estoppel**, where there is a verbal agreement which has been acted on by the parties – Lyon *v* Reed (1844) 13 M and W 285; Phene *v* Popplewell (1862) 12 CBNS 334; Beall *v* White,

94 US 382. When a tenant accepts a new lease during the currency of his existing lease which is inconsistent with the existing lease, he is deemed to have surrendered the existing lease – Dodds *v* Acklom (1843) 6 Man. and G 672.

The surrender of an intermediate or sandwich lease does not put an end to a sub-lease; the sub-lessee effectively steps into the place of the former intermediate tenant as if the original lease had not been surrendered (Law of Property Act 1925, s. 150).

cf. **merger**. See also **remise**, **renunciation**.

Real Property, by William E. Burby, 3 edn., pp. 181–187.

Adkin's Landlord and Tenant 18 edn, pp. 228–232.

Landlord and Tenant Law, by David Yates and A.J. Hawkins, pp. 245–249 (1981).

The Law of Landlord and Tenant, by David Lloyd Evans, 2 edn., pp. 200–203.

Hill and Redman's Landlord and Tenant, 17 edn, pp. 429–441.

Woodfall's Landlord and Tenant, 28 edn, paras. 1–1841 to 1–1875.

27 Halsbury's Laws of England, 4 edn, paras. 444–452.

surrender-back clause

A clause in a lease which provides that should a tenant seek to assign his interest he must first offer to surrender that interest to his landlord. Only if the landlord refuses to accept a surrender can the application to assign be considered in the manner prescribed in the lease. Such a clause may be considered an unreasonable **restraint on alienation** – Allnat London Properties Ltd. *v* Newton (1981) 257 EG 243. See also **assignment**.

surrender value

1. The consideration that may be realised by a tenant surrendering his rights under a lease. A tenant who holds a property at a rent that is below the current market value, i.e. one who has the benefit of a realisable **profit rent**, may be able to obtain a capital payment for surrendering that lease and giving the landlord the benefit of reletting the property (to the original or a new tenant) at a higher rent. See also **surrender, leasehold value, marriage value**.

2. In insurance, a cash sum paid by an insurance company to the insured when he decides to surrender his rights under an insurance policy.

surrogate

A person appointed to act in another's place e.g. a deputy. One who stands in for another; a substitute. cf. **agent**. See also **novation**.

survey

1. The process by which the boundaries of a property are determined and the area contained therein is measured. See also **ordnance survey, surveying**.

2. A formal and critical examination of a site, building, structure, or other tangible property. An inspection of a property in order to ascertain its present condition, situation, use, value, tenure, etc.; or to determine the precise position of the boundaries or the dimensions of a property. See also **right of entry, 'subject to survey', valuation report**.

3. The collection, recording, compilation and interpretation of information; especially when this information is required prior to preparing or proceeding with a plan or project of development. See also **feasibility study, project appraisal, structure plan**.

surveying

1. The action of preparing a **survey**.

2. The science of making large scale, accurate, geometrical measurement in order to produce, in graphical or numerical form, a representation of an area of the earth's surface, in both horizontal and vertical form, together with a representation of the natural and man-made features of that area. The principal forms of surveying real property are **cadastral surveying**, to show property boundaries; **topographical surveying**, to produce maps or plans; **geodetic surveying**, to take account of the curvature of the earth's surface; as well as more specialised fields such as engineering and mine surveying.

Land Surveying, by R.J.P. Wilson, 2 edn.

Surveying, by J.B. Evett, (1979).

Surveying, by R.H. Dugdale, 3 edn.

Principles of Surveying, by J.G. Olliver and Clendenning, 4 edn.

surveyor

A person who prepares a **survey**. A person who undertakes the science (or art) of surveying including a land, building, mining, or hydrographic surveyor; a **quantity surveyor**; a **valuer**; **estate manager**; a town planner; land economist or an **estate agent**. See also **chartered surveyor**.

survivorship

The fact of living longer than another person or persons. See also **joint tenancy**, *jus accrescendi*, **tenancy by the entireties**.

suspensive condition

A condition that must be fulfilled before a contract comes into effect. A term used in the civil law to refer to a **'condition precedent'**.

sweetner
An inducement to someone to enter into a contract or to make a financial commitment. A gift, reward or bribe given to mollify someone. See also **equity kicker, kickback**.

swing loan
1. See **bridging loan**.
(US) 2. A loan made on the basis of the security of a property owner's assets, without being secured by a charge or mortgage on any of those assets.

synallagmatique (F)
synalagmatic; **bilateral contract**.
cf. **unilateral contract**.

synallagmatic contract
A contract by which the parties exchange promises thereby creating mutual promises, as compared to a **unilateral contract** in which a promise is exchanged for an act. "If the consideration required of the offeree is a promise, the giving of that promise is said to result in a bilateral or synallagmatic contract, under which both sides initially exchange promises; but, if the requested consideration is an act other than a promise, its performance is said to make a unilateral contract, whereupon the offeror becomes bound by his offer." (9 Halsbury's Law of England 4, ed., p. 82). A term used more in the civil law. See also **bilateral contract**.

syndic (F)
syndic. An organisation, or agent, appointed to manage a business, or property for another; for example, to manage a property held in **co-ownership**. The officially appointed agent of a *syndicat*, or collection of co-owners as formed into a legal body.
(*syndic de faillite* – trustee, or receiver in bankruptcy).

syndicat (F)
syndicate.

syndicat de copropriétaires
An organisation or trust established to hold property held in co-ownership (*copropriété*).
La Copropriété, by Francois Givord et Claude Giverdon, pp. 226–252 (1968).
Dictionnaire Permanent: Gestion Immobilière, pp. 1253–1269.

syndicate
An association or body of persons established for the purpose of a business venture or undertaking that is essentially too large for the individuals; or by individuals who wish to subject a venture to common management. A group of investors or financiers who combine together for the purpose of a particular transaction or in order to promote a new business; in particular, when such persons combine together for a limited or specific duration. The association may take the form in law of a **society**, **partnership**, or **company**. In the US called also 'syndication'. See also **joint ownership**.

syndication
1. A means by which an investment is made available to a wide range of investors. A syndication brings together a larger number of investors or financiers than would make a particular investment. Usually a professional investment manager undertakes to provide the services that are not available to the individual investors

and offers the investors the opportunity to acquire a share in an investment that would otherwise be too large for their own more limited resources. For example, the sponsor of the syndication provides the corporate, legal and tax advice and the extensive managerial resources that it would not be practical or economic for the individuals to provide. The sponsor forms a **syndicate**, to acquire and manage the investment, and invites a group of private investors, or the public as a whole, to acquire shares, or any other apropriate participating interest, in that syndicate. Called also 'securitisation' or in the UK, especially when used as a means of investing in one or a limited number of properties, 'unitization' – the investor acquiring a right to a 'unit' share in the investment. See also **blind-pool offering, limited partnership, mutual fund**.

Real Estate Syndication: Tax, Securities and Business Aspects, by Stephen Jarchow, (1985).

(US) 2. See **syndicate**.

T

'T' mark
> A mark, in the form of a T, placed on a plan to indicate who owns a boundary fence, hedge, wall or any other form of **boundary line**. The mark is placed along the boundary line on the side of the owner of the form of demarcation. A 'T' mark is used for identification purposes only and has no legal significance.

tables
> see **valuation tables**.

tâcheron (F)
> **sub-contractor.** Especially one paid for a specific service (usually on a daily basis).

tacit approval
> Approval to a course of action by implication, especially as a result of silence on the part of the person affected by the result. See also **implied term, estoppel**.

tacit relocation
> In the civil law and Scottish law, the renewal of a lease by operation of law when the landlord and tenant have failed to take steps to end the lease after it has reached the end of its term. See also **hold over, tenancy at will**.

tacite (F)
> **implied**; tacit; inferred.
> (*tacite reconduction, d'un contrat* – tacit renewal, of a contract; i.e. the renewal of a contract which arises from the implied or inferred action of the parties)
> (*relocation tacite* – tacit renewal of a lease – French Civil Code, art. 1738).

tack
> 1. see **tacking**.
> 2. In Scottish law, a contract for the hire of goods; or a lease. See also **hire**.

tack rent (or duty)
> In Scottish law, rent under a lease.

tacking
> 1. 'Adding on'. The joining of a subsequent **mortgage** to an existing mortgage so as to defer the **priority** of an intervening or second mortgage. Or, a process by which a mortgagee who makes a further advance to the mortgagor is allowed to demand that both loans are paid from the proceeds of sale of the land that has been mortgaged before any other mortgagee shall have any claim, even though the latter may have obtained his security before the further advance was made. In English common law the holder of the **legal estate** (or the best claimant to the legal estate) had priority over any other mortgagee so that he could make a further advance secured on that estate and obtain priority for the total sum advanced, ahead of any subsequent mortgagee; provided that at the time of the further advance he had no **notice** of the subsequent mortgage. Also if an equitable mortgagee acquired the legal estate from the first mortgagee, he could join these claims together and squeeze out any intermediate mortgagee. This doctrine of tacking, and automatically postponing the priority of a mortgagee who might otherwise have a prior claim to a property, was partly abolished by the Law of Property Act 1925. However, in the following cir-

cumstances, a further advance may be tacked onto an existing advance so that the total loan has priority (regardless of whether the mortgage is legal or equitable): (i) if the consent of the subsequent mortgagee is obtained (this is unlikely to be forthcoming unless the secured property is of sufficient value to cover all the monies advanced); (ii) at the time the further advance is made the mortgagee does not have **notice** of the subsequent mortgage (which generally means that the subsequent mortgage is not registered); or (iii) when there is a provision in the prior mortgage (a **further advances clause**) that the mortgagee is bound to make further advances if called upon so to do (although the mortgagee must be obliged, and not just be empowered, to make a further advance) (Law of Property Act 1925, s. 94). Accordingly, a second or subsequent mortgagee should enquire fully as to whether a prior mortgagee has accepted an obligation to make a further advance.

In the US, the doctrine of tacking no longer applies; priority of mortgages being dependent on their dates of registration.

cf. **consolidation**.

Megarry's *Manual of the Law of Real Property*, 6 edn, pp. 512–515.
The Law of Real Property, by Robert Megarry and H.W.R. Wade, 5 edn., pp. 1008–1012.
Cheshire's Modern Law of Real Property, 13 edn, pp. 668–669 & 680–682.
32 Halsbury's Laws of England, 4 edn, paras. 549–550.
Fisher & Lightwood's Law of Mortgage, 9 edn, pp. 455–463.
2. Adding or combining successive periods of possession in order to establish a title to land by **adverse possession**. As a rule, to establish a title to property by adverse possession the possession must be continuous (unless interrupted by periods of recognised disability, fraud, etc.,). But, because adverse possession is a means of barring an existing title, successive periods of adverse possession by successors in title may be added together. Thus tacking of periods of adverse possession by parties between whom there is **privity of estate** (vendor and purchaser, ancestor and heir, landlord and tenant) is permitted when barring a title to property; provided that the periods are not interrupted by one party giving up possession before the other takes over – Asher *v* Whittlock (1865) LR 1 QB 1. If a succession of squatters occupy land they may bar the initial owners title to the land; although they may in turn establish competing claims between themselves.
3. The adding of terms or conditions to a contract, e.g. as a **rider**. See also **supplementary deed (or instrument)**.

tail
see **entailed interest, fee tail**.

tail after possibilities
see **tenant in tail after possibilities**.

taille
An estate in tail, i.e. a **fee tail**.

tailzie
In Scottish law, an **entailed estate**.

takedown
see **draw-down**.

take-out commitment
see **forward commitment**.

take-out financing
Long-term financing obtained to
replace an interim loan. Commonly
used to refer to a **long-term loan**
taken out on completion of a new
development to replace a construction loan. In the US, called also an
'end loan'. See also **forward commitment**.

taking-off
A process in **quantity surveying** by
which the quantity of materials
required for a building contract is
assessed. Detailed measurements are
taken from the drawings and plans
prepared by the architect and these
measurements are used for the purpose of determining the detailed
quantities of materials required to
construct the buildings. The measurements 'taken off' the plans usually are set out in the **bill of quantities**
prior to assessing the cost of the building works. In the US, called also 'figuring'. See also **abstracting, billing**.

taking possession
Obtaining a right to **possession** of
property. The vesting of property, or
a title to real property, in someone.
Upon the completion of the purchase
of real property 'possession' does not,
of itself, mean personal occupation. If
a property is tenanted and a purchaser is "placed in a position to
receive rents and profits he will be
given a right to 'possession'" – Lake *v*
Dean (1860) 28 Beav. 607. Under the
Statutes of Limitation mere entry on
to land is not taking possession.
cf. **access**. See also **acquisition,
adverse possession, vacant possession**.

tangible property
Property that has a physical or sen-
sory existence and is necessarily corporeal, i.e. land, buildings, goods and
chattels; but not any form of property
that is represented by a right of action
(choses-in-action) and any **incorporeal hereditament**. Cash is considered
to be tangible property although it
represents an intangible claim.
cf. **intangible property**. See also **corporeal property**.

tantième (F)
proportion; percentage; a payment
based on a share of profits. Interest,
i.e. a partial right to property.
(*tantième copropriété* – co-owner's
share, of common charges).

target-cost contract
see **cost-plus contract**.

target rate of return
A rate of return that an investor sets
out to achieve from a particular
investment. Normally this is represented by the annualised return projected for the life of the investment,
i.e. the expected **redemption yield** or
internal rate of return. A target rate of
return may be based on the return
required (a) to provide the investor
with a return that exceeds the cost of
his capital by a margin that is sufficient to provide a reward commensurate with the risk involved in parting
with that capital; or (b) to equal, or
exceed, the anticipated return from a
comparable investment. Called also a
'criterion rate of return' or an 'opportunity – cost rate of return'.

taudis (F)
slum.
(*lutte contre les taudis* – **slum
clearance**).

taux (F)
rate; charge; duty.

(*taux d'accroissement* – growth rate)
(*taux d'actualisation* – **discount rate**, to arrive at a **present value**)
(*taux d'amortissement* – **amortisation rate, redemption yield**)
(*taux de capitalisation* – **capitalisation rate** or factor)
(*taux d'escompte* – **discount rate**)
(*taux d'intérêt* – **interest rate**)
(*taux de capitalisation des bénéfices* – **price/earnings ratio**)
(*taux de rendement, taux de rentabilité* – **rate of return**)
(*taux interne de rentabilité* – **internal rate of return**).

tax

1. A compulsory contribution, usually of a pecuniary kind, made by the general body of subjects or citizens to a sovereign or government authority. A tax must be authorised for a public purpose; be enforceable at law; and the obligation to pay it must be imposed compulsorily on a group of persons or organisations. However, it need bear little relation to the benefit received by any payer of the tax. A tax may be levied against person or property and should be distinguished from any **assessment, charge** or **levy** imposed on one or a small group of individuals.

In a lease a liability to pay "taxes" does not include a liability to pay "**rates**". – Smith *v* Smith [1939] 4 All ER 312; nor does it impose a duty to pay taxes levied directly against the landlord. As a rule, a tenant is required to pay his rent gross (i.e. before deduction) of income tax. When a tenant covenants to pay rent free from all "rates, taxes, assessments, deductions or abatements", or to pay "all taxes, rates, duties, levies, assessments and payments what-

soever" in respect of the demised premises, then the tenant may not deduct any of these sums from the rent payable to the landlord. However, it is important to interpret each word in the covenant. For example, a clause to pay "all taxes, rates, duties and assessments whatsoever imposed, upon the said demised premises or any part thereof or upon the landlord or tenants in respect thereof" makes a tenant liable for the expense of abating a nuisance arising from the demised premises, e.g. the cost of drainage repairs – Budd *v* Marshall (1880) 5 CPD 481. But he is not liable for a like expense when he covenants to pay "all rates, taxes, and assessments whatsoever, which now are or during the said term shall be imposed or assessed upon the said premises, or the landlord or tenant in respect thereof, by authority of Parliament or otherwise (except the landlord's property tax)" – Lyon *v* Greenhow (1892) 8 TLR 457 See also **capital gains tax, capital transfer tax, development land tax, land tax, outgoings, property tax, value added tax**.
Landlord and Tenant Law, by David Yates and A.J. Hawkins, pp. 85–88 (1981).
Woodfall's Landlord and Tenant, 28 edn, para. 1–1327 *et seq.*
2. To assess the value of a property, particularly for official purposes. To make the subject of a **levy**. See also **rating**.

tax abatement
A reduction, in part or in total, in a local tax for a specific period of time; such as an **abatement** granted when access to a property is severely restricted by a government body. See also **rebate**.

tax base (US)

The **assessed value** of a property. Similar to the rateable value in the UK. See also **basis**.

tax basis (US)

see **basis**.

tax book (US)

see **tax roll**.

tax certificate (US)

see **tax sale**.

tax credit

A credit that may be offset against a future tax liability; generally a credit that arises from a previously over-taxed income. Unlike a **tax deduction**, a tax credit may be deducted from a tax liability in full, not merely from income that is taxable.

tax deduction

An amount which legally may be deducted from income or from a capital gain prior to calculating the tax to be charged thereon.

cf. **tax credit**. See also **capital allowance, depreciation, tax shelter**.

tax deed (US)

An instrument by which a tax authority undertakes to transfer a property from the owner to the purchaser of that property at a **tax sale**. Normally the authority retains a lien on the property, after it has been 'sold' at public auction, for a fixed period of time to permit the owner to pay the tax due and redeem his property. At the end of that time the deed automatically vests an unencumbered title in the purchaser.

tax-deferred exchange (US)

see **tax-free exchange**.

tax delinquency (US)

A failure to pay a tax when due, espe-cially when this results in a tax sale of the delinquent tax payer's property.

tax escalation clause (US)

see **escalation clause**.

tax foreclosure (US)

Seizure and sale of property to meet a liability for unpaid tax. See also **sequestration, tax sale**.

tax-free exchange (US)

The exchange of one real property for another in order to defer a potential tax liability. A property held for investment or to produce income may be exchanged for a 'like kind' of property without creating an immediate liability for capital gains tax. Any gain realised by the transfer of either property by way of exchange is not recognised, but is deferred until the newly acquired property is disposed of by way of a future taxable disposition (Internal Revenue Code, s. 1031). Any monies paid to balance the difference in values of the properties (called **boot**) are taxable. See also **tax shelter**.

tax haven

A country or state that levies no taxation, or very low levels of taxation, usually to attract foreign investors. A country that accepts, and normally encourages, foreign investment by charging far lower tax rates than would be payable by the investors in their own country. See also **off-shore trust**.

Tax Havens – A World Survey, by M. Grundy, 4 edn.

Using Tax Havens Successfully, by Edouart Chambost (1978).

Tax Havens Encyclopaedia, by Barry Spitz (ed.), (1975).

tax lien
see **lien**.

tax map
see **cadastral map**.

tax plat (US)
see **plat**.

tax roll (US)
An official list, published in each county, which contains details of all taxable property and the amounts levied against those properties. Called also a 'tax book'. See also **assessment roll**.

tax sale (US)
The sale of a property at the instigation of the tax authorities, when the owner of the property has failed to meet a tax liability. The sale is usually by public auction, but it may be arranged by tender or sealed bids. The purchaser may acquire an immediate title (**tax title**) and possession of the property offered for sale, or his right may be postponed in order to enable the delinquent tax payer a specified period of time in which to repay the tax. The proceeds of the sale are used to pay the unpaid tax and the balance, if any, is paid to the erstwhile delinquent tax payer. In some states when tax due on a property remains unpaid the tax authority may sell, at public auction, a lien they have obtained against the delinquent tax payer's property. A bidder who pays an amount equal to, or in excess of, the amounts due to the authority acquires a 'tax certificate' which may be converted into ownership of the property if the sums due are not paid by the delinquent taxpayer within a specified redemption period. See also **tax deed**.

tax shelter (US)
An investment that is used to reduce or defer a liability for tax; or, in broad terms, a **tax credit** or **tax deduction** that is available only to a particular group of taxpayers, e.g. those who pay mortgage interest. Real estate is one of the principal forms of tax shelter because depreciation, loan interest and tax losses from previous tax years may be deducted from income in order to reduce the owner's total tax liability. The 'sheltered' income is the amount that is free of tax.

tax-stop clause (US)
A clause in a lease which provides that the lessee will pay any taxes above a given level, usually above that payable at the start of the lease. See also **escalation clause**.

tax title (US)
The title granted to a person who has acquired a property at a **tax sale**. The title may grant a right to possession of the property and a right to accede to the owner's title; but usually it is subject to a condition that the delinquent tax payer has a right to recover the property provided he pays the tax due within a specified time. In the latter case the purchaser's claim is represented by a 'tax certificate' issued by the tax authority, which is converted into a title if the tax payer fails to meet his liability in full. See also **tax deed**.

taxe (F)
tax; **duty**; fee; fixed or controlled price.
(*taxe sur la valeur ajoutée* (TVA) – **value-added tax** (VAT)
(*taxe de transmission* – **transfer tax**)
(*taxe d'habitation* – a tax levied on the owner, tenant or occupier of a furnished property. Since 1974 repla-

ces *contribution mobilière*)
(*taxe foncières* – property tax, a tax that is similar to rates in the UK and is levied on the assumed rental value of a property. Since 1974 replaces *contributions foncières*: Law of 7 January 1959).
(*taxe foncière sur les propriétés bâties* – development land tax)
(*taxe hypothécaire* – mortgage duty)
(*taxe locale* – **rates**)
(*taxe locale déquipment* – local utility tax, a tax levied whenever a building is constructed, redeveloped or enlarged)
See also *contribution, droit, imposition, impôt, précompte, prélèvement, versement*.
Taxes in France, by Lionel Halpern, 3 edn., (adapted from Francis Lefebvre's *Les Impôts en France*.
Fiscalité Immobilière, by Louis Broet, 7 edn.

taxable gain
see **capital gains tax**.

taxable value
see **assessed value, rateable value**.

taxation of costs
The means by which a court determines the amount of costs that a person to an action is entitled.

tear
see **fair wear and tear**.

technical estoppel (US)
Estoppel by record or deed.

technical mortgage (US)
see **regular mortgage**.

technique d'évaluation et de contrôle de programme (F)
programme evaluation and review technique.

témoin (F)
witness; evidence.
(*appartement/maison témoin* – show flat/**show house**).

tempérament (F)
(*vente à tempérament* – credit sale or **instalment sale**. See also *vente*.)

temporary housing
Prefabricated or 'patched-up' dwellings that are provided by a local authority to meet an urgent housing need. For example, the Housing (Temporary Accommodation) Acts of 1944, 1945, and 1947 gave local authorities special powers to provide such houses to meet the urgent post-war housing needs in the UK.
West's Law of Housing, 4 edn, Ch. 16.

temporary planning permission
see **limited period permission, planning condition**.

tenancier (F)
tenant farmer; holder, of land.

tenancy
1. A right to hold land from another, while acknowledging the eventual right of that other to regain the land. A relationship, created by means of a contract (express or implied) termed a **lease**, by which one party (**landlord**) grants another (**tenant**) a right to possession of land for a defined or definable period of time, usually in exchange for a payment called **rent**. An essential element of a tenancy is that the landlord retains an interest in the land (called his **reversionary interest**); otherwise he will have made a grant or conveyance of his entire right to the land. A tenancy creates more than a contractual right; it is a right to land which, for the duration

of the contract, is enforceable against anyone.

A tenancy requires three other essential elements: (i) an identifiable landlord and tenant, i.e. a person cannot be a tenant of himself nor of land that has no known owner; (ii) the land demised (which may include buildings) must be clearly identifiable and the tenant must have a degree of **exclusive occupation** of that land; and (iii) the right to the land must be granted for a period of time that is certain, or capable of being made certain. Normally, the tenant is required to pay rent as an acknowledgement of a fealty to another, and to observe certain conditions, either as expressed in the lease or as implied by law. A tenancy may be created by a lease; a sub-lease or underlease; an **agreement for a lease**; or merely by implication as when a person enters into possession of another's land and pays rent.

In relation to a **business tenancy** tenancy has been defined to mean "a tenancy created immediately or derivatively out of a freehold, whether by a lease or underlease, by an agreement for a lease or underlease or in pursuance of any enactment (including this Act), but does not include a mortgage term or any interest arising in favour of a mortgagor by his attorning tenant to his mortgagee" (Landlord and Tenant Act 1954, s. 69(1)). In most statutes a tenancy created for the purpose of mortgage and any tenancy created by way of a trust under a settlement is excluded from the term 'tenancy' when used without further qualification. A **tenancy at will**, a **tenancy on sufferance** and a **statutory tenancy** are not considered as true tenancies (as they do not create interests in land that are cap-

able of onward transmission); although the Defective Premises Act 1972, s. 6(1) specifically includes a tenancy at will and a tenancy at sufferance in its definition of tenancy.

In common usage the word 'tenancy' is used to refer to a short term or periodic tenancy and the word 'lease', especially one created by deed, to refer to a tenancy for a fixed period. cf. **licence**. See also **agricultural tenancy, assured tenancy, controlled tenancy, long tenancy, minor tenancy, periodic tenancy, protected tenancy, regulated tenancy, secure tenancy, shorthold tenancy, statutory tenancy, tenancy by estoppel, tenancy by entireties, tenancy for a fixed term**.
2. The period of a tenant's right to occupation or possession of demised premises.
3. The holding of any form of title to land; especially a joint holding of land, as in '**joint tenancy**' and '**tenancy in common**', this usage being derived from **tenure**, i.e. a holding of land (it does not denote the modern relationship of landlord and tenant referred to in 1. above).

tenancy agreement
An agreement to create a **tenancy**. A term that refers especially to an informal or **parol lease**, or a written agreement to create a short-term lease. See also **agreement for a lease, periodic tenancy**.

tenancy at a low rent
see **low rent**.

tenancy at sufferance
see **tenancy on sufferance**.

tenancy at will
An arrangement whereby a person occupies land, with the consent of the owner, as if he were a tenant (and not

merely a servant or agent) but on the understanding that his occupation may be terminated at any time at the will of either party. A tenancy at will is a personal contract between the parties; it is created without any formal agreement; and it does not create any interest in land. It arises most frequently when a person enters into possession before a formal lease is entered into; or when a tenant retains possession at the end of a lease and the landlord impliedly consents to the continued occupation, as when a landlord is proposing to grant a new lease. "A tenancy at will, although called a **tenancy**, is unlike any other tenancy except a **tenancy at sufferance**, to which it is the next-of-kin. It has been properly described as a personal relationship between the landlord and his tenant; it is determined by the death of either of them or any of a variety of acts, even by an involuntary alienation, which would not affect the subsistence of any other tenancy" – Wheeler *v* Mercer [1957] AC 427. However, unlike a **licence** it has the characteristics of a proper tenancy, notably a right for the tenant to have exclusive occupation and the necessity for a valid **notice to quit** to bring it to an end, and if the landlord collects **rent** it is converted immediately into a periodic tenancy – Martin *v* Smith (1874) LR 9 Exch. 50. It is brought to an end if either party commits an act that is inconsistent with the relationship, e.g. a purported **assignment**, or an act of voluntary **waste** – Countess of Shrewsbury's Case (1600) 5 Co. Rep. 136. A tenancy at will cannot be a **business tenancy** (Wheeler *v* Mercer, *supra*). In the US, called also an 'estate at will'; although that term may be used

also to refer to any right to land that arises when a person retains possession at the will of another, especially for an uncertain and indeterminate estate. See also **copyhold, eviction, use and occupation**.

The Law of Landlord and Tenant, by David Lloyd Evans, 2 edn., pp. 33–34.

27 Halsbury's Laws of England, 4 edn, pp. 125–130.

Woodfall's Landlord and Tenant, 28 edn, paras. 1–0647 to 1–0657.

tenancy by coparcenary
see **coparcenary**.

tenancy by the curtesy
see **curtesy**.

tenancy by entireties
A form of **co-ownership** that arose when property was conveyed to a husband and wife as if they were a single fictitious entity, with equal unity of title, unity of possession and unity of control over the whole property; so that on the death of one spouse the other took the entire property to the exclusion of any heirs or other claimants. The property was conveyed in such a way that had the parties not been married they would have held a **joint tenancy**. Neither spouse could dispose of or assign his or her interest without the consent of the other party and no severance of ownership was possible unless both spouses agreed. In English law since 1882 it is not possible to create a tenancy by entireties (from that date a wife was entitled to hold land separately from her husband) and from January 1925 every tenancy by entireties was converted into a joint tenancy (Married Women's Property Act

1882, ss. 1, 5; Law of Property Act 1925, Sch. I, Part IV). In the US, (where it is now virtually obsolete), called also a 'tenancy by the entirety' an 'estate by entireties'. See also **community property, matrimonial property**.

The Law of Real Property, by Robert Megarry and H.W.R. Wade, 5 edn., pp. 460–462.
Real Estate Law, by Robert Kratovil and Raymond J. Werner, 8 edn., pp. 242–249.
Real Property, by William E. Burby, 3 edn., pp. 221–228.

tenancy by estoppel
A tenancy that comes into existence when a person who does not have a proper interest in land, so as to enable him to grant a lease, purports to create a tenacy, and, by virtue of the doctrine of **estoppel**, cannot deny to his 'tenant' that he has not created a contract of tenancy so that "even though the lessor's want of title is apparent to the parties, both the parties and their successors in title will be estopped from denying that the grant was effective to create the tenancy that is purported to create."(*The Law of Real Property*, by Megarry and Wade, 5 edn., p. 661). A tenant who takes premises knowing that his landlord has a defective title cannot at a later date deny that he has a tenancy; he is obliged to fulfil the obligations he has contracted for, especially to pay rent to the landlord; and he cannot escape a repairing obligation by claiming that there never was a tenancy – Industrial Properties (Barton Hill) Ltd. *v* Associated Electrical Industries [1977] QB 58. If the 'landlord' later acquires a proper title he is said to 'feed the estoppel' and to

create the form of tenancy originally envisaged.

tenancy by the entirety (US)
see **tenancy by entireties**.

tenancy by the rod
A **copyhold** tenure.

tenancy for a fixed term (or fixed period of time)
A **tenancy** for a fixed period of time or for a **term** or, at least, for a period that is capable of being fixed in time – the maxim being *id certum est quod certum reddi potest*, 'that is certain which can be rendered certain'. In particular, a 'fixed term' is "one which cannot be unfixed by notice. To be a 'fixed term', the parties must be bound for the term stated in the agreement and unable to determine it on either side". – BBC *v* Ioannu [1975] 2 All ER 999. A tenancy for a fixed term need not be brought to an end by **notice to quit**, but determines at the end of the fixed period (unless the tenant is entitled to remain in possession by virtue of some statutory provision). It is intended to end by effluxion of time; although it may be terminated by **forfeiture, surrender, merger, enlargement** and possibly **frustration**.
cf. **periodic tenancy**. See also **tenancy for a term of years**.

tenancy for one year certain and thereafter from year to year
see **tenancy from year to year**.

tenancy for life (or lives)
1. The estate held by a **tenant for life**, i.e. freehold tenure limited in duration for the life of some person. See also **life interest**.
2. A **tenancy** for a period fixed according to a person's (or persons'

life, whether the life of the tenant, or the life of another (*pur autre vie*). Such an interest (as well as any tenancy for a term of years determinable with a life or lives or on the tenant's marriage), if granted at a rent or for a fine, is converted automatically into a lease for 90 years. The lease may continue after the death of the tenant, but then can be terminated by either party giving one month's notice on a quarter day that is appropriate to the tenancy or if there is no quarter day applicable to the tenancy one of the usual **quarter days** (Law of Property Act 1925, s. 149(6)). Such tenancies are rarely created.

tenancy for a term of years
Strictly, a **tenancy** for a minimum of two years duration. However, a tenancy for a *fixed* period of one **year**, a period of less than a year, or parts of a year, may be called a tenancy for a term of years, provided the commencement and termination dates of the tenancy can be ascertained precisely when the lease comes into operation, and provided it is not a **periodic tenancy**. A 'tenancy for a term of years' is synonymous with 'tenancy for a fixed term' but the term is one that has reference to a year or a fixed portion of a year or years. A tenancy for a term exceeding three years must be in **writing** and signed, otherwise it takes effect as a **tenancy at will** only (Law of Property Act 1925, s. 54). A tenancy for a term of years normally starts at midnight of the day on which it is stated to commence and lasts until the end of the anniversary day upon which the fixed period comes to an end. Thus a term of "five years from 25 March 1985" commences at midnight of the 25/26 March and

ends at the end of 25 March 1990, unless the rent is payable 'on' 25 March, in which case that day must fall within the term of years and 25 March 1990 is excluded from the term. In the US, called also an 'estate for years'.
cf. **tenancy from year to year**. See also **term of years absolute**.

tenancy for years
see **periodic tenancy**, **tenancy for a term of years**.

tenancy from year to year
A **tenancy** that continues for one **year** and then another, for an indefinite number of years, until brought to an end by the landlord or the tenant serving a valid **notice to quit** to expire at the same time of the year as it started. A tenancy from year to year is treated as a tenancy for a minimum duration of one year and if it is not brought to an end after the first full year a tenancy for another year comes into existence – Gray v Spyer [1922] 2 Ch. 22: Gladstone v Bower [1959] 3 All ER 479.

A tenancy from year to year, or a 'yearly tenancy' unless there is an agreement to the contrary, may be terminated by notice given **half a year** (183 days, at least, or two **quarter days**) before the anniversary of the commencement date – Doe d. Shore v Porter (1789) 3 Term. 13; except in the case of an **agricultural holding** which may be terminated by only one year's notice. Literally construed, the end of a 'year' is the end of the day before the anniversary of the day on which the tenancy commenced; but a notice to quit which expires on the anniversary date itself is just as good – Sidebotham v Holland [1895] 1 QB 383. In English law, (unless there is anything expressly to the contrary) a yearly tenancy that starts on 1 January may be terminated by notice given on or before 1 July to expire on 1 January.

A tenancy from year to year may be created expressly using such words as "from year to year"; "yearly tenancy"; "to be terminated by six month's notice to expire on the anniversary hereof"; "annually thereafter". Also it may be created by implication when a person enters into possession of premises (or retains possession of premises) and rent is paid and accepted by reference to a year. The rent need not be payable yearly, provided the basis on which it is calculated is related to a year – Shirley v Newman (1795) 1 Esp. 266. A rent of £5000 per annum, payable quarterly implies a yearly and not a quarterly tenancy. A tenancy 'for one year certain, and thereafter from year to year' cannot be terminated by notice to quit until it has run at least two full years – although the notice could be served six full months before the end of the second year – Re. Searle [1912] 1 Ch. 610. Called also a 'year-to-year tenancy' or in the US, an 'estate from year-to-year'. See also **periodic tenancy**.

Woodfall's Landlord and Tenant, 28 edn, para. 1-0625.

27 Halsbury's Laws of England, 4 edn, pp. 137–154.

tenancy-in-chief
see **tenant in chief**.

tenancy in common
A form of co-ownership that arises when two or more persons have separate and distinct titles to the same property; titles that may be freely disposed of by grant or devise. (The word 'tenancy' in this context has nothing to do with the relationship of landlord and tenant as created by a lease, but is derived from **tenure** denoting a right to 'hold' or 'own' land). A tenancy in common is created normally by **words of severance** which indicate that each owner is to have an 'undivided share' in the property, so that for all practical purposes each tenant-in-common has sole or several ownership. Unlike a **joint tenancy** there is no *jus accrescendi* 'right of survivorship' (or 'coalescence' of interests'), between the owners, so that on the death of any one owner his interest passes to his personal representative and not to the surviving owners. A tenancy in common is said not to require 'unity of time': each owner can hold the land for a different duration; as when one has a fee simple interest and the other a life interest. It does not require 'unity of title', each owner can come by his interest by separate documents, e.g. a grant to one and a devise to another. It does not require 'unity of interest'; one owner can have a freehold interest and another a leasehold interest, or the owners can have a one-quarter and three quarters interest respectively. But, there must be **unity of possession**, i.e. any one of the owners must have the same rights over each and every part of the property as any other – no one owner can "point to any part of the land as his own to the exclusion of others; if he could, there would be separate ownership and not co-ownership".

(*The Law of Real Property*, by Megarry and Wade, 5 edn., p. 419).

In English law, a tenancy in common (or as it is referred to by statute an estate "in undivided shares") cannot exist as a **legal estate** (Law of Property Act 1925, s. 1(6)), but must be held upon **trust for sale**, i.e. the legal estate is held by trustees who ultimately have a duty (a duty that may be postponed) to sell the property and distribute the proceeds to the tenants in common. Thus the 'joint owners' have no more than a beneficial or **equitable interest** in the property.

A tenancy in common, as a rule, is construed to exist when there is co-ownership and the intention is to preclude the right of survivorship; or when the owners are granted separate shares in a property but without the 'four unities' that are essential to a joint tenancy, or without the use of 'words of severance' such as "to A and B equally". Unless there is evidence to the contrary, equity will generally construe that a tenancy in common exists if (a) ownership arises in favour of co-mortgagees; (b) the money to purchase the property is provided in unequal shares; or (c) land is held by a partnership – *jus accrescendi inter mercatores pro beneficio commercii locum non habet* – 'for the benefit of commerce, there can be no place for the right of survivorship' (Co. Litt. 182a).

A tenancy in common may be brought to an end by (i) **partition** – whereby the right to the property is divided severally among the co-owners, either voluntarily or compulsorily; (ii) sale – so that there is no longer any unity of possession and all the purchasers take the property free of the co-owners; and (iii) the unity of the beneficial interest in one person – whether by express grant or, when all the shares come into the hands of one co-owner, by operation of law.

In the US, called also an 'estate in common'. See also **coparcenary, constructive trust, resulting trust, severalty, severance.**

Introduction to Land Law, by J.G. Riddell, 3 edn., pp. 141–146.
Land Law, by Patrick J. Dalton, 3 edn., pp. 201–219.
Real Property and Real People, by K.J. Gray and P.D. Symes, pp. 237–242, (1981).
Megarry's Manual of the Law of Real Property, 6 edn, p. 299 *et seq.*
The Law of Real Property, by Robert Megarry and H.W.R Wade, 5 edn., p. 417 *et seq.*
Cheshire's Modern Law of Real Property, 13 edn, p. 241 *et seq.*
39 Halsbury's Laws of England, 4 edn, paras. 542–564.

tenancy in partnership (US)
A tenancy held in the name of a **partnership**. Strictly, a partnership, having no legal status, may not contract *per se* for a tenancy – the partners must be co-owners in their respective names. However, subject to the observance of strict rules, many states have adopted the Uniform Partnership Act which permits a partnership to enter into a tenancy as if it were a corporate entity. Under a tenancy-in-partnership the partners have the same right to possession for the purpose of the partnership; they have no interest that they may assign as individuals (except to another partner); and on the death of one partner his or her interest vests in the other partners (subject to payment of due compensation to the partner's estate). See also **joint tenancy.**

tenancy in severalty
see **several ownership.**

tenancy in tail
  see **entailed interest**.

tenancy in tail after possibilities
  see **tenant in tail after possibilities**.

tenancy on sufferance
  A tenancy that arises when a person wrongfully holds over at the end of a lease. A tenancy that comes into existence when a person, who had entered legally into possession of a property, remains there without the consent, or dissent, of the person entitled to possession; nor with statutory authority. A tenant on sufferance is "he that at first comes in by lawful demise and after his estate ended continueth in possession and wrongfully holdeth over" ... he has only "naked possession, stands in no **privity** to the landlord, and may, consequently be removed without notice to quit" (Co. Litt. 57b). A form of tenancy that is said to come into operation when a person fails to give up possession of demised premises when a lease comes, or is brought to an end; but, unlike a **tenancy at will**, an arrangement that is considered to constitute a wrongful act. A tenancy on sufferance may follow any form of tenancy (including a tenancy at will), but it cannot be created against the Crown; nor can it be created as a sub-letting by one who is himself a tenant on sufferance. If a tenant at sufferance is requested to leave the demised premises, and fails to do so, he becomes a trespasser; but if the landlord consents to his continued occupation he becomes a tenant at will. A tenant on sufferance may leave at any time without notice.
  A tenant on sufferance has no obligation to pay rent and the landlord cannot distrain for payment (it is not a true tenancy) but the tenant may be liable to pay **mesne profits**. A tenant on sufferance who has been requested to give up possession to his landlord and who wilfully holds over (and has not statutory right to retain possession) may be charged double the 'annual value' of the premises during his period of continuing possession (unless he is a weekly or quarterly tenant) (Landlord and Tenant Act 1730, s. 1). Alternatively, the landlord may bring an action for **trespass** and claim damages for any loss suffered as a result. If a tenant gives notice to quit (written or oral) and then retains possession (without statutory authority) he may be liable to pay "double the rent" that was due under the expired tenancy for his period of occupation, regardless of the duration of the expired tenancy (Distress for Rent Act 1737, s. 18). The acceptance of such payments normally would be made when the tenant finally vacates, or after the landlord obtains an order of the court for possession, because the acceptance by the landlord of any payment which could be construed as rent is likely to create a **periodic tenancy**. Called also a 'tenancy at sufferance' or in the US an 'estate at sufferance'.
  cf. **disseisin**.
  Woodfall's Landlord and Tenant, 28 edn, paras. 1–0662 to 1–0664.
  27 Halsbury's Laws of England, 4 edn, paras. 175–176.

tenant
  Derived from the Norman French *tenaunt*, 'holder'. One who holds or possesses real estate by any kind of right. In particular, one who holds land from another (**landlord**) for a certain period of time, in return for a

payment called rent. A person or body who is permitted, under the terms of a contract of **tenancy** (termed a **lease**) to hold, use and enjoy real property. In its primary and historical significance, a tenant is anyone who has a right to possession of land whether as a fee interest, or for life, or for a term of years, or at will, or for any certain period of time. In common usage a tenant is anyone who has been granted a lease, or an agreement for a lease or similar right or anyone who takes over the rights of an original grantee, whether as an assignee, a sub-tenant or otherwise. A tenant has a right to **exclusive possession** which may take the form of a right to actual occupation, or he or she may forego that right in return for a right to rents and profits.

cf. **licensee**. See also **landlord and tenant**, **lessee**, **tenure**.

tenant by copy of court roll
see **copyhold**.

tenant by curtesy
see **curtesy**.

tenant-cooperator (US)
see **cooperative ownership**.

tenant for a term of years
One entitled to possession of land under a **tenancy for a term of years**. Called sometimes a 'termor'.

tenant for life
The holder of a **life estate (or interest)** in land, i.e. a freeholder who has the right to possession of land for his life or the life of another. When the length of the interest is determined by the life of a person other than the holder of the estate in land, the former is called the *cestui que vie* and the holder of the estate is called a tenant *pur autre vie*

(Bl. Comm. vol. ii p. 120 – Blaydes *v* Selby (1891) 7 TLR 567). (The word 'tenant' is used to refer to a person who has **tenure**, i.e. 'holds', land; it is not used in the sense of a person who is a party to a contract of tenancy). The interest of a tenant for life ceases on his or her death and does not pass to the holder's personal representative.

In the case of **settled land** the tenant for life is "the person of full age who is for the time being beneficially entitled under a settlement to possession of settled land for his life" (Settled Land Act 1925, s. 19(1)). This definition includes not only a person entitled to a life interest but any person who is competent to hold the legal estate in the settled land and who has the accompanying powers to manage and eventually dispose of that land. For example, a tenant in tail; the holder of a fee simple or term of years absolute whose interest fails if there is no longer an issue; a person entitled to a base or determinable fee; a tenant for a term of years determinable on life (provided he does not hold the settled land under a lease at a rent); and various other persons considered to be in a similar position (1925 Act, s. 20). If there is no tenant for life of settled land, then the legal estate and powers of administration are vested in a **statutory owner**. There can be only one tenant for life for the purpose of the Settled Land Act, but the 'tenant' may be constituted by two or more persons of full age acting as joint tenants (1925 Act, s. 19(2)).

A tenant for life has extensive powers over the settled land and is effectively a trustee for all the parties entitled under the settlement (1925 Act, s. 107(1)). He has powers of sale

or exchange (1925 Act, ss. 38, 39, 40); powers to grant or accept leases (1925 Act, ss. 41–48); to borrow money by grant of a mortgage or charge on the settled land, including money required to discharge an incumberance on the settled land (1925 Act, s. 71); to make certain authorised improvements (as defined in the 1925 Act, Sch. 3); and power to effect "any transaction" under an order of the court. He is not entitled to commit voluntary **waste**, unless made unimpeachable for such waste; and is not liable for permissive waste, unless made responsible expressly for repairs. These powers are usually subject to the prior approval of a court or the trustees of the settlement and the money arising therefrom will have to be treated, wholly or partly, as **capital money**, i.e. invested in securities authorised by the settlement or used for repairs to the settled land, etc. See also **estate owner, emblements, mansion house, vesting document**.
Real Property and Real People, by K.J. Gray and P.D. Symes, pp. 162–164, 176–180 (1981).
Megarry's Manual of the Law of Real Property, 6 edn, pp. 262, 266–276.
The Law of Real Property, by Robert Megarry and H.W.R. Wade, 5 edn., p. 350 *et seq.*
Cheshire's Modern Law of Real Property, 13 edn, p. 173 *et seq.*, 755 *et seq.*
42 Halsbury's Laws of England, 4 edn, pp. 379–467.

tenant from year to year
One entitled to possession of land under a **tenancy from year to year**.

tenant *in capite*
see **tenant in chief**.

tenant in chief
Under the **feudal system** of land tenure, one who held land direct from the King. Called also a 'tenant in capite'.
cf. **mesne lord, tenant in demesne**.

tenant in common
The holder of a **tenancy in common**.

tenant in demesne
Under the feudal system of land tenure the person who actually occupied the land, as distinguished from a **tenant in chief** who held the land from the King or a **mesne tenant** who stood between the King and the tenant in demesne.

tenant in fee
see **fee**.

tenant in tail
One who is entitled to an **entailed interest**, whether as an immediate or a future right to possession, i.e. one who "holdeth certaine lands or tenements to him or to his heirs of his body begotten" — Termes de La Ley. See also **fee tail, tenant in tail after possibilities**.

tenant in tail after possibilities
A person who comes to hold a virtual life interest when an interest in land cannot pass, as was intended, to a special class of heir(s) owing to the premature death of a spouse who is intended to beget the heir(s). When an interest in land has been given to a man and his wife, or to either of them solely, with the intention that the interest (which is called a 'tail special') should pass only to *their* issue and either of them dies without leaving such issue (or the survivor outlives any issue) then the surviving party is termed a 'tenant in tail after possi-

bilities of issue extinct' – the terminology vividly demonstrating that the surviving owner of the land holds it for his or her life, but thereafter the interest returns to the grantor (or the heirs thereof). Such a tenant is holder of the land only for his or her own life and, therefore, cannot bar the entail (Fines and Recoveries Act 1833, s. 18). Like any other tenant for life, he or she is not impeachable for voluntary **waste**. A tenancy in tail after possibilities is an estate that is carved out of a 'special entail', just as an entailed estate is carved out of a fee simple.

tenant *pur autre vie*
see **tenant for life**.

tenant's contribution
see **rent escalation, service charges**.

tenant's default insurance
An insurance policy taken out to indemnify a landlord against a loss of rent in the event of the tenant's default; for example, on the liquidation or bankruptcy of the tenant. Called also 'tenant's insurance' or 'lease insurance'.
cf. **loss of rent insurance**.

tenant's fixture
see **agricultural tenant's fixture, fixture, trade fixture**.

tenant's improvement
An **improvement** to a property made at a tenant's expense. See also **compensation for improvements, fixture**.

tenant's insurance
see **tenant's default insurance**.

'tenant-like manner'
When a tenant is required to use a house in a 'tenant-like manner' he "must take proper care of the place ... he must do the little jobs about the

place which a reasonable tenant would do. In addition, he must not, of course, damage the house wilfully or negligently; ... but, apart from such things, if the house falls into disrepair through **fair wear and tear** or lapse of time or for any reason not caused by him, the tenant is not liable to repair it" – Warren *v* Keen [1953] 2 All ER 1121. (Wycombe Health Authority *v* Barnett (1982) 264 EG 619). This obligation is, therefore, less onerous than **tenantable repair**; it is the form of obligation imposed as an implied covenant upon a weekly tenant of a dwelling-house. A requirement to use premises in a **'husband-like manner'** conveys a similar obligation on an agricultural tenant. See also **weekly tenancy**.

tenant mix
The manner in which units in a shopping centre are allocated to tenants; or the letting of shop units selectively to different trades according to the type of business, size, pedestrian flow, rent level, etc. A well-balanced distribution of uses in a shopping centre is considered a prerequisite to the success of the centre in terms of its ability to draw and keep customers, and as a means of insuring healthy competition between retailers without causing friction between conflicting users. *Tenant Mix for Small Centers*, International Council of Shopping Centres.
Rent Assessment and Tenant Mix in Planned Shopping Centres, CALUS, (1975).
Enclosed Shopping Centres, by Clive Darlow (ed.), pp. 15–26 (1972).
Analysis and Valuation of Retail Locations, by Edwin M. Rams, pp. 151–165 (1976).

Shopping Centre Management, by
Peter Martin, p. 129 *et seq* (1982).

tenant-right

The right to compensation that an
outgoing tenant has from his landlord
for **improvement** or **amelioration** left
to the landlord's benefit. In particular, in England the right of a tenant of
agricultural land to claim compensation, upon the termination of a
tenancy or upon quitting a farm, for
the benefit of work expended on cultivating, sowing, and manuring land.
This right was originally founded on
custom or agreement (based on the
principle that it was usual to grant a
new tenancy to an existing occupier in
preference to a stranger and, therefore, an outgoing tenant should be
paid for any benefit that might
accrue to an incoming tenant). However, this right is now contained predominately in statutory regulations.
The items for which compensation
may be claimed are set out in the
Agricultural Holdings Act 1948, Sch.
4., Pt. II (as amended by the Agricultural Holdings Act (Variation of the
Fourth Schedule) Orders 1951 and
1978). This statute provides compensation for such matters as the value of
growing crops or crops harvested but
not removed, together with the cost
of ploughing, seeding and cultivation
and certain costs of laying down
pasture. See also **compensation for
improvements**.
*Agricultural Valuations: a Practical
Guide*, by P.G. Williams (1985).

tenantable repair

Such repairs as a tenant might reasonably be required to carry out by
virtue of the fact that he has been
granted a right to use and occupy
another's property and it is to be
expected that he would not return the
premises at the end of the tenancy in
an unduly deteriorated state. The
type of **repair** that an incoming tenant
would expect an outgoing tenant to
have carried out; "such repair as, having regard to the age, character and
locality of the house, would make it
reasonably fit for occupation of a
reasonably-minded tenant of the class
who would be likely to take it.... The
house need not be put into the same
condition as when the tenant took it;
it need not be put into perfect repair".
– Proudfoot *v* Hart (1890) 25 QBD
52. In that case the lease was granted
for three years, so a stricter interpretation is likely to apply to a longer lease
(and conversely a lesser obligation to
a shorter lease). Even though premises
are in a very poor state at the outset, a
tenant is not absolved from carrying
out 'reasonable repairs'. Words such
as 'repair', 'repair reasonably and
properly', 'keep in good repair', 'sufficient repair', 'habitable repair', or
'tenantable repair' all convey similar
meanings. "The tenant must when
necessary restore by reparation or
renewal of subsidiary parts of the subject matter demised to a condition in
which it is reasonably fit for the purposes for which such a subject matter
would ordinarily be used." – Cal-
thorpe v McOscar [1924] 1 KB 729.
However, all such words should be
interpreted in the context of the lease
and with due regard to the condition
and locality of the property at the
start of the lease. A tenant is not
required to redecorate completely (a
requirement to "redecorate completely" normally would be stated as a
specific covenant in a lease) if an
incoming tenant would be happy to
take the premises without complete

redecoration, providing there would be no undue adverse effect on the rent the incoming tenant might pay. A tenant is not obliged to repair or restore that which has worn out by age – Crawford *v* Newton 36 WR 54; he is not responsible for **fair wear and tear**; but he must not commit **waste**. cf. '**tenant-like manner**'.

tenantry (US)

1. Property occupied by tenants.
2. A body of tenants.

tender

1. An unqualified **offer** of goods or services to fulfil a demand or obligation. An actual proffering of the exact amount of money required to pay a debt at the time and place where the obligation is due, especially in order to avoid a penalty or forfeiture or a right. A tender represents an expression of willingness to pay a debt or discharge an obligation; it is a means by which a penalty, or the forfeiture of a right, may be avoided; but it does not discharge the debt or obligation – that is accomplished only by payment or complete performance: "there is a great difference between payment and tender; payment extinguishes the debt; tender does not" – Hogg *v* Smyth 32 LRK 191. However, "the law considers a party, who has entered into a contract to deliver goods or pay money to another, as having substantially performed it if he has tendered the goods or the money" – Startup *v* Macdonald (1843) 6 Man G 610. Traditionally, an expressed rent has to be tendered, in the same way as an offer of goods or the supply of services, and the tenant was required to seek out and pay over that which was due to the landlord. However, this requirement normally

is dispensed with by a provision in a lease as to the time, place and means required for the payment of rent. If an obligation to pay rent is not express, but arises by implication, then the payment should be made at the demised premises and the landlord is required to present himself to collect the rent. See also **bilateral contract, legal tender**.

2. A response to an invitation to supply goods or services. A tender usually constitutes an offer which the invitor is at liberty to reject or accept. However, whether the party who calls for a tender is obliged automatically to accept the offer made by the tenderer depends on the language of that invitation. "One knows that these tenders are very often in a form under which the purchasing body is not bound to give the tenderer any order at all, in other words the contractor offers to supply goods at a price, and if the purchasing body chooses to give him an order for goods during the stipulated time, then he is under an obligation to supply the goods in accordance with the order; but apart from that nobody is bound" – Percival Ltd *v* LCC Asylums and Mental Deficiency Committee (1918) 87 LJKB 677. 'Tender' may refer also to an invitation to submit offers for goods or services i.e. an **invitation to tender**, which does not constitute an offer and does not form any part of a contract until an offer is made and then accepted by the invitor – Spencer *v* Harding (1870) LR 5 CP 561.

tenement

1. Anything of a permanent nature that can be held (Bl. Comm. vol. ii p. 17). That which is the subject of **tenure**; everything that may be held,

provided it is of a sustantial and permanent nature, including the right to
anything that issues out of or is a part
of real property, such as rent, estovers, or other profits – Martyn v Williams (1857) 1 H and N 827 – but not a
leasehold interest which in English
common law, represents personal
property. In English law, real property is a right to land, but not land
itself; a tenement is the subject of that
right – "... 'tenement' means the
physical entity which is the subject
matter of the demise, and not any
interest therein ..." – Jeroome v
Fordhla Printing Co. Ltd [1943] IR
405. The term 'tenement' is used frequently in conjunction with **hereditament** and may be considered as
synonymous therewith. However,
'hereditament' more particularly refers to that which is capable of inheritance and 'tenement' to any right to
land; so that "tenements and hereditaments" includes all species of **real
estate**, whether corporeal or incorporeal (Jarman on Wills 8 ed., vol. ii p.
1270; Co. Litt. 19b). Tenement may
be used also to distinguish any freehold estate, in a corporeal or incorporeal hereditament, from a leasehold
estate. See also **dominant tenement,
servient tenement**.
2. A house divided into separate
dwellings, or any dwelling contained
within a building that contains a
number of similar dwellings. A term
applied commonly to any residential
building that contains a number of
rooms, flats, or apartments, with a
common access from the street –
M'Arthur v Edinburgh Magistrates
43 Sc. LR. 727); in particular, such a
building that is over-crowded and has
substandard amenities. In the US,
called also a 'community house'. See

also **apartment house**.
3. In a lease, a "part of a house so
structurally divided and separated as
to be capable of being a distinct property or a distinct subject of a lease" –
Russell v Coutts 19 Sc. LR 691.

tenement factory
1. A **factory** situated in a building
that contains similar premises at
different levels. For the purpose of
laws affecting the health and safety
of those employed in factory premises, a tenement factory means any
premises where mechanical power is
distributed from a central source in
the same building for use in manufacturing processes to "different parts of
the same premises occupied by
different persons in such a manner
that those parts constitute in law
separate factories" (Factories Act
1961, s. 176(1)). (The owner of a
tenement factory, not the occupier, is
responsible for any contravention of
the Factory Act 1961 in respect of
such matters as the health and safety
and conditions of employment of
those working in the building).
(US) 2. see **flated factory**.

tenement house
    see **tenement**.

tenemental land
    Land which, under the **feudal system**
of land tenure, was granted to be held
by a person other than the lord of the
manor or his servants. Called also
'outland'.
    cf. **demesne land**. See also **waste land**.

tenendum
    Originally a word used to signify that
land was held from a superior lord or
a clause in a document to the same
effect. In a lease the 'tenendum'
indicates the interest held by the

tenant. In practice usually it is combined with the **habendum** and starts with the phrase "to hold". See also **conveyance, tenure**.

tenets of rating
see **rateable occupation**.

tenure
A right to hold property, especially land; the manner or terms upon which land (and buildings) is held. The word tenure is a vestage of the **feudal system** under which all land was held of a superior lord and ultimately from the Sovereign; subject to the rendering of a service or the making of a payment for the privilege. The Sovereign was the only person who had an absolute right to the ownership of land and 'tenure' signified that something was held or possessed from another. "The thing holden is therefore stiled a **tenement**, the possessors thereof tenants, and the manner of possession a tenure."(Bl. Comm. vol. ii p. 59). Tenures were classified by the service required to enable the tenant to continue to hold the land. For example, tenure in chivalry or military tenure, including **knight-service** or military service; and grand **sergeanty** or service to the King; **spiritual service** or service by prayer; non-military service or **socage**, including petty sergeantry; as well as the servile tenure of **villeinage**. The person who held directly from the King was the **tenant in chief** (*in capite*) and one who held from any other person was the **mesne lord** or 'intermediary' tenant, or if he actually occupied the land the **tenant in demesne**. The tenant had a right to possession of the soil or **seisin**, i.e. an enjoyment of land based on title.

Most forms of feudal tenure were abolished or converted to free and common socage from 1660 (Tenures Abolition Act 1660). All remaining forms of tenure were converted to **freehold** (which is the name now given to free and common socage) from 1926 (Law of Property Act 1922, s. 128, Sch. 12 para (1), Sch. 13). Freehold is still referred to as a form of tenure as all land in England and Wales technically is held from the Crown.

In modern usage tenure means the manner in which land is held and may be qualified by being 'freehold' or 'leasehold'. Also it is used synonymously with tenancy, which signifies in the same way that land is held from another. (The terms 'tenure' and 'tenancy' have different origins, the former being a right to land held against another – to exclude another's seisin; the latter being a contractual right to **exclusive occupation** of land for a certain duration, in return for a payment called rent.) See also **copyhold, doctrine of tenure, gavelkind, manor, security of tenure, tenant for life**.

Real Property, by William E. Burby, 3 edn., pp. 1–4.
The Law of Landlord and Tenant, by David Lloyd Evans, 2 edn., pp. 7–8.
Introduction to Land Law, by J.G. Riddell, 2 edn., pp. 1–13.
Holdsworth's History of English Law, vol. iii pp. 37–46.
The Law of Real Property, by Robert Megarry and H.W.R. Wade, 5 edn., pp. 12–37.
39 Halsbury's Laws of England, 4 edn, paras. 305–328.
Littleton's Tenures in English, John Byrne & Co., 1903.

tenure (F)
tenure; tenancy.
(*tenure à bail* – **leasehold interest**).

term

1. A fixed period; a prescribed or limited period of **time**. The quantity or duration for which a lease or estate exists; or the period for which a right to use and occupy land may be enjoyed. The word 'term' may be used to signify the time for which a lease or estate will last, assuming that it will run the full period for which it was granted; but also it may mean the time within which it may be brought to an end; as by surrender, forfeiture, and the like (Bl. Comm. vol. ii p. 145).

A term of a lease must be expressed "with certainty or specifically or by reference to something which can, at the time when the lease takes effect, be looked to as a certain ascertainment of what the term is meant to be" – Lace *v* Chantler [1944] KB 368. A lease granted for an uncertain duration, e.g. 'for the duration of the war' is void. See also *habendum*, **tenancy for a fixed term, termination, unexpired term**.

2. A word or phrase; in particular one that has a known meaning in a science, art or profession. A part of an agreement that relates to a particular matter. A **condition, warranty**, or **limitation** in an agreement. The word 'term' does not have any legal import; it is used generally to refer to any clause or part of a contract that does not amount to a condition which if breached would give rise to a right to terminate the contract. See also **covenant, express term, implied term, term of art, terms and conditions**.

term date
The date on which a **tenancy for a**

fixed term (or fixed period of time) comes to an end by effluxion of time. See also **unexpired term**.

term days
see **quarter days**.

term (or word) of art
A term (or word) that has a meaning in a legal or technical context which may be different from, or more precise than, the meaning in common usage. A term of art in law is interpreted strictly, normally based on precedent, and as a rule, it is not altered by the context. (Sydall *v* Castings Ltd [1966] 3 All ER 774.) See also *ejudem generis, noscitur a sociis*, **words meaning of**.

term of years (or term for years)
see **tenancy for a term of years**.

term of years absolute
A phrase used in the Law of Property Act 1925 to refer to one of the two interests in land that can exist as a **legal estate**, provided it is created by the required formalities (in most cases by deed). "'Term of years absolute' means a term of years (taking effect either in possession or in reversion whether or not at a rent) with or without impeachment for **waste**, subject or not to another legal estate, and either certain or liable to determination by notice, re-entry, operation of law or by a provision for cesser on redemption, or in any other event (other than the dropping of a life, or the determination of a determinable life interest)". It includes a "term for less than a year, or for a year or years and a fraction of a year or from year to year" (Law of Property Act 1925, s. 205(1) (xxvii)). A 'term of years' means a valid **lease** for any term that has a fixed and ascertainable dura-

tion, including a **periodic tenancy** provided the periods are fixed and are of ascertainable duration; but not a lease for a life nor a lease (granted at a rent or in consideration of a fine) that does not take effect in **possession** for 21 years (1925 Act, s. 149(2)). However, neither a **tenancy at will** nor **tenancy on sufferance** can be a term of years, because their duration is wholly uncertain. The word 'absolute' appears only to emphasise that apart from the conditions outlined above the leasehold must not otherwise be limited or qualified. See also **legal lease, tenancy for a fixed term, term**.

Land Law: Cases and Materials, by R.H. Maudsley and E.H. Burns, 4 edn., p. 355 *et seq.*

Cheshire's Modern Law of Real Property, 13 edn, pp. 362–380.

39 Halsbury's Laws of England, 4 edn, paras. 316, 401–414.

term mortgage (or loan)

A mortgage (or loan) granted for a fixed period of time, especially for a number of years. See also **maturity date, redemption, standing loan**.

term policy

see **long-term insurance agreement**.

term and reversion method

The conventional method of assessing the capital value of a property that will generate a variable income. Each tranche of income is capitalised for the term for which it is receivable and these capital values are summated. For example, if a property is let at a rent of £10 000 per annum for 3 years and then it is estimated that the income will revert to a market rent of £15 000 per annum, the capital value may be assessed as:

'term rent'	£10 000 p.a.	
capitalisation rate,		
or **YP**, for 3 years		
at 5%	2.72	£27 232
'reversion' to	£15 000 p.a.	
capitalised in		
perpetuity at 6½%		
deferred 3 years	15.38	
at 6½%	0.83 12.77	£191 481
Total capital value		£218 713

(The 'term' rent is considered a more secure income and, therefore, is capitalised at a lower rate of interest – or higher capitalisation rate – than the market rent). Sometimes called the 'block income approach'.

cf. **hardcore method**. See also **income method of valuation**.

terme (F)

1. **term**; period; time; date.

(*terme de bail* – term (i.e. the length) of a lease).

(*bail à terme* – lease for a term of years)

(*emprunt à court terme* – short-term loan)

(*terme de grace* – days or period of grace).

2. term; clause; condition. "A *terme* is like a **condition** in that the event to which it refers is in the future, but it differs in that the event is certain to occur (though the moment at which it will occur may not be certain)" *French Law of Contract*, by Barry Nicholas, p. 153 (1982). A *terme* may be *suspensif* when an obligation is held in abeyance until the event occurs; or *extictif* when the event will bring an obligation to an end. (Thus a **condition** may have the English common law meaning of condition or may be used to refer to a contingency, but a *terme* is more limited in its meaning).

(*termes d'un contrat* – terms of a contract).

3. **quarter day**; quarter.

(*payer un term* – to pay a quarter's rent)

4. **instalment**.

(*le versement des termes échus d'annuité* – the payment of the instalment due on an annuity).

5. limit; boundary.

terms and conditions

The express basis upon which parties enter into a **contract**; the essential points or stipulations that make up and constitute the agreement contained therein, e.g. the subject matter, consideration, date of commencement, quantity of property, etc. A term may be classified as a 'material' term (usually called a **condition** in English law) or a 'non-material' term (usually called a **warranty** in English law). However, "the word 'terms' is not a word of art, and has no definite legal meaning." – Re Gillespie, Gillespie v Gillespie (1902) 2 NZLR 81; it may refer to any part or clause of a legal document. See also **term**.

terminable interest

An interest in land that will come to an end on the occurence of a specified event or on a specified date e.g. a tenancy for a life or a tenancy for a term of years.

cf. **periodic interest**. See also **term**.

terminal equity (US)

The value of an investor's interest, or **equity**, in a property at the end of an assumed period of ownership or at the time when all loans or debt capital will have been repaid. See also **equity build-up, redemption value**.

terminal value

see **redemption** value, **terminal equity**.

termination

The coming or bringing to an end, as with a lease or contract. In particular, the act of bringing to an end by mutual agreement, by effluxion of time, or by the exercise of a right of one of the parties. 'Termination' may have a transitive or intransitive meaning, according to the context. It may mean the act of coming to an end or the action of being brought to an end, by whatever means. In relation to a hire purchase agreement, termination has been described as an ambiguous word "since it may refer to a termination by a right under the agreement or by a condition incorporated in it or by a deliberate breach by one party amounting to a repudiation of the whole contract" – Bridge v Campbell Discount Co. [1962] AC 600. It may have similar meanings when used in relation to a lease, i.e. the bringing to an end before completion of the expected **term**; especially when brought about by service of notice to quit. Under the Agricultural Holdings Act 1948, s. 94, in relation to an agricultural tenancy, termination means, "the **cesser** of a contract of tenancy by reason of effluxion of time or from any other cause". See also **determination, frustration, merger, notice to quit, recission, surrender**.

termination clause

A clause that permits either party to nullify or terminate a contract. A clause that provides for a contract to be brought to an end by mutual agreement, e.g. by service of **notice to quit**, or when one party is in **breach of contract**. Called also a 'cancellation clause', especially when the cancelling party has a right to compensation for non-performance of the entire contract or an unperformed balance. See also **revocation, termination**.

terminus (L)
1. A **boundary line** or limit.
2. An **estate** for a term of years.

termor
An old word for one who holds land for a term of years (Bl. Comm. vol. ii p. 142; Co. Litt. 456); a **lessee**. See also **tenancy for a term of years**.

terra (L)
Earth; soil.

terrace house
A house annexed to another house on two sides, forming part of a row of similar houses. The house at each end of the row, being annexed only on one side, is called the end terrace house. "A terrace house is one in a row or series which has its own frontage to a public road or public place." – Holmes v Ryde Municipal Council [1969] 2 NSWR 139. In the US, more commonly called a 'row house'. cf. **back-to-back house, semi-detached-house**. See also **party wall, town house**.

terrain (F)
land; ground; parcel of land.
(*terrain à batir* – building land)
(*terrain à lotir* – building or development site; lot)
(*terrain bati* – developed or built-on land)
(*terrain et construction* – land and buildings; real property)
(*terrain vague* – **raw land**).

terre (F)
ground; **land**; estate.
(*terre assignée à un bénéfice* – **glebe land**)
(*terre vaine et vague* – **wasteland**)

(*fonds de terre* – **tenament**; landed property).

terre-tenant
1. One who has actual possession and enjoyment of land, as distinguished from one who has a future or conditional right to possession. Historically a person who had **seisin** of land i.e. "he who occupied the land" as distinguished from a superior lord (Bl. Comm. vol. ii p. 91). In certain states in the US, used also to refer to one who purchases a property subject to the prior right of a mortgage.
2. One who had the power to dispose of land on behalf of a *cestui que use* or beneficiary; the forerunner of a modern trustee of a legal estate – a *feoffee to uses*. See also **feoffment**.

terrier
A register used for setting down a schedule of land boundaries and interests in land as held by a person or body. An official register of real property – historically as maintained by a parish church.

testament
A written statement specifying the desired arrangement for the transfer of a person's property on his death; "the true declaration of our last will, of that wee would be done after our death" – Termes de La Ley. A testament may be distinguished from a **will** as the latter historically dealt only with real property whereas a testament dealt with personal property. However, in modern English law a will may be used to transfer personal property and real property. The word testament is now seldom used except as a formal introduction to a will. In effect, therefore, the words 'will' and

'testament' are interchangeable, and 'testament' includes a **codicil**.

testament (F)

will; testament.

testamentary disposition

A disposition of property, by will or deed, that does not take effect until after the grantor's death. See also **testament**.

testator (fem. **testatrix**)

One who makes a **will**; a deceased person who has made a will and is said to die testate.

testatum

The introduction to the operative parts of a deed, which comprises such words as "now this deed witnesseth ..." Called also the 'witnessing clause'.

testimonial clause (US)

see **testimonium**.

testimonium

The formal introduction to the final or **attestation clause** in a deed; the clause that precedes the signature and seal of the parties. A testimonium starts with words such as "IN WITNESS whereof the parties ...". In the US, called also the 'testimonial clause'.

testing clause

In Scottish law, a **testimonium**.

things

Permanent objects that may be perceived through the senses. In common usage, a 'thing is that which is tangible, being the object of property; but in legal usage it means any of the rights to **property** whether tangible – goods, chattels, land, etc. – or intangible – estates, interests, rights, claims, patents, etc. "By this word is understood every object, except man, which may become an active subject of a right" (Code du Canton de Berne, art. 322).

In English law, things are divided into *real* things and *personal* things. "Things real are such as are permanent, fixed, and immoveable, which cannot be carried out of their place; as lands and tenements: things personal are goods, money and all other moveables; which may attend the owner's person wherever he thinks proper to go." (Bl. Comm. vol. ii. p. 16). In the civil law, things are classified broadly as **corporeal property** or **incorporeal property**; or moveables or immoveables. An alternative classification of things is (i) land or real property; (ii) goods or 'choses-in-possession' i.e. moveable and tangible property; (iii) 'choses in action' i.e. moveable and intangible property; (iv) money, including legal tender, cheques or other readily acceptable means of exchange; and (v) funds, e.g. capital of a company or money held in trust being something which retains its identity but may change in content. cf. **effects**. See also **chose**, *ejusdem generis*.

The Law of Property, by F.H. Lawson and Bernard Rudden, 2 edn., pp. 14–39.

third party

A party who is a stranger to a contract, or action, but may be affected by it. One who is intended to benefit from a promise in a contract but is not a party to that contract. Any party other than the principal parties to a contract. A feature of real estate is that, more often than not, it is affected by rights held by parties other than the ostensible owner; such rights being enforceable against the real estate itself rather than owner, e.g. the rights of a mortgagee or the beneficiary of a trust; the rights appertaining to an easement or restrictive covenant. Such rights may benefit or burden those who are not parties to the contract by which they were created; for example, a purchaser of land affected by a mortgage or an assignee of a lease. See also **legal estate, notice, overriding interest, public liability, insurance, privity.**

third-party liability insurance
see **public liability insurance.**

third possessor (US)
One who purchases a property that is subject to a mortgage, but does not accept any obligation to the mortgagee. See also **assumption.**

third schedule development
Certain forms of development set out in the third schedule of the Town and Country Planning Acts of 1947 & 1962 that were not considered as new development and, therefore, did not require planning permission. Now superceded by the eighth schedule of the Town and Country Planning Act 1971 i.e. by 'eighth schedule development'. See also **existing use rights.**

thoroughfare
A **highway, street, bridleway,** or **footpath** used by the public; especially a 'throughway' that is subject to constant and regular use. A major highway or a way from one part of a town to another. A street or path that is open at both ends.
cf. **cul-de-sac.**

three months
Three consecutive periods of a

month; as a rule, three calendar months.
cf. **quarterly.**

throughput method
A method of valuing petrol filling stations, based on the volume of sales achieved. See also *profits' method valuation.*

tidal land
see **foreshore, shore.**

tied accommodation
Residential accommodation provided to an employee as part of his or her terms of employment; especially accommodation that is provided to enable a person to better perform his or her duties of employment. In general, an occupier of tied accommodation is granted a contractual right to remain in occupation only as long as the employment subsists; the employer reserving the right to put an end to the arrangement if the occupier leaves or is dismissed from the employment. In that event, if the occupier can establish that he or she had a **tenancy** as distinguished from a **licence,** the occupier may acquire a **statutory tenancy** entitling him or her to remain in occupation of the premises. However, if the arrangement is no more than a licence the employer may obtain possession, provided he obtains a prior order of the court (Protection from Eviction Act 1977, s. 3).

A forestry or agricultural worker who is housed by an employer, whether as a tenant or licencee, (called a 'protected occupier') and who 'qualifies', normally by having been in full-time agricultural employment for not less than 91 out of the last 104 weeks prior to the termination of his or her employment, has a

right basically to continue in occupation "if and so long as he occupies the dwelling house as his **residence**", i.e. he acquires a form of 'statutory tenancy' (The Rent (Agriculture) Act 1976, as amended by the Housing Act 1980, Sch. 25, ss. 32, 33). A protected occupier cannot be displaced unless the landlord obtains a court order on one of the statutory **grounds for possession** (1976 Act, Sch. 4). A landlord of agricultural tied accommodation may apply to the local authority for the tenant to be rehoused "in the interests of efficient agriculture" to enable a new worker to make use of the accommodation (1976 Act, Part IV). There are rights of succession on death provided to protect occupiers and statutory tenants who qualify under the 1976 Act. The rent of premises occupied by a protected occupier who accedes to a 'statutory tenancy' may be fixed by agreement between the parties and registered in the same way as for any other tenancy that is protected under the Rent Acts (1976 Act, ss. 11,13). See also **eviction**, **secure tenancy**, **service tenancy**.
The Law of Landlord and Tenant, by David Lloyd Evans, 2 edn., pp. 307–309.
Rent Control and Leasehold Enfranchisement, by Trevor Aldridge, 8 edn., Ch. 9.
Landlord and Tenant Law, by David Yates and A.J. Hawkins, pp. 361–369 (1981).
Housing Law, by Andrew Arden and Martin Partington, pp. 1097–1110 (1983).
27 Halsbury's Laws of England, 4 edn, paras. 802–823.

tied cottage
A cottage maintained by an emplo-
yer, especially a farmer or owner of a large estate, for occupation by an employee. See also **tied accommodation**.

tied house
A public house which, by virtue of a franchise or control over its ownership (in the form of outright ownership or a mortgage), may sell only those alcoholic or other beverages supplied by a particular brewer or distiller. A term that may be applied also to any business house which is obliged to purchase its goods from a particular concern. See also **equity of redemption**, **solus agreement**, **tied accommodation**.

tied loan
see **solus agreement**.

tiers, tierce (F)
third party.
(*tierce caution* – **contingent liability**)
(*assurance au tiers* – **third-party liability insurance**).

timber
In general, a growing **tree** or wood therefrom, especially wood that may be used for building, carpentry or joinery. In particular, wood derived from a tree that is suitable for repairing a house (Co. Litt. 63a). In English common law, timber could be derived only from an oak, ash or elm over twenty years old, and it had to be sufficient to make a good post. However, wood derived from other trees, that is capable of being put to the same use, may be considered as timber – Honeywood *v* Honeywood (1874) LR 18 Eq. 309. A local custom may extend the meaning of timber to wood derived from beech, hornbeam, lime, white-thorn, black-thorn, aspen and/or horse-chestnut. A minimum

diameter of six inches, a girth of two feet or a height of ten feet may be essential qualities. On the other hand larch, willow and fruit-trees have been held not to constitute timber – Re Harrison's Trusts, Harrison *v* Harrison (1884) 28 Ch. D227; Bullen *v* Denning (1826) 5 B and C 847. Similarly in the US saplings, brush, fruit trees, and trees that could be used only for ornament or firewood, are not classified as timber – W.T. Smith Lumber Co. *v* Jernigan, 185 Ala. 125).

19 Halsbury's Laws of England, 4 edn, para. 33.

timbre (F)

(*droit de timbres* – **stamp duty**).

time

A measure of change; the relative occurrence, or reoccurrence, of something. The instant at which an event takes place, or should take place; the moment stipulated for a condition to occur. (Traditionally, time was measured by reference to observed changes in nature, e.g. the phases of the moon, but in modern times it is calculated normally by reference to an ordained measure or 'clock'). In contract law time runs, as a rule, from the end of the **day** specified as the starting point and continues throughout the day specified as the finishing point. Thus, a lease for six calendar months from 20 February starts at midnight of that day and continues until midnight on 20 August – Winchester Court Ltd *v* Bignall [1924] 1 KB 124; Lemon *v* Lardeur [1946] KB 613. However, this strict rule is replaced frequently by the most practicable time based on the intention of the parties or any **custom** surrounding the type of contract. So a rent payable

'from' or 'since' 25 December is payable on that date (because that is one of the 'usual' **quarter days**). – Brakespear and Sons *v* Barton [1924] 2 KB 38. 'Commencing with', 'commencing on', or 'beginning with' a stipulated **date** includes that date. On the other hand, commencing on the date set by receipt of a notice would exclude that date and would effectively start the next day, leaving the entire date for the notice to be received. 'Commencing three days after receipt of a notice' refers to the end of the third clear day after the day during which the notice is received. By the same reasoning, "if the act done be an act to which the party against whom time is to run, is privy, then the day on which it is done is to be included; otherwise it is excluded" – Hardy *v* Ryle (1829) LJ(OS)MC 120. The party who is privy to the time in question has had the benefit of some part of the day included.

When performance of a contract is required 'before', 'within the period up to' or 'not later than' a specified date, the period for performance expires immediately before that date. On the other hand, a requirement to perform an obligation 'by' a specified date gives the whole of that day for performance: a date is "much more commonly descriptive of a day than of any smaller division of time" – Simpson *v* Marshall (1900) 37 SLR 316. The same rule applies to a requirement to perform 'on or before' a specified date, with the additional option for the obligor, or debtor, to perform, or discharge, the duty before the required date – Dagger *v* Shepherd [1946] KB 223. The word 'within' in relation to a period of time "does not usually mean 'during' or 'throughout the whole of'; it is more frequently used to delimit a period inside which certain events may happen" – Reynolds *v* Reynolds [1941] VLR 249 – and is used ordinarily to restrict that which precedes from that which follows. As a rule 'until' allows for that date it qualifies; until 20 January includes the 20th but no longer. However, 'till' and 'until' may be construed to include or exclude a specified date and should be qualified accordingly, e.g. 'until and including 21 December', 'until but excluding 3 January 1984'.

In computing the period for the service of a **notice to quit**, at common law, the first day upon which the notice is served is included and the last day excluded. When a periodic tenancy commences 'on' a particular date and may be terminated on the anniversary of that date, it should be brought to an end at the close of the anniversary date. "'At', 'on', 'from' and 'on or from' are for this purpose equivalent expressions." – Sidebotham *v* Holland [1895] 1 QB 384. (However, it is preferable to prefix such expressions with 'commencing' or 'ending' to emphasise that the specified date is included in the compilation of the term.)

In general, a specified time is the local time of the place (especially if that place is paramount to the contract), "but wherever any expression of time occurs in any Act of Parliament, deed, or other instrument, the time referred to shall, unless it is specifically stated, be held to be Greenwich mean time" (Statutes (Definition of Time) Act 1880). If summer time is in operation this usually takes preference (Summer Time Acts 1922–47). See also **half-year, limitation,** **month, prescription, Statutes of Limitation, term, 'time is of the essence', week, year.**
Odger's Construction of Deeds and Statutes, 5 edn, pp. 134–140.
45 Halsbury's Laws of England, 4 edn, paras. 1101–1200.

time bargain
A dealing in a future right to property. See also **option**.

time immemorial
see **prescription**.

'time is of the essence'
An expression inserted in a contract (either by these words or similar terms, denoting clearly or precisely that the same effect is intended) to indicate that performance of the contract within or by a specified time is essential to the contract; it makes time a **condition** of the contract, not a mere **warranty** for the better performance of the contract. Time may be expressed to be of the essence of a contract at the outset; or it may be expressly made a condition after reasonable notice has been issued to that effect. In the latter instance the consequences of any further delay must be seriously detrimental to the proper performance of the contract and the need for the time limit must stem from the construction of the contract at the outset or from the nature of the subject matter; it is not possible to make time of the essence merely because a breach of contract may arise, or has arisen. Even if time is stipulated to be of the essence of a contract, equity may look at the whole scope of the agreement and decide that the intention of the parties was only that the contract should be performed within a reasonable time –

Lennon v Napper (1802) 2 Sch. & Lef 684. "In short, time is of the essence of the contract if such is the real intention of the parties and an intention to this effect may be expressly stated or may be inferred from the nature of the contract or from its attendant circumstances. By way of summary it may be said that time is essential first, if the parties expressly stipulate in the contract that it shall be so – Hudson v Temple (1860) 29 Beav. 536; secondly, if in a case where one party has been guilty of undue delay, he is notified by the other that unless performance is completed within a reasonable time the contract will be regarded as at an end – Stickney v Keeble [1915] AC 386; and last, if the nature of the surrounding circumstances or of the subject matter makes it imperative that the agreed date should be precisely observed. Under this last head it has been held that a date fixed for completion is essential if contained in a contract for the sale of property which fluctuates in value with the passage of time, such as a public house – Lock v Bell [1931] 1 Ch. 35; business premises – Harold Wood Brick Co. v Ferris [1935] 2 KB 198; a reversionary interest – Newman v Rogers (1793) 4 Bro. CC 391; or shares of a speculative nature liable to considerable fluctuation in value – Hare v Nicoll [1966] 2 QB 130." Cheshire & Fifoot's Law of Contract 10 edn, p. 499. Also, time is of the essence in the case of a unilateral contract, such as an **option**, which requires one party to take action by a certain date in order that the other party is put under an obligation – United Scientific Holdings Ltd v Burnley [1978] AC 904. Failure to complete a contract when time is of the essence entitles the innocent party to elect to rescind the contract.

A contract for the sale of land (except in one of the special situations stated above) must be completed within a **reasonable** period of time from the date set for completion and the contract normally cannot be repudiated if completion is fairly delayed beyond a stipulated time; although in such a case there may still be a right to damages – Raineri v Miles and Another [1979] All ER 763. What is reasonable is a question of fact, taking account of such matters as investigation of title, searches and preparation of the requisite documents – Johnson v Humphrey [1946] 1 All ER 460.

In a building contract, work should be completed by the stipulated time; there is no implied covenant that a longer time is permitted, unless the employer renders it impossible or impracticable for the contractor to do his work within the stipulated time. In that event the work must be completed in a reasonable time – "that is, as a rule, the stipulated time plus a reasonable extension for the delay caused by his (the employer's) conduct" – Trollope and Colls v North West Metropolitan Regional Hospital Board [1973] 2 All ER 266.

In the case of a **rent review clause** in a lease, the provision therein is usually a form of machinery for reviewing the rent and the times stipulated for the service of notices are not of the essence; "I [Lord Diplock] would hold that in the absence of any contra-indication in the express words of the lease or in the interpretation of the rent review itself or other clauses or in the surrounding circumstances the presumption is that the time-table specified ... is not of the essence of the contract" – United Scientific Holdings Ltd. *v* Burnley Corporation, *supra.* at 930. On the other hand, if there is a procedure by which a landlord 'triggers-off' a rent review, and there is an option for a tenant to terminate a lease in the event that the tenant is unable to accept the new rent then, because time is of the essence in the exercising of an option to terminate a lease, there arises an implication that time is of the essence when fixing the reviewed rent – Coventry City Council *v* J. Hepworth and Son Ltd (1983) 265 EG 608. "Where a rent review clause is associated with a true option (a 'break' clause, for example), it is a strong indication that time is intended to be of the essence of the rent review clause – if not absolutely, at least to the extent that the tenant will reasonably expect to know what new rent he will have to pay before the time comes for him to elect whether to terminate or review the tenancy" – United Scientific Holdings case, *supra* at p. 946. Thus if there are no express words, nor extraneous or surrounding circumstances, time is not of the essence of a rent review; but, "since there is no magical formula it is possible that small differences of language will lead in some cases to the opposite" – Drebbond Ltd *v* Horsham (1979) 246 EG 1013. When a tenant has a right to bring the settlement of a rent review to fruition, for example by serving notice of a wish to refer the matter to an independent expert in accordance with a provision in the lease, then he may make time of the essence by exercising that right: if he does not take any such action, he cannot later declare that the landlord has been unreasonable in delaying the

service of notice of an intention to increase the rent, unless the delay is inordinately prolonged.

An undue delay in exercising a right, when time is of the essence, may amount to an **abandonment** of that right. See also **act of God, laches, rescission, waiver.**

time ownership
see **time sharing**.

time sale
see **instalment sale**.

time sharing
A term derived from a system devised to enable a number of parties to share the use of a computer for an allotted period of time, with each party having a vestige of ownership of the hardware. Subsequently applied to a form of property interest by which real property is made available in perpetuity, for life, or for a term of years, to a number of persons and each receive a right to one of a series of similar and exclusive rights to use or occupy a parcel or unit of the property. The interest may be granted by means of a membership of a club, a beneficial right under a trust, a sale as a tenancy in common, a lease or a licence. It may be a personal right, or a real right to property. The commonest forms of time sharing are (i) the property is held by a trustee on behalf of a club or association of which the members, as beneficiaries, have a right of occupation – the trustees and members may be one and the same (thus giving the members an interest in the property) or the trustees may be totally separate from the members; (ii) a series of leases are granted to each occupier, e.g. two weeks each year or a lease is granted to each party for a term of

years with a limited right of occupation; (iii) the property, or units in the property, are held in **co-ownership** (or as a **condominium** or **collective ownership**) by the timeshare owners and occupational leases are granted to each owner for specified periods of the year; (iv) the property is held by a company and each timeshare purchaser becomes a shareholder and is granted by the company a right to occupy a part of the property. The first two forms of timeshare are the more common under English law and the third and fourth forms are the more usual in countries operating under a system based on the civil law.
Valuing the Timeshare Property, by Kathleen Conroy, (1981).
International Timesharing, by J. Edmonds (1984).
Timeshare Properties, by Robert Irwin, (1983).

time value
see **future value, present value**.

time-weighted rate of return (TWR)
An **internal rate of return** calculated to take account of the changing capital values at different intervals during the life of an investment; a TWR also takes account of the time at which additional investments of capital are made. The geometric mean of the returns between the times of each addition or reduction in the capital invested.

tithe
1. A term derived from the Old English *teogotha*, 'a tenth'. A form of due, payable to an established Church, which was based on one tenth of a person's income or the yearly profit from land. "The tenth part of all fruits, praedial, personal and mixt which are due to God, and consequentially to his churches' ministers for their maintenance" (Cowel, Bl. Comm. vol. ii p. 23–32). The *Old Testament*, the *Mishna* and the *Talmud* each require the payment of tithes for the support of the poor, and the early Christian church came to demand similar payments. In the Middle Ages, in many European countries, tithes became common and compulsory and were annexed to the established Church. The Church purportedly had the right to raise money, for its own support and for its poor, from those who held a right to benefit from 'God's property' i.e. from land. Tithes were abolished in most European countries in the 19th century (in certain instances being replaced by another church tax). Tithes persisted in England (being converted into a monetary **rentcharge**, with the liability transferred from the occupier to the landowner) until the Tithe Act 1936 commuted all tithes to a single premium, 'tithe redemption annuity', payable to the Crown upon sale of the land affected by the charge. They were abolished finally by the Finance Act 1977, s. 56. In English law a tithe was an **incorporeal hereditament** in gross (analogous to a profit à prendre); in the civil law it was a **servitude**.
The Law of Real Property, by Robert Megarry and H.W.R. Wade, 5 edn., pp. 830–834.
14 Halsbury's Laws of England, 4 edn, paras. 1209–1223.
2. Any levy that amounts to one-tenth of the value of a property or service.

tithe redemption annuity
see **tithe**.

title

Derived from the Latin **titulus**, 'a label'; a cause of acquiring a right. The right to or the evidence of **ownership**. "The legal connection between a person and a right constituted by some act or event having legal significance" *The Oxford Companion to Law*, by D.M. Walker (1980). Title, if proven, is the means by which a person recovers or retains just **possession** of his property (Bl. Comm. vol. ii p. 195; Co. Litt. 345b). It constitutes all the elements that make up ownership: possession, a right to possession and a right to property. Title is demonstrated usually by an instrument that supports a valid claim to possession of property: *titulus est justa causa possidendi quod nostrum est* 'title is the just right to possess that which is ours'. Title is that right which is proper and will be defended by law; but cannot be created without due cause, "For truth it is that neither fraud nor might can make a title where there wanteth right" – Altham's Case (1610) 8 Co. Rep 153b.

Title may be used in two senses, either (i) to signify a right to enter and take possession of property; or (ii) to indicate the means or capacity in which the right comes about. It is used most commonly in the latter sense. Title to real estate may be acquired by descent, by purchase, by adverse possession or by gift. Also title may be considered to start as mere possession – actual occupation; progresses through a right to possession, even if physical possession is held by another; and arrive at the point where complete title arises, when the right and physical possession are combined (Bl. Comm. vol. ii p. 196). Title may be defective due to (i) uncertainty as to whether it satisfies the law; (ii) doubt as to the view the law might take when considering its validity; or (iii) doubt on a matter of fact; or a combination of any of those reasons. See also **absolute title, abstract of title, good leasehold title, good title, land registration, marketable title, possessory title, qualified title, root of title, Statutes of Limitation, title deeds, title insurance.**

42 Halsbury's Laws of England, 4 edn, paras. 96–122, 143–182.
Emmet on Title, 18 edn., 1983 with 1984 supplement.
William's Contract for the Sale of Land and Title to Land, 4 edn., with 1983 supplement.

title by occupation (or by occupancy)

Title to property that arises as a result of being the first to lay claim to the property — especially property that belonged to nobody. See also *jus possidendi*, **possessory title**, *res nullius*.

title by prescription

see **adverse possession**.

title certificate

see **certificate of title, land certificate.**

title closing (US)

see **closing**.

title cloud

see **cloud on title**

title, covenants for

see **beneficial owner, implied condition.**

title deeds

see **title documents**.

title documents

The documents that evidence the right to the ownership of land. Deeds, or one of a number of deeds or other documents, that are sufficient to substantiate a person's legal right to land. "Title deeds have been called the sinews of the land" (Co. Litt. 6a). The expression 'documents of title to lands' has been defined to include, "any **deed**, map, roll, register, instrument in writing being or containing evidence of the title or any part of the title to any land or any interest in or arising out of any land, or any authenticated copy thereof" (Forgery Act 1913, s. 18). Normally, on completion of a sale of property, the title deeds are retained by the purchaser (or any party who acquires a charge against the property); unless (a) the vendor retains any part of the land to which a document relates (Law of Property Act 1925, s. 45(9); or (b) a document relates to a subsisting trust. See also **abstract of title, equitable mortgage, forgery, land certificate, vesting instrument**.

title defect
see **defect of title**.

title guaranty
see **title insurance**.

title holder
One who holds a **title**; an **owner**. See also **tenure**.

title insurance
A contract of insurance provided to indemnify a purchaser, mortgagee or any other party with an interest in land against an unknown **defect of title** or against a loss due to any encumberance, lien, etc., that has not been disclosed. The policy usually covers such matters as defective or lost documentation, mistakes, forgeries, etc., but does not indemnify a purchaser who fails to make proper enquiries prior to purchase. Title

insurance is not provided normally against a totally defective title. It is intended to cover those risks that arise, for example, when a **marketable title** is acquired but the vendor cannot guarantee certain matters and, therefore, the title falls short of a **good title**. Thus, unlike most other forms of insurance, title insurance protects the policy holder against an event or act that has already occurred, rather than one that may occur in the future. In the US, called sometimes 'fee insurance' when the policy is intended to indemnify the insured if his title turns out not to be a fee simple interest but is, in some way, limited or qualified. Called also a 'guaranty title policy'. See also **certificate of title, contingency insurance, Torrens title system**.
Real Estate Law, by W.D. Milligan and Arthur G. Bowman, pp. 293–304 (1984).
Real Estate Principles, by Bruce Harwood, 2 edn., pp. 119–125.
Real Estate Law, by Robert Kratovil and Raymond J. Werner, 8 edn., pp. 206–209.

title opinion (US)
see **certificate of title**.

title paramount
see **paramount title**.

title registration
see **land registration**.

title report (US)
A preliminary report on an owner's title to land obtained for the purpose of **title insurance**.
cf. **abstract of title**.

title searches
Enquiries made to ascertain the validity, or otherwise, of a vendor's title to

a property. Usually the searches are made by an examination of the Land Registry or other public land registration offices; or, if the land is unregistered, by submitting a set of written questions to the vendor's solicitor (or any other interested party, e.g. a mortgagee), in order to verify that there is a **good title** to the property. In the US, a title search of the registry of deeds is made usually by a title abstractor or title company that specialises in such work. See also **abstract of title, certificate of title, searches**.

title theory (US)
see **mortgage**.

titre (F)
1. **instrument**; **title**; **deed**; document. (*titre authentique* – valid title) (*titre de propriété* – title to property; title deeds of property; proof of ownership) (*titre negotiables* – **negotiable instrument**) (*titre putatif* – presumed title, i.e a title which the possessor of a property presumes he has by the nature of **possession** cf. *just titre*. See also *prescription*) (*à titre onerous* – for (valuable) consideration; subject to payment) (*juste titre* – title obtained legally but not from the true owner e.g. title obtained by *prescription acquisitive* (**adverse possession**) cf. *titre putatif*. *Droit Civil – Les Biens*, by Jean Carbonnier, 11 edn., pp. 278–279, 289–291). (*propriétaire en titre* – legal owner) See also *propriété*.
2. **bond**; certificate. (*titre de père de famille* – gilt-edged security).
3. **right**; claim.

titulus est justa causa (L)
see **title**.

'to have and to hold'
see *habendum, tedendum*.

toll
1. A price or a fixed charge paid for a service rendered or privilege granted.
2. A sum payable for a right to offer goods for sale at a **market** or **fair**. See also **franchise, stallage**.
3. A right of a lord to levy a tax against a villein tenant. See also **villeinage**.

tone of the list
A phrase used in **rating valuation** to indicate that, when making an assessment for the purpose of altering an entry in the **valuation list**, rateable values are to be assessed on a 'uniform basis', as at the date that the current valuation list came into force. Thus when considering the value of an individual property or hereditament, consideration should be given to the general level of values in the valuation list. In theory, "equality of rating being the main object, a valuation officer ... should ... ascertain an assessment for each heraditament on a uniform basis" – Poplar Assessment Committee *v* Roberts [1922] 2 AC 207. A principle which is not easy to adopt when (as frequently happens in rating valuations) a value is to be based on prices several years ago and when any comparable property may subsequently have changed in character. This principle lapsed for a time and valuations were made at the date of any **proposal** to alter the assessment, rather than the earlier date when the list was first prepared. However, the Local Government Act 1966, s. 17 reintroduced the principle.

and it was re-enacted in the General Rate Act 1967, s. 20, which provides that the rateable value should be ascertained at the date of the preparation of the valuation list, but account should be taken of "relevant factors" such as the actual "mode or category of occupation", (taken as a general rule not a specific rule, i.e. occupation as a shop but not as a butcher's shop); as well as the locality of the property, as it exists, at the date of a **proposal** to alter or fix a rateable value. The result is that an assessment "should not exceed" the value based on the 'tone of the list' i.e. the prevailing level of values for comparable properties as established from the valuation list when it was compiled, subject to adjustment for the relevant factors. In summary, the physical state of the property and its locality are considered to be the same as when a proposal is made, but the value is to be based on comparable information adjusted "to reflect, as far as possible, the values prevailing at the time when the list was to take effect". – Reg. v Paddington Valuation Officer *ex parte* Peachey Property Corporation Ltd [1966] 1 QB 405. See also *rebus sic stantibus*.
Principles and Practice of Rating Valuation, by Roger Emery and Hector M. Wilks, 4 edn., pp. 143–146.
Encyclopaedia of Rating Law and Practice, paras. 2-070, 2-073.

tonnage royalty (or rent)
A **royalty** calculated by reference to the tonnage of mineral extracted from a mine or quarry, or manufactured articles produced from such minerals, or by reference to any similar system (Mineral Workings Act 1971, s. 7(2)(c)).

cf. **dead rent**. See also **mining lease**.

top-line, bottom-line commitment (US)
A commitment to provide a loan secured on an investment or development property, subject to a condition that no funds will be advanced until a minimum occupancy rate or net income return is achieved (the bottom-line), and the balance will be retained until the property is fully-let or has reached an agreed higher level of return (the top-line). See also **ceiling loan, floor loan**.

top loan
see **ceiling loan**.

top out
see **topping out**.

top-slice income
A portion or slice of the **net income** from a property investment over and above a stipulated level. In particular, the amount of income, if any, available after a **priority yield** has been paid. For example, if a property produces a return of 9 per cent on a cost of £2m, i.e. £180000, and it was agreed that an investor would receive a priority yield of 7 per cent, i.e. £140000, then the top-slice income is £40000. See also **equity participation, hardcore method, overage, profit rent**.

topographical surveying
The art, or science, of producing maps, charts or other graphical representations of natural or man-made features such as rivers, lakes, towns, roads, together with contours to delineate relief. A topographical map is intended primarily to show the relative position of objects on the earth's surface, in a horizontal and

vertical plane. See also **plan, surveying**.

topping off (US)
see **topping out**.

topping out (or top out)
The completion of a new building up to the stage of enclosing the main structure: usually an event calling for a minor celebration. In the US, called 'topping off'.

topping-up clause
A clause in a loan agreement which provides that the borrower will provide additional **security**, if required, to maintain the margin between the amount borrowed and property held by the lender as security.

top-slice participation
A form of **equity participation** whereby the partners in an investment project or joint venture share in different levels of cash flow received from the investment or venture. For example, the passive investor may receive the first share of the cash flow until his return equals an agreed percentage – a **priority yield**; the next share may go to the active or managing partner up to an agreed percentage; and any additional cash flow is shared equally. A lease that provides for the landlord with a share of the cash flow received by his tenant is called a 'top-slice' or 'horizontal' lease. Called also 'horizontal-slice participation'.
cf. **side-by-side participation**. See also **slice, top-slice income**.

Torrens title system
A system for the registration of titles to land, originally introduced in Australia in 1858 by Sir Richard Torrens and extended to Canada and many states in the US as well as forming the basis for the present system of land registration in England. The system is based on the principle that title to a parcel of land cannot pass, and no encumberance can be enforced, unless it is noted on a land register; title is then guaranteed or effectively insured by the State. The Torrens system, or any similar system, provides for the registration of a land title, as distinguished from any system which merely provides for the recording of evidence of title or encumberances that restrict a title. Title deeds are replaced by a **certificate of title** or **land certificate** issued by the registering authority. See also **land registration**.
Torrens in the United States, by Blair C. Shick and Irving H. Plotkin (1978).

tort
Derived from the Latin *tortus*, 'twisted', 'crooked'. In general usage any wrong or misdemeanour. In law, a private or civil wrong, independent of any contractual obligation or trust, whereby one person, by act or omission, causes injury to another person, or to his property or reputation, without any legal authority. The remedy for the wrong is an action at common law for **unliquidated damages**. A tort requires three essential elements: (i) a breach of a **duty of care** owed by one person to another; (ii) injury or loss which arises as a reasonable consequent of that breach, i.e. the **damage** must not be too remote; and (iii) the act or omission must not be authorised by law. The injury must not arise as a result of a breach of contract or breach of trust; although there may be a relationship of contract or trust between the parties. A

tort may arise, for example from (i) wrong to the body of a person e.g. assault; (ii) wrong to a reputation e.g. libel; (iii) interference with another's goods, e.g. **conversion**; or (iv) interference with another's right over real estate e.g. **trespass, nuisance, waste.** See also **injunction, negligence, strict liability, vicarious liability.**

An Introduction to the Law of Torts, by J.G. Fleming, 5 edn.

Law for Land Management Students, by Richard Card, John Murdoch and Peter Schofield, pp. 285–455 (1981).

Foundations of the Law of Tort, by G.L. Williams and B.A. Hepple (1976).

General Principles of the Law of Torts, by P.S. James 4 edn.

Tort Law, by R.W.M. Dias & B.S. Markesimis (1984).

Winfield and Jolowicz on Tort 12 edn.

The Law of Torts, by Harry Street, 7 edn.

Salmond and Hewson on the Law of Torts, 18 edn.

The Law of Torts, by J.F. Clerk and W.H. Lindsell, 15 edn.

45 Halsbury's Laws of England, 4 edn, paras. 1201–1256.

tort (F)

wrong; injury; error. See also *quasidélit.*

tortfeasor

One who commits a **tort**; a wrongdoer.

tortious

In the nature of a **tort**.

total cost

see **acquisition cost.**

total equity

see **equity, net worth.**

touching and concerning land

see **easement, restrictive covenant.**

tour d'échelle (servitude de) (F)

An easement to place a ladder on land adjoining a building, in separate ownership, for ease of repair and maintenance of the building. Called also a *droit d'échelle.*

town and country planning

A term applied to any form of planning directed towards controlling the free and unimpeded use of land by an individual in the interests of the community, especially the establishment of a system of laws, rules and guidelines to govern the **development** and the intensification of land use. A means of allocating the scarce resource of land to its best use, when full account is taken of all social and economic factors that affect the whole, rather than any particular sector, of society. "The art and science of ordering the use of land and the character and siteing of buildings and communication routes so as to secure the maximum practicable degree of economy, convenience and beauty" *Principles and Practice of Town and Country Planning,* by Lewis Keeble, 3 edn. p. 1. "A science, or art, and a movement of policy concerned with shaping and guiding of the physical growth and arrangement of towns in harmony with their social and physical needs" *Outline of Town and City Planning,* by Thomas Adams (1936). Town and country planning is concerned with guiding and regulating the growth and change of cities, towns, villages and rural areas. It goes beyond the physical form and arrangement of buildings, streets, parks, utilities or other specific parts of the environment; it combines these aspects with considerations of economic planning, communications, demography, and future development or redevelopment proposals, in a given area or district, in order to try and achieve a degree of harmony with the natural and man-made environment. In particular, town and country planning covers such aspects as (i) the lay-out of sites and the inter-relationship of land uses; (ii) the balanced distribution of buildings, open spaces, roads, etc., in terms of size and scale; (iii) the arrangement of communications so as to ensure the most efficient circulation of traffic; (iv) the housing, health, educational and recreational needs of a community; (v) the provision of adequate land for the agricultural, horticultural, commercial and industrial needs of a society, as well as general **amenity** or overall environmental 'quality of living'.

Some form of planning is evidenced in most early settlements. Hippodamus of Miletus (c. 480 B.C.) is credited with being one of the first architects to have combined the design of buildings, with a consideration of the street system. Most of the world's major cities evidence areas of preconceived control and design in their development; for example, Haussman's Paris, Wren's London. L'Enfant's Washington, Peter the Great's Petersburgh and countless other new towns or cities. Other areas of urban growth evidence less formal development; but planning in one form or another has usually been exercised, at least, so as to restrict building density, height, etc. and to ensure proper communications and areas for recreation. Modern western planning has tended to move away from the grand design to the consid-

eration of each individual proposal for development within a set of government rules and ordinances, with the supervisory role being taken away from the architect and entrusted to a specialist called a 'town planner' or to an engineer. In the US, the terms 'town and city planning', or 'city and regional planning', are more commonly used for this form of planning. See also **advertisement, compensation for planning restrictions, conservation area, development plan, garden city, land use planning, listed building consent, planning authority, planning permission, public participation, Radburn, site licence, Town and Country Planning Acts, tree preservation order, waste land, zoning**.

Town Planning and the Surveyor, by Gerard Burke (1980).
Introduction to Town and Country Planning, by John Ratcliffe, 2 edn.
Town Planning Made Plain, by Lewis Keeble (1983).
Town and Country Planning in Britain, by J.B. Cullingworth, 9 edn.
Urban Planning Law, by Malcolm Grant (1981).
46 Halsbury's Laws of England, 4 edn.
Encyclopaedia of Planning Law and Practice, by Desmond Heap, (looseleaf).

Town and Country Planning Acts

Acts of Parliament passed to exert extensive control over the planning, use and development of land. The first major Act affecting England and Wales was passed in 1947 (various Acts to control the use and development of land were passed before that date, the first being the Housing, Town Planning, etc., Act 1909, but

these did not contain a comprehensive code of town and country planning and essentially were extensions of the **Housing Acts** and the **Public Health Acts** exercising only minor controls on new development). Since 1947 a series of Acts have been passed to tighten the controls on development and extend the powers of local planning authorities (and various other authorities) over the planning of the area under their administration. The principal Act currently in force in England and Wales is the Town and Country Planning Act 1971 (as amended by the Town and Country Planning (Amendment) Acts of 1972 and 1977; the Town and Country Planning Amenities Act 1974 and the Local Government, Planning and Land Act 1980). (In Scotland comparable law is contained in the Town and Country Planning (Scotland) Act 1972.) The Town and Country Planning Acts, which are administered predominately by the local district council, cover such matters as development plans, structure plans and local plans; development control, including the grant or refusal of planning applications; listed buildings; conservation areas; and tree preservation orders. See also **town and country planning**.
Practical Planning Law, by J.F. Garner, pp. 61–66 (1981).
Introduction to Town and Country Planning, by John Ratcliffe, 2 edn., pp. 81–86.
Planning Law and Procedure, by A.E. Telling, 6 edn., pp. 1–20.
An Outline of Planning Law, by Desmond Heap, 8 edn., pp. 1–29.

town development
The development or expansion of an existing urban area to provide additional housing accommodation, and accompanying employment facilities, in order to relieve overcrowding, or to accept overspill, from another urban area. In particular, "development ... which will have the effect, and is undertaken primarily for the purpose, of providing accommodation for residential purposes ... (to) relieve congestion and over-population elsewhere" (Town Development Act 1952, s. 1). Town development is similar to **new town** development, but on a smaller scale, and is associated with the balanced expansion of an existing urban area. It is undertaken by an existing local authority, rather than a body appointed for the purpose. Most of the town development undertaken subsequent to the 1952 Act has now been completed.

town (or village) green
see **green**.

town house
A house in the town as compared to a house in the country; in particular, a term for a modern **terrace house** or 'row house', situated near the centre of a town or city. A dwelling-house on two levels linked in a row to other similar houses by a **party wall** or party walls.

town map
A form of **development plan** (or, strictly, a land use plan normally prepared to a scale of 6 inches to 1 mile (1: 10000)) which shows the zoning and future development proposals of a local authority for the area under its administration. In particular, the form of plan prepared by a local planning authority for a town or city

to meet the need for a development plan as required under the provisions of the Town and Country Planning Act 1947. However, such plans contained little more than a record of existing land uses overlaid with a demarcation for a few future schemes, such as an area for a new civic centre or the line of a new highway. "Too often, in fact, the town map does not really attempt to solve any problems at all, but merely records probable land needs over the next 20 years" *Town Planning at the Crossroad*, by Lewis Keeble, p. 87 (1961) (which contains a detailed analysis and critique of such plans). Since the Town and Country Planning Act 1968 this form of plan is being superceded by the structure plan.
Town Planning Made Plain, by Lewis Keeble (1983).

town planning
see **land use planning, town and country planning**.

tract
1. An expanse or parcel of land. A tract of land normally means a large undefined expanse of land or a number of contiguous plots of land; but it may refer also to a precisely defined or definable area of land.
(US) 2. A parcel of land that has been referenced and recorded at the office of the County Recorder. See also **plat**.

tract index (US)
An index or record kept by a county official showing the location, boundaries and owners of land in the county.

trade
An occupation, a commercial way of life, or a means of making a profit; usually involving the buying and selling, or manufacture for sale, of goods. A **business** or employment carried on principally by a skilled worker; a means of earning a living that requires a training or skill but does not demand the same level of education and training as is required by a **profession**. Trade is a word of extensive meaning and may be broadly used to refer to (a) an occupation or business conducted by a group of people; (b) the barter, exchange, buying and selling of goods for profit; or (c) a skilled form of employment. "The practice of some occupation, business or profession habitually carried on, especially when practiced as a means of livelihood or gain; a calling; formerly used very widely, including professions; now usually applied to a mercantile occupation and to a skilled handicraft, as distinct from a profession and specifically restricted to a skilled handicraft, as distinguished from a professional or mercantile occupation on the one hand and from unskilled labour on the other" (*Oxford English Dictionary*). It is not essential that the aim is to make a profit, although this is a common objective; in that respect a trade may be distinguished from a business. The word trade suggests "some form of mercantile enterprise or occupation, while 'business' connotes some type of commercial activity generally associated with the production of a person's livelihood" – Coleman *v* Grafton Greyhound Racing Club (1954) 55 SR (NWS) 218. However, trade is concerned primarily with buying and selling; it may include manufacture, especially when skill is required and the ultimate intention is the resale of the manufac-

tured goods – Grainger and Son *v* Gough [1896] AC 345–6. In the case of a **business tenancy** taking in lodgers and making only a meagre profit is not a "trade, profession or employment" within the meaning of s. 23 (2) of the Landlord and Tenant Act 1954. (Note: In relation to the expression 'trade union' the reference is to any occupation by which a person endeavours to make a living; the word in that case being used "in its widest application" – National Association of Local Government Officers *v* Bolton Corporation [1943] AC 185). See also **custom, goodwill, retail.**

trade area
see **catchment area.**

trade custom
see **custom, implied term, usage.**

trade cycle
see **cycle.**

trade fixture
A **fixture** that is necessarily installed for, and related directly to, a tenant's business or trade. For example, petrol pumps installed in a garage; dispensing equipment in a public house; shelves and counters in a shop. A trade fixture is installed primarily for the convenience of use, rather than as an addition or appendage to a property; accordingly it is likely to remain in the tenant's ownership at the end of his lease, providing that it is removed within a reasonable period after the end of the lease. Instances of trade fixtures are seats for the stalls in a theatre; wall brackets for lights; electric transformers or engines fixed to the floor.

A lease may provide that a tenant cannot remove any fixture at the end of his lease, but, "if the landlord wishes to restrict his tenant's ordinary right to remove trade fixtures attached to demised premises ... the landlord must say so in plain language. If the language leaves the matter doubtful, the ordinary right of the tenant to remove trade fixtures will not be affected" – Leschallas *v* Woolf [1908] 1 Ch. 641 and, "when an existing lease expires or is surrendered and is followed by another to the same tenant remaining in possession, the tenant does not lose his right to remove tenant's fixtures. He is entitled to remove them at the end of his new tenancy" – New Zealand Government Property Corporation *v* HM and S Ltd [1982] 1 All ER 624. In general, a trade fixture may not be distrained on by a landlord. See also **agricultural tenant's fixture, distress.**

trade property
see **business property.**

trade usage
see **custom, usage.**

trading area
see **catchment area.**

trading estate
1. An **industrial estate**; in particular, one where the main occupants are involved in manufacture.
2. A form of industrial estate first established by the government in Britain in the 1920's to provide cheap land and buildings in order to encourage industrial expansion, especially in areas of high unemployment. See also **development area.**

trading on the equity (US)
1. Increasing the rate of return on the equity invested in a property by borrowing funds at a rate of interest that

is lower than the return provided by the existing or projected net income from the property. See also **convertible mortgage**, **leverage**.

2. see **sub-sale**.

traditio (L)

'**Delivery**; the act of handing over'. In Roman or the civil law, the delivery of **possession** (*animo et corpore*) of a corporeal property combined with a cause or reason that supports the act; *traditio* being a means to secure the conveyance of goods.

tradition (F)

tradition; **delivery** (of property).

tranche

A **slice**, instalment, or portion. An instalment on a loan facility which has been actually borrowed or 'drawn-down'. See also **top-slice participation**.

tranche (F)

instalment; portion.

(*emprunt par tranches* – instalment loan).

transfer

1. The act of conveying or making over possession or control from one person to another. The process by which real or personal property is delivered from one person (transferor) to another (transferee) with the intention of passing ownership to the latter; a change in the party who has possession or title to a property. In general use, transfer may refer to any means of disposing or parting with property or an interest in property, including a **sale**, **mortgage**, **gift**, **devise** or otherwise. It may be conditional or unconditional, voluntary or involuntary – Gatherole *v* Smith (1875) 17 Ch. D1. In particular,

transfer is used to refer to a voluntary **conveyance** of property or an interest in property. A voluntary transfer may arise by way of sale, exchange or settlement. An involuntary transfer may arise by expropriation, compulsory purchase, or a similar form of compulsion; or by operation of law as when a person is declared bankrupt; dies intestate and without heirs; dies insolvent, or is sued for non-payment of a debt. A transfer may take place *inter vivos*, between living persons; or on death (either by will or by the laws of intestacy).

cf. **subrogation**. See also **assignment**, **assumption**, **bill of sale**, **cession**, **deed**, **delivery**, **grant**.

2. A conveyance of registered land; such land being transferred by the execution of an instrument in the statutory form and by an entry of the change of ownership on the land register. See also **dealing**.

transfer (F)

transfer; assignment. See also *acquisition*.

transfer deed

A deed or instrument that is used to effect a **transfer** of a right to property from one party to another. A term more commonly used with reference to a transfer of securities or shares in a company. See also **conveyance**, **delivery**.

transfer fee (US)

A fee charged by a mortgagee to cover the expenses involved in substituting one mortgagor for another, as when the mortgaged property is sold. See also **subject to mortgage**.

transfer *inter vivos*

A transfer of property 'between living persons'.

cf. **devise**. See also **conveyance**.

transfer stamp (US)
see **stamp duty**.

transfer tax
A tax payable on the transfer of property, whether corporeal or incorporeal property, frequently in the form of a **stamp duty**. See also **capital transfer tax, conveyance tax, estate tax, registration duty**.

transferable development right (TDR) (US)
A legal right to transfer consent to develop from one area of land to another. A right to develop property in accordance with zoning ordinances may be considered as a marketable item. Thus, if an owner of a site is deprived of his development rights, e.g. because they affect a landmark building, that right may be transferable to enable an adjoining site to be developed to a higher density, provided the overall zoning proposals for the surrounding area are not unduly affected. See also **planning agreement, windfalls and wipeouts, zoning**.
Handling the Land Use Case, by Frank Schnidman, Stanley D. Abrams and John J. Delaney, pp. 529–538 (1984).

transferee
One to whom something is transferred. See also **transfer**.

transferor
One who makes a **transfer**.

transformation et reparation (F)
alterations and repairs.

translation (F)
transfer; conveyance.

transmission
The passing of a title to registered land to a new proprietor on the death or bankruptcy of the existing proprietor.

travaux de transformation (F)
alteration works.

treasure trove
Derived from the French *tresor* or the Greek *thesauros*, – a 'store laid up'; and the French *trouvé* 'found'. A treasure that has been buried or hidden in a secret place; thereby is lost to the true owner; and when found is incapable of having an ascertainable owner. In English law treasure trove means gold or silver – in the form of plate or bullion – and coins made with a substantial quantity of gold or silver (3 Co. Inst. 132; Att. Gen. of the Duchy of Lancaster *v* G.E. Overton (Farms) Ltd [1982] Ch. 277). Such treasure belongs to the Crown. "A man that hides his treasure in a secret place, evidently does not mean to relinquish it, but reserves a right to claiming it again, when he sees occasion; and, if he dies and the secret also, dies with him, the law gives it to the King, [or Queen] in part of his [or her] royal revenue". (Bl. Comm. vol. i. p. 295). Treasure trove does not belong to the Sovereign unless no one knows who hid it and it is the hiding, and not merely the abandonment of the property, that entitles the Crown to it – A.G. *v* British Museum Trustees [1903] 2 Ch. 598. If the treasure is found in a secret hiding place or is buried it is presumed to have been hidden, and the finder must rebut the presumption that it is treasure trove. Similar property found on the surface of land is not treasure trove and title then passes to the finder, until his claim is rebutted by the true owner. It is an offence at common law not to disclose treasure trove when it is

discovered.

In the US, treasure trove is gold, silver or paper money that was intentionally hidden and has been found by someone other than the owner, the owner being unknown. In general, it may be retained by the finder; although some states require the finder to advertise publicly his find before he can claim title.

In French law, treasure trove (*tresor*) is any moveable property of particular value (including bullion, plate, coins or other chattels) that has been hidden or buried, is found by chance, and has no owner who can be identified. If found on one's own land it may be retained by the finder and, in general, if found on another's land it is shared equally between the finder and the land owner (French Civil Code, art. 716).

cf. **res nullius**.

Droit Civil – Les Biens, by Jean Carbonnier, 11 edn., pp. 349–351.

Precis Dalloz. *Droit Civil, Les Biens* (Alex Weill) 2 edn, pp. 373–376.

8 Halsbury's Laws of England, 4 edn, para. 1513.

treat

To deal, negotiate or consider terms for a bargain. See also **invitation to treat, negotiation, notice to treat**.

tree

In law, vegetation that, without question, is part of the real estate; in particular, a woody perennial plant that is suitable for building, i.e. it can be converted into **timber**. Traditionally in England, oak, elm, ash, and in certain localities beech, birch and pine are the primary trees for building, but other large plants that are used for this purpose may be classified at law as trees. On the other hand, willow and larch normally are not so classified – Re Hawker's WT. [1938] Ch. 323. It has been said that a 'tree' should be at least 7–8 inches in diameter – Kent County Council *v* Batchelor [1976] JPL 754; however, this should be taken as a general rather than a hard and fast rule. In a lease 'trees', without further qualification means trees that are "good for their wood" – Whindham *v* Way (1812) 4 Taunt. 318.

The owner of land upon which a tree is situated is responsible for an **encroachment** or **trespass** on to, or any forms of nuisance to, adjoining land. A branch of a tree which overhangs another's land does not, of itself, constitute a trespass; but a landowner may cut such branches without prior notice to the owner of the tree, provided he does not need to venture onto the adjoining land – Lemmon *v* Webb [1895] AC 1. Similarly, a person may cut roots of trees on his own land, even if that kills a tree on a neighbour's land, provided his action is not done with malicious intent and the tree is not serving as a boundary protection – Smith *v* Giddy [1904] 2 KB 448; Michaelson *v* Nutting (1931) 275 Mass. 232, 175 N.E. 490. However, fruit from trees are the property of the owner of the tree even if they overhang or fall on to neighbouring land. Highway authorities have powers to require the cutting of trees that obstruct a public highway (Highways Act 1980, s. 154). See also **encroachment,** *fructus*, **strict liability, tree preservation order, timber, waste**.

Trees, Some Points in Law, (contributed) 220 EG 355 (1971).

Tree Roots and Buildings, by D.F. Cutler and L.B.K. Richardson (1981).

tree preservation order (TPO)

An order made by a local planning authority, (normally the local borough or district council) in accordance with the provisions of the Town and Country Planning Act 1971, s. 60 (as amended by the Local Government Planning and Land Act 1980, Sch. 15, s. 13) and the Town and Country Planning (Tree Preservation Order) (Amendment) Regulations 1981) and Trees in Conservation Areas (Exempted Cases) Regulations 1975, for the purpose of preserving a **tree**, a group of trees, or an area of woodland. The order specifies that a tree or certain trees, as defined on a map attached to the order, may not be felled, lopped, topped, uprooted or wilfully destroyed or wilfully damaged, without the authority's consent. There is no statutory definition of 'tree' for this purpose and an order may be made to cover trees that are smaller in size to those defined as such at common law; but bushes, shrubs, and trees in a woodland under six inches in girth and under ten feet in height, are not normally covered by a TPO, although a hedgerow may well be covered. The order does not prevent thinning and it may be made to cover a **coppice**, even though by definition a coppice must be thinned out and pruned – Bullock v Secretary of State for the Environment (1980) 254 EG 1097). Such an order is made "in the interests of amenity" and the authority is not required to consider the economic value of the tree or trees. The order does not prevent the cutting of a tree that is dying, dead or dangerous; when it is necessary to prevent or abate a nuisance; or when required under a statutory obligation. However, this does not sanction wilful damage to a tree that is included in a TPO and any tree that is cut down in defiance of an order must be replaced, unless the authority waives that requirement. Consent to fell a tree included in a TPO is obtained in much the same way as planning permission and the consent may be granted conditionally, e.g. felled trees must be replaced by similar trees elsewhere on a site, or unconditionally. There is a right of appeal to the Secretary of State for the Environment against a refusal of consent to fell a tree, or against a condition imposed on such consent. Contravention of a TPO is an offence punishable by a fine (1971 Act, ss 59–62, 102, as amended by the Town and Country Planning Amenities Act 1974, s. 10). Compensation may be payable for a refusal of consent, or the grant of consent subject to a condition, to fell a tree covered by a TPO; although such compensation is limited normally to the timber value of the tree (1971 Act, s. 174). See also **conservation area, local land charge planning condition, purchase notice.**

Urban Planning Law, by Malcolm Grant, pp. 456–462 (1982).

Planning Procedure Tables, by R.N.D. Hamilton, 4 edn., pp. 112–117.

Planning Law and Procedure, by A.E. Telling, 6 edn., pp. 175–181.

An Outline of Planning Law, by Desmond Heap, 8 edn., pp. 197–202.

Urban Conservation & Historic Buildings – A Guide to Legislation, Royal Borough of Kensington and Chelsea (1984).

Encyclopaedia of Planning Law and Practice, by Desmond Heap, paras. 1–157 to 1–163.

46 Halsbury's Laws of England, 4 edn, paras. 382–391.

tréfoncier (F)
owner of soil or subsoil.
See also *superficie*.

tréfonds (F)
see *superficie*.

trésor (F)
treasure; **treasure trove**.
(*le trésor public* – the (French) Treasury)

trespass
An unlawful act or transgression that interferes with a person's property or rights, including an act that causes injury to a person or to his or her reputation, but does not constitute a crime. Historically, an act committed with force and violence (*vi et armis*), but now any misdemeanor that has the direct intention of depriving a person of his or her rights. "Every invasion of private property, be it ever so minute, is a trespass" – Entick *v* Carrington (1795) 19 St. Tr. 1066. Trespass to property may be instigated by taking physical, i.e. *de facto*, **possession**; or by taking away a legal right to possession, including taking away goods without consent.

In a popular sense trespass denotes an unlawful entry on to the property of another, whether by man or beast. Trespass to land (or buildings) may be committed on, over or under the land; it includes destroying anything attached to land or placed on land or placing anything on, over or under land; as well as any act or omission that interferes with possession of land, e.g. flooding land. A person may commit an act of trespass, even though he has an unrestricted right to enter land (or buildings), if he abuses his right or acts recklessly when in possession of land – R *v* Jones and R.

v Smith [1976] 3 All ER 54. A person may become a trespasser if he strays beyond the limits to which his right to possession was constrained either in terms of space or time; especially if he refuses to leave when required to do so.

A trespass may occur in the space above land or in the ground underneath – the maxim being that **land** extends *ad coelum usque ad infernos*, 'from the heavens to the centre of the earth'. Thus an advertising sign erected so as to project into adjoining air space constitutes a trespass – Kelsen *v* Imperial Tobacco Co. [1957] 2 QB 334; as does the swinging of the jib of a crane (or anything similar) over neighbouring land (Woollerton and Wilson Ltd *v* Richard Costain Ltd [1970] 1 All ER 483; Holmwood Realty Corp. *v* Safe Deposit and Trust Co. (1931) 154 Atl. 58.). However, this maxim is limited to a height that is reasonable for the proper enjoyment of land, so that the passage of aircraft "several hundred feet" above land, which does not cause any inconvenience, is not a trespass – Bernstein *v* Skyviews and General Ltd [1977] 3 WLR 136). An **encroachment** by the branch of a tree over, or roots of a tree under, land is not a trespass; although a landowner may top branches from trees that overhang his land and may bring an action for **nuisance** if the encroachment causes damage – Lemmon *v* Webb [1895] AC 1; Davey *v* Harrow Corporation [1958] 1 QB 60; Morgan *v* Knight [1964] 1 WLR 475). A person who enters land lawfully and then exceeds his authority, or refuses to leave when properly requested to do so, may be liable for the consequences of his trespass *ab initio*, 'from the beginning' – Six Carpenters' Case (1610) 8 Co. Rep. 146a. Trespass is actionable *per se*, without the necessity of proving damage or financial loss. Thus a person who brings an action for trespass may recover the property *in specie*, i.e. the object itself, or possession of land and not just damages; or he may obtain an *injunction* to prevent a further trespass on land without needing to prove a continuing financial loss.

An owner or occupier of land owes no true duty of care to a trespasser, especially if the trespasser's presence on the land is unknown; but he must not act callously or maliciously; for example, by setting man traps – R. Addie and Sons (Collieries) Ltd *v* Dumbreck [1929] AC 365. He should take reasonable steps to alert anyone who may stray on to his land of any potential danger or any inducement to injury. He may keep a domestic animal to repulse trespassers, even a fierce dog – Cummings *v* Grainger [1977] QB 367; but the animal must be properly controlled and due notice given to any unsuspecting party. On the other hand, an **occupier** may have a **strict liability** for any dangerous item kept on his land and he must "take such care as is reasonable in all the circumstances" to see that a trespasser does not suffer injury on premises by reason of a danger that is known to the occupier of those premises; in particular, when the occupier knows or has reasonable grounds to believe that there may be a trespasser on his land, unless the trespasser knowingly and willingly accepted the risk when he entered the land (Occupier's Liability Act 1984, s. 1). In addition, he should take special care of the possibility that children may enter on his property; "... the presence in a frequented place of some object of attraction, tempting him [a child] to meddle where he ought to abstain, may well constitute a trap, and in the case of a child too young to be capable of contributory negligence it may impose full liability on the owner or occupier, if he ought as a reasonable man to have anticipated the presence of a child and the attractiveness of the peril of the object" – Latham *v* Johnson (Richard) and Nephew Ltd [1913] 1 KB 416; Herrington *v* British Rail Board [1972] AC 877.

cf. **adverse possession, conversion.** See also **air right, damage feasant, ejectment, negligence, recovery, right of access, self-help, squatter, tenancy at sufferance, tort.**

The Law of Torts, by J.G. Fleming, 6 edn., pp. 15–23, 36–44.

The Law of Torts, by Harry Street, 7 edn, pp. 13–17, 58–65.

Salmond and Heuston on the Law of Torts, 18 edn, pp. 36–46.

Winfield and Jolowicz on Tort, 12 edn, pp. 359–376.

46 Halsbury's Laws of England, 4 edn, paras. 1384–1409.

triennal (F)
  every three years.
  (*bail triennal* – three yearly lease)
  (*période triennale* – each of the three periods of a *bail commercial*, a 3-6-9 year commercial lease).

trimestre (F)
  quarter.
  (*loyer par trimestre* – quarterly rent).
  See also *terme*.

trimestriel (paiement) (F)
  quarterly (payment).

triple A rating

A financial standing of the first order; derived from a system of corporate financial classification in the US made by credit rating agencies such as Dun and Bradstreet, Moody's or Standard and Poors. See also **blue chip company, covenant.**

triple net lease (US)

A lease that requires the tenant to pay all expenses of property ownership so that the landlord receives his rent clear of all outgoings or, at least, the three major expenses namely, repairs, taxes and insurance. A term used to refer to a lease that is more tightly drawn than a 'net lease or 'net-net lease', so as to place a greater contractual responsibility on the tenant for real estate outgoings. In certain triple net leases the tenant may even be responsible for the landlord's mortgage interest and amortisation costs. The tenant accepts responsibility for a property as if he were the owner; except, of course, that the landlord retains a **reversionary interest.** A ground lease, or a lease to a major shopping centre tenant (a pad tenant), usually takes the form of a triple net lease and such leases are granted normally for a long term (over 50 years). Called also a 'net-net-net lease', or sometimes an 'absolutely net lease'. See also **full repairing and insuring lease.**

triplex (US)

A building divided into three separate dwelling units or apartments.
cf. **duplex.**

trottoir (F)

footpath; footway; especially alongside a highway.

trover

1. An ancient common law action to recover damages when goods have been found (*trouvé*) and wrongfully used by another. The action sought to prove that the plaintiff had lost the goods and that the defendant had found them and wrongfully converted them to his own use. An action for trover was replaced in 1852 by an action of **conversion** (Common Law Procedure Act 1852, s. 49); although an action for conversion is still referred to sometimes as an action of trover.
2. A coming into **possession.**

true effective rate

see **effective annual interest rate.**

true interest rate

see **annual percentage rate, effective annual interest rate.**

true net yield (US)

see **net yield after tax.**

true owner

A person who is the **owner** of property notwithstanding a right, charge or claim of another. In particular, in bankruptcy, a person who has acquired the beneficial interest in personal chattels; to be distinguished from a vendor, mortgagor or grantor who has been allowed to retain possession and, therefore, to act as the apparent or reputed owner. A true owner "may, as owner, convey goods over which there exists rights of other persons, which qualify his own right and render him something less than absolute owner" – Re Tamplin and Son, *Ex. p.* Barnett (1890) 59 LJQB 195. See also **beneficial owner, trust.**

true rate of return

see **internal rate of return.**

true rent
see **virtual rate**.

true rental rate
see **effective rate**.

true yield
see **equated yield**.

trust

1. A fiduciary relationship that is created, or comes into existence, when a person (**trustee**) is compelled or required to hold or deal with property, over which he has control, on behalf of another (**beneficiary**) in such a way that the benefits to be derived from the property accrue not to the trustee, but to the beneficiary. To the rest of the world, other than the parties to the relationship, the trustee appears as the true or absolute owner of the property and has the apparent power of dealing with it; while the beneficiary, or *cestui que trust*, remains cloaked behind the arrangement. A trust is essentially a creature of English law; it imposes an equitable responsibility on the trustee to hold **title** to the property, but leaves the beneficiary with the right to keep the use, or retain the profit, to be derived therefrom. A trust is a product of **equity**; it is a relationship based on confidence; and it enables both parties to hold different, but simultaneous, interests in the same property. It owes its origin to the **use**, an arrangement that was unique to English law, by which land could be held *ad opus* or *al oes*, 'for the use' of another. A 'use' was created when a person did not wish to appear the legal owner, for example on religious grounds or even to avoid tax, but instead passed his property to another on the understanding it would be held beneficially for the true owner. "A trust is altogether the same as a use was before the Statute of Uses and they have ... the same nurse, a court of conscience" – A.–G. *v* Sands (1669) Hard. 488. Thus, even when English common law considered that the creator of the trust (the 'settlor') had made an outright transfer of his land to another, Equity – the Court of Conscience – recognised his intention and, therefore, his right to continue to benefit from the land. "A trust ... is a relationship which arises wherever a person called the trustee is compelled in Equity to hold property, whether real or personal, and whether by legal or equitable title, for the benefit of some persons (of whom he may be one and who are called *cestuis que trust*) or for some object permitted by law, in such a way that the real benefit of the property accrues, not to the trustees, but to the beneficiaries or other objects of the trust" (*The Law of Trusts*, by Keaton, 9 edn., p. 5).

A trust separates management and enjoyment of property, but leaves both the trustee and beneficiary with a form of ownership; the trustee has 'legal' ownership or title, and the beneficiary has 'beneficial' ownership or enjoyment – "the fundamental feature of a trust is that it separates the functions of administration and enjoyment which were so inseparably combined in the Roman law concept of *dominium*. Although the trustee is invested with the legal title (which, by definition, carries the administrative powers of management and disposition), his ownership is nominal and purely formal. The legal title is a 'paper title'; the trustee, a mere 'paper owner'. The substance of beneficial enjoyment is reserved at all times for the beneficiary ... The legal title is a matter of *form*; the rights of the beneficiaries represent the *substance*". *Real Property and Real People*, by Gray and Symes, p. 22 (1981). The trustee is said to have a right *in rem* – a real right against the property; and the beneficiary a right *in personam* – a personal right against the trustee or any other person who controls the trust property; unless that beneficial right is transferred to the proceeds of sale. (The civil law has created the right of *usufruct* by which the enjoyment of the profits from land are separated from the legal title, but that right merely creates separate rights to land, without the necessity for there to be any relationship between the 'usufructuary' and the 'bare owner').

The principle features of a trust are (a) a clear intention that the person who holds the trust property is to hold it for the use of another; (b) the subject matter of the trust is ascertainable and capable of forming the subject of a trust; (c) the trust property is transferred, expressly or by operation of law, so that it can be held by the trustee; (d) the trustees are able to administer the trust in accordance with the terms by which it was created; (e) the trust is workable within the law, so that it can be 'policed' by the courts; (f) there is certainty as to who is intended to benefit from the trust and clear arrangements for the profit and use to remain with the beneficiaries.

A trust may be created expressly or may arise by implication of law. It may be created expressly either (a) by the settlor transferring the property to another and declaring that the intention is that it will be held on trust; or (b) by the settlor declaring that he himself will hold property on trust for a particular purpose. An express or 'declared' trust must be a present and irrevocable disposition of property; even though the benefits do not accrue until a future time. It may be created between living persons, *inter vivos*, or by a testamentary disposition, i.e. a will. An express trust may be created by words which do not demonstrate clearly that the aim was to create a trust, provided it is apparent that a trust was intended; the maxim being "equity looks to the intent rather than the form". An **implied trust** arises when the court deems from the surrounding circumstances that there should be a trust. For example, when one person acquires title to property with another's money – Dyer *v* Dyer (1788) 2 Cox 92. A trust may be implied also by statute, sometimes called a **statutory trust**; in particular, when a **statutory trust for sale** arises.

A trust may be 'private' when the beneficiaries are individuals; or 'public' when the object is general welfare, i.e. a charitable trust. It may be partially constituted when the trust property remains to be vested in the trustees; or it may be completely constituted. It may be 'executed' when it is completely and finally declared, and no further instrument is required; or it may be 'executory' when some instrument remains to be completed to define the interest to be held in trust. It may be a 'naked', 'simple', 'passive' or **bare trust** when the trustee is required to do no more than hold the trust property, leaving the beneficiary with effective control and power over the property; or a 'spendthrift' or **protective trust** when the trustee has extensive control over the property in order to safeguard the beneficiaries' interest. In practice the trustee rarely has any such extremes of control, but has a range of powers laid down by a deed of trust or by statute.

A trust may be distinguished from a **power** by the existence of an obligation on the part of a trustee when dealing with the trust property, whereas the holder of a power has a discretion in such dealings. Thus the court may compel the performance of a trust, but will never compel the exercise of a power. A trust and **agency** both create a fiduciary relationship, but an agent has no title to the principal's property; an agent is governed by the terms of the agreement by which he or she is appointed; and the agent seeks to represent, and establish contractual relationships for, the principal. **Bailment** produces a delivery of goods to be held on trust, but bailment applies only to personal property; the bailor retains title to the property in question; and a bailee (unless he is a factor) normally cannot pass a good title to a third party without first acquiring title himself. Unlike a **contract** the beneficiary of a trust need not be a party to the transaction that creates the trust; and, as a rule, a third party to a contract cannot enforce rights or obtain benefits from that contract. An **escrow** is a form of contract and the person entitled to the property that is held in escrow usually does not have use or physical possession of the property. See also **constructive trust**, **discretionary trust**, **Massachusetts trust**, **resulting trust**, **special trust**.

The Law of Trusts, by J.G. Riddell, 2 edn.

Modern Equity, by Hanbury and Maudsley, 11 edn, p. 154 *et seq.*

Snell's Principles of Equity, 28 edn, pp. 90–196.

The Modern Law of Trusts, by D.B. Parker and A.R. Mellows, 5 edn.

48 Halsbury's Laws of England, 4 edn, pp. 272–542.

Cases and Commentary on the Law of Trusts, by David J. Nathan and R. Marshall, 8 edn.

2. A form of business organisation established when a number of persons entrust money to a manager for the purpose of investment. The investors or beneficiaries retain the right to the capital and all profit or income to be derived therefrom; but the management and administration of the organisation is left entirely to the managers. As with any other form of trust the managers have a **fiduciary** responsibility to the beneficiaries and their powers and duties are strictly controlled by a deed of appointment. The managers may receive a commission or fee for performing their duties, but may not share in the profits or proceeds of sale of the investments.

cf. **partnership**. See also **agency**, **housing trust**, **investment trust**, **unit trust**.

3. A combination of firms operating together, in the same sphere of business, for the purpose of creating a monopoly or a dominant market position.

trust beneficiary
see **beneficiary**

trust corporation
The Public Trustee, or a corporation either appointed by the court or entitled by statute to act as the Public Trustee (Settled Land Act 1925, s. 117(1) (xxx); Administration of Est-

ates Act 1925, s. 55(1)(xxvi); Law of Property Act 1925, s. 205 (1)(xxviii); Trustee Act 1925, s. 68(1)(18)). A trust corporation is appointed when a situation arises that requires two or more trustees and none has been so appointed. A 'trust corporation' may be also the Treasury Solicitor, the Official Solicitor, any other official prescribed by the Lord Chancellor, as well as a trustee in bankruptcy, trustees of a deed of arrangement and various other local or public authorities who administer charitable, ecclesiastical or public trusts. (Law of Property (Amendment) Act 1925, s. 3).

Snell's Principles of Equity, 28 edn, p. 198.

trust deed
>see **deed of trust, debenture, trust instrument.**

trust estate
>see **trust property.**

trust for sale
>An arrangement by which property, especially real property, is held on **trust** for another with express or implied instructions from the creator of the trust (trustor or settlor) that the property must be sold. In particular, a form of **settlement** that is created, or arises, when property is disposed of to a number of persons in such a way that they are intended to enjoy only a right to the proceeds of sale; rather than the benefit of using the property itself, as with a **strict settlement**. A trust for sale is created when the aim is to treat the property as an investment and a source of income for the beneficiaries of the settlement and not to keep the property in the family. Under a trust for sale the property is to be held by trustees who are under a binding *duty to sell* the property and hold the proceeds of sale upon trust for the beneficiaries, i.e. the settlement is said to be subject to the doctrine of **conversion**; it is not sufficient for the trustees to have a mere power to sell the property. The sale may be, and usually is, postponed but it must be intended that the property will be sold, so that the purchaser takes it free of the settlement and the beneficiaries are left with an interest in the proceeds of sale, not the property *per se*. A trust for sale, in relation to land, means, "an immediate binding trust for sale, whether or not exercisable at the request or with the consent of any person, and with or without a power at discretion to postpone the sale; 'trustees for sale' means the person (including a personal representative) holding land on trust for sale; and 'power to postpone' means power to postpone in exercise of a discretion" (Law of Property Act 1925, s. 205 (1)(xxix) – Administration of Estates Act 1925, s. 55(1) (xxvii); Land Registration Act 1925, s. 3 (xxviii).

>A trust for sale may be created expressly or may arise by implication. An express trust for sale is created when a settlor specifically vests land in persons as trustees to hold 'on trust for sale' with instructions that they are to provide an income for the beneficiaries of the settlor's estate (usually for members of his or her family). It is created usually by two instruments, a 'written assent' which vests the **legal estate** in the trustees and a **trust instrument** which expresses the settlor's intentions for the distribution of the proceeds of sale; however, (unlike a strict settlement) it may be created by one instrument alone, e.g. by a

will. An implied trust for sale arises normally under some statutory provision; it is then called a **statutory trust for sale**. A statutory trust for sale arises automatically when a person dies intestate (Administration of Estates Act 1925, s. 33(1)). It may arise also when land is held under a **joint tenancy** or sometimes as a **tenancy in common** (Law of Property Act 1925, s. 36(1); 34(2)); or when trustees foreclose on mortgaged property (Law of Property Act 1925, s. 31). A trust for sale continues in existence until the trust property has been sold and the proceeds of sale distributed to the beneficiaries (Law of Property Act 1925, s. 25).

The majority of modern settlements of land are created as a trust for sale, rather than as a strict settlement because (a) the management and disposition of the property can be controlled by the same trustees, while the interests of the beneficiaries change from one successor to another; (b) the legal and taxation treatment of trusts for sale is simpler; (c) it is easier for a purchaser to acquire the legal estate free of the trust or the rights of the beneficiaries; and (d) the legal estate need not be sold upon the death of any one of the beneficiaries. A trust for sale may be established so that the beneficiaries can, usually at the trustees' discretion, take occupation of the property in lieu of receiving rents and profits – such a trust for sale is called an 'occupation trust'. When there is no intention that occupation should be taken, the trust is referred to as a 'distribution trust'. See also **overreached interest, trustee for sale**. *Introduction to Land Law*, by J.G. Riddell, 3 edn, pp. 126–140. *Real Property and Real People*, by K.J. Gray and P.D. Symes, pp. 212–231.

Megarry's Manual of the Law of Real Property, 6 edn, pp. 277–283, 306 & 314–315.

Land Law: Cases and Materials, by R.H. Maudsley and E.H. Burn, 4 edn, pp. 185–217.

The Law of Real Property, by Robert Megarry and H.W.R. Wade, 5 edn, p. 385 *et seq.*

Cheshire's Modern Law of Real Property, 13 edn, pp. 78–90, 193 *et seq.*

trust, housing
see **housing trust**.

trust indenture (US)
see **indenture, trust instrument**.

trust instrument
1. The document or instrument that declares the existence of the trust by which a **strict settlement** is created; appoints or constitutes the trustees; sets out the powers, if any, to appoint new trustees; and sets out any powers or duties that are an extension of those provided by statute (Settled Land Act 1925, s. 4(3)). The purpose of a trust instrument is to set out the terms on which the settlement is made and the rights of the beneficiaries, but to leave details of the land that forms the subject of the settlement (the settled land) to be described in a separate **vesting document**. Thus, a purchaser of the settled land can obtain title by reference to the vesting document without requiring access to the terms of the settlement – referred to as the 'curtain principle' of a strict settlement. "'Trust instrument' means the instrument whereby the trusts of the settled land are declared, and includes any two or more such

instruments and a settlement or instrument which is deemed to be a trust instrument" (Settled Land Act 1925, s. 117(1) (xxxi)). When a strict settlement is made by will, the will is deemed to be the trust instrument, because it sets out the intended rights of the beneficiaries. The testator's/settlor's personal representative is then required to execute a vesting document (called a 'vesting assent') in order to transfer title to the settled land to the tenant for life or statutory owner. A trust instrument must bear *ad valorem* stamp duty for the value of the settlement being created.

A trust instrument may be used to create an express **trust for sale**, although there is no statutory definition of a trust instrument as used for the purpose of creating a trust for sale; the 'curtain principle' not being an inherent part of a trust for sale. cf. **deed of trust**.

(US) 2. Any **instrument** by which a trust is created. Called also a 'trust indenture'.

trust power
see **power of appointment**.

trust property
Property held under a **trust**; property that has been vested, i.e. the title thereto has been transferred to a trustee to hold for and on behalf of a beneficiary. See also **trust for sale**.

trustee
A person who has a right "which he is bound to exercise on behalf of another or for the accomplishment of some particular purpose" *Equity*, by F.W. Maitland, p.44 (1936). In particular, a person who holds the ownership or a right to property on behalf of and for the benefit of another (the beneficiary), holds that property in **trust** i.e. has only a nominal title; and is bound to permit the beneficiary to have the use or profit from the property. One who deals with a property as a principal or owner, but is under an equitable obligation to account to another: a *cestui que trust* or **beneficiary**. A trustee owns the property commited to his or her trust (usually the **legal estate**) and deals with it, "as principal, as owner, and as master, subject only to an equitable obligation to account to some person to whom he [or she] stands in the relation of trustee, and who are his [or her] *cestuis que trust*" – Smith *v* Anderson (1880) 15 Ch. D. 275. In general, any person may be a trustee provided he or she has the legal capacity to hold property. Also a corporation can act as a trustee. A trustee may be appointed (a) by a settlement or will (as a rule, if there is no declared trustee, the person in whom the trust property is vested is considered to be the trustee); (b) by an express provision in a **trust instrument**; (c) under statutory provisions (e.g. Trustee Act 1925, s. 36), especially when an existing trustee is unable or unwilling to act; (d) by the court. A trustee has a duty to take care of the property entrusted to him; to carry out the terms of the trust; and is controlled by statute law (especially the Trustee Act 1925) as to the manner in which he conducts his responsibilities, powers and duties. Trustees are restricted frequently as to the type of property that they may acquire or invest in. For example, in the UK a trustee must take professional advice before investing in certain types of securities or in real

property (Trustee Investment Act 1961, ss. 1–11; and in the US a trustee may grant mortgage loans but is prohibited usually from making direct investment in real estate because it is considered too speculative. For the purpose of administering settled land the 'trustees of a settlement' are defined in the Settled Land Act 1925, s. 30 as basically, the person with the power to sell the settled land or trustees as appointed by the deed of settlement. See also **strict settlement, tenant for life, trust corporation, trustees of a settlement**.
The Law of Real Property, by Robert Megarry and H.W.R. Wade, 5 edn., pp. 354–357.

trustee for sale
A person appointed to administer land held on **trust for sale**, including a personal representative when a person dies intestate. A trustee or trustees for sale have similar powers to a **tenant for life** under a strict settlement. The trustee for sale also has the power to postpone the sale of the trust property, unless there is a contrary intention (Law of Property Act 1925, s. 25).

trustor (US)
1. A person who creates a **deed of trust** in which he is nominated also as a beneficiary.
2. One who creates a **trust**. Called also a 'settlor', or 'donor' or 'grantor' of the trust property. See also **testator**.

truth-in-lending laws (US)
Laws that require a lendor to disclose full details of the true cost and conditions of a loan; in particular, Title I of the Federal Consumer Credit Protection Act 1969 (15 USCA para. 1601 *et*

seq.) and Regulation Z issued pursuant to that Act. The law does not control the terms upon which loans may be granted, but merely requires full disclosure to ensure that individual consumers (but not business or commercial entities) are aware of the cost of borrowing money and are able freely to compare one loan offer with another. The lender is required to disclose the **annual percentage rate**; details of the requirements for repayment of the principal; any conditions for refinancing or early repayment of the loan; any balloon payment; whether other property acquired by the borrower will be secured by the loan; and any conditions for payment by the borrower of insurance, taxes, etc. See also **usury**.

turbary, common of
A right to dig turves (peat, but not green turf) from the land of another for use as fuel. Turbary may be granted or acquired by prescription; it may be a right **in gross** (as a **profit à prendre**), or it may be **appurtenant**. If appurtenant (for the benefit and annexed to a property) it may be only a right to take turves for fuel in a house. See also **right of common**.
6 Halsbury's Laws of England, 4 edn, paras. 576–578.

turn-key contract
A building contract by which a developer or builder undertakes to complete a building up to the stage where the key is in the door. The contractor accepts full responsibility for and the risks of, completing the project; usually, the contract price is payable in total on completion. However, unlike a **package-deal contract**, the contractor owns the building and contracts to dispose of the entire project on com-

pletion. In the US called also a 'design and management contract'.

turnkey lease

A lease under which the landlord agrees to provide premises to the tenant's requirements or carry out alterations to meet the tenant's specification; a lease of property which enables the tenant to take possession and start trade or business from the start of the lease.
cf. **shell lease**.

turnover

1. The rate at which properties are sold.
2. The rate at which tenants change in leased premises.

turnover lease

A lease that provides for the payment of a **turnover rent**. Called also a 'percentage lease'.

turnover rent

Rent that is based on an agreed percentage of the sales turnover achieved by the tenant, especially a retail tenant. Normally a minimum or **base rent** is payable throughout the term of the lease and additional rent or 'overage' is payable when the agreed percentage of the turnover exceeds the base figure. However, the rent may be based entirely on a percentage of the tenant's turnover. The rent may be based also on a percentage of the tenant's net profit, but that is less common because of the difficulty of defining 'net profit'. The percentage rates for retail premises vary for different types of trade and may range from 1 to 2 per cent for a trade with a high sales turnover, e.g. a food supermarket, to over 10 percent for a trade with a low sales turnover, such

as a jeweller. Called also a 'percentage rent'.

turpis causa (L)

'An immoral cause'. See **illegal contract**.

twelve months

A period of twelve consecutive months or one **year**. However, "'a twelve-month' includes all the year according to the calendar; but 'twelve months' shall be reckoned according to twenty-eight days to each month" – Catesby's Case Co. Rep. 62a (Bl. Comm. vol. ii p. 141). (Hence a term that is likely to lead to misunderstanding, so that it is preferable to refer to a 'year', 'twelve calendar months', or to define the start and finish dates of the intended period of time). See also **month**.

twilight area (or zone)

An area of urban decay. An area where buildings are in an advanced state of deterioration, especially a predominately residential area that is in a state of transition so that many of the buildings have been adapted to a different and generally inferior use to that for which they were originally constructed. Such areas commonly are adjacent to a town or city centre and contain houses that, although not necessarily **unfit for human habitation**, have substandard amenities and, if no action is taken, are likely to degenerate into slums. See also **slum**, **urban renewal, urban development area**.

type (F)

type; standard form.
(*bail type* – standard lease)
(*contrat type* – standard form contract)

U

uberrimae fidei (L)
'Of the **utmost good faith**'.

ultra vires (L)
'Outside the scope; beyond the **power**'. An act of a public authority, company, or a person acting in a fiduciary authority, may be *ultra vires* if it is outside, or goes beyond, the powers entrusted to that party; although the act may not necessarily be illegal or contrary to public policy. For example, a corporation that is created by statute acts *ultra vires* if its powers are not "expressly conferred or derived by reasonable implication from its [the Statute's] provisions" – Baroness Wenlock *v* River Dee Co. (1885) 10 App. Cas. 354. A company incorporated under the Companies Acts acts *ultra vires* if it operates outside the powers conferred upon it by its memorandum of association (Ashbury Railway Carriage Company & Iron Company *v* Riche [1875] LR 7HL 653). A decision of a planning authority is *ultra vires* if it is outside the authority's statutory powers; or if it is a breach of natural justice, e.g. if it is clearly biased – R. *v* Hendon UDC *ex parte* Chorley [1933] 2 KB 696; Seddon Properties *v* Secretary of State for the Environment (1978) 248 EG 949. A **compulsory purchase order** may be *ultra vires* if it is not properly authorised; not carried out in accordance with the appropriate enabling Act; or if the land is acquired for a purpose that is not specified for in the enabling Act – Webb *v* Minister of Housing and Local Government [1964] 1 WLR 1295).

At common law, a contract entered into by a company acting outside its powers is null and void and it cannot be ratified by the company. However, if a director of a company decides to enter into a transaction and the person with whom he deals acts in good faith the transaction "shall be deemed to be one which it is within the capacity of the company to enter into" (European Communities Act 1972, s. 9 (1)). Therefore, the third party to the transaction can enforce it against the company even if it is not authorised by the memorandum of association. It is not necessary for the third party to inquire as to the company's capacity to act, he is entitled to rely on the representations of the director. If the contract is not *ultra vires* as far as the company is concerned, but the director has exceeded his powers, then the company has the ability to validate the contract by **ratification**. See also **restitution**.

Anson's Law of Contract, 26 edn, pp. 203–205.

Cheshire and Fifoot's Law of Contract, 10 edn, pp. 398–401.

Chitty on Contract, 25 edn, para. 625 *et seq.*

Company Law, by Robert R. Pennington, 4 edn., p. 93 *et seq.*

Encyclopaedia of Local Government Law, by Charles Cross (ed.), para. 1–08 (1980 looseleaf).

7 Halsbury's Laws of England, 4 edn., paras. 705–712.

umbrella insurance policy
An insurance policy that combines the indemnity of a **comprehensive**

insurance policy and a **public liability insurance policy**, i.e. a policy that covers all or most insurable risks associated with the ownership of a property.

umbrella lease (US)

A lease, granted to a key or **anchor tenant** in a shopping centre, in which the rent is based on the normal market rental value, plus a contribution to the landlord's debt service. In return the tenant obtains a right to a share of the net cash flow receivable from the centre. See also **equity participation, triple net lease**.

umpire

A person who acts to settle a dispute that cannot be resolved by two or more arbitrators. One who has authority to arbitrate and make a final decision. See also **arbitrator**.

unaccrued sum

A sum of money that is not yet due, but against which a payment has been made already, e.g. rent paid before the due date (but not rent paid properly in advance). See also **rent in advance (or in arrears)**.

unalienable

Incapable of being sold or alienated. See also **inalienable**.

unavoidable

That which cannot be prevented even by reasonable care and forethought; although it may result from a human act. An act that results from *force majeure* may be considered unavoidable. An unavoidable delay in proving title to land under a contract for sale does not permit the vendor to claim interest on the purchase monies. See also **act of God**, *cas fortuit*, 'time is of the essence'.

unconditional offer

An offer that is not subject to any condition, restriction, qualification or limitation.
cf. **counter offer**. See also **sealed offer**.

unconscionable bargain (or contract)

A bargain that is outside the limits of what is reasonable or acceptable. A bargain or contract that is so unfair or unreasonable that no one in his or her right mind would entertain it, or no honest person would enter into it. In particular, a contract made when the bargaining power of the parties is so patently unbalanced that one of the parties cannot be said to be acting of his or her own volition, or when one party is clearly advantaged by special or technical knowledge that is used to the detriment of an unsuspecting party. An unconscionable bargain is entered into usually when a person is in dire need; because, "necessitous men are not truely free men but, to answer a present exigency, will submit to any terms that the crafty will impose on them" – Vernon *v* Bethel (1761) 2 Ed. 113. An unconscionable bargain may result also from **undue influence** or **duress**.

The charging of **usury** (in the sense of an exhorbitant rate of interest) may be considered as an unconscionable bargain: taking an unfair advantage to extract an excessive charge for the use of money. Alternatively, a lender who is in an advantaged position, e.g. a trustee, may use that position to grant a loan on unreasonable or unconscionable terms. The court has an equitable power to examine any mortgage transaction; although this power is exercised only in exceptional cases. "Equity does not reform mortgage transactions because they are unreasonable. It is concerned to see two things: (i) that the essential requirements of a mortgage transaction are observed; and (ii) that oppressive and unconscionable terms are not enforced. Subject to this ... it does not interfere" – Knightsbridge Estates Trust Ltd *v* Byrne [1939] Ch. 441. The courts also have the power to reopen and examine any 'extortionate credit bargain' made with an individual (unless the loan is made by a building society or a local authority) (Consumer Credit Act 1974, s 137–40).

In the US, the Uniform Residential Landlord and Tenant Act, which has been adopted by a number of states, provides that the court has a discretion to refuse to enforce any unconscionable tenancy agreement. Also the Uniform Commercial Code, which has been adopted in whole or in part by most states, makes any unconscionable contract unenforceable. Called also a 'catching bargain'. See also **penalty, undervalue, Uniform Residential Landlord and Tenant Act**.
Anson's Law of Contract, 26 edn, pp. 248–249.
Chitty on Contract, 25 edn, para. 3128 *et seq.*
Unfair Contracts, by Sinai Deutch, (1977).
18 Halsbury's Laws of England, 4 edn, paras. 344–357.

under insurance
see **average, insured value**.

'under the hammer'
see **auction**.

under seal
see **seal**.

underground room
see **basement, unfit for human habitation**.

underimprovement
An **improvement**, or construction of a building on land, that does not represent the highest and best use of the land.
cf. **overimprovement**.

underlease
see **sublease**.

under-let
see **sub-let**.

underlying mortgage
1. A mortgage that has **priority** over another mortgage granted on the security of the same property. An underlying mortgage may be a **first mortgage** or any mortgage that takes priority over another mortgage. cf. **junior mortgage**.
2. (US) A mortgage that is covered by a **wraparound mortgage**, i.e. the 'in-place' mortgage.

under-tenant
see **sub-tenant**.

undertaker, statutory
see **statutory undertaker**.

undertaking
1. An agreement to perform an act or provide a service. A **promise** to do or to refrain from doing something. For example, an agent may undertake to use his best endeavours to find a purchaser '**ready, able and willing**' to buy a property. An undertaking may have the force of a binding contract; or it may represent no more than an expression of intent – binding only morally or by a code of conduct. See also **commission**.
2. A willingness to undertake a business enterprise or accept a risk.

undervalue
To value at less than the real worth.

To assess the value of a property at a figure well below its **market value** or its true worth. Generally to be undervalued, a property must be grossly below the just or proper value: everyone is permitted a reasonable tolerance in making an assessment of value. The court may set aside a transaction for the transfer of an interest in property "where a purchase is made from a poor and ignorant man at a considerable under-value, the vendor having no independent advice", unless the purchaser can show that in the circumstances the transfer was fair and reasonable – Fry v Lane (1888) 40 Ch. D 312. An executed conveyance, or a sale by a mortgagee exercising his **power of sale**, may be set aside by the court if there appears to have been a substantial under-estimate of the worth of the property and there is evidence of **fraud, undue influence** or **mistake** – Garrard v Frankel (1862) 30 Beav. 445; Davey v Durrant (1857) 26 LJ Ch. 830. The Law of Property Act 1925, s. 174 provides that the purchase of a **reversionary interest** in property may not be set aside "merely on the grounds of undervalue": the entire transaction needs to be considered, not just the price. However, this section does not affect the jurisdiction of a court to set aside or modify an **unconscionable bargain**. See also **fraudulent conveyance, negligence, mortgage value**.

undeveloped land
see **raw land**.

undisclosed principal
A **principal** whose existence is not disclosed by his agent. If an authorised agent makes a contract in his own name, without disclosing that he is merely a representative, he may sue

or be sued upon the terms of that contract – Saxon v Blake (1861) 29 Beav. 438. Under the 'doctrine of undisclosed principal', the principal, when his existence is made known, may intervene also as a party to the contract, provided the result is not unduly detrimental to the third party to the contract. An undisclosed principal may not intervene if the agent uses words which indicate that the agent is acting alone – Humble v Hunter (1848) 12 QB 310; nor can he seek to benefit from a contract if the third party to the contract proves that he intended to deal with the agent personally, believing him to be the principal – Greer v Downs [1927] 2 KB 238. An undisclosed principal may not ratify an unauthorised action of his agent – Keighley, Maxsted and Co. v Durant [1901] AC 240; although he may be estopped by his conduct from denying the agent's authority. As a general rule the third party to the contract may sue the agent or the principal, as and when he is disclosed, but he may not sue both; "if a man is entitled to one of two inconsistent rights it is fitting that where with full knowledge he has done an unequivocal act showing that he has chosen the one he cannot afterwards pursue the other, which after the first choice is by reason of the inconsistency no longer his to choose" – United Australia Ltd v Barclays Bank Ltd [1914] AC 30. In French law the doctrine of undisclosed principal is rarely admitted because "a person may not, in general, bind himself or stipulate in his own name, except for himself." (French Civil Code, art. 1119). If a person is intending to commit a third party he must make a clear stipulation to that effect (Civil Code, arts. 1121–2).

cf. **unnamed principal**. See also **agency, agency of necessity, election, estoppel, ratification**.

The Law of Estate Agency and Auctions, by J.R. Murdoch, 2 edn., pp. 85–90.

Bowstead on Agency, 15 edn, pp. 312–325.

undivided fee (US)

A **fee** interest in land that is held without any other estate or interest being held in the same land; a fee that is not subject to any **partial interest**.

undivided fractional interest (US)

An interest in property as held by a co-owner. The holder of an undivided interest has no right to any specific part of the property, but has a right to possession of the whole. An undivided interest in a property may be equal, as with a **joint tenancy**; or unequal, as (sometimes) with a **tenancy in common**. Called also an 'undivided fractional interest'. See also **undivided fee**.

undivided property

see **co-ownership**.

undivided share

see **tenancy in common**.

undue influence

Such influence as destroys a person's freedom to act at his or her own volition. Any form of moral or unreasonable pressure exerted by one party on another. An inequality of bargaining power that is used to persuade or entice another to enter into a contract. Basically, "to be undue influence there must be – to sum it up in one word – coercion" – Wingrove *v* Wingrove (1885) 11 PD 82. Undue influence is not capable of strict legal definition; the term is left "wide open for identification on the facts and in all the circumstances of each particular case as it arises." – *Re* Craig (Decd.), Meneces *v* Middleton [1970] 2 All ER 396. Any conduct that amounts to overpersuasion, or artful or fraudulent contrivance, to such a degree that a person's free will to act is destroyed, may amount to undue influence. On the other hand, undue influence is something more than unbounded influence or a mere desire to gratify the wishes of another; it must be affirmative and decisive. Undue influence may arise if a person uses a threat to disclose confidential information; plays upon another's fears or foibles; offers exceptional favours or gifts; or if a professional adviser exerts pressure on his client in order to coerce that party to enter into a contract. Normally a presumption of undue influence requires some form of special relationship between the parties, e.g. parent and child, doctor and patient, banker and borrower. In certain relationships – parent and child, doctor and patient – a presumption of undue influence arises automatically from the nature of the relationship. In other relationships the presumption of undue influence requires "some quality beyond that inherent in the confidence that can well exist between trustworthy persons who in business affairs deal with each other at arm's length" – Lloyds Bank Ltd *v* Bundy [1974] 3 All ER 767. "Undue influence consists in the use, by one in whom a confidence is reposed by another, or who holds a real or apparent authority over him, of such confidence or authority for the purpose of obtaining an unfair advantage over him; in taking an unfair advantage of another's weakness of mind; or in taking a grossly oppressive and unfair advantage of another's necessities or distress." (California Civil Code, para. 1575).

A contract that results from undue influence is voidable at the instigation of the influenced party, because any agreement depends on free consent. An **agent** (or a **trustee**) is expected to be able to demonstrate that he has not used his unique position to induce or coerce his principal (or a beneficiary) to enter into a contract. Independent professional advice tends to mitigate against proof of undue influence; "I [Lord Denning] do not mean to suggest that every transaction is saved by independent advice. But the absence of it may be fatal" – Lloyds Bank Ltd v Bundy *supra* at 765. Once a presumption of undue influence arises it continues until positively reubutted, usually by showing that the 'influenced' party acted of his own free will. Any transaction for valuable consideration which results in a benefit to one party out of all proportion to the amount of valuable consideration so given may be set aside on the basis that there was undue influence, even if the person who benefitted by the transaction is different from the one who exerted the influence.
cf. **duress**. See also **fraud, rectification, unconscionable bargain, undervalue, voidable contract.**
Anson's Law of Contract, 26 edn, pp. 243–2.
Chitty on Contract, 25 edn, paras. 502–51.
18 Halsbury's Laws of England, 4 edn, paras. 330–343.

unearned increment
An increase in the value of a property brought about by natural causes; by favourable changes in the neighbourhood; by a grant of consent to carry out new development; or a change of use; rather than by any intrinsic change in the property. An increase in the value of land arising from any cause other than an action of the owner. See also **betterment.**

unencumbered
Free of any **charge** or **burden.** A totally unencumbered property is free of any private condition, easement, restrictive covenant, mortgage, lien, servitude or other **encumberance**; although it may be subject to a lease or licence, and any public law that affects its use or alienability. See also **beneficial owner, vacant possession.**

unenforceable contract
A contract that cannot be enforced, by one or both parties, by direct legal proceedings based on the form or subject of the contract. An unenforceable contract may be defective because (a) there is a lack of a requisite formality e.g. it is not evidenced in **writing**; (b) the right of action is barred by the **Statutes of Limitation**; or (c) it is made with a foreign sovereign or his ambassador. Apart from such a defect the contract is valid in all other respects. Thus it may be possible to enforce or obtain a benefit from the contract in some other way. For example, a prospective vendor may refuse to return a deposit and thereby force the prospective purchaser to bring an action for its recovery. An unenforceable contract is not void and may be enforceable if the defect is cured.
cf. **voidable contract.** See also **agreement for a lease, Statute of Frauds, void contract.**

Cheshire and Fifoot's Law of Contract, 10 edn, pp. 174–198.
Chitty on Contract, 25 edn, para. 17.

unexhausted manurial value
see **tenant right**.

unexpended balance of established development value (UXB)
A sum of money, attached to a parcel of land, which represents the residue of an amount of compensation payable to a landowner as a result of the confiscation of **development value** under the Town and Country Planning Act 1947, (plus certain subsequent minor increases). The 1947 Act stated that the development of land, with certain minor exceptions, was no longer permitted without consent and, basically, that no compensation would be payable for any resultant loss. The only form of redress for this appropriation of development value was the right, for a freeholder or leaseholder who had a prospect of carrying out development as at 1 July 1948, to make a claim for the loss in the value of his land to a **Central Land Board** established for the purpose. Such a claim, if admitted, became known as an "established claim" and any person who had a prospect of a payment in respect of that claim had the "benefit of an established claim" or, as it was redesignated, a **claim holding** (Town and Country Planning Act 1954, s. 17). Any subsisting claim after any necessary adjustments for sums that had been paid out because a landowner had been refused development consent or to take account of aggregations or divisions of ownership, was increased in value by one seventh and renamed an "unexpended balance of established devel-

opment value" (Town and Country Planning Act 1971, ss 135–139). Such sums are attached to the relevant land in the event of a refusal of planning permission, or a grant of permission subject to conditions, compensation may be payable against this sum in the event of a refusal of planning permission. Details of these sums may be obtained from the Department of the Environment, although the subsisting amounts remain small because not many claims were accepted; the amounts of those that were accepted have been eroded by inflation; and those areas of land that had potential for development in 1947 but remain undeveloped are negligible. See also **compensation for planning restrictions**.
Modern Methods of Valuation, 7 edn., pp. 423–443.
Guide to Development and Planning, by R.N.D. Hamilton, 6 edn., pp. 374–378.
Law of Compulsory Purchase and Compensation, by Desmond Heap, 4 edn., pp. 296–300.
Encyclopaedia of Compulsory Purchase and Compensation, by Harold J.J. Brown, paras. 1–118, 1–130, 2–2075 *et seq.*
8 Halsbury's Laws of England, 4 edn, paras. 285–286.

unexpired term
The period of a lease that, at any point in time, remains until the lease terminates by lapse of time; especially the remaining term of a **tenancy for a term of years**.

unfair contract term
see **duress, exclusion clause, misrepresentation, rescission, unconscionable bargain, undue influence.**

unfit for human habitation

Unsuitable for living in by a normal human being; incapable of being used as a satisfactory place of residence by reason of the state or condition. In particular, a dwelling-house that is considered unfit when judged against a statutory standard. The Housing Act 1957, s. 4, as amended by the Housing Act 1969, s. 71, specifies that, in determining whether a house is unfit, the following matters are to be taken into account: (a) repair; (b) stability; (c) freedom from damp; (d) natural lighting; (e) ventilation; (f) water supply; (g) drainage and sanitary conveniences; (h) facilities for storage, preparation and cooking of food; (i) arrangements for the disposal of waste water; and (j) internal arrangement. If a house is "so far defective in one or more of the said matters" that it is not reasonably suitable for occupation in that condition it shall be deemed unfit for human habitation. Also, "if the state of repair of a house is such that by ordinary user damage may naturally be caused to the occupier, either in respect of personal injury to life and limb, or injury to health, then the house is not in all respects reasonably fit for human habitation" – Morgan *v* Liverpool Corporation [1927] 2 KB 131. For the purpose of serving a **closing order** a room may be deemed unfit if it is more than three feet below the surface of the street nearest the room (or any ground within nine feet of the room) and the average height of the room is under seven feet (Housing Act 1957, s. 18). Also a house may be unfit due to the presence of rats, bugs, disease, germs, etc., – Smith *v* Marrable (1843) 11 M and W 5), (although such causes are not referred to as factors under the Housing Acts).

cf. **fit for human habitation**. See also **back-to-back house, clearance area, cleared site value, demolition order, nuisance, repairs notice, standard amenities**.

West's Law of Housing, 4 edn, pp. 7–51.

Housing Law, by Andrew Arden and Martin Partington, pp. 383–398 (1983).

unfree tenure

Tenure by which a person is bound to the land. In particular, a form of tenure under the **feudal system** by which the tenant held land only so long as he provided certain services to the lord of the manor, e.g. the earlier forms of **villeinage**. Called also 'base tenure'. See also **customary freehold**.

The Law of Real Property, by R. Megarry & H.W.R. Wade, 5 edn, pp. 21–27.

unidentified principal

see **unnamed principal**.

Uniform Commercial Code (UCC) (US)

A body of law, based on the recommendation of the Commissioners of Uniform State Laws in conjunction with the American Law Institute, which has been adopted by all states, except Louisiana, as a means of regulating and controlling commercial and business practices throughout the United States. The Code was originally approved in 1952 and has been revised on a number of occasions since. The Code affects only personal property, with the exception of Section 9–313 which deals with fixtures. See also **unconscionable bargain.**

Handbook of Law under the Uniform Commercial Code, by James S. White & Robert S. Summers, 2 edn.

American Law Institute and National

Conference of Commissioners of Uniform State Laws, Uniform Commercial Code, Official Text (1972).

Uniform Partnership Act (UPA) (US)
A model statute, adopted in whole or in part by most states, which governs the establishment and running of a **partnership**.

Uniform Residential Landlord and Tenant Act (URLTA) (US)
A model statute, which has been prepared by the Commissioners of Uniform State Laws and adopted by several states, or used as the basis for similar legislation aimed at providing uniformity in tenancies of residential property. The Act sets out a number of conditions that are implied in residential tenancies, unless there is anything expressed to the contrary. In addition, it provides protection for tenants against unreasonable terms imposed by landlords, e.g. limiting the size of deposits that can be demanded, requiring the landlord to keep the premises fit for habitation; requiring the landlord to give proper notice to quit and permitting the courts to refuse to enforce an **unconscionable bargain**.

unilateral contract
A contract by which only one party is bound. A contract that arises when a person gives a one-sided promise or undertaking to another to perform an obligation "without any obligation on the part of the latter" (French Civil Code, art. 1103). A unilateral contract usually requires the other party to accept certain conditions or commitments, i.e. it creates rights in one party only and duties in the other. It is an 'if' contract – "if you provide ... then I will, or I undertake to ...", or

"if I wish to ... then you will agree to ...". "A promise on one side is exchanged for an act (or forbearance) on the other" (*An Introduction to the Law of Contract*, by P.S. Atiyah, 3 edn., p. 32). Instances of unilateral contracts include: an offer of a reward for the return of stolen goods; the grant of an **option** to purchase a property (at least until the option is exercised); the appointment of an estate agent to find a prospective purchaser for a property, provided his remuneration is based entirely on success; the making of a **promissory note**. See also **contingency fee, deed poll, open offer**.
Engaging an estate agent: is it really a unilateral contract? by Christopher R. McDonnell, 265 EG 547 (1983). Chitty on Contract, 25 edn, p. 13.

unilateral mistake
see **mistake**.

unimpeachable for waste
see **waste**.

unimproved land
Land that has not been tilled or cultivated. Land upon which no improvement or building has been placed or constructed. In particular, land that would be suitable for development but which has not been opened up by roads, services or utilities. A site that comprises unimproved or undeveloped land may be referred to also as a 'green field site'. See also **raw land**.

uninsurable title (US)
see **unmarketable title**.

union-mortgage clause (US)
A clause in an insurance policy by which a mortgagee effectively contracts directly with the insurer. The mortgagee becomes not only a party

interested in the insurance policy (as in a **mortgage clause**) but, in the event of a payment under the policy being made to the mortgagee, his rights are to be considered independently of, and are to be unaffected by, the rights or claims of any other party.

unit
see **planning unit, standard unit, unit cost (or value)**.

unit cost (or value)
The cost (or value) of a property related to an area or to a volume of measurement, e.g. pounds sterling per square foot, dollars per acre. The cost or value allotted to a given unit of property, e.g. the value of a standard unit. The average cost of a building expressed as a rate per unit area or unit volume.

unit-in-place method (US)
see **unit method**.

unit of value
The value of something that is taken as a standard or yardstick for comparing the value of other things.

unit method (US)
A method of assessing the cost of a development project or the replacement cost of a building by determining an appropriate unit cost for each component of the property and applying the appropriate unit cost to the number of components or units that make up the property. Called also the 'unit-in-place method' or the 'segregated cost method'. See also **quantity surveying, project valuation**.

unit mortgage (US)
A mortgage secured on one unit in a **condominium** property together with the rights of the owner of the unit over the common areas, as compared to a mortgage secured on the entire building.

unit owner (US)
The owner of an individual unit in a condominium property. A unit holder holds title to the area within the confines of the 'unit' (apartment, office area, etc.) and an undivided interest in the common areas. See also **condominium ownership**.

unit trust
A form of **trust** established to enable persons with funds for investment to join together in order to acquire a diversified block of stocks, shares or other forms of investment and thereby spread their risks. "Any arrangement made for the purpose, or having the effect, of providing facilities for the participation by persons, as beneficiaries under a trust, in profits or income arising from the acquisition, holding, management or disposal of securities or any other property whatsoever." (Prevention of Fraud (Investments) Act 1958, s. 26 (1); Charging Orders Act 1979, s. 6 (1)) (these statutes provide that such a trust must be authorised by the Department of Trade and Industry). A unit trust is constituted by a deed that sets out the terms of the trust, appoints the managers or trustees, and stipulates the permitted forms of investment. Units in the trust are not transferable but are bought and sold through the trustees or managers, and the price of those units is based on the underlying value of the investments (less a difference between the unit buying and selling price to cover the costs of administering the trust, including remuneration for the managers). The beneficiaries receive an income based on the return from the invested funds.

cf. **investment company (or trust)**. See also **mutual fund, property unit trust**.

Unit Trusts: the Law and Practice, by Martin Day and Paul Harris, 2 edn.

unities of time, possession, title, and interest
see **joint tenancy**.

unitisation
see **syndication, unit trust**.

unity of possession
1. Joint possession of two interests in land held by the same person. A situation that arises, for example, when a person holds a lease of land, then acquires the reversionary interest and thereby extinguishes the lease.
2. A temporary form of unity of a right to land that arises when an owner of a **dominant tenement** (land benefitting from an easement or restrictive covenant) acquires a lease of the **servient tenement** (the land burdened by the easement or restrictive covenant). During the term of that lease the easement or restrictive covenant is of no effect as it is held by one person against himself, but it is re-established when the lease terminates. If the right to the dominant and servient tenement comes into possession of the same person permanently there is said to be unity of **seisin** and the interest is extinguished (Co. Litt. 313).
3. A right to the same undivided **possession** of the whole of a property, as held by co-owners. A co-owner of land has unity of possession as he is entitled to possession and enjoyment of the whole; but he has no right to preclude any other co-owner from the land, because he cannot point to any part of the property as his own to the exclusion of the other co-owners; if he could there would not be **co-ownership** but separate ownership. See also **joint tenancy, tenancy in common**.

unity of seisin
see **seisin, unity of possession**.

unity of title
see **joint tenancy**.

universal agent
see **agent**.

unjust enrichment
see **quasi-contract, restitution**.

unlawful eviction
see **eviction, harrassment, security of tenure**.

unlawful user clause
see **user clause**.

unlimited mortgage
see **open-end mortgage**.

unlimited policy
An **all-risks insurance policy** that sets no ceiling on the amount of cover provided for the insured; the insurer provides an indemnity to cover the actual loss sustained by the insured. See also **blanket policy, unvalued policy**.

unliquidated damages
Damages that have not been fixed or determined; e.g. damages that are not stipulated in a contract but are left to be decided by a court of law or arbitrator.
cf. **liquidated damages**.

unmarketable title (US)
A title to property that is so far defective that it would expose a purchaser to the risk of litigation, or would reduce substantially the market value

of the property. A title may be treated as unmarketable if there is a reasonable doubt as to its validity – New York Investors *v* Manhattan Beach Bathing Parks Cor., 243 NYS 548. An unmarketable title is referred to as an 'uninsurable title' if the title is so far defective that a title insurance company would refuse to provide **title insurance**.
cf. **marketable title**.

unnamed principal

A **principal** whose identity is not revealed to a third party by an agent, although unlike an **undisclosed principal**, the agent makes it clear that he is acting for someone else. As a rule, an agent is not liable for a contract made by an unnamed principal, provided there is a principal who can consumate the transaction (either directly or through the agent) when called upon to do so. However, an agent may be liable when he does not disclose the identity of his principal if the custom of the trade dictates, or because of the nature and intention of the contract and the surrounding circumstances. A person buying at auction frequently does not know the identity of the vendor, but accepts that the **auctioneer** has the ability to contract and is contracting personally at the time of the sale; unless the auctioneer is selling specific chattels that are clearly known to be sold on behalf of another – Hanson *v* Roberdean (1792) Peake 162; Franklyn *v* Lamond (1847) 4 C.B. 637. See also **ratification**.
The Law of Estate Agency and Auctions, by J.R. Murdoch, 2 edn, pp. 130–134, 433–436.
Chitty on Contract, 25 edn, para. 2278.

unoccupied

Not inhabited or used for its intended purpose. An unoccupied property may be kept ready and available for **occupation**, e.g. by being furnished, but may not be used as such; it lacks animated occupancy, as distinguished from a **vacant** property which normally has no inanimate objects on the premises. In insurance, a residential property is unoccupied (and, therefore, probably not insured) when it has ceased to be used as a dwelling or place of abode, and not merely vacated for a short period. Whether a person has left a property unoccupied depends on the intention of the person who has the right to take up occupation; if a person leaves premises and takes up residence elsewhere the indication is that he or she has left the premises unoccupied (or ceded occupation to another).

A property may be unoccupied (in the normal sense of the word), but if a person is able to derive some benefit or value therefrom, i.e. has **beneficial occupation**, it is occupied for the purpose of a liability to pay rates. In addition, a rating authority may levy rates (sometimes called unoccupied or empty rates) on any unoccupied property if that is considered appropriate. It may not levy rates until the property has been unoccupied for a continuous period exceeding three months, or six months in the case of newly erected dwellings. The owners of various types of property are exempt from this liability; notably property that cannot be occupied legally, and factories, mills, and similar properties (General Rate Act 1967, s. 17, Sch. 1; Rating (Exemption of Unoccupied Industrial Hereditaments) Regulations 1984). See also

rateable occupation.
Ryde on Rating, 13 edn, pp. 801–810
(and 3rd Cumulative supplement:
30–32).

unpaid vendor's lien
see **general equitable charge, lien,
overriding interest.**

**'unreasonably withhold (or refuse)
consent'**
see **improvement, restraint on alienation.**

unsecured ground rent
A **ground rent** receivable for a site
upon which no buildings have yet
been erected.
cf. **secured ground rent.** See also
security of ground rent.

unsecured loan
A loan that is not protected by any
form of **security** other than the personal liability of the borrower. A loan
that is not secured by **collateral.**
cf. **secured loan.** See also **lien,
mortgage.**

unsightly land
see **derelict land, waste land.**

until
see **time.**

unusual covenant
A **covenant** or proviso that is unlikely
to have been intended to form part of
the terms and conditions of a lease,
because it negates the type of agreement entered into by the parties –
Church v Brown (1808) All ER Rep.
440. An 'unusual' covenant may be
expressly inserted in a lease, but it
cannot be implied in any way. Covenants that have been held to be
'unusual' include a covenant by a
tenant to insure the demised premises

or to repair or rebuild after fire; a
covenant not to carry on a particular
trade; a proviso for re-entry on bankruptcy – Hodgkinson v Crowe (1875)
LR 19 Eq. 591.
cf. **usual covenant.** See also **express
term.**

unvalued policy
An insurance policy in which the
value of the insured property is not
specified, but in the event of loss
payment is based on the actual loss
suffered, i.e. payment is based on the
strict principle of **indemnity,** or is
provided in a manner laid down in the
policy. Any sum that is referred to in
the policy is intended merely as an
upper limit to the insurer's liability;
not as a representation of the amount
for which the insured is covered.
Insurance policies on real estate are
made normally as unvalued policies.
The insured cannot recover any
monies unless he substantiates the
loss suffered, subject to any stipulated
ceiling. Blanket insurance policies,
which cover a number of properties,
are usually 'unvalued', with the upper
limit of indemnity stated as and when
properties are added or removed
from the policy. Called also an 'open
policy'.
cf. **valued policy.**
General Principles of Insurance Law,
by E.R. Hardy Ivamy, 4 edn., pp.
227–228.

uplift factor
An allowance applied to the value of a
property to reflect a special feature of
that property, e.g. a factor applied to
the value of a tenant's interest in a
property to reflect the fact that the
rent is fixed for a long period and,
therefore, protected against inflationary increases.

cf. **quantity allowance**. See also constant-rent factor, equated yield.

upon

At the time of. 'Upon' or 'on' the occurrence of a particular event or act may mean immediately 'before', 'simultaneously with', or immediately after the event or the act, according as "reason or good sense require with reference to the context and the subject-matter of the enactment" – R. v Arkwright (1848) 12 QB 970. Usually 'upon' means commencing with and includes the **date** to which it may refer.

upset date (US)

A date by which a contract, in particular a building contract, must be performed; after that date, if the contract is not substantially completed, it may be rescinded. See also **substantial completion, 'time is of the essence'**.

upset price

1. The **reserve price** set an auction. (US) 2. The minimum price that must be bid to acquire a property at a **foreclosure sale**.

upside leverage (US)

Borrowing funds at a rate of interest that is lower than the free and clear return from an investment and, thereby, increasing the return on **equity**. See also **leverage**.

upzoning (US)

A change of a **zoning ordinance** or **zoning classification**, so as to widen the use to which a property may be put.
cf. **downzoning**.

urban

From the Latin *urbanus*, 'of, or belonging to, a town or city'. A densely populated area.

cf. **rural**. See also **suburb, urban region**.

urban development area (UDA)

An area of land in a metropolitan district or in an inner London Borough, which the Secretary of State for the Environment has designated, in accordance with the provisions of the Local Government, Planning and Land Act 1980, s. 134, as an area that requires **urban renewal** or "regeneration" by "bringing land and buildings into effective use, encouraging the development of existing and new industry and commerce, creating a new environment and ensuring that housing and social facilities are available to encourage people to live and work in an area". The Secretary of State may create an **urban development corporation** to be responsible for this task.
46 Halsbury's Laws of England, 4 edn, paras. 531–543.

urban development corporation

A public corporation appointed by the Secretary of State for the Environment to undertake the "regeneration" of an **urban development area**. The corporation is modelled on the New Town **development corporation** and similarly has extensive powers to acquire, hold, manage, and dispose of land; to carry out most forms of development; and generally to ensure that a designated inner urban area, e.g. London docklands or the south docks of Merseyside, is improved, rebuilt or redeveloped.

urban development grant

Financial assistance provided for a development project in a deprived or declining urban area. In Great Britain urban development grants are provided by a local authority, a "designated district authority" (which reclaims 75 per cent of the cost from central government), and such grants normally take the form of top-up aid to meet part of the cost of a development project that would not otherwise be viable. Grants may be made also towards the cost of improving the amenity of the area (Inner Urban Areas Act 1978, ss. 5,6). See also **inner urban area**.

urban land economics
see **land economics**.

urban region
A town or city region, comprising an area of continuous and highly condensed development which includes, but extends beyond, the confines of a single town or city. A term that may be used also to refer to a group or cluster of towns or cities which have a degree of unity in terms of trade, population, communications, etc. An urban region is similar, but generally smaller than a **megalopolis**, and is larger than a **conurbation**.

urban renewal
The **renovation** or **rehabitation** of a run down area or district of a town or city by a series of measures designed to improve and remodel the existing buildings, but at the same time to conserve the environment. A process that may include improving the communication system; repairing the existing fabric; rebuilding certain buildings to a significantly higher standard; and landscaping or augmenting the landscape. The intention of urban renewal is to preserve, as far as possible, the basic character of the area rather than to carry out comprehensive redevelopment. In the US,

'urban renewal' may be used synonymously with **comprehensive development**; especially to refer to any combined activity designed to prevent urban decay, or blight, and to eliminate slum property. Urban renewal may be carried out by private landowners or by bringing land, wholly or partly, into public ownership.
An Introduction to Urban Renewal, by Gibson and Langstaff (1982).

urban servitude
In Roman, the civil and Scottish law a 'real' **servitude**, in particular a servitude that affects a building (wherever situated) and one that runs with the building so as to burden or benefit (as appropriate) a future owner of the building, e.g. a right of light or a right of support.

urbanisation
The conversion of a rural area to an urban area, especially by the spread of population from an existing urban area. The process of converting a district into a town or city, especially the latter by increasing the concentration of population.

urbanisme (F)
town planning. A term that is used in the same sense as **town and country planning** in English.

urbaniste (F)
town planner.

urbanity
Possessing the character of an **urban area**. A word in English town and country planning jargon used to describe a well ordered and controlled development. "For some years past 'urbanity' has been a blessed word and '**subtopia**' an accursed word ...

The concepts which are symbolised by these words are such an inextricable mixture of sound sense and abominable rubbish that they are hard to analyse … Urbanity … is, I suppose, a quality or qualities to be associated with development appropriate to a town, while subtopia, a useful though misused word, is an unpunctuated sprawl of ill-designed houses, and ill-sited shops, inefficient roads and unsightly poles, wires and roadside details" (*Town Planning at the Cross-roads*, by Lewis Keeble, p. 176 (1961). See also **town and country planning**.

usable area

1. The **net usable area**, either as let to one tenant or the total such area in a building, i.e. the area from which an occupier or occupiers effectively can derive benefit. See also **net internal area**.

2. In a building that is let to a number of tenants the area that each tenant occupies exclusively, as distinguished from the **common area** (or common parts) which are available for the joint use of two or more tenants.

usage

A habitual practice or **use**; a long and well established practice. A notorious, but legal, reasonable practice that is adopted and accepted by those in a particular form of business. "Usage may be broadly defined as a particular course of dealing or line or conduct generally adopted by persons engaged in a particular department of a business life" (29 Halsbury's Laws of England, 4 edn, p. 28). 'Usage' may encompass **custom** or **prescription**, although it differs from both; for if custom and prescription lose their being usage fails (*Coke's Complete Copyholder* 33 (1673)).

cf. **user, enjoyment**. See also **implied term**.

usage (F)

use; **usage**, a right to use property but unlike **usufruct** a right that cannot be hypothecated or alienated; **custom**.

(*droit d'usage* – right of user – a right to enjoy the fruits (*fruits*) of real property but only so far as is required to meet the needs of the beneficiary and his family. A limited form of **usufruct** that comprises a personal and inalienable right to real property. See also *habitation*. Précis Dalloz. *Droit Civil*, Les Biens (Alex Weill) 2 edn, pp. 522–527.)

(*valuer d'usage* – **going-concern value**.)

usance

1. The period of time allowed for the payment of a **bill of exchange**, excluding any days of grace.

2. Interest payable for the use of money, especially a usurous rate of interest. See also **usury**.

use

1. Derived from the Latin *opus* or Norman French *oes*, 'benefit'. The act of employing something for a purpose, especially a continuous or profitable purpose. The **enjoyment** or **benefit** to be derived from holding, occupying or manipulating something. In the case of land or buildings, use means particularly occupation and enjoyment of the fruits and profits to be derived therefrom. "The use of a thing does not mean the thing itself (i.e. possession), but means that the user is to enjoy, hold, occupy, or have in some manner the benefit thereof. If … real estate, the use thereof is its occupancy and cultivation … or the rent which can be obtained for its use. If it is money or its equivalent …

it is the interest which it will earn" – Elwell *v* Stewart (1922) Kan. 219. 'Use' represents one of the essential characteristics of property: an owner lives in a house, cultivates land, works in a factory and thereby is making use of that particular property. Use of property may change or destroy it; i.e. the property may be 'used up'; or it may provide profit or enjoyment without affecting its essential self, or *corpus*. Use to destruction is restricted primarily to an absolute **owner**. Use for profit or enjoyment makes it possible to separate the benefit of property from **ownership**.

A thing or object may be considered as having a double use; a proper or natural use and a derived or unnatural use. The natural use treats the object as it exists *in esse*; the derived use treats the object for any other purpose to which it can be put. For example, a piece of yarn may be used to make an article of clothing, or to measure a distance; a piece of metal may be used to make a vessel, or as a medium of exchange (that is as money); and land may be used to provide food, or as a means of deriving income or profit, especially by renting it to another. The extent to which land may be used, or any restriction placed on its use, is an important factor in determining its **value**.

An owner of land or real estate may retain the use entirely for himself or he may transfer that use, in whole or in part, to another. Such a transfer may be by gift, sale, lease, licence or, in the civil law, by a grant of the **usufruct**. If a person is given the 'use' of land, and nothing more, he is granted a mere **licence** – Warr *v* London County Council [1904] 1 KB 713. A covenant in a lease prohibiting a tenant from letting any other person 'use' the demised premises prohibits almost any activity on the land by another person, except a visitor or casual interloper.

In planning law a 'use' of land normally means a lawful use, in the sense of not being criminal – Glamorgan County Council *v* Carter [1963] 1 WLR 1. With reference to a **discontinuance order** served under the Town and Country Planning Act 1971, s. 51, 'use' means activities that are done in, on, or around land even if they do not "interfere with the actual physical characteristics of land" – Parkes *v* Secretary of State for the Environment [1978] 1 WLR 1311.

In assessing a liability for rates if land is kept in a virgin state it may still be 'used' for a particular purpose, provided there is a benefit derived therefrom, e.g. an area of land may be used and occupied as part of the grounds of a hospital and, therefore, as part of the hospital is exempt from rates – Newcastle City Council *v* Royal Newcastle Hospital [1959] AC 248.

cf. **occupation**. See also **existing use, highest and best use, material change in the use, usage, use and occupation, user clause, utility**.

2. To put something into practice, to put into action or service. To follow a practice or **custom**, especially as a matter of habit. A regular use or practice may well establish a custom; "for use almost can change the stamp of nature, and either curb the devil, or throw him out, with wondrous potency" (William Shakespeare, *Hamlet*, Act III, Scene IV).

3. The legal enjoyment of property, especially the benefits or profits aris-

ing in favour of a person other than the legal owner. In particular, an ancient term employed to indicate that a property was to be transferred to one person to be held 'on behalf of' (or *ad opus*, *ad oeps* or *ad eops*, 'to the use of') another. A use was a means in the late Middle Ages of transferring property to another in order to avoid 'escheat' i.e. the land falling back into the hands of a lord upon the death of the true owner. The system of 'uses' appears to have originated in England about 1225 as a means by which the Franciscan Order could retain the benefit of property without actually being the owner. The Order was given property, in particular land to establish monasteries, but as it was not permitted to own gold, silver, or money, nor any other form of wealth, the land was given to the municipality 'for the use of' the Order. Under the **feudal system** of land tenure, a similar arrangement was adopted to enable private citizens to pass land between themselves, either *inter vivos* or by will, without it passing automatically to the lord of the manor or the Sovereign on the death of the tenant. The land, or the right to the soil (**seisin**), was passed by a tenant, A, to another party, B, to be held on behalf of, 'to the use of', A, or a third party C. In this way upon the death of A, C obtained a right to the land (provided he acted in accordance with the wishes of A). A and C were known as the *cestui que uses*, 'he for whom the use was made', and B as the *feoffee to uses*, 'the party to whom the land was enfeoffed' (or conveyed). This arrangement, although prohibited after the Statute of Uses 1535, represented the forerunner of the modern **trust**, the *cestui que use* being the equivalent to a **beneficiary** and the *feoffee to uses* the equivalent to a **trustee**.

Cheshire's Modern Law of Property, 13 edn, pp. 43–55.
The Law of Real Property, by Robert Megarry and H.W.R. Wade, 5 edn., pp. 1164–1175.
39 Halsbury's Laws of England, 4 edn, paras. 329–340.

use and occupation

1. A form of action by which an owner of land claims that another has had the benefit of occupying and enjoying his land, with permission, but that no form of payment has been made for that benefit. An action for use and occupation may be brought when someone has enjoyed the same rights and benefits from land as can be enjoyed by a tenant, but when there has been no lease or agreement for a lease and, therefore, no liability to pay rent. The person bringing the action seeks damages or compensation for a loss of the right to 'use and occupy' the land, but acknowledges that he did not go so far as to create a tenancy. "The action for use and occupation does not necessarily suppose any **demise**; it is enough that the defendant used and occupied the premises by the permission of the plaintiff" – Rochester (Dean and Chapter) *v* Pierce (1808) 1 Camp. 466. No regular or specific form of payment or 'rent' is claimed, but only an amount of compensation based on the enjoyment or "reasonable satisfaction" obtained by the occupier (The Distress for Rent Act 1937, s. 14). A claim for use and occupation is based on an implied or tacit contract to pay for the use of the land; not a claim against a trespasser or illegal occupant. Thus, a tenant who remains

on demised premises after a writ has been served for ejectment is not liable for 'use and occupation': although he may be liable for **mesne profits**. Where a verbal contract to grant a lease has been made and the intending tenant takes possession he may be liable for use and occupation, and the amount of compensation payable is fixed usually at the level of the agreed rent.

The Law of Landlord and Tenant, by David Lloyd Evans, 2 edn., pp. 129–130.

Hill and Redman's Law of Landlord and Tenant, 17 edn, pp. 352–354.

Woodfall's Landlord and Tenant, 28 edn, paras. 1–1031 to 1–1070.

27 Halsbury's Laws of England, 4 edn, para. 254.

2. The combined benefit derived from the **use** and the **occupation** of land. "As occupation is a kind of user, it is difficult to envisage occupation of land or building which is not also a user. The reverse does not apply. Not every use is an occupation, and obviously many things capable of being used are incapable of being occupied. The words are not fully interchangeable but only interchangeable in some contexts" – Land Reclamation Co. Ltd *v* Basildon District Council [1978] 2 All ER 1166–7.

use and occupation insurance
see **rental value insurance**.

use classes
see **Use Classes order**.

Use Classes Order
An order, made by the Secretary of State for the Environment under the provisions of the Town and Country Planning Act 1971, s. 22 (2) (f), which sets out a number of categories of 'use

classes' within which a change of use may take place without there being **development** and, therefore, a need for planning permission. A change of use may be made to "any other purpose of the same class". The purpose of the order is to avoid the need for planning permission when there is merely a change from one use of property to another similar use; provided the change is not substantial or "material".

The Town and Country Planning (Use Classes) Order 1972 sets out eighteen use classes which may be summarised as: Class I – a **shop** used for any purpose, except for the sale of hot food, tripe, pet animals and birds, cat's meat and motor vehicles; Class II – any type of **office**; Class III – any type of light **industrial building**; Class IV – a general industrial building; Class V–IX – various special industrial buildings; Class X – a **warehouse** or repository used for the storage of any type of goods, except offensive or dangerous material; Classes XI–XVIII – these classes group together a number of similar specialised purposes, such as a boarding house or hotel; health centre, clinic, or creche; an art gallery, museum or exhibition hall; a theatre, cinema or concert hall; or a dance hall, skating rink, or sports hall.

A Use Classes Order should be distinguished from a **General Development Order**, as the former lists changes that do not constitute 'development' and the latter lists activities that are 'development' but do not require planning permission. Thus a change from a grocer to a butcher, to a tailor, to a shoe shop does not constitute development but a change from a hot food shop to a grocer is development, although it is 'permitted development'(Town and Country Planning General Development Order 1977 Class III). Similarly a change from assembly of radios to the assembly of computers is not development; but a change from a general industrial use to a light industrial use is 'permitted development'; although the reverse is not 'permitted'. See also **planning unit**.

Guide to Development and Planning, by R.N.D. Hamilton, 7 edn., pp. 132–136.
An Outline of Planning Law, by Desmond Heap, 8 edn., pp. 97–101.
Planning Law and Procedure, by A.E. Telling, 6 edn., pp. 74–79.
Encyclopaedia of Planning Law and Practice, by Desmond Heap, paras. 3B–122.

use density
The ratio of the number of building units used for a particular purpose (dwellings, shop units, warehouses) to a given unit area of land; e.g. dwellings per acre; retail units per hectare. See also **residential density**.

use district (US)
An area of a town or city within which the use of land and buildings is regulated by law. See also **zoning**.

use value
1. The **value** of a property for a particular **use**, as distinguished from the value for the **highest and best use**. The **utility** to be derived from something. See also **existing use value**.
2. The **reinstatement cost** of a property. Called also 'value-in-use'.

use variance (US)
see **variance**.

use zoning
see **land use planning, zoning**.

useful life
see **economic life**.

user
The continuous **use**, or the enjoyment of a right to property; the actual exercise or enjoyment of any right or interest.
cf. **usage**.

user as of right
see *nec vi, nec clam, nec precario*.

user clause
A clause or **covenant** in a lease limiting the **use** to which the demised property can be put e.g. "to use the premises only for the sale of shoes and footwear" or prohibiting certain uses of the premises, e.g. "not to use the premises for the storage of toxic materials", or "not to use the premises for any illegal or immoral purpose". Usually such a clause restricts the freedom of the tenant to use the premises for more than one purpose, without the consent of the landlord, and consequently may limit the rental value of the premises. If there is no restriction on user contained in the lease the tenant may make what use of the premises he wishes, within the confines of the law – Yelloly *v* Morley (1910) 27 TLR 20). However, a tenant is bound by any **restrictive covenant** that affects the freehold, and usually by any user clause contained in a superior lease; – Hill *v* Harris [1965] 2 QB 601. A user clause may be inserted in order to protect the value of the leased property or to protect the value of other property owned by the landlord.
cf. **non-competition clause**. See also **change of use**.

usine (F)
factory; plant.

usque ad coelum (L)
'To the heavens'. See **air rights, land**.

usque ad medium filum aquae (L)
see *ad medium filum aquae*.

usual covenant

1. A **covenant** that is deemed to have been inserted in a lease, either because an **agreement for a lease** specifies that the lease when formally granted will contain 'usual covenants', or when the agreement is silent as to the covenants to be included in the lease (as with an **open contract**). In the later instance the usual covenants are implied by law (Propert *v* Parker (1832) 3 My & K 280). 'Usual covenants' are such covenants as are to be expected in a lease "looking at the nature of the premises, their situation, the purpose for which they are let, the evidence of the conveyancers, and the books of **precedent**" – Chester *v* Buckingham Travel [1981] 1 WLR 101. Unless there is anything expressed to the contrary, the usual covenants on the part of the tenant are (a) to pay **rent**; (b) to pay the rates and property taxes (except those that are imposed on the landlord by statute); (c) to keep and deliver up the premises in **repair**; (d) if the landlord is liable to repair, to permit him to enter the demised premises to view the state of repair – Hodgkinson *v* Crowe (1875) 10 Ch. App. 622; (e) to permit the landlord a **right of re-entry** for non-payment of rent (but not for a breach of any other covenant). On the part of the landlord there is a usual covenant that he will grant the tenant **quiet enjoyment** – Hampshire *v* Wickens (1878) 7 Ch. D 561: In that case *Davidon's Prece-*

dents in Conveyancing, 13 edn., Vol. 5 pp. 51–54 was considered as appropriate in establishing the usual practice for the type of lease in question. It may be usual also to consider that a lease should contain some form of covenant as to user; not to create a nuisance; not to make structural alterations without the landlord's consent; and possibly in a modern office lease, a restriction on assignment or sub-letting without the landlord's reasonable consent. However, although these and many other covenants are usually inserted in a lease, they are not deemed to be 'usual' in the technical sense of the word unless, based on precedent, **custom** or trade **usage**, they are clearly usual for the type and duration of tenancy created, and the type of property; after all, "what is usual in Mayfair or Bayswater is not usual in some other part of London, such as, for instance Whitechapel" – Flexman *v* Corbett [1930] 1 Ch. 678. Thus a covenant providing for re-entry for breach of covenant (other than for nonpayment of rent) is not a "usual covenant", but is 'usually' inserted in a well drawn lease. Sometimes called a 'common covenant'.
cf. **implied covenant**. See also **recitals**.
Hill and Redman's Law of Landlord and Tenant, 17 edn, pp. 148–152.
27 Halsbury's Laws of England, 4 edn, paras. 62–63.
Woodfall's Landlord and Tenant, 28 edn, para. 1–0422 *et seq.*
(US) 2. A covenant for title that is implied in a **conveyance** to enable the purchaser to acquire the title he might expect. See also **beneficial owner**.

usual quarter days
see **quarter days**.

usucapion (F)
usucaption; prescriptive acquisition;
adverse possession. See also ***prescription acquisitive***.

usufruct or usufructuary right
A right to the use and enjoyment of the fruits or profits of another's property, without fundamentally changing its substance. "Usufruct is the right to enjoy things of which another is owner, in the same way as an owner, but subject to an obligation to conserve the substance"(French Civil Code, art. 589). Usufruct is a right usually granted for life, although it may be limited further by a period of years. "Usufruct is a real, but temporary and life time right that only grants the possibility to use a thing and receive the fruits therefrom; if one removes from property the use of a thing, there remains the complementary right called bare ownership (*nue propriété*). When the usufruct is extinguished the bare ownership again becomes absolute ownership (***plein propriété***)" *Droit Civil*, by Gabriel Marty and Pierre Raynaud, 2 edn., vol. i. p. 462). Usufruct may be granted over corporeal or incorporeal property, movable (*meubles*) or immoveable (*immeubles*) property (Civil Code, art. 581). Unlike a lessee the **usufructuary** takes and accepts the thing as he finds it, but is obliged to return the subject matter as he found it originally or to provide equivalent value. Although, if the property wears out through normal use, as with most goods, the usufructuary need not return them in the same condition as when he took them (French Civil Code, art. 589). The grantor or bare-owner (*nu-propriétaire*), is responsible primarily for

grosses réparations and the usufructuary for maintenance. Usufruct may be created by law (as with a surviving spouse of an intestacy); or by private grant, either by agreement or by will. A usufruct may come to an end (a) at the end of the life of the grantee; (b) at the end of a set period of limitation; (c) upon the expiration or exhaustion of the thing granted; (d) after a period of 30 years of non-user; or (e) by renunciation, merger or subrogation. It is a right that may be mortgaged, charged or otherwise alienated, unless there is a prohibition to the contrary in the terms of the grant. See also ***démembrement de la propriété, droit d'habitation, usage***.
Amos & Walton's Introduction to French Law, 3 edn, pp. 118–119, 299–301.
Dictionnaire Permanent: Gestion Immobilière, pp. 1287–1294.
Droit Civil – Les Biens, by Jean Carbonnier, 11 edn, pp. 137–153.
Manuel de Droit Civil, by Pierre Voirin and Gilles Goubeaux, 20 edn., pp. 290–298.
Précis Dalloz. Droit Civil, Les Biens (Alex Weill) 2 edn, pp. 475–527.
Droit Civil, by Gabriel Marty and Pierre Raynaud, 2 edn., vol. ii pp. 79–122.

usufructuary
A person who has a right of **usufruct**, i.e. a right to use (*usus*) property and reap profit (*fructus*) therefrom, provided he or she does not alter its substance. "A usufructuary has the right to enjoy all manner of fruits, whether natural, industrial or civil, which are capable of being provided by the object of the usufruct" (French Civil Code, art. 582).

usufruit (F)
usufruct.

(*usufruit viager* – life interest)
(*quasi-usufruit* – a usufructuary right to property that, by its nature, must be consumed e.g. grain; since the beneficiary of a usufruct is obliged to conserve the substance of such a right he is obliged to replace the consumed items in kind (in quality and quantity) or in value at the end of his period of enjoyment). See also **habitation, usage.**

usufruitier (F)
One who has a right of *usufruit* **(usufruct).**
cf. **nu-propriétaire.**

usure (F)
1. wear and tear.
(*usure normale; usure naturelle* – **fair wear and tear**).
2. **usury.**

usurpation
1. The unlawful use of another's authority or property; an **encroachment** on to the property of another. See also **usucapion.**
2. The use of a royal **franchise** without authority.

usurpation (F)
encroachment.

usury
Charging of **interest** for the use of money, or charging an amount of interest that is excessive, unconscionable, inordinate or malicious. A charge for the use of money. A charge for the mere use of money has been despised for centuries; "very much disliked also is the practice of charging interest; and the dislike is fully justified, for the gain arises out of currency itself, not as a produce of that for which currency was provided.

Currency was intended to be a means of exchange, whereas interest represents an increase in the currency itself" (Aristotle, *Politics* Book 1, Ch. 10). It has been prohibited as being a form of exploitation of those in need, especially of one's kith and kin; "thou shalt not lend upon usury to thy brother; usury of money, usury of victuals, usury of any thing that is lent on usury: Unto a stranger thou mayest lend upon usury; but unto thy brother thou shalt not lend upon usury (*Deuteronomy*, 23–19/20). It is considered contrary to the law of God; "those who swallow usury cannot arise except as he arises whom the devil prostrates by touch . . . Allah has permitted trading and forbidden usury" (*Koran* 2: 275). It was condemend by the Council of Nicea in 325 and Pope Innocent IV stated (c. 1250) that, "money bears no fruit and that the userer sells time which is common to all".

The Protestant Reformation, and the rise of modern capitalism, produced acceptance in the western world that there could be a 'just price' for money; a 'time value' of money; so that man should receive his "fair share of the profits, according to the degree in which God has blessed him by whom the money is used" (W. Aimes, *De Conscientia et eius iure vel Casibus* (1630). Jeremy Bentham argued in 1787 in his *Defense of Usury* that lending money was a trade like any other and William Blackstone argued that "unless money . . . can be borrowed, trade cannot be carried on: and if no premium were allowed to the hire of money, few persons would care to lend it" (*Commentaries on the Laws of England* vol. ii. p. 456, 1776). In modern commerce it is accepted that Mammon (or at least Caesar) should have rendered to him, by one who receives a pecuniary advantage, an equal and real advantage: not a diminutive thereof.

In the UK various statutes were passed prohibiting the charging of usury, which usually meant an interest rate above a given limit. These statutes were repealed by the Usury Laws Repeal Act 1854. The majority of mortgage loans can now bear interest at a rate of interest that is freely agreed between the parties. However, the court has power to examine and, if considered appropriate, set aside a mortgage agreement that is considered to constitute an **unconscionable bargain** or to have been made by the use of **undue influence**. On the other hand, the court does not upset a mortgage transaction simply because it appears unreasonable – Knightsbridge Estates Trust Ltd. *v* Bryne [1939] Ch. 441. If the interest rate is not stipulated in a mortgage agreement the court has power to fix a rate. For a consumer credit loan the court may also reopen an 'extortionate credit bargain' in order to do justice between the parties when the borrower is an individual (but not a corporation), i.e. a credit bargain that requires a payment that is "grossly exorbitant" or "grossly contravenes ordinary principles of fair dealing". In deciding whether the bargain is extortionate regard is had to such matters as (a) prevailing interest rates at the time the credit bargain was made; (b) factors relating to the debtor such as his or her age, experience, business capacity, state of health, and any financial pressure to take the loan; (c) factors relating to the creditor such as risk, relationship to the debtor, any special cash benefit attached to the loan; and (d) any other factor that might reasonably have affected the parties to the transaction (Consumer Credit Act 1974, ss. 137-140). The 1974 Act does not apply to building societies, local authorities and any body named in the Consumer Credit (Exempt Agreements) Order 1980. Those offering loans are normally required to make it clear what the true or **annual percentage rate** charged for credit is, taking into account such factors as the arrangements for the repayment of principal, revision of the interest rate and commission or discount charges (Consumer Credit Act 1974, s. 20(1); Consumer Credit (Total Charge for Credit) Regulations 1980).

In the US, most states had laws fixing the maximum rate of interest that could be charged; frequently at levels of 5 or 10 per cent. Such laws have been scaled down and 'usury laws' now apply only to loans to private individuals, in particular loans in the secondary mortgage market or for consumer credit. Most major institutions, including savings and loan associations, are excluded from these laws and are subject to separate state regulation. However, laws requiring clear disclosure of the terms of mortgage loans to private individuals and small businesses and to protect the borrower from moneylenders or 'loan sharks', are becoming more prevalent. See also *antichrèse*, **penalty**, **truth-in-lending laws**, *vivum vadium*. *Commercial and Consumer Credit: An Introduction*, by Audrey L. Diamond (1982).
The Scholastic Analysis of Usury, by John T. Norman Jr, (1957).
Modern Mortgage Law and Practice,

by R. Kratovil and R.J. Werner (1982).

usus (L)
usage. See **usufructuary**.

usus fructus (L)
'The use of the fruits'; **usufruct**. In the civil law, the right to enjoy the fruits and benefits of a thing, without impairing its substance.

utile (domain) (F)
use and enjoyment (of real property).

utilisation (F)
(*plan d'utilisation du terrain* – land use plan. See also *Plan d'Occupation des Sols*).

utilité (F)
utility; purpose.
(*expropriation pour cause d'utilité publique* - expropriation for a public purpose).

utility
1. Capable, or the quality, of being of **use**. The ability of property to satisfy a particular need or want, especially in a given situation and over a given period of time. Capable of being used beneficially either directly or as a substitute. See also **value**.
2. see **public utility**.

utility easement (US)
see **easement, wayleave**.

utility room (US)
A room in a dwelling-house used as a laundry, child's playroom, for the storage of machinery, of for any similar purpose.

utmost good faith
A principle which demands that the parties to certain types of contract should act openly and in all good conscience to one another. A party to a contract of utmost good faith, *uberrimae fidei*, must not supress facts that are material to the contract, nor fail to disclose facts that subsequently are known to have an adverse effect on the essential terms of the contract. A requirement that goes beyond the need for **good faith** as expected of many contracts. It demands a complete disclosure of facts or circumstances that are known to only one of the parties and might have influenced the other party's decision to enter into the contract. Contracts of **insurance** are the most important contracts of utmost good faith; "It has been for centuries in England the law in connection with insurance of all sorts, marine, fire, life, guarantee and every kind of policy that, as the underwriter knows nothing and the man who comes to ask him to insure knows everything, it is the duty of the assured, the man who desires to have the policy, to make a full disclosure to the underwriters without being asked of all the material circumstances, because the underwriters know nothing and the assured knows everything. This is expressed by saying that it is a contract of the utmost good faith, *uberrimae fidei* – Rozanes *v* Bowen (1928) 3 Ll. L. Rep. 102. Further, "... the proper question is whether any particular circumstance was in fact material, and not whether the party believed it to be so ... It will be in the interest of the assured to make a full and fair disclosure of all the information within their reach" – Lindenau *v* Desborough (1828) 8 B and C 592. An ordinary contract of **guarantee** is not one that requires 'utmost good faith' – Seaton *v* Heath, Seaton *v* Burnard [1899] 1 QB 792. A contract that requires such disclos-

ure is voidable at the option of the 'deceived' party, but it is not void. Contracts to subscribe for shares in a newly floated company; contracts between partners; contracts by which a party acts as surety; and contracts involving arrangements between members of a family, require a degree of honesty of intent that makes them akin to contracts of utmost good faith. See also **misrepresentation, voidable contract**.

V

vacancy allowance

An allowance or discount made when estimating the projected income from a property investment, or a proposed development, to take account of the anticipated loss of income due to vacant, but rentable, units. This allowance may be expressed as a ratio or a percentage of the total projected income. Called also a 'vacancy factor'.

cf. **vacancy rate**. See also **effective gross income**.

vacancy allowance ratio

see **vacancy allowance**.

vacancy clause

A clause in an insurance policy which enables the insured to leave a property **vacant** for a stipulated period of time without prejudicing the insurance cover. Called also a 'vacancy permit', especially when such a right is granted after the policy has been effected.

vacancy factor

see **vacancy allowance**.

vacancy permit

see **vacancy clause**.

vacancy rate

The ratio of the number of vacant units, or the area of vacant space, in a property to the total number of units, or total area of the property.

cf. **occupancy rate**, **vacancy allowance**.

vacant

Empty; devoid of occupation or use. A vacant property generally is one that is **unoccupied** and has been left

so for a reasonable period of time, especially when all the furniture and personal goods have been removed. In insurance, a 'vacant' property is one left empty with no immediate intention of reoccupation; thus, the term implies a degree of **abandonment** – Foley *v* Sonoma County Farmers' Mutual Fire Insurance Co. of Sonoma, Cal. App. 108 P. 2d 939.

The owner of a property that is left vacant may be subject to a liability to pay rates if there is **rateable occupation** (for example, if it is kept furnished); or, even when there is no rateable occupation, if the local authority exercises its right to levy a rate on an unoccupied property – General Rate Act 1967, s. 17. See also **vacant possession**.

vacant (F)

vacant.

(*bien vacant* – ownerless property). See also *res nullius*.

vacant land

Land without buildings or land that is not put to any use. See also **unimproved land, waste land**.

vacant possession

The right to the free unimpeded enjoyment of physical or actual **possession. Vacant** and available for use and occupation for an intended purpose. 'Possession' of land may be satisfied by the receipt of a right to the rents and profits; but "the phrase 'vacant possession' is no doubt generally used in order to make it clear that what is being sold is not an interest in reversion", i.e. it is not subject to any form of tenancy. And, "subject to the rule *de minimis* a vendor who leaves property of his own on the premises on completion cannot, in our opinion, be said to give vacant possession, since by doing so he is claiming a right to use the premises for his own purposes" – Cumberland Consolidated Holdings Ltd *v* Ireland [1946] KB 269, 271; Cook *v* Taylor [1942] Ch. 349. A vendor who contracts to sell a property with vacant possession must take all necessary steps to eject those not lawfully in possession and must remove any rubbish or furniture from the premises, unless the contract for sale indicates that something less will be accepted by the purchaser – Topfell Ltd *v* Galley Properties Ltd [1979] 1 WLR 447.

vacantia bona (L)
  see ***bona vacantia.***

vadium (L)
  In the civil law, a **pledge** or security. A pawn or pledge of a chattel, especially by **bailment**. See also ***mortuum vadium***, ***vivum vadium***.

vaine pâture (F)
  common land. Also in French law a right to graze land after a crop has been harvested until it is prepared for resowing.
  (*droit de parcours et vaine pâture* – common right of pasture)
  See also **enclosure**.

valeur (F)
  1. **value; worth**. asset.
  (*valeur à neuf* – **replacement cost**; replacement value)
  (*valeur actuelle* – **present value**; real value)
  (*valeur actualisée* – **capitalised value**; net asset value)
  (*valeur comptable* – **book value**)

(*valeur d'achat* – cost price)
(*valeur de l'actif* – **asset value**)
(*valeur de liquidation* – **break-up value**)
(*valeur de rachat* – **surrender value**)
(*valeur d'usage* – **going-concern value**)
(*valeur hypothécaire* – **mortgage value**)
(*valeur intrinsèque* – **instrinsic value** asset value)
(*valeur locative* – **rental value**)
(*valuer négotiable* – **market value**)
(*valeur nominale* – **nominal value; face value**)
(*valeur présente* – current value; realisable value)
(*valeur résiduelle* – **residual value**; net book value; scrap value)
(*valeur unitaire* – assessment, of a property value; rateable value)
(*valeur vénale* – **market value**; actual cash value; commercial value)
(*mettre en valeur* – to open up for development).

valeurs (F)
  securities; investments; shares; **value**.
  (*valeurs de tout repos*; *valeurs de père de famille* – gilt edged investment)
  (*valeurs au pair* – **par value**)
  (*valeurs immobilières* – real property shares)
  (*valeurs immobilisées* – fixed assets).

valid agreement
  see **contract**.

valid planning consent
  see **planning permission**.

valuable consideration
  see **consideration**.

valuable improvement
  An **improvement** to a property which adds permanent value, as distin-

guished from temporary work or a minor improvement that does not provide any benefit to the property or that can readily be removed. In the event that an improvement made to a property is claimed as an act of **part performance**, in general, that improvement should be substantial and add value to the property to which the claim relates. See also **compensation for improvements**.

valuation

The act or process of determining the **value** or **worth** of something. An **assessment** of the **market value** of a property, at a given point in time. The market price of monetary consideration placed on something as a determination of its value or worth. (Valuation differs from placing a price on a property in that the latter does not always afford a true measure of value, whereas the former is intended to do so. A price may be placed on a property as a result of an objective assessment, whereas a valuation remains a matter of subjective appraisal.) A valuation is a process normally carried out by an **expert** or **valuer** using his or her skill, experience and comparatively objective view of the subject property.

A valuation of a property may be made for a number of purposes, such as for (i) investment; (ii) sale by private treaty; (iii) compulsory purchase; (iv) insurance; (v) probate; (vi) a rating assessment or other property tax levy; (vii) an estimate of the going-concern value of a company; or (viii) a mortgage loan security. The value may differ depending on the purpose for which it is required. An insurance valuation may assess the cost of reinstatement of a property, whereas a valuation for sale may assess the 'open' market value.

A valuation may be made using a number of methods or approaches, in particular: (a) the comparative or **comparison method**; (b) the income or **investment method**; (c) the reinstatement or **replacement method**; (d) the **residual method**; (e) the **profits method**. More than one method of valuation may be used for any given property and the method used may vary depending on the purpose of the valuation. In the US, the term valuation is used usually to refer to the assessment of value for taxation purposes; otherwise the term **appraisal** is used. See also **before-and-after method of valuation, compensation, rating valuation, valuation report**.
A Guide to Institutional Property, by Angus P.J. McIntosh and Stephen G. Sykes, pp. 187–218 (1985).
Introduction to Valuation, by David Richmond, 2 edn.
An Introduction to Property Valuation, by A.F. Millington, 2 edn.
Complete Valuation Practice, by N.E. Mustoe, H. Brian Eve and Bryan Anstey, 5 edn.
The Valuation of Property Investments, by Nigel Enever, 3 edn.
Valuation: Principles into Practice, by W.H. Rees (ed.), 2 edn.
Guidance Notes on the Valuation of Assets, RICS, 2 edn.
Valuation and Investment Appraisal by Clive Darlow (ed.), (1983).
Modern Methods of Valuation, by William Britton, Keith Davies and Tony Johnson, 7 edn.
Property Valuation Handbook, by N. Stratton (ed.), (1979).

valuation by abstraction (US)
see **abstraction approach**.

valuation certificate

A formal certificate, signed by an expert or qualified **valuer**, stating the estimated value of a property. The certificate may be a separate document but is incorporated normally in a formal **valuation report**. In either case the certificate should state the valuer's qualification; outline details of the subject property; and state any factors that have a direct bearing on the valuation, such as planning or zoning consents. In the US, called usually a 'certificate of appraisal'. See also **appraisal report**.

valuation date

1. The date at which a valuation is placed on a property, i.e. the date applicable to a **valuation certificate**. In the US, referred to usually as the 'appraisal date'.

2. The date at which the value of a property is determined for the purpose of assessing **compulsory purchase compensation**. When **market value** is the basis for the assessment of compensation the date is either (a) the date when compensation is agreed or the date of a Lands Tribunal award; or (b) the date the acquiring authority takes possession, whichever is the earlier. When cost of **equivalent reinstatement** is the basis, the valuation date is the earliest practicable date at which reinstatement is possible or the date the authority takes possession, whichever is the earlier – Birmingham Corporation *v* West Midland Baptist (Trust) Association (Inc.) [1970] AC 874. See also **notice to treat**.

3. In rating, the date on which the **valuation list** comes into effect and, therefore, the base date used to determine the rateable value of a property. See also **tone of the list**.

valuation list

A list maintained, as a statutory requirement by a local authority in England and Wales, that is responsible for the collection of rates. The list provides details of each **hereditament** in its area of application and the **rateable value** of those hereditaments. It is prepared and kept up to date by the **valuation officer** of the Inland Revenue (Valuation List Rules 1972). A completely new valuation list should be prepared every five years and submitted to the appropriate rating authority for implementation (although this quinquennial revaluation frequently has been postponed). Once brought into effect the valuation list may not be changed, in respect of any individual property, except by a **proposal** submitted by an "aggrieved person" or by the **valuation officer** (General Rate Act 1967, ss. 67 and 68). The valuation list is available for inspection by members of the public at the offices of the local **rating authority**. Commonly called the 'rating list'. See also **tone of the list**.

Ryde on Rating, 13 edn., pp. 660–768.

Encyclopaedia of Rating – Law and Practice by Harry B. Sales (ed.) paras. 2–162 to 2–217.

valuation officer (VO)

An employee of the Commissioners of Inland Revenue who, *inter alia*, assesses the rateable value of properties for local authorities to enable the authority to collect rates on those properties. The valuation officer is responsible for the preparation and amendment of the **valuation list**. A valuation officer may be called also to give **expert** evidence before a local valuation court or the Lands Tribunal on the rateable value of a property in the officer's area of responsibility.

valuation report

A statement of the facts and opinions that have guided a **valuer** when assessing the worth of a property. The report sets out details of all data and information collated by the valuer, as well as setting out the basis for his opinion of value. In particular, it provides details of location; socioeconomic facts; a description of the property: its type, accommodation, condition and any such factor that especially affects its value; tenure; services or public utilities; town planning details; and for an investment property, details of occupiers, rental income, outgoings, etc. The report should state also the purpose of the valuation, give comparable valuation information, and conclude with a **valuation certificate** signed by the valuer. In the US, this type of report is called an **appraisal report**.

Pleased to Report by T.B. Stapleton (1983).
Real Estate Valuation Reports and Appraisals, by R.T.W. Whipple (ed.), (1984).

valuation table

A mathematical table that sets out a number of different factors to be used in the **investment method of valuation**. These tables provide figures for such factors as an **amount of one**; an **amount of one per period**; a **present value of one**; a **present value of one per period**; a **years' purchase** factor; a **mortgage constant**; an **equated yield**; an **Ellwood factor**; and life expectancy. The most frequently used books of tables are:-

i) Parry's Valuation and Conversion Tables, 10 edn., (1978);
ii) Financial Publishing Company Tables, edited by J.J. Mason (1981);
iii) Ellwood's Tables for Real Estate Appraising and Financing, 4 edn. (1977);
iv) Rose's Property Valuation Tables (constituting the 34 edn., of INWOOD's tables) (1975);
v) Bowcock Property Valuation Tables (1978).

Referred to also as a 'capitalisation table'. See also **interest table**.
Handbook of Mortgage Mathematics and Financial Tables, by Paul Goebel and Norman Miller (1981).
Modern Methods of Valuation, 7 edn, Ch. 8.
The Valuation of Property Investment, by Nigel Enever, 3 edn, Ch. 6.

valuator (US)
see **appraiser**.

value

1. That which is good or desirable, or the result of owning or using something that is good or desirable in itself. The relative benefit or satisfaction to be derived from something; either (a) by use or possession – its intrinsic good or usefulness; or (b) by exchange for something else – its extrinsic advantage or price. A subjective assessment of the merit, desirability, **worth** or **utility** of a property at any point in time. The word value has a variety of meanings according to the context; "it is not a crystal, transparent and unchanged; it is the skin of living thought, and may vary greatly in colour and content according to the circumstances and the time in which it is used" – Oliver Wendell

Holmes in Towne *v* Eisner, 245 US 418. In economics, value is given two meanings; it "sometimes expresses the utility of some particular object, and sometimes the power of purchasing other goods which the possession of that object conveys. The one may be called 'value in use'; the other 'value in exchange' *Wealth of Nations*, by Adam Smith, Book I, Ch. 4 (1776).

The value of a commodity at any point in time, is a function (i.e. depends on) four factors: (i) utility – its ability to satisfy human wants or to be of use to someone (especially 'marginal utility' i.e. the extra benefit to be derived from one more unit of the commodity, which in turn is a function, but normally an inverse function, of how much we already possess); (ii) scarcity – the inadequacy of the available quantity to meet demand, i.e. the supply relative to the desire for it; (iii) taste – the total quantity of the commodity that is preferred; (iv) transferability – the ease with which a commodity, or other commodities, may be converted or made available to provide a suitable substitute for the subject commodity. Alternatively value is governed by demand, which depends on the amount a consumer wishes to pay for the commodity (the price), the price of all substitute commodities, the total level of consumer income, and consumer tastes or preferences; and supply, which depends on the profitability of producing more of the commodity, the ability to produce substitutes, the price of the factors of production (i.e. the cost of land, labour and capital) required to increase the available quantity of commodity and producer tastes or preferences. Value is not dependent on any one factor, nor

even a group of factors, but on an interaction of objective and subjective, intrinsic and extrinsic, and determinable and determining factors. To Karl Marx the dominant factor is labour; "all commodities are only definite masses of congealed labour time" (*Das Kapital*, Pt. 1. Ch. 1 p. 1). To Stanley Jevons "value depends entirely on utility" (*Theory of Political Economy*, 4 edn., Ch. 1 p. 1). To Alfred Marshall it is "relative and expresses the relationship between two things at a particular place and time" (*Principles of Economics*, 7 edn., Book II, Ch. 2 p. 61). And to a modern real estate investor it is primarily a function of the total income or return that can be obtained from a property in the future; or the power that the ownership of the property represents as a medium of exchange, either for other property or for **money**.

The intrinsic factors that may affect the value of real estate include topography, soil, plot size and shape, improvements, utilities or services, title, property rights and interests. The extrinsic factors include accessibility, location, climate, zoning or land use planning, taxation, building restrictions, consumer preferences. When considering the 'value in use' the intrinsic factors may dominate; when considering the 'value in exchange' the extrinsic factors may dominate. In the final analysis the value of a plot of land or building, at any point in time, depends on the interreaction of these factors as assessed by individual wants and needs. A plot of land may be readily accessible, level, zoned for offices and in a tax free area but have little or no value if no one needs it; but it may be irregularly shaped, unsuitable for building, be held on a short lease but have a premium or **nuisance value** because it provides access to a major development site.

Value may have different meanings, even for the same property, according to the context or the use of the word. For example, to a landowner it may mean **market value**, or **replacement value**; to a mortgagee, **loan value**; to a tenant, **rental value** or **annual value**; to an insurer, **insurable value**; to a shareholder of a company, **asset value** or **going-concern value** and to an occupier who is liable for a property tax, **assessed value** or **rateable value**. However, unless qualified or varied by the context, value in real estate normally means market value. See also **book value**, **capital value**, **cash value**, **current use value**, **economic rent**, **fair market value**, **going-concern value**, **hope value**, **investment value**, **mortgage value**, **par value**, **present value**, **residual value**, **valuation**.

The Appraisal of Real Estate, AIREA, 8 edn., pp. 33–39.

2. In English land law 'value' is used as an abbreviation for valuable **consideration**; something of economic value that is given to support a simple contract. Thus in the phrase 'purchase for value' it means **money** or **money's worth** or a promise made in consideration of a future marriage; even if the amount is not equivalent to the full worth of that which is received. Good consideration (e.g. natural love and affection) or a promise made in respect of a past marriage is not value and, therefore, will not make a promise enforceable.

In the US, value may be said to be given "(a) in return for a binding commitment to extend credit ... or (b) as security for or in total or partial satisfaction of a pre-existing claim; or (c) by accepting delivery pursuant to a pre-existing contract for purchase; or (d) generally in return for any consideration sufficient to support a simple contract." (United States Uniform Commercial Code, (1972) para. 1–201(44)). See also **bona fide purchaser**.

value added tax (VAT)
A form of sales tax charged on the supply, by way of business or enterprise, of goods and services and on the importation of goods and services. VAT is payable by any entity that is subject to its liability (a 'taxable person') and therefore must be registered as such. It is payable on the supply of goods and services in the course or furtherance of any business, unless the supply is relieved from such liability. It is levied at each stage of the manufacturing, producing or selling of goods, or the provision of services, by way of a percentage of the increased value of the goods or services brought about by the business activity. It is levied in such a way that the tax is paid ultimately by the final 'consumer' as a percentage increase on the purchase price of the goods or services. The person adding value at each stage is the effective collector of the tax because that 'taxable person' charges tax on the increased value of goods or services supplied by him in the course of business and then accounts to the appropriate authority. VAT was first introduced in France in 1954 and was introduced in Britain in 1973 under the Finance Act 1972.

In the UK each taxable person, at

the end of a prescribed accounting period, deducts from the tax he has charged on goods or services supplied by him (his 'output tax') the tax he has paid on goods or services supplied to him for the purpose of his business (his 'input tax'). He is accountable then, or he may reclaim input tax paid on goods or services which he will have paid to suppliers to his business, through the Commissioners of Customs and Excise. The supply of goods or services may be (a) taxed at the standard rate (as fixed from year to year – 1986 at 15 per cent); (b) exempt; or (c) zero-rated. If a good or service is exempt the taxable person does not charge VAT on the item supplied but he cannot recover the input tax which he has paid. If the good or service is zero rated the taxable person calculates his output tax at zero and is entitled to recover the input tax he has paid.

The grant, assignment or surrender of any interest in, or right over, or any licence to occupy land (including buildings) is in general exempt (Finance Act 1972, Sch. 5 Gp. 1 as amended). There are exceptions to this rule, notably in the case of a builder who sells a building on land held freehold or on a lease for a term exceeding 21 years; in that case the transaction is zero-rated. The supply of services in the course of construction, reconstruction, or demolition of a building, or in the course of any civil engineering work, is zero-rated. These services exclude those of an architect, surveyor, engineer or any person acting as a consultant or in a similar capacity. Repairs, maintenance and most alterations to a building are subject to the standard rate of tax. An individual who builds a new house or garage may be able to reclaim VAT on goods used for that purpose. Rent received for accommodation is exempt or in some cases zero-rated, but a charge for repair, maintenance and any other services charge (when charged to the tenant separately rather than for a building as a whole is subject to VAT at the standard rate. The cost of an insurance premium for a building or its contents is exempt.

In France *la taxe sur la valeur ajoutée* (TVA) is payable by any person who carries on an independent commercial or industrial activity i.e. by most self-employed persons and legal entities. It is payable on delivery of most 'movable tangible property', i.e. the transfer of the ownership of goods whether by wholesale or retail. Services and imports also are subject to TVA, but exports are not. Property dealers, developers and those who act as intermediaries for the sale or purchase of buildings, businesses or shares in building companies pay an output tax based on their gross profit margin at a rate of 20 per cent; building contractors pay TVA at a rate of 17.6 per cent for most of their transactions; and those who are involved in the sale, letting or erection of a new building may be entitled to a reduced rate of TVA on the sale of the building-land element of a transaction. A person who leases land or buildings is subject normally to TVA. *VAT on property transactions*, by Stewart Urry, I, II, III, IV & V, 264, EG 230, 231, 518, 520, 904, 905; 265 EG 113, 114, 375, 378 (1982–83).
VAT on Construction and Development Work, by Philip S.D. King (1984).
Taxation of Land Transactions, by A.R. Mellows, 3 edn., pp. 17–186.

Value Added Tax, by Hugh Main Price (1978).
Land and Tax Planning, by Patrick C. Soares, 2 edn., pp. 217–252.
VAT Guide, by David D. Relf and Christopher A.L. Preston, (1981).
Tolley's Value Added Tax (annual).
Tolley's VAT Planning (Annual).
Encyclopaedia of Value Added Tax, by G.S.A. Wheatcroft and J.F. Avery Jones (updated).
Butterworth's Orange Tax Handbook, pp. 3001–3413 (1985–86).
De Voile's Value Added Tax, 1972 (updated).

value before-and-after taking (US)
see **before-and-after valuation**.

value-cost contract
A building contract which provides that the amount payable to the contractor as his fee or profit is in inverse proportion to the cost of the building work, i.e. he receives a higher profit the lower the total cost to the employer. See also **cost-plus reimbursement contract**.

value date
The date upon which a transfer of money becomes effective or a credit instrument becomes available for use as ready cash. From a given value date the recipient is able to earn interest on the money or use the cash.

value-in-use
1. see **cost-in-use, use value, value**.
(US) 2. see **equivalent reinstatement**.

valued policy
An **insurance policy** in which the amount to be paid in the event of total loss is an agreed sum as stipulated in the contract, without any assumed allowance for depreciation or appreciation. The stipulated figure is taken to be the true value of the subject matter of the policy or to be the amount of **liquidated damages** payable in the event of loss. The value placed on the subject-matter is binding between the parties and the insured does not have to prove the figure (except in the event of fraud, gross overvaluation or mistake). In the event of partial loss the insurer only pays for the actual loss suffered. This form of policy is not used generally for the insurance of real estate. In most states in the US valued policies are illegal, but in some states fire insurance policies are treated as valued policies if the policy refers to an insured value.
cf. **unvalued policy**. See also **first-loss insurance**.
The Law of Insurance, by Raoul Colinvaux, 4 edn., pp. 8–9.
General Principles of Insurance Law, by E.R. Hardy Ivamy, 4 edn., pp. 228–229.

valuer
A person who determines the worth of something; an **expert** who assesses the **value** of property. Someone who provides professionally a service by undertaking the **valuation** of properties. A valuer is an acknowledged expert in his field; "The term 'Valuer' (with a capital 'V' at any rate) is used nowadays to denote a member of a recognised profession comprising persons possessed of skill or experience in assessing the market price of a property, particularly real property" – Sudbrook Trading Estate Ltd v Eggleton and Another (1982) 265 EG 217. He or she is expected to exercise a reasonable degree of care and attention in collating and assessing the factors that are relevant to the subject

matter under consideration; the valuer's duty extends beyond merely "going and looking at the place". The valuer's ultimate conclusion as to the value of a property is a matter of opinion; he or she may be optimistic or pessimistic and accordingly be permitted that degree of latitude which is commensurate with the nature of the task. "The law does not require any man, valuer ... or any other expert agent to be perfect ... there is no absolute rule as regards the proper methods of ascertaining the value ... [if the methods of ascertaining the value in a particular case] are not perfect, if they are not the best, if they might have been improved upon, still [they] are methods which a man of position, endeavouring to do his duty, might fairly adopt without being said to be wanting in reasonable care and skill" – Lowe *v* Mack (1905) 92 LT 349, 350; a valuer "cannot be faulted for achieving a result which does not admit some degree of error" Singer and Friedlander Ltd. *v* John D. Wood and Co (1977) 243 EG 212. (It has been suggested that a latitude of ten per cent is reasonable, but twenty per cent leaves something to be desired.) However, a valuer of real property must assemble all those factors – planning, building construction, legal constraints, area measurements, special situations etc. – that might have a bearing on his final figure; such facts as he ought to know or have ascertained; and he should draw his client's attention to these factors, and any other matters that have affected his opinion of value – Old Gate Estates Ltd *v* Toplis [1939] 3 All ER 209. In the US, this person is called usually an **appraiser** or a 'valuator'. (Although in common usage)

an appraiser may be distinguished from a valuer as the former not only assesses the price or value of a property but may assess also its quality, worth or excellence.) See also **chartered surveyor**, **mortgage value**, **professional negligence**, **valuation report**. 49 Halsbury's Laws of England, 4 edn, paras. 1–17.
Valuers: A study on Professional Liability, by North, 29 Conv. 186, 275 (1965).

variable-amortisation mortgage (VAM)
see **variable-payment mortgage**.

variable operating expenses (US)
An **operating expense** that is directly related to the use and occupation of the building to which it relates.
cf. **fixed expense**.

variable-payment mortgage (VPM)
A mortgage loan in which the repayments of **principal** vary during the term of the loan; in particular, a mortgage which provides for the payments of principal in the early term of the loan to be below those required by an **amortisation mortgage**. Later payments are correspondingly higher than those required by an amortisation mortgage. A term commonly applied to a mortgage on a residential property when repayments are lower in the earlier years to assist first-time buyers; for example, when no capital repayment is required in the first five years. When the payments of capital are increased at fixed stages this form of mortgage may be termed a 'graduated-payment mortgage'. Called also a 'variable-amortisation mortgage', or a 'flexible-payment mortgage'.
cf. **variable-rate mortgage**. See also **deferred-payment mortgage**.

variable-rate mortgage (VRM)

A mortgage loan granted at a rate of **interest** that varies during the term of the loan. The rate may be varied in line with an autonomous interest rate, such as a rate determined from time to time by market conditions, e.g. a bank rate or 'prime rate'; or as expressly specified in the mortgage agreement, as when the rate is reduced during the initial term of the loan to assist the borrower in making the necessary payments and increased during the later period to compensate. In the latter instance if the rate varies at set stages during the period of the loan the arrangement may be called a 'graduated-rate mortgage' or if the rate may be varied as agreed between the parties, or as determined by the lender from time to time, a 'renegotiable-rate mortgage' or an 'adjustable-rate mortgage'.

cf. **variable-payment mortgage**. See also **price-level adjusted mortgage, roll-over mortgage, step-rate mortgage**.

variable (or varying) rent

A **rent** that may be changed by one of the parties (usually the landlord), or that varies according to a predetermined formula, during the term of a lease. See also **graded rent, graduated rent, indexed rent, rent review, turnover rent**.

variance

1. The difference in a project or scheme between a standard or budget cost and the comparable actual cost incurred.

(US) 2. A permitted change in a **zoning ordinance**. A zoning variance is intended to provide flexibility with zoning ordinances, especially when "a literal enforcement of the ordinance will result in unnecessary hardship, so that the spirit of the ordinance shall be served and substantial justice done." (U.S. Department of Commerce, Standard State Zoning Enabling Act 1926, para. 7). A variance may take the form of an 'area variance' by which the dimensional requirements of the ordinance are altered or waived, or a 'use variance' by which a different user is permitted. A variance is authorised normally by a 'board of adjustment' or 'board of zoning appeal' established by the local municipality for the purpose of considering requests for variances. An appeal against the decision of a board of adjustment may be made to a court of law.

variation of a contract

see **accord and satisfaction, discharge, estoppel, waiver**.

variation order

An order made under a **building contract** requiring a modification or variation to the terms of the contract; in particular, an order requiring an alteration to the quantity or quality of the work or a condition under which the work is carried out. The order is given normally by the **architect** (as an 'architect's instruction'), on behalf of the employer, and usually permits the contractor to request a modification of the contract price. A properly executed and written variation order should be the only means of altering any part of a building contract. A variation order may be made verbally on site but should be confirmed by a written order submitted at the earliest date thereafter and this order should be copied to all professional advisors directly concerned with the contract. Called, especially in the US, a 'change

order'. See also **waiver**.
The Architect's Guide to Running a Job, by Ronald Green, 4 edn., pp. 120–124.
Mitchell's Architectural Practice and Procedure, (1981) pp. 90–92.
The Architect in Practice, by Arthur J. Willis and W.N.B. George, 6 edn., pp. 109–117.

variations
see **variation order**.

variety store (US)
A retail store, usually on one level, that sells a wide variety of small goods, especially at a low price and by means of self-service. A variety store has a selling area usually between 1000 square metres (10000 square feet) and 8000 square metres (80000 square feet). Called sometimes a 'bazaar store'.
cf. **department store, specialty store**. See also **discount store**.

varying rent
see **variable rent**.

vendee
One who acquires property, especially real property. More commonly called a 'buyer' (of goods) or a 'purchaser' (of land). See also **purchase**.

vendeur (F)
vendor.
(*vendeur aux enchères* – auctioneer).

vendition
The act of selling.

vendor
One who sells property or offers property for **sale**; particularly real estate. (In English law, a **lessor** is not *prima facie* a vendor but is an assignor or cessor). See also **open contract, seller**.

vendor and purchaser summons
A document issued by the High Court requiring a party to a contract for the transfer of an interest in land to answer questions arising out of or connected with that contract. The summons may relate to requisitions, objects, or matters of compensation relating to the contract (but not a question relating to the validity or existence of the contract). It may be requested by the vendor or purchaser (Law of Property Act 1925, s. 49(1)).
See also **specific performance**.
42 Halsbury's Laws of England, 4 edn, paras. 229–241.

vendor's lien
see **lien**.

vente (F)
sale; selling; auction. In French law *vente* is used principally for the sale of a tangible asset or a corporeal property; the sale of a personal right or an incorporeal hereditament, including a lease, is referred to usually as *cession*.
(*vente à credit; vente à tempérament* – credit sale or **instalment sale**. If the purchaser defaults, the vendor can reclaim the property in a similar way to foreclosure under a mortgage. French law does not recognise **hire purchase** as found in English law whereby ownership is retained by the seller until the last instalment of the total consideration is paid. See also *crèdit-bail*)
(*vente à réméré* – conditional sale; such as when a sale is made with a right for the vendor to buy-back the property)
(*vente aux enchères* – sale by auction)
(*vente de gré à gré; vente à l'amiable* – sale by private treaty)
(*vente d'immeuble à construire* – sale

'off-plan', e.g. sale of a property that is to be constructed by a builder, especially individual units in a block of apartments. It may take the form of a *vente à terme* whereby the property is paid for and ownership transferred upon completion; or, a *vente en l'état futur d'achèvement* whereby the land is sold immediately and the work paid for as the building proceeds. The use of either form of contract for the sale of a residential property, as distinguished from a *vente clé en main* – sale under a 'turn-key contract', is controlled by a French Law of 3 January 1967).
(*vente forcée* – forced sale)
(*vente publique* – public sale; public auction)
(*acte de vente* – **bill of sale**)
(*agent de vente* – selling agent)
(*salle de vente* – auction room).

ventilation (F)
allocation. The apportionment of a purchase price when a single price is paid for several properties.

venture capital
see **risk capital**.

verba accipienda sunt secundum subjectum materiam (L)
'Words are to be interpreted according to the subject matter'.

verba chartarum fortius accipiuntur contra proferentem (L)
'The words of deeds are to be taken more strongly against those who chose them'. See *contra proferentem*.

verbal (F)
verbal; by word of mouth.
(*convention verbale* – oral or *simple contract*). See also *procès-verbal*.

verbal contract
A contract expressed in words,

spoken or written, but not made under seal. A contract that is written but not signed or not set down formally. An **oral contract**.

verbatim
'Word for word'; precisely.

verificateur (F)
surveyor.
See also *éxpert*.

versement (F)
payment; deposit.
(*versement à compte* – payment on account)
(*versement à titre gracieux* – ex-gratia payment)
(*versement par anticipation; versement anticipé* – payment in advance).

versus (L)
'Against'. Abbreviated to *v*. In English law when used in the name of a civil case *v* is referred to as 'and' – not *versus*.

vertical lease
see **side-by-side participation**.

vertical-slice participation
see **side-by-side participation**.

vest
1. To bestow or endow with an immediate and fixed right, privilege or authority. To confer a legal right on someone; in particular, to grant or bestow an estate, interest or right to land that is not subject to a contingency. For the purpose of the **rule against perpetuities** an estate or interest becomes vested when "(1) the person or persons, corporation or body to whom or to which it is limited is or are ascertained and in existence and capable of being an alienee; (2) the quantum of the estate and interest is ascertained; and (3) all other events

have happened to enable the estate or interest to come into possession at once, subject to the determination at anytime of the prior estates and interests." (35 Halsbury's Laws of England, 4 edn, p. 504). See also **vested interest, vesting declaration**.
Land Law: Cases and Materials, by R.H. Maudsley and E.H. Burn, 4 edn, pp. 291–293.
2. To give **seisin**; to deliver **possession**.

vested estate
    see **vested interest (or estate)**.

vested-in-interest
    see **vested interest (or estate)**.

vested-in-possession
    see **vested interest (or estate)**.

vested interest (or estate)
    1. An interest (or estate) in land that is held unconditionally; a right to possession of land that is not dependent on any contingent or uncertain event. A right that has accrued to, or is vested in, someone; as distinguished from one accompanied by an uncertainty as to whether it may or may not be acquired by someone or an uncertainty as to who will acquire that interest. An interest (or estate) that may be created at present but the right to possession is restricted to a future determinable period. For example, if an estate is conveyed to "A for life, remainder to B in fee simple", then A has a vested interest in possession (a right that is said to be 'vested-in-possession') and B a vested interest that comes into possession on the death of A. (B has an interest which during A's lifetime is said to be 'vested-in-interest' or is called a 'vested remainder'). When used by itself 'vested interest' means primarily

an interest vested-in-interest. An essential feature of a vested interest is that the person or persons entitled to the interest has been ascertained, but that, although the interest may be ready to take effect forthwith, it need not take effect until the determination of all preceeding estates and interest. "The test is always the same – is the owner absolutely entitled at the present moment to assume possession whenever it may fall vacant? If so, he owns a vested interest – he is invested with a portion of the fee simple – even though he may never obtain possession" (Cheshire's Modern Law of Real Property 13 edn). The holder of a vested interest has an interest in land that is readily saleable as compared to a **contingent interest** which may be lost, or may never arise, if the contingency arises upon which the interest depends.
cf. **inchoate interest**. See also **defeasible, remainder, rule against perpetuities, vest**.
The Law of Real Property, by Robert Megarry & H.W.R. Wade, 5 edn, p. 231 *et seq.*
2. An interest in a property, affair, or business, where the holder has a personal commitment, or is likely to receive a personal benefit from that interest. An involvement with a thing, person or body that is likely to produce a pecuniary benefit as a result of the actions of a third party. See also **arm's length transaction, undue influence**.

vested remainder
    see **remainder, vested interest**.

vesting assent
    see **vesting document**.

vesting declaration
    1. A declaration, contained in a deed

by which new trustees are appointed, to the effect that an estate or interest in trust property is to **vest**, i.e. be transferred, to the new trustees. A vesting declaration avoids the necessity for a separate conveyance for the trust property; except in the case of a mortgage, shares in a company, and a leasehold interest held subject to a covenant against assignment (Trustee Act 1925, s. 40). See also **general vesting declaration**.

2. A deed by which a local authority adopts a private sewer in order to enable the authority to carry out its responsibility for the proper provision of sewage facilities. (Public Health Act 1936, s. 17). See also **adoption**.

vesting deed

see **vesting document**.

vesting document

A formal document that confers or vests an estate or interest in land on someone. In particular, a document under seal used to transfer the **legal estate** in **settled land** to the tenant for life or statutory owner, i.e. to the person who holds the 'paper title' to land that is the subject of a **strict settlement**. A strict settlement of land is created normally by two deeds, a vesting document and a **trust instrument**; the former provides details of the title to the land and the latter sets out details of the settlement (Settled Land Act 1925, s. 4). The purpose of having separate documents is to enable a future purchaser of the land to obtain a valid title without concerning himself with the terms of the settlement – known as the 'curtain principle'.

When the settlement is made *inter vivos* (between living persons) the legal estate is conveyed by means of a 'vesting deed'. If the settlement is made by will, the **will** acts as the trust instrument and the personal representatives, after having paid any debts or death duties, are required to execute a 'vesting assent' which has the same effect as the vesting deed but need only be in writing (Settled Land Act 1925, s. 8). When settled land is vested in the tenant for life or statutory owner by order of a court, that order is called a 'vesting order'. A vesting deed, vesting assent, or a vesting order (provided the land remains settled land when the order has been made) may each be referred to as a 'vesting instrument' (1925 Act, s. 117 (1) (xxxi)).

A vesting deed (referred to in the Settled Land Act 1925 as the 'principal vesting instrument') must describe the settled land; name the trustees; name any person entitled to appoint new trustees; and describe any powers conferred on the tenant for life by the trust instrument beyond those provided by the Act. The deed must contain also a statement "that the settled land is vested in the person or persons to whom it is conveyed or in whom it is declared to be vested" (1925 Act, s. 5(1) (b)). A vesting deed is like any other **conveyance**, except that it states that there is a settlement affecting the land, and sets out such details of the settlement but no more, as may be required by the person to whom the land is conveyed. It signifies to a purchaser of the land that the purchase money must be paid to the trustees of the settlement.

Land Law: Cases and Materials, by R.H. Maudsley and E.H. Burn, 4 edn., pp. 251–255.

42 Halsbury's Laws of England, 4 edn, paras. 685–704.

vesting instrument
see **vesting document**.

vesting order
An order made by a court by which an interest in land is vested in such a person as the court considers appropriate as if a transfer of the interest had been made by a **conveyance**. A vesting order made for the purpose of vesting, conveying or creating a **legal estate** has the same effect as if it were made by the estate owner of the interest to which it relates (Law of Property Act 1925, s. 9). The Trustees Act 1925, ss. 44–56 sets out a number of instances in which the High Court may make such an order: for example, when it is necessary to transfer a legal estate to trustees because land has been granted as security for a mortgage to an infant or a person under a disability; when there is no personal representative of a deceased trustee; or in any other case where a court appoints, or has appointed, a trustee. See also **vesting document**.

vesture of land
Everything (other than trees) that is growing on land; "he who has the vesture of land has a right, generally, to exclude others from entering upon the **superficies** of the soil" (Co. Litt. 4b). See also **seisin**.

vétusté (F)
decay; wear and tear; depreciation.

viability study
see **feasibility study**.

viager (f.-ère) (F)
life.
(*propriété* or *bien viagère* – **life interest**)
(*rente viagère* – **life annuity**).

vi, clam, precario (L)
see *nec vi, nec clam, nec precario*.

vi et armis (L)
'By force of arms'. See **trespass**.

vicarious liability
An indirect legal liability; a liability for a **tort** committed by another, even though the person made liable is not directly culpable or is not a party to the tort. Vicarious liability normally arises from the relationship of employer (or master) and an employee (or servant) because the servant's acts, when carried out as part of his duties of employment, are considered as the acts of the master – *qui facit per alium facit per se*. The employee also may be liable for his acts, but a wronged person may prefer to claim against the employer. A person is liable for the tort of another if the former is able to control the method by which the latter performs his duties; but, in general, there is no similar liability for the acts of an **independent contractor** because, by definition, the contractor has a wide discretion as to how he acts. "It is trite law that an employer who employs an independent contractor is not vicariously liable for the **negligence** of that contractor. He is not able to control the way in which the independent contractor does the work, and the vicarious liability of a master for the negligence of his servant does not arise under the relationship of employer and independent contractor." – Salsbury v Woodland [1970] 1 QB 336. A similar liability may arise between a **principal** and his **agent**, the principal being liable if a relationship akin to master and servant exists but not if the relationship is that of employer and independent contractor. Such a liability may occur when the principal is aware of the facts put

forward by his agent and lets him make a **misrepresentation**, or a defamatory statement about a rival agent, to a prospective purchaser – Colonial Mutual Life Assurance Society Ltd *v* Producers and Citizens Assurance Co. of Australia Ltd (1931) 46 CLR 41.

Law for Land Management Students, by Richard Card, John Murdoch and Peter Schofield, pp. 429–442, (1981).

The Law of Torts, by John G. Fleming, 6 edn., pp. 338–363.

Clerk and Lindsell on Torts, 15 edn., pp. 156–198.

Salmond and Heuston on the Law of Torts, 18 edn., p. 425 *et seq.*

Winfield and Jalowicz on Tort, 12 edn., pp. 571–603.

Vicarious Liability in the Law of Torts, by P.S. Atiyah, 9 edn.

vicarious performance

1. The **performance** of all or part of a contractual obligation by a person who is not a party to a contract e.g. by a sub-contractor. See also **main contractor**.

2. An action carried out by a company using a human or mechanical agent. A company, being a intangible entity, must act through a tangible body, i.e. it acts vicariously; and thus may be 'vicariously liable' for its actions. See also **vicarious liability**.

vice

A defect or fault in something. See also **inherent defect**.

vice (F)

fault; defect.

(*vice caché* – hidden defect)

(*vice de consentement* – contractual defect, which may include a mistake (*erreur*); fraud (*dol*); duress or undue influence (*violence*)).

(*vice latent* – latent defect)

(*vice propre, vice inhérent* – inherent defect).

vicinage

An adjoining area; part of a neighbourhood. A **right of common** available to neighbouring tenants. "Common *because of vicinage*, or neighbourhood, is where the inhabitants of two townships which lie contiguous to each other, have usually intercommoned with one another: the beasts of one straying into the other's fields without any molestation from either" (Bl. Comm. vol. ii p. 34) – Newman *v* Bennett [1980] 3 All ER 452.

videlicet (viz) (L)

'Namely; that is to say'.

vie (F)

life.

(*bail à vie* – tenancy for life).

viellisement-vétusté (F)

obsolescence.

view

To take notice by eye; but not to go as far as to survey. See also **access**, **right of light**, **valuer**.

village green

see **green**.

ville (F)

town.

(*ville nouvelle* – new town)

villeinage or villein tenure

A form of feudal **tenure** by which a tenant was granted a right to use land in return for services of a servile or menial nature rendered to his lord. The tenant or villein was not quite a slave, but was tied to the land and was bound to render lowly services to the lord of the **manor**. To the outside world he was a freeman, but he retained his right to land solely at the will of the lord. Villeinage might be 'pure villeinage' or 'base tenure' by which the tenant was obliged to do all the lord commanded; or 'privileged villeinage' or 'villein socage' by which the services were certain and determinate (Bl. Comm. vol. ii. p. 61). This tie was gradually released as the **feudal system** collapsed and labour exerted its authority; the servile duties were replaced by money payments and villeinage by copyhold. "The Black Death (1348–9) destroyed a large proportion of villein tenants of the manors, and the ensuing competition for labour amongst lords brought into being a class of labourers prepared to hire out their services to the highest bidder they could find. By the middle of the fifteenth century the mass of villein tenants no longer laboured for their lords, but paid them a fixed sum in lieu of personal service." – *An Introduction to the History of Land Law*, by A.W.B. Simpson, pp. 150–151 (1961). cf. **freehold**. See also **socage**. *The Law of Real Property*, by Robert Megarry and H.W.R. Wade, 5 edn., pp. 23–27.

vindictive damages
see **damages**.

virtual rent
The **rent** paid under a lease plus the **annual equivalent** of any improvement to the leased property carried out at the tenant's expense, i.e. the true annual cost of the property itself, excluding property taxes or similar impositions. Called also 'sitting rent' or 'true rent'.
cf. **effective rental rate, improved rent**. See also **cost-in-use, occupancy cost**.

vis major (L)
'A greater or irresistable force'. A force of nature or man that cannot be avoided by reasonable precaution, e.g. a storm, a riot. A person is not liable normally for damage caused by *vis major*. See also **act of God,** *force majeure*.

vision splay
An area of land at the junction of two highways, or at an access point to a highway, which must be kept free of buildings or obstructions to afford adequate visibility for motor vehicles crossing or entering the highway. A highway authority may require a landowner to maintain a vision splay as a condition for authorising a development that could increase the volume of traffic entering a highway. See also **planning condition**.

visitor
A person who enters onto land, or into a building, with the leave and at the invitation of the owner or occupier, usually for a particular purpose, but with no intention to stay. "A person is a 'visitor' if, at common law, he would be regarded as an **invitee** or **licensee**, or be treated as such, as for instance, a person lawfully using premises provided for use of the public (e.g. a public park) or a person entering by lawful authority (e.g. a policeman with a search warrant): But a 'visitor' does not include a person who crosses land in pursuance of a public or private right of way. Such a person was never regarded as an invitee or licensee, or treated as such" – Greenhalf *v* British Railways Board [1969] 2 All ER 117 (Occupiers' Liability Act 1957, s. 2 (6)). An occupier of land owes a "common **duty of care**" to his or her visitors, that is a "duty to

take such care as in all the circumstances of the case is reasonable to see that the visitor will be reasonably safe in using the premises for the purposes for which he is invited or permitted by the occupier to be there." (Occupier's Liability Act 1957, s. 2(2)). A duty that is higher in the case of a child, but is not necessarily owed to a trespasser. See also **negligence, trespass**.

vitium reale (L)
'Inherent defect'.

vitrine (F)
shop window; shop front.

viva voce (L)
'By word of mouth' e.g. an oral testament.

vivum vadium (L)
'A living pledge'. A form of **mortgage** by which the borrower permitted the lender to enter onto land held as security in order to take the rents and profits until the principal and interest was discharged. It was so called because the lender did not receive only interest, unlike a **mortuum vadium** or 'dead pledge'. A *vivum vadium* was intended to avoid the disdainful act of **usury** by granting a lender of money a right to the rents and profits from land in place of interest; thus, "the profits went in reduction of the debt, and it was considered to be a fair and honourable bargain" (Holdsworth's History of English Law, 3 edn, vol. iii p. 128). Once the debt was paid in full the claim to the rents and profits automatically ceased. See also **antichrèse**.

void contract
An agreement that is devoid of legal effect; a **contract** that is completely 'nul' and cannot give rise to any legal right, duty, effect or obligation. Strictly 'void contract' is a contradiction in terms, because an agreement must have legal effect to constitute a contract. A void contract follows the rule *non est factum*, 'it has not been made' and, therefore, unlike a **voidable contract** it is not a contract at all; it never came into existence as such. Whether an agreement is null and void, or 'voidable' at the option of one of the parties, does not depend on the express provision of an agreement, but on the nature of the agreement. For example, when a licence is granted permitting a person to enter onto land to cut timber and it is specified that if certain conditions are breached the agreement is "null and void" then this agreement came into effect as a binding contract, but is voidable at the option of the landowner – Jardine *v* A-G for Newfoundland [1932] AC 275. A void contract may arise because the agreement is illegal or immoral. For example, if it is made (a) with the intention of committing a crime, tort or fraud against a third party; (b) in order to hamper the course of justice; (c) by a party who does not have any capacity to contract; (d) when there is a **mistake** as to the type of agreement being entered into, e.g. contract of sale in place of an option; or (e) the subject-matter of the contract does not exist – Couturier *v* Hastie (1856) 5 HL Cas. 673. A contract that is void need not be illegal or unenforceable; it is not 'illegal' in the sense that a contract to do a prohibited or immoral act is illegal; it is not 'unenforceable' in the sense that a contract within the **Statute of Frauds** is unenforceable for want of writing. A void contract is somewhere in between; the law

simply takes no notice of it; it is "invalid and unenforceable" – Bennett *v* Bennett [1952] 1 KB 260. A contract (a) in restraint of trade; (b) that seeks to oust the jurisdiction of the courts; (c) that is prejudicial to marriage; or (d) that is otherwise contrary to public policy is void, but it is not necessarily illegal. "The appelation 'void' has also been inaccurately used to describe an initially valid contract which ceases to have effect before its expiry in normal course, either automatically, or by **election** of one of the parties after breach" (9 Halsbury's Laws of England, 4 edn, p. 83).

A court of equity may hold that a void contract is enforceable by rectifying a mistake or granting a decree of **specific performance** when the intention of the parties can be ascertained. cf. **illegal contract**. See also **champerty, equity of redemption, rectification, solus agreement**.
Anson's Law of Contract, 26 edn, pp. 17–19, 295, 590.

void trust

A **trust** that cannot be enforced because it is against the policy of the law, e.g. a trust that offends the **rule against perpetuities**. See also **resulting trust**.

voidable contract

A contract that appears valid but, due to some defect or vitiating factor, may be repudiated or avoided by one or more of the parties; although it has not been so declared. A voidable contract, unlike a **void contract**, has legal effect but it may be avoided, or accepted as valid, by the **election** of one or more of the parties. A voidable contract may arise from **misrepresentation, mistake; duress; undue influence**; when there is a breach of a requirement for **utmost good faith**; or when one of the parties is legally incapable of contracting (due to drunkeness, age, soundness of mind or statute). A voidable contract remains valid until the party who has the power to negate or aver it takes the appropriate action to rescind it, to have it set aside in a court of law, or to affirm it. If it is not rescinded within a reasonable time, or if a benefit is accepted from it, the contract may cease to be 'voidable'.
cf. **unenforceable contract**. See also **estoppel, ratification, rescission**.

voie (F)

way; road; track.
(*voie routière; voie publique* – highway)
(*voie urbaine* – street).

voirie (F)

public **highway**.
(*servitude de voirie* – highway easement).

voisinage (F)
neighbourhood.

volenti non fit injuria (L)

'That to which a man consents cannot be considered an injury'. An action for damages arising from a tort may be defeated when it can be shown that the injured party expressly or impliedly assented, in whole or in part, to the act that caused the injury, i.e. is contributorily negligent, as by "voluntarily and rashly exposing himself to injury" – Smith *v* Baker and Sons [1891] AC 325. However, merely being aware of a risk, or a willingness to take a risk, is insufficient to support this defence; there must be full and free consent to accept the risk entailed – actual and not constructive knowledge – Nettleship *v* Weston

[1971] 3 All ER 581; (Unfair Contract Terms Act 1977, s. 2(3)). Consent is not deemed to exist when there is a legal or moral duty (as by a policeman) compelling the consent (Haynes *v* Harwood [1934] 1 KB 146). See also **contributory negligence, negligence, waiver**.

voluntary conveyance
see **voluntary disposition**.

voluntary disposition
1. A conveyance or other transfer of real estate made without the transferor receiving any valuable **consideration**; e.g. a **deed of gift** but not a marriage settlement, because a marriage is valuable consideration for a transfer of property. See also **fraudulent conveyance, voluntary transfer (or sale)**.
(US) 2. A transfer of mortgaged or secured property, by the mortgagor to the mortgagee, in order to extinguish an outstanding debt without the need to resort to **foreclosure** or a public sale.

voluntary improvement
An **improvement** that is made without obligation or that adds nothing to the value of a property. An improvement made purely for adornment. cf. **repair**.

voluntary settlement
A **settlement** that is not made for money or money's worth or in consideration of a future marriage, i.e. one that is not made for 'valuable' **consideration**.

voluntary transfer (or sale)
A **transfer** made when there is no constraint on the owner of the thing sold; a sale without **duress** or compulsion. cf. **compulsory purchase, involuntary**

transfer. See also **market value, willing seller**.

voluntary trust
1. A **trust** that arises from a confidence confined in another and voluntarily accepted, as distinguished from an involuntary trust which arises by operation of law. cf. **constructive trust, resulting trust**.
2. see **living trust**.

voluntary waste
see **waste**.

volunteer
One who acquires a property without paying valuable **consideration**; one who acquires land as a **gift**.

voucher plan (US)
A method of financing construction work by which the lender advances funds directly to those who have provided labour or materials based on order (vouchers) received from the employer or a principal contractor.

vu (F)
preamble; seen.

vue et jour (F)
A right of view and light. A *vue* is an opening in a wall giving the benefit of an uninterrupted right to air and light, but which is only exercisable at certain distance from a neighbouring property. A *jour* serves as a right to admit air only (French Civil Code, arts. 676–679).
(*droit de vue* – ancient light)
See also *jour*.
Précis Dalloz. *Droit Civil, Les Biens* (Alex Weill) 2 edn, pp. 105–106.
Droit Civil, Les Biens, by Jean Carbonnier, 11 edn., pp. 228–229.
Droit Civil, by Gabriel Marty and Pierre Raynaud, vol. ii, pp. 292–295 (1965).

W

'wait and see' rule
see **rule against perpetuities**.

waiver
The act of voluntarily giving up, or of intentionally relinquishing, a claim, benefit or interest. The unilateral **renunciation** of a remedy against a tort, or a right under a contract. The making of a concession by not insisting on the precise **performance** of some or all of the stipulations of a contract. Waiver requires that a person intends to give up a right; that he communicates his intention to the person who might benefit from it; and that the other person relies on the waiver and alters his position accordingly. "If one part, by his conduct, leads another to believe that the strict legal rights arising under a contract will not be insisted on, intending that the other should act on that belief, and he does act on it, then the first party will not afterwards be allowed to insist on the strict legal rights when it would be inequitable for him so to do. There may be no consideration moving from him who benefits by the waiver. There may be no detriment to him acting on it. There may be nothing in writing. Nevertheless, the one who waives his strict rights cannot afterwards insist on them. His strict rights are at any rate suspended so long as the waiver lasts" – W.J. Alan and Co Ltd *v* El Nasr Export and Import Co. [1972] 2 All ER 140. Waiver, being a unilateral right, may not be exercised in respect of a right that is of mutual benefit to both parties; the right must be for the sole

benefit of the party claiming that it has been waived – Lloyd *v* Nowell (1895) 2 Ch. 744. For example, if a contract for the sale of land is entered into subject to a condition that the purchaser obtains planning permission for a specified form of development, then if the planning permission is refused the purchaser cannot waive the condition when the vendor claims that there is no longer a binding contract, the condition having been inserted for both parties' benefit – Heron Garage Properties Ltd *v* Moss and Ano. [1974] 1 WLR 148.

In the context of a building contract waiver may mean "(1) an agreement to modify the original terms of the contract, or (2) some act or conduct whereby the innocent party recognises the continued existence of the contract after a serious breach by the other party which would otherwise have entitled the innocent party to bring the contract to an end, or (3) where there are circumstances from which the employer can be said to have 'accepted' defective or incomplete performance by the contractor." (4 Halsbury's Laws of England, 4 edn, p. 628).

Waiver applies only to a right and not to property *per se* and in that way differs from **abandonment**. It also has a slightly narrower meaning than abandonment; although it may ultimately result in an abandonment. Waiver can be described as "the abandonment of a right in such a way that the other party is entitled to abandonment by way of confession and avoidance if the right is thereafter asserted" – Banning v Wright [1972] 2 All ER 987.

A landlord may waive his right of forfeiture, when a tenant is in **breach of covenant**, if he *knows* (directly or through an agent) of the breach, but accepts rent; issues a demand, sues or distrains for rent; or "does some unequivocal act recognising the continued existence of the lease" – Matthews v Smallwood [1910] 1 Ch. 786. The acceptance of rent is evidence that the landlord acknowledges that the tenant has complied with the conditions of his lease; even if the acceptance is stated to be 'without prejudice', or is made by an authorised agent by mistake (Segal Securities Ltd v Thoseby [1963] 2 WLR 403; Central Estates (Belgravia) Ltd v Woolgar (No. 2) [1972] 3 All ER 610). Waiver of a right of **forfeiture** by acceptance of rent may arise even when a lease provides that no waiver shall have effect unless the waiver is in writing, as long as the landlord indicates that he has elected to accept that the lease shall subsist – R. v Paulson [1921] AC 271. Acceptance of rent after a landlord has served notice to quit does not necessarily amount to a waiver of that notice, and the consequent creation of a new tenancy, if there is evidence that the parties did not intend to create a new tenancy; the landlord may be claiming **mesne profits** for permitting the tenant to hold over, but have no intention to forego his right to possession at any time after the contract of tenancy has ended – Doe d. Cheny v Batten [1775–1802] All E.R. 594; Clarke v Grant [1950] 1 KB 104); nor does receipt of rent that was already unpaid prior to the breach of covenant – Marsh v Curtleys (1596) Cro. Eliz. 528.

The waiver of a covenant or of a condition only affects that particular term; it does not affect the right to enforce any other covenant or condition, just as consent for a tenant to vary one term of a lease does not affect the other terms. Similarly, a landlord who does waive his right to forfeit a lease does not give up any alternative right that he may have to take an action for damages – Stephens v Junior Army and Navy Stores Ltd. [1914] 2 Ch. 516; (Law of Property Act 1925, s. 148). A breach of a covenant that is 'continuing', e.g. an unauthorised change of user or repairing covenant, is not necessarily waived by the acceptance of rent because the landlord may, at any time, refuse further rent and revert to a position whereby the tenant is claimed anew to be in breach of covenant. If a tenant has failed to repair or insure the demised premises, in accordance with the terms of his lease, then the landlord will waiver his right to forfeiture if he accepts rent after he becomes aware of the breach. But he may start forfeiture proceedings afresh merely by proving that the tenant is again in breach of covenant – Doe d. Ambler v Woodbridge (1829) 9 B and C 376; Penton v Barnett [1898] 1 QB 276.

Waiver may be express or implied. An express waiver (which resembles a **release**) is given normally in **writing** and is required, as a rule, when the contract or the condition of the contract to be waived is in writing. A lease commonly contains a provision that it may not be waived, amended, or modified unless there is written evidence to that effect. An implied waiver may arise from an act that is inconsistent with the continuance of the right or benefit that might be claimed; or an act which indicates that a person no longer intends to rely on the right or benefit – provided the act is made knowingly, positively and intentionally – Perry v Davies (1858) CB (NS) 376.

'Waiver' is used also to refer to an **election** whereby one right is forgone by adopting an alternative, but inconsistent, course of action; although when an alternative right is 'waiver' it is preferable to refer to the 'election' for that which is accepted – Kammins Ballrooms Co Ltd v Zenith Investments (Torquay) Ltd [1970] 2 All E.R. 894. Waiver may refer also to the loss of a right by **laches** i.e. an unreasonable delay in asserting or enforcing a right. However, a waiver can only extinguish a right or claim, it can never act as a basis for a claim.

cf. **estoppel**. See also **discharge, imputed notice, rescission, surrender**. Woodfall's Landlord and Tenant, 28 edn, para. 1–1108.
9 Halsbury's Laws of England, 4 edn, para. 571.
27 Halsbury's Laws of England, 4 edn, para. 429.

waiver clause

A clause in an insurance policy which provides that the insurer will have the right to take such action as is necessary to minimise his loss, e.g. to demolish a dangerous building after a fire. See also **subrogation**.

walk-up apartment house (US)

A block of apartments or flats with two or more storeys and without a lift. A 'walk-up' is an apartment above ground floor level or one to which the entrance is reached only by a flight of stairs.

walking possession

see **distress**.

walkway

A passage way intended for walking, i.e. a **footpath**; especially a way that links a number of buildings at ground or upper levels. A local highway authority may enter into an agreement with an owner of land upon which buildings are, or will be, constructed to enable walkways to be provided for use by the public and for the authority to accept responsibility for maintaining such walkways (Highways Act 1980, s. 35).

wall

see **partition, party wall**.

warehouse

A building, usually of considerable size, used for receiving, storing and distributing merchandise or goods in bulk; but not one used primarily for processing or manufacturing goods and merchandise. A place where a person stores goods in large quantities that are not immediately needed for sale or manufacture. A warehouse may incorporate the ancilliary use of receiving tradesmen, or even limited public access to inspect goods for wholesale, but visits by the public at large would create a **retail store**. A building used for the business of selling where storage is only an accessory or ancilliary thereto is a **shop** – Haynes Ford [1911] 2 Ch. 257. (A builders merchants' warehouse cannot be used as a do-it-yourself supermarket nor can a building authorised for use as a wholesale or retail warehouse be used as a supermarket without separate planning permission – Monomart (Warehouses) Ltd and Others v Secretary of State for the

Environment and Others (1977) 34 P & CR 305; Calcaria Construction Co. (York) Ltd *v* Secretary of State for the Environment [1974] 27 P and CR 435.) As a rule a warehouse is a covered area, so an open yard used for the same purpose is not a warehouse. cf. **factory**. See also **industrial building**.

warehouse loan (US)

A loan secured by means of a number of mortgages held by the same borrower. The borrower (usually a mortgage bank) is holding or 'warehousing' the mortgages until they can be sold in the secondary mortgage market.

warehousing

see **warehouse loan.**

warrant

1. A document that authorises someone to do something, especially to pay or receive a sum of money, or to deliver or receive goods.
2. A certificate delivered under seal, or an authority in writing, authorising or requiring an action; especially an action that would not otherwise be permitted. A document by which an officer of the law is authorised to enter premises and conduct a search thereon when that would otherwise be an act of trespass.
3. Something given as a **pledge, guaranty** or assurance.
4. A **receipt** for deposited goods.

warrant (F)

warrant; authority.

warrantor

One who gives a **warrant.**

warranty

1. An **indemnity** against loss. A **promise** or assurance, express or implied, to the effect that a certain fact is true or that a property is in a stipulated condition. In particular, a statement that induces a person to enter into a contract and thus comes to form part of the terms upon which the contract is created. A warranty as to the state or condition of a property may relate to the title or the physical state of the property. In the traditional sense warranty meant to 'give one's word', but "during the last hundred years, however, the lawyers have come to use the word 'warranty' ... to denote a *subsidiary* term in a contract as distinct from a vital term which they call a **condition**" – Oscar Chess Ltd *v* Williams [1957] 1 All ER 328. However, whether a term of a contract is intended as a warranty or as a condition depends on what the parties intended, i.e. on "the conduct of the parties, on their words and behaviour, rather than on their thoughts. If an intelligent bystander would reasonably infer that a warranty was intended, that will suffice. And this, when the facts are not in dispute, is a question of law" – *supra*, at p. 328. In the final analysis whether it is intended to create a warranty or a condition is a matter for the courts – Wickman Machine Tools Sales Ltd *v* L. Schuler AG [1974] AC 235 HL. A warranty should be distinguished from a **representation** (or misrepresentation), as the former is a promise to be honoured, an indemnity upon which a person relies without further need of investigation, whereas a representation is an inducement that leads to a promise; an intention relied on by another. The remedy for breach of warranty, given as **collateral** to a contract, is damages, not (as with a breach of a condition) a right to repu-

diate the contract. "'Warranty' (as regards England and Wales and Northern Ireland) means an agreement with reference to goods which are the subject of a contract of sale, but collateral to the main purpose of such contract, the breach of which gives rise to a claim for damages, but not a right to reject the goods and treat the contract as repudiated." – Sale of Goods Act 1977, s. 61(1). The remedy for a false representation by a seller is an election to repudiate the contract and recover any monies paid. The word warranty is used frequently, but incorrectly, as synonymous with **guaranty**. See also **pledge**, **proposal**, **repair**, **security**, **warranty deed**.

2. In common usage, a contract, or any term of a contract, that guarantees the quality of a property or the suitability of work or of a product. An undertaking, express or implied, that a statement that forms part of, or is incidental to, a contract is true or is then as represented – Mitchell *v* Rudasill, (Mo. App.) 332 SW 2d 91. In insurance, warranty is used when the insured gives an undertaking that a particular fact does or does not exist or that something will or will not be done and in that circumstance the warranty constitutes a fundamental **term** or **condition** of the contract of insurance (Lane *v* Spratt [1970] 2 QB 486–7. See also *caveat emptor*, **covenant**.

warranty deed (US)

1. A **deed** by which a vendor of real property guarantees that he has a good and unencumbered title. This form of deed transfers similar rights to those implied by a **beneficial owner** in English law, i.e. that the vendor has

a right to convey the property; is selling free of any encumberances *except those specified in the deed*; will grant quiet enjoyment; and will take any steps in his power to secure a good title for the purchaser, including bearing the cost of defending the purchaser's title. A deed may be called a 'special warranty deed' if the grantor covenants only against claims arising directly from his or her own rights. It may be called a 'general warranty deed' if the grantor is liable for a defect of title arising through a third party. In some states a special warranty deed is called a 'grant deed' and arises if the grantor uses words such as "grant" or "warrants particularly". (In old English law a warranty deed or 'warranty' meant that the grantor of a freehold estate warranted the title and if the title was defective he undertook to provide other lands to those that were lost by the paramount title (Co. Litt 365a). This form of warranty was abolished by the Real Property Limitation Act 1833.

(US) 2. A deed that contains a covenant of warranty i.e. a covenant for **quiet enjoyment**.

waste

1. An action that results in loss or deterioration, whether from use, misuse, neglect, or wear and tear. Spoil or destruction that results in a marked and lasting alteration to the nature or condition of land (including any building or fixture thereon); sometimes for better but usually for worse. In particular, an act or omission that alters property, or impairs its value, to the detriment of a person who comes into possession of the property in the future, e.g. a landlord at the end of a lease or a remainder-

man who follows a tenant for life; "unlawful damage caused to land and buildings by tenants whereby the value of property is depreciated to the detriment of the person who is entitled to the immediate **reversion** or **remainder**" (Adkin's Landlord and Tenant, 18 edn, p. 158; Bl. Comm. vol. ii p. 281 – Keogh v Peck, 316 III. 318, 147 NE 266).

Waste may be classified as: (a) 'permissive' waste – negligence or omission by which a property is permitted to fall into a state of decay, e.g. not repairing a roof damaged by storm or allowing decay to continue due to a lack of protective paint; (b) 'voluntary' waste – actual or positive damage to a property falling short of an act of wanton damage or destruction, e.g. converting meadow into arable land, cutting down **timber** or opening up a new mine or quarry; (c) 'ameliorating' or 'meliorating' waste – an act of voluntary waste that has the effect of improving property, e.g. restoring a dilapidated building; (d) 'equitable' waste – wanton or malicious damage or destruction; "that which a prudent man would [definitely] not do in the management of his own property." – Turner v Wright (1860) 2 De GF and J 243, e.g. cutting down ornamental trees or demolishing a good building. Waste is a **tort** (not a breach of any contract between the tenant and the person who follows him) and a reversioner or remainderman who is prejudiced by an act of waste may obtain damages for the depreciation in the value of his reversion or remainder, or seek an injunction to restrain the act (except against permissive waste).

A **tenant for a term of years** is liable for permissive or voluntary waste (unless precluded by agreement or by obtaining the consent of the landlord – Davies v Davies (1888) 38 Ch. D 499). A **tenant from year to year** (or less) is liable for voluntary, but not permissive waste beyond (probably) keeping the premises **wind and water tight** – Warren v Keen [1954] 1 QB 15. A **weekly tenant**, however, need do no more than take proper care of the premises e.g. clean gutters, tidy the garden etc. (The liability of a short-term tenant for repair is more usually governed by the covenants of his lease, express or implied, than by any possible liability for waste.) A **tenant at will** is not liable for permissive waste, but an act of voluntary waste automatically terminates his right to continued occupation and he is liable for the consequential damage – Countess of Shrewsbury's Case (1600) 5 Co. Rep. 360.

A **tenant for life** is not liable for permissive waste (unless he is made responsible for repairs as a condition of his holding the estate), but is liable, or 'impeachable', for voluntary waste. In certain cases a tenant for life may be granted consent to commit what would otherwise be waste, e.g. cut timber on a non-timber estate, and he is then said to be 'unimpeachable' for waste; although he may be restrained from committing equitable waste – Vane v Lord Barnard (1716) 2 Vern. 738. It is unlikely that a court would restrain or grant damages for an act of ameliorating waste (especially if the lease has a long unexpired term), even though it is strictly a prohibited act, because a landowner must show that he has suffered financial loss or that the nature of the land has changed to his detriment – Doherty v Allman (1878) 3 App. Cas. 709. An action cannot be waste if it is authorised by the landlord – Meux *v* Cobley [1892] 2 Ch. 262; nor if the action is one that accords with local **custom** or **usage** – Dashwood *v* Magniac [1891] 3 Ch. 357.

cf. **fair wear and tear, improvement**. See also **assart, dilapidations, estovers, grounds for possession**.

Real Property, by William E. Burby, 3 edn., pp. 33–39.

Cheshire's Modern Law of Real Property, 13 edn, pp. 261–265.

Megarry's Manual of the Law of Real Property, 6 edn, pp. 52–56, 363.

Land Law: Cases and Materials, by R.H. Maudsley and E.H. Burn, 4 edn., pp. 18–23.

The Law of Real Property, by Robert Megarry and H.W.R. Wade, 6 edn., pp. 96–102.

Hill & Redman's Landlord and Tenant, 17 edn, pp. 213–219.

Woodfall's Landlord and Tenant, 28 edn, paras. 1–1513 to 1–1532.

27 Halsbury's Laws of England, 4 edn, paras. 279–283.

2. see **wasteland**.

waste land

Land that formed part of a **manor** and upon which the tenants of the manor had rights of common. "The open, uncultivated and unoccupied lands parcel of the manor, or open lands parcel of the manor other than the **demesne lands** of the manor" – A-G *v* Hammer (1858) 27 LJ Ch. 837 (Commons Registration Act 1965, s. 22(1); *Re* Britford Common [1977] 1 WLR 39). Waste land was owned by the lord of the manor, but was used by the tenants in such a way that the lord of the manor obtained little or no profit from it. See also **common land, enclosure, wasteland**.

wasteland

An area of open and uncultivated, barren or unproductive land. Unoccupied and unused land. A local planning authority has power to serve notice on a land owner to require the "proper maintenance" of wasteland (or strictly "a garden, vacant site or other **open land**") if it appears to the authority that the **amenity** of the land, or any adjoining land, is seriously injured by its condition. If the notice is not complied with, the authority has power also to impose a fine on the landowner, against which the landowner has certain grounds of appeal. (Town and Country Planning Act 1971, s. 65, as amended by the Local Government and Planning (Amendment) Act 1981, s.1). Also local authorities have extensive statutory powers to require the tidying up of wasteland on the grounds of danger to public health, or to abate a public nuisance (Public Health Act 1931, ss. 92–100; Public Health Act 1961, s. 34). Called also 'waste'.

cf. **derelict land**.

wasting asset

An asset with a limited or predictable **economic life** or an asset that is intended to be consumed or used up. Anything that diminishes in value due to time, e.g. a leasehold interest; obsolescence or wearing out, e.g. buildings, plant, machinery; or use or depletion, eg. mines and quarries. Called also a 'depleting asset'. See also **depreciation, sinking fund**.

water gavel

Rent paid for a right to water or to fish. See also **gavel**.

water, right to

A right to take water on or below, or

running on or below, land; especially a right that is appropriated, as distinguished from a littoral or riparian right. Water on **land**, as in a pond or lake, is part of the land and belongs to the owner of the land; he or she may use it without limit (subject to any restriction or limitation that may apply to the land on which it stands). A **conveyance** of land is deemed to include *inter alia* ditches, waters, watercourses and, if the land includes a building, sewers, gutters, drains and watercourses appertaining thereto; unless a contrary intention is expressed in the conveyance (Law of Property Act 1925, s. 62). Water that runs off land no longer belongs to the landowner, the water being considered as personal property so that the landowner can only have a transient, usufructuary right therein; "if a body of water runs out of my pond into another man's, I have no right to reclaim it." (Bl. Comm. vol. ii p. 18 – Race v Ward (1855) 4 E and B 702).

Water running over or under land, whether in a defined channel or percolating freely, is strictly the property of no one; it is *res nullius* – Mason v Hill (1833) 5 B and Ad. 1. However, it may be appropriated in certain circumstances. Water flowing in an undefined channel, especially water that percolates underground, may be appropriated by any landowner (unless restrained by statute law) and, therefore, no landowner can claim a right to a continuous flow of such water to his land from another's land (unless he has an **easement** for that purpose) – Acton v Blundell (1843) 12 M and W 324; Bradford Corpn v Pickles [1895] AC 587). Water flowing in a *defined* channel (which it is unlikely to do underground) must be

left to run in its natural state, so a riparian owner can sue an upper riparian owner if the **stream** is dammed or diverted – Swindon Waterworks Co. Ltd v Wilts and Berks Canal Navigation Co. (1875) LR 7 HL 697); although a right to dam or divert the stream may be acquired as an easement. A person whose land is intersected or bounded by water flowing in a defined channel may take water for "ordinary use" connected with the land itself (such as for reasonable domestic purposes or for watering cattle kept on the land), even if this has the effect of exhausting the supply to a landowner down stream (unless restrained by an easement granted to a lower riparian owner). He may not take water for "extraordinary purposes" (such as spray irrigation or manufacturing) "without returning it . . . substantially undiminished in quantity" – Rugby Joint Water Board v Walters [1966] 3 All ER 507. The drawn water must be used for a reason connected or associated with the land (or buildings thereon) and when returned must not be diminished in quality – McCartney v Londonderry and Lough Swilly Rly Co. [1904] AC 306–7. However, a licence is required from a river authority (formerly called a water authority) to extract water "from any source of supply". Exceptions to this rule are single extractions of up to 1000 gallons of water; water extracted in the course of land drainage or to prevent interference with mining, building or engineering operations; water used for a domestic household; or water taken for agricultural use, excluding spray irrigation, provided the water is used on land adjoining the water supply (Water Resources

Act 1963, s.23–25, 135(1), as amended by the Water Act 1973, s. 9).

In the US, most states follow the principles of English common law in respect of rights to water, except as modified by charter, statute, statute usage or federal law or the constitution – Shively *v* Bowlby, 152 US 1). However, some states follow the civil law rule that a lower riparian owner has a **servitude** to receive a natural flow of surface water. Also in a number of states statutes have been passed to limit the right to extract percolating water to an amount that is reasonable for a riparian owner and not detrimental to other landowners. In a few states water is treated as the property of the state government and may be allocated according to its rules and regulations. See also *ad medium filum aquae*, **foreshore, general words, littoral rights, profit à prendre, right of support, right to fish, riparian rights, strict liability**.

Real Property, by William E. Burby, 3 edn., pp. 45–61.

14 Halsbury's Laws of England, 4 ed., p. 90–100.

49 Halsbury's Laws of England, 4 edn, pp. 83–246.

The Law of Easements and Profits, by Paul Jackson, pp. 178–188 (1978).

Cheshire's Modern Law of Real Property, 13 edn, pp. 156–161.

The Law of Rivers and Watercourses, by A.S. Wisdom, 4 edn., pp. 1–8, 89–94.

Aspects of Water Law, by A.S. Wisdom, (1981).

watercourse

The passage of water over land, in a more or less defined channel, e.g. between banks, and including a **river**, **stream**, creek or ditch. The channel may be man-made or naturally formed as long as water flows continuously, or regularly (e.g. seasonally). The term watercourse may be used to refer to the water, the channel in which it runs (even when dry), or the land over which the water flows; according to the context – Taylor *v* St. Helens Corp (1877), 6 Ch. D 264). English statutory definitions of watercourse are fairly broad. It may include "all rivers, streams, ditches, drains, cuts, culverts, dykes, sluices, sewers (other than sewers vested in a local authority or joint board of local authorities) and passages, through which water flows" (Water Act 1945, s. 59 (1) Sch. 3, s. 1; The Water Resources Act 1963, s. 135(1) and the Land Drainage Act 1976, s. 116(1) contain similar definitions). A watercourse may form an **easement** if it exists by virtue of a right to receive water from one person's land for the benefit of another's land. See also **drain, foreshore, overriding interest, quasi-easement, riparian rights, right to fish, water right to**.

watercourse, right of
see **watercourse, water right to**.

way, right of
see **right of way, easement of necessity**.

way-going crop
A crop that has been sown or planted during the course of an agricultural tenancy, but is not ripe until after the termination of the tenancy. Generally **custom** permits a tenant to harvest such crops. Called also 'away-going crops'. See also **compensation for improvements, emblements**.

way of necessity
see **easement of necessity**.

wayleave

Originally a **right of way** to a mine or quarry for the purpose of carrying away extracted minerals, or a right to extend a mine on to or under adjoining land in separate ownership. The term was applied also to a payment for such a right and in the US it is still used in this sense. In the UK, a wayleave is a right of way over, under, or across land, used as a means for transferring material; including a right for the passage of wires, ducts, pipes, cables or sewers. Normally a wayleave is a species of **easement**, although in the case of a public utility easement the dominant and servient tenements may be some distance apart. However, a wayleave may be a mere **licence** for the passage of such a conduit or, in some cases, a right granted by **lease** permitting the exclusive use of the land over which the conduit passes for as long as the right is exercised. See also **outstoke**.

Agricultural Valuations: A Practical Guide, by R.G. Williams, pp. 81–83 (1985).

Modern Methods of Valuation, 7 edn., Ch. 32.

The Valuation of Pipe-line Easements and Wayleaves, by R. Poole and P.M. Poole, (1962).

wayleave rent (or fee)

A rent (or fee) paid for a **wayleave**. See also **outstoke**.

wealth

Derived from Middle English *welthe*, health, well-being or prosperity. In modern usage an abundance of worldly goods or possessions; that which contributes to a well-being, even to the extent of opulence. The total value of all that is possessed, whether by an individual, an association, or a nation. The quantity of one's possessions, especially those possessions that exceed what is needed for self-sufficiency. Traditionally wealth was measured by the hoarding of **money**: "and wealth is often regarded as being a large quantity of coins, because coin is what the techniques of acquiring goods and of trading are concerned with" (Aristotle, *Politics*, Book I, Ch. 9). However, anything hoarded for its own sake may be classified as wealth. In modern usage wealth can mean any form of **private property** held as a store of value, or all material objects that contribute to human comfort and enjoyment. "All wealth consists of things that satisfy wants, directly or indirectly. All wealth consists of desirable things or things that satisfy human wants; but not all desirable things are reckoned as wealth." *Principles of Economics*, by Alfred Marshall, p. 123 (1898). See also **capital**.

wear and tear

see **fair wear and tear**.

week

Any period of seven successive days, from midnight to midnight. Unless there is an express statement or custom to the contrary, a week runs from immediately after midnight on Saturday to immediately after midnight the following Saturday. (Shops Act 1950, s. 74; Offices, Shops and Railway Premises Act 1963, s. 90 – Ronkendorff v Taylor, 29 US 349). As a rule of English common law fractions of a **day** are excluded and, therefore, 'one week's notice' is seven 'clear days'. So a notice given on 17 November to expire on 24 November is not a proper week's notice – Weston v Fidler (1903) 88 LT 769. However, when terminating a weekly tenancy, as a rule and unless there is anything expressed to the contrary, the day of the notice is excluded, but the day for which the notice is given is included. Thus, notice given on or before a Monday to expire at midnight the following Sunday is a valid notice – Newman *v* Slade [1926] 2 KB 328. However, to avoid doubt a notice may be given in such a form that it expressly terminates the tenancy at the end of the stipulated week (or weeks), or at the end of the next completed week (or weeks), as the case may be – Queen's Club Gardens Estates Ltd *v* Bignell [1924] 1 KB 126.

weekly tenancy

A **periodic tenancy** that continues from **week** to week until terminated by notice to quit. A weekly tenancy is terminable by not less than seven days notice which expires at the "end of the current period", which may be either on the anniversary of the date of commencement or the previous day – Crate *v* Miller [1947] KB 946. If the tenancy is weekly because it is implied that it should run from week to week it is not necessary to give seven 'clear' days notice; but if it is to be expressly terminated by 'one week's notice' there must be seven clear days between the day the notice is given and the day from which it takes effect. Also, a weekly tenancy runs from immediately after midnight on Saturday to immediately after midnight on the following Saturday, unless there is an express or implied alternative e.g. a different day for the payment of rent; in practice weekly tenancies usually start on Monday and thus may be brought to an end by notice given on or before Monday to expire the following Sunday night. Unless there is evidence to the contrary, a letting at a weekly rent is a weekly tenancy. A weekly tenancy of a dwelling-house may not be terminated by less than four weeks notice given to include the first day and exclude the last day (Rent Act 1957, s. 16 – Schnabel *v* Allard [1966] 3 All ER 816.). See also **rent book**.

weekly tenant

The holder of a **weekly tenancy**.

weighted aggregate index

An index that reflects relative changes in a number of cost or expenditure items. These items are weighted to take account of their relative importance in the overall index. For, example, a cost of construction index may be compiled from the cost of labour and materials, in order to reflect their relative importance in a building contract. If materials are considered to account for $\frac{2}{3}$ of the total cost and labour $\frac{1}{3}$ of the total cost, then materials would be allocated a weight of 66.66 and labour 33.33. Expenditure of £1000 on materials and £500 on labour would produce a weighted cost of £1000 × 66.66 + £500 × 33.33 = £83 325, so that if materials increased by 25 per cent and labour by 10 per cent the weighted cost or index would increase to £1250 × 66.66 + £550 × 33.33 = £101 656.50, or by 22 per cent. A formula for calculating such an index is:

$$\text{Index} = \frac{(P_i \times w)}{(P_o \times w)}$$

where:

P_i = new price
P_o = old price
w = weight.

See also **indexation**.

weighted average cost of capital

The average cost of capital (whether equity or debt), taking account of the relative proportion of each source of capital. For example, if £1.5m is provided as equity capital on the basis of an expected return of 5 per cent, and £5m is provided as debt capital at an interest rate of 12 per cent, the weighted average cost is:

$[(1.5/6.5 \times 5\%] + [(5/6.5 \times 12\%] = 10.38$ per cent

When capital is obtained from a number of sources, the weighted average cost may be obtained from the formula:

$$\text{cost} = \frac{\Sigma\, iw}{\Sigma\, w}$$

where i = interest rate for each source; and w = weight allocated to each source of capital, usually based on its proportion of the total. See also **composite rate**, **gearing**.

well-maintained payment

An amount of additional compensation paid, in accordance with the provisions of the Housing Act 1957 ss 30,60 (as modified by the Housing Act 1974, s. 108 and extended by the Housing Act 1969, ss 65–69), to an owner (whether a freeholder or leaseholder) of a dwelling-house that is deemed **unfit for human habitation** and, therefore, is compulsorily acquired at **cleared site value** or is made the subject of a demolition order or closing order. A well maintained payment is made by a local authority when that authority considers the house to have been 'well-maintained' even though it is 'unfit', the intention being to recompense in some measure an interested party for the loss of the building itself when the occupier has carried out work or expended money on maintaining the house. The amount of compensation is based normally on four times the rateable value of the house, provided such an amount does not exceed the difference between the market value of the site with the house standing on it and the cleared site value. If the house is let the payment may be divided between the landlord and the tenant. See also **owner-occupier payment**.

West's Law of Housing, 4 edn, pp. 240–241.

welsh mortgage

A form of mortgage by which the mortgagee is given possession of the rent and profits but only in order to pay interest. The mortgagor has no obligation to make any repayment of principal and may redeem the mortgage at any time. The mortgagee has no corresponding right to compel redemption or foreclose. A form of mortgage that is now obsolete in the UK. See also *vivum vadium*.

white elephant

Something that has lost the high esteem in which it was held by its owner. An investment made with high expectations but one that has turned out to be a financial disaster or fiasco. A building erected at considerable expense that has lost its attraction to potential users or occupiers. Something acquired by a speculator whose crystal ball has turned frosty. The term is derived from a rare albinic elephant found in India, Sri Lanka, Burma and Thailand. Such an animal was acquired at considerable expense by P.T. Barnum of Barnum and Bailey's circus; but it drew few extra people to the circus, proved expensive to keep and subsequently was difficult to dispose of.

white land

An area demarcated on a statutory **land use plan**, or development plan, to remain as agricultural land or to remain undisturbed: the area is left white (or uncoloured) on the plan. The type of land use plan that uses this form of designation is now almost obsolete. See also **certificate of appropriate alternative development**

white rent

Rent reserved or payable in silver.

widow's quarantine

A right granted under Magna Carta for a widow to remain in her deceased husband's home for a period of time, without an obligation to pay rent to the heirs; "and she may remain in her husband's house for forty days after his death, within which time her dower shall be assigned to her" (*Magna Carta* (1215) Ch. 7; Co. Litt. 92b). This right was abolished in 1925 (Administration of Estates Act 1925, s. 45). See also **matrimonial home**.

wild animals

see **game**, *res nullius*, **strict liability**.

wilful waste

see **waste**.

will

An instrument by which a person expresses an intention for the disposition of his or her property on death. Historically a will was used to express a person's intention for real property and personal property was dealt with in a **testament**. However, a will is now used to deal with real and personal property (except in some states in the US). A will is an 'ambulatory' decla-ration; that is, it does not take effect until after the death of the person (testator or testatrix) who made it and, therefore, it may be revoked or changed at any time during a person's life – Vynor's Case (1610) 8 Co. Rep. 81b.

A will is not valid unless it is in writing, signed by the testator (who must be of sound mind and of age) or on his behalf by some other person in the presence of the testator. It must appear that the testator intended by his signature to give effect to the will and the signature must be made or acknowledged by the testator in the presence of two or more witnesses present at the same time. Each witness must attest and sign the will; or acknowledge his signature in the presence of the testator (but not necessarily in the presence of the other witness), and no particular form of attestation is required provided a signature appears on the face of the will and the testator intended that signature to validate the will (Administration of Justice Act 1982, s. 17, inserting a revised section 9 in the Wills Act 1837). A will need not take any particular form or use any special wording, provided the intention of the testator can be clearly ascertained; if it cannot, it fails for uncertainty. (Also, if not drawn with professional advice it may fail to meet the true wishes of the testator.) In the US, most states require similar formality to that required in English law, but some states require three witnesses to attest a will.

A person is at liberty to dispose of property by will in any manner he or she chooses, subject to making reasonable provision out of his or her estate for a surviving spouse, a former spouse who has not remarried, any child of the family and any person who immediately before the death of the deceased was being wholly or partly maintained by the deceased (which may extend to a mistress – Malone *v* Harrison [1979] 1 WLR 1353. (Inheritance (Provisions for Family and Dependants) Act 1975, s. 1).

The term 'will' may be used also to refer to a **codicil** to a will, although 'will' usually signifies a testamentary document that is complete in itself and any subsequent document is called a codicil. A codicil is subject to the same formalities as a will (Wills Act 1837, s. 1).

cf. **settlement**. See also **devise, signature, words of limitation**.

Megarry's Manual of the Law of Real Property, 6 edn, pp. 158–171.

Cheshire's Modern Law of Real Property, 13 edn, pp. 767–802.

The Law of Real Property, by Robert Megarry and H.W.R. Wade, 5 edn., pp. 499–539.

Wills, Administration and Taxation: A Practical Guide, by Barlow, King and King, (1983).

The Law of Succession, by A.R. Mellows, 4 edn.

Law relating to Wills, by W.J. Williams, 5 edn.

50 Halsbury's Laws of England, 4 edn, paras. 201–655.

will, tenancy at
see **tenancy at will**.

willing seller (or buyer)
One who is not under any obligation, duress or pressure to contract for the sale (or purchase) of a property. A person who has a reasonable time to conclude a settlement; has time to negotiate the best terms; and, if necessary, to await changes in market con-

ditions that favour his or her best interests. When considering a claim for **compulsory purchase compensation**, anyone who is selling an interest in property to the acquiring authority is assumed to be a "willing seller" (Land Compensation Act 1961, s. 5(2)). "A willing seller means one who is prepared to sell, provided a fair price is obtained under all the circumstances of the case. I do not think it means only a seller who is prepared to sell at any price and on any terms and who is actually at the time wishing to sell. In other words, I do not think it means an anxious seller" – Inland Revenue Commissioners *v* Clay and Buchanan [1914] 3 KB 466. A willing seller is a "hypothetical character. There is no justification from attaching to him, so as to increase or reduce the assessment of compensation, any special characteristics. He is to be assumed to be willing to sell at the best price which he can reasonably get in the open market" – Trocette Property Co. *v* Greater London Council (1974) 28 P and CR 408. Similarly, a willing buyer does not have to purchase a property unless he can obtain it at what he considers a fair price; although he wishes to purchase, he only does so on terms that are reasonable having regard to the conditions of the market at a given point in time. See also **market value**.

'willing to purchase'
see **'ready, able and willing'**.

'wind and water tight'
Words used to imply that a tenant should repair and maintain the skin or fabric of a building to an extent that is sufficient to keep out the elements, e.g. to cover up holes in windows; replace roof titles; repair exter-

nal doors; patch up gaps around a window frame; or replace a chimney pot. However, it is a term of uncertain definition and "I (Lord Denning) think that the expression 'wind and water tight' is of doubtful value and should be avoidable" – Warren *v* Keen [1954] 1 QB 15.
cf. **tenantable repair**. See also **waste**.

windfall

A **tree**, or fruit therefrom, blown down by the wind. Generally these belong to the owner of the land from whence they came, unless they are decayed. As between landlord and tenant windfalls of **timber** belong to the landlord if the wood is sound and to the tenant if they are dead or rotten – Herlakender's Case (1589) 4 Co. Rep. 92.

windfalls and wipeouts (US)

Extraneous or unexpected gains or losses in the value of land, especially when these arise from the activities of a public authority. A windfall or a wipeout may have a direct or indirect effect and it may arise as a result of a positive activity, e.g. the construction of a new highway, a grant of planning or zoning consent; or as a result of a negative activity, e.g. a refusal of planning permission, closure of vehicular access to a site. In the UK more commonly referred to as **betterment** and **worsenment**. See also **transferable development rights**.
Windfall for Wipeouts, by Donald G. Hayman and Dean J. Misczynski (eds), (1978).

winkling

Seeking to evict or dispossess a person from property. In particular, seeking out property to be acquired in order to secure a site for development or redevelopment or to resell at an immediate profit. Commonly applied to harassing an owner or tenant in order to entice him or her to sell or vacate a property. See also **harassment**.

wipeouts (US)

see **windfalls and wipeouts**.

with recourse

see **recourse**

withholding tax

A tax on income deducted at source.

within

see **time**.

without impeachment for waste

see **waste**.

without prejudice

Without intending to be bound or committed; especially when one does not intend to sacrifice a right or claim. Without intending to suffer any consequential injury. Negotiations conducted 'without prejudice', whether by an exchange of correspondence or any legal document, as a rule cannot be used as evidence in a court of law or in any quasi-judicial hearing, unless the parties concerned give their consent, a binding agreement results therefrom, or it is necessary to use the document to decide whether negotiations have taken place between the parties – Tomlin *v* Standard Telephones and Cables Ltd [1969] 3 All ER 201. The intention of marking a letter or document 'without prejudice' is to enable negotiations to be held without either party being bound. In other words "before bloodshed let us discuss the matter, and let us agree that for the purpose of this discussion we will be more or less frank; we will try to come to terms, and that nothing that each of us says shall ever be used against the other so as to interfere with our rights at war, if unfortunately, war results" – Kurts and Co. *v* Spence and Sons (1887) 57 LJ Ch. 241. The words 'without prejudice' are not intended to totally exclude the use of the text to which they refer; nor do they apply in respect of a document which, from its character, may prejudice the person to whom it is addressed. Also, if there is no dispute between the parties the words have no application. Thus, an offer made 'without prejudice' is capable of being accepted and forming the subject of a contract (it does not, as is sometimes thought, have any semblance to the result of using the words '**subject to contract**'). On the other hand, a proposal of a revised rent, put forward under the provisions of a lease, when made 'without prejudice' may be devoid of effect because the subject-matter is capable of dispute and the proposal amounts to an equivocation – *In re* Daintry *ex parte* Holt [1893] 2 QB 116. In the same way, a notice of an intention to rescind a contract may be void if it is marked 'without prejudice' – *Re* Weston and Thomas' Contract [1907] 1 Ch. 244. An agreement reached or negotiations held 'without prejudice' remain so unless or until the parties express their intention to waive or concede this reservation – Oliver *v* Nautilus Steam Shipping Co [1903] 2 KB 639. 'Without prejudice' letters or documents are not intended to be admissible if a dispute is submitted to **arbitration**, but it is not certain whether legally they may be submitted to an expert or valuer for his consideration (although the submission of 'without prejudice' negotiations or correspondence without the consent of both parties to the dispute could be considered as a breach of a professional institution's rules of conduct).

without recourse
see **non-recourse loan**.

without reserve
The sale of a property at auction when there is no **reserve price** fixed and, therefore, it it intended that the property will be sold to the highest bidder. "When a property is offered for sale without reserve the meaning, and the only meaning that can be attached to it, is that of the bidders – the public – who choose to attend the sale, whoever bids the highest shall be the purchaser" – Robinson *v* Wall [1847] 2 Ph. 375. If an auctioneer does not stipulate that a sale is subject to a reserve price "it seems to us [the judges in the Court of Exchequer Chamber in an *obiter dicta*] that the highest *bona fide* bidder at an auction may sue the auctioneer as upon a contract that the sale shall be without reserve. We think that an auctioneer who puts the property up for sale upon such a condition pledges himself that the property shall be without reserve; or, in other words, contracts that it shall be so; and that this contract is made with the *bona-fide* bidder and that in the case of a breach of it, he has a right of action, against the auctioneer" – Marlow *v* Harrison (1858) 1 E and E316. The auctioneer implies that he is making a public offer, when he sets the property up for sale or strictly that he will be bound to accept any offer made, but it would appear that he is at liberty to withdraw the property up to the last moment set for auction, or even up to the time immediately before the first

bid is made. A vendor of property being sold at auction 'without reserve' cannot bid or employ anyone else to bid at the sale; the presumption is that the auctioneer will offer it without constraint or interference to anyone who cares to bid and will accept the highest *bona-fide* bid (Robinson *v* Wall *supra*). If a sale is not expressed to be "without reserve" it is probable that there is a reserve price and a prospective purchaser should make inquiry of the auctioneer. In the US, a sale at auction 'without reserve' is referred to also as an 'absolute auction'.
Anson's Law of Contract, 26 edn, pp. 27–28.
Cheshire and Fifoot's Law of Contract, 10 edn, pp. 28–29.
The Law of Estate Agency and Auctions, by J.R. Murdoch, 2 edn., pp. 387–492, 499–504.

witness
1. An affirmation of a fact or event. Subscribing one's name to a deed to indicate that a **signature** is genuine or that the signature was placed with a free will. Most real estate contracts do not require a witness; with the exception of a **will** and a form for the **transfer** of title to registered land. See also **attest**.
2. One who gives evidence under oath at a hearing. See also **expert witness**.

wood
see **timber**.

woodland
An area of land covered with trees or substantially covered with woody vegetation, especially an area where trees are grown for the production of timber, as compared to a coppice

which is intended to be cut and pruned after a short period of time. Woodland includes all "land used primarily for growing trees" (Agricultural Act 1967, s. 57 (1)). See also **tree preservation order**.

words, general
see **general words**.

words of art
see **term of art**.

words of limitation
Words used in a deed or instrument to mark out the limit or **quantity** of an estate that is granted or settled. In particular, words used in a conveyance or will by the holder of a **freehold** estate to indicate that it is not to be transferred, but that the interest is to be cut down in some way. For example, a conveyance or testamentary grant to "A for life and thereafter to B" limits A's interest by the words of limitation "for life". Prior to 1925 it was necessary to use words of limitation to transfer a fee simple *inter vivos* (between living persons), a transfer "to A" granted only a life interest to A. Since 1925 a conveyance of freehold land passes a fee simple estate, or the entire estate of the grantor, unless there is an express limitation to the contrary (Law of Property Act 1925, s. 60). Before 1837, no formal words of limitation were required in a will to pass a fee simple estate, provided the testator's intention was made clear; thus using words such as "to A for ever" or "to A and his heirs" was sufficient. Since 1837 the onus of proof is reversed and a will passes a fee simple, or the testator's entire estate, unless there is an express intention to the contrary (Wills Act 1837, s. 28). Accordingly, words of limitation are

now used to indicate that an estate of limited inheritance, an entailed estate, is to pass. Words of limitation may be of direct limitation, e.g. "for life" or of determinable limitation, e.g. "upon the death of A".

cf. **words of purchase**. See also **heirs, limitation, qualified estate.**

Megarry's Manual of the Law of Real Property, 6 edn, pp. 33–39.

The Law of Real Property, by Robert Megarry and H.W.R. Wade, 5 edn., pp. 48–58.

words of procreation

Words used to designate the person or persons entitled to an **entailed interest** in land, e.g. "to A and the male heirs of his marriage to B". An entailed interest cannot be created without words of procreation. The words indicating who shall receive land after the grantee are called sometimes 'words of inheritance'. See also **heirs, words of limitation.**

words of purchase

The words in a contract for the transfer of an interest in real property, defining who shall take the interest. For example, if a grant is made "to A and his heirs" "to A" indicates who shall purchase the property; the words "and his heirs" place a limitation on the grant and are **words of limitation**. See also *habendum*, **purchase.**

words of severance

see **severance, tenancy in common.**

words, meaning of

In English law, a word is given its ordinary or literal meaning in its context; "it is only when that meaning leads to some result which cannot reasonably be supposed to have been

the intention of the legislature that it is proper to look for some other permissible meaning of the word or phrase" – Pinner *v* Everett [1962] 3 All ER 257. See also *ejusdem generis*, **term of art.**

words, operative

see **operative parts (or words).**

work letter

An addendum or schedule to a lease (or an agreement for a lease) setting out details of the works to be carried out at the commencement of the contract by the landlord or tenant. In particular, work to be carried out at the landlord's expense.

working capital

Liquid assets available for the day-to-day running of a company or for meeting immediate liabilities. The monetary difference between current assets and current liabilities; the 'net current assets'. Working capital is defined to include stocks (inventories) plus debts (accounts receivable) and cash, less creditors (accounts payable). Called also 'circulating capital'.

cf. **fixed capital.**

working drawing

A drawing, or large scale plan, containing details of a proposed building; especially one of the drawings prepared by an architect, setting out sufficient details for the workmen on site.

working-up

A process in **quantity surveying**, that follows **taking-off**, by which the total quantity of materials required for the performance of a building contract is added up. This total is then used to ascertain the price of these materials. "The traditional preparation of a bill of quantities divides itself into three distinct stages: (1) the measurement of the dimensions from the drawing by the 'taker off'. (2) working out volumes, area, etc. (known as squaring the dimensions), the casting up of their totals and the entering of all the results on the abstract, which collects and classifies them in a recognised order preparatory to the writing of the bill. (3) The casting up of the abstract, the reducing of totals to recognised units, and transferring the results to a schedule or bill having money columns ready for pricing out" (*Elements of Quantity Surveying*, by Arthur J. Willis and Christopher J. Willis, 7 edn, p. 2).

work-out agreement (US)
see **rescheduling agreement**.

workshop
A small building or establishment where goods are manufactured or a craft is conducted, usually with the objective of producing, repairing, altering, maintaining or finishing goods. Commonly, premises occupied by a service industry. See also **factory, industrial property**.

worldly goods (or estate)
All those goods (or the total estate) owned by a person. "All my worldly goods" does not necessarily include real estate, unless the context so admits (Wright *v* Shelton (1853) 18 Jur. 445).

worsement or worsenment
A reduction or depreciation in the value of a parcel or plot of land caused by an external factor, in particular by the activities or decisions

of a public authority, e.g. by the construction of an airport or sewage works.
cf. **betterment**. See also **blight, injurious affection, nuisance, windfalls and wipeouts**.

worth
The measure of **value**; commonly of monetary value. The value of one's possessions; "that 'value' which is acknowledged" (*Crabb's English Synonyms*, 1816). See also **price, wealth**.

wraparound mortgage (US)
A mortgage loan granted against the security of a property that is already mortgaged whereby a new mortgagee assumes, that is, takes over, the obligation to pay interest and principal on the existing or 'in-place' mortgage and makes a further 'wrap-around' advance to the mortgagor. The face value of the wraparound mortgage is equivalent to the amount outstanding on the 'in-place' mortgage, plus the additional funds advanced. The mortgagor undertakes to make payments to the new or subordinate mortgagee that are sufficient to cover the cost of servicing both the existing mortgage and the new advance. The wraparound mortgage is a type of mortgage which may be taken out when an in-place mortgage is held at a favourable interest rate and, therefore, the mortgagor does not wish to refinance the entire mortgage arrangements. The interest rate on the wraparound mortgage is fixed at a rate between the in-place mortgage rate and the rate that would be charged if only a new advance was to be made. Called sometimes an 'all-inclusive mortgage'. See also **assumption**.

writ

A formal written document. In particular, an order under seal issued by the Crown, a court or an officer of the court, commanding the person to whom it is sent to do, or to refrain from doing, something. In medieval England, an order from the Sovereign requiring a defendant in a case to show why a plaintiff should not be put in a position to enjoy the right he claims; a writ being an essential prerequisite to starting an action in a court of common law. Writs were classified into two types, prerogative writs (now called prerogative orders) and writs of right: the former arose as part of the Crown's prerogative and the latter as part of the general administration of justice when the court was satisfied that there was a *prima facie* case to answer. No action could be brought unless a plaintiff could find a writ and used the correct writ for his case; such as a 'writ of detinue', 'writ of trespass', 'writ of ejectment', 'writ of replevin'. The medieval writ has been superseded by an **action**.

In modern English law a writ is a summons in the name of the Crown submitted, in civil proceedings, by a plaintiff to a defendant or defendants, requiring the named party or parties to answer a case alleged against him, her or them. The summons is first sealed by Supreme Court in London, or a District Registry in the Provinces, and then served on the defendant's solicitor. There is no longer a need for a special form of writ; the same form can be used for any action, thus leaving a plaintiff free to state his claim in his own words. See also **attachment, Land Charges Register, prerogative order, service warrant, writ of entry, writ of execution, writ of possession, writ of right**.

writ of attachment

see **attachment**.

writ of certiorari

see *certiorari*.

writ of ejectment

see **ejectment**.

writ of entry

A **writ** used to enable a person to go on to land in order to assert a legal right to possession of that land. Abolished in England, but still used in some states in the US. See also **recovery**.

writ of execution

A court order or writ instructing an official or sheriff of the court to implement a decision of the court, e.g. regain possession of property. In English law there is no writ of execution as such but the term may be used to refer to a number of writs by which the judgement or orders of a court of justice are enforced by a public office, including a writ of *fieri facias*, of possession, of delivery, of sequestration and various related writs (Rules of the Supreme Court Order 46, r.1). See also **attachment**.

writ of *fieri facias*

see *fieri facias*.

writ of possession

A decree or order from a court directing possession to be given or authorising a sheriff to reclaim possession of land. See also **possessory action, writ of execution**.

writ of replevin

see **replevin**.

writ of right

1. A form of writ used by a person

who wished to reclaim a freehold right to land which had been taken from him illegally. The plaintiff sought to prove that he had a better claim to possession or **seisin** of the land. If successful he was able to eject the possessor of the land, although he did not necessarily then establish a title that was good against the whole world. Abolished in England in 1833, (Real Estate Limitations Act 1833).
2. A writ that is granted as of right, as distinguished from a **prerogative writ** which is granted as a matter of discretion.

write down

To reduce in value an amount specified against an asset in a financial statement, e.g. to reduce the book value.
cf. **write up**. See also **depreciation, write-off**.

write-off

1. A cost that may be **set off** against a tax liability.
2. A debt that has been accepted as uncollectable and is so recorded in a book of accounts.
3. To write down or depreciate an asset to nil in a book of accounts. See also **depreciation**.

write up

To increase the value of a property, as shown in a financial statement, usually to its **market value**.
cf. **write down**. See also **revaluation**.

writing

The forming of letters on any suitable surface. "'Writing' includes typing, printing, lithography, photography, and other modes of representing or reproducing words in visible form" (Interpretation Act 1978, Sch. 1).

In English law most contracts relat-ing to real property must be evidenced in writing if they are to be capable of enforcement in a court action. "No action may be brought upon any contract for the sale or other disposition of land or any interest in land, unless the agreement upon which such action is brought, or some **memorandum** or **note** thereof, is in writing and signed by the person to be charged or by some other person thereunto by him lawfully authorised" (Law of Property Act 1925, s. 40(1)). (This does not make an oral contract void or invalid, but means that it is unenforceable in a court of law. A similar requirement was first introduced by the **Statute of Frauds**, 1677, s. 4. to discourage fraud, falsehood and deceit. This provision does not affect the law relating to **part performance**, or sales by a court of law: 1925 Act, s. 40(2).)

Any interest in land, noteably a tenancy that is created by word of mouth only, and not put in writing and lawfully signed, even if granted for proper consideration, creates an interest at will only, i.e. there is no more than a personal contract between the parties. This provision does not apply to the creation of a **parol lease** which (a) takes effect immediately; (b) is for a term not exceeding three years and (c) is created at the **best rent** obtainable without the payment of a **fine** or **premium** (1925 Act, s. 54). With the exception of such a parol lease "no interest in land can be created or disposed of except by writing signed by the person creating or conveying the same, or by his agent thereunto lawfully authorised in writing, or by will, or by operation of law" (1925 Act, s. 53(1) (a)). Further, a disposal of an

equitable interest must be in writing and be signed by the person disposing of the same, or his agent authorised in writing; and a **declaration of trust** (but not an implied, resulting, or constructive trust) cannot be enforced in a court unless it is evidenced in writing and signed by the person declaring the trust (1925 Act, s. 53 (1)(b), (c)).

In most states in the US, agreements for the sale of real estate and leases for more than one year must be in writing.

In French law documents that must be in writing, and evidenced by a notary, include agreements to make a gift, marriage contracts and mortgages. In addition, an agreement to set a rate of interest that is different from a rate permitted by law must be evidenced by a signed document. See also **bill of exchange, bond, deed, guarantee, legal assignment, signature, unenforceable, will.**

writing-down allowance

A form of **capital allowance** by which certain capital expenditure, such as the cost of constructing an industrial building or an agricultural building, may be set off against a tax liability over a number of years (Finance Act 1971, s. 44; Finance Act 1976, s. 39).

To be distinguished from an **initial allowance**, whereby the capital expenditure is set against a tax liability in the year it is incurred. See also **industrial building allowance.**

written contract

see **express contract, writing.**

written statement

1. A document that accompanies a **structure plan**, in order to set down the future planning proposals for the area covered by that plan as well as the reasoning behind the proposals in the plan.
2. Submissions that a local planning authority propose to put forward at a planning inquiry; including a list of all documents it intends to submit to the inquiry.

wrong

An action that is unjust, inequitable or injurious. An illegal or immoral act. An infringement or violation of the legal rights of another, either the rights of an individual – a private wrong or **tort**; or of the community – a public wrong or crime. See also **breach of contract, delict, *quasi-délit*, void contract.**

wrongful conversion

see **conversion.**

Y

year

The period of just over 365 consecutive solar days required for the earth to make one revolution around the sun. In English common law and the civil law, a period measured by the Gregorian calendar which has 365 clear days in a 'common year' and 366 days in a 'leap year' – Guaranty Trust and SD Co. *v* Buddington, 27 Fla. 215, 9 So. 246. A year is normally twelve calendar and not lunar months. A year commences on 1 January, unless an alternative start date is designated. Normally 29 February is treated as an extension of 28 February when subdividing a year. A period from a moveable feast in one year, e.g. Whitsuntide, to a moveable feast in the next year may constitute one year, even though the number of intervening days is less than 365 – R. *v* Inhabitants of Newstead (1769) Burr. S.C. 669; although that would normally require evidence of the intent to establish such a time span. A 'year' in case of a **weekly tenancy** usually means 52 weeks and not 365 (or 366) days – Lamb *v* Boyden [1961] CLY 4406. See also **half year**, *per annum*, **quarter year, tenancy for a term of years, tenancy from year-to-year, time**.

year certain and thereafter from year to year

see **tenancy from year-to-year**.

yearly, or year-to-year, tenancy

see **tenancy from year-to-year**.

yearly value

see **annual value**.

years' purchase (YP)

A sum of money which if invested now will produce an annual return of one unit of value for a given number of years. The present capital value of the right to receive one unit of value per annum over an appropriate term at a required rate of return i.e. the **present value of one per period (or per annum)**. When the appropriate period is indefinite, i.e. the income is receivable in perpetuity, the year's purchase is equivalent to the reciprocal of the required rate of return expressed as a decimal. Thus, a years' purchase at: $5\% = 100/5 = 20$; at $6\% = 100/6 = 16.66$ A year's purchase is usually applied in reverse, as a **capitalisation factor**, so that capital value = income × year's purchase – the income then provides the requisite return on that capital value. In the US, this capitalisation factor is called a 'present worth factor' or 'Inwood factor'. See also **dual-rate capitalisation factor (or year's purchase)**.

yield

1. The return or net income from an investment over a period of time (normally a year), expressed as a percentage of its total cost. The actual **rate of return** on capital. See also **all-risks yield, capitalisation rate, cash-on-cash yield, dividend yield, earnings yield, equated yield, equity yield rate, equivalent yield, initial yield, net yield, redemption yield, reversionary yield, running yield, yield to maturity**.
2. To give up or **surrender**, especially possession. In old English law, to pay a sum due to the lord of the manor. In

real property contracts, in particular in a lease, the words 'yielding and paying' are followed by the sum due as consideration i.e. the **rent**. See also **cede**.

yield capitalisation (US)
see **annuity capitalisation**.

yield gap
The difference between the rates of return on two alternative forms of investment, or between the immediate and long-term returns from the same investment. Thus the yield gap may refer to (a) the difference between the yield on long-dated fixed interest government securities and an equity investment, whether in company shares (dividend yield) or an investment in property; (b) the difference between the return from an equity investment in a property (**equity yield**) and the cost of servicing the debt used to purchase that investment; or (c) the difference between the **initial yield** and the **redemption yield** on a given investment. Historically equity shares provided higher returns than debentures or government securities; in recent times this situation has been reversed, so that in that context the difference may be referred to as a 'reverse yield gap'. See also **deficit financing**.

yield to maturity
The annual return from an investment (or loan) taking account of total expenditure, income and capital appreciation (or depreciation) calculated up to the date that the investment is resold (or a loan matures). The yield to maturity is equivalent to the **redemption yield** on an investment, or the **annual percentage rate** of interest on a loan. See also **internal rate of return**.

yielding and paying
see *reddendum*, **yield**.

Z

zero-lot line (US)
A **boundary line** of a plot of land that corresponds to the **building line**.
cf. **set-back**.

zero-rated
see **value-added tax**.

zonage (F)
zoning.

zone
1. An area of land that has been designated by a planning authority for a specific use. See also **zoning**.
2. An area or district set aside for a different purpose from the surrounding area. See also **variance**.

zone (F)
zone; district; area.
(*zone artisanale* – light industrial or workshop area)
(*zone d'activité* – area zoned for industrial use)
(*zone de concentration urbaine* – urban region; conurbation)
(*zone de dévelopement* – **development area**)
(*zone de rénovation* – rehabilitation area; area of comprehensive development)
(*zone industrielle* – industrial area; **industrial estate**)
(*zone piétonnière*; *zone piéton* – **pedestrian area**)
(*zone urbaine* – urban area; central business district).

'**zone A**'
see **zoning method**.

zone à urbaniser par priorité (ZUP) (F)
priority urban development area. A

housing area that a public authority considered should be redeveloped as a matter of urgency (similar to an **action area** in English planning law). Since 1975, superseded by a *zone d'intervention foncière*.

zone d'aménagement concerté (ZAC) (F)
comprehensive development area; area for concerted development. An area of land that has been designated by a planning authority for comprehensive development, but not as a matter of immediate priority. A ZAC is controlled essentially by a collective or a public authority that aims to acquire land to facilitate comprehensive development (French Law of 3 January 1968, art. 16; *Code de l'Urbanisme, art. L 311 et seq.*).
Précis Dalloz. *Droit Civil, Les Biens* (Alex Weill) 2 edn, p. 163.
Petits Codes Dalloz, *Code de l'Urbanisme*, 3 edn, pp. 99–102, 366–379.

zone d'aménagement différé (ZAD) (F)
deferred or future development area. An area that is likely to be designated a *zone d'intervention foncière* at a future date, but is currently not considered as one that requires priority treatment. The purpose of designating a ZAD is to prevent land speculation by giving a public authority a *droit de préemption* (right of preemption) on any land in the area that is offered for sale (Law of 26 July 1962, arts 7–12; *Code de l'Urbanisme, art. L 212-1 et seq.*).
Petits Codes Dalloz, *Code de l'Urbanisme*, 3 edn, pp. 84–94, 349–359.

zone d'environnement protégé (ZEP)
(F)
environmental protected area; conservation area. A rural area that is protected from development (*Code de l'Urbanisme, art. L 143-1*).

zone d'intervention foncière (ZIF) (F)
An urban area that is designated so that a public authority has the power to acquire any property that is offered for sale (a *droit de préemption*). Such an area is designated to enable an authority to acquire land that may come onto the open market and is required for a public purpose, e.g. open space, social housing (Law of 31 December 1975; *Code de l'Urbanisme, art. L 211 et seq.*). The designation of a ZIF frequently supersedes the designation of a **zone** *d'aménagement différé*.
Petits Codes Dalloz, *Code de l'Urbanisme*, 3 edn, pp. 76–84

zone exemption (US)
see **variance**.

zone non-aedificandi
see *non-aedificandi*.

zoning
1. A method of **land use planning** by which different areas of a town or city are allocated, or zoned, on an official map for different uses, either to indicate the present use or a proposed future use. Zoning is concerned primarily with controlling the use and development of land by setting down density controls, rules for the height, size, type and shape of new buildings and the grouping together of complementary land uses. The zoning of land aims also to limit or exclude any incompatible user: a **non-conforming user**. However, it is not as extensive a means of development control as is exerted by modern British town and country planning; the function of zoning is to guide the use and development of land without unduly fettering the scope for individual expression in terms of new building design. Zoning formed the essence of town planning in Britain until around the 1950's; it was used particularly in preparing a **town map** prepared under the provisions of the Town and Country Planning Act 1947.

In the US, zoning forms the basis of development control in most states and cities. "In its generic sense, zoning embraces all aspects of land use regulation, from the basic legislative act of adopting an ordinance and establishing use districts on the zoning map to the various administrative activities essential to the land use regulatory process. In its basic legal sense, however, zoning is regarded as a legislative act by a legislative body, representing its judgement of how land within a municipality should be utilised and where the lines of demarcation between various zoning or use districts should be drawn" – *Handling the Land Use Case*, by Schidman, Abrams and Delaney, p. 15 (1984). See also **cluster zoning**, **density**, **exclusionary zoning**, **master plan**, **police power**, **spot zoning**, **zoning classification**, **zoning ordinance**.
Real Estate Law, by W.B. Milligan and Arthur G. Bowman, pp. 323–328 (1984).
Zoning and Planning Law Handbook, by Frederic A. Strom (1982).
Urban Planning and Land Development Control Law, by Donald Hagman, (1975).
Handling the Land Use Case, by Schnidman, Abrams and Delaney, pp. 15–21, 564–565 (1984).

The Zoning Game, by R.F. Babcock (1966).

American Law of Zoning, by Robert M. Anderson, 2 edn.

Zoning Law and Practice, by E.C. Yokley, 4 edn.

2. see **zoning method**.

zoning classification (US)

A system of designation given by a planning commission to indicate the permitted use for an area of land. Commonly used designations are (A) – agriculture; (C) – commerce; (I) – general industry; (M) – manufacturing or heavy industry; (P) – parking; (R) – residential. A numerical designation limits the use more strictly e.g. (M3) – heavy industry. See also **zoning**.

zoning exception (US)

see **variance**.

zoning map (US)

see **zoning ordinance**.

zoning method

A method of analysing or assessing the rental value of a shop. The zoning method is based on the principle that the rent a trader will pay for retail premises is highest at the front of the property and decreases the greater the distance from the shop front or entrance. A shop is divided therefore into notional areas or zones for which it is assumed different rental values will be paid.

To apply the zoning method of analysis the front area of the shop, or 'Zone A' is given a value of x, the next zone half that value, the next a quarter, and so on as necessary: a process called 'halving back'. Ancillary or non-retail space is normally excluded from the analysis and assessed separately and the halving-back process

discontinued after the third zone; the principle of zoning is that "the rental value of the sales space of a shop diminishes as its depth increases, subject to their coming a point at which any further reduction in value would offend common sense" – Trevail v C & A Modes Ltd [1967] RA 132. The depth of each zone is commonly taken as 15, 20 or 25 feet (or 5, 7 or 8 metres), the width corresponding to the actual width of the premises. Then the total area of the shop is reduced to a factor of x and by dividing the rental value of the shop by that factor the quotient represents the rate per square foot (or per square metre) appropriate to the 'zone A' area, i.e. it represents the 'zone A rate'. For example, if a shop has a rental value of £49500 p.a., a frontage, and width throughout, of 25 feet and a depth of 52 feet, the 20ft zone A rate would be:

$$20 \times 25 \times x \quad = 500x$$
$$20 \times 25 + \tfrac{1}{2}x = 250x$$
$$12 \times 25 \times \tfrac{1}{4}x = \underline{\quad 75x}$$
$$825x$$

so that, $x = 49,500 \div 825 = £60$ per sq. ft for zone A. This rate may be applied to assess the rental value of a shop that is considered of comparable value but has different dimensions. Thus, if the shop being valued has a frontage of 18 feet and a depth of 65 feet, based on the zone A rate of £60 its rental value is $(20 \times 18 \times 60) + (20 \times 18 \times 30) + (20 \times 18 \times 15) + (5 \times 18 \times 7.5) = £38475$ or, say, £38500 p.a. The particular zone A depth used in the analysis is not of considerable importance, provided that same depth is used when assessing the value of another shop – "as one analyses so should one value" – Marks and Spencer Ltd v Hall (1960) R and IT 154; Marks and Spencer v Collier

VO [1966] RA 107. See also **comparison method of valuation, quantity allowance**.

Analysis of Shop Rent, 'Mainly for Students' (1984) 269 EG 333-6.

Site Value of Shops, by G.S. Brownlow, (1956).

Modern Methods of Valuation, 7 edn., pp. 379-383.

Handbook of Business Tenancies, by D.W. Williams, paras. 11-33 (1985).

zoning ordinance (US)

An **ordinance** governing the permitted use or development for a given area of land. A zoning ordinance normally comprises a text containing regulations for the use of land and a 'zoning map' which delineates the boundaries for various permitted uses and shows such items as a proposed highway, an area of special use, open space, etc. Zoning ordinances normally specify such matters as density limits (called 'density zoning'); zoning classification; parking standards; landscaping requirement; building or improvement lines, etc. A zoning ordinance that controls the overall envelope or 'bulk' of the building permitted on a site is called a 'bulk zoning ordinance'.

cf. **master plan**. See also **variance, zoning**.

Real Estate Law, by Robert Kratovil and Raymond J. Werner, 8 edn., pp. 439-442. See also Appendix B.

Appendix A: Abbreviations

REAL ESTATE

AAA rating	Triple A rating
AAR	Average annual return
a/c	air conditioning
AI	All inclusive
AIA	American Institute of Architects
AIP	American Institute of Planners
AIREA	American Institute of Real Estate Appraisers
ALTA	American Land Title Association
AMC	Agricultural Mortgage Corporation
ANOB	Area of outstanding natural beauty
ANSI	American National Standards Institute
app	Appreciation
APR	Annual percentage rate
ARIBA	Associate of the Royal Institute of British Architects
ARICS	Associate of the Royal Institution of Chartered Surveyors
ARM	Adjustable-rate mortgage
ARR	Average rate of return
ASA	American Society of Appraisers
asf	Annual Sinking Fund
ASREC	American Society of Real Estate Counselors
BFP	Bona fide purchaser
BOMA	Building Owners and Managers Association
BONM	National Association of Building Owners and Managers
BPN	Building preservation notice
BRR	Book rate of return
C	Mortgage co-efficient
CALUS	Centre for Advanced Land Use Studies
CAP rate	Capitalization rate
CBA	Cost-benefit analysis
CBD	Central business district
CD	Certificate of Deposit
CGT	Capital gains tax
CM	Construction management
CO	Certificate of Occupancy
CPA	Critical path analysis
CPI	Consumer price index
CPM	Certified property manager
CPM	Critical path method

CPO	Compulsory purchase order
CRV	Certificate of reasonable value
CTT	Capital transfer tax
CUV	Current use value
DCF	Discounted cash flow
DCR	Debt-coverage ratio
dep	Depreciation
DGC	Development gains charge
DGT	Development gains tax
DIM	Deferred-interest mortgage
DLT	Development land tax
DOE	Department of the Environment
DPM	Direct-payment mortgage
DRC	Depreciated replacement cost
DRM	Direct reduction mortgage
EGI	Effective gross income
EPA	Environmental Protection Agency
ERISA	Employee Retirement Income Security Act
ERV	Estimated rental value
EZ	Enterprise zone
FAR	Floor area ratio
FHA	Federal Housing Administration
FHLB	Federal Home Loan Bank
FHLMC	Federal Home Loan Mortgage Corporation (Freddie Mac)
FIABCI	Fédération Internationale des Administrateurs de Biens Conseil Immobiliers (The International Real Estate Federation)
FIG	Fédération International des Géomètres (The International Federation of Surveyors)
FMV	Fair market value
FNMA	Federal National Mortgage Association (Fannie Mae)
FRI lease	Full repairing and insuring lease
FRICS	Fellow of the Royal Institution of Chartered Surveyors
FRM	Fixed-rate mortgage
FRV	Full rental value
FSI	Floor space index
FV	Future value
GBA	Gross built area
GDO	General development order
GEA	Gross external area
GIA	General improvement area

GIA	Gross internal area
GIM	Gross income multiplier
GLA	Gross lettable (or leasable) area
GNMA	Government National Mortgage Association (Ginnie Mae)
GPM	Graduated-payment mortgage
GRM	Gross rent multiplier
GV	Gross value
GVD	General vesting declaration
HUD	(United States) Department of Housing and Urban Development
IBA	Industrial building allowance
ICSC	International Council of Shopping Centres
in perp	In perpetuity
IRC	Internal revenue code
IREF	International Real Estate Federation
IRR	Internal rate of return
IRS	Internal Revenue Service
JCT	Joint Contracts Tribunal
'k' factor	A mortgage factor
l/c	Letter of credit
LS	*Locus sigilli*
LVT	Local Valuation Tribunal
L/V ratio	Loan to value ratio
MAI	'Member of the Appraisal Institute' A member of the American Institute of Real Estate Appraisers
MRC	Major retail centre
NAR	National Association of Realtors
NAREB	National Association of Real Estate Brokers
NAV	Net annual value
NHBC	National House Building Council
NIA	Net internal area
NIM	Net income multiplier
NIREB	National Institute of Real Estate Brokers
NLA	Net lettable (or leasable) area
NOI	Net operating income
NPV	Net present value
NRV	Net realizable value

OAR	Overall rate
ODP	Office development permit
OE & T	Operating expenses and taxes
OER	Operating expense ratio
OL & T insurance	Owner's, landlord's and tenant's public liability policy
OS	Ordnance Survey
pa	per annum
PAR	Plan d'aménagement rural
PAZ	Plan d'aménagement de zone
pc sum	prime-cost sum
P/E ratio	Price-earnings ratio
PERT	Project evaluation and review technique
PGI	Potential gross income
PHA	Public Housing Administration
P & I	Principal and interest
PITI	Principal, interest, taxes and insurance
PLD	Plan légal de densité
POS	Plan d'occupation des sols
PSA	Property Services Agency
PUD	Planned unit development
PUT	Property unit trust
PV	Present value
PW	Present worth
qv	*quod vide*, 'which see'
R	A capitalisation rate
®	Realtor
RAM	Reverse annuity mortgage
REIT	Real Estate Investment Trust
RIBA	Royal Institute of British Architects
RICS	Royal Institution of Chartered Surveyors
ROM	Roll-over mortgage
RM	Residential Member, of the Appraisal Institute
RRM	Renegotiable-rate mortgage
SAM	Shared-appreciation mortgage
SDAU	Schèma Directeur d'Aménagement et d'Urbanisme
SDO	Special development order
SEC	Securities and Exchange Commission
sf	square foot
SF	Sinking fund
SI	Statutory Instrument
SICOMI	Société Immobilier pour le Commerce et l'Industrie

S & L association   Savings and loan association
sm   square metre
SOYD   Sum of the years' digits
SREA   Senior Real Estate Analyst
SREA   Society of Real Estate Appraisers
SSSI   Site of special scientific interest
SYD depreciation   Sum-of-the-years' digits depreciation

TDR   Transferable development rights
TPO   Tree preservation order
TVA   Taxe sur la valuer ajoutée
TWR   Time-weighted rate of return

UCC   Uniform Commercial Code
UDA   Urban development area
ULI   Urban Land Institute
UPA   Uniform Partnership Act
URA   Urban Renewal Administration
URLTA   Uniform Residential Landlord and Tenant Act
UXB   Unexpended balance of established development value

VA loan   Veterans Administration loan
VAM   Variable-amortisation mortgage
VAP   Variable-payment mortgage
VAT   Value added tax
VO   Valuation officer
VRM   Variable-rate mortgage

YP   Years' purchase

ZAC   Zone d'aménagement concerté
ZAD   Zone d'aménagement différé
ZER   Zone d'environnement protégé
ZIF   Zone d'intervention foncière
ZUP   Zone à urbaniser par priorité

GENERAL

A	Atlantic Reporter (USA)
A 2d	Atlantic Reporter, Second Series (USA)
AB	Anonymous Reports at the end of Benloe Reports, 1515-1628
AC	Law Reports, Appeal Cases, 1891-date
AD 2d	Appelate Division Reports, Second Series, New York (USA)
A and E/ Ad and E	Adolphus and Ellis's English King's Bench Reports, 1834-1840
Ala	Alabama Reports (USA)
All ER	All England Law Reports, 1936-date
All ER Rep	All England Law Reports, Reprinted, 1558-1935
ALR	American Law Reports, Annotated (USA)
ALR	Argus Law Reports, 1895-1973 (Australia)
ALR	Australian Law Reports, 1973-date, formerly Argus Law Reports
amb	Ambler's Chancery Reports, 1737-1784
App Cas	Law Reports, Appeal Cases, 1875-1890
art	article
ATR	Australasian Tax Reports, 1969-date
Att Gen/ A-G	Attorney General
B and Ad	Barnewall and Adolphus's King's Bench Reports 1830-1834
B and Ald	Barnewall and Alderson's King's Bench Reports, 1817-1822
B and C	Barnewall and Cresswell's King's Bench Reports, 1822-1830
Barb (NY)	Barbour's Supreme Court Reports, New York, 1847-1877 (USA)
Barn Ch Rep	Barnardiston's Chancery Reports, 1740-1741
BC	Borough Council
Beav	Beavan's Rolls Court Reports, 1838-1866
Bing	Bingham's Common Pleas Reports, 1832-1834
Bl Com	Blackstone's Commentaries on the Laws of England (see Appendix B, bibliography)
Bos and PNR	Bosanquet and Puller's English Common Pleas Reports, 1796-1804
Bro CC	Brown's Chancery Reports, 1778-1794
Brownl and Golds	Brownlow and Goldsborough's Common Pleas Reports, 1569-1624
B and S	Best & Smith Reports

Burr	Burrows's King's Bench Reports, 1757-1771
Burr SC	Burrow's Settlement Cases, 1733-1736
c	chapter (Act of Parliament)
C 2d	California Supreme Court Reports, Second Series (USA)
CA	Court of Appeal
CA 3d	California Appelate Reports, Third Series (USA)
Cal	California Reports (USA)
Cal 2d	California Reports, Second Series (USA)
Cal App	California Appelate Reports (USA)
Cal Rptr	California Reporter (USA)
Camp	Campbell's Nisi Prius Reports, 1807-1816
Car and M	Carrington and Marshan's Nisi Prius Reports, 1840-1842
Cas in Ch	Selected Cases in Chancery, 1660-1697
Cass Civ	*Cassation Chambre Civile*–Court of Cassation (France)
CB	English Common Bench Reports, Manning, Granger & Scott, 1845-1856
CB(NS)/CBNS	English Common Bench Reports, New Series by John Scott, 1856-1865
CC	County Council
cf	confer-compare with
Ch	Law Reports Chancery Division, 1891-date
Ch App	Law Reports, Chancery Appeal Cases, 1865-1875
Ch D	Law Reports Chancery Division, 1875-1890
CL	English Common Law Reports, American Reprints, 1875-1890
	Current Law, 1947-date
CLR	Canada Law Reports, 1923-date
	Commonwealth Law Reports, 1903-date (Australia)
CLY	Current Law Year Book, 1947-date
Co Inst	Coke's Institutes (see Appendix B, bibliography)
Co Litt	Coke on Littleton (see Appendix B, bibliography)
Colo	Colorado Supreme Court Reports
Com	Comerback's King's Bench Reports, 1685-1699
Comm R	Commonwealth Arbitration Reports, 1905-date (Australia)
Conv	Conveyancer
Co Rep	Coke's Reports, 1572-1616
Cowell	Cowell's Law Dictionary
Cowp	Cowper's King's Bench Reports, 1774-1778
Cox	Cox's Chancery Cases, 1783-1796
C and P	Craig & Philips Chancery Reports, 1840-1841
CPD	Law Reports, Common Pleas Division, 1875-1880
CPR	Canadian Patent Reporter, 1941-date
CPR	Common Pleas Reporter, Pennsylvania (USA)
Crim LR	Criminal Law Review

Cro Eliz	Croke's King's Bench Reports, tempore Eliz I Cro, 1582-1603
Cro Jac	Crooke's King's Bench Reports, tempore James, 1603-1625
D and C	Deacon & Chitty's Bankruptcy Reports, 1852-1835
	Dow & Clark's House of Lords Appeals, 1827-1832
DC La	District Court, Louisiana (USA)
DC LR	Dominion Companies Law Reports, 1949-date (Canada)
DC NY	District Court, New York (USA)
DC WVa	District Court, West Virginia (USA)
DeGf and J	DeGex, Fisher and Jones's Chancery Reports, 1859-1862
DeGM and G	DeGex, Macnaghten and Gordon's Chancery Reports, 1851-1857
Digest (Repl)	English and Empire Digest Replacement Volumes (Blue Band)
DLR	Dominion Law Reports, 1912-date (Canada)
DPD	Law Reports, Common Pleas Division, 1875-1880
Drew	Drewry's Chancery Reports, 1852-1859
Drew and SM	Drewry and Smale's Vice Chancellor's Reports, 1859-1865
Dy/Dyer	Dyer's King's Bench Reports, 1513-1582
Ea	East's Term Reports, King's Bench, 1880-1812 Eastern Reporter (USA)
East	East's Term Reports, King's Bench, 1800-1812
E and B	Ellis and Blackburn's Queen's Bench Reports 1851-1858
E and E	Ellis and Ellis's Queen's Bench Reports, 1858-1861
ed	edition
EG	Estates Gazette, 1858-date
EGD	Estates Gazette Digest of Cases, 1902-date
ER/Eng Rep	English Reports, 1220-1865
Esp	Espinasse's Nisi Prius Reports, 1793-1807
et seq	*et sequentes* – and those following
Ex	Exchequer Reports, 1847-1856
Ex D	Law Reports, Exchequer Division, 1875-1880
F/Fed	Federal Reporter, 1880-date (USA)
F 2d	Federal Reporter, Second Series (USA)
F and F	Foster and Finlason's Nisi Prius Reports, 1856-1867
Fla	Florida Supreme Court Reports, 1846-1948 (USA)
F Supp	Federal Supplement, 1932-date (USA)
Ga App	Georgia Appeals, 1807-date (USA)

H and C	Hurlstone and Coltman's Exchequer Reports, 1862-1866
H and N	Hurstone and Norman's Exchequer Reports, 1856-1862
Har L Rev	Harvard Law Review (USA)
HL Cas	House of Lords Cases, 1847-1866
HMSO	Her Majesty's Stationery Office
Hob	Hobart's King's Bench Reports, 1603-1625
Howard	Howard's Supreme Court Reports, 1834-1843 (USA)
	Howard's Mississippi Supreme Court Reports, 1834-1843 (USA)
Ill	Illinois Supreme Court Reports, 1819-date (USA)
Ill App	Illinois Appelate Cases, 1877-date (USA)
Ind App	Indiana Appelate Cases, 1890-date (USA)
IR	Irish Reports, 1838-date
Ired (NC)	Iredell's North Carolina Law Reports, 1840-1852
Johns and Hem	Johnson and Hemming's Chancery Reports, 1859-1862
JP	Justice of the Peace and Local Government Reports, 1837-date
JPL	Journal of Planning and Property Law, 1954-1972
	Journal of Planning and Environmental Law, 1973-date
JR	Juridical Review (Scotland), 1889-date
Jur	The Jurist, London
Jurid Soc	Juridical Society's Papers (Scotland)
Just Inst	Justinian's Institutes
Kans	Kansas Supreme Court Reports, 1862-date (USA)
KB	Law Reports, King's Bench Division, 1901-1952
Kent	James Kent's Commentaries on American Law, 1826-1830
K and J	Kay and Johnson's Vice Chancellor's Reports, 1854-1858
Ky	Kentucky Supreme Court Reports, 1879-1951 (USA)
Lea	Lea's Tennessee Reports (USA)
Leach	Leach's Crown Cases, 1730-1814
L Ed	Lawyer's Edition Supreme Court Reports (USA)
LGR	Knight's Local Government Reports, 1903-date
	Local Government Review
LGRA	Local Government Reports of Australia
Litt	Coke on Littleton (see Appendix B, bibliography)
LJ	Law Journal, 1866-1965 (newspaper)
LJCh	Law Journal, Chancery, New Series, 1831-1946

LJCP	Law Journal Reports, Common Pleas, New Series
LJEq	Law Journal, Chancery, New Series, 1831-1946
LJExch	Law Journal, Exchequer, New Series
LJExEq	Law Journal, Exchequer in Equity, 1835-1841
LJKB	Law Journal, King's Bench, New Series, 1831-1946
LJMC	Law Journal, Magistrates Cases, 1866-1892
LJOS	Law Journal, Old Series, 1822-1831
LJ(OS)MC	Law Journal, Magistrates Cases, Old Series, 1826-1831
LJQB	Law Journal, Queen's Bench, New Series, 1831-1946
Ll LL R	Lloyd's List Law Reports, 1919-date
LL Rep/Ll L Rep	Lloyd's List Law Reports, 1919-date
Lloyd's Rep	Lloyd's List Law Reports, 1919-date
Lloyd's LR	Lloyd's List Law Reports, 1919-date
LQR	Law Quarterly Review
LR	Law Reports, 1865-date
LR Ch App	Law Reports, Chancery Appeal Cases,1865-1875
LRCP	Law Reports, Common Pleas Cases, 1865-1875
LREq	Law Reports, Equity Cases, 1866-1875
LREx	Law Reports, Exchequer Cases, 1865-1875
LRHL	Law Reports, English and Irish Appeals, 1866-1875
LRIr	Law Reports, Ireland, 1878-1893
LRK	Kenya Law Reports, 1897-1956
LRQB	Law Reports, Queen's Bench, 1865-1875, 1891-date
LSG	Law Society Gazette
LT	Law Times, Pennsylvania (USA)
LT/LTR/LT Rep	Law Times Reports, New Series, 1859-1947
Macq HL	Macqueen's Scotch Appeals, House of Lords, 1849-1865
Macq (Scot)	Macqueen's Scottish Appeal Cases
Mad	Madras High Court reports
Man and G	Manning and Granger's Common Pleas Reports, 1840-1844
Mass	Massachusetts Reports (USA)
M and W	Meeson and Welsby's Exchequer Reports, 1836-1847
Md	Maryland Supreme Court Reports (USA)
Me	Maine Reports (USA)
Mer	Merivale's Chancery Reports, 1815-1817
Mich	Michigan Supreme Court Reports, 1847-date (USA)
Mich LR	Michigan Law Review (USA)
Misc 2d	Miscellaneous New York Reports, Second Series, (USA)
MLR	Modern Law Review, 1937-date
Mod Rep	Modern Reports, 1669-1775
Mood and R	Moody and Robinson's Nisi Prius Reports, 1830-1844
MR	Master of the Rolls

My and K	Mylne & Keen's Chancery Reports, 1832-1835
NC	North Carolina Supreme Court Reports, 1968-date (USA)
NE	North Eastern Reporter (USA)
NE 2d	North Eastern Reporter, Second Series (USA)
NJ Eq	New Jersey Equity Reports, 1830-1835
NJ Super	New Jersey Superior Court Reports, 1948-date (USA)
NLJ/New LJ	New Law Journal, 1965-date
NR	New Reports, 1883-1865
NSWR	New South Wales Reports, 1960-date (Australia)
NW 2d	North Western Reporter, Second Series (USA)
NY	New York Court of Appeals Reports, 1847-date (USA)
NYS	New York Supplement, 1887-1937 (USA)
NYS 2d	New York Supplement, Second Series, 1938-date (USA)
NZLR	New Zealand Law Reports, 1883-date
Okl	Oklahoma Supreme Court Reports, 1890-1956 (USA)
OLR	Ohio Law Reporter, 1903-date (USA)
	Ontario Law Reports, 1901-1930 (Canada)
Or	Oregon Supreme Court Reports, 1953-date (USA)
OR	Ontario Supreme Court Reports, 1882-1900, 1931-date (Canada)
OS	Old Series
p.pp	page (s)
P	Law Reports, Probate, Divorce and Admiralty Division, 1891-1971
	Pacific Reporter (USA)
P 2d	Pacific Reporter, Second Series (USA)
Pac	Pacific Reporter (USA)
P and CR	Planning (Property from 1968) and Compensation Reports, 1949-date
PD	Law Reports, Probate Division, 1875-1890
Peake	Peake's Nisi Prius, 1790-1794
Ph	Philip's Chancery Reports, 1841-1849
Pl	Plowden's Commentaries, 1550-1580
Plow/Plowd/Plwd	Plowden's King's Bench Reports
Prec Ch	Precedents in Chancery, 1689-1722
PW/PWms	Peere William's Chancery Reports (24ER), 1695-1735
QB	Law Reports, Queen's Bench Division, 1891-1901, 1952-date
QBD	Law Reports, Queen's Bench Division, 1875-1890
R	*Rex* (King) or *Regina* (Queen)
RA	Registration Appeals (USA)

Rep Coke's	Coke's King's Bench Division, 1572-1616
RI	Rhode Island Supreme Court Reports, 1828-date (USA)
Russ	Russell's Chancery Reports, 1823-1829
s/ss (plural)	section(s)
Salk/Salkeld	Salkeld's English King's Bench Reports
SASR	South Australian State Reports, 1921-date
SC	Session Cases, 1906-date (Scotland)
Sch	Schedule
Sch and Lef	Schoales and Lefroy's Irish Chancery Reports
ScLr	Scottish Law Reports, 1865-1924
SCt	Supreme Court Reports (USA)
SE	South Eastern Reporter (USA)
SE 2d	South Eastern Reporter, Second Series (USA)
SI	Statutory Instument
SJ/Sol Jo	Solicitor's Journal
SLT (Sch Ct)	Scots Law Times Reports, Sheriff Court, 1893-date
So	Southern Reporter (USA)
So 2d	Southern Reporter, Second Series (USA)
Sol Jo	Solicitor's Journal
SR(NWS)	New South Wales, State Reports, 1901-date (Australia)
S R & O	Statutory Rules and Orders
Star	Starkie's Nisi Prius Reports, 1814-1823
STC	Simon's Tax Cases
St Tr	Howell's State Trials, England, 1163-1820
supra	above
SW/SW Rep	South Western Reporter (USA)
SW 2d	South Western Reporter, Second Series (USA)
Swans	Swanston's Chancery Reports, 1818-1819
SWL REV	Southwestern Law Review, 1916-1918 (USA)
Taunt	Taunton's Common Pleas Reports, 1808-1819
Term/Term Rep	Dunford and East's Term Reports, 1775-1800
Termes de La Ley	Terms of the Common Law and Statutes of England Expounded and Explained by John Rastell, 1624 reprinted 1641 and 1708
Tex Civ App	Texas Civil Appeals Reports
TLR	Times Law Reports, 1884-1952
UCC	Uniform Commercial Code
UDC	Urban District Council
US	United States Supreme Court Reports, 1790-date
USCA	United States Code Annotated
Utah	Utah Supreme Court Reports, 1855-date (USA)

Utah 2d	Utah Reports, Second Series (USA)
v	*versus*
Va	Virginia Supreme Court Reports, 1880-date (USA)
Vern	Vernon's Chancery Reports, 1680-1719
Ves	Vesey Junior's Chancery Reports, 1789-1817
VLR	Victoria Law Reports, 1875-date (Australia)
Vt	Vermont Supreme Court Reports 1826-date (USA)
Wall	Wallace Reports (USA)
WALR	Western Australia Law Reports, 1898-date
Wash App	Washington Appelate Reports (USA)
WLR	Weekly Law Reports, 1953-date
WN	Law Reports, Weekly Notes, 1866-1951
WN (NSW)	Weekly Notes, New South Wales, 1884-date (Australia)
WR	Weekly Reports, 1853-1906
WWR	Western Weekly Reports, 1912-1950 (Canada)
YB	Year Books (followed by year of King's reign, initials of his or her name, and the folio and number of the *placita*)

Appendix B: Bibliography

APPRAISAL, AND PRINCIPLES AND PRACTICE OF U.S. REAL ESTATE
See also: Land Economics, Valuation, Financial Analysis and Report Writing

Akerson, Charles B. *Capitalisation Theory and Techniques: Study Guide (with financial tables computed by the Financial Publishing Company)*. Chicago: American Institute of Real Estate Appraisers, revised edition 1984.

Akerson, Charles B. *The Internal Rate of Return in Real Estate Investments*. Chicago: American Institute of Real Estate Appraisers and American Society of Real Estate Counsellors, 1976.

Akerson, Charles B. *An Introduction to Mortgage-Equity Capitalisation*. Chicago: American Institute of Real Estate Appraisers, 1975.

American Institute of Real Estate Appraisers. *Reading in the Appraisal of Special Purpose Properties*. Chicago: American Institute of Real Estate Appraisers, 1981.

American Institute of Real Estate Appraisers. *Readings in the Income Approach to Real Property Valuation. Vol 1*. Chicago: American Institute of Real Estate Appraisers, 1977.

American Institute of Real Estate Appraisers. *Readings in Market Value*. Chicago: American Institute of Real Estate Appraisers, 1981.

American Institute of Real Estate Appraisers. *The Appraisal of Real Estate*. 8th edn. Chicago: American Institute of Real Estate Appraisers, 1983.

American Institute of Real Estate Appraisers. *The Appraisal of Rural Property*. Chicago: American Institute of Real Estate Appraisers, 1983.

Barash, Samuel T. *Complete Guide to Appraising Condominiums and Cooperatives*. Englewood Cliffs, New Jersey: Prentice-Hall, Inc., 1981.

Barrett, Vincent G. and Blair, John P. *How to Conduct and Analyse Real Estate Markets and Feasibility Studies*. New York: Van Nostrand Reinhold Co., Inc., 1982

Betts, Richard and Ely, S.J. *Basic Real Estate Appraisal*. New York: John Wiley & Sons, Inc., 1982.

Bloom, George F., Weiner, Arthur M. and Fisher, Jeffery D. *Real Estate*. 8th edn. New York: John Wiley & Sons, Inc., 1982.

Conroy, Kathleen. *Valuing the Timeshare Property*. Chicago: American Institute of Real Estate Appraisers, 1976.

Dombal, Robert M. *Residential Condominiums: A Guide to Analysis and Appraisal*. Chicago: American Institute of Real Estate Appraisers, 1976.

Ellwood, L.W. *Ellwood's Tables for Real Estate Appraising and Financing.* 4th edn. Chicago: American Institute of Real Estate Appraisers, 1977.

Everett, E.R. and Kinnard, William N. Jr. *A Guide to Appraising Apartments.* 5th edn. Chicago: Society of Real Estate Appraisers, 1979.

Friedman, Edith J. (editor). *Encyclopedia of Real Estate Appraising.* Englewood Cliffs, New Jersey: Prentice-Hall, Inc., 1978.

Friedman, J.P. and Ordway N. *Income Property Appraisal and Analysis.* Reston, Va.: Reston Publishing Company, 1981.

Foreman, Robert L. *Communicating the Appraisal: A Guide to Report Writing.* Chicago: American Institute of Real Estate Appraisers, 1982.

Garrett, Robert L. et al. *The Valuation of Shopping Centres.* Chicago: American Institute of Real Estate Appraisers, 1976.

Gibbons, E. *Mortgage-Equity Capitalisation: Ellwood Method.* Chicago: American Institute of Real Estate Appraisers, 1980.

Harwood, Bruce. *Real Estate Principles.* 4th edn. Englewood Cliffs, New Jersey: Prentice-Hall, Inc., 1986.

Irwin, Robert (editor). *The McGraw-Hill Real Estate Company Handbook.* New York: McGraw-Hill Book Company, 1984

Jaffe, Austin and Sirmans, C.F. *Real Estate Investment Decision Making.* Englewood Cliffs, New Jersey: Prentice-Hall, Inc., 1982.

Johnson, Irvin E. *Instant Mortgage-Equity.* Lexington, Mass.: Lexington Books, 1980.

Johnson, Irvin E. *Selling Real Estate by Mortgage-Equity Analysis.* Lexington, Mass.: Lexington Books, 1976.

Kahn, Sanders A. and Case, Frederick E. *Real Estate Appraisal and Investment.* 2nd edn. New York: John Wiley & Sons, Inc., 1977.

Kinnard, William N. Jr. *Income Property Valuation.* Lexington, Mass.: Lexington Books, 1971.

Kinnard, William N. Jr. and Boyce, Bryl N. *An Introduction to Appraising Real Property.* Chicago: American Institute of Real Estate Appraisers, 1978, revised edition 1984.

Lukens, Reaves C. Jr. *The Appraiser and Real Estate Feasibility Studies.* Chicago: American Institute of Real Estate Appraisers, 1972.

Mason, James J. (editor). *American Institute of Real Estate Appraisers Financial Tables (with financial tables computed by Financial Publishing Company).* Chicago: American Institute of Real Estate Appraisers, 1982.

Rams, Edwin M. *Analysis and Valuation of Retail Locations.* Reston, Va.: Reston Publishing Company, Inc., 1976.

Reynold, Judith. *Historic Properties: Preservation and Valuation Process*. Chicago: American Institute of Real Estate Appraisers, 1983.

Ring, Alfred A. and Dasso, Jerome. *Real Estate Principles and Practice*. 10th edn. Englewood Cliffs, New Jersey: Prentice-Hall, Inc., 1985.

Ring, Alfred A. *Valuation of Real Estate*. 2nd edn. Englewood Cliffs, New Jersey: Prentice-Hall, Inc., 1970

Roca, Ruben A. *Market Research for Shopping Centres*. New York: International Council for Shopping Centres, 1980.

Rushmore, Stephen. *Hotels, Motels and Restaurants: Valuation and Market Studies*. Chicago: American Institute of Real Estate Appraisers, 1983.

Shenkel, William M. *Modern Real Estate Appraisal*. New York: McGraw-Hill Book Company, 1978.

Wendt, Paul F. and Cerf, Alan R. *Real Estate Investment Analysis and Taxation*. 2nd edn. New York: McGraw-Hill Book Company, 1979.

Woolery, Arlo. *The Art of Valuation*. Lexington, Mass.: Lexington Books, 1978.

ARCHITECTURE AND BUILDING DESIGN

See Also: Building Construction and Control

Beddington, N. *Design for Shopping Centres*. London: Butterworth Scientific, 1982.

Centre for Advanced Land Use Studies. *Rent Assessment and Tenant Mix in Planned Shopping Centres*. Reading, Berkshire: College of Estate Management, 1975.

Darlow, Clive (editor). *Enclosed Shopping Centres*. London: Architectural Press, 1976.

Dawson, John A. *Shopping Centre Development*. London & New York: Longman Group Ltd., 1983.

Drury, Jolyon. *Factories: Planning, Design and Modernisation*. London: Architectural Press, 1982.

Gosling, David and Maitland, Barry. *Design and Planning of Retail Systems*. London: Architectural Press, 1976.

Hines, M.A. *Shopping Centre Investment and Design*. New York: John Wiley & Sons, Inc., 1983.

Longman's Directory of Official Architecture and Planning. London: Longman Professional, annual.

Maitland, Barry. *Shopping Malls: Planning and Design*. London: Longman Scientific & Technical, 1985.

Marber, Paul and Paula (editors). *Office Development*. London: Estates Gazette, 1985.

Martin, David. *Specification*. London: Architectural Press, annual.

Munn, David. *Shops: A Manual of Planning and Design*. London: Architectural Press 1983.

Northen, Ian and Hoskoll, M. *Shopping Centres: A Developer's Guide to Planning and Design*. Reading, Berkshire: College of Estate Management, 1977. See also: Jolly, Brian (editor) *Property Development Library*.

Salata, Antony. *Offices Today and Tomorrow*, See: Jolly, Brian (editor), *Property Development Library*, vol.1., 1983.

Scott, J. J. *Architectural Practice*. London: Butterworth & Co. (Publishers) Ltd., 1985.

Spink, Frank H. Jr. (editor). *Shopping Center Development Handbook*. Washington D.C.: Urban Land Institute, 1976.

Willis, Arthur J. and George, W.N.B. *The Architect in Practice*. 6th edn. William Collins Sons & Co. Ltd., 1981.

BUILDING CONSTRUCTION AND CONTROL

See also: Architecture and Building Design

The ACQUA Group. *Fire and Building: A Guide for the Design Team*. London: Granada Publishing Ltd., 1984

Antill, J.M. *Critical Path Methods in Construction Practice*. Chichester, Sussex: John Wiley & Sons Ltd., 1982.

Ashworth, A and Heath, B.C. *Advanced Quantity Surveying*. 3rd edn. London: Butterworth & Co. (Publishers) Ltd., 1983.

Battersby, Albert. *Network Analysis for Planning and Scheduling*. 3rd edn. London: Macmillan Publishers Ltd., 1970.

Bennett, J. *Construction Project Management*. London: Butterworth, 1985.

Burchess, D. *Specification and Quantities*. 2nd edn. London: George Godwin Ltd, 1980.

Burgess, R.A. and White, G. *Building Production and Project Management*. London: Longman Scientific & Technical, 1979.

Cleland, David I. and King, William R (editors). *Project Management Handbook*. New York: Van Nostrand Reinhold Co., Inc., 1983

Elder, A.J. *Guide to the Building Regulations 1976*. 7th edn. London: Architectural Press, 1981 with 1982 supplement.

Fryer, Barry. *Practice of Construction Management.* New York: Sheridan House, Inc., 1985.

Greater London Council. *Handbook for Clerks of Works.* 3rd edn. London: Architectural Press, 1983.

Green, Ronald. *The Architect's Guide to Running a Job.* 4th edn. London: Architectural Press, 1986.

Halpin, D.W. and Woodhead, R. *Construction Management.* New York: John Wiley & Sons, Inc., 1980

Hughes, G.A. *The Anatomy of Quantity Surveying.* 2nd edn. Lancaster: Construction Press, 1982.

Knight's Building Regulations, by G.D. Binns, J.I'A. Nelson and E.Thompson. First published in 1966, subsequently updated to cover Building Regulations 1976. Croydon, Surrey: Charles Knight Publishing.

Knight's Building Regulations (with approved documents), by H.W. Clarke, J.I'A. Nelson and E.Thompson. Croydon, Surrey: Charles Knight Publishing. 1985, looseleaf with updating service.

Lock, D. *Project Management.* 3rd edn. Aldershot, Hampshire: Gower Publishing Company Limited, 1984.

Lockyer, K.G. *An Introduction to Critical Path Analysis and Project Analysis Network Techniques.* 4th edn. London: Pitman Publishing Ltd., 1984

Moder, Joseph J., Philips, Cecil R. and Davis, Edward W. *Project Management with CPM, PERT, and precedence diagramming.* 3rd edn. New York: Van Nostrand Reinhold Co., Inc., 1983.

Peart, Alan T. *Design of Project Management Systems and Records.* Epping, Essex: Gower, 1971.

Pitt, P.H. and Dufton, J. *Building Controls in Inner London.* London: Architectural Press, 1983.

Powell-Smith, V. and Billington, N.J. *The Building Regulations Explained and Illustrated.* 7th edn. London: William Collins Sons & Co. Ltd., 1986.

Redgrave, Alexander. *Health and Safety in Factories.* New edition by Ian Fife and Antony Machin. London: Butterworth & Co. (Publishers) Ltd, 1976 with 2nd cumulative supplement 1981.

Redgrave's Offices and Shops. 2nd edn. by Ian Fife and Antony Machin. London: Butterworth & Co. (Publishers) Ltd., 1973.

Rosenfeld, Walter. *The Practical Specifier: A Manual of Construction Documentation for Architects.* New York: McGraw-Hill Book Company, 1985.

Scott, J.J. *Specification Writing: An Introduction.* London: Butterworth & Co. (Publishers) Ltd., 1984.

Seeley, Ivor H. *Building Quantities Explained.* 3rd edn. London: Macmillan Publishers Ltd., reprinted 1985.

Skinner, D.W.H. *The Contractor's Use of Bills of Quantity.* Ascot, Berkshire: Chartered Institute of Building, 1981.

Stallworthy, E.A. and Kharabanda, O.P. *Total Project Management.* Aldershot, Hampshire: Gower Publishing Company Limited, 1983.

Stasiowski, Frank and Burstein, David. *Project Management for the Design Professional.* London: Architectural Press, 1983.

Stephenson, John. *Building Regulations 1976 in Detail,* with 1st, 2nd & 3rd amendments. London: Northwood Publications, 1984.

Stephenson, John. *Building Regulations 1985 Explained.* London: International Thompson Publishing, 1985.

Stewart, Edwin, P. *Techniques for Preparing a Bill of Quantities.* London and New York: E.& F.N. Spon Ltd., 1971

Taylor, Jane and Cooke, Gordon. *The Fire Precautions Act in Practice.* London: Architectural Press, 1978.

Turner, D.F. *Design and Build Contract Practice.* London: Longman Scientific & Technical, 1986.

Turner D.F. *Quantity Surveying: Practice and Administration.* 3rd edn. London: George Godwin Ltd., 1983.

Underdown, G.W. *Practical Fire Precautions.* 2nd edn. Aldershot, Hampshire: Gower Publishing Company Limited, 1979.

Walker, Antony. *Project Management in Construction.* London: William Collins Sons & Co., Ltd., 1984.

Whyte W.S. and Powell-Smith, Vincent. *The Building Regulations Explained and Illustrated.* 6th edn. London: Granada Publishing Ltd., 1982.

Willis, Arthur J. and George W.N.B. *The Architect in Practice.* 6th edn. London: Granada Publishing Ltd., 1981.

Willis, Arthur J. and Willis, Christopher J. *Elements of Quantity Surveying.* 7th edn. London: William Collins Sons & Co. Ltd., 1978.

Willis, Arthur J. and Willis, Christopher J. *Practice and Procedure for the Quantity Surveyor.* London: William Collins Sons & Co. Ltd., 1978.

Willis, Arthur J. and Willis, Christopher J. *Specification Writing for Architects and Surveyors.* 8th edn. London: Granada Publishing Ltd., 1982.

Willis, Christopher J. and Moseley, Leonard. *More Advanced Quantity Surveying.* London: William Collins Sons & Co. Ltd., 1984.

Wood, R.D. *Principles of Estimating.* 6th edn. London: Estates Gazette, 1982.

Wright, Graham J.H. *Building Control by Legislation: The U.K. Experience.* Chichester, West Sussex: John Wiley & Sons Ltd., 1983.

BUILDING CONSTRUCTION LAW

Ashworth, Allan. *Contractual Procedures in the Construction Industry.* London: Longman Scientific & Technical, 1985.

Douglas, B.J. *Latent Defects: Some Legal and Insurance Considerations*, Technical Information Service no.41. Ascot, Berkshire: Chartered Institute of Building, 1984.

Emden, A. and Gill, W.H. (editors). *Building Contracts and Practice.* 8th edn. London: Butterworth & Co. (Publishers) Ltd., 1980.

Healey, P.E. *Force Majeure.* Ascot, Berkshire: Chartered Institute of Building, 1979.

Hudson, A.A. *Building Contracts, including Duties of Architects, Engineers and Surveyors.* 10th edn. London: Sweet & Maxwell, 1970 with 1979 supplement by I.N. Duncan Wallace.

Keating, D. *The Law and Practice of Building Contracts, including commentary on the JCT standard form of contract.* 4th edn. London: Sweet & Maxwell, 1978 with 1982 and 1984 supplements.

Powell-Smith, Vincent and Pymont, Stephen J. *Design and Build Contracts.* London: William Collins Sons & Co. Ltd., 1985

Turner, D.F. *Building Contracts: A Practical Guide.* 4th edn. Harlow, Essex: George Godwin Ltd, 1983.

Uff, J. *Construction Law: Law and Practice relating to the Construction Industry.* 4th edn. London: Sweet & Maxwell, 1985.

COMPULSORY PURCHASE AND COMPENSATION
See: Planning Law and Compulsory Purchase.

FINANCE, BANKING AND INVESTMENT
See also: Valuation, Financial Analysis and Report Writing, Appraisal, and Principles and Practice of Real Estate.

Adams, J. and Pritchard Brown, K.V. *Franchising.* 2nd edn. London: Butterworth & Co. (Publishers) Ltd., 1986.

Arnaud, A.A. *Investment Trusts Explained.* 2nd edn. Cambridge: Woodhead-Faulkner (Publishers) Ltd., 1984

Berman, Daniel S. *How to Put Together a Real Estate Syndicate or Joint Venture.* Englewood Cliffs, New Jersey: Prentice-Hall, Inc., 1984.

Beaton, William R. *Real Estate Finance.* 2nd edn. Englewood Cliffs, New Jersey: Prentice-Hall, Inc., 1982.

Boddy, M. *The Building Societies.* London: Macmillan Publishers Ltd., 1980.

Boleat, Mark. *The Building Society Industry.* London: George Allen & Unwin (Publishers) Ltd., 1982.

Boykin, J.H. *Financing Real Estate.* Lexington, Mass.: Lexington Books, 1979.

Brueggerman, William B, and Stone, Leo D. *Real Estate Finance.* 7th edn. Holmwood, Ill.: Richard D. Irwin, Inc., 1981.

Clarke, T.M. *Leasing.* Maidenhead, Berks: McGraw-Hill Book Company (UK) Ltd., 1978.

Cummings, Jack. *Complete Guide to Real Estate Financing.* Englewood Cliffs, New Jersey: Prentice-Hall, Inc., 1978.

Dasso, Jerome and Kuhn, Gerald W. *Real Estate Finance.* Englewood Cliffs, New Jersey: Prentice-Hall, Inc., 1983.

Day, Martin and Harris, Paul. *Unit Trusts: The Law and Practice.* 2nd edn. London: Longman Professional, 1986

Diamond, Audrey L. *Commercial and Consumer Credit: An Introduction.* London: Butterworth & Co. (Publishers) Ltd., 1982.

Epley, Donald and Millar, J. *Basic Real Estate Finance and Investments.* 2nd edn. New York: John Wiley & Sons, Inc., 1984.

Fanning, David and Pendlebury, Maurice. *Company Accounts: A Guide.* London: George Allen & Unwin (Publishers) Ltd., 1984.

Findlay, Chapman M., Messner, Stephen D. and Tarantello, Rocky A. *Real Estate Portfolio Analysis.* Lexington, Mass.: Lexington Books, 1983.

Gilcrist, Christopher. *Unit Trusts.* 3rd edn. Cambridge: Woodhead-Faulkner (Publishers) Ltd., 1980.

Goode, R.M. *Hire Purchase Law and Practice.* 2nd edn. London: Butterworth & Co. (Publishers) Ltd., 1970.

Hines, Mary Alice. *Income Property Development, Financing and Investment.* Lexington, Mass.: Lexington Books, 1983.

Hines, Mary Alice. *Real Estate Finance.* Englewood Cliffs, New Jersey: Prentice-Hall, Inc., 1978.

Holmes, Geoffrey and Sugden, Alan. *Interpreting Company Reports and Accounts.* 3rd edn. Cambridge: Woodhead-Faulkner (Publishers) Ltd., 1986.

Hopkins, Leon. *Business Ratios: A Guide to Interpretation.* 2nd edn. London: I.C.C. Publications Ltd., 1980.

Hubbard, Graham. *Finance Leasing*. London: Institute of Cost and Management Accountants, 1980.

Hull, J.C. *The Evaluation of Risk in Business Investment*. Oxford: Pergamon Press, 1980.

Irvin, George, with assistance of Richard Brown. *Modern Cost-Benefit Methods: An Introduction to Financial, Economic & Social Aspects*. New York: Harper & Row Publishers, 1978.

Jachow, Stephen R. *Real Estate Syndication: Tax, Securities and Business Aspects*. New York: John Wiley & Sons, Inc., 1985.

McIntosh, Angus P.J. and Sykes, Stephen G. *A Guide to Institutional Property*. London: Macmillan Publishers Ltd., 1981.

Maisel, Sherman J. *Financing Real Estate: Principles and Practice*. New York: McGraw-Hill Book Company, 1976.

Maisel, Sherman J. and Roulac, Stephen E. *Real Estate Investment and Finance*. New York: McGraw-Hill Book Company, 1976.

Mendelsohn, M. *The Guide to Franchising*. 4th edn. Oxford: Pergamon Press, 1984

Merrett, A.J. and Sykes, Allen. *The Finance and Analysis of Capital Projects*. 2nd edn. London: Longman Group Ltd., 1973.

Mishan, E.J. *Elements of Cost-Benefit Analysis*. London: George Allen & Unwin (Publishers) Ltd., 1972.

National Association of Real Estate Investment Trusts. *The R.E.I.T. Fact Book*. Washington, D.C.: National Association of Real Estate Investment Trusts, annual.

Norman, John T. Jr. *The Scholastic Approach to Usury*. Cambridge, Mass.: Harvard University Press, 1957.

Paice, D.A. *Critical Path Analysis: Basic Techniques*. London: Longman Group Ltd., 1982.

Pearce, D.W. *Cost-Benefit Analysis*. 2nd edn. London: Macmillan Publishers Ltd., 1983.

Pollack, W.A.J. and Goldzen, G. *Franchising for Profit: A Guide for Professional Advisors and Businessmen*. Milton Keynes, Buckinghamshire: Chartac Books, 1985.

Pyhrr, Stephen A. and Cooper, James R. *Real Estate Investment*. New York: John Wiley & Sons, Inc., 1982.

Richardson, Dudley. *Guide to Negotiable Instruments and Bills of Exchange*. 7th edn. London: Butterworth & Co. Ltd., 1981.

Sarna, L. *Letters of Credit*. Toronto: Carswell Legal Publications, imported by Sweet & Maxwell, 1984.

Sirman, C.F. *Real Estate Finance*. New York: McGraw-Hill Book Company, 1985.

Sirota, David. *Essentials of Real Estate Finance.* 3rd edn. Chicago: Real Estate Finance Company, 1983.

Sugden, R. and Williams, A. *The Principles and Practice of Cost-Benefit Analysis.* Oxford: Oxford University Press, 1978.

Wainman, David and Brown, Howard. *Leasing: The Accounting and Taxation Implications.* 2nd edn. London: Institute of Chartered Accountants, 1979.

Weidermar, John D. *Real Estate Finance.* 4th edn. Reston, Va.: Reston Publishing Company, 1983.

Weist, Jerome D. and Levy, Ferdinand K. *A Management Guide to P.E.R.T./C.P.M.: with Gert-PDM, DCPM & Other Networks.* 2nd edn. Englewood Cliffs, New Jersey: Prentice-Hall, Inc., 1977.

Whitehouse, Brian P. *Partners in Property: a history and analysis of the provision of institutional property finance for property development.* London: Birn Bros, 1964.

Wurtzburg, G.F.A. and Mills, John. *Building Society Law.* 14th edn. London: Sweet & Maxwell, 1976.

GENERAL LAW, England and Wales
See also: Housing Law, Real Property Law

Anson's Law of Contract. 26th edn., by A.G. Guest. Oxford: Oxford University Press, 1984.

Atiyah, P.S. *An Introduction to the Law of Contract.* 3rd edn. Oxford: Oxford University Press, 1981.

Atiyah, P.S. *The Sale of Goods.* 7th edn. London: Pitman Publishing Ltd., 1985.

Atiyah, P.S. *Vicarious Liability in the Law of Torts.* London: Butterworth & Co. (Publishers) Ltd., 1967.

Baker, C.D. *Tort.* 4th edn. London: Sweet & Maxwell, 1986.

Barlow, J., King, L. and King, A. *Wills, Administration and Taxation: A Practical Guide.* 2nd edn. London: Sweet & Maxwell, 1986.

Bennion, Francis. *Statute Law.* 2nd edn. London: Longman Professional, 1983.

Birks, Peter. *An Introduction to the Law of Restitution.* Oxford: Clarendon Press, 1985.

Blackstone, Sir William. *Commentaries on the Laws of England.* 4 vols. Oxford: Oxford University Press, 1765-1769.

Bowden, Gerald F. and Morris, Alan S. *An Introduction to the Law of Contract and Tort.* London: Estates Gazette, 1978.

Bowstead's Law of Agency. 15th edn. by F.M.B. Reynolds. London: Sweet & Maxwell, 1985.

Burgess, R. and Morse, G. *Partnership Law and Practice.* London: Sweet & Maxwell, 1980.

Butterworth's Encyclopaedia of Forms and Precedents. 4th edn. London: Butterworth & Co. (Publishers) Ltd., 1964, with cumulative noter-up.

Calnan, R. *Law of Set-off.* London: Sweet & Maxwell, 1986.

Caplin, Charles and Wexler, Arnold. *Powers of Attorney.* 4th edn. London: Longman Professional, 1971 reprinted 1976.

Card, Richard, Murdoch, John and Schofield, Peter. *Law for Land Management Students.* 2nd edn. London: Butterworth & Co. (Publishers) Ltd., 1986.

Carter, John. *Breach of Contract.* London: Sweet & Maxwell, 1985.

Charlesworth, I.J. and Percy, R.A. *The Law of Negligence.* 7th edn. London: Sweet & Maxwell, 1983 with 1986 supplement.

Charlesworth, I.J. *Mercantile Law.* 14th edn., by Clive M. Schmitthoff and David A.G. Sarre. London: Sweet & Maxwell, 1984.

Cheshire, Fifoot & Furmston's Law of Contract 11th edn. London: Butterworth & Co. (Publishers) Ltd, 1986.

Chitty on Contract. 25th edn., by A.G. Guest. London: Sweet & Maxwell, 1983 with 1986 supplement.

Clerk, J.F. and Lindsell, W.H. *The Law of Torts.* 15th edn., by R.W.M. Dias. London: Sweet & Maxwell, 1982 with 1985 supplement.

Clarke, P.H. *The Surveyor in Court.* London: Estates Gazette, 1985.

Coke, Sir Edward. *The First Part of the Institutes; or, A Commentary upon Littleton,* 3 vols. 13th edn. London: Francis Hargrave, 1775, first published 1628.

Coke, Sir Edward. *Institutes of the Laws of England in four parts, or Institutes,* 1628-1644.

Craies, W.F. *Statute Law.* 7th edn., by S.G.G. Edgar. London: Sweet & Maxwell, 1971.

Cross, Charles (general editor). *Encyclopaedia of Highway Law and Practice.* 3 vols. London: Sweet & Maxwell, looseleaf with updating service.

Cross on Local Government Law. 7th edn., by Charles Cross and Stephen Bailey. London: Sweet & Maxwell, 1986.

Cross, Rupert. *Precedent in English Law.* Oxford: Oxford University Press, 1983.

Crossley Vaines' Personal Property. 5th edn., by E.L.G. Tyler and N.E. Palmer. London: Butterworth & Co. (Publishers) Ltd., 1973.

Davies, F.R. *Contract*. 5th edn. London: Sweet & Maxwell, 1986.

Davies, Keith. *Local Government Law*. London: Butterworth & Co. (Publishers) Ltd., 1983.

Denning, The Rt.Hon. Lord. *The Discipline of Law*. London: Butterworth & Co. (Publishers) Ltd., 1979.

Denyer-Green, Barry. *Compulsory Purchase and Compensation*. 2nd edn. London: Estates Gazette, 1985.

Dixon, S.F. *Subrogation: Substituted Liabilities*. Philadelphia: G. W. Childs, 1862

Drake, C.D. *Law of Partnership*. 3rd edn. London: Sweet & Maxwell, 1983.

Dugdale, A.M. and Stanton, K.M. *Professional Negligence*. London: Butterworths & Co. (Publishers) Ltd., 1982.

Fleming, J.G. *An Introduction to the Law of Torts*. 6th edn. London: Sweet & Maxwell, 1983.

Fridman, G.H.L. *The Law of Agency*. 5th edn. London: Butterworth & Co. (Publishers) Ltd, 1983.

Fry, S.P. *A Treatise on the Specific Performance of Contracts*. 6th edn., edited by George Russell Northcotte. London: Sweet & Maxwell, reprinted 1985.

Gill, G.H. *The Law of Arbitration*. 3rd edn., by Enid A. Marshall. London: Sweet & Maxwell, 1982.

Ginnings, A.T. *Arbitration: A Practical Guide*. Aldershot, Hampshire: Gower Publishing Company Limited, 1984.

Goff, R. and Jones, G. *The Law of Restitution*. 3rd edn. London: Sweet & Maxwell, 1986.

Halsbury's Laws of England. 4th edn. 56 vols. London: Butterworth & Co. (Publishers) Ltd., 1973-1986 with cumulative supplements.

Halsbury's Statutes of England. 3rd edn. 54 vols. London: Butterworth & Co. (Publishers) Ltd., 1968-1972 with cumulative supplements. 4th edn. being published vol. by vol. 1985- .

Halsbury's Statutory Instruments: being a companion to Halsbury's Statutes of England, prepared by Butterworths Legal Editorial Staff. 23 vols. 4th reissue. London: Butterworth & Co. (Publishers) Ltd., 1979 with updating service.

Hanbury, H.G. and Maudsley, R.H. *Modern Equity*. 12th edn., by Jill Martin London: Sweet & Maxwell, 1985.

Holdsworth, Sir William. *A History of English Law*. 16 vols. London: Methuen & Co., Ltd., 1903, 7th revised edition published by Sweet & Maxwell, 1956.

Jackson, R. and Powell, J. *Professional Negligence*. London: Sweet & Maxwell, 1982.

James, Philip S. *General Principles of the Law of Tort.* 4th edn. London: Butterworth & Co. (Publishers) Ltd, 1982.

James, Philip S. *Introduction to English Law.* 11th edn. London: Butterworth & Co. (Publishers) Ltd, 1985.

Jones, Gareth and Goodhart, William. *Specific Performance.* London: Butterworth & Co. (Publishers) Ltd, 1986.

Josling, J. F. *Periods of Limitation.* 6th edn. London: Longman Professional, 1986.

Kay, M. *Arbitration.* London: Sweet & Maxwell, 1979.

Keaton, George W. Professor. *The Law of Trusts.* 9th edn. London: Pitman Publishing Ltd, 1968 reprinted 1972.

Kemp, D. A. McI. and Kemp, M.S. *The Quantum of Damages.* 2 vols. London: Sweet & Maxwell, 1975, looseleaf with updating service.

Lawson, Frederick Henry. *A Common Lawyer Looks at Law: five lectures delivered at the University of Michigan.* Ann Arbor, University of Michigan Law School, 1953.

Lawson, R. *Exclusion Clauses.* 2nd edn. London: Longman Professional, 1983.

Leach, W.A. *Legal Interpretation for Surveyors.* London: Estates Gazette, 1966.

Leigh, L.H. *Strict and Vicarious Liability.* London: Sweet & Maxwell, 1982.

Lewin, T. *The Law of Trusts.* 17th edn. London: Sweet & Maxwell, 1986.

Lindley, Lord. *The Law of Partnership.* 15th edn. by E.H. Scamell and R.C. I'Anson Banks. London: Sweet & Maxwell, 1984.

Maitland, Frederick W. *Constitutional History of England.* Cambridge: Cambridge University Press, 1908.

Mann, F.A. *Legal Aspects of Money.* 4th edn. Oxford: Oxford University Press, 1982.

Markesenis, B.S. and Munday, R.J.C. *Outline of the Law of Agency.* 2nd edn. London: Butterworth & Co. (Publishers) Ltd., 1986.

McGregor on Damages. 14th edn. by Harvey McGregor. London: Sweet & Maxwell, 1980.

Mellows, A.R. *Law of Succession.* 4th edn. London: Butterworth & Co. (Publishers) Ltd., 1983.

Mildred, R.H. *The Expert Witness.* London: Longman Scientific & Technical, 1982.

Milman, D. and Flanagan, T. *Modern Partnership.* Beckenham, Kent: Croom Helm, 1983.

Munkman, John. *Employer's Liability at the Common Law.* 10th edn. London: Butterworth & Co. (Publishers) Ltd., 1985.

Mustill, Sir Michael J. and Boyd, S. *Commercial Arbitrations*. London: Butterworth & Co. (Publishers) Ltd., 1982.

Nathan and Marshall's Cases and Commentaries on the Law of Trusts. 8th edn. by D.J. Hayton. London: Sweet & Maxwell, 1986.

Nicholas, Barry. *An Introduction to Roman Law*. Oxford: Oxford University Press, 1976.

Oakley, T. *Constructive Trusts*. 2nd edn. London: Sweet & Maxwell, 1986.

Odger's Construction of Deeds and Statutes. 5th edn. London: Sweet & Maxwell, 1981.

Ogus, Antony, Ian. *The Law of Damages*. 2nd edn. London: Butterworth & Co. (Publishers) Ltd., 1973.

Parker, D.B. and Mellows, A.R. *The Modern Law of Trusts*. 5th edn. London: Sweet & Maxwell, 1983.

Parris, H. *The Law Relating to Private Street Works*. Chichester, West Sussex: Barrie Rose (Publishing) Ltd., 1979.

Parris, John. *Arbitration: Principles and Practice*. London: Granada Publishing Ltd., 1983.

Parry, Sir D.H. and Clarke, J.B. *The Law of Succession*. 8th edn. London: Sweet & Maxwell, 1983.

Pennington, Robert R. *Company Law*. 5th edn. London: Butterworth & Co. (Publishers) Ltd., 1985.

Pettit, Philip H. *Equity and the Law of Trusts*. 5th edn. London: Butterworth & Co. (Publishers) Ltd., 1984.

Pollock, F. and Maitland, F.W. *History of English Law*. 2nd edn. Cambridge: Cambridge University Press, 1898.

Radcliffe, G.R.Y. and Cross, Lord. *The English Legal System*. 6th edn. Butterworth & Co. (Publishers) Ltd., 1977.

Ranking and Spicer on Company Law. 11th edn. edited by R.E.G. Perrins and A. Jeffreys. London: H.F.L. (Publishers) Ltd, 1970.

Riddell, J.G. *The Law of Trusts*. 2nd edn. London: Butterworth & Co. (Publishers) Ltd., 1982.

Rose, F. and Birks, P. *Restitution*. London: Sweet & Maxwell, 1986.

Russell on The Law of Arbitration. 20th edn., by A. Walton and M. Victoria. London: Sweet & Maxwell, 1982.

Salmond, Sir J.W. and Hewston, R.F.V. on the Law of Torts. 18th edn. by R.F.V. Hewston and R. Chambers. London: Sweet & Maxwell, 1981.

Sandys-Winsch, Godfrey. *Animal Law*. 2nd edn. London: Shaw & Sons Ltd., 1984.

Sandys-Winsch, Godfrey. *Garden Law*. London: Shaw & Sons Ltd., 1982.

Smith, J.C. and Thomas, J.A.C. *A Casebook on Contract*. 7th edn. London: Sweet & Maxwell, 1982.

Smith, K. and Keenan, D. *Mercantile Law*. 6th edn. London: Pitman Publishing ·Ltd., 1985.

Snell's Principles of Equity. 28th edn. by P.V. Baker and P.St J. Langan. London: Sweet & Maxwell, 1982.

Statutes in Force. London & Norwich: HMSO Books, looseleaf with updating service.

Street, Harry. *The Law of Torts*. 7th edn. London: Butterworth & Co (Publishers) Ltd., 1982.

Theobald, Sir H.S. *The Law of Wills*. 14th edn. London: Sweet & Maxwell, 1982 plus 1984 supplement.

Treitel, G.H. *The Law of Contract*. 6th edn. London: Sweet & Maxwell, 1983.

Treitel, G.H. *An Outline of the Law of Contract*. 3rd edn. London: Butterworth & Co. (Publishers) Ltd., 1984.

Tyler, E.L.G. *Cases and Statutes on Land Law*. 2nd edn. London: Sweet & Maxwell, 1986.

Underhill's Principles of the Law of Partnership. 12th edn. by E.R. Hardy Ivamy. London: Butterworth & Co. (Publishers) Ltd., 1986.

Underhill and Holt's Professional Negligence. 2nd edn., by Hilton Harro-Griffiths and Jane Bennington, (consulting editor Ashley Underwood). London: Fourmat Publishing, 1985.

Underhill, A. *Law relating to Trusts and Trustees*. London: Butterworth & Co. (Publishers) Ltd., 1984.

Walker and Walker on The English Legal System. 6th edn. by R.J. Walker. London: Butterworth & Co. (Publishers) Ltd., 1985

Walker, David M. *The Law of Delict in Scotland*. 2nd edn. published under the auspices of The Scottish Universities Law Institute. London: Sweet & Maxwell, 1981.

Walker, M. (editor). *Oxford Companion to the Law*. Oxford: Oxford University Press, 1980.

Watson, John A.F. *Nothing But The Truth; or expert evidence in principle and practice for surveyors, valuers and others*. 2nd edn. London: Estates Gazette, 1975.

Williams, Glanville and Hepple, B.A. *Foundations of the Law of Tort*. 2nd edn. London: Butterworth & Co. (Publishers) Ltd., 1984.

Williams on Wills. 6th edn. by C.H. Sherrin and R.F.D. Barlow. London: Butterworth & Co. (Publishers) Ltd., 1985.

Yates, David. *Exclusion Clauses in Contracts.* 2nd edn. London: Sweet & Maxwell, 1985.

GENERAL LAW, United States

See also: Real Estate Law, United States

American Law Institute and National Conference of Commissioners of Uniform State Law. *Uniform Commercial Code: Official Text.* Philadelphia: American Law Institute Publishers, 1972.

Bogert, George T. *Law of Trusts.* 5th edn., reprint of 1973 edition. St Paul, Minnesota: West Publishing Co., 1985.

Deutch, Sinai. *Unfair Contracts.* Lexington, Mass.: Lexington Books, 1977.

Dorram, Peter. *The Expert Witness.* Chicago: APA Planners Press, 1982.

White, James J. and Summers, Robert S. *Handbook of Law under the Uniform Commercial Code.* 2nd edn. St Paul, Minnesota: West Publishing Co., 1980.

HOUSING LAW, England and Wales

See also: Real Estate Law, England and Wales

Alder, J. and Handy, C. *Housing Associations.* London: Sweet & Maxwell, 1986.

Aldridge, Trevor. *The Law of Flats.* London: Longman Professional, 1982.

Allen, Patrick. *Shared Ownership–a stepping stone to home ownership.* London: Her Majesty's Stationery Office, 1982.

Arden, Andrew, and Cross, C. (consulting editors). *Encyclopaedia of Housing Law and Practice.*, 4 vols. London: Sweet & Maxwell, 1985, looseleaf with updating service.

Arden, Andrew, and Partington, Martin. *Housing Law.* London: Sweet & Maxwell, 1983 with 1986 supplement.

Arden, Andrew. *Manual of Housing Law.* 2nd edn. London: Sweet & Maxwell, 1983.

Baker, Charles Vivian. *Housing Associations.* London: Estates Gazette, 1976.

Brand, Clive. *Mobile Homes and the Law.* London: Sweet & Maxwell, 1986.

Cawthorn, J. *Sale and Management of Flats: Practice and Precedents.* London: Butterworth & Co. (Publishers) Ltd. 1985.

Davies, Keith. *West's Law of Housing*. 4th edn. London: Estates Gazette, 1979.

George, E.F. and George, A. *The Sale of Flats*. 5th edn. London: Sweet & Maxwell, 1984.

Gordon, R.J.F. *Caravans and the Law*. London: Shaw & Sons Ltd., 1978.

Hawkins, N. *Housing Grants*. 2nd edn. London: Kogan Page Ltd., 1983.

Her Majesty's Stationery Office (Department of the Environment). *Housing Booklet Number 14: Housing Improvement Grants*. London: Her Majesty's Stationery Office, 1983.

Hoath, David. *Council Housing*. 2nd edn. London: Sweet & Maxwell, 1978.

Hughes, David J. *Public Sector Housing Law*. London: Butterworth & Co. (Publishers) Ltd., 1981.

Macpherson, J. *Leasehold Enfranchisement, Property Valuation Handbook* C3. Reading, Berkshire: College of Estate Management, 1985.

Merrett, Stephen. *State Housing in Britain*. London: Routledge & Kegan Paul Limited, 1979.

Tapping, A.P de B. and Rolfe, R. *Guarantees for New Homes: A Guide to the N.H.B.C. Scheme*. 2nd edn. London: Longman Professional, 1981.

West's Law of Housing. 4th edn. by Keith Davies. London: Estates Gazette, 1979.

Wright, C. *Housing Improvement*. London: Sweet & Maxwell, 1979.

INSURANCE

Association of Insurance and Risk Managers in Industry and Commerce (AIRMIC). *Company Insurance Handbook*. 2nd edn. Aldershot, Hampshire: Gower Publishing Company Limited, 1984.

Bird, John. *Modern Insurance Law*. London: Sweet & Maxwell, 1982.

Carter, R.L. (editor). *Handbook of Insurance*. Brentford, Middlesex: Kluwer Publishing Ltd., 1973, looseleaf with updating service.

Collinvaux, R. *The Law of Insurance*. 5th edn. London: Sweet & Maxwell, 1984.

Dinsdale, W.A. *Elements of Insurance*. 5th edn., revised by D.C. McMurdie. London: Pitman Publishing Ltd., 1980.

Dobbyn, John F. *Insurance Law in a Nutshell*. St. Paul, Minnesota: West Publishing Co., 1981.

Eagle, M.G. *Special Perils Insurance: Chartered Insurance Institute Handbook No. 15*. London: Pitman Publishing Ltd. 1963.

Eagletone, F.N. *Insurance for the Construction Industry.* Harlow, Essex: George Godwin Ltd., 1979.

Hall, Chas E. *Property and Pecuniary Insurance.* London: Longman Professional, published in association with The Chartered Insurance Institute, 1981 reprinted 1984.

Hanwell, D.S. *Elements of Insurance.* 4th edn. Plymouth: Macdonald & Evans Ltd., 1985.

Hardy Ivamy, E.R. *General Principles of Insurance Law.* 5th edn. London: Butterworth & Co. (Publishers) Ltd., 1986.

Hickmott, G.J.R. *Principles and Practice of Interruption Insurance.* London: Witherby & Co. Ltd., 1982.

Huebner, S.S., Black, Kenneth and Cline, Robert S. *Property Liability Insurance.* 3rd edn. Englewood Cliffs, New Jersey: Prentice-Hall, Inc., 1982.

Jess, Digby J. *A Guide to Insurance of Professional Negligence.* London: Butterworth & Co. (Publishers) Ltd., 1982.

Keeton, Robert E. *Keeton's Basic Text on Insurance.* St. Paul, Minnesota: West Publishing Co., 1971.

MacGillivray, E.J. and Partington, Michael. *Insurance Law.* 7th edn. London: Sweet & Maxwell, 1981.

O'Dowd, A. *Encyclopaedia of Insurance Law.* London: Sweet & Maxwell, 1985, looseleaf with updating service.

Piper, L.P. *Contractor's All-Risks and Public Liability Insurance.* Brentford, Middlesex: Buckley Press, 1976.

Riegel, Robert, Miller, Jerome S. and Williams, Arthur C. *Insurance Principles and Practices: Property and Liability.* 6th edn. Englewood Cliffs, New Jersey: Prentice-Hall, Inc., 1975.

Riley on Business Interruption and Consequential Loss Insurances and Claims. 3rd edn. by David Cloughton. London: Sweet & Maxwell, 1986.

Steele, John T. *Principles and Practice of Insurance.* 2nd edn. London: Longman Professional, published in association with The Chartered Insurance Institute, 1984.

LAND ECONOMICS

American Institute of Real Estate Appraisers. *Readings in Highest and Best Use.* Chicago: American Institute of Real Estate Appraisers, 1973.

Balchin, Paul N. and Kieve, Jeffrey L. *Urban Land Economics.* 3rd edn. Basingstoke, Hampshire: Macmillan Publishers Ltd., 1985.

Barlowe, Raleigh. *Land Resource Economics: The Economics of Real Estate.* 3rd edn. Englewood Cliffs, New Jersey: Prentice-Hall, Inc., 1978.

Button, K.J. *Urban Economics: Theory and Policy.* London: Macmillan Publishers Ltd., 1976.

Centre for Advanced Land Use Studies. *Urban Development in France and Germany.* Reading, Berkshire: College of Estate Management, 1974.

Chapin, Stuart Francis and Kaiser, Edward J. *Urban Land Use Planning.* 3rd edn. Urbana, Illinois: University of Illinois Press, 1979.

Cox, R. *Retail Site Assessment.* London: Business Books Ltd., 1968.

Dumke, Glenn S. *The Boom in the 'Eighties in Southern California.* San Marion, California: Huntington Library, 1944.

Evans, Alan. *Urban Economics.* Oxford: Basil Blackwell Ltd., 1985.

Goldberg, Michael and Chinloy, Peter. *Urban Land Economics.* New York: John Wiley & Sons, Inc., 1984.

Harrison, A.J. *Economics and Land Use Planning.* Beckenham, Kent: Croom Helm Ltd., 1977.

Harvey, J. *The Economics of Real Property.* London: Macmillan Publishers Ltd., 1981 reprinted 1985.

Kinnard, William N. and Society of Industrial Realtors. *Industrial Real Estate.* 3rd edn. Chicago: Institute of Real Estate Management & National Association of Realtors, 1979.

Lean, William and Goodall, Brian. *Aspects of Land Use Planning.* London: Estates Gazette, 1966.

Lean, William. *Economics of Land Use Planning.* London: Estates Gazette, 1969.

Lichfield, Nathaniel. *The Economics of Planned Development.* London: Estates Gazette, 1956 4th reprint 1969.

Marlow, Joyce. *Captain Boycott and the Irish.* London: André Deutsch, 1973.

Marriot, Oliver. *The Property Boom.* London: Hamish Hamilton Ltd., 1967.

Newell, Martin. *An Introduction to the Economics of Urban Land Use.* London: Estates Gazette, 1977.

Ratcliff, Richard U. *Urban Land Economics.* New York: McGraw-Hill Book Company, 1949, reprint edn. Connecticut: Greenwood Press, 1972.

Richardson, H.W. *Urban Economics.* 2nd edn. Illinois: Dryden Press, 1978.

Richardson, H.W. *The New Urban Economics: and alternatives.* London: PION Ltd., 1977.

Royal Institution of Chartered Surveyors. *The Property Boom and its Collapse:*

1968-1975. London: Royal Institution of Chartered Surveyors, 1978.

Turvey, Ralph. *The Economics of Real Property.: An Analysis of Property Values and Patterns of Use.* London: George Allen & Unwin (Publishers) Ltd., 1957.

Urban Land Institute. *Industrial Development Handbook.* Washington, D.C.: Urban Land Institute, 1976.

Wallwork, Kenneth L. *Derelict Land.* Newton Abbot: David & Charles (Publishers) Ltd., 1974.

Willis, K. G. *The Economics of Town and Country Planning.* London: Granada Publishing Ltd., 1980.

LANDLORD AND TENANT

See also: Housing Law, Real Estate Management, Real Property Law

Adkin's Landlord and Tenant. 18th edn. by The Hon. Sir Raymond Walton and Michael Essayan. London: Estates Gazette, 1982.

Aldridge, Trevor M. *Leasehold Law.* London: Longman Professional, 1983 with updating service.

Aldridge, Trevor M. *Letting Business Premises.* 5th edn. London: Longman Professional, 1985.

Aldridge, Trevor M. *Rent Control and Leasehold Enfranchisement.* 8th edn. London: Longman Professional, 1980.

Arden, Andrew and Partington, Martin. *Quiet Enjoyment: Law and Practice Guide No. 5.* 2nd edn. London: Legal Action Group, 1985.

Bennett, Charles. *Residential Leases: A Draftsman's Handbook.* London: Longman Professional, 1984.

Bernstein, Ronald and Reynolds, Kirk with Nicholas Dowding. *Handbook of Rent Review.* London: Sweet & Maxwell, 1981, looseleaf with updating service.

Brahams, D. and Pawlowski, M. *Casebook on Rent Review and Lease Renewal.* London: William Collins Sons & Co. Ltd., 1986.

Brahams, Malcolm. *Commercial Leases.* London: William Collins Sons & Co. Ltd., 1985.

Clarke, D.N. and Adams, J.E. *Rent Reviews and Variable Rents.* 2nd edn. London: Longman Professional, 1984.

Evans, David Lloyd. *The Law of Landlord and Tenant.* 2nd edn. by P. Smith. London: Butterworth & Co. (Publishers) Ltd., 1985.

Farrand, J.T. and Arden, A. *Rent Acts and Regulations.* 2nd edn. London: Sweet & Maxwell, 1981.

Freeman, P., Shapiro, E. and Mass, R. *Service Charges: Law and Practice.* London: Henry Stewart Publications, 1986.

Green, Shirley. *Rachman.* London: Hamlyn Paperbacks, 1981, originally published by Michael Joseph Ltd., London, 1979.

Hague, N.T. *Leasehold Enfranchisement.* 2nd edn. London: Sweet & Maxwell, 1986.

Hill & Redman: Landlord and Tenant Law. 17th edn. edited by Michael Barnes. London: Butterworth & Co (Publishers) Ltd., 1982.

Institute of Real Estate Management. *Lease Escalators and Other Pass-Through Clauses.* Chicago: Institute of Real Estate Management, 1979.

Lewison, K. *Drafting Business Leases.* 2nd edn. London: Longman Professional, 1986.

McMichael, Stanley L. and O'Keefe, Paul T. *Leases: Percentage, Short and Long Term.* 6th edn. Englewood Cliffs, New Jersey: Prentice-Hall, Inc., 1974.

Macpherson, J. *Leasehold Enfranchisement, Property Valuation Handbook C3.* Reading, Berkshire: College of Estate Management, 1985.

Muir Watt, J. *Agricultural Holdings.* 12th edn. London: Sweet & Maxwell, 1967 with 1978 supplement.

Nelkin, David. *The Limits of Legal Process: A Study of Landlords, Law and Crime.* London: Academic Press Ltd., 1983.

Pettit, Philip. *Private Sector Tenancies.* 2nd edn. London: Butterworth & Co. (Publishers) Ltd., 1981.

Prophet, J. *Fair Rents: A Practical Guide.* 3rd edn. London: Shaw & Sons Ltd., 1985.

Realtors National Marketing Institute. *Percentage Leases.* 13th edn. Chicago: Realtors National Marketing Institute, 1973.

Reynolds, Kirk and Clarke, Wayne. *Renewal of Business Tenancies: Law and Practice.* London: Henry Stewart Publications, 1985, looseleaf with updating service.

Rogers, C.P. with C.V. Margrave-Jones. *Agricultural Tenancies: Practice and Precedents.* London: Butterworth & Co. (Publishers) Ltd., 1985.

Ross, Murray J. *Drafting and Negotiating Commercial Leases.* 2nd edn. London: Butterworth & Co. (Publishers) Ltd., 1984.

Scammell W.S. and Densham, H.A.C. *Law of Agricultural Holdings.* 6th edn. London: Butterworth & Co. (Publishers) Ltd., 1978 with 1980 supplement.

West, W.A. *The Law of Dilapidations.* 8th edn. London: Estates Gazette, 1979.

Williams, D.W., Brand, C. and Hubbard, C. *Handbook of Business Tenancies.* London: Sweet & Maxwell, 1985, looseleaf with updating service.

Williams, D.W. *Landlord and Tenant Casebook*. London: Sweet & Maxwell, 1985.

Woodfall's Landlord and Tenant. 4 vols. 28th edn. by L.A. Blundell and V. G. Wellings. London: Sweet & Maxwell, 1978, looseleaf with updating service.

Yates, David and Hawkins, A.J. *Landlord and Tenant Law*. London: Sweet & Maxwell, 1981.

MANAGEMENT

See: Real Estate Management

PERSONAL PROPERTY LAW

See also: General Law, England and Wales, Real Property Law

Benjamin's Sale of Goods. 2nd edn. London: Sweet & Maxwell, 1981.

Chalmer's Sale of Goods. 18th edn. London: Sweet & Maxwell, 1981.

Crossley Vaines' Personal Property. 5th edn. by E.L.G. Tyler and N.E. Palmer. London: Butterworth & Co. (Publishers) Ltd., 1973.

Palmer, N.E. *Bailment*. London: Sweet & Maxwell, 1979.

PLANNING LAW AND COMPULSORY PURCHASE, England and Wales

See also: Real Property Law, Valuation, Financial Appraisal and Report Writing, Zoning and Condemnation, United States.

Blundell, L.A. and Dobry, George. *Planning Appeals and Inquiries*. 3rd edn. by Robert Carnwath. London: Sweet & Maxwell, 1982.

Boynton's Guide to Compulsory Purchase and Compensation. 5th edn. by Sir John Boynton and David J. Hawkins. London: Longman Professional, 1983.

Brand, Clive. *Mobile Homes and the Law*. London: Sweet & Maxwell, 1986.

Brown, H.J.J. (general editor). *Encyclopaedia of Compulsory Purchase and Compensation*. 2 vols. London: Sweet & Maxwell, 1960, looseleaf with updating service.

Corfield, Sir Frederick and Carnworth, R.J.A. *Compulsory Purchase and Compensation*. London: Butterworth & Co. (Publishers) Ltd., 1978.

Corfield, Sir Frederick. *A Guide to the Community Land Act*. London: Butterworth & Co. (Publishers) Ltd., 1976.

Davies, Keith. *Law of Compulsory Purchase and Compensation*. 4th edn. London: Butterworth & Co. (Publishers) Ltd., 1984.

Denyer-Green, Barry. *Compulsory Purchase and Compensation*. 2nd edn. London: Estates Gazette, 1980.

Denyer-Green, Barry. *Development and Planning Law*. London: Estates Gazette, 1980.

Emlyn-Jones, J.H. *The Lands Tribunal: A Practical Guide*. London: Hubert Bewlay Fund, 1982.

Garner, J.F. (editor). *Planning Law in Western Europe*. Amsterdam: North-Holland Publishing, 1975.

Garner, J.F. *Practical Planning Law*. Beckenham, Kent: Croom Helm, 1981.

Gordon, R.J.F. *Caravans and the Law*. London: Shaw & Sons Ltd., 1978.

Grant, Malcolm. *Urban Planning Law*. London: Sweet & Maxwell, 1982.

Hamilton, R.N.D. *Guide to Development and Planning Law*. 7th edn. London: Longman Professional, 1981.

Hamilton, R.N.D. *Planning Procedure Tables*. 4th edn. London: Longman Professional, 1981.

Heap, Sir Desmond (general editor). *Encyclopaedia of Planning Law and Practice*. 4 vols. London: Sweet & Maxwell, 1982.

Heap, Sir Desmond. *An Outline of Planning Law*. 8th edn. London: Longman Professional, 1981.

Howell James' Notes on the Need for Planning Permission. 3rd edn. by C.M. Brand and D.W. Williams. London: Longman Professional, 1984.

Keeble, Lewis. *Fighting Planning Appeals*. London: Construction Press, 1985.

Leach, W.A. *Disturbance on Compulsory Purchase*. 3rd edn. London: Estates Gazette, 1975 with 1976 supplement.

Little, A.J. *Planning Controls and Their Enforcement*. 5th edn. London: Shaw & Sons Ltd., 1983.

McAuslan, Patrick. *The Ideologies of Planning Law*. Oxford: Pergamon Press Ltd., 1980.

Purdue, M. *Cases and Materials on Planning Law*. London: Sweet & Maxwell, 1977.

Stephenson, John. *Planning Procedures*. London: Northwood Publications Ltd., 1982.

Suddards, R.W. *Listed Buildings: The Law and Practice*. London: Sweet & Maxwell, 1982.

Telling, A.E. *Planning Law and Procedure*. 7th edn. London: Butterworth & Co. (Publishers) Ltd., 1986.

REAL PROPERTY LAW, England and Wales
(including Estate Agency, Conveyancing Sales of Land, and Land Registration)

See also: General Law, Housing Law, Landlord and Tenant, Real Property Law, United States.

A'Court, M. *Estate Conveyancing*. Oxford: Pergamon Press, 1984.

Adkin, Benaiah, W. and Bowen, D. *The Law Relating to Fixtures*. 3rd edn. London: Estates Gazette, 1947.

Aldridge, Trevor. *Boundaries, Walls and Fences*. 6th edn. London: Longman Professional, 1986.

Aldridge, Trevor. *Guide to Enquiries before Contract*. London: Longman Professional, 1978.

Aldridge, Trevor. *Guide to Enquiries of Local Authorities*. 2nd edn. London: Longman Professional, 1982.

Annaud, Ruth and Cain, Brian. *Modern Conveyancing*. London: Sweet & Maxwell, 1984.

Anstey, Brian and Chavase, Michael. *The Right of Light*. London Estates Gazette, 1963.

Barnsley's Conveyancing Law and Practice. 2nd edn. by D.G. Barnsley and P.W. Smith. London: Butterworth & Co. (Publishers) Ltd., 1982.

Barnsley, D.G. *Land Options*. London: Oyez Publishing Ltd., 1978.

Bourne, E. *Handbook of Conveyancing Searches and Enquiries*. London: Sweet & Maxwell, 1984.

Brand, Clive. *Mobile Homes and the Law*. London: Sweet & Maxwell, 1986.

Butterworths' Property Law Handbook by E.H. Scamell. London: Butterworth & Co. (Publishers) Ltd., 1984.

Campbell, Denis (editor). *Legal Aspects of Alien Acquisitions of Real Property*. Netherlands: Kluwer Law and Taxation, 1980.

Cawthorn, John. *Practical Time-Sharing: U.K. and Overseas*. London: Butterworth & Co. (Publishers) Ltd., 1986.

Cheshire's Modern Law of Real Property. 13th edn., by E.H. Burn. London: Butterworth & Co. (Publishers) Ltd., 1982.

Challis, H.W. *Law of Real Property Chiefly in Relation to Conveyancing*. 3rd edn. by C. Sweet. London: Butterworth & Co (Publishers) Ltd., 1911 reprinted 1963.

Clayden, Paul. *Our Common Land: The Law and History of Commons and Village Greens*. Henley-on-Thames, Oxfordshire: The Open Spaces Society, 1980.

Clayden, Paul and Trevelyan, John. *Rights of Way–A Guide to Law and Practice.* Henley-on-Thames, Oxfordshire: Commons, Open Spaces and Footpath Preservation Society and Ramblers Association, 1983.

Dalton, Patrick J. *Land Law.* 3rd edn. London: Pitman Publishing Ltd., 1983.

Davies, Keith. *Law of Property in Land.* London: Estates Gazette, 1979.

Dawson, I.J. and Pearce, Robert A. *Licences Relating to the Occupation and Use of Land.* London: Butterworth & Co. (Publishers) Ltd., 1979.

Digby, K.E. and Harrison, W.H. *An Introduction to the History of the Law of Real Property.* 5th edn. Oxford: Oxford University Press, 1897.

Duckworth, Peter. *Matrimonial Property and Finance.* 2nd edn. London: Longman Professional, 1984 reprinted 1985 with supplement.

Edmonds, J. *International Timesharing.* London: Sweet & Maxwell, 1984.

Emmet on Title. 19th edn., by J.T. Farrand. London: Longman Group UK Ltd, 1986, looseleaf with updating service.

Fairest, Paul B. *Mortgages.* 2nd edn. London: Sweet & Maxwell, 1980.

Farrand, J.T. *Contract and Conveyance.* 4th edn. London: Longman Professional, 1983.

Fisher and Lightwood's Law of Mortgages. 9th edn. London: Butterworth & Co. (Publishers) Ltd., 1977.

Gale's Law of Easements. 15th edn. by Spencer G. Maurice, assisted by Robert Wakefield. London: Sweet & Maxwell, 1986.

Garner, J.F. *Law of Allotments.* 4th edn. London: Shaw & Sons Ltd., 1984.

Garner, J.F. *Law of Sewers and Drains.* 6th edn. London: Shaw & Sons Ltd., 1981.

Garner, J.F. *Local Land Charges.* London: Shaw & Sons Ltd., 1982.

Garner, J.F. *Rights of Way and Access to the Countryside.* 4th edn. London: Longman Professional, 1982.

Gibson, A. *Conveyancing.* 21st edn. London: Law Notes Lending Library, 1980, with 1981 supplement.

Gonner, E.C.K. *Common Land and Inclosure.* 2nd edn. London: Frank Cass & Co., Ltd., by arrangement with Macmillan & Co., 1966.

Gray, K.J. and Symes, Pamela. *Real Property and Real People.* London: Butterworth & Co. (Publishers) Ltd., 1981.

Hamilton, Susan. *The Modern Law of Highways.* London: Butterworth & Co. (Publishers) Ltd., 1981.

Harris, B. and Ryan G. *Law Relating to Common Land.* London: Sweet & Maxwell, 1967.

Harvey, Brian W. and Meisel, F. *Auctions: Law and Practice*. London: Butterworth & Co. (Publishers) Ltd., 1985.

Harvey, Brian W. *Settlement of Land*. London: Sweet & Maxwell, 1973.

Harwood, Michael. *Cases and Materials on English Land Law*. Abingdon, Oxfordshire: Professional Books, 1977.

Harwood, Michael. *Modern English Land Law*. 2nd edn. London: Sweet & Maxwell, 1982.

Hayton, D.J. *Registered Land*. 3rd edn. London: Sweet & Maxwell, 1981.

Ing, Noël D. *Bona Vacantia*. London: Butterworth & Co. (Publishers) Ltd., 1971.

Jackson, Paul. *Law of Easements and Profits*. London: Butterworth & Co. (Publishers) Ltd., 1978.

Lawson, F.H. and Rudden, B. *The Law of Property*. 2nd edn. Oxford: Oxford University Press, 1982.

Littleton's Tenures in English. Washington, D.C.: John Byrne & Co., 1903. First published in Law French c.1450.

Macrory, Richard. *Water Law: Principles and Practice*. London: Longman Professional, 1985.

Maudsley, R.H. and Burn, E.H. *Land Law: Cases and Materials*. 5th edn. London: Butterworth & Co. (Publishers) Ltd., 1986.

Mellows, Anthony R. *Conveyancing Searches*. London: Longman Professional, 1975.

Megarry, Sir Robert and Wade, H.W.R. *The Law of Real Property*. 5th edn. London: Sweet & Maxwell, 1984.

Megarry, Sir Robert. *Megarry's Manual of the Law of Real Property*. 6th edn., by David J. Hayton. London: Sweet & Maxwell, 1984.

Moeran, Edward. *Introduction to Conveyancing*. 2nd edn. London: Longman Professional, 1983.

Moeran, Edward. *Practical Conveyancing*. 9th edn. London: Longman Professional, 1984.

Morris, J.H.C. and Leach M.B. *The Rule against Perpetuities*. 2nd edn. London: Stevens & Sons, 1962, reprinted with 1964 supplement by Sweet & Maxwell, 1986.

Morris, J.H.C. (advisory editor). *Sweet & Maxwell's Property Statutes*. 4th edn. London: Sweet & Maxwell, 1982.

Murdoch, J. *The Law of Estate Agency and Auctions*. 2nd edn. London: Estates Gazette, 1984.

Pease and Chitty's Law of Markets and Fairs. Looseleaf edition by Edward F.

Cousins and Robert Antony. Croydon, Surrey: Tolley Publishing Ltd., 1984 with updating service.

Pollock, Sir Frederick and Wright, R.S. *An Essay on Possession in the Common Law*. Oxford: Oxford University Press, 1888.

Powell-Smith, Vincent. *Boundaries and Fences*. 2nd edn. London: Butterworth & Co. (Publishers) Ltd., 1972.

Pratt and Mackenzie's Law of Highways. 21st edn., by Harold Parrish and Lord DeMauley. London: Butterworth & Co. (Publishers) Ltd., 1967.

Preston, C.H.S. and Newson, G.H. *Restrictive Covenants affecting Freehold Land*. 7th edn., by G.H. Newson and G.L. Newson. London: Sweet & Maxwell, 1982.

Pritchard, A. *Squatting*. London: Sweet & Maxwell, 1981.

Riddell, J.G. *Introduction to Land Law*. 3rd edn. London: Butterworth & Co. (Publishers) Ltd., 1983.

Rowton-Simpson, S. *Land Law and Registration*. Cambridge: Cambridge University Press, 1982.

Royal Institution of Chartered Surveyors. *Party Wall Legislation and Procedure*. London: Surveyors Publications Ltd., 1985.

Ruoff, T.B.F. and West, C. *Concise Land Registration Practice*. 3rd edn. London: Sweet & Maxwell, 1982.

Ruoff, T.B.F. and Ropper, R.B. *The Law and Practice of Registered Conveyancing*. 5th edn., by T.B.F. Ruoff et al. London: Sweet & Maxwell, 1986.

Silverman, Frances. *Searches and Enquiries–A Conveyancer's Guide*. London: Butterworth & Co. (Publishers) Ltd., 1985.

Silverman, Frances. *Standard Conditions of Sale–A Conveyancer's Guide*. 2nd edn. London: Butterworth & Co. (Publishers) Ltd., 1986.

Simpson, A.W.B. *A History of the Land Law*. 2nd edn. Oxford: Clarendon Press, 1986.

Speight, Antony and Stone, Gregory. *The Law of Defective Premises*. London: Pitman Publishing Ltd., 1982.

Stephens, N.B.B. *The Practice of Estate Agency*. London: Estates Gazette, 1981.

Stephenson, Ian. *The Law Relating to Agriculture*. Aldershot, Hampshire: Gower Publishing Company Limited, 1975.

Storey, I.R. *Conveyancing*. London: Butterworth & Co. (Publishers) Ltd., 1983.

Wilkinson, H.W. *Pipes, Mains Cables and Sewers*. 4th edn. London: Longman Professional, 1984.

Wilkinson, H.W. *Standard Conditions of Sale of Land*. 3rd edn. London: Longman

Professional, 1982 with 1985 supplement.

Williams, William James. *Williams' Contract for the Sale of Land and Title to Land.* 4th edn. London: Butterworth & Co. (Publishers) Ltd., 1975 with 1983 supplement.

Wontner, J.J. and Quickfall, F. *Wontner's Guide to Land Registry Practice.* 15th edn., by P.J. Timothy. London: Longman Professional, 1985.

REAL ESTATE LAW, United States
See also: Real Estate Law, England and Wales

American Law Institute. *First Restatement of the Law of Property.* Philadelphia: American Law Institute Publishers, 1936.

American Law Institute. *First Restatement of the Law of Contract.* Philadelphia: America Law Institute Publishers, 1932.

American Law Institute and Casner, James A. *Second Restatement of the Law of Property.* Philadelphia: American Law Institute Publishers, 1983.

Burby, William E. *Cases on Community Property.* 4th edn. St Paul, Minnesota: West Publishing Co., 1955.

Burby, William E. *Handbook of the Law of Real Property.* 3rd edn. St Paul, Minnesota: West Publishing Co., 1965.

Clurman, David, Jackson, Scott C. and Hebard, Edna L. *Condominiums and Cooperatives.* 2nd edn. New York: John Wiley & Sons, Inc., 1984.

Cunningham, Roger A., Stoebruck, William B. and Whitman, Dale A. *The Law of Real Property.* St. Paul, Minnesota: West Publishing Co., 1984.

Friedman, Milton R. *Contracts and Conveyances of Real Property.* 4th edn. New York: Practising Law Institute, 1984 with 1986 supplement.

Friedman, Milton R. *Friedman on Leases.* 3 vols. 2nd edn. New York: Practising Law Institute, 1983 with 1985 supplement.

Gibson, Frank, Karp, James and Klayman, Elliot. *Real Estate Law.* Chicago: Real Estate Education Company, 1983.

Gray, J.C. *The Rule against Perpetuities.* 4th edn., by R. Gray. Boston, Mass.: Little Brown & Co., 1942.

Irwin, Robert. *Timeshare Properties: What Every Buyer Must Know!* New York: McGraw-Hill Book Company, 1983.

Kratovil, Robert and Werner, Raymond J. *Modern Mortgage Law and Practice.* 2nd edn. Englewood Cliffs, New Jersey: Prentice-Hall, Inc., 1981.

Kratovil, Robert and Werner, Raymond J. *Real Estate Law.* 8th edn. Englewood Cliffs, New Jersey: Prentice-Hall, Inc., 1983.

Lynn, Theodore S. and Goldberg, Harry F. *Real Estate Limited Partnerships*. 2nd edn. New York: John Wiley & Sons, Inc., 1983.

Lefcoe, George. *An Introduction to American Land Law: Cases and Materials*. Indianapolis, Ind.: Bobbs-Merrill Company , Inc., 1974.

Lindeman, Bruce. *Real Estate Brokerage Management*. Reston, Va.: Reston Publishing Company, 1981.

Milligan, W.D. and Bowman, Arthur G. *Real Estate Law*. Englewood Cliffs, New Jersey: Prentice-Hall, Inc., 1984.

Osborne, George E., Nelson, S. and Whitman, Dale A. *Real Estate Finance Law*. St Paul, Minnesota: West Publishing Co., 1979.

Seidel, George J. *Real Estate Law*. St. Paul, Minnesota: West Publishing Company, 1979.

Shick, Blair C. and Plotkin, Irving H. *Torrens in the United States*. Lexington, Mass.: Lexington Books, 1978.

Simes, Lewis H. *Future Interests*. 2nd edn. St Paul, Minnesota: West Publishing Co., 1966.

Thompson, George W. *Thompson on Real Estate Law*. Revised by John S. Grimes. 24 vols. Charlottesville, Va.: The Mitchie Company, with 1981 supplement by Patrick K. Hetrick.

REAL ESTATE MANAGEMENT

See also: Appraisal and Principles and Practice
of U.S. Real Estate; Architecture and Building Design;
Valuation, Development Analysis and Report Writing; Landlord and Tenant.

Aldridge, Trevor M. and Johnson, T.A. *Managing Business Property: A Legal Handbook*. London: Longman Professional, 1978.

Boisot Waters Cohen Partnership. *Business Property Handbook*. Aldershot, Hampshire: Gower Publishing Company Limited, 1981.

Carpenter's Shopping Center Management: Principles and Practices, edited by Robert J. Flynn. New York: International Council of Shopping Centers, 1984.

Downs, James C. Jr. *Principles of Real Estate Management*. 12th edn. Chicago: Institute of Real Estate Management, 1982.

Grear, A.C.L. and Oxborough, J. *Commercial Property Management*. Aldershot, Hampshire: Gower Publishing Company Limited, 1970.

Holeman, J.R. *Condominium Management*. Englewood Cliffs, New Jersey: Prentice-Hall, Inc., 1980.

Institute of Real Estate Management. *Income/Expense Analysis: Apartments, Condominiums and Cooperatives*. Chicago: Institute of Real Estate Management, annual.

Institute of Real Estate Management. *Income/Expense Analysis: Suburban Office Buildings*. Chicago: Institute of Real Estate Management, annual.

Institute of Real Estate Management. *Managing the Shopping Center*. Chicago: Institute of Real Estate Management, 1983.

Irwin, Robert (editor). *The McGraw-Hill Handbook of Property Management*. New York: McGraw-Hill Book Company, 1986.

Jaffe, Austin J. and Sirmans, C.F. *Property Management in Real Estate Investment Decision Making*. Lexington, Mass.: Lexington Books 1980.

Johnson, T.A. (editor). *The Management of Urban property: Property Studies in the United Kingdom and Overseas, study no. 8*. Reading, Berkshire: College of Estate Management Publications, 1972 reprinted 1976.

Macey, John P. and Baker, Charles V. *Housing Management*. 4th edn. London: Estates Gazette, 1983.

McGee, Tristan. *Service Charges in Property*. 4 reports. Reading, Berkshire: College of Estate Management Publications, 1984-1985.

Martin, Peter G. *Shopping Centre Management*. London and New York: E.& F.N. Spon, 1982.

Scarrett, D. *Property Management*. London and New York: E.& F.N. Spon, 1983.

Shenkel, William M. *Modern Real Estate Management*. New York: McGraw-Hill Book Company, 1980.

Stapleton, Tim. *Estate Management Practice*. 2nd edn. London: Estates Gazette, 1986.

Thorncroft, M. *Principles of Estate Management*. London: Estates Gazette, 1965.

Urban Land Institute. *Dollars and Cents of Shopping Centers*. Washington,D.C.: Urban Land Institute. 1984, revised triannually.

Walmsley's Rural Estate Management. 6th edn., by C.W.N. Miles, H.A.R. Long and W. Seabrooke. London: Estates Gazette, 1979.

SURVEYING

Bannister, A. and Raymond, S. *Surveying*. 5th edn. London: Pitman Publishing Ltd., 1984.

Dale, P.F. *Cadastral Surveys in the Commonwealth*. London: Her Majesty's Stationery Office, 1976.

Davies, R. Anderson, J. and Mikhail, E. *Surveying Theory and Practice*. 6th edn. New York: McGraw-Hill Book Company, 1981.

Dugdale, R.H. *Surveying*. 3rd edn. London: George Godwin Ltd, 1980.

Evett, J.B. *Surveying*. Chichester, Sussex: John Wiley & Sons Ltd., 1979.

Olliver, J.G. and Clendinning, James. *Principles of Surveying*. 4th edn. Wokingham, Berkshire: Van Nostrand Reinhold (UK) Co. Ltd., 1978.

Seymour, W.A. (editor). *A History of the Ordnance Survey*. Folkstone, Kent: Wm. Dawson & Sons, 1980.

Wilson, R.J.P. *Land Surveying*. 2nd edn. Plymouth: Macdonald and Evans Ltd., 1977.

TAXATION, England and Wales

Bagnall, K.R. and Lewison, Kim. *Development Land Tax*. London: Shaw & Sons Ltd., 1978, looseleaf with updating service.

Barlow, J., King, L. and King, A. *Wills, Administration and Taxation: A Practical Guide*. 2nd edn. London: Sweet & Maxwell, 1986.

Blakeway-Webb, Hugh. *Stamp Duty Guide*. London: Butterworth & Co (Publishers) Ltd., 1985.

Butterworths' Orange Tax Handbook 1985-86. edited by Moiz Sadikali. London: Butterworth & Co. (Publishers) Ltd., 1986.

Chambost, Edouard. *Using Tax Havens Successfully*. London: Institute for International Research, 1978.

Chapman, A.L. *Capital Transfer Tax*. 6th edn. London: Longman Professional, 1985.

Cox, C. and Ross, H.J. *Capital Gains Tax on Business*. London: Sweet & Maxwell Ltd., 1986.

De Voil's Value Added Tax, 1973, looseleaf with updating service.

Dobry, George, Stewart-Smith, W.R. and Barnes, Michael. *Development Gains Tax*. London: Butterworth & Co. (Publishers) Ltd., 1975.

Dymond's Capital Transfer Tax. 3rd edn., by Roy R. Greenfield. London: Longman Professional, 1986, looseleaf with updating service.

Goy, D. *Development Land Tax*. 2nd edn. London: Sweet & Maxwell, 1985.

Grundy, M. *Tax Havens: A World Survey*. 4th edn., by John Walters. London: Sweet & Maxwell, 1983.

Heap, Sir Desmond (editor). *Encyclopaedia of Betterment Levy and Land*

Commission: Law and Practice. London: Sweet & Maxwell, 1967, looseleaf with updating service.

Jackson, Joseph and Davies, D.T.A. *Matrimonial Finance and Taxation*. 4th edn. London: Butterworth & Co. (Publishers) Ltd., 1986.

Joseph, Clifford. *Development Land Tax: A Practical Guide*. 3rd edn. Longman Professional, 1986.

King, Philip S. *V.A.T. on Construction and Development*. London: Granada Publishing Ltd., 1984.

Maas, Robert W. *Development Land Tax*. 4th edn. Croydon, Surrey: Tolley Publishing Company Ltd., 1982.

Maas, Robert W. *Tolley's Property Taxes*. Croydon, Surrey: Tolley Publishing Company Ltd., 1986.

Matthews, J., Johnson, T. and Westlake, E.F. *Development Land Tax Guide*. London: Butterworth & Co. (Publishers) Ltd., 1984.

Mellows, A.R. *Taxation of Land Transactions*. 3rd edn. London: Butterworth & Co. (Publishers) Ltd., 1982.

Monroe, J.G. and Nock, R.S. *The Law of Stamp Duties*. 6th edn., by Reginald Nock. London: Sweet & Maxwell, 1986.

Ray, Ralph P. and Redman, John E. *Practical C.T.T. Planning*. 3rd edn. London: Butterworth & Co. (Publishers) Ltd., 1985.

Relf, David D. and Preston, Christopher, A.L. *V.A.T. Guide and Casebook*. London: Longman Professional, 1981, looseleaf with updating service.

Ryde on Rating: The Law and Practice. 13th edn. London: Butterworth & Co. (Publishers) Ltd., 1976 with 1984 supplement.

Sales, Harry (editor). *Encyclopaedia of Rating Law and Practice*. London: Sweet & Maxwell, 1985, looseleaf with updating service.

Sergeant and Simms's Stamp Duties and Capital Duties. 8th edn., by B.J. Simms et al. London: Butterworth & Co. (Publishers) Ltd., 1982 looseleaf with updating service.

Shock, J. *Capital Allowances*. 2nd edn. London: Sweet & Maxwell,1984.

Soares, Patrick C. *Land and Tax Planning*. 2nd edn. London: Longman Professional, 1984.

Soares, Patrick C. *VAT Planning for Property Transactions*. London: Longman Professional, 1985.

Tolley's Capital Gains Tax, by Robert Wareham and Patrick Noakes. Croydon, Surrey: Tolley Publishing Company Ltd., annual.

Tolley's Capital Transfer Tax, by Robert Wareham and Jane Scollen. Croydon,

Surrey: Tolley Publishing Company Ltd., annual.

Tolley's Stamp Duties. 2nd edn. Croydon, Surrey: Tolley Publishing Company Ltd., 1980.

Tolley's Value Added Tax, by Eric L. Harvey and Robert Wareham. Croydon, Surrey: Tolley Publishing Company Ltd., annual.

Tolley's VAT Planning. Croydon, Surrey: Tolley Publishing Company Ltd., 1986.

Whiteman, P. and Wheatcroft, G.S.A. *Capital Gains Tax.* 3rd edn., by Mark Herbert and Brian Green. London: Sweet & Maxwell, 1980 with 1985 supplements.

TAXATION, United States

Almy, Richard R. *Improving Real Estate Assessment: A Reference Manual.* Chicago: International Association of Assessing Officers, 1978.

Conroy, Kathleen. *Timeshare Property Assessment and Taxation.* American Land Development Association, 1983.

Halperin, Jerome Y. et al. *Tax Planning for Real Estate Transactions.* Chicago: Coopers & Lybrand for the Farm and Land Institute of the National Association of Realtors, 1978.

International Association of Assessing Officers. *Assessing and the Appraisal Process.* 5th edn. Chicago: International Association of Assessing Officers, 1974.

International Association of Assessing Officers. *Property Assessment Valuation.* Chicago: International Association of Assessing Officers, 1977.

TOWN AND COUNTRY PLANNING
See also: Planning Law and Compulsory Purchase, Zoning and Condemnation

Aldridge, Meryl. *The British New Towns.* London: Routledge & Keegan Paul, 1979.

Burke, Gerald L. *Town Planning for the Surveyor.* London: Estates Gazette, 1980.

Cherry, G.E. *The Evolution of British Town Planning.* Leighton Buzzard, Bedfordshire: Leonard Hill, 1974.

Cullingworth, J.B. *Town and Country Planning in Britain.* 9th edn. London: George Allen & Unwin (Publishers) Ltd., 1985.

Fedden, Robin and Joekes, Rosemary (editors). *The National Trust Guide.* 3rd edn. London: Jonathan Cape Ltd., 1984.

Gibson, Michael and Langstaff, Michael. *An Introduction to Urban Renewal.* London: Hutchinson & Co. (Publishers) Ltd., 1982

Glasson, John. *Introduction to Regional Planning.* 2nd edn. London: Hutchinson & Co. (Publishers) Ltd., 1978.

Healey, P. *Local Plans in British Land Use Planning.* Oxford: Pergamon Press, 1983.

Howard, Ebenezer. *Garden Cities of Tomorrow.* London: George Allen & Unwin (Publishers) Ltd., 1946, first published 1898.

Keeble, Lewis. *Principles of Town and Country Planning.* 4th edn. London: Estates Gazette, 1979.

Keeble, Lewis. *Town Planning at the Crossroads.* London: Estates Gazette, 1961.

Keeble, Lewis. *Town Planning Made Plain.* London: Construction Press, 1983.

Merlin, Pierre. *New Towns: Regional Planning and Development.* First published as *Les Villes Nouvelles*, 1969 by Presses Universitaires de Paris. London: Methuen & Co., Ltd., 1971.

Mumford, Lewis. *The City in History.* London: Martin Secker & Warburg Ltd., 1961.

Osborne, F. and Whittick, A. *The New Towns.* Leighton Buzzard, Bedfordshire: Leonard Hill, 1977.

Ratcliffe, J.S. *An Introduction to Town and Country Planning.* 2nd edn. London: Hutchinson & Co. (Publishers) Ltd., 1981.

Royal Borough of Kensington and Chelsea. *Urban Conservation and Historic Buildings: A Guide to the Legislation.* London: Architectural Press, 1984.

Schaffer, F. *The New Town Story.* London: MacGibbon & Kee, 1970.

Waller, P.J. *Town, City and Nation: England 1850-1914.* Oxford University Press, 1983.

VALUATION, DEVELOPMENT ANALYSIS AND REPORT WRITING

See also: Appraisal and Principles and Practice of US Real Estate

Baum, Andrew and Mackin, D. *The Income Approach to Property Valuation.* 2nd edn. London: Routledge & Keegan Paul, 1983.

Baum, Andrew. *Statutory Valuations.* London: Routledge & Keegan Paul, 1983.

Bowcock, P. *Property Valuation Tables.* London: Macmillan Publishers Ltd., 1978.

Britton, William, Davies, Keith and Johnson, Tony. *Modern Methods of Valuation of Land, Houses and Buildings.* 7th edn. London: Estates Gazette, 1980.

Byrne, Peter and Cadman, David. *Risk, Uncertainty and Decision-making in*

Property Development. London & New York: E.& F.N. Spon Ltd., 1984.

Cadman, David and Catalano, Alex. *Property Development in the U.K. - Evolution and Change.* See: Jolly, Brian (editor), *Property Development Library*, vol. 1., 1983.

Cadman, David and Austin Crowe, Leslie. *Property Development.* 2nd edn. London and New York: E.& F.N. Spon Ltd., 1983.

College of Estate Management. *Property Valuation Handbook*, a series of handbooks on valuation. Supervisory editor, Strathon, R.N. Reading, Berkshire: College of Estate Management, 1979.

Darlow, Clive (editor). *Valuation and Development Handbook.* London: Estates Gazette, 1982.

Darlow, Clive (editor). *Valuation and Investment Appraisal.* London: Estates Gazette, 1983.

Davidson, A.W. *Parry's Valuation and Conversion Tables.* 10th edn. London: Estates Gazette, 1978.

Davidson, A.W. and Leonard, J.E. (editors). *The Property Development Process.* Reading, Berkshire: Centre for Advanced Land Use Studies, College of Estate Management, 1976.

Emeny, R. and Wilkes, H.M. *Principles and Practice of Rating Valuation.* 4th edn. London: Estates Gazette, 1984.

Enever, Nigel. *The Valuation of Property Investments.* 3rd edn. London: Estates Gazette, 1984.

Jolly, Brian A. (editor). *Property Development Library*, a series of over 20 handbooks published in 2 volumes. Vol.1. Property Development in the U.K. – Evolution and Change; Offices Today and Tomorrow; Building Regulations and Control; Taxing the Profit; Trouble with Neighbours; Vol 2. Shopping Centre Development; Building Costs and Contracts; Acquisition and Marketing; Property Company Accounts. Reading, Berkshire: College of Estate Management, 1983 & 1984.

Karslake, Howard H. and Nichols, A. D. *Industrial Valuations*, London: Estates Gazette, 1974.

Millington, A. F. *An Introduction to Property Valuation.* 2nd edn. London: Estates Gazette, 1982.

Mustoe, N. E., Eve, Brian H. and Anstey, Bryan. *Complete Valuation Practice.* 5th edn. London: Estates Gazette, 1960 reprinted 1963.

Parry's Valuation and Conversion Tables. 10th edn., by A.W.Davidson. London: Estates Gazette, 1978.

Poole, R. and Poole, P.M. *The Valuation of Pipeline Easements and Wayleaves.* London: Estates Gazette, 1962.

Rees, W.N. (editor). *Valuation: Principles into Practice.* 2nd edn. London: Estates Gazette, 1984.

Richmond, David. *Introduction to Valuation.* 2nd edn. London: Macmillan Publishers Ltd., 1985.

Rose's Property Valuation Tables, constituting the 34th edition of INWOOD'S TABLES, reconstructed and explained by J.J. Rose. Oxford: The Freeland Press Ltd., 1977.

Rose, J. J. *Tables of the Constant Rent* Aldershot, Hampshire: Gower, The Technical Press Ltd., 1979.

Royal Institution of Chartered Surveyor's and Incorporated Society of Valuers and Auctioneers. *Code of Measuring Practice.* 2nd edn. London: Surveyors Publications, 1987.

Royal Institution of Chartered Surveyors. *Guidance Notes on the Valuation of Assets*, prepared by The Asset Valuation Standards Committee. 2nd edn. London: Royal Institution of Chartered Surveyors, 1982, updated 1986.

Stapleton, T.B. *Pleased to Report.* 2nd edn. London: Estates Gazette, 1983.

Strathon, R.N. (supervisory editor). *Property Valuation Handbook*, an evolving series of handbooks. Reading, Berkshire: College of Estate Management, 1979-

Westbrook, R.W. *The Valuation of Licenced Premises.* London: Estates Gazette, 1967, revised 1983.

Westbrook, R.W. *The Valuation of Petrol Filling Stations.* 2nd edn. London: Estates Gazette, 1969.

Westbrook, R.W. *Valuer's Casebook of Approved Valuations.* 2 vols. London: Estates Gazette, 1968 and 1973.

Williams, D. and Hubbard, C. *Leasehold Valuations.* London: Sweet & Maxwell, 1986, looseleaf with updating service.

Wood, L.S. *Principles and Practice of Farm Valuations.* 7th edn. London: Estates Gazette, 1970.

ZONING AND CONDEMNATION, United States

See also: Planning Law and Compulsory Purchase.

Abrams, Stanley D. *How to Win the Zoning Game.* Charlottesville, Va: The Mitchie Company, 1982 with supplement.

American Institute of Real Estate Appraisers. *Condemnation Appraisal Practice, volume II.* Chicago: American Institute of Real Estate Appraisers, 1973.

Anderson, Robert M. *American Law of Zoning.* 3rd edn. Rochester, New York: Lawyers Cooperative Publishing, 1986.

Babcock, Richard F. *The Zoning Game: Municipal Practices and Policies*. Madison, Wisconsin and London: University of Wisconsin Press, 1966.

Eaton, James D. *Real Estate Valuation in Litigation*. Chicago: American Institute of Real Estate Appraisers, 1982.

Hagman, Donald G. and Misczynski, Dean J. *Windfalls and Wipeouts*. Washington, D.C.: Planners Press, 1978.

Harrison, Harold S. *Harrison on Eminent Domain: A Guide for Appraisers and Others*. Chicago: Society of Real Estate Appraisers, 1980.

Hind, Dudley, Carn, Neil G. and Ordway, Nicholas. *Winning at the Zoning Game*. New York: McGraw-Hill Book Company, 1979.

Mandelker, Daniel R. *The Zoning Dilemma*. Charlottesville, Va.: The Mitchie Company, 1971.

Nichol's Law of Eminent Domain. 3rd edn. 18 vols. Edited by Julius L. Sackman and Patrick J. Rohan. Albany, New York: Matthew Bender & Co., 1956, looseleaf with updating service.

Peterson, Craig A. and McCarthy, Claire. *Handling Zoning and Land Use Litigation: A Practical Guide*. Charlottesville, Va. The Mitchie Company, 1982 with 1984 supplement.

Rams, Edwin. *Valuation for Eminent Domain*. Englewood Cliffs, New Jersey: Prentice-Hall, Inc., 1973.

Schmindman, F. et al. *Handling the Land Use Case*. Boston, Mass.: Little, Brown and Company, 1984.

Schmutz, George L. *Condemnation Appraisal Handbook*. Revised and enlarged by Edwin M. Rams. Englewood Cliffs, New Jersey: Prentice-Hall, Inc., 1963.

Strom, Frederick A. *Zoning and Planning Law Handbook*. New York: Clark Boardman Co., 1982.

Yokley's Law of Subdivisions. 2nd edn. by the Publisher's editorial staff. Charlottesville, Va: The Mitchie Company, 1981.

Yokley, E.C. *Zoning Law and Practice*. 8 vols. Charlottesville, Va.: The Mitchie Company, 1978-1980, with 1984 supplement.

FRENCH LAW AND TAXATION

Amos & Walton's Introduction to French Law. 3rd edn., by F.H. Lawson, A. Anton and L. Neville Brown. Oxford: Oxford University Press, 1967 reprinted 1974.

Auby, J-M. and Ducos-Ader, R. *Droit Administrative: L'Expropriation pour Cause d'Utilité Publique*. 4th edn. Paris: Dalloz, 1980.

Aubry, C and Rau, C-F *Droit Civil Français*. 12 vols with updating service. 7th ed., 1936–1958.

Bey, El Mokhtar and Gavalda, Christian. *Le Crédit-Bail Immobilier*. Paris: Press Universitaire de France, 1983.

Bouysson, Fernard and Hugot, Jean. *Code de L'Urbanisme*. 3rd edn. Paris: Litec, 1984.

Broet, Louis. *La Practique de La Fiscalité Immobilière*. 7th edn. Paris: Masson, 1981.

Calfan, Henri and Doublier, Roger. *La Copropriété: Leurs Droits, Leurs Obligations*. 2nd edn. Paris: Librairie Generale de Droit et de Jurisprudence, 1980.

Carbonnier, Jean. *Droit Civil. Vol. 3: Les Biens*. 11th edn. Paris: Press Universitaire de France, 1983.

Cotton, Guy and Randier, Robert. *Baux Ruraux: tout les litiges entre preneur et bailleur*. 2nd edn. Paris: Masson, 1978.

Cremieux-Israel, Danièle. *Leasing et Crédit Bail: Aspects Juridiques, Comptables et Fiscaux*. Paris: Dalloz, 1975.

Dalloz. *Code Général des Impôts*. Paris: Dalloz, 1983, with updating service to March 1984.

David, R. and Vries, H.P. de. *The French Legal System*. New York: Oceana Publishing Inc., 1958.

Gilli, Jean-Paul and Lanversin, Jacques de. *Lexique: Droit de L'Urbanisme*. Paris: Press Universitaire de France, 1978.

Gilli, Jean-Paul and Hubert, C. *Les Grands Arrêts du Droit de L'Urbanisme*. 2nd edn. Paris: Edition Sirey, 1981.

Giovandi, Mario. *Le Crédit-Bail (Leasing) en Europe: Développement et Nature Juridique*. Paris: Litec, 1980.

Givord, François and Giverdon, Claude. *La Copropriété*. 12th edn. Paris: Librairie Dalloz, 1968.

Halpern, L. *Taxes in France*, 4th edn. based on *Les Impôts en France* by Francis Lefebvre. London: Butterworth & Co. (Publishers) Ltd, 1985.

Homont, André. *L'Expropriation pour Cause d'Utilité Publique* Paris: Litec, 1980.

Kahn-Freund, O., Levy, C. and Rudden, B. *A Source-book of French Law*, 2nd edn. Oxford: Oxford University Press, 1978.

Kischinewsky-Broquisse, E. *La Copropriété des Immeubles Bâtis*. 3rd end. Paris: Litec, 1978.

Laubadère, A. de, Venezia, J-C. and Gaudement, Y. *Manuel de Droit Administratif.*

12th edn. Paris: Librairie Générale de Droit et de Jurisprudence, 1982 with updating service from June 1984.

Le Gall, J. *French Company Law.* edited by R. Pennington, London: Oyez Publishing Ltd, 1974.

Linotte, D. in collaboration with C. Atias. *Le Remembrement Rural.* Paris: Litec, 1980.

Marty, Gabriel and Raynaud, Pierre. *Droit Civil.* 2nd edn. 3 vols. Paris: Sirey, 1961-76.

Nicholas, Barry. *French Law of Contract.* London: Butterworth & Co. (Publishers) Ltd., 1982.

Pace, Gilbert. *Crédit-Bail (Leasing)* Paris: J. Delmas et Cie, 1974.

Pace, Gilbert. *Financière du Crédit-Bail (Leasing): Practique et Technique.* Paris: Masson, 1974.

Petit Code Dalloz, *Code de L'Urbanisme.* 3rd edn. Paris: Dalloz, 1985.

Planiol, M. and Ripert, G. *Traité Pratique de Droit Civil Français.* 13 vols. 2nd edn. Paris: Librairie Générale de Jurisprudence, 1952-60.

Précis Dalloz. *Droit Administrative* (J.-M. Auby et R. Ducos-Ader). 6th edn. Paris: Dalloz, 1984.

Précis Dalloz. *Droit Civil, Les Biens.* 2nd edn., by Alex Weill. Paris: Dalloz, 1974 with updating service.

Saint-Alary, Roger, editor in chief. *Dictionaire Permanent: Gestion Immobilière.* Paris: Editions Legislatives et Administratives, 1981 with updating service.

Ripert, G. and Boulanger, J. *Traité de Droit Civil.* 4 vols. Paris: Librairie Générale de Droit et de Jurisprudence, 1984.

Starck, Boris. *Droit Civil: Obligations,* Paris: Litec, 1972 with 1976 supplement.

Voirin, Pierre. *Manuel de Droit Civil.* 20th edn., by Gilles Goubeaux. Paris: Librairie Générale de Droit et de Jurisprudence, 1981 with updating service.

Voulet, Jacques. *Baux d'Habitation et Professionnels.* 10th edn. Paris: Masson, 1982.

Weisman, M. and Debled, R. *Tous les problèmes de la Copropriété.* 12th edn. Paris: Masson, 1981.

Appendix C

Tables of measures of length, area and volume, including metric/imperial conversions

LAND LINEAR MEASURE
3 inches (in.) = 1 foot (ft.)
3 feet = 1 yard (yd.) = 36 inches
1760 yards = 1 mile (mi.) = 5280 feet

$5\frac{1}{2}$ yards = 1 rod, pole or perch = $16\frac{1}{2}$ feet
40 rods = 1 furlong (fur.) = 220 yards
8 furlongs = 1 mile = 80 chains

7.92 inches = 1 link (Gunter's or surveyor's chain)
100 links = 1 chain = 66 feet
80 chains = 1 mile = 5280 feet

12 inches = 1 link (engineer's chain)
100 links = 1 chain = 100 feet
52.8 chains = 1 mile = 5280 feet

0.3937 inches = 1 centimetre
3.9370 inches = 1 decimetre
3.2808 feet = 1 metre
1.0936 yards = 1 metre
0.6214 miles = 1 kilometre

25.40 millimetres (mm) = 1 inch
2.54 centimetres (cm) = 1 inch
0.3048 metres (m) = 1 foot
0.9144 metres = 1 yard
1.6093 kilometres (km) = 1 mile

LAND AREA MEASURE
144 square inches = 1 square foot (sq. ft.)
9 square feet = 1 square yard (sq. yd.)
4840 square yards = 1 acre (ac.)
10 acres = 1 square furlong
640 acres = 1 square mile

36 square miles or sections = 1 United States Township

30.25 square yards = 1 square rod, pole or perch
625 square links = 1 square rod, pole or perch
16 square rods, poles or perches = 1 square surveyor's chain
10 square surveyor's chains = 1 acre

0.155 square inches = 1 square centimetre (cm2)
10.764 square feet = 1 square metre (m2)
1.1960 square yards = 1 square metre
0.3861 square miles = 1 square kilometre
2.47 acres = 1 hectare (ha.)

10,000 m2 = 100 acres = 1 hectare or square hectometre

6.452 square centimetres (sq. cm.)   =   1 square inch
0.0929 square metres (sq. m.)   =   1 square foot
0.83613 square metres   =   1 square yard
2.590 square kilometres (sq. km.)   =   1 square mile

0.4047 hectares   =   1 acre = 4,4046 square metres

VOLUME MEASURE
1728 cubic inches (cu. in.)   =   1 cubic foot (cu. ft.)
27 cubic feet   =   1 cubic yard (cu. yd.)
128 cubic feet   =   1 cord

1.734 cubic inches   =   1 British fluid ounce
28.32 litres   =   1 cubic foot

4.5460 litres   =   1 gallon (U.K.)
3.7853 litres   =   1 gallon (U.S.A.)

277.42 cubic inches   =   1 gallon (U.K.)
231 cubic inches   =   1 gallon (U.S.A.)
1 gallon (U.K.)   =   1.20094 gallons (U.S.A.)

1 cubic inch   =   16.387 cubic centimetres (cm3)
1 cubic foot   =   0.2832 cubic metres (m3)
                =   28.32 litres

1 m3 = 1000 litres   =   35.31445 cubic feet
                     = 1 tonne of water
0.0610 cubic inches   =   1 cm3

WEIGHT OR MASS
1 ounce (oz.)   =   28.35 grams (g.)
16 ounces   =   1 pound
            =   454 grams
2.2046 pounds   =   1 kilogram (kg.)
2240 pounds   =   1 ton
              =   1016 kilograms

100 pounds   =   1 short hundredweight   =   45.359 kilograms
112 pounds   =   1 long hundredweight   =   50.802 kilograms

1 short ton   =   20 short hundredweights   =   0.907 metric tons
1 long ton   =   20 long hundredweights   =   1.016 metric tons